BUILDING *the* PERFECT PC

Second Edition

**Robert Bruce Thompson
and Barbara Fritchman Thompson**

O'REILLY®

BEIJING · CAMBRIDGE · FARNHAM · KÖLN · PARIS · SEBASTOPOL · TAIPEI · TOKYO

Building the Perfect PC, Second Edition

by Robert Bruce Thompson and Barbara Fritchman Thompson

Published by O'Reilly Media, Inc., 1005 Gravenstein Highway North, Sebastopol, CA 95472.

O'Reilly books may be purchased for educational, business, or sales promotional use. Online editions are also available for most titles (*safari.oreilly.com*). For more information, contact our corporate/institutional sales department: 800-998-9938 or *corporate@oreilly.com*.

Print History:		Editor:	Brian Jepson
August 2004:	First Edition.	**Production Editor:**	Philip Dangler
December 2006:	Second Edition.	**Cover Designer:**	Karen Montgomery

The O'Reilly logo is a registered trademark of O'Reilly Media, Inc. The *MAKE: Projects* series designations, *Building the Perfect PC*, and related trade dress are trademarks of O'Reilly Media, Inc.

Many of the designations used by manufacturers and sellers to distinguish their products are claimed as trademarks. Where those designations appear in this book, and O'Reilly Media, Inc. was aware of a trademark claim, the designations have been printed in caps or initial caps.

While every precaution has been taken in the preparation of this book, the publisher and authors assume no responsibility for errors or omissions, or for damages resulting from the use of the information contained herein.

Cover photograph features:

    Antec NSK1300 case
    Gigabyte GeForce 7600GS video adapter
    Hauppauge WinTV-PVR 150 TV capture card
    Intel D946GZIS motherboard
    Intel Core 2 Duo E6300 processor
    Seagate Barracuda 7200.10 750 GB hard drive
    Thermalright XP-120 CPU cooler

 This book uses RepKover™, a durable and flexible lay-flat binding.

ISBN-10: 0-596-52686-5
ISBN-13: 978-0-596-52686-3
[F]

*To Mark Brokering, who came up with the idea
and kept the ball rolling.*

✳

Contents

Foreword to the Second Edition

I was asked to revise the Foreword I wrote for the first edition of this book, but I found there was no need. A few details have changed, but the principles haven't.

However, the details are important. My main systems at Chaos Manor now mostly run with dual core (both Intel and AMD) CPU chips. Since the first edition of *Building the Perfect PC*, the video card scene has changed several times. Intel lost its dominance as the maker of the fastest desktop CPUs for the money. AMD took advantage of the Intel stumble and surged ahead to its highest market share yet. AMD and nVIDIA joined forces, and now AMD has bought ATI. Case designs have changed. We have both DDR and DDR2 RAM to contend with.

If you have the first edition, you know how important the book is, and when you contemplate building a new system, you'll be wise to upgrade. And if you don't have the first edition, this remains the best book you can buy if you're building or planning to build a PC. Now read the Foreword to the first edition.

—Jerry Pournelle
Chaos Manor
December 2006

Foreword to the First Edition

I presume you're reading this because you've either just bought this book, or you're thinking of buying it; so let's get that out the way now. Should you buy this book, or, having bought it, should you be happy you did? The answer is yes. If the subject of building your own computer interests you —and why in the world are you reading this if it doesn't?—then you need this book.

That out of the way, we can look at the broader question of whether you should build your own computers.

As I look around Chaos Manor (*http://www.jerrypournelle.com*) I see that I have over 20 computers, all networked, and I built nearly every one of them myself. The exceptions are Princess, an ancient Compaq desktop Professional Workstation running Dual Pentium Plus 200 MHz CPUs; a Mac; a Tablet PC; and another laptop. No one in his right mind builds his own laptop or Tablet. I keep Princess because I've had her for a decade, and she hasn't been shut down in more than a year, and I haven't the heart to scrap her; besides, she's still useful for doing long web searches. Until fairly recently I had a Compaq Professional Workstation (Dual 750 MHz Pentium III) as my communications system, but I retired it a few months ago in favor of a new 3 GHz built here, and since then every server and workstation added to the Chaos Manor network was built here. Clearly I must like building systems and using them.

It wasn't always this way. Until a few years ago I had at least as many brand-name systems as home-built "white boxes." Then came the consumerization of the PC industry. Manufacturers were forced to make cost reduction after cost reduction. Some of those cost reductions were not wise. Some were disasters. Worse, component makers were themselves competing on cost. It became more and more difficult to build a quality line of PC's to sell at any realistic price.

It is still possible to buy quality computers. You'll pay for them, though, and sometimes having paid an arm and a leg you still won't know what quality you have bought. There are still big companies with mission-critical tasks who are well advised to buy the very best machines from top-of-the-line companies; but most users and small businesses would be better advised to consider building their own, or having them built to specs by a trustworthy local shop—and this book is indispensable when it comes to writing out those specifications.

In general there are two reasons why you build your own systems. First is if you want the *highest possible performance* using only the latest and greatest components. When new and better components come out, it takes a while for commercial system builders to change over, and the first ones to come out with the latest in high performance demand and get premium prices. If you're interested in building a really screaming machine, you need this book, because building that kind of system is tricky. Components like power supplies, cases, and fans are important, and information about why they are important is often hard to come by. You'll find all the information you need in this book.

The other reason for building your own system is to get *the best performance and quality for your money, and to customize your high-performance system for your specific needs*. You probably don't need the very best performance available, and often you can get more than good enough systems at dramatically lower prices. These are known as "sweet-spot" systems, and once again, if that's your goal, you need this book, because that too can be tricky. Sometimes saving money isn't a good idea at all. You can fudge on some components, but you're better off paying premium for others. Bob and Barbara Thompson offer great advice on which is which.

So. If you're thinking of building your own system, you need this book to give you some notion of how difficult it's likely to be, and help you decide if it's a good idea; and if you're determined to build a PC, you need this book because most of us who build PCs have picked up a number of techniques and tricks over the years, and the Thompsons know nearly all of them. Learn from our mistakes. It's a lot easier.

—Jerry Pournelle
Chaos Manor
August 2004

Preface

When we sat down to write the Preface for this second edition, we realized that, as they say, the more things change the more they remain the same.

In one sense, things have changed a lot in two years. Almost none of the components we used in the first edition are still available. They've been replaced by bigger, faster, better, cheaper parts. But those are mere details. In a fundamental sense, nothing has changed. The reasons for building your own PC are the same. The decisions you need to make differ only in details. The skills you need to master are the same, and the satisfaction you'll gain from designing and building your own PC is as great as ever.

So, on with the original preface, which we found it necessary to modify only to update information about the system configurations in the book and other similar details.

Building PCs isn't just for techies any more.

It used to be, certainly. Only gamers and other geeks actually built their PCs from the ground up. Everyone else just called the Dell Dude and ordered a system. That started to change a few years ago. The first sign was when general merchandisers like Best Buy started stocking upgrade components. If you wanted to expand the memory in your PC or install a larger hard drive or add a CD writer, you could now get the components you needed at the local big-box store.

A year or two ago, things changed again. Big-box retailers started carrying PC components like cases and motherboards—parts seldom needed by upgraders, but necessary to build a new PC from scratch. Nowadays, although CompUSA, Best Buy, and other local retailers may not carry as broad a range of PC components as some online specialty retailers, you can get everything you need for a new PC with one visit to a big-box store.

Specialty PC component superstores like Fry's carry a full range of components at extremely good prices. We wish we had a Fry's within driving distance. Then again, maybe not. There's too much good stuff there. Our credit cards are smoking already, and a trip to Fry's might be the last straw.

And you can bet that big-box stores don't allocate shelf space to products that aren't selling. Building your own PC has become mainstream. Nowadays, even regular nontechnical people build their own systems and have fun doing it. Instead of settling for a mediocre, cookie-cutter system from Dell or Gateway, they get a PC with exactly the features and components they want, at a good price, and with the pride that comes from knowing they built it themselves. They also get a faster, higher-quality PC with much better reliability than any mass-market system. No small thing, that.

Robert visited Best Buy one day and spent some time hanging out in the PC component aisles. He watched a lot of regular people comparing hard drives, video adapters, DVD writers, and other PC components. Some of them were buying components to upgrade their current systems, but many of them were buying components to build new systems.

Robert watched one grandmotherly woman fill her shopping cart. She chose an Antec case and power supply, a Maxtor hard drive, an Abit motherboard, an AMD Athlon XP processor, an *n*VIDIA graphics adapter, a couple sticks of DDR memory, and a Lite-On DVD writer. He approached her, and the conversation went something like this:

> Robert: "Looks like you're building a new computer."
>
> Woman: "Yes, I'm building my granddaughter a new PC for her birthday."
>
> Robert: "Are you worried about getting everything to work?"
>
> Woman: "Oh, no. This is the third one I've built. You should try it. It's easy."
>
> Robert: "I may do that."

If she'd had this book, she might have made different choices for one or two of her components. Still, Dell may have something to worry about.

Goals of This Book

This book is your guide to the world of building PCs. Its goal is to teach you—even if you have no training or prior experience—everything you need to know to select the best components and assemble them into a working PC that matches your own requirements and budget.

We present six projects, in as many chapters, each of which details design, component selection, and assembly instructions for a particular type of PC. You can build any or all of these systems as presented, or you can modify them to suit your own requirements.

Every project system in this book can be built entirely from components available at your local big-box store. If some of the components we recommend aren't in stock, one or more of the alternative components we recommend almost certainly will be. If you buy this book on a Friday, you can buy your components Saturday morning, assemble the new system Saturday afternoon, test it Sunday, and have it up and running Monday morning.

Rather than use a straight cookbook approach, which would simply tell you *how* to build a PC by rote, we spend a lot of time explaining *why* we made particular design decisions or chose certain components or did something a certain way. By "looking over our shoulders" as we design PCs and choose components, you'll learn to make good decisions when it comes to designing and building your own PC. You also learn how to build a PC with superior quality, performance, and reliability.

Not that we skimped on the how-to. Each project system chapter provides detailed assembly instructions and dozens of photographs that illustrate the assembly process. Even if you've never seen a hard drive, after reading this book you should be completely comfortable sitting down with a bunch of components to build your own PC.

If you have never built a PC, we hope this book will inspire you to build your first system. If you have some PC building experience, we hope this book will provide the ideas and advice that you need to make the next PC you build the perfect PC for your needs.

Audience for This Book

This book is intended for anyone who wants to build a PC for personal or business use. System builders of any experience level will find this book useful because it explains the concepts used to design a PC to fit specific needs and budgets, and provides the information needed to choose the best components. First-time system builders will also find this book helpful because it provides detailed step-by-step instructions for building a PC, supplemented by numerous photographs that illustrate each step in detail.

Organization of This Book

The first two chapters of this book are a short but comprehensive course in planning the perfect PC and choosing and buying components for it.

Chapter 1, *Fundamentals*, focuses on things you need to know, things you need to have, and things you need to do before you start to buy components and build your new PC. This chapter explains the advantages of building a PC versus buying one (YOU control quality, performance, reliability, and quietness of your components); provides design guidelines; and explains the inevitable trade-offs in performance, price, size, and noise level. We list tools and software you'll need, and provide a detailed tour of the motherboard, the most important and complex PC component. Finally, we provide detailed troubleshooting information in this chapter, because it's easier to avoid problems if you know from the beginning what to look out for. After you read this chapter, you'll be prepared for the next step, actually buying the components for your new PC.

Chapter 2, *Choosing and Buying Components*, tells you everything you need to know about how to choose and buy the components you need to build your new PC.

> When you design and build your own PC, you get something that money can't buy if you purchase a preassembled machine: total control of quality, reliability, performance, and noise level.

We explain the important characteristics of each component and how to choose among alternatives. We also recommend specific components by brand and model number, and provide alternative recommendations for those with different requirements or smaller budgets.

The final six chapters detail project systems, any of which you can build as-is or modify to suit your particular needs. The introductory section of each project chapter is a design guide that explains the choices we made (and why) and how we decided to implement them. Following that is a detailed section on selecting components, with specific products listed by brand name, and a bill of materials at the end of the section. In each case, we list alternatives for those with different needs or budgets. The bulk of each chapter is a detailed guide, with numerous photographs, that shows you step-by-step how to build the system.

> As this book went to press, Windows Vista was still in beta testing. We designed all of the project systems in the book to be capable of running Windows Vista, based on the Vista hardware requirements published by Microsoft. We also verified that each system was in fact able to load and run the most recent Vista beta release we had access to, subject to limitations such as buggy or missing drivers. It's likely that any of the systems will run the release version of Vista perfectly, but obviously we can't guarantee that until Vista actually ships, whenever that may be. At worst, the most any of these project systems should require to run the release version of Vista flawlessly are some additional memory and perhaps a more capable video adapter. Either of those upgrades is easy and inexpensive, so it's unlikely you'll paint yourself into any corners with regard to Vista if you build any of these systems as specified.

Chapter 3, *Building a Mainstream PC*, teaches you how to build a general-purpose PC that is a jack of all trades and a master of...well, quite a few, actually. In the standard configuration, this system combines high performance, top-notch reliability, and moderate cost. Depending on the components you choose—and how much you're willing to spend—you can make this system anything from an inexpensive entry-level box to a do-it-all powerhouse. And it's also quiet, particularly if you build it in a midrange configuration. In a normal office or home environment, you can barely hear it running.

Chapter 4, *Building a SOHO Server*, focuses on building a reliable, high-performance SOHO (Small Office/Home Office) server, appropriate for anything from an inexpensive server for a home office to a serious server for a small-business network. Because these requirements span a vast range, we take particular pains to detail alternative choices and configurations that are appropriate for different environments. We emphasize reliability and data safety regardless of configuration, because a server failure is as disruptive for a home office as for a small business. Accordingly, we emphasize such features as redundant disk storage and reliable backup.

Chapter 5, *Building a Gaming PC*, is all about building a gaming PC on a reasonable budget. Some devoted gamers spend $3,000, $4,000, $5,000, or more to buy or build a fire-breathing PC optimized for games. That's fine if you've just won the lottery, but most gamers can't justify spending that much on their systems. We set out to design and build a seriously fast gaming system that's a lot easier on the wallet. By paying careful consideration to component choices, we were able to design and build a system that offers about 90% of the performance of the extreme systems for about a third of the price.

Chapter 6, *Building a Media Center PC*, shows you how to build a PC that provides TiVo-like DVR (Digital Video Recorder) functions, without the monthly subscription or the DRM (Digital Restrictions Management) "features" common to commercial PVR units. For not much more than the price of a combination TiVo/DVD writer and program guide subscription, this PC substitutes not only for a commercial DVR unit, but also for an AV receiver, CD-ROM player, DVD-ROM player, DVD recorder, 5.1 home-theater speaker system, *and* a gaming console. Talk about bang for the buck.

Chapter 7, *Building a Small Form Factor (SFF) PC*, shows you how to build a full-featured PC that is small enough and quiet enough to fit in almost anywhere. Depending on the components you choose, you can make the SFF PC anything from an inexpensive secondary system suitable for a dorm room or child's bedroom to a primary general-purpose system to a home theater or PVR system to a barn-burner of a portable gaming system to a dedicated "appliance" system or small server.

Chapter 8, *Building a Budget PC*, shows you how to build a fast, reliable PC on a minimum budget. For only $300 or so (not counting external peripherals), it's possible to build a system with high quality components that matches or exceeds the performance of last year's mainstream models. We designed this budget system to be capable of running Windows Vista with at most one or two minor, inexpensive upgrades. It's ideal as a secondary system—or even a primary system, if your needs are modest—and can be upgraded incrementally to add additional features.

Each project chapter is full of tips, many of which are useful no matter what type of system you build. Accordingly, we suggest you read the entire book, including all project system chapters, before you start building your new system.

Acknowledgments

The first edition of this book was conceived one day in late 2003, when Robert received a phone call from Mark Brokering, vice president of sales and marketing for O'Reilly Media. Mark had decided to build a new PC rather than buy one, and he'd picked up a copy of Robert and Barbara's book, *PC Hardware in a Nutshell*.

Mark had lots of good questions about which components to choose and, later on, questions about assembling his new system. At some point during the back-and-forth of emails and phone calls, Mark commented, "You know, we really need to do a book about building a PC." And so this book was born.

The working title was *Build Your Own Computer*. None of us thought that was a great title, but none of us could come up with a better one. Then one day Tim O'Reilly weighed in. "Why don't we call it *Building the Perfect PC*?," Tim asked. Duh. It always seems so obvious after the fact.

In addition to Mark, Tim, and the O'Reilly production staff, who are listed individually in the Colophon, we want to thank our technical reviewers. Ron Morse has been building PCs for more than 20 years. Jim Cooley has built and repaired computers from San Francisco to Athens (Ohio), with the occasional stop in Bangalore. Brian Bilbrey started with vacuum tubes and wire wrap, passed through S-100, ISA, and PCI buses, and was last seen tunneling into a quantum future. All of them did yeoman duty in finding mistakes we made and in making numerous useful suggestions, all of which helped make this a better book. We're entirely responsible for any errors that remain.

We also want to thank our contacts at the hardware companies, who provided technical help, evaluation units, and other assistance. There are far too many to list individually, but they know who they are. We also want to thank the readers of our books, web sites, and message boards, many of whom have taken the time to offer useful suggestions for improvements to this book. Thanks, folks. We couldn't have done it without you.

Finally, we want to thank our editor, Brian Jepson, who contributed numerous useful comments and suggestions.

We'd Like to Hear from You

We have tested and verified the information in this book to the best of our ability, but we don't doubt that some errors have crept in and remained hidden despite our best efforts and those of our editors and technical reviewers to find and eradicate them. Those errors are ours alone. If you find an error or have other comments about the book, you can contact the publisher or the authors.

How to Contact O'Reilly

Please address comments and questions concerning this book to the publisher:

O'Reilly Media, Inc.
1005 Gravenstein Highway North
Sebastopol, CA 95472
(800) 998-9938 (in the United States or Canada)
(707) 829-0515 (international or local)
(707) 829-0104 (fax)

There is a web page for this book, which lists errata and other information. You can access this page at:

http://www.oreilly.com/catalog/9780596526863/

You can also send us email. To be put on our mailing list or to request a catalog, send email to:

info@oreilly.com

For comments on the book, send email to:

bookquestions@oreilly.com

For more information about books, conferences, Resource Centers, and the O'Reilly Network, go to:

http://www.oreilly.com

How to Contact the Authors

To contact one of the authors directly, send mail to:

barbara@hardwareguys.com

robert@hardwareguys.com

We read all mail we receive from readers, but we cannot respond individually. If we did, we'd have no time to do anything else. But we do like to hear from readers.

There is also a web site for the book, which includes updated hardware recommendations, buying guides, and articles, as well as errata, archived older material, and so on:

http://www.hardwareguys.com

We also maintain a message board, where you can read and post messages about PC hardware topics. You can read messages as a guest, but if you want to post messages you must register as a member of the message board. We keep registration information confidential, and you can choose to have your email address hidden on any messages you post:

http://forums.hardwareguys.com/

When you see a Safari® Enabled icon on the cover of your favorite technology book, it means that book is available online through the O'Reilly Network Safari Bookshelf.

Safari offers a solution that's better than eBooks. It's a virtual library that lets you easily search thousands of top tech books, cut and paste code samples, download chapters, and find quick answers when you need the most accurate, current information. Try it for free at:

http://safari.oreilly.com.

We each maintain a personal journal page, updated daily, which frequently includes references to new PC hardware we're working with, problems we've discovered, and other things we think are interesting. You can view these journal pages at:

Barbara: *http://www.fritchman.com/diaries/thisweek.html*

Robert: *http://www.ttgnet.com/thisweek.html*

Disclaimer

Much of the information contained in this book is based on personal knowledge and experience. While we believe that the information contained herein is correct, we accept no responsibility for its validity. The hardware designs and descriptive text contained herein are provided for educational purposes only. It is the responsibility of the reader to independently verify all information. Original manufacturer's data should be used at all times when implementing a design.

The authors, Robert Bruce Thompson and Barbara Fritchman Thompson, and O'Reilly Media, Inc., make no warranty, representation, or guarantee regarding the suitability of any hardware or software described herein for any particular purpose, nor do they assume any liability arising out of the application or use of any product, system, or software, and specifically disclaim any and all liability, including, without limitation, consequential or incidental damages. The hardware and software described herein are not designed, intended, nor authorized for use in any application intended to support or sustain life or any other application in which the failure of a system could create a situation in which personal injury, death, loss of data or information, or damages to property may occur. Should the reader implement any design described herein for any application, the reader shall indemnify and hold the authors, O'Reilly Media, Inc., and their respective shareholders, officers, employees, and distributors harmless against all claims, costs, damages and expenses, and reasonable solicitor fees arising out of, directly or indirectly, any claim of personal injury, death, loss of data or information, or damages to property associated with such unintended or unauthorized use.

Thank You

Thank you for buying *Building the Perfect PC*. We hope you enjoy reading it as much as we enjoyed writing it.

Fundamentals

The idea of building their first PC intimidates a lot of people, but there's really nothing to worry about. Building a PC is no more technically challenging than changing the oil in your car or hooking up a DVD player. Compared to assembling one of those "connect Tab A to Slot B" toys for your kids, it's a breeze.

PC components connect like building blocks. Component sizes, screw threads, mounting hole positions, cable connectors, and so on are standardized, so you needn't worry about whether something will fit. There are minor exceptions, of course. For example, some small cases accept only microATX motherboards and half-height or half-length expansion cards. There are important details, certainly. You must verify, for example, that the motherboard you intend to use supports the processor you plan to use. But overall there are few "gotchas" involved in building a PC. If you follow our advice in the project system chapters, everything will fit and everything will work together.

> Most compatibility issues arise when you mix new components with older ones. For example, an older video card may not fit the video slot in a new motherboard, or a new processor may not be compatible with an older motherboard. If you build a PC from all-new components, you are likely to encounter few such issues. Still, it's a good idea to verify compatibility between the motherboard and other major components, particularly CPU, video adapters, and memory. The configurations in this book have been tested for compatibility.

Nor do you need to worry much about damaging the PC—or it damaging you. Taking simple precautions such as grounding yourself before touching static-sensitive components and verifying cable connections before you apply power are sufficient to prevent damage to all those expensive parts you bought. Other than inside the power supply—which you should *never* open—the highest voltage used inside a modern PC is 12V, which presents no shock hazard.

This chapter doesn't cover the nuts-and-bolts details of assembling a PC, because that's covered exhaustively in text and images in the project system chapters. Instead, this chapter explains the fundamentals—everything you need to prepare yourself properly. It examines the advantages of building your own PC and explains how to design a PC that is perfect for your needs. It tells you what you need to know and do before you start the project, and lists the components, hand tools, and software tools you'll need to build your system. Because the motherboard is the heart of a PC, we include a "motherboard tour" section to illustrate each major part of the motherboard. Finally, because the best way to troubleshoot is to avoid problems in the first place, we include a detailed troubleshooting section. Let's get started.

Why Build a PC?

With entry-level PCs selling for less than $500 and fully-equipped mainstream PCs for $1,000, you might wonder why anyone would bother to build a PC. After all, you can't save any money building one, can you? Well, yes you can. But that's not the only reason to build a PC. There are many good reasons to build your own PC.

Lower cost

PC makers aren't in business for charitable reasons. They need to make a profit, so they need to sell computers for more than they pay for the components and the labor to assemble them. Significantly more, in fact, because they also need to support such expensive operations as research and development departments, toll-free support numbers, and so on.

But PC manufacturers get big price breaks because they buy components in huge volume, right? Not really. The market for PC components is extremely efficient, with razor-thin margins whether you buy 1 unit or 100,000. A volume purchaser gets a price break, certainly, but it's a lot smaller than most people think.

Mass-market PCs are inexpensive not because the makers get huge price breaks on quality components, but because they generally use the cheapest possible components. Cost-cutting is a fact of life in mass-market, consumer-grade PCs. If mass-market PC makers can save a few bucks on the case or the power supply, they do it every time, even though spending a few dollars more (or even a few cents more) would have allowed them to build a noticeably better system. If you compare apples to apples—a home-built system versus, say, a business-class PC from Micron, Dell, or HP—you'll find you can build it yourself for less, sometimes a lot less. Our rule of thumb is that, on average and all other things being equal, you can build a midrange PC yourself for about 75% to 85% of what a major manufacturer charges for an equivalent top-quality system.

Cheaper by the Dozen?

For example, when AMD announces price reductions or a faster new version of the Athlon 64, the news stories often report "Quantity 1000" pricing for the OEM or "tray" versions. This is what a computer maker who buys processors 1,000 at a time pays. A maker who buys 100,000 at a time may pay a few dollars less per processor. If you buy just one OEM processor, you'll typically pay a couple bucks more than the Quantity 1000 pricing. You may even pay less, because PC makers often order more processors than they need to take advantage of price breaks on larger quantities, and then sell the unneeded processors at a slight loss to distributors who then sell them to retailers.

More choice

When you buy a PC, you get a cookie-cutter computer. You can choose such options as a larger hard drive, more memory, or a better monitor, but basically you get what the vendor decides to give you. If you want something that few people ask for, like a better power supply or quieter cooling fans or a motherboard with more features, you're out of luck. Those aren't options.

And what you get is a matter of chance. High-volume direct vendors like Dell and HP often use multiple sources for components. Two supposedly identical systems ordered the same day may contain significantly different components, including such important variations as different motherboards or monitors with the same model number but made by different manufacturers. When you build a PC, you decide exactly what goes into it.

Flexible design

One of the best things about building your own PC is that you can optimize its design to focus on what is important to you and ignore what isn't. Off-the-shelf commercial PCs are by nature jacks of all trades and masters of none. System vendors have to strike a hapy medium that is adequate, if not optimum, for the mythical "average" user.

Want a small, quiet PC for your home theater system? There are three options. You can use a standard PC despite its large size and high noise level, you can pay big bucks for a system from a specialty builder that does just what you want, or you can build your own. Need a system with a ton of redundant hard disk storage for editing video or a professional audio workstation? Good luck finding a commercial system that fits your requirements, at least at a reasonable price. When you build your own PC, you spend your money on things that matter to you and ignore those that don't.

Better component quality

Most computer vendors cut costs by using cheaper OEM versions of popular components if they're "visible" and no-name components if they're not. By "visible" we mean a component that people might seek out by brand name even in a prebuilt PC, such as an ATI or nVIDIA video adapter. Invisible components are ones that buyers seldom ask about or notice, such as motherboards, optical and hard drives, power supplies, and so on.

OEM components may be identical to retail models, differing only in packaging. But even if the parts are the same, there are often significant differences. Component vendors usually do not support OEM versions directly, for example, instead referring you to the system vendor. If that system vendor goes out of business, you're out of luck, because the component maker provides no warranty to end users. Even if the maker does support OEM products, the warranty is usually much shorter on

Quality Costs Money

Not all commercial PCs are poorly built. Business-class systems and gaming systems from "boutique" vendors are well engineered with top-quality components and high build quality. Of course, they also cost a lot more than consumer-grade systems.

OEM Software Bargains

OEM software prices are striking. For example, when we priced motherboards for a new system in October 2006, with the motherboard we could have bought full OEM versions of Windows XP Home for $64, Windows XP Pro for $95, or Office Pro 2003 for $89. Full OEM versions sell for a small fraction of the price of full retail versions and significantly less than even upgrade-only versions, so if you need the software this is a cheap way to get it.

OEM parts, often as little as 30 to 90 days. The products themselves may also differ significantly between OEM and retail-boxed versions. Major PC vendors often use downgraded versions of popular products, for example, an OEM video adapter that has the same or a very similar name as the retail-boxed product, but runs at a lower clock rate than the retail version. This allows PC makers to pay less for components and still gain the cachet from using the name-brand product.

It's worse when it comes to "invisible" components. We've popped the lid on scores of consumer-grade PCs over the years, and it never ceases to surprise us just how cheaply they're built. Not a one of them had a power supply that we'd even consider using in one of our own systems, for example. They're packed with no-name motherboards, generic memory, the cheapest optical drives available, and so on. Even the cables are often shoddy. After all, why pay a buck more for a decent cable? In terms of reliability, we consider a consumer-grade PC a disaster waiting to happen.

No bundled software

Most purchased PCs include Microsoft Windows, Microsoft Office, or other bundled software. If you don't need or want this software, building a PC allows you to avoid paying the "Microsoft tax."

If you *do* want commercial software, you can buy OEM versions at a bargain price when you buy your hardware components. Buying a hard drive or a motherboard entitles you to buy full OEM versions of the software you need at a large discount. OEM software includes a full license rather than an upgrade license, so you needn't own the product already to benefit from OEM software pricing. OEM software is one of the best-kept secrets in the retail channel. If you need Windows or Office, when your order components ask the vendor if it has OEM versions of the titles you want. OEM versions of Windows and Microsoft applications are "For sale only with a new PC," but Microsoft takes a liberal view of what constitutes a new PC. Buying a hard drive, motherboard, or processor entitles you to buy OEM software.

YOU CAN'T TAKE OEM WITH YOU

OEM versions are "locked" to the system upon which you first install them, so they can't be moved to a new system later on. Full-retail and retail upgrade-only versions can be moved to a new system, as long as you delete them from the old system.

Warranty

The retail-boxed components you'll use to build your own PC include full manufacturer warranties, which may run from one to five years or more, depending on the component. PC makers use OEM components, which often include no manufacturer warranty to the enduser. If something breaks, you're at the mercy of the PC maker to repair or replace it. We've heard from readers who bought PCs from makers who went out of business shortly thereafter. When a hard drive or video card failed six months later, they contacted the maker of the item, only to find that they had OEM components that were not under manufacturer warranty.

Experience

If you buy a computer, your experience with it consists of taking it out of the box and connecting the cables. If you build the computer, you know exactly what went into it, and you're in a much better position to resolve any problems that may occur.

Upgradability

If you design and build your own PC, you can upgrade it later using industry-standard components. That's sometimes not the case with commercial systems, some of which are intentionally designed to be incompatible with industry-standard components. PC makers do this because they want to force you to buy upgrade and replacement components from them, at whatever price they want to charge.

INTENTIONAL GOTCHAS

These designed-in incompatibilities may be as trivial as nonstandard screw sizes, or as profound as components that are electrically incompatible with standard components. For example, in the late '90s some Dell PCs used motherboards and power supplies with standard connectors but nonstandard pin connections. If you replaced a failed Dell power supply with a standard ATX power supply—or if you connected the nonstandard Dell power supply to a standard motherboard—the power supply and motherboard were destroyed as soon as you applied power to the system.

Designing the Perfect PC

A sign you'll see in many repair shops says, "Good. Cheap. Fast. Pick any two." That's also true of designing a PC. Every choice you make involves a trade-off, and balancing those trade-offs is the key to designing a PC that's perfect for your needs. Each of the project system chapters has a graphic that looks something like what's shown to the right.

Ah, if it were only true. Reality, of course, is different. One can't put the highest priority on everything. Something has to give. As Frederick the Great said of designing military defenses, "He who defends everything defends nothing." The same is true of designing a PC.

If you focus on these elements while designing your PC, you'll soon realize that compromises are inevitable. If small size is essential, for example, you

Save Those Receipts

Keep receipts together with the "retain this portion" of warranty cards and put them someplace they can be found if required for future warranty service. This goes for software, too.

DESIGN PRIORITIES	
Price	☆☆☆☆☆
Reliability	☆☆☆☆☆
Size	☆☆☆☆☆
Noise level	☆☆☆☆☆
Expandability	☆☆☆☆☆
Processor performance	☆☆☆☆☆
Video performance	☆☆☆☆☆
Disk capacity/performance	☆☆☆☆☆

must make compromises in expandability, and you may very well have to compromise in other respects. The trick is to decide, before you start buying components, which elements are essential, which are important, which would be nice to have, and which can be ignored.

Once you have the priority of those elements firmly fixed in your mind, you can make rational resource allocations and good purchasing decisions. It's worth looking at each of these elements in a bit more detail.

Price

We put price first, because it's the 900-pound gorilla in system design. If low price is essential, you'll be forced to make compromises in most or all of the other elements. Simply put, high performance, reliability, low noise, small size, and other desirable characteristics cost money. We suggest you begin by establishing a ballpark price range for your new system and then play "what-if" with the other elements. If you've set too low a price, it will soon become clear that you'll need to spend more. On the other hand, you may well find that you can get away with spending less and still get everything you want in a system.

Reliability

We consider high reliability essential in any system, even the least expensive entry-level PC. If a system is unreliable, it doesn't matter how feature-laden it is, or how fast, or how cheap. We always aim for 5-star reliability in systems we design for ourselves and others, although sometimes price and other constraints force us to settle for 4-star reliability. The best mass-market systems may have 3-star reliability, but most deserve only a 1- or 2-star rating.

What does reliability mean, and how do you design for it? A reliable system doesn't crash or corrupt data. It runs for years with only an occasional cleaning. We are always amused when people claim Windows is crash-prone. That is true of Windows 9X, of course, but Windows NT/2000/XP has never blue-screened on us except when there was a hardware problem, and that's going back to the early days of Windows NT 4. We're not Microsoft fanboys—far from it—but the truth is that the vast majority of system crashes that are blamed on Windows are actually caused by marginal or failing hardware.

There are a few simple rules for designing a reliable system. First, use only top-quality parts. They don't have to be the fastest available—in fact high-performance parts often run hotter and are therefore less reliable than midrange ones—but top-quality components may be a full order of magnitude more reliable than run-of-the-mill ones. Use a motherboard built around a reliable chipset and made by a top-notch manufacturer. For Intel processors, Intel motherboards and chipsets are the standard by which we judge, and for AMD processors the same is true of ASUS motherboards and nVIDIA chipsets. Use a first-rate power

A Dissenting View

Our technical reviewer Jim Cooley says, "I disagree. *You* don't load the crap on your machines that Average Joe does, but if you did you'd find most crashes were software related, not hardware."

Jim is right. Years ago, before we migrated to Linux, we were very careful to avoid Windows Rot, going as far as to reinstall Windows from scratch every few months. A fresh Windows install with current drivers is reasonably stable (although not remotely in the same class as Linux), but as you use a Windows system over weeks and months, its stability degrades gradually (or not so gradually).

supply and the best memory available. Avoid cheap cables. Keep the system cool and clean out the dust periodically. That's all there is to it. Following this advice means the system will cost a bit more, but it will also be significantly more reliable.

Size

Most people prefer a small PC to a large one, but it's easy to design a system that's too small. Albert Einstein said, "Everything should be made as simple as possible, but not simpler." In other words, don't oversimplify. Use the same rule when you choose a size for your PC. Don't over-smallify.

Choosing a small case inevitably forces you to make compromises. A small case limits your choice of components, because some components simply won't fit. For example, you may have to use a different optical drive than you'd prefer because your first choice is too long to fit into the case. A small case also limits the number of components you can install. For example, you may have to choose between installing a card reader and installing a second hard drive. Because a small case can accept fewer (and smaller) fans, it's more difficult to cool the system properly. To move the same amount of air, a smaller fan must spin faster than a larger fan, which generates more noise. The limited case volume makes it much harder to work inside the case, and makes it more difficult to route cables to avoid impeding air flow. All other things being equal, a small PC will cost more, run slower, produce more heat and noise, or be less reliable than a standard-size PC, or all of those.

For most purposes, the best choice is a standard mini- or mid-tower case. A full-tower case is an excellent choice for a server, or for an office system that sits on the floor next to your desk. Choose a microATX or other small form factor case only if size is a high priority.

Noise level

Noise level has become a major issue for many people. If you think PCs are getting louder, it's not your imagination. As PCs get faster and faster, they consume more power and produce more heat. The most convenient way to remove heat is to move a lot of air through the case, which requires fans. Fans produce noise.

Just a few years ago, most PCs had only a power supply fan. A typical modern PC may have half a dozen or more fans—the power supply fan, the CPU fan, a couple of supplemental case fans, and perhaps fans for the chipset, video card, and hard drive. All of these fans are needed to keep the components cool, but all of them produce noise. Fortunately, there are methods to cool a PC properly while minimizing noise. We'll look at some of those methods later in this section.

Determining Quality

Of course, this raises the question, how does one tell great from good from bad? Discriminating among companies and brands is difficult for someone who doesn't know which companies have an established reputation for quality and reliability, which purvey mostly junk, and which are too new to have a track record. All of the components and brands we recommend in this book are safe choices, but the proliferation of brands makes it easy to choose inferior components.

If you must use components other than those we recommend, the best way to avoid inferior components is to do your homework. Visit the manufacturers' web sites. A good web site doesn't guarantee that the products are also good, but a poor web site almost certainly means the products are also poor. Check online reviews of products you are considering, and visit discussion forums for those components. In the end, trust your own judgment. If a component appears cheap, it probably isn't reliable. If the documentation is sparse or isn't written in good English, that tells you something about the likely quality of the component as well. If the component has a much shorter warranty than similar components from other manufacturers, there's probably good reason.

Finally, although price is not invariably a perfect predictor of component quality, it's usually a very good indicator. The PC component business is extremely competitive, so if a product sells for much less than similar competing products, it's almost certain that that product is inferior.

Expandability

Expandability is worth considering when you design a PC. For some systems, expandability is unimportant. You design the system for a particular job, install the components you need to do that job, and never open the case again except for routine cleaning and maintenance. For most general-purpose systems, though, expandability is desirable. For example, if you need more disk space, you might prefer to add a second hard drive rather than replace the original drive. You can't do that unless there's a vacant drive bay. Similarly, integrated video might suffice originally, but you may later decide that you need faster video. If the motherboard you used has no AGP or PCI Express (PCIe) video slot, you're out of luck. The only option is to replace the motherboard.

Keep expandability in mind when you choose components, so you won't paint yourself into any corners. Unless size constraints forbid it, choose a case that leaves plenty of room for growth. Choose a power supply that has sufficient reserve to support additional drives, memory, and perhaps a faster processor. Choose a motherboard that provides sufficient expansion slots and memory sockets to allow for possible future expansion. Choose less flexible components only if you are certain that you will never need to expand the system.

Processor performance

Most people worry too much about processor performance. Here's the truth. Midrange processors—those that sell for $150 to $225—are noticeably faster than $50 to $100 entry-level processors. The most expensive processors, which sell for up to $1,000, are noticeably faster than midrange processors. Not night-and-day different, but noticeable. For casual use—browsing the Web, checking email, word processing, and so on—choose a $75 "value" processor from AMD or Intel. For a general-purpose system, choose a Pentium D, Core 2, or Athlon 64 processor that sells for $150 to $225 in retail-boxed form. It makes little sense to choose a high-end processor unless cost is no object and performance is critical.

Video performance

Video performance, like processor performance, usually gets more attention than it deserves. It's probably no coincidence that processors and video adapters are two of the most heavily promoted PC components. When you design your PC, be careful not to get caught up in the hype. If the PC will be used for intense 3D gaming or similarly demanding video tasks, you need a high-end video adapter (or dual video adapters). Otherwise, you don't.

Integrated video—a video adapter built into the motherboard—is the least expensive video solution, and is perfectly adequate for most uses. The incremental cost of integrated video ranges from $0 to perhaps $10, relative to a similar motherboard without integrated video. The next step up in video performance is a standalone video adapter, which requires that the motherboard have a slot to accept it. Standalone video adapters range in price from $25 or so up to $500 or more. The old 80/20 rule applies to video adapters, which is to say that a $100 video adapter provides most of the performance and features of a $500 adapter.

More expensive video adapters provide incrementally faster 3D video performance and may support more recent versions of Microsoft DirectX, both of which are of interest to serious gamers. Expensive video adapters also run hot and are generally equipped with dedicated cooling fans, which produce additional noise.

When you design your PC, we recommend using integrated video unless you need the faster 3D performance a standalone video adapter can provide. If you choose integrated video, make sure the motherboard has an AGP or PCIe slot available in case you later decide to upgrade the video.

Disk capacity/performance

A mainstream 7,200 RPM ATA or Serial ATA hard drive is the best choice for nearly any system. Such drives are fast, cheap, and reliable. The best models are also relatively quiet and produce little heat. When you design your system, use one of these drives (or two, mirrored for data protection) unless you have good reason to do otherwise. Choose a 10,000 RPM ATA drive if you need the highest possible disk performance—as for a server or personal workstation—and are willing to pay the price. Avoid 5,400 RPM ATA drives, which cost only a few bucks less than 7,200 RPM models, but have noticeably poorer performance.

See Chapter 2 for specific component recommendations.

Balanced Design

Novice PC builders often ignore the important concept of balanced design. Balanced design means allocating your component budget to avoid bottlenecks. If you're designing a gaming PC, for example, it makes no sense to spend $50 on the processor and $500 on the video card. The resulting system is nonoptimal because the slow processor is a bottleneck that prevents the expensive video adapter from performing to its full potential.

The main enemy of balanced design is the constant hype of manufacturer advertising and enthusiast web sites (which sometimes amount to the same thing). It's easy to fixate on the latest "must-have" component, even though its price may be much too high to justify. Many people just can't help themselves. Despite their best intentions, they end up spending $700 for a premium LCD display when a $400 model would have done just as well, or they buy a $400 video adapter when a $150 adapter would suffice. If your budget is unlimited, fine. Go for the latest and best. But if you're building a

AGP Versus PCIe

AGP is an older video adapter interface that is gradually being replaced by the newer PCIe interface. Many AGP motherboards and video adapters are still available—and are likely to remain so for quite some time—but AGP is a dying standard. For example, when we searched the NewEgg site in November 2006, we found 150 AGP video adapter models available, versus 356 PCIe models. When we did that search a few months earlier, there were about 200 AGP models, versus about 300 PCIe models.

AGP video adapters and motherboards, with few exceptions, are restricted to older technology. The latest and fastest video and motherboard chipsets and support for the fastest memory are available only in PCIe models. Although it may seem a bad idea to buy into an obsolescent technology like AGP, an AGP-based motherboard is often a good and economical choice, particularly for a system you are building on a tight budget.

system to a fixed budget, every dollar you spend needlessly on one component is a dollar less you have to spend somewhere else, where it might make more difference.

Balanced design does not necessarily mean giving equal priority to all system components. For example, we have built servers in which the disk arrays and tape backup drive cost more than $10,000 and the rest of the system components totaled less than $2,000. A balanced design is one that takes into account the tasks the system must perform and allocates resources to optimize performance for those tasks.

But balanced design takes into consideration more than simple performance. A truly balanced design accommodates nonperformance issues such as physical size, noise level, reliability, and efficient cooling. You might, for example, have to choose a less expensive processor or a smaller hard drive in order to reserve sufficient funds for a quieter case or a more reliable power supply.

The key to achieving a balanced design is to determine your requirements, look dispassionately at the available alternatives, and choose accordingly. That can be tougher than it sounds.

Designing a Quiet PC

The ongoing PC performance race has had the unfortunate side effect of making PCs noisier. Faster processors use more power, which in turn requires larger (and noisier) power supplies. Faster processors also produce more heat, which requires larger (and noisier) CPU coolers. Modern hard drives spin faster than older models, producing still more noise and heat. Fast video adapters have their own cooling fans, which add to the din. The days when a high-performance PC sat under your desk making an unobtrusive hum are long gone.

Fortunately, there are steps you can take to reduce the amount of noise your PC produces. No PC with moving parts is completely silent, but significant noise reductions are possible. Depending on your requirements and budget, you can build a PC that is anything from quietly unobtrusive to nearly silent. The key to building a noise-reduced PC is to recognize the sources of noise and to minimize or eliminate noise at the source.

The major sources of noise are typically the power supply, CPU cooler fan, and supplementary case fans. Minor sources of noise include the hard drive, chipset fan, video adapter fan, and optical drive. As you design your PC, focus first on major noise sources that can be minimized inexpensively, then minor noise sources that are cheap to deal with, then major noise sources that are more expensive or difficult to minimize, and finally (if necessary) minor noise sources that are expensive or difficult to fix. Use the following guidelines:

Choose a low-power processor

The amount of power consumed by the processor has a direct effect on the noise level of the system. The peak power consumption of mainstream processors ranges from less than 70W to more than 130W. That power ends up as waste heat that must be exhausted from the case. Using a lower-power processor produces less waste heat, which in turn allows you to use a quieter CPU cooler, fewer and quieter case fans, and so on.

Power consumption isn't necessarily proportional to processor performance. For example, an AMD Athlon 64 X2 that draws 70W peak power may be faster than an Intel Pentium D that draws 130W, and an Intel Core 2 Duo processor that draws only 60W may be faster than either, at least for some tasks. None of this is to say that there's anything wrong with choosing a high-wattage processor, but doing so complicates cooling and noise issues.

Choose a quiet case

Inexpensive cases are designed with little thought to noise abatement. Better cases incorporate numerous design features that reduce noise, including large, slow-spinning exhaust fans, sound-absorbing composite panels, rubber shock mounts for drives that isolate vibration, and so on. We cover case considerations thoroughly in the next chapter.

Choose a quiet power supply

In most systems, the power supply is potentially the first or second largest noise source, so minimizing power supply noise is critical.

- At the first level, choose a noise-reduced power supply, such as the Antec TruePower (*http://www.antec.com*) or PC Power & Cooling Silencer (*http://www.pcpowercooling.com*) models we recommend in the next chapter. Such power supplies cost little or no more than competing models of equivalent capacity and quality, and are noticeably quieter. A system that uses one of these power supplies can be quiet enough to be unobtrusive in a normal residential environment.

- The next step down in noise level is a power supply that is specifically designed to minimize noise, such as the Antec NeoHE series, Enermax NoiseTaker series (*http://www.enermaxusa.com*), or Seasonic S12 series (*http://www.seasonicusa.com*). These power supplies cost a bit more than comparable noise-reduced power supplies, but produce as little as 18 dB at idle, and not much more under load. A system that uses one of these power supplies (and other similarly quiet components) can be nearly inaudible in a normal residential environment.

- Finally, there are power supplies that substitute huge passive heatsinks for cooling fans. These power supplies, such as the

Monitoring CPU Temperature

Most modern motherboards provide temperature sensors at important points such as the CPU socket. The motherboard reports the temperatures reported by these sensors to the BIOS. You can view these temperatures by running BIOS Setup and choosing the option for temperature reporting, which can usually be found under Advanced Hardware Monitoring, or a similar menu option. Alternatively, most motherboards include a monitoring utility–Intel's, for example, is called the Intel Active Monitor–that allows you to monitor temperatures from Windows rather than having to run BIOS Setup.

CPU temperature can vary dramatically with changes in load. For example, a CPU that idles at 30°C may reach 50°C or higher when it is running at 100% capacity. A hot-running modern processor such as a fast Pentium D may reach temperatures of 70°C or higher under load, which is perilously close to the maximum acceptable temperature for that processor. It is therefore very important to verify that your CPU cooler and system fans are doing their jobs properly.

An idle temperature of 30°C or lower is ideal, but that is not achievable with the hottest processors, which idle at 40°C or higher with any but the most efficient CPU coolers. In general, a CPU cooler that produces an idle temperature of 40°C or lower suffices to cool the CPU properly under load.

(continued)

Antec Phantom 350 and the Silverstone ST30NF (*http://www.silverstonetek.com*), have no moving parts, and the only noise they produce is a slight buzz from the electronic components. (The Antec Phantom 500 includes an "emergency" fan that runs only if the power supply begins to overheat. Up to 200W or so, the fan doesn't run and the power supply is completely silent; above 200W, the fan kicks in, and this power supply becomes a bit louder than the best quiet fan-based power supplies.)

Choose an efficient power supply

Power supply efficiency has a direct bearing on system noise level. Every power supply requires higher input power than the output power it provides, and that power difference is converted to heat within the power supply. For example, if the system actually requires 200W from the power supply, a 67% efficient power supply draws 300W of input power to provide that 200W of output power (200W/0.67 = 300W). That extra 100W is converted to heat within the power supply. An 85% efficient power supply requires only about 235W of input power to provide 200W of output power. The difference between 300W input and 235W input power translates to an extra 65W of heat within your system. The efficiency of mainstream power supply models ranges from about 65% to about 85%.

Choose a quiet CPU cooler

As processor speeds have increased over the last few years, manufacturers have gone from using passive heatsinks to using heatsinks with slow, quiet fans to using heatsinks with fast, loud fans. Current processors differ greatly in power consumption from model to model. At the lower end of the range—less than 50W—nearly any decent CPU cooler can do the job with minimal noise, including the stock CPU coolers bundled with retail-boxed processors and inexpensive third-party units. At the middle of the range—50W to 90W—standard CPU coolers begin to produce intrusive noise levels, although specialty quiet CPU coolers can cool a midrange processor with little or no noise. At the upper end of the range, even the quietest fan-based CPU coolers produce some noise.

- For a processor with low to moderate power consumption, try using the stock CPU cooler supplied with the retail-boxed processor. If it produces too much noise, install an in-line resistor to reduce the voltage supplied to the fan, which reduces fan speed and noise. Resistor kits (sometimes called voltage or fan speed controllers) are sold by quiet-PC vendors such as FrozenCPU (*http://www.frozencpu.com*), QuietPC USA (*http://www.quietpcusa.com*), and Endpcnoise.com (*http://www.endpcnoise.com*).

- For processors with high power consumption, there are several alternatives. Some of the CPU coolers bundled with Intel Pentium D processors are reasonably quiet in stock form, and can be quieted further while still providing adequate cooling by using an in-line resistor to drop the supply voltage to 7V. However, Intel uses different CPU cooler models and changes them without notice, so which you get is hit or miss. For the quietest possible fan-based cooler, you can install a premium CPU cooler from manufacturers such as Thermalright (*http://www.thermalright.com*) and Zalman (*http://www.zalmanusa.com*).

- To minimize noise for any processor, install a Thermalright or Zalman unit. For processors with low to midrange power consumption, some of these premium coolers can be run in silent (fanless) mode, which completely eliminates CPU cooler noise.

Choose quiet case fans

Most modern systems have at least one supplemental case fan, and some have several. The more loaded the system, the more supplemental cooling you'll need to use. Use the following guidelines when selecting case fans:

- Case fans are available in various sizes from 60mm to 120mm or larger. All other things being equal, a larger fan can move the same amount of air with less noise than a smaller fan, because the larger fan doesn't need to spin as fast. Of course, the fan mounting positions in most cases are of fixed size, so you may have little choice about which size fan(s) to use. If you do have a choice—for example, if the case has two or three fan positions of different size—use the largest fan that fits.

- Case fans vary significantly in noise level, even for the same size and rotation speed. Many factors come into play, including blade design, type of bearings, grill type, and so on. In general, ball bearing fans are noisier but more durable than fans that use needle or sleeve bearings.

- The noise level of a fan can be reduced by running it at a lower speed, as long as it moves enough air to provide proper cooling. The simplest method to reduce fan speed is to install an in-line resistor to reduce the supply voltage to 7V. These are available from the sources listed above, or you can make your own with a resistor from RadioShack or another electronics supply store. Some fans include a control panel, which mounts in an available external drive bay and allows you to control fan speed continuously from zero to maximum by adjusting a knob. Finally, some fans are designed to be controlled by the power supply or a motherboard fan connector. These fans vary their speed automatically in response to the ambient temperature, running at high speed when the system is heavily loaded and producing lots of heat, and low speed when the system is idle.

Monitoring CPU Temperature *(continued)*

If you want to verify temperature under load, run an application that loads the CPU with intense calculations, ideally with lots of floating-point operations. Two such applications we have used are the SETI@home client (*http://setiathome.ssl.berkeley.edu*) and the Mersenne Prime client (*http://mersenne.org*). Run the application for an hour to ensure that the CPU has reached a steady-state temperature, and then use the temperature monitoring application to view the temperature while the application is still running.

CPU Coolers and Motherboard Compatibility

If you choose an aftermarket CPU cooler, verify that it is physically compatible with your motherboard. Quiet CPU coolers often use very large heatsinks, which may conflict with protruding capacitors and other motherboard components. Most premium CPU cooler manufacturers post compatibility lists on their web sites.

- The mounting method you use makes a difference. Most case fans are secured directly to the chassis with metal screws. This transfers vibration directly to the chassis panels, which act as sounding boards. A better method is to use soft plastic snap-in connectors rather than screws. These connectors isolate vibration to the fan itself. Better still is to use the soft plastic snap-in connectors in conjunction with a foam surround that insulates the fan frame from the chassis entirely.

The preceding six elements are the major steps required to quietize your PC. Once you minimize noise from those major sources, you can also take the following steps to reduce noise from minor sources. Some of these steps cost little or nothing to implement, and all contribute to quieting the PC.

Put the PC on a mat

Rather than put the PC directly on your desk or the floor, put a sound-deadening mat between it and the surface. You can buy special mats for this purpose, but we've used objects as simple as a couple of mouse pads, front and rear, to accomplish the same thing. The amount of noise reduction from this simple step can be surprisingly large.

Choose a quiet hard drive

Once you've addressed the major noise sources, hard drive noise may become noticeable, particularly during seeks. The best way to reduce hard drive noise is to choose a quiet hard drive in the first place. Seagate Barracuda ATA and SATA models are the quietest mainstream hard drives. To reduce hard drive noise further you can use a Smart Drive Enclosure or the Zalman Hard Drive Heatpipe, both of which are available from the sources listed above.

Choose a video card with a passive heatsink

All video adapter chipsets produce significant heat, but most use a passive heatsink rather than a fan-based cooler. If possible, choose a video adapter with a passive heatsink. If you must use a high-end video adapter with a fan-based cooler, consider replacing that cooler with a Zalman Video Heatpipe. The small fans used on video adapters typically run at high speeds and are quite noisy, so replacing the cooler with a passive device can reduce noise noticeably.

Choose a motherboard with a passive heatsink

The north bridge chip of modern chipsets dissipates significant heat. Most motherboards cool this chip with a large passive heatsink (see, for example, Figure 1-5), but some use a fan-based cooler. Again, these coolers typically use small, fast fans that produce significant noise. If you have a choice, pick a motherboard with a passive heatsink. If you must use a motherboard with a fan-based chipset cooler, consider replacing that cooler with a Zalman Motherboard Heatsink.

Silent PC Review

Silent PC Review (*http://www.silent-pcreview.com*) is an excellent source of information about quiet PC issues. The site includes numerous articles about reducing PC noise, as well as reviews of quiet PC components, a forum, and other resources.

Designing a Small PC

At the beginning of the millennium, some forward-thinking PC builders and manufacturers began to design and build PCs smaller and/or more portable than traditional mini-tower systems. Small PCs have become extremely popular, and it's no wonder. These systems are small, light, easily portable, and fit just about anywhere. In order of decreasing size, small/portable PCs fall into four broad categories:

LAN party PC

A LAN Party PC is essentially a standard ATX mini- or mid-tower system with a handle and other modifications to increase portability, port accessibility, and other factors important in a "totable" PC. Most LAN party cases are constructed largely of aluminum to minimize weight and maximize cooling efficiency. LAN party PCs are often "tricked-out" with colorful motherboards, clear side panels, fluorescent lights, fans, and cables, and similar visual enhancements. Despite the customizations, LAN party PCs are based on industry-standard components and are as capable as any standard PC.

microATX PC

A microATX PC is basically a cut-down version of a standard ATX PC. The microATX case and motherboard are smaller and provide less expandability, but are otherwise comparable in features and functionality to a standard ATX system. The great advantage of microATX PCs relative to the smaller styles described next is that microATX PCs use industry-standard components. microATX cases are available in two styles. Slimline cases are about the size and shape of a VCR. "Cube" cases are typically 8" tall and roughly a foot wide and deep. The relatively small case capacity makes cooling more difficult and puts some restraints on the number and type of hard drives, expansion cards, and other peripherals you can install, but it is possible to build a reliable, high-performance PC in the microATX form factor.

Small Form Factor (SFF) PC

Small Form Factor (SFF) means different things to different people. We use the term to mean the cube-style form factor pioneered by Shuttle (*http://us.shuttle.com*) with their XPC models. In fact, Shuttle says that SFF stands for Shuttle Form Factor. Other companies, including Soltek, Biostar, and others, now produce cube-style SFF systems. These true SFF systems use proprietary cases, power supplies, I/O templates, and motherboards, which limits their flexibility. In effect, "building" an SFF system consists of buying a bare-bones system with case, power supply, and motherboard, and adding your choice of memory, drives, video adapter, and so on. SFF PCs are typically more expensive, slower, and less reliable than standard-size or microATX PCs, but they are noticeably smaller.

Small Outside Means Small Inside

The limited space available in cube-style SFF cases restricts component choice. For example, you may have to purchase special low-profile memory modules and you may not be able to install full-length, standard-height expansion cards. The tiny case volume also makes heat dissipation critical. For example, you may not be able to use the fastest available processors because the case is not capable of cooling them sufficiently.

Mini-ITX PC

Mini-ITX is a semi-proprietary form factor pioneered by VIA Technologies. Although a few minor third-party manufacturers supply Mini-ITX components, VIA products dominate the Mini-ITX market. Mini-ITX motherboards are 170mm (6.7") square, and are in effect smaller versions of microATX motherboards. Although Mini-ITX motherboards are available that accept Socket 479 Intel Pentium M and Intel Celeron M processors, the majority of Mini-ITX systems use VIA motherboards with embedded processors.. These processors are very slow relative to modern AMD and Intel processors, and Mini-ITX motherboards are relatively expensive. Even so, Mini-ITX has its place, for systems that do not require high performance but need to be small and very quiet. Mini-ITX motherboards are so small that they can be built into enclosures as small as a cigar box (literally), and the flip side to low processor performance is that these processors consume little power and produce little heat. Most Mini-ITX systems use passive cooling and "wall-wart" power supplies, which eliminates fan noise and allows the system to be almost totally silent. Mini-ITX is most appropriate for such "appliance" applications as small Linux servers, routers, and satellite DVR playback-only systems.

Table 1-1 lists the characteristics of each of these system types relative to a standard mini/mid-tower desktop system, using the rankings of Excellent (E), Very Good (VG), Good (G), Fair (F), and Poor (P).

Table 1-1 presents best-case scenarios for each of the form factors. For example, not all standard desktop systems have excellent performance, nor are all of them extremely quiet.

Table 1-1. Small system strengths and weaknesses

	Desktop	LAN party	microATX	SFF	Mini-ITX
Typical case volume (liters)	35 to 60	25 to 40	12 to 20	8 to 12	2.5 to 9
Size	P to F	F to G	G to VG	VG to E	E
Cost efficiency	E	VG	E	P to F	P to F
Reliability	E	F to VG	VG to E	F to VG	F to VG
Portability	P	VG to E	F to VG	VG to E	VG to E
Noise level	VG to E	F to VG	VG to E	P to VG	E
Cooling	E	G to E	G to VG	P to F	F to E
Upgradability/expandability	E	VG to E	F to VG	F to G	P
Processor performance	E	E	VG to E	VG to E	P
Graphics performance	E	E	VG to E	F to E	P
Disk capacity/performance	E	E	G to VG	G to VG	P

Rather, this table presents the best that can be done within the limitations of each form factor, which may vary according to the specific components you select.

If you need to design a small PC, recognize that each step down from standard mini-tower size involves additional compromises in performance, cost, reliability, noise level, and other key criteria. Reducing case size limits the number and type of components you can install and makes it more difficult to cool the system effectively. It also makes it harder to quiet the PC. For example, small cases often use relatively loud power supplies. Because the power supply is proprietary, installing an aftermarket quiet power supply is not an option. Similarly, using a small case forces you to trade off performance against cooling against noise. For example, you may be forced to use a slower processor than you'd like, because the necessary CPU cooler for a faster processor is too large to fit in the available space or is louder than acceptable.

When it comes to designing small PCs, our rule is to use a standard mini-tower system whenever possible. If that's too large, step down to a micro-ATX system. If a microATX system is too large, we suggest you rethink your priorities. Perhaps you could free some additional space by moving things around, or perhaps you could place the PC in a different position. Try hard to avoid using any form factor smaller than microATX.

Then, if and only if you are certain that the trade-offs are worth it, buy a bare-bones SFF system and build it out to meet your requirements. We don't think of Mini-ITX systems as direct competitors to traditional PCs at all. They're simply too slow to be taken seriously as a mainstream PC. Instead, we suggest you consider Mini-ITX systems to be special, relatively expensive, low-performance computing appliances that are suitable only for very specialized applications.

Things to Know and Do Before You Start

We've built many systems over the years, and we've learned a lot of lessons the hard way. Here are some things to keep in mind as you begin your project.

Make sure you have everything you need before you start

Have all of the hardware, software, and tools you'll need lined up and waiting. You don't want to have to stop in mid-build to go off in search of a small Phillips screwdriver or to drive to the store to buy a cable. If your luck is anything like ours, you won't find the screwdriver you need and the store will be closed. In addition to tools and components, make sure you have the distribution CDs for the operating system, service packs, device drivers, diagnostics utilities, and any other software you'll need to complete the build.

Missing Pieces

Don't assume that every box contains what it's supposed to. Before you begin the build, open every box and verify its contents against the packing list. Quite often, we open a new component box only to find that the driver CD, manual, cable, or some other small component that should have been included is missing. On one memorable occasion, we opened a new, shrink-wrapped video adapter box only to find that everything was present except the video adapter itself!

Don't Forget the Manuals

While you're at it, download all of the documentation you can find for each component. Quite often, the detailed documentation intended for system builders is not included in the component box. The only way to get it is to download it.

RTFM

Read the fine manuals, if only the Quick Start sections. Surprisingly, while system manuals are notoriously awful, many component manuals are actually quite good. You'll find all sorts of hints and tips, from the best way to install the component to suggestions on optimizing its performance.

DO AS WE SAY...

Okay, we admit it. We almost never read the manuals, but then we can just about build a system blindfolded. Until you're proficient, reading the manuals before you proceed is the best way to guarantee that your new PC will, um, work.

Download the latest drivers

Although PC component inventories turn over quickly, the CDs included with components usually don't contain the most recent drivers. Some manufacturers don't update their driver CDs very often, so the bundled drivers may be a year or more out of date, even if the component itself was made recently. Before you begin building a PC, visit the web site for each of your components and download the most recent driver and BIOS updates for each. (Bookmark the URLs so you can easily find updates later.) Unpack or unzip them if necessary, burn them to CD, and label the CD. You may choose to install drivers from the bundled CD—in fact, at times it's necessary to do so because the downloadable updates do not include everything that's on the CD—but you want to have those later drivers available so that you can update your system immediately.

Ground yourself before touching components

Processors, memory modules, and other electronic components—including the circuit boards in drives—are sensitive to static shock. Static electricity can damage components even if the voltage is too low for you to see or feel a static spark. The best way to avoid static damage to components is to get in the habit of grounding yourself before you touch any sensitive component. You can buy special antistatic wrist straps and similar devices, but they're really not necessary. All you need do is touch a metal object like the chassis or power supply before you handle components.

Keep track of the screws and other small parts

Building a PC yields an incredible number of small pieces that need to be kept organized. As you open each component box, your pile of screws, cables, mounting brackets, adapters, and other small parts grows larger. Some of those you'll need, and some you won't. As we can attest, one errant screw left on the floor can destroy a vacuum cleaner. Worse, one unnoticed screw can short out and destroy the motherboard and other components. The best solution we've found is to use an egg carton or old ice cube tray to keep parts organized. The goal is to have all of the small parts accounted for when you finish assembling the PC.

A SNAKE IN THE WOODPILE

Some PCs use a variety of screws that look very similar but are in fact threaded differently. For example, the screws used to secure some case covers and those used to mount some disk drives may appear to be identical, but swapping them may result in stripped threads. If in doubt, keep each type of screw in a separate compartment of your organizer.

Use force when necessary, but use it cautiously

Many books tell you never to force anything, and that's good advice as far as it goes. If doing something requires excessive force, chances are a part is misaligned, you have not removed a screw, or something similar. But sometimes there is no alternative to applying force judiciously. For example, drive power cables sometimes fit so tightly that the only way to connect them is to grab them with pliers and press hard. (Make sure all the contacts are aligned first.) Some combinations of expansion card and slot fit so tightly that you must press very hard to seat the card. If you encounter such a situation, verify that everything is lined up and otherwise as it should be (and that there isn't a stray wire obstructing the slot). Then use whatever force it takes to do the job, which may be substantial.

Check and recheck before you apply power

An experienced PC technician building a PC does a quick scan of the new PC before performing the smoke test by applying power to the PC (if you don't see any smoke, it passes the test). Don't skip this step, and don't underestimate its importance. Most PCs that fail the smoke test do so because this step was ignored. Until you gain experience, it may take several minutes to verify that all is as it should be—all components secure, all cables connected properly, no tools or other metal parts shorting anything out, and so on. Once you are comfortable working inside PCs, this step takes 15 seconds, but that may be the most important 15 seconds of the whole project.

Static Guard

To minimize problems with static, wear wool or cotton clothing and avoid rubber-soled shoes. Static problems increase when the air is dry, as is common in winter when central heating systems are in use. You can reduce or eliminate static with a spray bottle filled with water to which you've added a few drops of dishwashing liquid. Spritz your work area thoroughly immediately before you begin working. The goal is not to get anything wet, but simply to increase the humidity of the air. (Whatever you do, avoid wetting the case or components themselves, especially the connectors and slots, which must be kept clean and dry at all times.)

A Screw Loose Somewhere

After we build a system, we pick it up, shake it gently, and tilt it front-to-back and side-to-side. If something rattles, we know there's a screw loose somewhere.

This Probably Won't Happen to You

Don't let this warning put you off building a PC. If you choose good components, assemble them carefully, and double-check everything before you apply power, the probability of catastrophic failure is probably about the same as the probability you'll be hit by lightning or win the lottery.

Start small for the first boot

The moment of greatest danger comes when you power up the PC for the first time. If the system fails catastrophically—which sometimes happens no matter how careful you are—don't smoke more than you have to. For example, the SOHO Server project system we built for this book uses four hard drives and two memory modules. When we built that system, we installed only one drive and one memory module initially. That way, if something shorted out when we first applied power, we'd destroy only one drive and memory module rather than all of them. For that reason, we suggest starting with a minimum configuration—motherboard, processor, one memory stick, video, and one hard drive. Once you're satisfied that all is well, you can add your optical and other drives, additional memory, expansion cards, and so on.

Leave the cover off until you're sure everything works

Experts build and test the PC completely before putting the lid back on and connecting the external cables. Novices build the PC, reassemble the case, reconnect all the cables, and *then* test it.

COVER UP

The corollary to this rule is that you should *always* put the cover back on the case once the upgrade is complete and tested. Some believe that leaving the cover off improves cooling. Wrong. Cases do not depend on convection cooling, which is the only kind you get with the cover off. Cases are designed to direct cooling air across the major heat-generating components, processors, and drives, but this engineering is useless if you run the PC uncovered. Replace the cover to avoid overheating components.

Another good reason to replace the cover is that running a system without the cover releases copious amounts of RF to the surrounding environment. An uncovered system can interfere with radios, monitors, televisions, and other electronic components over a wide radius.

Things You Need to Have

The following sections detail the items you should have at hand before you actually start building your new system. Make a checklist and make sure you check off each item before you begin. There are few things more frustrating than being forced to stop in mid-build when you belatedly realize you're missing a cable or other small component.

Components

Building a PC requires at least the following components. Have all of them available before you start to build the system. Open each component box and verify the contents against the packing list before you actually start the build.

- ❏ Case and power supply, with power cord
- ❏ Motherboard, with custom I/O template, if needed
- ❏ Processor
- ❏ CPU cooler, with thermal compound or pad
- ❏ Memory module(s)
- ❏ Hard drive(s), cable(s) (and SATA power adapter(s), if applicable)
- ❏ Optical drive, with data cable (and audio cable, if applicable)
- ❏ Floppy drive and cable (if applicable)
- ❏ Tape drive, cable, and tape cartridge (if applicable)
- ❏ Card reader and cable (if applicable)
- ❏ Video adapter, unless embedded
- ❏ Sound adapter, unless embedded
- ❏ Network adapter, unless embedded
- ❏ Any other expansion cards (if applicable)
- ❏ Supplementary case fan(s)
- ❏ Keyboard, mouse, display, and other external peripherals
- ❏ Screws, brackets, drive rails, and other connecting hardware

Hand Tools and Supplies

You really don't need many tools to build a PC. We built one PC using only our Swiss Army knife, just to prove it could be done. Figure 1-1 shows our basic PC-building toolkit. Yep. It's true. You can build every PC in this book using only a #1 Phillips screwdriver. It's a bit small for the largest screws and a bit large for the smallest, but it works.

Figure 1-1. A basic PC toolkit

It's helpful to have more tools, of course. Needle-nose pliers are useful for setting jumpers. A flashlight is often useful, even if your work area is well lit. A 5mm (or, rarely, 6mm) nutdriver makes it faster to install the brass standoffs that support the motherboard. A larger assortment of screwdrivers can also be helpful.

Non-Fatal Attraction

Don't worry about using magnetized tools. Despite the common warnings about doing so, we've used magnetized screwdrivers for years without any problem. They are quite handy for picking up dropped screws and so on. Use commonsense precautions, such as avoiding putting the magnetized tips near the flat surface of a hard drive or near any floppy disk, tape, or other magnetic media.

You may also find it useful to have some nylon cable ties (not the paper-covered-wire type of twist tie) for dressing cables after you build the system. Canned air and a clean microfiber dust cloth are useful for cleaning components that you are migrating from an older system. A new eraser is helpful for cleaning contacts if you mistakenly grab an expansion card by the connector tab.

Software Tools

In addition to hand tools, you should have the following software tools available when you build your system. Some are useful when you build the system, others to diagnose problems. We keep copies of our standard software tools with our toolkit. That way, we have everything we need in one place. Here are the software tools we recommend:

Operating system distribution discs

OS distribution discs are needed when you build a system, and may also be needed later to update system software or install a peripheral. We always burn copies of the distribution discs to CD-R or DVD+R and keep a copy with our toolkit. If you use Windows or another nonfree operating system, remember to record the initialization key, serial number, and other data you'll need to install the software. Use a felt-tip permanent marker to record this data directly onto the disc immediately after you burn it. It also helps to record the same information on a small piece of paper so that you'll have it available while the disc is in the drive.

Service packs and critical updates

Rather than (or in addition to) updating Windows and Office online, download the latest service packs and critical updates and burn them to CD-R. In addition to giving you more control of the process, having these updates on CD-R means you can apply them even when the system has no Internet connection, such as when you're building it on your kitchen table.

USE SOME PROTECTION

It's a very bad idea to connect a PC directly to the Internet, and that's especially true for an unpatched system. Several of our readers have reported having a new system infected by a worm almost instantly when they connected to the Internet, intending to download patches and updates. Patch the new system *before* you connect it to the Internet, and never connect it directly to the Internet. Use a NAT/router between any PC and your broadband modem.

Major applications discs

If your system runs Microsoft Office or other major applications that are distributed on CDs, keep a copy of those discs with your toolkit. Again, don't forget to record the serial number, initialization keys, and other required data on the disc itself and on a supplementary note.

Driver CDs

Motherboards, video adapters, sound cards, and many other components include a driver CD in the box. Those drivers may not be essential for installing the component—the Windows or Linux distribution CD may (or may not) include basic drivers for the component—but it's generally a good idea to use the driver CD supplied with the component (or an updated version downloaded from the web site) rather than using those supplied with the OS, if any.

FIRST THINGS FIRST

Pay close attention to the instructions that come with the driver. Most drivers can be installed with the hardware they support already installed. But some drivers, particularly those for some USB devices, need to be installed *before* the hardware is installed.

In addition to basic drivers, the driver CD may include supporting applications. For example, a video adapter CD may include a system tray application for managing video properties, while a sound card may include a bundled application for sound recording and editing. We generally use the bundled driver CD for initial installation and then download and install any updated drivers available on the product web site. Keep a copy of the original driver CD and a CD-R with updated drivers in your toolkit.

Hard drive installation/diagnostic utility

We're always amazed that so few people use the installation and diagnostic software supplied with hard drives. Perhaps that's because many people buy OEM hard drives, which include only the bare drive. Retail-boxed drives invariably include a utilities CD. Most people ignore it, which is a mistake.

Seagate, for example, provides DiscWizard installation software and SeaTools diagnostic software. If you're building a system, you can use the bootable floppy or bootable CD version of DiscWizard to partition, format, and test the new drive automatically. If you're adding a drive, you can use the Windows version of DiscWizard to install, prepare, and configure the new drive automatically. You can configure the new drive as a secondary drive, keeping the original drive as the boot drive. You can specify that the new drive be the sole drive in the system, and DiscWizard automatically migrates your programs and data from the old drive. Finally, you can choose to make the new drive the primary (boot) drive, and make the old drive the secondary drive. DiscWizard does all of this automatically, saving you considerable manual effort.

Driver Education

Keep original driver CDs stored safely. They may be more valuable than you think. More than once, we've lost track of original driver CDs, thinking we could always just download the latest driver from the manufacturer's web site. Alas, a company may go out of business, or its web site may be down just when you desperately need a driver. Worse still, some companies charge for drivers that were originally freely downloadable. That's one reason we don't buy HP products.

HARD DRIVE DIAGNOSTICS

All hard drive makers provide installation and diagnostic utilities. Maxtor, for example, distributes MaxBlast installation software and Powermax diagnostic utilities. If you buy an OEM hard drive or lose the original CD, you can download the utilities from the manufacturer's web site. For obvious reasons, many of these utilities work only if a hard drive made by that manufacturer is installed.

Diagnostic utilities

Catch-22. Diagnostic utilities are of limited use in building a new system, because if the PC works well enough to load and run them, you don't need to diagnose it. Conversely, when you need to diagnose the PC, it's not working well enough to run the diagnostic utility. Duh. (Diagnostic utilities can be helpful on older systems; for example, to detect memory problems or a failing hard drive.) The only diagnostic utility we use routinely when building systems is a Knoppix Live Linux CD (*http://www.knoppix.com*). With Knoppix, you can boot and run Linux completely from the CD, without writing anything to the hard drive. Knoppix has superb hardware detection—better than Windows—and can be useful for diagnosing problems on a newly built system that refuses to load Windows.

TEST YOUR MEMORY

Many system builders routinely run a memory diagnostic to ensure the system functions before installing the operating system. One excellent utility for this purpose is MEMTEST86 (*http://www.memtest86.com*). It's free, and self-boots from a CD-ROM or floppy drive, and can also be loaded via a Linux bootloader. Best of all, it does a great job testing the otherwise difficult to diagnose memory subsystem. The Knoppix Live CD can run MEMTEST86 from its boot menu.

Burn-in utilities

PC components generally fail quickly or live a long time. If a component survives the first 24 hours, it's likely to run without problems for years. The vast majority of early failures are immediate, caused by DOA components. Something like 99% of the remaining early failures occur within 24 hours, so it's worth "burning in" a new system before you spend hours installing and configuring the operating system and applications.

Many people simply turn on the system and let it run for a day or two. That's better than nothing, but an idling system doesn't stress all components. A better way is to run software that accesses and exercises all of the components. One good (and free) ad hoc way to burn in a system is to repeatedly compile a Linux kernel, and we sometimes use that method. We generally use special burn-in software, however, and the best product we know of for that purpose is BurnInTest from PassMark Software (*http://www.passmark.com*).

Getting to Know Your Motherboard

A motherboard is so complex and has so many components and connections that it can be overwhelming to someone who is not used to working inside PCs. All of the other system components connect to and are controlled by the motherboard, so it's important to be able to identify the major parts of the motherboard. As is true of many things, the easiest way to understand the working of the whole is to understand the working of the individual parts. So let's take the $2 tour of a modern motherboard, where you'll learn the functions of each important component and how to identify those components visually.

This section includes photographs of each of these components to help you visually identify items. The details and layout vary from model to model, but all modern motherboards include these or similar components. Once you're able to locate and identify the major components on any motherboard you should be able to do the same on any other motherboard.

To begin, let's examine a block diagram of a chipset. Figure 1-2 shows the major components and functions of the Intel 925XE chipset. (Other modern chipsets are similar.) The 925XE chipset uses two physical chips. The north bridge chip, which Intel calls the MCH (Memory Controller Hub), is the blue box labeled 82925X MCH. The MCH arbitrates and coordinates communications between the processor, memory, and the PCI Express video adapter. The MCH provides very high bandwidth channels: 6.4 GB/s between the MCH and processor; 8.0 GB/s between the MCH and the video adapter; and 8.5 GB/s between the MCH and memory.

Once You Label Me, You Negate Me

Most motherboards include a reference label to show the location of connectors, jumpers, and other key components. Place this label inside the case after assembly so you'll have key configuration information readily available if you open the case to install additional components or troubleshoot problems.

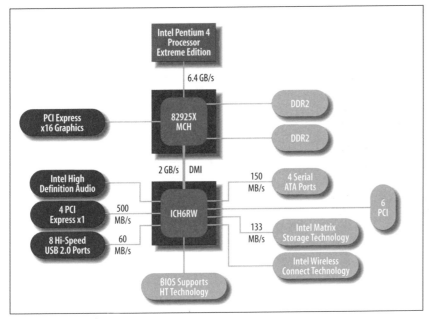

Figure 1-2. Block diagram of the Intel 925X chipset (graphic courtesy of Intel Corporation)

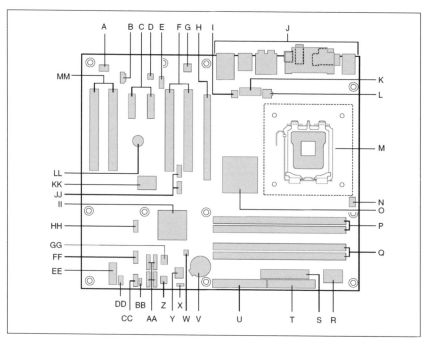

Figure 1-3. Component layout on a typical motherboard (graphic courtesy of Intel Corporation)

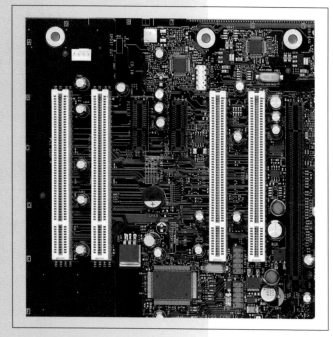

Figure 1-4. Left-rear quadrant of the D925XECV2 motherboard (graphic courtesy of Intel Corporation)

The south bridge chip, which Intel calls the ICH (I/O Controller Hub), is the blue box labeled ICH6RW. The ICH handles input/output functions, which function at much lower data rates than the processor, memory, and video channels. These channels include four 150 MB/s Serial ATA ports, six PCI slots with a cumulative 133 MB/s bandwidth, eight USB 2.0 ports with 60 MB/s bandwidth each, and four 500 MB/s PCI Express x1 slots. The ICH also handles such functions as embedded audio, the interface with the system BIOS, and wireless networking.

Figure 1-3 maps these chipset features to the component layout on a real-world motherboard. For illustrative purposes, we've used an Intel D925XECV2 motherboard, but any recent motherboard has similar features and layout. Not all of the components shown are present on all motherboards, and the exact positioning of some components may differ, but the essentials remain the same.

Figure 1-4, the left-rear quadrant of the motherboard, is dominated by expansion slots—two pairs of white PCI slots bracketing a pair of PCI Express x1 slots, with a black PCI Express x16 video adapter slot at the far

Ⓐ Auxiliary rear fan connector
Ⓑ ATAPI CD-ROM audio
connector
Ⓒ PCI Express x1 expansion slots
Ⓓ Audio codec
Ⓔ Front-panel audio connector
Ⓕ PCI expansion slots
Ⓖ Gigabit Ethernet PCI Express
controller chip
Ⓗ PCI Express x16 video adapter
slot
Ⓘ Rear case fan connector
Ⓙ Back panel I/O connectors
Ⓚ Alternate power connector
Ⓛ ATX12V power connector
Ⓜ Processor socket
Ⓝ CPU fan connector
Ⓞ MCH (north bridge)
Ⓟ Channel A memory slots
Ⓠ Channel B memory slots
Ⓡ Supplemental I/O controller
chip
Ⓢ ATX main power connector
Ⓣ Diskette drive interface
connector
Ⓤ ATA (IDE) interface connector
Ⓥ Battery

Ⓦ Chassis intrusion connector
Ⓧ BIOS Setup configuration
jumper block
Ⓨ Firmware Hub (FWH)
Ⓩ Front case fan connector
ⒶⒶ Serial ATA interface connectors
ⒷⒷ Auxiliary front-panel power
LED connector
ⒸⒸ Front-panel connector
ⒹⒹ SCSI hard disk activity
indicator LED
ⒺⒺ Auxiliary power output
connector
ⒻⒻ Front-panel USB interface
connector
ⒼⒼ Trusted Platform Module
(TPM) chip
ⒽⒽ Front panel USB interface
connector
ⒾⒾ ICH6R (south bridge)
ⒿⒿ Front-panel IEEE-1394a
(FireWire) interface connectors
ⓀⓀ IEEE-1394a (FireWire)
controller chip
ⓁⓁ Speaker
ⓂⓂ PCI expansion slots

right. The white auxiliary rear fan connector is visible centered above the left pair of PCI slots. The yellow connector at top center is the front-panel audio connector, with the audio codec chip to its upper left. The gigabit Ethernet controller chip is visible centered between the two mounting holes on the upper right. The round object below the PCI Express x1 slots is the system speaker. The large chip at bottom center is the FireWire controller, and the two blue header-pin connectors to its right are the front-panel FireWire interface connectors.

The right-rear quadrant of the motherboard, shown in Figure 1-5, is dominated by the processor socket (lower right), the heatsink for the north bridge chip (bottom left), and a top view of the rear I/O panel (top). The group of three white connectors at the upper left are, from left to right, the rear case fan connector, the alternate power connector—used to provide additional current to the motherboard if the power supply has a 20-pin main power connector rather than a 24-pin connector—and the ATX12V power connector.

Figure 1-5. Right rear quadrant of the D925XECV2 motherboard (graphic courtesy of Intel Corporation)

Figure 1-6 shows the rear I/O panel connectors. Legacy PS/2 mouse (top) and keyboard connectors are visible at the far left. The second group of connectors includes a parallel (LPT) port at the top and a 9-pin serial port at the lower left. At the bottom right of this group are coax (round) and optical (square) digital audio-out ports. The third group of connectors are all audio connectors, which can be configured for various functions. The fourth group of connectors has a FireWire connector at the top, with two USB 2.0 connectors beneath it. The fifth group of connectors has a gigabit Ethernet connector at the top, with two more USB 2.0 connectors beneath it.

It took longer than it should have, but the I/O connectors on many motherboards now use a more-or-less standardized color code, shown in Table 1-2.

Figure 1-6. Rear I/O panel connectors (graphic courtesy of Intel Corporation)

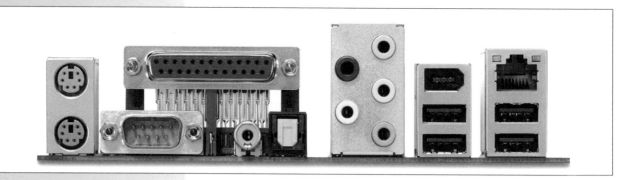

Obviously, manufacturers make some case-by-case exceptions. The coax digital audio-out connector on this motherboard, for example, is orange, which should make it a speaker out/subwoofer. Similarly, one of the audio connectors is bright yellow, which should make it a video-out connector. Oh, well.

Table 1-2. I/O connector color codes

Connector	Color	Connector	Color
Analog VGA	Blue	PS/2-compatible keyboard	Purple
Audio line-in	Light blue	PS/2-compatible mouse	Green
Audio line-out	Lime	Serial	Teal/turquoise
Digital monitor/ flat panel	White	Speaker out/sub-woofer	Orange
IEEE 1394	Gray	Right-to-left speaker	Brown
Microphone	Pink	USB	Black
MIDI/gameport	Gold	Video-out	Yellow
Parallel	Burgundy	SCSI, LAN, telephone, etc.	Not defined

The left-front quadrant of the motherboard is shown in Figure 1-7. The round object at the lower right is the battery. The large chip immediately to its left is the Firmware Hub (FWH), with the orange BIOS Setup Configuration jumper block below it. The white object to the left of the jumper block is the front case fan power connector. Above that power connector is the Trusted Platform Module (TPM) chip, and a group of four Serial ATA interface connectors appears to the left of the TPM chip and power connector. The large silver object at right center is the heatsink for the ICH6 south bridge chip. The black header pin connector to the left of the south bridge heatsink is one front-panel USB connector, with a second identical connector below it. The multicolored jumper block at the center bottom edge of the motherboard is the front-panel connector.

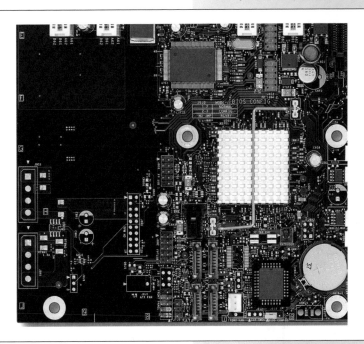

Figure 1-7. Left-front quadrant of the D925XECV2 motherboard (graphic courtesy of Intel Corporation)

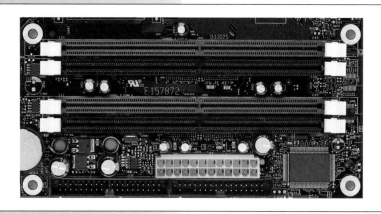

Figure 1-8. Right-front quadrant of the D925XECV2 motherboard (graphic courtesy of Intel Corporation)

Figure 1-8 shows the right-front quadrant of the motherboard, with the two Channel A memory slots at the top and two Channel B memory slots beneath them. The large chip at the lower right is the supplemental I/O controller chip, with the white ATX main power connector to its left. The black ATA interface connector is at the bottom-left edge of this image, with the floppy drive interface connector immediately to its right.

Troubleshooting

Many first-time system builders are haunted by the question, "What if it doesn't work?" Or, worse still, "What if it goes up in flames the first time I turn it on?" Set your mind at ease. This isn't rocket surgery. Any reasonably intelligent person can build a system with a high degree of confidence that it will work normally the first time it is turned on. If you use good components and assemble them carefully, you're actually less likely to encounter problems with a home-built system than with a prebuilt mail-order system or one off the shelf from your local superstore.

CONTENTS MAY SETTLE DURING SHIPPING

Shipping can be tough on a computer. We always pop the cover of PCs that have been shipped, and often find something has been jarred loose. Our editor reports that when he shipped a PC to his parents, it arrived with the video card completely out of its slot. Not good.

Even worse, shipping can cause the CPU cooler to break loose. A heavy heatsink rattling around can do some serious damage to other components. If someone ships a system to you, always open it up and verify that everything is properly connected before you apply power to the system.

Still, it can happen. So, while it would take a whole book to cover troubleshooting in detail, it's worth taking a few pages to list some of the most likely problems and solutions. Fortunately, it's easier to troubleshoot a newly built system than a system that's been in use for some time. Fewer things can go wrong with a new system. You can be certain that the system is not infected with a virus or malware, for example, and driver problems are much less likely on a new system because you have all the latest drivers installed.

The best time to troubleshoot is while you build the system. A good carpenter measures twice and cuts once. Take the same approach to building your system, and you're unlikely to need any of this troubleshooting advice. As you build the system, and then again before you apply power for the first time, verify that all cables are oriented and connected correctly. Make sure expansion cards, memory modules, the processor, and so on are fully seated, and that you haven't left a tool in the patient. Each project system chapter includes a final checklist. Verifying the items on that checklist eliminates about 99% of the potential problems.

Possible problems fall into one of four categories, easy versus hard to troubleshoot and likely versus unlikely. Always check the easy/likely problems first. Otherwise, you may find yourself replacing the video card before you notice that the monitor isn't plugged in. After you exhaust the easy/likely possibilities, check the easy/unlikely ones followed by hard/likely and, finally, hard/unlikely.

Other than sheer carelessness—to which experienced system builders are more prone than are novices—most problems with new systems result from one or more of the following:

Most problems that occur during repairs and system upgrades result from one or more of the following:

Cable problems

> Disconnected, mis-connected, and defective cables cause more problems than anything else. The plethora of cables inside a PC makes it very easy to overlook a disconnected data cable or to forget to connect power to a drive. It's possible to connect some cables backward. Ribbon cables are a particularly common problem, because some can be connected offset by a row or column of pins. And the cables themselves cannot always be trusted, even if they are new. If you have a problem that seems inexplicable, always suspect a cable problem first.

Configuration errors

> Years ago, motherboards required a lot more manual configuration than do modern motherboards. There were many switches and jumpers, all of which had to be set correctly or the system wouldn't boot. Modern motherboards auto-configure most of their required settings, but may still require some manual configuration, either by setting physical jumpers on the motherboard or by changing settings in CMOS Setup. Motherboards use silk-screened labels near jumpers and connectors to document their purposes and to list valid configuration settings. These settings are also listed in the motherboard manual. Always check both the motherboard labels and the manual to verify configuration settings. If the motherboard maker posts updated manuals on the Web, check those as well.

Cables Are Commonplace

Fortunately, most problems with defective cables involve ribbon cables, and those are pretty easy to come by. For example, when we recently assembled a new PC, the motherboard came with two IDE cables and a floppy drive cable. The floppy drive came with a cable, the hard drive with another IDE cable, and the optical drive with still another IDE cable. That gave us four IDE cables and two floppy cables, so we ended up with two spare IDE cables and a spare floppy cable. Those went into our spares kit, where they'll be available if we need to swap cables to troubleshoot another system.

DON'T FORGET THE FLASHLIGHT

One of our technical reviewers observes, "A good flashlight with a tight beam (I use a mini Maglight) really helps to spot offset ribbon connector problems, even if workspace lighting is otherwise adequate. I've done systems where a handheld magnifier became an indispensable tool."

Incompatible components

In general, you can mix and match modern PC components without worrying much about compatibility. For example, any IDE hard drive or optical drive works with any IDE interface, and any ATX12V power supply is compatible with any ATX12V motherboard (although a cheap or older power supply may not provide adequate power, which means you need to visit Chapter 2). Most component compatibility issues are subtle. For example, you may install a 1 GB memory module in your system. When you power it up, the system sees only 256 MB or 512 MB because the motherboard doesn't recognize 1 GB memory modules properly. It's worth checking the detailed documentation on the manufacturers' web sites to verify compatibility.

Dead-on-arrival components

Modern PC components are extremely reliable, but if you're unlucky one of your components may be DOA. This is the least likely cause of a problem, however. Many novices think they have a DOA component, but the true cause is almost always something else—usually a cable or configuration problem. Before you return a suspect component, go through the detailed troubleshooting steps we describe. Chances are the component is just fine.

Here are the problems you are most likely to encounter when you repair or upgrade a system, and what to do about them:

Problem: When you apply power, nothing happens

The Happy Noise

A healthy PC finishes the POST (Power-On Self-Test) with one happy-sounding beep. If you hear some other beep sequence during startup, there is some sort of problem. BIOS beep codes provide useful troubleshooting information, such as identifying the particular subsystem affected. Beep codes vary, so check the motherboard documentation for a description of what each code indicates.

Note that some recent motherboards do not generate beep codes. Also, unless the motherboard has a built-in speaker, you'll have to connect the case speaker to hear the beep codes.

- Verify that the power cable is connected to the PC and to the wall receptacle, and that the wall receptacle has power. Don't assume. We have seen receptacles in which one half worked and the other didn't. Use a lamp or other appliance to verify that the receptacle to which you connect the PC actually has power. If the power supply has its own power switch, make sure that switch is turned to the "On" or "1" position. If your local mains voltage is 110/115/120V, verify the power supply voltage selector switch, if present, is not set for 220/230/240V. (If you need to move this switch, disconnect power before doing so.)

- If you are using an outlet strip or UPS, make sure that its switch (if equipped) is on and that the circuit breaker or fuse hasn't blown.

- If you installed a video adapter, pop the lid and verify that the adapter is fully seated in its slot. Even if you were sure it seated fully initially—and even if you thought it snapped into place—the adapter may still not be properly seated. Remove the card and reinstall it, making sure it seats completely. If the motherboard has a retention mechanism, make sure the notch on the video card fully engages the retention mechanism. Ironically, one of the most common reasons for a loose video card is that the screw used to secure it to the chassis may torque the card, pulling it partially out of its slot. This problem is rare with high-quality cases and video cards, but is quite common with cheap components.

- Verify that the 20- or 24-pin main ATX power cable and the 4-pin ATX12V power cable are securely connected to the motherboard and that all pins are making contact. If necessary, remove the cables and reconnect them. Make sure the latch on each cable plug snaps into place on the motherboard jack.

- Verify that the front-panel power switch cable is connected properly to the front-panel connector block. Check the silk-screened label on the motherboard and the motherboard manual to verify that you are connecting the cable to the right set of pins. Very rarely, you may encounter a defective power switch. You can eliminate this possibility by temporarily connecting the front-panel reset switch cable to the power switch pins on the front-panel connector block. (Both are merely momentary on switches, so they can be used interchangeably.) Alternatively, you can carefully use a small flat-blade screwdriver to short the power switch pins on the front-panel connector block momentarily. If the system starts with either of these methods, the problem is the power switch.

- Start eliminating less likely possibilities, the most common of which is a well-concealed short circuit. Begin by disconnecting the power and data cables from the hard, optical, and floppy drives, one at a time. After you disconnect each, try starting the system. If the system starts, the drive you just disconnected is the problem. The drive itself may be defective, but it's far more likely that the cable is defective or was improperly connected. Replace the data cable, and connect the drive to a different power supply cable.

- If you have expansion cards installed, remove them one by one. Remove all but the video adapter. If the motherboard has embedded video, temporarily connect your display to it and remove the video card as well. Attempt to start the system after you remove each card. If the system starts, the card you just removed is causing the problem. Try a different card, or install that card in a different slot.

- Remove and reseat the memory modules, examining them to make sure they are not damaged, and then try to start the system. If you have two

Swapping Power Supplies

If you have a spare power supply—or can borrow one temporarily from another system—you might as well try it as long as you have the cables disconnected. A new power supply being DOA is fairly rare, at least among good brands, but as long as you have the original disconnected, it's not much trouble to try a different power supply.

memory modules installed, install only one of them initially. Try it in both (or all) memory slots. If that module doesn't work in any slot, the module may be defective. Try the other module, again in every available memory slot. By using this approach, you can determine if one of the memory modules or one of the slots is defective.

- Remove the CPU cooler and the CPU. Check the CPU to make sure there are no bent pins (some newer CPUs don't have pins). If there are, you may be able to straighten them using a credit card or a similar thin, stiff object, but in all likelihood you will have to replace the CPU. Check the CPU socket to make sure there are no blocked holes or foreign objects present.

- Remove the motherboard and verify that no extraneous screws or other conductive objects are shorting the motherboard to the chassis. Although shaking the case usually causes such objects to rattle, a screw or other small object may become wedged so tightly between the motherboard and chassis that it will not reveal itself during a shake test.

- If the problem persists, the most likely cause is a defective motherboard.

Problem: The system seems to start normally, but the display remains black

- Verify that the display has power and the video cable is connected. If the display has a noncaptive power cable, make sure the power cord is connected both to the display and to the wall receptacle. If you have a spare power cord, use it to connect the display.

- Verify that the brightness and contrast controls of the display are set to midrange or higher.

- Disconnect the video cable and examine it closely to make sure that no pins are bent or shorted. Note that the video cable on some analog (VGA) monitors is missing some pins and may have a short jumper wire connecting other pins, which is normal. Also check the video port on the PC to make sure that all of the holes are clear and that no foreign objects are present.

- If you are using a standalone video adapter in a motherboard that has embedded video, make sure the video cable is connected to the proper video port. Try the other video port just to make sure. Most motherboards with embedded video automatically disable it when they sense a video card is installed, but that is not universally true. You may have to connect the display to the embedded video, enter CMOS Setup (usually by pressing a key such as F2 or Delete while the system is booting), and reconfigure the motherboard to use the video card.

Use New Thermal Goop Every Time

Before you reinstall the CPU, always remove the old thermal compound and apply new compound. You can generally wipe off the old compound with a paper towel, or perhaps by rubbing it gently with your thumb. (Keep the processor in its socket while you remove the compound). If the compound is difficult to remove, try heating it gently with a hair dryer. Never operate the system without the CPU cooler installed.

- Try using a different display, if you have one available. Alternatively, try using the problem display on another system.

- If you are using a video card, make certain it is fully seated. Many combinations of video card and motherboard make it very difficult to seat the card properly. You may think the card is seated. You may even feel it snap into place. That does not necessarily mean it really is fully seated. Look carefully at the bottom edge of the card and the video slot, and make sure the card is fully in the slot and parallel to it. Verify that installing the screw that secures the video card to the chassis did not torque the card, forcing one end up and out of the slot.

- If your video card requires a supplemental power cable, be sure to connect it and make sure it snaps into place.

- If the system has PCI or PCIe expansion cards installed, remove them one by one. (Be sure to disconnect power from the system before you remove or install a card.) Each time you remove a card, restart the system. If the system displays video after you remove a card, that card is either defective or is conflicting with the video adapter. Try installing the PCI or PCIe card in a different slot. If it still causes the video problem, the card is probably defective. Replace it.

Problem: When you connect power (or turn on the main power switch on the back of the power supply), the power supply starts briefly and then shuts off

---

DANGER, WILL ROBINSON

All of the following steps assume that the power supply is adequate for the system configuration. This symptom may also occur if you use a grossly underpowered power supply. Worse still, doing that may damage the power supply, motherboard, and other components.

- This may be normal behavior. When you connect power to the power supply, it senses the power and begins its startup routine. Within a fraction of a second, the power supply notices that the motherboard hasn't ordered it to start, so it shuts itself down immediately. Press the main power switch on the case and the system should start normally.

- If pressing the power switch doesn't start the system, your power supply may have another switch on the back that's set in the off position. Switch it on and then try pressing the front power switch again.

- If pressing the main power switch still doesn't start the system, you have probably forgotten to connect one of the cables from the power supply or front panel to the motherboard. Verify that the power switch cable is connected to the front-panel connector block, and that the 20-pin or 24-pin main ATX power cable and the 4-pin ATX12V power cable are connected to the motherboard. Connect any cables that are not connected, press the main power switch, and the system should start normally.

- If the preceding steps don't solve the problem, the most likely cause is a defective power supply. If you have a spare power supply, or can borrow one temporarily from another system, install it temporarily in the new system. Alternatively, connect the problem power supply to another system to verify that it is bad.

- If the preceding step doesn't solve the problem, the most likely cause is a defective motherboard. Replace it.

Problem: When you apply power, the floppy drive LED lights solidly and the system fails to start

- The FDD cable is defective or misaligned. Verify that the FDD cable is properly installed on FDD and on the motherboard FDD interface. This problem is caused by installing the FDD cable backward or by installing it offset by one row or column of pins.

- If the FDD cable is properly installed, it may be defective. Disconnect it temporarily and start the system. If the system starts normally, replace the FDD cable.

- If the FDD cable is known-good and installed properly, the FDD itself or the motherboard FDD interface may be defective. Replace the FDD. If that doesn't solve the problem and you insist on having an FDD, either replace the motherboard or disable the motherboard FDD interface and install a PCI adapter that provides an FDD interface, or, if your motherboard allows you to boot from USB devices, purchase a USB external floppy drive for the purpose.

Problem: The optical drive appears to play audio CDs, but no sound comes from the speakers

- Make sure the volume/mixer is set appropriately, i.e., the volume is up and CD Audio isn't muted. There may be multiple volume controls in a system. Check them all.

- Try a different audio CD. Some recent audio CDs are copy-protected in such a way that they refuse to play on a computer optical drive.

- If you have tried several audio CDs without success, this may still be normal behavior, depending on the player application you are using. Optical drives can deliver audio data via the analog audio-out jack on the rear of the drive or as a digital bit stream on the bus. If the player application pulls the digital bit stream from the bus, sound is delivered to your speakers normally. If the player application uses analog audio, you must connect a cable from the analog audio-out jack on the back of the drive to an audio-in connector on the motherboard or sound card.

SPECIAL AUDIO CABLES

Few optical drives or motherboards include an analog audio cable, so you will probably have to buy a cable. In the past, audio cables were often proprietary, but modern drives and motherboards all use a standard ATAPI audio cable. However, most modern optical drives will send audio over the ATAPI data cable.

- If you install an audio cable and still have no sound from the speakers, try connecting a headphone or amplified speakers directly to the head-phone jack on the front of the optical drive (if present). If you still can't hear the audio, the drive may be defective. If you can hear audio via the front headphone jack but not through the computer speakers, it's likely the audio cable you installed is defective or installed improperly.

Problem: SATA drives are not recognized

- How SATA (Serial ATA) drives are detected (or not detected) depends on the particular combination of chipset, BIOS revision level, SATA interface, and the operating system you use. Failing to recognize SATA devices may be normal behavior.

- If you use a standalone PCI SATA adapter card, the system will typi-cally not recognize the connected SATA drive(s) during startup. This is normal behavior. You will have to provide an SATA device driver when you install the operating system.

- If your motherboard uses a recent chipset, e.g., an Intel 865 or later, and has embedded SATA interfaces, it should detect SATA devices during startup and display them on the BIOS boot screen. If the drive is not recognized and if you have not already done so, update the BIOS to the latest version. Restart the system and watch the BIOS boot screen to see if the system recognizes the SATA drive. Run BIOS Setup and select the menu item that allows you to configure ATA devices. If your SATA drive is not listed, you can still use it, but you'll have to provide a driver on diskette during OS installation.

- Recognition of SATA drives during operating system installation varies with the OS version and the chipset. The original release of Windows 2000 does not detect SATA drives with any chipset. To install Windows 2000 on an SATA drive, watch during the early part of Setup for the prompt to press F6 if you need to install third-party storage drivers. Press F6 when prompted and insert the SATA driver floppy. Windows XP may or may not recognize SATA drives, depending on the chipset the moth-erboard uses. With recent chipsets, e.g., the Intel 865 series and later, Windows XP recognizes and uses SATA drives natively. With earlier

Why Only 128GB or 137GB?

If you install Windows XP from an early distribution disc, it will recognize at most 137 GB (decimal) or 128GB (binary) of hard drive capacity, even if the drive is much larger. You can use the remaining space after Windows is installed, but only if you format it as a separate volume. If you want the entire capacity of a large hard drive to be used as a single volume by Windows XP, you'll need a more recent distribution disc that includes Service Pack 2 (SP2) or later.

chipsets, e.g., the Intel D845 and earlier, Windows XP does not recognize the SATA drive natively, so you will have to press F6 when prompted and provide the SATA driver on floppy. Most recent Linux distributions (those based on the 2.4 kernel or later) recognize SATA drives natively.

- If the SATA drive is still not recognized, pop the lid and verify that the SATA data and power cables are connected properly. Try removing and reseating the cables and, if necessary, connecting the SATA drive to a different motherboard interface connector. If the drive still isn't accessible, try replacing the SATA data cable. If none of this works, the SATA drive is probably defective.

Problem: The monitor displays BIOS boot text, but the system doesn't boot and displays no error message

- This may be normal behavior. Restart the system and enter BIOS Setup (usually by pressing Delete or F1 during startup). Choose the menu option to use default CMOS settings, save the changes, exit, and restart the system.

- If the system doesn't accept keyboard input and you are using a USB keyboard and mouse, temporarily swap in a PS/2 keyboard and mouse. If you are using a PS/2 keyboard and mouse, make sure you haven't connected the keyboard to the mouse port and vice versa.

- If the system still fails to boot, run BIOS Setup again and verify all settings, particularly CPU speed, FSB speed, and memory timings.

- If the system hangs with a DMI pool error message, restart the system and run BIOS Setup again. Search the menus for an option to reset the configuration data. Enable that option, save the changes, and restart the system.

- If you are using an Intel motherboard, power down the system and reset the configuration jumper from the 1-2 (Normal) position to 2-3 (Configure). Restart the system, and BIOS Setup will appear automatically. Choose the option to use default CMOS settings, save the changes, and power down the system. Move the configuration jumper back to the 1-2 position and restart the system. (Actually, we routinely run the configuration option—when such an option is offered—and reset BIOS values to default every time we first use a new motherboard, regardless of make, model, or chipset. It may not be absolutely required, but we've found that doing this minimizes problems.)

- If you are still unable to access BIOS Setup, power down the system, disconnect all of the drive data cables, and restart the system. If the system displays a Hard Drive Failure or No Boot Device error message, the problem is a defective cable (more likely) or a defective drive.

Replace the drive data cable and try again. If the system does not display such an error message, the problem is probably caused by a defective motherboard.

Problem: The monitor displays a Hard Drive Failure or similar error message

- This is almost always a hardware problem. Verify that the hard drive data cable is connected properly to the drive and the interface and that the drive power cable is connected.

- Use a different drive data cable and connect the drive to a different power cable.

- Connect the drive data cable to a different interface.

- If none of these steps corrects the problem, the most likely cause is a defective drive.

Problem: The monitor displays a No Boot Device, Missing Operating System, or similar error message

- This is normal behavior if you have not yet installed an operating system. Error messages like this generally mean that the drive is physically installed and accessible, but the PC cannot boot because it cannot locate the operating system. Install the operating system.

- If the drive is inaccessible, verify that all data and power cables are connected properly. If it is a parallel ATA drive, verify that master/slave jumpers are set correctly, and that the drive is connected to the primary interface.

- If you upgrade your motherboard, but keep your original hard drive (or use a utility such as Norton Ghost to clone your original), your operating system installation may not have the drivers necessary to function with your new hardware. If you're upgrading your motherboard, chances are good that enough things are different that Windows won't be able to boot. You'll need to reinstall Windows.

Problem: The system refuses to boot from the optical drive

- All modern motherboards and optical drives support the El Torito specification, which allows the system to boot from an optical disc. If your new system refuses to boot from a CD, first verify that the CD is bootable. Most, but not all, operating system distribution CDs are bootable. Some OS CDs are not bootable, but have a utility program to generate boot floppies. Check the documentation to verify that the CD is bootable, or try booting the CD in another system.

- Run CMOS Setup and locate the section where you can define boot sequence. The default sequence is often (1) floppy drive, (2) hard drive, and (3) optical drive. Sometimes, by the time the system has decided it can't boot from the FDD or hard drive, it "gives up" before attempting to boot from the optical drive. Reset the boot sequence to (1) optical drive, and (2) hard drive. We generally leave the system with that boot sequence. Most systems configured this way prompt you to "Press any key to boot from CD" or something similar. If you don't press a key, they then attempt to boot from the hard drive, so make sure to pay attention during the boot sequence and press a key when prompted.

- Some high-speed optical drives take several seconds to load a CD, spin up, and signal the system that they are ready. In the meantime, the BIOS may have given up on the optical drive and gone on to try other boot devices. If you think this has happened, try pressing the reset button to reboot the system while the optical drive is already spinning and up to speed. If you get a persistent prompt to "press any key to boot from CD," try leaving that prompt up while the optical drive comes up to speed. If that doesn't work, run CMOS Setup and reconfigure the boot sequence to put the FDD first and the optical drive second. (Make sure there's no diskette in the FDD.) You can also try putting other boot device options, such as a Zip drive, network drive, or boot PROM ahead of the optical drive in the boot sequence. The goal is to provide sufficient delay for the optical drive to spin up before the motherboard attempts to boot from it.

- If none of these steps solves the problem, verify that all data cable and power cable connections are correct, that master/slave jumpers are set correctly, and so on. If the system still fails to boot, replace the optical drive data cable.

- If the system still fails to boot, disconnect all drives except the primary hard drive and the optical drive. If they are parallel ATA devices, connect the hard drive as the master device on the primary channel and the optical drive as the master device on the secondary channel and restart the system.

- If that fails to solve the problem, connect both the hard drive and optical drive to the primary ATA interface, with the hard drive as master and the optical drive as slave.

- If the system still fails to boot, the optical drive is probably defective. Try using a different drive.

Problem: When you first apply power, you hear a continuous high-pitched screech or warble

- The most likely cause is that one of the system fans either has a defective bearing or a wire is contacting the spinning fan. Examine all of the system fans—CPU fan, power supply fan, and any supplemental fans—to make sure they haven't been fouled by a wire. Sometimes it's difficult to determine which fan is making the noise. In that case, use a cardboard tube or rolled up piece of paper as a stethoscope to localize the noise. If the fan is fouled, clear the problem. If the fan is not fouled but still noisy, replace the fan.

- Rarely, a new hard drive may have a manufacturing defect or have been damaged in shipping. If so, the problem is usually obvious from the amount and location of the noise and possibly because the hard drive is vibrating. If necessary, use your cardboard tube stethoscope to localize the noise. If the hard drive is the source, the only alternative is to replace it.

Choosing and Buying Components

2

The components you choose for your system determine its features, performance level, and reliability. How and where you buy those components determines how much the system costs.

Sometimes it is a good idea to spend more for additional features or performance, but often it is not. The trick is to figure out where to draw the line—when to spend extra money for extra features and performance, and when to settle for a less expensive component. Our years of experience have taught us several lessons in that regard:

- Benchmarks lie. Buying PC components based solely on benchmark results is like buying a car based solely on its top speed. It's worse, actually, because no standards exist for how benchmarks measure performance, or what aspect of performance they measure. Using one benchmark, Component A may be the clear winner, with Component B lagging far behind. With another benchmark, the positions may be reversed. When you select components for your new system, we suggest you regard benchmarks with suspicion and use them only as very general guidelines, if at all.

- Performance differences don't matter if it takes a benchmark to show them. Enthusiast web sites wax poetic about a processor that's 10% faster than its competitor or a video card that renders frames 5% faster than its predecessor. Who cares? A difference you won't notice isn't worth paying for.

- It's easy to overlook the really important things and focus on trivialities. The emphasis on size and speed means more important issues are often ignored or at best given short shrift. For example, if you compare two hard drives you might think the faster drive is the better choice. But the faster drive may also run noticeably hotter and be much louder and less reliable. In that situation, the slower drive is probably the better choice.

Vista and Integrated Video

The one exception to the general suitability of integrated video is systems that will run Windows Vista. The fastest integrated video currently available is fast enough for running Vista, but only just. If you plan to use Vista, particularly if you will place additional demands on the video adapter other than just running the interface, consider installing a standalone video adapter that is approved to run the Vista Aero Glass interface.

Bang for the Buck

To find the sweet spot, just compare the price of a component to its performance or capacity. For example, if one processor costs $175 and the next model up is 10% faster, it should cost at most 10% more. If it costs more than that, you've reached the wrong part of the price/performance curve, and you'll be paying a premium for little additional performance. Similarly, before you buy a hard drive, divide the price by the capacity. At the low end, you may find that a small hard drive costs more per gigabyte than a larger drive. At the high end, a very large drive probably costs significantly more per gigabyte than a medium capacity model. The sweet spot is in the middle, where the cost per gigabyte is lowest. Make sure, though, that you compare apples to apples. Don't compare a dual-core processor to a single-core processor, for example, or a 5,400 RPM hard drive to a 7,200 RPM model.

- Integrated (or embedded) components are often preferable to stand-alone components. Many motherboards include integrated features such as video, audio, and LAN. The integrated video on modern motherboards suffices for most purposes. Only hardcore gamers and others with special video requirements need to buy a separate video adapter. The best integrated audio—such as that on motherboards that use Intel and nVIDIA chipsets—is good enough for almost anyone. Integrated LAN adapters are more than good enough for nearly any desktop system.

- The advantage of integrated components is three-fold: cost, reliability, and compatibility. A motherboard with integrated components costs little or no more than a motherboard without such components, which can save you $100 or more by eliminating the cost of inexpensive standalone equivalents. Because they are built into the motherboard, integrated components are usually more reliable than standalone components. Finally, because the motherboard maker has complete control over the hardware and drivers, integrated components usually cause fewer compatibility issues and device conflicts.

- Buying at the "sweet spot" is almost always the best decision. The sweet spot is the level at which the price/performance ratio is minimized—where you get the most bang for your buck. For example, Intel sells a broad range of processors, from $50 Celerons to $1,000 Core 2 Duo Extreme Editions. Celerons are cheap, but slow. Extreme Edition processors are fast, but hideously expensive. There must be a happy medium. The sweet spot for Intel processors is around $175 for a retail-boxed CPU. If you spend much less, you get less performance per dollar spent. If you spend much more, you get only a slight performance increase. This sweet spot has stayed the same for years. That $175 buys you a faster processor every time Intel cuts prices. But that $175 processor has always been the bang-for-the-buck leader.

- It's almost always worth paying more for better quality and reliability. If the specs for two components look very similar but one sells for less than the other, it's a safe bet that someone cut corners to reduce the price of the cheaper component. The cheaper component may use inferior materials, have shoddy build quality, or poor quality control, or the manufacturer may provide terrible tech support or a very short warranty. If it's cheaper, there's a reason for it. Count on it. The best way to avoid the trap of poor-quality components is to be willing to pay a bit more for quality. The price difference between a mediocre product and a top-quality one can be surprisingly small. Throughout this book, we recommend only high-quality products. That's not to say that products we don't list are bad, but those we do recommend are good.

- Brand names really do mean something, but not all brands are good ones. Brand names imply certain performance and quality characteristics, and most manufacturers take pains to establish and maintain those links in consumers' minds. Different brand names are often associated with different quality and/or performance levels in a good/better/best hierarchy, in the same way that General Motors sells their inexpensive models as Chevrolets and their expensive models as Cadillacs.

  For example, ViewSonic makes several lines of LCD displays, including their high-end Pro Series, their midrange Graphics Series, and their entry-level E2 Series. Like many vendors, ViewSonic also maintains a separate brand name for their cheapest products, which they call OptiQuest. If you buy a Pro Series monitor, you know it's going to cost more than the lower-end models, but you also know it's going to have excellent performance and will likely be quite reliable. Conversely, if you buy an OptiQuest monitor, you know it's going to be cheap and not very good. Some manufacturers also have a "high-end" brand name, although that practice has declined as margins have eroded throughout the industry.

- If you're on a tight budget, shop by brand name rather than by performance specifications. For the same price, it's usually better to choose a component that has less impressive specifications but a better brand name rather than a component with better specifications but a poor brand name. For example, if you can't afford a high-end 19" Samsung LCD display with 4 ms response time, but an 8 ms Samsung model or a similarly priced Brand-X 19" LCD display with 4 ms response time is within your budget, choose the 8 ms Samsung model. It may be a bit slower than the Brand-X display, but the Samsung will almost certainly have better display quality and be more reliable. In other words, if you have to choose between better quality and higher performance, choose quality every time.

In this chapter, we tell you what we've learned based on more than 20 years of buying PC hardware components. In the first edition of this book, we recommended specific brands and models. The obvious downside to doing that is that products change in Internet time. A product that is leading edge when we proof the final galleys may be midrange by the time the book arrives in bookstores and discontinued by the time you read it.

So, rather than a detailed discussion of such ephemera, this chapter focuses instead on important characteristics of hardware components—the things you need to understand to make good decisions. But we recognize that many people want detailed recommendations, so we also include links to our online forums, where we post our current recommendations for specific products by brand name and model that are reliable and offer good value for money. If you hew closely to our advice when you make your buying decisions you won't go far wrong.

A Rose by Any Other Name

It's not uncommon for several manufacturers to relabel identical or closely similar products from the same Pacific Rim factory. For example, the factory that makes many of the cases that Antec sells under its brand names also makes similar cases that are sold under other brand names such as Chieftec and Chenming. Contrary to web wisdom, that doesn't mean those similar products are identical to the Antec case. Different companies can specify different levels of finish, quality control, and so on. A case with the Antec name on it meets Antec's quality standards. An "identical" case with a different brand name may not be of the same quality.

With so many alternatives, it's easy to buy the right part from the wrong source. Accordingly, the last part of this chapter distills what we've learned about how and where to buy PC hardware components. When you finish reading this chapter, you'll have all the information you need to make the right buying decisions.

Choosing Components

The biggest advantage of building your own PC is that you can choose which components to use. If you buy a cookie-cutter system from Dell or HP, most of the decisions are made for you. You can specify a larger hard drive, more memory, or a different monitor, but the range of options is quite limited. Want a better power supply, a quieter CPU cooler, or a motherboard with built-in FireWire and enhanced RAID support? Tough luck. Those options aren't on the table.

When you build from scratch, you get to choose every component that goes into your system. You can spend a bit more here and a bit less there to get exactly the features and functions you want at the best price. It's therefore worth devoting some time and effort to component selection, but there are so many competing products available that it's difficult to separate the marketing hype from reality.

On your own, you might find yourself struggling to answer questions like, "Should I buy a Seagate hard drive or a Western Digital?" (hint: Seagate), or "Does Sony or HP make the best DVD writers?" (hint: neither; Plextor makes the best optical drives, but there are "bargain" brands that are quite good). We've done all that research for you, and the following sections in conjunction with our online forums distill what we've learned in testing and using hundreds of products over many years.

We recommend products by brand name, and we don't doubt that some people will take issue with some of our recommendations. We don't claim that the products we recommend are "best" in any absolute sense, because we haven't tested every product on the market and because "best" is inherently subjective. What's "best" for us may be just "very good" from your point of view, but it almost certainly won't be "awful."

So, keeping all of that in mind, the following sections describe the products we recommend.

Case

The case (or chassis) is the foundation of any system. Its obvious purpose is to support the power supply, motherboard, drives, and other components. Its less-obvious purposes are to contain the radio-frequency interference produced by internal components; to ensure proper system cooling; and to subdue the noise produced by the power supply, drives, fans, and other components with moving parts.

A good case performs all of these tasks well, and is a joy to work with. It is strongly built and rigid. Adding or removing components is quick and easy. All the holes line up. There are no sharp edges or burrs. A bad case is painful to work with, sometimes literally. It may have numerous exposed razor-sharp edges and burrs that cut you even if you're careful. It is cheaply constructed of flimsy material that flexes excessively. Tolerances are very loose, sometimes so much so that you have to bend sheet metal to get a component to fit, if that is even possible. Using a cheap case is a sure way to make your system-building experience miserable.

Use the following guidelines when choosing a case:

- Choose the proper size case, taking into account the original configuration and possible future expansion. For a general-purpose system, choose a mini- or mid-tower case. For a small PC, choose a microATX case. Choose a case that leaves at least one drive bay—ideally a 5.25" external bay—free for later expansion.

- Get a case with supplemental cooling fans, or space to add them. Heat is the enemy of processors, memory, drives, and other system components. Cooler components last longer and run more reliably.

The cases we recommend are listed at *http://www.hardwareguys.com/picks/ cases.html*.

Power Supply

The power supply is one of the most important components in a PC, and yet most people give it little consideration. In addition to providing reliable, stable, closely-regulated power to all system components, the power supply draws air through the system to cool it. A marginal or failing power supply can cause many problems, some of which are very subtle and difficult to track down. Most problems are not subtle, however. A poor or marginal power supply is likely to cause system crashes, memory errors, and data corruption, and may fail catastrophically, taking other system components with it.

Use the following guidelines to choose a power supply appropriate for your system:

- Above all, make sure the power supply you buy fits your case and has the proper connectors for your motherboard. Most cases use ATX power supplies, and any ATX power supply fits any ATX case. SFF and microATX cases often use SFX or proprietary power supplies. We avoid using those whenever possible.

- Size your power supply according to the system configuration. For an entry-level system, install a 300W or larger power supply. For a mainstream system, install a 400W or larger power supply. For a high-performance system, install a 500W or larger power supply. If you're installing dual video adapters in an nVIDIA SLI (Scalable Link

BTX

The latest case form factors are BTX (Balanced Technology eXtended) and its smaller variants microBTX and picoBTX, which until late 2006 Intel had been pushing strongly as the eventual replacement for ATX and microATX. Relative to ATX-family cases, BTX-family cases offer superior ventilation and cooling and other improvements. BTX-family cases use ATX-family power supplies, but are physically incompatible with ATX-family motherboards.

As of August 2006, when we completed the final draft manuscript for this book, Intel had announced its intention to convert fully to BTX in 2007 and 2008, abandoning the ATX standard. In mid-October 2006, as this book was about to go to press, Intel abruptly reversed course, announcing that it would cease producing BTX components in 2007, and return to producing only ATX and microATX products. Most industry observers believe that this abrupt change was caused by Intel's fast transition from the hot-running, power-hungry Pentium 4/D architecture to the cool, low-power Core 2 architecture. Suddenly, Intel processors no longer had a heat problem, and BTX was a solution in search of a problem.

Interface) or AMD/ATi CrossFire configuration, make sure to use a power supply that is certified for operation with dual video adapters.

- Buy only an ATX12V 2.0 or higher compliant power supply.

- Make sure the power supply provides Serial ATA power connectors.

The power supplies we recommend are listed at *http://www.hardwareguys. com/picks/power.html*.

Processor

Most people spend too much time dithering about which processor to install. The two choices you have to make are, first, Intel versus AMD, and, second, how much to spend. Here are the considerations for each of the processor price ranges:

Low-end (under $150)

At the bottom of this range—sub-$100 processors—inexpensive AMD Sempron models are generally faster than comparably-priced Intel Celerons. At the upper end of this range are the least expensive processors that we consider mainstream models—the slower Athlon 64, Athlon 64 X2, Pentium 4, and Pentium D processors, all of which offer similar price/performance ratios.

Midrange ($150 to $250)

This is the mainstream. The bottom half of this range includes fast Pentium D and Athlon 64 X2 processors, any of which are good choices for a mainstream system, as well as the entry-level Core 2 Duo processors. At the upper end of this range are the fastest Pentium D and Athlon 64 X2 processors and midrange Core 2 Duo models. Midrange processors as a group are generally noticeably faster than low-end processors and cost only a little more, while at the same time they are only a bit slower than high-end processors and cost a lot less.

High-end ($250+)

AMD is no longer competitive in this segment. At the lower end, this range is the realm of midrange Core 2 Duo models. At the high end—which may approach or exceed $1,000—you'll find the Intel Core 2 Duo Extreme Edition. This range is characterized by a rapidly decreasing bang-for-the-buck ratio. A $150 processor might be 50% faster than a $75 processor, but a $500 processor may be only 10% faster than a $250 processor, and a $1,000 processor only 5% faster than a $500 one.

Also consider the following issues when you choose a processor:

- Even the slowest current processor more than suffices for office productivity applications. If you never load the system heavily, you'll not notice much difference between an inexpensive processor and a more expensive model.

- Low-end processors are hampered by small secondary caches, which cripple performance, particularly if you work with large data sets, such as multimedia, graphics, or video.

- Processors in the "sweet spot" range—$150 to $225 for a retail-boxed processor—usually represent the best bang for the buck.

- Buy the processor you need initially, rather than buy a slower processor now and plan to upgrade later. Processor upgrades, AMD and Intel, are a minefield of compatibility issues.

The processors we recommend are listed at *http://www.hardwareguys.com/ picks/processors.html*.

THE GREAT PROCESSOR SHAKEUP

In July 2006, Intel introduced its long-awaited Core 2 Duo line of processors and obsoleted its existing single-core Pentium 4 processors and dual-core Pentium D processors overnight. At introduction, even the entry-level $185 Core 2 Duo E6300 processor was as fast as existing AMD and Intel processors that had been selling for $350 to $600. In addition to very high performance, Core 2 Duo processors feature very low power consumption and correspondingly low heat production. For Core 2 Duo, Intel claims a 40% increase in performance at 40% lower power consumption, and our testing confirms those claims.

Core 2 Duo was a devastating blow to AMD's single-core Athlon 64 and dual-core Athlon 64 X2 processor line. AMD took a meat-ax to its processor price list, cutting prices on many models by 60% or more. Even that wasn't enough to give AMD price/performance parity with Core 2 Duo. In effect, Core 2 Duo knocked AMD back into K6 days, when all it had to sell was "value" processors. Or, more accurately, AMD is now selling what we consider "mainstream" and "performance" processors at "value" prices. Intel again owns the high end, and is likely to keep that crown at least through late 2007. In the interim, Intel and AMD will compete strongly in the midrange $150 to $250 segment, with Intel selling its slowest processors in that price range, and AMD selling its fastest. All of us benefit, because we're now able to get what amounts to a performance processor for a mainstream price.

As we write this in August 2006, Intel's plans for the Core 2 processor line are unclear. We expect Intel to release single-core Core 2 Solo models in late 2006 as a replacement for the aging Celeron series. If that occurs, Intel will own the low-end segment as well as the midrange and high-end segments unless AMD makes extraordinary pricing cuts on its single-core Athlon 64 line. We expect that to happen as well, because otherwise AMD will find itself unable to sell any processors.

Whither Pentium D?

Although Intel has not yet discontinued the Pentium D, and in fact introduced new models in July 2006, Pentium D is really just a bridge processor. Intel will continue to offer it as they ramp up Core 2 Duo production, but will almost certainly discontinue it as soon as they are able to meet demand for Core 2 Duo. While it remains available, which will probably be well into 2007, Pentium D remains an excellent choice. Intel has priced it competitively in terms of price/performance against the Core 2 Duo, and certainly against the AMD Athlon 64 X2. The only downside of Pentium D is that it draws a lot of power and produces a lot of heat. Still, that can be dealt with, so don't rule out Pentium D when you're designing your own system.

Heatsink/Fan Units (CPU Coolers)

Modern processors consume 50W to 100W or more. Nearly all systems deal with the resulting heat by placing a massive metal heatsink in close contact with the processor and using a small fan to draw air through the heatsink fins. This device is called a heatsink/fan (HSF) or CPU cooler. Use the following guidelines when choosing an HSF:

- Make certain the HSF is rated for the exact processor you use. An HSF that physically fits a processor may not be sufficient to cool it properly. In particular, be careful with newer Intel Pentium 4 and Pentium D processors, which produce much more heat than the earlier models that ran at similar speeds.

- Make sure the HSF is usable with your motherboard. Some HSFs are incompatible with some motherboards because clamping the HSF into position may crush capacitors or other components near the processor socket.

- Pay attention to noise ratings. Some high-efficiency HSFs designed for use by overclockers and other enthusiasts have very noisy fans. Other HSFs are nearly silent.

- Use the proper thermal compound. When you install an HSF, and each time you remove and replace it, use fresh thermal compound to ensure proper heat transfer. Thermal compound is available in the form of viscous thermal "goop" and as phase-change thermal pads, which melt as the processor heats up and solidify as it cools down. Make sure that the thermal compound you use is approved by the processor maker.

The CPU coolers we recommend are listed at *http://www.hardwareguys. com/picks/cpu-coolers.html*.

Motherboard

The motherboard is the main logic board around which a PC is built. The motherboard is the center of the PC in the sense that every system component connects to the motherboard, directly or indirectly. The motherboard you choose determines which processors are supported, how much and what type of memory the system can use, what type of video adapters can be installed, the speed of communication ports, and many other key system characteristics.

Use the following guidelines when choosing a motherboard:

- For a general-purpose system, choose an ATX motherboard. For a small system, a microATX motherboard may be a better choice, although using the smaller form factor has several drawbacks, notably giving up several expansion slots and making it more difficult to route cables and cool the system.

- For a Pentium D or Core 2 Duo system, choose a Socket 775 (Socket T) motherboard that is compatible with your choice of processor. For an Athlon 64 X2 system, choose a Socket AM2 motherboard.

- For an Intel processor, choose an Intel or ASUS motherboard that uses an Intel 946/955X/963/965/975X-series chipset. For an AMD processor, choose an ASUS motherboard that uses an *n*VIDIA *n*Force 5-series chipset.

- Make sure the motherboard supports the exact processor you plan to use. Just because a motherboard supports a particular processor family doesn't mean it supports all members of that family. You can find this information on the motherboard maker's web site or in the release notes to the BIOS updates. It's also important to know exactly what revision of the motherboard you have, because processor support may vary by motherboard revision level.

- Make sure the motherboard supports the type and amount of memory you need. Do not make assumptions about how much memory a motherboard supports. Check the documentation to find out what specific memory configurations are supported.

- Before you choose a motherboard, check the documentation and support that's available for it, as well as the BIOS and driver updates available. Frequent updates indicate that the manufacturer takes support seriously.

The motherboards we recommend are listed at *http://www.hardwareguys. com/picks/motherboards.html*.

Memory

The only real decisions are how much memory to install, what size and type of modules to use, and what brand to buy. Consider the following factors when choosing memory modules (DIMMs):

- For budget systems, install no less than 512 MB. If the system will run Windows Vista, install 1 GB or more. For mainstream systems, install 1 GB or more. For performance systems, workstations, and multimedia/graphics systems, install 2 GB or more. If you use a Core 2 Duo, Pentium D or Athlon 64 X2 dual-core processor, double these amounts.

- Memory manufacturers like Crucial (*http://www.crucial.com*), Kingston (*http://www.kingston.com*), Corsair (*http://www.corsairmemory.com*), and Mushkin (*http://www.mushkin.com*) provide online memory configurators that allow you to enter the brand and model of your motherboard and return a list of compatible memory modules. Before you buy memory, use these configurators to make sure the memory you order is compatible with your particular motherboard.

- For motherboards that use 184-pin DDR memory, buy only PC3200 or faster DDR-SDRAM memory modules. Choose modules that support fast CAS latency timings only if they cost little or no more than modules that support standard timings.

- For motherboards that use 240-pin DDR2 memory, buy DDR2 memory modules of at least the speed required by your motherboard/processor combination. DDR2 memory is available in PC2 3200, PC2 4200, PC2 5300, PC2 6400, and PC2 8000 variants. Choose the fastest modules that do not sell at a significant price premium over slower modules. Once again, choose modules that support fast CAS latency timings only if they cost little or no more than modules with standard timings.

- For higher performance, use DIMMs in pairs to enable dual-channel memory operation.

- It's generally less expensive to buy a given amount of memory in fewer modules. For example, if you are installing 2 GB of memory, two 1 GB DIMMs will probably cost less than four 512 MB DIMMs. Using fewer but larger DIMMs also preserves memory slots for future expansion. However, the largest capacity modules often sell at a substantial premium. For example, a 2 GB DIMM may cost five times as much as a 1 GB DIMM, rather than only twice as much.

- Verify the memory configurations supported by your motherboard. For example, a particular motherboard may support 1 GB DIMMs, but not 2 GB DIMMs. One motherboard may support 1 GB DIMMs in all four of its memory slots, but another may support 1 GB DIMMs in only two of its four slots. Check the motherboard documentation to determine the memory configurations your chosen motherboard supports.

- Nonparity memory modules provide no error detection or correction. ECC modules detect and correct most memory errors, but are slower and more expensive than nonparity modules. Use ECC memory if you install more than 2 GB of memory and the motherboard supports ECC memory. For 2 GB or less, use nonparity modules.

The memory modules we recommend are listed at *http://www.hardwareguys. com/picks/memory.html*.

Floppy Disk Drive (FDD)

Every time we build a PC without an FDD we regret doing it when we need to load a driver from floppy. (But we keep doing it anyway...) Accordingly, we recommend installing an FDD. At $8 or so, it's cheap insurance. If you want an FDD, buy any brand. FDDs are commodity items, and the brand makes little difference. If you're short on external drive bays and want both an FDD and a card reader, install a combination FDD/card reader such as the Mitsumi FA402A.

ADVICE FROM BRIAN BILBREY

Almost all new motherboards support booting from a USB floppy these days. Buy one of these, and your days of installing a new FDD in a box, or migrating an FDD from a retired system to a new one are over.

Hard Drive

It's easy to choose a good hard drive. Several manufacturers produce drives at similar price points for a given size and type of drive. That said, we prefer Seagate hard drives because they are fast, quiet, cool-running, and competitively-priced, and because we and our readers have experienced poor reliability with drives made by some other manufacturers.

Compatibility is not an issue for hard drives. Hard drives are plug-and-play devices. Any recent hard drive coexists peacefully with any other recent hard drive or optical drive, regardless of manufacturer. (But see the warning about Serial ATA optical drives in the next section.)

Use the following guidelines when you choose a hard disk:

- Hard drives are available in standard ATA (Parallel ATA or PATA) and Serial ATA (SATA) interfaces. PATA drives are suitable only for upgrading older systems that lack SATA interfaces. For a new system, choose a drive that uses the SATA interface. Choose a model that supports the 3.0 Gb/s SATA interface—which is often (incorrectly) described as SATA-II—and native command queuing (NCQ).

- It's tempting to buy the highest-capacity drive available, but high-capacity drives often cost more per gigabyte than midrange drives, and the highest-capacity drives are often slower than midrange models. Decide what performance level and capacity you need, and then buy a drive that meets those requirements. Choose the model based on cost per gigabyte. You may need to buy the largest drive available despite its higher cost per gigabyte and slower performance, simply to conserve drive bays and ATA channels.

- Choose a 7,200 RPM SATA drive for a general-purpose system. 10,000 RPM drives cost more than 7,200 RPM models, are not all that much faster, and are much noisier and hotter running than 7,200 RPM models.

- Get a model with larger buffer/cache if it doesn't cost much more. Some drives are available in two versions that differ only in buffer size. One might have a 2 MB buffer and the other an 8 MB buffer. The larger buffer is worth paying a few extra dollars for.

The hard drives we recommend are listed at *http://www.hardwareguys. com/picks/harddisk.html*.

Optical Drive

Every system needs an optical drive of some sort, if only for loading software. There are several types of optical drives available. Some can use only CDs, which typically store about 700 MB of data. Other optical drives can use DVDs, which typically store between 4,700 MB and 8,500 MB of data. CD-ROM and DVD-ROM drives are read-only (the "ROM" part of the name). CD writers and DVD writers (also called burners or recorders) can write optical discs as well as read them. DVD is backward compatible with CD, which means that a DVD drive can also read CD discs, and all DVD writers can also write CD discs.

CD drive speeds are specified as a multiple of the 150 KB/s audio CD rate, which is called 1X. For example, a 52X CD drive transfers data at 52 times 150 KB/s, or 7,800 KB/s. DVD drives use a different "X-factor." A 1X DVD drive transfers data at about 1.321 MB/s, or about nine times faster than a 1X CD drive.

Choose an optical drive for your system based on the capabilities you need and the price you are willing to pay. In the past, there were many different types of optical drives, with a wide range of prices and capabilities, including such variants as hybrid DVD-ROM/CD writers. Most of those drive types have fallen by the wayside, victims of the rapidly declining prices of more capable drives. Nowadays, only two optical drive types make sense for use in new systems.

DVD-ROM drive

> DVD-ROM drives read CD and DVD discs, cannot write discs, and sell for $20 or less. Install a DVD-ROM drive only when budget is the top priority and you don't need a drive that can write discs. Choose any current model made by Lite-On, Mitsumi, NEC, Samsung, or Toshiba. If you need to read writable DVD discs, make sure the model you choose explicitly lists compatibility with the formats you use. If you need to read DVD-RAM discs, buy a Toshiba model. Otherwise, buy on price.

DVD writer

> DVD writers read and write both CDs and DVDs. Inexpensive DVD writers such as those made by BenQ and NEC sell for $35, and are perfectly acceptable for casual use. Midrange and premium models made by Plextor are a better choice for heavy use and when reliability counts, such as making backups.

DON'T BUY AN SATA OPTICAL DRIVE

Nearly all optical drives use the PATA interface. A few models are available with the SATA interface, but we suggest you avoid those. SATA optical drives are plagued with compatibility problems. If you must have an SATA optical drive, make absolutely sure it is certified to be compatible with the exact motherboard model you use.

DON'T BUY A PATA OPTICAL DRIVE

Of course, if you're building an Intel Core 2 system based on a motherboard built around the Intel ICH8 south bridge, you have no choice. ICH8 does not provide PATA interfaces, so your only option is to use an SATA optical drive. The only SATA model we can recommend is the Plextor PX-755SA. Just make sure the motherboard is explicitly listed on Plextor's supported motherboards list.

The optical drives we recommend are listed at *http://www.hardwareguys.com/picks/optical.html*.

Video Adapter

The video adapter, also called a graphics adapter, renders video data provided by the processor into a form that the monitor can display. Many motherboards include embedded (integrated) video adapters. You can also install a standalone video adapter, also called a video card or graphics card, in a motherboard expansion slot. Keep the following in mind when you choose a video adapter:

- Unless you run graphics-intensive games, 3D graphics performance is unimportant. Any recent video adapter is more than fast enough for business applications and casual gaming.

- Choose integrated video unless there is good reason not to. Integrated video adds little or nothing to the price of a motherboard, and generally suffices for anyone except hardcore gamers or those with other special video requirements. Make sure any motherboard you buy allows integrated video to be disabled and provides an AGP or PCI Express slot. That way, you can upgrade the video later if you need to.

- Make sure that the video adapter you choose uses the type of interface provided by your motherboard. Older motherboards and some current models use the obsolescent AGP (Accelerated Graphics Port) interface. Most current motherboards use the newer PCI Express (PCIe) interface. When you buy a motherboard for a new system, always choose a PCIe model unless you already have an AGP video adapter that you want to migrate to the new system.

WHAT ABOUT VISTA AND AERO GLASS?

Much has been made of the fact that Windows Vista is the first version of Windows to use a 3D graphical interface. While it's true that the Aero Glass interface requires 3D graphics support, we have verified that recent integrated video adapters including Intel GMA 950, Intel GMA 3000, and nVIDIA 6100/6150 have sufficiently powerful 3D acceleration to handle Aero Glass. Any video adapter, standalone or integrated, that supports DirectX 9 and PS (Pixel Shader) 2.0 and has 128 MB of memory (on-board or shared) should suffice to run Aero Glass, albeit not with top performance.

ADVICE FROM BRIAN JEPSON

And even then, trying to keep the old one locks you into some unpleasant trade-offs. I had a great AGP adapter that I handed down to my brother because I couldn't find a decent AGP motherboard that supported a dual core Pentium. It seems that trying to get AGP support on a modern system leads to some motherboards that are real mongrels in terms of chipsets.

- Make sure that the video adapter you choose (or the integrated video on your motherboard) provides the type of video output connector you need. CRT monitors and some LCD displays use the 15-pin analog VGA connector; other LCD displays use the digital DVI connector.

- If you plan to use dual displays, make sure that your integrated video or video adapter supports dual displays, and that it provides the type of video connectors you need for both displays. Note that some video adapters provide one analog and one digital video connector, but allow only one of those to operate at a time. The most flexible choice is a card with dual DVI-I hybrid video connectors, which support both analog and digital displays.

ADVICE FROM JIM COOLEY

Even if you plan to use a separate video adapter, having integrated video available is a good diagnostic resource. For that reason alone I'd never buy a board without one.

- If you need a 3D graphics adapter, don't overbuy. A $400 video adapter is faster than a $100 adapter, but nowhere near four times faster. As with other PC components, the bang-for-the-buck ratio drops quickly as the price climbs. If you need better 3D graphics performance than integrated video provides but you don't have much in the budget for a video adapter, look at "obsolescent" 3D video adapters—those a generation or two out of date. If you buy an older adapter, make sure the level of DirectX it supports is high enough to support the games you play.

- Make sure that the adapter you choose has drivers available for the operating system you intend to use. This is particularly important if you run Linux or another OS with limited driver support.

The video adapters we recommend are listed at *http://www.hardwareguys. com/picks/video.html*.

Advice from Brian Jepson

I find the user reviews on NewEgg to be helpful in determining whether a given card might be a hassle under Linux.

Display

You spend a lot of time looking at your display, so it's worth devoting some time and effort to choosing a good one. The first decision to make when you choose a display is whether to buy a traditional "glass bottle" CRT monitor or a flat-panel LCD display.

WHITHER CRTS?

Our editor comments that CRTs are becoming more difficult to find and the selection more limited, which is true. For that matter, CRT-based televisions are fast waning in popularity. But we believe that CRT monitors will continue to be widely available at least through 2007, and probably into 2008 or later.

Relative to CRTs, LCDs have several advantages. LCDs are brighter than CRTs and have better contrast. Short of direct sunlight impinging on the screen, a good LCD provides excellent images under any lighting conditions. LCDs are much lighter than CRTs, and are only a few inches deep, which makes them more convenient when space is limited. Finally, LCDs consume only 20% to 60% as much power as typical CRTs.

LCDs also have many drawbacks relative to CRTs. Not all LCDs suffer from all of these flaws. Newer models are less likely than older models to suffer from any particular flaw, and inexpensive models are more likely than premium models to suffer from these flaws, both in number and in degree.

The primary drawback of LCDs is their high price, 50% to 100% more than CRTs of comparable size and quality. (Yes, you can buy a $200 19" LCD, but to match the display quality and durability of a $200 19" CRT LCD you'll have to spend $350 or more on an LCD.) LCDs are optimized for one resolution, usually 1024×768 for 15" LCDs and 1280×1024 for 17", 18", and 19" LCDs. LCDs backlight the image with an array of cold cathode ray tubes (CCRTs), which are similar to fluorescent tubes and are subject to failure and to gradual dimming over time. An out-of-warranty CCRT failure means you might as well buy a new LCD, because it's very costly to repair.

LCDs have other drawbacks as well. Only fast LCD displays—those with black-white-black response of 8 ms or less—are acceptable for displaying fast-motion video and games, because on slower models the image smears and ghosts. LCDs have a limited viewing angle. Most graphic artists we've spoken to refuse to use LCDs, because the appearance of colors and the relationship between colors change depending on the viewing angle. LCDs provide less vibrant color than a good CRT monitor. This is particularly evident in the darkest and lightest ranges, where the tones seem to be compressed, which limits subtle gradations between light tones or dark tones that are readily evident on a good CRT. Also, some LCDs add a color cast to what should be neutral light or dark tones. LCDs, particularly inexpensive models, suffer from image persistence, which causes temporary "ghost images."

Pay Me Now or Pay Me Later

Their lower power consumption means that an LCD costs less to run than a CRT. The amount you save on your power bill depends on how much you pay for power and how many hours your display is used each day, but saving $25 or more per year is typical for a SOHO system. Over a four- to five-year period, lower power bills may offset the higher initial cost of an LCD display. Against this advantage, however, is the fact that even a high-quality LCD display is unlikely to last as long as a good CRT display.

Finally, some LCDs have one or more defective pixels. ISO Standard 13406-2 defines rules for defective pixels, including their number, type, and locations relative to each other. Defective pixels may be always-on (white, called a Type 1 defective pixel) or always-off (black, called a Type 2 defective pixel). A defective subpixel, called a Type 3 defective pixel, is always on, but displays a color other than white. In general, Type 3 defective pixels are more intrusive visually than Type 1 defective pixels, which in turn are more intrusive than Type 2 defective pixels.

ISO standard 13406-2 defines the four classes of panels listed in Table 2-1.

Table 2-1. ISO Standard 13406-2 panel classes (defects per million pixels)

Class	Type 1	Type 2	Type 3
I	0	0	0
II	2	2	5
III	5	15	50
IV	50	150	500

A Class I panel must be perfect—zero dead pixels of any type—regardless of its size or resolution. Such panels are extremely expensive, so nearly all high-quality LCD displays use Class II panels. Some of the very cheapest LCD displays use Class III panels. As far as we know, no one sells a Class IV panel for computer use.

The actual number of defective pixels in a panel of a specific class depends on the resolution of that panel. For example, a 17" LCD display with 1280×1024 resolution has $1280 \times 1024 = 1{,}310{,}720$ pixels = 1.31072 million pixels. If the panel is Class II, it can have at most the following number of dead pixels of each type:

Type 1 = $1.31072 \times 2 = 2.62144$ dead pixels = 2 dead pixels
Type 2 = $1.31072 \times 2 = 2.62144$ dead pixels = 2 dead pixels
Type 3 = $1.31072 \times 5 = 6.5536$ dead pixels = 6 dead pixels

So, for example, a 1280×1024 panel that had as many as 10 dead pixels—two Type 1, two Type 2, and six Type 3—could qualify as a Class II panel. Defective pixels cannot be "traded" among types. For example, if this panel had three Type 1 defective pixels, it would not qualify as a Class II panel, even if it had zero Type 2 and Type 3 defective pixels. Also, some manufacturers voluntarily exceed ISO 13406-2 requirements. For example, Samsung offers a "Zero Bright Pixel Defect Warranty" on some of its premium models. Although these models use Class II panels, Samsung warrants them to be free of Type 1 defective pixels (although the Class II standards for Type 2 and Type 3 defective pixels remain in effect).

People vary in their reaction to defective pixels. Many people won't even notice a few defective pixels, while others, once they notice a defective pixel, seem to be drawn to that pixel to the exclusion of everything else. Some manufacturer warranties specifically exclude some number of defective pixels, typically between 5 and 10, although the number may vary with display size and, sometimes, with the location of the defective pixels and how closely they are clustered. As long as the display meets those requirements, the manufacturer considers the display to be acceptable. You may or may not find it acceptable.

We formerly suggested that LCDs should be used only if their size, weight, low power consumption, or portability outweighed their higher cost and other disadvantages. Otherwise, we recommended choosing a good CRT and allocating the money saved to other system components. But current LCD displays are better, faster, more reliable, and much less expensive than earlier models. In the 17" and 19" range, a midrange name-brand LCD can cost as little as $100 to $150 more than a comparable CRT, and that differential is soon made up, at least in part, by the LCD's lower power consumption. We currently recommend LCD displays for any mainstream or higher system, and recommend CRTs only for budget systems or for those to whom the color accuracy of CRTs is important.

If you've decided that a CRT monitor is right for you, use the following guidelines to choose one:

- Remember that a CRT display is a long-term purchase. Even with heavy use, a high-quality CRT can be expected to last five years or more, so buy quality and choose a model that's likely to keep you happy not just for your current system, but for one or even two systems after that.

- Make sure the CRT is big enough, but not too big. We consider 17" models suitable only for casual use or those on the tightest of budgets. For not much more, you can buy a 19" model that you'll be much happier with. Conversely, make sure your desk or workstation furniture can accommodate the new CRT. Many people have excitedly carried home a new 21" CRT only to find that it literally won't fit where it needs to. Check physical dimensions and weight carefully before you buy. Large CRTs commonly weigh 50 lbs. or more, and some exceed 100 lbs. That said, if you find yourself debating 17" versus 19" or 19" versus 21", go with the larger model. But note that if your decision is between a cheap larger CRT and a high-quality smaller one for about the same price, you may well be happier with the smaller CRT. A $130 17" CRT beats a $130 19" CRT every time.

- Stick with good name brands and buy a midrange or higher model from within that name brand. That doesn't guarantee that you'll get a good CRT, but it does greatly increase your chances. The CRT market is extremely competitive. If two similar models differ greatly in price, the cheaper one likely has significantly worse specs. If the specs appear similar, the maker of the cheaper model has cut corners somewhere, whether in component quality, construction quality, or warranty policies.

Recommended Brands

Our opinion, which is shared by many, is that NEC-Mitsubishi, Samsung, and ViewSonic make the best CRTs available. Their CRTs, particularly midrange and better models, provide excellent image quality and are quite reliable. You're likely to be happy with a CRT from any of these manufacturers.

- If possible, test the exact CRT you plan to buy (not a floor sample) before you buy it. Ask the local store to endorse the manufacturer's warranty—that is, to agree that if the CRT fails you can bring it back to the store for a replacement rather than dealing with the hassles of returning it to the manufacturer. Mass merchandisers like Best Buy usually won't do this—they try to sell you a service contract instead, which you shouldn't buy—but small local computer stores may agree to endorse the manufacturer's warranty. If the CRT has hidden damage from rough handling during shipping, that damage will ordinarily be apparent within a month or two of use, if not immediately.

- Most mainstream CRT manufacturers produce three—Good, Better, and Best—models in 17", 19", and 21". In general, the Good model from a first-tier maker corresponds roughly in features, specifications, and price to the Better or Best models from lower-tier makers. For casual use, choose a Good model from a first-tier maker, most of which are very good indeed. If you make heavier demands on your CRT—such as sitting in front of it 8 hours a day—you may find that the Better model from a first-tier maker is the best choice. The Best models from first-tier makers are usually overkill, although they may be necessary if you use the CRT for CAD/CAM or other demanding tasks. Best models often have generally useless features like extremely high resolutions and unnecessarily high refresh rates at moderate resolutions. It's nice that a Best 17" model can display 1600×1200 resolution, for example, but unless you can float on thermals and dive on rabbits from a mile in the air, that resolution is likely to be unusable. Similarly, a 17" CRT that supports 115 MHz refresh rates at 1024×768 is nice, but in practical terms offers no real advantage over one that supports 85 or 90 MHz refresh.

- Choose the specific CRT you buy based on how it looks to you. Comparing specifications helps narrow the list of candidates, but nothing substitutes for actually looking at the image displayed by the CRT.

- Make sure the CRT has sufficient reserve brightness. CRTs dim as they age, and one of the most common flaws in new CRTs, particularly those from second- and third-tier manufacturers, is inadequate brightness. A CRT that is barely bright enough when new may dim enough to become unusable after a year or two. A new CRT should provide a good image with the brightness set no higher than 50%.

Like all other component manufacturers, CRT makers have come under increasing margin pressures. A few years ago, we felt safe in recommending any CRT from a first-tier maker, because those companies refused to put their names on anything but top-notch products. Alas, first-tier makers have been forced to make manufacturing cost reductions and other compromises to compete with cheap Pacific Rim CRTs.

Accordingly, low-end models from first-tier makers may be of lower quality than they were in the past. The presence of a first-tier maker's name plate still means that CRT is likely to be of higher quality than a similar no-name CRT, but is no longer a guarantee of top quality. Many first-tier CRTs are actually made in the same Pacific Rim plants that also produce no-name junk, but don't read too much into that. First-tier CRTs are still differentiated by component quality and the level of quality control they undergo. There is no question in our minds that the first-tier CRTs are easily worth the 10% to 20% price premium they command relative to lesser brands. In fact, we think it is worth the extra cost to buy not just a first-tier CRT, but a midrange first-tier CRT.

If you've decided that an LCD display is right for you, use the following guidelines to choose one:

- Current LCDs are available in analog-only, digital-only, and models with both analog and digital inputs. Analog input is acceptable for 15" (1024 × 768) models, but for 17" (1280 × 1024) models analog video noise becomes an issue. At that screen size and resolution, analog noise isn't immediately obvious to most people, but if you use the display for long periods the difference between using a display with a clean digital signal and one with a noisy analog signal will affect you on almost a subconscious level. For a 19" (1280 × 1024) LCD, we regard a digital signal as extremely desirable but not absolutely essential. For a larger display or above 1280 × 1024, we wouldn't consider using analog signaling.

- Insist on true 24-bit color support, which may be described as support for 16.7 million colors. Most current LCDs support 24-bit color, allocating one full byte to each of the three primary colors, which allows 256 shades of each color and a total of 16.7 million colors to be displayed. Many early LCDs and some inexpensive current models support only six bits per color, for a total of 18-bit color. These models use extrapolation to simulate full 24-bit color support, which results in poor color quality. If an LCD is advertised as "24-bit compatible," that's good reason to look elsewhere. Oddly, many LCDs that do support true 24-bit color don't bother to mention it in their spec sheets, while many that support only 18-bit color trumpet the fact that they are "24-bit compatible."

- Most LCD makers produce three or more series of LCDs. Entry-level models are often analog-only, even in 19" and 21" sizes, and have slow response times. Midrange models usually accept analog or digital inputs, and generally have response times fast enough for anything except 3D gaming and similarly demanding uses. The best models may be analog/digital hybrids or digital-only, and have very fast response times. Choose an entry-level model only if you are certain that you will never use the display for anything more than word processing, web

Buy CRTs Locally

After shipping costs, it may actually cost less to buy locally, but that is not the main reason for doing so. Buying locally gives you the opportunity to examine the exact CRT you are buying. Except for LCDs, CRTs vary more between samples than other computer components. Also, CRTs are sometimes damaged in shipping, often without any external evidence on the CRT itself or even the box. Damaged CRTs may arrive DOA, but more often they have been jolted severely enough to cause display problems and perhaps reduced service life, but not complete failure. Buying locally allows you to eliminate a "dud" before you buy it, rather than having to deal with shipping it back to the vendor or manufacturer.

browsing, and similarly undemanding tasks. If you need a true CRT-replacement display, choose a midrange or higher model with a digital interface and the fastest response time you are willing to pay for.

- Decide what panel size and resolution is right for you. Keep in mind that when you choose a specific LCD model, you are also effectively choosing the resolution that you will always use on that display.

- Buy the LCD locally if possible. Whether or not you buy locally, insist on a no-questions-asked return policy. LCDs are more variable than CRT monitors, both in terms of unit-to-unit variation and in terms of usability with a particular graphics adapter. This is particularly important if you are using an analog interface. Some analog LCDs simply don't play nice with some analog graphics adapters. Also, LCDs vary from unit to unit in how many defective pixels they have and where those are located. You might prefer a unit with five defective pixels near the edges and corners rather than a unit with only one or two defective pixels located near the center of the screen.

- If you buy locally, ask the store to endorse the manufacturer's warranty—that is, to agree that if the LCD fails you can bring it back to the store for a replacement rather than dealing with the hassles of returning the LCD to the maker.

- If possible, test the exact LCD you plan to buy (not a floor sample) before you buy it. Ideally, in particular if you will use the analog interface, you should test the LCD with your own system, or at least with a system that has a graphics adapter identical to the one you plan to use. We'd go to some extremes to do this, including carrying our desktop system down to the local store. But if that isn't possible for some reason, still insist on seeing the actual LCD you plan to buy running. That way, you can at least determine if there are defective pixels in locations that bother you. Also, use a neutral gray screen with no image to verify that the backlight evenly illuminates the entire screen. Some variation is unavoidable, but one or more corners should not be especially darker than the rest of the display, nor should there be any obvious "hot" spots.

- Stick with good name brands and buy a midrange or higher model from within that name brand. That doesn't guarantee that you'll get a good LCD, but it does greatly increase your chances. The LCD market is extremely competitive. If two similar models differ greatly in price, the cheaper one likely has significantly worse specs. If the specs appear similar, the maker of the cheaper model has cut corners somewhere, whether in component quality, construction quality, or warranty policies.

The CRT monitors and LCD displays we recommend are listed at *http://www.hardwareguys.com/picks/displays.html*.

Recommended Brands

Our opinion, confirmed by our readers and colleagues, is that NEC-Mitsubishi, Samsung, Sony, and ViewSonic make the best LCDs available. Their LCDs, particular midrange and better models, provide excellent image quality and are quite reliable. You're likely to be happy with an LCD from any of these manufacturers.

Audio Adapter

Audio adapters, also called sound cards, are a dying breed. Nearly all motherboards provide integrated audio that is more than good enough for most people's needs. In particular, the integrated audio provided by *n*VIDIA and Intel chipsets is excellent, with good support for six-channel audio. Only gamers, those who work professionally with audio, and those who have purchased a motherboard without integrated audio need consider buying a standalone audio adapter.

Use the following guidelines when choosing an audio adapter:

Don't buy too much audio adapter
> When you add or replace an audio adapter, don't pay for features you won't use. Don't buy an expensive audio adapter if you'll use it only for playing CDs, casual gaming, VoIP telephony, and so on. Even $25 sound cards include most of the features that more expensive cards provide, and are more than adequate for most purposes.

Don't buy too little audio adapter
> If you use your sound card for 3D gaming, buy one with hardware acceleration and other features that support what you use the card for. Capable consumer-grade audio adapters like the M-AUDIO Revolution and Creative Labs Audigy2-series sound cards sell for under $75, and are suitable for anything short of professional audio production.

Avoid no-name audio adapters
> Stick to name-brand audio adapters. We frequently hear horror stories from readers who have purchased house-brand audio adapters—outdated drivers, missing or inadequate documentation, poor (or no) tech support, shoddy construction, incompatibilities with Windows, and on and on. What's particularly ironic is that you may pay more for a house-brand audio adapter than for a low-end name-brand card. You can buy decent name-brand audio adapters for $25 from reputable companies. Don't buy anything less.

The audio adapters we recommend are listed at *http://www.hardwareguys. com/picks/soundcard.html*.

Speakers

Computer speakers span the range from $10 pairs of small satellites to $500+ sets of six or seven speakers that are suitable for a home theater system. Personal preference is the most important factor in choosing speakers.

Speakers that render a Bach concerto superbly are often not the best choice for playing a first-person shooter like Unreal Tournament. For that matter, speakers that one person considers perfect for the Bach concerto (or the UT game), another person may consider mediocre at best. For that reason, we

External USB Sound Adapters

Several companies, including Creative Labs, M-Audio, and Turtle Beach, manufacture external audio adapters that connect to a PC via a USB port. The advantage of these devices is easy installation–you just connect the box to a USB port and install the drivers; no need to open the case. The disadvantage is that you have one more box cluttering up your desk.

strongly suggest that you attempt to listen to speakers before you buy them, particularly if you're buying an expensive set.

Speaker sets are designated by the total number of satellite speakers, followed by a period and a "1" if the set includes a subwoofer (also called a low-frequency emitter or LFE). Speaker sets are available in the following configurations:

- 2.0: Front left and right satellites
- 2.1: 2.0 with a subwoofer
- 4.1: 2.1 with a rear left/right satellite pair added
- 5.1: 4.1 with a front center-channel speaker added
- 6.1: 5.1 with a rear center-channel speaker added
- 7.1: 5.1 with a side left/right satellite pair added
- 8.1: 7.1 with a rear center-channel speaker added

6.1, 7.1, and 8.1 speaker sets are used primarily by gamers. Some manufacturers have begun to produce "wireless" 5.1 and higher speaker sets. These speaker sets are wireless in the sense that the audio signal is communicated wirelessly; the remote satellite speakers still must be connected to AC power. Wireless speakers use the 2.4 GHz band that is shared with wireless networks, cordless telephones, microwave ovens, and innumerable other devices, so interference is always a consideration. Still, the absence of speaker wires makes it much easier to install these speakers, particularly in a living room, den, home theater, or other residential environment.

The price of a speaker set doesn't necessarily correspond to the number of speakers in the set. For example, there are very inexpensive 5.1 speaker sets available, and some 2.1 sets that cost a bundle. We recommend that you decide on the number of speakers according to your budget. If you have $75 to spend, for example, you're better off buying a good 2.1 speaker set than a cheesy 5.1 set.

The speakers we recommend are listed at *http://www.hardwareguys.com/picks/speakers.html*.

Keyboards

The best keyboard is a matter of personal preference. A keyboard we really like, you may dislike intensely, and vice versa. Ultimately, your own preferences are the only guide.

Keyboards vary in obvious ways—layout, size, and style—and in subtle ways like key spacing, angle, dishing, travel, pressure required, and tactile feedback. People's sensitivity to these differences varies. Some are keyboard agnostics who can sit down in front of a new keyboard and, regardless of layout or tactile response, be up to speed in a few minutes. Others have strong preferences about layout and feel. If you've never met a keyboard you didn't like, you can disregard these issues and choose a keyboard based on other factors. If love and hate are words you apply to keyboards, use an identical keyboard for at least an hour before you buy one for yourself.

That said, here are several important characteristics to consider when you choose a keyboard:

- Keyboards are available in two styles, the older straight keyboard and the modern ergonomic style. Some people strongly prefer one or the other. Others don't care. If you've never used an ergonomic keyboard, give one a try before you buy your next keyboard. You may hate it—everyone does at first—but then again after you use it for an hour or so you may decide you love it.

- The position of the alphanumeric keys is standard on all keyboards other than those that use the oddball Dvorak layout. What varies, sometimes dramatically, is the placement, size, and shape of other keys, such as shift keys (Shift, Ctrl, and Alt), function keys (which may be across the top, down the left side, or both), and cursor control and numeric keypad keys. If you are used to a particular layout, purchasing a keyboard with a similar layout makes it easier to adapt to the new keyboard.

- Most current keyboards use the USB interface natively, and are supplied with an adapter for those who need to connect them to a PS/2 keyboard port. We use mostly USB keyboards, but it's a good idea to have at least one PS/2 keyboard available (or a PS/2 adapter) for those times when Windows shoots craps and won't recognize USB devices.

- Some keyboards provide dedicated and/or programmable function keys to automate such things as firing up your browser or email client or to allow you to define custom macros that can be invoked with a single keystroke. These functions are typically not built into the keyboard itself, but require loading a driver. To take advantage of those functions, make sure a driver is available for the OS you use.

- The weight of a keyboard can be a significant issue for some people. The lightest keyboard we've seen weighed just over a pound, and the heaviest nearly eight pounds. If your keyboard stays on your desktop, a heavy keyboard is less likely to slide around. Conversely, a heavy keyboard may be uncomfortable if you work with the keyboard in your lap.

- Some manufacturers produce keyboards with speakers, scanners, and other entirely unrelated functions built in. These functions are often clumsy to use, fragile, and have limited features. If you want speakers or a scanner, buy speakers or a scanner. Don't get a keyboard with them built in.

- Wireless keyboards are ideal for presentations, TV-based web browsing, or just for working with the keyboard in your lap. Wireless keyboards use a receiver module that connects to a USB port or the PS/2 keyboard port on the PC. The keyboard and receiver communicate using either radio frequency (RF) or infrared (IR). IR keyboards require direct line-of-sight between the keyboard and receiver, while RF keyboards do not. Most IR keyboards and many RF keyboards provide limited range—as little as five feet or so—which limits their utility to working around a desk without cables tangling. Any wireless keyboard you buy should use standard AA, AAA, or 9V alkaline or NiMH batteries rather than a proprietary battery pack.

Logitech and Microsoft both produce a wide range of excellent keyboards, one of which is almost certainly right for you. Even their basic models are well built and reliable. The more expensive models add features such as RF or Bluetooth wireless connectivity, programmable function keys, and so on.

The keyboards we recommend are listed at *http://www.hardwareguys.com/picks/keyboards.html*.

Mice

Choosing a mouse is much like choosing a keyboard. Personal preference is by far the most important consideration. If possible, try a mouse before you buy it.

Use the following guidelines when choosing a mouse:

- Mice are available in various sizes and shapes, including small mice intended for children, notebook-sized mice, the formerly standard "Dove bar" size, the mainstream ergonomic mouse, and some oversize mice that have many buttons and extra features. Most people find standard-size mice comfortable to use for short periods, but if you use a mouse for longer periods small differences in size and shape often make a big difference in comfort and usability. Although oversize mice provide attractive features and functions, people with small hands may find such mice too large to use comfortably. Pay particular attention to mouse shape if you are left-handed. Although asymmetric ergonomic mice are often claimed to be equally usable by left- and right-handers, many lefties find them uncomfortable and resort to right-handed mousing. Some manufacturers, including Logitech, produce symmetric ergonomic mice.

- Get a wheel mouse. Although some applications do not support the wheel, those that do are the ones most people are likely to use a great deal—Microsoft Office, Internet Explorer, Firefox, and so on. Using the wheel greatly improves mouse functionality by reducing the amount of mouse movement needed to navigate web pages and documents. Mice with a tilt-wheel allow you to scroll vertically and horizontally.

Small Hands, Big Mouse

Don't assume that hand size and mouse size are necessarily related. For example, Barbara, who has small hands, prefers the Microsoft IntelliMouse Explorer, which is an oversize mouse. She found that using a standard or small mouse for long periods caused her hand to hurt. Changing to a large mouse solved the problem.

- Standard two-button mice (three, counting the wheel) suffice for most purposes. However, five-button mice are ideally suited to some applications, such as games and web browsing. For example, the two extra buttons can be mapped to the Back and Forward browser icons, eliminating a great deal of extraneous mouse movement.

- Mice have cords ranging in length from less than 4 feet to about 9 feet. A short mouse cord may be too short to reach the system, particularly if it is on the floor. If you need a longer mouse cord, purchase a PS/2 keyboard or USB extension cable, available in nearly any computer store.

- Consider buying a cordless mouse. The absence of a cord can make a surprising difference.

- Buy an optical mouse. Optical mice use a red LED or chip LASER light source and do not require any special mousing surface. Because they are sealed units, optical mice seldom need cleaning. Robert had to take his mechanical mice apart and clean them literally every few days, but his optical mice go for months without cleaning. Fortunately, only the cheapest mice nowadays are mechanical.

Logitech and Microsoft both produce a wide range of excellent optical mice, in corded and cordless models. One of them is almost certainly right for you. Even their basic models are well built and reliable. The more expensive models have more features, are more precise, and are probably more durable. We used Microsoft optical mice almost exclusively for many years, and continue to recommend them. However, when we tested the superb Logitech MX-series optical mice, we found that we preferred their shape and feel. We now use Logitech optical mice on most of our primary systems.

Avoid cheap, no-name mice. If someone tries to sell you a mechanical "ball" mouse, run.

The mice we recommend are listed at *http://www.hardwareguys.com/picks/mice.html*.

Network Adapters

A network adapter—also called a LAN (Local Area Network) adapter, or NIC (Network Interface Card)—is used to connect a PC to a home or business network. A network adapter provides a relatively fast communication link—100 megabits per second (Mb/s) or 1,000 Mb/s—between the PC and other devices connected to the network. Network adapters are available in wired and wireless versions. A network may use all wired network adapters, all wireless network adapters, or some combination of the two.

Mouse Alternatives

Consider using a trackball or touch-pad, particularly if you experience hand pain when using a mouse.

Wired network adapters

In a typical wired network, the network adapters in each PC connect to a central hub or switch that allows any connected device to communicate with any other connected device. In a home or SOHO setting, a wired network adapter may also be used to connect an individual PC directly to a cable modem or xDSL modem.

Nearly all wired network adapters support one or more of a family of networking standards that are collectively called Ethernet. Current Ethernet adapters use unshielded twisted pair (UTP) cable, which resembles standard telephone cable, and communicate at 100 Mb/s (100BaseT or "Fast Ethernet") or 1,000 Mb/s (1000BaseT or "Gigabit"). Wired Ethernet adapters use an 8-position, 8-connector (8P8C) jack that resembles an oversized telephone jack, and is usually (although incorrectly) called an "RJ-45" connector.

Many motherboards include integrated wired Ethernet adapters, which are typically 10/100 or 10/100/1000 hybrid devices. You can add wired Ethernet to a system that lacks an integrated NIC by installing an inexpensive PCI expansion card. Integrated network adapters are reliable and add little or nothing to the cost of a motherboard. Standalone desktop PCI network adapters typically cost from $15 to $40, depending on manufacturer and speed. PCI network adapters are often more efficient and fully featured than integrated adapters.

WARNING

Most Ethernet adapters are backward compatible with slower Ethernet versions. For example, most 100BaseT adapters can also communicate with old 10BaseT devices, and most 1000BaseT adapters can also communicate with 100BaseT and 10BaseT devices. This is not invariably true, however. Some Ethernet devices support only one or two standards. That can cause problems if, for example, you connect a 10BaseT adapter (for example, in an old notebook system) to a hub or switch that supports only 100BaseT or 100BaseT and 1000BaseT. Although the devices can be physically connected, they do not communicate. Components that support multiple speeds, called hybrid components, are usually labeled in the form 10/100BaseT, 100/1000BaseT, or 10/100/1000BaseT.

Apples and Oranges

Make sure you know what you're getting when you order a motherboard. Many motherboards are available in several variants, which may provide different levels of integrated Ethernet. For example, the Intel D945GNT motherboard is available in five variants. The D945GNTL and the D945GNTLR provide integrated 10/100 Ethernet. The D945GNTLK, D945GNTLKR, and the LAD945GNTLKR provide integrated 10/100/1000 Ethernet.

The best rule of thumb for most desktop systems is to use an integrated network adapter, if your chosen motherboard offers that option and if you do not require the additional management and other features available only with standalone adapters. For servers, use a standalone 100BaseT PCI network adapter, unless you are using a special server motherboard that incorporates one or more server-class 100BaseT or 1000BaseT network adapters. For 1000BaseT on a server, use only an integrated adapter. A PCI 1000BaseT adapter simply consumes too much of the available PCI bandwidth to be usable in such an environment.

If you need wired connectivity, choose a motherboard that provides an integrated 10/100, 100/1000, or 10/100/1000 Ethernet adapter. 10/100 is acceptable for most people's current needs, but Gigabit models provide "future-proofing" at small additional cost.

If your motherboard does not provide an integrated LAN adapter or if you prefer to use a separate LAN adapter, choose one of the wired network adapters we recommend at *http://www.hardwareguys.com/picks/lan.html*.

Wireless network adapters

Wireless network adapters—also called WLAN (wireless LAN) cards, 802.11 cards, or Wi-Fi (Wireless Fidelity) cards—use radio waves to communicate. WLAN adapters communicate with a central device called an access point (AP) or wireless access point (WAP). In a mixed wired/wireless network, the AP connects to the wired network and provides an interface between the wired and wireless portions of the network. One AP can support many WLAN adapters, but all of the adapters must share the bandwidth available on the AP. In a large network, multiple APs may be used to extend the physical reach of the wireless network and to provide additional bandwidth to computers that connect to the network with WLAN adapters.

WLAN adapters are commonly used in notebook computers, either in integrated form or as a PC card. WLAN adapters are also available as PCI expansion cards that can be installed in desktop systems to provide a network link when it is difficult or expensive to run a cable to a system. The original 1997-era WLAN adapters used the 802.11 standard, which supported a maximum data rate of only 2 Mb/s. Those adapters are long obsolete. Current WLAN adapters support one or more of the following standards.

802.11b

> 802.11b supports a maximum data rate of 11 Mb/s, comparable to 10BaseT Ethernet, and has typical real-world throughput of 5 Mb/s. 802.11b uses the unlicensed 2.4 GHz spectrum, which means it is subject to interference from microwave ovens, cordless phones, and other devices that share the 2.4 GHz spectrum. The popularity of 802.11b is waning because components that use the faster 802.11g standard, described shortly, are now available at low cost, and because most 802.11b components support only the compromised WEP authentication and encryption rather than trustworthy WPA or WPA2. Millions of 802.11b adapters remain in use, primarily as integrated or PC Card adapters in notebook computers.

Warning

Running at 1,000 Mb/s, a PCI Gigabit Ethernet adapter can swamp the 133 MB/s (1,067 Mb/s) PCI bus, so it's a bad idea to use a PCI Gigabit adapter. Instead, look for a motherboard that provides integrated Gigabit LAN that keeps LAN traffic off the PCI bus by using a dedicated high-speed bus, such as Intel's CSA or Communications Streaming Architecture bus, or a PCIe channel. Alternatively, install a Gigabit Ethernet card that uses the PCIe bus.

802.11a

802.11a supports a maximum data rate of 54 Mb/s, and has typical real-world throughput of 25 Mb/s. It uses a portion of the 5 GHz spectrum that until late 2003 was licensed, but is now unlicensed. 5 GHz signals have shorter range and are more easily obstructed than 2.4 GHz signals, but are also less likely to interfere with other nearby devices. 802.11a is incompatible with 802.11b because they use different frequencies. The higher cost for 802.11a devices means they are used almost exclusively in business environments. Most 802.11a components have business-oriented features such as remote manageability that add cost but are of little interest to home users.

802.11g

The most recent WLAN standard is 802.11g, which combines the best features of 802.11a and 802.11b. Like 802.11b, 802.11g works in the unlicensed 2.4 GHz spectrum, which means it has good range but is subject to interference from other 2.4 GHz devices. Because they use the same frequencies, 802.11b WLAN adapters can communicate with 802.11g APs, and vice versa. Like 802.11a, 802.11g supports a maximum data rate of 54 Mb/s, and has typical real-world bandwidth of about 25 Mb/s. That is sufficient to support real-time streaming video, which 802.11b cannot. 802.11g devices now sell for little more than 802.11b devices, so 802.11g has effectively made 802.11b obsolete.

WARNING

802.11b and 802.11g components are standards-based, so devices from different manufacturers should interoperate. In practice, that is largely true, although minor differences in how standards are implemented can cause conflicts. In particular, some high-end 802.11b/802.11g components include proprietary extensions for security and similar purposes. Those components do generally interoperate with components from other vendors, but only on a "least common denominator" basis—that is, using only the standard 802.11 features. The best way to ensure that your wireless network operates with minimal problems is to use WLAN adapters and APs from the same vendor.

"802.108g"

Several manufacturers, including D-Link and NetGear, produce APs that claim to provide 108 Mb/s bandwidth. In fact they do, but only by "cheating" on the 802.11g specification. Such APs, colloquially called "802.108g" devices, work as advertised, but using them may cause conflicts with 802.11g-compliant devices operating in the same vicinity.

802.11g defines 11 channels (13 in Europe), each with 22 MHz of bandwidth. Each 22 MHz channel can support the full 54 Mb/s bandwidth of 802.11g. But these channels overlap, as shown in Figure 2-1. Three of the channels—1, 6, and 11—are completely nonoverlapping, which means that three 802.11g-compliant APs in the same vicinity—one assigned to each of the three nonoverlapping channels—can share the 2.4 GHz spectrum without conflicts. Alternatively, two 802.11g-compliant APs can be assigned to two channels that do not overlap each other, for example, Channels 2 and 8.

An 802.108g device claims two of the three completely nonoverlapping channels, typically either 1 and 6 or 6 and 11, although it could in theory use 1 and 11. That leaves only one channel available for other 802.11g devices. To make matters worse, although 802.11g APs detect other nearby 802.11g APs and adjust themselves to use nonconflicting channels, many 802.11g APs fail to detect 802.108g APs operating nearby. The 802.11g devices wrongly assume that the channels being used by the 802.108g devices are available, and so may choose to operate on those "available" channels. The upshot is that it's possible, even likely, to end up with an 802.11g device and an 802.108g device attempting to use the same channel at the same time, which means neither device works properly.

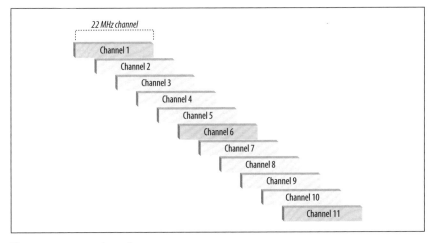

Figure 2-1. 802.11g channels

If you are building a new wireless network, use a D-Link 802.11g or 802.108g WLAN adapter and AP. Choose 802.11g if channel conflicts are possible, e.g., if you live in an apartment or if your business is in close proximity to other businesses. Choose 802.108g if there are no 802.11b/g APs nearby, but note that you may have to replace 2.4 GHz cordless phones with models that use a different frequency band. If you are expanding a wireless network, use an 802.11g adapter from the same company that made the existing components.

Avoid no-name network adapters and other components. Avoid mixing components from different manufacturers, if possible, particularly in a wireless network. Avoid 802.11a unless you need SNMP remote manageability and other business-oriented features.

Run a Router

If you need to purchase an 802.11g or 802.108g AP, consider buying a model that also incorporates a hardware firewall/router. Using a hardware firewall/router on a home or SOHO network is the single most important thing you can do to improve security and reduce the likelihood that your systems will be infected by a worm.

Buying Components

We've bought hundreds of thousands of dollars' worth of PC components over the last 20 years, for ourselves and on behalf of employers and clients. In the following sections, we'll tell you what we learned along the way.

Buying Guidelines

Until the early 1990s, most computer products were bought in computer specialty stores. Retail sales still make up a significant chunk of computer product sales—although the emphasis has shifted from computer specialty stores to local "big-box" retailers like Best Buy, CompUSA, Fry's, Wal-Mart, and Costco—but online resellers now account for a large percentage of PC component sales.

Should you buy from a local brick-and-mortar retailer or an online reseller? We do both, because each has advantages and disadvantages.

Local retailers offer the inestimable advantage of instant gratification. Unless you're more patient than we are, when you want something, you want it Right Now. Buying from a local retailer puts the product in your hands instantly, instead of making you wait for FedEx to show up. You can also hold the product in your hands, something that's not possible if you buy from an online reseller. Local retailers also have a big advantage if you need to return or exchange a product. If something doesn't work right, or if you simply change your mind, you can just drive back to the store rather than dealing with the hassles and cost of returning a product to an online reseller.

Online resellers have the advantage in breadth and depth of product selection. If you want the less-expensive OEM version of a product, for example, chances are you won't find it at local retailers, most of which stock only retail-boxed products. If an online reseller stocks a particular manufacturer's products, they tend to stock the entire product line, whereas local retailers often pick and choose only the most popular items in a product line. Of course, the popular products are usually popular for good reasons. Online resellers are also more likely to stock niche products and products from smaller manufacturers. Sometimes, if you must have a particular product, the only option is to buy it online.

Online resellers usually advertise lower prices than local retailers, but it's a mistake to compare only nominal prices. When you buy from a local retailer, you pay only the advertised price plus any applicable sales tax. When you buy from an online retailer, you pay the advertised price plus shipping, which may end up costing you more than buying locally.

WARNING

Ah, but you don't have to pay sales tax when you buy online, right? Well, maybe. In most jurisdictions, you're required by law to pay a *use tax* in lieu of sales tax on out-of-state purchases. Most people evade use taxes, of course, but that free ride is coming to an end. States faced with increasing budget problems, which is to say all of them, are starting to clamp down on people who buy from online resellers and don't pay use tax. States are using data-mining techniques to co-ordinate with each other and with credit card companies and online retailers to uncover unpaid use taxes. If you don't pay use taxes, one day soon you're likely to hear from the audit division of your state department of revenue, asking what these credit card charges were for and why you didn't report the use taxes due on them. Count on it.

Although online resellers *may* have a lower overall price on a given component, it's a mistake to assume that is always the case. Local retailers frequently run sales and rebate promotions that cut the price of a component below the lowest online price. For example, we bought a spindle of 100 CD-R discs on sale from a local retailer for $19.95 with a $10 instant rebate and a $20 mail-in rebate. After the cost of the stamp to mail in the rebate form, they *paid* us $9.68 to carry away those 100 discs, which is pretty tough for an online reseller to match. Similarly, we bought an 80 GB hard drive for $79.95, with a $15 instant rebate and a $30 mail-in rebate. Net cost? About $35 for a retail-boxed 80 GB hard drive, which no online vendor could come close to matching.

In particular, local retailers are usually the best place to buy heavy and/or bulky items, such as monitors, cases, UPSs, and so on. Local retailers receive these items in pallet loads, which makes the cost of shipping an individual item almost nothing. Conversely, online resellers have to charge you, directly or indirectly, for the cost of getting that heavy item to your door.

Whether your purchase your PC components from a local brick-and-mortar store or a web-based retailer, here are some guidelines to keep in mind:

- Make sure you know exactly what you're buying. For example, a hard drive may be available in two versions, each with the same or a similar model number but with an added letter or number to designate different amounts of cache. Or a hard drive maker may produce two models of the same size that differ in price and performance. Always compare using the exact manufacturer model number. Before you buy a product, research it on the manufacturer's web site and on the numerous independent web sites devoted to reviews. We usually search Google with the product name and "review" in the search string.

- Vendors vary greatly. Some we trust implicitly, and others we wouldn't order from on a bet. Some are always reliable, others always unreliable, and still others seem to vary with the phases of the moon. We check *http://www.resellerratings.com*, which maintains a database of customer-reported experiences with hundreds of vendors.

- The list price or Suggested Retail Price (SRP) is meaningless. Most computer products sell for a fraction of SRP, others sell for near SRP, and for still others the manufacturer has no SRP, but instead publishes an Estimated Selling Price (ESP). To do meaningful comparisons, you need to know what different vendors charge for the product. Fortunately, there are many services that list what various vendors charge. We use *http://www.pricescan.com*, *http://www.pricewatch.com*, *http://www.pricegrabber.com*, and *http://www.froogle.com*. These services may list 20 or more different vendors, and the prices for a particular item may vary dramatically. We discard the top 25% and the bottom 25% and average the middle 50% to decide a reasonable price for the item.

- Many components are sold in retail-boxed and OEM forms. The core component is likely to be similar or identical in either case, but important details may vary. For example, Intel CPUs are available in retail-boxed versions that include a CPU cooler and a three-year warranty. They are also available as OEM components (also called tray packaging or white box) that do not include the CPU cooler and have only a 90-day warranty. OEM items are not intended for retail distribution, so some manufacturers provide no warranty to individual purchasers. OEM components are fine, as long as you understand the differences and do not attempt to compare prices between retail-boxed and OEM.

- The market for PCs and components is incredibly competitive and margins are razor-thin. If a vendor advertises a component for much less than other vendors, it may be a "loss leader." More likely, though, particularly if its prices on other items are similarly low, that vendor cuts corners, whether by using your money to float inventory, by shipping returned product as new, by charging excessive shipping fees, or, in the ultimate case, by taking your money and not shipping the product. If you always buy from the vendor with the rock-bottom price, you'll waste a lot of time hassling with returns of defective, used, or discontinued items and dealing with your credit card company when the vendor fails to deliver at all. Ultimately, you're also likely to spend more money than you would have by buying from a reputable vendor in the first place.

- The actual price you pay may vary significantly from the advertised price. When you compare prices, include all charges, particularly shipping charges. Reputable vendors tell you exactly how much the total charges will be. Less reputable vendors may forget to mention shipping charges, which may be very high. Some vendors break out the full manufacturer pack into individual items. For example, if a retail-boxed hard drive includes mounting hardware, some vendors will quote a price for the bare drive without making it clear that they have removed the mounting hardware and charge separately for it. Also be careful when buying products that include a rebate from the maker. Some vendors quote the net price after rebate without making it clear that they are doing so.

- Some vendors charge more for an item ordered via their 800 number than they do for the same item ordered directly from their web site. Some others add a fixed processing fee to phone orders. These charges reflect the fact that taking orders on the web is much cheaper than doing it by phone, so this practice has become common. In fact, some of our favorite vendors do not provide telephone order lines.

- It can be very expensive to ship heavy items such as CRTs, UPSs, and printers individually. This is one situation in which local big-box stores like Best Buy have an advantage over online vendors. The online vendor has to charge you for the cost of shipping, directly or indirectly, and that cost can amount to $50 or more for a heavy item that you need quickly. Conversely, the big-box stores receive inventory items in truckload or even railcar shipments, so the cost to them to have a single item delivered is quite small. They can pass that reduced cost on to buyers. If you're buying a heavy item, don't assume that it will be cheaper online. Check your local Best Buy or other big-box store and you may find that it actually costs less there, even after you pay sales tax. And you can carry it away with you instead of waiting for FedEx to show up with it.

- Most direct resellers are willing to sell for less than the price they advertise. All you need do is tell your chosen vendor that you'd really rather buy from them, but not at the price they're quoting. Use lower prices you find with the price comparison services as a wedge to get a better price. But remember that reputable vendors must charge more than the fly-by-night operations if they are to make a profit and stay in business. If we're ordering by phone, we generally try to beat down our chosen vendor a bit on price, but we don't expect them to match the rock-bottom prices that turn up on web searches. Of course, if you're ordering from a web-only vendor, dickering is not an option, which is one reason why web-only vendors generally have better prices.

- Using a credit card puts the credit card company on your side if there is a problem with your order. If the vendor ships the wrong product, defective product, or no product at all, you can invoke charge-back procedures to have the credit card company refund your money. Vendors who live and die on credit card orders cannot afford to annoy credit card companies, and so tend to resolve such problems quickly. Even your threat to request a charge-back may cause a recalcitrant vendor to see reason.

- Some vendors add a surcharge, typically 3%, to their advertised prices if you pay by credit card. Surcharges violate credit card company contracts, so some vendors instead offer a similar discount for paying cash, which amounts to the same thing. Processing credit card transactions costs money, and we're sure that some such vendors are quite reputable, but our own experience with vendors that surcharge has not been good. We always suspect that their business practices result in a high percentage of charge-back requests, and so they discourage using credit cards.

- Good vendors allow you to return a defective product for replacement or a full refund (often less shipping charges) within a stated period, typically 30 days. Buy only from such vendors. Nearly all vendors exclude some product categories, such as notebook computers, monitors, printers, and opened software, either because their contracts with the manufacturer require them to do so or because some buyers commonly abuse return periods for these items, treating them as "30-day free rentals." Beware of the phrase, "All sales are final." That means exactly what it says.

- Check carefully for any mention of restocking fees. Many vendors who trumpet a "no questions asked money-back guarantee" mention only in the fine print that they won't refund all your money. They charge a restocking fee on returns, and we've seen fees as high as 30% of the purchase price. These vendors love returns, because they make a lot more money if you return the product than if you keep it. Do not buy from a vendor that charges restocking fees on exchanges (as opposed to refunds). For refunds, accept no restocking fee higher than 10% to 15%, depending on the price of the item.

- If you order by phone, don't accept verbal promises. Insist that the reseller confirm your order in writing, including any special terms or conditions, before charging your credit card or shipping product. If a reseller balks at providing written confirmation of their policies, terms, and conditions, find another vendor. Most are happy to do so. If you're ordering from a vendor that uses web-based ordering exclusively, use a screen capture program or your browser's save function to grab copies of each screen as you complete the order. Most vendors send a confirming email, which we file in our "Never Delete" folder.

- File everything related to an order, including a copy of the original advertisement; email, faxed, or written confirmations provided by the reseller; copies of your credit card receipt; a copy of the packing list and invoice; and so on. We also jot down notes in our PIM regarding telephone conversations, including the date, time, telephone number and extension, person spoken to, purpose of the call, and so on. We print a copy of those to add to the folder for that order.

- Make it clear to the reseller that you expect them to ship the exact item you have ordered, not what they consider to be an "equivalent substitute." Require they confirm the exact items they will ship, including manufacturer part numbers. For example, if you order an eVGA GeForce 7900GT graphics card with 512 MB of RAM, make sure the order confirmation specifies that item by name, full description, and eVGA product number. Don't accept a less detailed description such as "graphics card," "eVGA graphics card," or even "eVGA 7900 graphics card." Otherwise, you'll get less than you paid for—a lesser GeForce card, a card with a slower processor or less memory, or even a card with a GeForce processor made by another manufacturer. Count on it.

A Cunning Plan

Nearly all retailers refuse to refund your money on opened software, DVDs, etc., but will only exchange the open product for a new, sealed copy of the same title. One of our readers tells us how he gets around that common policy. He returns the open software in exchange for a new, sealed copy of the same product, keeping his original receipt. He then returns the new, sealed copy for a refund. That's probably unethical and may be illegal for all we know, but it does work. Recently, though, some stores including Best Buy and CompUSA have begin annotating the original receipt when you make an exchange. Oh, well. It was too good to last.

- Verify warranty terms. Some manufacturers warrant only items purchased from authorized dealers in full retail packaging. For some items, the warranty begins when the manufacturer ships the product to the distributor, which may be long before you receive it. OEM products typically have much shorter warranties than retail-boxed products—sometimes as short as 90 days—and may be warranted only to the original distributor rather than to the final buyer. Better resellers may endorse the manufacturer warranty for some period on some products, often 30 to 90 days. That means that if the product fails, you can return the item to the reseller, who will ship you a replacement and take care of dealing with the manufacturer. Some resellers disclaim the manufacturer warranty, claiming that once they ship the item dealing with warranty claims is your problem, even if the product arrives DOA. We've encountered that problem a couple of times. Usually, mentioning phrases like *merchantability and fitness for a particular purpose* and *revocation of acceptance* leads them to see reason quickly. We usually demand the reseller ship us a new replacement product immediately and include a prepaid return shipping label if they want the dead item back. We don't accept or pay for dead merchandise under any circumstances, and neither should you.

- Direct resellers are required by law to ship products within the time period they promise. But that time period may be precise (e.g., "ships within 24 hours") or vague (e.g., "ships within three to six weeks"). If the vendor cannot ship by the originally promised date, it must notify you in writing and specify another date by which the item will ship. If that occurs, you have the right to cancel your order without penalty. Make sure to make clear to the reseller that you expect the item to be delivered in a timely manner. Reputable vendors ship what they say they're going to ship when they say they're going to ship it. Unfortunately, some vendors have a nasty habit of taking your money and shipping whenever they get around to it. In a practice that borders on fraud, some vendors routinely report items as "in stock" when in fact they are not. Make it clear to the vendor that you do not authorize them to charge your credit card until the item actually ships, and that if you do not receive the item when promised you will cancel the order.

Even if you follow all of these guidelines, things may go wrong. Even the best resellers sometimes drop the ball. If that happens, don't expect the problem to go away by itself. If you encounter a problem, remain calm and notify the reseller first. Good resellers are anxious to resolve problems. Find out how the reseller wants to proceed, and follow their procedures, particularly for labeling returned merchandise with an RMA number.

If you seem to have reached a dead end with the vendor, explain one last time to the vendor why you are dissatisfied, and ask them to resolve the problem. Tell them that unless they resolve the matter you will request a charge-back from your credit card company. Mail-order and Internet

Another Cunning Plan

If you buy from a local retailer, open the box from the bottom rather than the top. If you need to return a non-defective item, that makes it easier to repackage the product with the manufacturer's seals intact, which keeps the retailer happy and can help you avoid restocking fees.

vendors live and die on credit card revenue, so keeping a good relationship with the credit card companies is critically important to them. Finally, but only as a last resort, contact your bank or credit card issuer and request a charge-back. Be prepared to provide a full explanation of the problem with documentation.

Recommended Sources

The question we hear more often than any other is, "What company should I buy from?" When someone asks us that question, we run away, screaming in terror. Well, not really, but we'd like to. Answering that question is a no-win proposition for us, you see. If we recommend a vendor and that vendor treats the buyer properly, well that's no more than was expected. But Thor forbid that we recommend a vendor who turns around and screws the buyer.

So, which online resellers do we buy from? Over the years, we've bought from scores of online vendors, and our favorites have changed. For the last few years, our favorite has been NewEgg.com (*http://www.newegg.com*). NewEgg offers an extraordinarily good combination of price, wide product selection, support, shipping, and return or replacement policies. We know of no other direct vendor that even comes close.

NewEgg's prices aren't always rock-bottom, but they generally match any other vendor we're willing to deal with. NewEgg runs daily specials that are often real bargains, so if you're willing to consider alternatives and to accumulate components over the course of a few weeks you can save a fair amount of money. NewEgg ships what they say they're going to ship, when they say they're going to ship it, and at the price they agreed to ship it for. If there's a problem, they make it right. It's hard to do better than that.

WARNING

All of that said, if you buy from NewEgg and subsequently your goldfish dies and all of your teeth fall out, don't blame us. All we can say is that NewEgg has always treated us right. Things can change overnight in this industry and, while we don't expect NewEgg to take a sudden turn for the worse, it could happen.

As to local retailers, we buy from—in no particular order—Best Buy, CompUSA, Target, Office Depot, OfficeMax, and our local computer specialty stores, depending on what we need and who happens to have advertised the best prices and rebates in the Sunday ad supplements. Wal-Mart used to sell only assembled PCs. It has recently started stocking PC components, such as ATi video adapters, so we'll add Wal-Mart to our list as well.

Loot, Pillage, and Burn

Thor? Yes, it's true. Robert the Red is of Viking extraction. On government forms, he describes himself as "Viking-American." And, no, he doesn't wear a funny helmet. Except among friends. And he hasn't pillaged anything in months. Years, maybe. In fact, he's not absolutely certain what pillaging is, although it does sound like fun.

Final Words

We've done our best in this chapter to tell you what components to buy for your new PC and where and how to buy them. The specific components you need differ according to the type of system you plan to build. We describe how to make component-specific decisions in the "project system" chapters later in the book. So, before you actually start ordering components, you might want to read some (or all) of those chapters.

When the components arrive, restrain yourself. Don't start building your system before the FedEx truck even pulls out of your driveway, particularly if this is your first system build. Read or reread the relevant project chapter.

One thing you should do immediately, though, is check the contents of the boxes that were just delivered. Verify what you ordered against the packing list and invoice, and verify what's actually in the box against those documents. Usually everything will be right, but if you have components coming from different sources, you don't want to wait a week or two before you find out that an early shipment was wrong or incomplete.

Take it a step further. Once you've verified that everything is correct with the order, start opening the individual component boxes. Look for a packing list in the front of the manual, and make sure that you actually received everything that was supposed to be in the box. It's not uncommon for small parts—mounting hardware, cables, driver CDs, and so on—to be missing. If that happens, call the vendor immediately and tell them what's missing from your order.

At this point, you should have everything you need to start building your new PC. It's kind of like being a kid again, on Christmas morning.

Building a Mainstream PC 3

A mainstream PC is one that seeks balance at a reasonable price point. A mainstream PC uses top quality (but midrange performance) components throughout, because that is where you find the best value for your dollar. What differentiates a mainstream PC from a budget PC is that the former makes fewer compromises. Whereas price is always a very high priority for a budget PC, it is less important for a mainstream PC. If spending more money yields better performance or reliability, or adds desirable features, a mainstream PC gets those extra dollars, whereas a budget PC probably doesn't.

Relative to the budget PC, that means the mainstream PC gets more expensive components, particularly where they pay off in additional performance, convenience, or data safety; more memory; a fast dual-core processor; redundant disk storage; better peripherals; and additional features. Considered individually, the incremental cost of better components is typically quite small. But taken collectively, the difference adds up fast. Depending on which components you choose, a mainstream system may cost 50% to 100% more than a budget system. That extra money buys you higher performance now and down the road, and extends the period between upgrades. If a budget PC will meet your needs for 12 to 18 months without upgrades, a mainstream PC may suffice for 24 to 36 months or longer, depending on the demands you put on it.

In this chapter, we'll design and build the perfect mainstream PC.

Many consumer-grade systems, particularly those sold in office superstores and big-box stores and by some large OEMs, masquerade as mainstream PCs but are really budget PCs with a few extra bells and whistles. These PCs have faster CPUs and more memory—components whose specifications are easily visible—but use the same low-end motherboards, marginal power supplies, and inferior optical drives found in their less expensive budget lines. True mainstream PCs, at least as we define them, are a vanishing breed. Marketers believe that spending $5 more on a better power supply or $10 more on a better motherboard will only boost the price of their systems, making them uncompetitive with other brands, without increasing sales or profit. From their point of view, consumers are too ignorant to appreciate the difference between cheap components and good components that cost only slightly more. The best way to prove them wrong is to build your own mainstream PC from top-notch components.

Determining Functional Requirements

We sat down to think through our own requirements for a mainstream PC. Here's the list of functional requirements we came up with:

Reliability

First and foremost, the mainstream PC must be reliable. We expect it to run all day, every day, for years without complaint. The key to reliability is choosing top-quality components, particularly the motherboard, memory, hard drive, and power supply. Those components don't need to be the largest or fastest available, but they do need to be of high quality.

Balanced performance

A mainstream PC is a jack of all trades and master of none. We expect it to perform any task we might give it, at least competently if not better. But, because this is not a cost-no-object system, we need to balance component performance against price. For example, we expect this system to be capable of serious number crunching, but the fastest processors cost more than we can justify for this system. Accordingly, we aimed for a balanced design that allows the system to do most things very well and everything else at least acceptably well.

Data safety

Although most of our data resides on our network server, which is backed up six ways to Sunday, a hard drive failure in our mainstream system could still wipe out local configuration files and cost us hours to rebuild and reconfigure the system. We decided that the small incremental cost of RAID (Redundant Array of Inexpensive Disks) was justified to protect against a hard drive failure.

Video capture

Although we built a full-feature dual-tuner media center system as another of the projects for this book, there are times when that system may be fully occupied, recording one program while we watch another. For those rare occasions when we need to record yet another program at the same time, we decided it made sense to add basic PVR capabilities to this system. The cost to do so is less than the cost of a standalone DVD recorder, and a PC-based solution provides much more flexibility.

Noise level

Most mainstream PCs are used in environments where noise is an issue. Accordingly, we designed this system for quiet operation, but we didn't spend much extra money to do so. That means, for example, that we chose the hard drive, case, and power supply based on noise level, but we did not spend $50 extra to replace the stock CPU cooling fan with a silent unit or $100 extra for a fanless power supply. Our goal is a quiet PC, not a silent PC (if there can truly be such a thing).

Hardware Design Criteria

With the functional requirements determined, the next step was to establish design criteria for the mainstream PC hardware. Here are the relative priorities we assigned for our mainstream PC. Your priorities may of course differ.

As you can see, this is a well-balanced system. Other than reliability, which is of primary importance, all of the other criteria are of similar priority. Here's the breakdown:

Price

Price is moderately important for this system, but value is more so. We won't attempt to match the low price of commercial systems built with low-end components, but we won't waste money, either. If spending a bit more noticeably improves performance, reliability, or usability, or if it adds features we want, we won't begrudge the extra cost.

Reliability

Reliability is the single most important criterion. A mainstream PC that is not built for reliability is not worth building.

Size

Size is somewhat important in the sense that it must fit in an already crowded office, so we don't want the system to be any larger than it needs to be to do its job. So, although we will not compromise other criteria in exchange for smaller size, we will choose the smallest case that meets other system requirements.

Noise level

Noise level is at least moderately important for nearly any mainstream PC. Our goal is to build a reasonably quiet PC at little or no incremental cost rather than to build a very quiet PC using expensive special components. Accordingly, when we choose components we'll keep noise level in mind, but we won't pay much extra for a marginally quieter component.

Expandability

Expandability is relatively unimportant for a mainstream PC. Fewer than 5% of commercial mainstream PCs are ever upgraded, and those upgrades are usually of a minor nature such as adding memory or replacing a video card or hard drive. Self-built mainstream PCs are more likely to be upgraded, but even then the upgrades are unlikely to require more than perhaps a spare drive bay or two, an expansion slot, or a couple of available memory sockets. We'll choose a case, power supply, and motherboard that are adequate to support such minor upgrades.

DESIGN PRIORITIES	
Price	★★★☆☆
Reliability	★★★★★
Size	★★★☆☆
Noise level	★★★☆☆
Expandability	★★☆☆☆
Processor performance	★★★☆☆
Video performance	★★☆☆☆
Disk capacity/performance	★★☆☆☆

Silence Is Golden

This system is destined to be Robert's secondary office desktop system. His office is already home to four other systems, so it's important that this system contribute as little additional noise as possible.

Processor performance

Processor performance is moderately important for a mainstream PC, both initially and to ensure that the system can run new software versions without requiring a processor upgrade. Midrange mainstream single- and dual-core processors are the "sweet spot" in price/performance ratio. At a given price point, a single-core processor is slightly faster than a dual-core model for people who single-task (do pretty much one thing at a time). A dual-core processor comes into its own on systems like ours that tend to have many windows open simultaneously and many tasks in progress. With a dual-core system, one core is always devoted to the foreground task, so the system doesn't "bog down" under load.

Although economy single-core processors like the Intel Celeron and AMD Sempron may suffice initially, spending a bit more on a mainstream processor buys you more horsepower and a larger cache, both of which increase the time during which the processor will provide subjectively adequate performance. The slow and midrange variants of the Intel Pentium D processors are the most cost-effective dual-core processors available. They are aggressively priced and fast enough that you probably won't need to upgrade the processor anytime soon.

Video performance

3D video performance is critical for a mainstream PC only if you use it to run 3D games or Microsoft Vista. Otherwise, integrated video suffices. In fact, current-generation integrated video such as Intel GMA 950 and nVIDIA 6150 is good enough for casual gaming, the Vista Aero interface, and will even support Vista's Aero Glass user interface effects (at the expense of using more shared memory than usual).

2D video quality is important for any mainstream PC, because it determines display clarity and sharpness for browsers, office suites, and similar 2D applications. Intel integrated video provides excellent 2D quality and reasonably good 3D performance. To future-proof the system, we'll choose a motherboard that provides a PCI Express x16 video card slot. That way, we can always add an inexpensive or midrange video adapter if we need better 3D performance or other features not supported by the integrated video.

Disk capacity/performance

Disk capacity is unimportant for this particular mainstream system, because it connects to a network that has more than 3,000 GB of available storage. For a standalone mainstream system, or one that connects to a network with insufficient shared storage, disk capacity may be a key consideration. Fortunately, with hard drives currently available in capacities ranging from 80 GB to 750 GB, it's easy enough to accommodate nearly any storage requirements simply by installing one or more hard drives of whatever capacity are needed.

Disk performance is unimportant for most mainstream systems in the sense that any standard 7,200 RPM ATA or Serial ATA hard drive is fast enough to avoid noticeable storage bottlenecks for most applications. For those few systems that do require higher performance disk subsystems, a variety of solutions are available, including 10,000 RPM ATA/SATA drives, RAID 0, or, when cost is no object, 15,000 RPM SCSI drives. But standard 7,200 RPM ATA/SATA hard drives are fine for most systems, including this one.

For this system, we're less concerned with disk capacity and performance, and more concerned with reliability. Modern ATA/SATA hard drives are extremely reliable, particularly Seagate models, but any hard drive is destined to fail eventually, usually at the worst possible time. When we designed this system, we had just suffered a hard drive crash in one of our secondary desktop systems and spent hours rebuilding and reconfiguring the system, so we had hard drive reliability firmly in mind.

In years past, there was no practical, inexpensive way to insure against a hard drive failure. But nowadays, RAID is easy and inexpensive to implement. Most midrange and higher motherboards provide integrated RAID support, so the only incremental cost is the cost of a second hard drive.

ADVICE FROM RON MORSE

RAID does not insure against hard drive failure. It mitigates/limits data loss resulting from a hard drive failure. In fact, the added drive to support RAID slightly increases the probability you will experience a hard drive failure.

<soapbox> And I still contend it is a very narrow attempt to deal with a much broader problem. The idea is to prevent inadvertent data loss. The vast majority of reasons people lose data have nothing to do with drive failure. On the other hand, RAID does complicate installation and maintenance so you do get something for your money.

RAID on servers is great. Ought to be mandatory, even. But on a desktop? It promises a false sense of security while dealing directly with only the most unlikely source of data loss. It would be better to hammer home the backup message. </soapbox>

Component Considerations

With our design criteria in mind, we set out to choose the best components for the mainstream PC system. The following sections describe the components we chose, and why we chose them.

WARNING

Although we tested the configuration we used to build our own mainstream PC, we did not test permutations with the listed alternatives. Those alternatives are simply the components we would have chosen had our requirements been different. That said, we know of no reason the alternatives we list should not work perfectly.

Case and Power Supply

Antec BK640B microBTX Case (*http://www.antec.com*)

Intel introduced the ATX form factor more than a decade ago, with the smaller Mini-ATX and microATX form factors introduced soon thereafter. Although Mini-ATX never caught on, ATX and microATX became immensely popular. Most commercial systems and nearly all home-built systems use ATX or microATX cases and motherboards to this day.

But ATX was designed at a time when a typical processor or video adapter consumed only a few watts and used a passive heatsink. As the power consumption of processors and video adapters continued to grow by leaps and bounds—reaching as much as 130W or more—the limitations of ATX became obvious. Getting rid of the heat became a major problem, despite such workarounds as the Intel TAC (Thermally Advantaged Chassis) initiative, which was a fancy name for a simple air duct between the processor and the side panel of the case. In addition to the CPU fan and power supply fan, ATX systems are usually equipped with at least one case fan to aid cooling. All of these fans inevitably add to the noise level of the system.

Intel addressed the problem by introducing a new form factor called BTX (Balanced Technology eXtended). BTX cases feature a redesigned component layout, greatly improved air flow, and other measures designed to optimize cooling while minimizing the number, size, and speed of cooling fans needed.

Despite the demonstrable superiority of BTX, manufacturers of motherboards and other components ignored BTX in droves. Intel had originally forecast that 40% of new systems would use BTX by the end of 2004. That turned out to be wildly optimistic, to put it kindly. With very few exceptions, system and component makers ignored BTX entirely, ridiculing BTX as a jerry-built fix for the notoriously high power consumption of Prescott-core Pentium 4 processors. ExtremeTech listed BTX in its *Ten Failed Tech*

Trends for 2005 article. They weren't alone. By the end of 2005, most industry pundits had written off BTX as a dead technology.

But then something odd happened. Beginning in early 2006, BTX rose from the dead. Major OEMs, including Dell, HP, and Gateway, introduced new BTX models. Online vendors like NewEgg began offering BTX components, albeit in limited variety.

Ironically, this revival began just as Intel began shipping the Core Solo and Core Duo processors, which consume much less power than earlier models and produce much less heat. If anything, these new, cooler-running processors should have been the final nail in the coffin of BTX. Instead, system makers apparently finally realized that if BTX could cool even hot processors with minimal noise, it could cool the newer low-current processors at extremely low noise levels.

ExtremeTech reversed its opinion, saying in an April 2006 article, "If you're building an Intel system, it's worth considering moving to the BTX form factor." We agree. It's nice to see ExtremeTech belatedly endorse our conclusion.

Although BTX appears to be gaining traction, its long-term viability is not yet assured. BTX cases and motherboards are now widely available, although the selection is quite limited. Despite these facts, we decided that the advantages of BTX were worth pursuing, so we decided to build our mainstream system around a BTX case and motherboard.

We began by evaluating the BTX cases available at the time we built this system. We considered BTX cases from various manufacturers, including Antec, Casetek, CoolerMaster, InWin, Thermaltake, and others. We had several checklist items, the most important of which were:

- Mini-tower or micro-tower form factor

- Two or more optical drive bays

- Two or more hard drive bays

- Front-panel audio, USB, and FireWire ports

- Provision for a standard ATX12V v2.0 power supply

The three remaining ATX form factors are all small. TFX12V is a "thin" form factor, used in some small commercial systems. LFX12V is a "low-profile" form factor, also used in some small commercial systems. CFX12V is a "compact" form factor, and is used in the smallest commercial systems. For more details about power supply form factors, visit *http://www.formfactors.org*.

Dead Again

As we mentioned in the previous chapter, just as the BTX zombie was staggering to its feet, Intel drove a stake through its heart, announcing that it would discontinue BTX components in 2007. Oh, well. That just means BTX components will be available at firesale prices. The case, motherboard, and CPU cooler are the only BTX-specific components in a BTX system, so we wouldn't hesitate to build this mainstream BTX system even in the face of BTX being discontinued.

Which Power Supply Fits Which Case?

There is no such thing as a BTX power supply. ATX-family cases and BTX-family cases both accept ATX-family power supplies. There are five ATX power supply form factors. Standard-size ATX and BTX cases use full-size ATX12V power supplies, and may also use the small form factor SFX12V power supplies. Nearly all home-built systems use an ATX12V power supply, although a few use SFX12V.

Figure 3-1. Antec BK640B microBTX case (image courtesy of Antec, Inc.)

ALTERNATIVES: CASE & POWER SUPPLY

For a BTX system, none we'd choose. For an ATX or microATX mainstream system, the Antec New Solution Series NSK3300 micro-tower, NSK4400 mini-tower, or NSK6500 mid-tower. If you're willing to spend a bit more, the premium Antec P150 and P180 cases are superb choices.

Most of the cases we considered were too small, had too few drive bays, were too expensive, or otherwise failed to meet one or more of our requirements. The Antec BK640B, shown in Figure 3-1, met all of our requirements.

The Antec BK640B belongs to Antec's mainstream line. It lacks some of the costly features included in premium Antec cases, but, like all Antec cases we have used, the BK640B is solidly built, has no sharp edges, and has excellent fit and finish. It is also an attractive case, and sells for only $75 or so, including a solid ATX12V v2.0 380W power supply. Finally, the Antec BK640B is an extremely quiet case.

Motherboard

Intel D945GCZLR (*http://www.intel.com*)

Intel motherboards set the standards by which we judge all other motherboards for construction quality, stability, and reliability. We chose the rock-solid Intel D945GCZLR, shown in Figure 3-2, which supports a socket 775 Intel Pentium 4, Pentium D, or Celeron D processor. Note the markedly different layout of a BTX motherboard, with the processor set at an angle near the front edge of the motherboard, the memory slots at the far left side, and the positions of the expansion slots and rear I/O panel reversed relative to ATX.

---

945 OR 946?

We built this system in Summer 2006. The Intel Core 2 Duo processor and motherboards that support it were not yet widely available. In anticipation of their new processors and motherboards, Intel deeply discounted their older products, pricing them too attractively for us to refuse. If we were building this system now, we'd probably use an Intel Core 2 Duo and an Intel 946- or 965-series motherboard.

The Intel D945GCZLR provides integrated Intel GMA 950 video, which suffices for anyone other than serious gamers, and excellent integrated high-definition audio. The D945GCZLR has four DIMM slots—which makes future memory upgrades easy—and supports up to 4 GB of DDR2-400, -533, or -667 memory. It also provides a plethora of interfaces and ports,

including two PCI slots, a PCI Express x16 video card slot, a PCI Express x1 general-purpose expansion slot, one dual parallel ATA-100 interface, four Serial ATA interfaces with RAID support, an FDD interface, PS/2 mouse and keyboard ports, serial and parallel ports for compatibility with legacy peripherals, a 10/100-BaseT Ethernet port, three FireWire ports, eight USB 2.0 ports, a digital optical out (S/PDIF) port, and a partridge in a pear tree.

MAKE SURE YOU KNOW WHAT YOU'RE GETTING

If you buy a D945GCZ, make sure you know exactly what you're getting. Like most Intel motherboards, the D945GCZ is available in several variants that have different feature sets. Some models, for example, include 7.1 audio, while others have 5.1 audio. Some models include RAID support, and others do not. One model does not include FireWire ports, and only the D945GCZLR model we chose provides the S/PDIF connector. For available configurations, see *http://developer. intel.com/design/motherbd/cz/cz_available.htm.*

ALTERNATIVES: MOTHERBOARD

For an Intel BTX system, you can use any Intel BTX motherboard that fits the case you choose. Very few BTX motherboards are made for AMD processors, and those motherboards are not generally available in retail channels, at least in the U.S. For an Intel ATX system, choose any Intel motherboard that offers the features you want and fits the case you choose, or any similar ASUS motherboard that uses an Intel chipset. For an AMD ATX system, choose an ASUS motherboard with an nVIDIA nForce-series chipset.

Processor

Intel Pentium D 940 (*http://www.intel.com*)

A mainstream PC deserves a dual-core processor. Although a fast single-core processor can hold its own against a dual-core processor on a lightly loaded system, a dual-core processor really shines on a more heavily loaded system. As you add more background tasks and open more windows on a single-core system, the processor bogs down. With a dual-core processor, one core is always allocated to the foreground task, so the system appears just as responsive when it is heavily loaded as when it is running only one or two tasks.

At the time we built this system, we had three dual-core technologies to choose from. We considered using the Intel Core Duo, which is essentially a desktop version of the Intel mobile processor, and was chosen by Apple as the basis of their Intel-based Mac systems. We rejected Core Duo for two reasons. First, although Core Duo processors were reasonably fast, they were also quite expensive compared to other dual-core processors with similar performance. Second, the selection of motherboards available for Core Duo was very limited, both in terms of the number of models available and the features supported by those motherboards. Core Duo was obviously an interim processor, introduced by Intel as a stopgap until they could ramp up production of their Conroe Core 2 desktop CPUs in late 2006 and into 2007.

That left us with the AMD Athlon 64 X2 and the Intel Pentium D, both of which are excellent dual-core processors. The Athlon 64 X2 features an elegant design, low power consumption, and superior gaming performance. The Pentium D draws more power and is less suitable for gaming, but offers top-notch multimedia performance. Dollar-for-dollar, the Athlon 64 X2 and Pentium D are pretty evenly matched in performance at the high end. But at the time we built this system, the least expensive Athlon 64 X2 sold for about $300, a $75 premium over an Intel Pentium D model with similar overall performance. We chose to use the Intel Pentium D, shown in Figure 3-3, which in turn allowed us to build the BTX system we really wanted to build.

Figure 3-3. Intel Pentium D (image courtesy of Intel Corporation)

MORE POWER

If you wonder why we chose an Intel Pentium D processor despite its notoriously high power consumption, it's because power consumption differences are much less important than most people believe.

The processor in most systems spends nearly all of its time at idle (even when the system is being used). At idle, the Pentium D 940 consumes only about 20W more than a comparable AMD Athlon X2 processor, or about 480 watt-hours per day for a system that runs 24×7. We pay about $0.10 per KW-hour for electricity, which means that using the Pentium D instead of the Athlon 64 X2 boosts our power bill by about 4.8 cents a day, or less than $20 per year.

Or it would, if both systems were always running at idle. But what about when they're running under load? Running at 100% CPU utilization, the Pentium D draws as much as 60W more than the Athlon 64 X2, so if both systems ran constantly at 100% load, the Pentium D system might cause our power bill to skyrocket... by nearly 15 cents a day. But of course most systems average more like 3% to 5% CPU utilization over the course of day, which brings the incremental cost of power back down to very close to five cents a day.

That small difference is dwarfed by other factors, including the relative prices of the processors and motherboards and particularly the relative strengths and weaknesses of the two processors. So, while the AMD Athlon 64 X2 is a superb processor and there are many good reasons to choose it, its lower power consumption probably shouldn't be a major factor in your decision.

**ALTERNATIVES:
PROCESSOR**

An ATX AMD Athlon 64 X2 system offers equal or better performance, albeit at a somewhat higher price. By late 2006 and into 2007, Intel Conroe processors will become an increasingly attractive solution, as more full-feature motherboards become available and prices fall.

Figure 3-4. Intel Pentium D retail box cooler, with square white thermal pad visible on base

CPU Cooler

Intel Pentium D 940 retail-box cooler

Ordinarily, the bundled CPU cooler supplied with a retail-boxed processor is quite a bargain. Bundled coolers are not as effective or as quiet as the best aftermarket CPU coolers, but they ordinarily add only $10 or $15 to the cost of the processor. At the time we built this system, that was not true of the bundled Pentium D BTX cooler, shown in Figure 3-4. (Two AA batteries are shown for scale.) Although the retail-boxed ATX version of the processor cost only a few dollars more than the bare OEM processor, the version with a BTX cooler sold for $30 to $40 more. (In addition to the bundled cooler, the retail-boxed version includes a much longer warranty on the processor.)

Intel supplied us with a retail-boxed BTX processor for this project, so we used the bundled CPU cooler. If we had bought the processor ourselves, we would probably have used an OEM processor with an aftermarket cooler.

**ALTERNATIVES:
CPU COOLER**

Any good third-party Type I BTX Thermal Module. Our first choice would be the Thermaltake CL-P0030 or the CoolerMaster CB5-NPFSA-02-GP.

It's quite possible, though, that by the time you read this retail-boxed BTX processors will have achieved price parity with ATX models. Compare prices on a retail-boxed BTX processor versus the same processor in OEM form with a third-party cooler before you decide what to buy.

BTX COOLER TYPES

There are two types of BTX coolers, which Intel imaginatively designates Type I and Type II. Our CPU uses a Type I cooler. Type II coolers are physically smaller, use smaller fans, are designed to be used in compact cases, and are less efficient and somewhat louder than Type I coolers. Both types of BTX cooler fit the same mounting holes, occupy the same motherboard real estate around the processor, and are otherwise interchangeable. The retail-boxed Intel Type I cooler supplied with our processor compares favorably in cooling efficiency and noise level with aftermarket coolers in the $25 to $30 range.

Memory

Kingston 2GB PC2-5300 DDR2 memory kit (1 GB × 2)
(http://www.kingston.com)

Memory costs little enough that it is senseless to hamper a system by installing insufficient memory. We consider 1 GB appropriate for most single-core mainstream systems, although you may want more if you run Photoshop or other memory-intensive applications on your system. But using a dual-core processor is, for all intents and purposes, the same as using two processors. That means a dual-core system really needs twice as much memory as a single-core system, so we elected to install 2 GB of memory in our mainstream system.

**ALTERNATIVES:
MEMORY**

Any compatible name-brand memory modules. Memory from different companies can vary dramatically in quality and reliability. For 20 years, we've depended on memory from Kingston and Crucial, and have never had cause to regret that decision. Whatever you do, avoid house-brand memory or any memory that's offered at a "bargain" price.

The Intel D945GCZLR motherboard has four DIMM slots and a dual-channel memory controller that provides faster memory performance when DIMMs are installed in pairs. Installing a pair of 1 GB DIMMs, for a total of 2 GB, leaves two DIMM slots available for future expansion. If you need more memory later on, you can fill that second pair of DIMM slots with 1 GB modules, taking the system to 4 GB of total memory. That should suffice for the expected lifetime of the system.

The Intel D945GCZLR supports DDR2-400 (PC2-3200), DDR2-533 (PC2-4200), and DDR2-667 (PC2-5300) memory. Although PC2-3200 modules would have been fast enough for our processor, we elected to install the faster PC2-5300 modules. The cost difference was small, and using the faster memory means we can later upgrade to a processor that uses a faster front-side bus without replacing the memory.

Video Adapter

Integrated Intel Graphics Media Accelerator (GMA) 950

A mainstream PC needs excellent 2D video quality and, if it is to be used for casual gaming or running Windows Vista, support for DirectX 9 and reasonable 3D graphics performance. Intel GMA 950 video easily meets the first requirement, and even suffices for casual gaming and running Vista's Aero Glass effects, depending on your expectations.

We had no intention of running Vista on this system—although we did install Vista to test compatibility—nor did we plan to use this system for anything more than casual gaming. Accordingly, we chose a motherboard that included integrated graphics, but with an available PCIe x16 slot in case we later decide to upgrade the graphics.

Video Capture Adapter

Hauppauge WinTV-PVR-150 (*http://www.hauppauge.com*)

Although this system is not a full-blown media-center PC, we wanted it to have video capture capability, if only to serve as a backup to our primary media-center system when it was busy doing something else. We needed only a single-tuner analog capture card, so we chose the inexpensive and reliable Hauppauge WinTV-PVR-150 card. The PVR-150 provides hardware-accelerated MPEG compression, so the system can be used for other tasks while it is recording a TV program without any degradation of either task.

The WinTV-Scheduler and WinTV-Editor utilities included with the card more than suffice for casual TV recording and editing. If you prefer to use a more featureful PVR application, the PVR-150 is supported by nearly every Windows and Linux PVR application available.

ADVICE FROM RON MORSE

Consider the Hauppauge Win-PVR-USB2 model. Slightly more expensive, comparable feature set. External means another box on the desk, but connections are extremely easy to make. Can be moved to another computer/location (say, your laptop) with ease. Works well. Needs USB 2.0 high speed port.

Sound Adapter

Integrated Intel High Definition Audio

The integrated Intel High Definition Audio is more than sufficient for anything other than serious gaming. The Intel D945GCZ model we used supports 7.1 audio, but other models support only 5.1 audio. We recommend using the integrated audio unless you require additional channels or you play games that benefit from hardware-accelerated audio.

ALTERNATIVES: VIDEO ADAPTER

We recommend using integrated video unless you require faster video performance or additional features. If you need better 3D graphics performance, install an appropriate nVIDIA or ATI PCI Express video adapter in the x16 video slot on the Intel D945GCZ motherboard. The Intel motherboard provides only a single standard 15-pin VGA analog video connector. If you need a DVI video connector for an LCD display or support for dual displays, install a PCI Express video card with a DVI connector. If you need only one DVI connector, even a $25 video adapter suffices. If you need a dual-head card, shop carefully. The least expensive dual-DVI adapters sell for more than $100. A few can use two standard DVI cables, but some require a special dual-DVI cable, which is often "optional" and may add $100 or more to the price of the card.

ALTERNATIVES: VIDEO CAPTURE ADAPTER

Not many, really. Hauppauge video capture cards are the gold standard in terms of image capture quality and compatibility with capture applications. ATI All-In-Wonder and TV Wonder cards provide video capture functions, but their software compatibility is much more limited and some of our readers have reported them to be less reliable than Hauppauge video capture cards. The Hauppauge WinTV-PVR-150 is inexpensive and extremely reliable. If you want your mainstream system to support basic video capture functions, use the Hauppauge WinTV-PVR-150 unless you have good reason to choose something else.

If your motherboard model provides only 5.1 audio and you need 7.1 audio, or if you need a hardware-accelerated sound card, install a standalone M-Audio or Creative Labs sound adapter. The M-Audio Revolution 7.1 has superb sound quality and good gaming support. The Creative Labs Audigy2 ZS and X-Fi sound cards have good sound quality and superb gaming support. If sound quality is your top priority, install the Revolution 7.1. If hardware-accelerated gaming support is your top priority, install an Audigy2 ZS or one of the X-Fi cards, depending on your budget.

If your motherboard model provides only 10/100BaseT and you require 1000BaseT, install a D-Link DGE-560T PCI-Express Gigabit Network Adapter. PCI gigabit adapters are a poor choice, because under load they use enough bandwidth to swamp the PCI bus. A PCI Express gigabit adapter uses a PCI Express x1 slot with its own dedicated bandwidth, which isolates the network traffic from the PCI bus.

ADVICE FROM RON MORSE

I would not recommend the Creative Labs Audigy X-Fi series at this time. They have serious driver issues, which CL has been reluctant to address... starting with a "Problem? What problem?" attitude and then going downhill from there. I understand there has been some progress, but there is still a long way to go. The Audigy 2ZS is a very solid card with mature, reliable drivers.

Network Adapter

Integrated Intel Ethernet adapter

Intel D945GCZ motherboards provide an embedded 10/100 or 10/100/1000BaseT network adapter, which you should use unless you have good reason for installing a standalone network adapter.

Hard Disk Drive

Seagate Barracuda 7200.9 SATA (two) (*http://www.seagate.com*)

A mainstream PC needs a mainstream hard drive, and you can't get much more mainstream than a Seagate Barracuda 7200.9 SATA drive. The Barracuda 7200.9 is inexpensive, fast, very quiet, and extremely reliable. It is available in capacities from 80 GB to 500 GB. We chose the 80 GB model because this system connects to our home network, which has more than 3,000 GB of network storage. There was no point to spending any more than necessary for local storage. If you need more local disk space, choose one of the larger models.

We decided our mainstream system deserved two hard drives, not to increase storage capacity but to reduce the risk of losing data to a hard drive failure. Seagate hard drives are extremely reliable, but as mechanical devices they are destined to fail, sooner or later. The best way to protect your data against a hard drive failure is to run two hard drives in a RAID 1. With RAID 1, all data is written to both hard drives. If one drive fails, data can be accessed from the second drive until you replace the failed drive and rebuild the RAID. The motherboard we chose includes built-in RAID 1 support, so the only additional cost for this protection is the $51 we paid for the second hard drive. That's cheap insurance by any reckoning.

RAID IS NOT BACKUP

RAID 1 protects against a hard drive failure, but it is not a substitute for backing up. There are any number of things that cause data loss, from viruses to accidental deletions to fires and other catastrophes. RAID protects against none of these. To protect your data properly, you must make backup copies on removable media such as tapes or optical discs.

Optical Drive

BenQ DW1650 DVD writer (*http://www.benq.us*)

DVD writers are now available for as little as $30, so it's pointless to choose a less capable optical drive. Although DVD writer manufacturers continue to make minor tweaks to their product lines, the technology is essentially mature. Nearly every model has similar features and writes the various types of discs at the same or similar speeds. More expensive models generally have larger buffers and provide a few bells and whistles that are of little practical importance. What counts is the durability of the drive and the quality of the discs it writes, and many current models, even some inexpensive ones, do well in both respects.

In the past, we used and recommended Plextor optical drives exclusively. Plextor still makes the best drives available, but the gap has narrowed. It's not that Plextor drives have declined in quality, but that inexpensive drives are now much better than they used to be.

The BenQ DW1650 is among the best of the inexpensive drives, so we decided to use one for our mainstream system.

TORTURE-TESTING DRIVES

Periodically, we torture-test optical drives by burning discs continuously. As soon as one disc finishes writing, we start writing another disc until we've burned through a spindle of 25 or 50 discs. We then run detailed surface scans on several discs from each batch to check write quality, focusing most of our attention on discs written late in the sequence.

In the past, inexpensive drives simply didn't stand up to this kind of abuse. As they heated up after burning several discs, many of them started burning coasters or refusing to load a disc. Even those that completed the torture test generally produced poor quality writes, particularly late in the process. Only Plextor drives came through with flying colors.

We repeated our torture test in mid-2006. The bad news is that premium-series Plextor drives were still the only models that survived unscathed. The good news is that several inexpensive drives we tested did remarkably well. The NEC ND-3550A and BenQ DW1655 were both able to write a spindle of 25 discs without failing, although both generated several poor quality discs late in the sequence. The Plextor PX-716A wrote an entire spindle of 50 discs, all of which were nearly perfect from first to last.

The moral here is that if you use your optical drive very heavily, pay the extra money and get a Plextor premium-series drive. If you use your drive less intensively, an NEC or BenQ model is adequate.

ALTERNATIVES: HARD DISK DRIVES

We use only Seagate hard drives in our systems, and recommend our readers do the same.

ALTERNATIVES: OPTICAL DRIVE

We were torn among the BenQ DW1650, DW1655, and DQ60, along with several competing models from Lite-On. All are excellent drives with similar features, and we consider them essentially interchangeable. We also considered the otherwise-excellent NEC ND-3550A, but were forced to choose another drive because of the compatibility problem we experienced with the ND-3550A, described at the end of this chapter. If you use a different motherboard, the ND-3550A is an excellent alternative.

If you need a drive that also writes DVD-RAM discs, choose the BenQ DQ60 or the Lite-On SHM-165P6S. If you need a drive with LightScribe support, choose the BenQ DW1655. If you want the best, most durable optical drive available, choose one of the Plextor premium series drives.

Floppy Disk Drive

Since before the turn of the century, Microsoft and Intel have claimed that the humble floppy disk drive is a "legacy" device that should not be installed in modern systems. We took them at their word, more fool us. For five years, we've been building systems without floppy drives, and for five years we've frequently had cause to regret it. All too often, we ended up popping the cover on a PC to install a floppy disk drive because that was the easiest way to solve one problem or another.

Intel at least provides motherboard BIOS updates that can be run from within Windows rather than requiring booting the system with a floppy disk to update the BIOS. That's fine for those who run Windows on an Intel system. Most of our systems run Linux, though, and the only way to update the Intel BIOS on a Linux system is to boot from a floppy disk. And many other motherboard manufacturers provide BIOS updates only as *.bin* files that must be loaded from a floppy.

Microsoft is worse. When we install Windows, we frequently encounter the dreaded prompt to insert a floppy disk with a driver that Windows Setup requires for a RAID card or some other component. You'd think Microsoft would join the '90s and support loading drivers from a CD during Setup, but no. Windows Setup demands drivers on a floppy disk and will accept nothing else.

We ran into the "can't get there from here" problem while testing the budget system, which had no floppy drive. Windows XP installed and ran perfectly on the budget system. After testing Windows, we blew away Windows and installed Linux. Then we realized that we needed to update the motherboard BIOS. Ooops. ASRock had a Windows BIOS updater, but we were no longer running Windows. ASRock also had a floppy-based BIOS updater, but we had no floppy drive. Arrrrrghhh.

If we were smart, we'd ignore Microsoft and Intel and install a floppy disk drive on every system we build. That drive may be used only a few times over the life of the system, but at $6 or so an internal floppy disk drive is cheap insurance. Instead, while we had the system open, we temporarily installed an old FDD that was gathering dust on our workbench. We needed the FDD only long enough to install the Intel RAID drivers during Windows setup. After the system was up and running, we shut it down, disconnected the FDD, and reassembled the system.

If you decide to install a floppy drive permanently in your system, don't worry about brand name. Buy whichever 3.5" FDD happens to be cheapest. It will probably run for literally only a few minutes over the life of the system, so durability is of little concern.

**ALTERNATIVES:
FLOPPY DISK DRIVE**

If you want to save drive bay space, install the Mitsumi FA404M combo floppy disk drive, which also incorporates a card reader. Note that the FA404M uses the USB interface for both the FDD and the card reader. That means that it can be used to load BIOS updates only if the motherboard supports booting from a USB floppy drive, which nearly all current motherboards do although that option is often disabled by default in BIOS setup. If your system does support booting from a USB FDD, consider buying an external USB FDD, which can be moved from system to system as needed.

Keyboard

Logitech Media Elite (*http://www.logitech.com*)

Personal preference outweighs all else when choosing a keyboard. So many personal factors determine the usability of a keyboard—straight versus ergonomic, layout, key size, cup depth, angle, stroke length, corded versus cordless, and so on—that no one can choose the "best" keyboard for someone else. That said, we had to pick a "mainstream" keyboard for our mainstream PC, and our favorite mid-priced keyboard is the Logitech Media Elite, although we also like several of the other Logitech models. Microsoft also offers many excellent standard and ergonomic keyboard models, but we generally prefer the feel of Logitech models.

Mouse

Logitech LX7 cordless optical mouse (*http://www.logitech.com*)

Personal preference is also the most important factor in choosing a mouse. Subtle differences in size, shape, button position, and so on can have a major effect on how comfortable a mouse is to use. What someone else loves, you may hate, and vice versa.

Years ago, Microsoft sent us prototype samples of their first "red light" optical mouse. We fell in love with optical mice, and used Microsoft optical mice exclusively for years. Several years ago, we tried a Logitech optical mouse and soon began replacing our Microsoft cordless mice with Logitech models. At the midrange and high-end, we actually prefer the feel of the Logitech mice. They feel more precise than the Microsoft models, and seem to fit our hands better. At the low end, Logitech and Microsoft optical mice seem comparable, but the Logitech models generally cost a bit less for models with features similar to competing Microsoft models.

Speakers

Logitech Z-2300 speaker system (*http://www.logitech.com*)

A mainstream PC deserves a decent set of speakers, but we can realistically spend no more than $100 on speakers for a mainstream PC. There are scores of speaker systems available within that range, including sets with 6 or even 8 speakers. We decided it was better to spend our $100 on a good 2.1 system—two satellites and a subwoofer—rather than spending the same amount on a cheesy, tinny-sounding speaker system with a half dozen satellites.

At 120W RMS for the subwoofer and 40W RMS for each satellite, the Z-2300 can rattle the walls when you're gaming, but at lower volume it's also fine for listening to anything from classical music to DVD soundtracks. The satellites do a good job on the midrange and highs, and the subwoofer provides excellent bass response for this price level.

ALTERNATIVES: KEYBOARD

Many. Decide which features and layout you want, and then look for an appropriate Logitech model. If Logitech doesn't offer a model that suits you, look next to one of the many models sold by Microsoft.

Brian Bilbrey Warns

Cordless keyboards. The more I think about them, the less happy I am. You're typing in your online banking password. Can I sit at the top of a neighborhood and use a high-gain directional antenna to cherry-pick usernames and passwords? There aren't THAT many banks...

Small Hands, Big Mouse

Conventional wisdom is not always reliable. For example, because Barbara has small hands, most ergonomics experts would recommend a small mouse for her. She used a small mouse for years, but began experiencing hand pain when using it. On a whim, she decided to try a Microsoft Explorer 5-button mouse, which was one of the largest standard mice available. Her hand pain went away, and she's been using large mice ever since. The moral is that if you're at all unhappy with your current mouse, try something else. You may well like it much better.

**ALTERNATIVES:
MOUSE**

Many. We used a Logitech LX7 Cordless Optical Mouse for the mainstream PC based on price and feel, but you might prefer another model. We recommend limiting your choices to Logitech and Microsoft models. Whatever you do, get a cordless optical mouse. The absence of a mouse cord is worth the small additional cost. Early cordless mice ate batteries quickly, but current Logitech and Microsoft models run for a month or more on one set of batteries. We keep a set of NiMH rechargeable batteries in the charger, ready to swap out when our mouse batteries die.

**ALTERNATIVES:
SPEAKERS**

In this price range, the Logitech Z-2300 is head and shoulders above any competing 2.1 system. If you prefer a $100 2.0 speaker system that's superior to the Z-2300 for listening to music, consider the Klipsch ProMedia Ultra 2.0 speaker system. We listened to several sub-$100 5.1 and 7.1 speaker systems, and decided none of them were worth having. We prefer decent sound from two or three speakers to terrible sound from six or eight speakers.

The THX-certified Z-2300 speakers are solidly built, and are attractive enough to use in your living room or den. The subwoofer includes an 8" long-throw woofer and the built-in amplifier. The satellites each use one 2.5" midrange/tweeter driver, and are brushed aluminum with removable grilles. The Z-2300 includes a wired remote with volume control, mute button, and headphone jack.

Display

NEC MultiSync FE992 19" CRT (*http://www.necmitsubishi.com*)
Samsung SyncMaster 997MB 19" CRT (*http://www.samsung.com*)
ViewSonic G90FB 19" CRT (*http://www.viewsonic.com*)

A mainstream PC should have a 19" display, and we allocated $200 to this component. That $200 buys us a top-notch 19" CRT monitor like the NEC MultiSync FE992, Samsung SyncMaster 997MB, or ViewSonic G90FB, or a mediocre 19" LCD display. In that price range, the CRT monitor wins hands down in every respect, including image quality and durability.

Table 3-1 summarizes our component choices for the mainstream PC system.

Table 3-1. Bill of materials for mainstream PC

Component	Product
Case	Antec BK640B microBTX micro-tower case
Power supply	Antec 380W (bundled)
Motherboard	Intel D945GCZLR
Processor	Intel Pentium D 940
CPU cooler	(Bundled with retail-boxed CPU)
Memory	Kingston PC2-5300 DDR2-SDRAM (two 1 GB DIMMs)
Video adapter	(Integrated)
Video capture adapter	Hauppauge WinTV-PVR-150
Sound adapter	(Integrated)
Network adapter	(Integrated)
Hard disk drive	80 GB Seagate Barracuda 7200.9 SATA (two)
Optical drive	BenQ DW1650 DVD writer
Floppy disk drive	(See text)
Keyboard	Logitech Media Elite
Mouse	Logitech LX7 Cordless Optical Mouse
Speakers	Logitech Z-2300 2.1 speaker system
Display	(See text)

Building the Mainstream PC

Figure 3-5 shows the major components of the mainstream PC. The Intel D945GCZLR motherboard is to the left of Antec BK640B case, with the Intel Pentium D 940 processor and Hauppauge PVR-150 video capture card to the right. Front and center are the two 80 GB Seagate Barracuda 7200.9 hard drives, just behind the NEC ND-3550A optical drive and the Kingston 2GB memory kit.

Before you proceed, make sure you have everything you need. Open each box and verify the contents against the packing list.

Figure 3-5. Mainstream PC components, awaiting construction

Preparing the Case

To begin, remove the two screws that secure the side panels, as shown in Figure 3-6. We call them "shipping screws" because they're there primarily to keep the side panel securely in place during shipping. Although you can insert these screws after you finish building the system, it really isn't necessary. The side panel latch by itself is sufficient to secure the side panel during routine use.

Assembly Order

Although by necessity we describe building the system in a particular order, you don't need to follow that exact sequence when you build your own system. Some steps—for example, installing the processor and memory before installing the motherboard in the case—should be taken in the sequence we describe, because doing otherwise makes the task more difficult or risks damaging a component. Other steps, such as installing the CPU cooler after you install the motherboard in the case, must be taken in the order we describe, because completing one step is a prerequisite for completing another. But the exact sequence doesn't matter for most steps. As you build your system, it will be obvious when sequence matters.

WARNING

The first step in building any system is always to make sure that the power supply is set to the correct input voltage, if necessary. Some power supplies, including the unit in the Antec BK640B, set themselves automatically. Others must be set manually using a slide switch to select the proper input voltage.

If you connect a power supply set for 230V to a 115V receptacle, there's no harm done. The PC components receive half the voltage they require, and the system won't boot. But if you connect a power supply set for 115V to a 230V receptacle, the PC components receive *twice* the voltage they're designed to use. If you power up the system, that overvoltage destroys the system instantly in clouds of smoke and showers of sparks.

Figure 3-6. Remove the screws that secure the side panels

After you remove the screws, remove the side panels, as shown in Figure 3-7 by sliding them slightly toward the rear of the case and then tilting the panels away from the chassis.

Figure 3-7. Press the latch and lift the side panel off

Chapter 3, Building a Mainstream PC

With the side panels removed, place the case flat on your work surface. The BK640B has two removable hard drive cages, one on each side of the violet BTX air duct. It's almost impossible to work on the motherboard with these cages in place, so for the time being we'll remove the cages and set them aside. Each cage is secured to the chassis by one screw. Remove both of those screws, as shown in Figures 3-8 and 3-9.

With the screws removed, you can remove each of the drive cages by sliding it toward the rear of the case and lifting it free, as shown in Figure 3-10. Each drive cage connects to the chassis with a slot-and-tab arrangement. If the cage doesn't release easily, wiggle it slightly until it slides freely toward the rear of the case.

With the drive cages removed, the interior of the case is completely open and uncluttered, as shown in Figure 3-11. The power supply is visible at the lower-right corner, and the optical drive bay at the upper-right corner. The large violet plastic box at the top left is the BTX air duct, which will guide cool air from the front case vent directly to the CPU cooler once the motherboard is installed.

The stamped metal structure visible at the lower center of the image is the BTX SRM (Support and Retention Module). The SRM provides a rigid mounting point for the heavy BTX CPU cooler, which is secured with four screws that pass through the motherboard and are threaded into the screw holes visible as a rectangular pattern on the SRM. The SRM transfers the weight of the CPU cooler directly to the chassis, instead of requiring the relatively fragile motherboard to support that weight. This allows BTX systems to use massive CPU coolers, which can be quieter and more efficient than the smaller CPU coolers used in ATX systems.

Most cases include a generic I/O template, which never seems to fit the I/O panel of the motherboard. The Antec BK640B case doesn't include a generic I/O template, so there's no need to pop out the old template before proceeding.

Most motherboards, including the Intel D945GCZLR, come with a custom I/O template designed to match the motherboard I/O panel. Before you install the custom I/O template, compare it to the motherboard I/O panel to make sure the holes in the template correspond to the connectors on the motherboard.

Figure 3-8. Remove the screw that secures one hard drive cage

Figure 3-9. Remove the screw that secures the second hard drive cage

Figure 3-10. Slide each drive cage toward the rear of the case and lift it free

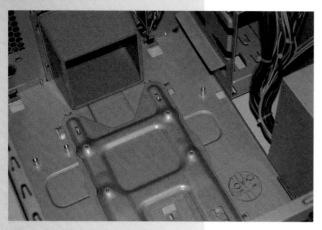

Figure 3-11. The case interior after removing the drive cages

Figure 3-12. Press the custom I/O template into place

Figure 3-13. Use a tool handle to snap the I/O template into place

Once you've done that, press the custom I/O template into place. Working from inside the case, align the bottom, right, and left edges of the I/O template with the matching case cutout. When the I/O template is positioned properly, press gently along the edges to seat it in the cutout, as shown in Figure 3-12. It should snap into place, although getting it to seat properly sometimes requires several attempts. It's often helpful to press gently against the edge of the template with the handle of a screwdriver or nut driver, as shown in Figure 3-13.

ADVICE FROM JIM COOLEY

It's often easiest to start in one corner. Once that snaps into place, move to an adjacent corner and continue to work your way around.

After you install the I/O template, make a "test run." Carefully slide the motherboard into place, making sure that the back panel connectors on the motherboard are firmly in contact with the corresponding holes on the I/O template.

WARNING

Be careful not to bend the I/O template while seating it. The template holes need to line up with the external port connectors on the motherboard I/O panel. If the template is even slightly bent it may be difficult to seat the motherboard properly.

Compare the positions of the motherboard mounting holes with the standoff mounting positions in the case. One easy method is to place the motherboard in position and insert a felt-tip pen through each motherboard mounting hole to mark the corresponding standoff position beneath it.

LET THERE BE LIGHT

If you simply look at the motherboard, it's easy to miss one of the mounting holes in all the clutter. We generally hold the motherboard up to a light, which makes the mounting holes stand out distinctly.

The Intel D945GCZLR motherboard has seven mounting holes. The Antec BK640B, like many cases, is shipped with several standoffs already installed. The BK640B had seven standoffs installed, all of which corresponded to the mounting holes in the motherboard, so we didn't need to install or remove any standoffs.

WARNING

If your case comes with preinstalled standoffs, make absolutely certain that each standoff matches a motherboard mounting hole. If you find one that doesn't, remove it. Leaving an "extra" standoff in place may cause a short circuit that may damage the motherboard and/or other components.

If necessary, install additional standoffs in your case until each motherboard mounting hole has a corresponding standoff. Although you can screw in the standoffs using your fingers or needle-nose pliers, it's much easier and faster to use a 5mm or 6mm nut driver. Tighten the standoffs finger-tight, but do not overtighten them. It's easy to strip the threads by applying too much torque with a nutdriver.

Once you've installed all the standoffs, do a final check to verify (a) that each motherboard mounting hole has a corresponding standoff, and (b) that no standoffs are installed that don't correspond to a motherboard mounting hole. As a final check, we usually hold the motherboard in position above the case and look down through each motherboard mounting hole to make sure there's a standoff installed below it.

Preparing and Populating the Motherboard

It is always easier to prepare and populate the motherboard—install the processor and memory—while the motherboard is outside the case. In fact, you must do so with some systems, because installing the heatsink/fan unit requires access to both sides of the motherboard. Even if it is possible to populate the motherboard while it is installed in the case, we always recommend doing so with the motherboard outside the case and lying flat on the work surface. More than once, we've tried to save a few minutes by replacing the processor without removing the motherboard. Too often, the result has been bent pins and a destroyed processor.

WARNING

Each time you handle the processor, memory, or other static-sensitive components, first touch the power supply to ground yourself.

Pen and Paper

Another method we've used to verify that all standoffs are properly installed is to place the motherboard flat on a large piece of paper and use a felt-tip pen to mark all motherboard mounting holes on the paper. We then line one of the marks up with the corresponding standoff and press down until the standoff punctures the paper. We do the same with a second standoff to align the paper, and then press the paper flat around each standoff. If we've installed the standoffs properly, every mark will be punctured, and there will be no punctures where there are no marks.

Figure 3-14. Lift the socket lever to
unlock the metal retention plate

Installing the processor

To install the Pentium D processor,
press the lever slightly away from
the socket to unlatch it, as shown
in Figure 3-14. Then lift the lever
straight up until it comes to a stop
vertical or slightly past vertical.

With the lever vertical, the metal
retention plate is unlocked and free
to swing up and away from the socket. Pivot the retention plate up and
remove the plastic socket protector,
as shown in Figures 3-15 and 3-16.
Ours required quite a bit of pressure
to snap out. Keep the plastic socket
protector in the motherboard box, in
case you ever remove the processor.
The exposed Socket 775 connectors
are very fragile, and should never be
left unprotected.

Figure 3-15. Lift the metal retention plate to expose the socket contacts

Figure 3-16. Snap the plastic socket protector out of the retention plate

With the plastic retention plate removed, as shown in Figure 3-17, the socket is prepared to receive the processor.

Figure 3-17. The socket prepared to receive the processor

Figure 3-18. Remove the plastic protector from the processor

Figure 3-19. Dropping the processor into place

Figure 3-20. Closing the retention plate

Remove the processor from its plastic blister-wrap container. The contact side of the processor is covered by a plastic protector. Hold the processor by its edges, as shown in Figure 3-18, and peel the plastic protector away from the processor. Store that protector with the motherboard or processor box, in case you ever remove the processor. Always reinstall the protector when you store a bare processor.

Keying is indicated on the processor by a small triangle and on the socket by a corresponding beveled edge, both visible in Figure 3-19. The socket also has two protruding nubs that correspond to notches in the processor, one of which is visible in the figure just to the right of the gold arrow at the lower-left corner of the processor.

With the metal retention plate vertical, align the processor with the socket and drop the processor into place, as shown in Figure 3-19. The processor should seat flush with the socket just from the force of gravity. If the processor doesn't simply drop into place, something is misaligned. Remove the processor and verify that it is aligned properly. **Never** apply pressure to the processor. You'll bend one or more pins, destroying the socket (and the motherboard).

With the processor in place and seated flush with the socket, lower the metal retention plate, as shown in Figure 3-20. If the processor is fully seated in its socket, the retention plate should freely seat flush with the top of the processor. Note the lip on the lower right of the retention plate and the corresponding cammed area of the clamping lever. When the retention plate is properly closed, the cammed portion of the clamping lever should engage that lip as the clamping lever is moved to the latched position.

With the retention plate closed, close the socket latching lever, as shown in Figure 3-21. Make certain that the lever is locked in place by the hook on the side of the socket.

Figure 3-21. Locking the processor into the socket

Installing memory

Installing memory is easy enough, but before you begin plugging in memory modules willy-nilly, take a moment to determine the best memory configuration. The Intel D945GCZLR motherboard has a dual-channel memory controller that provides better memory performance than a single-channel controller, but it's possible to force the motherboard to operate in single-channel mode if you're not careful about where you install the memory modules. Dual-channel operation requires using DIMMs in pairs, one per channel.

Examining the D945GCZLR motherboard, we see that it has four DIMM slots in two pairs. The slot nearest the processor is Channel A, DIMM0; followed by Channel A, DIMM1; Channel B, DIMM0; and Channel B, DIMM1. We want to install one memory module in Channel A and the second in Channel B. We could use either slot, but as a matter of good practice we decided to install our DIMMs in the first (DIMM0) slot of each channel.

Having decided where to install the memory modules, the first step in actually installing them is to pivot the locking tabs on both sides of the DIMM socket outward. To install the first DIMM, orient it with the notch in the contact area of the DIMM aligned with the raised plastic tab in the Channel A, DIMM0 slot and slide the DIMM into place, as shown in Figure 3-22.

Figure 3-22. Orient the DIMM with the notch aligned properly with the socket

Figure 3-23. Seat the DIMM by pressing firmly until it snaps into place

With the DIMM properly aligned with the Channel A, DIMM0 slot and oriented vertically relative to the slot, use both thumbs to press down on the DIMM until it snaps into place, as shown in Figure 3-23. The locking tabs should automatically pivot back up into the locked position when the DIMM snaps into place. If they don't, close them manually to lock the DIMM into the socket.

To install the second DIMM, orient it with the notch in the contact area of the DIMM aligned with the raised plastic tab in the Channel B, DIMM0 (blue) slot and slide the DIMM into place. Use your thumbs to press down on both sides of the DIMM, as shown in Figure 3-24, until the DIMM seats fully in the slot and the locking tabs snap into place.

Before you proceed, verify that the locking tabs on both sides of both DIMMs are locked into place, as shown in Figure 3-25.

With the processor and memory installed, you're almost ready to install the motherboard in the case. Before you do that, check the motherboard documentation to determine if any configuration jumpers need to be set. The Intel D945GCZLR has only one jumper, which sets operating mode. On our motherboard, that jumper was set correctly by default, so we proceeded to the next step.

Figure 3-24. Insert the second DIMM in the Channel B, DIMM0 slot

Figure 3-25. Verify that both DIMMs are fully seated and locked in place

Installing the Motherboard

Installing the motherboard is the most time-consuming step in building the system because there are so many cables to connect. It's important to get all of them connected right, so take your time and verify each connection before and after you make it.

Before you begin installing the motherboard, use a paper towel to polish the processor, as shown in Figure 3-26. You want to remove any smudges or skin oil from the processor surface to make sure the CPU cooler can make good contact with the processor.

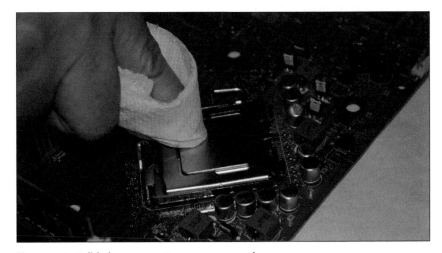

Figure 3-26. Polish the processor to remove any smudges

Figure 3-27. Slide the motherboard into position

Seating and securing the motherboard

To begin, slide the motherboard into the case, as shown in Figure 3-27. Carefully align the back panel I/O connectors with the corresponding holes in the I/O template, and slide the motherboard toward the rear of the case until the motherboard mounting holes line up with the standoffs. Also verify that the four CPU cooler mounting holes that surround the processor socket are aligned with the corresponding holes in the Support and Retention Module (SRM).

MEASURE TWICE, CUT ONCE

Check one more time to make sure that there's a standoff installed for each mounting hole, and that no standoff is installed where there is no mounting hole. One of our technical reviewers suggests installing white nylon standoffs, trimmed to length, in all unused standoff positions covered by the motherboard, particularly those near the expansion slots. Doing so provides more support to the motherboard, making it less likely that you'll crack the motherboard if you seat a recalcitrant expansion card.

Although the image shows Barbara grasping the motherboard by the northbridge heatsink, she was using it only to guide the motherboard into position. Be careful not to put any pressure on that heatsink. It is not firmly connected to the motherboard, and can easily be torn loose.

Before you secure the motherboard, verify that the back-panel I/O connectors mate cleanly with the I/O template, as shown in Figure 3-28. The I/O template has metal tabs that ground the back-panel I/O connectors. Make sure none of these tabs intrude into a port connector. An errant tab at best blocks the port, rendering it unusable, and at worst may short out the motherboard.

After you position the motherboard and verify that the back-panel I/O connectors mate cleanly with the I/O template, insert a screw through one mounting hole into the corresponding standoff, as shown in Figure 3-29. You may need to apply pressure to keep the motherboard positioned properly until you have inserted two or three screws.

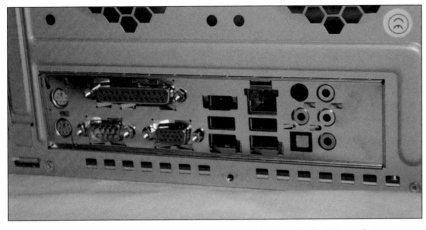

Figure 3-28. Verify that the back panel connectors mate cleanly with the I/O template

Figure 3-29. Install screws in all mounting holes to secure the motherboard

If you have trouble getting all the holes and standoffs aligned, insert two screws but don't tighten them completely. Use one hand to press the motherboard into alignment, with all holes matching the standoffs. Then insert one or two more screws and tighten them completely. Finish mounting the motherboard by inserting screws into all standoffs and tightening them. If you're still having difficulty getting everything aligned, try installing all of the mounting screws before you tighten any of them completely.

Less Power

People sometimes ask us why we don't use power screwdrivers. Because they're large, clumsy, and the batteries are always dead when we want to use the driver. Worse still, we once watched someone crack a motherboard by over-torquing the mounting screws with a power screwdriver. A clutched driver eliminates that objection, but we still find power screwdrivers too clumsy to use, even when we've built many identical systems on an ad hoc production line.

With first-rate products like the Antec BK640B case and the Intel D945GCZLR motherboard, all the holes usually line up perfectly. With second- and third-tier brands, that's not always the case. At times, we've been forced to use only a few screws to secure the motherboard. We prefer to use all of them, both to physically support the motherboard and to make sure all of the grounding points are in fact grounded, but if you simply can't every hole lined up, just install as many screws as you can.

After you've inserted all of the motherboard mounting screws, make one final check to verify that all of the ports on the back-panel I/O connector are clear of the metal grounding tabs on the I/O template.

Installing the CPU Cooler

Modern processors draw as much as 130W of power and must dissipate a correspondingly large amount of heat. Our Pentium D 940 processor has a TDP (Thermal Design Power) rating of 95W, and can actually exceed that figure under heavy load. All of that wattage is converted to waste heat. The processor must rid itself of that heat over the surface of its heat spreader, which is about the size of a large postage stamp. Without a good CPU cooler, the processor would almost instantaneously shut itself down to prevent damage from overheating.

To install the CPU cooler, position it over the processor, as shown in Figure 3-30. Make sure that the cylindrical finned-metal heatsink portion of the cooler is toward the rear of the case and that the front of the CPU cooler (the part with the fan) mates cleanly to the violet plastic air duct just visible behind Barbara's hand. Check the four holes in the base of the CPU cooler to verify that they are aligned with the corresponding screw holes in the SRM.

Correct Cooling

Using a proper CPU cooler is critical. A retail-boxed processor includes a CPU cooler that is designed for that processor. If you buy an OEM processor, it's up to you to install a CPU cooler that can keep the processor operating within its design temperature range.

Just because a CPU cooler fits doesn't guarantee it's usable. Even apparently identical processors may differ widely in their power consumption and heat production. For example, our Pentium D 940 is a later model that is rated at 95W TDP. Earlier Pentium D 940 models were rated at 130W TDP. If you choose a third-party CPU cooler, make certain that it is rated to cool the exact processor you use, not just by model number but by the S-spec number or a similar detailed specification number.

Figure 3-30. Position the CPU cooler over the processor

The Intel CPU cooler includes a preapplied thermal pad, visible as a square white patch on the copper base of the heatsink shown earlier in Figure 3-4. A thermal pad uses phase-change media, which is a fancy way of saying that it melts when it gets hot and solidifies when it cools down again. This thermal compound greatly improves heat transfer between the CPU heat spreader plate and the base of the heatsink by eliminating air gaps and filling in tiny pits in the smooth surfaces of the heat spreader and heatsink base.

WARNING

Always check the thermal pad before you install the CPU cooler to verify that there is no protective paper or plastic film covering it. Some thermal pads have protective film; others are supplied bare. If the pad has protective film, peel it off before you position the CPU cooler.

If you remove the heatsink, you must replace the thermal compound or pad when you reinstall it. Before you reinstall, remove all remnants of the old thermal pad or compound. That can be difficult, particularly for a thermal pad, which can be very tenacious. We use an ordinary hair dryer to warm the thermal material enough to make it easy to remove. Sometimes the best way is to warm up the compound and rub it off with your thumb. (Use rubber gloves or a plastic bag to keep the gunk off your skin.)

Alternatively, one of our technical reviewers says that rubbing gently with #0000 steel wool works wonders in removing the gunk, and is fine enough not to damage the surface. Another of our technical reviewers tells us that he uses Goof-Off or isopropyl alcohol to remove the remnants of the thermal goop or thermal pad. Whatever works for you is fine. Just make sure to remove the old thermal compound and replace it with new compound each time you remove and reinstall the processor.

When we replace a heatsink, we use Antec Silver Thermal Compound, which is widely available, inexpensive, and works well. Don't pay extra for "premium" brand names like Arctic Silver. They cost more than the Antec product and our testing shows little or no difference in cooling efficiency.

With the CPU cooler in position, secure it by driving the four provided screws through the holes in the base of the CPU cooler and into the SRM, as shown in Figure 3-31. Intel says you can drive those screws in any order. We drove them as we'd install the lug nuts on a tire. We drove all four screws to a loose fit and then tightened them down, alternating diagonally. You want these screws to be tight enough to force the CPU cooler into tight contact with the heat spreader plate on the processor, but not tight enough to risk cracking the motherboard. Finger-tight is good enough.

The thermal mass of the heatsink draws heat away from the CPU, but the heat must be dissipated to prevent the CPU from eventually overheating as the heatsink warms up. To dispose of excess heat as it is transferred to the heatsink, most CPU coolers use a fan to continuously draw air through the fins of the heatsink. Some CPU fans use a drive power connector, but most are designed to attach to a dedicated CPU fan connector on the motherboard. Using a motherboard fan power connector allows the motherboard to control the CPU fan, reducing speed for quieter operation when the processor is running under light load and not generating much heat, and increasing fan speed when the processor is running under heavy load and generating more heat. The motherboard can also monitor fan speed, which allows it to send an alert to the user if the fan fails or begins running sporadically.

Figure 3-31. Secure the CPU cooler with four screws

To connect the CPU fan, locate the header connector on the motherboard labeled CPU Fan, and plug the keyed cable from the CPU fan into that connector, as shown in Figure 3-32.

Figure 3-32. Connect the CPU cooler fan power lead to the CPU fan header

Connecting front-panel switch and indicator cables

With the CPU cooler installed, the next step is to connect the front-panel switch and indicator cables to the motherboard. Before you begin connecting front-panel cables, examine the cables. Each is labeled descriptively, e.g., "Power," "Reset," and "HDD LED." Match those descriptions with the front-panel connector pins on the motherboard to make sure you connect the correct cable to the appropriate pins. The motherboard header pins are color-coded. Figure 3-33 shows the pin assignments for the Hard Drive Activity LED (yellow), Reset Switch (purple), Power LED (green), and Power Switch (red) connectors.

- The Power Switch and Reset Switch connectors are not polarized and can be connected in either orientation.

- The Hard Drive Activity LED is polarized and should be connected with the ground (black) wire on Pin 3 and the signal (red) wire on Pin 1.

- The Power LED connector on the Intel motherboard accepts a two-position Power LED cable. Like other Intel motherboards, the D945GCZLR also provides an alternative three-pin Power LED connector with pins in positions one and three. The Power LED connector is dual-polarized, and can support a single-color (usually green) Power LED, as is provided with the Antec BK640B case, or a dual-color (usually green/yellow) LED. If you are using a case that has a dual-color Power LED, check the case documentation to determine how to connect the Power LED cable.

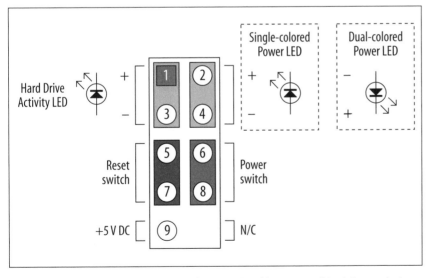

Figure 3-33. Front panel connector pin assignments (graphic courtesy of Intel Corporation)

Despite Their Best Intentions

Intel has defined the standard front-panel connector block shown in Figure 3-33, and uses that standard for its current motherboards. Unfortunately, few other motherboard makers adhere to that standard. Accordingly, rather than provide an Intel-standard monolithic connector block that would be useless for motherboards that do not follow the Intel standard, most case makers, including Antec, provide individual one-, two-, or three-pin connectors for each switch and indicator. A few cases provide both a monolithic Intel connector block and individual wires for nonstandard motherboards. If your motherboard provides the monolithic connector block, use it to minimize the possibility of connecting the cables incorrectly.

Once you determine the proper orientation for each cable, connect the Hard Drive Activity LED, Reset Switch, Power LED, and Power Switch cables to the motherboard, as shown in Figure 3-34. Not all cases have cables for every connector on the motherboard, and not all motherboards have connectors for all cables provided by the case. For example, some cases provide a speaker cable. The Intel D945GCZLR motherboard has a built-in speaker, but no connector for an external speaker, so that cable goes unused. Conversely, the Intel D945GCZLR has a Chassis Intrusion Connector, for which no corresponding cable exists on the Antec BK640B case, so that connector goes unused.

Figure 3-34. Connect the front-panel switch and indicator cables

When you're connecting front-panel cables, try to get it right the first time, but don't worry too much about getting it wrong. Other than the power-switch cable, which must be connected properly for the system to start, none of the other front-panel switch and indicator cables is essential, and connecting them wrong won't damage the system. Switch cables—power and reset—are not polarized. You can connect them in either orientation, without worrying about which pin is signal and which ground. LED cables may or may not be polarized, but if you connect a polarized LED cable backwards the worst that happens is that the LED won't light. Most cases use a common wire color, usually black, for ground, and a colored wire for signal.

Connecting front-panel USB ports

The Antec BK640B case provides two front-panel USB 2.0 ports, for which the Intel D945GCZLR motherboard provides corresponding internal connectors. Both front-panel USB 2.0 ports are routed through a single cable that terminates in an Intel-standard 10-pin monolithic USB connector block.

TWO BY TWO

The D945GCZLR actually provides four internal USB 2.0 connectors, in two sets of two header pin groups. One of those connectors serves the two front-panel USB 2.0 ports on the BK640B, leaving the second connector free for other uses, such as connecting an internal USB card reader or routing additional USB ports to the rear of the system.

Other cases provide individual wires rather than a monolithic USB connector block. If your case has individual wires, refer to Figure 3-35 for the pin assignments for the dual front-panel internal USB connectors.

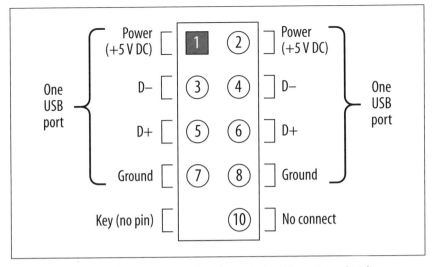

Figure 3-35. Front panel USB connector pin assignments (graphic courtesy of Intel Corporation)

To route USB to the front panel panel of the BK640B, you simply connect the USB cable to the corresponding internal connector, as shown in Figure 3-36.

Figure 3-36. Connect the front-panel USB cable

Connecting the front-panel IEEE-1394a (FireWire) port

The Antec BK640B case provides one front-panel FireWire (IEEE-1394a) port, for which the Intel D945GCZLR motherboard provides a corresponding internal connector (actually, it provides two). To route FireWire to the front panel, you must connect a cable from the front-panel FireWire port to this internal connector.

Although the Antec BK640B case provides a front-panel FireWire cable with an Intel-standard monolithic connector block, many cases provide only individual wires that must be connected one by one to the FireWire header on the motherboard. Figure 3-37 shows the pinouts for the internal FireWire connector.

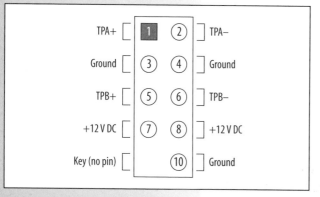

Figure 3-37. Front-panel IEEE-1394a (FireWire) connector pin assignments (graphic courtesy of Intel Corporation)

Connect the FireWire cable, as shown in Figure 3-38. A second set of FireWire pins is visible immediately below Barbara's finger in the figure. You can connect the front-panel FireWire cable to either of these sets of pins. With the standard back-panel FireWire port, that gives you two available FireWire connectors. If you need a third FireWire connector, you can install a "cliffhanger" bracket with a FireWire port and run its cable to this unused connector. Such brackets are available from most online computer parts vendors.

Figure 3-38. Connect the front-panel FireWire cable

Connecting the front-panel audio ports

The Antec BK640B case provides two front-panel audio ports, Line Out and Mic In. These ports are very convenient for connecting a headset to use Skype or simply to listen to music on your headphones. Some earlier Intel motherboards forced you to make a decision: to connect the front-panel audio port cable, you had to disable the corresponding rear-panel ports. Fortunately, the D945GCZLR requires no such decision. You can connect the front-panel audio ports and still use Line Out and Mic In on the back panel. To enable the front-panel audio ports, connect the Audio cable to the front-panel audio header pins near the rear I/O panel, as shown in Figure 3-39.

Figure 3-39. Connect the front-panel audio cable

Installing the Tuner Card

As long as we have the system on its side, we might as well install the Hauppauge WinTV-PVR-150 tuner card. To begin doing so, remove the screw that secures the expansion slot cover bracket, as shown in Figure 3-40.

With the screw removed, slide the expansion slot cover bracket up and tilt it toward the inside of the case, as shown in Figure 3-41. (Our bracket required a light tap with the screwdriver handle to free it.) Remove the bracket completely and set it aside for now.

Figure 3-40. Remove the screw that secures the expansion slot cover bracket

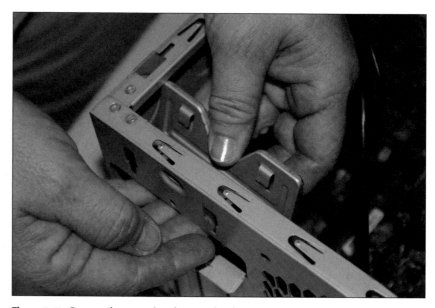

Figure 3-41. Remove the expansion slot cover bracket

Choose one of the expansion slot covers that corresponds to a PCI expansion slot on the motherboard. (If you're not sure which cover to remove, temporarily align the Hauppauge PVR-150 card with the expansion slot you intend to install it in and see which expansion slot cover needs to be removed.)

Slide the expansion slot cover upward, as shown in Figure 3-42, and remove it. Be careful while doing so. Antec cases are renowned for their absence of sharp edges and burrs, but expansion slot covers are thin metal and may have sharp edges.

Figure 3-42. Remove the selected expansion slot cover

Slide the Hauppauge WinTV-PVR-150 card into position, making sure that the card contacts are aligned with the expansion slot. Using your thumbs, press down on the card, as shown in Figure 3-43, until you feel the card snap into place in the expansion slot.

Figure 3-43. Align the tuner card and press down until it snaps into the expansion slot

Replace the expansion slot cover bracket, as shown in Figure 3-44, working from inside the case. Press the bracket down until the keyed tabs on the bracket slide into place in the corresponding cutouts in the case. Insert the screw that secures the expansion slot cover bracket, and then insert the screw to secure the tuner card in place. (That second screw passes through the expansion slot cover bracket first, then through the card bracket itself, and then into the case frame.)

Figure 3-44. Reinstall the expansion slot cover bracket

Figure 3-45. Connect the main ATX power connector

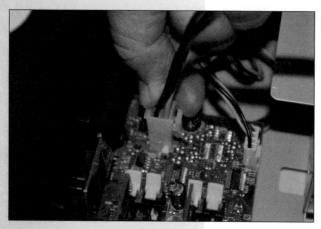

Figure 3-46. Connect the ATX12V power connector

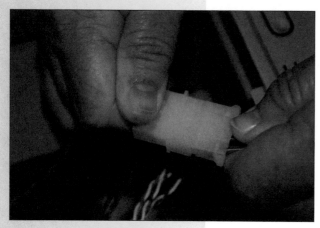

Figure 3-47. Connect the front-panel blue LED to a power supply connector

Connecting the ATX Power Cables

The next step in assembling the system is to connect the two power cables from the power supply to the motherboard. The main ATX power connector is a 24-pin connector located near the rear of the motherboard, adjacent to the rear I/O connector panel. Locate the corresponding cable coming from the power supply. The main ATX power connector is keyed, so verify that it is aligned properly before you attempt to seat it.

Once everything is aligned, press down firmly until the connector seats, as shown in Figure 3-45. It may take significant pressure to seat the connector, and you should feel it snap into place. The locking tab on the side of the connector should snap into place over the corresponding nub on the socket. Make sure the connector seats fully. A partially seated main ATX power connector may cause subtle problems that are very difficult to troubleshoot.

Modern processors require more power to the motherboard than the standard ATX main power connector supplies. Intel developed a supplementary connector, called the ATX12V connector, that routes additional +12V current directly to the VRM (Voltage Regulator Module) that powers the processor. On most current Intel (and AMD) motherboards, including the D945GCZLR, the ATX12V connector is located very near the processor socket. The ATX12V connector is keyed. Orient the cable connector properly relative to the motherboard connector, and press the cable connector into place until the plastic tab locks, as shown in Figure 3-46.

WARNING

Failing to connect the ATX12V connector is one of the most common causes of initial boot failures on newly built systems. If nothing happens the first time you power up the system, chances are it's because you forgot to connect the ATX12V connector.

As long as we're connecting power cables, let's connect power to the blue LED that illuminates the front of the case. Locate a female Molex (hard drive) power connector among the other wires coming from the front panel. Connect that to one of the Molex connectors coming from the power supply, as shown in Figure 3-47.

Installing the Drives

The Antec BK640B case provides two externally-accessible 5.25" bays, each of which is covered by a snap-in plastic bezel. We decided to install the NEC ND-3550A DVD writer (our initial choice for the burner) in the upper bay. Before installing the drive, you have to remove the bezel. The easiest way to do that on the BK640B case is to press out on the bezel from inside the case until the bezel snaps out, as shown in Figure 3-48.

Before you install the optical drive, verify the master/slave jumper settings. Like most optical drives, the NEC ND-3550A DVD writer is set by default to be the master device on the ATA channel. Our hard drives are S-ATA, so the optical drive will be the only parallel ATA device in the system, and should be set as the master device on the ATA channel. If you use a different optical drive, verify that its jumper is set to master.

It's usually easier to connect the ATA cable to the drive before you install the drive in the case. The Intel D945GCZLR motherboard comes with an 80-wire Ultra ATA cable, which we used. Because optical drives have relatively slow transfer rates, they can use the older 40-wire ATA cable rather than the 80-wire Ultra-ATA cable used for ATA hard drives. (An 80-wire cable works fine if that's all you have, but it's not necessary.)

To connect the cable, locate pin 1 on the drive connector, which is usually nearest the power connector. The pin-1 side of the cable is indicated by a colored stripe, usually red or blue. Align the cable connector with the drive connector, making sure the colored stripe is on the pin-1 side of the drive connector, and press the cable into place, as shown in Figure 3-49.

To mount the optical drive in the case, feed the loose end of the ATA cable through the drive bay from the front, align the drive with the corresponding tracks in the case, and slide the drive into the bay, as shown in Figure 3-50. Make sure the front panel of the drive is flush with the front bezel of the case.

Figure 3-48. Remove the bezel to prepare the bay to receive the optical drive

Figure 3-49. Connect the ATA cable to the optical drive

Figure 3-50. Slide the optical drive into the drive bay

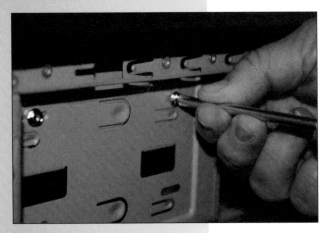

Figure 3-51. Secure the optical drive with four screws

Figure 3-52. Connect the power cable to the optical drive

Figure 3-53. Slide the top hard drive cage into place

With the optical drive aligned flush with the front case bezel, secure the drive in the bay by inserting four screws, two on each side of the drive, as shown in Figure 3-51. The front mounting position on each side of the bay provides three discrete screw holes, one of which should align properly with the drive screw hole when the drive is aligned flush with the front panel. (For our drive and case, the middle screw hole is the proper one.) The rear mounting position is a slot that allows some slack to account for minor manufacturing variations in the position of the screw hole.

The next step in installing the optical drive—one we forget more often than we should—is to connect power to the drive. Choose one of the power cables coming from the power supply and press the Molex connector onto the drive power connector, as shown in Figure 3-52. It may require significant pressure to get the power connector to seat, so use care to avoid hurting your fingers if the connector seats suddenly. The Molex power connector is keyed, so verify that it is oriented properly before you apply pressure to seat the power cable.

With the optical drive installed, the next step is to install the hard drives. We had the choice of mounting both of our hard drives in one of the removable drive cages, or one drive in each cage. At first, we were inclined to split the drives between cages so that each drive would run cooler.

Then we noticed the vent arrangement on the BK640B case. The drive cage that connects to the optical drive bay has no vent of its own, while the bottom drive cage is positioned directly behind a front-panel vent. We decided that mounting both of our hard drives in the bottom cage would actually provide better drive cooling, so we decided to leave the top cage unused.

We might need that top cage later, though, if we decide to add hard drives to the system, so the next step was to reinstall the top hard drive cage (we removed them back in the "Preparing the Case" section). To do so, position the hard drive cage so that it is aligned with the bottom of the optical drive bay, and slide the cage into position, as shown in Figure 3-53. Make sure the locking tabs engage and that the screw hole in the cage aligns with the screw hole in the optical drive bay.

Once the drive cage is seated, secure it by driving a single screw through the drive cage and into the optical drive bay, as shown in Figure 3-54.

The next step is to mount the hard drives in the bottom hard drive cage. To do so, first position the empty cage against the chassis as though you were reinstalling it. Note the orientation of the cage to make sure you don't install the hard drives upside-down or backward. You want to install the drives with the label side facing up and the power and data connectors toward the rear.

You don't need to set configuration jumpers for Serial ATA drives, because each drive connects to a dedicated interface. Set aside four screws for each of the two hard drives. Verify that the screws are the proper size by threading one screw into the drive before you begin mounting the drives, and then selecting seven identical screws. Once you have done so, insert each drive into the cage and secure it with four screws, as shown in Figure 3-55.

After you mount both drives in the drive cage, connect an S-ATA data cable to each drive, as shown in Figure 3-56. The S-ATA connector is keyed with an L-shaped slot. Make sure the cable is oriented properly to the drive connector, and then slide the connector onto the drive until it seats completely. Be careful not to apply any sideways torque to the connector, which is relatively fragile and may snap off if you're not careful.

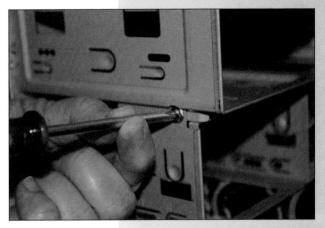

Figure 3-54. Secure the hard drive cage with a screw

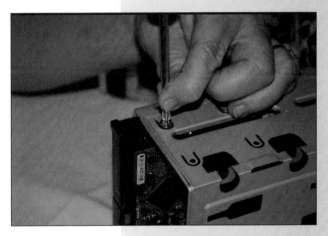

Figure 3-55. Secure each drive in the cage with four screws

ADVICE FROM JIM COOLEY

Once both the S-ATA and ATA cables are inserted, I use a Wite-out pen to paint a stripe across both cable and connector, making it much easier to identify the correct orientation if I disconnect them at some point in the future.

MINOR VARIATIONS

Although an S-ATA data cable can have the same connector on both ends, our S-ATA cables had slightly different connectors on each end. These S-ATA cables were included with the Intel motherboard. One end of each cable includes a metal locking tab that is designed to mate with a special matching connector on the motherboard S-ATA interface connector. Even so, we could have connected either end of the cable to our hard drive, because the S-ATA part of the connector body is identical on each end.

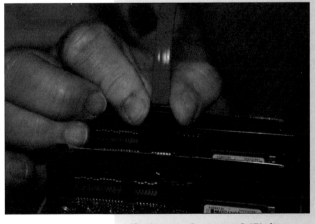

Figure 3-56. Connect an S-ATA data cable to each drive

Figure 3-57. Connect an S-ATA power cable to each drive

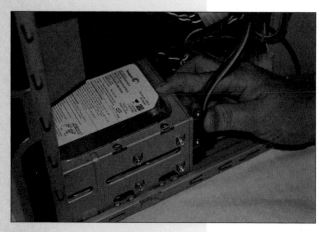

Figure 3-58. Slide the hard drive cage into the case

Figure 3-59. Secure the drive cage to the chassis with one screw

After you have the data cables connected to both drives, place the drive cage assembly near the bottom front of the case. Connect an S-ATA power cable to each drive, as shown in Figure 3-57. Once again, the S-ATA power connectors use an L-shaped keying slot, and are relatively fragile. Be careful as you attach the connectors.

Slide the hard drive cage assembly into the case, as shown in Figure 3-58. Make sure that the locking tabs on the cage and chassis align and seat properly, and that the screw hole in the chassis aligns with the screw hole in the cage. Drive one screw through the chassis and into the drive cage to secure it, as shown in Figure 3-59.

JIM COOLEY WARNS

DO NOT SKIP THIS STEP. If you don't lock the hard drive cage down you'll forget it's not secure and only find out the hard way when you move the computer at some point in the distant future, quite possibly causing much damage in the process.

The final step in installing the drives is connect their data cables to the motherboard. The S-ATA data cable from each hard drive can be connected to any of the four S-ATA ports on the motherboard. As a matter of good practice, we prefer to connect the hard drives in sequence to the S-ATA ports. We connected the first hard drive—which by convention we designate the top of the two drives—to the first S-ATA port, labeled S-ATA 0. We then connected the second (bottom) hard drive to the second S-ATA port, labeled S-ATA 1, as shown in Figure 3-60.

Once again, the S-ATA connectors are keyed with an L-shaped slot and the connectors are relatively fragile. Make sure the cable connector is aligned properly with the motherboard connector, and then press the cable connector firmly onto the motherboard connector until it seats fully. Do not apply any sideways torque.

After you've connected the S-ATA data cables, it's time to connect the P-ATA data cable from the optical drive. The Intel D945GCZLR motherboard has only one ATA interface, which is visible in Figure 3-60 just below the S-ATA connectors.

Orient the motherboard end of the P-ATA data cable so that its keying tab is aligned with the keying notch in the motherboard connector, and press the P-ATA cable firmly into place, as shown in Figure 3-61.

Figure 3-60. Connect the S-ATA data cables to the motherboard

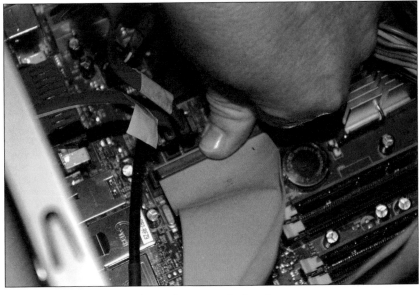

Figure 3-61. Connect the ATA data cable to the motherboard

What About the Audio Cable?

Speaking of connecting cables, one of our technical reviewers pointed out that we'd forgotten to connect the audio cable to the optical drive in all of the project systems. We hadn't forgotten; we just don't do it any more.

Years ago, connecting an audio cable from the optical drive to the motherboard audio connector or sound card was an essential step, because systems used the analog audio delivered from the optical drive by that cable. If you didn't connect that cable, you didn't get audio from the drive. All modern optical drives and motherboards support digital audio, which is delivered across the bus rather than via a dedicated audio cable.

To verify the setting for digital audio, which is ordinarily enabled by default, use the Windows XP Device Manager to display the Device Properties sheet for the optical drive. The Enable digital CD audio… checkbox should be marked. If it is not, mark the checkbox to enable digital audio.

Final Assembly Steps

Congratulations! You're almost finished building the system. Only a few final steps remain to be done, and those won't take long.

Before you go any further, dress the cables. That simply means routing the cables away from the motherboard and other components and tying them off so they don't flop around inside the case. Chances are that no one but you will ever see the inside of your system, but dressing the cables has several advantages other than making the system appear neater. First and foremost, it improves cooling by keeping the cables from impeding air flow. It can also improve system reliability. More than once, we've seen a system overheat and crash because a loose cable fouled a fan.

After you dress the cables, take a few minutes to double-check everything. Verify that all cables are connected properly, that all drives are secured, and that there's nothing loose inside the case. If your power supply is not auto-sensing, check one last time to verify that it is set to the correct input voltage. It's a good idea to pick up the system and tilt it gently from side to side to make sure there are no loose screws or other items that could cause a short. Use the following checklist:

- ❑ Power supply set to proper input voltage (the built-in power supply on the Antec BK640B sets itself automatically)
- ❑ No loose tools or screws (shake the case gently)
- ❑ CPU cooler properly mounted; CPU fan connected
- ❑ Memory modules full seated and latched
- ❑ Front-panel switch and indicator cables connected properly
- ❑ Front-panel I/O cables connected properly
- ❑ Hard drive data cable(s) connected to drive(s) and motherboard
- ❑ Hard drive power cable(s) connected
- ❑ Optical drive data cable connected to drive and motherboard
- ❑ Optical drive power cable connected
- ❑ Optical drive audio cable connected, if applicable
- ❑ Floppy drive data and power cables connected (if applicable)
- ❑ All drives secured to drive bay or chassis, as applicable
- ❑ Expansion card(s) fully seated and secured to the chassis
- ❑ Main ATX power cable and ATX12V power cable connected
- ❑ Front and rear case fans installed and connected (if applicable)
- ❑ All cables dressed and tucked

Once you're certain that all is as it should be, it's time for the smoke test. Leave the cover off for now. Connect the power cable to the wall receptacle and then to the system unit. Unlike some power supplies, the Antec unit has a separate rocker switch on the back that controls power to the power supply. By default, it's in the "0" or off position, which means the power supply is not receiving power from the wall receptacle. Move that switch to the "1" or on position. Press the main power button on the front of the case, and the system should start up. Check to make sure that all fans are spinning. You should also hear the hard drive spin up and the happy beep that tells you the system is starting normally. At that point, everything should be working properly.

Turn off the system, disconnect the power cord, and take these final steps to prepare the system for use:

Set the BIOS Setup Configuration jumper to Configure mode
> The BIOS Setup Configuration jumper block on the Intel D945GCZLR motherboard is used to set the operation mode. This jumper is located at the rear center of the motherboard, near the speaker and the Main ATX Power connector. By default, the jumper is in the 1-2 or "normal" position. Move the jumper block to the 2-3 or "configure" position.

Reconnect the power cord and restart the system
> When the configuration jumper is set to configure mode, starting the system automatically runs BIOS Setup and puts the system in maintenance mode. This step allows the motherboard to detect the type of processor installed and configure it automatically. When the BIOS Setup screen appears, reset the system clock and load the system defaults. Save your changes, exit, and power down the system. Disconnect the power cord.

Set the BIOS Setup Configuration jumper to Normal mode
> With the power cord disconnected, move the BIOS Setup Configuration jumper block from 2-3 (Configure mode) to 1-2 (Normal mode).

Replace the side panels and reconnect power
> With the jumper set for Normal operation, replace the side panels and reconnect the power cord. Your system is now completely assembled and ready for use.

Post-Assembly

This system was as easy to build as any system we've ever assembled. Counting only actual construction time, it took only about 30 minutes from start to finish. (Of course, counting the time to shoot images, reshoot images, re-reshoot images, tear down for re-shoots and re-reshoots, rebuild and re-rebuild after the re-shoots and re-reshoots, and so on, it took a couple days.) A first-time system builder should be able to assemble this system in an evening with luck, and certainly over a weekend.

Initial Problems

When we fired up our mainstream PC for the first time, we were surprised when it refused to boot. The system started up normally enough, with all fans spinning and the BIOS boot text appearing onscreen. The access light on the NEC ND-3550A optical drive came on, and we expected the system to boot into Windows XP Setup. Alas, after a few seconds, the light on the

False Starts

When you turn on the rear power switch, the system will come to life momentarily and then die. That's perfectly normal behavior. When the power supply receives power, it begins to start up. It quickly notices that the motherboard hasn't told it to start, and so it shuts down again. All you need to do is press the front-panel power switch and the system will start normally.

NEC optical drive went out. After a minute or two, we concluded that the system had hung.

Our first thought was that the Windows XP distribution disc was bad. We had some Linux distribution discs handy, so we tried booting one of them. Same thing: the light on the optical drive would come on, the drive would read the disc for a few seconds, and then the light would go out. Hmmmm.

When we have problems like this, we always suspect the cable. We replaced the ATA cable and restarted the system. Same problem. Apparently, the drive itself was bad. We happened to have another NEC ND-3550A drive on the work bench, so we tried swapping it in. Same problem. Double hmmmm. Thinking that perhaps we'd just been unlucky enough to get two bad samples of the NEC ND-3550A, we pulled an ND-3550A from another system. Despite the fact that that third drive had been working normally in the other system, it exhibited exactly the same symptoms in our new system.

Once is happenstance. Twice is coincidence. Three times is enemy action. It seemed that the only possible explanations were that the motherboard ATA interface was bad or that the NEC ND-3550A drives were somehow incompatible with the motherboard. We'd never had a dead ATA interface out of the box on an Intel motherboard, but then we'd never seen an optical drive that was incompatible with a motherboard, either. An ATA optical drive should Just Work.

So we went back to the stock room and pulled a selection of other optical drives. We swapped them in one after the other, and every one worked perfectly. The system booted normally with several models of DVD-ROM drives, a selection of Plextor optical drives, and a BenQ DW-1650 DVD writer. Obviously, the motherboard ATA interface was working just fine. Whatever incompatibility caused our initial problems was apparently related to some interaction between the NEC ND-3550A and our D945GCZ motherboard. Oh, well. The ND-3550A is a nice optical drive, and quite inexpensive, but there are numerous other alternatives that cost about the same.

We left the BenQ DW-1650 drive in the system and went back to modify our recommended optical drive section earlier in the chapter. That's why the text recommends the BenQ DW-1650 but the images show us installing the NEC ND-3550A.

Configuring RAID

Intel supplies a RAID driver floppy with the D945GCZLR motherboard. During Windows XP Setup, you insert that floppy when Setup prompts you for a third-party disk subsystem driver. But before you install Windows, you must configure your RAID in BIOS Setup. To do so, restart the system and watch the screen as the system boots. When the Intel Matrix Storage Manager setup screen shown in Figure 3-62 appears, press Ctrl-I to enter the Configuration Utility.

```
Intel (R) Matrix Storage Manager option ROM v5.1.1.1002 ICH7R wRAID5
Copyright (C) 2003-05 Intel Corporation.  All Rights Reserved.

RAID Volumes:
None Defined.

Physical Disks:
Port Drive Model     Serial #           Size     Type/Status(Vol ID)
 0   ST3808110AS     5LR0JTLS           74.5GB   Non-RAID Disk
 1   ST3808110AS     5LR0JTMP           74.5GB   Non-RAID Disk

Press <CTRL-I> to enter Configuration Utility..
```

Figure 3-62. Intel Matrix Storage Manager setup screen

The Intel Matrix Storage Manager Main Menu shown in Figure 3-63 appears. This screen displays the current RAID configuration, if any, and information about the disks and volumes available on the system. At this point, no RAID has been configured. Make sure the first option, Create RAID Volume, is highlighted, and press Enter to begin the process of creating the RAID.

```
Intel (R) Matrix Storage Manager option ROM v5.1.1.1002 wRAID5
Copyright (C) 2003-05 Intel Corporation.  All Rights Reserved.
=========================[ MAIN MENU ]=========================
                      1.  Create RAID Volume
                      2.  Delete RAID Volume
                      3.  Reset Disks to Non-RAID
                      4.  Exit

===================[ DISK/VOLUME INFORMATION ]===================
RAID Volumes:
None defined.

Physical Disks:
Port Drive Model     Serial #           Size     Type/Status(Vol ID)
 0   ST3808110AS     5LROJTLS           74.5GB   Non-RAID Disk
 1   ST3808110AS     5LROJTMP           74.5GB   Non-RAID Disk


      [↑↓]-Select        [ESC]-Exit        [ENTER]-Select Menu
```

Figure 3-63. Creating the RAID

The next step is to specify the level of your new RAID. We have only two hard drives installed, so the RAID10 and RAID5 options cannot be selected. We can choose RAID0, which offers the fastest performance at the expense of reduced data safety, or RAID1, which offers high performance and data safety at the expense of total disk capacity. We chose RAID1 to mirror our two drives, as shown in Figure 3-64.

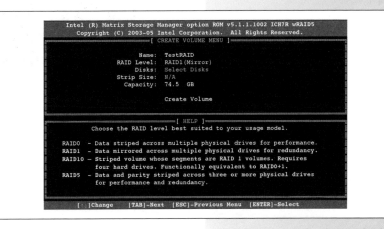

Figure 3-64. Choosing the RAID level

You Can't Get There from Here

The "screen shots" in this section are dummies. We couldn't use our usual screen-capture utility, because when these RAID configuration screens are visible, the system hasn't finished booting yet.

At first, we tried shooting literal screenshots. That didn't work very well with our little point-and-shoot digital camera, so we set up Barbara's Pentax DSLR on a tripod. We figured that using a telephoto lens from a distance would give us reasonably good images. It didn't, or at least it didn't during several trial passes. We probably could have made it work, given enough time and effort, but we decided it'd be easier and cleaner just to create dummy "screen shots" in OpenOffice Writer to use for the illustrations. If you notice any minor differences between these illustrations and what you see onscreen, that's why.

Chapter 3, Building a Mainstream PC

RAID1 writes the same data to two drives, so if one drive fails, no data is lost.

By default, Intel Matrix Storage Manager assigns all available disk space to the new array. If you want to change the amount of disk space allocated to your RAID, move the cursor to the Capacity field and enter a new value for volume size, as shown in Figure 3-65.

Gigabytes Versus Gibibytes

You might wonder why our two 80 GB drives show up as only 74.5 GB. It's because Seagate, like all drive makers, uses decimal notation. Seagate defines a gigabyte as 1,000,000,000 (10^9) bytes. Intel, Microsoft, and nearly everyone else uses binary notation, defining a gigabyte as 1,073,741,824 (2^{30}) bytes. Seagate is correct. A binary gigabyte should properly be called a gibibyte, although almost no one uses that term.

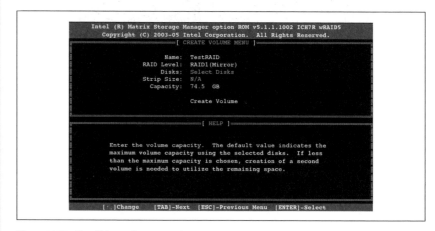

Figure 3-65. Specifying volume capacity

After you select the RAID level and specify the volume size, press Enter to create the new RAID volume. The Main Menu is redisplayed, as shown in Figure 3-66, updated to show the new RAID configuration.

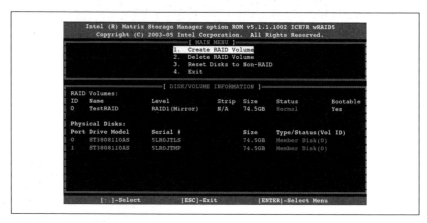

Figure 3-66. The Main Menu displaying the final RAID configuration

Installing Software

With RAID configured, we booted the Windows XP SP2 distribution disc to install the OS. Early in Setup, we were prompted to press F6 if we had a third-party driver floppy. Oops. We hadn't installed a floppy drive in this system, so we pulled one off the bench, shut down the system, and temporarily connected it. Once we install the Intel RAID drivers, we'll never need that floppy drive again, and we didn't want it messing up the appearance of the front panel.

Windows XP installed uneventfully. We installed the various drivers from the Intel CD, and then used the Passmark BurnInTest utility (*http://www. passmark.com*) to burn in the system. The system passed with no problems. We installed the applications disc provided with the Hauppauge WinTV-PVR-150 tuner card to test TV capture functions, which worked as expected. (In fact, the Hauppauge bundled utilities are surprisingly complete; if your needs are modest, the Hauppauge utilities may be all you need for capturing TV programs.)

With Windows installed and running on this system, it was a good time to check for firmware updates. We visited the Intel web site to check for BIOS updates. We found that we already had the most recent BIOS version available, so there was no need to run the Intel Express BIOS Update utility. There was a firmware update available for the BenQ optical drive, so we downloaded and installed it.

With all of that done, we blew away our Windows installation and installed the operating system we'll really run on this system, Ubuntu 6.06 LTS Linux (*http://www.ubuntu.com*).

UBUNTU AND RAID

Brian Bilbrey queried us about Intel Matrix RAID support under Ubuntu Linux. As far as we know, Ubuntu doesn't support Intel Matrix RAID, which, although it's often described as hardware RAID, is in fact hybrid RAID that depends on Windows-only drivers.

We disabled Intel Matrix RAID and installed Ubuntu on the system. During Ubuntu setup, we had the choice to partition manually, and setting up RAID is one of the options. We're sure that Ubuntu software RAID is slower than hardware RAID and perhaps even Matrix RAID, but it does the job.

Final Words

Overall, we're happy with our new mainstream PC system, although it's a bit louder than we hoped it would be. The problem isn't the Antec power supply or the Seagate Barracuda hard drive, both of which are nearly inaudible. The culprit is the CPU cooler fan, which produces a noticeable buzz.

That surprised us, because recent Intel ATX CPU coolers we've used have been quiet enough to be inaudible in a typical home office environment. This one is definitely audible, although not loud enough to be intrusive. Still, others who have built similar systems have commented about how quiet this BTX cooler is, so we wonder if our CPU cooler fan is defective. When we get a chance, we may disassemble the system and replace the CPU cooler fan with a Panaflo or similar quiet model.

The other thing that surprised us was the CPU temperature. Running in a room at 23°C ambient temperature, the sensor on the Intel motherboard reports the CPU temperature as 58°C at idle and 75°C or more under load. Although those temperatures are within acceptable limits, they're about 20°C higher than we'd like to see.

Still, there's no doubt that the Pentium D 940 is a hot processor in every sense of the word, so perhaps we'll just have to get used to it. Also, motherboard temperature sensors are notoriously unreliable. In the past, we've used a thermal probe on various systems and found that the actual CPU temperature was as much as 10°C or 15°C lower than the temperature reported by the CPU temperature sensor. We hope that's the case here, although there's no convenient way to test it because the humongous BTX CPU cooler leaves us no way to get a temperature probe in contact with the processor.

But those are mere niggles. Sure, we'd like the system to run a bit quieter and a bit cooler, but its performance is top-notch. It's also rock-solid stable, as we proved by running the Passmark burn-in utility for 72 hours without a single glitch. We can't ask for much more.

For updated component recommendations, commentary, and other new material, visit *http://www.hardwareguys.com/guides/mainstream-pc.html*.

Building a SOHO Server

4

One day in early 2004, our server started making funny noises. It was no big deal, as it turned out. A bearing in the supplemental case fan was failing. That was cheap and easy to fix, but it started us thinking.

Our server, that anonymous beige box where all our data lived, was an antique. As we blew the dust off it, literally and figuratively, we took stock of the hardware upon which so much of our working lives depended. An ancient Intel RC440BX motherboard. A Slot 1 Pentium III/550 processor with 128 MB of Crucial PC133 memory (we could have sworn we'd upgraded that to 256 MB). A 10 GB 7,200 RPM hard drive that Maxtor had sent us for evaluation before that drive was commercially available. A Travan tape drive from Tecmar, a company that departed the tape drive business years ago. And Windows NT Server 4. Ugh.

Although we'd made a few minor upgrades—including mirroring the 10 GB Maxtor to a larger Seagate drive—we realized that we were several years into the 21st century and still depending on a server that dated from the late 20th century. That was good in the sense that a server should be so reliable that one simply forgets it's there. And, despite all the nasty things people say about Windows stability, that server often ran for months on end without a reboot. That's what happens when you build a machine with top-notch components, put it on a good UPS, and blow out the dust dinosaurs from time to time.

But, although that box had been a good and faithful servant, it was clearly time for a change. So we set out to design and build a server that would meet our needs then and (we hoped) for several years to come. We decided from the start that we would look to the future rather than to the past. Accordingly, we designed our server to run Linux rather than a legacy Microsoft OS. Linux is fast, free, easier to install and maintain than Windows, immensely stable, and suffers from few of the security flaws endemic to Microsoft operating systems.

Shared Versus Dedicated

If yours is a typical SOHO environment, you may wonder if you need a dedicated server. After all, it's easy enough to set up a share on a desktop system and use that box as a shared desktop/server, just as we did until mid-2006. If you have only a couple users and make few demands on a network, that may be a viable alternative. Otherwise, the security, reliability, and other advantages of a dedicated server are worth the relatively low cost.

Advice from Brian Bilbrey

One real downside of using a workstation as a shared server is instability. That is, a server isn't usually running a GUI, and even if it is, you're not running any of the userland apps that might cause even a Linux system to be less than stable. Not that the running OS will keel over, but if you're transferring files when the person using the shared server decides to reboot because the browser doesn't want to get un-hung... that's a bad thing.

We described the design and construction of that new server in the first edition of this book. Our new server turned out to be fast and reliable, but it was also much more than we really needed for our small home business—particularly because we were using it only as a file and print server—and it was much noisier than we would have liked. Barbara had recently converted to using Xandros Linux on her main desktop system, and we decided that Barbara's desktop system was perfectly adequate as a dual-function desktop/server. So we donated our new server to a local nonprofit agency that needed a real server.

A couple of years passed, we signed a contract to write this new edition, and we decided it was again time to build a dedicated server for our own use. We work in a typical SOHO (Small Office/Home Office) environment—half a dozen desktop systems, some printers and other shared peripherals, and a cable-modem Internet connection. Of necessity, we designed our new SOHO server to meet our own needs. Your needs may differ from ours, though, and a SOHO server isn't a one-size-fits-all proposition. Accordingly, we've made every attempt to explain why we chose to configure our new server as we did, and how you might want to alter our configuration to suit your own requirements. In this chapter, you'll look over our shoulders as we design and build the perfect SOHO server.

ADVICE FROM RON MORSE

I'm not sure printers should be shared with an active workstation. A single machine can easily share workstation and file server duties, but add a printer to that mix and every incoming print job will tie up that machine totally until it is fully spooled, and the workstation will still suffer noticeably as the job spools to the printer.

Determining Functional Requirements

The problem with defining a "SOHO server" is that both words mean different things to different people. SOHO might encompass anything from 1 to 25 or more users, and a simple file and print server has very different requirements from a system that also functions as an application, database, web, and/or email server. In short, a "SOHO server" can be just about anything.

At one extreme, a SOHO server can be just a repurposed older desktop system, perhaps with a larger hard drive added. At the other extreme, a SOHO server can be a $15,000 box that uses such technologies as multiple processors, ECC memory, SCSI RAID, redundant power supplies, and so on.

As much as we believe in the advantages of building your own, we think it's a mistake to build the latter type of server, except perhaps for medium or larger companies that will have several such servers in use. A small company can no more afford extended server downtime than can a larger company, and avoiding downtime means having spares on hand. If you're running a dozen such servers, it's no great hardship to maintain a reasonable spares kit. If you're running only one server, the cost of spares can nearly double the cost of building the server.

Accordingly, for a "larger" small company that requires a powerful, sophisticated server, we recommend buying rather than building. Call IBM, buy a server that meets your requirements, and sign up for the best on-site service plan they offer. The cost of 20 people sitting around drawing their salaries while they're unable to work adds up quickly. Even a short server outage may cost the company more than you "saved" by building your own server.

Most SOHO servers fall between the extremes, and it's such servers that this chapter focuses on. Tables 4-1 and 4-2 list some starting points for configuring a SOHO file or application server appropriate for your own requirements. (In reality, we'd probably not build either of the 11–20 user or 20+ user configurations; we'd buy an IBM server instead.)

Buy Blue

If you're going to do it, do it right. Don't buy from Dell or another second-tier server vendor. Don't buy HP. Buy IBM, period. We know we'll get mail from people with horror stories about their IBM servers. It happens, but not often. And we'd hear lots more horror stories if we recommended anything but IBM servers.

Table 4-1. Suggested SOHO file server configurations

	1–5 users	6–10 users	11–20 users	20+ users
CPU	Celeron Sempron	Pentium 4 Athlon 64	Pentium D Core 2 Duo Athlon 64 X2	Opteron Dual Opteron
Memory	512 MB	1 GB	2 GB (1 GB/core)	2 GB/CPU
Disk subsystem	S-ATA S-ATA RAID 1	S-ATA RAID 1 S-ATA RAID 5 S-ATA RAID 0+1	S-ATA RAID 0+1 SCSI RAID 1 SCSI RAID 5	SCSI RAID 5 SCSI RAID 0+5
Ethernet interface	100BaseT 1000BaseT	1000BaseT	1000BaseT dual 1000BaseT	1000BaseT dual 1000BaseT
Backup hardware	DVD+R external hard drives	DVD+R external hard drives	tape drive/changer external hard drives	tape drive/changer external hard drives

Table 4-2. Suggested SOHO application server configurations

	1–5 users	6–10 users	11–20 users	20+ users
CPU	Pentium D Core 2 Duo Athlon 64 X2	Pentium D Core 2 Duo Athlon 64 X2	Opteron Dual Opteron	Dual Opteron Quad Opteron
Memory	2 GB (1 GB/core)	4 GB (2 GB/core)	application dependent	application dependent
Disk subsystem	S-ATA S-ATA RAID 1	S-ATA RAID 1 S-ATA RAID 5 S-ATA RAID 0+1	S-ATA RAID 0+1 CSSI RAID 1 SCSI RAID 5	SCSI RAID 5 SCSI RAID 0+5
Ethernet interface	100BaseT 1000BaseT	1000BaseT	1000BaseT dual 1000BaseT	dual 1000BaseT
Backup hardware	DVD+R external hard drives	DVD+R external hard drives	tape drive/changer external hard drives	tape drive/changer external hard drives

All of these configurations assume you are running Linux, which for most situations is the best OS choice for a SOHO server. If you run a Microsoft server OS, these configurations may be marginal, particularly CPU and memory. There's no getting around it; Windows server is a pig. When it comes to server hardware, Linux takes tiny sips whereas Windows server takes great gulps.

Although we specify number of users, all users are not equal. One user who runs a CPU-intensive server-based application may put more load on an application server than a dozen users who simply retrieve and save a document or spreadsheet occasionally. The type of load also varies. A shared database that resides on the server may stress the disk subsystem but place fewer demands on CPU and memory. A client/server application that ships large amounts of data to clients may stress the network interface. A server-based application may hammer the CPU and memory but not the disk subsystem. And so on.

When you design a SOHO server, it's important to determine which server subsystems are likely to be bottlenecks and design accordingly. For example, if the server functions primarily as a database server, you might spend a significant part of your budget on a stacked SCSI RAID disk subsystem and lots of memory, and correspondingly less on CPU, the network interface, and other components. If network throughput is the bottleneck, you might install multiple Gigabit Ethernet adapters on the server and use Gigabit Ethernet switches rather than 10/100BaseT hubs or switches. Designing a SOHO server is all about balance—allocating your budget to eliminate the most important bottlenecks. Of course, each time you eliminate one bottleneck, you uncover another.

We sat down to think through our own requirements for a SOHO server. Here's the list of functional requirements we came up with:

Reliability

> First and foremost, the SOHO Server must be reliable. Our server will run 24/7/365. Other than periodic downtime to blow out the dust, upgrade hardware, and so on, we expect our server to take a licking and keep on ticking.

Massive storage capacity

> In the past, we routinely used lossy compression formats to cut down file sizes, storing our audio as MP3s and our digital camera images as JPEGs. Hard disk space is so inexpensive nowadays that it's no longer necessary to use lossy compression for many types of files. For example, instead of storing important digital camera images as 3 MB JPEG files, we now store them in RAW format, which produces 20 MB files. Similarly, when we rip one of our audio CDs, we no longer store the tracks in lossy MP3 format. Instead, we simply store the original, uncompressed WAV files, or convert them to FLAC files, which use lossless compression, but produce files significantly larger than MP3 or

SCSI Versus SATA

We recommend SCSI hard drives for any server whose disk subsystem is very heavily accessed. SATA hard drives, particularly in a performance-enhancing RAID, are suitable for servers that experience light to moderate disk activity. In fact, under such conditions, SATA is often faster than SCSI. But when the disk subsystem is being hammered by a flood of disk requests, SCSI simply leaves SATA in the dust. Also, the fastest hard drives are available only in SCSI interfaces.

OGG files. Also, we have begun experimenting with a DV camcorder, which requires 13 GB of storage per hour of video. Obviously, we need a lot of disk space on our server. We decided that 2 TB (2000 GB) would suffice, at least to get started.

Data safety

We've never lost any data other than by our own stupidity, and we want to keep it that way. Accordingly, our initial thought was to configure our server with RAID storage. Just because it's possible to do something, though, doesn't mean it's always the best solution.

RAID prevents data loss when a hard drive fails, and can increase disk subsystem performance on a heavily loaded server. Weighed against those advantages, using RAID requires buying more hard drives (and perhaps a special RAID adapter) and doesn't protect against the more common causes of data loss, such as accidental deletion, data being corrupted by a virus or malfunctioning hardware, or catastrophic loss caused by theft or fire. Even if you have a full RAID storage system, you must still back up your data frequently to protect against loss.

We're paranoid about backup. We do daily backups of our server data directories to the local hard drive of Robert's main desktop system, and copy those backups to DVD+RW discs daily and DVD+R discs weekly. We use rsync to replicate our data continuously from the server drives to networked volumes on other systems, and we capture a snapshot of all our working data every day to external hard drives, which also contain multiple copies of our archived data. All of our video is duped to backup DV tapes. Even a catastrophic server failure would cost us at most a few minutes' work.

So, after considering the advantages and disadvantages of using RAID, we decided to use nonredundant S-ATA hard drives in our SOHO server. By giving up the small additional safety factor provided by RAID, we gain much more available hard disk space and free up at least a couple of drive bays that can be used for later expansion.

Flexibility

Initially, our SOHO server will be almost exclusively a file and print server. It will run Linux, though, so it's likely that at some point the server will transmogrify to an application server of some sort. To allow for that possibility with minimum disruption, we'll configure the server initially with enough processor and memory to allow adding functions incrementally without upgrading the hardware.

Expandability

When we set out to design our new SOHO server, we originally considered building an "appliance" system with a microATX board and a low-power processor in a small form factor case. There are a lot of advantages to such a server. It's small and so can be put anywhere. It doesn't consume much power, produces little heat, and doesn't make much noise. But as we thought about it, we realized that for us the disadvantages of a small system outweighed the advantages. However flexible our initial configuration, it's likely that at some point we will want to expand the server by adding disk space or other additional hardware. The microATX form factor is simply too limiting. With a full ATX motherboard and a larger case, we have room to grow.

Television capture

Although we have a full-blown media center system with complete PVR functionality, there may be times when it would be useful to have additional PVR capability in another system. For example, if we are watching one program on the media center system using "live-pause" while recording a second program, both tuner cards are occupied. If we need to record a second program simultaneously, we're out of luck. The SOHO server system is an ideal "backup PVR." It's lightly loaded, particularly during nonworking hours when we're most likely to want to record programs. It has plenty of disk storage, and is protected by an industrial-grade UPS.

Hardware Design Criteria

With the functional requirements determined, the next step was to establish design criteria for the SOHO server hardware. Here are the relative priorities we assigned for our SOHO server. Your priorities may of course differ.

Here's the breakdown:

Price

Price is moderately important for this system. We don't want to spend money needlessly, but we will spend what it takes to meet our other criteria.

Reliability

Reliability is the single most important consideration.

Size

Size is unimportant. Our SOHO server will reside in Barbara's office, which has more than enough room for a full tower or even a double tower system.

Noise level

Noise level is unimportant for a server that sits in a server room, but in a residential or small-business environment it can be critical. Because the SOHO server will be installed in Barbara's office, it's important to minimize noise level. We'll choose quiet components whenever possible.

Jim Cooley Warns

Jim commented, "Dumb idea. Why add the risk of corrupting the OS with recording software? Use it on the client and store to the server." And he has a point. But Jim is a Windows guy and we're Linux guys. We agree that installing a TV capture card on a Windows server would be a dumb idea. But Linux is much more stable than Windows. If our TV recording application crashed under Windows, there's a very good chance it would crash the server. Under Linux, if the TV recording application crashes, there's very little chance it would crash anything but itself.

DESIGN PRIORITIES

Price	★★★☆☆
Reliability	★★★★★
Size	★☆☆☆☆
Noise level	★★★★☆
Expandability	★★★☆☆
Processor performance	★★☆☆☆
Video performance	☆☆☆☆☆
Disk capacity/performance	★★★★☆

Expandability

Expandability is moderately important. Our server will initially have four hard drives and an optical drive installed, but we may want to expand the storage subsystem later. Similarly, although we'll use the integrated S-ATA and network interfaces initially, we may eventually install additional disk adapters, network interfaces, and so on.

Processor performance

Processor performance is relatively unimportant, at least initially. Our SOHO server will run Linux for file and print services, which place little demand on the CPU. However, we expect the server eventually to run at least some server-based applications, perhaps X11 apps that display on workstations or server-based applications such as mailman or squirrelmail. The incremental cost of installing a moderately fast dual-core processor and sufficient memory to support those expected software upgrades is small enough that we'll do it now and have done with it.

Video performance

Video performance is of literally zero importance, because we'll run our SOHO server headless. That is, we'll temporarily install a monitor while we install and configure Linux, but we'll subsequently manage the server from a desktop system elsewhere on the network. We'll either use a motherboard with integrated video, or install a video card just long enough to get Linux installed and working.

Disk capacity/performance

Disk capacity and performance are very important. Our SOHO server has only one or two simultaneous users, so standard 7,200 RPM S-ATA hard drives provide more than adequate performance. Capacity is the more important consideration for our server. We want at least 2 TB of hard disk space initially, and we'd like to be able to expand that to 4 TB or more without making major changes to the case or the existing drive subsystem. That means we'll need to use relatively few high-capacity hard drives instead of many lower-capacity drives.

RAID for SOHO Servers

Although we elected not to use RAID on our SOHO server, that doesn't mean RAID isn't right for your SOHO server. RAID is an acronym for Redundant Array of Inexpensive Disks. A RAID stores data on two or more physical hard drives, thereby reducing the risk of losing data when a drive fails. Some types of RAID also increase read and/or write performance relative to a single drive.

Five levels of RAID are defined, RAID 1 through RAID 5. RAID levels are optimized to have different strengths, including level of redundancy, optimum file size, random versus sequential read performance, and random

Warning

We can't say it often enough. RAID does not substitute for backing up. RAID protects against data loss as a result of a drive failure, and may increase performance. But RAID does not and cannot protect against data loss or corruption caused by viruses; accidental or malicious deletions; or catastrophic events such as a fire, flood, or theft of your server.

versus sequential write performance. RAID 1 and RAID 5 are commonly used in PC servers. RAID 3 is used rarely. RAID 2 and RAID 4 are almost never used. The RAID levels typically used on SOHO servers are:

RAID 1

RAID 1 uses two drives that contain exactly the same data. Every time the system writes to the array, it writes identical data to each drive. If one drive fails, the data can be read from the surviving drive. Because data must be written twice, RAID 1 writes are a bit slower than writes to a single drive. Because data can be read from either drive in a RAID 1, reads are somewhat faster. RAID 1 is also called mirroring, if both drives share one controller, or duplexing, if each drive has its own controller.

RAID 1 provides very high redundancy, but is the least efficient of the RAID levels in terms of hard drive usage. For example, with two 500 GB hard drives in a RAID 1 array, only 500 GB of total disk space is visible to the system. RAID 1 may be implemented with a physical RAID 1 controller or in software by the operating system.

RAID 5

RAID 5 uses three or more physical hard drives. The RAID 5 controller divides data that is to be written to the array into blocks and calculates parity blocks for the data. Data blocks and parity blocks are interleaved on each physical drive, so each of the three or more drives in the array contains both data blocks and parity blocks. If any one drive in the RAID 5 fails, the data blocks contained on the failed drive can be re-created from the parity data stored on the surviving drives.

RAID 5 is optimized for the type of disk usage common in an office environment—many random reads and fewer random writes of relatively small files. RAID 5 reads are faster than those from a single drive, because RAID 5 has three spindles spinning and delivering data simultaneously. RAID 5 writes are typically a bit faster than single-drive writes. RAID 5 uses hard drive space more efficiently than RAID 1.

In effect, although RAID 5 uses distributed parity, a RAID 5 array can be thought of as dedicating one of its physical drives to parity data. For example, with three 500 GB drives in a RAID 5 array, 1,000 GB—the capacity of two of the three drives—is visible to the system. With RAID 5 and four 500 GB drives, 1,500 GB—the capacity of three of the four drives—is visible to the system. RAID 5 may be implemented with a physical RAID 5 controller or in software by the operating system. Few motherboards have embedded RAID 5 support.

RAID 3

RAID 3 uses three or more physical hard drives. One drive is dedicated to storing parity data, with user data distributed among the other drives in the array. RAID 3 is the least common RAID level used for PC servers, because its characteristics are not optimal for the disk usage patterns typical of small office LANs. RAID 3 is optimized for sequential reads of very large files, and so is used primarily for applications such as streaming video.

Then there is the so-called RAID 0, which isn't really RAID at all because it provides no redundancy:

RAID 0

RAID 0, also called striping, uses two physical hard drives. Data written to the array is divided into blocks, which are written in an alternating fashion to each drive. For example, if you write a 256 KB file to a RAID 0 that uses 64 KB blocks, the first 64 KB block may be written to the first drive in the RAID 0. The second 64 KB block is written to the second drive, the third 64 KB block to the first drive, and the final 64 KB block to the second drive. The file itself exists only as fragments distributed across both physical drives, so if either drive fails all data on the array is lost. That means data stored on a RAID 0 is more at risk than data stored on a single drive, so in that sense a RAID 0 can actually be thought of as less redundant than the zero redundancy of a single drive. RAID 0 is used because it provides the fastest possible disk performance. Reads and writes are very fast, because they can use the combined bandwidth of two drives. RAID 0 is a poor choice for desktops and workstations, which typically do not load the disk subsystem heavily enough to make RAID 0 worth using. Heavily loaded servers, however, can benefit from RAID 0 (although few servers use bare RAID 0 because of the risk to the data stored on a RAID 0 array).

Finally, there is stacked RAID, which is an "array of arrays" rather than an array of disks. Stacked RAID can be thought of as an array that replaces individual physical disks with subarrays. The advantage of stacked RAID is that it combines the advantages of two RAID levels. The disadvantage is that it requires a lot of physical hard drives.

Stacked RAID

The most common stacked RAID used in PC servers is referred to as RAID 0+1, RAID 1+0, or RAID 10. A RAID 0+1 uses four physical drives arranged as two RAID 1 arrays of two drives each. Each RAID 1 array would normally appear to the system as a single drive, but RAID 0+1 takes things a step further by creating a RAID 0 array from the two RAID 1 arrays. For example, a RAID 0+1 with four 500 GB drives comprises two RAID 1 arrays, each with two 500 GB drives. Each RAID 1 is visible to the system as a single 500 GB drive. Those two RAID 1 arrays are then combined into one RAID 0 array, which is visible to the system as a single 1,000 GB RAID 0. Because the system "sees" a RAID 0, performance is very high. Because the RAID 0 components are actually RAID 1 arrays, the data is very well protected. If any single drive in the RAID 0+1 array fails, the array continues to function, although redundancy is lost until the drive is replaced and the array rebuilt.

RAID 1 Versus RAID 0+1

If your storage subsystem has four hard drives, there is no point to using RAID 1 rather than RAID 0+1, assuming that your motherboard or RAID adapter supports RAID 0+1. A RAID 1 uses two of the four drives for redundancy, as does the RAID 0+1, so you might just as well configure the drives as a RAID 0+1 and get the higher performance of RAID 0+1. Either RAID level protects your data equally well.

HARDWARE VERSUS SOFTWARE VERSUS HYBRID RAID

RAID can be implemented purely in hardware, by adding an expansion card that contains a dedicated RAID controller, processor, and cache memory. Hardware RAID, if properly implemented, offers the highest performance and reliability and places the fewest demands on the main system processor, but is also the most costly alternative. True hardware RAID adapters cost several hundred dollars and up, and are generally supplied with drivers for major operating systems including Windows and Linux.

Software RAID requires only standard ATA or S-ATA interfaces, and uses software drivers to perform RAID functions. In general, software RAID is a bit slower and less reliable than hardware RAID and places more demands on the main system processor. Most modern operating systems, including Windows Server and Linux, support software RAID—usually RAID 0, RAID 1, and RAID 5—and may also support RAID 0+1. We believe that well-implemented software RAID is more than sufficient for a typical SOHO Server.

Hybrid RAID combines hardware and software RAID. Hybrid RAID hardware does not contain the expensive dedicated RAID processor and cache memory. Inexpensive RAID adapters have limited or no onboard processing, and instead depend on the main system processor to do most or all of the work. With very few exceptions, motherboards that feature onboard RAID support, such as Intel models, use hybrid RAID, although it is sometimes incorrectly called hardware RAID. If you choose a hybrid RAID solution, make certain that drivers are available for your operating system.

Until a few years ago RAID 0+1 was uncommon on small servers because it required SCSI drives and host adapters, and therefore cost thousands of dollars to implement. Nowadays, thanks to inexpensive S-ATA drives, the incremental cost of RAID 0+1 is very small. Instead of buying one $200 hard drive for your small server, you can buy four $100 hard drives and a $50 RAID adapter. You may not even need to buy the RAID adapter, because some motherboards include native RAID 0+1 support. Data protection doesn't come much cheaper than that.

ADVICE FROM SCOTT KITTERMAN

Linux 2.4 kernels had support for hybrid RAID, but it was dropped in 2.6, so unless a distributor has specifically added it or the hybrid RAID card vendor supplies Linux-specific drivers/kernel patches, a 2.6-based distro won't support hybrid RAID.

I discovered this the hard way when converting my old dual Pentium III 450 box with a Promise IDE RAID controller from Win2K to Ubuntu Server.

Chapter 4, Building a SOHO Server

And what if you choose not to use any form of RAID, as we did? We decided to install four 500 GB hard drives in our SOHO server, configured as a JBOD (Just a Bunch of Drives). All four drives function independently as ordinary drives, and we get the full 2 TB combined capacity of the four drives. Just because we chose not to use RAID doesn't mean you should do the same. With our four 500 GB drive configuration, you can choose any of the following disk configurations without making any hardware changes.

JBOD

All four drives operate independently. The operating system "sees" 2 TB of disk capacity. Performance and data safety are determined by the performance and reliability of the individual drives. Note that, with four drives spinning, the failure of one drive is four times more likely to occur than when only one drive is spinning. If a drive fails, you lose whatever data was stored on that drive, but the data on other drives is not affected.

RAID 5

All four drives are assigned to the RAID 5. The operating system sees 1.5 TB of disk capacity. (The equivalent of one drive's capacity is used to store parity data, although that data is actually distributed across all four drives.) Read and write performance for small files is the same or slightly faster than with individual drives. Read and write performance for large files is slightly slower than with individual drives. RAID 5 offers moderate redundancy. Any one drive may fail without loss of data. If two drives fail simultaneously, all data on the array is lost.

RAID 0+1

All four drives are assigned to the RAID 0+1, as in effect a RAID 0 pair of RAID 1 mirrored drives. The operating system sees 1 TB of disk capacity. Read performance for any size file is noticeably faster than JBOD or RAID 5, particularly when the drives are heavily loaded. Write performance is slower. RAID 0+1 offers very high redundancy. Any two drives may fail without loss of data, as long as they are not both members of the same RAID 1. If both drives in a RAID 1 fail simultaneously, all data on the array is lost.

With the hardware configuration we detail later in this chapter, you can choose any of these disk configurations during setup. You don't even need to pop the lid or move any cables. But give some serious thought to which configuration to use. If you change your mind later, you can reconfigure the disk subsystem, but you'll need to back up all of your data and re-store it after you set up the new configuration.

Component Considerations

With our design criteria in mind, we set out to choose the best components for the SOHO server system. The following sections describe the components we chose, and why we chose them.

Your Mileage May Vary

Although we tested the configuration we used to build our own SOHO server, we did not test permutations with the listed alternatives. Those alternatives are simply the components we would have chosen had our requirements been different. That said, we know of no reason the alternatives we list should not work perfectly.

Case

Antec P180 Advanced Super Mid-Tower Case (*http://www.antec.com*)

SOHO servers can be built in anything from full-tower cases specifically designed to house servers down to the smallest of small form factor cases. True server cases are usually large, heavy, and expensive—overkill for a typical SOHO server. Either that, or they are rack-mount (or blade) cases, and few homes or small offices have need of an equipment rack. (Robert tried to convince Barbara that an equipment rack was just what we needed, but she put her foot down.)

To fill the void, many case manufacturers offer so-called "SOHO server cases," which are usually just standard tower or mini/mid-tower cases with lockable front panels. Whether you're building a SO server or a HO server, you probably don't need the small additional security provided by a lockable front panel, so we suggest you also consider more mainstream case styles.

The key considerations for a SOHO server case are the number of drive bays it provides and its cooling efficiency. In a residential or small business environment, noise level and appearance may also be important. For us, all four of those factors were important. We wanted at least half a dozen hard drive bays to accommodate our initial disk configuration while leaving drive bays available for future expansion. Effective cooling is critical for obvious reasons. Noise level is important because this server will live in Barbara's office, which is across the hall from our master bedroom. Appearance is important because Barbara refuses to have an ugly box sitting in her office.

For all of these reasons, we chose the Antec P180 case, shown in Figure 4-1.

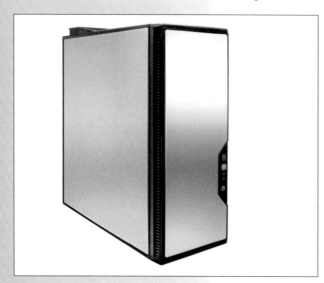

Figure 4-1. The Antec P180 case

The Antec P180 provides a total of 11 drive bays—four external 5.25" bays, one external 3.5" bay, and six internal 3.5" bays. Allocating one 5.25" bay to the optical drive leaves room for as many as nine hard drives, which should suffice for the life of the system.

The Antec P180 offers the best cooling of any case we have ever tested. It uses dual interior chambers, isolating the power supply from the rest of the system, which simplifies cooling. (The downside is that you must choose a power supply that is compatible with the P180; not all power supplies have cables long enough to reach the motherboard and drive connectors from the location of the power supply in the bottom chamber.) The P180 comes standard with three 120mm fans—one rear, one top, and one in the lower chamber to cool the power supply. There are mounting positions for two optional 120mm fans, one in front and one in the middle to cool the graphics card.

The P180 is also the quietest case we've ever tested, despite its effective cooling. Antec engineered this case to be as quiet as possible, incorporating such features as silicone grommets to isolate the hard drives from the chassis and aluminum-plastic-aluminum composite panels to absorb noise.

Appearance is a matter of taste, but we think the P180 is the most attractive case we've ever used. We wouldn't hesitate to have it in our den, library, or living room, let alone our offices. If you prefer something darker than the aluminum-and-black color scheme of the P180, consider the P180B, which is the same case in all-black.

The only real downside to the Antec P180 is the price. It sells for about $125, not including a power supply. A good power supply suitable for our SOHO server costs $75 to $100, taking the total price to $200 or more. But for that price, you get what we consider to be the best case on the market, with top-notch expandability, cooling, and noise level.

Power Supply

Antec NeoHE 550 (*http://www.antec.com*)

The P180 case does not include a power supply, which gave us the opportunity to choose the power supply best suited for our SOHO server. The power supply is a critical component for a server that will run 24 hours a day, every day, year after year. Although reliability was paramount, we also wanted a power supply that was quiet and efficient. Quiet, because this server will reside in Barbara's office, which is directly across the hall from our master bedroom. Efficient, because high efficiency reduces power consumption, which makes it easier to cool the system and allows the fans to run slower and quieter.

Figure 4-2. Antec NeoHE power supply

We also decided to oversize the power supply, because a power supply that runs at a fraction of its rated output is more efficient, quieter, and much more reliable than one that runs near its rated output. An oversize power supply also makes upgrades easier. If in the future we decide to add more hard drives, expansion cards, memory, or a faster processor, the existing power supply will suffice to carry the extra load. Accordingly, although a 400W unit might have been adequate, we decided to look for a 500W or 550W unit.

ALTERNATIVES: CASE

If you're building a SOHO server on a tighter budget but you still need lots of drive bays, consider using the Antec Titan550 or Atlas server cases or the TX1088AMG SOHO tower case. If a mid-tower case is large enough, consider the Antec P150. All of these cases include Antec TruePower power supplies, which are of excellent quality. Do not underestimate the importance of a high-quality power supply when you build a server. You can buy less expensive cases, but they include inferior power supplies.

We looked at quiet, high-efficiency power supplies from Antec, Enermax, PC Power & Cooling, Seasonic, and others, keeping in mind the need for long cables for use in the P180 case. Many of those units are excellent power supplies, but we chose the Antec NeoHE 550 power supply for its combination of high quality, very low noise, and reasonable price.

Processor

Intel Pentium D 820 (*http://www.intel.com*)

Processor performance is a minor consideration for a file/print server. In fact, if this server were to be used only for file/print duties, even the slowest current processor would do the job with Linux. But, although this server will provide only file and print services initially, we expect it to last for years with few upgrades, and we may eventually run some applications on it. Accordingly, it made sense to choose a faster processor that would give us some horsepower in reserve.

At the time we built this server, Intel had just introduced their new-generation Core 2 Duo (Conroe) processors. Usually, Intel sets a significant price premium on such new products, but in this case Intel priced their new processors at mainstream levels. That left no "price umbrella" for the older models, which began selling at fire sale prices.

We were able to pick up a retailed-boxed Pentium D 820 dual-core processor for about $100, so for the price of a "value" processor we obtained a very capable dual-core processor. (Although Intel has de-emphasized its older models, it did not discontinue them; we expect this processor or a similar model to be available well into 2007.) The retail-boxed Pentium D processor comes with a three-year warranty and a surprisingly effective and quiet CPU cooler.

It may seem strange to choose an obsolescent processor for our SOHO server, but cutting-edge technology is the last thing we want for a server. We want proven technology, and the Pentium D provides that in spades. The fact that the Pentium D costs less than newer models with similar performance is just a nice bonus.

Motherboard

Intel D945PVSLKR (*http://www.intel.com*)

Choosing the Intel Pentium D processor means we need a compatible Socket 775 motherboard. We wanted an Intel-branded motherboard, because we have found Intel motherboards to be the most reliable of any brand we have tested. Intel-branded motherboards also offer top-notch compatibility and driver support, whether you run Linux or Windows Server.

945 OR 946?

We built this system in Summer 2006. The Intel Core 2 Duo processor and motherboards that support it were not yet widely available. In anticipation of their new processors and motherboards, Intel deeply discounted their older products, pricing them too attractively for us to refuse. If we were building this system now, we'd probably use an Intel Core 2 Duo and an Intel 946- or 965-series motherboard.

Any Intel-branded motherboard based on the 945P or 945G chipset would probably have worked well, but we chose the Intel D945PVSLKR model. Although the D945PVS lacks integrated video and costs more than 945G models like the D945GNT, we chose it for two reasons. First, we happened to have a new D945PVS sitting unused in our inventory room. More important, we plan to run the Server Edition of Ubuntu 6.06 LTS (Long Term Support) on our SOHO Server. Robert ran the Desktop Edition of Ubuntu 6.06 LTS extensively on his main workstation, which uses—you guessed it—an Intel D945PVSLKR motherboard and a Pentium D processor. Based on that experience, we knew with absolute certainty that Ubuntu 6.06 was fully compatible with the D945PVSLKR and fully supported its hardware features. We decided that the $30 higher cost of the D945PVSLKR relative to the D945GNT was cheap insurance.

CHECK COMPATIBILITY

If we'd chosen a different motherboard, we might have used the Pentium D 805 processor, which is a bit slower than the Pentium D 820 model we used, but which cost $20 less. Fortunately, we checked the processor compatibility list for the D945PVSLKR motherboard before we ordered the processor. We found that the D945PVSLKR supported every Pentium D processor *except* the 805.

In fact, no Intel-branded motherboard listed the Pentium D 805 as compatible, and the Intel compatibility page for the Pentium D 805 listed only one MSI-branded motherboard as supported. We suspect that's because the Pentium D 805 is a "special" processor. Intel introduced it primarily to allow Dell and other OEMs to build inexpensive systems that could be advertised as "dual-core" models.

Before you order your motherboard and processor, make sure that the motherboard you intend to use supports the *exact* processor model you are ordering. Significantly different processor models may have similar names or model numbers, so always check the full model number for compatibility.

Also verify that the BIOS version installed on the motherboard supports the processor you install. Quite often, a more recent processor is supported by a particular motherboard, but not unless you install an updated BIOS. Of course, that often introduces a "can't get there from here" problem, because you can't update the BIOS without a working processor, and the processor isn't supported by the existing BIOS. In that situation, either return the motherboard and ask for one with a current BIOS, or temporarily install a supported processor, update the BIOS, and then remove that processor and install the one you intend to use.

**ALTERNATIVES:
MOTHERBOARD**

If you're on a tight budget, consider one of the Intel D945GNT models, which are available with or without integrated RAID support, with 100BaseT versus 1000BaseT integrated LAN, and so on. For an AMD-based SOHO server, choose an ASUS Socket 939 motherboard that uses an nVIDIA chipset.

What Does PVSLKR Mean, Anyway?

Intel and some other motherboard manufacturers use trailing letters or numbers or some similar means of designating slightly different variants of a motherboard model. For example, although the Intel D945PVS motherboard is available in only one variant, the similar D945GNT motherboard is available in three models, all with the same basic features, but each with different options.

The D945GNTL includes only integrated 10/100 Ethernet. The D945GNTLKR adds 1000BaseT Ethernet support, as well as three IEEE-1394a (FireWire) ports, a Trusted Platform Module, and support for Intel Matrix RAID. The D945GNTLR drops back to the 10/100 Ethernet and eliminates the Trusted Platform Module, but includes the FireWire ports and Matrix RAID support, and adds better integrated audio and a digital optical-out connector.

When you order a motherboard, make sure to check available options and variants. Otherwise, you may find you've ordered a motherboard that doesn't include the options you thought you were getting.

Memory

Crucial CT6464AA40E PC3200 DDR2 DIMMs (512 MB × 4)
(http://www.crucial.com)

We could analyze the memory requirements of a Linux SOHO server all day long, but what's the point? Memory is inexpensive, so it's a false economy to install too little. In our 20 years of dealing with servers, we've never heard anyone complain that his server had too much memory.

In terms of memory requirements, using a dual-core processor is essentially the same as using dual processors. To avoid memory bottlenecks, it's a good idea to install twice as much memory for a dual-core processor as you would for a single-core processor. Our Linux SOHO server could probably get along initially with 1 GB (512 MB/core), but the incremental cost of installing 2 GB (1 GB/core) was less than $100, so we decided to install 2 GB.

The Intel D945PVS motherboard provides four memory slots, and supports a maximum of 4 GB of memory. We could have installed two 1 GB modules for 2 GB total—which would leave two memory slots available for future expansion—or four 512 MB modules. At the time we ordered memory for this system, two 1 GB modules cost about $30 more than four 512 MB modules. After thinking about it, we decided that we were unlikely to upgrade the memory in this server beyond 2 GB, so we decided to save the $30 and install four 512 MB modules.

We chose four 512 MB Crucial CT6464AA40E PC3200 DDR2 memory modules, using the online Crucial product selector to ensure compatibility with our D945PVS motherboard. The motherboard supports DDR2-400 (PC3200), DDR2-533 (PC4200), and DDR2-667 (PC5300) memory modules. Although Crucial offers PC4200 and PC5300 modules for this motherboard, those modules are more expensive. PC3200 is fast enough for the processor we chose and for any upgrade processor we're likely to install later.

**ALTERNATIVES:
MEMORY**

Any Crucial or Kingston DDR2 memory modules that are compatible with the motherboard. Compare prices for modules of various capacities before you decide which modules to install.

TV Tuner

Hauppauge WinTV-PVR-500MCE *(http://www.hauppauge.com)*

Although it is not a primary function, we wanted our server to function as a backup to our primary media center system. The media center system has two analog tuner cards and one HDTV tuner card, which should suffice for most of our television recording needs. Still, there may be times when we want to record additional programs when the media center system is fully occupied.

So we decided to add a TV tuner card or cards to our server. The only question was which model to install. Because our server will run Linux, we needed a tuner card that was supported by MythTV, the most popular and featureful PVR application available for Linux. Obviously, we required top-notch video quality. To minimize the load on the CPU we wanted a card that provided hardware-based MPEG encoding.

After comparing the specifications and reviews of several tuner cards, we decided to use a Hauppauge WinTV-PVR-500MCE, shown in Figure 4-3.

Hauppauge is the gold standard in TV tuner cards. Hauppauge tuner cards have the best capture quality of any we have used, and are supported by nearly every PVR application available, under both Windows and Linux.

Hauppauge offers several models, including some that bundle a remote control that is compatible with Windows Media Center Edition (MCE). We don't intend to run MCE, and we have no need of a remote control because this system will function only as a "back end" for recording. (Remember, our server runs headless, so we'll control recording setup from another system elsewhere on the network.) We narrowed our choices to the WinTV-PVR-150 single-channel tuner card and the WinTV-PVR-500 dual-channel tuner card.

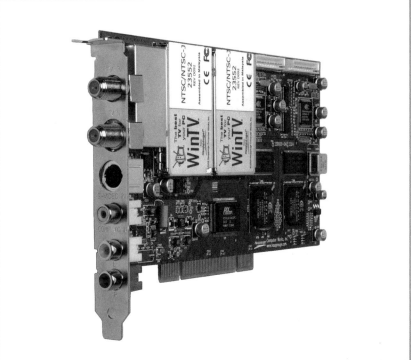

Figure 4-3. Hauppauge WinTV-PVR-500 tuner

The PVR-150 is less expensive and by some reports offers very slightly better recording quality. (The PVR-500 splits a single TV-in cable connector; the second F-connector visible in the image is FM-in.) Conversely, the PVR-500 costs less than *two* PVR-150 cards, and occupies only one expansion slot. We decided the small additional cost of the PVR-500 was worthwhile in exchange for the additional flexibility of having a second tuner available. When we're on vacation, for example, we can shut the rest of the house down, leaving only the server running, and still be able to record two programs simultaneously.

ALTERNATIVES

Whether you run Linux or Windows, Hauppauge tuner cards are the best choice. If you decide to equip your server with a tuner card, choose whichever Hauppauge model best suits your own requirements.

Hard Disk Drives

Seagate Barracuda 7200.9 Serial ATA (500 GB × 4)

(http://www.seagate.com)

The disk subsystem of our SOHO server must be capacious, fast, and reliable. Capacious, because this server will store all of the data we want to keep online, including large DV video files. Fast, because the server will sometimes be hammered by clients accessing large amounts of data. Reliable, well, for obvious reasons.

Capacity

Our target for capacity was 2 TB (2,000 GB). The largest hard drives available when we built this system held 750 GB, so clearly we needed multiple hard drives to meet our capacity requirement. We decided to use four 500 GB drives. For about $100 more, we could have installed three 750 GB drives, and used only three drive bays. For about $100 less, we could have used five 400 GB drives, at the expense of using one more drive bay. But doing that would have required adding an S-ATA interface card for the fifth hard drive, which would have reduced the cost benefit of using five drives to about $50. The economics will be different when you build your system, so balance the cost versus the number of drive bays and S-ATA interfaces required when you order your drives.

The Intel D945PVS motherboard provides four Serial ATA interfaces, just enough for our purposes, and allows the drives connected to those interfaces to be configured as standard drives or a RAID. If we need the entire capacity of all drives to appear as one volume, we can use the operating system disk management utilities to concatenate those four physical drives into one logical volume. If multiple volumes are acceptable, we can simply install the four drives normally and partition and format them as separate volumes.

Performance

In olden days, we used SCSI hard drives on all but the smallest servers. Nowadays, although SCSI is still desirable for large, heavily loaded servers, most SOHO servers can use standard Serial ATA drives with little or no performance hit. Modern S-ATA drives like the Seagate 7200.9 and 7200.10 Barracuda models provide performance features such as large caches and NCQ (Native Command Queuing) that were formerly available only on SCSI models. For our purposes, Serial ATA drives provide more than enough performance, particularly with the load distributed among four spindles.

Reliability

For a desktop system, we sometimes use the RAID support integrated on many motherboards to build a RAID 1 (mirrored) array. All that is required is a second hard drive, at the small cost of $50 to $75, to eliminate the risk of data loss from a hard drive failure.

But RAID 1 is impractical for our 2 TB server, for which a RAID 1 would require four additional hard drives. In addition to the significant expense of four additional 500 GB hard drives, we'd have to install a separate RAID adapter to provide additional S-ATA interfaces, and we'd end up with nearly all of our drive bays occupied. Also, that add-on RAID adapter, unless we were able to find a PCI Express model, would put an unacceptably high load on the PCI bus of our server. Accordingly, we decided to risk running a standard disk configuration, with no redundancy.

There are different kinds of reliability. First, of course, is the inherent reliability of the hardware itself. Seagate Barracuda S-ATA drives are extremely reliable, as any data recovery firm knows. We (and our readers) have had fewer failures with Seagate drives than with any other brand. A clean, well-ventilated system with reliable power protection contributes further to drive reliability. And, although we could nearly eliminate the small risk of data loss caused by a drive failure by using RAID, that protection comes at a very high price for a 2 TB drive configuration.

Which brings up the final type of reliability, procedural reliability. Our procedures replicate our data, both manually and automatically, to numerous locations, from network shares to optical discs to external hard drives. A failed hard drive on the server might cost us at most a few minutes' work, depending on which drive failed. Chances are that a drive failure will lose no work at all, but simply require replacing the failed drive and restoring the data to it from backup. We can live with that.

External Hard Drives

Build-them-yourself

The first decision is whether to buy purpose-built external hard drives or to build them yourself using bare hard drives and external enclosures. Each has advantages, although on balance we've come to prefer home-built external drives.

Commercial external hard drives are available from Seagate, Maxtor, Western Digital, and many other companies. Their major advantage over a home-built external hard drive is that they typically bundle Dantz Retrospect, CMS Bounceback Express, or similar backup software that allows you to initiate a backup just by pressing a button on the external drive. (Of course, that software works only if you run Windows on your server, and in some cases the software is limited to workstation versions of Windows rather than Windows Server.) The major drawbacks of commercial external hard drives are limited choice of configuration, relatively high cost, and short warranties—often a year or less versus five years on a standard hard drive.

Strength in Numbers

One of the advantages of having several hard drives installed is that it gives you a great deal of flexibility. With four drives, for example, we can easily configure our disk subsystem as a RAID 0, RAID 1, RAID 5, RAID 10, or JBOD.

Several of our readers who reviewed early drafts of this book questioned our sanity when they read of our plans to run a server without disk redundancy. To that, we plead long experience with the reliability of Seagate hard drives and our rigorous backup procedures. Still, they got us thinking about RAID 5. Perhaps we'll settle for a 1.5 GB RAID 5. Better still, we may upgrade to four 750 GB hard drives and set up a 2.25 TB RAID 5.

If you prefer commercial external hard drives, we recommend Seagate models. As an alternative to external hard drives, consider a frame-carrier system, such as those made by StorCase (*http://www.storcase.com*). The frame mounts in a standard drive bay, and accepts carriers that contain a standard hard drive. In the past, these frame-carrier systems had a real advantage. Although they were more costly than external enclosures, they used the standard ATA interface, which transfers data faster than USB 2.0. The availability of FireWire and e.SATA external drives has eliminated this advantage, so frame-carrier systems are no longer as popular as they were. Still, many people prefer them and there's certainly nothing wrong with using one.

Home-built external hard drives have many advantages. By choosing the appropriate enclosure, you can have a USB 2.0, FireWire, or e.SATA external interface—or any of the two, or all three in one device. (We generally use USB 2.0 for maximum compatibility with any system we might need to restore to in an emergency, but it's nice to have the choice.) Enclosures are available to support old-technology ATA hard drives as well as current S-ATA models, so you can use an enclosure to convert an otherwise useless older ATA drive into a useful backup device. External enclosures offer complete flexibility because they accept essentially any standard hard drive. That means you can build an external hard drive using anything from a small, slow, inexpensive drive to the latest high-capacity barn burner. Giving up the one-touch convenience of commercial models can save you a lot of money, particularly if you need several external drives. The total cost of a new hard drive and enclosure may be only 50% to 75% the cost of a commercial model of similar capacity. Finally, with a home-built external drive, you get the standard five-year warranty on the hard drive instead of a one-year warranty. (Presumably, hard drive manufacturers offer shorter warranties on external drives because their mobility makes them more subject to damage than a similar hard drive installed internally in a nice, safe computer case.)

If you decide to roll your own, choose your external enclosure carefully. The first decision is which internal and external interfaces to use. A few enclosures support both ATA and S-ATA internal interfaces, although most have only one or the other. (Some are designed for SCSI hard drives, but that is beyond the scope of this book.) Any enclosure provides one or more external interfaces, which may be USB 2.0, FireWire, or e.SATA, in any combination. If high data transfer rates are important to you, choose a model that provides FireWire and/or e.SATA external interfaces. Otherwise, USB 2.0 is sufficient and has the advantage of compatibility with any computer built in the last several years.

There is a strong correlation between the price of an external enclosure and its quality. Cheap enclosures are of mostly plastic construction, and are quite flimsy and unreliable. Better enclosures use a metal chassis and generally have better quality connectors and power bricks. Some enclosures, particularly more expensive models, provide very robust internal power and data connectors, which means you can swap drives in and out of them as necessary. Others, including every inexpensive model we've seen, use less robust internal connectors. They're fine if all you plan to do is install the drive and use it until it drops, but they're not really intended to allow drives to be swapped in and out frequently.

Our "default" choice is the KingWin TL-35CS Night Hawk model. At $40 or so, it's twice as expensive as the cheapest models, but it's built like a tank and extremely reliable. It has only a USB 2.0 external interface, which suffices for our needs. We don't use FireWire for external drives, and so have no experience upon which to base a recommendation. For an e.SATA enclosure, we recommend the Vantec NST-360SU, which includes an external USB 2.0 interface.

Backing Up the Beast

If you're concerned about how to back up a 2 TB disk subsystem, you're not alone. For us, the problem actually isn't as bad as it first appears. Not all of the data on our server needs to be backed up. For example, we may eventually have hundreds of gigabytes of digital video stored on our server. That data is already "backed up" in the sense that we still have the original DV tapes, as well as duplicates of those tapes, so it is not in danger of being lost if a hard drive fails. Similarly, Barbara's collection of several hundred audio CDs will be stored as *.wav* files on the server. If those files are lost, they can easily be retrieved from the original CDs. Some of the files on the server, such as copies of television programs recorded by our media center system, are really just backup copies anyway.

Still, that leaves a significant amount of data that *does* need to be backed up. Optical drives are neither large enough nor fast enough to back up this amount of disk space. Although tape changers with sufficient speed and capacity are available, we'd have to sell our yacht to afford one. And we don't own a yacht.

So what's left? External e.SATA/FireWire/USB 2.0 hard drives, which we suggest you look at not as hard drives, but as funny-looking backup tapes. Using compression, a 500 GB external hard drive can typically store between 750 GB and 1 TB—depending on the compressibility of the data—which is more than sufficient to store the critical data from our 2 GB disk subsystem. If the disk subsystem is of smaller capacity or the amount of data stored on the server does not exceed the capacity of the external drive, you can make an exact copy without compression, which makes it trivially easy to restore.

A USB 2.0 external drive can transfer about 25 MB/second, which translates to about 90 GB/hour. FireWire 400 is nearly twice as fast, although the transfer rate of the hard drive itself may limit you to something less than the 40+ MB/s rate of the FireWire interface. An e.SATA external drive is limited only by the transfer rate of the hard drive. With any of these interfaces, you can transfer a terabyte or more of data overnight, which is sufficient for all but the largest SOHO servers. And, at well under $0.50/GB, the cost of hard drive space is the same or lower than the cost of backup tapes.

We recommend buying (or building—see the "External Hard Drives" section) at least two or three e.SATA/FireWire/USB 2.0

external hard drives and using them, just as you would tapes, to back up your server. If you gulp at spending a few hundred dollars on external drives, just think for a moment about the cost of losing all of your data. You might think RAID is sufficient protection for your data. It isn't. RAID prevents data loss when a drive fails, period. It doesn't prevent accidental deletions or corrupted files. Nor does it prevent catastrophic data loss caused by fire or theft. The only way to protect against such dangers is to have an off-line, off-site copy of your data, ideally more than one copy. e.SATA/FireWire/USB 2.0 external hard drives are the only affordable solution we know of for backing up a large SOHO array.

But external hard drives are only part of the solution. A weekly full backup is a good start, but a proper backup plan requires backing up changed files at least daily. Such incremental backups are much smaller than full backups, but are essential to recovering files changed since the previous full backup. As for full backups, it is important that these incremental backups be stored off-line and off-site. We recommend one of the following methods, depending on how much data you need to back up daily:

- **DVD writer**—A DVD writer stores about 4 GB (6 GB to 8 GB with compression) to a $0.20 DVD+R disc, or about 8 GB (11 GB to 15 GB with compression) to a $3 DVD+R/DL disc. A 16X or 18X writer, such as the Plextor PX-760A, fills a disc in just a few minutes. A DVD writer is appropriate for incremental backups if your server has many small files or several relatively large files changed on a daily basis.

- **External hard drive**—external e.SATA/FireWire/USB 2.0 hard drives are as good a solution for incremental backups as they are for full backups. We keep several, one or another of which is always connected to Robert's desktop system, where it used frequently during the working day to make quick backups of our working data directories. When we leave the house, the current external hard drive goes with us, as well as the external hard drive that contains the most recent full backup. If disaster happens, at least we won't lose any data.

When it comes to preventing data loss, we recommend the belt-and-suspenders method. In addition to backing up to external hard drives and optical discs, we frequently copy changed files to other network volumes using Windows batch files or rsync. If you value your data, you should do the same.

ADVICE FROM BRIAN JEPSON

Our editor, Brian Jepson, comments, "I have seen these wonderful nonenclosures (*http://www.wiebetech.com*) that are nothing more than the FireWire to ATA bridge, no case. So, if you're buying a pile of drives and want to avoid paying for an enclosure for each of them, you can just snap the drive into the drive dock when you need to use it and put the drive on the shelf when you are done."

Optical Drive

NEC ND-3550A DVD writer (*http://www.necus.com*)

Our SOHO server runs headless, so in theory it doesn't really need a DVD writer. We'll back it up across the network and to removable hard drives. The only reason we'll use the optical drive in this system is for installing software and perhaps for infrequent periodic maintenance. Still, the NEC DVD writer costs only $30, so it was pointless to install a read-only optical drive. Although we can't foresee the circumstances, one day having that writable optical drive installed might be a lifesaver. (As our old friend Mandy frequently says, "It could happen.")

ALTERNATIVES: OPTICAL DRIVE

Any good name-brand DVD-ROM drive or DVD writer. We generally use models from BenQ, Lite-On, Pioneer, Plextor, or NEC. After several bad experiences, we avoid models from HP, LG, and Sony.

Keyboard, Mouse, and Display

Because this SOHO server runs Linux, we need a keyboard, mouse, and display only for initial installation and configuration. Once the server is running, we can manage it remotely from one of our desktop systems.

WINDOWS VERSUS LINUX

Yes, we know about Windows Remote Desktop, but it's not the same. Remote Desktop provides limited remote management functions, but some management tasks must still be done from a monitor and keyboard physically connected to the server. Linux remote management tools allow us to do almost anything remotely that doesn't require changing hardware.

UPS

Falcon Electric SG Series 1 kVA On-Line UPS (*http://www.falconups.com*)

Running a server without a UPS is foolish. Even a momentary power glitch can corrupt open databases, trash open documents, and crash server-based apps, wiping out the work of everyone connected to the server. A UPS may literally pay for itself the first time the power fails.

We used and recommended APC UPSs for many years. Then, after we experienced several premature failures of APC units and received numerous messages from readers about their increasingly frequent problems with

APC units, we decided to look elsewhere. On the advice of our friend and colleague Jerry Pournelle, we looked at Falcon Electric UPSs, which turned out to be as good as Jerry said they were. (Years ago, an earthquake rattled Chaos Manor, knocking everything over. All of Jerry's equipment failed, except the Falcon Electric UPS, which just kept running, lying on its side amidst the debris of his computer room.) We've now used Falcon Electric units exclusively for a couple of years, without so much as a hiccough.

Falcon Electric units are built to industrial standards. They cost more than consumer-grade systems, although we found the actual price difference surprisingly small. You won't find them at online resellers or big-box stores, but they are readily available from numerous distributors. Check the Falcon Electric web site for details.

Our server connects to the 1 kVA Falcon Electric SG Series On-Line UPS that was already located in Barbara's office, protecting her desktop system. That unit has plenty of reserve capacity to protect the server as well, so there was no need to install a separate UPS for the server. Note that the Falcon Electric SG is a true online UPS. Falcon also sells less expensive line-interactive models that offer similar functionally to mass-market models from APC and others, but are substantially better built. Table 4-3 lists our component choices for a SOHO Server system.

Table 4-3. Bill of materials for SOHO server

Component	Product
Case	Antec P180
Power supply	Antec NeoHE 550
Motherboard	Intel D945PVSLKR
Processor	Intel Pentium D 820 (retail boxed)
CPU Cooler	(Bundled with processor)
Memory	Crucial PC2-3200 DDR2 (4 × 512 MB)
TV tuner	Hauppauge WinTV-PVR-500MCE
Video adapter	(None permanent; integrated or temporary for setup only)
Sound adapter	(Integrated)
Hard drive	Seagate Barracuda 7200.9 SATA (four 500 GB)
External hard drives	Seagate 500 GB drives in Kingwin USB 2.0 enclosures
Optical Drive	NEC ND-3550A DVD writer
Keyboard	(None)
Mouse	(None)
Speakers	(None)
Display	(None)
UPS	Falcon Electric 1 kVA SG Series On-Line UPS

ALTERNATIVES: UPS

We think it's worth spending some additional time and effort to get a Falcon Electric UPS. Even though they cost a bit more than consumer-grade units with similar capacity and features, the Falcon Electric units really are better built and more reliable. If the Falcon Electric units are out of your price range, we think the APC Smart-UPS units remain the best of the mass-market UPSs, despite the problems we've had with them. (We've had more problems with other brands.) For those on an even tighter budget, the APC Back-UPS Pro and Back-UPS units are reasonable choices.

If you've decided to forego a UPS entirely, we suggest you think again. Any power protection is better than none at all. Even the inexpensive units that look like outlet strips are better than nothing. Their runtime is very short, but even a few seconds of backup power is often sufficient. If you buy one of these inexpensive units, just make sure that the VA rating is high enough to support the draw of your server. Also be aware that the built-in surge and spike suppression in these units is often very poor, so it's worthwhile to install a good surge protector between the power receptacle and the UPS.

Building the SOHO Server

Figure 4-4 shows the major components of the SOHO server. The Antec P180 case is flanked on the left by the Intel Pentium D processor and Intel D945PVS motherboard. To the right of the case, a Kingwin external drive enclosure sits atop the Falcon Electric UPS and the Antec NeoHE power supply. Four 500 GB Seagate Barracuda 7200.9 hard drives are visible at the lower left. The NEC ND-3550A DVD writer is front and center, with four 512 MB sticks of Crucial DDR2 memory sitting on top of it. Finally, the Hauppauge WinTV-PVR-500 dual tuner card is visible at the lower right.

Make sure you have everything you need before you start building the system. Open each box and verify the contents against the packing list.

Figure 4-4. SOHO server components, awaiting construction

HE GOT UP, GOT DRESSED, AND TOOK A SHOWER

As always, you needn't follow the exact sequence of steps we describe when you build your own SOHO server. Always install the processor and memory before you install the motherboard in the case, because doing otherwise risks damaging the processor, memory, or motherboard. The exact sequence doesn't matter for most other steps. Some steps must be taken in the order we describe, because completing one step is required for completing the next, but as you build your system it will be obvious when sequence matters.

Preparing the Case

As much as we like the Antec P180 case, using it involves a bit more work than a typical case requires. To begin preparing the case, remove both thumbscrews from the left side panel, as shown in Figure 4-5, and then slide the panel to the rear and remove it from the case, as shown in Figure 4-6.

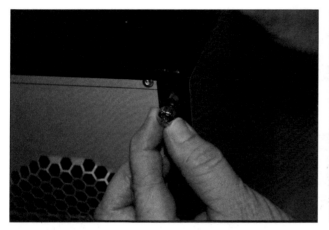

Figure 4-5. Remove both thumbscrews from the left side panel

Figure 4-6. Slide the panel to the rear and remove it from the case

For some reason, Antec decided to use ordinary screws rather than thumbscrews on the right side panel. Remove the three screws that secure the panel, as shown in Figure 4-7. Remove the panel and set it aside.

Figure 4-7. Remove the three screws that secure the right side panel

The Antec P180 has two hard drive cages. One, located in the upper chamber of the case, holds three hard drives. The second, located in the lower chamber, holds four hard drives. We decided to install our hard drives in the lower cage. The number of positions happens to match the number of hard drives we are installing, but that wasn't the main reason for our decision. Putting the four hard drives at the bottom of the case places the center of gravity lower, which makes the system easier to move around safely. Most

Figure 4-8. Remove the thumbscrew that secures the lower hard drive cage

important, the lower drive cage is very well ventilated, with both the power supply fan and a supplemental fan constantly drawing cool outside air over the drives.

To remove the lower drive cage, remove the one thumbscrew that secures it, as shown in Figure 4-8, and then slide the drive cage out of the chassis, as shown in Figure 4-9. (We used a screwdriver because the thumbscrew was very tight.)

Figure 4-9. Pull the drive cage out of the chassis

Remove the parts box, as shown in Figure 4-10. When we pulled out this box, we assumed it would contain screws and other small parts. Not so. It contains the spoiler for the fan mounted on the top of the case.

Figure 4-10. Remove the parts box from the hard drive cage

Remove the screws that secure the black plastic VGA ventilation duct and drive rail holder, as shown in Figure 4-11. Pull the duct straight out, as shown in Figure 4-12, and set it aside for now.

Figure 4-11. Remove the screws that secure the VGA ventilation duct and drive rail holder

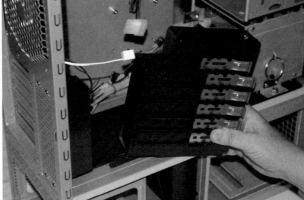

Figure 4-12. Remove the VGA ventilation duct and set it aside

Removing the ventilation duct reveals the black plastic sliding panel assembly shown in Figure 4-13. Loosen both of the thumbscrews that secure this panel and slide the panel all the way toward the rear of the case to clear the opening into the power supply bay, as shown in Figure 4-14.

With these steps complete, it's time to install the power supply.

Figure 4-13. Loosen the two thumbscrews that secure the sliding panel

Figure 4-14. Slide the panel fully to the rear of the case to open the access hole to the power supply bay

Assembling and installing the power supply

It still seems strange to us to talk about "assembling" a power supply. Most power supplies are ready to use out of the box, with all of their cables permanently attached. Several Antec power supply models, including our NeoHE, are different. They use a patented cable-management system that allows you to connect only the cables you actually need for your system, eliminating the rats' nest of unused cables.

WARNING

The Antec NeoHE power supply is auto-sensing, which means that it automatically detects the input voltage and sets itself accordingly. Many power supplies are not autosensing, and must be set manually for 120V or 240V input. If you use such a power supply, make certain to set the input voltage switch correctly.

If the switch is set to 240V and you connect the power supply to a 120V receptacle, nothing bad happens. The motherboard and other components get half the voltage they require, and simply don't run. But if the switch is set to 120V and you connect the power supply to a 240V receptacle, the components get twice the voltage they require. You'll realize your mistake immediately, as your new system disappears in a shower of sparks and clouds of smoke.

Figure 4-15 shows the NeoHE power supply and a selection of optional cables. Only the main ATX power cable and the ATX12V power cable are permanently connected. All other cables are optional. These optional cables use a proprietary plug on one end that connects to a matching proprietary jack on the power supply.

Figure 4-15. Antec NeoHE power supply with optional cables

Our system has four S-ATA hard drives, so we'll need to install two of the optional S-ATA power cables, each of which provides two connectors. We'll also install one or two Molex cables, which use the old-fashioned Molex hard drive connectors. We'll need those to power the optical drive as well as the case fans. Finally, we'll install one of the two optional PCI Express power cables that Antec includes with this power supply. We probably won't need that cable, but we'd prefer to have it available in case the video card we install temporarily to use while we do the initial software installation requires a PCI Express power cable.

Figure 4-16. Connect the optional cables to the power supply

Figure 4-16 shows Barbara connecting one of the optional cables to the power supply. One of the proprietary jacks is visible immediately to the right of the cable she's connecting. Note that the connector is keyed both by the shapes of the individual holes in the connector and by the keying tab visible at the top of the jack. Press each optional cable into a jack until it seats completely, which may require some pressure. After you seat each cable, tug gently on it to make sure that it's locked into place.

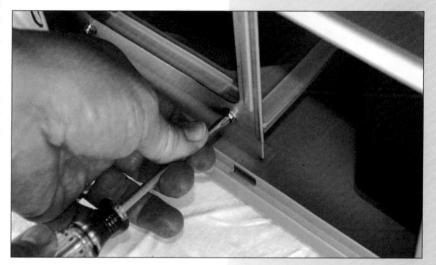

Figure 4-17. Remove the four screws that secure the retaining cage

With the power supply prepared, the next step is to remove the power supply retaining cage. The retaining cage is secured by four screws, two on each side of the case. Remove those screws, as shown in Figure 4-17, and then slide the retaining cage out of the case, as shown in Figure 4-18.

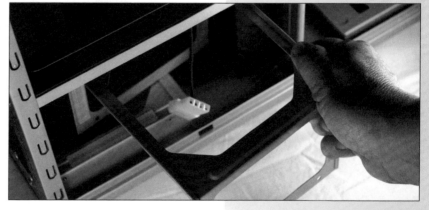

Figure 4-18. Slide the retaining cage out of the case

Figure 4-19. Place the retaining cage over the power supply

Figure 4-20. Feed all of the cables through the large (rear) hole into the upper chamber

Orient the power supply so that its rear screw holes correspond with those in the back of the case, and then place the retaining cage over the power supply, as shown in Figure 4-19. This bracket was a very tight fit on our power supply. When we pressed the bracket down flush on the top of the power supply, the bottom of the retaining cage was forced outward, as is visible in Figure 4-19. At first, we thought we'd have to assemble the system without the retaining cage, but as it turned out we were able to use it, although it was a very tight fit.

Don't install the power supply and retaining cage assembly in the case quite yet. Instead, place the assembled unit near the rear of the case, with the cable side of the power supply toward the case. Feed all of the power cables up through the rear access hole into the upper chamber, as shown in Figure 4-20. Feed the main ATX power cable (the one with the largest connector) through first. We learned this by experience. We'd fed all the other cables through first, and attempted to feed the main ATX power cable through last. With the other cables already in place, there wasn't room for the main ATX power cable to fit through the access hole.

Slide the assembled power supply and retaining cage assembly into the case, as shown in Figure 4-21. As you do so, take up the slack in the cables by pulling them gently into the upper chamber of the case. The goal is to have as little of the cables as possible remaining in the lower chamber, where they would block the air flow.

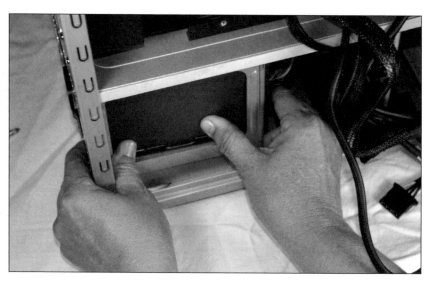

Figure 4-21. Slide the assembled power supply and retaining cage into position

Once the power supply and retaining cage assembly are in place, secure the retaining cage with four screws, as shown in Figure 4-22. (The white box on the white cable visible at the front of the power supply is a temperature sensor.)

To complete installation of the power supply, insert the four mounting screws provided with the power supply to secure the power supply to the rear panel of the case. (With eight screws securing it, that power supply isn't going anywhere.)

Installing the hard drives

With the power supply installed, the next step is to install the hard drives in the lower hard drive cage. This cage requires special mounting screws, which Antec supplies. For years, we've played the hide-the-screws game with Antec. Once or twice, we were convinced Antec hadn't included them, but each time we eventually found the cunningly concealed storage box.

We spent a couple of minutes looking around for the secret storage box this time, but without success. Where had they put it this time? Finally, we admitted defeat and looked in the manual, which told us the storage box was attached to the "back of the upper HDD cage." Hmmm. "Back" to us meant the open part of that cage, visible in Figure 4-24 with metal drive mounting rails protruding. Obviously, it wasn't there. Perhaps they meant the front of the hard drive cage, visible as a black plastic assembly to the right of the cage.

Accessing that area requires removing the hard drive cage. To do so, remove the one thumbscrew securing the upper hard drive cage, as shown in Figure 4-23, and then slide the cage out of the case, as shown in Figure 4-24. (Once again, the thumbscrew was tightened enough that we found it easier to use a screwdriver to remove it.)

As it turns out, the secret storage box is attached to the right side of the upper hard drive cage assembly. It's actually visible from the right side of the case when the panel is removed. We spotted it there after reading the manual, but with the limited clearance around the box, Robert wasn't able to open the latch, nearly breaking a fingernail in the attempt. With the upper hard drive cage removed, the secret storage box is easily accessible.

Figure 4-22. Secure the power supply retaining bracket to the case with four screws

Figure 4-23. Remove the thumbscrew that secures the upper hard drive cage

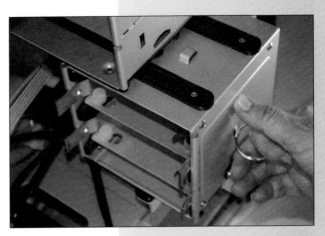

Figure 4-24. Slide the upper hard drive cage out of the case

Figure 4-25. Open the secret storage box and remove the baggie of screws

Figure 4-26. Feed the S-ATA power cables from the upper chamber to the front lower chamber

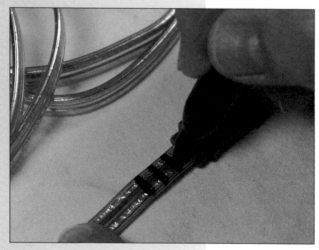

Figure 4-27. Label the S-ATA data cables to identify the port and drive they connect

Open the latch, as shown in Figure 4-25, and remove the plastic baggie of screws and other small parts.

Once you've retrieved the baggie, close the latch, slide the upper hard drive cage back into place, and reinsert the thumbscrew to secure it.

The next step, as shown in Figure 4-26, is to feed the S-ATA power cables from the upper chamber down through the front (smaller) access hole in the sliding panel assembly and into the area of the lower hard drive cage. For the time being, feed the full lengths of the S-ATA power cables down into the lower hard drive cage area. You'll need as much slack as possible when you connect the drives.

With four hard drives in this system, it's a good idea to do a little advance planning. The Seagate Barracuda 7200.9 drives are remarkably reliable. Chances are they'll all keep running until years from now when you decide to replace them with larger drives. Still, hard drives are mechanical devices, and even the most reliable mechanical devices sometimes fail.

If the hard drive fails in a typical system, there's no ambiguity. There's only one hard drive, and it failed. Even if the system has two hard drives, chances are good that one was installed as an upgrade and they're of different models or capacities. Identifying the failed drive is usually straightforward.

But we have four identical hard drives in this system. What happens if one fails? The operating system or BIOS tells us that, say, hard drive #2 has failed. Great. Which one is #2? They all look the same, so the only way to identify the failed drive is to trace the cable from the motherboard interface port to the drive. That can be easier said than done in an assembled system.

Spending an extra 30 seconds now can save you an hour of aggravation if a drive does fail. Simply use a permanent felt-tip marker to label both sides of both ends of all four cables, as shown in Figure 4-27. We keep it simple. The S-ATA interfaces are designated 0, 1, 2, and 3. We simply draw 0, 1, 2, or 3 bars across each cable to match it to an interface and drive. If a drive does fail, it's immediately clear which drive it is.

After you label the cables, feed them through the access hole from the upper chamber of the case into the lower front chamber, as shown in Figure 4-28. Just leave them dangling for now.

The next step is to mount the four hard drives in the lower hard drive cage, as shown in Figure 4-29. Use the special screws from the baggie that was in the secret storage box. These screws have a very wide head and a long shaft, of which only the lower part is threaded. Secure each drive with four of these screws, driving them through the white silicone grommets. (These grommets fall out

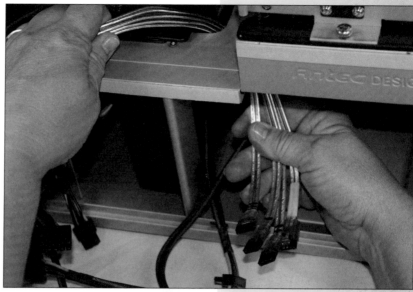

Figure 4-28. Feed the S-ATA data cables from the top chamber to the lower chamber

of the cage easily. If you lose one, locate the spare grommets in the secret storage box baggie.) Drive the screws in far enough to compress the grommets slightly. Driving them in too far squishes the grommet and eliminates its ability to isolate drive vibrations from the chassis structure.

Once you have secured all four drives in the lower hard drive cage, connect an S-ATA data cable to each drive, as shown in Figure 4-30. The S-ATA data cable is keyed with an L-shaped notch. Align the cable connector with the drive connector and press firmly to seat the cable connector. S-ATA data connectors are relatively fragile. Avoid putting any torque on the connectors, or they may break off. Press the cable connector straight in to seat it. If you need to remove a cable, pull straight out on the connector.

Figure 4-29. Secure each hard drive with four special mounting screws

Figure 4-30. Connect an S-ATA data cable to each drive

ADVICE FROM JIM COOLEY

Because the connectors are so fragile, I use a white-out pen to draw a stripe across the connector and its block to make reconnecting them easier in the future.

By convention, we mount multiple drives with drive 0 in the topmost or left-most bay. In fact, when we are using only two drives, we sometimes forget to label the cables (as we did when we built the Mainstream PC).

Figure 4-31. Connect an S-ATA power cable to each drive

With all four S-ATA data cables connected, the next step is to connect the S-ATA power cables, as shown in Figure 4-31. Like the S-ATA data cables, the S-ATA power cables are keyed with an L-shaped slot. The power cables are also at least as fragile as the data cables, so take care when connecting or disconnecting them.

With all of the S-ATA data and power cables connected, the next step is to reinstall the lower hard drive cage, as shown in Figure 4-32. Guide the cage into the chassis, using your left hand to press the excess cable lengths up into the upper chamber. Once again, the goal is to minimize the amount of cable in the lower chamber to provide as little impediment as possible to air flow. Once the drive cage is fully seated, secure it with one thumbscrew, as shown in Figure 4-33.

Figure 4-32. Slide the lower hard drive cage into position, feeding the cables into the upper chamber

Figure 4-33. Secure the lower hard drive cage with one thumbscrew

Installing the I/O template and standoffs

Like most cases, the Antec P180 comes with a generic back-panel I/O template installed. We're not sure why case makers bother, because the generic template almost never matches the motherboard back-panel I/O ports. Remove the installed template by pressing gently along its edges from the outside of the case until the template pops loose. If the template is well and truly stuck, as sometimes happens, don't worry too much about bending it. You won't need it later.

With the original template removed, the next step is to install the template supplied with the motherboard. Before you do so, hold the template up against the motherboard rear-panel I/O ports to verify that the holes are in the right places. Although it doesn't happen often, we've received motherboards that included an incorrect template.

Working from inside the case, position the I/O template in the cutout, as shown in Figure 4-34, making sure that the lip on the edge of the template seats against the edge of the cutout. Once the I/O template is aligned, press gently against its edges until it snaps into place. If you have trouble seating the I/O template, use a screwdriver handle to apply even pressure until one corner seats, and then run the handle along the edges of template to seat it.

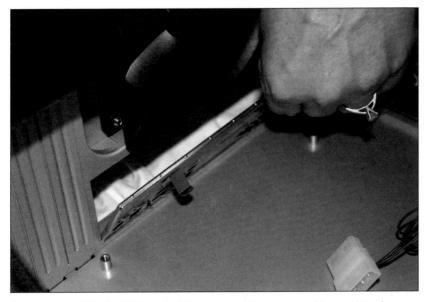

Figure 4-34. Position the I/O template in the case cutout and press until it snaps into place

The final step in preparing the case is to install standoffs to support the motherboard. Although the standoff positions are standardized, different motherboards use different subsets of the available standoff positions. Also, different cases come with standoffs preinstalled in various positions.

Pen and Paper

One of our technical reviewers recommends another method. Place the motherboard flat on a large sheet of paper and use a felt-tip pen to make a large dot on the paper under each mounting hole. Then place the paper in the case with two of the dots aligned with two corresponding standoffs. Press the paper down until the standoffs puncture the paper. Continue pressing the paper down until it is flat against the bottom of the case. Each of the large dots on the paper should have a standoff protruding through it, and there should be no standoff protruding where there is no dot.

In addition to supporting the motherboard physically, standoffs provide electrical grounding points, so it's important to install a standoff that corresponds to each motherboard mounting hole. It's just as important to make sure that no standoffs are installed that don't have a matching motherboard mounting hole. An "extra" standoff can cause a short circuit in the motherboard. If that happens, the best outcome is that the system just won't boot. If you're unlucky, a short circuit may damage the motherboard, processor, memory, or other components.

The best way to ensure that there's a standoff for every mounting hole and a mounting hole for every standoff is to count the preinstalled standoffs and then count the mounting holes in the motherboard. With the clutter of components on the motherboard, it's easy to miss a mounting hole. We hold the motherboard up to a light, which makes the mounting holes stand out. (Don't include the CPU cooler mounting holes in your count. These four holes form a square pattern around the CPU socket, and don't require standoffs.)

Once you have located all of the mounting holes, slide the motherboard into position, with the back-panel I/O ports mated to the corresponding holes in the I/O template, and examine each mounting hole to see if a standoff is visible. Count the visible standoffs, and compare that number with the number of preinstalled standoffs you counted earlier. The numbers should match. If they don't, one or more of the preinstalled standoffs needs to be removed. If no standoff is visible beneath a mounting hole, install a standoff as shown in Figure 4-35.

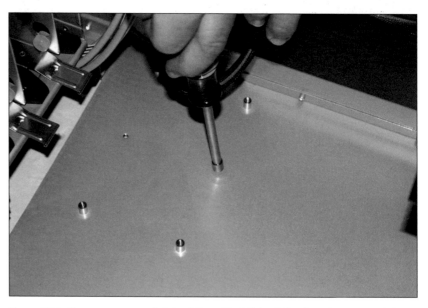

Figure 4-35. Remove any unneeded standoffs and install standoffs where they are needed

The Intel D945PVS motherboard has 11 mounting holes. The Antec P180 case has nine standoffs preinstalled, all of which correspond to mounting holes in the motherboard. If you use this case and motherboard you need install only two standoffs.

Populating the External Drive Bays

The Antec P180 case provides four externally accessible 5.25" bays and one externally-accessible 3.5" bay. We'll fill one of the 5.25" bays with the NEC ND-3550A optical drive, and the 3.5" bay with the port-expander supplied with the Intel D945PVS motherboard.

Installing the optical drive

We decided to install the NEC ND-3550A DVD writer in the upper bay. Before installing the drive you have to remove the plastic bezel that covers the drive bay and the metal RF shield plate that is concealed by the bezel. To remove the bezel, simply pull gently with your finger until it snaps out, as shown in Figure 4-36. With the plastic bezel removed, the metal RF shield plate is visible. Twist that plate back and forth until the metal tabs snap, and then remove it from the case.

Figure 4-36. Remove the bezel to prepare the bay to receive the optical drive

---

ADVICE FROM JIM COOLEY

Save those bezels! If you remove an optical drive, replacing the bezel will help maintain proper air circulation inside the case.

Figure 4-37. Install the drive rails on the optical drive

The P180 case uses drive rails for mounting the optical drive. Locate the white cardboard box that was stored in the lower hard drive bay. In addition to the spoiler for the top vent, this box contains a pair of 5.25" drive rails. Install the drive rails on the ND-3550A drive, as shown in Figure 4-37, using two screws to secure each rail. Position the metal spring tabs forward and angled outward, with the front lip of the spring tab flush with the rear surface of the drive bezel. The drive rails should be just above the centerline of the drive, which you can accomplish by driving the screws into the rear hole in each group of three holes in the rails.

Before you install the optical drive, verify the master/slave jumper settings, and slide the drive partway into the bay to verify you've positioned the rails correctly. Like most optical drives, the NEC ND-3550A DVD writer is set by default to be the master device on the ATA channel. Our hard drives are S-ATA, so the optical drive will be the only parallel ATA device in the system, and should be set as the master device on the ATA channel. If you use a different optical drive, verify that its jumper is set to master.

It's usually easier to connect the ATA cable to the drive before you install the drive in the case. The Intel D945PVS motherboard comes with a round 40-wire ATA cable, which we used. Because optical drives have relatively slow transfer rates, they can use the older 40-wire ATA cable rather than the 80-wire Ultra-ATA cable used for ATA hard drives. (An 80-wire cable works fine if that's all you have, but it's not necessary.)

Figure 4-38. Connect the ATA cable to the optical drive

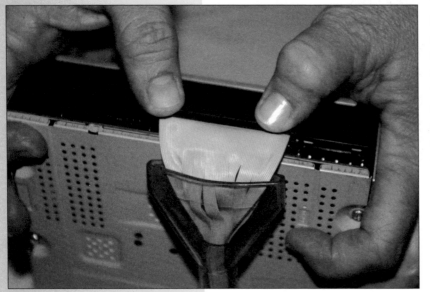

To connect the cable, locate pin 1 on the drive connector, which is nearest the power connector. The pin 1 side of the cable is indicated by a red stripe. Align the cable connector with the drive connector, making sure the red stripe is on the pin 1 side of the drive connector, and press the cable into place, as shown in Figure 4-38. Nowadays, most optical drives and ATA cables are keyed with a protruding tab on the cable connector and a corresponding notch on the drive connector.

ADVICE FROM JIM COOLEY

Pin 1 is almost always positioned closest to the power connector. I've never seen this otherwise.

To mount the optical drive in the case, feed the loose end of the ATA cable through the drive bay from the front, align the drive rails with the corresponding tracks in the case, and slide the drive into the bay, as shown in Figure 4-39. Make sure the drive rails snap into place to secure the drive.

The final step in installing the optical drive is to connect power to the drive. Choose one of the power cables coming from the power supply and press the Molex connector onto the drive power connector, as shown in Figure 4-40. It may require significant pressure to get the power connector to seat, so use care to avoid hurting your fingers if the connector seats suddenly. The Molex power connector is keyed, so verify that it is oriented properly before you apply pressure to seat the power cable.

Figure 4-39. Slide the optical drive into the drive bay until the rails snap into place

Color Contrast

Most people would choose a black optical drive for the P180 case. We chose a silver model instead. The silver drive bezel closely matches the silver portions of the P180 case, and the silver drive bezel makes it easier to locate the drive in the dimly lit area under Barbara's desk.

Figure 4-40. Connect the power cable to the optical drive

Installing the front-panel port expander

The Antec P180 case provides five front-panel ports: two USB, one IEEE-1394 (FireWire), one audio-in, and one audio-out. The Intel D945PVS motherboard provides port connectors for four USB ports, two FireWire ports, one audio-in, and one audio-out. That means two USB ports and one FireWire port for which connections are available on the motherboard go unused in a standard configuration.

For a server, we don't care about audio, but more USB ports are always welcome—particularly if they're easily accessible from the front—and a second FireWire port might be very handy indeed. Fortunately, Intel includes a front-panel port expander with the motherboard. The port expander installs in a 3.5" external drive bay, and provides two USB ports, one FireWire port, and a pair of audio ports. The audio ports are superfluous, but the other ports match up nicely with the "extra" port connectors on the Intel motherboard.

The Antec P180 has only one externally accessible 3.5" drive bay, so installing the port expander rules out installing a floppy drive or card reader (although we could use an adapter to mount any of those devices in an available 5.25" bay). We didn't plan to install a floppy drive or card reader in this server, so using the bay for the port expander was no sacrifice.

To install the port expander, use the same procedure you used to install the optical drive. Remove the plastic bezel that covers the 3.5" bay and twist the metal RF shield back and forth until it breaks loose. The white cardboard box that contained the rails for the optical drive also contains a set of 3.5" rails. Attach these rails to the port expander, as shown in Figure 4-41, positioning the metal spring tabs forward and angled outward. Secure the rails with two screws on each side, using the rear set of screw holes in the port expander and the rear of each group of three screw holes in the rails. When the rails are properly installed, the bottom of each rail should be flush with the bottom of the port expander, and the metal spring clips should be flush with the front bezel.

Figure 4-41. Install drive rails on the optical drive

Feed the cables on the back of the port expander through the bay from the front and then slide the port expander into the bay, as shown in Figure 4-42. Make sure that the rails snap into place to secure the port expander. With the port expander installed, our SOHO server now has four front USB 2.0 ports, two front IEEE-1394a (FireWire) ports, and two pairs of audio ports, one pair of which will remain disconnected. (Later, we'll apply tape over the unused audio port pair to provide a clear indication that those ports are unusable.)

Preparing and Populating the Motherboard

It is always easier to prepare and populate the motherboard—install the processor and memory—while the motherboard is outside the case. In fact, you must do so with some systems, because installing the CPU cooler requires access to both sides of the motherboard. Even if it is possible to populate the motherboard while it is installed in the case, we always recommend doing so with the motherboard outside the case and lying flat on the work surface. More than once, we've tried to save a few minutes by replacing the processor without removing the motherboard. Too often, the result has been a damaged processor or motherboard.

Installing the Processor

To install the Pentium D processor, press the lever slightly away from the socket to unlatch it, as shown in Figure 4-43. Then lift the lever straight up until it comes to a stop vertical or slightly past vertical.

Figure 4-42. Slide the port expander into the bay until it snaps into place

WARNING

Each time you handle the processor, memory modules, or any other static-sensitive components, first touch the power supply to ground yourself.

Figure 4-43. Lift the socket lever to unlock the metal retention plate

With the lever vertical, the metal retention plate is unlocked and free to swing up and away from the socket. Pivot the retention plate up and remove the plastic socket protector, as shown in Figures 4-44 and 4-45. Keep the plastic socket protector in the motherboard box, in case you ever remove the processor. The exposed Socket 775 connectors are very fragile, and should never be left unprotected.

Figure 4-44. Lift the metal retention plate to expose the socket contacts

Figure 4-45. Snap the plastic socket protector out of the retention plate

With the plastic retention plate removed, as shown in Figure 4-46, the socket is prepared to receive the processor.

Remove the processor from its container. The contact side of the processor is covered by a plastic protector. Hold the processor by its edges, as shown in Figure 4-47, and snap the protector away from the processor. Store that protector with the processor box, in case you ever remove the processor. Always reinstall the protector when you store a bare processor.

Figure 4-46. The socket prepared to receive the processor

Figure 4-47. Remove the plastic protector from the processor

Keying is indicated on the processor by a small gold triangle and on the socket by a matching beveled edge. The socket also has two protruding nubs that correspond to notches in the processor, one of which is visible in the figure just to the right of the gold triangle at the lower-left corner of the processor.

With the metal retention plate vertical, align the processor with the socket and drop the processor into place, as shown in Figure 4-48. The processor should seat flush with the socket just from the force of gravity. If the processor doesn't simply drop into place, something is misaligned.

Figure 4-48. Drop the processor into place

Remove the processor and verify that it is aligned properly. **Never** apply pressure to the processor. You'll bend one or more pins, destroying the socket (and the motherboard).

With the processor in place and seated flush with the socket, lower the metal retention plate, as shown in Figure 4-49. If the processor is fully seated in its socket, the retention plate should freely seat flush with the top of the processor. Note the lip on the lower right of the retention plate and the corresponding cammed area of the clamping lever. When the retention plate is properly closed, the cammed portion of the clamping lever should engage that lip as the clamping lever is moved to the latched position.

With the retention plate closed, close the socket latching lever, as shown in Figure 4-50. Make certain that the lever is locked in place by the hook on the side of the socket.

Figure 4-49. Close the retention plate

Figure 4-50. Lock the processor into the socket

Figure 4-51. Polish the processor heat spreader with a paper towel

Installing the CPU cooler

With the processor locked in its socket, the next step is to install the CPU cooler. We used a retail-boxed Intel Pentium D processor, which includes a quiet and effective CPU cooler. Before you install the CPU cooler, use a paper towel to polish the surface of the CPU heat spreader, as shown in Figure 4-51. The idea is to remove any skin oil or other foreign matter that might prevent the CPU cooler from making good thermal contact with the processor.

The stock Intel cooler has a pre-applied thermal pad on the surface that contacts the CPU. Our cooler had a bare pad, but we have seen Intel coolers with a plastic or paper film covering the thermal pad. If there's film covering the thermal pad on your cooler, peel it off before you proceed.

Position the CPU cooler over the processor socket, aligning the four posts of the cooler mounting assembly with the four corresponding holes in the motherboard, as shown in Figure 4-52. The four mounting holes form a square, so you can orient the CPU cooler any way you please. We generally orient the cooler so that the CPU fan cable has as little slack as possible after it's connected to the power header pins on the motherboard. Once you have aligned the CPU cooler with the mounting holes, press down each of the four mounting posts and rotate them until they lock into place, as shown in Figure 4-53.

Figure 4-52. Align the CPU cooler over the processor socket

Figure 4-53. Press down all four mounting posts and rotate them to the locked position to secure the CPU cooler

The last step required to install the CPU cooler is connecting the CPU fan power lead to the 4-pin CPU fan connector on the motherboard, as shown in Figure 4-54. The cable connector and motherboard connector are keyed to prevent misaligning the pins or connecting the cable backward. Align the cable connector with the motherboard header pins and press the connector into place until it seats completely.

Installing memory

Installing memory is always easy, but this time it's easier than usual. Because we're populating all four memory slots in the D945PVS motherboard with identical memory modules, we don't have to make any decisions about which modules should be installed in which slots. (If you're using a different motherboard or installing only two memory modules, make sure you install the modules in the proper slots to enable dual-channel memory operation. See the motherboard manual.)

To install the memory modules, pivot the locking tabs on both sides of all four DIMM sockets outward. Examine the contact side of a DIMM to locate its keying notch. Position the DIMM vertically above a memory slot, with the keying notch in the DIMM aligned with the keying tab in the slot, and slide the DIMM into place, as shown in Figure 4-55.

With the DIMM properly aligned with the slot and oriented vertically relative to the slot, use both thumbs to press down on the DIMM until it snaps into place, as shown in Figure 4-56. The locking tabs should automatically pivot back up into the locked position when the DIMM snaps into place. If they don't, close them manually to lock the DIMM into the socket. Install the three remaining DIMMs the same way.

With the processor and memory installed, you're almost ready to install the motherboard in the case. Before you do that, check the motherboard documentation to determine if any configuration jumpers need to be set. The Intel D945PVS has only one jumper, which sets operating mode. On our motherboard, that jumper was set correctly by default, so we proceeded to the next step.

Figure 4-54. Connect the CPU cooler fan lead to the motherboard CPU fan header

Figure 4-55. Orient the DIMM with the notch aligned properly with the socket

Figure 4-56. Seat the DIMM by pressing firmly into the slot until it snaps into place

Figure 4-57. Slide the motherboard into position

Figure 4-58. Verify that the back panel connectors mate cleanly with the I/O template

Figure 4-59. Install screws in all mounting holes to secure the motherboard

Installing the Motherboard

Installing the motherboard is time consuming because there are so many cables to connect. It's important to get them all connected properly, so check each connection before and after you make it.

Seating and securing the motherboard

To begin, slide the motherboard into the case, as shown in Figure 4-57. Carefully align the back panel I/O connectors with the corresponding holes in the I/O template, and slide the motherboard toward the rear of the case until the motherboard mounting holes line up with the standoffs.

Do one final check to make absolutely certain that there's a standoff installed for each mounting hole and that no extra standoffs are installed. Before you secure the motherboard, make sure the back panel I/O connectors mate cleanly with the I/O template, as shown in Figure 4-58. Make sure none of the metal grounding tabs on the I/O template intrude into a port connector. Although we've never seen a system actually damaged by an errant tab, we have worked on a few systems that exhibited mysterious boot failures that turned out to be caused by a tab protruding into a USB port.

After you position the motherboard and verify that the back panel I/O connectors mate cleanly with the I/O template, insert a screw through one mounting hole into the corresponding standoff. You may need to apply pressure to keep the motherboard positioned properly until you have inserted two or three screws.

If you have trouble getting all the holes and standoffs aligned, insert two screws but don't tighten them completely. Use one hand to press the motherboard into alignment, with all holes matching the standoffs. Then insert one or two more screws and tighten them completely. Finish mounting the motherboard by inserting screws into all standoffs and tightening them, as shown in Figure 4-59.

With high-quality products like the Antec P180 case and the Intel D945PVS motherboard, all the holes line up perfectly. With cheaper brands, that's not always the case. At times, we've been forced to use only a few screws to secure the motherboard. We prefer to use all of them, both to physically support the motherboard and to make sure all of the grounding points are in fact grounded, but if you can't get all of the holes lined up, simply install as many screws as you can.

After you've inserted all of the motherboard mounting screws, make one final check to verify that all of the ports on the back-panel I/O connector are clear of the metal grounding tabs on the I/O template.

Connecting front-panel switch and indicator cables

With the motherboard secured, the next step is to connect the front panel switch and indicator cables to the motherboard. Before you begin connecting front panel cables, examine the cables. Each is labeled descriptively, e.g., "Power," "Reset," and "HDD LED." Match those descriptions with the front panel connector pins on the motherboard to make sure you connect the correct cable to the appropriate pins. The motherboard header pins are color-coded. Figure 4-60 shows the pin assignments for the Hard Drive Activity LED (yellow), Reset Switch (purple), Power LED (green), and Power Switch (red) connectors.

- The Power Switch and Reset Switch connectors are not polarized, and can be connected in either orientation.

- The Hard Drive Activity LED is polarized, and should be connected with the ground (black) wire on Pin 3 and the signal (red) wire on Pin 1.

- The Power LED connector on the Intel motherboard accepts a two-position Power LED cable. Like other Intel motherboards, the D945PVS also provides an alternative three-pin Power LED connector with pins in positions one and three. The Power LED connector is dual-polarized, and can support a single-color (usually green) Power LED, as is provided with the Antec P180 case, or a dual-color (usually green/yellow) LED. If you are using a case that has a dual-color Power LED, check the case documentation to determine how to connect the Power LED cable.

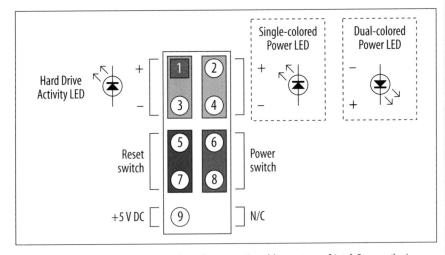

Figure 4-60. Front panel connector pin assignments (graphic courtesy of Intel Corporation)

Chapter 4, Building a SOHO Server

Once you determine the proper orientation for each cable, connect the Hard Drive Activity LED, Reset Switch, Power LED, and Power Switch cables to the motherboard, as shown in Figure 4-61. Not all cases have cables for every connector on the motherboard, and not all motherboards have connectors for all cables provided by the case. For example, some cases provide a speaker cable. The Intel D945PVS motherboard has a built-in speaker, but no connector for an external speaker, so that cable goes unused. Conversely, the Intel D945PVS has a Chassis Intrusion Connector, for which no corresponding cable exists on the Antec P180 case, so that connector goes unused.

Despite Their Best Intentions

Intel has defined the standard front-panel connector block shown in Figure 4-61 and uses that standard for its current motherboards. Unfortunately, few other motherboard makers adhere to that standard. Accordingly, rather than provide an Intel-standard monolithic connector block that would be useless for motherboards that do not follow the Intel standard, most case makers, including Antec, provide individual one-, two-, or three-pin connectors for each switch and indicator. A few cases provide both a monolithic Intel connector block and individual wires for nonstandard motherboards. If your motherboard provides the monolithic connector block, use it to minimize the risk of connecting the cables incorrectly.

Figure 4-61. Connect the front-panel switch and indicator cables

When you're connecting front-panel cables, try to get it right the first time, but don't worry too much about getting it wrong. Other than the power switch cable, which must be connected properly for the system to start, none of the other front-panel switch and indicator cables is essential, and connecting them wrong won't damage the system. Switch cables—power and reset—are not polarized. You can connect them in either orientation, without worrying about which pin is signal and which ground. LED cables may or may not be polarized, but if you connect a polarized LED cable backward, the worst that happens is that the LED won't light. Most cases use a common wire color, usually black, for ground, and a colored wire for signal.

Connecting front-panel USB ports

The Antec P180 case provides two front-panel USB 2.0 ports. Both are routed through one cable that terminates in an Intel-standard 10-pin monolithic USB connector block. The Intel D945PVS motherboard provides two internal dual-USB ports, which are black connectors located at the left front of the motherboard, near the S-ATA connectors. The two front-panel USB ports on the case require only one of these internal connectors, leaving the second one available to connect the front-panel port expander we installed earlier.

Other cases provide individual wires rather than a monolithic USB connector block. If your case has individual wires, refer to Figure 4-62 for the pin assignments for the dual front-panel internal USB connectors.

To route USB to the front panel of the P180, simply connect the USB cables from the front of the case and from the port expander to the corresponding internal connectors, as shown in Figures 4-63 and 4-64. It doesn't matter which cable you connect to which internal USB connector.

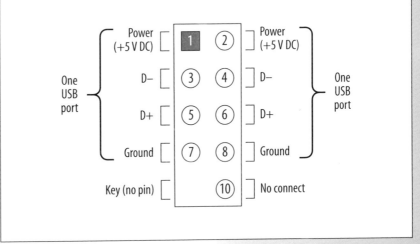

Figure 4-62. Front-panel USB connector pin assignments (graphic courtesy of Intel Corporation)

Figure 4-63. Connect the front-panel USB cable from the case

Figure 4-64. Connect the front-panel USB cable from the port extender

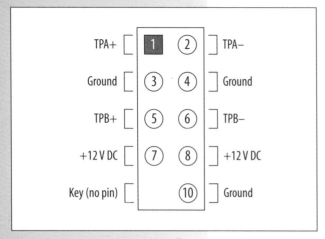

TPA+ — 1 2 — TPA–

Ground — 3 4 — Ground

TPB+ — 5 6 — TPB–

+12 V DC — 7 8 — +12 V DC

Key (no pin) — 10 — Ground

Figure 4-65. Front panel IEEE-1394a (FireWire) connector pin assignments (graphic courtesy of Intel Corporation)

Connecting the front-panel IEEE-1394a (FireWire) ports

The Antec P180 case provides one front-panel FireWire (IEEE-1394a) port. The Intel D945PVS motherboard provides two internal FireWire connectors. We'll connect the front-panel FireWire cable to one of those internal FireWire connectors, and the port expander FireWire cable to the second one.

Although the Antec P180 case provides a front-panel FireWire cable with an Intel-standard monolithic connector block, many cases provide only individual wires that must be connected one by one to the FireWire header on the motherboard. Figure 4-65 shows the pinouts for the internal FireWire connector.

Connect one of the FireWire cables to one of the blue internal FireWire connectors, as shown in Figure 4-66, and the second FireWire cable to the second connector visible immediately below Barbara's finger, as shown in Figure 4-67. Once again, it doesn't matter which FireWire cable you connect to which FireWire internal connector. With the standard back-panel FireWire connector, our system now has three available FireWire ports, which should be more than enough for our purposes.

Figure 4-66. Connect the front-panel FireWire cable from the case

Figure 4-67. Connect the front-panel FireWire cable from the port

Connecting the front-panel audio ports

The Antec P180 case provides two front-panel audio ports, line out and mic in. The port expander adds a second set of audio ports. Obviously, audio is unimportant on a server, but we decided to connect one set of ports (the set on the case itself) just for completeness. To enable the front-panel audio ports, connect the audio cable to the front-panel audio header pins at the back-left corner of the motherboard, as shown in Figure 4-68. That leaves the audio ports on the port expander unconnected. As a matter of good practice, we used a piece of tape to cover those disabled ports.

Figure 4-68. Connect the front-panel audio cable

Installing the Tuner Card

As long as we have the system on its side, we might as well install the Hauppauge WinTV-PVR-500 tuner card. To begin, remove the four screws that secure the black plastic vent shroud above the expansion slot covers, as shown in Figure 4-69. Pull the shroud off and put it aside.

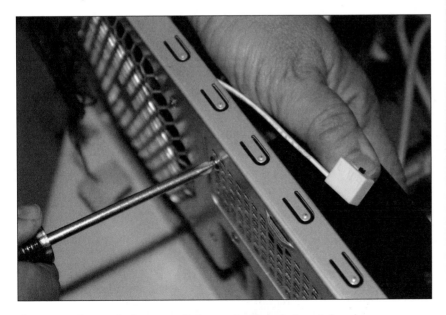

Figure 4-69. Remove the four screws that secure the black plastic vent shroud

The next step is to choose an expansion slot in which to install the card. Position the card temporarily to determine which slot cover bracket it aligns with. Once you're sure you're removing the correct slot cover bracket, remove the screw that secures the bracket, as shown in Figure 4-70.

With the screw removed, slide the expansion slot cover bracket up and tilt it toward the inside of the case, as shown in Figure 4-71. Remove the bracket completely and set it aside for now.

Figure 4-70. Remove the screw that secures the expansion slot cover bracket

Figure 4-71. Remove the expansion slot cover bracket

Slide the Hauppauge WinTV-PVR-500 card into position, making sure that the card contacts are aligned with the expansion slot. Using your thumbs, press down on the card, as shown in Figure 4-72, until you feel the card snap into place in the expansion slot. After you seat the card, reinsert the slot cover screw to secure it.

Figure 4-72. Align the tuner card and press down until it snaps into the expansion slot

At this point, we also installed a PCI Express video adapter temporarily. We'll use it to install the operating system and other software, and then remove it.

Replace the expansion slot cover shroud, as shown in Figure 4-73, using four screws to secure it.

Figure 4-73. Reinstall the expansion slot cover shroud

Connecting the Remaining Motherboard Cables

All that remains is to connect the final few cables to the motherboard. Begin by connecting the Serial ATA data cables, as shown in Figure 4-74.

The four motherboard S-ATA ports are labeled 0 through 3. Connect each S-ATA cable to a port, making sure to align the keying notch on the cable connector with the corresponding tab on the S-ATA port. Also make sure to connect each cable to the correct port, cable 0 to port 0, and so on. Once you have aligned each cable connector, press it down firmly until it snaps into place. The motherboard S-ATA connectors are more robust than those on the drives, but they are still relatively fragile. Be careful not to put any sideways pressure or torque on the cable connector as you insert it.

Figure 4-74. Connect the Serial ATA data cables

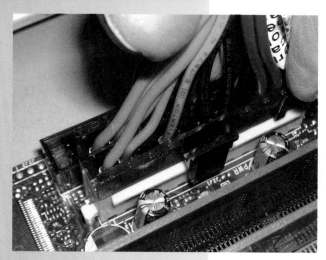

Figure 4-75. Connect the Main ATX Power Connector

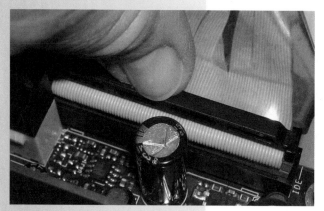

Figure 4-76. Connect the ATA data cable

The next step is to connect the main power cable from the power supply to the motherboard. The main ATX power connector is a 24-pin connector located near the front edge of the motherboard. Locate the corresponding cable coming from the power supply. The main ATX power connector is keyed, so verify that it is aligned properly before you attempt to seat it.

Once everything is aligned, press down firmly until the connector seats, as shown in Figure 4-75. It may take significant pressure to seat the connector, and you should feel it snap into place. The locking tab on the side of the connector should snap into place over the corresponding nub on the socket. Make sure the connector seats fully. A partially seated main ATX power connector may cause subtle problems that are very difficult to troubleshoot.

As long as you're working near the front edge of the motherboard, locate the 40-pin ATA connector (labeled "IDE") adjacent to the main ATX connector. Align the data cable from the optical drive with the ATA interface connector, making sure that the cable keying nub aligns with the keying slot in the motherboard connector. Once the cable is aligned, press straight down to seat it, as shown in Figure 4-76.

Modern processors require more power to the motherboard than the main ATX power connector can provide. Intel developed a supplemental connector, called the ATX12V connector, that routes additional +12V current directly to the VRM (Voltage Regulator Module) that powers the processor. There are actually two forms of ATX12V connector, the older 4-pin version and the newer 8-pin version. Both versions are still used. Which one a motherboard uses is determined by its current requirements. The 8-pin connector is a superset of the 4-pin connector—the 8-pin connector simply supplies more current at the same voltages and the pin assignments are compatible—so a power supply with an 8-pin supplemental power connector can be used with a motherboard that has either an 4-pin or 8-pin connector.

As it happens, the Antec NeoHE 550 has an 8-pin supplemental power connector, and our Intel D945PVS motherboard has a 4-pin connector. That means we need to take care to align the four proper pins on the 8-pin power cable with the 4-pin connector on the motherboard. (Because both connectors are keyed with square and rounded sockets, it's impossible to seat the connector unless it's aligned properly.)

Examine the motherboard and cable connectors to determine how to orient them, and then press the cable connector into the motherboard socket, as shown in Figure 4-77. Make sure the plastic tab on the cable connector snaps into place over the motherboard socket to lock the connectors.

Only one cable connection left. Well, two. Each of the two case fans has a Molex connector for power. The Molex cable you ran to the optical drive has two spare connectors. Connect each fan to one of those connectors, as shown in Figure 4-78.

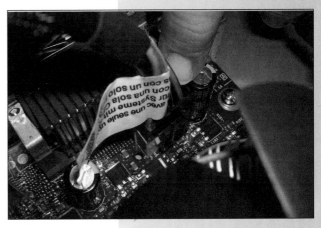

Figure 4-77. Connect the ATX12V Power Connector

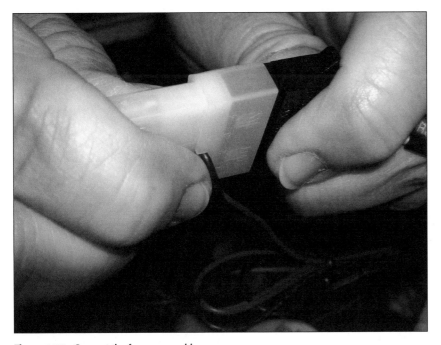

Figure 4-78. Connect the fan power cables

Final Assembly Steps

Congratulations! You're almost finished building the system. Only a few final steps remain to be done, and those won't take long.

Before you go any further, dress the cables by routing them away from the motherboard and other components—particularly fans—and tying them off so they don't flop around inside the case. Install the spoiler for the top vent (it's in the white cardboard box that contained the rails you used to mount the optical drive and port expander).

If you intend to run your server headless, as we do, leave the cover off for now. You can install the operating system and other software with the case open. Once the software is installed and tested, you can shut down the system and remove the video card. Slide the black plastic assembly that separates the upper and lower chambers of the case to seal the gap as well as possible and tighten both thumbscrews to secure it. Reinstall the VGA ventilation duct (the black plastic assembly that holds extra drive rails), and replace the side panels.

Before you proceed, take a few minutes to double-check everything. Verify that all cables are connected properly, that all drives are secured, and that there's nothing loose inside the case. If your power supply is not auto-sensing, check one last time to verify that it is set to the correct input voltage. It's a good idea to pick up the system and tilt it gently from side to side to make sure there are no loose screws or other items that could cause a short. Use the following checklist:

- ❑ Power supply set to proper input voltage (the Antec NeoHE power supply is auto-sensing)
- ❑ No loose tools or screws (shake the case gently)
- ❑ CPU cooler properly mounted; CPU fan connected
- ❑ Memory modules full seated and latched
- ❑ Front-panel switch and indicator cables connected properly
- ❑ Front-panel I/O cables connected properly
- ❑ Hard drive data cables connected to drives and motherboard
- ❑ Hard drive power cables connected
- ❑ Optical drive data cable connected to drive and motherboard
- ❑ Optical drive power cable connected
- ❑ Floppy drive data and power cables connected (if applicable)
- ❑ All drives secured to drive bay or chassis, as applicable
- ❑ Expansion card(s) fully seated and secured to the chassis
- ❑ Main ATX power cable and ATX12V power cable connected
- ❑ Front and rear case fans installed and connected
- ❑ All cables dressed and tucked

Once you're certain that all is as it should be, it's time for the smoke test. Connect the power cable to the wall receptacle and then to the system unit. Unlike some power supplies, the Antec unit has a separate rocker switch on the back that controls power to the power supply. By default, it's in the "0" or off position, which means the power supply is not receiving power from the wall receptacle. Move that switch to the "1" or on position. Press the main power button on the front of the case, and the system should start up. Check to make sure that all fans are spinning. You should also hear the hard drive spin up and the happy beep that tells you the system is starting normally. At that point, everything should be working properly.

FALSE STARTS

When you turn on the rear power switch, the system will come to life momentarily and then die. That's perfectly normal behavior. When the power supply receives power, it begins to start up. It quickly notices that the motherboard hasn't told it to start, and so it shuts down again. All you need to do is press the front-panel power switch and the system will start normally.

Turn off the system, disconnect the power cord, and take these final steps to prepare the system for use:

Set the BIOS Setup Configuration jumper to Configure mode
The BIOS Setup Configuration jumper block on the Intel D945PVS motherboard is used to set the operation mode. This jumper is located at the rear center of the motherboard, near the speaker and the main ATX power connector. By default, the jumper is in the 1-2 or "normal" position. Move the jumper block to the 2-3 or "configure" position.

Reconnect the power cord and restart the system
When the configuration jumper is set to configure mode, starting the system automatically runs BIOS Setup and puts the system in maintenance mode. This step allows the motherboard to detect the type of processor installed and configure it automatically. When the BIOS Setup screen appears, reset the system clock and load the system defaults. Save your changes, exit, and power down the system. Disconnect the power cord.

Set the BIOS Setup Configuration jumper to Normal mode
With the power cord disconnected, move the BIOS Setup Configuration jumper block from 2-3 (Configure mode) to 1-2 (Normal mode).

Final Words

Our SOHO server took longer to build than we expected. The Antec P180 case is the quietest case we have ever used, and has superb cooling. But those benefits come at the small price of some additional complexity during the build process. That's a trade-off we were more than happy to make. The system runs cooler than any comparable system we have built, and is nearly inaudible even in a quiet room.

If this is the first system you've built, expect to spend a full weekend building it. Even if you've built systems before, the SOHO server will probably be more than a one-evening project. Still, once it's complete, you've built something worth having.

Installing Software

Choosing the operating system for a SOHO server involves several trade-offs. We considered the following operating systems for our own SOHO server.

Microsoft Small Business Server

Microsoft Small Business Server (SBS) is a turnkey server OS aimed squarely at small businesses. It is designed to be easy to install and administer, although many small businesses choose to pay a consultant to install it and sometimes to manage it. SBS Standard sells for about $400 for a one-server license with five Client Access Licenses (CALs). Additional CALs cost about $450 per five-pack, and are needed for additional users or machines. SBS Premium costs about $800 for a one-server license with 5 CALs. Additional CALs cost about $850 per five-pack. Both versions support file and print sharing, email, shared calendaring, and other basic features. SBS Premium adds limited versions of SQL Server and ISA Server.

Xandros Server

Xandros Server is, in effect, a Linux-based superset of Microsoft SBS Premium. A one-server license costs about $300, and no CALs are required for basic client access. (Some of the bundled third-party utilities, such as the Scalix groupware server, the BRU Backup Server, and the Helix Streaming Media Server include some number of bundled CALs, but require additional CALs for additional users.) Xandros Server is, if anything, easier to set up and maintain than SBS. (That's fortunate, because Xandros Server consultants are still relatively thin on the ground compared to SBS consultants.) We think Xandros Server is the best choice for SOHO administrators who need a "full-function" server OS.

Ubuntu Server

Ubuntu Server is free-as-in-beer and free-as-in-speech. It uses text-based installation and maintenance, so it's unlikely to be suitable for anyone who's not comfortable with command-line Linux. On the other hand, this is serious server software. It's stripped down to essentials, whence the absence of a default GUI, and it's far faster than any of the other products we considered. One wonderful feature of Ubuntu Server is its scripted setup of a LAMP (Linux, Apache, MySQL, PHP/Perl/Python) server. Setting up a LAMP server manually may take hours, even for an experienced Linux administrator. With Ubuntu Server, setting up a LAMP server is a single menu option. Frankly, we think Ubuntu Server is a pretty good choice for nearly any SOHO environment, provided you're already a moderately experienced command-line-savvy Linux administrator (or have access to a Linux guru for advice and assistance).

A desktop Linux distribution

If your functional requirements are modest, don't rule out using a standard desktop Linux distribution like Xandros 4 or Ubuntu/Kubuntu on your server. In theory, there are a lot of disadvantages to doing that, but in practice many of those objections disappear. For example, a desktop Linux distribution is usually slower than a purpose-built server distribution. So what? We'll never notice any tiny performance difference that may exist. A desktop distribution may not support software RAID. Again, we don't care, because we plan to run JBOD on our SOHO server. Desktop Linux distributions also have advantages relative to server distributions. The biggest advantage for most people is that the desktop distro uses a familiar graphic interface. Setting up a shared disk volume or printer is usually a matter of a few clicks.

We ruled out Microsoft SBS for our SOHO server based on cost, if nothing else. Based on how Microsoft calculates CAL requirements, we would have had to spend more than $800 for SBS Standard or $1,600 for SBS Premium. That was simply more than we could justify based on the features and benefits of SBS. We also distrust the business policies and security of Microsoft software, so we took SBS off our list immediately.

Ubuntu Server was the next candidate we eliminated. We simply don't know Linux well enough to maintain a command-line server, nor do we need the LAMP stack that is the real reason Ubuntu Server was created. For a small business that has an experienced Linux administrator, Ubuntu Server might be an excellent and economical choice. For us, it was a nonstarter.

We looked next at Xandros Server. This product is reasonably inexpensive, extremely full-featured, and by default uses a Windows-like graphical interface, shown in Figure 4-79. (There is the option to run it in text mode for higher performance.) Xandros sent us an evaluation copy, which we spent some time evaluating.

The core of Xandros Server is the Xandros Management Console, shown in Figure 4-80 only three minutes after we'd installed Xandros Server and before we'd installed and enabled any but the default functions. Anyone who has even a bit of experience managing Windows servers will immediately feel right at home in Xandros Server.

Figure 4-79. The Xandros Server administrator desktop

Figure 4-80. Xandros Management Console

We concluded that Xandros Server was fast, reliable, and very easy to manage. If we needed even one or two of the advanced features of this product—such as the groupware server or the streaming media server—or if we needed to manage multiple servers, we'd choose Xandros Server in a heartbeat.

But all we really need our SOHO Server to do is share files, printers, and other resources. For those simple tasks, even the minimal $300 street price of Xandros Server was more than we wanted to pay. We decided to do what we really intended to do all along—install a desktop Linux distro and set it up as our server OS. The choice came down to Xandros 4 Home Edition Premium or Ubuntu 6.06 LTS, both of which we were already running on other systems.

We looked first at Ubuntu 6.06 LTS Linux, which Robert runs on his primary office desktop system. Unfortunately, although Ubuntu has good support for Windows Networking as a client, setting up a Windows Networking server turned out to be nontrivial.

We read the Samba documentation and various Ubuntu help pages until we were confident that we could set up network shares properly. After an hour or two of mucking about, we got it working, or so we thought. Unfortunately, we soon encountered some strange problems with Windows clients authenticating to the server, sporadically dropped connections, and so on.

We turned next to Xandros 4 Home Edition Premium, which Barbara runs on her primary office desktop. Xandros 4 Premium retails for $80, but is available from online merchants for $55 or so. Although it is licensed for use on only one business system, the license allows it to be installed on unlimited personally owned systems for personal use.

In contrast to our struggles to configure Ubuntu to work properly as a server, Xandros 4 is trivially easy to set up as a server. Sharing a disk volume or printer with other Linux and Windows users on the network requires only a few clicks, and Just Works. In fact, it's easier to set up Xandros to share resources in either direction than it is to set up Windows to do the same.

The desktop version of Xandros lacks the Management Console and third-party server applications bundled with Xandros Server, but for our purposes it was perfect. Inexpensive, reliable, and easy to use. We couldn't ask for more.

For updated component recommendations, commentary, and other new material, visit *http://www.hardwareguys.com/guides/soho-server.html*.

Building a Gaming PC 5

In the first edition of this book, we built a LAN party PC—one designed for high performance and maximum portability. When we built that system in the summer of 2004, it was faster than any system we were likely to encounter at a LAN party. Even today, its Pentium 4 Extreme Edition processor and RADEON 9800XT are fast enough for any but the most intense recent games.

But after more than two years, it was time to update our gaming system. We call this version a gaming PC rather than a LAN party PC because we designed this system to be appropriate both for LAN parties and for gaming at home. We found ourselves traveling less than we expected and playing more at home, so for our new gaming PC we decided to deemphasize the portability aspects and pay more attention to issues that bear on home use.

Of course, our gaming PC is useful for much more than just gaming. Gaming demands more from a PC than any other common task, so a PC that's configured for gaming is by definition good for nearly any other job you throw at it. For most people, our gaming PC configuration will also serve as an ideal general-purpose system.

In the first edition of this book, we described our LAN party PC as a "kick-ass" system, which it indeed was for the time. It used a $1,000 processor and a $600 video adapter, for example. This time, we decided to set our sights a bit lower, for two reasons.

First, many of our readers expressed their desire for a configuration that could be built on a reasonable budget and still provide decent gaming performance. Getting that last few percent of performance isn't cheap, and many people will never notice the difference. Fanatic gamers for whom cost is no object will still want expensive options like dual video adapters (along with the costly extras they require, such as SLI-certified power supplies and extreme cooling solutions). But for most of us, a solid gaming system that can be built on a reasonable budget is a more realistic option.

Second, the price of performance has dropped remarkably in the last couple of years. Certainly, you can still spend $1,000 for a processor or $600 for a video adapter, but you probably don't need to. Today's $175 processor is faster than last year's $1,000 processor, and fast enough is fast enough.

That's also true when it comes to video. For example, we actually recycled an older video adapter for our own gaming PC. That video adapter was a $600 card little more than a year before we built this system, but comparable video adapters are now available for under $125. No, that older video adapter won't provide the fastest frame rates with the newest, most intense games, but who cares? It's playable even for the most demanding current games, and it's as fast as ever on less demanding titles. Nowadays, all but the most rabid gamers will be quite happy with the performance of a $200 video adapter, and many will be content with a $100 model.

Manufacturer hype aside, the truth is that serious gaming is now accessible for those on mainstream budgets. So we set out to design a gaming PC on that basis, and what we came up with is, for us at least, the perfect gaming PC.

Determining Functional Requirements

We sat down to think through the project. Here's the list of functional requirements we came up with:

Gaming utility

Most important, this system must have all of the resources necessary to be a good gaming platform. It must be fast enough to handle any current game at least reasonably well, have enough ports (and conveniently located) to handle any combination of game controllers, and so on. It must have audio and video support suitable for any game we decide to play on it.

General utility

This system must have all of the resources necessary for use as a general purpose system. No one who builds this system for gaming should have to own a second system for other purposes. That means, for example, that the system must have a FireWire port for downloading DV video from a camcorder (and sufficient disk space to edit that video). It must have a display and other external peripherals that are suitable for general use, as opposed to only peripherals optimized for gaming. This system must be capable of handling all but the most specialized tasks with aplomb. Two plombs, even.

Portability

Although portability is a secondary issue, it remains important for the gaming PC to be easily portable. Size and weight are both considerations. We set our upper size limit at a standard mini-tower case, which is small enough to be easily portable but large enough to contain several drives and whatever other components we might wish to add later and with enough volume to eliminate any problems with ventilation and cooling. We set our upper weight limit at 30 pounds, give or take, for the system unit, which is light enough for Barbara to pick up with one hand.

Hardware Design Criteria

With the functional requirements determined, the next step was to establish design criteria for the gaming PC hardware. Here are the relative priorities we assigned for the gaming PC.

Here's the breakdown:

DESIGN PRIORITIES	
Price	★★★☆☆
Reliability	★★★★☆
Size	★★☆☆☆
Noise level	★★★★☆
Expandability	★★☆☆☆
Processor performance	★★★★☆
Video performance	★★★★☆
Disk capacity/performance	★★★☆☆

Price

Price is moderately important for this system. Our goal is to spend as little as possible above the cost of a general purpose system to create a system that's suitable for gaming. Reasonable gaming performance is now available for not much more than mainstream performance, so we'll keep a close eye on the prices of the processor, video adapter, and other components. We'll use only top-notch components in this system, particularly those that most affect gaming performance, but we'll use integrated components when they're capable of doing the job.

Reliability

Reliability is very important for this system, and we're willing to spend a bit extra to make the system as reliable as possible within reason. That means, for example, using a premium power supply and premium memory, and using cool-running components wherever possible.

Size

Size is relatively unimportant. Ultimately, what matters is that the gaming PC be easy to move from one location to another, and that it be large enough to facilitate ventilation and cooling.

Noise level

Noise level is very important. Although this system will go on the road with us periodically, it will spend most of its time at home. Quiet operation is a nonissue at a LAN party, but critical for residential use. We won't use radical quiet PC techniques like water cooling or added insulation, but we will use the quietest mainstream components available. To some extent, the goal of having a quiet system is at odds with portability. For example, it's impossible to use elastic suspension to mount the hard drives in a portable system.

Expandability

Expandability is relatively unimportant relative to other factors. We may upgrade our gaming PC from time to time, but those upgrades are likely to be things like a faster processor or video adapter, a high-capacity optical drive (if Blu-Ray or HD-DVD ever becomes affordable), larger hard drives, or more memory. Any of those upgrades simply replaces a component already installed or uses an otherwise vacant bay or slot. The one exception is dual video adapters. We decided not to use dual video adapters initially, but we also decided to choose an SLI motherboard (one with dual video slots) to leave that option open for the future.

Processor performance

In one sense, processor performance is very important to any gaming PC. Even with a fast video adapter, most games play poorly on a system with a slow processor. Fortunately, Intel's July 2006 introduction of their new Core 2 Duo processor family and AMD's dramatic price cuts on their Athlon 64 X2 dual-core processors have pretty much rendered the issue of processor horsepower moot. In the new world order, very fast processors now sell for mainstream prices, and the fastest (and most expensive) models are no longer needed even for extreme gaming. Unless your budget is unlimited, there's no longer any point to spending more than $175 to $250 for a processor, particularly if you are willing to overclock less expensive processors, as many gamers are.

Video performance

Again, although video performance is very important for a gaming PC, even midrange video adapters are now fast enough to deal with all but the most demanding 3D games played at high resolutions with all the eye candy enabled. A current $200 video adapter is faster than last year's $600 model, and even a $100 model compares favorably with the top-of-the-line model from 18 months prior. Video adapter makers have been on a 6-month refresh schedule for years. In general the current Better model matches the Best model from six months previous, and the current Good model matches the Best year-old model. What all that means is that most gamers will be happy with a $100 video adapter and delighted with a $200 model. Once again, the price of performance has fallen dramatically, and only the most devoted gamers will find it worth spending more than $200 to $250 on a video adapter.

Disk capacity/performance

We assigned moderate importance to this factor because our friends who are serious gamers tell us that drive performance matters in gaming, both for hard drives and optical drives. So, apparently, does disk capacity, as many serious gamers copy entire CDs and DVDs to their hard drives for faster access while gaming. Accordingly, we'll aim for fast performance from our hard drives and optical drives, and high disk capacity. All keeping within a reasonable budget, of course.

SLI and CrossFire

nVIDIA developed SLI (Scalable Link Interface) to allow two video adapters to function as one. ATi soon followed with its similar but incompatible CrossFire system. (In dual mode, an SLI motherboard accepts only nVIDIA SLI-compatible video cards; a CrossFire motherboard accepts only ATi CrossFire-compatible video adapters. Either type of motherboard can use a single video adapter from either company.)

In theory, you can install two identical $150 video adapters in an SLI-compatible or CrossFire system and have noticeably higher video performance than a single $300 video adapter would provide.

In practice, the cost advantage is diminished by the need for a relatively expensive SLI motherboard and a high-wattage SLI-compliant power supply, and the performance gain is not always as great as expected. Unstable and buggy drivers have also been a problem for dual-adapter systems, although those problems have become less severe recently as ATi and nVIDIA continue to polish their dual-adapter drivers.

The real cost benefit with dual video adapters occurs only when you install two midrange or better adapters that cost enough to offset the extra $100 to $150 cost of building a dual-capable system. For example, installing two $200 adapters totals $400 for the adapters and, say, a $125 incremental cost for the SLI motherboard and power supply, for a total of $525. That combination may outperform a single $700 adapter. Similarly, dual adapters are useful when even the fastest single model isn't fast enough. Instead of using one $700 adapter, you use two. (Yes, some gamers are both rich and foolish enough to do this.)

For our Gaming PC, we decided to leave the door open for SLI, but not to implement it initially. We chose a top-of-the-line SLI-compatible motherboard, but installed just one video adapter (in our case, a year-old nVIDIA 6800 Ultra that was still fast enough to do the job for us.) That motherboard cost about $50 more than a comparable non-SLI motherboard, which we considered a reasonable insurance premium. Six months or a year from now, when it's time to replace the 6800 Ultra, we'll consider the options. It's quite possible that we'll decide to install two low-end or midrange adapters in SLI mode.

Component Considerations

With our design criteria in mind, we set out to choose the best components for the gaming PC system. We took advice from our readers, because Barbara doesn't game at all and Tux Racer is Robert's idea of a challenging game. The following sections describe the components we chose, and why we chose them.

Case

Antec P150 (*http://www.antec.com*)

We could have built the gaming PC in just about any case. For the LAN party PC we built for the previous edition of this book, we chose the aluminum Antec Super LANBOY for portability.

But portability turned out to be less important than we'd thought. When we went on a road trip to visit friends over the Labor Day weekend, Robert didn't think about the LAN party system. He took along his primary office desktop system instead. That system was a loaded mid-tower box, with a dual-core processor, 2 GB of memory, dual optical drives, and a 2.5 TB of hard disk space. It was much more capable than the LAN party PC, and, as it turned out, just as portable. So we decided to build our gaming PC in a standard mini- or mid-tower case, confident that it would be as easily portable as a system built in a special LAN party case.

With a blank sheet of paper, so to speak, we set out to choose the perfect case for our gaming PC. We wanted a case that was attractive, provided excellent cooling, and was as quiet as possible. After considering numerous alternatives, we settled on the Antec P150. The P150 uses a gloss white and brushed aluminum color scheme that looks good anywhere. Mike Chin of Silent PC Review (*http://www.silentpcreview.com*) helped Antec design the P150, so we were confident that it would provide excellent cooling at a very low noise level.

The P150 includes an Antec NeoHE 430 power supply, which is a premium unit. The only downside to the P150 is that the NeoHE 430 is not SLI-certified for use with dual video adapters. That wasn't a problem for us, because we don't intend to use dual video adapters, and the NeoHE 430 is otherwise a superb choice. If you plan to use SLI (or CrossFire), choose a case that doesn't include a power supply or one that includes an SLI-certified power supply. Otherwise, we think you'll also be delighted with the P150.

Advice from Jim Cooley

Cases made more cheaply than Antec are liable to use thinner steel or aluminum in the frame and side panels, so if portability is an issue double-check the case integrity. I've seen cases mangled and bent out of shape from a drop of less than two feet, something that wouldn't happen with an Antec.

ALTERNATIVES: CASE

Nearly any mini- or mid-tower case. If the case includes a power supply, make sure that it is ATX v2.x-compliant and of sufficient wattage to support your configuration. If you plan to use dual video adapters, make sure the power supply is SLI-certified. If the case does not include a power supply, purchase a high-quality unit such as the Antec NeoHE separately. For SLI systems, we recommend the Antec NeoHE 550.

Processor

AMD Athlon 64 X2 4200+ (*http://www.amd.com*)

Intel's July 2006 introduction of its new-generation Core 2 Duo processor line wreaked havoc with processor pricing. To make room in the price list for the Core 2 Duo models, Intel took a meat-ax to the prices of their older Pentium D dual-core processors. Literally overnight, the price of performance was cut in half. AMD had no choice but to respond with similar price cuts, chopping the price of some of their Athlon 64 models by more than 60%.

In the past, a serious gaming system typically used a processor that cost $350 to $1,000, versus the $150 to $225 cost of mainstream processors. The most rabid gamers happily coughed up $1,000 for "extreme" processors like Athlon FX-series models. Happily, the processor price war kicked off by Intel means that even a serious gaming system can now use a $200 processor.

We considered three processor families for our gaming system, the Intel Pentium D, the Intel Core 2 Duo, and the AMD Athlon 64 X2. All of these are dual-core processors. Although dual core is of limited benefit for most games, there's really no alternative. Nowadays, only "value" processors are single core. Here are the issues we considered.

Intel Pentium D

> The Intel Pentium D doesn't get much respect as a gaming processor, but that has more to do with pricing than any real problems with the processor itself. Intel had priced the Pentium D against the AMD Athlon 64 X2 for comparable general performance at a comparable price. But the Athlon 64 X2 architecture is more efficient for gaming. That meant that, for similar gaming performance, a less expensive Athlon 64 X2 matched a significantly more expensive Pentium D. Gamers abandoned Intel in droves. When Intel cut Pentium D prices dramatically, the equation shifted in favor of the Pentium D, dollar for dollar. Even AMD's July 2006 price cuts on the Athlon 64 X2 didn't completely close the gap, so the Pentium D suddenly became an excellent choice for a gaming system, particularly for a gamer on a tight budget.

Intel Core 2 Duo

> The first benchmark tests on the Core 2 Duo made it clear that this new processor family simply blew the doors off the older Pentium D and Athlon 64 X2. That might not have mattered if Intel had priced the Core 2 Duo models as premium products, but they didn't. Intel wanted to transition to the Core 2 Duo as quickly as possible, so they priced the Core 2 Duo models extremely aggressively. How aggressively? At introduction, the $316 Core 2 Duo E6600 matched or beat the overall performance of the $1,000+ AMD Athlon 64 FX-62, and even the entry-level $224 Core 2 Duo E6300 outpaced all but the fastest AMD

Athlon 64 X2 Power Consumption

AMD produces several Athlon 64 X2 models in two variants. The model designations are identical, but the more expensive variants use noticeably less power and produce less heat. At the time we built this system, the low-power version of the Athlon 64 X2 4200+ sold at a $60 premium. We didn't consider the benefit worth the cost, so we used the standard version. As time passes, we expect that AMD will improve its production processes and eventually begin producing only the low-power variants.

processors. The Core 2 Duo also shifted the playing field in terms of gaming performance, with benchmark tests showing that Core 2 Duo was at least on a par with AMD's best. Core 2 Duo is a superb choice for a gaming system. But not the only superb choice, as we found.

AMD Athlon 64 X2

The introduction of the Intel Core 2 Duo knocked AMD down, but not out. At the very highest reaches of gaming performance, the AMD Athlon 64 X2 was no longer competitive with Intel Core 2 Duo, but very few systems, even dedicated gaming systems, use extreme processors. In the sweet spot for gaming processors, AMD could again be competitive with Intel simply by reducing its prices for the Athlon 64 X2, and that is exactly what they did. Suddenly, a fast X2, which not long before had sold for $400, now cost $200, and AMD was right back in the ballgame.

We were faced with making the choice among three excellent processor families. Talk about an embarrassment of riches. For $125, we could have chosen a Pentium D that offered sufficient performance for a mainstream gaming system. For $50 or so more, we could choose a Core 2 Duo or a fast Athlon 64 X2, either of which had noticeably better gaming performance.

If we had been on a tight budget, we wouldn't have hesitated to use the Pentium D, despite its somewhat lower performance and higher heat. We might have chosen the Core 2 Duo for our gaming PC except that availability was tightly constrained soon after its introduction, with Intel shipping every available Core 2 Duo processor to Dell and other large OEMs. Fortunately, the AMD Athlon 64 X2 was widely available, and provided excellent bang for the buck.

For our gaming PC, we chose the AMD Athlon 64 X2 4200+ in the new Socket AM2, which at the time was selling for about $185. Admittedly, it seemed odd to pay only a mainstream price for a high-performance processor like the 4200+, but we could get used to that. The simple truth is that any but the most extreme gaming PC no longer needs a $350+ processor. The Athlon 64 X2 4200+ is just as fast priced at $185 as it was when it sold for twice that much, and fast enough is fast enough.

We chose a retail-boxed Athlon 64 X2 4200+, which includes a decent CPU cooler. The stock AMD cooler appears to be an AVC Z7U7414001 heatpipe model, which is reasonably efficient and quiet. If you prefer to use a quieter or more efficient cooler, consider premium models from Thermalright (Ultra-90/K8, XP-90, or XP-120) or Zalman (CNPS7xxx- or 9xxx-series). Socket AM2 uses the same mounting arrangements for the CPU cooler as Socket 939, so nearly any Socket 939 cooler that fits your motherboard and case should work properly with a Socket AM2 processor.

Motherboard

ASUS M2N32-SLI Deluxe (*http://www.asus.com*)

Like Intel, AMD made a major change to its processor line in mid-2006 by introducing a new socket that will eventually replace Socket 754 and Socket 939. The announcement of Socket AM2 also presaged AMD's shift from DDR memory to DDR2 memory. Unlike Intel's shift from Netburst architecture to Core 2 architecture, AMD's shift from Socket 939 to Socket AM2 had little impact on performance. A Socket AM2 Athlon 64 processor with DDR2 memory is little or no faster than the same model for Socket 939 with DDR memory, and AMD makes no claims of increased performance.

But the processor and memory are not the sole determinants of performance. The motherboard and, more particularly, the chipset, can have a dramatic impact on system performance. Years ago, it was common for benchmark tests for a particular processor model to differ widely depending on the motherboard and chipset used for testing. Around the time Intel introduced the 440BX chipset for the Pentium III, those differences began to disappear. In recent years, the performance differences between motherboards and chipsets had become relatively minor, at most a few percent either way.

nVIDIA changed that when they introduced the nForce 590 SLI chipset. nVIDIA nForce chipsets had always been the premium choice for AMD processors, offering top-notch performance and stability. We expected nVIDIA's chipset for Socket AM2 to be more of the same—fast and reliable, and little different from their nForce 4 series chipsets for Socket 939. Boy, were we wrong.

We benchmarked AMD Athlon 64 X2 4200+ processors in Socket 939 and Socket AM2 on similar nForce motherboards, expecting similar results. We were surprised to find that the Socket AM2 processor on an nForce 590 motherboard was faster than the Socket 939 processor on an nForce 4 motherboard. And not just a little faster. In some benchmarks, the nForce 590 SLI motherboard was as much as 30% faster, which is an incredible difference for a chipset to make. To put this in perspective, the $175 Athlon 64 X2 4200+ in an nForce 590 SLI motherboard gave faster performance benchmarks than we'd expect to see from an Athlon 64 FX-62 processor in an nForce 4 motherboard. nVIDIA really hit a home run with the nForce 590 SLI chipset.

Perhaps that performance difference isn't all attributable to the chipset. The motherboard itself may have something to do with it. At the time we built our gaming PC, Socket AM2 motherboards were still pretty thin on the ground. We were fortunate enough to get our hands on an ASUS M2N32-SLI Deluxe motherboard, which is what we used for benchmark-testing the Socket AM2 processor. We've always sworn by ASUS motherboards for their quality, performance, and reliability, so on that basis we chose the top-of-the-line ASUS M2N32-SLI Deluxe motherboard as the foundation of our gaming PC.

ALTERNATIVES: MOTHERBOARD

For an Intel Pentium D processor, choose any compatible Intel or ASUS motherboard based on an Intel 946-, 963-, 965-, or 975X-series chipset that provides a PCI Express video adapter slot. For an Intel Core 2 Duo processor, choose any compatible Intel or ASUS motherboard based on a 946-, 963-, 965-, or 975X-series chipset that provides a PCI Express video adapter slot. For a less expensive alternative to the ASUS M2N32-SLI for a Socket AM2 Athlon 64 X2 processor, choose the ASUS M2N-E or M2N-SLI Deluxe. Based on our performance testing, we do not recommend using a Socket 939 processor.

Memory

Kingston KVR667D2N5K2/2G PC2 5300 DDR2-SDRAM (1 GB × 2)
(*http://www.kingston.com*)

If you want a stable system, install a premium power supply and top-quality memory. Using cheap memory almost guarantees frequent system crashes. We've used premium, name-brand memory in all of our systems for more than 20 years, and it has seldom let us down.

When determining memory requirements, it's important to remember that a dual-core processor like our AMD Athlon 64 X2 4200+ is effectively two processors. Each of those processors needs as much memory as a single-core processor does. We consider 1 GB the sweet spot for gaming on a single-core processor, so we decided to install 2 GB of memory in our dual-core gaming PC. Because the AMD Athlon 64 X2 4200+ has a dual-channel DDR2 memory controller, we decided to install two 1 GB memory modules.

As we always do when we're configuring a new system, we visited the Kingston and Crucial web sites and used their configurators to display lists of memory modules compatible with our ASUS M2N32-SLI Deluxe motherboard. As it happened, Kingston memory was a bit less expensive than comparable Crucial memory that day, so we opted for the Kingston modules.

Kingston listed three compatible 2 GB memory kits, each of which contained two matched 1 GB modules. The only differences in those kits were the speed and CAS latency (CL) of the modules and their price. At the time we built this system, a PC2 5300 CL5 memory kit sold for $161. We could instead have chosen a PC2 4200 CL4 kit that had slower access time but faster latency for about $190. That kit would have offered somewhat faster random memory access at the expense of slower sequential memory access, so we ruled out the CL4 kit. The third alternative was a 2 GB PC2 6400 CL5 kit for $346. That kit would have offered faster sequential memory access than the PC2 5300 kit, but at more than twice the cost. The PC2 6400 kit would have boosted performance by at most a few percent. That gain wouldn't be perceptible other than when running memory benchmark tests, so we decided to use the less expensive PC2 5300 kit.

**ALTERNATIVES:
MEMORY**

Any compatible premium memory modules. We recommend a minimum of 2 GB of memory for a Gaming PC, and we recommend using only Kingston or Crucial modules.

Why "Performance" Memory Usually Isn't Worth Paying Extra For

Companies like Corsair and Mushkin sell "high-performance" memory to the enthusiast market. We're sometimes asked if it's worth paying more for such memory rather than using standard Kingston or Crucial modules. The short answer is that it's usually not.

Even nominally identical memory chips vary from one to the next. Some are faster than others, and performance memory packagers take advantage of that fact. They order large numbers of memory chips and use a process called *binning* to hand-select the fastest chips from that batch. After they've cherry-picked the fastest 5% or 10%, they resell the remaining chips to other memory packagers. They assemble those hand-picked chips into high-performance modules and test the finished modules to verify that they function at higher speeds and tighter memory timings than standard memory.

Many gamers happily pay substantial premiums for such memory, on the assumption that faster memory must translate to faster system performance. Alas, that's not necessarily true. If one type of memory is fast enough to keep up with the processor, or nearly so, substituting faster memory has very little effect on overall system performance.

Some might object that the benchmarks show the difference. Sure they do, when they test memory subsystem performance in isolation. But memory performance is only one aspect of overall system performance, and using faster memory helps only if memory speed is the bottleneck. For most gaming systems, it is not.

The one exception is overclocked systems. If you boost the bus speed to run your CPU at higher than nominal speed, which we do not recommend, you're also pushing other system components, including the memory, to speeds they were not designed to support. In such cases, it's a good idea to use hand-picked performance memory rather than depend on the tolerances built into standard memory modules.

Video Adapter

Pick one (or two)

Choosing a video adapter (or adapters) for a gaming system is the most complex decision you'll have to make. You have to weigh your budget against the minimum level of 3D graphics performance that is acceptable to you. You have to take into account the specific games you play, because some games are faster on nVIDIA adapters and others on ATi adapters. You have to decide whether it's better to install one expensive adapter or two midrange adapters. You have to weigh the advantages and drawbacks of buying an expensive adapter now and using it for a year versus installing a less expensive adapter now and upgrading every six months.

For our own configuration, we had no need of a new video adapter. Instead, we migrated a year-old nVIDIA GeForce 6800 Ultra from an older system to our new gaming PC. That formerly high-end card is now midrange in terms of performance against current models, but it's still more than fast enough for the games we play. We could have matched its performance with a current model that sold for $125, but there was no point to doing that. Instead, we'll wait until we actually need a faster graphics adapter, and then upgrade to what by then will probably be a midrange model.

When you choose a graphics adapter for your own gaming PC, we suggest using the following guidelines:

- Video adapters change in Internet time. Get the latest information and benchmarks from enthusiast sites such as AnandTech (*http://www.anandtech.com*), Sharky Extreme (*http://www.sharkyextreme.com*), and Tom's Hardware (*http://www.tomshardware.com*).

- ATi versus nVIDIA is a religious issue. Both companies produce excellent video chipsets, and overall performance is comparable between similarly priced adapters that use either company's chipsets. That said, we prefer to use nVIDIA adapters on motherboards that use nVIDIA system chipsets. Because we prefer nVIDIA-based motherboards for AMD systems, we generally use nVIDIA-based video adapters in AMD systems. For Intel-based systems, we've historically used mostly ATi adapters, although nVIDIA adapters work just as well. With AMD's buyout of ATi and the introduction of Intel's new-generation Core 2 Duo processors and new chipsets to support them, the graphics landscape will change significantly in late 2006 and into 2007. Only experience will tell which combinations are optimum in this new environment.

- Make sure the adapter you choose has sufficient onboard memory for the games you play. For casual gaming, particularly with older titles, 128 MB may suffice. A mainstream gaming adapter should have 256 MB, and if you play the latest, most intense games, you'll want 512 MB or more.

- Pay close attention to performance with the specific games you play. Some games play better on nVIDIA adapters, and others on ATi adapters. In the most extreme cases, a particular game may be faster on a midrange adapter from nVIDIA than on a high-end adapter from ATi, or vice versa.

- Unless your budget is effectively unlimited, give careful thought to your upgrade strategy. Quite often, you're better off upgrading every six months to the latest mid-range adapter than spending a lot of money on a high-end adapter initially and having to use it for a year or more.

- No matter which card or cards you install, play close attention to driver updates. ATi and nVIDIA both release driver updates frequently. Those updates may fix bugs, but often they are primarily performance tweaks for the most recent games. The performance delta between the current driver and an old version can be extraordinary.

- Consider carefully before you buy into the dual adapter concept. In theory, nVIDIA's SLI (Scalable Link Interface) and ATi's CrossFire are very attractive. You can install two less expensive adapters instead of one more expensive adapter, and get higher performance for less money. In practice, dual adapters may not work particularly well. Driver problems are common, and performance is not always as high as expected. If you do decide to use dual adapters, verify everything carefully. In particular, make absolutely certain that your motherboard is compatible with the adapters you choose and that the power supply you use is SLI-certified and can provide the required current to both adapters.

- Decide what is reasonable to spend, and then limit yourself to that amount. If you set a $150 budget, don't let the marketing hype convince you to walk out of the store with a $300 adapter. The 80/20 Rule definitely applies to graphics adapters. A $150 adapter provides 80% of the performance of a $750 model, give or take, and all but the most avid gamers will probably be happy with the performance of that $150 adapter.

- If you do decide to buy a high-end adapter, be aware that at the very high end the 80/20 Rule is replaced by the Law of Diminishing Returns. For example, a $750 adapter costs 50% more than a $500 adapter, but may be only 10% (or less) faster. Super-premium adapters are more often bought for bragging rights than for any perceptible performance benefit.

Sound Adapter

Integrated

When we sat down to design this system, we fully intended to install a standalone sound adapter. Then we started reading reviews of the ASUS M2N32-SLI Deluxe motherboard and its integrated ADI SoundMax HD Audio, and decided just to use the integrated audio.

Gamers install standalone sound adapters for two reasons. First, integrated audio can put a heavy burden on the main system processor, resulting in lower frame rates. Second, integrated audio typically lacks hardware acceleration for positional audio.

The integrated ADI codec answers the first objection easily. Frame rates with ADI audio enabled are only 2% to 3% lower than frame rates with ADI audio disabled (versus a 25% to 33% drop with many integrated audio solutions) and the audio quality is excellent. Unfortunately, ADI accomplished this feat by not including support for Creative's EAX positional audio. We don't care about EAX support, so the integrated audio is sufficient for us.

Hard Disk Drive

Seagate 7200.9 Barracuda SATA (500 GB × 2) (*http://www.seagate.com*)

We've used and recommended Seagate hard drives for many years, and have never had cause to regret it. Seagate Barracuda-series drives are fast, extremely reliable, quiet, and reasonably priced. So, when we configured our gaming PC, the only real decisions were which model of Barracuda drive to install, and how many.

Several of our gaming friends convinced us to try a RAID 0 once again, swearing that RAID 0 provided better gaming performance. We didn't really believe that. We've tested RAID 0 (and the similar RAID 0+1) many times over the years. While RAID 0/0+1 indeed boosts disk performance on a heavily loaded server, we've never seen much performance benefit on desktop systems. Weighed against the risk—one drive failing in a RAID 0 causes all data on both drives to be lost—using RAID 0 on our gaming PC seemed like a sucker bet. Still, why not? It was worth testing again, and if the tests turned out as we expected, we could simply pull the second drive and use it in another system.

ADVICE FROM BRIAN BILBREY

In transitioning from one texture map to another, load times are significant. I might expect to see much better performance from *hardware* RAID 0 than from a JBOD configuration. Software RAID, not so much.

RIGHT AGAIN

The tests turned out just as we expected. By choosing benchmarks that exercised the disk subsystem heavily, we could "prove" that RAID 0 gave better performance than a single drive. But those benchmarks hammered the drives with access patterns typical for a file server, not for a single-user desktop system. For real-world single-user use, including gaming, RAID 0 offered very little performance benefit. So, although we illustrate the build process using two drives, you can safely install just one drive in your own gaming PC.

The same objection holds true for using faster drives. We tried a Western Digital Raptor 10,000 RPM ATA drive and Seagate Cheetah 15,000 RPM SCSI drives, alone and in a RAID 0. While the faster drives made program loading faster and heavy disk operations noticeably snappier, they had little perceptible effect on game play once the game was loaded.

Optical Drive

BenQ DW1650 DVD writer (*http://www.benq.us*)

Many gamers install two optical drives in their systems—a DVD writer for general use and a DVD-ROM drive for faster read access to game DVDs. Fast DVD writers, such as the BenQ DW1650 model we chose for our gaming PC, make this strategy obsolete. In our testing, the BenQ DW1650 proved to have true random access times as fast as or faster than the several DVD-ROM models we also tested.

WHEN SLOWER IS FASTER

Take published random access times with a grain of salt. There are many ways to test random access time, and they are not standardized. A drive with a published 120 ms random access time may actually be faster than another drive that claims 85 ms random access. Other than testing specific drives with a utility like Nero CD-DVD Speed, there's no way to tell which claims are conservative and which are exaggerated.

For example, we tested the NEC ND-3550A (rated at 140 ms random access) and indeed found it to be slightly slower than the BenQ DW1650 (120 ms). However, the Plextor PX-740A and PX-716AL, both rated at 150 ms, were faster than the BenQ DW1650. We tested several DVD-ROM drives, with rated access times ranging from 85 ms to 120 ms, and found no correlation between rated access times and actual performance. One of the DVD-ROM models listed at 85 ms was the slowest drive we tested, and the 150 ms Plextor DVD writers were among the fastest.

ALTERNATIVES: OPTICAL DRIVE

Any DVD writer from BenQ, Lite-On, NEC, Pioneer, or Plextor. If you use DVD-RAM discs, make sure to choose a model with DVD-RAM support. If you decide to install a DVD-ROM drive in addition to or instead of a DVD writer, choose a current model from ASUS, Lite-On, Pioneer, Samsung, or Teac.

Advice from Brian Bilbrey

DVD for faster read access...I don't agree. I *always* load the whole game onto disk. The only need for the DVD is to validate that I am allowed to run the game.

Mouse and Keyboard

If you plan to take your gaming PC on the road, you'll probably want two mice and two keyboards, one set for home and one for away.

Home mouse and keyboard

Logitech cordless mouse/corded keyboard (*http://www.logitech.com*)

At home, we use cordless mice and corded keyboards on most systems. We have tested numerous cordless mice from Logitech and Microsoft. We much prefer the design and feel of the Logitech models, particularly those that include a receiver that doubles as a recharging cradle. Logitech cordless keyboards have reasonably long battery life, but we use them only when cordlessness is really important, because swapping cordless keyboard batteries is a pain in the begonia.

We particularly dislike recent Microsoft cordless mice, whose scroll wheels make it too easy to click accidentally while scrolling. Also, although battery life in the recent Microsoft cordless mice we have used is reasonably good, keyboard battery life is terrible. (In one test, we exhausted a fresh set of three AA heavy-duty alkaline batteries in less than one day of constant use.)

As to a corded keyboard, choose whichever model feels best to you. Again, we generally prefer the design and feel of the Logitech models, but Microsoft also offers several very good corded keyboards.

Away mouse and keyboard

Logitech MX-series corded optical mouse (*http://www.logitech.com*)
Zippy EL-715 illuminated keyboard (*http://www.zippy.com.tw*)

We love the freedom of a cordless mouse for home use, but for away use corded devices are almost mandatory. Cordless keyboards and mice use radio frequency (RF) communications. Some provide an A-B switch to prevent conflicts by using different frequencies, but a choice of only two frequencies is wholly inadequate at a crowded LAN party. If you doubt that, just wait until the first time you watch the cursor moving across your screen in response to someone else's mouse movements. Until someone comes up with frequency-agile, stealthed cordless input devices, corded it is.

For a corded mouse, we prefer a Logitech MX-series optical mouse. The $25 six-button MX 310 can be used with either hand, and is precise enough for most gamers. The $35 eight-button MX 518 offers higher tracking resolution and is specifically designed for gaming (although it's also excellent for general use). The MX 518 is available only for right-handers.

Although your regular corded keyboard may serve for away use, it's worth considering a specialty keyboard designed for use on the road, particularly at LAN parties. Our favorite travel keyboard is the Zippy EL-715. The EL-715 is a medium-size, notebook-style, 105-key keyboard with electroluminescent backlighting that is quite useful at dimly-lit LAN parties. At just over a pound and about 0.75" thick, the EL-715 is extremely portable. We find it a bit too cramped to use as our primary keyboard, but it's unsurpassed as a portable LAN party keyboard. The blue backlighting is bright enough to see what you're doing, but not so bright that it becomes intrusive in a dimly lit environment.

Game Controllers

Choose your own

As with keyboards and mice, personal preference is the most important factor in selecting the best game controllers for your own needs. Cordless controllers are very nice for use at home or small LAN parties, but if you attend large LAN parties corded is the only way to go.

MAY THE FORCE BE WITH YOU

One downside to cordless models is that none we know of incorporates full force feedback, which apparently requires too much juice to run from batteries. The best cordless controllers can provide is limited vibration feedback. Full force feedback uses small motors within the game controller to provide tactile response to gaming actions. For example, as you maneuver your F-16 Falcon onto the six of a MiG-29 Fulcrum and begin hosing him down with your Vulcan rotary cannon, a force feedback joystick jitters and jerks to simulate recoil. Games that implement force feedback well are much more immersive than games that do not.

The first step is to decide which type or types of game controller you need, which is determined by the types of games you play. For example, we play mostly flight simulation and air combat games, so our primary controller is a joystick. For first-person shooter (FPS) games, most people consider a gamepad to be the optimum controller. For racing games, you'll want a wheel game controller. Although different types of controllers can substitute for each other to some extent, using an inappropriate game controller can put you at a severe disadvantage relative to players who are using controllers better suited to the type of game being played.

Once you determine which types of game controller you need, decide how to allocate your budget among them. If you regularly play games that require all three types of game controller, allocate your budget evenhandedly among them. That doesn't mean spending a third of your budget on each, because different types of controllers have different price points. It

---

ALTERNATIVES: MOUSE AND KEYBOARD

Thousands. Well, hundreds anyway. Personal preference is the most important factor in choosing a keyboard, mouse, game controller, display, or other I/O peripheral. What we hate you may love, and vice versa. For a cordless or corded mouse or keyboard, we suggest you try a Logitech model first. If you don't like it, exchange it for a similar model from Microsoft. If you want the best gaming mouse and are willing to pay a premium price, the $45 Logitech G5 Laser Mouse is the best choice we know of.

ALTERNATIVES: GAME CONTROLLERS

Many, some of which you'll love and some you'll hate. The trick is to figure out which is which before you pay for them. If you have no idea which controller(s) to buy, buy something inexpensive to start with and then try as many midrange and high-end controllers as you can get your hands on.

does mean you should buy all three high-end, all three midrange, or all three low-end, depending on your budget. When you play a racing game, for example, a $70 wheel controller is better than a $250 joystick. On the other hand, if you spend most of your time playing flight sims, play FPS games occasionally, and never play racing games, put most of your budget into the joystick, and spend whatever is left on a decent gamepad. And so on.

Before you buy a game controller, see if you can play with someone else's for at least a short session. If you ask nicely, most gamers are happy to let you try their rigs. Of course, the flipside is that if you do buy that $250 joystick, you can expect to be very popular at LAN parties.

Speakers and Headphones

Logitech Z-5500 5.1 speaker system (*http://www.logitech.com*)
Zalman ZM-RS6F 5.1 surround headphones (*http://www.zalman.co.kr*)

A gaming system needs good, high-power speakers, and the Logitech Z-5500 5.1 speaker system is the best we know of for the purpose. With four 62W RMS satellite speakers, a 69W center-channel speaker, and a 188W subwoofer, the Z-5500 produces a wall-rattling 505W RMS. You don't just *hear* the bass, you *feel* the bass vibrating your internal organs. Nor is the Z-680 limited to gaming. At lower volume, it's also excellent for anything from listening to background music to playing DVDs.

As nice as the Logitech Z-5500 is, it's overkill for a road trip, not to mention for playing games at home while the spousal unit is trying to sleep. For those situations, you need headphones, and the Zalman ZM-RSF6F 5.1 surround headphones are the best we know of for gaming. They're light, durable enough to stand up to LAN party use, fold up into a self-contained unit, and their 3-meter cord gives you plenty of slack to move around.

The Zalman headphones use three separate drivers per ear to produce a surround sound field comparable to that provided by a 5.1 speaker system. The importance of positional audio may not be apparent at first glance, but it can mean the difference between winning and losing. When you play an FPS, knowing where your opponents are is critical. Stereo headphones just don't cut it. By the time you figure out where shots are coming from, you're dead meat. The Zalman headphones make it easy to discriminate not just left and right but front and rear. The difference is amazing.

Display

Samsung 930BF 19" FPD (*http://www.samsung.com*)

In the first edition of this book, we specified two displays. For road trips, a CRT monitor was simply too bulky and heavy to take along. On the other hand, the flat-panel LCD displays of the time were too slow for gaming. So

If the $275 Z-5500 speaker set is a bit rich for your taste, consider the $125 Logitech Z-5300e 5.1 set. The Z-5300e has a combined RMS output of "only" 280W, but the sound quality is comparable to its more expensive sibling. If the Z-5300e is still beyond your budget, consider the $50 Logitech X-530 5.1 set. The combined output is a modest 70W RMS, and the sound quality is noticeably inferior to the better Logitech sets, but still reasonably good. (Ordinarily, we don't recommend inexpensive 5.1 speaker sets, but for gaming, support for surround sound deserves priority even at the expense of sound quality.)

We've found nothing we like nearly as much as Zalman ZM-RSF6F headphones for gaming. The bad news is that these are not general-purpose headphones. The bass is weak, although for gaming that is more than made up for by the excellent 3D imaging. Used for music and other stereo sources or for DVDs, the Zalman headphones boom and echo pretty badly. For general-purpose listening, buy a decent set of Grado or Sennheiser headphones.

we compromised, specifying a good CRT for use at home and a light, easily portable LCD display to take on the road.

Nowadays, although CRT monitors still have a few advantages—primarily low price and off-axis color fidelity—there's no real reason not to use an LCD display as the only display for a gaming system. Slow LCD display response time and the associated ghosting were the main problem with early LCD displays. Many current LCD display models are more than fast enough to use for gaming. Robert uses a 19" Samsung 930BF on his own system.

Table 5-1 summarizes our component choices for the gaming PC.

Table 5-1. Bill of materials for gaming PC

Component	Product
Case	Antec P150
Power supply	Antec NeoHE 430 (bundled with case)
Motherboard	ASUS M2N32-SLI Deluxe
Processor	AMD Athlon 64 X2 4200+
CPU cooler	AMD (bundled with processor)
Memory	Kingston KVR667D2N5K2/2G (two 1 GB PC2 5300 DDR2 DIMMs)
Video adapter	(See text)
Sound adapter	(Integrated)
Hard drive	Seagate Barracuda SATA 7200.9 (two 500 GB in RAID 0)
Optical drive	BenQ DW1650 DVD writer
Home mouse and keyboard	Logitech cordless mouse/corded keyboard
Away mouse	Logitech MX-series corded optical mouse
Away keyboard	Zippy EL-715 illuminated keyboard
Game controller(s)	(See text)
Speakers	Logitech Z-5500 5.1 speaker system
Headphones	Zalman ZM-RS6F surround headphones
Display	Samsung 930BF 19" LCD

ALTERNATIVES: DISPLAY

Any 17" or larger LCD display from NEC, Samsung, or ViewSonic that has response time fast enough to suit you. For most gaming, a 12ms BWB response time is adequate, and 8ms or faster ideal. For a 17" model, either VGA (analog) or DVI/HDMI (digital) input is sufficient. For 19" and larger models, we recommend digital input. (Make sure your video adapter provides an output that's compatible with the display you choose.)

Some models are available with built-in speakers. Although their sound quality isn't as good as standalone speakers, many LAN partiers choose one of these models to eliminate the need to carry separate speakers. You can always use the built-in speakers on the road and a better set of speakers at home. We prefer to use standalone speakers at home and headphones on the road.

Building the Gaming PC

Figure 5-1 shows the major components of the gaming PC. The Antec P150 case is flanked on the left by the nVIDIA video adapter, and on the right by the ASUS motherboard. In front, left to right, are the two 500 GB Seagate hard drives, the BenQ optical drive, the AMD CPU cooler, and the Kingston DDR2 memory modules. The Samsung display, Logitech speakers, and the other external peripherals are not shown.

Figure 5-1. Gaming PC components, awaiting construction

Before you start building the system, verify that all components are present and accounted for. We always remind readers to do that, but for some reason we often forget to do it ourselves.

Preparing the Case

To begin preparing the case, place the Antec P150 upright on the work surface and loosen the captive thumbscrews that secure the left side panel, as shown in Figure 5-2.

Figure 5-2. Loosen the thumbscrews that secure the left side panel

Sequencing the Build

Although by necessity we describe building the system in a particular order, you don't need to follow that exact sequence when you build your own system. Some steps—for example, installing the processor and memory before installing the motherboard in the case—should be taken in the sequence we describe, because doing otherwise makes the task more difficult or risks damaging a component. Other steps, such as installing the video adapter after you install the motherboard in the case, must be taken in the order we describe, because completing one step is a prerequisite for completing another. But the exact sequence doesn't matter for most steps. As you build your system, it will be obvious when sequence matters.

WARNING

Before you do anything else, check the back of the power supply to see if it has an input voltage switch. Auto-sensing power supplies (like the Antec NeoHE 430 we used) automatically detect the input voltage and set themselves for 120V or 240V operation. Other power supplies must be set manually for the correct input voltage. If you see a voltage switch, make sure it's set for the correct voltage.

If you connect a power supply set for 240V to a 120V receptacle, no harm is done. The PC components receive half the voltage they require, and the system won't boot. But if you connect a power supply set for 120V to a 240V receptacle, the PC components receive *twice* the voltage they're designed to use. If you power up the system, that overvoltage destroys the system instantly in clouds of smoke and showers of sparks.

Figure 5-3. Remove the left side panel and set it aside

Swing the rear of the panel away from the case, as shown in Figure 5-3, and lift it free. Place the side panel aside, where it won't be scratched.

You'll see a large plastic bag in the drive bay. This bag contains various cables and small parts. Antec apparently wants to make very sure that bag stays in place during shipping, because they secure it with a plastic cable tie. Use your diagonal cutters or a sharp knife to sever the cable tie, as shown in Figure 5-4. Remove the plastic bag from the drive bay and unseal it. Some of the parts you'll need right away. Others you'll need later, or not at all.

The front bezel of the case is held in place by three plastic tabs along the inside left-front edge of the chassis. Press each one of these tabs toward the outside of the case to unlatch the bezel, as shown in Figure 5-5.

Figure 5-4. Snip the cable tie that secures the plastic parts bag

Figure 5-5. Press the three locking tabs to unlatch the front bezel

With all three plastic tabs unlatched, the bezel is free to rotate. Swing the left side of the bezel away from the case until it is at about a 45° angle, as shown in Figure 5-6. Then lift the right side of the bezel straight up about an inch, as shown in Figure 5-7, and pull the bezel free from the case.

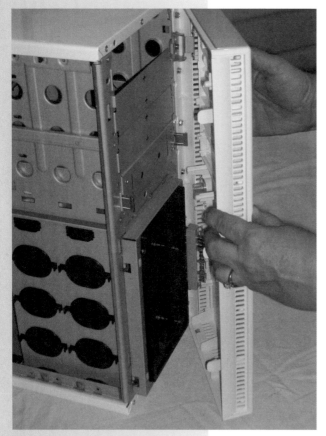

Figure 5-6. Swing the left side of the front bezel away from the chassis

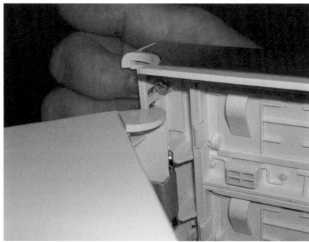

Figure 5-7. Lift the right side of the bezel up about an inch and then remove it

ADVICE FROM JIM COOLEY

DO NOT FORCE plastic bezels during removal because it's all too easy to break a latch or hinge mount. They are designed to be removed with a minimum of force, IF you are doing it correctly. If you have trouble, take a deep breath and examine the case more closely.

The NeoHE 430 power supply arrives installed in the P150 case. The NeoHE 430 uses Antec's patented cable management system. Only the main ATX power cable and the ATX12V power cable are permanently attached to the power supply. All other cables are optional, so you can install only the cables you need.

The optional power cables plug into one of the five proprietary 6-pin sockets on the power supply, as shown in Figure 5-8. Any of the optional cables can be connected to any of the sockets. Antec supplies three types of optional cables, which are stored in the large plastic bag you removed earlier:

1. Two cables with a 6-pin power supply plug on one end and two S-ATA power connectors on the other.
2. Two cables with a 6-pin power supply plug on one end and three Molex power connectors on the other.
3. One cable with a 6-pin power supply plug on one end and a 6-pin PCI Express power connector on the other.

Antec also provides a short Y-adapter cable that connects to a Molex (hard drive) power connector on one end and provides two Berg (floppy drive) power connectors on the other. We had no need of that adapter, because we didn't install a floppy drive or any other component that uses the Berg connector in our gaming PC.

Our system requires one of each type of cable. The two S-ATA Seagate hard drives will receive power from one of the optional S-ATA power cables. The optical drive and rear case fan will receive power from one of the optional Molex power cables. The video adapter requires supplemental power, which it receives from the optional PCI Express power cable. We connected those three cables, as shown in Figure 5-8, leaving two of the proprietary 6-pin power supply connectors unused.

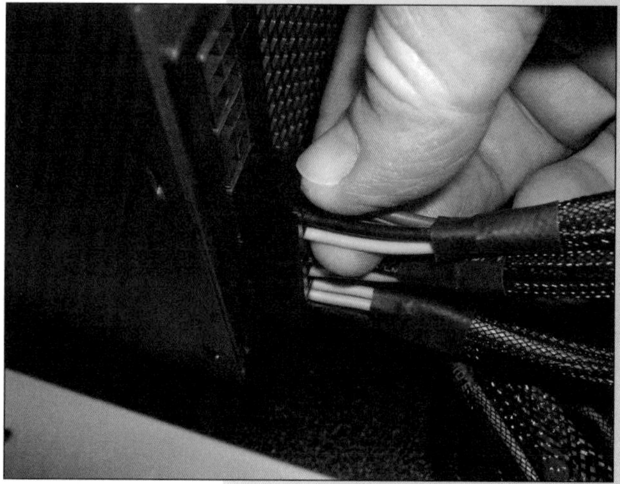

Figure 5-8. Connect the optional cables to the power supply

ADVICE FROM JIM COOLEY

Always get a couple spare cables (they're cheap) and leave one in the case if there's any chance you'll add another HD at some point down the road. Ditto for SATA adapter cables. There's nothing more infuriating than getting a new drive and not being able to install it at 11 P.M. on a Saturday night.

More Cables

If we add one or two hard drives later, we'll install the second S-ATA power cable, which gives us two more S-ATA power connectors. Antec sells these optional power cables separately, so we could install as many as six S-ATA hard drives in this system if we ordered a third S-ATA power cable. Actually, we could install as many as eight hard drives by using the 3-connector Molex cables with Molex-to-SATA adapters.

Also, although Antec doesn't claim SLI compatibility for the NeoHE 430 power supply, we might use it to power two PCI Express video adapters by buying a second PCI Express power cable. If we did that, we'd have to be very careful to choose a pair of video cards that had relatively low current draw to keep within the current limits of the NeoHE 430.

Like nearly all cases, the Antec P150 comes with a generic back-panel I/O template installed. As usual, this generic template doesn't match the back-panel I/O ports on the motherboard, so the next step is to remove that template. The template installed in our case was wedged in very tightly. We eventually were able to pop it out using a screwdriver handle. Start in one corner, and be careful not to hurt yourself if the template suddenly pops free. The template is thin metal and has sharp edges.

We didn't bend the template, but it was a near thing. Of course, it's not really the generic template we're concerned about. We have stacks of generic templates in a box in our workroom. (Robert never throws anything out.) But that template was well and truly stuck, and we were worried that we might bend the edge of the template cutout in the case. Fortunately, with a bit of patience we were able to remove the generic template without damaging the case.

With the original template removed, the next step is to install the custom back-panel I/O template that's supplied with the motherboard. Before you do that, verify that the holes in the custom template match the ports on the motherboard I/O panel. Although it's rare, we have seen custom templates that don't match the motherboard they were supplied with. Once you've verified that you have the correct I/O template, install it in the template cutout in the case, working from inside the case. Align the template with the cutout and use a screwdriver handle to press gently along the edges and corners until it snaps into place, as shown in Figure 5-9.

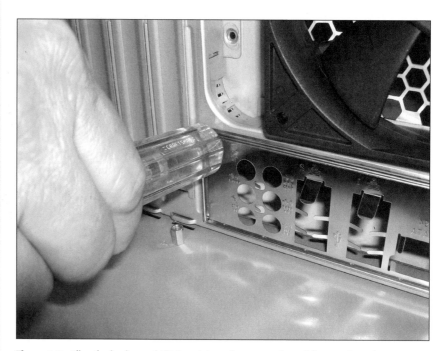

Figure 5-9. Align the back-panel I/O template and press gently until it snaps into place

The next step is to install brass standoffs in the case to support the motherboard once it is installed. Examine the motherboard to locate all of the mounting holes. It's easy to miss a mounting hole or two in all the clutter on a typical motherboard, so we generally hold the motherboard up to a bright light, which makes the mounting holes stand out.

Once you've located all the mounting holes (the ASUS M2N32-SLI Deluxe motherboard has nine), you need to make sure that standoffs are installed in each corresponding position on the motherboard tray. The easiest way to check this is to hold the motherboard in position above the case, as shown in Figure 5-10, and look straight down through each mounting hole to determine which motherboard screw holes should receive standoffs.

What's All That Copper?

That structure of copper pipes and fins that extends from near the rear I/O panel around the processor socket and toward the front edge of the motherboard is the ASUS Stack Cool 2, their unique solution to cooling the chipset and other heat-generating motherboard components. Unlike most high-end motherboards, which use active cooling (noisy fans), ASUS designed a completely passive cooling solution using heatpipes and copper radiators.

This passive cooling solution is very effective, and of course completely silent. It's also reliable, in the sense that there are no moving parts to fail. More than one owner of a motherboard with chipset cooling fans has had to replace that motherboard because a fan failed and the chipset burnt itself to a crisp. That's not possible with this passive cooling system.

Figure 5-10. Hold the motherboard above the case to determine where standoffs should be installed

The Antec P150 case comes with four standoffs installed, all of which correspond to mounting holes in the ASUS M2N32-SLI Deluxe motherboard. That means we need to install five more standoffs in the vacant positions that match the mounting holes in the motherboard.

Locate the plastic parts bag that contained the power supply cables you installed earlier. You'll find a small plastic bag with screws, standoffs, and other small parts. Set aside the five standoffs you'll need to install. While you're at it, locate nine motherboard mounting screws and set them aside as well. (You can verify you have the right screws by temporarily inserting one into a standoff.)

Figure 5-11. Install standoffs in each mounting position required by the motherboard

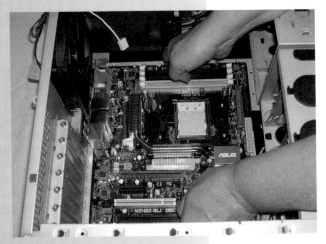

Figure 5-12. Verify that every mounting hole has a standoff and that no extra standoffs are installed

Install the five additional standoffs into the positions you determined earlier. You can use your fingers to install the standoffs, but using a 5mm nutdriver as shown in Figure 5-11 makes the job much easier. If you do use a nutdriver, be careful not to apply too much torque. The standoffs are made of soft brass that is easily stripped. Tighten the standoffs only finger-tight.

After you've installed the standoffs, temporarily slide the motherboard into position, as shown in Figure 5-12. Make sure that there's a standoff visible under each mounting hole, and that no extra standoffs are installed. After you've done that, remove the motherboard and set it on your work surface.

ADVICE FROM JIM COOLEY

Make sure the standoffs are tight enough that you won't unscrew them along with the motherboard screws if you ever remove the motherboard.

Populating the Motherboard

It is always easier to populate the motherboard—install the processor and memory—while the motherboard is outside the case. In fact, you must do so with some systems, because installing the heatsink/fan unit requires access to both sides of the motherboard. Even if it is possible to populate the motherboard while it is installed in the case, we always recommend doing so with the motherboard outside the case and lying flat on the work surface. More than once, we've tried to save a few minutes by replacing the processor without removing the motherboard. Too often, the result has been bent pins and a destroyed processor.

Installing the processor

To install the Athlon 64 X2 processor, lift the ZIF (zero insertion force) lever until it reaches vertical. With the arm vertical, there is no clamping force on the socket holes, which allows the processor to drop into place without requiring any pressure.

Pin 1 is indicated on the processor and socket by small triangles. With the socket lever vertical, align pin 1 of the processor with pin 1 of the socket and drop the processor into place, as shown in Figure 5-13. The processor should seat flush with the socket just from the force of gravity, or perhaps with very gentle pressure. If the processor resists being seated, something is misaligned. Remove the processor and verify that it is aligned properly and that the pattern of pins on the processor corresponds to the pattern of holes on the socket. **Never** force the processor to seat. You'll bend one or more pins, destroying the processor.

Figure 5-13. Drop the processor into the socket

With the processor in place and seated flush with the socket, press the lever arm down and snap it into place, as shown in Figure 5-14. You may have to press the lever arm slightly away from the socket to allow it to snap into a locked position.

When Pressure Is Good

Sometimes closing the ZIF lever lifts the processor slightly out of the socket. It does no harm (once the processor is already fully seated) to use gentle pressure to keep it in place as you close the ZIF lever.

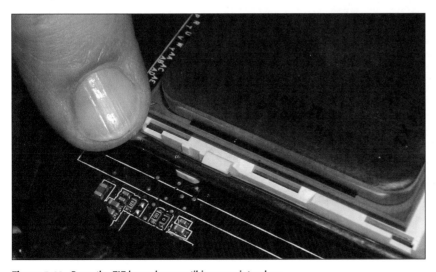

Figure 5-14. Press the ZIF lever down until in snaps into place

Installing the CPU cooler

Current processors draw from 30 W to 130 W of power. Our Athlon 64 X2 4200+ processor is just below the middle of that range, so it produces about as much heat as a 60W incandescent light bulb. The processor must dissipate that heat over the surface of its heat spreader, which is about the size of a large postage stamp. Without a good CPU cooler, the processor would almost instantaneously shut itself down to prevent damage from overheating.

We used the stock AMD cooler included with the retail-boxed Athlon 64 processor, which is reasonably efficient and as quiet as any but the best aftermarket coolers. If you install a third-party cooler, make absolutely certain it is rated for the exact processor model you use and follow the installation instructions included with the cooler.

To install the stock AMD CPU cooler, begin by removing the plastic cover from the base of the heatsink, as shown in Figure 5-15. (We verified that it is possible to install the CPU cooler with the plastic cover still in place, but of course it won't function properly that way.)

Polish the heat spreader surface on top of the processor with a paper towel or soft cloth, as shown in Figure 5-16. The goal is to remove any grease, grit, or other material that might prevent the heatsink from making intimate contact with the processor surface.

Figure 5-15. Remove the plastic cover from the heatsink base

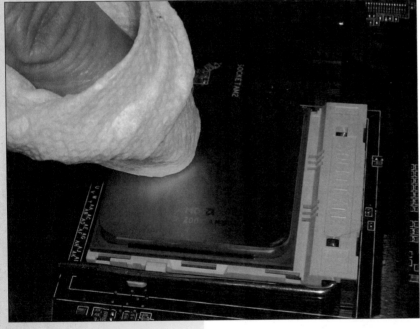

Figure 5-16. Polish the CPU heat spreader to remove skin oil and other foreign material

WARNING

If you're using a third-party CPU cooler, also check the base of the heatsink. If the heatsink base is bare, that means it's intended to be used with thermal compound, usually called "thermal goop." In that case, also polish the heatsink base. Some heatsinks, including our stock AMD model, have a square pad made of a phase-change medium, which is a fancy term for a material that melts as the CPU heats and resolidifies as the CPU cools. This liquid/solid cycle ensures that the processor die maintains good thermal contact with the heatsink If your heatsink includes such a pad you needn't polish the base of the heatsink. (Heatsinks use *either* a thermal pad *or* thermal goop, not both.)

The CPU cooler secures to the socket by two spring steel retention brackets, one on either side of the heatsink. One of those brackets floats freely, and the other is linked to a camming lever that is used to lock the CPU cooler in place.

Position the free-floating retention bracket over the plastic nub on one side of the black plastic retention module base, as shown in Figure 5-17. (The CPU cooler can be mounted in either direction. We generally connect the free-floating bracket to the side of the retention module base nearer the center of the motherboard, which is usually more cramped for space.)

With the first retention bracket in position, make sure the cammed locking lever on the other bracket is in the fully open position shown in Figure 5-18 (rotated fully counterclockwise as you face it). Press the second bracket into position over the plastic nub on the retention module base. You may have to press down on the CPU cooler with one hand while guiding the bracket into position with the other.

Backward Compatibility

The new AM2 socket uses the same retention-clip CPU cooler mounting arrangement as the older Socket 939, so nearly any third-party retention-clip CPU cooler designed for Socket 939 can also be installed on a Socket AM2 motherboard.

That's not true of Socket 939 coolers that mount with screws rather than the retention clips. Socket 939 uses a two-screw retention bracket versus the four-screw arrangement used for Socket AM2, so a Socket 939 screw-mount CPU cooler won't fit a Socket AM2 motherboard.

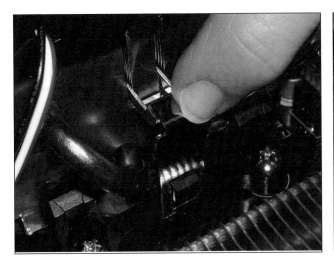

Figure 5-17. Position the free-floating retention bracket over the plastic nub on the retention module base

Figure 5-18. Position the latching retention bracket over the plastic nub on the retention module base

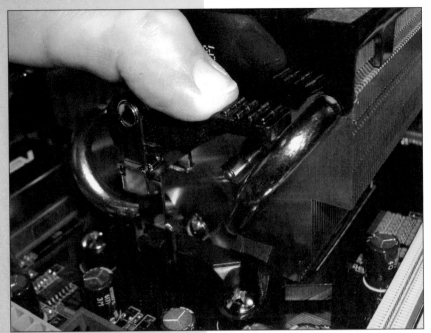

Figure 5-19. Rotate the latching lever and press down firmly until it locks into place

Figure 5-20. Connect the CPU fan power lead to the CPU fan power header on the motherboard

Verify that both sides of the retention bracket are in position, and then pivot the cammed locking lever fully clockwise into the locked position, as shown in Figure 5-19. It takes significant pressure to lock this lever, so be prepared to press firmly if necessary.

The thermal mass of the heatsink draws heat away from the CPU, but the heat must be dissipated to prevent the CPU from eventually overheating as the heatsink warms up. To dispose of excess heat as it is transferred to the heatsink, most CPU coolers, including this one, use a fan to continuously draw air through the fins of the heatsink. Some CPU fans use a drive power connector, but most are designed to attach to a dedicated CPU fan connector on the motherboard. Using a motherboard fan power connector allows the motherboard to control the CPU fan, reducing speed for quieter operation when the processor is running under light load and not generating much heat, and increasing fan speed when the processor is running under heavy load and generating more heat. The motherboard can also monitor fan speed, which allows it to send an alert to the user if the fan fails or begins running sporadically.

To connect the CPU fan, locate the 4-pin header connector on the motherboard labeled CPU Fan, and plug the keyed 3-pin cable from the CPU fan into that connector, as shown in Figure 5-20. (The newer-style 4-pin CPU fan connector on the ASUS motherboard is backward compatible in pin assignments and keying with 3-pin fans.)

WARNING

If you ever remove the CPU cooler, don't reuse the old thermal compound or pad when you reinstall it. Remove all remnants of the old thermal compound or pad, using a hair dryer or solvent if necessary, and reapply new thermal compound before you reinstall the heatsink.

Installing memory

The Athlon 64 X2 processor includes an embedded dual-channel memory controller that provides better memory performance than a single-channel controller. You must take care when installing memory, though. The system defaults to single-channel memory operation unless you install memory modules in pairs in the proper slots.

The ASUS M2N32-SLI Deluxe motherboard makes it hard to go wrong. The motherboard has four DDR2 memory slots in two color-coded pairs. If you're installing one matched pair of DIMMs, as we are, they both go in the yellow memory slots. If you add memory later, install another matched pair of DIMMs (which may differ in speed or capacity from the first pair) in the black memory slots.

To install a DIMM, pivot the locking tabs on both sides of the DIMM socket outward. Align the DIMM, as shown in Figure 5-21, making sure that the keying notch in the DIMM is oriented properly with the keying tab in the slot.

Once the DIMM is aligned and vertical relative to the slot, use both thumbs to press down firmly until the DIMM seats, as shown in Figure 5-22. When the DIMM seats, both locking tabs should automatically pivot back into the locked position, engaging the notches in the side of the DIMM. If the tabs don't fully engage the notches, press the tabs into place manually. Install the second DIMM in the other yellow slot in the same manner.

It may take significant pressure to seat a DIMM, depending on the combination of the particular modules you install and the slot. The combination of the ASUS M2N32-SLI Deluxe motherboard and the Kingston DDR2 memory modules proved to be a very tight fit.

When you seat the memory modules, make certain you are pressing straight down on them. Any sideways force may damage the module or the socket. DIMMs that are difficult to seat are one reason we always install memory with the motherboard outside the case and resting on a firm, flat surface. We have seen more than one motherboard cracked when a technician who was in too much of a hurry to remove the motherboard attempted to install memory modules with the motherboard still in the case.

Figure 5-21. Align the keying notch and slide the first memory module into the slot

Figure 5-22. Press down firmly with both thumbs until the memory module seats completely

It's very important to make absolutely sure that the memory modules are fully seated. If necessary, use a strong light and a magnifier to examine the junction between the module and the slot to verify that the module is fully and evenly seated. Partially seated memory modules can cause very subtle problems that are difficult to troubleshoot. Also, although we have never seen it ourselves, we have read credible reports of motherboards being damaged when they were powered on with a memory module only partially seated.

ADVICE FROM JIM COOLEY

I still prefer to make certain I have the notch lined up, then partially insert one side and then the other, then seat the whole module by firmly pressing down on both ends simultaneously. It's often a really tight fit, and this method avoids using too much pressure, which can be considerable if you do the whole module at once.

Installing the Motherboard

Installing the motherboard is the most time-consuming step in building the system because there are so many cables to connect. It's important to get all of them connected right, so take your time and verify each connection before and after you make it.

Seating and securing the motherboard

Figure 5-23. Slide the motherboard into position

To begin, slide the motherboard into the case, as shown in Figure 5-23. Carefully align the back-panel I/O connectors with the corresponding holes in the I/O template, and slide the motherboard toward the rear of the case until the motherboard mounting holes line up with the standoffs you installed earlier.

It's helpful to keep the front edge of the motherboard slightly raised as you slide the motherboard into position. As the back-panel I/O connectors on the motherboard come into contact with the back-panel I/O template, lower the front edge of the motherboard until the motherboard is level and then press gently to seat the back-panel ports in the template. In theory, at least, this prevents the metal grounding tabs on the I/O template from intruding into the ports.

Before you secure the motherboard, verify that the back-panel I/O connectors mate properly with the I/O template. Make sure none of the grounding tabs intrude into a port connector. An errant tab at best blocks the port, rendering it unusable, and at worst may short out the motherboard.

After you position the motherboard and verify that the back-panel I/O connectors mate cleanly with the I/O template, insert a screw through one mounting hole into the corresponding standoff. You may need to apply pressure to keep the motherboard positioned properly until you have inserted two or three screws.

If you have trouble getting all the holes and standoffs aligned, insert two screws but don't tighten them completely. Use one hand to press the motherboard into alignment, with all holes matching the standoffs. Then insert one or two more screws and tighten them completely. Finish mounting the motherboard by inserting screws into all standoffs and tightening them, as shown in Figure 5-24.

Chicken and Egg

It may be easier to connect the front-panel switch/indicator and port cables before you install the motherboard in the case. The trade-off is that if you install the motherboard first, you have plenty of cable length, but the pins you must connect those cables to are deep in the case and hard to get to. If you install the cables first, the pins are more easily accessible, but you have very little cable slack to work with, both when you connect the cables and when you slide the motherboard into the case. We generally install the motherboard first and worry later about getting all the cables connected.

Figure 5-24. Install screws in all nine mounting holes to secure the motherboard

WARNING

When you install motherboard mounting screws, you're also putting torque on the standoffs. Tighten the motherboard screws gently, using a standard screwdriver. When you feel tension, stop turning the driver. If you overtorque the mounting screws, you're also overtorquing the standoffs, which may strip. Don't even think about using a power screwdriver with an *aluminum* case.

Figure 5-25. Everything looked fine at first glance...

Figure 5-26. ...but two ports were fouled by grounding tabs...

Before we installed the motherboard screws, we took a quick glance at the rear I/O panel, shown in Figure 5-25, to make sure that none of the metal ground tabs were protruding into ports. At first glance, everything looked fine, so we installed all nine motherboard screws.

After we finished securing the motherboard, we planned to shoot an image of the rear I/O panel to show that none of the grounding tabs were obstructing ports. Ruh-roh. When we got down to shoot a close-up, we were surprised to see that both Gigabit Ethernet ports were obstructed, as shown in Figure 5-26. Although the grounding tabs weren't contacting any of the pins in the ports and so wouldn't cause a short circuit, the tabs made it impossible to connect a cable to either Ethernet port.

If we'd been building this system for someone else (or if we weren't on a short deadline), we'd have removed the nine motherboard screws, pulled the motherboard, and started over. But this system was for us, and we had only a few days left until deadline, so we decided to use the quick-and-dirty method shown in Figure 5-27. Barbara carefully inserted a small flat-blade screwdriver under each of the problem grounding tabs, and bent them outward to clear the ports.

Figure 5-27. ...so we used a small flat-blade screwdriver carefully to bend the grounding tabs out of the way

Connecting front-panel switch and indicator cables

Once the motherboard is secured, the next step is to connect the front-panel switch and indicator cables to the motherboard. Before you begin connecting front-panel cables, examine the cables. Each is labeled descriptively, such as "Power SW" and "Reset SW" on the connector body. Match the descriptions with the front-panel connector pins on the motherboard to make sure you connect the correct cable to the appropriate pins. Figure 5-28 shows the pin assignments for the ASUS M32N32-SLI Deluxe motherboard front-panel switch/indicator connector, which is located on the left-rfront corner of the motherboard.

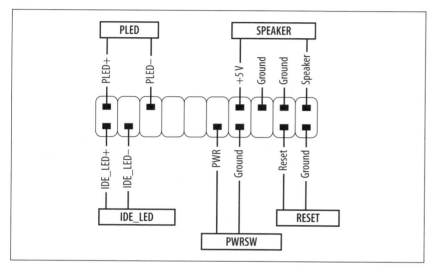

Figure 5-28. M2N32-SLI Deluxe front-panel connector pin assignments (graphic courtesy ASUSTeK Computer, Inc.)

- The power switch (PWRSW) and reset switch (RESET) connectors are not polarized, and can be connected in either orientation.

- The hard drive activity LED (IDE_LED) is polarized, and should be connected with the ground (white) wire to the pin labeled IDE_LED− on the connector.

BLACK AND WHITE

Conventionally, the ground/common connection uses a black wire. For some reason, Antec uses a white wire for ground/common (−) and a colored wire for the signal (+) lead.

- The power LED (PLED) connector uses two contacts in a 3-pin connector. Insert this cable with the white wire on the pin labeled PLED− on the motherboard.

ASUS Q-Connector

Retail versions of the ASUS M2N32-SLI Deluxe motherboard include ASUS Q-Connector blocks for the front-panel switch/indicator, USB, and FireWire cables. These blocks are small color-coded plastic devices that on one side have pins to accept the individual 2- and 3-pin connectors for the front-panel switches, indicators, and ports. The opposite side of the Q-Connector blocks have holes that match the appropriate sets of header pins on the ASUS motherboard. The Q-Connector converts the many individual front-panel connectors into one monolithic connector block. We used an engineering sample motherboard for this system, which did not include the Q-Connector blocks.

We regretted the lack of Q-Connector blocks only while we were installing the front-panel switch/indicator cables, for which the Antec P150 case provides individual 2- and 3-pin connectors. The Antec P150 case provides Intel-standard monolithic connector blocks for the front-panel USB, FireWire, and Audio cables. The ASUS motherboard uses the same Intel-standard pin assignments and keying for those cables.

Once you determine the proper orientation for each cable, connect the power switch, reset switch, power LED, hard drive activity LED, and speaker cables, as shown in Figure 5-29. When you're connecting front panel cables, try to get it right the first time, but don't worry too much about getting it wrong. Other than the power switch cable, which must be connected properly for the system to start, none of the other front-panel switch and indicator cables is essential, and connecting them wrong won't damage the system. LED cables may or may not be polarized, but if you connect a polarized LED cable backward the worst that happens is that the LED won't light.

Figure 5-29. Connect the front-panel switch and indicator cables

---

TRANSGENDERED CONNECTORS

The usual practice is to refer to the connector on the end of a cable as a plug, and the connector on a motherboard or device as a jack. Historically, plugs have been male (such as the plug on the end of a lamp cord) and jacks have been female (such as a standard electrical receptacle). Some computer connectors ignore that convention, instead using female plugs and male jacks. Alternatively, you can think of it as placing the jack on the cable and the plug on the device.

Connecting the front-panel USB ports

The Antec P150 case provides two front-panel USB ports. Both of those ports share one cable, which terminates in an Intel-standard 10-pin USB dual-port connector. The ASUS M2N32-SLI Deluxe motherboard provides three sets of USB dual-port connector pins, for a total of six USB ports in addition to the four USB ports on the back-panel I/O connector. (The motherboard we used for this system is the M2N32-SLI Deluxe Standard Edition; the M2N32-SLI Deluxe Wireless Edition has only two sets of dual USB connectors.)

To enable the front-panel USB ports, locate the cable coming from the front panel that terminates in a black 10-pin 5X2 connector labeled USB. Plug that cable into either of the shrouded blue plastic USB connectors near the left-rear edge of the motherboard, as shown in Figure 5-30. The connection is keyed with a blocked hole on the cable and a missing pin on the motherboard connector, so be careful to orient the connectors properly before applying pressure.

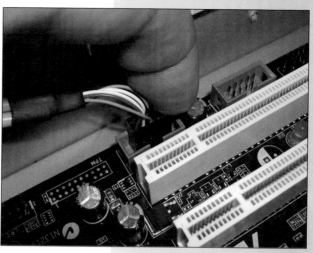

Figure 5-30. Plug the front-panel USB cable into a motherboard USB jack

---

WARNING

The USB and FireWire connectors on the ASUS M2N32-SLI Deluxe motherboard are shrouded and keyed. Some cases and port extender cables have oversize keyed connectors, which shrouded motherboard connectors must be large enough to accept. (If the motherboard uses bare header pins, any connector will fit as long as the pin keying is correct). Antec uses simple block connectors for its front-panel USB and FireWire cables, which means there's extra space in the shrouded motherboard connectors, as shown in Figures 5-30 and 5-32. When you connect the front-panel USB and FireWire cables, be careful to orient the cable connector correctly and not to offset the connector by one set of pins.

Advice from Jim Cooley

If your case has individual wires, bundling them with a cable tie to combine them into one connector block makes it much easier to get all of the wires connected.

The front-panel USB ports use one of the three available sets of internal USB dual-port connectors, leaving two of those connectors free for other purposes, such as connecting a card reader or USB floppy drive. ASUS provides a dual-port USB port extender, shown in Figure 5-31, which you can use to extend one dual USB port to an expansion slot cover on the back panel. To install the port extender, simply remove an expansion slot cover and connect the cliffhanger bracket as you would a standard expansion card, then connect the cable to one of the motherboard USB connectors.

You can purchase a second USB port extender from ASUS or another supplier to reach a total of ten USB ports, eight rear and two front. We decided that the standard four rear USB ports and two front USB ports were sufficient for our purposes, so we left two of the dual-USB internal connectors free for future use.

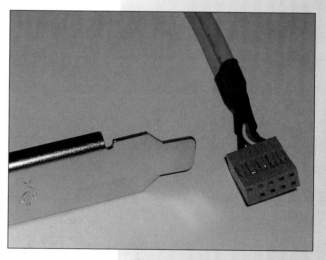

Figure 5-31. The USB port extender (note blocked hole at lower left of blue connector)

Connecting the front-panel IEEE-1394a (FireWire) port

The Antec P150 case provides one front-panel IEEE-1394a port, with a cable that terminates in an Intel-standard 10-pin IEEE-1394a connector block. The ASUS M2N32-SLI Deluxe motherboard provides one IEEE1394a connector on the rear I/O panel and an internal FireWire connector that can be routed to the front or rear panel.

To enable the front-panel FireWire port, locate the cable coming from the front panel that terminates in a black 10-pin 5X2 connector labeled IEEE-1394. Plug that cable into the shrouded red plastic IEEE-1394 connector near the left-rear edge of the motherboard, as shown in Figure 5-32. The connection is keyed with a blocked hole on the cable and a missing pin on the motherboard connector, so be careful to orient the connectors properly before applying pressure.

If you'd rather route the second FireWire port to the rear of the case, use the FireWire port extender that is included with the motherboard, shown in Figure 5-33. To install the port extender, remove an expansion slot cover and connect the cliffhanger bracket as you would a standard expansion card, then connect the cable to the motherboard FireWire connector.

Figure 5-32. Plug the front-panel FireWire cable into the motherboard FireWire jack

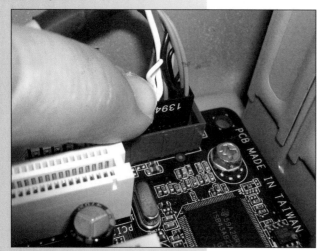

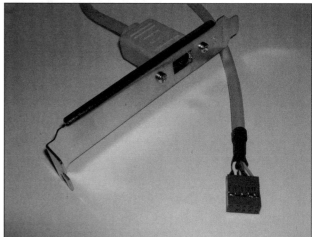

Figure 5-33. The FireWire port extender

Connecting the front-panel audio ports

The Antec P150 case provides front-panel audio-in and audio-out connectors, with a cable that terminates in an Intel-standard 10-pin audio connector block. The ASUS M2N32-SLI Deluxe motherboard provides a full set of audio connectors on the back panel and an internal audio connector that can be routed to the front panel.

To enable the front-panel audio ports, locate the cable coming from the front panel that terminates in a black 10-pin 5X2 connector labeled Audio. Plug that cable into the black front-panel audio connector near the center PCI expansion slot, as shown in Figure 5-34. The connection is keyed with a blocked hole on the cable and a missing pin on the motherboard connector, so be careful to orient the connectors properly before applying pressure.

Figure 5-34. Plug the front-panel audio cable into the motherboard audio jack

Installing the Optical Drive

The next step is to install the optical drive. The upper two 5.25" drive bays in the Antec P150 case include a universal drive door that conceals the front bezel of the optical drive. That means you can use any color of optical drive without the mismatch being visible. That's fortunate, because the gloss-white surface of the P150 bezel is very difficult to match with an off-the-shelf optical drive. We used a standard black optical drive for our system.

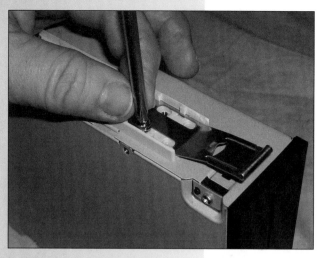

Figure 5-35. Install drive rails on the optical drive

Figure 5-36. Connect the ATA cable to the optical drive

To begin installing the optical drive, locate a pair of the drive rails shown in Figure 5-35. If you are installing the optical drive in one of the bays with a universal drive door, use the rear set of screw holes. If you are installing the drive in a lower bay, use the front set of screw holes. (Using the rear set recesses the drive slightly, making room for the universal drive door; using the front set puts the drive flush with the front bezel of the P150.)

Although there are four screw holes available for each drive rail, using two screws per rail is sufficient. We generally insert the front screw in the lower hole and the rear screw in the upper hole, but any arrangement with one screw in a front hole and one in a back hole works as well.

The screw holes in the drive rails are slightly oblong, providing a couple millimeters of slack. This is done to allow you to adjust the drive seating depth slightly to make sure that the pass-through button on the universal drive door can successfully operate the eject button on the actual drive bezel. We centered the screws in the screw holes, and found that they work fine with the BenQ DW1650 optical drive. If you use a different optical drive, you may have to play with the seating depth a bit to get the eject button to work properly.

With the drive rails mounted, slide the drive at least partway into the bay to verify that the rails are installed properly for correct vertical alignment of the drive in the bay. The next step is to install the ATA cable. ASUS supplies an 80-wire UltraATA cable intended for use with a hard drive. Our hard drives are both Serial ATA, so we used this cable for our optical drive. (A 40-wire ATA cable is sufficient for an optical drive, but it does no harm to use the 80-wire cable.)

Align the keying tab on the cable with the keying notch on the drive, and press firmly to seat the cable in the connector on the drive (Figure 5-36). If you are using an unkeyed ATA cable, make sure that pin 1 on the cable connector, indicated by a color stripe on the cable, is aligned with Pin 1 on the drive connector, which is nearly always toward the power connector on the drive.

To install the drive in the case, feed the loose end of the ATA cable into the drive bay and then slide the drive partially into the bay, making sure that both drive rails are aligned with the matching slots in the case body. Place your thumbs on either side of the drive bezel and press firmly until the drive slides fully into the bay, as shown in Figure 5-37. When the drive seats, the drive rails snap into the locked position.

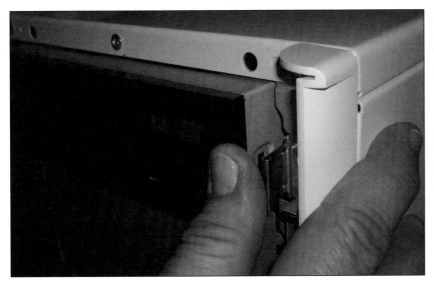

Figure 5-37. Slide the drive into the bay and press firmly to snap the drive rails into the locked position

Feed the loose end of the ATA cable down toward the front edge of the motherboard. Keeping it clear of other cables will make your job easier during the final assembly steps when you neaten up the cables. Align the cable connector with the shrouded ATA connector on the motherboard, making sure that the keying tab on the cable connector is oriented properly with the keying notch on the motherboard connector. Press the ATA cable firmly into place, as shown in Figure 5-38, until it fully seats in the motherboard connector.

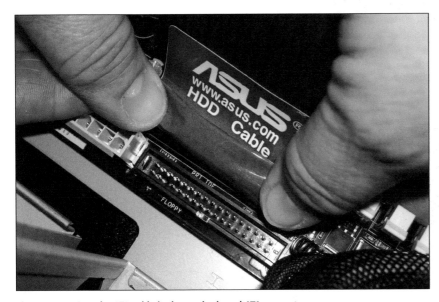

Figure 5-38. Seat the ATA cable in the motherboard ATA connector

Master and Slave

With standard (parallel) ATA devices, it's necessary to set a jumper to configure the device as the master (first) or slave (second) device on the channel. If only one device is connected to the cable, it should be set as master. The optical drive is the only ATA device in our gaming PC, so we'll make sure it's configured as the master device.

Some optical drives are set by default as master, and others as slave. As it happens, our BenQ DW1650 optical drive arrived from the factory jumpered as master, so we didn't need to change the setting. If you use a different model of optical drive, verify that it is set as master before you install it. If it is set as slave, simply move the jumper to the master position. Most optical drives have a figure illustrating the positions for master and slave settings printed on the drive label or stamped into the metal body of the drive itself.

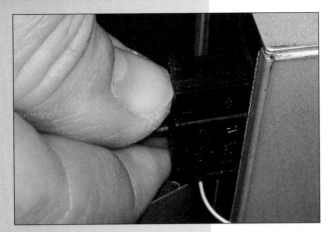

Figure 5-39. Connect power to the optical drive

Figure 5-40. Connect the ATX12V power cable

Figure 5-41. Connect the main ATX power cable

Locate the Molex power cable you installed earlier on the power supply. Again, make sure you route that cable to avoid other cables as much as possible, and then press one of the Molex connectors into the power connector on the back of the optical drive, as shown in Figure 5-39. The Molex connector is keyed with two beveled corners on one side of the connector. Those beveled edges match similar bevels on the upper side of the drive power connector. Once you're sure the connectors are aligned properly, press firmly to seat the power cable in the drive connector.

Connecting the ATX Power Cables

Ordinarily, we connect the two ATX power cables to the motherboard as one of the final assembly steps. With this motherboard and case, it's easier to make those connections before the hard drives or video adapter is installed.

The ASUS M2N32-SLI Deluxe motherboard has what we consider to be an almost ideal component layout. All of the connectors are well-placed and easily accessible, with one exception. The ATX12V supplemental power connector, shown in Figure 5-40, is so close to the blue PCI Express video card slot that it's very difficult to install the ATX12V cable with a video card already installed.

Locate the ATX12V cable, which is one of the two cables that are permanently attached to the power supply. The ATX12V cable connector and the corresponding motherboard jack are keyed using square and beveled holes. Orient the cable connector properly against the ATX12V socket, as shown in Figure 5-40, and press the cable connector firmly until it seats completely in the socket. When the cable is fully seated, the latch visible in Figure 5-40 snaps over a projection on the socket, locking the cable in place.

The next step is to connect the 24-pin main ATX power cable, as shown in Figure 5-41. Align the cable connector with the socket, making sure that the latch on the cable connector is toward the front of the system. Press down firmly until the cable connector seats fully in the socket and the latch snaps into place. Make sure to complete this step before you install the hard drives, which obstruct access to the main ATX power socket.

Installing the Hard Drives

We're in the home stretch now. All that remains is to install the hard drives and video adapter and do a bit of cleanup. The first step in installing the hard drives is to loosen the two front-panel thumbscrews that secure the door that covers the hard drive bays, as shown in Figure 5-42.

Swing the hard drive bay door open, as shown in Figure 5-43. With the door open, the mounting arrangements are clearly visible. The Antec P150 provides two methods for mounting hard drives. (Antec cautions to use one or the other, but not both.)

Four drive trays are visible, each secured by a pair of drive rails similar to those used to mount the optical drive. The first, and more traditional, mounting method is to secure the hard drives to those trays using screws. Antec provides soft silicone shock-mount pads, visible as the small circular white items in Figure 5-43, that isolate the drive physically from the case structure, minimizing the transfer of vibration and sound from the drive to the case.

Figure 5-42. Loosen the two thumbscrews that secure the hard drive bay door

The second mounting method, popular among quiet PC enthusiasts, is to use suspension mounting. Antec provides elastic bands, visible just below the front edge of each of the top three drive trays, for those who want to use this method. (If you use suspension mounting, you can install only three hard drives instead of four.)

The advantage of suspension mounting is that it is the best way to minimize hard drive noise. The disadvantage is that the hard drives are not securely connected to the case. If the system is moved, the drives may escape their mountings and rattle around inside the case, damaging the drives and other system components.

Figure 5-43. Swing open the hard drive bay door

BELT AND SUSPENDERS

Our friend and colleague Jerry Pournelle built a similar system in an Antec P150 case, which he carries to and from his beach house. Jerry opted for suspension mounting despite the fact that he hauls this system around in the back of his SUV. His solution is to open the case each time he transports the system and stuff the drive bays full of bubble-wrap packaging, which protects the drives during transport. Needless to say, forgetting to install the bubble wrap might have catastrophic consequences, as might forgetting to remove it when he reaches his destination. Still, he seems happy with the arrangement.

Figure 5-44. Remove the hard drive bay door

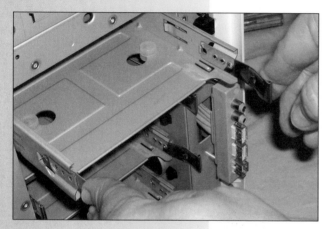

Figure 5-45. Remove a hard drive tray

Figure 5-46. Insert four screws to secure the drive

With the drive bay door open fully, lift it slightly to disengage it from its hinges and lay it flat in front of the case, as shown in Figure 5-44. Note the cable that joins the door to the case, and be careful not to put any stress on it.

ON THE RAILS

The three plastic items visible at the bottom of the case in Figures 5-43 and 5-44 are spare drive rails for the external 5.25″ drive bays. Three more rails are located inside the case. When we first opened the Antec P150 case, we were puzzled to find only three drive rails in a holder that was clearly designed for four. We were further puzzled because there should have been six rails available for the three external 5.25″ drive bays. When we opened the hard drive bay cover, we realized that Antec had supplied six rails, but split three and three between two storage locations.

Our system will be portable, and we're not as brave as Pournelle, so we decided to screw-mount our hard drives. To begin, remove a drive tray, as shown in Figure 5-45. To do so, press inward on both drive rails to disengage the latches, and slide the hard drive tray out of the case.

Secure the drive with four screws driven through the bottom of the drive tray and into the drive, as shown in Figure 5-46. Antec supplies special screws for this purpose, with wide heads and shafts that are only partially threaded. Place the drive upside down on the work surface, with the inverted drive tray over it. Align the screw holes and install the four screws finger-tight. Do not overtorque the mounting screws. You want them to apply some pressure to the silicone shock-mount pads, but not enough to deform them.

With the drive secured to the tray, slide the tray into the drive bay until it latches, as shown in Figure 5-47. It doesn't matter greatly which bays you use. We were installing only two drives in the four-drive bay, so we decided to use the top and bottom drive bays to keep the drives as far apart as possible for better air flow and cooling.

Figure 5-47. Slide the mounted drive into the drive bay until it latches

With both drives installed in the hard drive bay, reinstall the hard drive bay cover, as shown in Figure 5-48. Align the pins on the cover with the corresponding holes in the hinges on the case body, and slide the cover down into place. Then close the cover and retighten the thumbscrews, as shown in Figure 5-49.

Figure 5-48. Reinstall the hard drive bay cover

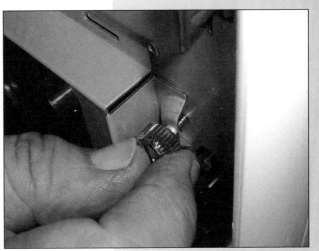

Figure 5-49. Tighten the thumbscrews to secure the hard drive bay cover

Figure 5-50. Connect the S-ATA power cables to the hard drives

Figure 5-51. Connect the S-ATA data cables to the hard drives

FRONT FANS

The hard drive bay cover has mounting positions for two optional 92mm fans. If you're going to install one or two front fans, now is the time to do so. Install them as intake (blowing in) fans and route their power cables to the case interior before you reinstall the hard drive bay cover.

Locate the S-ATA power cable you connected to the power supply. Route that cable down to the back of the hard drives, again making sure to keep it clear of other cables to simplify things when you bundle and tie off the cables later. The S-ATA power connector uses an L-shaped connector body to ensure that it can't be connected backward. Orient the cable connector properly relative to the drive connector and then press the cable connector firmly until it slides completely onto the drive connector, as shown in Figure 5-50.

ADVICE FROM JIM COOLEY

Use a white-out pen to paint a swath across the data and power cable and drive connectors to make re-attaching the S-ATA cables easier in the future, especially when you might not have ideal lighting.

With power connected to both hard drives, the next step is to connect the data cables. Like S-ATA power cables, S-ATA data cables use an L-shaped connector body to prevent installing them backward. Align the cable connector with the drive connector, and press firmly until the cable connector slides into place, as shown in Figure 5-51.

WARNING

S-ATA power connectors and data connectors are quite fragile. When you insert or remove an S-ATA connector, avoid putting any sideways pressure or torque on the connector. Slide the connector straight in to insert it, and pull it straight out to remove it.

Route the S-ATA data cables to the front edge of the motherboard, again avoiding entangling the cables with other cables. The ASUS M2N32-SLI Deluxe motherboard provides six S-ATA data connectors, labeled SATA-1 through SATA-6. Connect the primary hard drive to SATA-1 and the secondary drive to SATA-2, as shown in Figure 5-52.

On systems with several S-ATA hard drives, we generally label both ends of each S-ATA cable to make it easier to determine which drive is connected to which interface. In this case, with only two hard drives, we didn't bother to label the cables. Our standard practice is to install the first hard drive in the top position with the secondary hard drive below it. We followed that practice here, which makes labeling the cables unnecessary.

S-ATA RAID

In addition to the six S-ATA ports shown in Figure 5-52, the ASUS M2N32-SLI Deluxe motherboard provides an External S-ATA (eSATA) connector on the back panel and a seventh S-ATA connector near the right rear corner of the motherboard.

The six standard ports are provided by the nVIDIA nForce 590 SLI chipset, and support RAID 0, RAID 1, RAID 0+1, RAID 5, and JBOD configurations. The two rear SATA ports are provided by a separate Silicon Image Sil3132 SATA controller chip. The external port includes a port multiplier function (SATA-On-The-Go). Both rear ports support RAID 0, RAID 1, and JBOD configurations. We elected to use two of the standard S-ATA ports, leaving the Sil3132 ports available for future use.

Figure 5-52. Connect the S-ATA data cables to the motherboard S-ATA interfaces

Installing the Video Adapter

As an SLI motherboard, the ASUS M2N32-SLI Deluxe provides two PCI Express x16 slots for video adapters. If you're installing only one video adapter, as we are, you can install it in either slot.

WARNING

If you're installing two video adapters, read the motherboard and video adapter manuals carefully to learn how to configure them properly. Also remember to connect the SLI Bridge cable to the golden fingers connectors on both video adapters. An SLI Bridge cable is supplied with the motherboard, and with most SLI-capable video adapters. You can use either SLI Bridge cable.

To begin installing the video adapter, temporarily slide it into position above the video adapter slot to determine which slot cover you need to remove. (We used the blue PCIe slot for our system.) Remove the screw that secures the expansion slot cover, as shown in Figure 5-53, and set it aside. Remove the slot cover and discard or store it.

Figure 5-53. Remove the screw that secures the slot cover

Figure 5-54. Attach the PCIe power cable to the video adapter

Figure 5-55. Align the video adapter with the slot and press firmly to seat it

There's not much clearance once the video adapter is installed in its slot, so we recommend connecting the PCIe power cable before you install the video adapter. Not all PCI Express video adapters require supplemental power, but if yours does it's very important to remember to connect the supplemental power cable. If you forget, best case, the video adapter simply won't work. Worst case, the video adapter and motherboard may be damaged.

Many older PCI Express video adapters and a few current models have a Molex (hard drive) power connector on the card. If your video adapter provides a Molex socket, connect a Molex power supply cable to it (don't use a connector labeled "fan only," as it won't supply enough power). Most PCI Express video adapters use the special 6-pin PCI Express power connector, shown in Figure 5-54. If your video adapter provides this socket, connect the PCI Express power cable you attached to the power supply earlier.

Slide the video adapter into position above the PCI Express slot, making sure the rear bracket is aligned properly with the open expansion slot cover. Once you're sure everything is properly aligned, press down on the video card with both thumbs, as shown in Figure 5-55, until the card seats firmly in the slot. Verify visually that the video card is fully seated. You may feel or hear the card snap into place, but that is no guarantee that it is fully seated. Make sure that the card is flush with the slot and level, and that the retention mechanism on the front edge of the PCIe slot is fully engaged with the matching cutout on the base of the video adapter.

Once the video adapter is seated properly, reinsert the screw to secure the card, as shown in Figure 5-56. Make sure that tightening the screw doesn't torque the far end of the video card contacts out of the video card slot. If that happens, you may need to bend the video card bracket slightly to release the pressure that causes it to torque out of the slot.

Figure 5-56. Insert the screw to secure the video adapter

Finishing Up

It's all over but the shouting now. All we need to do is connect power to the rear case fan and do some tidying up of the cables. The rear case fan is an Antec 120mm TriCool, so called because it can be set to run at low, medium, or high speed. The speed control switch is a small white box at the end of a short, stiff cable.

By default, the TriCool is set to run at low speed, which moves the least air but is also produces the least noise. For most systems, including this one, the low setting moves enough air to keep the system cool. Set the TriCool to medium or high speed only if the processor or motherboard temperature sensors report unacceptably high temperatures.

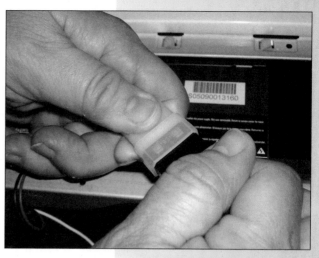

Figure 5-57. Connect power to the rear case fan

To enable the TriCool rear case fan, connect its power lead to a standard Molex power connector, as shown in Figure 5-57. The fan draws very little current, even at high speed, so it's safe to use the same Molex cable that you use to power the optical drive or ATA hard drives.

WARNING

Some power supplies, including many Antec units, provide "Fan-Only" Molex connectors. If you power the TriCool fan with such a connector, we recommend setting the fan speed to high. Otherwise, the reduced voltage available on the Fan-Only Molex connector may be insufficient to start the fan spinning.

The final step in building a PC is always to dress the cables, which simply means organizing, bundling, and tying them off so that they don't clutter up the case interior, impeding air flow and possibly fouling a fan. The P150 case has built-in cable organizers for just this purpose. To reveal them, remove the right side panel from the case.

Figure 5-58. Use the cable organizer hooks to bundle and tie off excess cable lengths

Gently feed the excess cable lengths through to the right side of the case and wrap them around the cable organizer hooks, as shown in Figure 5-58. Be careful not to pull too hard on the cables. Leave just a bit of slack to avoid putting undue stress on the connections.

In addition to using the cable organizer, look for opportunities to tuck and bundle the ATA data cable and the cables coming from the power supply. The drive bay immediately beneath the optical drive provides a convenient niche for tucking cables into. Don't forget to dress the ATX12V cable and the rear fan power cable. Use cable ties or plastic twist-ties to secure the cable bundles to the chassis frame or other convenient tie points. Don't hesitate to disconnect cables temporarily if you need to disentangle them from other cables or to route them around parts of the case structure.

Advice from Brian Bilbrey

Most twist-ties are paper-over-thin-wire, and not suitable for system internal use, in my opinion. Of course, I buy cable-ties by the 200–500 count, so... But even a small pack at any home center shouldn't be too expensive, and it's worth it in reliability and suitability for the job at hand.

Figure 5-59 shows the case interior immediately after we finished building the system. Figure 5-60 shows the case interior after we spent five minutes dressing the cables. Your goal should be a system that looks at least as well organized as Figure 5-60. Actually, because we built this system for ourselves, we spent less time dressing the cables. If we'd been building it for someone else, we'd have spent a few more minutes to make things even neater; for example, by bundling the cables visible near the front of the system and by tying off the gray front-panel cables to the frame at the upper right of the image.

Figure 5-59. The case interior before dressing the cables

Figure 5-60. The case interior after dressing the cables

The Smoke Test

After you finish building the system, take a few minutes to double-check everything. Verify that all cables are connected properly, that all drives are secured, and that there's nothing loose inside the case. Check one last time to verify the power supply is set for the correct input voltage, if applicable. It's a good idea to pick up the system and tilt it gently from side to side to make sure there are no loose screws or other items that could cause a short. Use the checklist:

- ❏ Power supply set to proper input voltage (the Antec NeoHE 430 is auto-sensing)
- ❏ No loose tools or screws (shake the case gently)
- ❏ Heatsink/fan unit properly mounted; CPU fan connected
- ❏ Memory modules fully seated and latched
- ❏ Front-panel switch and indicator cables connected properly
- ❏ Front-panel I/O cables connected properly
- ❏ Hard drive data cable connected to drive and motherboard
- ❏ Hard drive power cable connected
- ❏ Optical drive data cable connected to drive and motherboard
- ❏ Optical drive power cable connected
- ❏ Optical drive audio cable(s) connected, if applicable
- ❏ Front-panel voltage/fan controller connected (if applicable)
- ❏ Floppy drive data and power cables connected (if applicable)
- ❏ All drives secured to drive bay or chassis, as applicable
- ❏ Expansion cards fully seated and secured to the chassis
- ❏ Video adapter power connected (if applicable)
- ❏ Main ATX power cable and ATX12V power cable connected
- ❏ Front and rear case fans installed and connected (if applicable)
- ❏ All cables dressed and tucked

Once you're certain that all is as it should be, it's time for the smoke test. Leave the cover off for now. Connect the power cable to the wall receptacle and then to the system unit. Unlike many power supplies, the Antec NeoHE 430 has a separate rocker switch on the back that controls power to the power supply. By default, it's in the "0" or off position, which means the power supply is not receiving power from the wall receptacle. Move that switch to the "1" or on position. Press the main power button on the front of the case, and the system should start up. Check to make sure that the power supply fan, CPU fan, and case fan are spinning. You should also hear the hard drive spin up and the happy beep that tells you the system is starting normally. At that point, everything should be working properly.

Only the Good Die Young

When you turn on the rear power switch, the system will come to life momentarily and then die. That's perfectly normal behavior. When the power supply receives power, it begins to start up. It quickly notices that the motherboard hasn't told it to start, and so it shuts down again. All you need to do is press the front-panel power switch and the system will start normally.

BIOS Updates

Our ASUS M2N32-SLI Deluxe motherboard arrived with the latest BIOS version already installed. When you first boot your system, check the installed BIOS version. Visit the ASUS web site to see if there's a later version available. If so, install it, following the instructions supplied with the updated BIOS file.

Once the system passes the smoke test, connect your keyboard, mouse, display, and any other external peripherals. Start the system and run BIOS Setup. Read the ASUS motherboard manual carefully, and follow the directions for initial system configuration exactly. Once you have completed BIOS Setup configuration, save your changes, shut the system down, and restart it with the operating system distribution disc in the optical drive. Install the OS, updated drivers, and your applications software, and you're ready to roll. Oh, and don't forget to replace the side panel.

Final Words

This system went together easily. Actual construction took about 90 minutes, spread out over several days (as usual in our case) as we photographed each step. If this is the first time you've built a system, leave yourself a full weekend to build it, install software, and so on.

We're quite pleased with the performance of this system. It's noticeably faster than our old LAN party PC, which used a Pentium 4 Extreme Edition 3.4 GHz processor. Our new gaming PC is small enough and light enough to make it easy to transport.

The system is a bit louder than we hoped, but is still much quieter than typical gaming systems with similar performance. Nearly all of the noise is produced by the stock AMD CPU cooler and the fan on the nVIDIA GeForce 6800 Ultra video adapter.

We could make this system nearly inaudible with only two changes, one minor and one major. Replacing the stock AMD CPU cooler with a Zalman or Thermalright cooler would cost $30 to $75, and would greatly reduce or eliminate CPU cooler fan noise. Replacing the noisy, actively cooled GeForce 6800 Ultra video adapter with a modern fanless video adapter (or two) would eliminate the high-pitched drone of the video card fan while maintaining or increasing video performance. With both of these upgrades, the gaming PC would be quiet enough to use even in the den or living room—a mild-mannered general purpose PC by day, and a kick-ass gaming PC by night.

Robert was thinking about putting the gaming PC in his office as his new primary system. Unfortunately, while he was thinking about it, Barbara grabbed the gaming PC. It now sits in her office as her primary desktop system. Oh, well.

For updated component recommendations, commentary, and other new material, visit *http://www.hardwareguys.com/guides/gaming-pc.html*.

Lugging All This Stuff

The gaming PC is easily luggable, but that raises the question, "What about all my other stuff?" You need a lot of accessories when you attend a LAN party, and it makes sense to organize them in one place. The best solution we know of—albeit an expensive one—is to use a deep, oversize aluminum case with cut-to-fit foam liners, such as those available from Zero Halliburton. You can arrange the interior so that every accessory has its own place, making it evident at a glance if something is missing. Such cases are expensive, particularly in large sizes, so those on a budget may have to compromise on a large nylon backpack, such as those available from L.L. Bean and Lands' End. (You can also buy purpose-built LAN Party accessory cases from many online vendors. Google for "LAN party accessories" and you'll turn up a bunch of hits. We have no experience with any of those, so we can't comment.)

As to what to carry, here's our list:

- Flat-panel display (wrapped in foam unless you use a rigid case)

- Display cable (and a spare)

- Keyboard and mouse (with spare batteries, if applicable)

- Wrist rest, mouse pad, and any other ergonomic accessories you use

- Headphones and/or speakers

- Category 6 Ethernet drop cable, 10-foot (and a spare)

- Extra USB cables (standard, 4-pin mini, and 5-pin mini) and FireWire cables

- Power cables for the PC and display (and spares). An outlet-strip surge protector is also handy. There are seldom enough electrical receptacles.

- Cable ties to keep everything neat. The last thing you want is someone tripping over your power cable.

- Copies of all the games you plan to play, including any that you haven't installed on the hard drive. The best way to carry CDs and DVDs is in a zippered nylon audio CD case, available at Best Buy and similar retailers. Make sure you also have patches, cheat sheets, and similar items, either on the hard drive or on CD.

- A minimal toolkit. Include at least a #2 Phillips screwdriver, needle-nose pliers, a flashlight with batteries, and spare screws and other small connectors. It's also a good idea to include a small first-aid kit, with adhesive bandages, disinfectant, and so on.

- Spare glasses or contact lenses, medications, etc.

- Emergency stock of munchies and caffeinated beverages.

That's a lot of stuff, including some things you may never need, but Murphy's Law says whatever you leave at home will turn out to be what you need at the LAN party.

Building a Media Center PC

6

We admit it. We're audio/video Luddites. Our home audio system is a dozen years old. The receiver has Dolby Pro Logic, but we've never gotten around to hooking more than two speakers to it. We use it only for playing CDs and occasionally an elderly cassette tape. We have a standard 27" Panasonic television, analog cable, no premium channels, no satellite receiver, and we didn't buy our first DVD player until 2005. TiVo? We've heard of it.

The only movies we watch are DVDs we rent from Netflix or borrow from the library or friends. We sometimes watch "Mystery!", "Masterpiece Theatre," or other PBS programs. Other than infrequent viewing of local news, sports, and weather, that's about it. We often go for literally months on end without watching a network television program or seeing a television commercial. And we like it that way.

For nearly 20 years, we've made it a practice never to watch television in real time if we can avoid it. We record everything, including commercial-free programs, and watch them later at our convenience. That way, we can watch multipart programs without waiting a week between episodes, and if the phone rings we can simply pause the program. The only change we've made over the years was to replace our VCRs as they died with inexpensive DVD recorders, which simply substitute inexpensive, convenient, reliable optical discs for bulky, inconvenient, unreliable VHS tapes.

Despite the very limited amount of time we devote to watching television, it sometimes happens that two programs we want to record are on simultaneously or that we want to watch a recorded program at the same time another program needs to be recorded. To avoid such conflicts, we have DVD recorders all over the house. One in the den. One in the master bedroom. One in the guest suite downstairs.

So why do we need a media center PC? We don't, really. In fact, we built a very capable home theater PC for the first edition of this book. After we verified that everything worked as it should, we found that we never used the system. We turned it off. It gathered dust, and eventually we salvaged its parts for other systems. There was nothing wrong with that system, mind you. It worked perfectly. We simply had no need for its capabilities.

But we freely admit that our television viewing habits (or lack thereof) are far outside the norm. Most people watch several hours of television every day, and have access to scores or hundreds of channels. If you're in that group (it's OK; you can admit it...), building a media center PC makes a lot of sense. It's not necessarily the easiest or least expensive alternative, but rolling your own media center PC offers a lot of advantages. Consider the alternatives:

Commercial Windows Media Center Edition (MCE) PC

> Dell, HP, Gateway, Sony, and others offer purpose-built media center PCs that run Microsoft Windows Media Center Edition (MCE). The lure of these systems is that the integration work has been done for you and that everything is supposed to just work, more or less.

> But there are many downsides to buying an MCE system. Although some MCE systems are advertised in the sub-$1000 range, these systems are minimally configured and often lack even such basic functions as the ability to record TV programs. Reasonably equipped MCE systems sell in the $1,200 to $1,500 range and up, and fully equipped systems may cost $2,500 or more. Even expensive models may have limited expandability. Windows MCE itself is problematic. It is crash-prone, even when running on fully certified equipment, and is unreliable. For example, many of our readers have reported such problems as MCE inexplicably failing to record a scheduled program or crashing reproducibly while playing back a recorded program. Finally, MCE is loaded with DRM (Digital Restrictions Management), which limits your freedom to use your recorded audio and video data as you wish.

TiVo

> TiVo remains very popular, although we don't understand why. Perhaps it's because TiVo is simple and reliable. It's easy to specify the programs you want to record, and TiVo always works as expected. The TiVo interface is attractive and functional. So why don't we like TiVo? First, it's expensive. A basic TiVo unit with dual tuners costs about $1,000 over five years after you factor in the monthly service charge. TiVo uses high compression with correspondingly low video quality. TiVo panders to the movie studios, networks, and advertisers, for example, by displaying special commercials when you fast-forward to avoid other commercials. Finally, TiVo also enforces DRM measures that make it difficult to view your recorded programs on other devices.

Cable/satellite PVR

Many cable and satellite providers rent basic set-top PVR systems, sometimes for as little as $5/month. The lure of these set-top PVR boxes is their low cost and tight integration with the cable or satellite feed. These devices offer little functionality, less flexibility, and poor reliability, but may suffice if your needs are limited and you don't want to archive recorded programs or view them on other devices.

DVD recorder

The VHS VCR is dead, replaced by inexpensive devices that record to optical discs instead of tapes. Basic DVD recorders cost less than $100. (We paid $78 for our CyberHome DVR-1600 unit.) Recording time on a $0.25 DVD+R disc or $1.00 DVD+RW disc typically varies from one hour (better than DVD quality) to six or eight hours (VHS quality). DVD recorders with built-in hard drives range in price from $275 to $1,000+, and typically store from 20 to 50 hours of DVD-quality recordings, which can easily be written out to DVD recordable discs. Current models enforce no DRM, although that may change as the movie studios and television networks continue to push for legislation such as the Broadcast Flag that mandates DRM in consumer recording equipment.

If your only requirement is to record television programs for later viewing, a basic optical-only DVD recorder or one of the less expensive hard disk models is the best choice. These units don't have an Electronic Program Guide (EPG), so you have to program recording times and channels yourself, but that is not unduly burdensome for most people.

Other than Windows MCE systems, which have problems of their own, none of these options offers anything more than basic television recording functions. If you need (or want) more, it's time for Plan B: rolling your own media center PC.

Determining Functional Requirements

We started our design of the media center PC by pretending that we were heavy consumers of audio and video media and deciding which functions were essential or desirable. Our goal was to design a media center PC that we could build for about the same price as a commercial Windows MCE PC, but with additional features and functionality.

Here's the list of functional requirements we came up with:

Analog cable-ready, 125-channel tuners

Our cable TV service is standard analog that uses no channels above 99, but our televisions can tune channels through 125. Because our cable company sometimes adds channels—and sometimes adds higher-numbered channels while leaving lower channels unused—we need tuners that support analog cable channels at least through Channel 125.

Digital OTA tuner

Although we don't yet own an HDTV, that could change at any time. We want our media center PC to record OTA (over-the-air) digital broadcasts, which requires a digital tuner. Also, with Broadcast Flag legislation looming, we wanted to acquire a DRM-free digital tuner card while they were still available. Most digital tuner cards can also tune digital cable signals, but only those that use unencrypted QAM-64 or QAM-256, which is usually limited to local channels, if that.

Time-shifted video recording

We use our DVD recorders primarily for time shifting. Other than sporting events, news, weather, and similar live programming, we haven't watched a program in real time for 15 years or more. We record everything and zap the commercials, if any. It is essential that the media center PC provide similar functionality, including commercial zapping.

Video recording quality

We record everything in DVD-quality mode unless we're recording a movie that requires higher compression to fit on one disc. Accordingly, although lower-quality recording modes are desirable for additional flexibility, DVD-quality mode is essential.

Capacity

We tend to accumulate recorded programs and watch them in batches. For example, if "Masterpiece Theatre" is running a four-part series, we don't begin watching the series until we've recorded all four episodes. Sometimes we don't watch a series until months after we recorded it. We decided we needed an absolute minimum of 100 hours of DVD-quality video storage, and 250 hours or more would be better.

Watch-while-record

The system must allow us to watch one live analog program while recording another analog and/or digital program.

Record multiple programs simultaneously

The system must allow us to record two analog programs simultaneously. We decided to settle for the ability to record only one digital program at a time, because to do otherwise would require additional digital tuners. That would be overkill for our system, but perhaps not for yours.

Live-pause and real-time commercial zapping

The system must allow us to "live-pause" a program while it is being recorded. That is, if we begin watching a program in real time, the system must allow us to press a pause button when the phone rings and continue recording the program. When we have dealt with the interruption, the system must allow us to resume watching the program at the point we paused it. Because live-pause buffers video for later viewing, this feature also allows us to zap commercials in a live program by waiting several minutes after the program starts to begin watching it.

Online program guide

The system must feature a free, interactive program guide, customized to the channels provided by our cable system. Selecting a program to be recorded should be a simple matter of pointing to that program on the guide menu and pressing a button. Ideally, the program guide should be customizable to hide channels we never watch.

Video archiving

The media center PC must make provision for archiving recorded programs to writable DVD discs that can later be played back in the media center PC or on an ordinary DVD player.

Standard file formats

The media center PC must record video data as standard file formats without DRM copy protection or other impediments to copying and editing those recordings. Ideally, the media center PC would also be able to translate various standard file formats to other file formats.

CD and DVD player

The media center PC must function as a standard CD player and DVD player, capable of playing CD-DA audio discs and DVD-Video discs. Ideally, the media center PC should also be capable of ripping the content of CD and DVD discs to its hard drive.

Media library and audio/video server

The media center PC should provide a media library management function, allowing us to store, organize, and play back video and audio data, including the MP3, OGG, FLAC, and WAV audio file formats, as well as digital camera images in JPEG and RAW formats and DV camcorder video. The media center PC should also function as a multimedia server for other systems throughout the house, by allowing those other systems to access stored audio/video via a network share.

Gaming console replacement

The media center PC should function as a gaming PC, within the limitations of using a standard television for display. We're only casual gamers, so even an entry-level 3D graphics card suffices for our needs. Dedicated gamers can install the latest fire-breathing gaming video card instead.

Casual PC replacement

The media center PC should be usable for casual PC functions such as checking email or browsing the Web, again within the limitations of using a television as a display device. Don't overestimate the abilities of a standard-definition TV. Our 27" CRT standard-definition TV supports 640 × 480 resolution at best, which makes it marginally usable for web browsing and email. When we replace that old 27" Panasonic, we'll choose a 32" or 35" LCD model that supports at least 720p, if not 1080p. Such a display has sufficient resolution to use for any PC function, including gaming.

Extensibility

As we thought about the functions a media center PC could provide, we realized that it could support other unrelated functions in the future. For example, we may eventually use the media center PC to control a home weather station or provide automated attendant and voice mail functions for our home telephone system. Because the media center PC is a standard PC, making provision for these possible future functions is a simple matter of making sure that the media center PC has plenty of processor, memory, hard drive capacity, USB ports, and so on.

Ease of use

Although the media center PC is a PC and will sometimes be used as such, ease-of-use is a major consideration for the core multimedia functions. For example, scheduling a program to be recorded or playing a DVD should be a matter of punching a few buttons on a remote control rather than navigating menus with keyboard and mouse.

Upgradable to HD-DVD and/or Blu-Ray

Consumers initially ignored the rollout of high-definition video discs based on the competing HD-DVD and Blu-Ray standards, and rightly so. The first players were slow, crash-prone, and overpriced by an order of magnitude. Only a handful of titles were available, and they sold at a 50% to 100% premium over standard DVDs. Still, those initial teething pains will eventually be dealt with, and either HD-DVD or Blu-Ray (not both) will become the new standard. We wanted our media center PC to be easily upgradable to support whichever HD standard eventually wins.

At first glance, it might seem that adding high-definition support would be as easy as replacing the existing optical drive with an HD-DVD or Blu-Ray model. There's more to it than that, though. HD playback requires a lot of processing power, memory, and video bandwidth, which is why early Blu-Ray players were essentially thinly disguised Pentium 4 PCs. We'll design our media center PC to have sufficient resources to be easily upgradable to support high-definition optical discs. At most, we'll need to upgrade the optical drive and video adapter.

That laundry list is a lot to ask of a system, but even at that one of our original wish-list items didn't make the final cut:

Streaming video/RF-out

We originally intended to design a media center PC capable of outputting an RF signal that could be received by any television in the house. We concluded that, although it was possible to do that, it would require significant cost and effort for little return. As an alternative, we decided it would be easy enough to burn any programs we wanted to watch elsewhere to a DVD and watch them on a standard DVD player.

Hardware Design Criteria

With the functional requirements determined, the next step was to establish design criteria for the media center PC hardware. The table to the right shows the priorities we assigned for the media center PC.

Here's the breakdown:

Price

> Price is an issue in that we'd like the total price of the system to be lower than that of a commercial Windows MCE system with similar functionality, or, alternatively, that the price be the same but the functionality of our system be higher. Accordingly, we'll use only first-rate components in this system, and if spending a few extra dollars buys us additional performance, reliability, or functionality, we'll spend the extra money.

Reliability

> Reliability is important for this system. Not, perhaps, in the same sense that reliability is critical for a departmental file server, but Robert never wants to have to explain to Barbara why our fancy new media center PC failed to record a program she was looking forward to watching. We won't use RAID disk storage, ECC memory, and other server technologies for cost, space, and other reasons, but we will attempt to design as reliable a system as possible within those constraints by using top-notch components, emphasizing cooling even at the expense of noise level, using an oversize power supply, and so on.

Size

> Size is relatively unimportant for our media center PC, but we would like it to resemble a standard home-audio component in size, shape, and appearance. Accordingly, rather than simply using the smallest available case, we evaluated cases that were designed for use as media center PCs.

DESIGN PRIORITIES	
Price	☆☆☆☆☆
Reliability	☆☆☆☆☆
Size	☆☆☆☆☆
Noise level	☆☆☆☆☆
Expandability	☆☆☆☆☆
Processor performance	☆☆☆☆☆
Video performance	☆☆☆☆☆
Disk capacity/performance	☆☆☆☆☆

DEPTH MATTERS

Many media center PCs have been built in standard mini-tower cases, and we've even seen one or two in full-tower cases standing beside the television. If your media center PC is to reside in an entertainment center, make sure that the case you use fits. In particular, if your entertainment center has an enclosed back, make sure the case is not too deep to fit.

Ron Morse adds that in addition to case dimensions, you need to allow for the big, fat, long video connector and its thick cable, and the AC power cord, too. Also, many media center PC cases exhaust warm air through side or top vents, so to prevent overheating it's important to maintain an inch or more of clearance near those vents.

Running Your Own TV Station

If you want to distribute RF throughout your home, you can do so by using an RF modulator. In theory it is possible to distribute that signal on the existing cable by filtering the channel used by the RF modulator at the cable demarc, but in practice attempting to do so risks poor image quality and interference on that channel, not just for you, but for your neighbors. If that happens, expect a visit from an angry cable company employee.

The alternative, which we would choose, is to run a separate coax cable to each TV and provide some means of switching between the two RF inputs. We decided that wasn't worth the trouble. It's easier just to transfer video files, either on a DVD or across the network to a set-top PC connected to the remote TV.

Noise level

Perhaps surprisingly, noise level is only moderately important for our media center PC. That's true because this system is destined to reside in an entertainment center across the room from the sofa. When the system is being used to view a movie or listen to music, even moderately loud system noise is swamped by the sound coming from the speakers. Of course, the system is not always active, so it must be reasonably quiet to avoid interfering with other uses of the room. Achieving low noise levels always involves trade-offs among cost, performance, cooling, and reliability. All other things being equal, a quiet system costs more, is slower, runs hotter, or is less reliable (or all of those.) Accordingly, we decided to compromise by using quiet standard components, but not by using radical quiet-PC technologies such as a very slow processor, an insulated enclosure, fanless coolers, water cooling, and so on.

Expandability

Expandability is moderately important, but only in the sense that we want our system to be easily upgradable to newer technologies like HD-DVD or Blu-Ray. Any new component we install will likely replace an old component, so we have no real need for many spare drive bays, expansion slots, and so on. We want provision for one optical drive and at least two hard drives. We'll choose a motherboard with integrated everything except video, so the only expansion slots we'll need are one PCIe slot for the video adapter and two or three PCI slots for the tuners. We do want to make provision for adding unrelated functions to the system, such as controlling a home weather station or functioning as an automated attendant and voice mail controller for our telephone system, but we can accommodate that requirement by having one or two spare expansion slots.

Processor performance

Processor performance is moderately important. Simple functions such as playing a CD or DVD or playing recorded video are undemanding; the slowest mainstream processor is more than sufficient for such functions. Recording video is a different matter, because real-time video compression is extremely CPU intensive—particularly HD video—but we intend to use analog tuners with hardware compression support and a digital tuner that offloads compression duties to the video adapter GPU. But we still need a capable processor because the media center PC will at times function as a normal PC—for gaming, web browsing, and so on—and we want to build the system initially with enough processor horsepower to handle an HD-DVD or Blu-Ray optical drive, either of which places heavy burdens on the main system processor.

Older Standards Make Life Easier

Sometimes the old ways are the good ways, and this is certainly true for someone who wants to build a media center PC. Broadly speaking, there are two types of television signaling protocols and two delivery methods.

The current standard-definition television signaling protocols are NTSC (National Television System Committee), which is used in North America and Japan, and PAL (Phase Alternating Line), which is used in most of Europe, China, and Africa. NTSC and PAL are analog protocols. They may be transmitted over-the-air or via cable using analog transmission or via cable or satellite using digital transmission. The second type of signaling protocol used in the United States is called ATSC (Advanced Television Systems Committee). ATSC is comparable to the DVB (Digital Video Broadcasting) standard used in Europe and the ISDB (Integrated Services Digital Broadcasting) standard used in Japan. ATSC is purely digital and may be transmitted over-the-air or via cable or satellite, using digital transmission methods. Although Digital Television (DTV) and HDTV (High-Definition Television) are inextricably linked in the public mind, ATSC standards also define standard-definition DTV modes.

There are several other standards in limited use. France uses SECAM (a French acronym for Sequential Color with Memory). Brazil uses a hybrid of NTSC and PAL called M-PAL. Argentina, Paraguay, and Uruguay use a lower bandwidth version of PAL called N-PAL. Many former Soviet-bloc and Middle Eastern countries use a variant of SECAM called MESECAM. But if you're reading the English-language version of this book, you're almost certainly using NTSC or PAL, and most capture cards are available in versions for either of those standards.

Although digital transmission and HDTV have real advantages in terms of bandwidth and image quality, both have severe drawbacks for anyone contemplating building a media center PC. A standard NTSC signal delivered by analog cable is easy for a media center PC to deal with. You can simply connect the cable to the tuner card and allow the PC to change channels as needed.

Using digital cable or satellite as a program source makes matters more complex. Although digital tuner cards for PCs exist, various laws and differing cable/satellite standards limit their utility. A digital tuner card can freely tune OTA digital broadcasts (standard-definition or high-definition), but probably cannot tune digital signals supplied by cable or satellite, unless those signals are unencrypted (rare) and use a standard modulation method such as QAM-64 or QAM-256.

In practical terms, if your signal source is digital cable or satellite, you will probably be limited to using the satellite receiver or digital cable box to tune the signal. To record programs on different channels, you must change channels on the satellite box or digital cable receiver rather than on the media center PC. That makes it difficult, although not impossible, to select the channel to be recorded under programmatic control.

Some satellite receivers and digital cable boxes are programmable to change channels at specific times. If you have such a box, programming recordings becomes a two-step process: program the cable/satellite box to tune the proper channel at the proper time, and program the media center PC to begin recording at that time on the output channel of the cable/satellite box. If you don't have a programmable cable/satellite box, the best solutions to the digital tuning problem are Rube Goldberg arrangements.

One solution is a programmable remote control for your satellite receiver or digital cable box. To record a program, you set the remote control to change to the proper channel at the proper time and leave it pointed at the satellite receiver or digital cable box. You also set the media center PC to begin recording at the proper time. The media center PC records whatever signal the satellite box or digital cable box happens to be delivering, so if someone moves the remote or the dog walks in front of it at just the wrong time, you may end up recording something other than what you intended.

Another solution is to equip the media center PC with an IR emitter that can mimic the remote control for your satellite receiver or digital cable box. The IR emitter works under control of a scheduling program running on the media center PC. When it's time to record a program, the media center PC sends a series of commands to the IR emitter, which turns on the satellite receiver or digital cable box and tunes it to the correct channel.

Either of these methods is awkward at best, but some solutions, such as the IR Blaster described later in this chapter, are reported to work well enough to get the job done.

257

Video performance

Video performance is moderately important overall, but there are several aspects of video performance in a media center PC that must be considered individually. Video capture quality is critical, so it's important to choose tuner/capture cards with excellent native video quality. Video playback quality is also critical, but any decent video adapter can easily handle video playback. When the media center PC is being used as a PC—as for browsing the Web or checking email—2D display quality is important, particularly because even high-definition televisions are not designed to be used as computer displays. Fortunately, the nVIDIA video adapters that are required to assist the HDTV tuner card in compressing the video stream also have excellent image quality when a television is used as the display. The final aspect of video performance is 3D acceleration for gaming. Our media center PC will be used for only casual gaming, so very high 3D graphics performance is unnecessary.

Disk capacity/performance

Disk capacity and performance are moderately important. Years ago, we'd have ranked these aspects as critically important, because hard drives of the time were smaller and slower than today's models. Fortunately, current hard drives have huge capacities and even mainstream models are fast enough to keep up with the demands of a media center PC. At first glance, capacity might seem more important than performance, but in fact both are equally important. On a lightly loaded media center PC, even a slow, 5,400 RPM "near-line" drive might be fast enough. But our system is designed to support many activities concurrently, all of which require disk access. For example, our system might have to play back one analog stream while it records a second stream on the second analog tuner while it records a third stream on the digital tuner while it streams audio to Barbara's office. To make sure the drive can keep up without dropping any frames, we'll choose a 7,200 RPM S-ATA drive that supports NCQ (Native Command Queuing) and has a large buffer.

Choosing Software

The traditional advice is to choose software before choosing the hardware to run it, and that holds true in spades for a media center PC. The PVR and related software applications that will run on the media center PC are fundamental. So, before we made specific hardware selections, we had to decide which PVR software to use. That in turn requires deciding which operating system to run. There are three practical choices:

- Microsoft Windows Media Center Edition (MCE)

- Microsoft Windows XP or Vista with a third-party PVR application

- Linux with MythTV or another Linux-based PVR application

We examine each of these three options in the following sections.

Microsoft Windows Media Center Edition 2005

At first, Microsoft MCE 2005 seemed the leading candidate. MCE is pretty, provides all the basic functions we want, has an excellent integrated electronic program guide (EPG), and has one of the best "10-foot interfaces" available. MCE also supports Studio RGB, which defines white as 235, 235, 235 and black as 16, 16, 16. Most third-party PVR applications use Computer RGB, which defines white as 255, 255, 255 and black as 0, 0, 0. That difference means that for recorded video MCE provides more accurate color rendering, particularly in the dimmest and brightest parts of the image.

Despite all of these advantages, we decided not to use MCE 2005, for the following reasons:

- Although it is possible to buy an OEM copy of MCE 2005 for $125 or so, Microsoft doesn't position MCE as a consumer product. Instead, they target MCE at OEMs that use it as the basis of a turnkey media center system. Accordingly, Microsoft does not offer direct support for MCE, which is a significant drawback for people who want to roll their own PVR systems.

- Microsoft plans to discontinue MCE as a separate product, instead bundling MCE features with Windows Vista Home Premium and Vista Ultimate, which were unavailable when this book went to press. We tested Vista Beta 2, but found the MCE functions to be unusable.

- MCE provides few customization choices other than basic setup options. With MCE, what you see is what you get.

- MCE records video in the proprietary DVR-MS format rather than an industry-standard format such as MPEG.

- MCE incorporates entirely too many DRM (Digital Restrictions Management) features for our taste. We want PVR software that does what we want it to do, not PVR software that does only what Microsoft decides to allow us to do. For example, MCE honors the proposed broadcast flag (which as we write this has not yet been approved or implemented, but appears to be inevitable). If the broadcast flag is set to prohibit copying, MCE allows you to view the programs you record only on the computer that originally recorded them. Similarly, if your video adapter has component output connectors, MCE restricts viewing of DVDs to 480p by prohibiting upscaling to native HDTV resolutions.

So, although we really wanted to like MCE—using it would certainly have made things easier—we reluctantly concluded that MCE wasn't the best choice for us. That doesn't mean MCE isn't the best choice for you, if you don't consider any of the objections we list as showstoppers. MCE is probably the most popular choice among those who build their own media center PCs, and for good reason. There's a lot to like about MCE, if you can get past its significant drawbacks.

Measure Twice, Cut Once

If you decide to use Microsoft Windows MCE (or a version of Vista with MCE features), be very careful when you select hardware. MCE has very specific hardware requirements. Attempting to use unsupported hardware components can cause various problems, from minor glitches to MCE refusing to load, record programs, or play them back. Also pay close attention to the revision levels of device drivers and other supporting software. (We had already ruled out MCE when we designed our system, so we made no attempt to verify compatibility of the components we selected with the MCE approved-hardware list.)

Of course, hardware and driver compatibility is an issue for any PVR application, but Windows MCE has tighter requirements than most. Before you order components for a Windows MCE system, verify that each component is certified for use with MCE. We don't include a URL because Microsoft reorganizes its web site frequently, but a Google search of microsoft.com for "Media Center edition" and "hardware compatibility" should return the pages you need.

Third-Party Windows PVR Applications

When we looked at third-party PVR applications for the first edition of this book in 2004, there weren't any ideal choices. We looked at half a dozen competing PVR apps, every one of which had significant drawbacks. We ended up using the PVR application that ATi bundled with its All-In-Wonder series cards. Although we weren't completely happy with it, it did the job.

Nowadays, it's a different story. There are many competing third-party PVR applications, most of which are quite polished, and many of which compare favorably with Microsoft Windows MCE. There are still differences, of course, in terms of feature sets, hardware requirements, and other factors. We won't presume to recommend a specific PVR application, because each of them has strengths and weaknesses. But if you want your media center PC to run Windows, one of these applications will almost certainly fulfill most or all of your requirements.

Beyond TV

Beyond TV 4 (*http://www.snapstream.com*) is the latest in a long series of PVR applications from SnapStream. BT4 supports unlimited analog tuners, and can record over-the-air HDTV if you install a supported digital tuner. BT4 supports a wide variety of tuner cards, including the popular Hauppauge models (but not ATi All-In-Wonder models.) You can store recorded video in MPEG-2 format (which can be burned directly to DVD), in the space-efficient DIVX format, or in WMV format for transfer to a Pocket PC or other other device that supports Windows Media. The optional Beyond TV Link software allows you to stream recorded video to other PCs on your network. The EPG (Electronic Program Guide), formerly weak, is greatly improved, although searching is still weaker than with some competing products. Intelligent conflict resolution minimizes recording conflicts. For example, if two programs are scheduled to record at the same time, BT4 records the higher-priority program, automatically searches for a later airing of the lower-priority program, and sets that program to record later. You can download a time-limited, full-function demo from the SnapStream web site to test the product before you buy it.

GB-PVR

GB-PVR (*http://www.gbpvr.com*) is a reasonably full-featured PVR application that's free for the download. GB-PVR supports multiple tuners from a wide range of compatible models. The core application provides basic PVR functions, which can be supplemented by numerous available plug-ins that support extended features such as weather forecasts, RSS feeds, theater listings, video transcoding, and so on. Although GB-PVR doesn't offer all the bells and whistles available with competing commercial applications, it's all many people will need.

SageTV

SageTV (*http://www.sagetv.com*) is another full-featured commercial PVR application that's been around for years and is now a mature, polished product. SageTV supports multiple tuners from a broad list of analog and over-the-air HDTV models. SageTV records natively in MPEG-2 format, which can be written directly to a DVD, and can also be configured to use MPEG-4 or DivX formats to minimize the size of recordings. The EPG is attractive and makes it easy to locate programs and schedule them to be recorded. Its intelligent recording and scheduling feature works much like the TiVo recommended viewing option. You can download a time-limited trial version from the web site.

We recommend that you begin by checking the feature sets of all of these products. Spend some time on the web sites of the various products, comparing features and looking at the screenshots until you have narrowed the field to two or three products that appear to be the best fit for your personal needs. Download the manuals if you need more detail. If one or two of these products look suitable, download the demo versions and try them out.

Linux PVR Applications

The two best-known Linux-based PVR applications, MythTV (*http://www. mythtv.org*) and Freevo (*http://freevo.sourceforge.net*), are, like most Linux applications, works in progress. When we reviewed them in mid-2004 for the first edition of this book, we concluded that, although both were impressive, neither was ready for primetime.

Things have changed a lot in two years. MythTV and Freevo have both improved dramatically since 2004, and Linux itself is now much more new-user friendly than it was back then. Linux, and Linux-based PVR applications, are now reasonable candidates for our media center system.

We spent some time looking at the features and capabilities of MythTV and Freevo, and concluded that MythTV had every feature we wanted, not to mention several features we hadn't even thought about wanting. Some MythTV features, such as its fully automatic commercial detection and skipping, are ones you'll never see on Windows MCE, let alone TiVo. (ReplayTV tried that and got sued out of business.) Even the third-party Windows PVR application companies tread lightly to avoid the attack-lawyers of the MPAA, television networks, and advertisers. Not so MythTV. Its feature set is designed to appeal to users, not to movie studios and television networks. There's no DRM, and no attempt to restrict what you can do with the programs that you record.

MythTV is more complicated to install and configure than the Windows-based alternatives, but we think it's worth trying even if you eventually settle on another PVR application. After all, Linux and MythTV can both be downloaded at no cost, and you may find they do the job as well as or better than competing Windows PVR applications.

Meedio RIP?

Of all the PVR applications we looked at, Meedio (*http://www.meedio.com*) came closest to being an exact clone of Microsoft Windows MCE. In fact, it's hard to tell the difference at first glance when Meedio uses default settings. Once you start configuring Meedio, though, the differences become clear. In contrast to the "have-it-our-way" approach of MCE, Meedio offers almost complete flexibility in configuring the appearance and functioning of the application to suit your own preferences. The basic package, Meedio TV, provides standard PVR functions and has one of the most comprehensive feature sets available. Meedio Pro bundles Meedio TV with Meedio Essentials to provide full media center functionality. If Meedio has a weakness, it's the search function, which is limited by the remote-centric design of the software. Alas, the future of Meedio is uncertain. In April 2006, Yahoo! bought Meedio and discontinued the Meedio products and EPG service. We hope that Yahoo! will decide to offer Meedio again under its own brand. It would be a shame to lose such a good product.

Dual Booting

There's no law that says you can have only one operating system installed on your media center PC. Many media center PC owners dual-boot Linux and Windows (which our Technical Reviewer Brian Bilbrey calls "Gaming OS.") Linux runs by default, and handles the PVR and other main system functions. When you want to play a game on the media center PC, reboot it into Windows. When you're finished gaming, reboot the system into Linux and it's immediately ready to record programs, serve audio streams, and perform its other primary functions.

If you decide to try MythTV, you'll find that much of the work has already been done for you by others. Search Google for the name of your preferred Linux distribution and MythTV. For example, we searched for Ubuntu and MythTV, and found several sites that provided detailed step-by-step instructions for installing and configuring MythTV under Ubuntu. But be prepared to do some research and a lot of tweaking before you have MythTV working to your satisfaction.

Component Considerations

With our design criteria in mind, we set out to choose the best components for the media center PC system. The following sections describe the components we chose, and why we chose them.

Case and Power Supply

Antec Fusion or Antec NSK2400 (*http://www.antec.com*)

You can, of course, build a media center PC in a standard mini-tower case. But the critical Spousal-Unit Approval (SUA) criterion (otherwise known as, "You're not putting *that* in my den!") demands a case that matches standard home-audio components in size and appearance as closely as possible. Barbara has a sense of humor about these things. Many spouses do not, so it's worth checking before you purchase a case. As we learned, there are a lot of media center PC cases available, but most have one or more drawbacks.

Silverstone (*http://www.silverstonetek.com*) is perhaps the best-known maker of media center cases. We looked at several of their LaScala-series media center cases, but found none that we considered ideal for our media center PC. Some were too cramped, others too expensive, and still others had inadequate power supplies or insufficient cooling.

We also looked at media center cases from Cooler Master and several other manufacturers. Some were very nice cases, but all had one or more drawbacks. We found several models we'd love to have used—until we saw the price tag. Budget was not a high priority for this system, but we had no intention of paying several hundred dollars for just the case and power supply.

As usual, Antec came to the rescue. We initially considered two Antec cases, the Fusion and Overture II models, both of which Antec positions as media center cases. Fortunately, as we were browsing the Antec site, we happened across their NSK2400 case. Antec classifies the NSK2400 as a desktop case, but its appearance and features make it an obvious choice for a media center PC.

We soon eliminated the Overture II from consideration. Although it's an attractive, reasonably-priced case, its only real advantage relative to the Fusion and NSK2400 is that it accepts full-size ATX motherboards. Two or three years ago, that would have been a key consideration. The selection of microATX motherboards was quite limited, and they often lacked important features that were present on full-size ATX models. Nowadays, many microATX motherboards are functionally identical to their larger cousins, differing only in having two or three fewer expansion slots.

That left us with the Fusion, shown in Figure 6-1, and the NSK2400, both of which incorporate design suggestions from Mike Chin of silentpcreview. com. Either is an excellent choice for a Media PC case, but there are differences. The $100 NSK2400 is an entry-level case. Although its fit and finish are up to Antec's usual high standards, few costly features are present. The $219 Fusion is a premium case, and it shows. The fit and finish are as good as we've seen with any case, including models that sell for much more. The included 430W power supply is a good step up in capacity and quality from the 380W unit included with the NSK2400. The Fusion also includes a large volume control knob and an expensive VFD (Vacuum Fluorescent Display) that is compatible with Windows MCE and some other PVR applications. If you're on a tight budget, choose the NSK2400. But if you have a bit more to spend, the Fusion won't disappoint you.

Figure 6-1. The Antec Fusion media center case

Processor

Intel Core 2 Duo E6400 (*http://www.intel.com*)

Dedicated PVRs like the TiVo or the set-top PVRs rented by cable companies use very slow processors. Playback (real-time video decoding) places little burden on the processor. Recording (real-time video encoding) requires substantial processing power, but a dedicated PVR offloads that task to a specialized co-processor that is optimized for video compression. As a result, dedicated PVRs consume little power, generate little heat, and require few or no fans.

Drive It Until It Drops

A subtle point is that a media center PC is likely to be upgraded much less frequently than a desktop PC. Once a media center PC system is built, configured, connected, and tested, it should reasonably be expected to live quietly in the home-audio rack for several years between upgrades. Accordingly, when the choice is between "just enough" and "more than I'll ever need," we suggest you choose the latter.

ALTERNATIVES: PROCESSOR

We think the Intel Core 2 Duo is the standout choice for a media center PC. If you prefer to use an AMD processor, we recommend the Athlon 64 X2 4200+ or faster. AMD offers low-power variants of some X2 models that consume much less power than the standard models. Although they are more costly than the standard models of the same speed, we recommend using the low-power variants in a media center PC.

Dedicated PVRs also have very limited functionality; for example, being limited to recording one SDTV stream. Our media center PC is different. We expect it to juggle many tasks, to handle difficult tasks like encoding HDTV or playing and recording multiple streams simultaneously, and to do all that without ever dropping the ball even momentarily.

That means our media center PC needs a serious processor, one with horsepower to spare. Because heavy multitasking is common on a media center PC, we need a dual-core processor with excellent support for multimedia functions. Our media center PC is an appliance that sits in our entertainment center, so we'd like the processor to consume little power and generate little heat.

Based on those requirements, one desktop processor immediately comes to mind. The dual-core Intel Core 2 Duo is fast, has excellent multimedia support, and has low power consumption. Even the entry-level Core 2 Duo E6300 is more than fast enough to handle all of the demands of the media center PC, but we decided to do a little "future proofing." On that basis, we chose the Core 2 Duo E6400 for our media center PC.

Motherboard

Intel D946GZIS (*http://www.intel.com*)

Our choice of the Antec Fusion case dictates a microATX motherboard. Core 2 Duo is a Socket 775 processor, but not all Socket 775 motherboards are compatible with Core 2 Duo. At the time we built this system, microATX motherboards with Core 2 Duo support were thin on the ground. Fortunately, Intel offered a microATX Core 2 Duo motherboard that was nearly perfect for our purposes, the D946GZIS Isleton. The D946GZIS supports up to 4 GB of DDR2 memory in two slots. It includes embedded GMA3000 video, but also provides a standard x16 PCI Express video adapter slot. The integrated 5.1 audio and 10/100 Ethernet are sufficient for our purposes.

The only minor drawbacks of this motherboard are its lack of integrated IEEE-1394 (FireWire) and that it provides only two PCI expansion slots. The lack of FireWire isn't a major issue. If we want to watch raw camcorder video, we can plug the camcorder into one of our DVD recorders or PCs. We're unlikely to want to edit video on the media center PC. Having only two PCI expansion slots was more problematic. We originally planned to install three tuner/capture cards in this system, one HDTV and two SDTV. As it turned out, that problem was easily solved. We simply installed one dual-tuner SDTV card instead of two single-tuner cards.

Memory

Kingston KHX6400D2LLK2/2G 2GB PC6400 DDR2 Memory Kit
(1 GB× 2) (*http://www.kingston.com*)

The Intel D946GZIS has two DDR2 memory slots and supports dual-channel memory operation with PC2-4200, PC2-5300, or PC2-6400 modules in capacities up to 2 GB. When we built this system, PC2-6400 modules were selling for far more than PC2-4200 or PC2-5300 modules. We decided to use the faster memory anyway, mainly because we were concerned about the demands that HDTV recording and playback will place on the system.

Obviously, we wanted to populate both slots for better memory performance, so we checked the prices of paired PC2-6400 memory modules. We didn't attempt to analyze the actual memory requirements of the media center PC. A pair of 512 MB DIMMs "felt" too small. Even with a dual-core processor, the media center PC would certainly have been fully functional with 1 GB of total memory, but that would have left little spare memory for running games and other secondary functions. As much as we'd have liked to install 4 GB of memory, at the time we built this system, a pair of 2 GB modules cost $1,600, and they were available only in PC2-3200 speed. A pair of 1 GB PC2-6400 modules cost only $325, so that's what we chose.

Media Center Video Components

A media center PC system requires four separate video functions:

Display

The media center PC must display computer output on a television. That requires a standard PCIe or AGP video adapter or a motherboard with embedded graphics that is capable of outputting a video signal that can be displayed by a television set (rather than a computer monitor). Depending on the type of connector used by the television set, you will need one of the following output connectors on the video adapter, listed in order of increasing video quality:

RF

Older televisions and inexpensive current models may provide only an RF input, the familiar F-connector to which you connect the cable TV feed. If your television has only an RF connector, you will need to use a video adapter that provides an RF-out connector. Such connectors can generally be configured to output on TV channel 3 or 4. To receive the signal from the adapter, you tune the television to whatever channel the adapter is configured to use. If you want to watch TV from both the cable and the PC, you'll need a splitter to allow the TV to accept RF input from both sources. Note that many RF splitters, particularly amplified models, are designed to accept one RF input and split it to two or more devices, and do not necessarily work "backward" to allow two sources to be delivered to one device.

ALTERNATIVES: MOTHERBOARD

For a microATX Core 2 Duo system, there were no other motherboard choices when we built this system. By the time this book reaches print, there will likely be numerous choices. Any microATX motherboard made by Intel or ASUS with a suitable feature set should work fine. For a microATX Socket AM2 Athlon 64 X2 system, choose any compatible ASUS motherboard based on an nVIDIA chipset.

If you build your media center PC in a full ATX case, your motherboard options are much broader. For a Core 2 Duo or other Intel processor, choose any compatible motherboard made by Intel or ASUS with the feature set you need. For a Socket AM2 Athlon 64 X2 system, choose any compatible ASUS motherboard with the feature set you need.

ALTERNATIVES: MEMORY

Any compatible name-brand memory modules. Memory from different companies can vary dramatically in quality and reliability. For 20 years, we've depended on memory from Kingston and Crucial, and have never had cause to regret that decision.

Composite

A composite video-out connector supplies an analog video signal and connects to the television using a standard RCA cable. All video data is transferred on a single cable. Conventionally, a yellow cable is used for video. Most analog television sets—at least those that are likely to be used in a home theater setup—include an analog video-in connector. (You can use a set that does not provide analog video-in by connecting the video-out connector on the PC to an RF modulator and thence to the RF-in connector on the television.) Some PC video adapters provide an RCA video-out connector or a VIVO (Video-In Video-Out) connector. You'll need one of those if you intend to connect your media center PC to an analog television that has only a composite video input.

S-Video

An S-Video-out connector (Separate Video) supplies an analog video signal, and connects to the television using an S-Video cable. S-Video devotes separate wires to luminance (brightness) and chroma (color), and so offers better video quality than a composite video connection. Use a video adapter that provides an S-Video output if your television has an S-Video input. S-Video connectors are notoriously fragile. If you use S-Video on your media center PC, be very careful not to put any undue pressure on the connectors.

DVI

A DVI (Digital Visual Interface) connector supplies a digital video signal, and connects to the television using a standard DVI cable. Most older digital television sets and some current models provide a DVI connector. Many current PCIe and AGP video adapters provide a DVI connector, which is used by many digital flat-panel computer displays. You'll need a video adapter with DVI output if you intend to connect your media center PC to a digital television, either an EDTV or HDTV model.

HDMI

The HDMI (High-Definition Multimedia Interface) connector is the latest standard for connecting a digital signal to a digital television. HDMI is essentially DVI with the addition of HDCP (High-Bandwidth Digital Content Protection) DRM. For unprotected content, HDMI works just like DVI, with which it is backward compatible. For protected content, at the option of the content owner, HDMI can enforce a protected signal path. If the HDMI source is connected to a DVI display that does not support HDCP, the HDMI source may refuse to display the content or display it at low resolution. At the time we built our media center PC, there were no PC video adapters available that supported HDMI output with HDCP.

TV tuning

A television signal can originate from many sources. The original signal may be analog or digital. It may arrive at the media center PC as an over-the-air (OTA) broadcast signal, analog or digital, or via cable or satellite. The original signal type—analog or digital—does not determine the signal type you receive. For example, we have analog cable television service. Some of the channels we receive originate as analog signals; others originate as digital signals, but are converted by our cable television company to analog before it retransmits those signals to us. A satellite receiver receives all digital signals, but may provide an analog output, a digital output, or both for your television.

The type of signals you receive determine the type of tuner card you need. If your signal is delivered via satellite or digital cable, your options are very limited. There's no convenient way for a PC to tune the raw signals provided by these types of services, so the only alternative is to use the cable or satellite box to choose the channel you want to record. Fortunately, that process can be automated by using an IR Blaster or similar device to change channels on the cable/satellite box under the control of the media center PC. Conversely, for OTA (analog and/or digital) or analog cable, tuner cards are available to process these types of signals, which means the media center PC itself can change channels directly as needed to record the programs you specify.

Video capture

Television video uses standards and protocols that differ from those used by PC video. The media center PC must have the ability to capture a television video stream and process it into a form that can be stored and played back by the PC.

Video encoding/decoding

A raw, uncompressed video stream would fill even the largest hard disk very quickly. All practical video storage methods use some form of compression, such as MPEG-1, MPEG-2, or MPEG-4, to reduce the size of stored video data. In order to make playback practical in devices with limited processing power, such as DVD players, MPEG compression algorithms place the processing burden on compression (encoding), while making decompression (decoding) as easy as possible. So, although even a slow processor can decode and play video without straining, the process of capturing, encoding, and storing video requires a lot of CPU ticks.

Some adapters simply deliver a raw video stream to the main system processor, which must compress the data itself. Because real-time video compression is extremely demanding, using such an adapter means the media center PC must have a very fast CPU, and even the fastest CPU may drop frames during real-time encoding. Other adapters include special MPEG compression hardware that delivers a precompressed video stream to the media center PC for storage. Still other adapters

"HDMI-Ready" Does Not Guarantee HDCP Support

In 2005, some video adapter manufacturers began advertising their video adapters as "HDMI-ready" or "HDMI-capable" or "HDMI-compatible." Those adapters were in fact HDMI-ready, but only in the sense of being physically and electronically compatible with HDMI televisions. These adapters do not support HDCP, and cannot be upgraded to support it, short of being returned to the manufacturer and having new chips soldered onto them.

Needless to say, many of the people who bought these video adapters with the understanding that they would be capable of displaying HDCP-protected content at full resolution were not amused to learn that these adapters could not and never would be able to display HDCP-protected content. ATI in particular earned the ire of many customers, who believed it had misrepresented its products. nVIDIA never claimed that its chipsets offered full support for HDMI/HDCP, although some nVIDIA OEMs did make such claims. The result has become a gigantic mess, and we expect class action lawsuits to result from it.

At this point, it is unclear to us whether PC video adapters with full HDMI/HDCP support will ever be available. The movie studios intensely distrust PC technology, and it is possible they may block any attempt to bring full HDMI/HDCP support to the PC platform.

use the video GPU to encode the video stream. Adapters with MPEG compression in hardware place very little burden on the main system CPU, which allows you to use a slower, cooler, quieter CPU for the media center PC.

Adapters may provide any combination of these functions. For example, some adapters provide video capture and TV tuning functions, but require a separate graphics card to display the video. Other adapters provide display and capture functions, but have no tuner, and so are useful only for capturing direct video signals such as the output from a camcorder. Still other adapters may provide display, tuning, and capture functions, but offload encoding functions to the main system processor. Choosing the proper adapter(s) is a major consideration for any media center PC.

TV tuner/capture card

Hauppauge WinTV-PVR-150 analog tuner
(*http://www.hauppauge.com*)

pcHDTV HD-5500 Hi Definition Television digital tuner
(*http://www.pchdtv.com*)

We want our media center PC to handle two signal sources, analog cable and OTA digital. We decided that the ability to record one digital channel at a time was sufficient, but wanted the option to record two analog channels simultaneously, or to watch one analog channel using "live pause" while recording another analog channel. That means we need three tuners, two analog and one digital.

For the analog tuners, we initially decided to use a pair of Hauppauge WinTV-PVR-150 cards, shown in Figure 6-2. The PVR-150 offers the best video quality available, has excellent hardware-based MPEG encoding, and is supported by nearly every PVR application. The retail-boxed PVR-150 includes an IR remote control with receiver and an IR Blaster (transmitter) that can be used to control a satellite or digital cable box. (We don't need to do that right now, but that may change shortly, and it's always best to be prepared.) With two PVR-150s, we have a remote control for each of us, which is no small aid to domestic tranquility.

Analog TV tuner cards have been available for years, but digital TV tuner cards are a relatively new product category. HDTV tuners are available from several companies, including ATI and AVerMedia, but most have only Windows drivers, and some work only under Windows MCE. We consider Windows a poor choice of operating system for a media center PC, so we continued our search for a Linux-based HDTV tuner card. On the recommendation of our technical reviewer Brian Bilbrey, we chose the pcHDTV HD-5500 Hi Definition Television digital tuner card, which offers full Linux support.

The HD-5500 supports all 18 ATSC-compliant digital formats. It also supports unencrypted QAM 64 and QAM 256 cable signals; that is of little use to us, because we plan to capture only OTA HDTV signals. The HD-5500 also supports capturing NTSC (analog) television signals. We won't use that capability, because our HD-5500 card will connect only to an OTA HDTV antenna.

The HD-5500 does not have onboard compression hardware, but it can offload compression tasks to an nVIDIA video adapter. For that reason, we'll install an nVIDIA video adapter in our media center PC.

As you might have noticed, we had a slight problem. We planned to install three PCI tuner/capture cards in our media center PC, but it has only two PCI slots. Hmmmm.

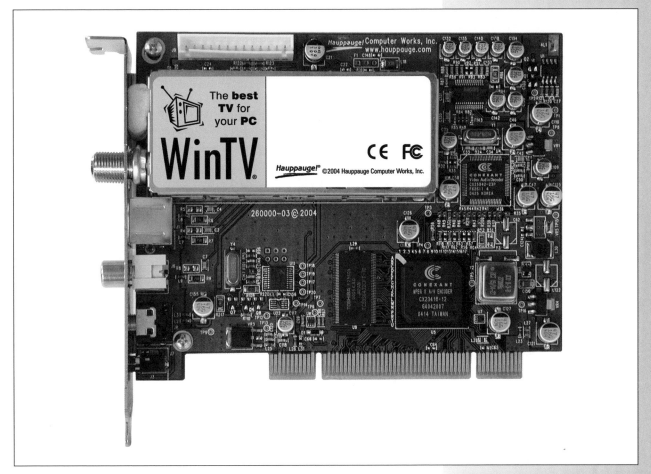

Figure 6-2. The Hauppauge WInTV-PVR-150 tuner/capture card

Chapter 6, Building a Media Center PC

Remote Controls and IR Blasters

Hauppauge sells their tuner/capture cards in various bundles. Some include only the bare card and drivers. Others include a remote control and receiver, some also an IR Blaster. The IR Blaster connects to the media center PC, and can output infrared signals that mimic those produced by a remote control. By pointing the output of the IR Blaster toward the remote receiver on a set-top box or similar device, the media center PC can send commands to that device.

For example, if you receive your television signal via a cable or satellite system that requires selecting the channel via a set-top box, you can point the IR Blaster at the set-top box. To schedule and record a program, you set the media center PC to record whatever signal is present on the wire at the required time. Under programmatic control, the IR Blaster sends a signal to the set-top box at the appropriate time to turn it on and change to the proper channel. It's a kludge, but it generally works pretty well, or so we're told. We have analog cable, so our analog tuner cards can select the proper channel directly. Similarly, we use OTA for digital reception, so all available digital channels are on the wire simultaneously, and can be tuned directly by the pcHDTV tuner card.

Instead of using the WinTV-PVR-150 single-tuner card, we could use the similar Hauppauge WinTV-PVR-500 dual-tuner card. With two PCI slots available, we could use any one of the tuner/capture card configurations shown in Table 6-1.

Table 6-1. Possible tuner/capture card configurations

Total tuners	Analog tuners	Digital tuners	Hauppauge PVR-150	Hauppauge PVR-500	pcHDTV HD-5500
1	1	-	1	-	-
1	-	1	-	-	1
2	1	1	1	-	1
2	2	-	2	-	-
2	2	-	-	1	-
2	-	2	-	-	2
3	2	1	-	1	1
3	3	-	1	1	-
4	4	-	-	2	-

We decided to install one Hauppauge WinTV-PVR-500 tuner/capture card to provide two analog tuners, and one pcHDTV HD-5500 tuner/capture card to provide one HDTV tuner.

Video adapter and capture/tuner Card

Gigabyte GV-NX73G128D-RH (*http://www.giga-byte.com*)

Although we list the Gigabyte GV-NX73G128D-RH video adapter we used, we won't recommend a specific video adapter for your system, because so much depends on your own situation and needs. Consider the following factors when you choose a video adapter:

Internal interface

The first consideration is the internal interface. If your motherboard has an AGP slot, you need an AGP video adapter. If your motherboard provides a PCI Express slot, you need a PCIe video adapter. We chose a PCIe model for compatibility with the motherboard we selected.

External interface

Make sure the video adapter you choose provides external interface(s) that match your television. Video adapters are readily available with a DVI connector, composite video connector, S-Video connector, or some combination. We chose an adapter that provides DVI and S-Video outputs.

Performance

For simple TV playback and basic computer functions, any current video adapter is sufficient. If you plan to use your media center PC for serious gaming, you'll need a fast video adapter. We don't plan to use our media center PC for gaming, so we chose an inexpensive PCIe video adapter.

Noise level

Many low-end video adapters use passive cooling. Most midrange and high-performance video adapters use cooling fans, which may be too loud for a media center PC. If you install a fast video adapter for gaming, give preference to one of the fanless models.

Compatibility with tuner card(s)

Nearly any video adapter is compatible with nearly any tuner card, in the sense that the two do not conflict. However, some tuner cards (such as the pcHDTV model we are using for HDTV support) do not have on-board hardware video acceleration, but instead depend on the video adapter GPU to accelerate the video stream. If your card is one of those, make sure that the video adapter you choose can provide hardware acceleration support to your tuner card.

We chose the Gigabyte GV-NX73G128D-RH video adapter—we'll call it the GV-RH for short—for the following reasons.

- Obviously, we needed a PCI Express model to fit the PCIe slot in our Intel D946GZIS motherboard.

- We needed a video adapter that provided connections for video-out and HDTV-out, which the GV-RH does.

- We wanted a passively cooled video adapter, both to avoid the noise of a video adapter fan and to increase reliability. When a video adapter fan fails, the results are not pretty. Realistically, a media center PC stuffed into an entertainment center is unlikely to get much in the way of periodic maintenance or cleaning, which makes a fan failure more likely.

- The pcHDTV HD-5500 Hi Definition Television digital tuner can use an nVIDIA video adapter as a co-processor to accelerate HDTV streams.

- We wanted a video adapter with enough graphics processing power to support Vista and for casual gaming. The GV-RH uses the nVIDIA GeForce 7300 GS chipset, which, although it is no speed demon, is perfectly adequate for Vista and light gaming.

- We wanted to keep the price below $100, and ideally below $50.

We chose the Gigabyte GV-RH based on those criteria. (Note that the RH on the end of the product number is significant; Gigabyte also sells a GV-NX73 model without the RH postfix that lacks HDTV support.) Your priorities may differ from ours. Choose accordingly.

Hard Disk Drive

Seagate Barracuda 7200.10 ST3750640AS 750GB (two)
(*http://www.seagate.com*)

Hard drive capacity, performance, noise level, and reliability are critical for a media center PC system.

Capacity

The most obvious consideration is capacity. Depending on the characteristics of the video stream and the compression type used, standard-definition video eats disk space at a rate of 700 MB to 5 GB per hour. At the low end, 700 MB/hour stores only VHS-quality video. We'll probably want to store most of what we record at DVD quality, which means we have to plan for the 2.5 to 5 GB/hour rate that typical DVD-quality SD video streams require. That means 100 GB of disk space translates to only 20 to 40 hours of video storage. Recording HDTV is even more demanding. Depending on capture resolution and compression method, one hour of HDTV may consume up to 30 GB of disk space.

We also need to store more than just video. The media center PC will also store and serve CD audio discs ripped and compressed in OGG or MP3 format at a high-quality setting or FLAC (Free Lossless Audio Codec). OGG and MP3 use variable bit-rate compression, but it's safe to assume that an average audio CD will require at least 150 MB of storage space when compressed at a quality level acceptable to us, and FLAC requires even more disk space. Barbara has several hundred CDs she'll want to rip, which may require another 100 GB or more of storage space.

Performance

Hard drive performance is another important criterion. The media center PC will spend much of its time idling, but at times it may need to do many things simultaneously, such as record one video stream while playing back another while also serving an audio stream. Accordingly, large cache and fast rotation rate are important. On that basis, we concluded that we needed a 7,200 RPM hard drive with an 8 MB or larger buffer.

SLOW AND STEADY

Dedicated PVRs like the TiVo often use 5,400 RPM drives with small buffers, but they're able to use such slow drives only because they are doing a limited number of things simultaneously.

Noise level

Modern 7,200 RPM hard drives differ greatly in noise level. Seagate Barracuda models are the quietest drives available that have acceptable performance.

Reliability

Seagate drives are extremely reliable, but even so we were concerned about the possibility of drive failure. As Barbara sometimes points out, Robert has to sleep sometime, and the thought of losing a week's or a month's worth of stored programs to a drive failure was not a pleasant one. Our first thought was to install two Serial ATA drives and mirror them using RAID 1. The obvious downside to that is that mirroring cuts drive capacity in half, and we need all the capacity we can get. Then we realized we already had a solution. The media center PC system will be connected to our internal network and, via our firewall, to the Internet. It has to be connected so that it can download program guide updates, periodically reset its clock against an SNTP time server, and so on. We have literally terabytes of disk spinning elsewhere on our network, so it'd be easy enough to set up a cron job to periodically check the media center PC hard drives and copy any new files to a hard drive elsewhere on the network. Problem solved.

We concluded that we wanted at least 1000 GB (1 TB) of available drive space on the media center PC system, and more would be better. The Antec Fusion case we chose has two hard drive bays, so the obvious decision was to install two of the largest high-performance hard drives available. On that basis, we chose two Seagate Barracuda SATA 750 GB drives.

> **ALTERNATIVES: HARD DISK DRIVE**
>
> None, really. The Seagate 750 GB drives are huge, fast, quiet, and extremely reliable. At the time we built this system, there were no other drives available that came even close to matching the combination of desirable characteristics of the Seagate Barracuda drives.

RAID 0

With two hard drives, we have the option of using RAID 0 striping for increased disk performance. We don't expect to need it, but many commercial Windows MCE PCs use RAID 0, presumably for good reason. Our testing has shown the RAID 0 has little or no real performance benefit on typical desktop systems, but is useful on servers that experience heavy disk access. In some respects, the disk access patterns of a media center PC more resemble a server than a desktop PC, so we'll leave the RAID 0 option open.

At first glance, it might appear that we can't use RAID on this system. The Intel D946GZIS motherboard does not include Intel Matrix RAID, and we have no free slots to add a RAID controller. Fortunately, both Windows and Linux provide software RAID 0 support. Software RAID is a bit slower than Intel Matrix RAID or RAID implemented with a dedicated RAID controller, but it should be more than fast enough for our purposes.

Optical Drive

NEC ND-3550A DVD writer (*http://www.necam.com*)

At $35 or so, DVD writers are so inexpensive nowadays that it's senseless to install any other type of optical drive. The optical drive in the media center PC is used for everything from loading software to watching DVDs to writing recorded programs to a burnable DVD for archiving, so it's important to choose a reliable model that supports all of the types of media you want to read and write.

We chose the NEC ND-3550A DVD writer for the media center PC, but any similar model from BenQ, Lite-On, NEC, Pioneer, or Plextor would serve as well. The Antec Fusion case has a universal optical drive door that hides the front bezel of the optical drive, so there's no need to match the color of the optical drive to the case.

WHAT ABOUT HD-DVD OR BLU-RAY?

We considered installing a high-capacity HD-DVD or Blu-Ray optical drive in the media center PC, but decided to bide our time. This system has the bandwidth and processor power to handle these new-generation drives, but the drives are still extremely expensive and there are few titles available on HD-DVD or Blu-Ray discs. Also, there's the small matter that when HD-DVD or Blu-Ray wins the war, the other will be orphaned. We have no intention of spending $1,000 on an optical drive that may become useless in a year or two.

Also, it's unclear to us at this point exactly what DRM hardware would be required to allow a PC-based media center system to play high-capacity discs, if indeed that is possible at all. Presumably, a PC-based media center system would require at least full HDMI/HDCP support, which is not yet available on the PC platform. It may also require Trusted Platform Module (TPM) support "married" to the optical drive and video subsystem.

So we decided to ignore high-capacity DVD for now. Eventually, the price of HD-DVD and Blu-Ray optical drives will fall into the $50 range and blank discs to $0.50 apiece, by which time "DVD Jon" Johansen will have cracked the encryption used by HD-DVD and Blu-Ray discs. We'll wait until those things happen before we install any type of high-capacity optical drive in this system.

Keyboard and Mouse

Logitech diNovo Media Desktop (*http://www.logitech.com*)

The type of keyboard and mouse you need for a media center PC depends on how you use the system. If you don't intend to use it as a standard PC—for example, for checking email, browsing the Web, or playing games—you need a keyboard and mouse only for initial system configuration and infrequent changes to the system. All other functions are handled with the remote control via the "10-foot interface" of MythTV or whatever PVR application you're running.

Although we won't do much serious gaming on our media center PC, we do intend to use it for browsing the Web, checking email, and similar tasks. That meant we needed a cordless keyboard and mouse that would work reliably at across-the-room distances. Most cordless keyboards and mice have very short range, a meter or so at most. There are some long-range

Out of Sight, Out of Mind

Many media center PC owners leave an inexpensive wired mouse and keyboard connected to the system, stored on top of or behind the case. Alternatively, you can temporarily connect a keyboard and mouse to front-panel USB ports when you need them, and store them elsewhere when you don't.

keyboard/mouse combos available, intended for corporate presentations and similar functions, but those we looked at cost several hundred dollars.

The best option we found was the Logitech diNovo Media Desktop. At $140 or so street price, this isn't an inexpensive desktop combo, but it is ideal for a media center PC. Logitech claims a range of up to 60 feet. We didn't test at anything like that distance, but the diNovo Media Desktop does work reliably at the 10- to 15-foot ranges typically needed for a media center PC.

Speakers

Home audio speakers

Logitech Z-5500 speaker system (*http://www.logitech.com*)

Most people who build a media center PC install it in their home entertainment center and connect the PC audio outputs to their receiver or amplifier. Obviously, if you already have a good receiver and speakers, you might as well use them.

Of course, not everyone has a suitable receiver and speaker set. When we built the Home Theater PC system for the first edition of this book, we'd decided to move our elderly JVC receiver and speakers to the downstairs guest suite and replace them with a high-power PC speaker system. At that time, the best PC speaker set available was the Logitech Z-680 5.1 speaker system, which we used.

Logitech has since replaced the Z-680 with the Z-5500, which has similar specifications and equal sound quality. The street price of the Z-5500 is $260 or so, about half the price of a traditional home audio receivers and speakers with comparable power and sound quality. The Z-5500 incorporates four satellite speakers for left/right and front/rear audio, a center-channel speaker, and an LFE (low-frequency emitter) subwoofer. The satellite speakers are rated at 62W RMS each, the center-channel speaker at 69W RMS, and the LFE at a massive 188W RMS, for a total RMS output of 505W.

PEAK VERSUS RMS

Two methods are commonly used to specify the output power of amplifiers. Peak Power is often specified for computer speakers, particularly inexpensive ones, but is essentially meaningless. Peak Power specifies maximum instantaneous power an amplifier can deliver, but says nothing about how much power it can deliver continuously. The RMS (Root Mean Square) Power rating is more useful because it specifies how much power the amplifier can deliver continuously.

The Z-5500 speaker system includes Dolby Digital and DTS hardware decoding and is THX certified. We confess that we don't understand what all that means, but our audiophile friends tell us those are Good Things. And, although admitting it may label us as audio barbarians, we have to say that the audio from our older Z-680 speaker system sounds as good to us as anything else we've listened to, and the Z-5500 audio quality is just as good. If the Z-5500 speaker set is a bit expensive for your budget, consider the Z-5300e, which costs less than half as much, provides 280W RMS total power, and has very good sound quality.

YOUR MILEAGE MAY VARY

One of our technical reviewers makes a good point. He writes:

"Speakers are probably the most subjective elements of the system. While I certainly have no argument with your selection there are many fine alternatives in the same price range. It's also an area where more dollars doesn't always mean better performance or better sound. I think it appropriate to urge readers to make the effort to personally audition speakers where possible rather than rely solely on reviews and recommendations... and given that room interactions play such a major role in speaker performance they should buy from an outlet with a liberal return policy."

Table 6-2 summarizes our component choices for the media center PC system.

Table 6-2. Bill of materials for media center PC

Component	Product
Case	Antec Fusion
Power supply	Antec 430W (included)
Processor	Intel Core 2 Duo E6400
Motherboard	Intel D946GZIS
Memory	Kingston KHX6400D2LLK2/2G 2GB PC6400 DDR2 Memory Kit (1 GB × 2)
Video adapter	Gigabyte GV-NX73G128D-RH GeForce 7300GS
SDTV tuner card	Hauppauge WinTV-PVR-500 (dual tuner)
HDTV tuner card	pcHDTV HD-5500
Hard drives	Seagate ST3750640AS Barracuda 7200.10 750 GB Serial ATA (two)
Optical drive	NEC ND-3550A DVD+R/RW writer
Keyboard and mouse	Logitech diNovo Media Desktop
Speakers	Home audio speakers or Logitech Z-5500 speaker system

When we built this system in August 2006, the total component cost was under $2,000, excluding speakers. Every commercial Windows MCE system we looked at in the $2,800 range had specifications that were noticeably inferior to our configuration.

A typical $2,800 commercial MCE system used a Pentium D processor rather than a Core 2 Duo, had half as much and slower memory, and only a fifth to a third as much disk space. Most $2,800 MCE systems had dual tuners, usually two analog models, but sometimes one analog and one digital. Eyeballing it, we concluded that we could have effectively matched the performance and functionality of a typical $2,800 commercial MCE system for about $1,400. Clearly, MCE systems are high-margin products.

Those systems did, of course, come with Windows MCE preinstalled and pre-configured. For someone who wants a turnkey system, it may be worth paying the 50% to 100% price premium for a commercial MCE system. But if you're willing to get your hands dirty, you can build your own media center PC for a lot less money, and end up with a better, more flexible, and much more reliable system.

Building the Media Center PC

Figure 6-3 shows the major components of the media center PC. The Logitech diNovo keyboard and mouse are on top of the Antec Fusion case at the rear, with the NEC ND-3550A and the Seagate Barracuda hard drives at the left front, and the Gigabyte video adapter at the right front. The Intel D946GZIS motherboard is in front of the Antec Fusion case, surrounded by the Intel Core 2 Duo processor and CPU cooler to the left, the Kingston HyperX memory modules in front, and the Hauppauge WinTV-PVR-500 and pcHDTV HD-5500 tuner cards to the right.

Figure 6-3. Media center PC components, awaiting construction

Before you proceed, verify that you have all of the necessary components. Open each box and confirm that all items on the packing list are present.

Choosing a Work Surface

We build systems on the kitchen table because it provides plenty of work room, easy access from front and rear, and plenty of light, all of which are important. Barbara isn't happy about having her kitchen table thus occupied, but when Robert explained that the alternative was using her antique dining room table, she grudgingly agreed that the kitchen table was the better choice. Whatever location you choose to build your system, make sure it provides sufficient workspace, easy access, and good lighting. Spousal approval is optional, but highly recommended.

SEQUENCING THE BUILD

You needn't follow the exact sequence we describe when building your own system. For example, some people prefer to install the drives before installing the motherboard while others prefer the converse. The best sequence may depend on the case you use and the components you are installing. For example, some case and motherboard combinations make it difficult or impossible to connect the ATX power cable after drives have been installed. Use your best judgment while building the system and you won't go far wrong.

Preparing the Case

The Antec Fusion case is extremely quiet and well ventilated, but with those virtues come more complexity than is usual for a PC case. The Antec Fusion divides the components into three chambers. The motherboard resides in the largest of these chambers, with the hard drives in another and the power supply and optical drive in the third. This means, as we found by experience, that it pays to think through what you're doing before you do it.

For example, Antec uses a sliding door pass-through to route cables from the power supply chamber to the motherboard chamber. Once you install expansion cards in the motherboard, access to that pass-through is constricted. We actually installed the expansion cards twice before we got it right. The first time, we forgot to pass through a Molex power cable, thinking that the only component that required a Molex connector was the optical drive, which is in the same chamber as the power supply. Alas, we'd forgotten the case fans in the motherboard chamber, which also require a Molex power cable. So we had to uninstall all the expansion cards, route the Molex cable into the motherboard chamber, and reinstall all of the expansion cards.

AVOID FIREWORKS

Before you do **anything** else, make sure that the power supply is set to the correct input voltage. Some power supplies, including the unit bundled with the Antec Fusion case, autodetect input voltage and set themselves automatically. Other power supplies require moving a slide switch to indicate the correct input voltage.

If your mains voltage is 115V and the power supply is set for 230V, no damage occurs. The system simply won't start. However, if your mains voltage is 230V and the power supply expects 115V, you will see a very short and expensive fireworks show the first time you plug the system in. The motherboard, processor, memory, expansion cards, and drives will all be burnt to a crisp within a fraction of a second.

To begin preparing the Antec Fusion case, place it on a flat surface and remove the single thumbscrew at the top rear, as shown in Figure 6-4, and then slide the top panel to the rear and lift it off, as shown in Figure 6-5.

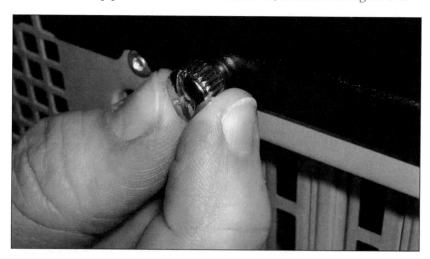

Figure 6-4. Remove the thumbscrew that secures the top panel

Figure 6-5. Slide the top panel to the rear and lift it off

Like most cases, the Antec Fusion comes with a generic rear-panel I/O template. Generic templates never fit any motherboard we've ever used, so we're not sure why case makers bother to include them. Removing the generic template simply adds one more task.

To remove the generic template, press gently inward on it with a screwdriver handle, as shown in Figure 6-6. Don't worry about bending the template, because you'll discard it anyway. Do take care not to bend the cutout area of the case, which would make it very difficult to install the proper template. Support the edge of the cutout area with your fingers, and press on the generic template until it snaps out.

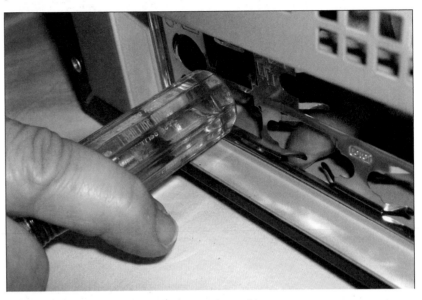

Figure 6-6. Press gently on the generic I/O template until it snaps out

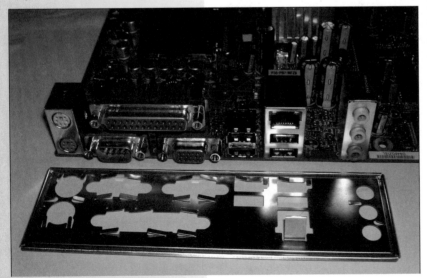

Figure 6-7. Compare the custom I/O template with the I/O panel of the motherboard

Every motherboard comes with a custom I/O template that matches the ports on its rear I/O panels. The included template is nearly always correct, but we have infrequently received a motherboard with an incorrect template. Before you install the custom I/O template supplied with the motherboard, compare it against the motherboard I/O panel, as shown in Figure 6-7. If you received the wrong template, contact the motherboard manufacturer to request a replacement.

To install the custom I/O template, first make sure that it's oriented properly relative to the motherboard ports. Working from inside the case, align the template with the cutout. Using a screwdriver handle, start at one corner, as shown in Figure 6-8, and press gently until the template snaps into place. Run the screwdriver handle around the edges and corners of the template to ensure that it's fully seated.

Figure 6-8. Press gently to seat the custom I/O template

After seating the I/O template, hold the motherboard aligned in position directly over the case, as shown in Figure 6-9. Compare the positions of the motherboard mounting holes with the standoff mounting positions in the case.

Figure 6-9. Determine which positions require standoffs

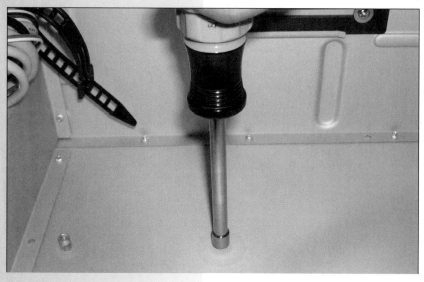

Figure 6-10. Install a standoff in each position that corresponds to a motherboard mounting hole

The Intel D946GZIS has eight mounting holes. The Antec Fusion case has six standoffs preinstalled, all of which correspond to mounting hole positions in the motherboard. Locate and note the two positions that require standoffs to be installed.

Install a brass standoff in each required position, and then use the motherboard again to verify that a standoff is installed at each of the required eight positions. Although you can screw in the standoffs using just your fingers, it's much easier and faster to use a 5mm nut driver, as shown in Figure 6-10.

Be careful not to overtorque the standoffs as you install them. The standoffs are made of soft brass, and the motherboard tray, although steel, is relatively thin. Applying too much torque can strip the standoff or the screw hole. Finger-tight is good enough.

WARNING

Make absolutely sure that every standoff installed corresponds to a motherboard mounting hole. An extra standoff can contact the bottom of the motherboard, causing it to short and possibly damaging or destroying the motherboard and other components.

Populating the Motherboard

It is always easier to populate the motherboard—install the processor and memory—while the motherboard is outside the case. In fact, you must do so with some systems, because installing the CPU cooler requires access to both sides of the motherboard. Even if it is possible to populate the motherboard while it is installed in the case, we always recommend doing so with the motherboard outside the case and lying flat on the work surface.

When the motherboard is flat on a firm surface, it's completely supported. When it is installed in the case, it's supported only by the standoffs. Installing a CPU cooler or memory may require significant pressure, which runs the risk of cracking an installed motherboard. Play it smart and populate your motherboard before you install it in the case.

Installing the processor

To install the Intel Core 2 Duo E6400
processor, begin by unlatching and
lifting the socket arm, as shown in
Figure 6-11. Swing the socket arm
past vertical until it reaches the end
of its travel.

With the socket lever open, the
retention plate is unlatched and can
be lifted upward, away from the
socket, as shown in Figure 6-12.
The retention plate has a black plastic cover that protects the delicate
contacts inside the socket when no
processor is installed.

Figure 6-11. Lift the socket lever
to prepare the socket to receive the
processor

Figure 6-12. Lift the retention plate away from the socket

Snap this protective plastic cover off, as shown in Figure 6-13, and store it in a safe place. If you ever remove the processor from the motherboard, reinstall the cover to protect the socket until you install another processor.

Figure 6-13. Remove the protective plastic cover

Figure 6-14. The socket prepared to receive the processor

Figure 6-14 shows the LGA775 socket prepared to receive the processor. In this state, the delicate contacts of the socket are fully exposed, and the socket is easily damaged. Take care to avoid touching the contacts or dropping anything on the exposed socket. If the socket is damaged, the only alternative is to replace the motherboard.

The processor is also protected by a plastic snap-on cover. When you are ready to install the processor in its socket, remove the plastic cover, as shown in Figure 6-15. Handle the processor only by its edges, and make sure the contact surface of the processor does not touch anything except the socket. If you ever remove the processor from the socket, reinstall the protective cover before you store the processor.

Figure 6-15. Remove the protective plastic cover from the processor

Pin 1 is indicated on the processor by a small golden triangle and on the socket by a beveled corner, both visible at the lower-right corner of the socket in Figure 6-16. The processor also has two keying notches that correspond with two nubs in the socket, both of which are also visible in Figure 6-16.

Hold the processor by its edges, align pin 1 of the processor with pin 1 of the socket and drop the processor into place, as shown in Figure 6-16. The processor should seat flush with the socket without any pressure being applied to it. If seating the processor requires more than a gentle nudge, the processor is not aligned properly with the socket. Remove the processor, align it properly, and drop it back into the socket.

Figure 6-16. Align the processor with the socket and drop it into place

Processor Markings

In case you're wondering, normal Core 2 Duo processors aren't labeled with a felt-tip pen. The processor shown in Figure 6-16 is an early Engineering Sample provided to us by Intel before the Core 2 Duo processors were officially released. Ordinarily, it's possible to identify an Intel processor by the S-Spec number on it. However, at the time we received this processor, Intel hadn't yet published S-Specs for the Core 2 Duo. Our contact at Intel kindly hand-labeled the processor before sending it to us.

After the processor is seated, lower the retention plate into place, as shown in Figure 6-17. Note the lip on the retention plate and the matching cammed section of the socket lever. As you press the socket lever down to latch it in place, make sure that the cammed section engages the lip on the retention plate and presses it firmly into position, as shown in Figure 6-18.

Figure 6-17. Lower the retention plate into position

Figure 6-18. Make sure the cam on the socket lever engages the lip on the retention plate

With the retention plate closed, press down firmly on the socket lever and snap it into the latched position, as shown in Figure 6-19. Once the socket lever is latched, the processor is secured in the socket and protected by the metal socket body.

Installing the CPU cooler

The Intel Core 2 Duo is a low-current processor, but low current is a relative term. Under heavy load, the Intel Core 2 Duo consumes about as much power as a 60W light bulb and turns that power into waste heat—about as much heat as a 60W light bulb produces. To prevent the processor from overheating and shutting down, that waste heat must be removed by a CPU cooler. Intel supplies a good CPU cooler with the retail-boxed Core 2 Duo processor. The bundled cooler isn't quite as efficient or quiet as the best after-market coolers, but it's not far behind. We received a stock Intel CPU cooler with the processor, so we decided to use it. If we later decide we want a better CPU cooler, we can always buy and install one.

Polish the CPU heat spreader to remove any foreign material. If there is no thermal pad installed on the heatsink base, polish it as well and apply thermal compound to the CPU heat spreader. Orient the CPU cooler above the processor, as shown in Figure 6-20. The cooler base has four expanding posts for which the motherboard has four corresponding mounting holes. Position the CPU cooler so that the posts are aligned with the mounting holes. You can orient the CPU cooler in any position that matches the square mounting hole pattern.

Figure 6-19. Close the socket lever and snap it into the latched position

Figure 6-20. Align the CPU cooler over the four mounting holes

Don't Forget Thermal Compound

The stock Intel CPU cooler comes with a thermal pad already installed. If you use a CPU cooler that does not include a thermal pad, apply thermal compound before you install the CPU cooler. Follow the instructions supplied with the thermal compound. A CPU cooler used without a thermal pad or thermal compound cannot cool the processor properly.

We recommend positioning the CPU cooler to minimize the amount of slack in the fan power lead. With the expanding posts aligned with the motherboard mounting holes, press down each post, as shown in Figure 6-21, until it snaps into the locked position.

Figure 6-21. Press down each locking post until it snaps into place

---

WARNING

Intel recommends installing the CPU cooler after the motherboard is installed in the case, but more than one person has cracked a motherboard by following that advice. Usually, the expanding posts seat and lock easily, but at times it requires significant pressure to get them seated and locked.

For that reason, we prefer to install Socket 775 CPU coolers with the motherboard outside the case. With other sockets, we prefer to install the cooler with the motherboard on a flat, firm surface, but it's not possible to do that with Socket 775 coolers because the expanding posts protrude through the motherboard. The safest way to install a Socket 775 cooler is shown in Figure 6-21. Support the underside of the motherboard with your fingers as you press each expanding post through the motherboard.

Don't forget to connect the fan power lead to the fan power header pins on the motherboard, as shown in Figure 6-22. (We did forget until after we installed the memory, which is why you can see one corner of a Kingston HyperX memory module peeking out at the upper-left corner of the image.) If there's excessive slack in the CPU fan power cable, secure it to make sure it can't foul the CPU fan.

Figure 6-22. Connect the CPU fan cable to the CPU fan connector

---

WARNING

If you remove the CPU cooler, you must use new thermal compound or a new thermal pad when you reinstall it. Before you install new thermal compound, remove all vestiges of the old thermal compound or pad, using friction from the ball of your thumb or another means. Follow the directions supplied with the new thermal compound precisely when you install it.

Installing memory

Installing memory in the Intel D946GZIS motherboard is easy. There are two memory modules to be installed, and two memory slots available. Pivot the white plastic locking tabs on both sides of both DIMM sockets outward to prepare the slots to receive DIMMs. Orient each DIMM with the notch in the contact area of the DIMM aligned with the raised plastic tab in the slot and slide the DIMM into place, as shown in Figure 6-23.

Figure 6-23. Orient the DIMM with the notch aligned properly with the socket

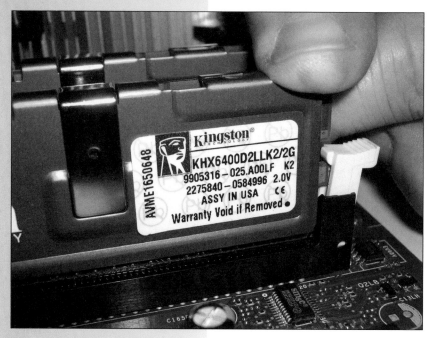

Figure 6-24. Seat the DIMM by pressing straight down with both thumbs until it snaps into place

With the DIMM properly aligned with the slot and oriented vertically relative to the slot, use both thumbs to press down on the DIMM until it snaps into place. The locking tabs should automatically pivot back up into the locked position, as shown in Figure 6-24, when the DIMM snaps into place. If they don't, close them manually to lock the DIMM into the socket.

With the processor and memory installed, you're almost ready to install the motherboard in the case. Before you do that, check the motherboard documentation to determine if any configuration jumpers need to be set. The Intel D946GZIS has only one jumper, which sets operating mode. On our motherboard, that jumper was set correctly by default, so we proceeded to the next step.

Installing the Motherboard

Installing the motherboard may take as long as all other assembly steps combined, because there are so many cables to connect. It's important to get all of them connected right, so take your time and verify each connection before and after you make it.

Seating and securing the motherboard

Figure 6-25. Slide the motherboard into position

To begin, slide the motherboard into the case, as shown in Figure 6-25. Carefully align the back panel I/O connectors with the corresponding holes in the I/O template, and slide the motherboard toward the rear of the case until the motherboard mounting holes line up with the standoffs you installed earlier.

The I/O template has metal grounding tabs that make contact with various back-panel I/O connectors. Make certain that the tabs are positioned correctly and do not intrude into one or more of the port connectors. More than once, we've mounted a motherboard, inserted all the screws, and connected all the cables before we noticed that there was a metal tab sticking into one of our USB or LAN ports. Before you secure the motherboard in place, verify that the back-panel I/O connectors are mated properly with the I/O template, as shown in Figure 6-26.

Figure 6-26. Back panel connectors should mate cleanly with the I/O template

Once the motherboard is positioned properly and you have verified that the back-panel I/O port connectors are mated cleanly with the I/O template, insert a screw through each motherboard mounting hole into the corresponding standoff, as shown in Figure 6-27. For the first two or three screws, you may have to apply pressure with one hand to keep the holes and standoffs aligned while driving the screw with the other.

At times it's difficult to get all the holes and standoffs aligned. If that occurs, insert two screws into easily accessible positions but don't tighten the screws completely. You should then be able to force the motherboard into complete alignment, with all holes matching the standoffs. At that point, insert one or two more screws into less-accessible standoffs and tighten them completely. Finish mounting the motherboard by inserting screws into all standoffs and tightening them. Don't put excessive force on the screws, or you may crack the motherboard. Finger-tight is plenty.

Figure 6-27. Securing the motherboard

SCREWED

With cheap motherboards and cases, it's sometimes impossible to get all of the mounting holes aligned with the standoffs. With high-quality products like the Antec case and Intel motherboard, everything usually lines up perfectly. But if you find yourself unable to insert all of the motherboard mounting screws, don't despair. We like to get all the screws installed, both for physical support and to make sure all of the grounding points on the motherboard are grounded, but getting most of the screws installed—say six or seven of the eight—is normally good enough.

If you are unable to install all of the screws, take the time to remove the brass standoffs where no screw will be installed. A misaligned standoff may short something out. In positions where you cannot use brass standoffs because of alignment problems, you can substitute white nylon standoffs, a few of which are usually included in the parts package. (If not, you can get them at most computer stores.) You may have to trim the nylon standoffs to length to make them fit. Jim Cooley suggests using double chopsticks, which are the right thickness to support the motherboard and are made of nonconducting wood.

It's particularly important to provide some support for the motherboard near the expansion slots, where significant pressure may be applied when installing cards. If the motherboard is unsupported, pressing down may crack it.

Connecting the front-panel switch and indicator cables

Once the motherboard is secured, the next step is to connect the front panel switch and indicator cables to the motherboard, as shown in Figure 6-28. Although Intel has defined a standard front panel connector block and uses that standard on its own motherboards, few other motherboard makers adhere to that standard. Accordingly, rather than provide an Intel-standard monolithic connector block that would be useless for motherboards that do not follow the Intel standard, most case makers provide individual two- or three-pin connectors for each switch and indicator.

The only essential front-panel connector is the power switch, which must be connected for you to be able to start the system. You'll probably also want to connect the reset switch and the hard disk activity LED (shown in Figure 6-28). Your case may have front-panel cables for which no corresponding pins exist on the motherboard. For example, many cases include a speaker cable, but most motherboards have embedded speakers and so may not include pins to connect to the case speaker. Conversely, your motherboard may have pins for which the case has no corresponding cable. For example, the Intel D946GZIS motherboard has pins for a Power LED, which the Antec Fusion case does not provide a cable for. (Instead of using a traditional power LED powered by the motherboard, the Antec Fusion uses front-panel illumination powered directly by the power supply. When the system is turned on, the front panel is illuminated.)

Before you begin connecting front-panel cables, examine the cables. Each should be labeled descriptively, e.g., "Power SW," "Reset SW," and "H.D.D. LED." Match those descriptions with the front-panel connector pins on the motherboard to make sure you connect the correct cable to the appropriate pins. Switch cables—power and reset—are not polarized. You can connect them in either orientation, without worrying about which pin is signal and which ground. LED cables may or may not be polarized, but if you connect a polarized LED cable backward the worst that happens is that the LED won't light. Antec cases use white wires for ground and colored wires for signal. Most cases use a black ground wires, and few use green.

Figure 6-28. Connect the front-panel switch and indicator cables

When you're connecting front-panel cables, try to get it right the first time, but don't worry too much about getting it wrong. Other than the power switch cable, which must be connected properly for the system to start, none of the other front-panel switch and indicator cables is essential, and connecting them wrong won't damage the system.

Connecting the front-panel USB ports

The Antec Fusion case provides two front-panel USB ports with cables that terminate in one Intel-standard dual-USB connector. Locate that cable, which is labeled USB, and connect it to one of the dual-USB motherboard connectors located near the left-front edge of the motherboard, as shown in Figure 6-29. The motherboard connector is keyed with a missing pin that corresponds to a blocked hole on the cable connector, so it's difficult to connect the cable incorrectly. Note, however, that it is possible to offset the cable connector against the motherboard connector and still seat the connector.

Figure 6-29. Connect the front-panel USB cable to a motherboard dual-USB connector

Connecting the vacuum fluorescent display and volume control

The Antec Fusion case provides a vacuum fluorescent display (VFD) and a volume control knob that work with Windows Media Center and (we hope) other media center applications. The VFD/volume cable terminates in a standard external USB connector. Antec supplies an adapter to convert the external USB connector to an internal 4-pin single USB connector. (The adapter is visible as the large black item at the bottom of Figure 6-30.)

Where's the FireWire?

The Antec Fusion case provides a front-panel FireWire port, but the Intel D946GZIS motherboard does not provide a FireWire interface. Tie off the FireWire cable neatly and tuck it out of the way. Alternatively, if you have a free expansion slot and want FireWire support, install a FireWire expansion card. All such cards provide one or more FireWire ports on the back panel, but many also include an internal FireWire port, which can be connected to the Fusion front-panel FireWire cable.

Unfortunately, in our configuration we have no available PCI slots. We do have an unused PCI Express x1 slot, but weren't able to locate a FireWire adapter that would fit that slot. Perhaps that will have changed by the time you build your media center PC.

Figure 6-30. Connect the VFD/Volume cable to a motherboard USB connector

The VFD/Volume connector is a 4-pin single-USB connector that can be connected to any available motherboard USB connector. Note that the 4-pin connector is not keyed, so it's easy to connect it incorrectly. Orient the cable connector as shown in Figure 6-30, with the GND pin nearest the missing pin on the motherboard connector, and press it into place.

Connecting the front-panel audio ports

The Antec Fusion case provides two front-panel audio ports with a cable that terminates in an Intel-standard front-panel audio connector. Locate that cable, which is labeled Audio, and connect it to the yellow FP Audio motherboard connector located near the left-rear corner of the motherboard, as shown in Figure 6-31. The motherboard FP Audio connector is keyed with a missing pin that corresponds to a blocked hole on the cable connector, so align the cable connector and motherboard connector properly before you press the cable connector into place.

In addition to the Intel-standard monolithic front-panel audio connector block, the Antec Fusion front-panel audio cable provides seven individual signal wires that match the signals on the connector block. You can use these individual wires to connect the front-panel audio if your motherboard provides a front-panel audio connector block that does not conform to the Intel standard.

If you don't need these individual wires, we recommend taping them off to the cable. We neglected to do that initially, and those tiny wires made things very difficult when we installed expansion cards.

Figure 6-31. Connect the front-panel audio cable to the motherboard FP Audio connector

Connecting the serial ATA data cables

As long as we're connecting cables to the motherboard, we might as well connect the Serial ATA data cables for the hard drives. The Intel D946GZIS motherboard provides four S-ATA data connectors, which are located on the left-front corner of the motherboard. Intel properly labels these connectors SATA 0 through SATA 3. (Some motherboards begin numbering at SATA 1.)

Locate two S-ATA data cables, which may be supplied with the motherboard, the hard drives, or both. Connect two of those S-ATA data cables to the first two motherboard S-ATA ports (SATA 0 and SATA 1), as shown in Figure 6-32. Align the cable connector with the motherboard connector, making sure that the L-shaped keys on both connectors are oriented properly, and then press the cable connector straight down until it seats in the motherboard connector.

Figure 6-32. Connect the Serial ATA data cables to the motherboard ports

WARNING

Both ends of an S-ATA cable are identical in terms of pin assignments and keying, so it usually doesn't matter which end you connect to the motherboard and which to the drive. Many S-ATA cables have simple plastic connectors on both ends, but some, including those supplied with the Intel motherboard, have metal latching connectors on one or both ends (visible in Figure 6-32) that are designed to lock the cable to the connector.

If you subsequently remove such a cable, make sure to press the latch to disconnect it before you pull the cable or you may damage the motherboard connector and/or the cable. Back in the days when latching S-ATA connectors were still very uncommon, we once pulled an S-ATA cable from a motherboard without watching what we were doing. We heard a loud cracking noise. Fortunately, it was the cable we damaged rather than the motherboard, but it might easily have been otherwise.

Route and Connect Power to the Motherboard

The next step is to route the necessary power cables from the power supply chamber to the motherboard chamber and connect those cables. Locate the sliding access panel between the power supply chamber and the motherboard chamber. Loosen the screw that secures it, as shown in Figure 6-33, and slide the panel all the way toward the rear of the case.

You'll need to route most or all of the following cables through the access panel:

❑ Main ATX power cable (always needed)
❑ ATX12V power cable (needed for most modern motherboards)
❑ Serial ATA power cable (always needed)
❑ Molex (hard drive) power cable with Berg (floppy drive) connector (always needed)
❑ PCI Express power cable (needed if your video adapter requires it)

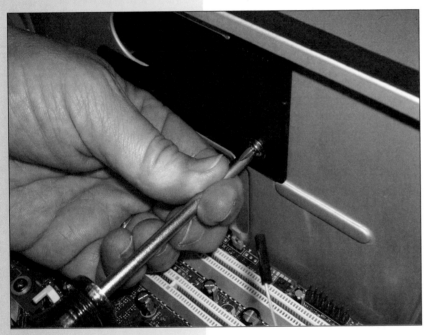

Figure 6-33. Loosen the screw that secures the access panel

Unfortunately, we spent too much time doing and too little time thinking, and it cost us. It took several iterations until we got the correct group of cables routed through the access panel.

The first time, we didn't route a Molex cable to the motherboard chamber because the optical drive is located in the same chamber as the power supply. We forgot we'd need a Molex cable in the motherboard chamber for the fans.

The second time, we routed a Molex cable to the motherboard chamber, but we chose the longer Molex cable, which doesn't include a Berg (floppy drive) connector. We later realized we needed a Berg connector for the front-panel illumination.

The third time, we finally got it right. Unfortunately, each time we'd already installed all of the expansion cards, and we had to pull every card to get to the access panel. Arrrrghhh.

Once you've routed the proper power cables through the access panel, slide the door closed and tighten the screw, as shown in Figure 6-34. If you forget a cable, don't say we didn't warn you.

Figure 6-34. Route the necessary cables from the power supply chamber and resecure the access panel

If you're paying close attention, you may have noticed that we forgot yet one more cable. Yep. The ATA ribbon cable has to be routed from the optical drive in the power supply chamber to the ATA motherboard connector in the motherboard chamber.

We'll confess that we actually did forget about the ATA data cable, but we couldn't face ripping out the expansion cards for a fourth attempt. Once is unfortunate. Twice is coincidence. Three times is enemy action. Four times begins to look like rank stupidity. Fortunately, we're very good at rationalizing.

If we'd had a round ATA cable, we probably would have bit the bullet and pulled all the expansion cards again (although we were beginning to wonder how many insertions their connectors were rated for...) But we had a flat ATA ribbon cable, and it seemed a bad idea to route it through that roundish hole in the access panel. As a matter of good practice, we try to avoid folding or crimping ribbon cables, and getting a flat ATA cable through that access panel would require crushing it severely. So we decided just to route the ATA ribbon cable over the top edge of the divider that separates the chambers. Once the side panel is reinstalled the ATA cable will be wedged between the divider and the side panel, but that will do it no harm.

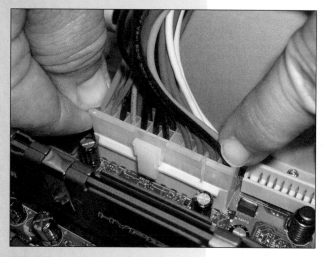

Figure 6-35. Connect the main ATX power cable

Figure 6-36. Connect the ATX12V power cable

Figure 6-37. Remove the screws that secure the expansion slot covers

Once you have the cables routed from the power supply chamber to the motherboard chamber, the next step is to connect the main ATX power cable, as shown in Figure 6-35. Align the cable with the motherboard connector and press down firmly until it snaps into place. Examine the connection visually to verify that the connectors are fully mated. A partially seated Main ATX power connector can cause subtle problems that are very difficult to troubleshoot.

The next step is to connect the ATX12V power cable, as shown in Figure 6-36. The ATX12V motherboard connector is located between the CPU socket and the rear I/O panel. Orient the ATX12V cable properly, and press down firmly until it snaps into place. Examine the connection to make sure that the latch is engaged.

Installing the Expansion Cards

The next step is to install the expansion cards and video adapter. We're installing the pcHDTV HDTV tuner and the Hauppauge dual analog tuner, each of which uses a PCI slot, and the Gigabyte video adapter, which uses the PCI Express x16 slot. To begin, remove the screws that secure the three slot covers, as shown in Figure 6-37.

Align each expansion card carefully with its corresponding slot. Press down firmly with both thumbs, as shown in Figure 6-38, until the card seats completely in the slot. Verify visually that each card is fully seated. Video adapters are particularly problematic. The video adapter may appear to seat. You may even feel it snap into place. That doesn't guarantee that it's completely seated. Always verify visually that the video adapter is fully seated and level in the slot, with the top edge of the video adapter contacts flush with the top edge of the slot.

WARNING

PCI Express video adapters (and the earlier AGP models) use a plastic retention mechanism to secure the video adapter in the slot. When you install a video adapter, make sure the retention mechanism latches. When you remove a video adapter, make sure to unlatch the retention mechanism before you attempt to remove the card from the slot.

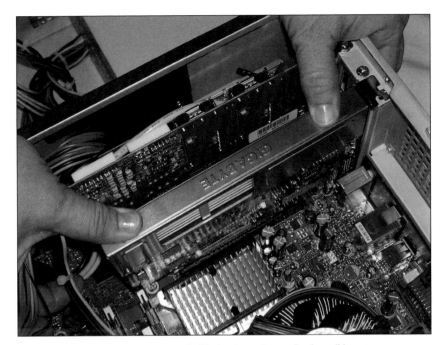

Figure 6-38. Align each expansion card with the slot and press firmly until it seats

After you seat each expansion card, reinsert the screw to secure the bracket to the chassis, as shown in Figure 6-39. After you've screwed in the retaining bracket, double-check to make sure the card is fully and completely seated in its slot. (Sometimes, driving the screw into the bracket can twist the card up and out of the slot slightly.)

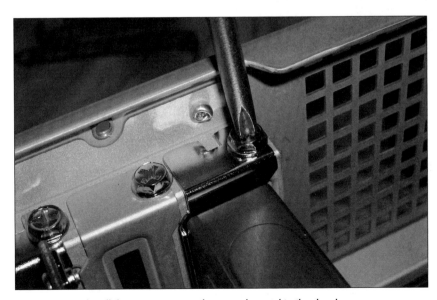

Figure 6-39. Reinstall the screw to secure the expansion card to the chassis

Figure 6-40. The back panel of the Media Center PC

With both tuner cards and the video adapter installed, the back panel of the media center PC is quite crowded, as shown in Figure 6-40. Also, this image doesn't show the breakout "octopus" box that we'll later connect to the analog tuner card to split out the audio/video I/O ports.

Installing the Optical Drive

The next step is to install the optical drive. The Antec Fusion case provides a dedicated optical drive bay with a universal drive door that conceals the bezel of the optical drive itself, so you can use any color of optical drive without concern for matching the front bezel of the case. To begin installing the optical drive, pivot the drive bay upward, as shown in Figure 6-41, and then lift it free of the case.

WARNING

Although the optical drive bay apparently has room for two optical drives, you can install only one drive, in the lower position. The upper position is unusable because the VFD protrudes back into the drive bay assembly. Note that at least early revisions of the Antec Fusion manual correctly said to mount the optical drive in the lower bay, but used an illustration that incorrectly showed the drive being mounted in the upper bay.

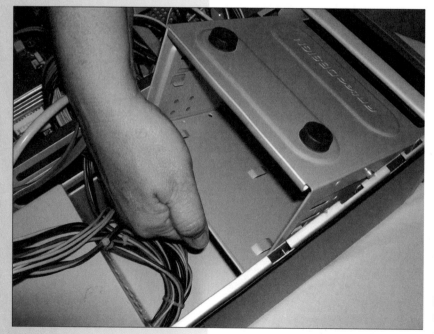

Figure 6-41. Remove the optical drive bay

Slide the optical drive into the bottom opening of the drive bay. Align the drive screw holes with the rear set of screw holes in the drive bay, as shown in Figure 6-42. Once the drive is aligned properly, secure it to the drive bay with four screws, as shown in Figure 6-43.

Figure 6-42. Align the drive screw holes with the rear set of screws holes in the bay

Figure 6-43. Secure the optical drive with four screws

The next step is to connect the cables to the optical drive. Before you proceed, check the jumper on the back of the optical drive to make sure it's configured properly. This is the only parallel ATA device in the system, so it should be jumpered as master. Our NEC ND-3550A optical drive was set as master by default, but some optical drives are set as slave by default. Check the jumper and change it if necessary to make the drive master.

Once you've verified that the drive is configured correctly, connect the ATA data cable to the drive, as shown in Figure 6-44. We used the 80-wire UltraATA cable supplied with the motherboard, which works properly but is a better cable than the drive actually requires. A standard 40-wire ATA cable is sufficient for an optical drive, so don't hesitate to use a 40-wire cable

Figure 6-44. Connect the ATA data cable to the optical drive

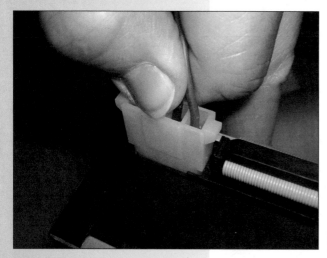

Figure 6-45. Connect a Molex power cable to the optical drive

Please Be Seated

Make sure the optical drive bay seats completely. When we first assembled our media center PC, we were unable to reinstall the top panel. As we tried to figure out the problem, we finally noticed that the optical drive bay was protruding just a couple millimeters too high to allow the top panel to slide into place. With the drive bay reseated properly, the top panel slid easily into place.

if that's what you have. Before you seat the cable, make sure that pin 1 on the cable (indicated by a color stripe) is aligned with pin 1 on the drive (usually toward the power connector, and always labeled). Once the cable is aligned properly with the drive socket, press firmly to seat it completely.

Locate a Molex (hard drive) power cable, and connect it to the optical drive, as shown in Figure 6-45. Molex connectors are keyed with beveled corners on the plug and socket. Align the plug with the socket and press firmly to seat the connector, which may require significant pressure.

After you've connected the data and power cables to the optical drive, replace the drive bay in the chassis, as shown in Figure 6-46. Align the front posts on each side of the drive bay with the corresponding notches on the chassis, and pivot the drive down into the latched position, with the rear posts fully seated in the chassis cutouts.

The next step is to install the hard drives. The Antec Fusion case uses a unique method for mounting the hard drives. Hard drives are usually mounted rigidly, secured by screws on both sides or on the bottom. The Fusion case instead allows the hard drives to "float" by suspending them from only one side.

Figure 6-46. Reinstall the optical drive bay in the case

To begin installing the hard drives, remove the four screws that secure the hard drive mounting plate, as shown in Figure 6-47.

With the screws removed, pivot the hard drive mounting plate upward, as shown in Figure 6-48, and pull it free from the case. Note the soft silicone grommets, visible as small white doughnuts in Figure 6-48. The four grommets on top of the hard drive mounting plate isolate the hard drives from the mounting plate, preventing hard drive vibrations from being transferred to the chassis structure. There are four corresponding grommets at the bottom of the drive bay, two of which are visible in the image. The hard drives are not screwed to these bottom grommets, but rest freely against them.

Figure 6-47. Remove the four screws that secure the hard drive mounting plate

Figure 6-48. Pivot the hard drive mounting plate upward and pull it free of the case

Bass Ackward

Note the orientation of the hard drive mounting plate relative to the chassis. The hard drive mounting plate appears to be symmetric, but it's not. The position of the screw holes for mounting the hard drive makes the mounting plate chiral, like a glove. If you reverse the mounting plate, the hard drives will not fit properly. When properly oriented, the hard drive screw holes are offset toward the front of the case, as shown in Figure 6-48.

Locate the special hard drive mounting screws in the parts bag supplied with the Fusion case. These screws have a very wide flange that bears against the silicone shock-mounting grommets. Align the drives with their connectors facing left when the mounting plate is oriented normally relative to the case. Secure each drive with two of the special hard drive mounting screws, as shown in Figure 6-49.

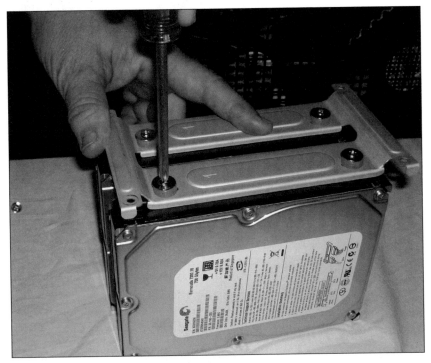

Figure 6-49. Secure each hard drive to the mounting plate with two screws

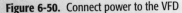
Figure 6-50. Connect power to the VFD

With the hard drives not yet installed in the case, now is a good time to connect power to the VFD. (The VFD is controlled by its USB connection but does not receive power from it.) Locate the short cable coming from the front panel that has a Berg (floppy drive) power connector. Route the power supply cable that has a Berg connector through the access hole to the hard drive bay area and connect power to the VFD cable, as shown in Figure 6-50.

The next step is to connect the data and power cables to the hard drives. Antec recommends connecting these cables after the hard drives are installed in the case, but we found it easier to connect them first. (Make sure to route the data and power cables through the access hole to the hard drive chamber before you connect the cables to the drives.)

Align the data cable with the hard drive connector, making sure the L-shaped keying notches match, and then press the cable connector firmly until it seats on the hard drive connector, as shown in Figure 6-51. Repeat this process to connect the power cables to the hard drives, as shown in Figure 6-52, again making sure that the keys are aligned properly before you seat the cables.

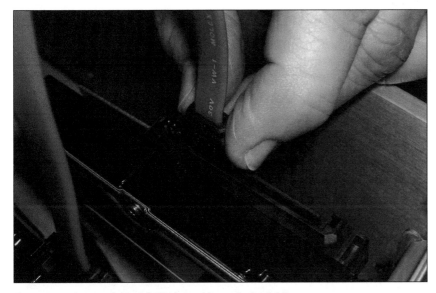

Figure 6-51. Connect the Serial ATA data cables to the hard drives

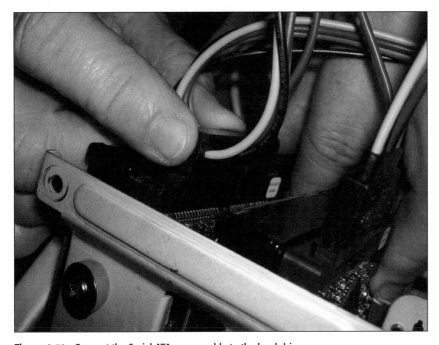

Figure 6-52. Connect the Serial ATA power cable to the hard drives

Figure 6-53. Reinstall the hard drive mounting plate and secure it with four screws

The final step in installing the hard drives is to reinstall the mounting plate, as shown in Figure 6-53. Make sure that all four tabs on the mounting plate seat in the corresponding cutouts in the chassis, and then secure the mounting plate with the four screws you removed earlier. When the mounting plate is correctly installed, the drives should be vertical, as shown in the illustration, with their lower sides resting on the silicone grommets at the bottom of the hard drive chamber. (If the hard drives are tilted, you've installed them backward on the mounting plate. Remove it and start over.)

Finishing Up

Only a few steps remain to complete your media center PC assembly. We haven't yet connected the optical drive data cable to the motherboard interface, so do that now. Align pin 1 on the cable (the side with the color stripe) with pin 1 on the motherboard interface, and press the cable connector firmly into place until it fully seats in the motherboard socket, as shown in Figure 6-54.

Figure 6-54. Connect the optical drive data cable to the motherboard ATA interface

Locate the Molex cable with the blue and white wires coming from the front-panel area. This connector supplies power to the front-panel LED. Connect this cable, as shown in Figure 6-55, to one of the Molex connectors on the cable coming from the power supply.

Finally, connect the two side fans to the power supply Molex cable, as shown in Figure 6-56. Each of these fans has a selector switch on the end of a short white cable. By default, the switch is set to run the fan at low speed, which should suffice. For better airflow, you can move the switch on one or both fans to the medium or high setting. On low speed, the fans are nearly inaudible. At medium speed, they move considerably more air, but produce noticeable (although not intrusive) sound. At high speed, they move still more air, but produce more noise than most people will find acceptable.

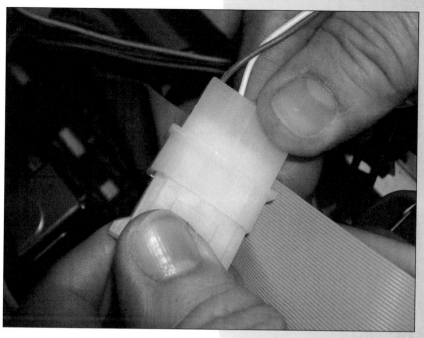

Figure 6-55. Connect power to the front-panel LED

BAFFLING

The Antec Fusion case includes a black plastic air baffle, visible in Figure 6-25, near the rear I/O panel that is designed to direct air across the CPU cooler. That baffle as supplied worked fine in our system, and will probably work well in most systems that use different components.

We could have installed the baffle extensions provided with the case to route more air directly to the CPU cooler, but doing that would have reduced the air flow around the expansion cards, which are very tightly grouped. The Core 2 Duo processor is a low-current, cool-running processor anyway, so we elected not to extend the baffle.

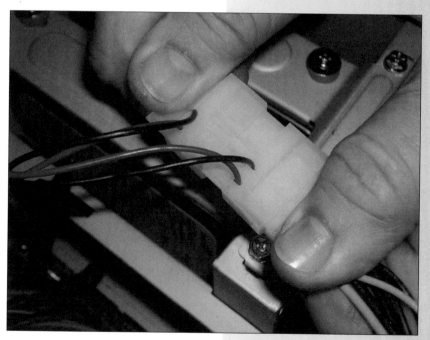

Figure 6-56. Connect power to the two side fans

All that remains is to dress the cables, configure BIOS Setup, and reinstall the top panel. Once you have the cables dressed, take a few minutes to double-check everything one last time before you apply power to the system. Use the following checklist:

- ❏ No loose tools or screws (shake the case gently)
- ❏ CPU cooler properly mounted; CPU fan connected
- ❏ Memory modules fully seated and latched
- ❏ Front-panel switch and indicator cables connected properly
- ❏ Front-panel cables connected properly
- ❏ Hard drive data cables connected to drive and motherboard
- ❏ Hard drive power cables connected
- ❏ Optical drive data cable connected to drive and motherboard
- ❏ Optical drive power cable connected
- ❏ All drives secured to drive bay or chassis, as applicable
- ❏ Expansion cards fully seated and secured to the chassis
- ❏ Main ATX power cable and ATX12V power cable connected
- ❏ All cables dressed and tucked

Only the Good Die Young

When you turn on the rear power switch, the system will come to life momentarily and then die. That's perfectly normal behavior. When the power supply receives power, it begins to start up. It quickly notices that the motherboard hasn't told it to start, and so it shuts down again. All you need to do is press the front-panel power switch and the system will start normally.

Once you're certain that all is as it should be, it's time for the smoke test. Leave the cover off for now. Connect the power cable to the wall receptacle and then to the system unit. Press the main power button on the front of the case, and the system should start up. Check to make sure that the power supply fan and CPU fan are spinning. You should also hear the hard drive spin up and the happy beep that tells you the system is starting normally. At that point, everything should be working properly.

Turn off the system, disconnect the power cord, and take these final steps to prepare the system for use:

Set the BIOS Setup Configuration jumper to Configure mode
The BIOS Setup Configuration jumper block on the Intel D946GZIS motherboard is used to set the operation mode. This jumper is located near the center of the left edge of the motherboard, near the front edge of the expansion slots. By default, the jumper is in the 1-2 or "normal" position. Move the jumper block to the 2-3 or "configure" position.

Reconnect the power cord and restart the system
When the configuration jumper is set to configure mode, starting the system automatically runs BIOS Setup and puts the system in maintenance mode. This step allows the motherboard to detect the type of processor installed and configure it automatically. When the BIOS Setup screen appears, choose the menu option to clear all BIOS data and then reset the system clock. Save your changes and exit. The system automatically shuts down. Disconnect the power cord.

Set the BIOS Setup Configuration jumper to Normal mode
> With the power cord disconnected, move the BIOS Setup Configuration jumper block from 2-3 (Configure mode) to 1-2 (Normal mode).

Replace the side panel and reconnect power
> With the jumper set for Normal operation, replace the side panel and reconnect the power cord. Your system is now completely assembled and ready for use.

Final Words

We finished building the Media Center PC with the book deadline approaching like an oncoming train. We'd already tested and compared various PVR applications on other hardware, so we were pretty sure we wanted to run MythTV on our Media Center PC. We downloaded and installed Ubuntu 6.06 LTS Linux (*http://www.ubuntu.com*), updated it to the SMP kernel, and then downloaded and installed MythTV (*http://www.mythtv.org*) with all of its optional packages and plug-ins.

As the book went to press, we were still playing with the software. Everything lights up and all of the hardware is recognized. But MythTV, while much more polished than the version we looked at two years ago, is still rough. (As Barbara observed while we were struggling to configure MythTV, "Well, here's another nice mess you've gotten us into.")

We'll continue fighting with MythTV for a while, but if it beats us there are several fall-back alternatives. First, of course, our hardware is completely compatible with Windows XP and Windows Vista. (Even the pcHDTV card has Windows drivers.) If worse comes to horrible, we can always install Windows and one of the Windows-based PVR apps. But it probably won't come to that.

SageTV (*http://www.sagetv.com*), which produces one of the finest Windows-based PVR applications available, also offers a Linux-based version of that software. Installing the SageTV Linux software on an existing system appears to be quite complex, although perhaps not as difficult as installing MythTV. Fortunately, SageTV also offers a turnkey version of their software based on Gentoo Linux. By all reports, installing this version is a simple matter of booting the distribution CD and following the prompts. Can it really be as easy as that? We don't know, but we intend to find out.

For updated component recommendations, commentary, and other new material, visit *http://www.hardwareguys.com/guides/media-center.html*.

Building a Small Form Factor (SFF) PC

When the discussion turns to Small Form Factor (SFF) PCs, the first question that comes to our minds is how the term is being used. SFF means different things to different people. For some, it's any PC smaller than the norm. For others, it's specifically the "shoebox" form factor—the so-called "cube" systems—pioneered by Shuttle. (In fact, Shuttle says SFF means Shuttle Form Factor.) Still others consider any PC built around a microATX motherboard and case to be an SFF system. Some True Believers claim that only systems based on Mini-ITX motherboards—which are so small they can be built into a teddy bear or cigar humidor—qualify as SFF PCs.

We think the best way to define SFF is by case volume. The cubic capacity of standard mini/mid-tower ATX cases ranges from 30 to 50 liters. Typical microATX cases range from 10 to 20 liters. The small Shuttle SFF case is 200mm × 300mm × 185mm, or just under 8" × 8" X 12", and has a volume of about 11 liters. Cases designed for Mini-ITX motherboards are smaller still, from 6 to 9 liters. Most people perceive a 20-liter or smaller case as "small" and a 10-liter or smaller case as "tiny." Any case with a volume of 20 liters or less fits our definition of SFF.

SMALL, SMALLER, SMALLEST

To provide an idea of scale, a cube that contains 20 liters is about 27 cm (10.7″) on a side. A cube that contains 6 liters is about 18 cm (7.2″) on a side. An NBA basketball has a volume of just under 7.5 liters.

Although Shuttle introduced the "shoebox" form factor, it was by no means the first company to produce SFF computers. Soon after Intel introduced the ATX form factor in the mid-'90s, they recognized the need for smaller systems. ATX was soon followed by smaller variants—Mini-ATX, micro-ATX, and finally FlexATX. Although Intel produced some Mini-ATX

Believe It or Not...

Intel heavily promoted at least two FlexATX computers, although they probably now wish they hadn't. An arrangement with Mattel resulted in the Hot Wheels PC and the Barbie PC, neither of which set any sales records.

and FlexATX motherboards, those form factors were generally ignored by third-party manufacturers, leaving ATX as Intel's answer for standard-size systems and microATX for small systems.

Shuttle's first shoebox PC immediately struck a chord with gamers, hobbyists, and other PC enthusiasts. It was expensive, ran hot, didn't have much room for drives or expansion cards, and was noisy. But it was small.

Shuttle followed that first SFF system with a continuing stream of new SFF systems based on various proprietary motherboards for the Athlon XP, Pentium 4, Athlon 64, and, most recently, the Core 2 Duo. Shuttle devotes significant engineering and design resources to their SFF systems, and it shows. Until recently, Shuttle SFF systems were the standard by which all other SFF systems were judged.

In the last few years, many manufacturers have jumped on the SFF bandwagon, trying to horn in on the market niche that Shuttle developed. Until recently, most of these clones were pale imitations of the original product. Recently, several of these other makers, including ASUS, Biostar, and EPoX, have begun shipping SFF systems comparable in quality and features to those made by Shuttle. Shuttle no longer has the SFF market to itself.

A lot of people love Shuttle SFF PCs and their clones. We don't, for several reasons. Most of them use proprietary (or at least semiproprietary) components, including the motherboard and power supply. If you want to upgrade your motherboard or power supply, tough luck. You're stuck with whatever the system manufacturer offers in the way of upgrade options, which often isn't much. We might have been able to live with that, but what we couldn't live with was the very high cost of proprietary SFF "bare-bones" systems. SFF systems typically sell for a 50% to 100% premium over the price of an industry-standard motherboard, case, and power supply of comparable quality.

But merely because we don't much like Shuttle SFF bare-bones systems and their clones doesn't mean we think there is no place for small systems. On the contrary, small systems are perfect for many situations, namely anywhere you need a PC that a standard mini-tower system won't fit or would be intrusive. An SFF system is an ideal candidate for a dorm room, a bedroom set-top box, a home theater system, or a portable LAN party system. For that matter, many people prefer to use an SFF PC as a primary desktop system.

In this chapter, we'll design and build the perfect SFF PC.

Determining Functional Requirements

The problem with determining functional requirements for an SFF PC is that the SFF umbrella covers a broad range of systems. An SFF PC can be anything from an inexpensive "appliance" PC with a slow processor and embedded video to a fire-breathing gaming system—or anything in between. The only thing these systems have in common is small size.

Accordingly, although we had to choose one SFF PC configuration to build for ourselves and to illustrate this chapter, we specify numerous alternative choices in components that we might have used if we had been designing the SFF PC for a different purpose. When we sat down to think through our own requirements for an SFF PC, here's what we came up with:

Size

Well, that's the whole point, isn't it? A large SFF PC is an oxymoron. Still, although we wanted a small system, we didn't want to make too many compromises in features, performance, cooling, or reliability. We decided that we'd settle for "medium-small."

Reliability

One of our concerns about SFF PCs is that the small case volume makes it difficult to cool the system properly. Running components at high temperatures reduces their service life and makes them less reliable and more crash-prone. The keys to building a reliable system are to choose top-quality components—particularly motherboard, memory, hard drive, and power supply—and to keep them cool. In the interests of keeping the system as cool and therefore as reliable as possible, we considered the thermal characteristics of the various components, and chose accordingly.

Performance

We wanted our SFF PC to be small, but not slow. High performance goes hand in hand with higher temperatures, of course, so we had to strike a balance between performance and cooling/reliability. Fortunately, new-generation processors draw as little as half the current of preceding models, which makes it easier to use a high-performance processor while keeping the system cool and reliable. We decided that 3D graphics performance was unimportant for our particular SFF PC, so we elected to use integrated graphics. We did, however, want a system that would support a fast 3D graphics card (if we decide to install one later), which meant the case must accept full-size cards and have sufficient cooling to run at reasonable temperatures with a hot-running graphics adapter installed.

Noise level

SFF PCs are popular because they are unobtrusive. But unobtrusiveness requires more than small size. A tiny PC that sounds like a leaf blower fails the unobtrusiveness test. The SFF PC must be quiet as well as small. Unfortunately, that introduces yet another trade-off. Quiet PCs are quiet because they minimize fan noise, which impedes cooling, or because they use insulation to deaden sound, which also impedes cooling. Once again, we'll need to strike a balance between sound level, performance, and cooling/reliability. We decided that it was a reasonable goal to build a system that was quiet (but not inaudible) while providing midrange or better performance and reasonable temperature levels.

This is a very demanding set of requirements, and one we weren't sure we'd be able to meet. Small, fast, cool, quiet, and reliable. Pick any four. Achieving all five in one system wouldn't be easy.

Hardware Design Criteria

With the functional requirements determined, the next step was to establish design criteria for the SFF PC hardware. Here are the relative priorities we assigned for our SFF PC. Your priorities may, of course, differ.

Our SFF PC configuration is a well-balanced system. Other than expandability and video performance, which are unimportant to us for this system, all of the other criteria are of similar priority. Here's the breakdown:

Price

> Price is moderately important for this system, but value is more so. We won't try to match the price of mass-market consumer-grade systems, but we won't spend money needlessly, either. If spending a bit more noticeably improves performance, reliability, or cooling, we won't begrudge the extra few dollars.

Reliability

> Reliability ties for top importance with size. We'll make compromises in cost, performance, noise level, or any other criterion to make this system as reliable as it is possible to make an SFF PC. The case volume of an SFF PC makes it difficult to achieve reliability comparable to a larger system using similar components, but we'll do everything possible to build the most reliable system we can within the inherent limits of the small case.

Size

> Size is matched in importance only by reliability. If it isn't small, the whole exercise is rather pointless. Still, we didn't award this category the absolute highest possible priority, because there are some compromises we simply won't make. Bare-bones "shoebox" PCs are available that have literally half the case volume of the SFF system we eventually decided to build, but those tiny systems simply give up too much in return for saving a few inches.

Noise level

> Noise level is moderately important for an SFF PC. Our goal is a system that is unobtrusive in both size and noise level. Accordingly, we'll choose the quietest available mainstream components that otherwise meet our requirements for performance, thermal characteristics, and reliability.

DESIGN PRIORITIES

Price	★★★☆☆
Reliability	★★★★☆
Size	★★★★☆
Noise level	★★★☆☆
Expandability	★☆☆☆☆
Processor performance	★★★☆☆
Video performance	★★☆☆☆
Disk capacity/performance	★★★☆☆

Expandability

Expandability is unimportant for our SFF PC. We may at some point want to make minor system upgrades, such as adding a PCI Express video adapter, an expansion card or two, more memory, and perhaps a second hard drive. To the extent that we can provide for such future expansion without compromising higher-priority considerations, we'll do so. But we consider expandability dead last in priority.

Processor performance

Processor performance is moderately important for our SFF PC. Our goal was performance indistinguishable from a similarly-priced desktop system, which meant we needed a dual-core processor with mainstream performance. Ventilation and cooling considerations limited our processor choices to one of the new-generation low-current processors—an Intel Core 2 Duo or a low-current AMD Athlon 64 X2 model.

Video performance

3D video performance is relatively unimportant for our SFF PC because we do not intend to use it for gaming. We want enough graphics horsepower to run the Windows Vista Aero Glass user interface effects smoothly, but no more. The most recent Intel, ATI, and nVIDIA integrated video chipsets are sufficient for our purposes, and produce much less heat than a high-performance video adapter.

We recognize, though, that many people may decide to build an SFF gaming system, so we tested various video configurations, from integrated video to a midrange nVIDIA 7600 GT. Although it is possible to install a high-end video adapter in an SFF case, a fast video adapter generates too much heat for the SFF case and draws more current than the typical SFF power supply can provide. We concluded that the realistic top-end for a video adapter in an SFF case is a midrange model, ideally one that is passively cooled.

Disk capacity/performance

Disk capacity and performance are moderately important for a SFF PC. This is an easy criterion to meet, because current Serial ATA hard drives are huge, fast, cheap, and reliable. Fortunately, the best models are also relatively quiet and produce little heat.

Component Considerations

With our design criteria in mind, we set out to choose the best components for the SFF PC. The following sections describe the components we chose and why we chose them. For the SFF PC, we had to reverse our usual practice of choosing the components and then building the system. As strange as it sounds, we had to build the SFF PC and then choose the components.

By that, we mean that component choice is constrained when you build a small system. With a standard system, you needn't worry about components fitting the case. With an SFF PC, component size is a constant concern. For example, the CPU cooler you really want to use may be too tall to fit between the motherboard and drive bay; the optical drive you really want to use may be half an inch too deep to seat fully in the drive bay; or the fan on your video adapter may intrude on the PCI slot, making it unusable.

For example, Figure 7-1 shows two optical drives, an NEC ND-3550A DVD writer on the bottom and a Lite-On DVD-ROM drive on top. In a standard case, the half inch or so difference in depth is immaterial. In an SFF case, that extra half inch may mean the larger drive won't fit the case. (As it happened, we were able to use the NEC ND-3550A DVD writer, but it was a tight fit.)

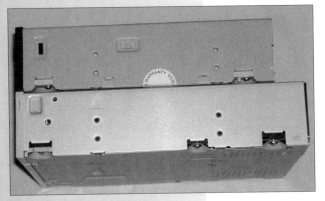

Figure 7-1. NEC ND-3550A DVD writer (bottom) and Lite-On DVD-ROM drive

Such factors as motherboard layout and cable flexibility may also come into play. For example, the motherboard you want to use may have the front-panel connectors in an inaccessible location, or the S-ATA connectors may have insufficient clearance to allow the S-ATA cable to be seated without breaking off the connector.

Configuring any PC involves trade-offs, but this is doubly true when you configure an SFF PC. The small case volume makes cooling more difficult and component dimensions critical, and the smaller power supply limits your choices for high-current devices like fast video adapters. Any PC requires compromises between performance and noise, but this is even more apparent with an SFF PC. Many "quiet PC" technologies—such as using large passive heatsinks and multiple large, slow fans—simply cannot be used with an SFF PC because there isn't room for them. If you want a fast SFF PC, it's going to be loud. If you want a quiet SFF PC, you'll have to make compromises.

Measure First, Buy Later

If you use components other than those we specify, you may encounter problems with fit or function. To minimize potential problems, buy the case before you buy other components. Measure the available space, and compare your measurements carefully against the component sizes listed on their web sites. Note that the sizes given for components are usually accurate, but may not include protruding connectors and do not include clearances required for cables. With the case in front of you, you can also get a reasonably good idea of layout issues, component clearance issues, and so on. Without the case, you'll find it's impossible to make even reasonable guesses about whether particular components will fit.

WARNING

Although we tested the configuration we used to build our own SFF PC, we did not test permutations with the listed alternatives. Those alternatives are simply the components we would have considered using if our requirements were different. We would still have had to verify fit and function and perhaps would have been forced to substitute other components. We can't guarantee that these alternative components will fit or function reliably, individually or together.

Case and Power Supply

Antec NSK1300 microATX case
(*http://www.antec.com*)

The SFF PC we built for the first edition of this book used an Antec Aria case. We liked the Aria case enough that we planned to use it again for our new SFF PC configuration. Alas, as we were choosing components for this system, we found that Antec had discontinued the Aria. Fortunately, as we browsed the Antec site, we found the NSK1300 case, shown in Figure 7-2. We think of it as the "Aria II."

At first glance, it's difficult to tell them apart. The only discernible differences we found were that the NSK1300 has round power and reset buttons instead of square ones, adds a top vent for the power supply, and doesn't include the card reader that was bundled with the Aria. Oh, and the NSK1300 sells for $20 or so less than the Aria did.

Figure 7-2. Antec NSK1300 microATX case

We actually had a new Aria in the stock room, and intended to use it for our new SFF PC. Then we realized that all of the motherboards we were considering using required a 24-pin ATX 2.2 main ATX power connector, but the Aria had the older-style 20-pin main ATX power connector. That sent us off to the Antec web site in search of an updated Aria with a 24-pin power supply, where we eventually discovered that the NSK1300 had replaced the older Aria.

Although we considered other microATX cases, we pretty much knew ahead of time that we were likely to go with the NSK1300, based on our experiences with the Aria. The NSK1300 accepts any microATX motherboard and full-height expansion cards. It has a robust 300W ATX 2.2 power supply rather than the marginal 160W to 220W power supplies provided with most bare-bones "shoebox" SFF systems. The Antec Aria is one of the quietest cases we have ever used, and yet it provides cooling sufficient to run midrange components at reasonable temperatures. We expected no less from the NSK1300. Finally, the NSK1300's reasonable price meant we could build an SFF system without breaking the bank on an overpriced proprietary SFF bare-bones system.

The NSK1300 is by no means the only microATX case available, but most microATX cases use the slimline "pizza-box" form factor rather than the "cube" form factor of the NSK1300. Slimline cases are useful for some "appliance" applications, but have too many limitations for a general-purpose system. For example, many of them accept only one optical drive and one hard drive, have proprietary (expensive) low-wattage power supplies, accept only two or three half-height expansion cards, and so on.

The NSK1300 addresses all of those issues, with its four drive bays, 300W power supply, and ability to accept four full-height expansion cards.

The NSK1300 is roughly the same height and depth as a typical "shoebox" SFF PC—within half an inch or so either way. The real difference is width. The NSK1300 is a couple inches wider than most SFF PCs, but don't blame Antec. The additional width is needed to accommodate a microATX motherboard, with its full complement of expansion slots. The relatively small increase in width also pays off in case volume. The volume of the Antec NSK1300 is about 18 liters, 20% or so larger than the largest shoebox models and nearly twice the 11-liter volume of smaller SFF cases. That additional volume makes the NSK1300 easier to work on, and contributes to more efficient cooling and a lower noise level.

Table 7-1 compares the Antec NSK1300 with the Shuttle SN27P2, a typical "large" bare-bones SFF system for Socket AM2 AMD processors.

Table 7-1. Antec NSK1300 case versus Shuttle SN27P2

	Antec NSK1300	**Shuttle SN27P2**
Height	7.9" / 200mm	8.3" / 210mm
Width	10.6" / 269mm	8.7" / 220mm
Depth	13.2" / 335mm	12.8" / 325mm
Case volume (liters/cubic inches)	18.1 / 1,105	15.1 / 924
External drive bays (5.25"/3.5")	1 / 0	1 / 1
Internal drive bays (5.25"/3.5")	0 / 3	0 / 2
Expansion slots	1 PCIe x16 + 3 PCI	1 PCIe x16 + 1 PCI
Motherboard included	None	Proprietary nForce 570 Ultra
Other motherboards accepted	Any microATX	none
Power supply	300W PFC	400W PFC
Street price (with motherboard)	$175 (typical)	$375

The Antec NSK1300 wins the comparison easily. The NSK1300 is a bit larger than the SN27P2, but uses industry-standard components and has three PCI expansion slots versus one. The Shuttle has a 400W power supply, but, frankly, we don't think it's a good idea to cram enough components into an SFF PC to require that larger power supply. The real killer is price. The Shuttle SN27P2 SFF case with motherboard sells for about $375. The Antec NSK1300 with a typical motherboard sells for about $175, or less than half the price.

Most SFF bare-bones systems we've seen use thin aluminum panels, which weigh little and help cooling, but do nothing to reduce sound emissions. In fact, most of them seem to resonate with a high-pitched buzz or whine that originates in the power supply fan and CPU fan. The NSK1300 is different.

Its side panels use composite construction, with two thin aluminum plates sandwiching a central plastic layer. The top panel is similar, but uses one aluminum plate facing the inside of the system, with an exposed corrugated plastic layer on the outside.

Although Antec gave up the minor cooling advantage of using thin single aluminum panels, their composite panels are acoustically inert. When we tapped on them, all we heard was a dull thud rather than the metallic sound generated by simple aluminum panels. We suspect that these composite panels contribute a great deal to the low noise level of the NSK1300.

Although the Antec NSK1300 isn't perfect, it does a excellent job of balancing size, accessibility, cooling efficiency, noise level, and price. For our purposes, the NSK1300 was the ideal SFF case.

Processor

Intel Core 2 Duo E6300 (*http://www.intel.com*)

Although our SFF PC is physically small, we want it to be fast. The small case and 300W power supply put some real limitations on processor choice. An older-generation, high-current processor would overload the power supply and make it very difficult to cool the system. Short of using a mobile processor—which introduces problems of its own, not least motherboard availability—that effectively limits our choices to a modern low-current desktop processor like the Intel Core 2 Duo or one of the special energy-efficient AMD Athlon 64 X2 models, either of which draws only 65W.

At the time we built this system, the Intel Core 2 Duo was the hands-down winner in both absolute performance and price/performance ratio. The so-called "entry-level" Core 2 Duo E6300 offers extremely high performance at a very reasonable price, so we chose that model for our SFF PC.

Motherboard

Intel D946GZIS (*http://www.intel.com*)

Our choice of the Antec NSK1300 case dictates a microATX motherboard. Core 2 Duo is a Socket 775 processor, but most Socket 775 motherboards are not compatible with Core 2 Duo. At the time we built this system, the Intel D946GZIS was the only microATX motherboard available that supported Core 2 Duo, so that's what we chose.

Fortunately, the D946GZIS suits our requirements perfectly. It supports up to 4 GB of DDR2 memory in two slots. It includes integrated GMA3000 video, which is fast enough to run the Windows Vista Aero Glass user interface effects, but also provides a standard x16 PCI Express video adapter slot. The integrated 5.1 audio and 10/100 Ethernet are sufficient for our purposes. The board layout is clean, and is as easy to work with as we could hope, given the constrained spaces of an SFF case.

ALTERNATIVES: CASE/POWER SUPPLY

When we checked NewEgg, we found 799 cases listed. More than 100 of those were microATX cases of one form or another, so you should be able to find an SFF case that's suitable for your needs. We ruled out the pizza-box and micro-tower form factors for our system, but one of those may be suitable for yours. Of the "cube"-style cases, we liked the Antec NSK1300 best, but there are numerous alternatives, including the Chenming 118, the JPAC 901, the Apevia (Aspire) X-QPACK models, and the Lian Li PC-V300 models. We haven't used any of those alternatives, so we can't comment on their quality or usability, but all are popular with SFF builders.

ALTERNATIVES: PROCESSOR

We think the Intel Core 2 Duo is the standout choice for the SFF PC. If you prefer AMD, we recommend an Athlon 64 X2 4200+ or faster. AMD offers low-power variants of some X2 models that consume much less power than the standard models. Although they are more costly than the standard models of the same speed, the low-power variants are much better suited for an SFF PC.

Memory

Kingston 2GB PC5300 DDR2 Memory Kit (1 GB× 2)
(*http://www.kingston.com*)

The Intel D946GZIS has two DDR2 memory slots and supports dual-channel memory operation with PC2-4200, PC2-5300, or PC2-6400 modules in capacities up to 2 GB. At the time we built this system, PC2-4200 modules sold for about the same price as PC2-5300 modules, but PC2-6400 modules sold at a 50% premium. We'd have liked to use PC2-6400 memory, but the slight performance bump wasn't worth the additional cost.

We consider 2 GB of memory about right for any but budget or high-end configurations. That's 1 GB per processor, and our dual-core Intel Core 2 Duo is effectively two processors. Accordingly, we checked the price of 1 GB memory modules on the Crucial and Kingston web sites, intending to install a pair of 1 GB modules for better memory performance. Kingston happened to have a better price that day than Crucial, so we ordered two 1 GB PC2-5300 Kingston modules.

Video Adapter

Integrated video

The Intel D946GZIS motherboard includes excellent integrated Graphics Media Accelerator 3000 (GMA 3000) video. Although serious gamers sniff at the 3D graphics performance of GMA 3000 video, it is more than sufficient for undemanding 3D video applications such as the Windows Vista Aero Glass effects and light gaming. Integrated video adds little to the heat burden inside the SFF case, and is perfectly adequate for anything we plan to do with this system.

ALTERNATIVES: VIDEO ADAPTER

The D946GZIS motherboard provides a standard x16 PCI Express slot for a graphics card, so it's possible to add some serious 3D graphics horsepower to the SFF PC, if you are so inclined. If you choose to install a standalone video adapter, keep in mind two limitations of the NSK1300.

- The small volume of any SFF case, including the NSK1300, makes it difficult to cool a hot-running video adapter, so installing a high-end video card is likely to cause cooling problems.

- The 300W power supply of the NSK1300 puts an upper limit on the current available to the video adapter. Make sure any video adapter you install in the NSK1300 case is within the ability of the 300W power supply to support. If you intend to install a high-end gaming video adapter, choose a case that provides a power supply capable of delivering the current that video adapter requires.

Note that the D946GZIS provides only analog VGA video output. If you need DVI digital output, install an inexpensive PCIe video adapter that provides DVI output.

Hard Disk Drive

Seagate ST3250620AS Barracuda 7200.10 (250GB)
(*http://www.seagate.com*)

An SFF PC needs a quiet, cool-running hard drive with mainstream performance. We've come to depend on Seagate Barracuda SATA drives based on years of good experiences with them. We chose a 250 GB 7200.10 model with 16 MB of cache for this system because it happened to be on sale at the time for $70. The similar ST3250820AS model with half as much cache sold for the same price. We could have saved $18 by using an 80 GB 7200.9 model, but three times the storage space for $18 more was too good a deal to pass up.

ALTERNATIVES: HARD DISK DRIVE

Any Seagate Barracuda 7200.9 or 7200.10 SATA drive, in any capacity. Choose a model with 16 MB of cache rather than 8 MB if the price difference is small.

Optical Drive

NEC ND-3550A DVD writer (*http://www.necam.com*)

With DVD writers selling for $35 or so, there's no point to installing a less capable optical drive. We chose the NEC ND-3550A DVD writer for the SFF PC, but any similar model from BenQ, Lite-On, NEC, Pioneer, or Plextor would also be a good choice, as long as it is not too deep for the case. The Antec NSK1300 case has a universal optical drive door that hides the front bezel of the optical drive, so there's no need to match the color of the optical drive to the case.

External Peripherals

We're going to wimp out here. Rather than make specific recommendations for keyboard, mouse, speakers, display, and other external peripherals, we'll refer you to the other project system chapters in this book and to the web site (*http://www.hardwareguys.com*).

It's not that we don't want to provide a list of recommended external peripherals for the SFF PC. It's that we can't, because an SFF PC can be built as anything from a $500 appliance system to a $1,000 mainstream system to an $1,800 gaming system. Accordingly, all we can recommend is that you choose external peripherals according to your budget and the purpose of the system.

Table 7-2 summarizes our component choices for the core SFF PC system.

Table 7-2. Bill of materials for SFF PC

Component	Product
Case	Antec NSK1300 microATX case (300W power supply included)
Motherboard	Intel D946GZIS
Processor	Intel Core 2 Duo E6300
CPU Cooler	(Bundled with retail-boxed CPU)
Memory	Kingston PC2-5300 DDR2-SDRAM (2 GB kit)
Video adapter	(Integrated)
Hard disk drive	Seagate ST3250620AS Barracuda 7200.10 (250GB)
Optical drive	NEC ND-3550A DVD writer

Building the SFF PC

Figure 7-3 shows the major internal components of the SFF PC. The Antec NSK1300 case is flanked on the left by the Seagate 7200.10 Barracuda SATA hard drive and the NEC ND-3550A DVD writer, and on the right by the Intel D946GZIS motherboard, with the Crucial DDR2 memory, the Intel Core 2 Duo processor, and the Intel CPU cooler already installed. Yep, that's everything. Not many components, but that's all it takes to build an SFF PC with some serious power.

Before you proceed, make sure you have everything you need. Open each box and verify the contents against the packing list. Make sure all driver discs, cables, screws, and other small components are present.

Figure 7-3. SFF PC components, awaiting construction

Preparing the Case

The first step in building any system is always to make sure that the power supply is set to the correct input voltage. Some power supplies, including the unit supplied with the Antec NSK1300, set themselves automatically. Others must be set manually using a slide switch to select the proper input voltage. If your case uses such a power supply, make sure that it's set to the proper input voltage before you proceed.

WARNING

If you connect a PC set for 230V to a 115V receptacle, nothing is damaged. The PC components receive half the voltage they require, and the system won't boot. But if you connect a power supply set for 115V to a 230V receptacle, the PC components receive twice the voltage they're designed to use. If you power up the system, that overvoltage destroys the system instantly in clouds of smoke and showers of sparks.

To begin preparing the Antec NSK1300 case, remove the thumbscrew that secures the top panel, as shown in Figure 7-4.

Figure 7-4. Remove the thumbscrew that secures the top panel

After you remove the thumbscrew, slide the top panel back slightly until the hooks that secure it disengage, and then lift the panel off, as shown in Figure 7-5.

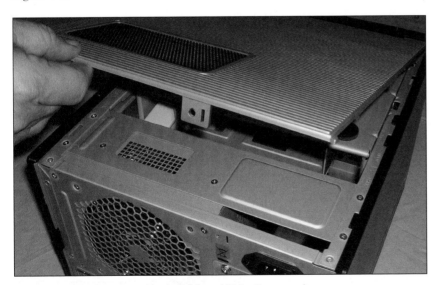

Figure 7-5. Slide the top panel back slightly and lift it off

Order Is Important

When you build a standard PC, the exact component installation sequence usually doesn't matter much. With an SFF PC, that's often not true. The small case means there's little room to work. One component may be inaccessible after you install another component. If you forget to connect a cable to the motherboard, for example, you may later have to partially disassemble the system to get to it.

The Antec NSK1300 case is much better than most SFF cases in this respect. The top panel and both side panels are removable, which means the interior is quite accessible, albeit a bit cramped. The disadvantage of the NSK1300 is that it doesn't include custom-length cables preinstalled and routed, as is the case with most "bare-bones" SFF systems. That means you need to take particular care to route and dress the cables appropriately to avoid restricting air flow or fouling a fan.

The side panels of the NSK1300 are secured by plastic latches at the rear center edges of the panels. To remove the side panels, press the plastic latch, as shown in Figure 7-6, to unlock the panel. Slide the panel slightly toward the front of the case and lift it off, as shown in Figure 7-7.

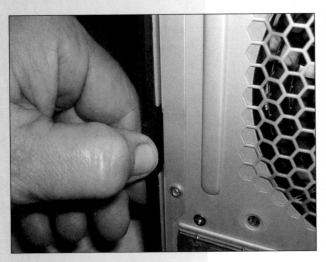

Figure 7-6. Squeeze the latch at the center rear of the side panel to release it

Figure 7-7. While squeezing the latch, slide the side panel forward slightly and then pull it away from the case

The Antec NSK1300 uses a swing-up removable drive bay that secures to the chassis using four posts on the drive bay that mate with corresponding notches in the chassis. To remove the drive bay, pivot the rear end upwards, as shown in Figure 7-8, until the two rear posts come free and then lift the drive bay straight up, sliding the front two posts out of the matching slots in the chassis.

Figure 7-8. Pivot the drive bay upward and lift it free of the chassis

Chapter 7, Building a Small Form Factor (SFF) PC

With the drive bay removed, the inside of the case is visible. The brown cardboard box contains mounting screws and other hardware. The white box contains the Cyclone Blower, a supplementary cooling fan that mounts in place of a PCI expansion card.

Nearly every case we've used, including the Antec NSK1300, comes with a generic I/O template. Every motherboard comes with a custom I/O template designed to fit its rear I/O panel. The generic I/O template supplied with the case never seems to fit the I/O panel of the motherboard, so you need to remove the stock I/O template and replace it with the one supplied with the motherboard. To remove the generic I/O template, use a tool handle to press against its corners and edges, as shown in Figure 7-9, until it snaps out.

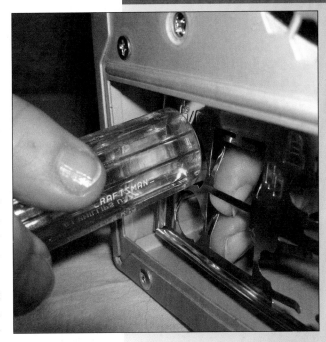

Figure 7-9. Remove the I/O template supplied with the case

Before you install the custom I/O template, compare it to the motherboard I/O panel to make sure the holes in the template correspond to the connectors on the motherboard. The inside of the template has several grounding tabs that project toward the inside of the case. We found by experience that because of the tight quarters inside the NSK1300 case, it is impossible to seat the Intel D946GZIS motherboard unless you first bend the grounding tab of the Ethernet port slightly upward. (We ended up doing this after the template was installed by using a long flat-blade screwdriver, but it's easier to do it before you install the template.)

Figure 7-10. Snap the custom I/O template into place

Once you've done that, press the custom I/O template into place. Working from inside the case, align the bottom, right, and left edges of the I/O template with the matching case cutout. When the I/O template is positioned properly, begin on one corner and press gently along the edges to seat it in the cutout, as shown in Figure 7-10. It should snap into place, although getting it to seat properly sometimes requires several attempts. As you apply pressure from inside the case against the template, use your finger to apply offsetting pressure on the outside of the template to avoid bending it.

Chapter 7, Building a Small Form Factor (SFF) PC

See the Light

If you simply look at the motherboard, it's easy to miss one of the mounting holes in all the clutter. We generally hold the motherboard up to a light, which makes the mounting holes stand out distinctly.

If your case comes with preinstalled standoffs, make absolutely certain that each standoff matches a motherboard mounting hole. If you find one that doesn't, remove it. Leaving an "extra" standoff in place may cause a short circuit that could damage the motherboard and/or other components.

WARNING

Be careful not to bend the I/O template when you seat the template. The template holes need to line up with the external port connectors on the motherboard I/O panel. If the template is bent even slightly it may be difficult to seat the motherboard properly. Except, of course, for the grounding tab for the Ethernet port, which must be bent slightly upward to provide room to seat the motherboard.

After you install the I/O template, place the motherboard atop the case, as shown in Figure 7-11, aligned and positioned as it will be when it is installed in the case. Look down through each motherboard mounting hole to locate the mounting positions on the base of the case. The goals are to make sure that there is a standoff installed that corresponds to each motherboard mounting hole, and that no extra standoffs are installed.

The Intel D946GZIS motherboard has eight mounting holes. The Antec NSK1300, like many cases, is shipped with several standoffs preinstalled. All six of the standoffs preinstalled in the NSK1300 corresponded with motherboard mounting holes, so we needed to install only two standoffs.

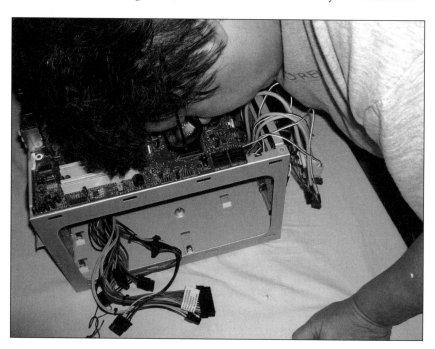

Figure 7-11. Look down through the motherboard mounting holes to verify standoff mounting positions

The Antec NSK1300 uses a mixture of standard brass standoffs and chrome-plated steel motherboard clips, shown in Figure 7-12. The top of each clip has a small, bent, protruding nipple that is small enough to pass through a motherboard mounting hole. Once the motherboard is dropped into place over these clips, sliding the motherboard slightly toward the back of the case causes the clips to clamp down on the top surface of the motherboard, securing it in place.

As the NSK1300 is shipped, there are brass standoffs in two positions and motherboard clips in four positions. For the two remaining required standoffs, we decided to use motherboard clips. They appear to secure the motherboard quite well, and we decided two screws were sufficient to lock the motherboard into place against the clips. If you're uncomfortable depending on the clips— for example, if this is to be a portable system—you can replace the motherboard clips with standard brass standoffs, which are provided in the parts bag.

To install the clips, press gently on the sides of the clip and slide it into the mounting position. Make sure that the bent nipple on the clip faces the same direction as

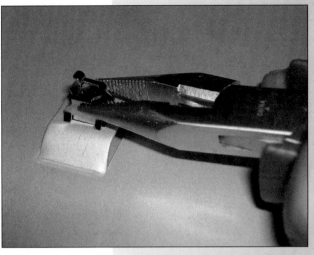

Figure 7-12. Insert a motherboard mounting clip in each position that corresponds to a motherboard mounting hole

the nipples on the clips that are already installed. Robert was able to insert the clips using only finger pressure to compress them, but Barbara found it easier to compress the clips with needle-nose pliers. Whichever method you use, make sure each clip snaps securely into the motherboard tray.

Once you've installed all the standoffs and motherboard clips, do a final check to verify that (a) each motherboard mounting hole has a corresponding standoff or clip, and (b) that no standoffs or clips are installed that don't correspond to a motherboard mounting hole. If you've removed the power supply, you can, as a final check, hold the motherboard in position above the case and look down through each motherboard mounting hole to make sure there's a standoff installed below it.

Installing the Processor and Memory

Even for a full-size system, it's easier to install the processor and memory while the motherboard is outside the case. An SFF system has so little working room that it's almost mandatory to do so.

WARNING

Each time you handle the processor, memory, or other static-sensitive components, first touch the power supply to ground yourself.

Installing the processor

To install the Core 2 Duo processor, place the motherboard on a flat surface. Lift the socket lever, as shown in Figure 7-13, until it swings past vertical and reaches the end of its travel.

Figure 7-13. Lift the socket lever to prepare the socket to receive the processor

With the socket lever open, the retention plate is unlatched and can be lifted upward, away from the socket, as shown in Figure 7-14. The retention plate has a black plastic cover that protects the delicate contacts inside the socket when no processor is installed. Snap this protective plastic cover off, as shown in Figure 7-15, and store it in a safe place. If you ever remove the processor from the motherboard, reinstall the cover to protect the socket until you install another processor.

Figure 7-14. Lift the retention plate away from the socket

Figure 7-15. Remove the protective plastic cover

Figure 7-16 shows the LGA775 socket prepared to receive the processor, with its delicate contacts exposed. The socket is easily damaged when it is in this state, so take care to avoid touching the contacts or dropping anything on the exposed socket. If the socket is damaged, the motherboard is scrap.

The processor also has a plastic snap-on cover that protects its contacts when it is not installed in a motherboard. When you are ready to install the processor in its socket, remove the plastic cover, as shown in Figure 7-17. Handle the processor only by its edges, and make sure the contact surface of the processor does not touch anything except the socket.

Figure 7-16. The socket prepared to receive the processor

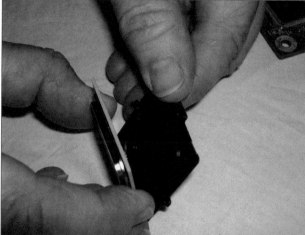

Figure 7-17. Remove the protective plastic cover from the processor

Pin 1 is indicated on the processor by a small golden triangle and on the socket by a beveled corner, both visible at the lower-right corner of the socket in Figure 7-18. The processor also has two keying notches that correspond with two nubs in the socket, both of which are also visible in Figure 7-18.

Holding the processor only by its edges, align pin 1 of the processor with pin 1 of the socket and drop the processor into place, as shown in Figure 7-18. The processor should seat flush with the socket just from the force of gravity. If seating the processor requires pressure more than a very gentle nudge, something is misaligned. Remove the processor and verify that it is aligned properly and that the pattern of holes on the processor corresponds to the pattern of pins on the socket.

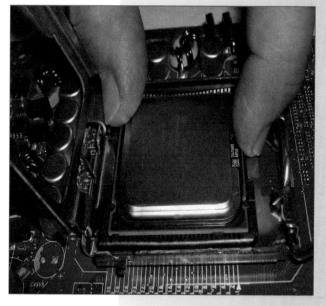

Figure 7-18. Align the processor with the socket and drop it into place

With the processor seated flush with the socket, lower the retention plate into place, as shown in Figure 7-19. Note the projecting lip on the retention plate and the corresponding cammed section of the socket lever. As you press the socket lever down to latch it in place, that cammed section engages the lip on the retention plate and presses it firmly into position.

With the retention plate in its closed position, press down firmly on the socket lever and snap it into the latched position, as shown in Figure 7-20. Once the socket lever is latched, the processor is secured in the socket and protected by the metal framework of the socket body.

Figure 7-19. Lower the retention plate into position

Figure 7-20. Close the socket lever and snap it into the latched position

Thermal Compound Is Required

The stock Intel CPU cooler comes with a preinstalled thermal pad on the base of the heatsink. As the processor heats up, that thermal pad melts, ensuring good thermal transfer between the processor and the heatsink base. If you use a different CPU cooler, one that does not include a thermal pad, make sure to apply thermal compound before you install the CPU cooler. Follow the instructions supplied with the thermal compound. (We use Antec Silver thermal compound, which is as good as anything and less expensive than many "premium" thermal compounds.)

Installing the CPU cooler

The Intel Core 2 Duo is a very cool-running processor, but it still consumes up to 65W of electrical power when it is running under heavy load. That power ends up as waste heat, which must be dissipated to prevent the processor from overheating. Intel supplies a decent CPU cooler with the retail-boxed Core 2 Duo processor, which is what we used.

Polish the CPU heat spreader to remove any foreign material. If there is no thermal pad installed on the heatsink base, polish it as well and apply thermal compound to the CPU heat spreader. Orient the CPU cooler above the processor, as shown in Figure 7-21. The cooler base has four posts that correspond to four mounting holes in the motherboard. Align those posts with the mounting holes. (It doesn't matter how you orient the CPU cooler, because the four motherboard mounting holes form a square. We generally orient the CPU cooler so that the fan power lead has as little slack as possible once it's connected to the motherboard fan power header pins.)

The CPU cooler is secured to the motherboard by four expanding posts that protrude through the motherboard. Align the posts with the motherboard mounting holes and then press down each post, as shown in Figure 7-22, until it snaps into the locked position.

Intel recommends installing the CPU cooler after the motherboard is installed in the case, but we prefer to install the CPU cooler with the motherboard still outside the case. If you do the same, note that you can't install the CPU cooler if the motherboard is lying flat on a firm surface because the mounting posts must protrude through the bottom of the motherboard in order to lock into place. Barbara solved that problem simply by raising one edge of the motherboard as she snapped the locking posts into place.

The final step in installing the CPU cooler is to connect the fan power lead to the fan power header pins on the motherboard, as shown in Figure 7-23. If there's excessive slack in the CPU fan power cable, secure it to make sure it can't foul the CPU fan.

Figure 7-21. Align the CPU cooler over the processor

Figure 7-22. Press down on all four locking posts to secure the CPU cooler

Figure 7-23. Connect the CPU fan cable to the CPU fan connector

As Simple As 3, 2, 1

Readers with sharp eyes may have noticed the edge of a memory module visible at the upper-left corner of Figure 7-23, which is odd because we haven't installed the memory yet. That's because the first images we shot of connecting the CPU fan power cable were blurred, so we came back and reshot this one later and forgot to remove the memory module when we reshot the image. Oh, well.

WARNING

If you remove the heatsink, you must replace the thermal compound or pad when you reinstall it. Before you reinstall, remove all remnants of the old thermal pad or compound. That can be difficult, particularly for a thermal pad, which can be very tenacious. We use an ordinary hair dryer to warm the thermal material enough to make it easy to remove. Sometimes the best way is to warm up the compound and rub it off with your thumb. (Use rubber gloves or a plastic bag to keep the gunk off your skin.) To protect the processor, keep it in the socket while you're removing remnants of the thermal compound or pad.

Alternatively, one of our technical reviewers says that rubbing gently with #0000 steel wool works wonders in removing the gunk, and is fine enough not to damage the surface. Another of our technical reviewers tells us that he uses Goof-Off or isopropyl alcohol to remove the remnants of the thermal goop or thermal pad. Whatever works for you is fine. Just make sure to remove the old thermal compound and replace it with new compound each time you remove and reinstall the processor.

When we replace a heatsink, we use Antec Silver Thermal Compound, which is widely available, inexpensive, and works well. Don't pay extra for "premium" brand names like Arctic Silver. They cost more than the Antec product and our testing shows little or no difference in cooling efficiency.

Installing memory

Installing memory in the Intel D946GZIS motherboard is straightforward. We have two memory modules to be installed, and two memory slots available. Pivot the white plastic locking tabs on both sides of both DIMM sockets outward to prepare the slots to receive DIMMs. Orient each DIMM with the notch in the contact area of the DIMM aligned with the raised plastic tab in slot and slide the DIMM into place, as shown in Figure 7-24.

Figure 7-24. Orient the DIMM with the notch aligned properly with the socket

With the DIMM properly aligned with the slot and oriented vertically relative to the slot, use both thumbs to press down on the DIMM until it snaps into place. The locking tabs should automatically pivot back up into the locked position, as shown in Figure 7-25, when the DIMM snaps into place. If they don't, close them manually to lock the DIMM into the socket.

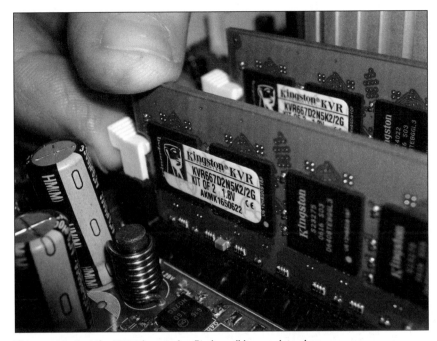

Figure 7-25. Seat the DIMM by pressing firmly until it snaps into place

With the processor and memory installed, you're almost ready to install the motherboard in the case. Before you do that, check the motherboard documentation to determine if any configuration jumpers need to be set. The Intel D946GZIS has only one jumper, which sets operating mode. On our motherboard, that jumper was set correctly by default, so we proceeded to the next step.

Installing the Motherboard

Installing the motherboard is the most time-consuming step in building the system because there are so many cables to connect. It's important to get all of them connected right, so take your time and verify each connection before and after you make it.

WARNING

Before you install the motherboard, tie off the front-panel and other cables to keep them out of the way. The limited working space inside an SFF case makes it easy to lose track of a cable and later find that it's caught underneath the mounted motherboard and can't be pulled free because the connector jams it in place.

Chapter 7, Building a Small Form Factor (SFF) PC

Figure 7-26. The ATX12V cable seated in its connector

Seating and securing the motherboard

Before you do *anything* else, locate the ATX12V power cable from the power supply and connect it to the motherboard. We forgot to do this before we installed the motherboard in the NSK1300 case. Doing it afterward was a royal pain in the petunia because there was almost no clearance. Figure 7-26 shows the ATX12V cable seated and latched (finally). Robert was able to guide it into position with his needle-nose pliers and press the cable into the connector with a flat-blade screwdriver. Next time, he'll remember to seat the ATX12V cable *before* he installs the motherboard.

Once you've connected the ATX12V cable, slide the motherboard into the case, as shown in Figure 7-27, carefully aligning the back-panel I/O connectors with the corresponding holes in the I/O template. As the motherboard I/O connectors seat, the protruding nipples on the motherboard clips should grasp the motherboard. Once the motherboard is in position, examine the rear I/O panel carefully to make sure that none of the grounding tabs are protruding into ports.

Figure 7-27. Slide the motherboard into position

SOMETIMES YOU NEED A SHOEHORN

As we mentioned earlier in this chapter, we had to bend the grounding tab for the Ethernet port slightly upward to allow the motherboard to seat. There is very little working room inside an SFF case, so you may have to take similar steps if you use a different motherboard. The important thing to remember is to check the rear I/O panel before you start driving screws to secure the motherboard. If a port is fouled, pull the motherboard out, fix the problem with the I/O template, and slide the motherboard back into position.

Keep pressure on the motherboard to align the two brass standoffs with the corresponding mounting holes, and drive screws into those two standoffs to secure the motherboard in place, as shown in Figure 7-28. After you secure the motherboard, verify once again that the back-panel I/O connectors mate properly with the I/O template and that the motherboard clips are correctly positioned to secure the motherboard.

Connecting motherboard cables

The final steps required to install the motherboard are to connect the various signal, data, and power cables. It doesn't much matter in what order you connect these cables, but make sure to get all of them connected.

To begin, locate the main ATX power connector near the front edge of the motherboard. The Antec NSK1300 power supply has a dual-purpose main power cable connector that can be configured as a 20-pin or 24-pin connector. By default, the main ATX power connector is configured as a 24-pin connector, which is used by most recent motherboards. If you're using a motherboard that is socketed for the older 20-pin main ATX power connector, examine the Antec power cable connector. You'll find that it has two segments, one with 20 pins and one with 4 pins, that can be separated. If you're using a 20-pin motherboard, remove the 4-pin segment from the main body of the connector.

Align the main ATX power cable connector as shown in Figure 7-29. Press it firmly into place until the latch on the cable connector snaps into place over the lip on the motherboard jack.

The ATA (IDE) motherboard interface connector is located on the front edge of the motherboard, adjacent to the main ATX power connector. Antec includes a round ATA cable with the NSK1300 case. Ordinarily, we prefer standard flat ATA ribbon cables to the round versions, but for a small form factor system the round cables are unarguably better at fitting in the cramped internal spaces and not blocking air flow.

Align the ATA cable with the motherboard connector, as shown in Figure 7-30, and press the connector firmly until it seats completely. Make certain the connectors are oriented properly. Most ATA cables and sockets are keyed in either or both of two ways: with a missing pin in the socket and a blocked hole in the cable connector, or with a cutout on the socket and

Figure 7-28. Secure the motherboard by driving screws into the brass standoffs

Figure 7-29. Align the main ATX power connector and press it firmly into place

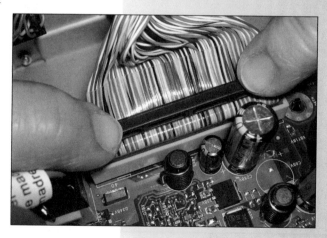
Figure 7-30. Align the ATA cable with the motherboard socket and press firmly to seat it

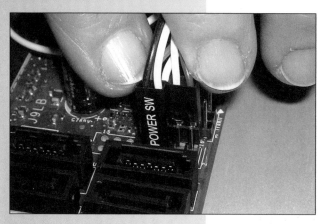

Figure 7-31. Connect the front-panel switch and indicator cables

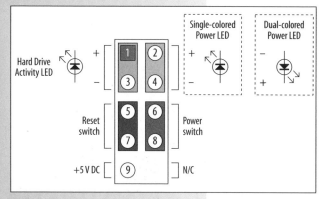

Figure 7-32. D946GZIS front-panel switch and indicator pin assignments (graphic courtesy of Intel Corporation)

Figure 7-33. Insert the S-ATA data cable

a corresponding nub on the cable connector. The ATA cable supplied by Antec is keyed in both ways, as is the socket on the Intel motherboard. If you use a different motherboard or cable, be aware that not all cables or motherboard sockets are keyed. If that's true of your components, make sure pin 1 on the cable is aligned with pin 1 on the socket before you seat the cable.

The next step is to connect the front-panel switch and indicator cables, as shown in Figure 7-31. The power switch and reset switch connectors are unpolarized, and so may be connected in either orientation, as long as you connect the cable to the correct pair of pins. The HDD activity LED cable is polarized, and should be connected with correct polarity. (If you get it wrong, though, the worst that happens is that the LED fails to illuminate.)

Each of the front-panel switch and indicator cables is labeled descriptively, e.g., "Power," "Reset," and "HDD LED." Match those descriptions with the front panel connector pins on the motherboard to make sure you connect the correct cable to the appropriate pins. The motherboard header pins are color-coded. Figure 7-32 shows the pin assignments for the Hard Drive Activity LED (yellow), Reset Switch (purple), Power LED (green), and Power Switch (red) connectors.

The Intel D946GZIS provides four Serial ATA interfaces, which are located in the extreme front left corner of the motherboard, adjacent to the front-panel connectors. Align the S-ATA data cable with the first S-ATA interface, and press it into place until it locks, as shown in Figure 7-33.

Intel begins numbering the S-ATA interfaces at 0. Some motherboards number the S-ATA interfaces beginning with 1. In either case, connect the S-ATA data cable to the lowest-numbered S-ATA interface connector on the motherboard.

The next step is to connect the front-panel USB ports to the motherboard. Most recent Antec cases provide a monolithic 10-pin (5×2) dual-port USB connector that matches the standard Intel USB pin assignments. The NSK1300 instead provides two single-port 5-pin (5×1) USB connectors on the dual front-panel USB cables. We decided to connect both of these cables to one of the dual-port motherboard USB connectors.

The Intel connector block is keyed with a missing pin on one end. The Antec cable connectors have all five pins open, which means it's possible to connect the cable backward. To avoid doing so, note which end of the motherboard connector has a missing pin. Connect the Antec cable with the two black ground wires toward that missing pin (toward the front of the case) as shown in Figure 7-34. If your case uses front-panel USB cables with individual connectors for each wire, refer to the pin assignment shown in Figure 7-35 to get those individual wires connected correctly.

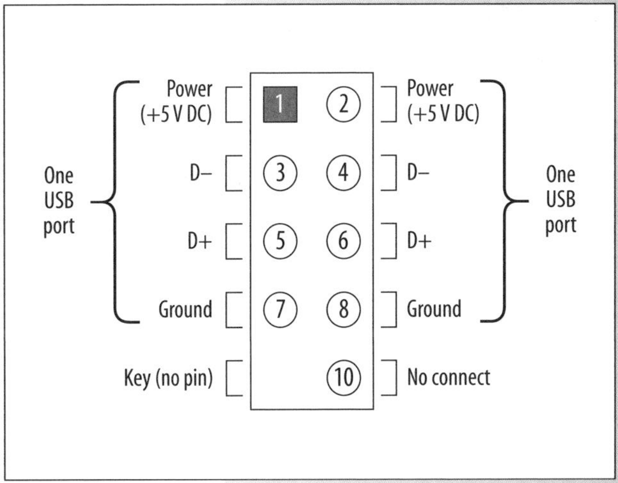

Figure 7-35. D946GZIS front-panel USB pin assignments (graphic courtesy of Intel Corporation)

Figure 7-34. Connect the front-panel USB cables to a motherboard USB interface

The final step in installing the motherboard is to connect the front-panel audio cable to the audio header pins, which are located at the left rear of the motherboard, behind the expansion slots. The NSK1300 case provides a monolithic front-panel audio cable that is keyed with a blocked hole that corresponds with a missing pin on the motherboard connector. Align the cable connector as shown in Figure 7-36, and press firmly to seat it.

NEATNESS COUNTS

In addition to the monolithic connector block, the Antec front-panel audio cable provides individual wires for use with motherboards that don't use the Intel-standard audio connector. If you don't need these individual wires for your motherboard, we recommend taping them off along the body of the cable. Otherwise, they simply flop around loose in the close vicinity of the expansion slots. The wires are quite thin, and if they were left loose one might easily foul an expansion slot.

Figure 7-36. Connect the front-panel audio cable to the front-panel audio connector pins

Installing the Low-Speed Cyclone Blower (Optional)

Antec bundles the Low-Speed Cyclone Blower with the NSK1300 case. ("Low-Speed Cyclone" sounds like an oxymoron to us, but there it is...) The Cyclone Blower occupies an expansion slot, exhausting warm air through the slot cover. It uses a low-speed fan that is so quiet it is difficult to hear it running even with your ear right up against the unit.

Installing the Cyclone Blower is optional. Antec provides it for configurations that require more cooling than the power supply fan can provide. We decided not to install it, because our final system configuration uses a low-current processor and integrated video and we wanted to see how well the system was cooled without the extra ventilation. If you decide to install the Cyclone Blower, Antec recommends the following placement:

- If no video card is installed, install the Cyclone Blower in the first slot (the slot that would otherwise be occupied by the video card).

- If a video card is installed but no other expansion card is installed, install the Cyclone Blower in the third slot, leaving one slot open between the video card and the Cyclone Blower.

- If a video card and one other expansion card are installed, install the Cyclone Blower in the third slot and the other expansion card in the fourth (last) slot.

- If a video card and two other expansion cards are installed, install the Cyclone Blower in the second slot, adjacent to the video card, and install the two other expansion cards in the third and fourth slots.

To install the Cyclone Blower, use the same procedure you would use to install an expansion card. Remove the two screws that secure the expansion slot cover bracket and the four screws that secure the four expansion slot covers and then pull the expansion slot cover bracket free. Remove the slot cover for the slot you select, and slide the Cyclone Blower into place. Reinstall the expansion slot cover bracket, and connect power to the Cyclone Blower.

Installing Drives

The Antec NSK1300 has one external 5.25" drive bay and three internal 3.5" drive bays. The external bay is for an optical drive, and the three internal 3.5" bays can each hold one hard drive.

To install the optical drive, align it with the guide slots inside the bay and slide it into place, as shown in Figure 7-37. If you are using the universal drive cover, slide the drive into the bay until the drive bezel is flush with the front of the drive bay. This seats the drive deeply enough to provide clearance for the "flapper" cover of the universal drive cover. If you are mounting the optical drive normally, with its front bezel flush with the front bezel of the case, seat the drive only until it protrudes half an inch or so beyond the face of the drive bay.

Align the drive screw holes with those in the drive bay. If you are using the universal drive cover, use the rear set of screw holes. If you want to mount the optical drive bezel flush with the front case bezel, use the front set of screw holes. Once you have the screw holes aligned, drive four screws to secure the drive, as shown in Figure 7-38. Insert two screws on each side of the drive, front and back. It doesn't matter if you use the top or bottom set of screw holes. We generally mix them up, using the front bottom screw holes and the rear top ones.

After you secure the optical drive, mount the hard drive. The Antec NSK1300 provides three hard drive bays, one horizontal underneath the optical drive bay, and one vertical on either side of it. We're installing only one hard drive in this system, so we took Antec's advice and mounted it in the horizontal hard drive bay.

To mount the hard drive, place the drive bay upside down on your work surface. Slide the hard drive—again, upside down, and with the drive power and data connectors toward the back (open) side of the bay—into the drive bay and align the screw holes in the bay and drive. Locate four of the special hard drive mounting screws with black rubber grommets, and use them to secure the hard drive to the bay, as shown in Figure 7-39.

Figure 7-37. Slide the optical drive into the drive bay

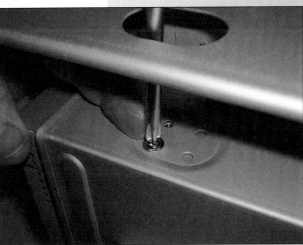

Figure 7-38. Secure the optical drive to the drive bay, using four screws

Figure 7-39. Secure the hard drive to the drive bay, using four screws

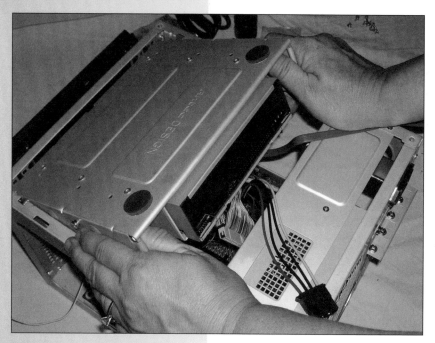

Figure 7-40. Slide the drive bay into the chassis

The final assembly step is to reinsert the drive bay in the chassis and connect the drive cables. To begin, locate the four cables you'll need to connect:

- ❏ Hard drive power cable
- ❏ Hard drive data cable
- ❏ Optical drive power cable
- ❏ Optical drive data cable

Pull these cables toward the upper rear of the system, near the power supply, and leave them dangling outside the case. The goal is to make sure the cables are accessible once you've reinstalled the drive bay. Slide the drive bay into the chassis, as shown in Figure 7-40, but don't seat it completely. Instead, leave it propped slightly open.

Connect the S-ATA data cable to the hard drive first, as shown in Figure 7-41. That cable has plenty of slack, but the drive connector will soon be obstructed by the optical drive cables, so we want to get it connected first. Connect the optical drive ATA data cable next, as shown in Figure 7-42, and then the optical drive power cable, as shown in Figure 7-43.

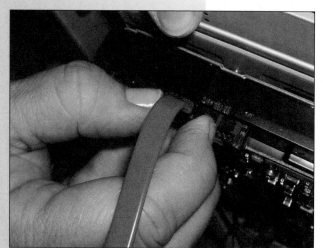

Figure 7-41. Connect the S-ATA data cable

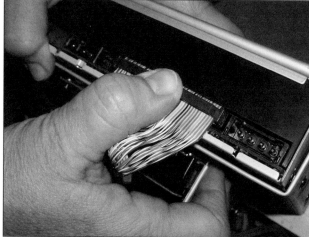

Figure 7-42. Connect the optical drive ATA data cable

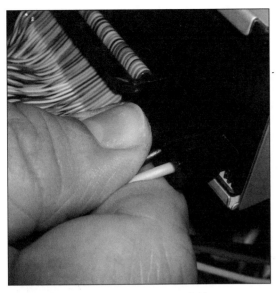

Figure 7-43. Connect power to the optical drive

The last cable is also the toughest. The S-ATA power cable has almost no slack to work with. To get it connected, first examine the back of the hard drive to determine the orientation of the short segment of the S-ATA power connector key. (With our drive, it was downward and to the right.) Do the same for the S-ATA power cable, and remember the relative orientations, or paint a stripe on both connectors with a Wite-out pen.

Pivot the drive bay assembly downward but not fully into place, until there is enough slack in the S-ATA power cable to reach the drive connector. Orient the cable connector key properly relative to the drive connector key and press the cable connector straight in until it seats, as shown in Figure 7-44.

With all four drive cables connected, seat the drive bay completely, as shown in Figure 7-45. Make sure that all four of the support pins are fully seated in the corresponding notches in the chassis frame, and slide the drive bay into position. Make sure that the drive bay is level and flush with the top of the chassis frame.

Figure 7-44. Connect the S-ATA power cable to the hard drive

Figure 7-45. Seat the drive bay completely

Chapter 7, Building a Small Form Factor (SFF) PC

Final Assembly Steps

The NSK1300 case doesn't use a traditional power LED. As a power indicator, it instead uses two blue LEDs that softly illuminate the front panel. These LEDs are powered directly by the power supply rather than from the motherboard Power LED connector. To enable them, locate the Molex connector with a white and a blue wire and connect it to a Molex power supply cable, as shown in Figure 7-46.

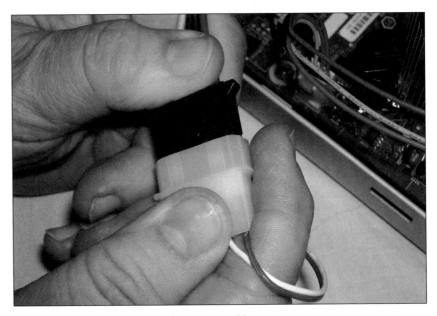

Figure 7-46. Connect the front-panel LED power cable

Figure 7-47. Label the top of the drive bay as a warning to yourself and others

Before you reinstall the side and top panels, we highly recommend putting a warning label on the top of the drive bay assembly, as shown in Figure 7-47. We learned this lesson by hard experience with the Aria SFF system we built for the first edition of this book.

A year or so after we built that system, we moved it to our workbench, intending to swap video adapters. We removed the top panel and side panels and lifted the drive bay assembly, intending to remove it. We heard something snap, and realized an instant too late what we'd done. With a sinking feeling, we examined the rear of the drives, hoping that what we'd heard snap was the S-ATA power cable ($50 for a power supply replacement) rather than the S-ATA power connector on the hard drive ($150 to replace the drive). Of course, it was the drive that was damaged, so we learned an expensive lesson: put a warning label on the drive bay or pay the price.

Congratulations! You're almost finished building the system. About all that remains is to dress the cables, configure BIOS Setup, and reinstall the top and side panels.

It's very difficult to dress the cables in an SFF system because there's so little room to work. Do the best you can, bundling and tying off excess cable lengths, tucking things into various nooks and crannies, and so on. The most important thing is to make sure that none of the cables can foul the CPU cooler fan. Once you have the cables dressed, take a few minutes to double-check everything one last time before you apply power to the system. Use the following checklist:

- ❏ No loose tools or screws (shake the case gently)
- ❏ Heatsink/fan unit properly mounted; CPU fan connected
- ❏ Memory modules fully seated and latched
- ❏ Front-panel switch and indicator cables connected properly
- ❏ Front-panel I/O cables connected properly
- ❏ Hard drive data cable connected to drive and motherboard
- ❏ Hard drive power cable connected
- ❏ Optical drive data cable connected to drive and motherboard
- ❏ Optical drive power cable connected
- ❏ Optical drive audio cable(s) connected, if applicable
- ❏ All drives secured to drive bay or chassis, as applicable
- ❏ Expansion cards fully seated and secured to the chassis
- ❏ Main ATX power cable and ATX12V power cable connected
- ❏ All cables dressed and tucked, if you choose to do that

Once you're certain that all is as it should be, it's time for the smoke test. Leave the cover off for now. Connect the power cable to the wall receptacle (or, better still, a UPS) and then to the system unit. Press the main power button on the front of the case, and the system should start up. Check to make sure that the power supply fan and CPU fan are spinning. You should also hear the hard drive spin up and the happy beep that tells you the system is starting normally. At that point, everything should be working properly.

Turn off the system, disconnect the power cord, and take these final steps to prepare the system for use:

Set the BIOS Setup Configuration jumper to Configure mode
> The BIOS Setup Configuration jumper block on the Intel D946GZIS motherboard is used to set the operation mode. This jumper is located near the center of the left edge of the motherboard, near the front edge of the expansion slots. By default, the jumper is in the 1-2 or "normal" position. Move the jumper block to the 2-3 or "configure" position.

Premature Death

When you turn on the rear power switch, the system will come to life momentarily and then die. That's perfectly normal behavior. When the power supply receives power, it begins to start up. It quickly notices that the motherboard hasn't told it to start, and so it shuts down again. All you need to do is press the front-panel power switch and the system will start normally.

Reconnect the power cord and restart the system

When the configuration jumper is set to Configure mode, starting the system automatically runs BIOS Setup and puts the system in maintenance mode. This step allows the motherboard to detect the type of processor installed and configure it automatically. When the BIOS Setup screen appears, choose the menu option to clear all BIOS data and then reset the system clock. Save your changes and exit. The system automatically shuts down. Disconnect the power cord.

Set the BIOS Setup Configuration jumper to Normal mode

With the power cord disconnected, move the BIOS Setup Configuration jumper block from 2-3 (Configure mode) to 1-2 (Normal mode).

Replace the side panel and reconnect power

With the jumper set for Normal operation, replace the side panel and reconnect the power cord. Your system is now completely assembled and ready for use.

Final Words

We built this system as a "pocket battleship"—small, but with more power than many systems twice its size. Even the entry-level Core 2 Duo processor we used is faster than about 99% of the processors that were sold at the time we built this system. The integrated GMA 3000 graphics adapter provides excellent display quality and sufficient 3D graphics power for Windows Vista and many games. With 2 GB of memory, this system handles everything we throw at it with a whole bunch of plombs.

Still, there are some upgrades we'd consider making. None are essential, but all would be useful.

First, although the integrated graphics are more than good enough for most purposes, we could easily upgrade this system to support moderately intense 3D games by adding a midrange PCI Express video adapter. We'd choose a passively cooled video card (for low noise) that drew as little current as possible (to stay within the limits of the 300W NSK1300 power supply). If we installed a video card, we'd also install the Cyclone Blower to provide additional air flow.

Second, as we've begun working more with camcorder video, we've come to appreciate the presence of a FireWire port. The Intel D946GZIS does not provide FireWire, but it would be easy enough to install a $15 FireWire card. If we did that, we might also upgrade the hard drive from 250 GB to 500 or 750 GB to provide more space for editing video footage.

Third, cooling. Like most SFF systems, this one runs 10°C to 15°C warmer than a typical desktop system with similar components. The stock Intel CPU cooler is reasonably efficient and quiet. At idle, it runs at 1,860 RPM. At that speed, although it is the loudest system component, it is still nearly

Advice from Jim Cooley

I have had so much trouble installing drivers for cheap no-name FireWire cards that I now use Adaptec FireWire cards exclusively. They cost more, but the savings in time and frustration is worth it.

inaudible. Under load, the CPU temperature increases, as does the CPU cooler fan speed. Under heavy load, the fan runs as fast as 3,360 RPM, which is fast enough to produce a noticeable whine.

One possible solution might be to install a premium third-party CPU cooler, such as a Thermalright or Zalman unit. Either of those might reduce the CPU temperature by as much as 5°C and would also be quieter than the stock Intel CPU cooler. The problem is that these third-party CPU coolers are typically quite large. As Figure 7-48 shows, there is very little room in the NSK1300 case for an oversize CPU cooler.

Figure 7-48. Clearance between the top of the CPU cooler and the bottom of the power supply

Antec provides another possible solution. The NSK1300 includes a bracket that allows you to mount a standard case fan on the side of the power supply. (Two of the four mounting holes are visible at the right-front edge of the power supply in Figure 7-48, with a third partially visible at the rear.) Substituting a large, quiet case fan for the stock CPU fan allows you to move lots of air at a relatively low fan speed, which reduces the noise level and improves cooling.

With or without these upgrades, we think the SFF PC is an excellent choice if you need a compact system that can fit just about anywhere. It's attractive, fast, reasonably quiet, and provides the same level of functionality as a typical mini-tower desktop system. It's an ideal system for a dorm room, the kids' bedroom, or as a secondary system. For that matter, many people would find it ideal as a primary system. With two PCI and one PCIe expansion slots as well as a video card slot, this system could easily be upgraded to function as a media center system. Finally, its compactness and portability make it a good "luggable" system for times when a notebook just isn't enough computer.

More Info

For updated component recommendations, commentary, and other new material, visit *http://www.hardwareguys.com/guides/sff-pc.html*.

Building a Budget PC

8

Inexpensive doesn't have to mean cheap. The myth persists that you can't save money building your own PC, particularly a budget system. In fact, it's easy to match the price of a mass-market commercial system with a home-built system that uses higher-quality components. Of course, you could instead match the quality level of a mass-market commercial system by buying the cheapest components available and save a few bucks by doing so, but we don't recommend doing that. We think there are good reasons to build inexpensive systems, but no reason at all to build cheap systems.

We define a budget PC as one that seeks the maximum bang for the minimum buck, consonant with good component quality, reasonable performance, and high reliability. A budget PC uses good-quality components throughout, but those components fall on the low end of the performance range. They may even be a generation or two out of date. That's not necessarily a bad thing, though. Last year's models are are every bit as good this year as they were 12 months ago, and you can save a lot of money if you don't insist on the very latest components.

In pursuit of low prices, we don't hesitate to buy components that are discontinued and on sale. There are few disadvantages to doing that. Discontinued products nearly always carry the full manufacturer warranty, and function as well as they did when they were the latest and greatest products available. Judicious shopping can easily knock $50 or more off the total cost of a budget system. That's nothing to sneeze at when your total budget is only a few hundred dollars.

In this chapter, we'll design and build the perfect budget PC.

Determining Functional Requirements

We sat down to think through our own requirements for a budget PC. Here's the list of functional requirements we came up with:

Reliability

Reliability is important for a budget PC, just as it is for any computer. Although our limited budget may force us to make minor compromises in reliability—such as using a lower-capacity power supply than we might otherwise choose—we'll still keep reliability firmly in mind as we select components. When we're forced to choose—as we inevitably will be—between performance, capacity, or features versus reliability, we'll always favor the latter.

Adequate performance

In order to be useful, a budget PC must have adequate performance. Cheap consumer-grade PCs are often obsolete the day they're unpacked. Most of them have slow processors, insufficient memory, small 5,400 RPM hard drives, and very poor integrated video. That's simply not good enough. For our budget PC, we aim for a performance level equal to what defined a mainstream or performance PC a year to 18 months prior. That means we need a processor in the 3 GHz class, 512 MB of memory, a 7,200 RPM hard drive, and either fast integrated video or an inexpensive standalone video adapter.

Usable peripherals

Cheap consumer-grade PCs always scrimp on peripherals. A typical cheap mass-market system is bundled with a $2 mouse, a $3 keyboard, a $3 set of speakers, a $12 CD-ROM drive, and a $65 17" monitor, none of which are good for anything but the trash bin. We can do better than that, even within the constraints of our tight budget. We'll have to spend an extra $5 here and $20 there, but we'll end up with solid, usable peripherals that are likely to last the life of the system.

Vista compatibility

Vista compatibility is a moving target, and means different things to different people. Technically, many current consumer-grade systems are Vista-compatible in the sense that Vista is likely to load and run on them. But there are different levels of Vista, and cheap systems are likely to support only the basic Vista feature set—no advanced graphics nor many of the other features that differentiate Vista from Windows XP. Although Vista hardware requirements had not yet been finalized when we designed this system, we made some assumptions based upon the best information then available with the goal of designing a budget system that would be able to run a full-feature Vista configuration with few or no hardware upgrades.

Noise level

There's little room in the budget for special quiet components, but that doesn't mean a budget PC must necessarily be noisy. We'll choose the quietest components available in our price range, always giving price and reliability high priority, but keeping noise level in mind as well. For example, two hard drives may be priced identically, but one may be literally twice as loud as the other. The same is true of other components such as cases, power supplies, and CPU coolers. By choosing carefully, we can build a budget PC that is much quieter than a similar but noisier configuration that costs the same.

Hardware Design Criteria

With the functional requirements determined, the next step was to establish design criteria for the budget PC hardware. Here are the relative priorities we assigned for our budget PC. Your priorities may of course differ.

As you can see, this is a well-balanced system. Price and reliability are our top concerns, with everything else secondary. Here's the breakdown:

DESIGN PRIORITIES	
Price	☆☆☆☆☆
Reliability	☆☆☆☆☆
Size	☆☆☆☆☆
Noise level	☆☆☆☆☆
Expandability	☆☆☆☆☆
Processor performance	☆☆☆☆☆
Video performance	☆☆☆☆☆
Disk capacity/performance	☆☆☆☆☆

Price

Price is the 900-pound gorilla for a budget system. We set our target price for this system at $350 excluding external peripherals ($500 with keyboard, mouse, speakers, and display), and tried very hard to stay within that budget. That meant making many trade-offs and giving up some "nice to have" features, but we were able to configure a solid system at that price.

Reliability

Reliability is as important as price. A unreliable budget system is not worth having. To get that reliability, we used good brand-name components throughout.

Size

Size is unimportant, so we paid it no mind. As it turned out, the best case for our purposes was a standard mini-tower unit.

Noise level

We'd like a quiet system, but had no extra money for noise reduction. We decided to do what we could to choose the quietest possible inexpensive components, but otherwise to let the chips fall where they may.

Expandability

Expandability is unimportant, except in terms of making the system upgradable to be compatible with Vista. In essence, that meant making sure that at least one slot was available for memory expansion and that there was a video slot available in case we needed to install a standalone video adapter later. Otherwise, this system will never be expanded or upgraded.

Processor performance

Processor performance is moderately important for our budget PC, both initially and to ensure that the system will have enough horsepower to run Vista without requiring a processor upgrade. We'd love to use a dual-core processor in this system, but there's simply no room in the budget. We can afford to spend perhaps $85 on the processor, which limited our choices to the AMD Sempron or the Intel Celeron.

Video performance

2D video quality is important for our budget PC, because it determines display clarity and sharpness for browsers, office suites, and similar applications that this system will run. A budget PC is not intended for serious gaming, so 3D video performance is a non-issue except to the extent that we need adequate 3D performance to run at least the Vista Aero interface, and preferably with Vista's Glass effects. That means we'll need either an inexpensive standalone video adapter or the latest and fastest integrated video, such as Intel GMA 950 or nVIDIA 6100/6150. If we opt for integrated video, we'll make sure to choose a motherboard that provides a PCI Express x16 video slot, just in case we need to upgrade the video later.

Disk capacity/performance

Disk capacity and performance are relatively unimportant for the budget system. We won't use one of the small 5,400 RPM drives typically found in cheap consumer-grade systems, but we won't break the bank, either. The smallest mainstream 7,200 RPM drives available store 80 GB, which is sufficient for our budget system.

Component Considerations

With our design criteria in mind, we set out to choose the best components for the budget PC system. The following sections describe the components we chose, and why we chose them.

Case and Power Supply

Antec SLK-1650B Mini-Tower Case (*http://www.antec.com*)

It's easy to spend too little on the case and power supply for a budget system. We've seen cases with 350W power supplies advertised for as little as $25, but we wouldn't even consider using such shoddy products. Cheap cases are bad enough. Things don't fit properly, and they're full of burrs and sharp edges that make working on them dangerous. But cheap power supplies are worse. It's simply not possible to build a reliable system using a cheap power supply.

Your Mileage May Vary

Although we tested the configuration we used to build our own budget PC, we did not test permutations with the listed alternatives. Those alternatives are simply the components we would have chosen had our requirements been different. That said, we know of no reason the alternatives we list should not work perfectly.

Plan to spend at least $65 or so on a decent case and power supply for a budget system. (Most of that cost is in the power supply.) We looked at budget cases from several manufacturers, but as usual we found that Antec had the best product for the money. We chose the Antec SLK-1650B mini-tower case, which includes a good 350W ATX 2.0 power supply.

We knew that Antec was about to discontinue the Solution Series SLK-1650B case in favor of the New Solution Series NSK4400 model, but we chose the SLK-1650B anyway. We think the SLK-1650B is a very attractive case, although the NSK4400 is prettier and includes a 380W power supply (versus 350W in the SLK-1650B). But we were able to find the SLK-1650B on sale for $62, about $10 less than the NSK4400. The 350W power supply in the SLK-1650B is perfectly adequate for the modest hardware configuration we planned to use, and the case features are otherwise suitable, so we decided to save the $10 for use elsewhere.

Motherboard

ASRock K8NF4G-SATA2 (*http://www.asrock.com*)

As always, the first decision to make in choosing a motherboard is which processor you intend to use. Our budget was $85 for the processor, which limited us to an AMD Sempron or Intel Celeron model. Dollar for dollar, the Sempron outperforms the Celeron significantly, so decided to buy the fastest Sempron we could find for $85. That meant we needed a Socket 754 motherboard.

Although AMD has de-emphasized Socket 754 in favor of Socket 939 and the new Socket AM-2, there were still many Socket 754 motherboards to choose among. Our requirement for integrated video fast enough to support Vista narrowed our choices down to motherboards that provided nVIDIA 6100 or 6150 integrated video. Among those, the ASRock K8NF4G-SATA2 was the standout choice.

ASRock is the value brand of ASUS, whose motherboards we've used for years and come to depend on. We had no experience with ASRock products, so we did a great deal of research before deciding to use this motherboard. We found that ASRock products were generally well thought of among their users, and that relatively few problems had been reported. Based on our confidence in ASUS, we decided to give the ASRock board a try. (Our subsequent torture-testing on three samples proved the ASRock board was indeed very stable.)

Although the ASRock K8NF4G-SATA2 motherboard lacks many of the features popular among performance enthusiasts and gamers, it has exactly the feature set we were looking for: nVIDIA GeForce 6100 integrated video with support for DX9 and Pixel Shader 3.0, a PCI Express x16 slot for future video upgrades, two SATA ports with RAID 0/1 support, good multichannel audio, an integrated 100BaseT network adapter, four USB 2.0 ports, etc. At about $60, it was a perfect fit for our needs and budget.

ALTERNATIVES: CASE/POWER SUPPLY

There are many competing cases in the same price range, but most of them include power supplies that are mediocre at best. Of those few inexpensive cases that include solid power supplies, our next choice after the Antec SLK/NSK models would be the Enermax Pandora CA3030.

ALTERNATIVES: MOTHERBOARD

If you build a Celeron system, any Intel or ASUS Socket 775 motherboard with integrated GMA 950 graphics. In Socket 939, any of the following GeForce 6100 motherboards: ASRock 939NF4G-SATA2; ASUS A8N-VM; EPoX EP-9GF6100-M; Gigabyte GA-K8N51GMF-9; MSI K8NGM2-L (6100), -FID (6150), or -NBP (6150). GeForce 6150 graphics should be slightly faster than GeForce 6100 graphics, but testing shows no real difference. The 6150-based motherboards typically cost $10 to $15 more than similar 6100-based models, so we recommend choosing one of the latter.

**ALTERNATIVES:
PROCESSOR**

No good ones. The Sempron processor is really the only game in town for a budget system. If we could afford to spend $125 for the processor, we'd choose a low-end dual-core Intel Pentium D model, but doing that would take us well beyond our $350 base budget for this system.

Processor

AMD Sempron 3100+ (*http://www.amd.com*)

With $85 allocated to the processor, our choices are limited to single-core "value" processors. Intel sells several Celeron models in that price range, but Celeron processors simply can't compete with comparably priced AMD Sempron processors. Semprons are noticeably faster than Celerons for most tasks, consume less power, and run cooler.

AMD produces two classes of Sempron processors. The so-called K7 Semprons are really just rebadged Athlon XP processors. They use the obsolete Socket A (462), and are a poor choice for a new system (although they are excellent upgrade processors for older systems). Conversely, K8 Semprons are essentially Athlon 64 processors with smaller L2 caches, and are an excellent choice for a new budget system.

CPU Cooler

Spire SP792B12-U KestrelKing V (*http://www.spirecoolers.com*)

The Spire SP792B12-U KestrelKing V is the CPU cooler you want for this project. Unfortunately, it's not the CPU cooler we ended up using. We originally intended to order the retail-boxed version of the Sempron processor, which includes a bundled CPU cooler. But, while the bundled CPU cooler is reasonably effective at cooling the processor, there are third-party coolers available that are much quieter and cool more efficiently than the stock unit.

We'd used the Arctic Cooling ACS64U Silencer 64 Ultra successfully on other Sempron systems. When we checked prices, we found that the ACS64U with an OEM Sempron processor together cost only $4 more than a retail-boxed Sempron. We decided that better cooling and quieter operation was worth the $4 difference, so we ordered the ACS64U and thought nothing more about it.

Until, that is, it was time to build the system. As we installed the processor and cooler, we found another motherboard component was so close to the processor socket that the ACS64U wouldn't fit. Ordinarily, we'd simply have ordered a replacement heatsink, such as the Spire SP792B12-U KestrelKing V. But this time we were stuck. We desperately needed a Windows box to run some Windows-only software that was required for another book project. Deadlines were looming. It was Sunday afternoon, and our editor was expecting a chapter from us the next day.

We decided to do the best we could with what we had to work with. We were able to make the Arctic Cooling ACS64U fit, but only by doing some minor surgery on the motherboard. We ended up with a functional system, although there was no way to hide the surgery we'd done. We almost didn't bother to shoot images of the build, because Robert intended to order a new motherboard and rebuild the budget system from scratch. Then, as Robert started hacking on the motherboard, Barbara starting shooting images. When Robert asked why she was bothering to shoot images of a project we wouldn't be using in the book, Barbara replied that she thought we should show the project, warts and all. "Nothing wrong with letting people know that we sometimes screw up, too."

So we decided not to gloss over the ugly parts, and to show our readers what we really did. And it turned out well, too. The CPU temperature at idle is only 5°C over ambient, and the system runs cool even under heavy load. It's also very quiet, barely audible from less than a meter away in a quiet room. Even so, we don't recommend you do what we did. Building the system is much simpler if you use the Spire cooler.

Memory

Crucial PC3200 DDR-SDRAM (*http://www.crucial.com*)

Although many low-end mass-market systems are equipped with only 256 MB of RAM, that's insufficient even for a budget system. You can load and run Windows XP and one or two applications in 256 MB, but having so little memory noticeably hampers performance and reduces stability. Doubling the memory to 512 MB pays big dividends for little additional cost.

Unlike Intel processors, which really need dual-channel memory to provide their best performance, the AMD Sempron is quite happy with single-channel PC3200 DDR-SDRAM. Like the Athlon 64, the Sempron has a built-in memory controller, but the Sempron memory control is single-channel (versus dual-channel for the Athlon 64). That means there's no advantage to installing memory modules in pairs in a Sempron system. That's fortunate, because the motherboard we chose has only two memory slots, and we'd like to leave one of them open for future expansion.

So we decided to install one 512 MB PC3200 DDR-SDRAM DIMM in our budget system. If we install Windows Vista on this system later, we can fill the second memory slot with another 512 MB DIMM—a total of 1 GB—to accommodate the higher memory requirements of Vista.

Crucial memory is fast, reliable, inexpensive, and readily available. We've used Crucial memory for more than a decade in hundreds of systems, and it's never let us down. Accordingly, we chose one Crucial CT6464Z40B PC3200 512 MB DIMM for this system.

ALTERNATIVES: MEMORY

For a budget system, Kingston ValueRAM is the only other memory we'd consider using.

Video Adapter

Integrated nVIDIA GeForce 6100

The nVIDIA GeForce 6100 video integrated on the ASRock motherboard provides excellent 2D display quality and reasonably good 3D performance for casual gaming and similar tasks. The ASRock motherboard includes a PCI Express x16 video adapter slot, so if necessary we can upgrade the video down the road by installing an inexpensive PCIe video adapter. We don't expect that to be necessary, even if we decide at some point to replace Windows XP with Vista. But if it does turn out that Vista requires more horsepower than the GeForce 6100 video provides, even a $30 standalone video adapter is likely to be more than sufficient.

Hard Disk Drive

Seagate Barracuda 7200.9 SATA 80 GB (*http://www.seagate.com*)

Many inexpensive consumer-grade systems use 5,400 RPM hard drives, which are noticeably slower than mainstream 7,200 RPM units. If we were attempting to cut costs to the bone, we might have chosen something like a 20 GB Seagate ST320014A U Series X drive for $30 or so.

We decided it was sensible to spend an extra $20 to get a 7,200 RPM 80 GB Seagate Barracuda 7200.9 SATA drive. That $20 is significant on a system with a base budget of $350, but the extra $20 buys us four times as much disk space and about twice the speed. It would be foolish to cripple system performance to save so little money.

Optical Drive

NEC ND-3550A DVD writer (*http://www.nec.com*)

DVD burners are so inexpensive nowadays that it seldom makes sense to install a less capable optical drive, even in a budget system. Among the many inexpensive DVD writers available, we chose the NEC ND-3550A for its combination of features, performance, reliability, and price.

Keyboard and Mouse

Logitech Internet Pro Desktop (*http://www.logitech.com*)

Personal preference outweighs all else when choosing a keyboard and mouse. No one can choose the "best" keyboard and mouse for someone else. That said, we had to pick a "budget" keyboard and mouse for our budget PC. We wanted something in the sub-$20 range that included a decent keyboard and a reliable optical mouse. Our favorite among inexpensive keyboard/mouse combos is the Logitech Internet Pro Desktop, for which we paid $17. If you prefer a cordless keyboard/mouse combo, buy the Logitech Cordless Internet Pro Desktop, which costs $25 or so.

ALTERNATIVES: HARD DISK DRIVE

Various models from Maxtor, Samsung, and Western Digital. But our advice is to buy the Seagate Barracuda, in whatever capacity is appropriate for your needs. Our readers and tech reviewers have rarely had a Seagate drive fail, which can't be said for other brands.

ALTERNATIVES: OPTICAL DRIVE

The BenQ DW1650 is an excellent alternative to the NEC ND-3550A, comparable in features, performance, reliability, and price. The BenQ DQ60 is a similar model that sells for about the same price and adds support for DVD-RAM, but is somewhat slower than the DW1650 or ND-3550A.

If you don't need a DVD writer, install a $20 LITE-ON SOHD-16P9S DVD-ROM drive.

Don't pass up thrift stores or garage sales. Quite often a brand-new keyboard which someone else doesn't like will be perfect for you and can be got for just a couple bucks.

Speakers

Logitech S-100 2.0 speaker system (*http://www.logitech.com*)

Even a budget PC needs a decent set of speakers, but we can realistically spend no more than $10 or $12 on speakers. In that price range, the Logitech S-100 2.0 speaker set has the best sound quality we've heard.

Display

NEC AS700 17" CRT (*http://www.necmitsubishi.com*)
Samsung 793DF 17" CRT (*http://www.samsung.com*)
ViewSonic E70 17" CRT (*http://www.viewsonic.com*)

As much as we'd love to have a 19" LCD display, budget limits us to a 17" CRT monitor. We allocated $120 to the display, and there are three standout choices in that price range. The NEC AS700, Samsung 793DF, and ViewSonic E70 all provide excellent display quality and (something rare with inexpensive displays) a 3-year warranty on the tube, parts, and labor. All three of these models are excellent. They're comparable in features and performance, so choose whichever is most easily available or least expensive.

Table 8-1 summarizes our component choices for the budget PC system.

ALTERNATIVES: KEYBOARD AND MOUSE

Many. Decide which features and layout you want, and then choose the appropriate Logitech model. If Logitech doesn't offer a model that meets your needs, look next to one of the many models sold by Microsoft.

ALTERNATIVES: SPEAKERS

The Creative Labs SBS240 and the Altec-Lansing 120i 2.0 speaker sets are priced similarly to the Logitech S-100 set and have similar sound quality.

ALTERNATIVES: DISPLAY

None we'd recommend, other than similar NEC, Samsung, and ViewSonic models.

Table 8-1. Bill of materials for budget PC

Component	Product
Case	Antec SLK1650B Mini-Tower Case
Power supply	Antec SmartPower 2.0 350W (bundled)
Motherboard	ASRock K8NF4G-SATA2
Processor	AMD Sempron 3100+
CPU cooler	Spire SP792B12-U KestrelKing V
Memory	Crucial PC3200 DDR-SDRAM (one 512 MB DIMM)
Video adapter	(Integrated nVIDIA GeForce 6100 IGP)
Hard disk drive	Seagate Barracuda 7200.9 SATA (80 GB)
Optical drive	NEC ND-3550A DVD writer
Keyboard and mouse	Logitech Internet Pro Desktop
Speakers	Logitech S-100 2.0 speaker set
Display	NEC AS700, Samsung 793DF, or ViewSonic E70 17" CRT monitor

Building the Budget PC

Figure 8-1 shows the components of the budget PC. The ASRock K8NF4G-SATA2 motherboard is at the left front, with the Seagate Barracuda 7200.9 hard drive and the NEC ND-3550A DVD writer front and center. At the right are the AMD Sempron 3100+ processor, the Crucial 512 MB DIMM, and the Arctic Cooling Silencer 64 Ultra CPU cooler, with the Antec SLK1650B case backing everything up.

Before you proceed, make sure you have everything you need. Open each box and verify the contents against the packing list. Once you're sure everything is present and accounted for, it's time to get started.

Figure 8-1. Budget PC components, awaiting construction

Preparing the Case

Antec must get a lot of support calls from people wondering why the SLK1650B rear fan isn't running. They stuck a warning label on the back of the power supply, shown in Figure 8-2, to tell people that the fan runs only when necessary. Unfortunately, they applied that label before they installed the power supply in the case, leaving part of the label clamped into place by the power supply. For the time being, just rip the label off. We'll remove the remnants of paper later.

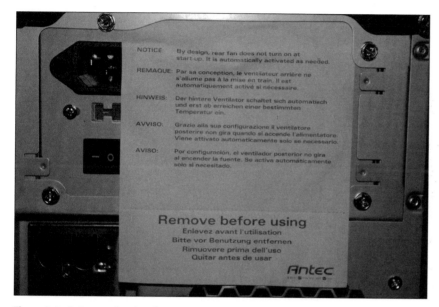

Figure 8-2. Antec warning that the rear case fan runs only when needed

The first step in building any system is always to make sure that the power supply is set to the correct input voltage. Some power supplies set themselves automatically. Others, including the Antec SmartPower 2.0 power supply in this system, must be set manually using a slide switch to select the proper input voltage, as shown in Figure 8-3. Bundled power supplies are nearly always set properly by default, but there are rare exceptions, so it's always a good idea to verify the input voltage setting before you proceed.

It's As Easy As 2, 1, 3

Although by necessity we describe building the system in a particular order, you don't need to follow that exact sequence when you build your own system. Some steps—for example, installing the processor and memory before installing the motherboard in the case—should be taken in the sequence we describe, because doing otherwise makes the task more difficult or risks damaging a component. But the exact sequence doesn't matter for most steps. As you build your system, it will be obvious when sequence matters.

Figure 8-3. Verify that the power supply is set for the proper input voltage

Figure 8-4. Remove the thumbscrews that secure the top panel

AVOID FIREWORKS

If you connect a power supply set for 230V to a 115V receptacle, there's no harm done. The PC components receive half the voltage they require, and the system won't boot. But if you connect a power supply set for 115V to a 230V receptacle, the PC components receive *twice* the voltage they're designed to use. If you plug in the system, that overvoltage destroys the system instantly in clouds of smoke and showers of sparks.

After you've verified that the power supply is set correctly, remove the two thumbscrews that secure the top panel, as shown in Figure 8-4.

After you remove the thumbscrews, slide the top panel slightly toward the rear, as shown in Figure 8-5, and then lift it off, as shown in Figure 8-6.

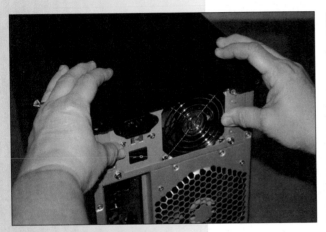

Figure 8-5. Slide the top panel to the rear to release it

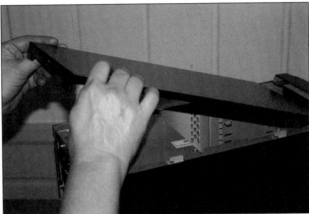

Figure 8-6. Lift the top panel off

Figure 8-7. Remove the side panels and set them safely aside

With the top panel removed, tilt the left side panel down and remove it, as shown in Figure 8-7. Be careful not to damage the TAC shroud, which is the black plastic duct attached to the side panel. Remove the right side panel in the same manner. Put the top and side panels safely aside, where they won't be scratched while you are building the system.

With the power supply exposed, it's time to remove the remnants of the Antec warning label we mentioned earlier, shown in Figure 8-8. To do so, remove the four screws that secure the power supply, and slide the power supply slightly forward.

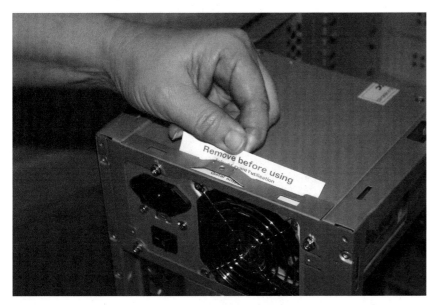

Figure 8-8. Remove the remnants of the Antec warning label

Remove the paper scraps, slide the power supply back into position, and reinsert the four screws to secure it.

Every case we've ever seen, including the Antec SLK1650B, comes with an I/O template. So does every motherboard. The generic I/O template supplied with the case never seems to fit the I/O panel of the motherboard, so you need to remove the stock I/O template and replace it with the one supplied with the motherboard.

I/O templates are made of thin metal that is easily bent. The best way to remove an I/O template without damaging it, as shown in Figure 8-9, is to use a tool handle to press gently against the panel from outside the case, while using your fingers to support the panel from inside the case. (We don't know why we care about damaging the generic I/O template supplied with the case. We have a stack of them sitting around, and have never needed one.)

Most motherboards, including the ASRock K8NF4G-SATA2, come with a custom ATX I/O template

Figure 8-9. Remove the I/O template supplied with the case

designed to match the motherboard I/O panel. Before you install the custom I/O template, compare it to the motherboard I/O panel to make sure the holes in the template correspond to the connectors on the motherboard.

Avoid Brute Force

Be careful not to bend the I/O template while seating it. The template holes need to line up with the external port connectors on the motherboard I/O panel. If the template is even slightly bent it may be difficult to seat the motherboard properly.

Once you've done that, press the custom I/O template into place. Working from inside the case, align the bottom, right, and left edges of the I/O template with the matching case cutout. When the I/O template is positioned properly, press gently along the edges to seat it in the cutout, as shown in Figure 8-10. It should snap into place, although getting it to seat properly sometimes requires several attempts. It's often helpful to press gently against the edge of the template with the handle of a screwdriver or nutdriver.

Figure 8-10. Snap the custom I/O template into place

After you install the I/O template, carefully slide the motherboard into place, making sure that the back-panel connectors on the motherboard are firmly in contact with the corresponding holes on the I/O template. Compare the positions of the motherboard mounting holes with the standoff mounting positions in the case. One easy method is to place the motherboard in position and insert a felt-tip pen through each motherboard mounting hole to mark the corresponding standoff position beneath it.

The ASRock K8NF4G-SATA2 motherboard has six mounting holes. Many cases are shipped with several standoffs already installed. The Antec SLK1650B has only one standoff preinstalled, which happens to be in one of the positions required by the ASRock K8NF4G-SATA2 motherboard. That means we needed to install standoffs in the five remaining positions required by the motherboard.

Seeing the Light

If you simply look at the motherboard, it's easy to miss one of the mounting holes in all the clutter. We generally hold the motherboard up to a light, which makes the mounting holes stand out distinctly.

Install additional brass standoffs until each motherboard mounting hole has a corresponding standoff. Although you can screw in the standoffs using your fingers or needle-nose pliers, it's much easier and faster to use a 5mm nutdriver, as shown in Figure 8-11. Tighten the standoffs finger-tight, but do not overtighten them. It's easy to strip the threads by applying too much torque with a nutdriver.

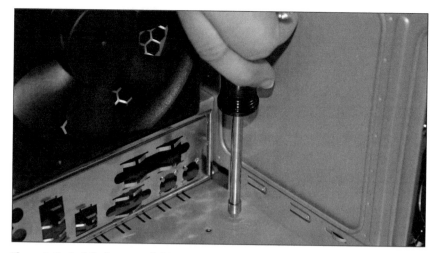

Figure 8-11. Install a brass standoff in each mounting position

Once you've installed all the standoffs, do a final check to verify that (a) each motherboard mounting hole has a corresponding standoff, and (b) that no standoffs are installed that don't correspond to a motherboard mounting hole. As a final check, we usually hold the motherboard in position above the case, as shown in Figure 8-12, and look down through each motherboard mounting hole to make sure there's a standoff installed below it.

Figure 8-12. Verify that a standoff is installed for each motherboard mounting hole and that no extra standoffs are installed

Avoid Grounding Problems

If your case comes with preinstalled brass standoffs, make absolutely certain that each standoff matches a motherboard mounting hole. If you find one that doesn't, remove it. Leaving an "extra" standoff in place may cause a short circuit that may damage the motherboard and/or other components, or at least cause a boot failure.

Also, if you use a case that uses stamped raised areas in the motherboard tray instead of standoffs, be aware that some motherboards, including this ASRock model, may fail to boot in such cases because the raised areas ground parts of the motherboard that were not intended to be grounded.

Pen and Paper

Another method we've used to verify that all standoffs are properly installed is to place the motherboard flat on a large piece of paper and use a felt-tip pen to mark all motherboard mounting holes on the paper. We then line one of the marks up with the corresponding standoff and press down until the standoff punctures the paper. We do the same with a second standoff to align the paper, and then press the paper flat around each standoff. If we've installed the standoffs properly, every mark will be punctured, and there will be no punctures where there are no marks.

Preparing and Populating the Motherboard

It is always easier to prepare and populate the motherboard—install the processor and memory—while the motherboard is outside the case. In fact, you must do so with some systems, because installing the heatsink/fan unit requires access to both sides of the motherboard. Even if it is possible to populate the motherboard while it is installed in the case, we always recommend doing so with the motherboard outside the case and lying flat on the work surface. More than once, we've tried to save a few minutes by replacing the processor without removing the motherboard. Too often, the result has been bent pins and a destroyed processor.

Preparing the motherboard

Ground Yourself

Each time you handle the processor, memory, or other static-sensitive components, first touch the power supply to ground yourself.

We decided to install an inexpensive third-party CPU cooler, because we wanted a cooler that was quieter and more efficient than the stock AMD cooler. We'd used the $13 Arctic Cooling Silencer 64 Ultra, shown in Figure 8-13, on several earlier systems, and were pleased with its noise level and cooling performance. We also considered using the Arctic Cooling Silencer 64 UltraTC, which has a temperature-controlled variable-speed fan, but at $20 it was a bit much for our budget. So, without thinking much about it, we ordered an Arctic Cooling Silencer 64 Ultra for this system.

That turned out to be a mistake, because fitting that CPU cooler to the motherboard required some minor surgery. Our first inclination was simply to order a different CPU cooler and let our readers remain ignorant of our mistake. But mistakes can be instructive, so we decided to go ahead and build the system with the Arctic Cooling Silencer 64 Ultra CPU cooler. It wasn't the first time we'd had to do minor surgery on a motherboard to fit a CPU cooler to it, and it won't be the last. But you can avoid all of the hassle simply by choosing a compatible CPU cooler, such as the Spire model we recommended earlier in this chapter.

The ASRock motherboard comes with a CPU cooler retaining bracket installed. Presumably, that bracket fits many standard CPU coolers, but it did not fit any of the AMD CPU coolers we had available, including one retail-boxed AMD cooler. The problem was the protruding vertical posts visible in Figure 8-14.

Figure 8-13. The Arctic Cooling Silencer 64 Ultra CPU cooler

Like many aftermarket CPU coolers, the Arctic Cooling Silencer 64 Ultra comes with its own retaining bracket. To install the Arctic Cooling bracket, you must first remove the bracket supplied with the ASRock motherboard. To do so, use a small flat-blade screwdriver to lift the four white posts, as shown in Figure 8-14. Lifting the posts releases the pressure on the plastic expansion clamps on the underside of the motherboard. After you lift all four posts, pull the retaining bracket straight up to remove it, as shown in Figure 8-15. If the bracket does not pull free easily, use the flat part of the screwdriver blade to press gently on the expansion clamps on the bottom side of the motherboard until they release.

Figure 8-14. Lift the white plastic posts to release the standard bracket

Figure 8-15. Lift the retaining bracket straight up to remove it

With the standard retaining bracket removed, the four retaining bracket mounting holes are visible, as shown in Figure 8-16, at the four corners of the processor socket.

The Arctic Cooling CPU cooler comes with a two-part custom retaining bracket made of heavy plastic. One part is installed on the top of the motherboard, where the heatsink can be clamped to it. The second part is installed beneath the motherboard, to distribute the weight of the heatsink over the processor socket area of the motherboard, rather than putting all

Figure 8-16. With the standard bracket removed, the four mounting holes are visible

of that weight on a couple of screw holes. To begin installing the bracket, remove the two screws that secure the two parts, as shown in Figure 8-17.

Align the four posts on the bottom of the top portion of the retaining bracket with the corresponding holes in the motherboard, and drop the retaining bracket into place. Align the bottom portion of the retaining bracket under the motherboard, with the screw holes lining up with the corresponding holes in the motherboard. Partially drive one screw, as shown in Figure 8-18, to secure the two parts of the retaining bracket together loosely.

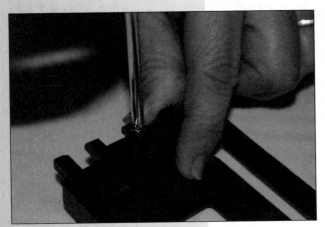

Figure 8-17. Disassemble the retaining bracket

Figure 8-18. Partially drive one screw to loosely connect the two parts of the retaining bracket

Tilt the motherboard upward, as shown in Figure 8-19, and align the second screw hole in the bottom part of the retaining bracket. Drive the second screw in to align the two parts of the bracket completely, and then finish driving both screws to clamp the bracket tightly into position. Drive both screws in completely, but do not overtighten them. Finger-tight is sufficient.

Figure 8-19. Align the bottom portion of the bracket and drive a second screw to secure it

Installing the processor

To install the AMD Sempron processor, lift the arm of the ZIF (zero insertion force) socket, as shown in Figure 8-20, until it reaches vertical. With the arm vertical, there is no clamping force on the socket holes, which allows the processor to drop into place without requiring any pressure.

Pin 1 is indicated on the processor and socket by a small triangle. With the socket lever vertical, align pin 1 of the processor with pin 1 of the socket and drop the processor into place, as shown in Figure 8-21. The processor should seat flush with the socket just from the force of gravity, or at most with the slightest fingertip pressure. If the processor doesn't seat easily, something is misaligned. Remove the processor and verify that it is aligned properly and that the pattern of pins on the processor corresponds to the pattern of holes on the socket. **Never** apply any significant pressure to the processor. You'll bend one or more pins, destroying the processor.

With the processor in place and seated flush with the socket, press the lever arm down and snap it into place, as shown in Figure 8-22. You may have to press the lever arm slightly away from the socket to allow it to snap into a locked position. Closing the ZIF lever may cause the processor to lift slightly out of its socket. Once you are sure the processor is fully seated, it's safe to maintain gentle finger pressure on the processor if necessary to keep it fully seated as you close the ZIF lever.

Installing the CPU cooler

Modern processors draw as much as 130W of power and must dissipate that power as heat over the surface of their heat spreaders, which are about the size of a large postage stamp. Without a good CPU cooler, also called a heatsink/fan (HSF) unit, the processor would immediately shut itself down to prevent damage from overheating. Our Sempron 3100+ has a design thermal power of only 62W, but even that relatively low wattage produces considerable waste heat.

Like all microATX motherboards, the ASRock K8NF4G-SATA2 crams in many components with very little clearance. The small size of microATX motherboards means they have to make a lot of compromises in where to position components, and it's often problematic to mount the CPU cooler, particularly if it's a third-party model.

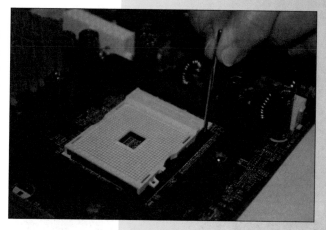

Figure 8-20. Lift the socket lever to prepare the socket to receive the processor

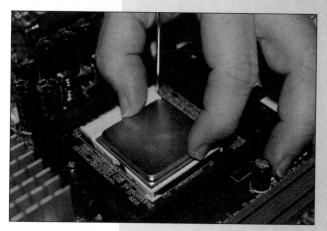

Figure 8-21. Dropping the processor into place

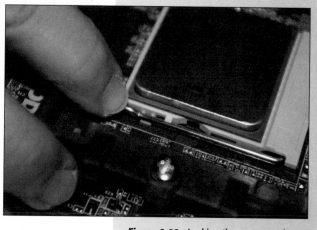

Figure 8-22. Locking the processor into the socket

Make Sure Your CPU Cooler Is Good Enough

Using a proper CPU cooler is critical. Retail-boxed AMD and Intel processors include a CPU cooler that is adequate for the task. If you buy an OEM processor, it's up to you to install a CPU cooler that is sufficient to keep the processor operating within the design temperature range. Just because a CPU cooler fits the doesn't guarantee it's adequate to cool the processor properly. Faster processors consume more power and generate more heat. A CPU cooler designed and rated for a slower processor may be woefully inadequate for a faster version of that processor.

An Easier Way

The Spire SP792B12-U CPU cooler we recommend doesn't use cammed clamping levers. Instead, it uses a one-piece slotted metal bracket that fits over the three protruding nubs on the plastic base. You secure the cooler by pulling up on the metal bracket and pressing it toward the heatsink, where a protruding metal tab engages one of the slots in the bracket. If you use the Spire cooler or a similar model, you can avoid performing surgery on your motherboard.

In this case, the problem was severe, as shown in Figure 8-23. The clamping bracket on the CPU cooler intruded into the space used by the northbridge heatsink, visible at the lower right of the image as a finned aluminum assembly. Some CPU coolers use a cammed clamping lever on only one side of the cooler, with a simple metal bracket on the other side. The Arctic Cooling CPU cooler uses two clamping levers, one on either side of the cooler, so we couldn't simply reverse the cooler to avoid the problem.

Figure 8-23. The CPU cooler cannot be seated fully because the northbridge heatsink interferes

Donning our kamikaze headband, we began by removing the northbridge heatsink. To do that, we used our needle-nose pliers to release the two expanding clamping posts that secure the northbridge heatsink to the motherboard, as shown in Figure 8-24.

Figure 8-24. Release the northbridge heatsink clamping posts

As you squeeze the posts gently, press them toward the motherboard until they pop free. At that point, the northbridge heatsink is still loosely connected to the northbridge chip by thermal compound. Pull up gently on the heatsink until it comes free. The northbridge chip is exposed, as shown in Figure 8-25, and there is now enough clearance to install the CPU cooler.

Figure 8-25. The exposed northbridge chip

We're now ready to install the CPU cooler. To begin, use a paper towel or soft cloth to polish the CPU heat spreader, as shown in Figure 8-26. The goal is to remove any grease, grit, or other material that might prevent the heatsink from making intimate contact with the processor surface.

Figure 8-26. Polish the CPU heat spreader to remove any foreign material

Voiding Your Warranty

Obviously, removing the northbridge heatsink voids the warranty on the motherboard. We decided to take that chance, because we had the Arctic Cooling CPU cooler in hand and didn't want to wait for a replacement.

If you decide to modify your motherboard and end up breaking it, don't blame us. After any such modification, there's always a chance the motherboard will no longer work. If that happens, you're out of luck.

Don't Recycle Thermal Compound

If you ever remove the heatsink, you must replace the thermal compound or pad when you reinstall it. Before you reinstall, remove all remnants of the old thermal pad or compound. That can be difficult, particularly for a thermal pad, which can be very tenacious. We use an ordinary hair dryer to warm the thermal material enough to make it easy to remove. Sometimes the best way is to warm up the compound and rub it off with your thumb.

Alternatively, one of our technical reviewers says that rubbing gently with #0000 steel wool works wonders in removing the gunk, and is fine enough not to damage the surface. Another of our technical reviewers tells us that he uses Goof-Off or isopropyl alcohol to remove the remnants of the thermal goop or thermal pad. Whatever works for you is fine. Just make sure to remove the old thermal compound and replace it with new compound each time you remove and reinstall the processor.

When we replace a heatsink, we use Antec Silver Thermal Compound, which is widely available, inexpensive, and works well. Don't pay extra for "premium" brand names like Arctic Silver. They cost more than the Antec product and our testing shows little or no difference in cooling efficiency.

After you polish the CPU, check the surface of the heatsink. If the heatsink base is bare, as is true of the Arctic Cooler model we used, that means it's intended to be used with thermal compound, sometimes called "thermal goop." In that case, also polish the heatsink base, as shown in Figure 8-27. Some heatsinks have a square or rectangular pad made of a phase-change medium, which is a fancy term for a material that melts as the CPU heats and resolidifies as the CPU cools. This liquid/solid cycle ensures that the processor die maintains good thermal contact with the heatsink. If your heatsink includes such a pad you needn't polish the base of the heatsink. (Heatsinks use *either* a thermal pad *or* thermal goop, not both.)

Figure 8-27. Polish the base of the CPU cooler heatsink

At this point during our actual build, we made a mistake. We used the syringe of thermal compound supplied with the Arctic Cooling CPU cooler (visible in Figure 8-13). That thermal compound turned out to be the most obnoxious we'd ever used. It was dry, excessively tacky, and refused to spread evenly. After making a mess with it, we ended up cleaning it all off, repolishing the CPU heat spreader and heatsink, and doing what we should have done originally. We went to our workbench, retrieved our tube of Antec Silver Thermal Compound (shown in Figure 8-28), and applied a small amount to the heat spreader.

Use your finger to spread the thermal compound evenly over the surface of the heat spreader, as shown in Figure 8-29. (We've always found thermal compound to be harmless, but if you're nervous about it, you can use a talc-free rubber glove or plastic wrap between your finger and the compound.) The goal is to use just enough thermal compound to provide a thin, even layer over the entire surface of the heat spreader. Remove any excess compound before you proceed to the next step.

Figure 8-28. Applying Antec Silver Thermal Compound

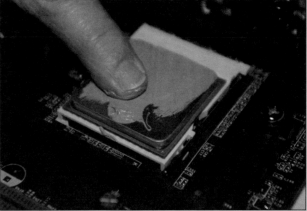

Figure 8-29. Spread the thermal compound evenly over the surface of the heat spreader

Orient the CPU cooler above the processor, as shown in Figure 8-30, keeping it as close to horizontal as possible. Slide the CPU cooler down into the retaining bracket. Press down gently and use a small circular motion to spread the thermal goop evenly over the surface of the processor.

Advice from Ron Morse

There is more goop on that CPU than I've used in my entire lifetime! I use an amount about equal to a half-grain of rice.

I'd consider using Zalman ZM-STG1 thermal compound (*http://www.zalmanusa.com*). It applies like contact cement or nail polish, with the small included brush. Just paint the goop on both the CPU and heatsink mating surfaces and assemble. I haven't tested it yet, so I don't have the slightest idea if it is any good as a thermal compound—but Zalman stuff is usually pretty good, and the concept sure looks promising!

Figure 8-30. Insert the CPU cooler into the retaining bracket

With the CPU cooler resting loosely in place, the next step is to clamp it tightly against the processor to ensure good thermal transfer between the CPU and heatsink. To do so, hold the metal retaining bracket in place, as shown in Figure 8-31, while you press down the cammed locking lever with the other hand until the clamp locks into place. Make sure that all three of the plastic protrusions have engaged the holes in the bracket. Repeat this step for the second locking lever. With both levers locked, the CPU cooler is secured firmly and clamped into tight contact with the processor.

Figure 8-31. Clamp the CPU cooler into firm contact with the processor

The next step is to reinstall the northbridge heatsink. We had hoped to be able to do that without modifying the heatsink, but that turned out to be impossible. In order to clear the locking lever on the CPU cooler, we had to bend some of the northbridge heatsink fins, as shown in Figure 8-32. Fortunately, the fins are made of soft aluminum, which is quite easy to bend with your needle-nose pliers.

Figure 8-32. Modify the northbridge heatsink to fit by bending one set of fins

Before you reinstall the northbridge heatsink, you must remove the old thermal pad from the heatsink base and from the northbridge chip itself. Do that by rubbing gently with your thumb to remove the bulk of the thermal pad, and then polishing gently with a paper towel. If the thermal pad material is difficult to remove, use your fingernail to peel it off the surface of the heatsink and northbridge chip. Apply a thin layer of thermal compound to the northbridge chip and spread it evenly. Place the northbridge heatsink in position, as shown in Figure 8-33, rotate it slightly to spread the thermal compound evenly, and then press the two locking posts back into place to secure the heatsink.

Figure 8-33. Replace the northbridge heatsink

Figure 8-34 shows the northbridge heatsink reinstalled, with the bent fins clearing the CPU cooler clamping lever. The northbridge heatsink has six rows of fins, so we'd have reduced its cooling efficiency by about 16% if we'd removed one row of fins entirely rather than simply bending them. As modified, we estimate the northbridge cooling efficiency has been reduced by no more than 5%, if that. The fins are still well exposed to the air flow from the rear chassis fan. (When the system is running, the northbridge heatsink fins become noticeably warm to the touch, indicating that they are doing their job well.)

The thermal mass of the CPU cooler heatsink draws heat away from the CPU, but the heat must be dissipated to prevent the CPU from eventually overheating as the heatsink warms up. To dispose of excess heat as it is transferred to the heatsink, most CPU coolers use a fan to continuously draw or push air through the fins of the heatsink. Some CPU fans use a drive power connector, but most are designed to attach to dedicated CPU fan connector on the motherboard. Using a motherboard fan power connector allows the motherboard to control the CPU fan, reducing speed for quieter operation when the processor is running under light load and not generating much heat, and increasing fan speed when the processor is running under heavy load and generating more heat. The motherboard can also monitor fan speed, which allows it to send an alert to the user if the fan fails or begins running sporadically.

Figure 8-34. The modified northbridge heatsink

Figure 8-35. Connect the CPU fan cable to the CPU fan connector

To connect the CPU fan, locate the 3-pin header connector on the motherboard labeled CPU Fan, and plug the keyed cable from the CPU fan into that connector, as shown in Figure 8-35.

Figure 8-36. Pivot the locking tabs on both sides of both DIMM sockets outward

Figure 8-37. Orient the DIMM with the notch aligned properly with the socket

Installing memory

Installing memory takes only a few seconds. The ASRock motherboard provides two memory slots, but we're installing only one Crucial 512 MB DIMM, leaving the second slot free for later memory expansion.

To begin installing the memory, pivot the locking tabs on both sides of both DIMM sockets outward, as shown in Figure 8-36. (We're installing memory in only one socket, but having both sets of locking tabs open makes it easier to ensure that the one DIMM we're installing is properly seated.)

We'll install our DIMM in the first memory slot, which is the one nearer the processor. To install the DIMM, orient it with the notch in the contact area of the DIMM aligned with the raised plastic tab in the slot and slide the DIMM into place, as shown in Figure 8-37, making sure that both ends of the DIMM slide straight into the slots on the locking tab brackets.

With the DIMM properly aligned with the slot and oriented vertically relative to the slot, use both thumbs to press down on the DIMM until it snaps into place, as shown in Figure 8-38. The locking tabs should automatically pivot back up into the locked position when the DIMM snaps into place. If they don't, make absolutely certain that the DIMM is well seated and then close the locking tabs manually to lock the DIMM into the socket.

When the DIMM is fully seated, the locking tabs should mate fully with the notches on the DIMM, as shown in Figure 8-39.

Figure 8-38. Seat the DIMM by pressing firmly until it snaps into place

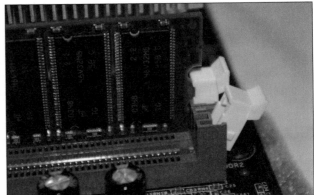

Figure 8-39. Make sure that the locking tabs on the bracket fully engage the cutouts on the DIMM

With the processor and memory installed, you're almost ready to install the motherboard in the case. Before you do that, check the motherboard documentation to determine if any configuration jumpers need to be set. The ASRock motherboard requires no additional configuration, so we proceeded to the next step.

Installing the Motherboard

Installing the motherboard is the most time-consuming step in building the system because there are so many cables to connect. It's important to get all of them connected right, so take your time and verify each connection before and after you make it.

Seating and securing the motherboard

To begin, slide the motherboard into the case, as shown in Figure 8-40. Carefully align the back-panel I/O connectors with the corresponding holes in the I/O template, and slide

Figure 8-40. Slide the motherboard into position

the motherboard toward the rear of the case until the motherboard mounting holes line up with the standoffs you installed earlier.

Before you secure the motherboard, verify that the back-panel I/O connectors mate properly with the I/O template, as shown in Figure 8-41. The I/O template has metal tabs that ground the back-panel I/O connectors. Make sure none of these tabs intrude into a port connector. An errant tab at best blocks the port, rendering it unusable, and at worst may short out the motherboard.

Final Check

Check one last time to make sure that there's a brass standoff installed for each mounting hole, and that no brass standoff is installed where there is no mounting hole. One of our technical reviewers suggests installing white nylon standoffs, trimmed to length, in all unused standoff positions covered by the motherboard, particularly those near the expansion slots. Doing so provides more support to the motherboard, making it less likely that you'll crack the motherboard when you are seating a recalcitrant expansion card.

Figure 8-41. Verify that the back-panel connectors mate cleanly with the I/O template

After you position the motherboard and verify that the back-panel I/O connectors mate cleanly with the I/O template, insert a screw through one mounting hole into the corresponding standoff, as shown in Figure 8-42. You may need to apply pressure to keep the motherboard positioned properly until you have inserted two or three screws.

Figure 8-42. Install screws in all mounting holes to secure the motherboard

If you have trouble getting all the holes and standoffs aligned, insert two screws in opposite corners but don't tighten them completely. Use one hand to press the motherboard into alignment, with all holes matching the standoffs. Then insert one or two more screws and tighten them completely. Finish mounting the motherboard by inserting screws into all standoffs and tightening them.

With first-rate products like the Antec SLK1650B case and the ASRock K8NF4G-SATA2 motherboard, all the holes usually line up perfectly. With cheap products, that's often not true. At times, we've been forced to use only a few screws to secure the motherboard. We prefer to use all of them, both to physically support the motherboard and to make sure all of the grounding points are in fact grounded, but if you can't get all of the holes lined up, simply install as many screws as you can.

Connecting front-panel switch and indicator cables

Once the motherboard is secured, the next step is to connect the front panel switch and indicator cables to the motherboard. Before you begin connecting front panel cables, examine the cables. Each is labeled descriptively, e.g., "POWER SW" and "H.D.D. LED." Match those descriptions with the front panel connector pins on the motherboard to make sure you connect the correct cable to the appropriate pins. Once you determine the proper orientation for each cable, connect it as shown in Figure 8-43.

Less Power

People sometimes ask us why we don't use power screwdrivers. Because they're large, clumsy, and the batteries are always dead when we want to use the driver. Worse still, we once watched someone crack a motherboard by overtorquing the mounting screws with a power screwdriver. A clutched driver eliminates that objection, but we still find power screwdrivers too clumsy to use, even when we've built many identical systems on an ad hoc production line.

Figure 8-43. Connect the front-panel switch and indicator cables

Keep these guidelines in mind as you connect the front-panel cables:

- Although Intel has defined a standard front-panel connector block and uses that standard for its own motherboards, few other motherboard makers adhere to that standard. Accordingly, rather than provide an Intel-standard monolithic connector block that would be useless for motherboards that do not follow the Intel standard, most case makers, including Antec, provide individual one-, two-, or three-pin connectors for each switch and indicator.

- Not all cases have cables for every connector on the motherboard, and not all motherboards have connectors for all cables provided by the case. For example, the ASRock K8NF4G-SATA2 motherboard provides connectors for front-panel audio and an infrared module, neither of which is provided by the Antec SLK1650B case. Conversely, the Antec SLK1650B case provides cables for secondary and tertiary hard drive activity LEDs, neither of which is supported by the ASRock K8NF4G-SATA2 motherboard.

- The power switch and reset switch connectors are not polarized, and can be connected in either orientation.

- LED connectors are usually polarized, and should be connected with the ground wire and the signal wire oriented correctly. Most cases use a common wire color—usually black, although sometimes white or green—for ground, and a colored wire for signal.

- The Power LED connector is often problematic, as it is for this system. There are two types of Power LED connector. The first has two pins. The second has three pins, but only two wires, with the middle pin unused. A motherboard may provide either or both types of Power LED connector, and a case may provide either or both types of Power LED cable. The ASRock K8NF4G-SATA2 motherboard provides only a two-pin Power LED connector, although solder patches for a three-pin Power LED connector are visible in Figure 8-43 just to the right of the upper red SATA connector. The Antec SLK1650B case provides only a three-pin Power LED cable. That leaves us with two options. We took the easy way by simply leaving the Power LED disconnected. If you want your Power LED to function, use a sharp knife or diagonal cutters carefully to cut the Power LED cable connector lengthwise, dividing it into two single-wire connectors. Connect each of those separately to the two Power LED pins on the motherboard.

- The Power LED connectors on some motherboards are dual-polarized, and can support a single-color (usually green) Power LED or a dual-color (usually green/yellow) LED. The Antec SLK1650B case and the ASRock K8NF4G-SATA2 motherboard both support only a single-color Power LED. If you are using a different case and motherboard that support a dual-color Power LED, check the case and motherboard documentation to determine where and how to connect the Power LED cable.

Advice from Brian Bilbrey

I prefer to use a knife tip to gently release (not break off) the plastic tab holding one of the end pins in the cable connector body in place, slide that pin out, and move it to the center location. Then I can install the connector onto the header with the empty location hanging out in space.

When you're connecting front-panel cables, try to get it right the first time, but don't worry too much about getting it wrong. Other than the power switch cable, which must be connected properly for the system to start, none of the other front-panel switch and indicator cables is essential, and connecting them wrong won't damage the system.

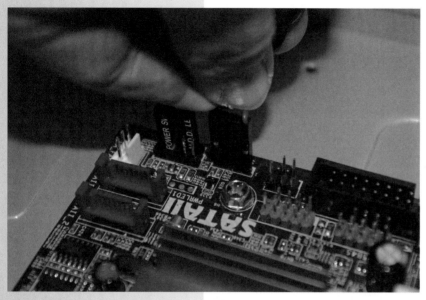

Figure 8-44. Connect the speaker cable

Figure 8-45. Connect the front-panel USB cable to a USB header pin set on the motherboard

Connecting front-panel switch and indicator cables

After you connect the front-panel switch and indicator cables to the motherboard, connect the speaker cable, as shown in Figure 8-44. Connect the cable with the signal wire (in this case, red) on pin 1 and the ground wire (black) opposite. If you use a motherboard that has a built-in speaker, there may be no speaker header pins on the motherboard. If so, just leave this cable disconnected. If the motherboard has both a built-in speaker and speaker header pins, we generally connect this cable because the case speaker usually provides better volume than a surface-mounted motherboard speaker.

Connecting front-panel USB ports

The ASRock K8NF4G-SATA2 motherboard provides four internal USB 2.0 connectors, in two sets of two header pin groups. The Antec SLK1650B case provides two front-panel USB 2.0 ports, which terminate in a single 10-pin USB connector cable. Connect this cable to one of the motherboard USB header pin sets, as shown in Figure 8-45.

Installing the Hard Drive

The Antec SLK1650B has three external 5.25" drive bays, two external 3.5" drive bays, and three internal 3.5" drive bays. The external bays are for devices like optical drives and floppy disk drives that use removable media, and can also be used for internal hard drives. The three internal 3.5" bays can each hold one hard drive. To begin installing the hard drive, remove the three screws that secure the internal drive bay, as shown in Figure 8-46.

After you remove the three screws, lift the drive bay free of the chassis, as shown in Figure 8-47.

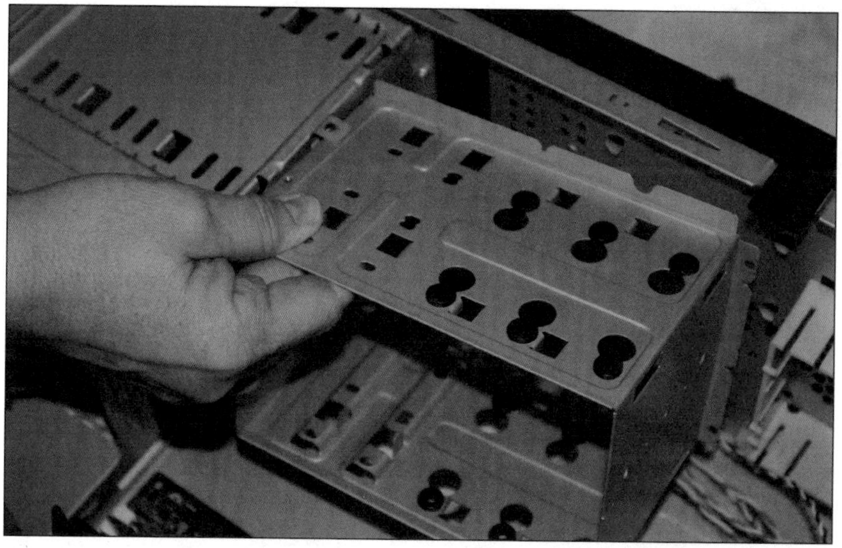

Figure 8-46. Remove the screws that secure the internal drive bay

Figure 8-47. Lift the internal drive bay free of the chassis

Advice from Brian Bilbrey (and Ron Morse)

If you have the option, choose the best position to install the hard drive. All other factors being equal, I prefer to make sure that the drive doesn't protrude out over the memory (first), and cable connection points (second). With only one drive being installed, and three install positions, one is bound to be a better choice than the others for any given case/motherboard combination.

Before you install the hard drive in the drive bay, verify that the drive is configured properly. We are using a Serial ATA hard drive in this system. Serial ATA drives do not require configuration because each S-ATA drive connects to a dedicated interface. If we had used a parallel ATA (P-ATA) hard drive, we'd have checked the jumpers on the drive to verify it was set as Master.

The Antec drive bay uses rubber shock-mounting pads to isolate the drive, which reduces the amount of vibration and noise transferred from the hard drive to the chassis. Several of these pads are visible in Figure 8-48, including one under the screw being driven. Secure the drive to the bay by installing four of the provided screws with oversize heads. Drive the screws finger-tight, but do not overtorque them.

Figure 8-48. Secure the hard drive to the bay using four of the provided large-head screws

With the hard drive secured in the bay, the next step is to reinstall the bay in the chassis, as shown in Figure 8-49. To do so, align the notches in the drive bay with the chassis tabs and slide the drive bay into the chassis.

With the drive bay fully seated, reinstall the three screws you removed earlier to secure the drive bay in the chassis, as shown in Figure 8-50.

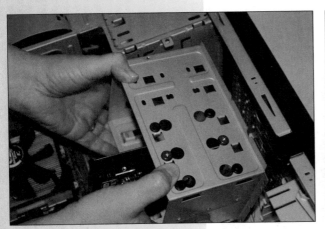

Figure 8-49. Slide the drive bay into the chassis, aligning the slots in the bay with the tabs on the chassis

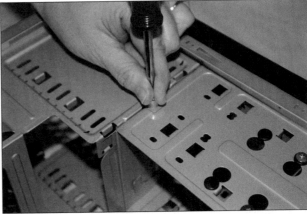

Figure 8-50. Reinstall the three screws you removed earlier to secure the drive bay to the chassis

With the drive bay reinstalled, the next step is to connect power to the hard drive. To do so, examine the various cables coming out of the power supply to locate a Serial ATA power cable. The Serial ATA power connector is keyed similarly to the Serial ATA data cable, using a slot and tab arrangement. Align the keying slot on the cable with the keying tab on the drive and slide the power cable into place, as shown in Figure 8-51.

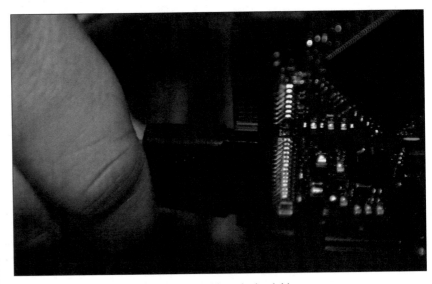

Figure 8-51. Connect the Serial ATA power cable to the hard drive

The next step is to connect the Serial ATA data cable to the drive. It doesn't matter which end of the Serial ATA cable you connect to the drive. The two ends are interchangeable. The Serial ATA data cable is keyed with a notch at one end that slides over a corresponding tab on the drive connector. Align the cable connector to the drive connector and press firmly until the cable connector slides into place, as shown in Figure 8-52.

Figure 8-52. Connect the Serial ATA data cable to the hard drive

The final step is to connect the Serial ATA data cable to the motherboard Serial ATA interface. The motherboard provides two Serial ATA interfaces, labeled SATA1 and SATA2. Although the drive functions properly connected to either interface, best practice is to connect the primary hard drive to the first interface, which is SATA1. The motherboard SATA connector is keyed in the same fashion as the hard drive SATA connector. Orient the Serial ATA data cable so that its keying slot corresponds to the keying tab on the motherboard connector, and press the cable into place, as shown in Figure 8-53.

Figure 8-53. Connect the Serial ATA data cable to the motherboard interface

What, No Floppy Drive?

We decided against installing a floppy disk drive (FDD) in this system, although we may come to regret it. We didn't skip the FDD to save money—they only cost $8 or so—but to avoid having one more dust collector and one more ribbon cable to block air flow.

Some years ago, Intel and Microsoft started telling everyone that the humble FDD was a "legacy" device. We doubted the wisdom of that statement at the time, and over the years we've frequently had cause to regret not installing an FDD. More than once, we've had to open up a system and install an FDD to load a driver that wouldn't load from CD or to update the BIOS.

But things have changed, and we now consider the FDD passé for new systems. Even if you don't have a network, it's easy to move files around on writable CDs, DVDs, or a USB 2.0 flash memory stick. ASRock provides a Windows-based BIOS updater utility, which eliminates the main reason for installing an FDD. And, although installing Windows XP Gold (the original release) on some early S-ATA motherboards requires a driver floppy, the ASRock motherboard supports pre-SP1 Windows XP directly.

So, although we won't install an FDD in our budget PC, we won't give you a hard time if you decide to install one in yours.

Installing the Optical Drive

Before you install the optical drive, verify the jumper settings. The NEC ND-3550A DVD writer ships with a jumper installed in the rightmost position, as shown in Figure 8-54. This default jumper setting configures the drive as master. We plan to use the optical drive as the master on the primary ATA channel, so the default jumper setting is correct.

Advice from Jim Cooley

If you are unsure, check the master/slave jumper setting against the legend usually imprinted in the metal on the top of the optical drive.

Figure 8-54. Verify that the optical drive jumper is set to master

Figure 8-55. Connect the ATA data cable to the optical drive, making sure pin 1 is oriented correctly

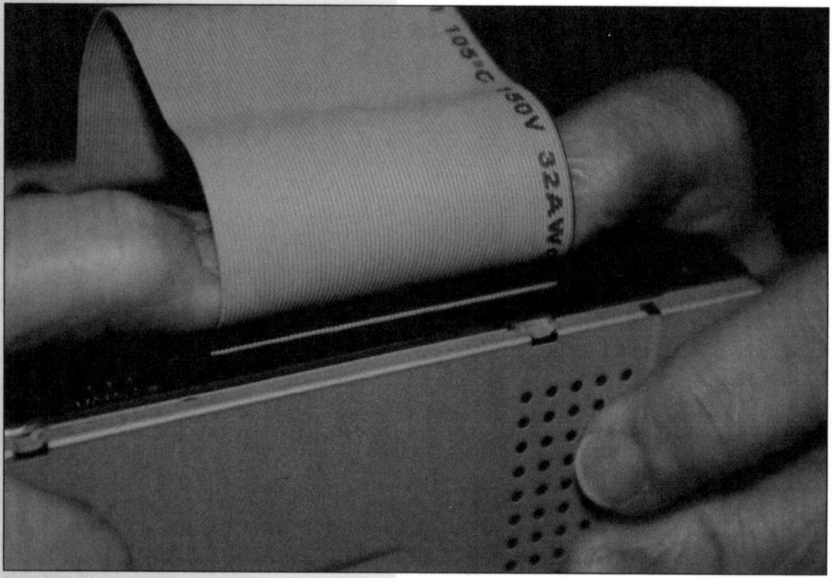

It's usually easier to connect the ATA cable to the drive before you install the drive in the case. The ASRock K8NF4G-SATA2 motherboard comes with an 80-wire Ultra ATA cable, which we used. Because optical drives have relatively slow transfer rates, they can use the older 40-wire ATA cable rather than the 80-wire Ultra-ATA cable used for ATA hard drives. (An 80-wire cable works fine if that's all you have, but it's not necessary.)

To connect the cable, locate pin 1 on the drive connector, which is usually nearest the power connector. The pin 1 side of the cable is indicated by a red stripe. Align the cable connector with the drive connector, making sure the red stripe is on the pin 1 side of the drive connector, and press the cable into place, as shown in Figure 8-55.

The Antec SLK1650B case provides three external 5.25" bays, each of which is covered by a snap-in plastic bezel. Before installing the drive you have to remove the bezel for the selected drive bay. The easiest way to do that on the Antec case is to press the bezel from behind, as shown in Figure 8-56, until it pops out. The two lower external 5.25" bays have metal RF shields installed, but the upper bay lacks that shield. For simplicity, we decided to leave the metal shields in place in the lower bays and install the NEC ND-3550A DVD writer in the upper bay.

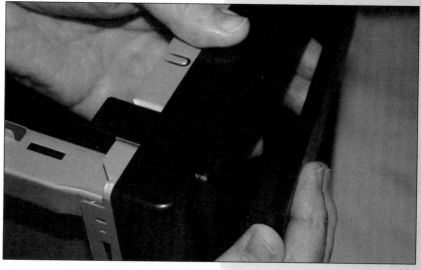

Figure 8-56. Pop the plastic bezel and remove it

Unlike some cases, the Antec SLK1650B self-aligns the optical drive both vertically and horizontally. To mount the drive in the case, feed the loose end of the ATA cable through the drive bay from the front, and feed the cable down into the case. Align the drive with the mounting rails inside the bay, and slide the drive into the case, as shown in Figure 8-57. Seat the front of the drive bezel flush with the case bezel, and install four screws—left and right, front and back—to secure the drive.

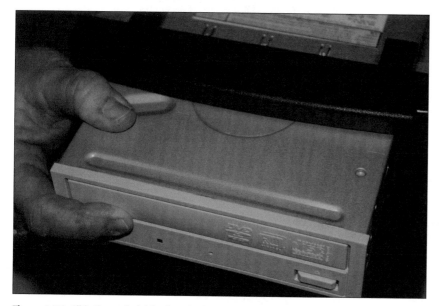

Figure 8-57. Slide the optical drive into the bay and set it flush

We want to connect the NEC ND-3550A optical drive as the master device on the primary ATA channel. In the past, we left the primary ATA channel unused in systems with S-ATA hard drives, because Windows sometimes

Ebony or Ivory?

Why use a beige drive in a black case? We admit that it looks strange, but we did it intentionally. For years, we installed beige drives in beige cases, black drives in black cases, and silver drives in silver cases. Then one day, Robert, who keeps his office quite dark, was fumbling around the front of one of his mini-tower units, trying to find the eject button on the optical drive. Robert had an AHA! moment, and began installing beige or white drives in his black mini-tower systems, which makes the drives much easier to locate in the dark. Barbara points out that she calls Robert's office the Black Hole of Calcutta for more than one reason, and that if he'd use something brighter than his single 15W desk lamp he wouldn't have these problems.

Figure 8-58. Connect the optical drive ATA cable to the primary ATA interface

Neatness Counts

After you connect the ATA cable, don't just leave it flopping around loose. That not only looks amateurish, but can impede air flow and cause overheating. Tuck the cable neatly out of the way, using tape, cable ties, or tie-wraps to secure it to the case. If necessary, temporarily disconnect the cable to route it around other cables and obstructions, and reconnect it once you have it positioned properly.

became confused if the master device on the primary ATA channel was an optical drive. With recent motherboards, that problem is much less likely, so we now connect the optical drive to the primary ATA channel.

The blue primary ATA interface and the black secondary ATA interface are located near the right-front edge of the motherboard near the DIMM slots. Locate pin 1 on the primary ATA interface, align the ATA cable with its red stripe toward pin 1 on the interface, and press the connector into place, as shown in Figure 8-58.

The final step in installing the optical drive—one we forget more often than we should—is to connect power to the drive. Choose one of the power cables coming from the power supply and press the Molex connector onto the drive power connector, as shown in Figure 8-59. It may require significant pressure to get the power connector to seat, so use care to avoid hurting your fingers if the connector seats suddenly. The Molex power connector is keyed, so verify that it is oriented properly before you apply pressure to seat the power cable.

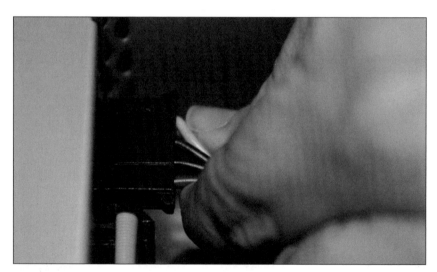

Figure 8-59. Connect the power cable to the optical drive

Connecting the ATX Power Connectors

The next step in assembling the system is to connect the two ATX power connectors from the power supply to the motherboard. The main ATX power connector supplies most of the power required by the motherboard. The ATX12V power connector provides supplemental (but required) power.

WHAT ABOUT THE AUDIO CABLE?

Speaking of forgetting to connect cables, for the last edition of this book one of our technical reviewers pointed out that we'd forgotten to connect the audio cable to the optical drive in all of the project systems. We hadn't forgotten. We just don't do it any more.

Years ago, connecting an audio cable from the optical drive to the motherboard audio connector or sound card was an essential step, because systems used the analog audio delivered from the optical drive by that cable. If you didn't connect that cable, you didn't get audio from the drive. All recent optical drives and motherboards support digital audio, which is delivered across the bus rather than via a dedicated audio cable. Few optical drives or motherboards include an analog audio cable nowadays, because one is seldom needed.

To verify the setting for digital audio, which is ordinarily enabled by default, use Windows XP Device Manager to display the Device Properties sheet for the optical drive. The Enable digital CD audio… checkbox should be marked. If it is not, mark the checkbox to enable digital audio. If the checkbox is grayed out, does not appear, or if the checkbox refuses to stay checked after a reboot, that means your optical drive and/or your motherboard do not support digital audio. In that case, you'll need to use an MPC analog audio to connect the drive to the CD-ROM audio connector on the motherboard or your sound card. Also, some older audio applications do not support digital audio, and so require that an analog audio cable be installed even if the system supports digital audio.

The NEC ND-3550A DVD writer, like many modern optical drives, provides two audio connectors. In addition to the 4-pin MPC analog audio connector, the ND-3550A includes a 2-pin digital audio connector that you can connect to a Sony Philips Digital Interface (SP/DIF) audio connector or a digital-in audio connector on your motherboard or sound card.

We suggest you install an audio cable only if needed. Otherwise, you can do without.

Broadly speaking, there are two types of main ATX power connector. Until recently, most ATX motherboards used the original 20-pin main ATX power connector. The higher current requirements of modern processors led Intel to revise the ATX standard to use a 24-pin main ATX power connector, with the extra four pins carrying additional current at standard voltages.

The 24-pin connector is a superset of the older 20-pin connector. The first 20 pins on a 24-pin connector use the same voltages and have the same keying as the 20 pins of the original connector. The extra four pins were simply added onto the end of the old connector. This similarity in layout confers a surprising degree of compatibility between 20-pin power supplies and 24-pin motherboards and vice versa.

Current (ATX12V 2.01 and higher) power supplies use the 24-pin connector, as do many (but not all) current motherboards. Most 24-pin motherboards can use a 20-pin power supply if you supplement that power by plugging a standard Molex (hard drive) power connector into a socket on the motherboard. Conversely, most 24-pin power supplies can be used with a 20-pin motherboard by using one of the following workarounds:

- Some 24-pin power supplies include a 24-to-20-pin adapter cable. Such adapter cables are also available from many online vendors.

- Some power supplies, including the Antec SmartPower 2.0 unit supplied with the SLK1650B case, provide a connector that can be configured as 24-pin or 20-pin by adding or removing a supplemental 4-pin section to the main 20-pin connector.

- Some 20-pin motherboards, including the ASRock K8NF4G-SATA2, have sufficient room around the 20-pin connector to allow a 24-pin cable to be connected, with the extra four pins simply left hanging off the end. This is the option we chose, even though the Antec power supply provides a detachable 4-pin section. Leaving the extra 4-pin section in place harms nothing, and avoids having yet another loose wire floating around inside the case. Those extra four pins are visible in Figure 8-60 between the white ATX power socket and the CPU cooler.

The main ATX power connector is located between the northbridge heatsink and the rear I/O panel. The main ATX power connector is keyed, so verify that it is aligned properly before you attempt to seat it.

Once everything is aligned, press down firmly until the connector seats. Figure 8-60 shows the connector in the process of being inserted, just before the black plastic latch on the cable connector snaps into place on the white socket body. It may take significant pressure to seat the connector. Make sure the plug mates completely with the socket, and that the latch snaps into place. A partially seated main ATX power connector may cause subtle problems that are very difficult to troubleshoot.

Figure 8-60. Connect the Main ATX Power Connector

Early Pentium 4 systems required more power to the motherboard than the standard 20-pin ATX main power connector supplied. As a stopgap measure, before they extended the ATX specification to use a 24-pin connector, Intel developed a supplementary connector, called the ATX12V connector. This 4-pin connector routes additional +12V current directly to the VRM (voltage regulator module) that powers the processor.

Nowadays, most motherboards—including 24-pin models for both Intel and AMD processors—require the additional current provided by the ATX12V connector. If you forget to connect the ATX12V cable, the system simply won't boot.

On most motherboards, including the ASRock K8NF4G-SATA2, the ATX12V connector is located near the processor socket. Unfortunately, the ASRock motherboard places this connector in a very inaccessible location, at the rear edge of the motherboard near the power supply, leaving almost no room to work. We had a difficult time connecting the ATX12V cable, let alone shooting an image of it. Barbara was finally able to get the connector oriented properly and seat it with one finger, as shown in Figure 8-61. When you seat this connector, make sure the locking tab snaps into place.

Figure 8-61. Connect the ATX12V power connector

Final Assembly Steps

Congratulations! You're almost finished building the system. Only a few final steps remain to be done, and those won't take long.

Connect the supplemental case fan

The Antec SLK1650B has one rear-mounted 120mm supplemental fan. To enable it, connect a four-pin Molex connector from the power supply to the connector on the fan, as shown in Figure 8-62.

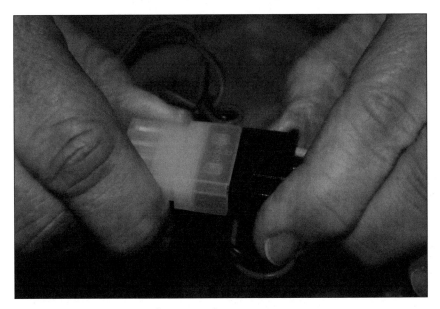

Figure 8-62. Connect power to the rear case fan

Dress the cables

The final step in assembling the system is to dress the cables. That simply means routing the cables away from the motherboard and other components and tying them off so they don't flop around inside the case. Chances are that no one but you will ever see the inside of your system, but dressing the cables has several advantages other than making the system appear neater. First and foremost, it improves cooling by keeping the cables from impeding air flow. It can also improve system reliability. More than once, we've seen a system overheat and crash because a loose cable jammed the CPU fan or case fan.

After you've completed these steps, take a few minutes to double-check everything. Verify that all cables are connected properly, that all drives are secured, and that there's nothing loose inside the case. Check one last time to verify the power supply is set for the correct input voltage. It's a good idea to pick up the system and tilt it gently from side to side to make sure there are no loose screws or other items that could cause a short. Use the following checklist:

- ❏ Power supply set to proper input voltage
- ❏ No loose tools or screws (tilt and shake the case gently)
- ❏ Heatsink/fan unit properly mounted; CPU fan connected
- ❏ Memory module(s) full seated and latched
- ❏ Front-panel switch and indicator cables connected properly
- ❏ Front-panel USB cable connected properly
- ❏ Hard drive data cable connected to drive and motherboard
- ❏ Hard drive power cable connected
- ❏ Optical drive data cable connected to drive and motherboard
- ❏ Optical drive power cable connected
- ❏ Optical drive audio cable(s) connected, if applicable
- ❏ Floppy drive data and power cables connected (if applicable)
- ❏ All drives secured to drive bay or chassis, as applicable
- ❏ Expansion cards (if any) fully seated and secured to the chassis
- ❏ Main ATX power cable and ATX12V power cable connected
- ❏ Front and rear case fans installed and connected (if applicable)
- ❏ All cables dressed and tucked

Now it's time for the smoke test. Leave the cover off for now. Connect the power cable to the wall receptacle and then to the system unit. Unlike many power supplies, the Antec SmartPower 2.0 has a separate rocker switch on the back that controls power to the power supply. By default, it's in the "0" or off position, which means the power supply is not receiving power from the wall receptacle. Move that switch to the "1" or on position. Press the main power button on the front of the case, and the system should start up. Check to make sure that the power supply fan, CPU fan, and case fan are spinning. (Remember that the case fan spins only when needed, so it may not be spinning when you first power up the system.) You should also hear the hard drive spin up and the happy beep that tells you the system is starting normally. At that point, everything should be working properly.

Final Words

Except for the CPU cooler problem, this system assembled easily. It took us about half an hour to build, or two days, depending on how you look at it. Counting only actual construction time, it took about 30 minutes from start to finish. Counting the time to shoot images, reshoot images, re-reshoot images, tear down for reshoots and re-reshoots, rebuild and re-rebuild after the re-shoots and re-reshoots, and so on, it took two days. A first-time system builder should be able to assemble this system in an evening with luck, and certainly over a weekend.

Installing Software

Microsoft declined our request for a beta copy of Windows Vista—we suspect we're on their Enemies List because we're vocal Linux advocates—so we installed Windows XP instead. We installed Windows XP uneventfully from a distribution disc that included SP2.

The next step was to install and update drivers. Like most motherboard makers, ASRock includes a driver CD that automates the process. Running the Drivers CD displays the dialog shown in Figure 8-63. We installed all of the drivers in the order shown.

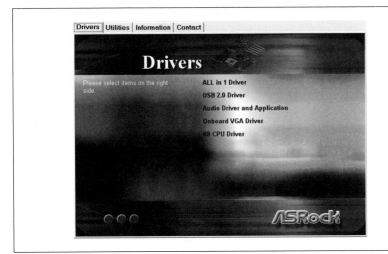

Figure 8-63. The ASRock Drivers CD main menu

After the Drivers CD installs the ASRock-provided drivers and utilities, install any necessary third-party drivers. For this system, no third-party drivers were needed. With all of the drivers installed, we restarted the system and installed our standard suite of applications, including Firefox and OpenOffice.org.

False Starts

When you turn on the rear power switch, the system will come to life momentarily and then die. That's perfectly normal behavior. When the power supply receives power, it begins to start up. It quickly notices that the motherboard hasn't told it to start, and so it shuts down again. All you need to do is press the front-panel power switch and the system will start normally.

Hasta La Vista, Baby

We actually weren't disappointed, when Microsoft refused to send us a Vista beta, because Vista has been gutted to the point that it is little more than a Windows XP service pack anyway. After we wrote this chapter, we downloaded a copy of Windows Vista Beta 2 during the public preview. Vista Beta 2 loads and runs fine on this system. Well, as fine as it runs on anything, which isn't very fine at all.

Optional Drivers

Some components include what we call "optional drivers." For example, there are drivers available for the Logitech keyboard and mouse. We generally don't install these drivers, although they are required to support enhanced functions such as programming the keyboard. We seldom use those enhanced functions, so we just use the default Microsoft drivers. If you want to enable those enhanced functions on your system, install the drivers.

But, as Jim Cooley notes, "beware, they often require significant memory and CPU resources with little apparent benefit except in specialized cases. The only exception to manufacturers' utilities that is of any real benefit is the Hardware Monitoring software, which can alert you should the system overheat in the event of a fan failure."

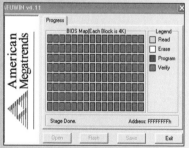

Figure 8-64. The ASRock Windows BIOS updater

Updating the BIOS

"If it ain't broke, don't fix it" is a good rule when it comes to updating the main system BIOS. We generally don't update the main system BIOS unless the later BIOS fixes a problem that actually affects us. The most recent BIOS available for the ASRock motherboard was only one version more recent than the one supplied with the motherboard, and included only a few minor fixes, none of which pertained to us. Still, for illustrative purposes, we decided to update our main system BIOS.

ADVICE FROM JIM COOLEY

That being said, readers of this book may, more often than not, want to tweak and update their system to include all the latest drivers and updates. I recommend updating the BIOS using the boot floppy method *before* installing an operating system because Windows, in particular, will force a reinstall (albeit mostly automatic) of every single device on the system when it detects a new BIOS and that introduces the chance for Murphy's Law to prove itself, often with spectacular results.

Like most motherboard makers, ASRock provides two methods to update the BIOS. The first is the traditional boot floppy method. You download the BIOS update as a binary file and copy it and the updater program to a floppy disk. Booting that floppy disk transfers the updated BIOS code to the system. The boot floppy method works on any system—at least any system that has a floppy drive—whether it runs Windows or some other operating system (or no operating system at all.) Most people use the second method, shown in Figure 8-64, which uses a Windows executable to update the BIOS. To update the BIOS using this method, you simply double-click the updater program icon and follow the prompts.

DON'T KILL YOUR MOTHERBOARD

Never interrupt the system while a BIOS update is in progress. If you turn off the system (or the power fails) during a BIOS update, the motherboard may be left in an unbootable state. For that reason, we recommend connecting the system to a UPS when you update the BIOS.

End Result

We're extremely happy with this system, particularly for the price. It sits under Robert's desk, and has the distinction of being the only computer in the house that runs Windows. (We have anything from half a dozen to a dozen other systems—the exact number varies from day to day—but all of them run Linux.)

We built this system because Robert needed a Windows system to run some Windows-only astronomy software he was using to generate charts for an astronomy book we were writing. We didn't want to spend much money on it, because it was needed only for as long as it took to complete the book. Once we finish that book, we'll donate this system to a local nonprofit and again have our home as a Microsoft-free zone.

Still, although it cost only $350 excluding external peripherals, many people would be happy with this system as their only system. It's slower than the fastest current systems, but it's more than fast enough for casual use, including even light gaming. It's also quiet enough that we wouldn't hesitate to use it in our den, living room, or bedroom.

All in all, this is the perfect budget PC for us.

For updated component recommendations, commentary, and other new material, visit *http://www.hardwareguys.com/guides/budget-pc.html*.

Index

SLI (Scalable Link Interface), 199
smoke test, 245
sound adapters
 EAX support, 208
 integrated audio, 208
 standalone, 208
speakers
 alternatives for, 212
 Logitech Z-5500 5.1 speaker system,
  212
transporting systems
 backpacks, use of, 247
 list of packing supplies, 247
 Zero Halliburton cases, use of, 247
video adapter installation, 241
Gentoo Linux, 309
GMA 950 integrated video, 84
graphics adapters. (See video adapters)
Graphics Media Accelerator 3000
  (GMA 3000), 320
grounding, 1

H

hand tools/supply list, 21–22
hardware design criteria
 2D video quality, 84
 3D video performance, 84
 disk capacity/performance, 84
 disk performance, 85
 expandability, 83
 noise level, 83
 price, 83
 processor performance, 84
 reliability, 83
 size, 83
 video performance, 84
hard disk drives
 500 GB Barracuda, 208
 alternative models, 354
 ATA/SATA drive, 85
 ATA (Parallel ATA or PATA), 53
 Barracuda 7200.9, 94
 BenQ DW-1650, 130
 buffer/cache, 53
 data loss, protect against, 85, 94
 diagnostics, 24
 drive failure, protect against, 94
 guidelines, 53
 high-capacity drives, 53
 IDE hard drive, 32

installation, 123–126
installation/diagnostic utility, 23
RAID 1, 94
recommended, 53
SATA drives, 37
Seagate Barracuda 7200.9 SATA, 94,
 208, 321, 354
Seagate Cheetah, 209
Seagate ST320014A U Series X, 354
Seagate ST3250620AS Barracuda
 7200.10, 321
Serial ATA (SATA) interface, 53–54
Smart Drive Enclosure, 14
Zalman Hard Drive Heatpipe, 14
hard drive activity LED (IDE_LED),
 229
Hard Drive Activity LED (yellow)
 connectors, 336
Hard Drive Failure error message, 38
Hauppauge dual analog tuner, 298
Hauppauge WinTV-PVR-150 tuner
 card, 119
HDD activity LED cable, 336
headphones, alternatives for, 212
heatsink/fan units (CPU coolers). (See
 HSFs [heatsink/fan units])
HSFs (heatsink/fan units)
 and motherboard compatibility, 13
 choosing a quiet cooler, 12
 cooling fans, 11
 emergency fans, 12
 Resistor kits (voltage or fan speed
  controllers), 12
 retail-boxed BTX processor, 91–93
 third-party CPU cooler, 362
 Type II cooler, 92
 Type I BTX Thermal Module, 92
 Type I cooler, 92

I

I/O panel, 28
ICH (I/O Controller Hub), 26
Intel CPU cooler, 344
Intel D945GCZLR, 88
Intel High Definition Audio, 93
Intel USB pin assignments, 336

K

keyboards
 alphanumeric keys, 65
 Bluetooth wireless connectivity, 66
 dedicated and/or programmable
  function keys, 65
 Dvorak layout, 65
 IR (infrared) keyboards, 66
 Logitech, 66
 Logitech Media Elite, 97
 Microsoft, 66
 programmable function keys, 66
 PS/2 keyboard, 65
 PS/2 keyboard port, 65
 recommended, 66
 RF (radio frequency) keyboards, 66
 styles, 65
 USB keyboards, 65
 wireless keyboard, 66
Kingston 2GB PC5300 DDR2 Memory
 Kit, 320
KingWin TL-35CS Night Hawk, 154
Knoppix Live Linux CD, 24

L

LAMP (Linux, Apache, MySQL, PHP/
 Perl/Python) server, 192
LAN (Local Area Network), 67
LAN (Local Area Network) adapter, 67
LED lights
 blue LED, 122
 Hard Drive Activity LED (yellow), 115
 HDD LED, 115
 Power LED (green), 115
 red LED, 67
Line Out audio ports, 119
Linux, 135
 distribution CD, 23, 193
 running from a CD, 24
 versus Windows, 135
Local Area Network. (See LAN [Local
 Area Network])
locked OEM versions, 4
Logitech LX7 Cordless Optical Mouse,
 97
Logitech Media Elite, 97
low-power processor, 11–12
low-speed Cyclone Blower installation,
 338

About the Authors

Robert Bruce Thompson is the author or co-author of numerous on-line training courses and computer books. Robert built his first computer in 1976 from discrete chips. It had 256 *bytes* of memory, used toggle switches and LEDs for I/O, ran at less than 1 MHz, and had no operating system. Since then, he has bought, built, upgraded, and repaired hundreds of PCs for himself, employers, customers, friends, and clients. Robert reads mysteries and non-fiction for relaxation, but only on cloudy nights. He spends most clear, moonless nights outdoors with his 10" Dobsonian reflector telescope, hunting down faint fuzzies, and is currently designing a larger truss-tube Dobsonian (computerized, of course) that he plans to build.

Barbara Fritchman Thompson worked for 20 years as a librarian before starting her own home-based consulting practice, Research Solutions (*http://www.researchsolutions.net*), and is also a researcher for the law firm Womble Carlyle Sandridge & Rice, PLLC. Barbara, who has been a PC power user for more than 15 years, researched and tested much of the hardware reviewed for this book. During her leisure hours, Barbara reads, works out, plays golf, and, like Robert, is an avid amateur astronomer.

Colophon

Our look is the result of reader comments, our own experimentation, and feedback from distribution channels. Distinctive covers complement our distinctive approach to technical topics, breathing personality and life into potentially dry subjects.

Philip Dangler was the production editor and copyeditor for *Building the Perfect PC*, Second Edition. Sada Preisch was the proofreader. Jimmie Young wrote the index.

Karen Montgomery designed the cover of this book using InDesign CS2. The cover image is a photograph by David Reavis. Emma Colby produced the cover layout with QuarkXPress 4.1 using Adobe's Formata Condensed font.

The series design is by David Futato. This book was converted from Microsoft Word to InDesign CS by Abby Fox. The text and heading fonts are Linotype Birka and Adobe Formata Condensed, and the code font is TheSans Mono Condensed from LucasFont. The illustrations and screenshots that appear in the book were produced by Robert Romano and Jessamyn Read using Macromedia Freehand MX and Adobe Photoshop CS.

MAKE KITS

⌄ Daisy MP3 Player

$114.95
makezine.com/daisy

In 2001, artist and designer Raphael Abrams went looking for a new challenge. After some long and careful consideration, he came upon the idea of designing and building his own open source MP3 player kit.

His criteria? First, it had to be easy to build. Second, it had to be open source. Finally, and most importantly, it had to be more than just a handheld device — it had to connect easily to many interfaces, everything from simple button-pushing to parallel ports to very powerful serial modes.

It took several iterations, but eventually he came up with the Daisy, an easy-to-build, pocket-sized MP3 player. Daisy sounds as good as an iPod, can access 65,000 tracks, and plays 48kHz WAV files as well as MP3s. And, unlike an iPod, you can change its battery.

But the big thing about Daisy is the ease with which it interfaces with so many devices, including the MAKE Controller. It is the perfect MP3 kit for makers, for it is easily integrated into kiosks, displays, art installations, or just about anything else.

« The MAKE Controller

$149.99
makezine.com/controller

Born in the fire and smoke issuing from Survival Research Labs' ramshackle compound near Potrero Hill in San Francisco, the MAKE Microcontroller traces its lineage to the digital controllers used to control SRL's robots and artistic weaponry.

Engineers Michael Shiloh and David Williams designed the hardware and software that controls SRL's robots and gives them savage intelligence. While brainstorming ideas for something more powerful and easier to use than available microcontrollers, they came up with what evolved into the MAKE Controller.

The MAKE Controller is a microprocessor unit, a computer-on-a-chip designed to handle a small set of related tasks. But the MAKE Controller has a more powerful processor than typically available on most microprocessors, plus built-in networking capabilities, an onboard USB port, and large memory. With the MAKE Controller, the maker's world opens up, enabling unlimited opportunities for automation, motion control, and artistic expression.

Straight out of the box, the controller is ready to connect to sensors, motors, and your own killer robot. It comes with common functions preprogrammed for immediate experimentation.

MiniPOV2

$17.99
makezine.com/minipov2

The MiniPOV2 is a persistence-of-vision device that rapidly blinks eight LEDs on and off so that when waved through the air, an image or message appears to float in front of the viewer.

MIT engineer Limor Fried originally cooked up the MiniPOV2 as an easy-to-build demonstration showing how microcontrollers work. She wanted something that was easy to make, inexpensive, and simple. This little kit, says Fried, teaches several not-so-little lessons:

· How to solder
· How to assemble simple kits
· How to program microcontrollers

The kit includes a microcontroller, sockets, resistors, LEDs, connectors, a battery case, and a printed circuit board. Add some basic tools, a PC with a parallel port, and a little programming, and the MiniPOV is ready to blink out your deepest thoughts.

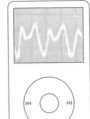

« The iBump

$99.95
makezine.com/ibump

"Freshman volume" is the sound level metric introduced to college students in their first year — it's the highest sound level possible at which there is nobody screaming at you to turn the music down. When Ben Anderson made his first attempt at freshman volume, he used his iPod, several guitar amps, and a regular stereo. Although loud, the sound fidelity was surprisingly low. What was wrong?

Big speakers work best with low notes; little speakers work best with high notes. Ben needed a way to separate lows from highs before amplifying his music.

Designed by Ben's dad, Wendell, the iBump is an audiophile-quality active crossover (which separates the highs from the lows). It is inserted between the source (iPod) and the amplifiers. Routing the iBump subwoofer output to a bass amp enables clear, earthmoving low notes. The iBump left and right channels provide high, undistorted volume.

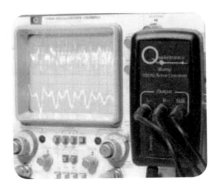

Now, Ben uses an iBump to make sure his neighbors understand the true concept of freshman volume. So can you.

» Minty Boost

$19.99
makezine/mintyboost

"People put a lot of interesting stuff in Altoids tins," says one maker. "Usually, it's either drugs or condoms." But besides such pedestrian uses, Altoids tins have been used in electronics projects for decades.

At Maker Faire last April, Limor Fried gave her latest spin on the Altoid box project concept. The Minty Boost is a small, simple, but powerful USB charger for MP3 players, cameras, cellphones, and other gadgets that plug into a USB port to charge.

The AA-cell-powered Minty Boost is the Cadillac of battery-powered USB chargers, lasting twice as long as most other Altoid tin chargers. Plus, it's a simple project requiring only easy soldering. All materials (except the Altoids box and batteries) are included.

Game of Life Board

In 2005 a group of brainy MIT students, the Dropout Design Team, decided to try something really novel and clever. They wanted to invent an electronics kit that would look cool, be simple to build, and be accessible to everyone.

At the time, some of them were toying around with the idea of "cellular automata" — a collection of cells on a grid whose colors change according to what's going on in adjacent cells. (The prime example is British math whiz John Conway's Game of Life, in which a collection of cells lives, dies, or multiplies based on a few mathematical rules.)

"Hey, let's build a huge wall of LEDs that would enact the Conway Game of Life rules," they said one night. "The wall could be split into identical modules, and each freshman could assemble their own module, then add the module to the collective wall."

DDT designed an easy-to-solder kit that is cheap and scalable. Each Game of Life board contains 16 LEDs in a 4×4 grid, a microcontroller, and a communications and power distribution network. Boards can act alone, or can be plugged together, border to border, to create a larger display.

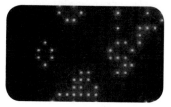

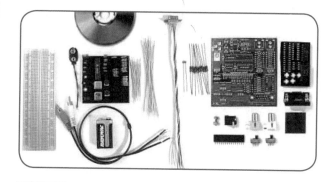

XGameStation Pico Edition 2.0

Twenty years ago, says Andre LaMonthe, game programming was a real art. LaMonthe, a programming maven, remembers when 32 kilobytes on machines with clock speeds of 1 MHz was state-of-the-art. Yet those programmers of the 1980s created classic video games with perfectly tuned mechanics and unbelievable details.

LaMonthe's XGameStation is a hardware platform developed for educating a new generation of hardware and software hackers in the nitty-gritty, low-level world of hardcore game development.

Combining modern technology with the bedrock-solid design philosophies of the past, the XGameStation Pico Edition 2.0 is a build-it-yourself game development kit based on the technologies of its bigger brother, the XGameStation Micro Edition.

Solder your unit together and you'll have a completely portable and reprogrammable embedded game system. Complete instructions covering assembly, architecture, and programming of the Pico Edition are included on CD.

The Pico Edition includes an 80MHz Ubicom SX28 microcontroller, a solderless breadboard, a 7-segment readout, 15-pin interface, A/V jacks, and a built-in directional game pad for a completely portable mini game console.

If you have a spare evening, weekend, or even an hour, there are projects here for you. No doubt about it, a year's worth of MAKE is a lot of information, discovery, and fun.

MAKE BOOKS

⏫ MAKE Magazine Collector's Edition Boxed Sets

$59.95 Each
MAKE Year 01 (Volumes 01-04)
MAKE Year 02 (Volumes 05-08)
makezine.com/store

With the publication of Volume 08, MAKE magazine has two full years under its belt. MAKE's famed projects run from practical to whimsical, to maybe even a little scary.

In each of the eight issues, we've showcased the great things people are making in their basements, garages, and backyards with the technology at hand. But most importantly, each issue contains hands-on instructions on how to build stuff yourself — practical or whimsical or scary, but always cool.

» MAKE Pocket Reference

$12.95
makezine.com/pocketreference

The perfect stocking stuffer for the workshop warrior, the *MAKE Pocket Reference* is both fun and useful.

Page through and you'll find data on everything from physical constants to bolt specifications to resistor color codes. Add in cool stuff such as first aid, crane hand signals, and the encyclopedia of knots, and you can see why it might take up permanent residence in your shirt pocket.

⏫ Makers: The Book

$24.95 MAKERS: All Kinds of People Making Amazing Things in Backyards, Garages, and Basements
makezine.com/makers

For more than ten years, Bob Parks has explored the world of the technology addicted, the gadget fetishists, the personalities behind the latest technologies.

In his book *Makers*, Parks profiles a brigade of citizen engineers and inventors, men and women who make their own HERF (High Energy Radio Frequency) guns, fusion reactors, night-vision scopes, and tree houses.

Makers celebrates digital tinkering, hardware hacks, and DIY of all stripes, profiling 100 people and their homebrew projects, in a handsome hardcover perfect for coffee breaks or coffee tables.

⏬ Backyard Ballistics

$16.95 Backyard Ballistics: Build Potato Cannons, Paper Match Rockets, Cincinnati Fire Kites, Tennis Ball Mortars, and More Dynamite Devices
makezine.com/backyardballistics

Sure, electronics projects are cool, but sometimes you just want to make something go ka-boom.

Well, *Backyard Ballistics* was written for just those times. William Gurstelle has been collecting information on build-it-yourself projects that go whoosh, boom, or splat for 20 years. From his trove comes this selection of 13 ballistic devices that people can build in their garage or basement workshops.

Instructions, diagrams, and photographs show how to build projects simple (a match-powered rocket), complex (a scale-model tabletop catapult), and wonderful (a combustion potato cannon). With an emphasis on safety, the book explains the physics behind the projects, and profiles experimenters such as Alfred Nobel, Robert Goddard, and Isaac Newton.

Better than e-books

Buy *Building the Perfect PC*, 2nd Edition, and access
the digital edition FREE on Safari for 45 days.

Go to www.oreilly.com/go/safarienabled
and type in coupon code YMKTLZG

Search thousands of top tech books

Download whole chapters

Cut and Paste code examples

Find answers fast

Search Safari! The premier electronic reference
library for programmers and IT professionals.

 Addison Wesley   Sun microsystems   ALPHA   Java Sun Microsystems   *Microsoft* Press   Peachpit Press

Adobe Press 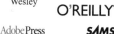 O'REILLY   New Riders   SAMS   que   Cisco Press   macromedia PRESS PRENTICE HALL PTR

Related Titles from O'Reilly

Hardware

Blackberry Hacks

Building Extreme PCs

Building the Perfect PC

Car PC Hacks

Designing Embedded Hardware, *2nd Edition*

Don't Click on the Blue E!

Hardware Hacking Projects for Geeks

Home Hacking Projects for Geeks

Make: Technology on Your Time

Makers: All Kinds of People Making Amazing Things
   in Their Backyard, Basement or Garage

Nokia Smartphones Hacks

Palm & Treo Hacks

PC Hacks

PC Hardware Annoyances

PC Hardware Buyer's Guide

PCs: The Missing Manual

Programming Embedded Systems, *2nd Edition*

Repairing & Upgrading Your PC

Smart Home Hacks

Talk Is Cheap

Treo Fan Book

Wireless Hacks, *2nd Edition*

The O'Reilly Advantage

Stay Current and Save Money

Order books online:
www.oreilly.com/order_new

Questions about our
products or your order:
order@oreilly.com

Join our email lists: Sign up
to get topic specific email
announcements or new
books, conferences, special
offers and technology news
elists@oreilly.com

For book content
technical questions:
booktech@oreilly.com

To submit new book
proposals to our editors:
proposals@oreilly.com

Contact us:
O'Reilly Media, Inc.
1005 Gravenstein Highway N.
Sebastopol, CA U.S.A. 95472
707-827-7000 or
800-998-9938
www.oreilly.com

Did you know that if you register
your O'Reilly books, you'll get
automatic notification and upgrade
discounts on new editions?

**And that's not all! Once you've registered
your books you can:**

» Win free books, T-shirts and O'Reilly Gear

» Get special offers available only to registered
O'Reilly customers

» Get free catalogs announcing all our new
titles (US and UK Only)

**Registering is easy! Just go to
www.oreilly.com/go/register**

CONTENTS

MAPS AND CHARTS

THE COURSE OF MEXICAN HISTORY

I PRE-COLUMBIAN MEXICO

1

The First Mexicans

There is in Mexican society a pervasive awareness of the ancients. The Indian presence intrudes on the national psyche; it suffuses the art, philosophy, and literature. It is stamped on the face of Mexico, in the racial features of the sturdy mestizo. It lies within the marvelous prehistoric ruins among whose haunted piles the Mexican seeks his origins. It has not always been so. Following the Spanish conquest of the sixteenth century, a combination of the conquerors' ethnocentrism and excessive Christian zeal reduced all things Indian to a level of shame. During the subsequent four centuries, until the cultural phase of the Revolution during the 1920s, the indigenous past lurked in the background as a mild embarrassment, save to a few enlightened scholars. This paradox existed among a people, the majority of whom had at least some Indian blood, because the minority of whites, insensitive to historical realities, looked to a European model. But the maturing Revolution sought the spirit of a Mexican cultural identity—*mexicanidad*—and what emerged was indeed revolutionary in its cultural implications. In the past several decades anthropologists, historians, painters, musicians, novelists, and craftsmen have bent their talents toward an exaltation of native values. If in its enthusiasm the movement took some liberties, it may be excused as following the natural path of cultural nationalism. More important, it revealed the stunning achievements of the past, for when, in 1519, Fernando Cortés and the Spanish host invaded, advanced civilization in Mexico was more than a thousand years old.

Pre-Agricultural and Proto-Agricultural Mexico

At what point the first Mexican appeared on the scene we shall, of course, never know. He was no doubt one of an obscure band of nomads descended from the intrepid hunters who crossed from the Asian mainland to Alaska. There appear to have been successive waves of migrants, the first perhaps as early as 50,000 B.C., with the beginning of the Wisconsin (Pleistocene) Ice Age. At this time much of the earth's water formed into gigantic ice caps, and the level of the oceans was reduced. Consequently, a land bridge over the Bering Straits facilitated the passage. When a melting trend began around 8000 B.C., the migrations very likely ceased.

"The story of Indian America," Pablo Martínez del Río used to tell his classes, "must be written with soft chalk, easily erased and corrected." Thus reference was made to our tenuous hold on knowledge of ancient Mexico. With increasing interest in anthropology, however, we may expect that many of our present conceptions will be altered, perhaps radically, in years ahead. For the moment, it is convenient to divide the history of pre-Hispanic Mexico into periods, which vary somewhat both in chronology and terminology according to the authority one consults. It will be noted that not all cultures fit within this chart, and there is inevitable overlapping on some dates.

STAGES OF PRE-HISPANIC INDIAN DEVELOPMENT

40,000–5000 B.C.	*Pre-Agricultural:* Nomadic hunters and food gatherers.
5000–1500 B.C.	*Proto-Agricultural* or *Archaic:* Agricultural beginnings; formation of crude but permanent villages; appearance of rudimentary political and social organization; development of primitive skills.
1500–200 B.C.	*Formative* or *Pre-Classic:* Elaboration of Proto-Agricultural achievements and refinement of techniques; artistry in ceramics; planned ceremonial sites, anticipating the Classic period.
200 B.C.–A.D. 900	*Classic:* The florescence of ancient Mexican civilization, with cities ruled by priests and kings; the apogee of artistic expression; monumental architecture; advancement in literacy and science.
A.D. 900–1521	*Post-Classic* or *Historical:* Societies increasingly yield to rule by warriors; emergence of conquest states; appearance of metallurgy; origin of authentic historical sources; an excess of human sacrifice; final destruction of the Indian states by Spanish Conquest.

Early man in America was a hunter, a food gatherer, and sometimes a fisherman. Contrary to recent popular assertions, his prominent trait was not aggressiveness but insecurity. It must be supposed that man spent an inordinate amount of his time merely struggling to survive and was almost constantly on the search for food. For thousands of years the Indian led a precarious existence, with no perceptible improvement in his condition.

Recent finds indicate that humans roamed northern Mexico at least forty thousand years ago, but our ignorance of their society is almost complete. We must, therefore, pass over at least twenty-five or thirty thousand years, during which time man's prospects remained essentially static. Although scattered indications of his presence in the interval exist, there is little substantive evidence of the nature of his society until the period of 10,000–8000 B.C. By these times of moist conditions, lush grasslands and full foliage provided ample fodder for strange animals—hairy mammoths, mastodons, giant armadillos, and early ancestors of the bison, camel, and horse. A large lake covered the floor of the Valley of Mexico, and to that watering place came the prehistoric beasts. In the congenial environment of the Valley man also lived. When animals became mired in the lakeshore marshes, primitive warriors assailed their prey with missiles—stone-tipped lances or darts propelled by the *atl-atl*, or spear thrower, the extension of which gave added velocity. Evidence of successful hunts was preserved in the muck. In the 1940s, the remains of a human were discovered at the village of Tepexpan, situated a few miles north of today's Mexico City on what was the edge of the old lake. The bones lay at a depth corresponding to a layer that also contained the bones of a mammoth, giving fragmentary evidence that the two were contemporaries. "Tepexpan Man" (who, it turned out, was a woman) is the first tangible clue to the early race. In 1952, not far distant at Santa Isabel Iztápan, another important discovery was unearthed: mammoth bones were found with a stone point lodged in the ribs, and there were clear indications that the beast had been butchered with flint knives that lay nearby. There is some dispute about the exact dating of these finds, but they seem to be from ten to twelve thousand years old.

Changes in climatic conditions reordered ancient man's routine. Around 7500 B.C. a drying-up phase began: rainfall was less frequent, and the rich plant life gradually yielded to sparse vegetation; the lake shriveled up; and the huge beasts that had provided a plentiful supply of meat eventually became extinct as their sources of food and water disappeared. Man was again back to eating insects, lizards, snakes, rodents, and anything else remotely edible, to supplement his diet of seeds, roots, nuts, berries, eggs, and shellfish. The audacious killer of mammoths gave way to the hunter of small game.

It appears that about the time large animals vanished—around 7000 B.C.—crude experimentations with agriculture began. It would be thousands of years before domesticated plants provided a reliable source of food, but no discovery of man in his long quest for security was more momentous than that of agriculture. The most important plant was maize, or corn, which responded well to human care and grew almost anywhere. It became the basis of the Mexican diet. As far as we know, the earliest successful planting was at Tehuacán in the modern state of Puebla; perhaps as early as 5000 B.C. primitive farmers there practiced the most rudimentary form of agriculture. In the many centuries that followed, other plants were domesticated to form the essential staples of the Mexican diet—corn, beans, and squash. It may be said that by at least 2500 B.C. they contributed an important part of man's sustenance, as indicated by the presence of grinding stones for the making of meal.

By the passage of the next millennium, when more moisture had returned to the land, the authentic farmer had evolved. Now, barring disasters common to all tillers of the soil, there was a fairly reliable source of food. The impact of this achievement can hardly be exaggerated. From having to devote almost all of his efforts to the desperate search for something to eat, man finally found some leisure time for experimentation, to develop and refine his skills and talents. Long a weaver of baskets and mats, he now—around 2000 B.C.—began to shape clay, a most important development.

The Formative Period

Ancient garbage dumps are to the archaeologist what documents are to the historian. From those piles of refuse scientific investigators patiently assemble pictures of primitive societies with a sophistication astonishing to the layman. Much has, of course, long been reduced to dust, and whatever use early man made of wood, hides, and woven reeds must be left to speculation. But instruments of flint, obsidian, and various kinds of stone survive, and when man began to fashion pottery he left behind indelible

Ceramic figurine of a dancer from Tlatilco, near Mexico City. The swollen thighs suggest an association with fertility.

traces of his culture. More often than not the vessels are found smashed, but these potsherds provide key links with the past. According to the way pots are made, shaped, and decorated, the archaeologist reconstructs and defines a way of life.

By 1500 B.C. the rough outlines of an existence with which we can identify had formed. Agriculture had enabled man to settle down and support larger population clusters, and he built huts of branches, reeds, and mud. A simple village life with incipient political and social orders evolved. Subsequently, cliques emerged to control both power and wealth. Increased exchange of goods among different cultures developed as a result of the distinctive techniques and specialties of local artisans. In addition, varied climate and geography yielded regional fruits, vegetables, woods, stone, and other items of value, such as shells, jade, cotton, and turquoise. This spreading trade naturally led to cultural exchanges as well.

Artists began to create ceramics that were both esthetically pleasing and functional. Clay figurines, usually of females and more often than not naked, were produced in great numbers. The most unusual were those of Tlatilco, in the Valley of Mexico, where, artists rendered charming figurines of the type known as "pretty lady," with delicate and beautiful faces. The eyes are almost Oriental and the hairdos sometimes elaborate. The figures have tiny waists, and their bulging thighs suggest that they were symbols of fertility. At the same time, a fascination with the deformed manifested early the Mexican idea of duality, for other small clay figures represented dwarfs, hunchbacks, and the diseased. Some figurines are of interest for their depiction of everyday life—nursing babies, dancing, playing, and performing acrobatics. Through them we gain some idea of popular pastimes, the use of jewelry, and clothing. Still other pieces were made in the forms of animals, birds, and fish. Art at this point was still an expression of curiosity, of the frivolous and innocent, devoid of the serious religious connotations it later acquired.

Agriculture advanced during the Formative period with the use of terracing and *chinampas*, or floating gardens. The chinampas were rafts made of branches onto which fertile mud from the lake bottom was piled. These made rich gardens for the raising of food, and irrigation was no problem. Farming implements of stone, horn, bone, and probably wood facilitated cultivation of fields.

Although textile manufacturing had evolved, it is likely that, in the more temperate zones anyway, people went about nude, or almost so. Clothing was apparently worn more among the upper classes than the lower, as were sandals, jewelry, and other adornments. Individual expression and vanity were evident in the dyed hair and elaborate coiffures of aristocratic women.

As villages grew in size and society became more complex, serious decisions had to be made by those who were most knowledgeable. Increasing reliance on agriculture made people aware that their security depended upon the blessings of nature. The mysteries of the universe were associated with the supernatural, and, as in other ancient cultures, gods of nature came to be worshipped. Vagaries of the elements were equated with capricious gods. When rain failed, for example, supplication was made to the angry deity through the agency of the priesthood. Among a **credulous people, the priest, with his special powers, acquired a predominant position. This presumed special relationship with the gods, astutely cultivated by the priests, gave them a certain** mystique and a hold over the community. In order to pay due reverence to the gods and to ensure their cooperation in providing rain and sunshine, priests ordered the construction of mounds, on top of which offerings were made. As the structures became larger and more elaborate, advanced permanent architecture evolved. By the late Formative, or Pre-Classic period, some impressive sites were already in evidence.

La Venta and Monte Albán

Because of the great diversity in aboriginal Mexico, it is perhaps misleading to refer to any group as the "mother culture." But the people with the best claim to being the first emerging civilization in Mexico are the Olmecs. "Civilization" here is meant to imply an urban, literate society. If La Venta, the main Olmec center, was not a true city, it at least displayed the pristine characteristics of urbanism; if its people were not truly literate, they at least drew hieroglyphs, the first step in writing. By 1200 B.C. the Olmecs flourished in western Tabasco and southern Veracruz. They reached the height of their development between 700 and 400 B.C., during which time they carved hieroglyphs and devised an early calendar. The most impressive of the Olmec sites, La Venta, was built in a swampy area in Tabasco, where a large pyramid, along with other painted structures, formed part of a ceremonial center. It served a nearby population of perhaps eighteen thousand.[1] La Venta was apparently destroyed around 400 B.C., having been subjected to violent desecrations.

Olmec origins are obscure; little, in fact, is known of the Olmecs except through their distinctive art. During this springtime of the Mexican world Olmec sculptors fashioned jade figurines whose elegance is unsurpassed. Their most spectacular pieces are colossal carved stone heads, some of which are over nine feet high and weigh up to forty tons. The facial features are strikingly Negroid, and the heads are covered with what seem to be helmets. Smaller pieces have facial characteristics designated as "baby face" and pudgy bodies that suggest infants or eunuchs.

Strongly established among the Olmecs was the jaguar cult, identified in some way with the rain god and fertility. Manifestations of the cult appear frequently in Olmec stone carvings, figures, and other artifacts. The obsession with feline forms, or "were-jaguars," was such that jaguars are even depicted in sexual union with women. The down-turned, snarling jaguar mouth is often seen in the sculptured faces of human forms, and it is

1. Michael D. Coe, *Mexico* (New York, 1967), p. 88.

This handsome basalt stone carving from the Gulf Coast Olmec culture is known as "The Wrestler."

possible that these strange faces actually represent masks. The mysterious Olmec civilization gradually declined, perhaps because of cultural pressures from the rising Maya to the south and the incipient Teotihuacán complex in the central highlands.

Developing at a time roughly parallel with La Venta was the important center at Monte Albán, situated on a mountain top outside of today's city of Oaxaca. Sometime before 200 B.C. the Indians of the Oaxacan civilization devised a calendar and a rudimentary form of writing expressed in carvings on stone markers. Both La Venta and Monte Albán anticipated the great civilizations to follow, having by the late Formative period already exhibited many of the characteristics associated with the Classic. There was unquestionably contact between the two sites. But while the Olmec influence was on the wane by the end of the Formative period, Monte Albán emerged as one of the great centers of the Classic world in Mexico.

It may be noted briefly that in the southern area of Chiapas and Yucatán, where the impressive Maya civilization would eventually rise, there were signs of advancing culture. These were, however, behind the development at La Venta and Monte Albán. Early achievement in the Valley of Mexico lagged somewhat; at Cuicuilco, located on the outskirts of Mexico City, the

Several colossal Olmec stone heads have been discovered. This one, more than eight feet high, is covered with what appears to be a helmet.

An Olmec jade figurine illustrates the skill of ancient artists.

Representing a pudgy baby, or perhaps a eunuch, this Olmec piece is 13½ inches in height.

oldest extant structure dates from approximately 600 B.C. A curious conical pyramid, it was built to a height of sixty feet, only to be buried in a later volcanic eruption.

Destined to become the most influential site of all was the developing center of Teotihuacán in the Valley of Mexico. By at least 200 B.C. the Teotihuacanos were formulating plans for what would later become a vast city. Before the birth of Christ work had begun on the great pyramids and mural paintings that may be seen today. A complicated polytheistic religion evolved. By the end of the Formative period there had emerged in that large civic-religious complex the technology and central authority necessary for the creation of one of the splendors of the ancient world.

Recommended for Further Study

Benson, Elizabeth P., ed. *The Olmec and Their Neighbors.* New York: Crowell, 1977.

Bernal, Ignacio. *The Olmec World.* Translated by Doris Heyden and Fernando Horcasitas. Berkeley: University of California Press, 1969.

Coe, Michael. *America's First Civilization: Discovering the Olmecs.* New York: Van Nostrand, 1968.

———. *The Jaguar's Children: Pre-Classic Central Mexico.* New York: Museum of Primitive Art, 1965.

———. *Mexico.* New York: Praeger, 1967.

Huddleston, Lee E. *Origins of the American Indians: European Concepts, 1492–1729.* Austin: University of Texas Press, 1970.

Litvak-King, Jaime. *Ancient Mexico, an Overview.* Albuquerque: University of New Mexico Press, 1985.

Miller, Mary Ellen. *The Art of Mesoamerica, from Olmec to Aztec.* London: Thames and Hudson, 1986.

Soustelle, Jacques. *The Olmecs: The Oldest Civilization in Mexico.* Translated by Helen R. Lane. Norman: University of Oklahoma Press, 1985.

Terra, Helmut de. *Man and Mammoth in Mexico.* Translated by Alan H. Brodrick. London: Hutchinson, 1957.

Wauchope, Robert. *They Found the Buried Cities: Exploration and Excavation in the American Tropics.* Chicago: University of Chicago Press, 1965.

Wicke, Charles R. *Olmec: An Early Art Style of Precolumbian Mexico.* Tucson: University of Arizona Press, 1971.

Willey, Gordon R., ed. *Prehistoric Settlement Patterns in the New World.* New York: Johnson Reprint, 1963.

Wolf, Eric. *Sons of the Shaking Earth: The People of Mexico and Guatemala—Their Land, History, and Culture.* Chicago: University of Chicago Press, 1974.

2

Mexico's Golden Age: The Classic Period

When, around 200 B.C., much of the Old World was being introduced to Roman ways, there was in the New World only a glimmer of high civilization. Six centuries later, when the Roman Empire crumbled and Europe entered its Dark Ages, Middle America was resplendent.

The Golden Age

The Classic period in pre-Columbian Mexico lasted about a thousand years (200/0 B.C. to A.D. 800/1000), of which some six hundred may be viewed as a Golden Age. Because of the many cultures under consideration, the Classic cannot be put into any simple chronological framework.[1] At some sites, such as Teotihuacán and Monte Albán, a Proto-Classic style began to evolve by 200 B.C., while at others it did not appear until a couple of centuries later. That transitional stage lasted until A.D. 200/300, at which time the splendor of the Full Classic emerged, flourishing until the declining stages between A.D. 650 to 800. There was a final, decadent phase, the Late Classic (or Epi-Classic), persisting in some areas as late as A.D. 1000.

One is struck by the grandiose scale of man's work in those centuries, most notable in the monumental architecture but also by the excellence of the ceramics, sculpture, and murals. Reli-

---

1. With about eleven thousand known archaeological sites in Mexico, of which perhaps no more than ninety have been scientifically excavated, the complexities of charting can be appreciated.

Why is this boy laughing? Such unrestrained joy is characteristic of the thousands of ceramic pieces found at the site of Remojadas in the state of Veracruz. Unique for their expressiveness, the figurines have triangular, flattened heads, and teeth that are often filed to points.

A howling coyote, another delightful piece from the Remojadas culture, A.D. 300–900. Indian artists frequently displayed a touch of whimsy in their works.

gion was the cohesive force in an increasingly stratified society, and the hierarchy of priests commanded the power to exact both labor and tribute from the masses. It was a time of great vigor, with the proliferation of crafts and skills necessary to provide for complex communities. The leadership was dedicated to a sense of order and progress, made possible by an apparently strict adherence to regimentation. Pressures to provide sustenance for a burgeoning population led to more careful consideration of planting cycles, which in turn produced exact calculations of the seasons. Consequently there developed a very sophisticated knowledge of astronomy and mathematics, which made possible precise calendrical markings. The Maya devised the world's most accurate calendar. Farming became scientific; abstract thinking soared. The intellectuals in ancient Middle America may have arrived at the revolutionary concept of the zero cipher even before its discovery by the fifth-century Hindus. Not until A.D. 1202 did Arab mathematicians introduce this concept to Europe. Yet, oddly enough, the accomplished scientists of the New World made almost no practical use of metals, nor had they stumbled onto the utility of the wheel!

It is therefore all the more admirable that these Middle Americans were able to raise structures to the height of 230 feet that have stood for some fifteen hundred years. The magnitude of their technical limitations was equaled by their ingenuity. Massive blocks of cut stone were most likely transported on river rafts from quarries to distant cities, and for lifting the pieces high in the air some clever engineering devices, however crude in appearance, were utilized. Nature had provided Mexico no beasts of burden, so armies of laborers toiled for years on public works projects.

Though we marvel that these structures remain after so many centuries (all the more remarkable in earthquake country), excellence of construction was not these early people's strongest suit. Rather, one finds in their work the origins of a fundamental, and not unattractive, Mexican trait—the subordination of technical perfection to the irresistible propensity for the esthetic. The affinity for that which is pleasing to the eye was uppermost. Though capable of exact measurements, they avoided harsh angles. If the result was agreeable to man, the purpose, it is clear, was to please the gods.

It was long believed that these building complexes were not true cities but only ceremonial centers inhabited by priests, rulers, and their retainers. Today it is generally agreed that these centers were true cities. They contained temples, pyramids, palaces, tombs, observatories, and acropoli, as well as ball courts, steam baths, and causeways. While the upper classes lived there in luxurious chambers, the artisans, petty officials, soldiers, merchants, laborers, farmers, and others of the commoner class lived in modest huts constituting cluster communities in outlying regions. There they farmed the land, hunted, fished, carried the burdens, and performed all sorts of tasks necessary to support the aristocracy. Apparently only during festivals, usually religious in nature, or on market days, did the masses gather in the central precincts. These marvelous stone cities were conceived for an impression of grandeur and laid out in breathtaking expanses. The architects were true artists, interposing grand courtyards to offset with horizontal lines the massive vertical projections. Vladimir Kaspé writes that "the early builders treated space . . . with remarkable intelligence and sensitivity. They achieved what modern architects and town planners continually advocate: to 'compose' with space." They blended their creations with nature, he adds, and "they knew how to obtain textures and could dress stone so that it not only fulfilled its function but also reflected the Mexican sunlight."[2]

Whether or not an "urban revolution" occurred is debatable, but there is no question that concentrated populations in so many sites had an incalculable impact on culture. The arts always thrive with greatest vigor in an urban milieu, and intellectual growth is enhanced as well. At the same time, the stratification of society is inevitable. So, too, is a central administration to maintain order, promote public works, provide justice, set regulations—to perform, in short, on a more simplified scale, the functions familiar to city administrators of our own times. And although the details of how these early people of Mexico accomplished all this still evade us, there are signs of considerable efficiency. Great plazas and avenues were paved, buildings were plastered and painted, subterranean tile drainage systems were provided, waste was disposed of, domestic water supplies were channeled, and the staggering problems of food supply were met. Over the centuries central authority was maintained, it seems, in an atmosphere of progress and relative tranquility, at least in central Mexico.

Traditionally, the Classic period was viewed as having been devoted to moderation and comparative serenity, with order imposed by dominant centers such as Teotihuacán and Monte Albán. These powers, like city-states, carved out spheres of influence that were tolerated by others. Allowing for some exceptions over the centuries, this impression may have been largely true for the non-Maya cultures. Conflict is, nevertheless, part of the human condition, and it would be unrealistic to assume that the Classic peoples had risen completely above it. But for central Mexico, indications of warfare during the Classic are relatively few. Little evidence exists to indicate that cities were planned with defense in mind, until later times. Moreover, the abundant examples of art present almost no battle scenes, nor are warriors prominently depicted. Where humans are shown, it is the priests who predominate. Certain works of art, especially toward the end of the period, do show soldiers, weapons, and slaves, as well as indications of human sacrifice. Then, too, one may reasonably ask if the wide dispersion of culture was simply the result of

2. Vladimir Kaspé, preface to Henri Stierlin, *Living Architecture: Ancient Mexican* (New York, 1968), pp. 4–5.

peaceful exchange or whether it was imposed by force. No doubt some fighting occurred in the central regions, but it appears that in no sense did a warrior elite dominate.

However, we can no longer accept scenes of relative tranquility for the Classic Maya. Because of important revelations as a result of improved deciphering of Maya hieroglyphic script, the character of these people has been dramatically reassessed. The Maya genius in art, architecture, and science remains clear; nevertheless, the romanticized version of a society ruled by a benevolent and intellectual priesthood, shunning violence and conquest, now rings hollow. Scholars have revealed that aggressive Maya kings during the Classic period regularly made war on their neighbors for both ritualistic and materialistic motives. The most valued prize was another king, who would be humiliated over a period of time, subjected to exquisite tortures, and finally decapitated. These kings, with a profound sense of history, erected monuments to commemorate their victories and to record their lineage. Nevertheless, despite their bloody campaigns, it appears that no Maya city was ever able to impose its will on a large area, as in the case of the more northern power centers. Instead, there were scattered, independent sites, with no dominant capital. One authority believes that there may have been twenty cities of fifty thousand inhabitants or more and that altogether some 2 million Maya existed.

The unifying element in Classic societies was religion. In the early centuries admission to the religious hierarchy seems to have been by talent, but over the years it became increasingly hereditary. The priestly ranks not only held political authority but also constituted the intelligentsia. Priests were the scientists and the cultural leaders, giving strong direction to those below. In the pantheon of gods the most ancient was the rain god Tláloc (Chac to the Maya). To the god of the sun and goddess of the moon were added deities to celebrate the beneficence of fire, corn, and the butterfly. Ultimately, however, the most powerful of gods was Quetzalcóatl, the Feathered Serpent.

In these theocracies social cleavage was implicit. There was an order in which everyone had his assigned place. The individual, unless of the aristocratic sacerdotal class, counted for little. In this respect social stratification was like that in other parts of the world, except that perhaps the individual in Mexico had more security. There is no reason to believe that the masses did not perform their obligatory duties willingly, but the evidence on which to construct a satisfactory examination of Classic society is

Small, hairless *techichi* dogs from Colima were bred for the table and were also used as foot-warmers. Molded in various poses, these ceramic pieces are usually in the form of a vessel.

Poised for action, another Colima figure may represent either a warrior or an athlete.

A bearded musician sings and keeps rhythm with rasps. The clay figure, from the state of Nayarit (A.D. 300–900) is about 20 inches in height.

lamentably slim. Enough disturbing signs exist to caution against painting a scene of pagan paradise. Still, it is not excessive to suggest that people fared well compared to their contemporaries in other parts of the world.

After a spectacular run of several centuries, the Classic world in Middle America began to deteriorate. Just why the great centers fell is still a mystery, although all sorts of theories abound. While some of the cities went into gradual decline, others, it appears, met a sudden, violent end. Pressures of various kinds impinged on ordered ways: aggressive nomadic tribes on the peripheries played a role in some cases; demand for increased food supplies, the result of population pressures, crop failures, and possibly soil exhaustion, was another cause. Perhaps an internal disruption was occasioned by a peasants' revolt against the ruling classes, bred by excessive demands or the parasitic priests' inability to mediate successfully with the all-important nature gods. Or were there plagues of some kind? Conceivably there was war between the different cultures. The reasons no doubt vary from place to place, and there may well have been a combination of factors. In any event, the Golden Age came apart after a long period that stands as one of the brightest in the history of man.

Teotihuacán and Its Successors

Classic Mexico had many important centers, but three dominant cultures exercised great influence over surrounding regions— Teotihuacán, Monte Albán, and the Maya. The most important Indian site of its time was the immense urban complex of Teotihuacán, "the Place of the Gods," as the Aztecs were to call it. The overall expanse measured at least twelve square miles, in the core of which was the ceremonial center occupying about two square miles. Surrounding this precinct were the sumptuous quarters of the priests and their retainers, and on the outer fringes the masses resided in the rude dwellings that have long since disappeared. The population of the city at its height of prosperity remains in dispute, but it probably had as many as 250,000 inhabitants, making it one of the largest cities in the world at the time. Long after its fall the site was held in reverence and awe by succeeding cultures, and owing to the grandiose dimensions of its structures, the Aztecs considered it to have been built by a race of giants.

The origins of the Teotihuacanos are unknown, but by 200 B.C. they had begun to emerge as a superior culture in the central

The Pyramid of the Sun at Teotihuacán dominates the extensive ruins of the ancient city.

Valley of Mexico. Their carefully planned city, conceived in a grid pattern, was laid out on a colossal scale. Its main thoroughfare was the Avenue of the Dead, 150 feet wide and stretching over two miles through the heart of the ceremonial center. The most striking monument is the splendid Pyramid of the Sun, measuring over 700 feet at the base lines and rising about 215 feet high. Like most Mexican pyramids, the truncated structure served merely as a base for the elevation of a temple on top. It contains no inner chambers[3] but is filled with over a million cubic yards of sun-dried bricks and rubble. The summit, reached after an ascent of 268 steps, offers the breathless viewer a commanding sweep of the surrounding Valley. Even so, what we see today is a pale replica of the former magnificence of the Pyramid of the Sun. Now stripped of its thick outer layer and violated by

3. In 1974, however, tunnels were discovered underneath the pyramid.

Carved stone images of the rain god Tláloc and Quetzalcóatl on the Temple of Quetzalcóatl at Teotihuacán.

Detail of a plumed serpent head. The eyes at one time held red jewels, long since plucked out by vandals.

a botched reconstruction many years ago, it was originally larger, its slope faced with cut stone. Its construction probably occupied ten thousand workers for two decades.

Teotihuacán must have been a bustling metropolis, teeming with porters carrying goods to the marketplace, laborers erecting temples, artisans busily engaged with their crafts, and here and there the sober presence of the elegant lords. Along the main avenue were various kinds of edifices covered with lime stucco, painted, and polished. Walkways and courts were paved. There were about one hundred palaces for priests, the largest of which had an estimated three hundred rooms. Some of the salons contained bright frescoes. A ceremonial plaza covering about thirty-eight acres, now known as the Citadel, was flanked by fifteen low pyramid mounds. Near one end is the Temple of Quetzalcóatl, its incline studded with carved stone projections of the Feathered Serpent and Tláloc that are as phantasmic as medieval gargoyles.

The dominance of Teotihuacán was so extensive that some scholars have discussed it in terms of an empire, believing its hegemony to have been as broad as that of the later Aztecs. In any event, its sway reached from parts of northern Mexico down into Guatemala. For the most part, however, Monte Albán and the Maya culture remained independent of Teotihuacán. Within its sphere the impact of that great city consisted not only in its cultural imperialism with respect to art and architecture but also in its religious dominance, for it was a shrine to which pilgrims traveled from far away. Ruling the pantheon of gods was Quetzalcóatl, by this time a deity almost universal in the Mexican world. Although there is some evidence that human sacrifice may have occurred in the city, the cult of the Feathered Serpent held that the god wished sacrifices of snakes and butterflies, not humans.

For some reason, very likely related to an agricultural debacle, decline set in, inviting incursions by barbarians on the northern frontier. About A.D. 650 a weakened Teotihuacán fell to its enemies, who desecrated and burned the city. The fall of the mightiest center was the first casualty in the gradual decay of the Classic world in Mexico.

With the Teotihuacano culture dissipated, central Mexico lost its focus. Three centers remained, however, to exert some influence: Cholula in the modern state of Puebla, Xochicalco in Morelos, and El Tajín in Veracruz. Although all three had probably been satellites of Teotihuacán, each had its own distinct character. There was almost certainly contact among them, but whether they shared power or were in conflict with each other is uncertain.

Cholula was a holy city and a large center of considerable importance. While tradition has it that 365 Christian chapels were later built over the ruins of pagan temples, the actual number is closer to seventy. The nature of the city's relationship with Teotihuacán is not entirely clear, but it seems to have been close. The center was dominated by its massive pyramid, the largest single man-made monument in Indian America. Begun in Pre-Classic times, it is now considerably reduced in size and stripped of its outer layers. Still, its total volume is greater than that of Egypt's Pyramid of Cheops. It was a sanctuary of Quetzalcóatl, and many of the refugees from Teotihuacán fled to Cholula, which continued to flourish for about another century and a half. By around A.D. 800 Cholula had fallen to invaders, and there began a five-hundred-year rule by a resurgent Olmec tyranny.

Xochicalco, first built around 200 B.C. atop small mountains, is of interest as a transition culture, exhibiting influences of both Teotihuacán and the Maya. The original purpose of its elevated

The Pyramid of the Niches, El Tajín, state of Veracruz.

site may not have been strategic, but it appears that with the later unleashing of the Olmec despotism Xochicalco was fortified with moats and parapets. It is the earliest known fortress site in central Mexico and is a manifestation of the alarming trend to militarism that developed there in the Late Classic period.

El Tajín had extensive influence along the Gulf coast. After the decline of Teotihuacán, it was very likely the most powerful culture of the three sites under discussion. A dramatic example of its unique architecture is the pyramid of niches, of which there is one for each day of the year.

The vigorous life at Tajín included bloody rites that anticipated the terror of the Post-Classic period. The ball game, *ollama*,

A ball court at Monte Albán. The ball game of *ollama* (*tlachtli*), was played in many different cultures, although the rules and courts varied somewhat.

was an ancient tradition that became an obsession with these lowland peoples. Most of the prominent centers in Mexico had ball courts, and Tajín had no fewer than eleven. Along each side of the court (which could vary considerably in length, according to the culture) was a wall on which a stone ring was fixed. Two teams played, the object being to keep the seven- to eight-inch solid rubber ball out of the opponents' possession and, if possible, to hit the ball through one of the rings. Scoring was exceedingly difficult, not only because the ring was small and high but also because the players could not hit the ball with their hands. Often they were allowed to use only their hips, although it seems that rules differed according to time and place. The athletes wore padding in vulnerable spots, as the flying ball could kill if struck with sufficient force. Contests were played with great enthusiasm, and on some occasions large sums were wagered. Ollama was more than a game, however; it was a sacred ritual in imitation of the movement of celestial bodies and associated with man's fate. On occasion the teams represented political factions. So serious was ollama taken that the losing captain was sometimes sacrificed, as scenes on the architectural friezes depict. A variation on the agreement was that the losers became slaves of the victors.

Monte Albán

From its lofty eminence thirteen hundred feet above the valley floor, Monte Albán, the creation of the Zapotecs, dominated surrounding Oaxaca for centuries. Less grand in scale than Teotihuacán, it was nevertheless spacious, poised on a rocky shelf over three thousand feet long and half again as wide. Urban construction was carried out at great cost in human effort because all materials, and even water, had to be hauled up the mountainsides. Grouped around its great paved plaza were many temples, platforms, and low pyramids, along with sunken patios. Unlike most of the other cultures of the Classic, the Zapotecs, with some two hundred sites, had kings, but the influence of the high priests was such, at least in domestic affairs, that government was more theocracy than monarchy. Monte Albán was one of the oldest of important Classic centers, for the Zapotecs were there by 600 B.C.

After A.D. 650 Monte Albán was possibly the single most powerful force in Mexico for some time, extending its influence into some areas formerly dominated by Teotihuacán. The extent to which its authority was challenged by the expansionist Tajín state has not been satisfactorily defined. Unaccountably, Monte Albán began to lose its cohesion sometime during the ninth century A.D. Whatever the reasons, whether from economic pressures or internal political problems, by A.D. 900 the great Zapotec center was abandoned. There is no indication, however, that the general populace served by that center left their homes. The region was ultimately invaded by the neighboring Mixtecs, with whom the Zapotecs coexisted for quite some time.

An overview of Monte Albán in Oaxaca, showing its platforms and expansive plazas.

Incised on stone slabs, curious figures who seem to be dancing are a feature of Monte Albán. They are called *danzantes*.

PRINCIPAL ARCHAEOLOGICAL SITES

The Maya

Of all the Classic groups, the Maya have generally been considered the most brilliant. But while their luster is not diminished, it now seems clear that they were not the first great civilization in Middle America and that, in fact, their rise to greatness
not only came considerably after that of the Olmecs but probably
later than that of Teotihuacán and Monte Albán as well. The
early history of the Maya is nebulous; however, by the beginning
of our era they were evolving into an advanced state, and by
A.D. 300 they were into their full Classic stage. Great expansion
and the florescence of Maya culture began around A.D. 600 and
lasted until about A.D. 900.

The Classic Maya had so many important centers, no one of
which completely dominated the others, that they must be dealt
with collectively. A good number of them, moreover, were outside of Mexico. If it can be said that Maya civilization had a

In dark hardwood, this unusual carving depicts a dignified worthy from the Tabasco Maya culture. It dates from the early Classic period.

heart, it would have to be considered the Petén, that northern-most region of Guatemala jutting up into southern Mexico. The area's isolation from the main corridors of migration allowed the Maya to achieve cultural stability with little foreign corruption. Their descendants were the last to be conquered by the Span-iards, not until 1697. But the Classic Maya also lived in the Mexi-can states of Chiapas, Tabasco, Campeche, and Yucatan, as well as in Quintana Roo.

The Petén was an unlikely region for settlement. Even today the forest, the inaccessibility, and unpleasant insects make it un-attractive, and it is very sparsely settled. But corn grew well enough in the soil, and there was an ample supply of limestone for constructing majestic buildings. Maya architecture was char-acterized by false fronts of mansard-style roofs and combs; the pyramids were more narrow and steep than those of other cul-tures. Like Teotihuacán and Monte Albán, the Maya had a vig-orous ceramic tradition and produced lovely polychrome bowls. In their exotic murals and bas-reliefs, however, they tended less to the geometric designs of central Mexico and more to the de-piction of the human form, often rendered with superb drafts-manship. Furthermore, there is an exuberance in the Maya style that stands much in contrast to the more restrained northern tra-dition. The great fluidity of Maya art gives it a baroque quality, whether in stone or stucco. Of the fascinating pictorial manu-scripts, only three survived the ravages of time, climate, insects, and the fires of Spanish clergymen.

The Maya stand as the premier scientists of ancient America, for if others invented calendars and writing, it was they who car-ried them to their highest expression. Like other Mexican calen-dars, theirs had 365 days; in addition, a ceremonial calendar had 260 days. The Maya did not, however, measure small units of time, like minutes and hours. Whereas we fix the beginning of our era with the birth of Christ, the Maya established theirs at the equivalent of 3133 B.C., apparently for mythical reasons. The preoccupation of the Maya with dates resulted in the pe-riodic chronological markings on stone pillars (stelae) that, in spite of the disputed correlations, allow us to convert them to our calendar. Because of their careful records, the descendants of the Post-Classic ruling Xiu family in Yucatán can trace their lineage back to the time of Charlemagne, that is, to about A.D. 800. Each date was assigned characteristics so distinctive that it would not recur in the records until the passage of 374,400 years. One of the Maya's mathematical units was the equivalent of 64 million.

The Temple of the Sun at Palenque is framed by thick jungle growth.

Although central Mexican pyramids are usually solid, without interior chambers, to the south temple-pyramids of the Maya sometimes contain tombs like the one shown here at Palenque's "Temple of the Inscriptions."

A superb stucco head with an elegant headdress found at the Temple of the Inscriptions at Palenque.

So puzzling are their hieroglyphs that it has taken years for scholars to master them.

The metropolis of the Maya Classic was Tikal, with a population in the nearby region estimated to have reached close to one hundred thousand. It is one of the earliest sites, having been settled by A.D. 292, the date of the earliest inscription. Set in a clearing of Guatemala's Petén jungle, Tikal is dominated by six great pyramids, including the tallest of any in the Maya civilization,

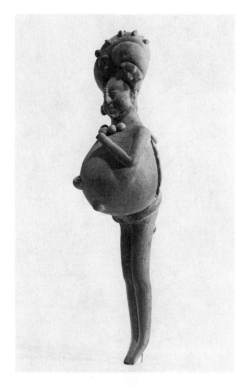

A pot-bellied, seed-filled ceramic rattle from the Maya culture on the small island of Jaina, off the coast of Campeche.

Of the same Maya culture is this whistle, in the form of an embracing couple.

towering 230 feet. The inner precinct covers more than a square mile, with other ceremonial edifices surrounding the core for a considerable distance. Aside from the usual temples, palaces, plazas, and ball courts, Tikal had ten reservoirs and was beautified by artificial lakes.

In a secondary category were other large cities. Uaxactún, a few miles north of Tikal, was apparently the oldest site, with a vault bearing the date A.D. 278. Yaxchilán, in the modern state of Chiapas, is known for its great central plaza, a thousand feet long. Palenque (Chiapas), though relatively small, is considered the gem of the Maya cities because of its exquisite sculpture. The bas-relief work there shows the art in its highest form. Although of minor importance in most respects, Bonampak (Chiapas) contains the most illustrious of the Maya murals. And Dzibilchaltún on the Yucatán Peninsula, long thought to be of less significance, now appears to have been one of the largest of the New World cities. With its multiple ceremonial precincts and numerous house mounds, it may have had fifty thousand structures. Dzibilchaltún was, moreover, populated continuously for three thousand years, from 1500 B.C. to the time of the Spanish conquest.

There may have been no common cause for the decline of all the Classic Maya centers, scattered as they were over considerable distances. Again, speculation suggests insufficient food supplies resulting from pestilence, locusts, earthquakes, or a confluence of these and other factors. There is also a reasonable chance that invaders from central Mexico introduced terror among the Maya, who themselves became more warlike toward the end. Equally credible is the thesis that the masses finally rose up in rebellion against the aristocracy in a social revolution. Although all sites did not fall simultaneously, by around A.D. 900 the cities were abandoned to the fecund jungle growth. They remained lost to the outside world until their lichen-mottled ruins were rediscovered almost a thousand years later. Thus the Classic world in Mexico folded, marking a turning point in history. What followed was distinctly different.

Recommended for Further Study

Adams, Richard E. W., ed. *The Origins of Maya Civilization.* Albuquerque: University of New Mexico Press, 1977.

Coe, Michael D. *The Maya.* London: Thames and Hudson, 1980.

———. *Mexico.* New York: Praeger, 1967.

Culbert, T. P., ed. *The Classic Maya Collapse.* Albuquerque: University of New Mexico Press, 1977.

Hammond, Norman. *Ancient Maya Civilization.* New Brunswick, N.J.: Rutgers University Press, 1982.

Kubler, George. *Art and Architecture of Ancient America.* Harmondsworth and Baltimore: Pelican, 1984.

Miller, Mary Ellen. *The Murals of Bonampak.* Princeton, N.J.: Princeton University Press, 1986.

Paddock, John, ed. *Ancient Oaxaca: Discoveries in Mexican Archaeology and History.* Stanford, Calif.: Stanford University Press, 1966.

Schele, Linda, and Mary Ellen Miller. *The Blood of Kings. Dynasty and Ritual in Maya Art.* Fort Worth: Kimbell Art Museum, 1986.

Weaver, Muriel Porter. *The Aztecs, Maya, and Their Predecessors. Archaeology of Mesoamerica.* New York: Academic Press, 1981.

Whitecotton, Joseph W. *The Zapotecs: Princes, Priests and Peasants.* Norman: University of Oklahoma Press, 1977.

3

Times of Trouble: Post-Classic Mexico

The order imposed by Teotihuacán's dominance during the Classic period gave way to a fragmentation of power among the transition centers. Details of history in the Valley of Mexico are nebulous from A.D. 650 to 900, but one has the impression of confusion and a great shifting of peoples in the waning decades of the Classic, when aggressive city-states—Cholula, Xochicalco, and El Tajín—vied for control, but none succeeding in bringing about unity and order. Then gradually a new period emerges, with very different characteristics.

The Post-Classic era began about A.D. 900 and lasted until the Spanish Conquest in the early sixteenth century. Culturally a plateau had been reached; indeed, in many respects the succeeding centuries were inferior to the Classic. Nor was there significant intellectual and scientific growth. Although metallurgy was introduced, probably from South America, its use was very limited. Gold and silver were fashioned into beautiful jewelry and copper was used in the manufacture of various tools and to cover the tips of arrow shafts.

The most striking change during the Post-Classic, especially for central Mexico, can be seen in the political systems, which became depressingly similar to those of the Old World. Now there appeared militaristic societies in which the prizes of war were no longer territorial but tributes to be exacted from the subject states. Political power was seized by a warrior elite whose ascendancy checked the traditional powers of religious leaders. Religion itself was cheapened with the rising importance of frightful gods thought to require ever-increasing quantities of the "divine liquid"—human blood. This orgy of human sacrifice was played out in the last bloody rites subsequent to the fall of the final Indian rulers of Mexico, the Aztecs.

Taking A.D. 900 as the pivotal date introducing the Post-Classic, we discern the emergence of historical central Mexico; for while earlier history must be deduced cautiously from archaeological evidence alone, there are in this period the beginnings of written records in which individuals appear with more clarity. But although there are now pegs upon which to drape our historical fabric, accounts are manifestly shot through with myths; thus some details vary with the telling, and many versions are vague and fragmentary at best.

The Toltecs

The great city of Teotihuacán, situated on the northern edge of the lake, had served as a buffer between civilized Mexico and the nomadic barbarians of the north. With the fall of that stronghold, however, the frontier was breached by vigorous warriors from the lands beyond. The northern tribes, consisting of many diverse groups, were known by the generic term *Chichimecs*, which meant, literally, "People of Dog Lineage" but carried none of the pejorative implications we might assign it. The most important of these were the Tolteca-Chichimeca, or Toltecs, whose origins were probably in southern Zacatecas. At the beginning of the tenth century they swept into the central valley led by Mixcóatl (Cloud Serpent), a Mexican Ghengis Khan who swifty scattered his demoralized opponents. After establishing his capital at Culhuacán and successfully extending his power, the resourceful Mixcóatl was assassinated by his brother, who seized leadership for himself.

Mixcóatl's pregnant wife fled into exile, where she died on giving birth to a son. The boy was given the name Ce Acatl Topiltzin (Ce Acatl meaning "One Reed," the year of his birth, perhaps A.D. 947, and Topiltzin meaning "Our Prince"), and he would become the cultural hero of foremost proportions in ancient Mexico. Reared in Tepoztlán, the boy completed his education at nearby Xochicalco, where he became a devotee of the ancient god Quetzalcóatl. Later, as a high priest of the cult, he assumed the name of his deity.

Upon reaching manhood, Topiltzin-Quetzalcóatl sought his destiny. With the support of his dead father's loyal partisans, he killed in single combat his uncle, Mixcóatl's assassin, and made himself lord of the Toltecs. Topiltzin-Quetzalcóatl eventually removed his capital some fifty miles northwest of the present Mexico City to a remote site on the frontier. There, around A.D. 968, he founded the splendid city of Tula, the most important city in the long interim between the fall of Teotihuacán and the later rise of Aztec Tenochtitlán. A semibarbarous people, the Toltecs only gradually absorbed the more advanced ways of central Mexico. From their new capital they asserted power over most of central Mexico and beyond. Although their hegemony lasted only about two centuries, their prestige was such that the name Toltec pervaded the consciousness of the land for five hundred years.

The legends of Tula that would so haunt the later Aztecs were at least in part pure confection. They began with the incredible benefactions attributed to Topiltzin-Quetzalcóatl, whose mythical achievements are interwoven with those of the Feathered Serpent god himself. According to tradition, Topiltzin-Quetzalcóatl, as the great leader of infinite knowledge, showed his people how to plant the "miraculous" corn, and under his tutelage all cultivated plant life yielded produce of gigantic size. Fields of cotton were a marvel, as the tufts of the plant emerged naturally in a variety of rich colors. Even the cacao trees (which, in fact, flourish in tropical lowlands) were said to be multihued. The ruler was also responsible for writing, the ritual calendar, and the architectural wonders of Tula. He was, indeed, the author of all benefits to mankind.

Less extensive than Teotihuacán, Tula was certainly more grandiose than its ruins today indicate. Palace interiors were decked with the brilliant plumage of exotic birds, while various salons were lined with sheets of gold, jewels, and rare seashells. Residents' ears were soothed by the sweet singing of pet birds. This version of paradise on earth, in which there was an abundance of all things, was embellished in the retelling over the centuries; it accounts, in part, for the curiously persistent Toltec mystique.

This honeyed tradition notwithstanding, all was not peace and light at Tula, for despite the undeniable prestige of Topiltzin-Quetzalcóatl, dissident factions existed within his capital. For one thing, diverse tribes, not yet amalgamated into a homogeneous society, lived in the city. Moreover, the ancestral supreme deity of the Toltecs was Tezcatlipoca (Smoking Mirror, or Shining Smoke), an invisible and unpredictable god who was feared—

The ingenuous Topiltzin-Quetzalcóatl is deceived by the crafty Tezcatlipoca.

and never crossed. His adherents resented the exaltation of the foreign god Quetzalcóatl introduced by Topiltzin. The priests of Tezcatlipoca bided their time, conspiring against the heresy.

The cult of the Feathered Serpent was the higher form of religion, as may be seen in its monotheism as well as by the wish of the god to be gratified only by modest sacrifices of butterflies, birds, or snakes, and offerings of jade, incense, or merely tortillas. Tezcatlipoca, on the other hand, demanded human hearts. His followers sought by various deceits to discredit the high priest of Quetzalcóatl. According to one account, Tezcatlipoca, in disguise, gained entrance to the house of Topiltzin, who was ill. At first the ruler refused an offer of "medicine," which was, in fact, the strong drink of *pulque*, made from undistilled cactus juice. Finally persuaded to take a sip, the innocent Topiltzin found it pleasing and asked for more. At length inebriated by five cupfuls, the lord of Tula awoke the next morning on a mat beside his sister. Having broken his priestly vows and disgraced himself by the sins of drunkenness and incest, he prepared to go into exile after almost twenty years of enlightened rule.

The benevolent reign of Topiltzin-Quetzalcóatl at Tula thus came to a close, but he does not disappear from history. He and his followers traveled to the holy city of Cholula, and in 987 they sailed across the Gulf of Mexico to the land of the Maya, where their impact was sharply felt. The legendary exit of the great Topiltzin-Quetzalcóatl is appropriate, if fantastic: he coasted

Giant stone warriors at Tula were manifestations of the militaristic spirit that came to dominate the Toltecs.

down a river to the sea in a raft of serpents, after which he flashed into the heavens to become the morning star.

A more prosaic denouement, though heavily laden with the most serious implications, is the more credible version. When Topiltzin and his partisans left Tula for their long odyssey, they marked their way by shooting arrows through saplings, leaving crosslike signs. Later he sent word that he would return from where the sun rose to take back his rightful throne in the year Ce Acatl, which recurred cyclically. Now, by tradition, he was of fair complexion and bearded. All of this would be of immense significance when, five centuries later, the Spaniards—white, bearded, and wearing crosses—appeared on the eastern horizon. The year was 1519—and Ce Acatl.

Meanwhile, with the success of the militant Tezcatlipoca faction at Tula, a new order of things evolved. While the reputation of the Toltecs as great architects was secure (the Aztecs named them Toltecs, meaning "Artificers"), a new and fearsome image of them was revealed in later works. Towering statues of impassive warrior figures, sixteen to eighteen feet tall, appeared on top of temples, and friezes symbolized the military orders of the jaguar and eagle, the latter of which were shown devouring human hearts. Tula nourished two traditions that persisted until the coming of the Spaniards—an excess of human sacrifice and the forceful conquest of other states. An aggressive expansionist policy led the Toltec legions to create an empire that in size approximated that of Classic Teotihuacán.

From the late eleventh century to 1156, drought and famine struck the Toltecs. Wars further weakened the state until, in desperation, the people even turned to the worship of their enemies' alien deities. Finally they abandoned Tula in despair, and the great Toltec diaspora began, with people spreading in many directions. The collapse of Tula was very significant for Mexico: once again the northern march between the sedentary peoples of the Valley and the northern barbarians was left unguarded. Not long after, new hordes descended upon this wonder of the Post-Classic world and subjected Tula to brutal desecration.

The Zapotecs and Mixtecs

To the south, following the abandonment of Monte Albán in Oaxaca, the Zapotecs remained a vigorous culture with many important centers. Their capital was at Zaachila, but the site

A palace at Mitla.

Detail of the palace showing the intricate geometric designs formed by precision stone cutting.

that interests us most is Mitla, built roughly the same time as Tula. Mitla was a comparatively small religious and military base. What one sees there, however, is a jewel of Mexican architecture. Surrounding a modest courtyard are white temples with walls of marvelous design—thousands of small pieces of cut stone, fitted together with a precision requiring no mortar, form mosaics of dazzling geometric patterns. Opening off the patios are subterranean passages leading to crypts. Although the site is in an exposed area, set apart some distance is the hill fortress, a grim reminder of the intense warfare that had overtaken Post-Classic Mexico.

To the areas west and north of the Zapotecs were a remarkable people who inhabited the mountainous regions, the Mixtecs, or Cloud People. The Mixtecs were certainly influenced by the Toltecs, some of whom apparently infiltrated after the fall of Tula. By the thirteenth century the Mixtecs were penetrating eastward into Zapotec territories, and, through open warfare and intermarriage, they eventually came to dominate their neighbors. At times they occupied many of the Zapotec sites, including Monte Albán and Mitla.

Mixtec artistic achievements are extraordinary. Among the treasures they gave us is the richest collection extant of picture *códices* in Mexico. These "books" are executed in brilliant colors on deerskin (the books of the Maya and others were made of vegetable fiber). They are also valuable historical sources. One gives data reaching back to A.D. 692, providing the earliest historical narrative of any society in the land. Mixtec *códices* also tell us that by the early years of the eighth century militaristic city-states had formed. Following the appearance of metallurgy around A.D. 1000, the Mixtecs became, in addition, the foremost jewelers in Mexico, fashioning delicate pieces in gold and silver.

The Post-Classic Maya

Coincident with the final distintegration of the Maya Classic period by around A.D. 900, there was a rising Maya cultural phenomenon on the peninsula of Yucatán. That peninsula is a limestone shelf, flat with some rolling, brush-covered hills, a land without surface rivers. With its thin soil and dependence for water on the *cenotes*, the sinkholes created by the collapse of underground caverns, it was an unlikely location for an agricultural people. Maya groups had inhabited Yucatán for many cen-

This unusual ceramic vessel, created in the Classic Period, is in the form of a stylized monkey wearing a startled expression.

A Mixtec vase from Zaachila. Representations of death were and still are common and are often treated lightly.

A Oaxacan gold pendant of a solar disk, with a bell.

turies B.C., but their achievements had not matched those of the southern Maya who flourished during the Classic era.

Beginning in the tenth century, the ancestral Yucatec Maya culture was adulterated by outside influences of peoples stigmatized as "foreigners." Some of the newcomers were undoubtedly refugees from the deserted Classic areas. But the invigorating force that gave impulse to the new hybrid style in Yucatán came from the northwest, with the dramatic appearance of Topiltzin-Quetzalcóatl and his Toltecs. Arriving in 987, the wanderers from Tula introduced the harsher traditions of the central highlands of Mexico. The Toltecs of Chichén Itzá made an alliance,

During the period of Toltec rule, curious Chacmool figures appeared at Chichén Itzá.

perhaps for mutual security, with the cities of Mayapán and
Uxmal. This triple alliance, the Mayapán League, was dominated by Chichén Itzá and, according to some accounts, lasted
for over two centuries.

The period of Toltec (or Mexican) rule was dynamic and prosperous, a time of great activity. The Maya region under the control of the Toltecs was much smaller than the broad dimensions
of the Classic Maya sphere. Tragically, the malaise that was
sweeping the northern regions of Mexico was insinuated in Yucatán. Under Toltec rule a military caste seized power, and
human sacrifice among the Yucatec Maya apparently became

A great ball court in the Maya style at
Chichén Itzá. Scores were seldom made
by knocking the ball through the high
ring. This city had six ball courts, one of
which, the largest in Middle America,
measures 480 by 120 feet.

Detail of the carved stone ring.

A heavily padded Maya ball player is portrayed in this graceful sculpture from Jaina.

more common. The new order of things was evident in the art
and architecture, both reflecting the militant spirit of the invaders: the ruins of Chichén Itzá are strikingly evocative of far-
off Tula. To the local Maya architecture dating from the sixth
century, a new style was joined. Thus, in the warrior motifs, images of the Feathered Serpent, the forest of columns, even in the
appearance of the quaint Chacmools (reclining stone figures),
an exotic cast is given to the city. Among the monuments of Post-
Classic Maya centers, those of Toltec Chichén Itzá are the most
widely known. Though distinctive, they are, in the words of
Eric Thompson, "showy, but unstable."[1] Like the sculptures, they
are esthetically less pleasing than works of the Classic Maya.
Uxmal, however, has structures of great beauty. Its Palace of the
Governor "is considered by many to be the most elegant of pre-
Hispanic architecture."[2]

With the arrival of the Toltecs in Maya lands, Quetzalcóatl
(called Kukulcán by the Maya) entered the pantheon of local
deities. Traditionally the most powerful of Maya gods was It-
zamná, while the rain god Chac and the gods of corn and the sun
were also important. Into the great Sacred Cenote, a well measuring some two hundred feet across at the mouth, victims (although infrequently the virgins so dear to modern tradition)
were cast, along with jewels and other valuables, to appease the
rain god. Human sacrifice continued to increase after the Toltec
phase had passed, but the practice never reached the excesses
that were to overtake central Mexico.

Some authorities believe that the elitist priestly class lost considerable political and cultural influence to rising utilitarian
merchants. Expanded commerce, some by sea, and increased production enhanced the peasants' lot.[3] But increasing repression by
the militarists led to rebellion. In the subsequent fighting between Chichén Itzá and Mayapán, the latter emerged the victor.
After some two centuries the Mayapán League broke apart, but
the wonder is that it lasted as long as it did, considering its conflicting economic and political interests.

Henceforth a dozen cities of northern Yucatán were dominated by Mayapán, and, from 1200 or so until about 1450, a period of general decline set in. The Toltecs were absorbed, and
their cultural influence disappeared. The new rulers established

1. J. Eric S. Thompson, *The Rise and Fall of Maya Civilization* (Norman, 1966),
   p. 141.
2. Justino Fernández, *Mexican Art* (London, 1965), p. 37.
3. Jeremy Sabloff and William Rathje, "The Rise of a Maya Merchant Class," *Scientific American* 233 (1975):72–82.

A reconstruction of Chichén Itzá shows the broad thoroughfare leading from the Temple of Kukulcán to the Sacred Cenote (well).

a strongly centralized regime maintained by Mexican merce-naries, by intermarriage, and by forcing all local chiefs from outlying areas to reside in Mayapán as hostages. Under this tyr-anny the capital was a walled city within which the inhabitants lived for security, while the economy was less oriented to agri-culture and trade than to the parasitical dependence on tribute paid by subject towns. In the two and a half centuries there was a general lowering of standards: building construction was not only shoddy but devoid of beauty, hieroglyphic inscriptions ceased, and it seems that athletes even stopped playing the sa-cred ball game.

The shattering of Mayapán hegemony resulted in the decen-tralization of the Yucatec Maya, in which some sixteen petty city-states clung feebly to the vestiges of the distant past. An-archy now became widespread as warfare among the various groups was almost constant. The neglected cities fell into ruin,

The Temple of Kukulcán, also known as "El Castillo."

sometimes hastened by vicious and wanton destruction by marauders. Indeed one finds few redeeming qualities in this final crumbling phase, a melancholy time with little ennobling or creative vitality. To the casualties of war were added, during the last half of the fifteenth century, the victims of plagues and a disastrous hurricane. When the first Spanish adventurers arrived in the Yucatán Peninsula a few decades later, they found only the demoralized and impoverished descendants of the grandeur that was the Maya civilization for so many centuries.

Despite their amazing skills, the Maya architects never developed the true arch; however, a corbeled vault of the type pictured here served much the same purpose. This is the magnificent Palace of the Governor at Uxmal, measuring more than 320 feet in length and 25 feet in height.

Recommended for Further Study

Castedo, Leopoldo. *A History of Latin American Art and Architecture from Precolumbian Times to the Present*. New York: Praeger, 1969.

Davies, Nigel. *The Toltecs: Until the Fall of Tula*. Norman: University of Oklahoma Press, 1977.

Fox, John W. *Maya Postclassic State Formation*. New York: Cambridge University Press, 1987.

Hardoy, Jorge. *Precolumbian Cities*. New York: Walker, 1973.

Katz, Friedrich. *The Ancient American Civilizations*. New York: Praeger, 1974.

Kelemen, Pál. *Art of the Americas, Ancient and Hispanic*. New York: Crowell, 1969.

Peterson, Frederick A. *Ancient Mexico: An Introduction to the Pre-Hispanic Cultures*. London: George Allen & Unwin, 1959.

Robertson, Donald. *Mexican Manuscript Painting of the Early Colonial Period*. New Haven, Conn.: Yale University Press, 1959.

Soustelle, Jacques. *Mexico*. Translated by James Hogarth. Cleveland: World, 1967.

Spores, Ronald. *The Mixtecs in Ancient and Colonial Times*. Norman: University of Oklahoma Press, 1985.

Thompson, J. Eric S. *The Rise and Fall of Maya Civilization*. Norman: University of Oklahoma Press, 1966.

Von Hagen, Victor W. *World of the Maya*. New York: Mentor, 1960.

4

The Rise of the Barbarians

The high Valley of Anáhuac—the Indian name for the Valley of Mexico, meaning "near the water"—was a compelling lure to rootless peoples seeking a more abundant life. With its equable climate and system of interconnecting lakes bordered by forests full of wild game, it was especially attractive to the nomads of the arid north. Because of its central location the Valley had been, from ancient times, a corridor through which tribes of diverse cultures passed—and sometimes remained. This cultural mélange produced a rich environment for the exchange of ideas and skills. Moreover, traders and merchants introduced exotic products from the coasts and other regions, thereby adding to the variety of life. At the same time, alien groups were frequently hostile, so that the lake country was periodically upset by violence. While there was little danger of cultural stagnation, the continual disruptions were not conducive to the relatively more settled traditions preserved in some of the more isolated Oaxaca and Maya lands for so many centuries. In the Valley of Anáhuac there was calm and order only when a dominant center such as Teotihuacán or Tula prevailed.

The Chichimecs and Tepanecs

With the power vacuum created by the collapse of Tula in the twelfth century, primitive Chichimecs again poured into the Valley from the north. By the early thirteenth century the Valley was teeming with activity and becoming increasingly crowded, with many of the attendant pressures so familiar to us today. It was an age of anxiety and tension. The first barbarian groups quickly staked out their claims, and later arrivals found no available space. The early Chichimecs settled in the proximity of established towns populated by remnants of Toltec refugees who had kept alive some semblance of a higher civilization. The phenomenon so familiar in history occurred: the militant savages gradually adopted the more advanced ways of their sedentary neighbors.

Most prominent of the early invader chieftains was Xólotl (Monster), who led his people into the northern reaches of the Valley in 1244. The "Chichimecs of Xólotl" entrenched themselves at their capital of Tenayuca and proceeded to dominate the immediate area. Their military successes owed much to the "revolutionary" weapon of the bow and arrow, used with devastating effect against the cruder atl-atl of ancient times, which the Toltecs still employed. The Chichimec archers were as significant in their way as were the English longbowmen in the military history of Europe.

During the long reign of Xólotl (1244–1304) Chichimec hegemony was established. In 1246 the Chichimecs conquered the prestigious city of Culhuacán, and, in order to give respectability to the Chichimec dynasty, Xólotl, with sure instinct, married his son Nopaltzin (Revered Prickly Pear) to a princess of the vanquished Toltecs. In other ways, too, contact with sedentary agricultural towns mellowed the crude northerners. Though they had at first preferred living in caves, the Chichimecs gradually built dwellings; they exchanged their animal skins for woven cloth garments; they ceased eating raw meat in favor of cooked meat; and they made wider use of agricultural foods, especially corn. The Chichimecs also adopted the Náhuatl language, which was becoming the *lingua franca* of the Valley.

While the followers of Xólotl at Tenayuca were improving their lineage, becoming more refined, and broadening their political influence, other cities in the Valley were emerging to prominence as well. Atzcapotzalco, originally settled long before by refugees from the ancient Teotihuacán, was infiltrated by a nomadic group known as the Tepanecs in the year 1230. Like others in the surrounding region, the Tepanecs ultimately recognized Xólotl as overlord and received land from him, and Xólotl gave his daughters in marriage to cement alliances.

At length the stronghold of Tenayuca went into decline, and, with the passing of Xólotl, the ascending power was Atzcapotzalco. Under the extended rule of Acolhua (1304–63) the Tepanecs of that thriving metropolis wrested important cities from their rivals. But the most domineering figure of his time was Acolhua's son, Tezozómoc, who lived from 1320 to 1427. Through deceit, dynastic marriages, violence, and treachery, this great tyrant made Atzcapotzalco the most powerful center in the Valley. Using the soldiery of the petty warlords as mercenaries, he was able to crush Tenayuca and take the important city of Culhuacán. In the last quarter of the fourteenth century, Tezozómoc and his allies extended the Tepanec dominions even further, conquering many centers, including Xochimilco, and spilling over the mountains southward to seize Cuauhnáhuac (now Cuernavaca).

Paralleling the rise of Atzcapotzalco was Texcoco, founded by Quinatzin, a great-grandson of Xólotl. From its modest beginnings (ca. 1318), the city made steady progress during the founder's reign, which lasted until 1377. But Texcoco gradually fell on hard times, owing to internecine strife. Then, under the rule of Ixtlilxóchitl (1409–18), the city was attacked by the forces of Tezozómoc. Defeated in battle, Ixtlilxóchitl retreated to a remote spot where he faced his pursuers alone. After a valiant struggle, he was impaled on the spears of his enemies in full view of his young son, Nezahualcóyotl (Fasting Coyote), who was concealed in a tree. This heir to the throne of Texcoco managed to escape the henchmen of Tezozómoc and finally found sanctuary across the mountains to the east. "In order to wipe out the memory of Ixtlilxochitl," writes Frederick Peterson, "Tezozomoc had his soldiers ask every child in Texcoco under the age of seven, 'Who is your king?' When the little children answered either 'Ixtlilxochitl' or 'Nezahualcoyotl,' they were immediately struck down with obsidian-edged clubs. In this way several thousand children were put to death before parents taught their children the name of Tezozomoc."[1]

Two years later, in 1420, at age one hundred, and having reigned since 1363, the hoary tyrant finally relinquished his rule. Through politics of terror, Tezozómoc had succeeded in unifying under one government most of central Mexico. And, as Wigberto Jiménez Moreno observes, Tezozómoc invites comparison with his contemporaries, the Italian princes of the Renaissance, so

---

1. Frederick A. Peterson, *Ancient Mexico: An Introduction to the Pre-Hispanic Cultures* (London, 1959), p. 79.

much so that the Tepanec ruler might have been inspired by *The Prince* of Machiavelli.[2] Yet, though he lived on for six or seven years, his territories were divided and Atzcapotzalco power vitiated.

The Aztec Rise to Power

The irruption of the Chichimecs from the dun wastelands of the north included one group that engages our attention above all others. While they called themselves the Mexica (pronounced "Mesheeka"), they have become more commonly known as the Aztecs. No tribe of record had more humble beginnings and rose to such heights in so short a time. Over the long view of pre-Hispanic Mexico, they must be regarded as upstarts, latecomers on the scene. The last of the important nomadic groups to enter the Valley, they were beginning to acquire some notoriety about two hundred years prior to the Spanish Conquest, but their rise to great power occurred less than a century before the advent of Cortés in 1519.

The origins of the Aztecs are apparently found on an island off the coast of the state of Nayarit, at Aztatlán or Aztlán, from which many tribes wandered southward. Historical accounts for the first decades following their departure from Aztlán, evidently in A.D. 1111, are fragmentary and unreliable, for, once secure, the Aztecs destroyed all the records and reconstructed their history with accounts favorable to themselves. Full of symbolism and myths, these official histories concede no Aztec defeats and are at pains to establish (however spuriously) Toltec roots. Eventually the Aztecs came to call themselves the Culhúa-Mexica, thus asserting a relationship with the prestigious Toltec culture of Culhuacán.

The Aztecs' great search for the promised land logically enough led them toward the verdant intermontane basin of Anáhuac, but they arrived there only after many decades of wandering. Somewhere along the way they came to conceive of themselves as a messianic people, the chosen of the gods. They pressed on, inspired by visions of their imperial destiny and by the persistent twitterings of their strange hummingbird god. Their su-

2. José Miranda et al., *Historia de México* (Mexico, 1971), p. 115. These chapters on Indian Mexico, especially the parts treating the Chichimecs, rely much on the various findings of Wigberto Jiménez Moreno.

The founding of the Aztec capital of Tenochtitlán, as depicted in the Codex Mendoza.

preme deity was the terrible Huitzilopochtli (Hummingbird of
the South), god of war and the sun.

At length these nomads made their way into the Valley of
Mexico, where they found a cold reception. To begin with, all
the lands were already carved up into various city-states. The
Aztecs became unwelcome squatters, a boorish, uncouth lot, disposed to all sorts of vulgarities. They were held in disdain by the
more refined farming residents of the Valley, who encouraged
the barbarians to keep moving. It seems as if the Aztecs purposely sought to anger others by their disgusting habits (which
included some gruesome human sacrifices) and their outrageous
practice of stealing their neighbors' wives. But however much
the farming peoples of the Valley were repulsed by the interlopers, they also learned (sometimes the hard way) to entertain
a healthy respect for them. The Aztecs were a young, vigorous
people, hungry and ambitious. They were also superb warriors,
whose fighting abilities did not go unnoticed by the ruling warlords of the Valley. Consequently, it was as mercenaries, exploiting the tenuous balance of power in Anáhuac, that the Aztecs
first achieved recognition.

From the 1270s to the year 1319 the Aztecs maintained a precarious existence, occupying the hill of Chapultepec (now a park
in Mexico City). They continued in their perverse ways, and the
leaders of some of the principal towns decided to deal with them
once and for all. They drove the intruders from Chapultepec and
sacrificed the Aztec chief and his daughter. The survivors escaped by concealing themselves in the rushes along the lake
shore until it was safe to come out.

Now subject to Coxcox (Pheasant), the ruler of Culhuacán,
the Aztecs were given some land to settle. But what land! They
found themselves living in a gully acrawl with rattlesnakes, no
doubt to the amusement of their enemies. But, as it turned out,
the Aztecs liked rattlesnake meat, and they devoured the vipers
with gusto. Still, it was not the promised land, and the restless
Aztecs bided their time. Their chance came when Coxcox agreed
to give them their liberty and better land in exchange for assistance in a war against the town of Xochimilco. Aztec leaders delivered to the shocked Coxcox proof of their deeds—sacks containing eight thousand ears cut from the slain Xochimilcas.

Although the king of Culhuacán hastily gave them their freedom, the Aztecs did not go away. They asked Coxcox for his
daughter, who would be made the Aztec queen and would be
treated as a goddess. Coxcox—who should have known better—

agreed. The perversity of the early Aztec mentality surfaced again, as the princess was sacrificed and flayed. When her father attended the banquet in his honor, he was horrified to find that the entertainment included a dancer dressed in the skin of his daughter. Having finally had enough of the Aztecs, Coxcox raised an army that scattered the barbarians, who took refuge once more among the reeds of the lake.

Again the Aztecs showed their adaptability and turned the situation to their advantage. They found that in the marshy edges of the lake no one bothered them, for the place was considered unsuitable for dwelling. It was, however, a region abundant in waterfowl, fish, and other edible creatures. Furthermore, it was of some strategic placement, located at a point where three kingdoms merged. Huddled in those swamps, the miserable Aztecs drew on their resources, and, finding strength and unity in adversity, they stiffened their resolve.

Unmolested, in 1345 (or 1325) the Aztecs occupied a small isle and began to acquire, through trade, the materials they needed to enlarge their foothold. They dredged the lake bottom to form more surface soil. From such inauspicious beginnings, and with considerable ingenuity and great labor, they eventually created the great city of Tenochtitlán. From that island redoubt they later built connecting causeways, which could easily be defended, to the mainland. It was an inspired defensive concept, flawed only by the eventual dependence on mainland Chapultepec for drinking water. Aqueducts conveying water could be cut.

Meanwhile the furious activity of the Aztecs and the development of the island came to the attention of Tezozómoc, the strongman of Anáhuac, who brought them under his sway and used them in their traditional role of mercenaries. Tezozómoc made unreasonable demands of tribute from the Aztecs, and even humiliated them, but he was astute enough not to push them too far. Gradually they were accepted as minor partners, and in 1376 Tezozómoc allowed Tenochtitlán to institute a monarchy. In that year the young Acamapichtli became the first king of the Aztecs. By the time Tezozómoc finally died in 1426, the Aztecs, his apt disciples, were flourishing.

About this time the Aztecs elected as their king Itzcóatl (Obsidian Snake), whose energetic rule led to Aztec independence. Following a power struggle, Tenochtitlán allied itself with the cities of Texcoco and Tlacopan. This Triple Alliance would soon control central Mexico. While the three were ostensibly equal partners, in fact, Tlacopan was inferior.

Although the feverish drive of the Aztecs ultimately carried them to dominance of the alliance, Texcoco maintained its position of equality for some time. To considerable extent Texcoco's strength was owing to the brilliance of Nezahualcóyotl (ruled 1418–72), one of the most remarkable figures in the history of Mexico. While so many are remembered for their military exploits, the illustrious Nezahualcóyotl is recalled for his cultural refinement. He was too much a man of his times to be a pacifist, and he steadily increased his influence through military force, but he had more positive redeeming qualities. Renowned for his philosophical verse, this "Poet King of Texcoco" was also a wise legislator and an impartial judge; he did not hesitate to condemn to death, for example, members of his own family who broke laws. In addition, he was an engineer who was instrumental in the construction of a great aqueduct, which brought water to Tenochtitlán from the mainland, and of a long dike across the lake. A scholar and bibliophile, his Texcoco, "the Athens of Anáhuac," had libraries housing thousands of manuscripts, which were, tragically, later destroyed. The city, with its gardens, royal baths, and beautiful temples, was the finest expression of civilization in an age otherwise marred by cruelty, intrigue, and almost constant warfare. When Nezahualcóyotl died in 1472, his son Nezahualpilli, who had many of his father's qualities, became ruler of Texcoco. But the city came increasingly under the influence of Tenochtitlán.

After Itzcóatl died, in 1440, his nephew, the mighty Moctezuma I (Moctezuma Ilhuicamina) became sovereign of the Aztecs. Even before taking power, Moctezuma was a prominent general, and during his reign of twenty-eight years he launched his armies to smashing victories, as the Aztec dominions were extended to the south and northeast. Beyond this explosive territorial growth, the Aztec state took on more formal characteristics and began to achieve remarkable cohesion. At the same time, a genuine Aztec art style evolved as one manifestation of fervent nationalism. On a less positive note, the pretension and arrogance for which the Aztecs were notorious became increasingly extravagant, as former allies were bullied and cheated in the extension of imperial ambitions.

Growth of the empire was checked in the middle of the fifteenth century by the onset in 1450–51 of a catastrophic famine occasioned by heavy snowfalls and rains that caused floods, which ruined crops. The food shortage persisted, leading the Aztecs to placate the gods with human sacrifices in ever-increasing num-

PRINCIPAL LAKE CITIES IN THE VALLEY OF MEXICO DURING THE AZTEC PERIOD

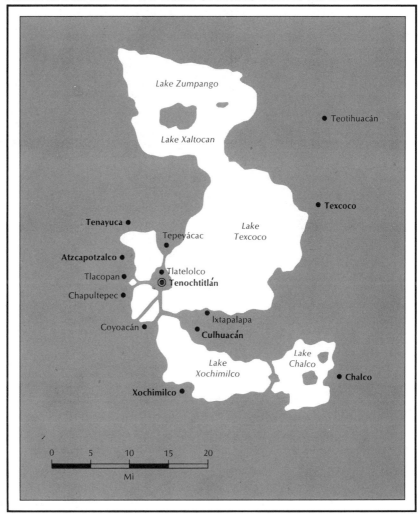

bers. Still they were not favored by nature, and the situation became even more desperate as wild beasts came out of the mountains to attack humans and vultures swarmed to feed on the dead. Great numbers of people sold themselves for a few ears of corn, becoming slaves to the Totonacs of the Gulf coast, where the famine had not occurred. When, after five years of near-starvation, food was again plentiful, the priests observed that the human sacrifices had been successful; the lesson had been learned, and the gods would never again be deprived of a regular diet of human hearts.

The sculpture of a female deity is reflected in an Aztec obsidian mirror with a wooden frame.

When Moctezuma I died in 1468, he was replaced by Axayácatl (ruled 1469–81), who faced rebellions of various tributary towns within the empire. Axayácatl cracked down on the rebels, and, in order to prevent future trouble, he established garrisons at frontier outposts. Like his predecessors he continued to conquer new provinces, and in the course of one furious battle he lost a leg. All Aztec kings were expected to be brave leaders, and one source of their immense authority derived from their presence in the thick of battle, where they shared dangers along with the lowliest common soldier.

The next lord of the Aztecs was the least distinguished of their number—Tizoc (Bloodstained Leg), brother of Axayácatl. Even though his armies enjoyed many victories (having taken a reported hundred thousand prisoners), Tizoc himself was considered a coward, anathema to the warriors of Tenochtitlán. It was no benefit to the hapless Tizoc that the armies were led by the extraordinary general Tlacaélel. This intrepid commander was the sinister power behind three different kings, and, while he never seized outright rule for himself, he had no need to, as he was in effect a king maker. It has been suggested that Tizoc's death by poisoning, after a short rule (1481–86), was contrived with the concurrence of Tlacaélel, who then saw to the election of Ahuítzotl (Water Dog), the third son of Moctezuma I to reign.

Much in contrast to his predecessor, Ahuítzotl was an extremely aggressive and fierce leader who unleashed the Aztec fury. He took his legions on wide-ranging expeditions, conquering the valley of Oaxaca, driving down the Pacific coast to Guatemala, and pushing up the Gulf coast. His merciless tactics subdued many provinces and increased the tributes paid to Tenochtitlán. Under his rule, in 1487, a great orgy of bloodletting was enacted as part of the dedication of an impressive new temple erected to honor the god Huitzilopochtli. In a ceremony lasting four days sacrificial victims taken during campaigns were formed in four columns, each stretching three miles. At least twenty thousand human hearts were torn out to please the god. Prominent guests, selected from allies and tributary towns, were invited to be impressed (and intimidated) by the might and glory of Tenochtitlán. In the frenzy of this ghastly pageant, the priests were finally overcome by exhaustion. The bloody reign of Ahuítzotl closed in 1502 when he accidentally struck his head on a stone lintel while trying to escape a flood. He had succeeded not only in knitting together a vast conglomeration of tribes under the Aztec yoke but also in imposing a tight bureaucratic control over the empire.

The Aztec Empire

By the beginning of the sixteenth century the Aztec system embraced most of central and much of southern Mexico, excluding the Maya regions. The north held little attraction, for the Aztecs were concerned with exacting tribute, not controlling land, especially not the semidesert area of the bellicose Chichimecs. There were areas along the southern Pacific coast that remained independent of the Aztec net, along with some in the northeast. Most notable among the independent states were those of the Tarascans and the Tlaxcalans.

The Tarascans lived in the scenic western state of Michoacán near Lake Pátzcuaro. Legends say that they were originally part of the Aztec migration from Aztlán. When the nomads reached the lake, some went in to bathe and came out of the water to find that their clothes and belongings had been stolen by the others,

A fine example of Aztec stone sculpture.

who had departed. The thieves (or pranksters) went on to establish Tenochtitlán, and the victims remained to become the Tarascans. From those early bathers of the remote past have emerged the tall, slender, fine-featured people regarded by many today as the most handsome of the land. Over the generations they prospered in their territory, isolated from the troubles of the Valley of Mexico. They built their capital at Tzintzuntzan. Eventually the Aztecs got around to attacking them, but the powerful Tarascans gave them a taste of copper weapons. In 1479 Axayácatl invaded Michoacán with the intention of capturing sacrificial victims to celebrate the carving of the great Aztec calendar stone, and of course to get tribute. His army of twenty-four thousand met a large Tarascan force, with disastrous consequences: the Aztecs left twenty thousand dead on the field. Thereafter few bothered the Tarascans.

The independent state of Tlaxcala was founded by one of the early Chichimec tribes in the region east of the mountains lining the Valley of Mexico. At various times the Tlaxcalans were allies of the Aztecs, but trouble erupted between the two in a curious way. During the great famine of the 1450s the Aztecs ran short of sacrificial victims to propitiate the gods. They dared not keep the gods waiting by undertaking campaigns in distant provinces, so they made an ingenious, if macabre, arrangement with the Tlaxcalans, who also needed victims. It was agreed that limited war would be waged for the precise purpose of taking live prisoners. It had a grim sort of logic, for lives would not be "wasted" in battlefield deaths but rather would be spent for the higher, "useful" purpose of pleasing the gods in order to lift the famine. Moreover, it would have the incidental goal of training young warriors. This concept of *Xochiyaoyotl* (Flowery Wars), which may have existed in earlier times, demonstrates the expediency of the Aztecs and their neighbors. But there was a ritualistic aspect to it as well; a Flowery War was defined by rules and had overseers. It began and ended by mutual consent. It appears, however, that such engagements, which had the ceremonial airs of a tournament, gradually got out of hand. Whatever the precise nature of the misunderstanding, the Aztecs and Tlaxcalans eventually got down to the real thing. They became exceedingly bitter enemies, a turn of events that would have ominous consequences with the arrival of the Spaniards in 1519.

The Aztecs never gained control of the Tlaxcalans, whose state was an island surrounded by Aztec dominions. But the Tlaxcalans were contained, and they were seriously disadvantaged when their trading was restricted, especially with the interdiction of their supplies of salt and cotton. Some speculate that the Aztecs purposely did not conquer the Tlaxcalans in order to maintain a state of war in which fledgling warriors could be tested and captives taken.

In 1502 the ill-starred Moctezuma II (Moctezuma Xocoyótzin), a son of Axayácatl, was elected to succeed Ahuítzotl. He reigned as the most absolute of Aztec lords, governing with great authority and enjoying the deference due a demigod. He was educated to be a high priest, but he later proved his valor on the field of battle. Moctezuma II undertook further expeditions to expand his suzerainty, and he laid the groundwork for an invasion of Central America. With the Aztec empire enjoying power and prosperity, there was a bustling commerce, a vigorous artistic style, and an advanced, well-organized society. From the brutish and pitiful beginnings, the Aztecs had created an astonishing capital city with a complex, sophisticated society. For seventeen years Moctezuma II ruled in splendor; then, quite suddenly, the Aztec world was turned upside down.

Recommended for Further Study

Barlow, Robert H. *The Extent of the Empire of the Culhua Mexica.* Ibero-Americana, no. 28. Berkeley: University of California Press, 1949.

Bernal, Ignacio. *Mexico before Cortez: Art, History and Legend.* Translated by Willis Barnstone. Garden City, N.Y.: Doubleday, 1975.

Brundage, Burr C. *A Rain of Darts: The Mexica Aztecs.* Austin: University of Texas Press, 1972.

Caso, Alfonso. *The Aztecs: People of the Sun.* Norman: University of Oklahoma Press, 1958.

Davies, Nigel. *The Aztec Empire: The Toltec Resurgence.* Norman: University of Oklahoma Press, 1987.

———. *The Aztecs: A History.* London: Macmillan, 1973.

———. *The Toltecs: Until the Fall of Tula.* Norman: University of Oklahoma Press, 1977.

Duran, Fr. Diego. *The Aztecs: The History of the Indians of New Spain.* Translated, with notes, by Doris Heyden and Fernando Horcasitas. New York: Orion Press, 1964.

Gillespie, Susan D. *The Aztec Kings: The Construction of Rulership in Mexican History.* Tucson: University of Arizona Press, 1989.

Rojas, Pedro. *The Art and Architecture of Mexico, from 10,000 B.C. to the Present Day.* Feltham, Eng.: Hamlyn, 1968.

Von Hagen, Victor W. *The Aztec: Man and Tribe.* New York: New American Library, 1961.

5

Aztec Society and Culture

It is one of the paradoxes of history that violence and artistic development are entirely compatible within the same society; brutality coexists with refinement and justice. Aztec society is a good case in point. We have seen the emergence of a state committed to a policy of war and hostage to a bloodthirsty religion; it is also true that Aztec society and culture embodied some remarkably enlightened codes of conduct and justice, sensitive accomplishments in the arts, an orderly administration, and behavior that was strangely puritanical in outlook. In some respects it was civilization of the highest order.

Aztec Religion

The negative aspects of late Aztec life bear some examination, not by way of apologia but rather because they inform a facet of thought central to Aztec policy. The rationale for human sacrifice finds its origin in a cosmic view of things. When the early Aztecs wandered in search of their homeland, they carried with them an effigy of their god Huitzilopochtli, lord of the sun and god of war. They believed that the sun and earth had been destroyed in a cataclysm and recreated four times, and that in their age of the fifth sun, final destruction was imminent. That fate was, understandably, to be avoided as long as possible, and the Aztecs believed that special intervention through Huitzilopochtli would serve their interests.

Furthermore, the Aztecs accepted the view of a natural cycle:

Modern re-enactment at Teotihuacán of the Aztec Fifth Sun Festival.

the sun, along with the rain, nourished the plant life that sustained man, and therefore man, in turn, should give sustenance to the sun and rain gods. Ancient deities had sacrificed themselves to the sun, and mere mortals could hardly decline the same honor. The greatest offering that could be made, the highest expression of piety, was the giving of life itself. In practice, the ritual offering to the sun god involved the removal of a palpitating human heart for presentation to Huitzilopochtli. Without such expressions of reverence, it was feared that the sun might not rise to make its way across the sky. Having accepted that warped premise, Aztec thought then progressed with considerable logic.

Human sacrifice was a stage through which many ancient cultures of the Old World passed on the way to becoming great civilizations. In many respects the New World schedule of development lagged centuries behind, so the practice persisted until a much later age. Sacrifice was to the Aztecs a solemn, and necessary, religious ceremony for the purpose of averting disaster. Victims were sent as messengers to the gods to demonstrate the reverence of the people, and it was often considered an honor to make the trip. With the same pious convictions priests occasionally indulged in ritual cannibalism[1] as a kind of pagan communion through which they might acquire the attributes of the enemy.

All was done in accordance with a strictly prescribed procedure. The most familiar sacrificial ceremony took place atop a high temple, where the victim was spread-eagled over a rounded stone, his back arched. While his limbs were held by four assistants, the priest went in under the rib cage with an obsidian knife to remove the heart. There were variations, according to the god to be honored. Those dispatched for Xipe Totec, the god of fertility, were bound and shot full of arrows, the falling drops of blood symbolizing the falling of spring rain. Those honoring the fire god were drugged with hashish and then placed in fire. There was also a kind of gladiatorial combat that amounted to sacrifice, in which a captured warrior, usually one who had shown great skill and bravery, was tied by the ankle to a great round, flat stone. He was given dull wooden weapons to face a series of well-armed Aztec warriors, one at a time. In the unlikely event that the captive survived, he could have his freedom, but, in at least one notable case, a survivor insisted that he be honored as a warrior with a sacrificial death.

Aztec successes seemed to justify their practices. Reversals in fortunes simply called for more sacrifices, which eventually brought about a shortage of the "god food." Hence the resort to Flowery Wars. In order to supply victims, an almost constant state of war was maintained; thus, for religious reasons, militarism was elevated to virtue.

1. Will Durant, *Our Oriental Heritage* (New York, 1935), p. 10, writes, "Cannibalism was at one time practically universal; it has been found in nearly all primitive tribes, and among such later peoples as the Irish, the Iberians, the Picts, and the eleventh-century Danes."

At the end of every fifty-two year cycle (the Indians' "century"), there was always the doubt that the sun would rise to begin a new cycle. Therefore, in fatalistic anticipation, on the last night of the cycle all dishes were broken and all fires put out. Then the priests assembled on a mountaintop to pray. When the sun did rise, a victim was sacrificed in appreciation and a New Fire ceremony was held; a new fire was kindled from which torches were carried to light all other fires.

The Aztecs perceived themselves as living in an insecure world, at the mercy of the elements and at the edge of doom. Natural calamities in their fragile universe were occasioned by the gods'

A temple is burned in this Indian painting, signifying the end of a 52-year cycle. From the Codex Telleriano-Remensis.

The New Fire ceremony is portrayed here much like a May Day frolic. The European artist had probably never seen an Indian in his native habitat.

displeasure. The Indians believed themselves surrounded by strange and harmful forces: as human beings were at one with nature, a person could suddenly be transformed into a hawk, a coyote, a fish, or even a tree or a rock. In such forms those who had passed on could haunt the living. There were demons and other strange apparitions in the nighttime, and in the dark one had to be especially careful of the noxious "airs." In an atmosphere heavy with symbolism, the apprehensive Aztec took no chances.

Huitzilopochtli was the predominant god, but there were many others to whom homage was paid. The ancient deities of Tláloc, Tezcatlipoca (the favorite of the warriors), and Quetzalcóatl (revered by the intellectual priests), were only a few of the more prominent gods worshipped for their special benefactions. Favored gods of conquered peoples were readily incorporated into a swelling Aztec pantheon of deities.

There was a version of afterlife, but it was not the same for all. Mothers who died in childbirth went to a special heaven. Warriors who fell in battle or who were sacrificed by the enemy went to a paradise with perfumed clouds, to accompany the sun in its daily passage; or they could find a new life as a hummingbird,

In old age the Aztecs confessed to the goddess Tlazoltéotl, whose effigy is shown here giving birth to the God of Corn.

destined to spend eternity among fragrant blossoms. Thus the warrior did not fear death any more than later Spanish priests feared the martyrdom that assured them a place in their heaven. Unless one was surprised by death, it was customary to confess late in life. Sins were related to the goddess Tlazoltéotl, "the Eater of Filth [sins]." After satisfying a penance imposed by a priest, the sinner was then cleansed.

Religion was all-pervasive in Tenochtitlán, and from birth to death there was daily religious observance. The Indians had many holy days during which celebrations, both solemn and joyful, took place. Some festivities included singing and dancing, along with children parading in garlands of flowers. Although religious fanaticism led to excesses among the Aztecs, the same can be said for their contemporaries in other parts of the world. If the Spanish Inquisition offers the most convenient comparison, we do not have to look far to find others.

Aztec Society

The early tribal society of the Aztecs was somewhat democratic. While they were nomadic and relatively few in number, Aztec social structure was simple; the majority were peasants or warriors, and the handful of priests and war leaders enjoyed comparatively few perquisites. Following the settlement of Tenochtitlán, however, a rapidly expanding population, a diversified economy, and the organizational demands of the imperial system led to a more complex class structure.

Naturally, the royal family was the most noble of all, and it was a large group. While the emperor had one principal (or "legitimate") wife, he had many others as well. The royal offspring were numerous, and they proliferated greatly. It is said that Nezahualpilli of Texcoco had two thousand wives and 144 children. Moctezuma II, with one thousand women, once had 150 pregnant at the same time. The royal wives had position and respect, and some were highly accomplished women whose views and talents were appreciated at court. Over a period of several generations the ruling dynasty had sufficient relations to be considered almost as a class apart. Emperors were always chosen from the royal family, but, unlike most monarchies, the heir apparent was not fixed. The best male candidate was chosen, whether he was a brother, nephew, or younger son of the previous emperor, a policy in keeping with Aztec recognition of merit over birth. Members of the royal family bore great responsibility; they were expected to serve as examples, to maintain dignity, and to lead warriors. Consequently, the moral fiber of Aztec leadership was strong. As Ignacio Bernal observes, "Excessive well-being had not made the imperial family either effeminate or degenerate,"[2] which was often the case with European royalty.

Others in the noble category included high priests, prominent military officers, and influential government leaders. Sons of nobles were in an advantageous position to achieve their fathers' rank, but nobility (outside of the royal family) was not an inherited right. One had to distinguish himself in service in order to enjoy the privileges of the aristocracy. Nobles wore fine clothing, had commodious houses, servants, jewelry, and prestige—in sum, the best of everything that was available. Such luxuries went with the office, however; they were a consequence of achievement and were not sought for their own sake. Little wealth could be passed on to children. In the late Aztec period, however, an elite class with landed estates, a kind of incipient feudal aristocracy, was apparently in process of formation. Whereas the noble had traditionally valued his reputation above all, it

2. Ignacio Bernal, "Mexico-Tenochtitlan," in *Cities of Destiny*, ed. Arnold Toynbee (New York, 1968), p. 208.

seems probable (had the Spanish Conquest not intervened) that within two or three generations a more materialistic class of nobility would have evolved.

Nobles had an acute sense of *noblesse oblige;* obligations and moral duties were not taken lightly, and commoners were treated with consideration, compassion, and mercy. The aristocratic tradition was hostile to open displays of frivolity; but, in spite of a public image of austerity, frugality, and modesty, in private the nobles were allowed some ostentation. The so-called Precepts of the Elders reflected a concern for courtly manners and behavior. One finds in it a startling similarity to the famous Renaissance manual, *The Courtier*, written by the Italian humanist Baldassare Castiglione at precisely the time Aztec nobility flowered in its most civilized state. The genteel Aztec courtier of the early sixteenth century was a far cry from his antecedents who had entered the Valley of Mexico several generations earlier. In Tenochtitlán, Leopoldo Castedo reminds, the "nobles were so extraordinarily refined that when they were forced to come near the Spaniards, they screened their nasal passages with branches of fragrant flowers."[3]

All able-bodied males were expected to bear arms, but soldiers came primarily from the lower class. Distinction in battle was one way in which a commoner might rise to the nobility. In order to achieve the cherished rank of warrior, a youth had to take a prisoner. If he succeeded in capturing or killing four of the enemy he was entitled to share in the booty. Perhaps more important, he was allowed to dress in the distinctive adornments of the military elite. Conceivably, he could become a member of the prestigious military orders—the Eagle Knights or Jaguar Knights—and thus enjoy the luxuries of noble status. By encouraging upward mobility through performance, Aztec society remained flexible and vigorous.

Access to high status might also be gained through the priesthood. However, there were a great many priests (five thousand were assigned to the main temple of Tenochtitlán alone), and most of them remained in minor positions. The sacerdotal life began with training young boys (or girls destined to be priestesses) in a monastery school, or *calmécac*. If suited to the life, a youth made the decision to enter the priesthood at about the age of twenty-one. Priests were expected to lead exemplary lives, and they spent long hours in prayer, fasting, and penance. The latter

3. Leopoldo Castedo, *A History of Latin American Art and Architecture from Precolumbian Times to the Present* (New York, 1969), pp. 38–39.

included scarification of the body, usually by drawing drops of blood with a thorn passed through the ear, tongue, or penis. Most of the priests led modest lives of service; those who advanced through the hierarchy, however, enjoyed the status of nobles and many of the perquisites that went with it. Like their European counterparts, the Aztec priests commanded the greatest knowledge, which gave them extraordinary power. Aside from routine religious duties, each priest had a specialty, such as music, painting, teaching, dancing, or assisting at sacrificial rites. Priests were the guardians of morality, and some of their admonitions are not unlike Scriptural injunctions: "He who looks too curiously on a woman commits adultery with his eyes."

Even though Tenochtitlán produced little for export, the merchants of that city ranged far and wide. These traders, the *pochteca*, were one of the most interesting groups in Aztec society. They organized and led caravans as far as Central America, often passing through hostile country. The pochteca were as brave as they were shrewd and often depended on both their wits and courage to evade dangers. Some of them knew foreign languages and customs and served as spies for the Aztec militarists.

The pochteca imported to the capital exotic and profitable goods, which were displayed in the markets. But while these merchants were prosperous, they took great care to avoid any show of opulence. Unlike any other groups in Aztec society, they were incipient capitalists; unlike Aztec nobles, they were little concerned about their reputations. They lived in their own district and formed a separate group altogether. They had their own guild, their special deities, and their own courts. Within their section of the city they frequently gave sumptuous banquets and enjoyed other luxuries. Not of the nobility, they nevertheless had influence and respect.

The great majority of the people formed the class of commoners (*maceguales*). These farmers, laborers, minor craftsmen, servants, vendors, and petty functionaries of the state were organized into wards or districts called *calpullis* (*barrios* to the Spaniards). A clan made up of many families, the calpulli was the basic social unit. It was a close-knit organization with loyalties much like those of an extended family. Each calpulli had lands apportioned to family heads who could use fields but did not own them. Members of the calpulli worked together, played together, and, in times of war, fought together as a unit. The people elected a captain who served as military commander of the district and was responsible for their welfare and good order.

Another group occupied still a lower position: those who rented their services out to the upper classes, to work their fields or to perform other labor for wages, were called *mayeques*. Though technically free, they were neither citizens nor identified with a calpulli and were considered socially and economically inferior to the commoners. These mayeques were often much like share-croppers, without real roots or traditions. In all probability they were conquered people from other areas.

At the bottom of the socioeconomic scale were the slaves. Az-tec slavery differed from the slave system most familiar to us in-asmuch as slaves had certain rights and bondage was not passed from parent to child. Some, in fact, served as slaves only for a specified term, either in payment of a debt or as punishment for a crime. In bad times people sometimes sold themselves or their children into slavery to avoid starvation. A gambler might bet his freedom on a ball game and end up as a slave. Some of the slaves were favored as concubines, and all slaves could inter-marry with free persons. Little stigma was attached to some con-ditions of slavery; the mother of the emperor Itzcóatl, in fact, had been a slave. In a different category were those captured in war and destined for sacrifice. The class of slaves was increasing at the time of the Spanish Conquest, another sign of the widen-ing social gap.

Aztec society's concern with education was singular for its time—school was compulsory for children. There were two main types of schools, and attendance at one or the other determined social and economic status. Children of the nobility usually at-tended the calmécac, run by the scholarly priests, in preparation for the priesthood or some high office in the state. Occasionally a talented son of a commoner gained entrance. To prepare stu-dents for future responsibilities, discipline was very strict and hours of study were long. In a vigorous intellectual regimen young boys studied religion, astronomy, philosophy, history, po-etry, rhetoric, and oratory, among other disciplines. Although the spoken language was rich and expressive and lent itself to fine subtleties, the picture writing was limited. History was passed on by oral traditions committed to memory. Written ac-counts depicted certain dramatic scenes that gave continuity and jogged the memory, but the fine details were transmitted from one generation to another by the retelling.

Most of the children attended one of the *telpochcallis* and found a more relaxed, less intellectual atmosphere. These stu-dents would become the class of commoners, or workers. Lay

600.

Prehispanic Mexican women ground their corn with stone *mano* and *metate*, and made tortillas much as many do today. From the Florentine Codex.

persons gave both boys and girls practical instruction in basic subjects. Here boys learned the rudiments of warfare, and those who went on to excel in the profession of arms could do very well for themselves; others had to be content with learning trades or lesser skills. Girls were instructed in the responsibilities of the household and motherhood. All were taught modesty, courtesy, and conformity. The humility and courtesy of so many Mexican Indians today are deeply rooted in the Aztec concept of virtue.

In the home parents imposed strict discipline. The birth of a child occasioned celebration and florid speeches. A child was named in hopeful anticipation of its character—the boys usually given names indicating military prowess and the girls names denoting beauty and delicacy, such as Rain Flower or Water Bird. In the home children were taught not only proper deportment but also the performance of daily tasks: girls learned to cook, sew, and embroider, while boys were taught agriculture and crafts. While children were very young some indiscretions were tolerated; but by the age of eight they were considered to be responsible, and infractions brought harsh punishment. Although parents were ordinarily tender and loving, wayward children were castigated by whippings, scratching with thorns, or by being forced to inhale the smoke of a fire into which chile peppers had been placed. It is reasonable to suppose that most children behaved themselves. Girls worked in the household until they were sixteen to eighteen, when they married; boys took mates in their early twenties.

Aztec society was curiously puritanical. Drunkenness could be a capital offense, although older people were allowed to become inebriated. The rule prohibiting excessive use of the strong pulque was rooted in the conviction that drunken behavior would undermine the good order of society and the economy. Oddly enough, there was no similar ban on drugs. Various kinds of hallucinogens were used, one of which was a fungus that produced powerful and graphic visions, to either the delight or the horror of the consumer. It appears, however, that such drugs were taken primarily by the upper classes, who did so privately and who could afford the luxury of the consequences. Both pulque and drugs were believed to have magical properties because they changed the personality.

Aztec society demanded moral conformity, and violators of the code, as well as criminal offenders, were dealt with firmly. For minor offenses punishment was correspondingly light. But since personal dignity was highly prized, any public humiliation, such as the cutting of one's hair, was a great insult to pride. Several offenses, including lying, theft, and treason, brought the death penalty. The heads of adulterers were crushed between stones, homosexuals were hanged, and the lips of slanderers were cut off. Such penalties may seem unduly harsh to us, but it must be recalled that sentences in other parts of the world at that time were also excessive.

The Aztec legal system was complex, with high judges seated at both Texcoco and Tenochtitlán and lesser judges in localities. The legalistic society had need for many judicial officials to prepare the multitude of carefully documented lawsuits. There were judges in the great marketplaces to maintain fairness in business transactions and to settle disputes. Appointed by the emperor, judges were selected for their integrity and virtue. They had great authority and could arrest even the highest dignitaries, for under the law all were equal. The judge was expected to be absolutely impartial; if he accepted a bribe or favored a noble over a plebeian he could be executed.

Duty and responsibility, as well as danger, increased with

one's rank, and they imposed special restraints. Because self-control was considered a mark of good breeding and nobility, the upper classes were subject to standards different from those of the lower classes. In contrast to most systems, where the upper classes have a favored position before the law, Aztec aristocrats were dealt with more harshly than plebeians. An offense that might bring a whipping or public humiliation for a commoner often brought death to a noble. Tax collectors, who had considerable rank, were executed for embezzlement, and the same fate awaited the lascivious priest. A salient example of justice for the wayward nobility may be observed in the notorious case of one of Nezahualpilli's wives (a daughter of Axayácatl) who was unfaithful. She and three of her lovers were publicly executed.

Aztec medical practices were generally on a par with those in Europe, and were in some respects superior. Doctors knew how to set broken bones and dislocations and to treat dental cavities. They even performed brain operations. Like their European counterparts, Aztec healers were ill informed on the causes of disease but adept at effecting cures. The bleeding of patients, accepted medical practice in Europe until the end of the eighteenth century, was practiced by Aztec physicians as well. Aztec medicines were essentially extractions from plant life (and some animal life), from which were prepared a bewildering variety of brews, powders, poultices, purges, and pastes. Years after the Conquest a Spanish physician cataloged some fifteen hundred different plants whose medicinal properties were utilized by the Indians. The conquerors adopted native medicines, many of which are still popular in rural Mexico today.

Because Aztec society was largely agricultural in character, the daily routine of most people was directly involved in the growing of food. Aside from the many floating gardens that ringed the island city, there were extensive plantings along the shores of the lakes. The diet remained much as it had been for centuries, with a base of corn, beans, chile, and squash. It also included a wide variety of other vegetables and melons, cactus fruit, and amaranth, in addition to many fruits imported from tropical regions. Commoners seldom ate meat, but the nobles, who liked to hunt for sport, consumed venison, peccary, pheasant, and turkey. A special treat was the small hairless dog fattened for the table. Cacao from the tropics was made into a chocolate drink, and avocados and many other exotic delicacies were brought in by the traders. Fish was a favorite when available.

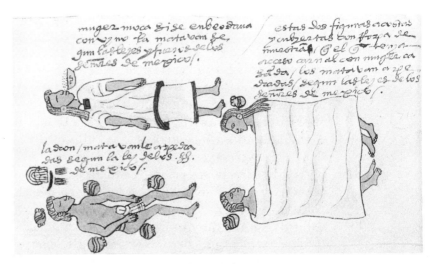

A girl has been put to death for drunkenness and a thief has been executed by stoning. Adulterers are shown wrapped together in a sheet and then stoned to death. From the Codex Mendoza.

An older woman is legally allowed to partake of the intoxicant *octli* (pulque). From the Codex Mendoza.

Aztec justice was strict, and it often imposed the harshest punishment on high officials. Here an erring functionary is being strangled. From the Florentine Codex.

The Aztec Political System

The limited resources of the Valley were not sufficient to meet the needs of Tenochtitlán, Texcoco, Tlacopan, and other Valley communities. Moreover, there was an increasing demand for luxuries from other provinces. To satisfy the necessities and desires for both raw materials and consumer goods, Aztec realms were extended. The so-called Aztec empire was really a loose coalition of subject city-states that paid tribute to the imperial center. The lords of Anáhuac were not particularly desirous of colonizing conquered areas with their own people or of imposing their own political system; nor were they cultural imperialists. Rather, the collection of tribute, which kept the Valley culture prosperous, was their main concern.

Tributes included a wide variety of commodities, among which were cacao, cotton, feathers, precious stones, jaguar skins, eagles, shells, dyes, cloth, gold, silver, sandals, and corn and other foodstuffs, as well as jewelry. Imperial tax collectors (*calpixquis*) were stationed in tributary towns to ensure prompt payment. Towns conquered by the Aztecs were expected to provide soldiers and slaves and were required to recognize the imperial courts of appeal. But they were also allowed considerable autonomy. If the conquered peoples agreed to submit to Aztec sovereignty, the Aztecs did not much interfere with their internal affairs and

their customs. Huitzilopochtli had to be recognized as the supreme deity; otherwise local religious practices and traditions
were usually respected.

Aztec political organization rested lightly on tributary towns,
provided they were cooperative. In fact, it may be said that the
Aztecs' policy of generous autonomy for subject provinces was a
weakness in their political system. The subject peoples continued
to be foreigners within the empire, which remained a conglomeration of tributaries with many different languages, customs,
and religions. The provinces paid tribute under duress but were
never assimilated into Aztec culture. Thus the empire lacked
genuine unity and was honeycombed with discontent, a circum-
stance that would be fatal in the years ahead.

After the death of Nezahualcóyotl of Texcoco in 1472, the
Triple Alliance had little significance, and Tenochtitlán gathered to itself almost all the power and most of the tribute. The
emperor was elected from among the royal family by a select
committee of about a hundred electors. The one chosen was considered to be the choice of the gods as well. Over the generations
the emperor came to dictate appointment to offices that had previously been elective. He grew increasingly powerful, and the
monarchy more absolute.

Aztec Art, Music, and Literature

The Aztecs borrowed much of their art from others. The Mixtecs
exerted strong influence on Aztec gold and silver work, pottery,
and pictographs. We have no examples of Aztec murals and little in the way of picture books. Aztec ceramic work was good but
not superior. The Aztecs did excel, however, in stone sculpture.
Although they lack the grace and loveliness of Olmec jade pieces,
Aztec carvings are, nevertheless, striking. They are monumental
in size and style and flawlessly executed. As Leopoldo Castedo
has observed, "Aztec art was imbued with the dread, drama, and
grandeur necessary to dazzle the subject peoples and convey the
image of an omnipotent and implacable state."[4]

The artisans who made the gold and silver jewelry were also
superb craftsmen. It is therefore lamentable that almost all of
their work was either lost or destroyed during the Spanish Conquest, for the conquerors valued raw gold but all too often did

4. Ibid., p. 39.

This fearsome image of the goddess Coatlicue, mother of Huitzilopochtli, stands over eight feet high.

A realistic stone sculpture of an Aztec Eagle Knight. His helmet is shaped like an eagle's head; knights of the orders of the Jaguar and Coyote wore appropriate headgear and pelts.

not appreciate the fine workmanship. Equally impressive was the art of the lapidarists; from precious jadeite, turquoise, and other stones they fashioned fine jewelry and mosaics. Most unusual were the artists who worked with feathers. The Aztecs put great value on the long green plumes of the quetzal bird that lived in the highlands of Chiapas and Guatemala, but the feathers of many other birds, too, were woven into mosaics of wonderful patterns and colors. Only rare examples remain, the most spectacular being the great headdress of Moctezuma II. The contemporary German artist Albrecht Dürer was lavish in his praise of Aztec artisans: "In all my life I have never seen anything that rejoiced my heart so much; I have found an admirable art in them, and I have been astonished by the subtle spirit of the men of these strange countries."[5]

Aztec music was composed primarily for ceremonial purposes, and its range was consequently limited. Instruments consisted of flutes, whistles, rasps, rattles, trumpets, conch shells, and drums vital for providing rhythm. The music itself was mournful and no doubt would seem monotonous to our ears. Musicians were highly regarded because of their accompaniment in the religious rituals. Powerful lords were patrons to composers who created ballads recounting the nobles' military exploits. If they had pres-

Musicians played important roles in religious observances. From the Florentine Codex.

Careless musicians were sometimes punished by death.

5. Quoted in Jacques Soustelle, *The Daily Life of the Aztecs on the Eve of the Spanish Conquest*, trans. Patrick O'Brian (London, 1961), p. 68.

tige, musicians also bore great responsibilities. As no written form for recording music had developed, musicians had to memorize a very wide repertoire for the many ceremonies that often went on for hours. At the same time, as Robert Stevenson points out, "Imperfectly executed rituals were thought to offend rather than appease the gods, and therefore errors in the performance of the ritual music—such as missed drum beats—carried the death penalty."[6]

Neither in music nor in poetry was romantic love a popular theme. Aztec lyrics were often eloquent, moving, and sentimental, though for most modern tastes perhaps too concerned with flowers, jade, feathers, and rain. In a verse praising a goddess, for example, a poet sings:

> The yellow flower has opened,
> Our mother has opened like a flower.
> She came from our Place of Beginning . . .
> Butterfly of Obsidian. . . .[7]

Poets sometimes addressed themselves to the proper role of artists and appealed to the public at large to assume a responsible and dignified posture. Like poets the world over, they often waxed philosophical and examined the meaning of life:

> Truly do we live on earth?
> Not forever on earth; only a little while here.
> Although it be jade, it will be broken,
> Although it be gold, it is crushed,
> Although it be quetzal feather, it is torn asunder.
> Not forever on earth; only a little while here.[8]

The City of Tenochtitlán

Aztec architecture, like Aztec art, was essentially derivative. Buildings were basically elaborations of forms that went all the way back to Teotihuacán. But while many pre-Aztec structures survive in amazingly good condition, Tenochtitlán was thought to have been completely demolished by the Spaniards. However, excavations since 1978 have revealed important archaeological findings, including parts of the main temple intact. We do have, moreover, enough descriptions of Tenochtitlán from both native

6. Robert Stevenson, *Music in Mexico: A Historical Survey* (New York, 1971), p. 18.
7. Quoted in Frances Gillmor, *Flute of the Smoking Mirror: A Portrait of Nezahualcoyotl, Poet-King of the Aztecs* (Albuquerque, 1949), p. 23.
8. Quoted in Miguel León-Portilla, *Aztec Thought and Culture: A Study of the Ancient Nahuatl Mind*, trans. Jack Emory Davis (Norman, 1963), p. 7.

and Spanish contemporary accounts to appreciate what the city looked like.

By the time Moctezuma II was elevated to power in 1502, the island capital of Tenochtitlán was a most impressive city. How large it was we do not know, but in the cautious opinion of Ignacio Bernal, there were about eighty thousand residents. Miguel León-Portilla writes that "beyond question the Aztec capital contained a quarter of a million people."[9] Even with the conservative estimate, the Aztec capital was one of the largest cities in the world. Only four cities of Europe—Paris, Venice, Milan, and Naples—had populations of one hundred thousand or more at the time. Seville, the city from which Spanish ships sailed for Mexico, had a population in 1520 of around forty thousand; and by 1580, when it was the largest city in Spain, it had only slightly over a hundred thousand. The amazement of the Spanish conquerors at their first sight of Tenochtitlán is therefore understandable. Cortés wrote of "the magnificence, the strange and marvelous things of this great city," which itself was "so remarkable as not to be believed."[10] In the Valley of Mexico, an area of some three thousand square miles, there were about fifty different cities by the second decade of the sixteenth century. If we take into account "greater" Tenochtitlán, with its many satellite communities on the lake shores (of which Texcoco was perhaps as large as the capital itself), the area surely held one of the heaviest concentrations of population in the world at the time.

By the early sixteenth century the island was an area comprising about five square miles, densely settled, and occupying much of the present center of Mexico City. It was a metropolis swarming with activity. Some sixty thousand people gathered daily in its buzzing market places to barter and gossip. The core of the city, corresponding to the extensive plaza of today (the Zócalo), had a great double pyramid dedicated to Huitzilopochtli and Tláloc, along with the royal palaces and other large structures. Among the shocks to the conquering Spaniards was a giant rack, the *tzompantli*, on which many thousands of human skulls were displayed.

From that central precinct enclosing about 125 acres, the city extended out to the residences of the nobles, which were often of

9. Bernal, "Mexico-Tenochtitlan," p. 204; Miguel León-Portilla, ed., *The Broken Spears: The Aztec Account of the Conquest of Mexico*, trans. Lysander Kemp (Boston, 1972), p. xix.

10. Hernán Cortés, *Hernán Cortés: Letters from Mexico*, trans. and ed. A. R. Pagden, introd. J. H. Elliott (New York, 1971), pp. 101–02.

The center of Tenochtitlán, reconstructed by Ignacio Marquina from descriptions of Spanish conquerors and surviving Aztec monuments.

two stories and contained as many as fifty rooms and patios. Beyond were districts with the modest dwellings of the commoners. The city was interlaced with stone-edged canals, which served as thoroughfares for thousands of canoes carrying people and goods. Paralleling the canals were streets for pedestrians. The Aztecs loved flowers, which with trees and other plants, decorated many luxurious gardens. Aside from the royal botanical gardens, which displayed almost all species of plant life in the empire, there were also zoos, in which were represented practically all the animals and snakes of the country, as well as a large aviary full of all varieties of domestic birds. Large ponds were maintained for swans, ducks, and egrets. In special cages were Moctezuma's snakes, eagles, and jaguars, which consumed five hundred turkeys daily. Hundreds of people were kept busy in the maintenance of these gardens and zoos.

Five shallow lakes interconnected to form a network—two fresh water lakes in the south drained into the brackish water of Lake Texcoco. Three long causeways joined the island city to the shores: one stretched southward to Ixtapalapa, branching off with a road to Coyoacán; another causeway went west to Tlacopan, with an offshoot to Chapultepec; and a third made a connection to the north with Tepeyácac. These broad thoroughfares, twenty-five to thirty feet wide, were cut at intervals by drawbridges. Within the city itself many canals were spanned by stout bridges across which, according to Cortés, ten horsemen could ride abreast.[11]

Compared to other cities in the world at the time, Tenochtitlán was very clean. There was good drainage, and night soil and garbage were hauled away in barges. A crew of a thousand men swept and washed down public streets every day. Cleanliness was considered essential, and people bathed often, many once a day. Owing at least in part to good sanitation and clean air, Aztec society was healthy.

Moctezuma II

Moctezuma II reigned over a territory roughly the size of Italy. His domains included the modern states of Mexico, Morelos, Puebla, Hidalgo, most of Veracruz, much of Oaxaca and Guerrero, as well as the coasts of Chiapas. They contained thirty-eight "provinces," stretching from arid highlands to the sweltering tropics. If, as some authorities believe, all of Mexico had a population approaching 30 million,[12] it was more populous than any country in Europe. France, the largest, had about 20 million, and Spain, 10 at most.

With his immense authority, prestige, and luxurious style of life, Moctezuma II was the equal of any Oriental despot. Three thousand servants attended him in his huge palace. Each day he was presented with a choice of one hundred different dishes, although he ate sparingly, taking his meals behind a screen. For his pleasure he had an unlimited number of concubines, and he was entertained by the antics of dwarfs, jesters, tumblers, acrobats, musicians, and dancers. No one dared look him in the face or touch him, and it was forbidden to turn one's back on him. Moctezuma was indeed the epitome of royalty, held as semidivine, exalted far above any of the earliest Aztec rulers. Never-

11. Ibid., p. 103.
12. Sherburne F. Cook and Woodrow Borah, *The Indian Population of Central Mexico, 1531–1610* (Berkeley, 1960); Cook and Borah, *The Aboriginal Population of Central Mexico on the Eve of the Spanish Conquest* (Berkeley, 1963).

A ceramic foot juggler from Oaxaca, ca.
A.D. 300.

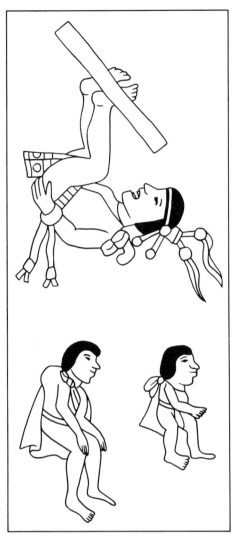

Some 1200 years later, a similar foot juggler appeared in the Florentine Codex.
Also shown are hunchbacks, a giant, and
a dwarf, for whom the Indians had affection.

theless, he was an ultimately tragic figure, undone by historical forces with which he could not cope.

Moctezuma reigned with great authority and popularity for many years. His deep knowledge of Mexican history and his respect for tradition were factors in his successful rule and in the collapse of the Aztec state as well. Aside from his religious convictions, Moctezuma was superstitious and sensitive; he was also an amateur "wizard" who dabbled in astrology. He lived in the shadow of historical inevitability; sometime, he knew, the great Quetzalcóatl would return, as he had promised, to take back his rightful throne.

Just when Moctezuma learned of the presence of white men in the New World is not entirely clear. It is no doubt true that word of the Spaniards, who had been in the Caribbean for several years, drifted to the mainland. Perhaps he was not yet unduly concerned. Cuba, in fact, lay dangerously near—but it was not part of the Aztec world. Moctezuma was almost certainly informed by his agents that Spaniards had landed on the Yucatán Peninsula in 1517 and that others the following year were making their way up the Gulf coast. Indians reported seeing "towers or small mountains floating on the waves of the sea." Meanwhile, strange phenomena, construed by the emperor's priests as evil portents, had occurred. Lightning, unaccompanied by thunder, "like a blow from the sun," damaged a temple; a strange bird was found with "a mirror in its head," in which Moctezuma saw a host of foreign warriors. In 1517 a comet appeared "like a flaming ear of corn . . . it seemed to bleed fire, drop by drop, like a wound in the sky."[13] These and other unexplained signs heightened general anxiety. Then, in the spring of 1519 (the Aztec year Ce Acatl), the emperor was filled with apprehension when a courier arrived bearing ominous paintings—they depicted the encampment on Aztec shores of bearded white men with crosses.

Recommended for Further Study

Anawalt, Patricia Reiff. *Indian Clothing Before Cortés: Meso-American Costumes from the Codices.* Norman: University of Oklahoma Press, 1981.

13. León-Portilla, ed., *The Broken Spears*, pp. 13, 5, 6, 4.

Anton, Ferdinand. *Women in Precolumbian America*. New York: Abner Schram, 1973.

Bernal, Ignacio. "Mexico-Tenochtitlan." In *Cities of Destiny*, edited by Arnold Toynbee, pp. 194–209. New York: McGraw-Hill, 1968.

Bierhorst, John, trans. *Cantares Mexicanos. Songs of the Aztecs*. Stanford, Calif.: Stanford University Press, 1985.

Cook, Sherburne F., and Woodrow Borah. *Essays in Population History: Mexico and the Caribbean*. Vol. 2. Berkeley: University of California Press, 1974.

———. *Essays in Population History: Mexico and California*. Vol. 3. Berkeley: University of California Press, 1979.

Gibson, Charles. *The Aztecs under Spanish Rule*. Stanford, Calif.: Stanford University Press, 1964.

Gillmor, Frances. *Flute of the Smoking Mirror: A Portrait of Nezahualcoyotl, Poet-King of the Aztecs*. Albuquerque: University of New Mexico Press, 1949.

———. *The King Danced in the Market Place*. Tucson: University of Arizona Press, 1964.

Keen, Benjamin. *The Aztec Image in Western Thought*. New Brunswick, N.J.: Rutgers University Press, 1971.

León-Portilla, Miguel. *Aztec Thought and Culture: A Study of the Ancient Nahuatl Mind*. Translated by Jack Emory Davis. Norman: University of Oklahoma Press, 1963.

———. *The Mind of Ancient Mexico*. Norman: University of Oklahoma Press, 1963.

Nicholson, Irene. *Firefly in the Night: A Study of Ancient Mexican Poetry and Symbolism*. London: Faber and Faber, 1959.

Offner, Jerome A. *Law and Politics in Aztec Texcoco*. Cambridge: Cambridge University Press, 1983.

Ortiz de Montellano, Bernard R. "Counting Skulls: Comments on the Aztec Cannibalism Theory of Harner-Harris." *American Anthropologist* 85 (1983): 403–6.

Price, Barbara J. "Demystification, Enriddlement, and Aztec Cannibalism: A Materialist Rejoinder to Harner." *American Ethnologist* 5 (1978): 98–115.

Sejourné, Laurette. *Burning Water: Thought and Religion in Ancient Mexico*. New York: Grove Press, 1960.

Smith, Bradley. *Mexico: A History in Art*. Garden City, N.Y.: Doubleday, 1968.

Stevenson, Robert. *Music in Mexico: A Historical Survey*. New York: Crowell, 1971.

Westheim, Paul. *The Sculpture of Ancient Mexico*. Garden City, N.Y.: Anchor Books, 1963.

Zantwijk, Rudolf van. *The Aztec Arrangement: The Social History of Pre-Spanish Mexico*. Norman: University of Oklahoma Press, 1985.

Zorita, Alonso de. *Life and Labor in Ancient Mexico: The Brief and Summary Relation of the Lords of New Spain*. Translated, with an introduction, by Benjamin Keen. New Brunswick, N.J.: Rutgers University Press, 1963.

II THE SPANISH CONQUERORS

6

The Spanish Invasion

"Let us try for a moment to imagine," the late Ramón Iglesia wrote, "the astonishment of the inhabitants of a small island called Guanahaní one morning when they beheld three shapes out there in the water, three immense hulks, out of which issued several absurd beings who seemed human only in their eyes and movements, of light complexion, their faces covered with hair, and their bodies—if indeed they had bodies—covered with fabrics of diverse pattern and color."[1] As they had never conceived the existence of such people, it was natural enough that, in 1492, the natives of the Caribbean fancied Columbus and his Spaniards had descended from the sky. The white men, on the other hand, were aware that beings of different racial characteristics existed. Indeed, they had expected to find people of dark skins and black hair, and, thinking (or at least hoping) that they were in the East Indies, the Spaniards subsequently referred to the natives as Indians. In spite of the natural beauty of the islands and the naked innocence of their handsome natives, the discoverers' joy was restrained, for they found little sign of the precious metals, valuable spices, and other wealth they had sought, and no indication of the civilized and exotic kingdoms of the Orient they had anticipated.

Spanish Exploration and Settlement in the Caribbean

Later voyages to the New World (or the "Indies") dampened even the most optimistic spirits. Consequently the Caribbean

1. Ramón Iglesia, *Columbus, Cortés and Other Essays*, trans. and ed. Lesley B. Simpson (Berkeley, 1969), p. 8.

95

Islands attracted relatively few settlers, and even these became
more disgruntled at each passing year, as hopes of finding either
wealth or fame dwindled. Columbus, who was always happier
sailing about than governing waspish colonists, let administrative matters slide, thus giving the Spanish crown a pretext for
removing him as governor of Santo Domingo, as the New World
colony was called, and revoking the generous terms earlier
granted him. Ultimately, the great discoverer was sent back to
the mother country in chains.

Royal officials then took charge, but the bickering continued.
Nearby islands were explored, some were settled, and Indians
were put to work washing the streams for gold, which provided
good income for a few. Beyond that, and small profits from agriculture, there seemed little opportunity. By 1516 Spaniards had
planted sugarcane in the islands with some success; but that enterprise rewarded only those with sufficient capital to finance
the costly operation. As it slowly dawned on the Spaniards that
they were not, in fact, on the rim of the Orient, they reasoned
that they were at least close to it, and, if a strait through the land
mass to the west could be found, they would soon be rich. With
this vision dancing before them, several expeditions set forth to explore in various directions—up to the coast of Florida, to Central
America, and down to South America.

The seat of royal government was on the island of Santo Domingo, but the larger island of Cuba held out more promise.
Easily conquered in 1511, Cuba proved disappointing. But Spaniards remained in the islands, not only because they continued to
hope that something exciting would turn up but also because
they had little waiting for them back in Spain. At least in the
Indies they had natives working their modest farms or, if they
were lucky, mining for gold. However, one of the tragic consequences of the European occupation of the islands was a catastrophic loss of life among the Indians, partly because of fatigue
and mistreatment but mostly because of their vulnerability to
diseases to which they had no previous exposure or immunity.
Epidemics of smallpox, measles, and other illnesses spread
quickly among the natives, causing widespread death. With the
great decline in the Indian population, a labor shortage ensued.

Governor Diego Velázquez of Cuba sent out an expedition in
1517 for the purpose of trading and finding other Indians to be
enslaved. Under the command of Francisco Hernández de Córdoba, the party of three ships sailed west and touched the coast
of Yucatán, thought at first to be an island. Further exploration

The chapel-de-fer, or kettle-hat, was a helmet popular with the Spanish infantry.

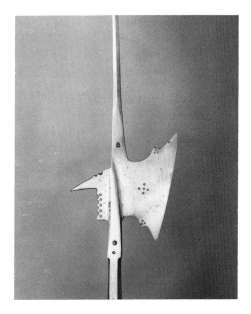

A halberd of the type used by the conquistadores.

An elaborate Spanish stirrup of the seventeenth century.

A warhorse of the sixteenth century was sometimes fitted with a chamfron, like the one shown here.

revealed the existence of cultures higher than those of the Caribbean, with people dressed in cotton fabric who tilled prosperous fields and lived in stone houses. In their brief contact with the natives the Spaniards understood that there was gold and silver in the land, and they also saw the first signs of human sacrifices. After a cautious initial reception, the Spaniards were attacked by a large and very fierce army of warriors, and in the ensuing battle fifty of the Europeans were killed and almost all were wounded. Accustomed to engagements with less bellicose Caribbean Indians, in which few Spaniards were killed, the invaders had a rude awakening. Córdoba was badly wounded by ten arrows, and he returned to Cuba to report his findings. He later died from his injuries, as did several more of his companions.

Despite the ferocity of the Yucatec warriors, the tantalizing references to gold fired the Spaniards' cupidity, and Governor Velázquez prepared to pursue the encouraging prospects. In 1518 he dispatched his nephew, Juan de Grijalva, with four ships and two hundred eager men to investigate further. Making for Yucatán, they sailed up the Gulf side. At a place called Champotón (Tabasco) they met the natives in a furious battle, which again left most of the Spaniards nursing wounds. Now convinced that Yucatán was not an island, Grijalva sailed up the coast to the present state of Veracruz, stopping occasionally to trade European baubles for local goods. By the time they reached the area of Pánuco, the Spaniards were discouraged, and, having been absent from Cuba for five months, they longed to go home. One of the ships returned first, with some small gold objects and rumors of Amazons. Of more interest, however, were the stories of a wealthy lake kingdom to the interior dominated by the great "Lord of Culhúa," by which title coastal Indians knew Moctezuma of the Aztecs. In Cuba this report was greeted with much excitement, but when Grijalva finally arrived home, the governor, disgusted with his nephew's timorous actions, refused to receive him. Grijalva lacked the daring and imagination for a great enterprise and thereby let slip the opportunity that was reserved for another. Sensing the potential for riches and power, Velázquez sought a bolder captain to explore and conquer the new land. Even before Grijalva returned to Cuba, Velázquez had commissioned the thirty-four-year-old Fernando[2] Cortés to undertake this venture.

2. Cortés's first name is often shown as Hernán or Hernando, but he seems to have preferred Fernando.

Fernando Cortés

Cortés was a native of the arid Spanish province of Extrema-
dura, the region from which so many of the prominent conquistadores came. Born in 1485 into an old, honorable family of
slender means, the frail boy grew into a robust youth. At fourteen he was sent to the city of Salamanca to study grammar in a
private home, in preparation for a career in law. But the youth
was restless and often into mischief, finally choosing to seek his
fortunes with the Spanish army at Naples. Subsequently he
changed his mind, and, deciding there was more opportunity in
the Spanish Indies, he prepared to sail with a large fleet. An
amorous adventure frustrated his plans, however; he fell off a
wall outside a bedroom and narrowly escaped death from a
wrathful husband. Injured and ill, he missed the sailing. Later,
when he did catch a ship to the New World, it was 1504, and
Cortés was nineteen.

Benefiting from his acquaintance with the governor of Santo
Domingo, Cortés received a job as notary and a grant of Indians
to work for him. For five or six years his life was uneventful
enough, aside from accompanying Diego Velázquez on an expedition to the interior of the island.

When Velázquez was sent to conquer Cuba in 1511, he asked
Cortés to go along as clerk of the treasurer, and during the campaign the youthful Cortés demonstrated his abilities and re-
sourcefulness. Velázquez, who subsequently became governor of
the island, rewarded him with another grant of Indians, along
with various positions of trust. Cortés settled in the first Spanish
town in Cuba, Santiago de Baracoa, where he raised livestock.
His Indians mined enough gold for him to enter into a trading
partnership, and he looked forward to a promising career as a
merchant. With an official position in local government, Cortés
was a secure and respected member of the community. Had it
not been for the indecision of the governor's nephew, Fernando
Cortés would very likely have ended his days in obscurity.

As Cortés began recruiting men and acquiring ships and supplies for the expedition to Yucatán, Velázquez grew apprehensive about mounting expenses. Worse, the ambitious Cortés
assumed pretentious airs, leading the governor to wonder if he
could control the headstrong captain. When an agent of Velázquez sought to dissuade Cortés from accepting the command,
Cortés quickly raised anchors in November 1518. In western

Cuba he gathered more supplies and was joined by many former companions of Grijalva. But a messenger from the governor ordered the expedition canceled; and, meanwhile, deputies of Velázquez were on their way to arrest Cortés.

Alerted to the danger, Cortés addressed his men, promised them riches and glory, and then prepared to sail immediately. At muster, he counted 550 men, perhaps a hundred of whom were sailors, along with several Cuban Indians and some blacks. The soldiers were divided into eleven companies, each with a captain, and put aboard eleven vessels. The flagship was only one hundred tons, and the other ships were even smaller. Sixteen scarce and expensive horses were put on board, as well as some small cannons. All of this had put Cortés heavily in debt, and there was no money to pay the men wages. But on February 18, 1519, they set sail as adventurers, to gamble on the potentially lucrative outcome.

The Initial Reception

After weathering stormy seas, the ships put in at the island of Cozumel, where friendly natives told them of two white men who lived in nearby Yucatán. Cortés made contact with one of them, Jerónimo de Aguilar, a survivor of a ship wrecked in 1511 en route from Panama to Santo Domingo. The other was thoroughly assimilated into Indian society, but Aguilar was overjoyed to be among his own again. His knowledge of the native language and local customs would be of great assistance to the Spaniards in the months ahead.

Later, at Potonchán (Tabasco), the local natives resisted Cortés's overtures for peace and attacked with abandon. After a bloody contest, Cortés took the city by force. In this and other fights the Spaniards suffered many wounded, but only two men were killed. The Indians, on the other hand, lost two hundred men and were convinced that the Spaniards were invincible. Little gold was found, but the natives said that people to the west had great amounts of it. After lecturing the Indians on their need for salvation through Christianity and describing the mag-

Fernando Cortés (1485–1547) dressed in the half armor used in battle. Full armor was not as heavy as one might think, but it did make the wearer very warm. Most Spaniards eventually adopted use of Indian layered-cotton protection.

Doña Marina, or Malinche, and other Indian girls are given to Cortés and his men in this romanticized version of a European artist.

nificence of the king of Spain, Cortés accepted a gift of twenty young maidens and continued up the Gulf coast.

Reaching San Juan de Ulúa, near the present city of Veracruz, the Spaniards met people who spoke a tongue foreign to Aguilar. However, one of Cortés's young maidens, baptized Marina, understood the language. Her role in the Conquest proved to be of great significance. Doña Marina, as she became known to her contemporaries (and Malinche to Mexicans, who consider her part in the Conquest as treasonous) became Cortés's interpreter and adviser. More than that, she was later his mistress and bore him a son. As a small child she had been given to merchants who sold her to people of the south, and consequently she knew not only her native Náhuatl but the Maya language as well. She communicated with the Indians, passed on the words in Maya to Aguilar, who then translated into Spanish for Cortés.

Realizing that the Indians would report to Moctezuma, Cortés had his men perform a mock battle to impress them. He then asked the local chief to send greetings to Moctezuma and to tell the Indian ruler that the Spaniards had a disease of the heart which could be cured only by gold. Tenochtitlán lay two hundred miles to the interior, but, by swift relay runners, reports of the Spaniards reached the Aztec capital in a day and a half. Pictures of the ships had been sent as soon as they were spotted, so the presence of Cortés was by this time no surprise to Moctezuma. The cautious emperor, fearful that Quetzalcóatl, or his emissaries, had returned to take the throne, now gave careful thought to his next move. For the moment, he sent word that he rejoiced in the coming of the strangers. He sent rich presents and promised to send more; however, he was unable to meet with Cortés because he was ill and could not make the long journey. Moreover, it was out of the question for Cortés to come to see him because the trip through rugged mountains and deserts was too rigorous. Beyond these hardships, the Spaniards would have to pass through dangerous enemy territories. In this fashion Moctezuma wished Cortés well, as if to dismiss him—all of which disheartened the Spanish captain not one bit. He replied by message that he would not think of missing the opportunity of greeting the great Lord of Culhúa after traveling across a great sea and suffering privations that were surely worse than the ones ahead. Anyway, he had an important message from his king and had no choice but to deliver it in person.

Meanwhile, Cortés was well aware of the tenuous legal position in which he found himself. Spaniards were not allowed to go off exploring on their own, but only with royal permission. The administration in Santo Domingo had authorized Governor Velázquez to send out an expedition, but Cortés had ignored the revocation of the governor's commission to him. He was, therefore, something of an outlaw, and dangerously close to treason. Consequently, he sought to clothe his actions with a veneer of legality, gambling that all would be forgiven in the event of a glorious conquest.

With that in mind, he founded a settlement called La Villa Rica de la Vera Cruz (today Veracruz), according to established ceremony, in the king's name, with the procedure duly noted by witnesses. Cortés appointed town councilmen and other appropriate municipal officials and resigned his leadership. The officials of Veracruz then proceeded to elect him captain and *justicia mayor* with authority in military matters, pending royal orders to the contrary.

In order to gain the loyalty and affection of his men, Cortés

turned over to them all the supplies and equipment, which, he
said, had put him seven thousand ducats in debt. He already
had enemies among the troops, especially those adherents of Governor Velázquez, but by this magnanimous, if calculated, gesture
he gained considerable goodwill. In keeping with the generosity
of the moment, the men agreed that, after the king's share of 20
percent—the *quinto*—was deducted, their captain would receive
one-fifth of the remaining spoils.

The Totonacs and a Mutiny Suppressed

Pushing on to the Totonac city of Cempoala, the Spaniards were
enthusiastically greeted by citizens bearing flowers and fruit.
The obese ruler, who had sent regrets that he was too heavy to
travel to meet them, complained of the Aztec tyranny and gave
Cortés a detailed description of Tenochtitlán. He suggested an
alliance of the Spaniards with the victims of the oppressors.

Shortly thereafter an incident occurred that illustrates the
guile of the Spanish captain in his psychological warfare with
the perplexed Moctezuma. The appearance of five Aztec tribute
collectors threw fear into the fat *cacique* (chief), who thought
they would resent his hospitality to the Spaniards. These imperi-
ous agents of Moctezuma ignored the presence of the Spaniards,
reproached the cacique for receiving the strangers, and demanded twenty Totonacs for sacrifice in Tenochtitlán. On the
side, Cortés told the terrified chief to seize the tribute collectors.
When the Totonac leader protested that such an act was sure to
bring harsh retribution from Tenochtitlán, Cortés explained that
he would protect the Cempoalans should any trouble arise, but
that trouble was unlikely, for Moctezuma was, in fact, his friend.
And so the Aztec officials were arrested, roughed up when they
resisted, and bound, unaware that this treatment had been ordered by the Spaniard. That night, in secrecy, Cortés released
two of the Aztecs, posing as their friend. He gave them a message
of good wishes for their emperor and repeated his urgent request
for a meeting.

In the morning, when the Cempoalans discovered the escape
of the tribute collectors, they were frightened and so sure of Aztec vengeance that they decided to rebel against Tenochtitlán.
Cortés agreed to stand by them and told them to send word to
potential allies to be prepared. Cortés then directed other Indian
towns to stop tribute payments to the Aztecs. When an Aztec
garrison punished some Cempoalans, Cortés destroyed it and

The frontispiece illustration of Cortés's Second Letter to Charles V, printed in Seville in 1522.

then released the captives in a gesture intended to impress both the coastal Indians and Tenochtitlán.

His army strengthened by the arrival of a ship from Cuba bearing sixty Spaniards and nine horses, Cortés made plans to press inland. In order to maintain a coastal base, a fortress and houses were built at Veracruz, to be staffed by the ill, wounded, and older men. Cortés wrote the king, telling of his progress to date, assuring him of his devotion, and sending most of the treasure accumulated to that point. He added that he needed help, and he requested financial assistance. The town council wrote another letter to the king, asking that the election of Cortés be confirmed. A ship with the letters, treasure, and two delegates sailed for Spain in late July 1519.

Anticipating the dangers and hardships that lay ahead, some men, especially the followers of Velázquez, plotted mutiny. Their intention was to steal a ship and inform the governor of events so that he could seize the vessel dispatched to Spain. Cortés learned of the conspiracy, and, after a trial and confessions, he hanged two of the leaders and sentenced the pilot to have his feet cut off, while the others were given two hundred lashes. Minor participants, including a priest, were released unpunished.

The companions of Cortés were not soldiers but soldiers-of-fortune, and only firm leadership based on respect (and fear) could maintain discipline. As weaker Spanish captains discovered, such men were prone to mutiny under stressful conditions. Cortés was both intelligent and tactful, but his great authority stemmed most of all from his own fearlessness; he was in the front ranks of battle, and he shared with his men all the fatigues, privations, wounds, fevers, and narrow escapes from death and sacrifice. He was fearless in taking decisive action as well.

Now determined to drive to the highlands as soon as possible, Cortés arranged to give the weakhearted no alternative and the disloyal no opportunity to desert. Alleging the unseaworthiness of the ships, he instructed loyal pilots to strip the vessels and then scuttle them as quietly and quickly as possible. When the men, encamped inland at Cempoala, learned what had happened, they were shocked and angry. According to some versions, the men were told that one ship had been saved to take back to Cuba any who wished to go; then, taking careful note of those who indicated they would be on the vessel, Cortés had the ship sunk. His audacity brought the army close to mutiny, and some no doubt questioned his sanity; but by this bold stroke he cut off all means of retreat. There was now no question of the Spaniards' course—they would have to conquer the mighty Culhúa-Mexica or die in the attempt. So Cortés led his men into the heart of the Aztec empire, on one of the greatest epic adventures of all times.

The Tlaxcalans and Reports to Moctezuma

Moctezuma's depiction of the hardships before the Spaniards was only slightly exaggerated, for the march upcountry would take them some two hundred miles, on a rough and twisting path, from the steamy tropics to the chilling highlands, where they would find the Aztec capital at seventy-five hundred feet. Aside from the wild terrain, there was indeed danger from enemies— both those hostile to the Aztecs and those who acted under the orders of the wily emperor himself.

Leaving 150 men and two horses at Veracruz, Cortés returned to Cempoala with fresh assurances of friendship. He accepted some Indian nobles as hostages and a thousand carriers to bear supplies. The Spaniards departed the city in the middle of August with four hundred troops, the remaining horses, and three cannons. As they pushed inland they were well received by towns subject to Moctezuma, for the emperor had ordered them to be friendly. Cortés sent some of the Cempoalans ahead to make amicable contact with the Tlaxcalans, known to be dedicated enemies of the Aztecs. But the Tlaxcalans, aware of the communications between Cortés and Moctezuma, were suspicious. An advance party of Spaniards ran into a small band of Tlaxcalans, who closed with them and killed two horses. Although finally routed, these few warriors dramatically showed the ferocity and skill that, when they shifted sides, would give the Spaniards a crucial edge. For the moment, the skirmish was considered most unfortunate, for until that time no horse had been killed. The word now spread that the beasts were mortal, a loss of great psychological advantage for the invaders.

While Cortés was trying to win over the Tlaxcalans, noble envoys from Moctezuma arrived to reaffirm the emperor's friendship and willingness to pay a yearly tribute to the king of Spain, provided Cortés halted his ascent to the interior. Cortés thanked the envoys for their concern for his safety and urged them to observe how he would deal with the Tlaxcalans. Moctezuma remained fearful and perplexed as to the best way to treat with the strangers, for he was unsure of not only who but what they were. Hoping to appease the white men, who appeared to be some kind of invincible deities, the Aztec emperor ordered his agents to sacrifice captives whose blood the "gods" might wish to drink; but when the Spaniards reacted with revulsion, Moctezuma was reminded that Quetzalcóatl, too, abhorred human sacrifice.

The European animals with Cortés were terrifying to the natives. Indians could only equate horses with deer, but later descriptions graphically depicted creatures of a more fearful aspect, as beasts who snorted and bellowed and sweated heavily, whose muzzles spilled over with foam. Their running produced tremors, "as if stones were raining on the earth." Although Cortés seems to have utilized war dogs very little in battle, these animals, sometimes trained to kill Indians, accompanied the Spaniards. The very appearance of the swift greyhounds and huge mastiffs, which weighed as much as two hundred pounds, intimidated the natives, one of whom recorded that

> their dogs are enormous, with flat ears and long, dangling tongues. The color of their eyes is a burning yellow; their eyes flash fire and shoot off sparks. Their bellies are hollow, their flanks long and narrow. They are tireless and very powerful. They bound here and there, panting, with their tongues hanging out. And they are spotted, like an ocelot. . . . They raised their muzzles high; they lifted their muzzles to the wind. They raced on before with saliva dripping from their jaws.[3]

In order to frighten Moctezuma's messengers further, on one occasion Cortés tied them down and fired one of the guns, at which the Indians were deafened and fainted dead away.

Receiving descriptions of all these strange and unnerving things, the emperor ordered his magicians and warlocks to work their magic on the Spaniards, to send an evil wind their way. He called for more human sacrifices to the gods. And finally, when these strategies failed to halt the Spaniards' advance, he commanded his people to give the strangers whatever they desired. But Moctezuma was surrounded by warriors who counseled resistance, and the emperor had not ruled out force.

Seeing large numbers of Indians as they proceeded, the Spaniards themselves grew apprehensive about their situation. A potential mutiny was averted by a stirring speech from Cortés. Then came the cheering news that Xicoténcatl, the commander of the Tlaxcalan forces, had decided to deliver his people to the Spanish camp. He agreed to be an ally, after which he listened while Cortés scolded him for not accepting his initial offers of peace and chided him for attempts at deception. Cortés could never resist an opportunity to lecture.

The Cholula Massacre

Moctezuma, who had been kept abreast of these developments by his agents, now sent word requesting Cortés to travel to the city of Cholula to await his decision about a meeting. In fact, it seems

3. Miguel León-Portilla, ed., *The Broken Spears: The Aztec Account of the Conquest of Mexico*, trans. Lysander Kemp (Boston, 1972), pp. ix, 31, 41.

clear that he wanted the Spaniards away from the Tlaxcalans, who in turn warned Cortés of treachery. The lords of Cholula, at first reluctant to meet the Spanish captain, eventually appeared, pleading friendship and offering tribute. Cortés had their pledge interpreted and recorded by notaries and witnesses. His act was no mere formality, because if a people who had sworn fealty to the Spanish sovereign later rebelled, they could be dealt with as traitors. The inhabitants of the city turned out with great fanfare, showering food and flowers on the strangers and perfuming them with incense.

This pleasant interlude did not last long; shortly thereafter the Cholulans ignored their guests and brought no more provisions. Moctezuma had apparently determined to test at Cholula the belief of his militant advisers that the foreigners were simply men of flesh and blood. Secretly encamped in nearby ravines were thirty thousand warriors, and the Cholulans were to bottle up the Spaniards in the city.

Cortés's suspicions were confirmed by Cempoalans, who had noted fortifications and covered pits in the streets, evidently for the entrapment of horses. Then Doña Marina was informed by a friendly Cholulan woman of a plot. Summoned by a ruse to Cortés's quarters, nobles of the city, who had planned in such secrecy, were astonished when the Spanish captain angrily told them that he knew of their treachery. The nobles confessed, swearing that they acted under orders from Moctezuma. Cortés dispatched a message to the Aztec ambassadors, saying that he did not believe this story of the "lying" Cholulans, as he was sure that a great ruler like Moctezuma would never be party to such duplicity. Cortés then ordered the summary execution of some of the nobles as an object lesson.

The Spanish captain now moved to a preemptive strike; he gave a prearranged signal to his men, who were poised for the attack, and the guns raked the main plaza, cutting down the unsuspecting citizens. Cortés gave orders to spare women and children, but in the ensuing five-hour battle some six thousand Cholulan warriors were killed. Much of the ancient holy city was burned and then put to the sack by the Spaniards' Indian allies, who richly savored the defeat of their old enemies.

The massacre at Cholula was a turning point, for Moctezuma, stunned at the Spaniards' prescience, now despaired of stopping them, although more halfhearted attempts would be made. The tragedy of that day is the blackest mark against Cortés in the minds of most Mexicans, who believe that, without provocation,

The Cholula Massacre as depicted by a sixteenth-century Indian artist in the Lienzo de Tlaxcala.

he planned the slaughter. As with so many other events of the Conquest, it is difficult to ascertain the whole truth of the affair, especially since there are few Aztec sources.

Into the Valley of Anáhuac

Cheered by the utter defeat of the first Aztec allies with whom he fought, Cortés now summoned the ambassadors of Tenochtitlán and sternly informed them that, while he had wished to enter the imperial capital in peace, Moctezuma seemed determined to have the Christians killed. Therefore, matters were on a footing of war. Again the emissaries begged Cortés not to be angry but to await another message. Tenochtitlán lay only about sixty miles distant, but it took six days for word to come, along with

the usual gifts. The emperor denied any part of the Cholula conspiracy and, finally, invited Cortés to an audience. Pleased that
he would not have to fight his way into the capital, the Spanish
commander and his men made their way toward the Valley, observed by incredulous natives, one of whom later preserved the
striking impression made by the aliens.

> They came in battle array, as conquerors, and the dust rose in
> whirlwinds on the roads, their spears glinted in the sun, and their
> pennons fluttered like bats. They made a loud clamor as they
> marched, for their coats of mail and their weapons clashed and
> rattled. Some of them were dressed in glistening iron from head
> to foot; they terrified everyone who saw them.[4]

The Spaniards climbed to the snowy pass between the spectacular volcanic peaks of Popocatépetl and Iztaccíhuatl. As they
began the descent into the Valley, they saw laid out in the distance before them the grand prospect of the lake cities. In that
breathless moment, viewing one of the most awe-inspiring sights
man has ever seen, the soldiers had mixed emotions—a tense excitement from the drama of the occasion and all that it promised
but also a chilling realization of the audacity of their scheme,
the dimensions of which were now for the first time abundantly
clear. Cortés went among the men, optimistically soothing their
fears. But as they neared the heart of the Aztec empire none was

ROUTE OF CORTÉS

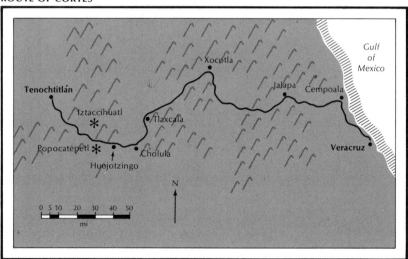

4. Ibid., p. 41.

more alive to the peril than the captain. He spread the rumor to impress the Indians that the Spaniards did not sleep at night or even remove their armor. The horses were kept saddled.

As the army moved toward the lake, an embassy of prominent lords, including the young Cacama, lord of Texcoco, approached to escort the Spaniards, expressing Moctezuma's regrets that he was unable to be there because of illness. The test of wills was not quite over; the lords insisted that Cortés give up, a suggestion that must have become tiresome to the Spanish leader by that point.

Cacama repeated that the Spaniards' way would be resisted and blocked, a threat that now rang hollow. Aside from the botched attempt at Cholula, there had been no serious military opposition on the part of the Aztecs. Since Moctezuma could quickly raise large armies in various parts of the empire, doubtless the Aztecs could have stopped the intruders on the beach, in the mountain passes, or other places suitable for ambush. But there had been the lingering fear that they were divine agents of Quetzalcóatl, a sentiment that Cortés did nothing to dispel. Had a large Aztec army confronted the Spaniards, Moctezuma would be held responsible; and therefore if the strangers were actually gods, as it appeared, the emperor would feel their wrath. Thus he resorted to deception, which could always be denied. Finally, however, the fatalistic emperor was demoralized and resigned to facing Cortés.

Indians of the Valley flocked to observe the entrance of the newcomers, who descended on Ixtapalapa, which anchored the longest causeway. From that beautiful city the Spaniards could look straight down the thoroughfare to where the red and white towers of Tenochtitlán rose out of the water and the torches of the temples shimmered on the lake. Proceeding down the causeway, the Spanish force of about four hundred, with their six thousand native allies, moved through throngs of the curious who lined the way with their canoes. At length the party crossed a drawbridge that gave access to the city, and there, under a canopy of green, gold, and silver, and attended by a splendid retinue, was the lord of the Aztec empire. Moctezuma leaned on the arms of two nephews. Clothed in gorgeous finery, the fifty-two-year-old emperor was of dignified mien, slender, of average height, with longish hair and a very sparse moustache and chin whiskers. As he walked forward, servants placed mantles on the ground so that the royal sandals did not touch the earth. Following him was a magnificent procession of two hundred courtiers.

For his part, Moctezuma must have been struck by the exotic appearance of the white captain, dressed in shiny armor and bright European fabrics and mounted on his war horse. As Cortés dismounted and strode forth to embrace Moctezuma, the nobles restrained him, signifying that the emperor's person was not to be touched. Instead, the leaders saluted each other, obeisance was made all around, and the two exchanged necklaces: the European piece of pearls and diamonds for the Aztec chain hung with several large golden shrimps. Then Moctezuma addressed the Spaniard, greeting him as Quetzalcóatl and welcoming him back to his throne. The "gods" were then domiciled in the palace of Axayácatl. It was November 8, 1519, and, by incredible good fortune, the Spaniards had made it safely into the stronghold of the Culhúa-Mexica.

Recommended for Further Study

Bancroft, Hubert H. *History of Mexico.* 6 vols. San Francisco: A. L. Bancroft, 1883.

Bishko, Charles Julian. "The Iberian Background of Latin American History: Recent Progress and Continuing Problems." *Hispanic American Historical Review* 36 (1956): 50–80.

Chaison, Joanne Danaher. "Mysterious Malinche: A Case of Mistaken Identity." *The Americas* 32 (1976): 514–23.

Collis, Maurice. *Cortés and Montezuma.* London: Faber and Faber, 1954.

Cortés, Hernán. *Hernán Cortés: Letters from Mexico.* Translated and edited by A. R. Pagden, with an introduction by J. H. Elliott. New York: Orion Press, 1971.

Davies, R. Trevor. *The Golden Century of Spain, 1501–1621.* New York: Harper & Row, 1961.

Díaz del Castillo, Bernal. *The True History of the Conquest of New Spain, 1517–1521.* Translated by A. P. Maudslay, with an introduction by Irving Leonard. New York: Farrar, Straus and Giroux, 1966.

Elliot, John H. *Imperial Spain, 1469–1716.* New York: St. Martin's Press, 1962.

Hassig, Ross. *Aztec Warfare: Imperial Expansion and Political Control.* Norman: University of Oklahoma Press, 1988.

Iglesia, Ramón. *Columbus, Cortés and Other Essays.* Translated and edited by Lesley B. Simpson. Berkeley: University of California Press, 1969.

Johnson, Harold R., ed. *From Reconquest to Empire: The Iberian Background to Latin American History.* New York: Knopf, 1970.

Kirkpatrick, F. A. *The Spanish Conquistadores.* New York: World, 1962.

León-Portilla, Miguel, ed. *The Broken Spears: The Aztec Account of the Conquest of Mexico.* Translated by Lysander Kemp. Boston: Beacon Press, 1972.

López de Gómara, Francisco. *Cortés: The Life of the Conqueror by His*

Secretary. Translated and edited by Lesley B. Simpson. Berkeley: University of California Press, 1964.

Lynch, John. *Spain Under the Habsburgs*. Vol. 1: *Empire and Absolutism, 1576–1598*. Vol. 2: *Spain and America, 1598–1700*. New York: Oxford University Press, 1964, 1969.

Merriman, Roger B. *The Rise of the Spanish Empire in the Old World and the New*. 4 vols. New York: Cooper Square Publishers, 1962.

Parry, John H. *The Age of Reconnaissance*. Cleveland: World, 1963.

Pike, Ruth. "Seville in the Sixteenth Century." *Hispanic American Historical Review* 41 (1961): 1–30.

7

The Fall of Tenochtitlán

The Spaniards spent several days wandering about the city, taking in the marvelous sights, much like any tourists in a foreign land. They admired the palaces with their cedar-lined chambers, the gardens, and the canals. Other scenes had quite the opposite effect: they were aghast at the great rack festooned with human skulls; and the priests, their long hair matted with dried blood, were repulsive to them. The visitors were properly fascinated by the zoo, as Bernal Díaz del Castillo noted, but, as for "the infernal noise when the lions and tigers roared, and the jackals and foxes howled, and the serpents hissed, it was horrible to listen to and it seemed like a hell."[1]

A Test of Wills

Moctezuma and his nobles visited their guests' quarters often to provide for all their needs. This attention and gracious hospitality notwithstanding, the peril of the situation was not lost on Cortés, who perceived with the greatest clarity that they were in fact trapped—if Moctezuma chose to make it so. Outside their luxurious palace the Spaniards were surrounded by a multitude of Indians who could rise on signal to ensnare them. The Spanish soldiers manifested their anxiety to Cortés, who now resolved on a bold and desperate course—he would seize as hostage Moctezuma himself.

1. Bernal Díaz del Castillo, *The True History of the Conquest of New Spain, 1517–1521*, trans. A. P. Maudslay, introd. Irving Leonard (New York, 1966), p. 213.

After the Tlaxcalan allies confirmed that the Aztecs were indeed planning to kill the Spaniards, Cortés found a convenient pretext: some of his men at the Spanish garrison at Veracruz had been killed, and Cortés accused Moctezuma of ordering their deaths and, worse, of preparing to massacre the Spaniards in Tenochtitlán. Despite the emperor's vehement denials, Cortés courteously but firmly told Moctezuma that he must remain in custody. The emperor would continue to rule his people and would be treated with the greatest respect. Meantime he was to counsel calm and patience among his people, because any outbreak of hostilities would result in his death.

This turn of events was inconceivable to the dignified lord of the Aztecs, who protested that his subjects would never suffer such an outrage, but he finally submitted. To check the rising anger among his people, Moctezuma announced that he was not a prisoner; rather, he resided with the strangers at his pleasure, because it was the will of the gods. Though kept under guard, Moctezuma was treated with kindness. His servants, women, and advisers were free to visit him, and he was allowed to leave his chambers to worship at the great temple. Cortés even gave him permission to go hunting with his own people, with the understanding that the Spanish guards would kill him if he attempted to bolt. The emperor, however, seemed strangely resigned to remaining with his captors. To a greater extent than previous rulers, he was an intellectual, like his grandfather, Nezahualcóyotl. He was a man of sentiment and reason, both of which Cortés played on with consummate skill. Woe to the Spaniards if they had arrived a few years earlier, during the reign of Ahuítzotl!

The general populace of Tenochtitlán abided by the ruler's wish for peace out of respect for his exalted rank, but some of the leaders did so only grudgingly. They were incensed at Cortés's demands that human sacrifice cease and pagan idols be smashed, to be replaced by crosses and images of the Virgin Mary.

Acts of Moctezuma attributed to pusillanimity may in fact have stemmed merely from his acceptance of a prophecy come true. If the gods had allowed this to happen, it was foolish, if not wrong, to resist. Other Aztecs, however, less devout and tradition bound, remained skeptical of the divine attributes of the strangers. The Spaniards remained about six months before the Aztecs reacted strongly. Outraged at the desecration of their religion, the priests roused the populace and joined the warriors in calling for an attack. Moctezuma advised Cortés, with the greatest urgency, to leave the city.

The Spanish captain agreed to depart whenever Moctezuma wished. The relieved ruler promised more gold and added that there was no great hurry in leaving. But even as the interpreter was translating the first words of the conversation, Cortés dispatched one of his men to alert the Spaniards to stand by. He told Moctezuma that, since his ships had been destroyed, he would need others to carry them away, and he requested Indian carpenters to help build them. At the same time, he instructed his own carpenters to stall for time and to stay alert. Cortés, of course, had no intention of departing.

However, this abrupt change in the state of affairs altered Cortés's plans to bring more men from the Caribbean in order to complete his take-over of Mexico and to introduce clergymen to effect the mass conversion of the Indians to Christianity. Under the ominous circumstances, the Spaniards nervously bided their time, planning and praying for a miracle. They did not get one, but a diversion of serious import did arise to break the tense atmosphere. Moctezuma asked to see Cortés, and the Spaniard, bearing in mind their recent meeting, feared the worst. Before leaving, he addressed his men, exhorting them to fight bravely, to commend themselves to God, and to die with dignity if this were to be the final act. But what Cortés learned from the emperor was news of a very different sort. The pleased ruler told Cortés that the Spaniards could leave immediately—a fleet of eleven ships, bearing nine hundred men, stood off the shore at Veracruz.

The Narváez Expedition

In Cuba, Diego Velázquez seethed with anger against Cortés and grew more bitter with news of his protégé's success. To Velázquez, Cortés's deeds represented a blatant act of rebellion. The governor's hand was strengthened, however, when the king, in ignorance of the Cortés venture, appointed Velázquez governor of whatever territories he could control in "Yucatán." Armed with this extended jurisdiction, Velázquez assembled a large force to pursue the rebel captain and arrest him. Under the command of Pánfilo de Narváez, the expedition included not only a very sizable complement of foot soldiers but also eighty horses.

Making port at Veracruz, Narváez ordered two soldiers and a priest to the garrison, now under the command of the capable Gonzalo de Sandoval, to demand submission. Sandoval arrested the three of them and sent them off to Cortés. Narváez then landed his troops and proceeded instead to Cempoala, where the Totonacs, assuming the newcomers to be associates of Cortés, lavished gifts and provisions on them. Narváez insinuated himself into the good graces of the Cempoalans, convincing them that Cortés and his men were traitors and adding that he intended to behead Cortés and send his men back to Cuba. He confided similar tidings to the agents of Moctezuma, with the assurances that, after Cortés was taken, all Spaniards would leave the country and the emperor would again rule as before. Moctezuma, unknown to Cortés, responded with presents and encouragement to Narváez. But the emperor was no fool; in actuality, he was exploiting the quarrel between the two Spanish forces. For the first time since the strangers arrived, the hapless ruler found himself in a favorable position, and now he was playing both sides against the middle. With good fortune, the white men might kill each other off.

On first learning of the large Spanish expedition on the coast, Cortés had a sense of foreboding—it was an army roughly twice as large as his own. If they were friends, he would have the strength necessary to take Mexico, but if, as he suspected, they were from Velázquez, his prospects were in the most serious jeopardy. After learning of Narváez's intent, Cortés sent his agents with gifts and instructions to inquire if Narváez had a commission from the king. Cortés would obey any royal orders, but if there were none, then he considered himself the authority in the land. In any case, he suggested a peaceful meeting to work out some compromise. But Narváez, believing he held the whip hand with his superior forces, was not disposed to parley.

Cortés mustered his men and told them that Narváez and his men had dishonored them by insults and were trying to steal what they had won with their sweat and blood. The captain selected some volunteers to accompany him to Veracruz and asked Moctezuma to assure the safety of the Spaniards left behind. The emperor agreed, offering the use of Aztec warriors to Cortés. Leaving Pedro de Alvarado in command of about 140 men in the city, Cortés departed for the coast with the same number. In Cholula he was joined by 120 of his men who had been settling a town on the lower Gulf coast.

In a rapid march Cortés soon put his men on the outskirts of

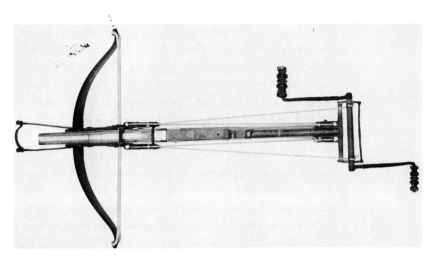

A crossbow with windlass of the type used in the Conquest. Because of its devastating force, popes forbade its use against Christians; but it was used very effectively in wars against Moslems and natives of the New World.

A wheel-lock pistol of the sixteenth century. This one belonged to Charles V.

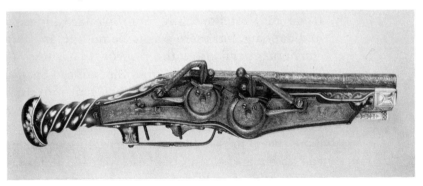

Cempoala, arriving under cover of darkness. He attacked suddenly, at midnight during a driving rainstorm, and in the confusion and darkness he gained the advantage. It appears that many of the newcomers were less than anxious to resist Cortés, and, in fact, some of the key people may well have been suborned. After a frenzied skirmish Narváez took a pike in the eye and surrendered.

The swift and decisive action of Cortés, which saw the ignominious rout of a much larger force, served to enhance his prestige among the Indians as well as with the men of Narváez. A diplomat of genius, Cortés now showed generosity to the defeated soldiers, most of whom he had known in Cuba. They were eager enough to join him when they were promised their share of the spoils. With his ranks now swelled and sanguine of the outcome, the captain was ready to seize the land. But as he set out for the return to Tenochtitlán, a battered messenger brought news of disaster—the Aztecs had risen up, and Alvarado and his companions were pinned down in their quarters.

The Spaniards Besieged and the Sad Night

The nobles of Tenochtitlán had received from Alvarado permission to celebrate their most important fiesta, that of Toxcatl, in honor of Huitzilopochtli. The Spaniard agreed to the singing and dancing, but there was to be no human sacrifice. There are conflicting versions of the tragedy that subsequently occurred. We assume, in any event, that the reduced Spanish garrison was edgy, especially since Narváez had sent provocative messages to the Aztecs, inciting them to rebel against the men of Cortés. Whatever the results of the confrontation at Veracruz, the Indians were presented with a tempting opportunity, as Cortés was absent and so few Spaniards were left in the city.

According to Alvarado, he was informed that the ceremonial dance to the war god was a prelude to an attack on the Spaniards, who were to be sacrificed. Therefore he determined to strike first. Others have maintained that he was moved by bloodlust, or that he simply overreacted to rumors without basis in fact. Whatever the truth, during the festivities the Spaniards blocked the four exits from the square, drew their swords, and rushed the celebrants. There followed a wild and bloody scene in which the Indians, caught unprepared and without escape, had little chance. In a short time some two hundred Aztec nobles fell under Spanish steel. After the Spaniards retreated to their quarters they were besieged by thousands of grief-stricken and enraged Indians.

Cortés, fearing the worst, made forced marches to the Valley in order to lift the siege. Approaching Tenochtitlán, he found a strangely silent city, showing little sign of activity. He fired a cannon and was heartened to hear a return boom. Later he learned that only the influence of Moctezuma had saved the defenders in the palace of Axayácatl. Oddly enough, the entrance of Cortés was unopposed. The Aztecs observing the return of Cortés saw a much larger force, consisting of about one thousand soldiers and one hundred cavalrymen. Counting those already in the city, Cortés now commanded an army about three times larger than his original force. Although he gained the palace without difficulty, it soon became clear that the Aztecs had simply allowed him to walk into a trap.

The Spaniards preferred fighting in wide open spaces where they could deploy their guns to advantage and charge their horses into enemy ranks. Confined in the city, hemmed in by buildings that afforded protection to the Indians, they were less effective. The Aztecs made repeated assaults on the Spanish position, finally resorting to what resembled suicide squads. The cannons put shot into them at close range, while the harquebuses, falconets, and crossbows took a frightful toll—and still they came. Cortés led a counterattack, but the swath he cut was immediately filled in. As fresh relays of Aztecs rushed the Spaniards, the defenders grew weary.

The Spaniards then began building three tall wooden barricades, mounted on rollers. With this protection they hoped to move forward with less risk, but before the vehicles were finished the enemy attacked with such recklessness that Cortés persuaded Moctezuma, who was still held hostage, to urge the Aztecs to desist. The ruler mounted the rooftop to draw attention and began to speak. In the confusion of battle not everyone saw him, and so it was apparently by accident that one of the stones thrown by the Aztecs struck him in the temple. He died three days later.

This version of his death is best documented, although some charge that Moctezuma was strangled or stabbed to death on orders from Cortés. Because he was irresolute in dealing with the Spaniards, refusing to rally his people in opposition—eventually, in fact, appearing to favor the white men—Moctezuma is viewed in Mexican histories as less than heroic. The ruler was not a coward (his bravery had been tested on the field of battle), but his true sentiments and motives remain enigmatic. In a crisis that called for a leader of visceral instincts, Mexico was ruled by a man of deliberation.

As the Indians resumed the offensive, the Spaniards put their mobile barricades to the test. The vehicles were soon smashed, and the soldiers beat a hasty retreat. Thereafter things went badly for the Christians, for while they could make offensive thrusts, they could not sustain a retreat from the city, surrounded as they were by tens of thousands of their adversaries. With food and powder almost depleted and his men badly mauled from the fighting, Cortés sought to make a truce. But the Aztecs, although suffering heavy casualties, rejected the offer with shrill hoots and insults.

Cortés, seeing the Spanish position as untenable and deteriorating, decided to make a break for it that night. The chosen avenue for escape was the Tacuba causeway, which, though said to have been two miles long, was the shortest of them. The Aztecs had removed the bridges spanning the gaps in the causeways, so Cortés ordered the construction of a portable bridge, which was to be carried by forty Tlaxcalan warriors. The treasure acquired earlier from Moctezuma was divided, with each man allowed to take what he wished for his share. Some, especially those who had come with Narváez, foolishly weighted themselves down with precious metals and jewelry, which later hampered their movements and contributed to their capture or death.

Sandoval, who had returned to Tenochtitlán with Cortés, was put in charge of the lead columns, while Alvarado was given command of the rear guard. Cortés elected to lead a flying squad of one hundred men, ready to shift to any weak point. At midnight they stole quietly out of the palace, the horses' hooves wrapped in cloth to muffle their movements. A heavy fog and light rain helped obscure the figures but made the footing treacherous. It was early in the morning of July 1, 1520, the *Noche Triste*, or Sad Night, as it has come down in history.

Moving carefully over the causeway the Spaniards were able to place their bridge over the first channel and cross. Then suddenly an old woman drawing water from a canal spotted them and cried out. Sentries sounded the alarm with blasts on their conch shells, and the Aztecs came pouring out of the darkness. Thousands of warriors fell on the escapees, and some Spaniards in the rear were cut off and seized. Other Indians flanked the causeway in their canoes and shot into the mass. The Aztecs emitted their customary loud whoops, which, taken with the

The Spanish retreat from the island city of Tenochtitlán was a great Aztec victory.

clang of metal, cries of the wounded, and the thrashings of horses, set up a din that made for utter chaos. The Spanish formations broke as each man tried to save himself.

With great effort the bridge was thrown across the second breach, and Cortés and four other horsemen galloped across, followed by a hundred scrambling foot soldiers. Under such strain the bridge collapsed, throwing into confusion and panic those who followed. Cortés and his cohorts raced for the mainland, forced to swim the remaining breaks in the causeway. Placing the hundred foot soldiers to hold the end of the avenue, Cortés and the other horsemen wheeled and spurred back to the melee. The unit in gravest danger was the rear guard, for it was taking the brunt of the Aztec charge. Alvarado, seeing his men overwhelmed, called to Cortés for help. Alvarado's mare had fallen under him, and he now stumbled over the masses of the dead choking the breaches and crossed on the bodies. As the enemy closed, Alvarado, who was a powerful athlete, sprinted toward the last open channel, placed the point of his lance, and, according to some contemporary accounts, made a tremendous vault that carried him over to safety. Some of his companions who attempted the same feat fell short and drowned in the dark waters.

In that terrifying night, the most drastic reversal of Spanish arms in the conquests of the New World, at least 450 of Cortés's men died[2] and more than four thousand of the steadfast Indian allies fell. Forty-six of the horses lay sprawled along the littered causeway. The survivors gained the mainland where, according to tradition, Fernando Cortés was so moved by the disaster that he sat under a great tree and wept.

The Spaniards Regroup

Because of their catastrophic defeat at Tenochtitlán, the Spaniards were uncertain of their reception from the various Indian groups that had previously sworn them allegiance. As the Spaniards neared Tlaxcalan territory, however, they were greeted by lords from Tlaxcala and Huejotzingo who offered consolation and warriors. Had it not been for these allies Cortés and his men would have been lost.

It required all of Cortés's force of personality and subtle blandishments to prevent mass defections and rebellion among his men. Cortés, who seems never to have wavered in his determination to retake Tenochtitlán, began to lay plans for the return. He conceived an ingenious plan for securing the island city: he would assault it by water as well as by land. To that end he set carpenters to work constructing launches in sections, which could be carried across the mountains by native porters and assembled on the lake shore. The vessels would be fitted for both sails and oars. Events proved this strategy to be an inspiration of tactical brilliance.

Following the victory in Tenochtitlán, the elated Aztecs raised to the throne a nephew of Moctezuma, Cuitláhuac, lord of Ixtapalapa. With the Aztecs now geared for total war and with no moderate voice at their court, the next confrontation with the Spaniards would be much different. Certain of the earlier advantages were now lost to the white men. The Indians knew that the strangers were not deities—they had slain them, sacrificed them to their gods, and even tasted of their flesh. Nor did the horses inspire the same terror; it was futile to attempt outrunning them, but they bled, too, and the Indians learned that they could be hamstrung. This time there would be no slick diplomacy on either side, no intrigue, no pleasant embassies pleading friendship and exchanging gifts. Now the mutual hatred was exposed, with each

---

2. Bernal Díaz del Castillo, who was present, wrote that on the Sad Night and in the next five days, during which the Aztecs pursued them, over 860 Spaniards died. Ibid., p. 321.

Cuauhtémoc (1502?–1525), the last Aztec emperor, as he appeared to a post-Conquest artist.

side bent on the destruction of the other. All things considered, it appeared that the Aztecs had gained the advantage.

But the Spaniards had a silent, deadly, and totally unexpected ally in the land: one of Narváez's men came to Mexico infected with smallpox, which spread quickly with devastating consequences to the Indians. Tens of thousands were carried off by the disease. It was, some Spaniards noted with satisfaction, only just, for the Indians had introduced them to syphilis.[3] The pox was contracted by Emperor Cuitláhuac within a short time, and when he succumbed, the lords chose the last Aztec ruler. He was the eighteen-year-old Cuauhtémoc, another nephew of Moctezuma. Cuauhtémoc has become a symbol of valor, the cultural hero of Indian Mexico. In the view of most Mexicans, he came to power two years too late.

The Final Assault

In late December 1520 the Spanish army crossed the mountains and re-entered the Valley of Anáhuac, opposed only by harassing feints of the Indians. Cortés made headquarters at Texcoco, where he found a calm reception. Waiting for the launches to be

3. Francisco López de Gómara, *Cortés: The Life of the Conqueror by His Secretary,* trans. and ed. Lesley B. Simpson (Berkeley, 1964), p. 205.

completed in Tlaxcala, Cortés set out to isolate the island city of Tenochtitlán by winning over the surrounding population with diplomacy or force. Both tactics were used with considerable success.

Sandoval proceeded to Tlaxcala to escort the launches. Sections of the thirteen vessels were carried over the mountains by eight thousand porters, while another two thousand bore provisions. The long procession, stretching out almost six miles, arrived at the Spanish camp at Texcoco after a four-day journey, without grave incident. By failing to attack the vulnerable column, the Aztecs lost the opportunity to destroy the cutting edge of the Spanish offense.

Ready at last to launch the invasion, Cortés reviewed his forces, now augmented by the arrival of additional adventurers from the Caribbean. He counted 900 Spaniards, of whom 86 had horses, 118 carried crossbows and harquebuses, and all were armed with swords and daggers. Some wielded pikes and halberds, most had shields, and many wore some form of protective armor. There were fifteen bronze cannons and three heavy guns of cast iron. Supporting the Spaniards were native legions numbering some hundred thousand warriors.

The small Spanish fleet was crucial to their strategy, for if the causeways could be commanded, all transportation and communication to the island could be cut off. Moreover, the Aztecs could be prevented from attacking the Spaniards from their canoes. Each launch had about a dozen men manning the oars, and other Spaniards aboard were armed with crossbows and additional weapons. Cortés chose to command the fleet in person. Those fighting on land were assigned to three commanders, each of whom was to secure a causeway, and on May 10, 1521, they moved to occupy their positions.

On the lake Cortés first overpowered a fortified rocky isle, at which smoke signals went up from various positions to alert Tenochtitlán. Five hundred Aztec canoes appeared before the Spanish vessels, but they stopped just short of harquebus range, as the Indians contented themselves with hurling insults at the Spaniards. Then, suddenly, a stiff breeze came up and caught the sails, and Cortés bore down on the canoes with such speed that many were swamped and crushed. Some Aztecs escaped to the city, but a large number were captured. The rout was important: it demonstrated that the canoes were no match for the launches, which gave the attackers control over the lake. Spanish boats penetrated canals on the edges of the city, after which the attack-

An Aztec Jaguar Knight dressed for battle, wearing a pelt and wielding an obsidian-edged war club.

A mounted Spaniard in full armor.

ers set fire to many houses. With the success of the operation on
water, Alvarado and Cristóbal de Olid charged down the causeways to engage the defenders of the barricades and bridges.

The Spaniards' early optimism proved unjustified. Furious
fighting continued for weeks, for although the attackers were
able to penetrate sections of the city, they could not easily hold
positions. They were assailed by warriors who rained arrows and
stones on them from the flat rooftops while others engaged them
in hand-to-hand combat. The advantages of horse and cannon
were greatly reduced in the close street fighting. Cortés concluded, to his regret, that he must level the city. Accordingly, his
men began the systematic destruction of the great temples and
palaces that afforded his adversaries protection.

Early on, the aqueducts had been cut, and the launches swept
the lake to prevent water, food, and reinforcements from reaching the besieged defenders. Still, in the face of heavy casualties,
illness, and a lack of food and drinking water, the Aztecs held
out, resigned to the warrior's death. Attempts to effect a truce
failed. Finally, in a last concerted offensive, the Spaniards and
their native allies overran the Aztec position. In the savage fi-
nale Cortés and Alvarado backed the survivors to the wall, and it
was all over. Tenochtitlán fell on August 13, 1521.

Cuauhtémoc had escaped in a large canoe, but he was captured on the lake. He was taken to Cortés, who treated the ruler
with courtesy. Cuauhtémoc then touched the dagger in Cortés's
belt and spoke: "I have done everything in my power to defend
myself and my people, and everything that it was my duty to do,
to avoid the pass in which I now find myself. You may do with
me whatever you wish, so kill me, for that will be best."[4]

When the tumult subsided and the dust settled, there remained a scene of desolation: the beautiful metropolis effectively
smashed, the gardens flattened, and the canals filled with rubble.
The destruction of one of history's grandest cities was accompanied by great heroism and suffering on both sides. Aside from
their superior weapons and armor, the Spaniards derived great
advantage from their horses, the spread of smallpox, and a favorable psychological atmosphere. They benefited, moreover,
from their practical application of a strategy that ignored the
ceremonial formalities inherent in Aztec warfare.

Brilliant as it was in certain respects, Aztec civilization thrived
on militarism; therefore, the character of its fall was consistent
with its rise. And it was poetically apt that its last great warrior-

4. Quoted in ibid., p. 292.

king was Cuauhtémoc, whose name translates "Falling Eagle" or, in another sense, "Setting Sun."

Recommended for Further Study

Cerwin, Herbert. *Bernal Díaz, Historian of the Conquest*. Norman: University of Oklahoma Press, 1963.

Denhardt, Robert M. "The Equine Strategy of Cortés." *Hispanic American Historical Review* 18 (1938): 550–55.

———. "The Truth about Cortés's Horses." *Hispanic American Historical Review* 17 (1937): 525–32.

Gardiner, C. Harvey. *The Constant Captain: Gonzalo de Sandoval*. Carbondale: Southern Illinois University Press, 1961.

———. *Martín López, Conquistador Citizen of Mexico*. Lexington: University Press of Kentucky, 1958.

———. *Naval Power in the Conquest of Mexico*. Austin: University of Texas Press, 1956.

Graham, R. B. Cunninghame. *The Horses of the Conquest*. London: Heinemann, 1930.

Kelly, John E. *Pedro de Alvarado, Conquistador*. Princeton, N.J.: Princeton University Press, 1932.

MacNutt, F. A. *Fernando Cortés and the Conquest of Mexico, 1485–1547*. New York: Putnam, 1909.

Madariaga, Salvador. *Hernán Cortés, Conqueror of Mexico*. Chicago: Regnery, 1955.

Padden, Robert C. *The Hummingbird and the Hawk: Conquest and Sovereignty in the Valley of Mexico, 1503–1541*. New York: Harper & Row, 1970.

Prescott, William H. *History of the Conquest of Mexico*. New York: Bantam Books, 1967. There are many other editions.

Scholes, France V. "The Last Days of Gonzalo de Sandoval, Conquistador of New Spain." In *Homenaje a Don José María de la Peña y Cámara*, pp. 181–200. Madrid: Ediciones José Porrúa Turanzas, 1969.

Vigil, Ralph H. "A Reappraisal of the Expedition of Pánfilo de Narváez to Mexico in 1520." *Revista de Historia de América* 77–78 (1974): 101–25.

Wagner, Henry R. *The Rise of Fernando Cortés*. Los Angeles: Cortés Society, 1944.

White, Jon Manchip. *Cortés and the Downfall of the Aztec Empire*. New York: St. Martin's Press, 1971.

8

The Settlement of New Spain

The conquerors withdrew to nearby Coyoacán, leaving the Aztecs to remove their dead. The Spaniards decided to build a new city over the ruins of Tenochtitlán, and soon armies of native laborers under the direction of Spanish architects and artisans laid the foundations for the splendid city of Mexico. It would be the capital of New Spain, by which name the country would be officially known for the next three centuries.

The Encomienda System

The Conquest had been the result of a great effort by individual adventurers who received no pay for their work. Many had gone into debt in order to outfit themselves for the enterprise; all had suffered great hardships and had seen companions die horrible deaths; almost all had been wounded. Those who survived thanked God and prepared to enjoy the fruits of victory. But the treasure for which they had endured so much proved to be a pittance. Some of the survivors of the Noche Triste had escaped with a few valuable objects, but the bulk of the riches had been lost in the lake waters.[1] Of the spoils, a horseman received as his share only about a hundred gold pesos, one-fifth of the cost of a horse. Foot soldiers, who constituted the bulk of the army, received even less. As the mood of his companions grew more ugly,

---

1. In 1981, several feet underground in Mexico City a crude gold bar was found. Quite possibly it was dropped on the retreat.

Cortés relented and allowed the torture of Cuauhtémoc and other lords, hoping thereby to learn the location of any remaining hoard of riches. The royal feet of the nobles were oiled and held over fire. Despite their agonies, they gave no information, for there was no cache—or at least none has ever been found.

One of Cortés's first concerns was to secure the tribute rolls of the Aztec treasurer, which contained paintings identifying the subject towns along with the kinds and amounts of tribute paid to Tenochtitlán. There were 370 such towns, each having yielded to the Aztec emperor one-third of its production. Thus the Spanish captain acquired knowledge of the population, the geography, and the economy—not to mention the tribute that the conquerors could now enjoy. In order to calm his irate soldiers, Cortés agreed, with some misgivings, to distribute the Indian towns to them as rewards.

There was a precedent for this practice; in the Caribbean Islands, Spaniards had been granted native villages for their profit. As originally conceived, this system, the *encomienda*, was seen as the best solution for all concerned. The individual deserving Spaniard (the *encomendero*) received the tribute of the Indians, as well as their free labor, in return for which the natives were commended to the encomendero's care. He was to see to their conversion to Christianity, to ensure good order in the village, and in all ways to be responsible for their welfare. It was hoped that by this system the Indians would be more easily acculturated, better controlled, and protected. What happened in practice was quite another matter, as the system, subjected to every imaginable abuse, kept the Indians in a state of serfdom and led to all sorts of horrors. Indians were overworked, separated from their families, cheated, and physically maltreated. The encomienda in early decades was responsible for demeaning the native race and creating economic and social tragedies that persisted in one guise or another into modern times.

The tremendous loss of Indian lives, attributable at least in part to this system, was a grim warning against awarding encomiendas in other lands. Moreover, the Spanish crown wanted the tribute for itself and thus sought to maintain direct control over the Indians to retain them as royal vassals. The thought of the conquered multitudes being subject to the whims of the conquerors was unsettling to the sovereign. Yet the crown could not —or would not—compensate those who had won extensive territories and millions of people for Spain. And so the king grudg-

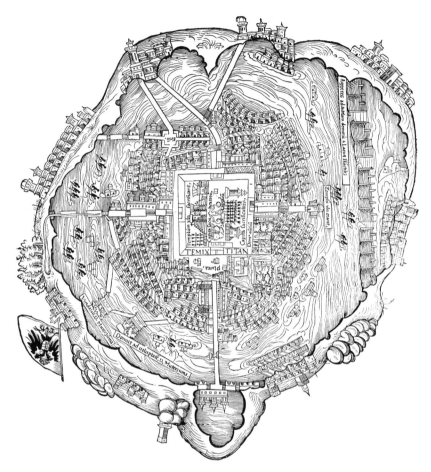

An early map of "Temixtitan" (Tenochtitlán). Probably drawn at the request of Cortés, it appeared in the Latin edition of his Second Letter, printed in Nuremburg in 1524. In order to ingratiate himself, Cortés wrote five long letters to the king in which he related the progress of the Conquest.

ingly allowed the awarding of encomiendas for New Spain. Nonetheless, he was never at ease with the arrangement and from the first sought the means to bring all Indian towns under royal control. The struggle between the crown and the individuals who held encomiendas was a dominant theme for much of the sixteenth century.

The Spread of Conquest

Even before the fall of Tenochtitlán, Cortés had sent small parties to explore the land's resources. They returned with information on sources of gold and silver and reported on the location of natural ports and timber for the construction of ships. Once he had secured the Valley, Cortés lost no time in dispatching expeditions in all directions to bring under Spanish control other inhabitants in the country. He was impelled to do so for various reasons: to gather more information about the people and the land, to satisfy a consuming interest in the existence of a strait through the continent to Asia, and to dominate as much territory as possible before rivals staked their claims. His time was short, for the crown had ordered an agent to take over the government and to arrest him. By August 1521 Cristóbal de Tapia had arrived, but he was intimidated by partisans of Cortés and withdrew. The conqueror meanwhile sent the king word of his defeat of the Aztecs, after which Cortés was forgiven his insubordination.

During the course of the next several years Spanish forces under many different lieutenants overran Mexico, parts of Central America, and much of what is now the southwestern United States. And although the Conquest of the Mexica-Aztecs had taken a relatively short time, the Spaniards soon discovered that bringing under their sway the entire land was a vastly more difficult enterprise.

Highly centralized states strongly dependent on a dominant capital are vulnerable, tending to disintegrate quickly when the center falls. Hence the collapse of the imperial capital of Tenochtitlán was tantamount to the surrender of almost all towns under the city's control, and, therefore, much of central Mexico automatically fell to the invaders. There were many other areas of Mexico, however, that had remained outside the Aztec pale. Some threw in with the Spaniards early, and some came around as the Spaniards gained in reputation. But others, which had successfully resisted the Aztecs, rejected Spanish overlordship as well. While none could command forces comparable to those of the Aztecs, their more fragmented political structure made conquest difficult. Fighting the loosely organized tribes of Mexico presented the same frustrations and vexing problems that confront those dealing with guerrilla tactics in modern warfare.

Cortés was eager to plant settlements with a view to legitimizing his actions. In 1521 he sent Gonzalo de Sandoval to Coatzacoalcos (later called Puerto México but now known also by its Indian name) to settle that region and establish better communications with the islands. The same year Luis Marín departed for Oaxaca, where he encountered little success in his attempt to pacify the Zapotecs in hill country. He was more fortunate far-

A Lacandón Indian by an altar at Bonampak. Now almost extinct, the Lacandones resisted Christian domination with great tenacity and ferocity.

ther south in Chiapas, remaining until 1524 to establish a town; but in 1527, the Chiapanecos rebelled, and the territory had to be reconquered by Diego de Mazariegos.

The governor of Jamaica, Francisco de Garay, had earlier been granted a royal commission to govern the Pánuco region north of Veracruz on the Gulf coast. Hoping to prevent what they considered an incursion, Cortés and Alvarado used force and diplomacy to convince Garay to withdraw. Meanwhile Cristóbal de Olid, one of Cortés's closest friends and confidants, was sent to western Mexico in 1522. After a cordial reception in Michoacán, he explored the Pacific coast, but in Colima he was stiffly opposed and forced to pull back.

Aware that expeditions from Panama were pushing northward up into Central America, Cortés moved to seize control first. Rumors circulated of cities rivaling Tenochtitlán in size and wealth, and in late 1523 Alvarado was ordered into the old Maya territory of Guatemala. After some arduous campaigns, he drove into El Salvador and conquered that region as well. For Alvarado's brilliant, though sanguinary, accomplishments, a grateful Spanish king appointed him governor and captain general of the lands he had won.

Shortly after Alvarado's departure from Mexico, Olid set sail

PRINCIPAL EXPLORATIONS AND CONQUESTS IN THE SIXTEENTH CENTURY

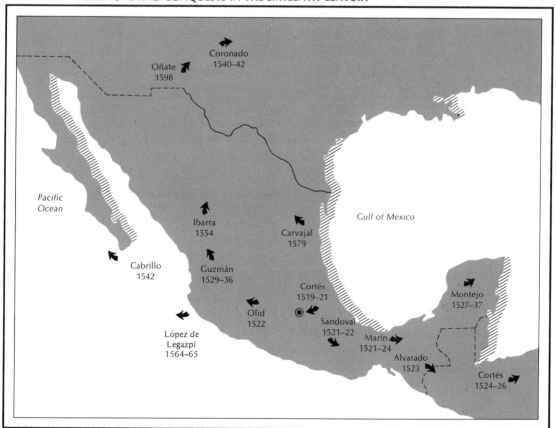

The flamboyant Pedro de Alvarado
(1485–1541), Cortés's lieutenant and the
conqueror of Guatemala.

to secure Honduras, stopping by Cuba for provisions. At this
point Olid threw off loyalty to his captain and made common
cause with the enemy, Governor Velázquez. When Cortés
learned that Honduras was to be taken in the name of Olid and
Velázquez, he was furious. He dispatched a punitive expedition,
then decided to go down himself. It was the most costly decision
the conqueror ever made.

Departing Mexico with a party of Spaniards mostly mounted,
along with many Indian allies, musicians, tumblers, acrobats,
and some young Spanish noblemen, Cortés headed to the Gulf
coast and then cut southward across unknown country. The journey took them through Tabasco, Campeche, and the base of Yucatán. Because they were not following native trade routes, they
encountered few settlements and had to survive off the wilderness. Great numbers of the porters collapsed from exhaustion,
and many of the horses perished also. Indians and Spaniards
alike contracted fevers and dysentery, and all suffered from near

starvation. Though lacking the drama of the Aztec Conquest, the Honduras march exceeded the earlier enterprise in sheer hardship. For months the expedition cut its way through thick jungles, waded in swamps, and crossed swollen rivers. Once, within a distance of fifty miles, the Spaniards were forced to build fifty bridges, one of which, by Cortés's account, required a thousand trees. During this disastrous march a tragic episode occurred. Cuauhtémoc and several other high Indian lords had been taken along as hostages lest, in the absence of Cortés from Mexico, they encourage a native rebellion. When they allegedly attempted to foment an uprising among the Indians on the expedition, all, including Cuauhtémoc, were summarily tried and hanged.

At last Cortés and his men stumbled into Honduras, only to find that all had been in vain, for the advance punitive party had beheaded the rebel Olid and returned to Mexico. After spending some time trying to establish a settlement in his name, the captain set about returning, this time wisely traveling by sea. The nineteen-month venture was a remarkable achievement of exploration and endurance but a fiasco in all else.

Cortés Is Discredited

Before departing for Honduras, Cortés had entrusted the government to the hands of royal treasury officials, with Alonso de Estrada in charge. Estrada was an honorable judge, but he found it difficult to govern the various factions that had formed, and he finally lost control. Because the expedition to Honduras remained out of contact with civilization so long, the rumor spread in Mexico that Cortés and the others had perished. Encouraged by word of Cortés's death, various factions moved to dispossess his followers of their encomiendas and other privileges, which were then handed over to supporters of corrupt treasury officials. It was a time of anarchy, as both Spaniards and Indians were maltreated.

The usurping governors ordered funeral ceremonies for Cortés and his men and then granted permission for the "widows" to remarry. When one of the wives, Juana Ruiz de Marcilla, criticized the action and heaped scorn on the officials, she was given one hundred lashes in public. Cortés later paid her great honors, carrying her on his horse and addressing her as "Doña." Most damaging for the captain (irreparably damaging, as it turned out) were the accusations made against him in dispatches sent to Spain, in which he was charged with having hidden Aztec treasure for himself, misusing crown funds, and cheating the royal treasury in other respects. The reports also cast doubt on his loyalty to the king. The dramatic news that Cortés was alive caused his men to rise up and seize the usurpers, who were thrown in cages and put on public display. Cortés's return to Mexico had a calming effect on political strife, but his reputation was not so easily restored.

The charges against the conqueror were never substantiated, but they planted seeds of suspicion, which were nourished by partisans of the treasury officials in Spain. Moreover, the allegations provided a convenient pretext for which the crown may well have been thankful. At precisely the time Cortés was campaigning against the Aztecs, Emperor Charles V, the king of Spain, faced a revolt of his nobles at home, and although he was able to prevail, he retained a distrust of the fractious Spanish nobility. Thus Charles viewed with some concern the concentration of so much prestige and power in the hands of a budding aristocracy in the New World, especially since these "nobles" were rough adventurers and far distant from his royal armies in Europe. Crown policy had been to ease explorers and conquerors from political power, but, for the sake of appearances, the crown sought pretexts to void earlier signed agreements. Hence, Columbus's maladministration of Española had given the crown an excuse to replace him. And now the accusations against Cortés would serve the same purpose.

Receiving word of the defeat of the Aztecs, the king had appointed the conqueror as governor and captain general of New Spain in 1522. As an administrator, Cortés demonstrated many attributes of a statesman and a responsible colonizer. In addition to moving energetically to explore the land and seek ports for further discoveries, he also began to develop the economy. He undertook the search for mines, introduced European plants and livestock, and promoted commerce. He issued intelligent ordinances for the good order of the colony, sought ecclesiastics and educators, promoted justice, and in most respects acted as an enlightened governor should. And while he probably commanded sufficient respect and fear among both Spaniards and Indians to seize the land as his own, the evidence is that he remained stoutly loyal to his sovereign. The king and his council could not, however, ignore the allegations made against the conqueror—after all, he had acted in a high-handed manner against Velázquez,

Charles V (1500–58), King of Spain and Holy Roman Emperor, reigned during the decades of the Spanish conquests of the New World.

Tapia, and Garay, and there were other disturbing incidents that left doubt as to his true character. His enemies had powerful support at court and gave advice prejudicial to Cortés. It would be best to suspend him, for the time being at least. Royal officials were sent to supplant Cortés's authority. Growing increasingly frustrated and disgusted, he resolved to lay his case before the king in person.

With a grand retinue of Indian nobles, exotic Mexican plants and animals, and rich gifts for Charles V, Cortés arrived in Spain in 1528. His entrance caused a great sensation, and he was received with considerable fanfare. Charles V, pleased with his gifts and charmed by the conqueror's gallant manner, was satisfied that most of the rumors of misconduct were false or exaggerated. He allowed Cortés to choose for his encomiendas twenty-two towns, and the captain proceeded to select some of the richest settlements in the land. He was granted twenty-three thousand Indians as his vassals, confirmed as captain general, and awarded the grand title of the marqués del Valle de Oaxaca.

Despite the king's generosity, however, Cortés was miffed; he had hoped to be made a duke. Moreover, although he was accorded wide privileges and powers within his private domains, he was not confirmed as governor of New Spain, and he took this slight as a special rebuke. Yet he might not have come off as well as he did had he not married (his first wife having died) the daughter of a count. She was also the niece of the duke of Béjar, whose influence on behalf of Cortés was helpful.

The Administration of New Spain

Prior to the settlement of Mexico there were few Spaniards in the
Indies. The territories under Spanish control were small and
required little attention from Spain. Ferdinand and Isabella appointed counselors for matters pertaining to the New World and
turned their full attention to more pressing matters in Europe. In
1503, shortly before her death, Isabella created the Casa de Contratación, a house of trade to deal with affairs of the Indies, especially with regard to commerce, shipping, and emigration to the
colonies. Juan Rodríguez de Fonseca, the bishop of Burgos, was
given prime authority for making overseas policy.

The situation changed considerably, however, following the
Conquest of Mexico, with its extensive lands and millions of people. Shortly thereafter Central America was penetrated, and
early reports on Peru and other South American lands promised
even more far-flung colonies. Affairs in the New World now
clearly required a more broadly organized administration. Consequently, in 1524 Charles V created a supreme body called the
Council of the Indies. This committee, composed of able, high-
ranking Spaniards, would oversee all aspects of the colonies, both
counseling the king and acting in his behalf.

Earlier, in 1511, there had been created in Santo Domingo a
court of appeals so that matters of justice could be handled in the
Indies instead of being referred to Spain. But the three judges of
that body, called the *audiencia*, came to have broader duties. Traditionally, audiencias in Spain were courts of justice only, but in
the New World they assumed executive and legislative functions
as well. The judges (*oidores*) in Santo Domingo were the most
powerful individuals in the Indies. With the lack of good government in New Spain, it was determined by the crown in 1527
that a similar court was needed in Mexico. Four experienced
judges in Spain were appointed, but two died before taking office.
The president of the audiencia was Nuño de Guzmán, a lawyer
from a noble family with powerful connections.

Guzmán joined the two surviving judges in Mexico in early
1529. The rule of these three judges proved to be of the worst sort
and a low point in the history of government in Spanish Mexico.
As an adherent of Governor Velázquez of Cuba, Guzmán was a
dedicated enemy of Cortés, and, with the conqueror absent in
Spain, the audiencia moved against his followers. Once again
their encomiendas were taken, and some were removed from offi-

Juan de Zumárraga (1468–1548), a Franciscan, was the first bishop and archbishop of Mexico.

cial positions. It was a time of graft, corruption, and injustice for
Indians and Spaniards alike.

Meanwhile, a bishop, Juan de Zumárraga, had arrived in Mexico City. Although he bore the title "Protector of the Indians,"
the judges refused to recognize his authority and prevented the
Indians from seeking help from him or any other clergyman.
Angered by the chaos and iniquities engendered by the misrule,
Zumárraga bravely preached a sermon condemning the oidores,
which brought threats against his life. All correspondence critical
of the government was intercepted before it reached Spain, until
the bishop traveled to Veracruz and entrusted a letter to the
crown to a faithful sailor who smuggled the message aboard a
departing vessel. As it became clear to Guzmán that his days were
numbered, and fearing imminent arrest by royal agents, he set
off in late 1529 for the west of Mexico, hoping to regain the royal
confidence by a spectacular conquest of new territories.

Guzmán invaded Michoacán with a large force of Spaniards
and thousands of native auxiliaries. He cut a bloody path through
the west, burning villages, murdering chiefs, enslaving the Indians, and abusing them in every manner. One of the most brutal
incidents saw the Tarascan king dragged behind a horse until he
was almost senseless and then burned alive. The soldiers pressed

north, lured by tales of a bountiful island ruled by attractive amazons, tales fabricated by the natives to induce their tormentors to move on. Quite aside from his depredations, Guzmán explored and conquered a large area, all the way up to southern Sonora. Altogether he founded five cities.

The extensive western region was isolated from central Mexico and was later created as the separate administrative territory of New Galicia, over which its conqueror was appointed governor. But Guzmán's dark deeds caught up with him at length. After his long odyssey, notable for its duration no less than its savagery, Guzmán was ordered in 1533 to appear before a new audiencia to answer charges. In 1538 he was sent to Spain, where he spent the next two decades of his life as a virtual prisoner of the court.

While Guzmán was terrorizing the hinterlands of the west, the southeast region of Yucatán, the areas first sighted in 1517 by Spaniards from Cuba, remained outside Spanish control. Its conquest had been unsuccessfully attempted in 1527 by Francisco de Montejo, an early companion of Cortés. The enterprise went badly because of unfavorable terrain and a lack of local provisions, but mostly because of the indomitable spirit of the Maya. In one lengthy battle they killed 150 Spaniards. Montejo, though not without talent, was deficient as a leader of men, and he failed to pacify the region of Yucatán and Tabasco. In 1536 he was made governor of Honduras, only to be eased out of that position by the redoubtable Pedro de Alvarado. After nine years of stalemate in Yucatán, the conquest was renewed in 1537, and Montejo's son and nephew, both of whom were also named Francisco, brought most of the region under Spanish control by 1542, when the city of Mérida was founded. In 1547 a serious insurrection broke out, and many Spanish settlers were killed before calm was restored. After two decades of conflict, the conquest of Yucatán was finally effected, but at the cost of an estimated five hundred Spanish lives.

After the fiasco of the first audiencia, the king and the Council of the Indies were more circumspect in their choice of oidores. They chose wisely in the appointment of Sebastián Ramírez de Fuenleal, who had served as both president of the Audiencia of Santo Domingo and bishop of that island. A man of highest integrity and proven abilities, he stood much in contrast to his predecessor in Mexico. He was joined in Mexico City by fellow judges of uniformly high quality, including Vasco de Quiroga, who would distinguish himself later in other undertakings. Within five years (1530–35) these learned magistrates wrought significant changes in the troubled colony. Bringing to bear the full weight and authority of the crown and maintaining a busy schedule, they proceeded to correct many abuses. A semblance of good order was restored, and ordinances were passed to improve the conditions of the Indians.

Cortés, now more commonly known as "the Marqués," had meantime returned to the colony in mid-1530 to a grand reception by the populace, somewhat to the discomfiture of the judges of the audiencia. Sorely disappointed in being deprived of political power, he had to be satisfied with the limited title of captain general. Problems with the audiencia began when the oidores undertook to investigate the actual number of Cortés's tributaries; he probably had three times the twenty-three thousand he was allowed. To make matters worse, he was deprived of various properties and privileges. Cortés remained the most prestigious individual in New Spain, but in 1535 even that status was challenged with the arrival of a viceroy.

The king and Council of the Indies had decided by 1528 that New Spain needed a ruler who would personify the dignity and authority of the crown and offset the affection of the people for Cortés. Such a person would have to be a great nobleman, jealous of his honor and above staining his name with acts of avarice and injustice, one whose competence and loyalty to the king were beyond question. After all, he would literally be a "vice-king." Many—and no doubt Cortés himself—assumed that the conqueror of New Spain would be the obvious choice for the post of viceroy. But Cortés had neither the desirable lineage nor the administrative experience for the high honor. Furthermore the very qualities that brought him success as a conqueror—audacity, independence of thought, and imagination—were anathema to the centralized bureaucracy of an absolute monarch. And there were too many disturbing and unanswered questions about his past actions.

The first three noblemen offered the august appointment declined the honor. The fourth, Don Antonio de Mendoza, the count of Tendilla, accepted, and he proved to be an excellent choice. An able ambassador to Rome, Mendoza was scion of one of Spain's most distinguished families and related to the royal house itself. He received his commission as viceroy in 1530, but the press of personal affairs prevented his arrival in Mexico until 1535. The viceroy's charge was to observe all matters of consequence affecting the colony except judicial matters, which would continue as the province of the audiencia. He had special orders

Don Antonio de Mendoza (1492?–1552), served as first viceroy in New Spain, from 1535–50.

to increase crown revenues and to ensure good treatment of the Indians. He was also vice-patron of the Church and responsible for the defense of New Spain. Allowing the viceroy a good salary as well as perquisites that included a palace and a personal guard, the crown purposely sought to enhance the prestige of the office.

In Search of Fabled Cities

During the 1520s and 1530s many fantastic tales circulated about wondrous lands in the New World. Among the more intriguing was the so-called Northern Mystery, which embraced not only the persistent myth of the amazons but also stories of the Seven (Golden) Cities of Cíbola. Speculation about fabulously rich kingdoms in other parts of the New World was rife, and it is not strange that men were ready to believe them. Had not the first rumors of Tenochtitlán and the dazzling Inca empire (conquered in the early 1530s) appeared just as fanciful?

Pánfilo de Narváez, the one-eyed casualty of Veracruz, commanded a fleet to Florida in 1528, hoping to discover the fabled lands of Apalachee. After an overland expedition, Narváez failed to make contact with his supply ships, and he and his men tried to reach Mexico by sailing makeshift boats down the Gulf coast. Most of them perished, but a few made the Texas coastline. In the end only four survived: Alvar Núñez Cabeza de Vaca, two other

Spaniards, and Estéban, a black slave. For years they wandered among the Indians of the present-day Southwest of the United States, sometimes as slaves, sometimes as respected medicine men. In 1536, after many travails, they reached the northern Mexican outpost of Culiacán, where they were received with astonishment by their fellow countrymen.

Having spent so much time in the north, they were plied with questions about the Seven Cities, of which they had heard vaguely. That was enough to cause excitement, and prominent men scrambled for the privilege of undertaking the great search. The viceroy sensed an opportunity for an expedition that might overshadow the achievements of Cortés, and so of course he kept the rights for himself. But he took the precaution of sending an advance party, guided by Estéban and under the command of a Franciscan friar named Marcos de Niza. Pushing ahead of the main party, Estéban met an ironic end, for, having survived so long among the northern tribes, he apparently angered some Indians, who killed him.

Distraught by this news, Marcos de Niza proceeded with extreme caution. He seems to have viewed from a distance one of the Zuñi villages in New Mexico, which he later reported as being larger than Tenochtitlán. Moreover—so he said—local chiefs told him that the city he saw was the smallest of the seven. In kindness to the friar, it must be said that sometimes, toward sunset, the fading light in that part of the country casts a rosy glow, and there may have been pieces of reflective quartz stuck in the adobe walls of the two-story dwellings he saw from afar; and so it is possible that he imagined he saw something truly marvelous. In any case, the Spaniards in Mexico wanted to believe the existence of such cities, and preparations were eagerly made for the adventure. Those who had missed the earlier conquests would now have their chance.

Mendoza chose his friend, Francisco Vázquez de Coronado, the governor of New Galicia, to lead the well-equipped expedition. In 1540, 336 Spaniards, with hundreds of Indian allies and about a thousand horses and swine, moved out with high expectations. When they saw the mud village at the end of a grueling march they must have cursed Friar Marcos. Their anger abated somewhat, however, when Indians told them of "the Land of Quivira," some distance away but even more wonderful than the legendary cities of Cíbola. Their hopes raised, off they went.

The natives, aware that the Spaniards were interested primarily in gold, soon found that the best way to get rid of the unwel-

ROUTE OF CORONADO'S EXPEDITION, 1540–42

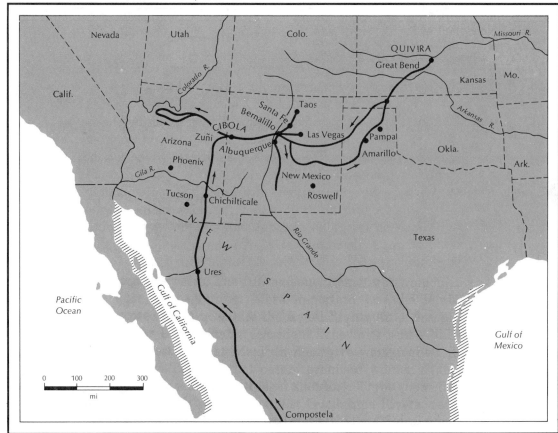

come intruders was to tell them that, while they had no wealth, there were abundant riches *más allá*—farther on. Because of such information the Spaniards wandered aimlessly for months, finally reaching the vicinity of Wichita, Kansas. Now greatly disheartened, having seen only squalid villages over a vast prairie, the miserable survivors dragged themselves back to Mexico. When they reached the capital in 1542 the viceroy, having not the slightest interest in their reports of the strange "shaggy cows" (buffaloes), refused to talk to his erstwhile friend Vázquez de Coronado. The captain had proved to be a less than ideal leader, but he was surely blameless for not discovering what was never there, in the land of más allá.

In 1542 a party commanded by Juan Rodríguez de Cabrillo sailed up along the beaches of California. The modern attractions of the area, however, had little appeal for the Spaniards, and they would not settle California for a very long time. That same year Mendoza dispatched Ruy López de Villalobos to the Philippines (named for prince Philip), but the expedition failed to return to Mexico.

The Vázquez de Coronado mission occasioned serious problems of another sort. When the expedition left western Mexico a good number of Spaniards who had settled New Galicia went along, **leaving the frontier sparsely occupied by Christians and militarily weakened.** Conscious of the situation, the Indians, who harbored resentments going back to the cruelty of Nuño de Guzmán, were roused by their priests to rebel. The ensuing Mixtón War (1540–41) was the most serious revolt prior to the struggle for Independence. The whole frontier was aflame. Natives attacked isolated Spanish ranches and then fortified themselves on well-stocked hilltops called *peñoles*, from which they could not be dislodged.

When the governor of New Galicia failed to subdue the rebels, he turned for assistance to Pedro de Alvarado, who had sailed up from Guatemala on his way to explore the Pacific. Courageous to a fault, Alvarado rashly ignored the advice to wait for reinforcements. A furious counterattack by the Indians produced a panicky Spanish retreat, during which a horse fell on Alvarado, crushing him. The great rebellion ended only after the viceroy himself took the field at the head of a strong army.

The Last Years of Cortés

Meanwhile Cortés, having been excluded from the search for the Northern Mystery and feeling insulted by his treatment from the viceroy and the audiencia, returned to Spain in 1540 to put his grievances once again before the king. Charles V was abroad, however, and crown representatives gave the Marqués a cool reception. The crisis of instability appeared to have been resolved in the colony, and with the royal bureaucracy entrenched and functioning well, government officials saw no need to humor the conqueror. Cortés volunteered his services for a Spanish expedition to Algeria in 1541, but his advice in military matters was ignored, and he became increasingly alienated. Beset by invidious rivals in Mexico and an indifferent sovereign in Spain, he spent his last years in frustration, then resignation. He was about to return to New Spain when, in 1547, he fell ill. Shortly thereafter, in his sixty-second year, he died in a village outside Seville. In 1556 his bones were deposited in Mexico, according to his wishes.

Though the last two decades of Cortés's life were fraught with disappointment, there is no greater example of rise to fame and fortune in the history of the New World. Through his diverse talents he gained immortality as one of the greatest military figures of the ages. He married into one of Spain's most noble families, was awarded a high title himself, and became one of the richest men in the Spanish empire. With all his defects (which were common to his time), Cortés was a captain who preferred diplomacy and persuasion to force. A disciplinarian who punished disloyalty with severity, he also, on many occasions, demonstrated compassion. He was the founder of Spanish civilization in Mexico and was clearly the most effective and capable person to establish the fledgling colony. But the defects remain. Three centuries after the Conquest of the Aztecs, when Mexico finally gained Independence from Spain, one of the first official acts of the new government called for the destruction of his bones. His remains were successfully hidden by the historian Lucas Alamán. Later in the nineteenth century his reputation was somewhat rehabilitated, but since the Revolution of 1910 his memory has been vilified. Revolutionary philosophy as conceived in the 1920s and 1930s was antiforeign and exalted native values. Thus, Cortés, the fair invader, the perpetrator of the Cholula massacre, the exterminator of Indian civilizations, the destroyer of Tenochtitlán, and the executioner of Cuauhtémoc, is viewed in Mexico in dark terms.

Stability under Viceroy Mendoza

Despite the reversals of the ill-fated Coronado expedition and the costly Mixtón War, by 1542 the colonial government was finally ready to achieve stability and order. There was good cause for optimism, for Mendoza was a firm and capable viceroy and the audiencia he worked with was responsible. Bishop Zumárraga was an energetic and positive complement to civil government. Yet there was brewing in Spain a reform movement that was destined to inflame passions once again. Bartolomé de Las Casas, a powerful Dominican friar and an indefatigable lobbyist on behalf of Indian liberties, had successfully convinced the crown to introduce legislation aimed at curtailing abuses of the natives, whose numbers had declined drastically. These New Laws of

1542–43 called for, among other things, the freedom of natives who had been unjustly enslaved and the easing of labor requirements. Most threatening from the standpoint of the Spanish conquerors, the laws eroded the encomienda system, for encomiendas awarded to conquerors and first settlers were to escheat to the crown on the death of the original encomendero. News of the provision caused a great outcry among the encomenderos, who remonstrated bitterly that they would have nothing to leave their children. Surely, they insisted, the king could not be so ungrateful to those who had won and settled lands larger than Spain itself.

The continuance of the encomienda system was regarded in Mexico, even by many royal officials, as vital to the maintenance of the colony's prosperity, for without it, it was feared, many Spaniards would leave. In fact, most ecclesiastics also favored its retention, seeing it as the best instrument for control of the Indians. Furthermore, tribute and labor helped support various charities, educational facilities, and religious institutions. The bishop himself held an encomienda. Many Spaniards agreed that natives under crown control were abused more by royal agents than by encomenderos. When an official investigator, Francisco Tello de Sandoval, was sent from Spain to help implement the New Laws, he found widespread opposition in the colony.

Tello de Sandoval and Viceroy Mendoza, assessing the situation and fearing a general revolt, exercised the prerogative of withholding the laws. Under the circumstances, they probably chose wisely: when the viceroy in Peru insisted on imposing the ordinances a serious insurrection ensued, which took his life and embroiled the colony in civil war for years. Finally giving way to the outraged encomenderos, the crown modified the laws in 1545 by removing the offending limitation to the encomiendas. For the moment, at least, the conquerors had won a victory.

Although the crown had retreated, it still intended to reform the encomienda system. In 1549 it ordered that encomenderos could no longer avail themselves of the free labor of their Indians but would have to be content with their tributes only. In the same year there was a flurry of excitement when a small group of Spaniards plotted to overthrow the government. But they were inept and persons of little consequence. They were tried, found guilty, and summarily hanged.

By 1550, as Mendoza's rule of nearly fifteen years came to a close, the colony was well implanted and thriving. In the crown's view Mendoza was the ideal administrator. His dreams of extending Spanish realms into rich areas (that did not exist) were unrealized, but his contributions in other respects were impressive. The part played by Mendoza was of crucial importance, because, as the first viceroy, he established patterns that would be followed by his successors. Although guilty of questionable profiteering and occasional lack of compassion, he was for the most part a wise, patient, and enlightened ruler. He left a flourishing economy and a capital that had already assumed the appearance of a beautiful city distinguished for its cultural life. He established order and stability; he founded schools, hospitals, and charitable foundations; he fostered religion and helped bring about a better measure of justice for all. Because of his government royal authority was firmly stamped on New Spain. The colony had survived the turbulent first three decades of its life.

Recommended for Further Study

Aiton, Arthur S. *Antonio de Mendoza, First Viceroy of New Spain.* Durham, N.C.: Duke University Press, 1927.

Bishop, Morris. *The Odyssey of Cabeza de Vaca.* New York: Century, 1933.

Blom, Frans. *The Conquest of Yucatan.* Boston: Houghton Mifflin, 1936.

Bolton, Herbert E. *Coronado: Knight of Pueblos and Plains.* Albuquerque: University of New Mexico Press, 1949.

Chamberlain, Robert S. *The Conquest and Colonization of Yucatán, 1517–1550.* Washington, D.C.: Carnegie Institute of Washington, 1948.

Chipman, Donald. *Nuño de Guzmán and Pánuco in New Spain, 1518–1533.* Glendale, Calif.: Clark, 1966.

Clendinnen, Inga. *Ambivalent Conquests: Maya and Spaniard in Yucatán, 1517–1570.* Cambridge: Cambridge University Press, 1987.

Hallenbeck, Cleve. *Alvar Núñez Cabeza de Vaca: The Journey and Route of the First European to Cross the Continent of North America, 1534–1536.* Glendale, Calif.: Clark, 1940.

Hirschberg, Julia. "Social Experiment in New Spain: A Prosopographical Study of the Early Settlement at Puebla de los Angeles, 1531–1534." *Hispanic American Historical Review* 59 (1979): 1–33.

Holmes, Maurice G. *From New Spain by Sea to the Californias, 1519–1668.* Glendale, Calif.: Clark, 1963.

Jones, Grant D. *Maya Resistance to Spanish Rule: Time and History on a Colonial Frontier.* Albuquerque: University of New Mexico Press, 1989.

Wagner, Henry R. *Spanish Voyages to the Northwest Coast of America in the Sixteenth Century.* San Francisco: California Historical Society, 1929.

Warren, J. Benedict. *The Conquest of Michoacán: The Spanish Domination of the Tarascan Kingdom in Western Mexico, 1521–1530.* Norman: University of Oklahoma Press, 1985.

III THE COLONY
OF NEW SPAIN

9

The Imperial System Entrenched

The Political Administration of New Spain

"Do little and do it slowly" had been Viceroy Mendoza's stated philosophy of administration. It was an attitude less than acceptable to reformers but consistent with royal wishes. The sixteenth-century viceroys, facing many crucial situations, were allowed considerable latitude, but their successors in the seventeenth century were reined in. Later kings and their councils increasingly gathered authority to themselves, discouraging the viceroys and audiencias from independence of thought and action.

Yet given the difficulty of communication and the time lapse between a request for instructions and the response from Spain, a certain amount of autonomy was implicit. Correspondence between colonial officials and the crown was necessarily slow, because for most of the colonial period ships sailed only once a year between Mexico and Spain. It was common for authorities in New Spain to wait many months, and even longer, for guidance. Consequently high officials often made important rulings on their own, pending royal approval. When a crown order seemed contrary to the best interests of the local situation, a viceroy sometimes noted, in all deference, *Obedezco pero no cumplo* (I obey but do not execute). The process of government was further bogged down by the endless detailed reports, requiring action, sent to Spain by officials, clergymen, and private subjects.

Colonial policy of the Hapsburgs (that is, up to the eighteenth century, when the new Bourbon dynasty instituted administrative reforms) was ponderous and inefficient. But sluggish as the

bureaucracy was, the crown concerned itself less with competence than with loyalty. The preoccupation with conformance
and fidelity manifested itself in the system of checks and bal-
ances. Officials were encouraged to comment on and criticize the
performance of others. The viceroy was the most powerful individual, but as the judges of the audiencia reported directly to the
king and the Council of the Indies and were often at odds with
the viceroy, they were a restraint on the viceroy's actions. Moreover, treasury officials and various other bureaucrats, as well as
clergymen, members of town councils, and private individuals,
contributed their complaints, and as a result, the crown was exposed to a wide spectrum of opinion on the operation of colonial
administration.

In order to ascertain the true state of affairs, the crown occasionally sent a royal inspector (*visitador*) to make an on-the-spot
investigation (*visita*). The crown visitador had great authority:
on arrival, he usually assumed rule of the colony for the tenure
of his inspection, which could take weeks or months. The visita
was sometimes undertaken in response to a specific set of charges
emanating from the colony, but in other instances it was more
routine in nature. In some instances the visitador traveled in-
cognito, taking officials by surprise, before adequate cover-ups
could be arranged. At other times the imminent arrival of the
inspector became known in time for precautionary measures on
the part of local officials.

Visitadores, usually men trained in the law, were responsible
for correcting abuses and instituting reforms. Moreover, their
charges included judging the performance of the viceroy and
other high functionaries. Such a judicial review, or trial, was
known as a (*juicio de*) *residencia*, so called because the official
being reviewed was required to remain in residence during the
trial. A residencia usually came at the end of an official's term of
office, although in the case of those who served for many years, a
review was sometimes taken periodically. Notice of an impending
review was made public, so that all within the official's jurisdiction with grievances could bring charges.

The admirable institutions of the visita and the residencia were
models that might well profit all governments. Unfortunately,
like so much in Spanish administration, there existed a wide
breach between theory and practice. Witnesses were sometimes
bribed or intimidated; perjury and obfuscation were common;
and judges were occasionally bought. Furthermore, despite the
long lists of allegations posted—and testimony that often con-

vincingly established the official's guilt—relatively few were punished in accordance with their crimes. Many of the higher functionaries were of the Spanish nobility, and the crown was reluctant to punish them with any severity.

Various restrictions were imposed on officials with a view to averting corruption. They were forbidden to hold encomiendas or to participate in commercial activities. They were to be circumspect in their social behavior and were to pick their company with care to avoid appearances of favoritism. In order to obviate conflicts of interest, they could not marry women from their jurisdictions without prior royal approval. In other ways, too, there were genuine attempts, at least on paper, to ensure honest government. Needless to say, the infractions were numerous, although certainly one finds many officials of integrity and humanity who died poor and were often unjustly treated for their honest attempts at good government.

Of the sixty-two viceroys who served in New Spain, almost all came from the high nobility and were born in Spain. Men born in the New World could attain this highest office (Mexico had three in the seventeenth century), but as sons of high nobles serving as viceroys themselves, they were not identified as locals. Most viceroys proved reasonably good rulers; a few were truly outstanding. The colony was fortunate that the first two viceroys, Mendoza (1535–50) and Luis de Velasco (1550–64), were wise

Luis de Velasco I (1511–64), the second viceroy of New Spain, served until his death. He continued the prudent policies established by his predecessor Mendoza.

administrators who set New Spain on firm footing. Mendoza was
a superb politician who carefully played off troublesome factions
to achieve order. Velasco abolished Indian slavery and in other
ways was so instrumental in easing the sufferings of the natives
that he is remembered as "the Father of the Indians." These first
two viceroys served many years, but there was no specified term
for a viceroy, and most remained in office for shorter periods.
The quality of the viceroys declined in the seventeenth century,
but the following century saw the emergence of some great talent
in the office. Not surprisingly, the abilities of the viceroys rose
and fell with the quality of Spanish monarchs.

It is more difficult to assess the character of the oidores of the
audiencias. As the functions of the courts expanded, more judges
were added. With the settlement of western lands, a new audiencia, that of Nueva Galicia, was created in 1548. It usually had
four or five oidores, while the Audiencia of Mexico counted ten
by late eighteenth century, plus other lawyers. Consequently,
during the colonial era a great many judges served, and since so
few have been studied in any detail, one cannot confidently offer
judgments on them as a whole. One has the impression, however,
that despite many individual cases of corruption, the majority of
the oidores were dedicated servants of the crown.

The same cannot be said for the provincial officials. As new
territories were colonized and towns founded, it became impossible to govern outlying provinces from the capital. Subdivisions
of administration were, therefore, formalized, and many smaller
administrative districts were created within the audiencia jurisdictions. Such districts were administered by officials known variously as *corregidores*, *alcaldes mayores*, or *gobernadores*, whose
territories of jurisdiction were called *corregimientos*, *alcaldías
mayores*, or *gobiernos*. There was little difference among the
duties of these officials, and a brief discussion of the position of
corregidor serves, in essence, to describe the others as well. Corregidores were responsible for the good order of their districts,
but their judicial and legislative responsibilities were limited, as
they were subject to higher authorities in all matters. In the
early years of the system these positions often went to conquerors
or their sons, or other early settlers, as a form of pension in lieu
of encomiendas. As can be imagined, most appointees had little
or no training for administrative posts, with the result that the
office was held in low esteem and was rewarded with a correspondingly low salary. It came to be accepted that these provincial officials would supplement their salaries where they could—

which usually meant cheating the natives or other lower-class groups. Gradually more qualified individuals often lawyers, from Spain took over, yet corregidores continued to be notorious as the crown agents who most abused the trust placed in them.

Least enlightened were those with the designation of *corregidor de indios*, whose responsibility it was to administer Indian towns. The natives had been gathered into new villages to facilitate their conversion and acculturation, and the corregidor de indios was charged with the good order of those under his jurisdiction, in those towns paying tribute to the crown rather than to individual encomenderos. These Spanish supervisors, or their agents, collected the king's tributes in the "crown towns" and supposedly guaranteed justice. In fact, they were the greatest enemies of the Indians, defrauding them in a variety of ways, often in collusion with the native chiefs.

Distinct from the royal authorities were those in municipal government. Beginning with the founding of Veracruz in 1519 by Cortés, as Spanish towns were established a town council was immediately formed. In the earliest years Cortés simply appointed many local administrators, but it became customary for them to be elected annually. The municipal council, called the *cabildo* (or *ayuntamiento*), consisted of members known as *regidores*. These councilmen numbered anywhere from four or five in smaller communities up to fifteen in late colonial Mexico City. A council usually had two senior officials, called *alcaldes ordinarios*, who had some judicial powers and more importance than the regidores, who were simply councilors.

The cabildos were responsible for such purely local matters as defending the town, keeping the peace, controlling prices, allocating lots, cleaning streets, and seeing to drainage, water supplies, public food, and a multitude of other concerns. Generally speaking, the cabildos of the various towns represented the interests of the local colonists, which were frequently in conflict with the wishes of the crown. But, with a corregidor close at hand, the pervasive royal influence was felt.

Although in early decades there was something of a democratic character to the cabildos, the crown took away even that small concession to popular representation. When Philip II became king in 1556, he inherited heavy debts from his father, and one of the ways in which he attempted to raise funds was through the sale of offices. Positions in the cabildos were awarded to the highest bidders, even though consideration was supposed to be given to those with the best credentials. Such posts were cherished because of the distinction they offered in the community, not to mention the opportunities for making profits on the side. The result was that membership in the cabildos came under the control of certain families, who held proprietary interest in them for generations. Since the seats were often sold in perpetuity, they were passed on from father to son. By the late colonial period fifteen regidores in Mexico City owned their positions.

It has sometimes been suggested that the cabildos were fairly representative because they were composed, by and large, of criollos, or Mexican-born Spaniards. Criollos on the cabildos, however, were from the leading families who controlled local affairs, and their rulings reflected the interest of the colonial elite. In addition, because the seats were so often inherited, or purchased by incompetents, the cabildos were frequently staffed by those who gave poor leadership and bungling administration. Administration of Indian towns was modeled after that of the Spanish communities, with regidores almost always chosen from among the Indian aristocracy. In practice, very strong influence was exerted by local clergymen or Spanish officials, whose wills were executed by the Indian leaders.

Disturbances during the "Colonial Siesta"

By the middle of the sixteenth century the Spanish imperial system was established, and the bureaucracy took control with a firm grip and imposed a good measure of order. Still, it is somewhat misleading to conclude that for the next two and a half centuries little of consequence disturbed the colony. Inevitably, from time to time, there were serious challenges to the authorities of New Spain. And although the decades of the seventeenth century, in particular, were calm, they were hardly the "colonial siesta" so often portrayed. There was very considerable expansion of settled territories, and a number of disorders afflicted the land.

One of the most dramatic episodes occurred in the 1560s, when the simmering feud between the encomenderos and the crown boiled over. Charles V had yielded after the fiery reactions to the New Laws, and in 1555 he extended encomiendas to a "third life"—that is, to the grandsons of the conquerors as well as to the sons. But by the early 1560s, when Philip II reigned, most of the conquistadores were aged or dead. It seemed safe enough to move against their less belligerent sons.

In contrast to their fathers, the first generation of Mexican-born Spaniards, the criollos, inherited status and incomes that made their lives comfortable. They were on the whole an amiable group, much given to the pursuits of the idle class. Underneath their insouciance, however, they were troubled, because their privileged positions were by no means secure. When rumors reached them in 1562 that the encomiendas were not, after all, to pass on to their heirs, their emotions ran from outrage to despair. Without a powerful leader their cause seemed lost. They were, therefore, elated to learn that the son of Cortés, the second marqués del Valle, was returning to Mexico. Fresh from the court of Philip II, the worldly young criollo, himself the greatest of encomenderos, was their natural leader. Or at least so they thought.

Don Martín Cortés, the only legitimate son of the conqueror and his heir, is a curious figure in Mexican history. Born probably in Cuernavaca in 1532, he was taken as a young boy to the royal court, where he was treated with all the respect and consideration due a child of high nobility. He became one of the favorites of Prince Philip, who later included him in his entourage. When at length Martín Cortés wished to return to the land of his birth, King Philip II generously confirmed—with some modifications—the rights and privileges previously conceded to Fernando Cortés.

Rich, educated, and famous, Don Martín at thirty was ambitious and haughty but not without charm. Yet he had inherited few of his father's good qualities and so posed no apparent threat to the crown. His own estates secured in perpetuity,[1] Martín Cortés could have lived out his life in honor and splendor. Instead, his pretentious manner was offensive to many, including the good Viceroy Velasco. Don Martín had his own seal with a crown on it (though, in modesty, the seal was somewhat smaller than the king's); he was preceded by a lance page when he went out on horseback; and, not content with being a marqués, he styled himself a duke.

The resident leader of the young criollos in Mexico City had been Alonso de Avila, the wealthy son of a prominent conqueror. He and his companions, anticipating the eventual losses of their encomiendas, talked loosely of assassinating the oidores and other high officials, throwing off allegiance to the crown, and making Martín Cortés king of Mexico. They claimed 120 followers. Mar-

---

1. The only other perpetual encomiendas conceded by the crown were those belonging to two daughters of Moctezuma.

tín's role in all this is not entirely clear—he seems to have done little to discourage the plotters from putting a crown on his head without, however, having the audacity to pledge himself to the cause. His temporizing combined with the bumblings of Avila to abort the conspiracy.

In a series of fascinating intrigues the patient and scheming judges of the audiencia strengthened their case against the rebels, who appeared to have abandoned whatever plans they had. Then, in one of the most poignant scenes ever enacted in the colonial capital, the elegant and popular young Alonso de Avila knelt before the headsman's axe in horror and disbelief. His decapitation was followed by that of his brother. The heads of both were exhibited on pikes as grisly reminders of the penalty for treason against the king. The citizens of the capital, believing that the criollo brothers and their friends had been merely foolish, were stunned.

The chastened Martín Cortés escaped with his life, thanks to his high station, but the severity with which many others were punished shocked the community and intimidated the criollo encomenderos. The Avila affair was their last convincing show of force, and its tragic result signaled the end of Conquest society. The age of heroes was past, and the time of the lawyers had arrived. Spanish attitudes were about to change even more: the year Fernando Cortés died Cervantes was born, and this genius of Spanish letters would ridicule the conceits so common to those who conquered the New World. Most of the sons of the conquerors were now in middle age, and they confined future actions to litigation through proper channels. They fed on the accomplishments of their fathers, seeking consideration for former deeds. The time of rebellion was past—at least for the white man.

Disturbances of a different kind upset the capital in the seventeenth century. In 1624, as a result of bitter animosities, the viceroy and the religious orders arrayed against a coalition of the archbishop and the audiencia. The archbishop excommunicated the viceroy, who responded by ordering the prelate banished from Mexico. The lower classes, fiercely loyal to their spiritual leader, formed a rampaging mob that threatened the viceroy. Their demonstration ended in violence and in some seventy deaths. So bitter were the denunciations that the viceroy was recalled.

A second great disturbance occurred in 1692. A crisis brought on by severe food shortages, the result of crop failures, was exacerbated by the rumor that authorities had connived to corner the grain market to their profit. The resentment of the Indians and mestizos—persons of mixed Spanish and Indian blood—burst into destructive riots in which the viceregal palace was burned and looted. Other government buildings were destroyed, along with 280 shops and stalls, before the viceroy's troops finally restored order through harsh measures.

These extreme examples of the breakdown of law and order were relatively few, but the government of New Spain had to cope continuously with widespread crime in both city and countryside as well as other threats to security. It was ill equipped to do so because for many years there was nothing resembling a large, well-organized professional force to maintain peace.

Authorities also had to contend with various natural calamities over which they had little control. Very destructive were the many floods that plagued the capital in the colonial period. The dike whereby the Aztecs had controlled the lake waters was destroyed by the Spaniards and never replaced. From the middle of the sixteenth century on, the city was inundated at intervals, with very serious losses. Officials were equally helpless in dealing with such periodical disasters as earthquakes, pestilences, and crop failures, even though some minimal precautions were taken.

Expansion into Northern Mexico

While much of central and southern Mexico was under Spanish control by the middle of the sixteenth century, the wide expanses of the north remained unsettled by the white man. Interest in the northern frontiers had quickened, however, with the discovery of silver ore in the 1540s, setting off a rush into the region. Within a few years mining camps appeared in many locations, but bellicose Chichimec warriors made supplying the camps difficult and dangerous. The long distances between Spanish settlements and the isolated mining camps offered the Indians ample opportunity to strike the wagon trains. For half a century the indomitable northern tribes resisted the Spanish advance, and the fighting subsided only in the last decade of the sixteenth century when Viceroy Luis de Velasco II, with the help of brave clergymen, inaugurated a policy of conciliation. In return for annual supplies of cattle and clothing, many of the natives were persuaded to put down their arms.

Missionaries braved the dangers of the hinterlands, and in the

Luis de Velasco II (1539–1617), the son of Mexico's second viceroy, went on to serve twice in the same office himself. He was instrumental in making peace with the Chichimecs in the 1590s.

seventeenth century the Jesuits, in particular, pushed northward, all the way to Baja California and Arizona. Following their trails, other Spaniards began to settle the northwest. Francisco de Ibarra explored and settled the areas of Durango and Chihuahua, which were formed into a distinct region known as New Biscay. In the 1570s Luis de Carvajal was given a commission to pacify the northeast of the country. Finding little of mineral wealth, the settlers of that land enslaved the local Indians, who were sold as miners to north central Mexico. Carvajal founded the city of Monterrey and settled other towns in the new province, which was named New León.

In the 1590s the viceroy of New Spain sent out more expeditions to the far north earlier traversed by Vázquez de Coronado. Following the march of Juan de Oñate in 1598, an outpost was established and Franciscan friars began converting Indians at Taos and other pueblos. In 1609, two years after the English colonized Jamestown, the northern capital was planted at Santa Fe. Nevertheless, the extensive region of New Mexico remained sparsely populated; there were some friars, a few soldiers, and a scattering of miners, traders, and ranchers, along with various officials. The harsh land yielded little revenue and offered hardly more to the imperial system than Indian souls and a tenuous hold on the land in the face of French expansion.

Expeditions by sea continued to explore new lands for the Spanish empire. After earlier attempts to plant colonies in the Pacific had failed, the historic voyage in 1565 by Miguel López de Legazpi and the friar Andrés de Urdaneta led to settlement. Most important, Urdaneta discovered a satisfactory route back to the western hemisphere, sailing for the California coast and then turning southward to Mexico. Manila was founded, and shortly thereafter the fabulous trade between the Orient and New Spain began, with one ship a year—the Manila Galleon—making its way from the Philippine capital to Acapulco and back.

The Manila trade piqued new interest in the coast of Califor-

The Pacific port of Acapulco in a 1671 Dutch engraving.

nia, where the galleons first sighted the mainland of America. In the 1590s Sebastián Vizcaíno explored the coastline with indifferent success. In 1602 another expedition under his command produced a commendable chart of California waters, and Vizcaíno founded the port of Monterey. Like others before him, he missed seeing the great bay of San Francisco. There was still no compelling reason to make serious attempts at colonizing California.

Rivals in the New World

A growing concern of Spanish authorities was the encroachment of foreigners on the fringes of New Spain, both by land and sea. A French force led by the Chevalier de La Salle journeyed southward from Canada in the 1680s into the region of Texas, where, it was rumored, a settlement was planted. In response Spaniards began to occupy Texas, and in 1698 a Spanish fort was established on the Gulf coast at Pensacola (Florida).

A more serious threat was posed by foreigners on the seas. North European powers had never accepted the pope's division of the New World, which gave most of it to Spain, and, especially following the growth of Protestantism, they challenged Spain's hegemony. Pirates, often with the blessings of their sovereigns, aggressively attacked Spanish property. French interlopers were cruising the eastern coastline of South America little more than a decade after Columbus's first voyage. The ship sent by Cortés carrying Aztec treasure to Charles V had been seized by French corsairs when it was in sight of Iberian shores. Later the French moved closer to the source, attacking Spanish ships in American waters and looting ports. Along the Gulf coast, from Yucatán to Tampico, French filibusters raided with little opposition. In 1561 they sacked the town of Campeche and a decade later seized valuable treasures from a Franciscan convent in Yucatán.

Somewhat later the English, too, appeared off Mexican shores. In 1567 John Hawkins sailed boldly into the port of Veracruz under pretext of repairing his ships, but he actually planned to sell his cargo of black slaves in defiance of laws that forbade Spanish trade with foreigners. Hawkins was trapped by an incoming Spanish fleet bearing a new viceroy. Despite a gentleman's agreement for a truce, the viceroy brought his ships to bear and peppered the English vessels, allowing only two of Hawkins's nine ships to escape. The captured English corsairs

A Spanish shield of the seventeenth century.

were given sentences at labor, and later some were tried and burned by the Inquisition, not for piracy but for heresy. The defeat of Hawkins was a great feather in the viceroy's cap, but the Spaniards would pay dearly for it, for escaping on one of the English ships was Hawkins's cousin, Francis Drake. Before long *El Draque* took his vengeance, becoming the terror of the Spanish Indies, raiding with considerable success in both the Caribbean and the Pacific, and driving the Spaniards to distraction.

From the middle of the sixteenth century until the end of the eighteenth century English and French corsairs attacked the coasts of Yucatán and Campeche many times, though the rewards were often modest. Some of the small, isolated ports were so poorly defended that they could be taken by a handful of pirates. In Pacific waters both the English and Dutch were active, the most successful being Thomas Cavendish, who captured a richly laden Manila Galleon.

The most vicious attack, however, was not on sea but on land. In 1683, after laying careful plans, a Frenchman known as Lorenzillo led a force of about a thousand ruffians of mixed nationalities to the strongly fortified port of Veracruz and invested the city under cover of night. Over six thousand local citizens were rounded up, held inside the churches, and denied food and water for three days and nights. Many were horribly tortured, and most of the females, of all ages, were raped. The pirates carried off about a million dollars worth of loot.

By the end of the seventeenth century the viceroyalty of New Spain stretched out over a vast expanse of territory. It embraced all land on the mainland north of Panama, extending up to New Mexico, the islands of the Caribbean, and even the Philippines. Ostensibly all these far-flung regions were under the control of the viceroy; in actual practice, his authority was nominal, for the more remote areas were effectively beyond his reach. Central America, the islands of the Caribbean, and the Philippines had their own audiencias, which were for all intents and purposes autonomous.

Spain itself, after boasting the richest and most powerful empire in the world during the sixteenth century, began to decline in the early decades of the seventeenth century. But the Spanish empire remained intact and relatively prosperous, thanks to an administrative system that, despite its flaws, held the immense territories together.

Recommended for Further Study

Bannon, John F. *The Spanish Borderlands Frontier, 1513–1821*. New York: Holt, Rinehart and Winston, 1970.

Benítez, Fernando. *The Century after Cortés*. Translated by Joan Maclean. Chicago: University of Chicago Press, 1965.

Bolton, Herbert E. *Rim of Christendom: A Biography of Eusebio Francisco Kino, Pacific Coast Pioneer*. New York: Macmillan, 1936.

Borah, Woodrow. *Justice by Insurance: The General Indian Court and the Legal Aides of the Half-Real*. Berkeley: University of California Press, 1983.

———. "Representative Institutions in the Spanish Empire in the Sixteenth Century: The New World." *The Americas* 12 (1956): 246–57.

Castañeda, Carlos E. "The Corregidor in Spanish Colonial Administration." *Hispanic American Historical Review* 9 (1929): 446–70.

Cline, S. L. *Colonial Culhuacan, 1580–1600: A Social History of an Aztec Town*. Albuquerque: University of New Mexico Press, 1986.

Farriss, Nancy M. *Maya Society under Colonial Rule. The Collective Enterprise of Survival*. Princeton, N.J.: Princeton University Press, 1984.

Fisher, Lillian Estelle. *Viceregal Administration in the Spanish American Colonies*. Berkeley: University of California Press, 1926.

Gerhard, Peter. *The North Frontier of New Spain*. Princeton, N.J.: Princeton University Press, 1982.

———. *Pirates on the West Coast of New Spain, 1575–1742*. Glendale, Calif.: Clark, 1960.

Gibson, Charles. *The Aztecs under Spanish Rule: A History of the Indians of the Valley of Mexico, 1519–1810*. Stanford, Calif.: Stanford University Press, 1964.

———. *Spain in America*. New York: Harper & Row, 1967.

Haring, Clarence H. *The Spanish Empire in America*. New York: Oxford University Press, 1947.

Jones, Oakah L. *Nueva Vizcaya: Heartland of the Spanish Frontier*. Albuquerque: University of New Mexico Press, 1988.

Liss, Peggy Korn. *Mexico under Spain, 1521–1556: Society and Origins of Nationality*. Chicago: University of Chicago Press, 1975.

Mecham, J. Lloyd. *Francisco de Ibarra and Nueva Vizcaya*. Durham, N.C.: Duke University Press, 1927.

Naylor, Thomas H., and Charles W. Polzer, eds. *The Presidio and Militia on the Northern Frontier of New Spain: A Documentary History*. Vol. 1: *1570–1700*. Tucson: University of Arizona Press, 1986.

Parry, John H. *The Audiencia of New Galicia in the Sixteenth Century: A Study in Spanish Colonial Government*. Cambridge: Cambridge University Press, 1948.

Pike, Frederick B. "The Cabildo and Colonial Loyalty to Hapsburg Rulers." *Journal of Inter-American Studies* 2 (1960): 405–20.

Poole, Stafford. "The Church and the Repartimientos in the Light of the Third Mexican Council, 1585." *The Americas* 20 (1963): 3–36.

Powell, Philip W. *Mexico's Miguel Caldera: The Taming of America's First Frontier, 1548–1597*. Tucson: University of Arizona Press, 1977.

———. *Soldiers, Indians, and Silver*. Berkeley: University of California Press, 1952.

Sluiter, Engel. "The Fortification of Acapulco, 1615–1616." *Hispanic American Historical Review* 29 (1949): 69–80.

Vigil, Ralph H. *Alonso de Zorita, Royal Judge and Christian Humanist, 1512–1585*. Norman: University of Oklahoma Press, 1987.

10

The Colonial Economy

Spain's Economic Policies

Mexico, as the colony of New Spain, existed for the benefit of the mother country. At least that was the view of the Spanish crown's economic advisers. Like other European colonial powers, Spain subscribed to the economic philosophy of mercantilism, which held that the purpose of a colony was to make the mother country stronger and more self-sufficient. If a colony did not return such advantages to the mother country it could be more of a liability than an asset. There were other considerations, both religious and strategic, but profit was no doubt the primary consideration.

Spain's colonial economic policies were protectionist in the extreme, which meant that the economy in New Spain was very much restricted by limitations imposed by the imperial system. Thus the natural growth of industry and commerce was significantly impeded, because manufacturers and merchants in Spain were protected from the competition of those in the colony. In accord with the classic pattern, the Spanish Indies were to supply Spain with raw products, which could be made into finished goods in the mother country and sold back to the colonists at a profit. As a consequence, the character of the colonial economy in Mexico was essentially extractive.

In early years of the colony whites lived parasitically off many Indians and a few blacks, but the picture changed considerably after a time. The importance of the encomiendas in the overall economy of New Spain did not last long, for few of those who came after the conquerors received grants of Indian villages. Within a short time the encomenderos formed but a small minority of the Spaniards in Mexico. At one time there were 934 encomenderos, but their numbers dropped to 537 by 1550, and in 1604 there were only about 50 left in central Mexico. Most of the encomienda towns escheated to the crown for lack of legitimate heirs, but some were confiscated for illegal activities. The system continued into the eighteenth century, but by then only a handful of villages remained in private hands.

In all events, even in the palmy decades of the sixteenth century the majority of the encomenderos had encomiendas that offered only modest incomes. It is true, however, that the more prominent conquerors had large numbers of tributaries, and such men were prosperous, especially if they diversified their interests. The wealthiest of all was Fernando Cortés, who had many rich towns. He held real estate and engaged in commercial transactions in New Spain as well as in other colonies; he raised blooded horses and other stock and experimented with the production of silk; and he had interests in mining, shipbuilding, sugar processing, and farming.

Meanwhile many more Spaniards poured into the colony, and, contrary to the view often held, most of them had to work. True, most had the preferred occupations in society; but as officials, clergymen, merchants, artisans, miners, ranchers, lawyers, physicians, teachers, sailors, or whatever, they were productive. While it was certainly advantageous to be white, a light complexion by no means guaranteed a life of ease. Indeed, some Spaniards of low socioeconomic status were reduced to menial labor and occasionally became beggars or brigands. Enterprising mestizos, on the other hand, might be more prosperous than the less energetic of lower-class Spaniards.

In spite of official attempts to encourage Spanish farmers and laborers to emigrate to America, almost none did. As a consequence, the necessary physical labor was performed by those of the colored classes. It has often been noted that the true wealth discovered by the Spaniards consisted of the millions of natives whose labor kept the colonies functioning. In the years following the Conquest a good number of Indians were slaves, either because they were already in that category in their own societies or because they were enslaved by Spaniards for continued resistance to Spanish authority. As chattel slaves, they were branded and became legally the property of their masters, who could buy and sell them. Slaves were often worked to the point of exhaustion and usually had short lives. Owing to the bitter protests of

Spaniards of conscience—most notably the Dominican friar Bartolomé de Las Casas—Indian slavery was finally abolished in the 1550s.

The percentage of Indians who were truly chattels was relatively small; those assigned to encomiendas constituted a far greater number. In addition to the tribute owed to their encomenderos, Indians were also required to contribute labor under a regulated system. When they could not provide the assessed tribute, they were allowed to work it off. Often the encomendero rented the services of his Indians to merchants and others who drove them mercilessly. In 1549 the labor obligation was abolished, and labor in lieu of tribute was forbidden. Without slaves and forced labor, who was then to carry out the necessary tasks of labor? The policy makers in Spain reasoned that if Indians were paid a fair wage for their work, and if they were treated humanely, they would volunteer. But few among the dwindling number of Indians stepped forward to assume the burden.

Consequently the crown decreed a system of forced labor called the *repartimiento*, or *cuatequil*. Under this system each adult male Indian had to contribute about forty-five days of labor a year, usually a week at a time at various intervals. Only a small percentage of the men from any village were to be absent simultaneously, and the head of a family was to have time free to cultivate his own fields. Provisions stipulated that each laborer was to be paid for his work and treated with consideration. In practice, however, Indians were forced to work twelve hours a day, and they were frequently mistreated and cheated of their pay. Numerous abuses of the system kept the natives in abject misery until, finally, in the early seventeenth century the cuatequil was abolished, except for mine labor.

There had been frequent labor shortages, especially following the devastating epidemics, but now there was increased pressure—at least insofar as cheap labor was concerned—for the decree of abolition coincided with the lowest point of Indian population. Black slaves had been introduced, but they were expensive and it was not feasible to use them in labor with low profit yield. As a result there was competition for Indian labor, and wages rose somewhat. Employers now induced Indians to work by offering them advances on their pay, which many were unable to resist. Enough money was advanced to the workers that they could never hope to pay off the debt, and since they could not legally leave their place of employment until accounts were settled, such workers sometimes became debt *peones*, tied to their

A Spanish overseer directs Indian laborers on a sugar plantation in this painting by the modern muralist Diego Rivera (1886–1957).

Indian *tamemes* were the traditional bearers of cargo, transporting goods to all corners of the colony. From the Florentine Codex.

employers for life. Their debts were inherited by their sons, thus perpetuating the system.

The economy of Indian Mexico was transformed by the Conquest. The Spaniards introduced European crops, draft animals, and technology. In some respects the benefits were slow in coming, as in transportation. In pre-Hispanic times everything that had to be moved was transported on the backs of porters, called *tamemes*, and the Spaniards continued to employ them. Despite a legal limit of fifty pounds for each load, it was not uncommon for tamemes to be forced to carry twice that weight over mountain passes. Prominent Spaniards arriving at Veracruz were conveyed to the capital two hundred miles distant in sedan chairs (*icpallis*) carried by Indians. One even reads of the conquerors' dogs being carried by tamemes. So many carriers succumbed to fatigue that a royal decree ordered the increased use of mules and horses and the opening of roads for carts. But the sight of men bent under staggering loads remained familiar.

Mining

The lands of the Spanish Indies belonged to the Spanish sovereigns personally, but their subjects were allowed to exploit the land at the pleasure of the rulers. The royal quinto of American riches applied to Indian treasure, precious metals and jewels, and the sale of slaves, to cite a few examples. The crown was, therefore, no less anxious to promote the search for gold and silver than the most avaricious colonist. The search for precious minerals continued unabated and ultimately succeeded. It was silver, however, not gold, that provided the great wealth of colonial Mexico. By the early 1530s silver was being mined in various locations, but not until a quarter century after the fall of Tenochtitlán was a great strike made. Between 1546 and 1548 the fabulous silver deposits of Zacatecas were revealed, and within a few years more rich mines were found at Guanajuato, San Luis Potosí, Pachuca, and other sites.

The great wealth of the mines dramatically transformed the economy of the colony. Mining camps, some of which became the important cities we see today, sprouted in many locations in north central Mexico. By the early years of the seventeenth century Zacatecas had become the third largest city in the colony,

A panoramic view of a silver-mining operation.

surpassed only by the capital and Puebla. A few miners became very wealthy and lived in ostentation. Other entrepreneurs made their fortunes by supplying those who flocked to the mining camps seeking silver. Commerce was profitable for merchants who risked taking their goods over the dangerous trails, past the Chichimecs. Others established stores and provided diverse services for the miners. Equally prosperous were farmers who furnished the food that was so much in demand in the barren north. At first cattle and sheep were driven north in herds, but eventually ranchers saw the wisdom of establishing ranches in the vicinity of the mines, and this was the genesis of the great livestock spreads of northern Mexico.

For decades Indians constituted most of the mine labor force. They labored far underground in the dark, damp shafts, breathing the noxious airs; some were drowned by floods or killed in explosions. They hauled ore out of the mines by climbing up notched logs that served as crude ladders, carrying their heavy loads in the same blankets with which they covered themselves at night. Poor diets, fatigue, and the unhealthful conditions in the mines made the workers susceptible to disease and early death. Yet, because the pay was good, at least in later years, there seems to have been enough labor for the mines. The mines of Zacatecas, producing one-third of Mexico's silver, required some five thousand laborers at the height of production and suffered no serious labor shortage.

Spaniards embraced the theory of bullionism—that is, they believed that true wealth consisted of precious metals. So intent were they on stockpiling bullion that they neglected other important aspects of the economy, to both their own and their colonies' detriment. And the ambitious European policies of the Spanish crown simply absorbed the income. Fabulous as the production of American mines was, the total impact is usually exaggerated; Spain's income from her various European sources was greater than the silver of the Indies. Ruinous economic policies placed Spain in a precarious posture by the early seventeenth century, when mining production began to decline.

Agriculture and Ranching

Although mining was the most salient enterprise, agriculture remained the basic occupation in all parts of New Spain. It was, of course, absolutely essential for the sustenance of the colony, and

This graceful aqueduct at Querétaro was built between 1729 and 1739. With seventy-four arches, it is 85 feet high at one point, and carried water to the city over a distance of five miles.

most agricultural production was for domestic consumption. To the variety of foods native to the land the Spaniards introduced an assortment of plant life—citrus and other fruits, wheat, sugarcane, and many edibles to enrich the colonial diet. Early Spanish settlers were given, in addition to town lots for residences, small garden plots outside of town for their own needs, to be cultivated by Indian farmers. The natives had their own personal lands, held privately or in common, to provide food for themselves.

Colonists were allowed to grow what they wished as long as their production did not conflict with interests in Spain. Often they ended up having to pay inflated prices for imported necessities that could easily have been grown in Mexico. Wine and olive oil, for example, were not luxuries, but staples. They were considered essential to the traditional Spanish table, and wine was necessary for mass. Yet so great were the profits to producers and middlemen in Spain that the growing of vines and olive trees was forbidden in the colonies. As a supplemental beverage, beer was brewed in Mexico as early as 1544.

Export crops were an important part of royal income. Essential to the booming textile industry in Europe were good dyes, and Mexico produced one of the best with the native product called cochineal. This red dye was of considerable value and convenient for export because of its compact nature. It was extracted from tiny insects found in the nopal cactus, which was soon planted in extensive tracts. Another profitable dye was the blue extracted from the indigo plant. Cacao, from which chocolate was made, had long been a favorite food with the Indians, and eventually it caught the fancy of Europeans, providing yet another valuable export for Spain. Both vanilla and henequen were additional products of some importance. Finally, sugar was introduced into Mexico by Cortés in 1524, and soon there were many plantations and mills in the warmer climes of the colony. Even though Mexican exports of sugar were comparatively modest, they added to the diversity of New Spain's economy.

The deleterious effects of labor in both sugar and indigo processing were such that the crown finally attempted to prohibit use of native laborers, but not altogether successfully. Nevertheless, black slaves were used more extensively, and by the seventeenth century they supplied the main labor for the numerous sugar mills, some of which employed as many as two hundred of them.

At the same time, the Mexican ranching industry evolved. Many great livestock spreads developed in the north because of the availability of land that was almost useless for cultivation. Multiplying herds were branded and regulated. Travelers reported seeing herds of as many as 150,000 head, and in the region of Zacatecas over two million sheep grazed in summer pastures. Even though beef was inexpensive, colonists consumed much more of the costlier mutton. Sheep thrived better in the north than cattle, and their wool brought very good returns on investments.

Stockmen in the mother country had acquired extraordinary influence, and some of it was transferred to Mexico in a controlled manner through their guild, the Mesta. This organization regulated the yearly migrations of flocks and herds and allowed ranchers special grazing privileges. In the dry season animals migrated to better grass, and later, during the annual *rodeo*, they were rounded up and separated according to brands.

Large Mexican estates are usually associated with the vast haciendas of the north, but in central and southern Mexico there were important, though smaller, landholdings devoted to the growing of sugar, henequen, and other agricultural products. The conquerors were often rewarded with tracts of land consisting of twenty to a hundred acres, and many were able to add to their holdings. With fewer encomiendas available, land titles were granted. Thus the acquisition of large estates began in the second half of the sixteenth century. Individuals with the capital necessary for an enterprise appealing to royal interests were either given land outright or allowed to purchase it at a low price. It was understood that for the grazing of livestock large acreage was essential. Foraging cattle and sheep, especially in the semidesert regions of the north, spread out over large areas. One entrepreneur of the northern frontier began putting together parcels in 1583, and by his death, in 1618, the family estates stretched over 11,626,850 acres.[1] In many instances ranchers acquired land from Indians, either by purchase, fraud, or coercion. While it is traditional to assume that a large percentage of Indian lands were lost to the Spaniards, in fact, the natives retained a good many of their ancestral holdings. They did, however, often lose their water rights to encroaching Spanish towns and private haciendas. The colonial court dockets were crowded with disputes over water and the Indians were at a decided disadvantage in litigation with the Spaniards. Gradually the mechanisms for conflict resolution were defined and water disputes were generally resolved by some form of compromise in which neither party suffered irreparable damage.

Industry and Commerce

With industry so closely regulated to prevent competition with Spain, Mexico produced very little in the way of manufactured goods for export. Almost all luxury goods had to be imported from Spanish merchants, even though most were not Spanish in origin, for Spain had neglected her own domestic industries and commerce. Expensive fabrics were imported by Spain from northern Europe, while the production of fine cloth was forbidden to the colonies. Silk, for example, flourished for a while in Mexico, especially during the sixteenth century. But its production was discouraged following objections of Spanish silk merchants in the mother country and ultimately by the competition of inexpensive silk from China.

Still there were many products for everyday use coming out of small industries in Mexico. Coarse cloth, for instance, was manufactured in *obrajes*, the textile mills that existed in various loca-

---

1. See Charles H. Harris, III, *A Mexican Family Empire: The Latifundio of the Sánchez Navarro Family, 1765–1867* (Austin, 1975), p. 6.

tions. Since few could afford imported finery, local mills were numerous, more than eighty by 1571. In 1604 there were twenty-five obrajes in the capital alone. These "sweatshops" were notorious for the unconscionable manner in which the Indian workers were treated. They were placed behind locked doors and forced to work long hours, breathing the lint that caused respiratory problems. Often they were locked in the mill at night, and married workers were allowed to see their families only on Sundays.

The city of Puebla was (and is) famous for its excellent ceramic products. Pots and tiles are richly decorated and glazed in the styles known as *majolica* and *talavera*. *Above right*, a typical seventeenth-century Puebla bowl. *Above left*, Moorish influence is evident in this vase. *Right*, this flowerpot is of a Chinese type.

Other manufactured items were produced by the many artisans in the colony—the tailors, blacksmiths, cobblers, candlemakers, goldsmiths, and so on. There were guilds, or *gremios*, for each of these crafts. Well established by the late sixteenth century, the guilds fixed both the quality of goods and the prices of work. People of the colored classes were allowed to join the gremios, but only whites were allowed to attain the rank of master, which followed successful completion of examinations and the presentation of the "masterpiece" that demonstrated the applicant's skill. In a more positive sense, the gremios were protective of their members, making provisions for those who suffered accidents and illness as well as extending help to widows. They were also active in promoting religious celebrations and philanthropic undertakings for the community. Eventually there were about a hundred guilds in Mexico City. A professional merchants' guild, the Consulado, was established in the capital in 1592. Its function was to arbitrate commercial disputes, to protect the interests of merchants, to establish rules of business conduct, and to foster the interests of the community.

Commerce was closely supervised by the imperial system

Muleteers (*arrieros*) were a familiar sight on the roads of New Spain.

through the agency of the Casa de Contratación. This house of trade was located in Seville, which served as the official entrepôt for all traffic with the Indies. As in industry, tight controls were imposed on commerce in order to benefit the merchants in Spain. Everything and everyone going to or coming from the colonies passed through officials who checked all papers with care. Traders in the city of Seville sent to the colonies a wide variety of goods—expensive fabrics, hats, wax for candles, wine, liquors, vinegar, olive oil, paper, steel and iron implements, fruit preserves, and other items. The masses rarely enjoyed such luxuries, however, and had to rely on native products sold in open markets. The main plaza of Mexico City was crowded with shoppers who could make their selections among the 323 stalls that existed in 1686.

All products destined for the Spanish Indies were required to go on Spanish ships with Spanish crews, and, to facilitate the collection of duties, cargoes were channeled through the one official port of Veracruz. Because of pirates, after the 1560s ships sailing to and from the New World went in annual convoys with armed escort vessels. One of the big events in New Spain was the arrival of the fleet in the spring, at which time merchants purchased their supplies for the coming months. The prevalence of yellow fever and malaria discouraged any sizable permanent population in Veracruz, but when the fleet arrived tents bristled on the beach almost overnight, as great numbers of buyers came to negotiate in the colorful trade fair that ensued. In some years the cargos were taken to Mexico City rather than remaining in the pestilential airs of the port. Eventually the fair was relocated inland at the higher, more salubrious climate of Jalapa, which had the added advantage of being a safer depository for silver destined for Spain.

A similar, though smaller, scene was presented on the Pacific coast at Acapulco. Once a year the Manila Galleon arrived at the port city laden with rich luxuries of the Orient, including silks, jade, ivory, perfumes, incense, and other goods. Merchants who escaped the fevers of Acapulco returned to Mexico City to sell their wares locally or to those buying for the market in Spain.

The Results of Spain's Policies

In addition to its profits through mining and agricultural exports, the Spanish crown realized revenues through retention for

A piece-of-eight minted in Mexico in 1609. Such coins were used mainly for trading with Spain for manufactured goods or purchase of Oriental spices and silks carried by the Manila Galleon.

itself of monopolies on such items as mercury, gunpowder, salt, pulque, and, in the eighteenth century, tobacco. The crown's quinto was eventually reduced to a tenth, but it still constituted a substantial source of royal income. As the encomienda system withered away, more Indian villages came under the crown, to whom tribute was paid. The king's treasury also benefited from the sale of licenses, offices, and land, and from the various taxes paid by the colonists. Altogether there were about sixty different taxes, of which the most detested was the *alcabala*, a sales tax payable on almost everything sold. At first only 2 percent of the item's value, the alcabala went as high as 14 percent during Spain's wars of the eighteenth century. The *almojarifazgo* was a tax of 7.5 percent on all imports and exports, so the crown was paid twice for goods moving between Spain and its colonies, for a total income of 15 percent.

The economic policies of the Hapsburg kings, who ruled up to 1700, were ultimately counterproductive. Excessive and arbitrary control of internal colonial economies stifled incentive and the natural growth of industry and commerce. Moreover local conditions, such as underdeveloped transportation, rural banditry, and, especially in the north, the attacks of Chichimecs, inhibited the evolution of a strong and diversified economy. Equally restrictive were the limitations imposed by an unrealistic imperial supply system. Colonists had little choice but to purchase some imported products; yet the supply seldom met the demand. It was bad enough that ships were dispatched from Spain only once a year, but they sometimes arrived late and there were years when no ships arrived at all. High prices and the irregular supply of essential goods drove colonists to contraband sources.

The general depression of the seventeenth century saw the colonists of New Spain withdrawing more and more from the mother country, becoming more introspective and self-reliant. It was a bleak time, with the wealth, power, and glory of the Spanish empire a fading memory. In the following century, however, Spain and its colonies would have a dramatic resurgence under the more dynamic rule of the Bourbon monarchs.

Recommended for Further Study

Bakewell, Peter J. *Silver Mining and Society in Colonial Mexico: Zacatecas, 1546–1700*. Cambridge: Cambridge University Press, 1971.

Barrett, Elinore M. *The Mexican Colonial Copper Industry*. Albuquerque: University of New Mexico Press, 1987.

Barrett, Ward. *The Sugar Hacienda of the Marqueses del Valle*. Minneapolis: University of Minnesota Press, 1970.

Bishko, Charles J. "The Peninsular Background of Latin American Cattle Ranching." *Hispanic American Historical Reivew* 32 (1952): 491–515.

Borah, Woodrow. *Early Trade and Navigation between Mexico and Peru*. Berkeley: University of California Press, 1954.

———. *New Spain's Century of Depression*. Berkeley: University of California Press, 1951.

———. *Silk Raising in Colonial Mexico*. Berkeley: University of California Press, 1943.

Boyd-Bowman, Peter. "Spanish and European Textiles in Sixteenth Century Mexico." *The Americas* 29 (1973): 334–58.

Boyer, Richard. "Juan Vázquez, Muleteer of Seventeenth-Century Mexico." *The Americas* 37 (1981): 421–44.

———. "Mexico in the Seventeenth Century: Transition of a Colonial Society." *Hispanic American Historical Review* 57 (1977): 455–78.

Brockington, Lolita Gutiérrez. *The Leverage of Labor: Managing the Cortés Haciendas in Tehuantepec, 1588–1688*. Durham, N.C.: Duke University Press, 1989.

Chevalier, François. *Land and Society in Colonial Mexico: The Great Hacienda*. Berkeley: University of California Press, 1963.

Dusenberry, William. *The Mexican Mesta: The Administration of Ranching in Colonial Mexico*. Urbana: University of Illinois Press, 1963.

Frank, Andre Gunder. *Mexican Agriculture, 1521–1630. Transformation of the Mode of Production*. New York: Cambridge University Press, 1979.

Hassig, Ross. *Trade, Tribute, and Transportation: The Sixteenth-Century Political Economy of the Valley of Mexico*. Norman: University of Oklahoma Press, 1985.

Israel, J. I. "Mexico and the 'General Crisis' of the Seventeenth Century." *Past and Present* 63 (1974): 33–57.

Kicza, John E. *Colonial Entrepreneurs: Families and Business in Bourbon Mexico City*. Albuquerque: University of New Mexico Press, 1983.

Konrad, Herman W. *A Jesuit Hacienda in Colonial Mexico: Santa Lucia, 1576–1767*. Stanford, Calif.: Stanford University Press, 1980.

Ladd, Doris. *The Making of a Strike: Mexican Silver Workers' Struggles in Real del Monte, 1766-1775*. Lincoln: University of Nebraska Press, 1988.

Lee, Raymond L. "Cochineal Production and Trade in New Spain to 1600." *The Americas* 4 (1948): 440–73.

Leiby, John S. *Colonial Bureaucrats and the Mexican Economy*. New York: Peter Lang, 1986.

Lockhart, James. "Encomienda and Hacienda: The Evolution of the Great Estate in the Spanish Indies." *Hispanic American Historical Review* 49 (1969): 411–29.

Meyer, Michael C. *Water in the Hispanic Southwest: A Social and Legal History, 1550–1850*. Tucson: University of Arizona Press, 1984.

Osborn, Wayne S. "Indian Land Retention in Colonial Metztitlán." *Hispanic American Historical Review* 53 (1973): 217–38.

Riley, G. Micheal. *Fernando Cortés and the Marquesado in Morelos: A Case Study in the Socioeconomic Development of Sixteenth Century Mexico*. Albuquerque: University of New Mexico Press, 1973.

Salvucci, Richard J. *Textiles and Capitalism in Mexico: An Economic History of the Obrajes, 1539–1840*. Princeton, N.J.: Princeton University Press, 1988.

Schurz, William L. *The Manila Galleon*. New York: Dutton, 1939.

Seeger, Martin L. "Media of Exchange in 16th Century New Spain and the Spanish Response." *The Americas* 35 (1978): 168–84.

Simpson, Lesley B. *The Encomienda in New Spain*. Berkeley: University of California Press, 1960.

Smith, Robert S. "Sales Taxes in New Spain, 1575–1770." *Hispanic American Historical Review* 28 (1948): 2–37.

Stein, Stanley J. "Bureaucracy and Business in the Spanish Empire, 1759–1804: Failure of a Bourbon Reform in Mexico and Peru." *Hispanic American Historical Review* 61 (1981): 2–28.

Super, John C. "Querétaro Obrajes: Industry and Society in Provincial Mexico." *Hispanic American Historical Review* 56 (1976): 197–216.

Taylor, William B. "Landed Society in New Spain: A View from the South." *Hispanic American Historical Review* 54 (1974): 387–413.

———. *Landlord and Peasant in Colonial Oaxaca*. Stanford, Calif.: Stanford University Press, 1972.

West, Robert C. *The Mining Community in Northern New Spain: The Parral Mining District*. Berkeley: University of California Press, 1949.

Young, Eric Van. *Hacienda and Market in 18th-Century Mexico. The Rural Economy of the Guadalajara Region, 1675–1820*. Berkeley: University of California Press, 1981.

11

The Colonial Church

A traveler in colonial Mexico approaching the outskirts of a town first saw in the distance a bell tower rising over all other structures. Before long he would hear the tolling of bells resounding over town and countryside. In the streets priests, friars, and nuns mingled prominently in the crowds. If the physical presence of the church was everywhere, in other ways, too, it was the most pervasive of colonial institutions, and none left its imprint more deeply on the culture.

Church Organization

Because of its expulsion of the Moslems in Spain and its discovery of the New World, the Spanish crown was granted extraordinary privileges by the papacy. In effect, through the royal patronage (*patronato real*) Spanish kings were heads of the Roman Catholic Church in their domains. While this conferred great power and prestige, it also imposed many responsibilities. And, significantly, it meant that the church became an arm of the state.

Church organization consisted of two distinct branches—the secular clergy and the regular clergy. The secular group was composed of priests who served under their bishops. The regulars were missionaries under the separate authority of the superiors of their various orders—the Franciscans, Dominicans, Augustinians, and others.

The Spanish conquerors were devout in their religious observances, confessing their sins and praying frequently, especially in times of danger. During the months of the Conquest five priests accompanied the Spaniards. Cortés demonstrated his pious fervor in his adamant insistence, even in threatening circumstances, that Indians cast down their idols, forbear human sacrifices, and abandon their old gods. His zeal more than once jeopardized the safety of the Spaniards, and he had to be restrained by his own priests.

Typical fortress-like construction is apparent in this sixteenth-century Dominican monastery at Tepoztlán, Morelos. There are some striking Renaissance details in this important structure.

As early as 1519 the crown created a bishopric for Cozumel and Yucatán, but later changed the location to Tlaxcala. In 1527 the Dominican Julian Garcés arrived in Tlaxcala to assume his duties as the first bishop in the land. That same year another bishopric was created for the city of Mexico, and the following year Juan de Zumárraga, a Franciscan friar, arrived as bishop. With the additional title "Protector of the Indians," Zumárraga not only established the form of the early secular church but also took an active part in alleviating the sufferings of the Indians, a policy that brought him into conflict with encomenderos and Spanish officials. A Christian humanist and wise administrator, Zumárraga was a stabilizing factor in the early years of the colony. He was elevated to archbishop of Mexico shortly before his death in 1548.

An event of considerable significance was said to have occurred in 1531. According to tradition, a newly converted Indian by the name of Juan Diego beheld a vision of the Virgin, who commanded him to have a temple built in her honor. Juan Diego's experience was seen as all the more miraculous because the Virgin was dark skinned, and so had a special meaning to the conquered peoples. Moreover, the apparition appeared on the hill of Tepeyac, just north of the capital, where Indians had always worshiped Tonantzin, mother of gods. A shrine was built to this Virgin of Guadalupe, and it is still of utmost importance to religious pilgrims as a symbol of cultural fusion.

As the Spaniards spread out over the land, new bishoprics were formed: seven were established in the sixteenth century, one in the seventeenth century, and two in the eighteenth. They were staffed by large numbers of priests who ministered to the needs of all segments of society.

The Religious Conquest

Meanwhile the important work of the regular orders had begun. In 1521 Cortés requested that missionaries be sent, and in 1523 three lay brothers arrived, the most remarkable of whom was Pedro de Gante. The following year twelve Franciscan friars landed at Veracruz and walked barefoot to the capital. One of them, lamed and tattered, was Father Toribio de Benavente, called affectionately by the Indians Motolinía, "the Poor Little One." He became one of the most renowned churchmen in Mexico's history. As monasteries were built to accommodate their ac-

The cathedral at Cuernavaca, built in 1529, was formerly a Franciscan monastery. In later years, the structure was altered extensively.

tivities, other Franciscans traveled to the colony. They were the most numerous of the various orders and probably the most popular with Spaniards and Indians.

Friars of the Dominican Order arrived in 1525. Distinguished for their intellectual discipline, the Dominicans had long been powerful in Spain, where they were associated with the Inquisition. In the colonies the Dominicans promoted the reformation of Indian legislation. Among their numbers was the militant and influential Bartolomé de Las Casas, later bishop of Chiapas and the most celebrated churchman in the Americas. The Dominicans were particularly important in southern Mexico, where they frequently dominated affairs, both civil and religious.

The Augustinians reached Mexico in 1533 and proceeded to construct some of the finest monasteries in the land. All of these orders flourished early: by 1559 there were thirty Franciscan houses with 380 religious; 210 Dominicans labored out of forty houses; and there were 212 Augustinians with forty houses.[1] Other orders had convents as well, in addition to those for nuns. The fruit of their activity is astounding; Motolinía claimed (no doubt with considerable exaggeration) that as early as 1537 some nine million Indians had been baptized, four million of them by the Franciscans alone.

Founded years after the Conquest of Mexico, the Jesuits entered the land only in 1571, when other religious groups were well established. In their first years they occupied themselves with teaching the sons of Spaniards and soon won the reputation of being superior teachers. But they also taught Indian children, and within a few years they undertook the arduous task of converting natives on the northern frontiers. In the late seventeenth century a number of very able Jesuits, such as Fathers Eusebio Francisco Kino and Juan Manuel de Salvatierra, labored in isolation to take Christianity and Spanish civilization to Indians in Sonora, Arizona, and Baja California. Like other missionaries, they taught their converts animal husbandry, better agriculture, and crafts in order to induce them to lead a more settled way of life and to enhance their security.

Spaniards thought their nation favored by God because of their discovery of the New World. The great conquests of Mexico, Peru, and other rich areas were seen as divine intervention— the millions of new converts in America would make up for those Europeans lost to the Protestant movement. The first half century of Spanish occupation in Mexico witnessed the phenomenon referred to as the Religious Conquest. Those were decades when selfless men of the church worked with great devotion and energy against heavy odds. Their task was an unparalleled opportunity but also an awesome challenge. Friars set out to learn local languages to facilitate communication, and they had to overcome hostility that remained because of Spanish excesses. Moreover many of the Indians clung with tenacity to their tra-

1. José Miranda et al., *Historia de México* (Mexico, 1971), p. 293.

An anonymous Mexican artist of the early eighteenth century rendered this St. Michael.

ditional religion and to certain social habits abhorrent to the Christians. Missionaries were in a hurry to accomplish their objective, and as a result many converts were superficially instructed and only vaguely conversant with the Christian religion. Similarities between aspects of pagan ritual and Christianity facilitated conversion but also led to the mingling of the two in religious syncretism. Though the church sought to discourage all manifestations of pagan practices, it gradually learned to accommodate some of the minor rituals. The obstacles notwithstanding, missionaries had notable success in their conversion of the New World natives, probably the greatest missionizing achievement in history.

Religious Disputes and Anticlericalism

From the beginning, clergymen in Mexico became embroiled in bitter disputes. Ecclesiastics and encomenderos competed for control of the Indians. Friars and priests tried to protect the natives from abuses of Spaniards, while the latter resented the

The glazed tile façade of the baroque eighteenth-century church of Santa María Tonantzintla, Puebla.

Detail of San Francisco Acatepec. The tiles are green, yellow, and blue, bordered by red brick.

interference of the clergymen in the encomienda towns. Men of the church saw the colonists as examples of bad Christians who corrupted Indian morals in addition to mistreating them physically and exacting exorbitant tributes. The encomenderos, in turn, regarded many of the ecclesiastics as hypocrites who were guilty of the same crimes of which they accused others. Within the church itself there were other quarrels, usually of a jurisdictional nature. The various orders differed over the assignment of territories, and the secular priests resented the preemption of some of their traditional functions by the regulars. On occasion the disputes ended in violence.

There were, moreover, some acrimonious quarrels between ecclesiastical and civil authorities, involving not only lesser figures in the provinces but even archbishops and viceroys. One of the most notorious and scandalous episodes took place in the 1640s between the Jesuits and the bishop of Puebla, Juan de Palafox, who also held a number of high civil posts and served as viceroy. This contest involving the wealth and power of the Jesuits became a *cause célèbre* in which several important people were excommunicated and a Jesuit school was almost burned. For the moment the Jesuits were victorious and the powerful bishop withdrew. Eventually, however, the secular arm of the church gained the upper hand in Mexico, as the crown consciously strove to weaken the influence of the regular orders.

The eighteenth-century baroque Sanctuary of Nuestra Señora de Ocotlán, Tlaxcala. Its richly decorated interior is a prime example of the Churrigueresque.

Finally, some clergymen felt discriminated against because of the social circumstances of their birth. As in the civil bureaucracy, those born in Spain were much favored in the religious hierarchy, and most of the higher positions were denied those of Spanish blood born in Mexico. One authority estimates that "in Mexico during the entire colonial period only 32 of the 171 bishops and archbishops were Mexican."[2] Yet, by the seventeenth century the majority of Franciscans, Augustinians, and Dominicans were criollos.

While almost all Spaniards were practicing Catholics, anti-

2. Antonine Tibesar, O.F.M., quoted in Richard E. Greenleaf, *The Roman Catholic Church in Colonial Latin America* (New York, 1971), p. 6.

clerical sentiment abounded in the colony. Aside from their conflicts with clergymen over the control of Indians, Spaniards were often critical of the personal behavior of churchmen. On the whole, those of the orders were of a higher moral type than most parish priests. More dedicated and better educated than the secular clergy, the regulars usually led more commendable lives; however, the cloistered tradition of the Old World gave way in America to a more open style of living, which led a few somewhat astray. But the majority of the regulars were of high caliber, for which reason a number of them were selected for bishoprics and important civil positions, including that of viceroy.

Complaints were more widespread against the secular priests; owing to their lower standards, they were sometimes poorly educated and lacking in commitment. The church had, indeed, become something of a haven for large numbers who were less than devoted to their vows. Reports accused the priests of taking mistresses, imbibing to excess, gambling, soliciting in the confessional, and engaging in commerce. Others were charged with exacting excessively high fees for the sacraments and subjecting the Indians to harsh punishment. Again, while there is a measure of truth in the allegations, it would be distortion to ignore indications that the majority of priests observed their vows, lived modestly, and performed good works for their parishioners.

Juan de Palafox y Mendoza (1600–59) was bishop of Puebla and also served as viceroy. He was involved in serious political disputes.

The tiled domes of Iglesia del Carmen in Mexico City.

The collective burst of energy and accomplishments of the first half century gradually waned. By 1570 there was a slump in missionary activity, accompanied by a moral lassitude on the part of the clergy. The humility and simplicity evident in earlier decades yielded to a more material and increasingly profane mode of behavior that may be attributed to a decline in interest as the novelty of the crusading spirit wore thin and routine set in. Then, too, in a practical sense the challenge was less in terms of numbers, for the Indian population had declined drastically. But it is also true that during the reign of Philip II (1556–98) there was an official check on the vigorous debate concerning Indian policy, which became institutionalized and less flexible. Thus the reforming clergy were frustrated in their desires to ease the conditions of the native peoples and less inclined to aspire to the elevated goals of their predecessors. No subsequent period would see the equal of the extraordinary clergymen of the first fifty years, the phase of the so-called primitive church in New Spain.

The early ideal of a priest for every 2,000 Indians proved impractical, especially in provincial areas. There were by 1650 no more than 2,000 secular priests in the colony, of whom about a quarter resided in Mexico City. At that time the capital had roughly 1,000 nuns. There were about 800 friars in New Spain in 1559; their numbers grew to 1,500 in the 1580s and to about 3,000 by 1600, some 1,000 of whom were in Mexico City. J. I. Israel concludes that Puebla had around 1,400 ecclesiastical personnel by 1650, including 600 nuns. "In Valladolid, capital of Michoacan," he adds, "there were in 1654 . . . more ecclesiastical personnel than white laity." Altogether, including 350 to 400 Jesuits, there were perhaps 6,000 ordained priests in New Spain by the 1640s.[3]

The Inquisition

Religious affairs assumed a more somber cast in 1571 with the entrance of the Holy Office of the Inquisition. With its roots in the Middle Ages, the Inquisition was employed in Spain when Ferdinand and Isabella were striving to achieve political and cultural unity in the state. Under those "Catholic Kings" conformity was seen as essential, Christianity was equated with the very soul of Spain, and heresy was akin to treason. Jews were forced to convert or leave, and later on Protestants were forbidden in Spanish realms. The essential function of the Inquisition was to maintain the purity of the faith, to preserve religious orthodoxy; it would, however, come to assume a much broader charge, not without sinister aspects.

Although emigrants to the New World were screened with care, some heretics slipped by. Particularly suspect were *conversos*, or New Christians, that is, those of Jewish origins who had converted to Christianity, and the Inquisition was determined to root out "crypto-Jews" in New Spain. Some unfortunate Protestant corsairs were also tried for heresy. Moreover,

3. J. I. Israel, *Race, Class and Politics in Colonial Mexico, 1610–1670* (London, 1975), p. 48.

Pedro Moya de Contreras (?–1591) who
arrived in the colony in 1571, established the formal Inquisition in Mexico,
became archbishop, and was appointed
viceroy in 1584.

many colonists, including clergymen and even persons in high
official positions, were tried for purely moral offenses.

Indians were not tried for heresy by the Inquisition as they
were considered childlike and irresponsible. In earlier years,
however, bishops had exercised inquisitorial powers, and some
natives had been brought before the court, usually for idolatry.
The most notorious case involved Don Carlos of Texcoco, who
was accused of idolatry, though his outspoken statements allegedly contained political and social overtones. Bishop Zumárraga found the noble guilty and, in 1539, had him burned at the
stake. This and other examples of excessive zeal helped convince
the crown that the conquered peoples should be allowed special
consideration. Of 131 trials presided over by Zumárraga, only
thirteen involved Indians. The prelate also tried twenty individuals for sorcery, of whom fifteen were women of various races.

The Inquisition also exercised control over printed matter that
entered the colony, being concerned primarily with works that
dealt with liberal, "dangerous" ideas, which, it was feared, would
corrupt and lead astray the unsophisticated Indians as well as
Spaniards. In fact, however, many prohibited writings, including those of the eighteenth-century French and English Enlightenment, found their way into the private libraries of educated
people, among whom were a good number of clergymen.

The Inquisition in colonial Mexico was much less active than
in Spain. Although it is often asserted that only about fifty pris-

oners were executed during the two and a half centuries of its existence in the colony, that figure is somewhat misleading. Deaths attributable to the Inquisition must include the many who died in prison of illness, neglect, torture, or suicide.

Those who paid the extreme penalty had been convicted, in most cases, of the serious crime of heresy, often compounded by "obstinacy"—that is, the refusal to recant. Prisoners sentenced to burning at the stake were often strangled first. Most of those

The Inquisition headquarters in Mexico City.

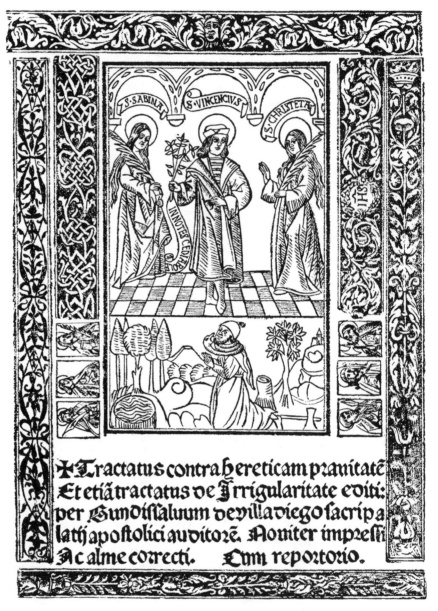

The frontispiece of a treatise against heresy printed in Spain in 1519. Much of colonial publishing dealt with religious subjects.

tried by the Inquisition were judged for lesser offenses, like adultery, bigamy, and blasphemy, and received sentences of floggings, fines, service in the galleys, or exile. Few who were arrested escaped without some punishment, for, as a saying went, "One can leave the Inquisition without being burned, but he will assuredly leave scorched." Those found guilty even of relatively minor crimes were made the objects of public shame and ridicule as an example to others. The solemnity of official proceedings notwithstanding, *autos de fé* assumed a carnival spirit for which elaborate preparations were made. People came from near and far to jeer the parade of those who carried candles and wore penitential garb with pointed hoods, as well as to regard the special ceremony reserved for those consigned to the stake. From the reviewing stand the viceroy, bishops, and other high dignitaries, with their ladies, viewed the macabre spectacle.

The first auto de fé in the colony took place in 1574. Sixty-three prisoners had been judged, of whom five were burned and most others flogged. Eight more autos occurred in the next twenty years. In 1528, long before the formal tribunal was established, two Spaniards died at the stake, accused of being crypto-Jews.[4] But perhaps the most sensational proceeding involving crypto-Jews concerned Don Luis de Carvajal, the colonizer and governor of Nuevo León, who was accused of harboring relatives who practiced Jewish rites. In an auto that included sixty-seven persons, some of his family were burned.

Always coercive in religious and moral affairs, the Inquisition became, in later times, less concerned with spiritual matters. As an instrumental of royal policy, it was utilized in the eighteenth century to check dissident political elements. Both of the liberal priests who led the struggle for Independence from Spain in the early nineteenth century were tried by the Inquisition before being turned over to secular authorities for execution. The tribunal persisted almost to the end of the colonial period and was not abolished until 1820.

The church touched the lives of those in New Spain from baptism to burial. Altogether some twelve thousand churches were built in the colony during the three centuries of Spanish rule. To the Spaniards the church was a link with the mother country, a familiar and comforting association that made them feel less alien in the New World. But perhaps it became even more im-

---

4. Richard E. Greenleaf, *The Mexican Inquisition of the Sixteenth Century* (Albuquerque, 1969), pp. 26, 169–71.

The seventeenth-century cathedral of Morelia, one of Mexico's most beautiful churches.

Carved wooden mask used in a dance celebrating the Christian victory over the Moors.

portant for the Indians, for religious services, soon an integral part of their lives, were a relief from drudgery. The Indians were entranced by the solemn ceremonies; the tolling of chimes and tinkling of bells, the incense, and the burning candles combined to inspire a sense of reverence and awe and to provide an interlude in an otherwise miserable existence. On the lighter side, the frequent religious festivals were usually holidays, offering an opportunity for celebration and relaxation. On a personal level, the Indians and impoverished mestizos considered men of the church to be about the only ones concerned with their welfare. All of these factors contributed to the essential conservatism and piety of the lower classes.

Recommended for Further Study

Adams, Eleanor. "The Franciscan Inquisition in Yucatán: French Seamen, 1560." *The Americas* 25 (1969): 331–59.

Braden, Charles. *Religious Aspects of the Conquest of Mexico.* Durham, N.C.: Duke University Press, 1930.

Dunne, Peter M. *Pioneer Jesuits in Northern Mexico.* Berkeley: University of California Press, 1944.

Farriss, Nancy. *Crown and Clergy in Colonial Mexico, 1759–1821.* London: University of London Press, 1968.

Friede, Juan, and Benjamin Keen, eds. *Bartolomé de Las Casas in History: Toward an Understanding of the Man and His Work.* De Kalb: Northern Illinois University Press, 1971.

Greenleaf, Richard E. *The Mexican Inquisition of the Sixteenth Century.* Albuquerque: University of New Mexico Press, 1969.

———. *Zumárraga and the Mexican Inquisition, 1536–1543.* Washington, D.C.: Academy of American Franciscan History, 1961.

Hanke, Lewis. *Bartolomé de Las Casas: Bookman, Scholar, and Propagandist.* Philadelphia: University of Pennsylvania Press, 1952.

Hordes, Stanley M. "The Inquisition as Economic and Political Agent: The Campaign of the Mexican Holy Office Against the Crypto-Jews in the Mid-Seventeenth Century." *The Americas* 39 (1982): 22–38.

Lamb, Ursula. "Religious Conflicts in the Conquest of Mexico." *Journal of the History of Ideas* 17 (1956): 526–39.

Lavrin, Asunción. "The Role of the Nunneries in the Economy of New Spain in the Eighteenth Century." *Hispanic American Historical Review* 46 (1966): 371–93.

Liebman, Seymour. *The Jews in New Spain: Faith, Flame and the Inquisition.* Coral Gables: University of Miami Press, 1970.

Liss, Peggy Korn. "Jesuit Contributions to the Ideology of Spanish Empire in Mexico." *The Americas* 29 (1973): 314–33, 449–70.

Morales, Francisco. *Ethnic and Social Background of the Franciscan Friars in Seventeenth Century Mexico.* Washington, D.C.: Academy of American Franciscan History, 1973.

Murray, Paul V. *The Catholic Church in Mexico: Historical Essays for the General Reader.* Mexico: Editorial E.P.M., 1965.

Phelan, John L. *The Millennial Kingdom of the Franciscans in the New World: A Study of the Writings of Gerónimo de Mendieta.* Berkeley: University of California Press, 1956.

Polzer, Charles W. *Rules and Precepts of the Jesuit Missions of Northwestern New Spain.* Tucson: University of Arizona Press, 1976.

Poole, Stafford. *Pedro Moya de Contreras: Catholic Reform and Royal Power in New Spain, 1571–1591.* Berkeley: University of California Press, 1987.

Ricard, Robert. *The Spiritual Conquest of Mexico.* Berkeley: University of California Press, 1966.

Riley, James D. "The Wealth of the Jesuits in Mexico, 1670–1767." *The Americas* 33 (1976): 226–66.

Schwaller, John F. *The Church and Clergy in Sixteenth-Century Mexico.* Albuquerque: University of New Mexico Press, 1987.

Shiels, William E. *King and Church: The Rise and Fall of the Patronato Real.* Chicago: Loyola University Press, 1961.

Simmons, Charles. "Palafox and His Critics: Reappraising a Controversy." *Hispanic American Historical Review* 46 (1966): 393–409.

12

Colonial Society: Race and Social Status

Racial Groups

The conquistadores of Mexico were adventurers, not true colonists. They sought no religious haven, nor were they searching for fields to cultivate or shops to tend. Heirs of a military tradition, they responded to the allure of danger and the promise of wealth in the New World. Not for them the prosaic toil of the pioneer.

The married among them left their wives and children in Spain; thus the restraints of domesticity were absent, and few felt any moral qualms about their sexual behavior in the Indies. From the beginning Spaniards mixed freely with female natives, leaving offspring of a new ethnic type. Just as readily they consorted with black women, fathering more progeny of mixed blood. Later cohabitation of the mixed children themselves resulted in additional racial distinctions, so that within a couple of generations the ethnic pattern was quite diverse.

Society in New Spain was composed of three basic ethnic groups: Spanish, Indian, and African. Miscegenation, however, produced offspring of mixed bloods who were called *mestizos*. Commonly, a mestizo is considered to be of Spanish–Indian parentage, but it is helpful to distinguish the racial categories more precisely:

> *Euromestizos:* those of a Spanish–Indian mixture, with European (Spanish) ethnic and cultural characteristics predominating. Such persons in the early colony were often considered as *Spanish* and later as *criollo*.

Indomestizos: persons of a Spanish–Indian mixture, with Indian ethnic and cultural characteristics predominating. They formed the bulk of those termed *mestizo.*

Afromestizos: persons of mixed bloods in which a black strain was evident. If Spanish–black, the designation was *mulatto;* if black–Indian, the designation was *zambo.*

Because all of the above combined in further strains, racial and cultural traits often became hopelessly confused; a minimum of sixteen different ethnic types were identified during the colonial period. Generalizations about the different groups of colonial society can be misleading, however, because conditions did not remain static. Some of the nonwhite castes could not hold official positions in royal government or become clerics, carry arms, serve in the military, or dress like Spaniards, but such prohibitions were by no means always in force. Anyone who relies extensively on published Spanish legislation will have a distorted view of the reality of colonial life; not only did laws change frequently, but in many instances they were not enforced. Although a fairly rigid class system was defined in the sixteenth century, by the eighteenth century society was quite different in several respects. The most notable change was the greatly increased number of those of mixed bloods, who were diverse in character and socioeconomic circumstances. The majority of the colored castes were in a depressed state, but enough of them achieved a measure of prosperity and recognition for their abilities and accomplishments to make facile generalizations invalid.

The Spaniards

The elite of society in the post-Conquest colony was made up of the more than two thousand Spaniards in Mexico in 1521. As the conquerors and first settlers, they were undisputed lords of the land; yet many were oddly cast in this role, coming as they did from humble origins. Some did indeed spring from the *hidalgo* class in Spain, that is, from the lower rung of nobility. Men in easy circumstances, however, seldom leave the comfort and security of family, friends, and familiar surroundings for the dangers, hardships, and uncertainties of alien shores—unless of course they are drawn by some noble cause. While some of the conqueror-hidalgos came from good families, more often than not they had little material wealth. In Spain property was passed on intact from one generation to the next, and it was customary for the eldest sons to inherit all. Under this practice of primogeniture, younger sons, as well as daughters, were left with no inherited wealth. The options open to penniless youths of good family were limited because their pretensions to hidalgo status prevented them from taking employment deemed unworthy of their class. A career in law might enable one to find a place in the royal bureaucracy, but it required a university education. So the best career possibilities lay in the church or the army. Owing to the long history of warfare in Spain, by the High Middle Ages the warrior was a figure of assured social standing, associated with the nobility. And as Lyle N. McAlister writes, "The bearing of arms was honorable while productive occupations—agriculture, trade, manufacturing—were dishonorable. Quality and honor, moreover, came to be conceived of not as individual attributes which could be acquired but as deriving from lineage."[1] The New World presented a rare opportunity—one of dubious distinction for a career-minded hidalgo, perhaps, but holding out the potential of great material rewards for the adventurer. Furthermore, the Spanish Indies offered those of ignoble birth the opportunity to acquire "quality and honor." Soon many expected to be called "Don" as if it were a birthright.

The majority of the conquerors, in fact, came from the working class, and many of them had trades. Suddenly, tailors, carpenters, masons, cobblers, seamen, and the like found themselves part of the new post-Conquest aristocracy. History offers few comparable examples of such rapid upward social mobility. Aside from the true hidalgos, the conquerors were an unlikely lot of "nobles." Many were coarse in speech, unrefined in manner, half literate (if indeed they were lettered at all), ignorant of the social amenities, and altogether possessing few of the attributes associated with even the minor nobility.

The needs of these Spaniards were taken care of by Indian servants and laborers, and their time was free to enjoy the simple diversions available in the developing society. Even though most of them groused about their pinched circumstances, individual economic well-being varied so much as to render generalizations difficult. Some of them ended up isolated in remote provinces with very few Indians, while others were favored with large Indian towns near one of the main Spanish settlements. A few

1. Lyle N. McAlister, "Social Structure and Social Change in New Spain," *Hispanic American Historical Review*, 43 (1963): 350.

found official positions, either in local government or in the royal bureaucracy, both of which could open the way to profiteering. It is probably safe to say that all enhanced their pre-Conquest socioeconomic status.

The natural leader of this early society was Fernando Cortés, who wielded great power and authority. He had a house in Coyoacán, another large residence built on the site of Moctezuma's demolished palace in Mexico City, a palace in Cuernavaca, a house in Oaxaca, as well as other dwellings. With his many tributaries and powers Cortés resembled one of the great feudal lords of Europe.

The heyday of the conquerors was short lived. Soon the colony was invaded by a different type of Spaniard, educated and well connected in the mother country. Royal officials with legal training entered to look after the crown's interests, and private lawyers (despite Cortés's plea that they be excluded) arrived to involve themselves with the interminable lawsuits that arose. Cultured men of the church came to set a higher moral and intellectual tone. Most of these newcomers were of a more elevated social status than the conquerors, and they were favored at the royal court. Crown favorites who had never faced a Mexican warrior were awarded encomiendas and official sinecures, while some veterans of the Conquest were in need. The men of Cortés bitterly resented this turn of affairs, seeing the late arrivals as grasping, officious types who were taking what rightfully belonged to those who had won the land. At the same time the more refined newcomers from Spain ridiculed the pretensions of the "hidalgos" of the Indies, some of whom had been given high titles and coats of arms. This was the germ of the long conflict between those who felt a deep bond to the land of Mexico and those from Spain who served the king's interest and whose real attachment was to the mother country. The permanent settlers observed that most officials and many clergymen were only temporary residents, passing a few years in the colony en route to bigger and better things and therefore insensitive to local concerns about the future.

A number of the conquerors, dissatisfied with the spoils in Mexico, left for the conquests of Central America and Peru and other ventures. Following the restraints imposed on Cortés, the symbol of encomendero power, and the seating of royal control through the audiencia and viceroy, the first settlers were further hurt by the passage of the New Laws of 1542. Although important parts of the legislation were not implemented, the laws were symptomatic of the trend to erode the encomenderos' position. After the clumsy attempt to assert themselves during the Avila-Cortés conspiracy, encomenderos were reduced to despair.

With the phasing out of Conquest society, the remainder of the colonial period would be dominated in circles of influence by men sent from the Spanish peninsula—the *peninsulares*, or *gachupines*, as they were derisively called by those born in Mexico. The peninsulares held the best positions in government and in the church, and they had the most prestige in the community. They were seen as attractive suitors for the daughters of conquerors; the gachupín gained an encomienda in such a match and the daughter rose in social stature. It is estimated that during the three centuries of colonial rule between 250,000 and 300,000 Spaniards entered Mexico, but their numbers were never large at any one time.

The Criollos

The second level of colonial society was formed by those of Spanish blood born in Mexico. These criollos were by physical appearance indistinguishable from the peninsulares, but the mere fact of their New World birth was sufficient to prejudice their status. It was commonly held by those born in Europe that America's environment was somehow detrimental, that the climate was enervating and corrosive, and that the atmosphere produced beings who were physically, mentally, and morally inferior. Thus the criollos were viewed by the peninsulares as innately lazy, effete, irresponsible, and lacking in both vigor and intelligence. To these defects were joined all the social and cultural limitations of life in the colony. Such opinions formed a convenient pretext for the gachupines to justify their favored position; and, although for various reasons the characteristics ascribed to the criollos were not entirely erroneous, they had nothing to do with geography. Nor were the criollos themselves completely wrong in considering the peninsulares arrogant, hypocritical, and rapacious. Both views were, of course, overdrawn.

The criollos, despite their secondary rank, were in a relatively favorable position in the society of New Spain; merely by virtue of their light skins they were considered superior to the darker masses below them. They could rise to respectable levels in church organization and to lower- and middle-rank posts in the royal bureaucracy, and they were able to dominate the cabildos.

WHITE POPULATION OF NEW SPAIN

Year	Whites	Comments
1521	2,329	peninsulares
1529	8,000	peninsulares
1560	20,211	peninsulares and criollos
1570	57,000	peninsulares and criollos
1646	114,000–125,000	mostly criollos
1770	over 750,000	mostly criollos
1793	1,095,000	70,000 of these were peninsulares

In fact some criollos were successful in attaining the highest offices of both church and government, and eventually a number also held high military rank. Nevertheless, although criollos were legally eligible to all offices, there is no question that they suffered discrimination. Distance from the power centers in Spain and the less prestigious academic degrees of the colony prevented their having equal opportunity.

Therefore many criollos devoted themselves to ranching, agriculture, and mining, and some prospered. Commerce, which had been held in low esteem by the socially conscious in Spain, was undertaken without hesitation by criollos. Accordingly, there emerged a criollo aristocracy, based on wealth, that lived in comfort, educated its sons (sometimes sending them abroad), and acquired considerable prestige, especially in regions outside the capital. The powerful criollo *hacendados*, or owners of large ranches, and mining barons felt in no way inferior to the presumptuous gachupines of the petty bureaucracy. Gradually the criollos (very few of whom, after all, had ever seen Spain) became alienated from the mother country. Traditional ties were especially weak in provincial areas, which were remote from the ceremonial and emotional trappings of church and state that symbolized royal authority and evoked mother Spain.

The Mestizos

During the Conquest friendly caciques gave women to the Spaniards, and other native females either joined the conquerors by choice or were taken forcibly. These women cooked for their men, nursed their wounds, carried their belongings, and shared their beds. Informal unions of Spaniard and native spawned the new physical type of the mestizo. Many such liaisons were fleeting, but others ripened into long, comfortable arrangements. In the early, hopeful years the conquerors visualized advantageous marriages with Spanish girls. But when, as happened in most cases, circumstances prevented their returning to Spain in desirable style, they remained in Mexico, where their relative positions were sounder. Other Spaniards already had wives in Spain or in the Caribbean, and, although by law they were obligated to send for them, by one pretext or another many avoided doing so. In 1551, according to the bishop of Mexico, there were five hundred married Spaniards in his diocese whose wives languished outside the colony. Meantime most of these men took native concubines, and some even remarried, thereby risking trial for bigamy.

Crown and church wanted Spaniards married and settled down in order to give the colony stability, and for that reason they encouraged Spaniards to marry Indian girls, through whom Spanish culture would more readily be transmitted to the conquered people. Mixed marriages involving Spaniards usually meant Spanish men and Indian women, because Spanish women seldom married outside their caste, except for an occasional mestizo of some prominence. In particular, the crown encouraged Spaniards to marry daughters of the Indian nobility and often compensated those who did so with encomiendas and official posts. Some of the conquerors found the proposition attractive, and those who took as wives the daughters or nieces of Moctezuma or other native aristocrats usually found themselves in comfortable circumstances.

But in the immediate post-Conquest years most Spaniards rejected marriage with Indian women as socially unacceptable. The shortage of Spanish women in the colony, however, made it difficult for many to find suitable wives. Encomenderos felt particular pressure, as they were required to marry within three years or lose their grants of Indians. So as time passed, quite a few Spaniards married their Indian mistresses, often legitimizing their children.

At the fall of the Aztec confederation the 2,329 people in the company of Cortés included only seven Spanish women, and between 1520 and 1540 no more than 6 percent of Spanish immigrants to Mexico were female. The problems arising from the shortage of women were real, but they have been somewhat exaggerated. Most of the married conquerors eventually sent for their wives. And, before long, more Spanish women arrived, for many of the early settlers, officials, and ecclesiastics brought their unmarried sisters, nieces, and other female relatives with them. In addition, by 1540 there were a good number of mestizo girls of marriageable age. They may not have been the preferred, pure Spanish types, but many were recognized daughters of prosperous and socially prominent conquistadores. As such, they often brought substantial dowries and position, along with names of distinction in the colony. The child of a Spaniard and a mestizo woman was classified as a *castizo* and often passed as criollo. Thus by late sixteenth century there seem to have been almost enough females considered white to go around. Consequently, few Spaniards or criollos of any social standing were still marrying Indian women.

Financial considerations were important factors in marriage; a woman of property had a decided advantage, often to the exclusion of certain other qualities. A widow of an encomendero, for example, seldom remained unmarried very long. If she happened to be an Indian or mestizo she might well be more attractive to a poor Spaniard than a penniless Spanish girl. If an encomendero died leaving no son or widow to inherit his Indian villages, the encomienda passed to his eldest daughter. If single, she was required to marry within a year in order to keep the encomienda—or, if a minor, within one year of reaching legal age. Women in these circumstances seldom lacked for suitors.

Mestizos formed a large, discrete group in society, and it is impossible to draw easy conclusions on their status. To take a notable case, Don Martín Cortés was the son of the captain and Doña Marina. Technically he was a mestizo, but such was the standing of his parents that he was certainly considered to be a Spaniard and entitled to every honor—except of course the inheritance of the estate of the marqués del Valle, which went to his younger but legitimate criollo brother (who was also named Martín). Fernando Cortés took his mestizo son with him to Spain when the boy was only five. While still a young child, Martín was made a knight of the prestigious Order of Santiago and a page to the prince (later Philip II). He fought with distinction in Spanish armies in Algeria and Germany and later he fell in crown service battling the Moriscos in Granada. Pedro de Alvarado's mestizo daughter also had high social status; she married a cousin of the duke of Alburquerque, one of Spain's most powerful nobles. Many less prominent mestizos likewise married well and achieved highly respectable places in society.

The majority of the mestizos, however, were much worse off. A high percentage were illegitimate, especially during the sixteenth century, when the term *mestizo* was almost synonymous with *bastard*. Unrecognized by their fathers, most stayed with their Indian mothers and so became culturally more Indian than Spanish. The mestizos were, by and large, poor, uneducated, and in a distinctly inferior socioeconomic class. For every mestizo who gained a comfortable place in society, there were a hundred others who remained culturally adrift, living in miserable circumstances and scorned by the upper class. For most of the colonial period they were grouped socially with Indians, blacks, and mulattoes.

The Indians

Central Mexico alone (roughly equal to the size of France) may have had a pre-Conquest population perhaps as high as twenty-five million, and for many decades the Indians of Mexico vastly outnumbered all other racial groups in New Spain. Then their numbers were catastrophically reduced. Waves of devastating plagues swept over the land, and after a century of Spanish occupation, during which many died from overwork and maltreatment, there were only about one million natives left. From their lowest number around 1630 they began to increase slowly. By the end of the colonial period the Indians were still the largest ethnic group, but not by so vast a percentage.

As a conquered people the natives were humbled and exploited by the victors. With the achievements of the Maya unknown and the splendor of Tenochtitlán a receding memory, the Spaniards saw the Indians as an inferior people. There were some enlightened ecclesiastics and a few royal officials who pleaded the Indian cause; they appealed to Christian ethics, emphasized the natives' positive qualities, and pressed for humane treatment. All too many Spaniards, however, considered the Indians simply pagans, cannibals, and sodomites. Natives were frequently described as lazy, disposed to vices, devious, and backward. Their capacities became such a subject of dispute that in 1537 the pope was moved to issue a bull (*Sublimis Deus*) declaring that the natives were indeed men and capable of reason! But by insisting on the low character of the conquered peoples,

INDIAN POPULATION OF CENTRAL MEXICO

Year	Indians	Plague Years	Comments
1519	25,200,000		
		1520	smallpox
		1529	measles
1532	16,800,000		
		1545	matlazáhuatl (typhus?); Indian deaths est. 800,000
1548	6,300,000		
1568	2,650,000		
		1576	matlazáhuatl; Indian deaths est. 2,000,000
1580	1,900,000		
1595	1,375,000		
1605	1,075,000		
1625–50	1,000,000 (or less?)		lowest point of Indian population
		1737	matlazáhuatl
		1779–80	smallpox? almost 20 percent of Mexico City's population died
		1784	respiratory infection plus famine; Indian deaths est. 1,300,000
1793	2,500,000		
1810	3,676,281		

Sources: Figures to the year 1605 are based on the researches of Sherburne F. Cook and Woodrow Borah: *The Indian Population of Central Mexico, 1531–1610* (Berkeley, 1960), and *The Aboriginal Population of Central Mexico on the Eve of the Spanish Conquest* (Berkeley, 1963). Their counts, especially those prior to 1568, are considered much too high by some scholars.

self-serving Spaniards justified keeping them in bondage, in line with Aristotelian philosophy that some men were the "natural slaves" of those "superior" to them.

Legally Indians were considered as minors and wards of crown and church. Their care and supervision were commended to clergymen, corregidores, and encomenderos. The church is sometimes criticized for keeping its wards childlike, but the crown must share the blame. Yet, because of their tutelary status, the Indians were, at least in some respects, protected and given consideration. There is little reason to doubt the genuine concern of the crown and church for the Indians' welfare, and many laws were passed for their benefit. Lawyers eagerly encouraged Indians to file lawsuits, and a surprisingly large number were settled in the Indians' favor. Ultimately, however, the colony's

Pre-Columbian dress of Mexican women. Modern versions of the blouses (*uipilli*) and skirts (*cueitl*) are still worn today in some regions.

welfare depended upon the labor of the Indians, and so they were doomed to serve the interests of the Spaniards.

Despite the cruelty of certain pre-Conquest practices and the ferocity of native warriors, when the fighting ended most of the Indians proved to be gentle, pliable people. Those within the Spanish pale converted to Christianity and Spanish ways with surprising ease. The process was facilitated by the shortage of strong Indian leaders, for many nobles had died from battle wounds or disease. They were replaced by lackeys of the Spaniards, who imitated Spanish ways and frequently exploited their own people.

The extent to which Indians were integrated into the society of New Spain depended upon their proximity to Spanish population centers. Those in isolated regions had little contact with the white men, aside from their clergymen, an occasional provincial official, and perhaps the overseer of their encomendero. They lived in small villages, called *pueblos*, preserved their customs, cultivated their small plots of land, and never learned Spanish. They paid tribute to their encomenderos and took their turns at required labor but otherwise lived in a world set apart.

Interestingly enough, by the seventeenth century quite a large number of Indians had willingly left their ancestral villages and migrated to the cities to work in Spanish homes or shops and even volunteered to labor on estates of white men. It appears that European culture came to have some attractions for them. Indians as individuals had not been acquisitive, but as they became acculturated to Christian ways, the promise of possessions and a more varied life drew some from their native villages. Another reason for the migrations, however, was the steady erosion of agricultural lands, which made life in some farming regions difficult. But life with the Spaniards was not easy either, and Indians were all too often overworked and abused in various ways. Tied to the land, without hope of anything better, many lost initiative and in their despair often turned to alcohol.

The Blacks

During the Conquest there were half a dozen blacks with the Spanish forces. In the Caribbean an expanding sugar economy resulted in the importation of large numbers of African slaves, and eventually many were taken to Mexico. At first most slaves were personal servants imported by prominent men, who often had three or four in their household staffs. Less fortunate were those slaves assigned to hard labor, especially in the mines. Indian laborers, both slave and free, had never been satisfactory in regimented labor, and it was commonly thought that one black could do the work of four Indians. And as a consequence of the declining Indian population, 120,000 or more slaves entered Mexico between 1519 and 1650. But blacks were expensive, while natives cost little. Accordingly, slaves from Africa used for labor were put where they could produce returns justifying their high purchase price, and because of their value some care had to be shown for their health. They produced well in the mines, but the dank shafts made them ill. On the other hand, they were well able to withstand enervating labor in the humid, fever-ridden tropics. They were often trained for important skilled positions and sometimes put in charge of Indian workers as overseers in mining operations, small factories, and ranches. Other blacks be-

BLACK POPULATION OF NEW SPAIN

Year	Blacks	Blacks and/or Afromestizos	Comments
1521	6		
1553	20,000		Afromestizos uncounted
1560	17,312		Afromestizos uncounted
1570	18,535	1,465	perhaps 2,000 blacks or mulattoes were escaped slaves
1580	18,500	1,500	figures are probably low
1600		140,000	
1646	35,089		Afromestizos uncounted
1650		130,000	including 20,119 black and mulatto slaves
1793	6,000		Afromestizos uncounted
1810	10,000	624,461	

came accomplished artisans, bringing their masters good profits. It was not uncommon for the slave to be given a share of the profits, which eventually allowed him to purchase his freedom.

Mulattoes, offspring of the union of Spaniards and blacks, were often able to improve their circumstances, both because they were thoroughly Hispanicized and because their Spanish fathers could ease the way for them by making sure they were free. Otherwise the mulatto would inherit the status of his mother according to law and would be a slave if she were one. By late sixteenth century there were many free blacks and mulattoes. The number of mulattoes increased as time passed because black women were attractive to the Spaniards, and, although marriage between them was infrequent (and officially discouraged), they certainly commingled freely. Over the generations, however, the church discouraged the practice of concubinage by pressuring Spaniards to marry their mistresses, of whatever color. Under threat of being deprived of absolution, for example, twenty Spaniards married black and mulatto slaves and free women in Puebla between 1690 and 1695.[2]

Perhaps two hundred thousand Africans entered Mexico during the colonial period. It appears that by around 1560 there

2. Magnus Mörner, *Race Mixture in the History of Latin America* (Boston, 1967), p. 66.

were almost as many blacks as whites in New Spain. The number of pure blacks was never great, however, while the number of mulattoes increased greatly. By 1650 there were over 35,000 blacks and about 130,000 Afromestizos. There was always a shortage of black women (the usual ratio of slaves introduced being two males for every female), which led many black men to take Indian wives. When blacks mated with Indian women the racial type of the zambo evolved. Despite official attempts to prevent it, contact between blacks and Indians was frequent, particularly in household staffs, where there were often numerous servants of various ethnic strains under one roof.

From the early years of Spanish occupation black slaves in Mexico had frequently run away from their masters, sometimes joining Indians in isolated regions. As more slaves were imported, free blacks were seen as a threat to the colony. There were apprehensions that blacks would incite a general rebellion, and many instances of black resistance worried settlers. As early as 1537, for example, blacks in Mexico City were rumored to have a "king" who was enlisting Indians to help them overthrow white authority. The viceroy arrested the leaders and had them hanged and quartered. In the 1540s other conspiracies produced grave concern and talk of limiting the importation of slaves. Blacks were forbidden to carry arms; they were forced to observe a curfew; and no more than three could gather in public. Despite such precautions in the 1560s and 1570s there were several slave insurrections, particularly in the northern mining and ranching areas. Often in alliance with natives, free blacks attacked ranches and assaulted wagon trains. In response, runaway slaves (maroons, or *cimarrones*) were hunted down by bounty hunters and punished with floggings, or hanging if they had committed serious crimes. And in spite of a royal order in 1540 that forbade the punishing of slaves by cutting off "parts that one cannot in modesty name," castration was revived when rebellions continued. By 1570 it was believed that some two thousand maroons were living outside the law and committing crimes.

Around the beginning of the seventeenth century the threat of black resistance centered in the eastern region, especially near Veracruz. There an elderly slave named Yanga had held out in the mountains for thirty years. In 1609 the viceroy sent an army of six hundred men against Yanga, whose camp had eighty men and some women and children. The viceroy's soldiers were given some lessons in guerrilla maneuvers by Yanga, and, when the skirmishing finally ended in a standoff, the government agreed to treat with the black rebel. It was an extraordinary concession on the part of royal authority, and Yanga's struggle was surely one of the most successful instances of black resistance in the New World. He and his followers remained free by agreeing to cause no more trouble and to help track down other runaways. Not long afterward an independent black town, San Lorenzo de los Negros, was founded near modern Córdoba.

Through miscegenation, manumission, and the purchase of freedom by slaves themselves black slavery declined considerably over the generations. Although toward the end of the colonial period there were many Afromestizos, only around ten thousand could be considered blacks. Of those, perhaps only six thousand or so were slaves by 1800, mainly congregated in the environs of Veracruz and Acapulco.

Other Groups

It may be noted briefly that there were other distinct groups in colonial Mexico. Despite the ban on foreigners for much of the three centuries, a substantial number of Portuguese entered along with Italians, a few Frenchmen, Germans, Middle Europeans, Englishmen, and Greeks. Some were specialists, such as scientists, who were in New Spain with royal approval, but others sneaked in, usually by bribing officials. Officials were more concerned with religious orthodoxy than with nationality. Yet there were many, especially among the Portuguese, of Jewish origin in the colony. Finally, a large number of Orientals— Filipinos and Chinese for the most part—entered the country on the Manila galleons. One authority believes that in some decades of the seventeenth century as many as six thousand may have arrived.[3]

The diversity of race in Mexico was well advanced before the close of the sixteenth century. White remained the color of privilege, but the typical colonist came to be one of various shades of brown. In a true fusion of races, the modern Mexican emerged. He became what has been called *la raza cósmica*—the cosmic race.

3. J. I. Israel, *Race, Class and Politics in Colonial Mexico, 1610–1670* (London, 1975), p. 76.

Population Figures

Tenochtitlán had a population of perhaps 250,000 at the advent of the Spaniards, but the Christian city that arose on its ruins began with far fewer people. In 1560 Mexico City had about 8,000 Spaniards. By 1574 there were around 15,000 Spaniards, in addition to a large Indian population and significant numbers of blacks and mixed bloods. By 1800 Mexico City had approximately 137,000 souls; it was the largest city in the western hemisphere, but still had perhaps less than half the population boasted by the Aztec capital at the time of the Conquest.

Population figures for the colony as a whole are especially suspect because of the difficulty of counting people in so many isolated villages. An estimate of 1560 showed a total of 20,211 Spaniards (which no doubt included criollos), 16,147 black slaves, 2,445 mestizos, and 1,465 mulattoes. Excluding the Indians, who still constituted the vast majority of the people of New Spain, the other racial groups totaled 40,268. Of those, around 50 percent were white, 40 percent were black, 6 percent were mestizos, and 3.5 percent were mulattoes.[4] This count almost certainly minimizes the numbers of the castes: doubtless many of the "Spaniards" were technically castizos and mestizos, and a good share of the blacks were probably mulattoes and zambos. The 1793 census reflects the slow recovery of the Indian population, from its lowest point of 1 million around 1630 to 2.5 million. The same count shows a mestizo figure that is probably much too

GENERAL POPULATION OF NEW SPAIN

1793

Racial Category	Number	Percentage (rounded)
Indians	2,500,000	52
Europeans (peninsulares)	70,000	1
Criollos	1,025,000	21
Mestizos (various mixes)	1,231,000	25
Blacks	6,000	0.1
Total population		
	4,832,000	

Source: Based on Agustín Cue Cánovas, *Historia social y económica de México (1521–1854)* (Mexico, 1972), p. 134.

4. C. E. Marshall, "The Birth of the Mestizo in New Spain," *Hispanic American Historical Review* 19 (1939): 184.

low. At Independence, in 1821, almost exactly three hundred years after the Conquest, the total population of Mexico was around 7 million, of many varied racial strains.

Recommended for Further Study

Aguirre Beltrán, Gonzalo. "The Slave Trade in Mexico." *Hispanic American Historical Review* 24 (1944): 412–31.

Anderson, Arthur J. O., Frances Berdan, and James Lockhart, eds. *Beyond the Codices: The Nahua View of Colonial Mexico.* Berkeley: University of California Press, 1976.

Ashburn, P. M. *The Ranks of Death: A Medical History of the Conquest of America.* New York: Coward-McCann, 1947.

Bacigalupo, Marvyn Helen. *A Changing Perspective: Attitudes Toward Creole Society in New Spain (1521–1610).* London: Tamesis, 1981.

Borah, Woodrow. "Race and Class in Mexico." *Pacific Historical Review* 23 (1953): 331–42.

Chance, John K. *Race and Class in Colonial Oaxaca.* Stanford, Calif.: Stanford University Press, 1978.

Cook, Sherburne F. "The Incidence and Significance of Disease among the Aztecs and Related Tribes." *Hispanic American Historical Review* 26 (1946): 320–25.

Cook, Sherburne F., and Woodrow Borah. *The Aboriginal Population of Central Mexico on the Eve of the Spanish Conquest.* Berkeley: University of California Press, 1963.

———. *The Indian Population of Central Mexico, 1531–1610.* Berkeley: University of California Press, 1960.

Cooper, Donald. *Epidemic Disease in Mexico City, 1761–1813.* Austin: University of Texas Press, 1965.

Crosby, Alfred W., Jr. *The Columbian Exchange: Biological and Cultural Consequences of 1492.* Westport, Conn.: Greenwood Press, 1973.

Davidson, David. "Negro Slave Control and Resistance in Colonial Mexico, 1519–1650." *Hispanic American Historical Review* 46 (1966): 235–53.

Dusenberry, William H. "Discriminatory Aspects of Legislation in Colonial Mexico." *Journal of Negro History* 33 (1948): 284–302.

Guthrie, Chester. "Riots in Seventeenth-Century Mexico." In *Greater America: Essays in Honor of Herbert Eugene Bolton*, edited by Adele Ogden and Engel Sluiter, pp. 243–58. Berkeley: University of California Press, 1945.

———. "Trade, Industry and Labor in Seventeenth-Century Mexico City." *Revista de Historia de América* 7 (1939): 103–34.

Hanke, Lewis U. *Aristotle and the American Indian: A Study in Race Prejudice in the Modern World.* Bloomington: Indiana University Press, 1970.

———. *The Spanish Struggle for Justice in the Conquest of America.* Philadelphia: University of Pennsylvania Press, 1949.

Hoberman, Louisa. "Bureaucracy and Disaster: Mexico City and the Flood of 1629." *Journal of Latin American Studies* 6 (1974): 211–30.

————. "Merchants in Seventeenth-Century Mexico City: A Preliminary Portrait." *Hispanic American Historical Review* 57 (1977): 479–503.

Israel, J. I. *Race, Class and Politics in Colonial Mexico, 1610–1670.* London: Oxford University Press, 1975.

Keen, Benjamin. *The Aztec Image in Western Thought.* New Brunswick, N.J.: Rutgers University Press, 1971.

Lavrin, Asunción, and Edith Couturier. "Dowries and Wills: A View of Women's Socioeconomic Role in Colonial Guadalajara and Puebla, 1640–1790." *Hispanic American Historical Review* 59 (1979): 280–304.

Love, Edgar F. "Legal Restrictions on Afro-Indian Relations in Colonial Mexico." *Journal of Negro History* 55 (1970): 131–39.

McAlister, Lyle N. "Social Structure and Social Change in New Spain." *Hispanic American Historical Review* 43 (1963): 349–70.

Marshall, C. E. "The Birth of the Mestizo in New Spain." *Hispanic American Historical Review* 19 (1939): 161–84.

Morales, Francisco. *Ethnic and Social Background of the Franciscan Friars in Seventeenth Century Mexico.* Washington, D.C.: Academy of American Franciscan History, 1973.

Mörner, Magnus. *Race Mixture in the History of Latin America.* Boston: Little, Brown, 1967.

Nunn, Charles F. *Foreign Immigrants in Early Bourbon Mexico, 1700–1760.* Cambridge: Cambridge University Press, 1979.

Palmer, Colin A. *Slaves of the White God: Blacks in Mexico.* Cambridge: Cambridge University Press, 1976.

Tutino, John. "Power, Class, and Family: Men and Women in the Mexican Elite, 1700–1810." *The Americas* 39 (1983): 359–82.

Zambardino, Rudolph. "Mexico's Population in the Sixteenth Century: Demographic Anomaly or Mathematical Illusions?" *Journal of Interdisciplinary History* 11 (1980): 1–27.

13

Culture and Daily Life in New Spain

Education

When Don Antonio de Mendoza arrived in Mexico fourteen years after the fall of Tenochtitlán, he was greeted by, among others, an Indian boy who recited in classic Latin. The amused viceroy soon learned that the energetic friars had already made a significant impact, Hispanicizing the natives through education. It was a plan devoutly encouraged by both crown and church, for quite aside from sentiments of altruism, there were practical considerations. The sincere desire to Christianize the conquered people was feasible only through their understanding Spanish; moreover, it hastened their assimilation of Spanish ways, which was essential to the goal of a more settled society.

In Spain a broad educational system was not seen as a responsibility of the state. Education was, rather, an individual concern, usually involving only those of the privileged class, while instruction itself was the province of the church. Only on the university level did the crown evince strong interest, primarily to prepare young men for careers in the bureaucracy. The church was equally concerned with higher education in order to instruct clergymen, who would in turn run the schools in the colonies, as in Spain. But in Mexico there developed the curious irony of at least a few well-educated Indians being held inferior by some illiterate Spaniards.

One is struck by the cultural vitality in the early years of a Conquest society that was in so many ways both turbulent and rustic. The impulse to refinement came from learned clergymen primarily because educated laymen were usually involved in

221

government, law, or other professional interests. Therefore the
debt owed to the intellectual and cultural attainments of the religious orders is immense.

The first prominent educator in Spanish Mexico was Pedro de
Gante, a Franciscan lay brother and illegitimate relative of
Charles V. By 1524 he was teaching Indian boys, and later he
founded the famous school of San José, where under his direction hundreds of native youths were given primary instruction
and adults were taught trades. While the children were drilled
in Latin, music, and other academic subjects, the elders became
the colony's masons, carpenters, blacksmiths, painters, and
sculptors. Their skills were put to good use by Gante, who
claimed to have supervised personally the building of one hundred chapels and churches.

The school of Santa Cruz de Tlatelolco was founded in 1536
by Viceroy Mendoza and Bishop Zumárraga. With such powerful patrons it became the outstanding Indian school and aimed at
the higher instruction for the sons of nobles, through whom it
was thought Spanish culture would more easily be passed on to
commoners. Aside from the fundamentals of reading and writing, courses were offered in Latin, rhetoric, logic, and philosophy, as well as music and native medicine. Taught by learned
humanists, the youths received excellent instruction, and they in
turn aided the friars in schools and church.

The most appealing figure in early education was Vasco de
Quiroga, whose practical approach to education was distinct. A

The Colegio de Santa Cruz de Tlatelolco.

Vasco de Quiroga (1470?–1565). A distinguished judge of the audiencia and later bishop of Michoacán, "Tata Vasco" successfully experimented with utopian Indian villages.

man of varied interests, Quiroga was a humanist, lawyer, and a judge in the second audiencia. But his fame rests on his personal crusade to benefit the conquered peoples. Using his own capital, the aging lawyer established his first hospital-school of Santa Fé in 1531–32, on the outskirts of Mexico City. Shortly thereafter he moved to Michoacán, near Lake Pátzcuaro in the area of the old kingdom of the Tarascans. There, in the region so troubled since the depredations of Núño de Guzmán, the benevolence of Quiroga inspired trust from the natives. Intrigued by Thomas More's *Utopia*, Quiroga attempted, with considerable success, to create an ideal society in the New World. He formed communities in which the Indians received training not only in religion but also in practical arts and crafts as well as in the rudiments of self-government. Each person worked six hours a day, sharing and contributing equally to the common welfare. Under Quiroga's tutelage the Indians became self-sufficient in agriculture and increased their prosperity through the preservation of traditional crafts. Appointed bishop of Michoacán in 1537, Quiroga continued to lead a productive life until past the age of ninety. With his death the utopian villages declined, but he had established some fine traditions that persisted, and descendants of his specialized artisans ply their crafts still.

There were various other Indian schools. The Jesuit San Gregorio Magno was started in 1586. Concern for abandoned or orphaned mestizos led to the opening in 1547 of the orphanage-school of San Juan de Letrán. But in the end the attempts to educate young Indians and mestizos, however congenial to the best interests of the young colony, were limited in scope. A small number of clergymen were involved, and, despite their intensive labors over the first half century, few of the natives learned to read and write. What had begun on such an auspicious note fell largely into neglect, as the cultural transition passed and apathy set in. After several decades of association with their conquerors, many of the Indians naturally absorbed the language and customs of the Spaniards, and the danger of large-scale rebellion seemed past. Now educating Indians and mestizos was perceived as not only unwarranted but socially undesirable.

The Franciscans are most identified with early education of Indians, and, similarly, the Jesuits and Augustinians were foremost in instructing criollos. Though many Spanish conquerors were uncultured, their sons inherited a social position that called for some measure of refinement. Consequently, there were primary schools, at least, in all Spanish communities of any size, and several advanced institutions in the colony. The most prestigious of such schools was the elite Jesuit Colegio de San Pedro y San Pablo, founded in 1576 and supported by profits from efficient Jesuit haciendas. Its graduates were equal, and sometimes superior, to those of the University of Mexico. An Augustinian institution, established a year earlier by the prominent intellectual Alonso de la Veracruz, also provided superior studies. There were in addition excellent seminaries where a high level of scholarship was maintained, perhaps the best being those of San Ildefonso and Tepotzotlán, both of which belonged to the Jesuits.

The most notable institution of learning was the Royal and Pontifical University of Mexico, created at the petition of Viceroy Mendoza and Bishop Zumárraga. The crown authorized it in 1551, and classes began in 1553, making it the first university to function in the New World. Founded with the aim of educating criollos for the clergy, the University was modeled on the Spanish University of Salamanca, with which it was supposed to be equal in rights and privileges. With an excellent faculty, it would produce many of New Spain's leading literary figures, scientists, lawyers, medical doctors, and theologians. During the colonial period the University granted around thirty thousand

bachelors' degrees, and over one thousand masters' and doc-
torates. Late in the colonial period, in 1791, another university
was founded in Guadalajara.

Girls were not completely ignored in the educational system,
although, to be sure, they were given fewer opportunities. As
early as 1534 women teachers arrived in Mexico and opened a
school for girls, and soon nuns of various orders continued the
tradition. Indian girls, under the tutelage of Gante, were taught
mainly how to be good wives in the Spanish manner. In 1548 the
Caridad school was established for orphaned *mestizas*, and in
the late sixteenth century schools were founded for young criollo
ladies.

Scholarship and Literature

Perhaps the most remarkable aspect of scholarship in the colony
began not long after the Conquest with the diligent studies made
by friars, among whom were a number of non-Spanish Europeans educated in France, Flanders, or other countries. Their in-
quiries into the nature of the native peoples and the land were
truly phenomenal.

The Conquest itself was described by Cortés in his famous letters to the king, which have been translated into several languages and appear in many editions. A more popular account,
however, remains the *Historia verdadera de la conquista de la
Nueva España*, written by Bernal Díaz del Castillo, a footsoldier
in Cortés's army. Díaz later moved to Guatemala, where he wrote
his delightful, personalized account years after the events. He has
left us a work that, with its simple prose and graphic descriptions, has become a classic of its kind.

Especially noteworthy are scholarly studies of the Indians:
Motolinía's *Historia de los Indios*; the Spanish judge Alonso de
Zorita's *Breve y sumaria relación de los señores de la Nueva España*; and the magisterial *Historia general de las cosas de la
Nueva España* by Father Bernardino de Sahagún, a compendium
of Aztec life that forms the basis for our knowledge of that people. Many other important works of the sixteenth century, including church histories, are eloquent testimony to the intellectual curiosity, industry, and painstaking scholarship of these
early historians.

Although the scholarly studies of the sixteenth century were
outstanding, valuable works were written in the seventeenth and
eighteenth centuries as well. The most significant work is the

Carlos de Sigüenza y Góngora (1645–1700) was an eminent scholar of wide-ranging scientific and historical interests.

Historia antigua de México by the celebrated Jesuit Francisco Javier de Clavijero, a native-born Mexican considered to be the founder of modern Mexican historiography. Another erudite Jesuit was Francisco Javier Alegre, accomplished in many fields but best known for his history of the Jesuits in New Spain.

Like early anthropologists and ethnohistorians, clergymen preserved Indian histories, customs, and languages. They created dictionaries and grammars so that Indians could read and write in their own languages. Many of the friars became proficient in three or four native tongues. There were fewer scholars of note in other disciplines, although some excelled in studies of the flora, fauna, and medicines of Mexico. Occasionally research was sponsored by the crown: in 1571 the royal cosmographer was ordered to take a census, study eclipses, and undertake both a general and a natural history. The towering figure in scientific thought was Carlos de Sigüenza y Góngora, a criollo of universal renown during the seventeenth century. He studied to be a Jesuit at Tepotzotlán but was expelled for an infraction of the strict rules. Poet, historian, mathematician, astronomer, and antiquarian, he exemplifies the scientific curiosity in the colonial period.

Leaving aside chronicles of the Conquest, the literary achievements in New Spain began with the *Dialogues* of Cervantes de Salazar, who extolled the beauty of Mexico City and the quality of the university. The brightest literary light of all, however, and holding first place in the hearts of Mexicans, was a woman, *Sor* (Sister) Juana Inés de la Cruz (1651–95). Sor Juana grew from a child prodigy who amazed intellectuals at the viceregal court into a beautiful, graceful young woman with astonishing talents. An early exponent of women's rights, she lamented the disdain with which female efforts were greeted and the subordinate position of women generally. Her disenchantment was well expressed in one of her poems:

> Hombres necios que acusáis
> a la mujer sin razón,
> sin ver que sois la ocasión
> de lo mismo que culpáis;
>
> · · · · · · · · · · ·
>
> ¿Cuál mayor culpa ha tenido,
> en una pasión errada:
> la que cae de rogada
> o el que ruega de caído?
> ¿O cuál es más de culpar,
> aunque cualquiera mal haga:
> la que peca por la paga,
> o el que paga por pecar?[1]

At the age of eighteen she stunned her admirers by ignoring favorable prospects of marriage and her privileged position at court and entering a convent. She devoted the rest of her life to contemplation, intellectual exercises, and the writing of prose and lyric poetry that was surpassed in the Spanish-speaking world at the time perhaps only by Calderón de la Barca. This

1. Ah stupid men, unreasonable
    In blaming woman's nature,
    Oblivious that your acts incite
    The very faults you censure.

    · · · · · · · · · · · ·
    Which has the greater sin when burned
    By the same lawless fever:
    She who is amorously deceived,
    Or he, the sly deceiver?
    Or which deserves the sterner blame,
    Though each will be a sinner:
    She who becomes a whore for pay,
    Or he who pays to win her?
    Translated by Robert Graves, in Joseph Sommers and Antonia Castañeda Shular, eds. *Chicano Literature: Text and Context* (Englewood Cliffs, N.J., 1972), pp. 10–11.

Colonial Mexico's greatest literary figure
was Sor Juana Inés de la Cruz (1651–
95). The portrait is by Miguel Cabrera.

nun-poetess, the first great poet in the New World, composed passionate, almost erotic, love poems of great beauty.

The eighteenth century, so full of conflicting ideologies and
intellectual ferment, did not produce creative writers comparable to those of the seventeenth century. Late in the colonial
period, however, Mexico had a major figure in José Joaquín Fernández de Lizardi. His satirical *El Periquillo Sarniento* (translated as *The Itching Parrot*) (1816), a picaresque depiction of
life in early nineteenth-century Mexico, is widely considered to
be the first true novel written in Spanish in Latin America.

Mexico City had a printing press by 1537–39. In the latter
year the first book was printed in the colony, a religious tract
written in both Náhuatl and Spanish by Bishop Zumárraga. Before the century was out, about 220 books had been produced in
the capital, although no other Mexican city had a press until a
century later. It is estimated that during the colonial period
some fifteen thousand books were printed in Mexico, among
them books in at least nine different Indian languages. In addition to many religious studies, there were dictionaries, gram-

mars, accounts of navigation, descriptions of natural phenomena like earthquakes, and works on medicine, methods of teaching reading, and simple arithmetic. In the second half of the sixteenth century at least twelve liturgical books containing music were published; in the same period only fourteen came out of presses in Spain.

Various obstacles were placed in the way of authors; permission for publication had to be obtained from both viceroy and bishop, and books treating American subjects required authorization from the Council of the Indies. Despite such impediments and the restrictions of the Inquisition, books were available in considerable variety, and there were some large and excellent private libraries in New Spain. When Vasco de Quiroga died in 1565, he had accumulated more than six hundred volumes, and in her convent Sor Juana was surrounded by four thousand of her own books. By the seventeenth century the College of Discalced Carmelites had twelve thousand volumes. Probably the finest library in the New World, however, at least by the eighteenth century, was the one originally started by Bishop Juan de Palafox y Mendoza in Puebla.

The literate public without means, however, had limited reading material, for there were no public libraries and, until late in the colonial period, no newspapers. Communication within the colony was, for the general populace, mainly rumor, gossip, and the information brought by travelers. In early times official announcements were made in the public square by a town crier, following the ringing of church bells, drum beats, or the blast of trumpets. Eventually broadsides were tacked up in public places. The curious were drawn to such places no more by official pronouncements than by the graffiti that showed up mysteriously. These *pasquines* were a way of venting displeasure with government or scoring personal enemies. Usually in rhyme, they were witty, sarcastic, and frequently risqué. No one was safe from these lettered shafts, and the more prominent the victim the sweeter the vengeance. Although illegal, they could no more be prevented than the scrawls that decorate our public walls today.

News from Spain and other parts of Europe came with the annual fleet, at which time enterprising printers published sheets with the "latest" information. For domestic events of high interest, such as a pirate attack in Campeche or a destructive earthquake in Oaxaca, a special sheet might be run off. Sigüenza y Góngora published a periodical, *Mercurio Volante*, beginning in

1693. It was not until 1805, however, that a daily newspaper—
the *Diario de México*—was offered to the public.

Music

Spanish musicians had entertained Cortés and his men during
the Conquest, and as life in the colony became more sedate, others performed more formally in the viceregal court and before
bishops and wealthy, cultured ladies and gentlemen of various
occupations. The clergymen, aside from using music in solemn
religious ceremonies, also staged plays written in prose in which
music had a place. The performers were often Indians.

Music had been important to the Aztecs, especially for ritual
ceremonies, and musicians had very respectable status in the
Indian community. Spanish clergymen soon found that the Indians' love of music was an expedient through which the natives
could be attracted to Christianity. Hearing the mass sung, neo-
phytes came to identify the Spaniards' religion with music. Natives were also pleased to perform, not only because of the enjoyment and the prestige involved but also because performers
were, at least part of the time, exempt from paying tribute. By
1576 there were about ten thousand Indians singing services.

In the beginning, Indians sang to the accompaniment of native flutes, but organs were later introduced from Spain. Before
long the variety of European instruments arrived, and local musicians became familiar with sackbuts, clarinets, rebecs, viols,
bassoons, lutes, guitars, cornets, and so forth. Indians quickly
learned to make such instruments, including even the great organs. Native artists also reproduced choirbooks, complete with
illuminated letters. In addition, Spanish masters encouraged Indians to compose music, which they did with considerable skill.

The church discouraged some Indian music identified with
paganism. Clergymen were horrified by the "obscene motions
and lewd gestures" of native dances, in which "the ultimate intricacies of the conjugal act" were pantomimed. To complicate
matters, uninhibited dancing found new life with the introduction by black slaves of dances, such as the *porto rico*, from the
Caribbean. And clerical admonitions notwithstanding, the
dances continued to be popular, especially in rural areas where
it was almost impossible to impose control. In the eighteenth
century the Inquisition protested the *jarabe gatuno*, "so indecent,
lewd, and disgraceful, and provocative, that words cannot en-

compass the evil of it. The verses and the accompanying actions, movements, and gestures, shoot the poison of lust directly into the eyes, ears, and senses."[2]

Yet the church did not discourage many forms of frivolous amusement, including some of the popular songs. Enjoying sensational popularity was the *villancico*. Originally a type of traditional Spanish Christmas carol usually sung in church, the villancico developed in Mexico as a popular song for festive occasions. While this lighter form was officially frowned upon during the sixteenth century, in the seventeenth century it emerged, like the contemporary baroque taste in art, as an exuberant display of lightheartedness. Felicitous lyrics celebrated not only saints' days but also the rites of spring and the emotions of profane love in startlingly modern form. There was at least a flirtation with a higher form of secular composition in the early eighteenth century when Manuel Zumaya wrote the New World's first opera, *La Parténope*, which was staged in 1711.

Architecture

The highest form of creative expression in colonial Mexico was achieved in architecture. Naturally enough, Spaniards tried to create buildings in the colony similar to those in Spain, and in the early years an essentially medieval style predominated. It was, nevertheless, modified in Mexico: churches assumed a fortresslike appearance because of the threats of Indian attacks; dangers of earthquakes called for buildings with very thick walls, often supported by great flying buttresses; and the humid tropics required provision for better ventilation. Moreover, architecture in Mexico took on a distinctively local character because building materials in the colony offered more color. In wide use was the red, porous *tezontle* pumice, the local whitish limestone, and a green stone found in Oaxaca. As the bright Puebla (*poblano*) style emerged, polychrome tiles came to be used extensively and in some cases dominated the façades of buildings. Indian influence crept in as native craftsmen insinuated their motifs in carvings and paintings. And because even the large churches could not accommodate the great crowds of Indian wor-

2. Robert Stevenson, *Music in Mexico: A Historical Survey* (New York, 1971), p. 184. The section in this chapter on music and dances is based to great extent on this excellent book.

The church and convent of San Agustín, Hidalgo.

shipers, broad courtyards, or "open-air chapels," were a familiar
sight.

The first decades of architecture in Mexico saw a *mestizaje* of
styles, in which features of the romanesque, Gothic, and *mudéjar*
(Moorish) merged. By the middle of the century, however, they
yielded to the influence of the Spanish Renaissance which, because its intricate plasterwork resembled the art of silversmiths,
was called plateresque. In line with the general philosophic outlook of their order, Franciscan churches had a simplicity that

contrasted with the massive, richly ornate Augustinian piles. The secular clergy, feeling fewer stylistic restraints, indulged a taste for even more elaborate architecture.

The great cathedrals stand out by virtue of sheer bulk, but those of Mexico City and Puebla, designed by the same architect and competing in excellence, are especially noteworthy structures. Begun in 1563, the cathedral of Mexico City occupied teams of craftsmen for a century and even then was not completed until the late colonial period. That of Puebla, considered by many to be the finer of the two, was laid out around 1575 and dedicated in 1649. Vasco de Quiroga's plan for a cathedral in Michoacán to match the dimensions of St. Peter's was obviously never realized.

Civil architecture fared less well over the centuries. We know that splendid buildings arose—palaces of the viceroy and bishops, offices of the audiencia and ayuntamiento, and various other

Cathedral of Mexico

A water tower at Teoloyucan, with its flared buttresses, one of the many remaining monuments to colonial artisans.

government structures. But some were destroyed, and the original forms of others were altered by later constructions. It is sad,
too, that the Renaissance mansions of the conquerors have almost
all disappeared, although we gain some appreciation of their
elegance from the residence of Francisco de Montejo in Mérida
and the modified palace of Cortés in Cuernavaca.

In the seventeenth century a style more distinctively Mexican
emerged. The moderate expression of the Spanish baroque gave
way in the colony to what is often referred to as "ultra" baroque
—that is, a style dominated by a profusion of decorative effects.
The trend began in Puebla, where one sees the best examples of
the form. In the eighteenth century the love of ornamentation
was carried to the ultimate in the Churrigueresque (for José
Churriguera, a Spanish architect). Surfaces were encrusted with
decoration, and façades and altarpieces were stifled with riotous
detail. It was, in a way, the glorious celebration of the optimism
and prosperity of criollo society; and, although too busy for some
tastes, it nevertheless produced some of the finest examples of

religious architecture and is held by many to be the highest form of the builder's art in colonial Mexico.

Such excesses inevitably exhaust the senses, and it is not surprising, therefore, that the next phase of architecture was a reaction. The severe, formal, neoclassic was a sober turn. Reflecting the stern realities of late colonial life, it was cold and devoid of the color and fantasy that have generally characterized Mexican art from the marvelous Maya façades to the brilliant murals of the twentieth century.

Sculpture and Painting

Sculpture was, to great extent, an adjunct to architecture. Sculptors, many of whom were Indians and mestizos, rendered in stone and plaster the incredibly complex designs of ceilings and façades, and they carved wooden altarpieces, images of saints, and other adornments that contributed to the grandeur of the art of New Spain. Most of these artists remain anonymous, but one prominent sculptor deserves mention. Manuel Tolsá, a Spaniard, created the admirable equestrian statue of Charles IV that is affectionately known as "the Caballito." Prominently on display in Mexico City today, it is regarded as one of the finest works of its kind in the world.

Second-story façade of the sixteenth-century residence of Francisco de Montejo in Mérida, Yucatán.

The first European painter in Mexico was a companion of Cortés who painted his captain at prayer. With the construction of churches and monasteries, frescoes were painted by friars and Indians trained in Gante's school. Good examples of these early efforts have been preserved at Acolman, Cuernavaca, and Actopan. Also to the first decades belong the post-Conquest códices, painted, with official encouragement, by Indian artists in the pre-Hispanic style. The códices that survive have not only invaluable historical importance but genuine artistic qualities as well. For the most part, however, native painters lost the traditions of their primitive, though charming, style as they were pressed into studios for training in the realism of the Spanish school.

Painting advanced in quality with the arrival in 1566 of the Flemish master Simón Pereyns. He gathered around him a talented group of criollo artists who painted canvases in the Spanish manner. By the seventeenth century, when Spain enjoyed a splendid period of art, their successors imitated Francisco de Zurbarán, José Ribera, Bartolomé Murillo, and other prominent Spanish artists. The seventeenth century saw the epitome of colonial painting. Whereas most of the earliest artists were associated with religious art, more opportunities now opened for the studio artist who prospered through rich patrons. The prominent and wealthy adorned their residences with paintings, and portraits were in great demand. One may weigh the skills of those portraitists in the paintings of the viceroys, most of whom stare down from the walls with grim and baleful countenance. Although the colony had many good and popular artists, it cannot be said that their work was comparable to the best being done in Europe. Yet by the eighteenth century such painters prospered, satisfying the egos of the silver barons and others who sought to be preserved for posterity.

As part of the "progressive" trend in Spain, the Art Academy of San Carlos was dedicated in Mexico City in 1785, and academic training was introduced to give equal opportunity to aspiring artists of all races. The stiff formal approach gave impulse to a controlled, less Mexican, school of art, consonant with the neoclassic in architecture.

Daily Life

The poverty, ugliness, injustices, and the general misery of the lower classes notwithstanding, colonial life was not a scene of unrelieved tragedy. It was indeed close to that for most of the Indians throughout the sixteenth century, but thereafter conditions eased somewhat. And while the daily routine of peasants in the provinces was mostly drudgery, urban life was more exciting.

Visitors to Mexico City who recorded their impressions usually commented on its fine buildings and broad, straight avenues. In the seventeenth century, travelers asserted that everything one could desire was available, including abundant supplies of foods that were both delicious and inexpensive. Daily more than one thousand boats and three thousand mules carried in provisions from outlying provinces. Foreigners remarked on the excellence of the city's construction, with its plazas, fountains, and sidewalks. An Englishman living in Mexico City in 1625 estimated that the capital had fifteen thousand coaches, some of which were trimmed with gold, silver, and Chinese silk.[3]

Color, of which Mexicans have always been almost excessively fond, was what struck the foreigner's eye. Color was everywhere, from the flower gardens and blossoming trees, to the textured hues of walls, to the kaleidoscope of the great open markets where bright exotic fruits and vegetables vied with polychrome tiles and pottery, brilliant native textiles, and jewelry. There was an astonishing variety of goods available in the marketplace, where thousands of people gathered to bargain and exchange gossip. A motley population thronged the streets, their rich skin tones adding to the mosaic of color. Dark habits of the ecclesiastics heightened the bright sashes of university students and the dress of criollo dandies who paraded in plumed, scarlet taffeta hats, ruffled laces, and velvet capes. A dignified worthy clothed in severe ebony might be accompanied by black slaves attired in blue or yellow breeches, with white silk stockings.

Both men and women wore jewels in the street, and it was not uncommon to see hatbands set with pearls and diamonds. Occasionally the procession of the viceroy or archbishop with his retinues passed, causing a mild sensation. Women, who were just as fashion conscious as men, flaunted exquisite cloths of the Orient and the richest textiles of Europe. Wealthy ladies frequently observed modesty by making their way through the streets in veiled palanquins, sedan chairs borne by slaves. But other females enjoyed the approval (or jealousy) provoked by scanty dress. Visitors were especially taken by beautiful mulatto women wearing expensive silks and sparkling gems, despite sumptuary

3. Irving A. Leonard, *Baroque Times in Old Mexico: Seventeenth-Century Persons, Places, and Practices* (Ann Arbor, 1971), pp. 73, 76.

laws that were passed from time to time to prevent them from
dressing like whites. Women of various classes applied rouge and
eye makeup.

Beneath all the finery and cosmetics, however, were people
who aged quickly and who enjoyed fewer of the beauty aids
available to serve the vanities of our times. In close conversation
with a colonist one would become aware of a strong musty odor,
a smile marred by missing or rotting teeth, and a face scarred

Glazed pottery was introduced to Mexico from Talavera de la Reina, Spain,
in the sixteenth century. In the first half of the seventeenth century, about
forty potters were registered in the city of Puebla. The informality of design and execution in Mexican ceramics make them appealing today, but
in colonial times Puebla pottery was mainly used by the poor; the rich
preferred their tables set with silver and Chinese porcelain. Examples are
shown below and on the facing page.

Late seventeenth-century ceramic fountain from Puebla suggesting Chinese
influence.

A Puebla vase decorated in Oriental style, late seventeenth century.

Flower pot of the style commonly used in the halls and patios of colonial houses.

Tiles from Puebla were commonly used on building façades.

and pitted. At least on social occasions some were considerate: a strong perfume might disguise the infrequency of bathing, and offensive breath could be tamed by chewing cloves or licorice.

Among the more pathetic elements of society were the many vagabonds who swarmed into the colony. They lounged around city streets, living by their wits and making a general nuisance of themselves in both urban and provincial areas. These *picaros*, so charmingly presented in literature, were in fact parasites infecting the society of New Spain, much to the dismay of the authorities and the general public. They were seen as a disruptive element, unsettling to the colony, and potentially dangerous.

Some of these beggars (later called *léperos*) were lads in their early teens who made their way to the Spanish Indies, where they picked up vices and venereal diseases. Much of their time was spent molesting Indian girls and spoiling for adventure, and they often ended up as petty criminals. Moreover the colony produced its own domestic vagabonds, of all racial groups. Many were syphilitic wretches, dressed in filthy rags, who hung about public places where they displayed open sores, grotesque tumors, and maimed limbs. Some were blind (or pretended to be) and joined other indigents outside churches to collect alms. Modest attempts were made to provide care for them and the church regularly dispensed food and small sums of money. In the countryside vagabonds often lived illegally in Indian villages, forcing villagers to support them and sometimes seizing their women. As early as 1560 there were three to four thousand of these parasites in New Spain without visible means of support.

All of these social types, elegant and rustic, were part of daily scenes in streets that were alternately muddy or dusty, depending on the season. Cursing mule drivers prodded their braying beasts along, stirring up clouds of dust or making quagmires, while other herders pushed swine, sheep, or turkeys through the crowds. Peddlers hawked their wares, Indian servant girls carried jugs of water from the public fountains, and tamemes bent under the loads that almost obscured them. Eventually some streets had cobblestones, but gutters remained like open sewers, strewn with garbage and an occasional dead dog. If color delighted the eye, stench assailed the nostril. But such aromas and unsanitary conditions were, after all, not much different from those in other parts of the world at the time. The filth did pose a serious health problem, however, and the government moved to keep the capital cleaner. The pigs that ran loose in the streets and scavenged for food were relied upon less fully after an ordinance of 1598 provided for twelve teams of two Indians, with mule carts, to collect refuse from city streets every day. Public buildings, including storehouses and jails, were to be cleaned every four months. There was little improvement in sanitary conditions throughout the colonial period, however, and swine, mongrel dogs, and vultures continued to be counted on to help keep streets clean.

A wide assortment of diversion was offered in the cities of New Spain, especially in the capital. At the center of social life was the viceregal court, although bishops and wealthy laymen often rivaled the court in extravagant entertainment. For the cultured elite there were the latest plays, music, and literature from Spain and clever conversation in the salons. Some recitals and performances were private, but a great many were for the general public. Dancing was popular with all, from the formal balls of the wealthy to the more spontaneous, often earthy, dances of the lower classes. Bullfighting, introduced shortly after the Conquest, found wide favor with all segments of society. An archbishop in early seventeenth century was such an *aficionado* that he had his own private bullring on the grounds of the archiepiscopal palace. The more intellectual enjoyed chess, and cards were played by all classes. Gambling was a vice to which almost everyone was addicted, as wagers were made at dice, cards, horse races, cockfighting, or any contest available for betting purposes. Such diversions were indulged in mainly by men, but new arrivals to the colony were shocked to see criollo ladies of presumed high social standing dealing cards with males. For the aristocrats there were jousting and other games played on horseback, and they rode to the hunt with their greyhounds and falcons.

Leisure time was abundant for most; colonists enjoyed many holidays, with eighty-five religious festivals annually. Each individual celebrated his saint's day, and towns had their special saints to be honored as well. These and other holy days were enjoyed to the fullest. Solemn religious rites, processions, and sometimes penance were followed by fireworks, feasting, singing, dancing, and no small amount of drinking—which in turn often led to fighting. Gentlemen might settle accounts of honor with a duel; the lower classes would more likely find satisfaction informally and im-

The picturesque Alameda Park in the center of Mexico City was first laid out in 1593 during the rule of Viceroy Luis de Velasco. Now much enlarged, it is still the scene of promenades under the tall trees and along the pathways past fountains and bright flower gardens.

mediately with knives or machetes. A favorite—and healthier—diversion at parties (during which daughters were watched by hawk-eyed chaperones) was the throwing of eggshells filled with confetti or of hollow wax balls containing perfumed water. All of this was conducted with great merriment and a consuming interest in sweet-meats and the opposite sex.

Other events demanded celebration. The birth of a royal child, a royal marriage, the coronation of a new king, the arrival of a new viceroy or archbishop, or a great victory over one of Spain's enemies, all called for displays and merrymaking. The most glorious of spectacles were the *mascaradas*, often planned far in advance and summoning the most creative talents to assure sensational (and sometimes bizarre) effects. The essential part of the show was the grand parade. It might lead off with Indian chiefs decked out in traditional native garb, followed by dignitaries of the church in their rich vestments, high royal officials mounted on superb horses with silver trappings, and faculty members of the university in their gaudy robes. There were also decorated floats, clowns, acrobats, jugglers, and musicians. Some individuals were masked (from which the ceremonies took their names), wearing costumes representing mythical or historical figures, while others personified Pride, Greed, Lust, or perhaps one of the virtues.

Sometimes the mascarada was sponsored, at great cost, by a wealthy individual and other times by the state, but the aim of the organizers was always to surpass previous extravaganzas. No expense or labor was spared—even to the extent of importing camels and ostriches for the parade, to the great delight of the spectators.

A cherished ritual of the elite youth was the daily *paseo*, in which the young men gathered around five o'clock in Mexico City's Alameda Park. These popinjays arrived in fancy carriages or perhaps mounted on blooded horses and were attended by black slaves suitably dressed to display their young masters' elegance. Young ladies arrived in much the same fashion, for the same purpose. The congregation indulged in what passed as witty repartee and strolled around the park, flirting with the opposite sex all the while. It was harmless enough, except when excesses of bravado led to drawn swords.

The impression should not be left that colonial society witnessed a continual round of parties and sport. The foregoing observations of colonists at play pertain mostly to large centers like Mexico City and Puebla. Smaller towns had similar amusements, but they were on a scale less grand and carried off with less flair. Occasions such as saints' days in small communities called for celebrations that were simple but lively, and the custom of the paseo—which has persisted into modern times—saw the gathering of young people of more humble aspect in village plazas. Local celebrations might consist of little more than a mass followed by fireworks and drinking to stupefaction.

Life in the colony also had its grim aspects. Throughout most of the colonial period streets were dark at night, with no provisions for lighting. Thus assaults were not unusual, and few went out late at night without arms and companions. Thievery was widespread, and so were crimes of passion. Rural brigandage was a plague to all. In the sixteenth century there were almost no inns, and Indian villages were required to furnish food and lodging for travelers. Later on, crude facilities for those on the road were maintained.

A common sight was that of criminals hanged by the roadside and left as a warning to others. Death by hanging was decreed for many crimes, and for especially serious offenses, such as treason, the body of the culprit was drawn and quartered, with the head and limbs prominently and gruesomely displayed. Mutilation of limbs, the severing of a hand or foot, the crushing of a foot in a diabolical device known as "the boot," and other tortures were employed on occasion. Floggings of one or two hundred lashes were not uncommon. Those of high social position, however, were usually spared humiliating and cruel punishment, escaping with fines or sometimes jail sentences. Nobles found guilty of treason, however, could not avoid the severest penalty, but they were given the preferred death of decapitation, for hanging was considered too undignified for one of high rank.

The plagues that so devastated the Indian population by no means left Spaniards untouched, even though they had better resistance. One of the most virulent of the diseases was *matlazáhuatl*. Known in Mexico apparently before the advent of the white man, the malady, similar to typhus, was thought by the Indians to have been caused by comets, volcanic eruptions, or earthquakes. Smallpox continued to be a great killer, and when it struck Mexico City in 1779–80, nearly 20 percent of the capital's population perished. Toward the end of the colonial period an extensive vaccination program succeeded in checking the spread of smallpox. But life expectancy for the colonists was half that of ours today.

When Spaniards landed at the port of Veracruz their first thought was to get out of the fever-ridden town and up into higher altitudes where the climate was more salubrious. The same unhealthful conditions prevailed at the Pacific port of Acapulco, and one colonial official described his assignment there as a sentence in hell. Both ports were populated in the majority by blacks and mulattoes. Colonists suffered from intestinal parasites and all sorts of digestive disorders, from leprosy, kidney stones, rheumatism, gout and a variety of other complaints that were only vaguely diagnosed. There was little to relieve suffering, although bleeding and purging were widely used as standard cures for many complaints.

Bishop Zumárraga established a hospital in the capital for those ailing from venereal diseases. Later an asylum for the insane was opened. At first there were hospital facilities for Spaniards only, but a royal order of 1553 made provision for a hospital for ill and indigent Indians. By 1580 Mexico City had six hospitals—four for Spaniards, one for Indians, and another for blacks and mestizos. Facilities were minimal, and these hospitals were actually what we might today call rest homes. Nuns operated seven convents that served as convalescent retreats, as did an equal number of monasteries.

Medical practitioners, identified as surgeons, were usually barbers as well and no doubt more skilled in the latter practice. Details of surgical operations may be left to the imagination— the doctors probably killed as many patients as they saved. They were, however, skillful in performing Caesarean sections. Medical doctors often had their own bags of tricks, with favorite cures of dubious merit. Spaniards sometimes resorted to Indian healers, who were apparently just as effective, if not more so.

At least some attempts were made by the crown to impose controls over the qualifications of doctors; after 1535 those practicing medicine were supposed to have been examined by university specialists. A professorship of surgery and anatomy was established at the University in 1621, and a medical board was formed a quarter century later. Medical inspectors were sent to the colony from time to time to improve medical practices, especially with regard to better training for surgeons and druggists. By 1790 there were fifty-one medical doctors in Mexico, along with 221 "surgeons and barbers," most of whom resided in the capital or other large centers. Despite modest attempts of authorities to improve medical services, the state of the profession advanced very little throughout the eighteenth century. People in Mexico learned to be familiar with death, to dwell upon it, and sometimes to make light of it; they were fatalistic and anxious to make their peace with God.

Far from being the vulgar backwater one might have supposed, New Spain had a vibrant and diverse cultural life, especially in the larger cities. From early years erudite clergymen introduced a strong tradition of scholarship, and refined Spanish immigrants spread their cultivated tastes. The cultural milieu was advanced with strong support from the viceroys and bishops. In summary, the society of New Spain during its first two centuries was a culture embodying the best and the worst of its times, more complex than colonial life in English colonies in America but more rustic than the European model it imitated.

246 it had a uniquely

By 1700 it had a uniquely Mexican character, with customs and traditions so firmly impressed on society that the patterns are still evident today.

Recommended for Further Study

Baird, Joseph H. *The Churches of Mexico, 1530–1810.* Berkeley: University of California Press, 1962.

Barth, Pius J. *Franciscan Education and the Social Order in Spanish North America (1502–1821).* Chicago: University of Chicago Press, 1945.

Castedo, Leopoldo. *A History of Latin American Art and Architecture from Precolumbian Times to the Present.* New York: Praeger, 1969.

Charlot, Jean. *Mexican Art and the Academy of San Carlos, 1785–1915.* Austin: University of Texas Press, 1962.

Estrada, Dorothy T. de. "The 'Escuelas Pias' of Mexico City, 1786–1820." *The Americas* 31 (1974): 51–71.

Fernández, Justino. *Mexican Art.* London: Spring Books, 1965.

Gage, Thomas. *Thomas Gage's Travels in the New World.* Edited by J. Eric S. Thompson. Norman: University of Oklahoma Press, 1969.

Gibson, Charles. "Writings on Colonial Mexico." *Hispanic American Historical Review* 55 (1975): 287–323.

Jacobsen, Jerome V. *Educational Foundations of the Jesuits in Sixteenth-Century New Spain.* Berkeley: University of California Press, 1938.

Keleman, Pál. *Art of the Americas: Ancient and Hispanic.* New York: Crowell, 1969.

Kubler, George. *Mexican Architecture of the Sixteenth Century.* 2 vols. New Haven, Conn.: Yale University Press, 1948.

Lanning, John Tate. *Academic Culture in the Spanish Colonies.* London: Oxford University Press, 1940.

Leonard, Irving. *Baroque Times in Old Mexico: Seventeenth-Century Persons, Places, and Practices.* Ann Arbor: University of Michigan Press, 1971.

———. *Books of the Brave.* Cambridge, Mass.: Harvard University Press, 1949.

———. *Don Carlos de Sigüenza y Góngora, A Mexican Savant of the Seventeenth Century.* University of California Publications in History, vol. 18. Berkeley: University of California Press, 1929.

McAndrews, John. *The Open-Air Churches of Sixteenth-Century Mexico.* Cambridge, Mass.: Harvard University Press, 1965.

Martin, Cheryl E. *Rural Society in Colonial Morelos.* Albuquerque: University of New Mexico Press, 1985.

Mathes, Michael. *The Americas' First Academic Library, Santa Cruz de Tlatelolco.* Sacramento: California State Library, 1985.

Mathes, Valerie. "Enrico Martínez of New Spain." *The Americas* 33 (1976): 62–77.

Mullen, Robert J. *Dominican Architecture in Sixteenth Century Oaxaca.* Tempe: Arizona State University's Center for Latin American Studies, 1975.

Paz, Octavio. *Sor Juana. Or, The Traps of Faith.* Translated by Margaret

Sayers Peden. Cambridge, Mass.: Harvard University Press, 1988.

Robertson, Donald. *Mexican Manuscript Painting of the Early Colonial Period: The Metropolitan Schools.* New Haven, Conn.: Yale University Press, 1959.

Rojas, Pedro. *The Art and Architecture of Mexico.* Translated by J. M. Cohen. Feltham, Eng.: Hamlyn, 1968.

Ronan, Charles E., S.J. *Francisco Javier Clavijero: His Life and Works.* Chicago: Loyola University Press, 1977.

Schurz, William L. *This New World: The Civilization of Latin America.* New York: Dutton, 1964.

Seed, Patricia. *To Love, Honor and Obey in Colonial Mexico. Conflicts over Marriage Choice, 1574–1821.* Stanford, Calif.: Stanford University Press, 1988.

Simpson, Lesley B. *Many Mexicos.* Berkeley: University of California Press, 1959.

Smith, Bradley. *Mexico: A History in Art.* Garden City, N.Y.: Doubleday, 1968.

Stevenson, Robert. *Music in Mexico: A Historical Survey.* New York: Crowell, 1971.

Taylor, William B. *Drinking, Homicide and Rebellion in Colonial Mexican Villages.* Stanford, Calif.: Stanford University Press, 1979.

Toussaint, Manuel. *Colonial Art in Mexico.* Translated and edited by Elizabeth W. Weismann. Austin: University of Texas Press, 1967.

Warren, Fintan B. *Vasco de Quiroga and His Pueblo Hospitals of Santa Fé.* Publications of the Academy of American Franciscan History, vol. 10. Washington, D.C.: Academy of American Franciscan History, 1963.

Weismann, Elizabeth W. "The History of Art in Latin America, 1500–1800: Some Trends and Challenges in the Last Decade." *Latin American Research Review* 10 (1975): 7–50.

IV REFORM AND REACTION:
THE MOVE
TO INDEPENDENCE

14

The Bourbons
Restructure New Spain

Early Bourbon Reforms

The nadir of Spain's fortunes by the late seventeenth century was nowhere better exemplified than in the person of the king himself. Inheriting the throne in 1665 at age four, Charles II was feeble in mind as well as body and was even in maturity clearly incompetent to rule. This wretched king, called in all kindness *El Hechizado*, "the Bewitched," sought desperately in off moments to hang himself with his bedclothes. His retainers, in dubious service to the nation, put a stop to that. He was, after all, the monarch; and so his idiosyncrasies were accommodated by an indulgent people. While exorcists tried to drive out his devil, advisers made policy of sorts.

Charles was the last of the Spanish Hapsburgs, and there was justifiable concern over the matter of succession. Despite two marriages, the king did not sire an heir. Who, then, would rule the Spanish empire after his anticipated early demise? While Spaniards weighed their fate with apprehension, others in Europe schemed to exploit the situation. Then, as now, there was considerable intermarriage among the various royal families of Europe, and relatives floated their pretensions to the Spanish throne. In the end the Austrian and French factions emerged as the two strongest claimants, and their diplomats maneuvered for years. To the exasperation of almost all concerned, Charles II refused to die. Finally, as his days grew short, he named as his successor Philip of Anjou, a grandson of Louis XIV of France. Charles joined his ancestors in 1700, and a new dynasty, the line of Spanish Bourbons, began with the rule of Philip V (1701–46).

Charles II (1661–1700). The death of this unfortunate king, the last
Spanish Hapsburg, precipitated the War of the Spanish Succession.

The Austrian party and their allies contested Philip's crowning during the long War of the Spanish Succession (1701–13), but the final outcome saw the Bourbons established in Spain.

Philip inherited a ruined Spain, a country wracked by foreign wars and internal revolts. The economy was in shambles, and the demoralized Spaniards lived in an age of cynicism, their proud intellectual and cultural tradition now barren. The new king was beset by further strains on revenues and manpower because of the war, but he approached the country's problems with vigor and intelligence. He applied many of the administrative policies that other Bourbons had used in France, and his centralization of authority proved effective. An immediate concern was the strengthening of the military forces. The Spanish infantry, invincible throughout the sixteenth century, had lost its incentive; the seventeenth century witnessed the spectacle of Spanish troops running from battle, and by the early years of the eighteenth century the army numbered only about twenty thousand soldiers. The nation that in 1588 had launched the great Spanish Armada now had a puny naval force of only twenty ships. Philip undertook a program of rehabilitation with some success.

Equally shattered at the time of Philip's coronation was the internal economy. Its treasury empty, its industry and agriculture deteriorated, Spain was beholden to foreigners. Trade with the colonies was to great extent in the hands of non-Spanish merchants who enjoyed extraordinary concessions from the Spanish crown. So dependent was the nation on others that two-thirds of the American silver went directly to foreign ports. The early Hapsburg bullionists must have rolled in their graves.

As his government began to bring some order to Spain, Philip also looked to his colonies with an eye to improving their economies for the financial benefit of the empire and as compensation for Spain's territorial losses in Europe. In 1702 a royal decree allowed two ships a year, instead of one, to sail from Manila to Acapulco. The antiquated trading system was further improved in 1717 when the official port for the New World trade was formally changed from Seville to Cádiz, which had better facilities. This was an important break in the monopoly of vested interests. Then, in 1740 the fleet system, which had operated so inefficiently for two centuries, was suspended. The threat of piracy having subsided, there seemed little point in restricting both merchants and consumers. In case of war, however, privateers could freely attack Spanish shipping, and, in fact, the fleets were revived later, sailing off and on until their final abolition in

1789. Although these colonial economic reforms were modest enough, along with other changes they were indicative of the Bourbon commitment to modernization.

Revival of the Colonial Economy

In the second half of the century momentous change took place. Following the relatively calm reign of Ferdinand VI (1746–59), Spain had a dramatic resurgence under one of its greatest sovereigns, Charles III (1759–88). A devotee of the Enlightenment philosophies then current in Europe, Charles not only introduced important reforms within Spain but also moved to restructure the colonies. To that end, in 1765 he dispatched to New Spain José de Gálvez with the powers of visitor general. Gálvez energetically undertook a long tour of the colony, and over the next five years he compiled important information on which he based sweeping economic and political reforms. He had two overriding concerns: the economy of New Spain and the defense of the colony's frontiers.

Not the least of New Spain's economic woes stemmed from the monopolies held by merchants and guilds of the two official ports of Veracruz and Acapulco. Their privileges were prejudicial to competition and kept prices unnaturally high; consequently, the economy was sluggish. In the 1760s Charles relieved this stifling situation by opening other official ports in Campeche and Yucatán, and before the end of the century additional ports in Mexico were given similar rights of trade. About the same time a different royal decree permitted New Spain to trade with other Spanish colonies. In 1764–65 the monopoly of Cádiz was broken when certain other ports in Spain were allowed to trade freely with the colonies. Finally, in 1790 the Casa de Contratación, having tightly controlled shipping and commerce for 287 years, was abolished. The crown also stimulated the economy by lowering some taxes, revising offensive customs duties, making quicksilver more easily available for miners, and organizing a miner's guild.

The cause of most rejoicing was the dramatic recovery of silver mining, and, except for a slight dip in the 1760s, production rose consistently throughout the century. The silver boom was partially attributable to more realistic royal policies but resulted from improved technology and the discovery of rich new mines as well. From slightly more than 3.25 million pesos in 1700, silver production rose to over 13.5 million by 1750, and by 1804 it had reached the substantial figure of 27 million pesos. Mexico alone produced about as much silver as the rest of the world. Between 1690 and 1822 Mexico minted over 1.5 billion pesos in silver and some 60 million in gold.

By the late colonial period there were about three thousand mines in the colony, although most had been abandoned and many of those being worked were small operations. In 1774 thirty-five sizable mining camps existed, of which only a few produced most of the silver. Mines could be worked with increased efficiency because of more scientific refining techniques and better drainage facilities. Modernized technology also permitted deeper mine shafts, and that of the great Valenciana (Guanajuato) reached into the earth some two thousand feet, deeper than any other mine in the world.

Important as precious metals were, however, the general production of the colony increased considerably in other ways, too. Always very profitable, cochineal dye was the second most valuable export during the eighteenth century. It was produced primarily in Oaxaca, where as many as thirty thousand Indians were employed in the industry. Another important commodity was sugar; by 1774 the town of Córdoba (Veracruz) alone had more than fifty sugar mills, employing mostly black slaves. Toward the close of the century the colony produced around twenty-five thousand tons of sugar annually, of which some two-thirds were exported. The city of Puebla was a manufacturing center of note, specializing in both textiles and ceramics. It sent more than a million pounds of cloth a year to the capital and in 1793 had forty-six shops producing pottery and glass. Native cotton had been cultivated over the centuries, and in 1803 Mexico exported more cotton to Europe than did the United States. A very lucrative crop by the late eighteenth century was tobacco; Mexico City and Querétaro each had factories employing about seven thousand workers. Among the many other export commodities were hemp, cacao, vanilla, and hides. Few manufactured goods were exported from the colony; 93 percent of exports consisted of silver, cochineal, and various agricultural products.

By the second half of the eighteenth century New Spain had become by far the most prosperous of Spain's holdings. Around 1800 the port of Veracruz had a trade in excess of thirty million pesos annually. By 1810 New Spain contributed three-fourths of the profits from all the Spanish American colonies. Nevertheless, the domestic economy had become more important than the export economy. More workers were employed in the production of goods for Mexican consumption—in agriculture, ranching, minor industry, and local commerce—than in export commodities.

Through its various taxes, duties, and monopolies the crown profited enormously from the improved colonial economy, as the following chart shows:

CROWN INCOME FROM NEW SPAIN, 1786–1789

Source	Value in Pesos (round figures)
Tobacco monopoly	16,000,000
Sales tax (alcabala)	15,500,000
One-tenth of precious metals	9,000,000
Coinage	6,000,000
Pulque monopoly	3,500,000
Indian tributes	3,500,000
Customs duties (almojarifazgo)	3,000,000
Total	56,500,000

Source: José Miranda et al., Historia de México (Mexico, 1971), p. 263.

What strikes one immediately is that, notwithstanding the considerable value of precious metals to the crown, royal income from the tobacco monopoly and sales tax was over three times as great. Of the revenues raised in the colony, part went to subsidize the administrative costs of New Spain, another portion contributed to the support of less prosperous colonies, and the remainder found its way to the royal treasury in Spain.

The state of the colony's overall economy toward the end of the colonial period, before fighting interrupted production, can be seen from the following estimates:

VALUE OF NEW SPAIN'S ANNUAL PRODUCTION, ca. 1810

Source	Value in Pesos	Percentage
Agriculture	106,285,000	56
Manufactures	55,386,000	29
Mining	28,451,000	15

Source: David A. Brading, Miners and Merchants in Bourbon Mexico, 1763–1810 (Cambridge, 1971), p. 18.

Reform of Colonial Administration

International rivalries among colonial powers in the eighteenth century led to wars that were fought in various theaters, including the New World. The power of Great Britain and its expanding colonies in North America was perceived in Madrid as a threat to the Spanish Indies, and not without reason. Thus, in 1762, during the Seven Years' War, Charles III authorized a professional standing army for New Spain. The troops were few in number, but the addition of various militia groups brought the armed forces in 1810 up to roughly thirty-three thousand, of whom no more than a third were regular soldiers.

During his inspection tour José de Gálvez became acutely conscious of the defenseless northern borders. Spanish settlement had pushed northward slowly during the seventeenth century, for, although the church generally had lost much of its early vigor, Jesuit and Franciscan missionaries on the frontiers continued in their selfless labors. In the late seventeenth century Fathers Kino and Salvatierra, both Jesuits, worked among the Indians of Baja California, Sonora, and Arizona. About the same time Fray Antonio Olivares and other missionaries began to establish missions in Texas, which was formally settled in 1718. The later and more famous Franciscan friar, Junípero Serra, was founding missions in California by 1769. These and other missionaries were followed by a few soldiers, ranchers, and miners, but the northern lands remained very sparsely settled and vulnerable to encroachments by other powers. Even though the French threat was no longer a reality, British expansion presented a menace, as did the appearance of Russian ships in California waters.

One result of the increasing international tensions was that viceroys and other high officials appointed in the last decades of the colonial period were often men with military training and experience. But even they were too far removed from the distant north to render effective defense of the frontiers. Therefore Gálvez planned an independent military government. After he returned to Spain and was appointed to the powerful post of minister of the Indies, he created, in 1776, the position of commandant general of the Interior Provinces. The new territorial organization of the commandancy general embraced the Interior Provinces of the present north Mexican states as well as Texas, greater New Mexico, and California. The commandant general oversaw the military and political administration of this large area, and he was independent of the viceroy, reporting directly to the king.

Operating out of Chihuahua City, he was responsible for establishing frontier forts (*presidios*) and patrolling the wilderness. While the foreign threats did not materialize in any important way, the Indian tribes who resisted fiercely Spanish expansion presented a real and continuing problem on the frontier.

The flaccid and corrupt bureaucracy of the colony also came under the careful scrutiny of Gálvez. He contemplated a drastic reorganization, even advocating the abolition of the viceregal position. He had to settle for less, but he did effect some profound changes for New Spain's administration at the provincial level. Since the first decades of settlement alcaldes mayores and corregidores had been notorious as the worst tormentors of the Indians. Their inadequate salaries had always encouraged extralegal commercial activities, and by the early eighteenth century these officials received no salaries at all. Instead they were expected to engage in business ventures. In effect, they were petty merchants who lived by purchasing the products and labor of the natives with cheap trinkets and forcing them to buy, at inflated prices, goods that they neither needed nor wanted.

Gálvez proposed that such officials be replaced by others called *intendants*. Intendants had served well in France and were subsequently utilized by the Bourbons in Spain. But Gálvez, who had enjoyed a cordial relationship with Viceroy Carlos Francisco de Croix, found that the succeeding viceroy, Antonio María de Bucareli, strongly opposed the substitution of intendants in the colony. So efficient and prosperous was Bucareli's rule that the crown deferred implementation of the reform for years. Finally, in 1786 Charles III agreed to the appointment of twelve intendants (of whom only one was a criollo) to replace some two hundred alcaldes mayores and corregidores in Mexico.

Implicit in the reforms decreed by the Bourbons was centralization and the imposition of unity, order, and efficiency. And paramount to the reorganization was the firm and effective management of crown revenues. The intendants sent to New Spain were charged with the control of royal monopolies, the collection of taxes, and overseeing the whole range of treasury interests in the colony, including suppression of smuggling. More than that, however, they had broad responsibilities to improve general administration in their districts, called intendancies, including such matters as justice, public facilities, and defense. Appointed from Spain, they were well paid, earning more even than the audiencia judges, and they were for the most part experienced, educated, and capable administrators. They enjoyed considerable

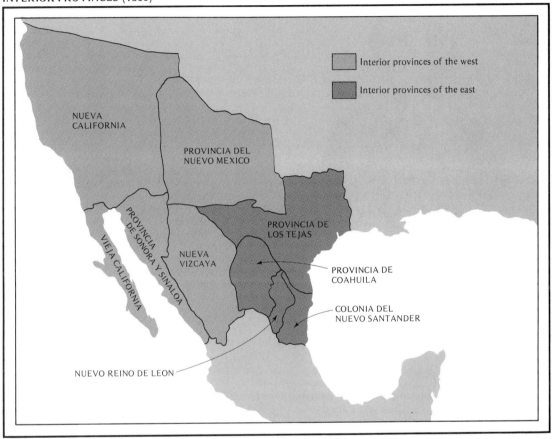

Interior provinces of the west

Interior provinces of the east

NUEVA CALIFORNIA

PROVINCIA DEL NUEVO MEXICO

PROVINCIA DE SONORA Y SINALOA

VIEJA CALIFORNIA

PROVINCIA DE LOS TEJAS

NUEVA VIZCAYA

PROVINCIA DE COAHUILA

COLONIA DEL NUEVO SANTANDER

NUEVO REINO DE LEON

prestige and had ample authority in their large districts. It was not unnatural, therefore, that the creation of the new offices engendered the resentment of both the oidores and the viceroys, many of whom saw their own authority vitiated as a consequence.

The Effects of Bourbon Reforms

A confluence of factors brought about significant change in the colony of New Spain by the time of the death of Charles III in 1788. Still, change is not necessarily progress, and the ultimate effects of the Bourbon reforms must be viewed in the light of recent findings. On the whole, the economic reforms had a positive effect on the colony. One must not, however, exaggerate the

Carlos Francisco de Croix (1730–?) was viceroy from 1766–71. Born in France, of Flemish extraction, Croix served with distinction in New Spain.

Antonio María de Bucareli (1717–79), the 46th viceroy, served from 1771 until his death. He was a popular ruler, renowned for his integrity.

benefits. It is true that wealth was somewhat redistributed as a result of the broken monopolies of Mexico City merchants and the Consulado interests. But the crown gave itself, at the same time, certain monopolies that inevitably hurt other groups. The king's exclusive control over tobacco, for instance, took great sums of money out of private hands and displaced a large number of individuals involved in its production and marketing. But the monopoly was an important part of the imperial policy of restructuring, since these new crown revenues went to the support of the professional army. The pulque monopoly also put local merchants out of business, while the surtax imposed on this drink of the plebeian class outraged the populace.

And one must not attach too much significance to the so-called free trade policies that emerged under the Bourbons. Despite the undeniable improvement of the Mexican economy, new strictures in the form of taxes were imposed. Moreover there was a flood of peninsulares to the colony, and they were the ones who all too often profited from the rejuvenated business climate. The redistribution of wealth to great extent merely created a new group of wealthy gachupín aristocrats. The essence of mercantilism survived; the Bourbons had simply made it more efficient. Mexico's economy was increasingly manipulated for the benefit of the mother country. Dependency of the colonists on the mother country remained a fundamental tenet of the imperial system.

Political reforms were equally mixed blessings. Although intendants were capable, they were not able to administer their extensive intendancies alone and, of necessity, appointed subdelegates for various districts. These agents were ill paid, poorly qualified, and corrupt, and, in effect, they tended to recreate the old system under a different guise. What had been envisioned as a more centralized, tighter colonial administration became in the end an expanded bureaucracy, in which the number of highly paid officials quadrupled. Furthermore almost all the intendants were Spaniards, and they replaced many criollos who were persons of importance in their localities and who had come to regard the positions as criollo sinecures. The result was increased resentment on the part of criollos against the peninsulares.

The commandancy general brought slightly better administration to the borderlands without, however, effecting any significant change. Increased military organization of the northern provinces may have discouraged foreign intrusions, but on reflection, the point is academic: French ambitions were blunted in the 1760s, and within two decades the British were out of the borderlands. By the late century the British threat was real, but it was more likely to come from the Gulf coast. The meager resources of the fledgling United States would not be sufficient to support a westward advance for decades, despite some blustering to the contrary. As it was, the commandant general had his hands full trying to cope with Comanches and Apaches. Power, like wealth, was redistributed, creating new vested interest groups. As the prerogatives of the viceroys and audiencia judges were diminished, the intendants, military men, and tax collectors assumed considerable influence.

In summary, it is fair to say that under the Bourbons much had improved. Spain under Charles III had made a remarkable recovery, to some extent because of intelligent reforms but also because of fluctuating international fortunes that for the moment favored it. Spain was once again a world power, and Mexico was the incidental beneficiary. As we have seen, however, the colonists paid a price for increased prosperity and improved administration. What appeared in the 1780s to have been promising for the future of the Spanish empire faded rather quickly. Charles III was succeeded by a son lacking in wisdom; political affairs on the European continent would ultimately engulf Spain;

The Mining College (Colegio de Minería), designed by Manuel Tolsá, was constructed at great cost between 1797 and 1813. One of Mexico's handsomest colonial buildings, it has 238 rooms, 13 stairways, 11 fountains, and 7 courtyards. Its grandeur is an indication of the importance of silver mining in the late Spanish period.

and these and other events would foster a growing disenchantment among the colonists in New Spain. For it has historically been true that the rising expectations of an aroused populace are not easily checked. Once conventions were relaxed in economic and political spheres, it was natural for colonists to hope for a shift in social attitudes. But the royal intent was to benefit Spain, not the colonists, and tradition-bound monarchs of the eighteenth century saw no plausible benefits in social reform. Quite to the contrary: the year following the death of Charles III the French masses rose up in the name of social justice, beheaded their king, and went on the rampage. The shudder that passed through the royal courts of Europe was felt in Madrid as well.

Recommended for Further Study

Archer, Christon I. *The Army in Bourbon Mexico, 1760–1810.* Albuquerque: University of New Mexico Press, 1977.
———. "Bourbon Finances and Military Policy in New Spain, 1759–1812." *The Americas* 37 (1981): 315–50.

Arnold, Linda. *Bureaucracy and Bureaucrats in Mexico City, 1742–1835.* Tucson: University of Arizona Press, 1988.

Bobb, Bernard E. "Bucareli and the Interior Provinces." *Hispanic American Historical Review* 34 (1954): 20–36.

———. *The Viceregency of Antonio Maria Bucareli in New Spain.* Austin: University of Texas Press, 1962.

Brading, David A. *Miners and Merchants in Bourbon Mexico, 1763–1810.* Cambridge: Cambridge University Press, 1971.

Brinckerhoff, Sidney B., and Pierce A. Chamberlain. *Spanish Military Weapons in Colonial America: 1700–1821.* Harrisburg, Pa.: Stackpole Books, 1972.

Burkholder, Mark A. "The Council of the Indies in the Late Eighteenth Century: A New Perspective." *Hispanic American Historical Review* 56 (1976): 404–42.

DePalo, William A., Jr. "The Establishment of the Nueva Vizcaya Militia during the Administration of Teodoro de Croix: 1776–1783." *New Mexico Historical Review* 48 (1973): 223–49.

Fisher, Lillian Estelle. *The Intendant System in Spanish America.* Berkeley: University of California Press, 1929.

Greenleaf, Richard E. "The Mexican Inquisition and the Masonic Movement: 1751–1820." *New Mexico Historical Review* 41 (1969): 93–177.

———. "The Nueva Vizcaya Frontier, 1787–1789." *Journal of the West* 8 (1969): 56–66.

Greenow, Linda. *Credit and Socioeconomic Change in Colonial Mexico: Loans and Mortgages in Guadalajara, 1720–1820.* Boulder, Colo.: Westview Press, 1983.

Hamnett, Brian R. *Politics and Trade in Southern Mexico, 1750–1821.* Cambridge: Cambridge University Press, 1971.

Howe, Walter. *The Mining Guild of New Spain and Its Tribunal General, 1770–1821.* Cambridge, Mass.: Harvard University Press, 1949.

McAlister, Lyle N. *The "Fuero Militar" in New Spain, 1764–1800.* Gainesville: University of Florida Press, 1967.

———. "The Reorganization of the Army of New Spain, 1763–1766." *Hispanic American Historical Review* 48 (1973): 223–49.

Priestley, Herbert I. *José de Gálvez, Visitor General of New Spain, 1765–1771.* Berkeley: University of California Press, 1916.

Thomas, Alfred B. *Teodoro de Croix and the Northern Frontier of New Spain, 1776–1783.* Norman: University of Oklahoma Press, 1941.

15

Society and Stress
in the Late Colonial Period

The Wealthy

In 1704 the royal treasurer in Mexico City gave a party for the viceroy that lasted several days and cost twenty thousand pesos. Among those in attendance, we may be sure, was a young lady of the capital whose dowry amounted to the incredible sum of six hundred thousand pesos. Affairs of this kind were part of the colonial social scene even before the later economic boom, for despite the general recession of the previous several decades, the small aristocracy of New Spain had maintained itself in luxury. Over the next few decades their numbers would increase significantly, as would their assets.

The poor did not get any poorer, but the rich certainly got richer. A disproportionate number of the wealthiest were peninsulares who had made good in America, but there were many prosperous criollos as well. Great fortunes were made in mining, such as those of the counts of Valenciana, Regla, and Bassoco. Regla's staggering wealth (the greatest fortune in the colony) is difficult to assess, but in the late eighteenth century Valenciana sometimes took a net profit of more than a million pesos annually, quite aside from his millions tied up in land and various other interests. Bassoco, elevated to count only in 1811 after a gift to the government of two hundred thousand pesos, accumulated assets worth some three million pesos.

These mining barons, along with some wealthy ranchers and merchants, frequently made generous gifts to the crown, which in gratitude conferred on the donors cherished titles of nobility—usually that of *conde*, less often that of *marqués*. Some prominent

Considered the most complete example of Mexican baroque is the exquisite church of Santa Prisca in Taxco. Built between 1751 and 1759, its cost was underwritten by the mining baron Don José de la Borda.

men had to be content with knighthood in one of the prestigious military orders. During the eighteenth century about fifty titles of nobility were granted to residents of New Spain, most of them after 1750.

But while these dignities appealed to the vanity of the recipients, many of the rich were philanthropic for less fatuous reasons. They contributed large sums of money to religious organiza-

This magnificent colonial residence, rising four stories, is a good example of the extravagant architectural style known as Churrigueresque. Built in the eighteenth century for the Count of San Mateo de Valparaíso, it was later used as a palace by Emperor Agustín I (Iturbide). Subsequently it served as a hotel and today it is beautifully maintained by a bank.

tions, funded charities, and financed the construction of schools, hospitals, and lovely churches. They also financed festivals and cultural events for the enjoyment of the community. In times of pestilence the rich often paid for medicines, and when famine struck they distributed large supplies of grain and other foods. Unfortunately these gestures were often little more than tokens, for some catastrophes were overwhelming. In 1784, for example, some three hundred thousand people in Mexico perished from starvation or illness induced by undernourishment. Thousands more died from a respiratory infection.

Among the most powerful men of Mexico were the rich hacendados in the north. As missionaries, miners, and soldiers penetrated the frontier, the Indians were gradually pushed back and the land came into the possession of wealthy and influential ranchers. Much of the region consisted of desert and could be acquired at low cost; in 1731 the marqués de Aguayo purchased 222,000 acres from the crown for a paltry 250 pesos. Within four decades his family controlled over fourteen and a half million acres, some of which were patrolled by the marqués's private

A rural scene of an hacendado and his foreman.

A spirited mount and fine clothing typify this scene of rural landowners in the early nineteenth century. The Mexicans' equestrian skill and love of fine horses have long been known.

cavalry to protect the livestock from marauding Indians. By the late colonial period the northern haciendas, sprawling and isolated, were like private fiefdoms. Yet the stereotype of the hacienda as an operation little concerned with profit and efficiency, a self-sufficient enterprise maintained primarily for the status inherent in the ownership of vast expanses of land, does not always survive examination. A study of the huge holdings of the Sánchez Navarro family, for example, shows the owners to have been capitalists who diversified their interests. Aside from running sheep, cattle, and horses, they were also involved in mining, agriculture, and commerce. They were hard-working men who were by no means cut off from the outside world, although their *latifundio*, eventually covering an area almost as large as the country of Portugal, was the largest ranch in Spanish America.[1]

The colony's increased prosperity was reflected not only in ornate religious edifices but also in the many impressive public buildings. In Mexico City today one can still see enough of those surviving to appreciate the grandeur of the capital in the late colonial era. There also remain about thirty of the magnificent mansions belonging to the wealthy of that period, some preserved either by the government or commercial firms. The spectacular House of Tiles, covered on the exterior and the interior with tiles said to have been brought expressly from China, is a modern landmark. Once the residence of the conde del Valle de Orizaba, it is today a restaurant. The stately townhouse of the counts of San Mateo de Valparaíso (also known as the Palace of Iturbide) has been restored by a bank, while the large residence of the counts of Santiago de Calimaya is now the interesting Museum of the City of Mexico.

The colony, and especially the capital, benefited from the improvements made by one of the greatest viceroys, the second count of Revillagigedo (1789–94). Among his many intelligent innovations was the lighting of streets, which lowered the rate of crimes and accidents. He also paved the streets and authorized the first public transportation system, and when that added to the crowded traffic in the capital, he set speed limits, restricted parking, and issued laws against shrill whistling and shouting imprecations at pedestrians and riders. He is remembered also for having ordered an important census and for improving the postal service. Sad to say, there were few public servants of his wisdom and vision.

1. See Charles H. Harris III, *A Mexican Family Empire: The Latifundio of the Sánchez Navarro Family, 1765–1867* (Austin, 1975).

This imposing residence, built in 1528, had been altered by the counts of Santiago de Calimaya by 1779. Today it is the Museum of the City of Mexico.

The Casa de Alfeñique ("Sugar-candy House"), an eighteenth-century showplace in Puebla, a city of many colonial treasures.

In rural territories, where Indians predominated, society had changed relatively little. Many of the natives in remote areas, and particularly in southern Mexico, had scarcely been acculturated into Spanish society, and to great extent they lived much as they had in pre-Hispanic times. Those who lived closer to Spanish centers, however, naturally took on many of the characteristics of the white society. As a result of generations of miscegenation, the mestizo population had increased enormously. By the late eighteenth century more than four-fifths of the population were nonwhite, most of them constituting the lower class. There existed a small, indistinct group that could be termed middle class, but perhaps the designation lower-upper class would be more accurate, for the people were considerably above the poverty level of the masses. Around 1810 a population in excess of six million included more than three and a half million Indians. Over a million were considered criollos, and only 15,000 were peninsulares. The remainder were mestizos of various mixes.

The aristocracy of the eighteenth century differed from its counterpart of the two preceding centuries primarily in the matter of style rather than attitude. Later aristocrats were wealthier and more cultured. Some had studied and traveled in Europe. They adopted continental fashions, the women appearing on festive occasions in expensive gowns and elaborate coiffures, the men in knee breeches, tricorn hats, and, on formal occasions, powdered wigs. To some extent Mexican high society had, like that of Spain, become "Frenchified" through tastes acquired with the Bourbon accession. Also in imitation of European styles were the fancy dress balls and salons in which the elite discoursed on

The second count of Revillagigedo (Juan Vicente de Güemes-Pacheco y Padilla) (1740–99). Viceroy from 1789–94, he is considered to have been one of the most outstanding rulers of New Spain.

A portrait of an aristocratic lady by Miguel Cabrera (1695–1768). A Zapotec Indian, Cabrera was New Spain's most successful and most prolific painter.

the new philosophies emanating from France and England and conversed about art, literature, music, and, inevitably, the economy and politics. Poetry was read (sometimes, mercilessly, the reader's own efforts), and scientific papers were presented. All this was spiced with gossip and expressions of horror at the vulgarities of the masses.

Criollo Discontent

The proliferation of wars during the eighteenth century, far from the shores of Mexico, occasioned little more than casual notice, enlivened perhaps by the personal account of a Spanish veteran. But interest increased with the successful revolt of the English colonists to the north and the outbreak of the French Revolution. Later came news of the astounding success of black slaves who overthrew their French masters in Haiti and declared their independence. Informed criollos could hardly fail to observe that in both revolts in the hemisphere, colonial populations smaller than Mexico's had thrown over imperial powers greater than Spain. But criollos also recognized that their own society was far more heterogeneous than either the United States or Haiti.

The opulent extreme of the rich was in glaring contrast to the majority, who lived in poverty. The lot of the colored castes had improved somewhat over the centuries. They were less abused physically and were usually paid for their labor. The encomiendas, long in decline, had finally been abolished in the eighteenth century, so the Indians were no longer subject to the abuses of

A typical scene along a provincial road.

that institution. But wages were niggardly, allowing only the barest necessities, and many were tied to the evils of peonage. There was little recourse for peones, who lacked the security and financial resources to risk a change in employment. Indians still bore the humiliating obligation of paying tribute to the crown, and they were forbidden to wear European clothing under pain of a hundred lashes and a month in jail. By the end of the colonial era there were few black slaves, but free blacks and mulattoes shared the indignities of the lowest classes. Illiterate, inhibited, and conditioned to their fate, the colored masses were generally ignorant of, and little affected by, imperial political and economic decisions. But they nursed a deep resentment against all whites, Spanish or criollo.

In the stratified society of New Spain there was little cohesion among the various groups. The lower classes were dispersed, the majority of them living and working in the provinces and having almost no communication outside their immediate acquaintances. Lacking organization and leadership, their occasional attempts to improve their conditions by violence were conceived in desperation and ended in tragedy. When time came for a political revolution, the impetus came not from any spontaneous uprising of the masses but rather from the actions of criollo conspirators. Criollo grievances combined with a succession of disruptive external circumstances to sever the colonial tie.

Criollos had from the beginning been forced into a secondary position by those born in Spain. The peninsulares, or gachupines, had always enjoyed special privileges and occupied the favored positions in church and state. There was a certain logic in this, for the peninsulares receiving high office were usually well educated and had more administrative experience and polish than the criollos. Beyond that, an official with strong ties to the mother country was likely to be more loyal to the interests of Spain. Few criollos, on the other hand, had ever seen Spain, and by birth, education, cultural milieu, property, and familial relationships they naturally identified strongly with the colony. As officials, they might succumb to the temptation of favoring their countrymen, perhaps at the expense of royal interests.

Still, the policy that apportioned relatively few good bureaucratic posts to criollos has perhaps been given more emphasis than it deserves. Criollos were not blind to the realities, and they did not aspire to the office of viceroy or archbishop. They did hope, however, that more of the important positions would go to the most competent among the Mexican-born. In the eighteenth century the Bourbons appointed some criollos to high office, and others were able to purchase posts put up for bidding. A few even served as judges in the audiencias as well as in other powerful positions. By 1769 at least eight of the twelve members of the Audiencia of Mexico were criollos. They were even more successful in obtaining rank in the church. This promising state of affairs came under some change during the reign of Charles III, who agreed with Gálvez that the colonists' participation in government should be restricted. As a result the number of criollos in the audiencia of the capital had declined by 1780 to only four of sixteen, and later there were even fewer. Criollos were, however, able to secure rank in the military; by the close of the eighteenth century of a total of 361 officers in the regular regiments 227 were criollos, and in the militia they held 338 commissions of 624 officer positions.[2]

The distinctions they perceived between the gachupines and themselves were increasingly galling to the criollos. Although no more than 10 percent of the former were legitimate hidalgos, all Spaniards in Mexico assumed nobility and expected to be addressed as "Don." The peninsulares, no matter how lacking in education and culture, considered themselves superior to all and disparaged the capacities of the criollos. These arrogant gachupines were greatly outnumbered, but they formed a small, tight circle, both in business and social affairs; only occasionally did they marry into criollo aristocracies. Far from accepting the stigma of congenital inferiority that Spaniards had placed on them, however, the criollos asserted their self-worth more vocally in the eighteenth century. They envied the privileges of the peninsulares and resented their pretentious manner, and they insisted that the demonstrable achievements of the Mexican-born were equal to those of the Spaniards. The criollos did not consider themselves Spaniards living in the Indies but rather as a distinct people. There was reason for pride in their land; foreign travelers had affirmed that Mexico City compared favorably with Spanish cities, even Madrid. Colonists extolled the unique charm of Mexico, a country with its own flavor and a society with its own character, more exotic and colorful than Spain.

One immediately noticeable difference was in the language, now losing its Castilian lisp and enriched by Indian words and

2. David A. Brading, *Miners and Merchants in Bourbon Mexico, 1763–1810* (Cambridge, 1971), pp. 40–42.

diminutives. The Mexican diet was distinctive; the architecture of Spain had been modified; customs and dress had acquired their own traits. The Mexican ambience had colored the literature, art, and music. The people, the landscape, the flora, and the fauna were all peculiar to Mexico. What was originally Spanish had been altered, and while the Spaniards showed disdain at the corruption of Spanish culture, the native-born began to celebrate their mexicanidad. Shunning the socially tainted designation of *criollo*, they considered themselves *americanos*.

Yet tradition takes a firm hold. Emotional ties to Spanish history and traditions, the felt personal relationship to the monarchy, the devotion to the Spanish church—all these bound tightly. Criollo discontent led at first not to a criticism of the crown so much as to a more profound consideration of the historical past in Mexico itself. In spite of the alert agents of the Inquisition, inflammatory literature from Europe circulated in the colony, provoking reflection on Spanish institutions. In guarded conversation—and ultimately in audacious published tracts—references were made to "the barbarity of Conquest" and "three centuries of slavery." The inequities and absurdities of colonial policies were satirized in popular verse and song.

In spite of the grumbling, serious consideration of rebellion against Spain was entertained by only the most radical of colonists. There were complaints about the imposition of new taxes, and the general tightening of administration pinched here and there. Colonists were displeased with the ubiquitous officials of the swollen bureaucracy, and some resented attempts to press them into the militia. But while some criollos had been hurt by royal economic policies, others had prospered, and, all things considered, the colonists were better off than ever before. Certainly conditions had been more ripe for rebellion in 1700 than in 1800.

What the criollos really wanted was to be on an equal footing with the peninsulares, or, better yet, somehow to replace them altogether. Aristocrats by virtue of complexion, the criollos wanted to maintain the class system. Their attitudes toward the lower masses were no less haughty than the peninsulares' opinion of the criollos. In no way did the criollos advocate social equality for those below them. As the visiting German scientist Alexander von Humboldt observed in the late colonial period, "In America, the skin, more or less white, is what dictates the class that an individual occupies in society. A white, even if he rides barefoot on horseback, considers himself a member of the nobility of the country."[3] Rebellion evoked the specters of anarchy and race war, in which the colored masses, who made little distinction between gachupín and criollo, might rise against all white persons.

Clerical Discontent

The provincial conservatism of the colonists was offended by the conscious crown policy of diminishing the traditional power, wealth, and prestige of the church. Long favored by Hapsburg monarchs, the religious establishment came under a cloud during the Bourbon period and was subjected to rigorous examination by Charles III. Above all, it was the Jesuits who stuck in the monarch's craw. The Society of Jesus had distinguished itself in various ways, especially in educating and missionizing, but it had also grown very powerful and wealthy. The king, wary of papal ascendancy, saw the Jesuits' allegiance to the pope as detrimental to the interests of Spain. Moreover, like other rulers of his time, he suspected the order of political intrigue and of spreading dangerous ideas.

In 1766 the Jesuits were accused of fomenting a riot against Spain's prime minister. The following year, without warning, they were suddenly expelled from all Spanish kingdoms. Sealed orders were opened throughout the Spanish empire on the same day in 1767, ordering the expulsion of the Jesuits forthwith and decreeing the confiscation of their properties. Colonists were stunned by this bold move of the crown. Initial shock gave way to outrage that exploded into violent demonstrations, especially by Indians, in half a dozen communities.

New Spain was notably affected by the expulsion. Of 678 Jesuits who left, some 400 were Mexican-born; of the 243 missionary houses, 114 had belonged to the Society of Jesus. The Jesuits had maintained the best schools in the colony, with twenty-three colleges and many seminaries that housed the most distinguished faculties. Their graduates, especially those of San Ildefonso, were some of the most prominent men in Mexico, including audiencia judges. Some of the Jesuit schools were turned over to the Franciscans, but the Franciscans were not prepared to carry on in the same way, nor could they sufficiently fill in the Jesuit missionary fields.

The crown charged the church with "excessive wealth," which

3. Quoted in Magnus Mörner, *Race Mixture in the History of Latin America* (Boston, 1967), pp. 55–56.

was, in fact, extensive, consisting of considerable urban real estate as well as latifundio. Beyond that, crown economic counselors emphasized that ecclesiastical properties were not being used to their potential, thus obstructing government efforts to stimulate the economy. Ironically, the Jesuit holdings had been among the best managed estates in the empire. In Mexico there were about eighty Jesuit estates worth some ten million pesos.

The steady pressure against the church continued to be a matter of concern to many in New Spain, not least among them the ecclesiastics themselves. In particular the lower echelon of parish priests became alienated, and they communicated their growing disillusionment with crown policies to their flocks. Exacerbating the already tender sensibilities of clergymen, in 1804 the crown decreed the Act of Consolidation, according to which assets of the church's charitable funds were sequestered. The huge sum involved was 44.5 million pesos, henceforth used to pay for Spain's misadventures in Europe rather than for the needy in Mexico. The church, formerly a major source of credit in the colony, was forced to call in notes and mortgages, thereby reducing some criollos to financial ruin. The disastrous Act crippled the activities of the church and embittered more priests, friars, and people throughout Mexico.

Conspiracies in New Spain and Confusion in Spain

It is sometimes the impression that there was comparatively little resistance to Spanish domination in Mexico until the outbreak of insurgency in 1810. This is erroneous; in fact, there were more than a hundred conspiracies and rebellions during the colonial period.[4] Some posed serious threats to Spain's hegemony, while others were trivial affairs. At least in a few there was mention of independence, but such movements were considered aberrations and slightly insane by the general populace. Most of the disturbances found their origins in local grievances and lacked broad support. Throughout most of the eighteenth century, except for some localized Indian revolts, there was relative calm.

In 1794, however, the popular Viceroy Revillagigedo was replaced by the vain, corrupt marqués de Branciforte. His appointment aroused anger that was ventilated in September, with posters appearing on walls in the capital. The messages acclaimed

4. These are listed in Agustín Cue Cánovas, *Historia social y económica de México (1521–1854)* (Mexico, 1972), pp. 183–87.

the ideals of the French Revolution, and rumors of a plot spread throughout the city. A conspiracy had, in fact, formed, with plans to seize the government, release eight hundred prisoners from jail, free the Indians from the tribute obligations, and liberate Mexico. The plotters, including a priest, were taken into custody, but the trials were delayed for years and in the end the prisoners were incarcerated in exile. Curiously enough, these intriguers were not criollos but peninsulares.

Hardly had their cases been disposed of when, in 1799, an ill-conceived conspiracy of criollos was discovered in Mexico City. Their plan was so naive that their cache of arms consisted only of machetes, and their plot became known, therefore, as the Machete Conspiracy. The plotters were arrested quietly to avoid a sensation. After languishing in prison, some died, but others were eventually released, escaping execution because of official fears that the affair would create criollo martyrs. The leniency toward rebels, including some Indian conspirators in 1801, suggests the crown's concern with the festering discontent in New Spain. Ironically, royal forbearance served only to underscore Spain's impotence. The weak response did little to discourage further plots.

Ultimately the deterioration of Spain's position in Europe brought on a crisis. At the death of his father in 1788, Charles IV had become king, and he quickly lent weight to the commonplace that great men seldom beget sons of their equal. He was inept and had little apparent interest in ruling the empire. His subjects grew weary of him and impatiently awaited the succession of Prince Ferdinand. The queen (no prize herself, if we trust the brush of Goya) also tired of him and found solace in the intimate company of a handsome provincial guardsman named Manuel de Godoy. The clever, ambitious Godoy maneuvered himself at the age of twenty-five into the rank of prime minister. He then proceeded to make a series of unwise alliances, which finally encouraged the invasion of Spain in 1808 by the troops of Napoleon Bonaparte. When Madrid fell to the French army, Charles IV and his son became prisoners, and shortly thereafter the king abdicated in favor of the prince. But the new Ferdinand VII was a king without a throne. Napoleon appointed his own brother Joseph to rule over Spain, while much of the country resisted. Some Spanish patriots formed a government in exile in the fortified city of Cádiz.

When news of the king's capture and the occupation of Spain by the French reached New Spain there was confusion as to who

María Luisa of Parma, the queen of Spain, at age fourteen married her cousin, who became Charles IV.

was to rule the colony. Joseph Bonaparte as sovereign was unthinkable, but what was the logical alternative? Although a few saw the situation as a golden opportunity to gain independence, the majority of the colonists advocated the formation of a caretaker government to run affairs in the name of Ferdinand VII until such time as the king was released. The viceroy seemed the obvious person to assume rule in Mexico, but the audiencia insisted on sharing power. Eventually, in cities throughout the Spanish American colonies, the cabildos asserted their own claims. They argued that historically, when a legitimate ruler was lacking, provisional bodies, or *juntas*, formed to manage local affairs. Following such a bold proclamation, several members of the Cabildo of Mexico City were arrested.

Viceroy José de Iturrigaray had shrewdly assessed the developments: if he played his cards right he might see a Mexican crown on his head. He decided that the criollos had the best prospects, and he played to their interests by allowing them to form a junta. A group of peninsulares now made their move, viewing Iturrigaray's actions as both stupid and treasonous. On the evening of September 15, 1808, a small band of Spaniards forcibly removed the viceroy from his palace and packed him off to Veracruz to await passage to Spain, where he was later imprisoned. The peninsulares also arrested half a dozen prominent criollo leaders. Replacing Iturrigaray was Pedro Garibay, a senile field marshal in his eightieth year who had to contend with various militant factions.

The instability of government in 1809 only added to the anxieties arising from a threatening economic picture. Insufficient rain fell that summer, and the resulting shortage of corn caused prices in some areas to inflate to four times their normal level. The consequences were far-reaching, affecting, for example, mining production, since there was too little food for draft animals, and workers had to be laid off. Interrupted commerce with the occupied mother country further dislocated the Mexican economy. Taken altogether, it was a time of confusion and stress, with all segments of society growing restless.

Among the more sophisticated criollos in Mexico City the mood remained conservative. They might espouse the principles of the French Revolution, but rebellion against the crown was a painful thought, especially amid reminders of rich Spanish traditions. Attitudes in the provinces were somewhat different. More isolated from ritual and pomp, more independent, and more closely identified with the land, the criollos in smaller communi-

The great central plaza of Mexico City, popularly known as the Zócalo. It is bordered by the cathedral, the viceregal (now the national) palace, the cabildo quarters, and other public buildings.

ties had a more fully developed sense of the *patria chica*—their own little world—where they wanted to run their own affairs. They were incensed by the thought of Joseph Bonaparte planning their destinies. Their surge of nationalism was triggered not so much by French philosophy as by French guns. Less worldly than criollos of the capital, less meticulous, and less pensive about the multiple consequences, the provincial criollos assumed a bolder stance. In many communities small groups had been meeting, sometimes under the guise of "literary clubs," to discuss what was to be done. Royal officials were cognizant of such gatherings, suspecting, correctly, that they were conspiratorial in nature. One plot, which included clergymen, military officers, and Indian groups, was exposed in Vallodolid in 1809. Although the principals were imprisoned for a while, most were in the vanguard of the insurrection that was to follow shortly.

In 1810 the important cities of southern Spain fell to French troops, compromising without question the sovereignty of the nation. The colonists were bewildered and apprehensive. In that same year it also came to the attention of royal authorities in Mexico City that a conspiracy had formed in Querétaro. Its ringleaders included an aging, dissident priest named Hidalgo. Once again troops were dispatched to deal with yet another provincial incident.

Recommended for Further Study

Anna, Timothy. "The Last Viceroys of New Spain and Peru: An Appraisal." *American Historical Review* 81 (1976): 38–65.

Arrom, Silvia Marina. *The Women of Mexico City, 1790–1857*. Stanford, Calif.: Stanford University Press, 1985.

Brading, David A. "Government and Elite in Late Colonial Mexico." *Hispanic American Historical Review* 53 (1973): 389–414.

———. *Haciendas and Ranchos in the Mexican Bajío: León, 1700–1860*. Cambridge: Cambridge University Press, 1978.

———. "Mexican Silver Mining in the Eighteenth Century: The Revival of Zacatecas." *Hispanic American Historical Review* 50 (1970): 665–81.

Cook, Sherburne F. "The Smallpox Epidemic of 1797 in Mexico." *Bulletin of the History of Medicine* 8 (1940): 937–69.

Cooper, Donald B. *Epidemic Disease in Mexico City, 1761–1813*. Austin: University of Texas Press, 1965.

Couturier, Edith R. "The Philanthropic Activities of Pedro Romero de Terreros: First Count of Regla (1753–1781)." *The Americas* 32 (1975): 13–30.

Fisher, Lillian Estelle. *The Background of the Revolution for Mexican Independence*. Gainesville: University of Florida Press, 1966.

Hamnett, Brian R. "The Appropriation of Mexican Church Wealth by the Spanish Bourbon Government: The Consolidation of Vales Reales, 1805–1809." *Journal of Latin American Studies* 1 (1969): 85–113.

———. *Roots of Insurgency, Mexican Regions, 1750–1824*. Cambridge: Cambridge University Press, 1985.

Humboldt, Alexander von. *Political Essay on the Kingdom of New Spain*. Edited, with an introduction, by Mary Maples Dunn. New York: Knopf, 1972.

Ladd, Doris M. *The Mexican Nobility at Independence, 1780–1826*. Austin: University of Texas Press, 1976.

Lafaye, Jacques. *Quetzalcóatl and Guadalupe: The Formation of Mexican National Consciousness, 1531–1813*. Translated by Benjamin Keen, with an introduction by Octavio Paz. Chicago: University of Chicago Press, 1976.

Lavrin, Asunción. "The Execution of the Law of Consolidation in New Spain: Economic Gains and Results." *Hispanic American Historical Review* 53 (1973): 27–49.

Lindley, Richard B. *Haciendas and Economic Development: Guadalajara, Mexico, at Independence.* Austin: University of Texas Press, 1983.

MacLachlan, Colin M. *Criminal Justice in Eighteenth Century Mexico: A Study of the Tribunal of the Acordada.* Berkeley: University of California Press, 1974.

Mörner, Magnus, ed. *The Expulsion of the Jesuits from Latin America.* New York: Knopf, 1965.

Motten, Clement. *Mexican Silver and the Enlightenment.* Philadelphia: University of Pennsylvania Press, 1950.

Probert, Alan. "The Real del Monte Partido Riots: 1766." *Journal of the West* 12 (1973): 85–125.

Scardaville, Michael C. "Alcohol Abuse and Tavern Reform in Late Colonial Mexico City." *Hispanic American Historical Review* 60 (1980): 643–71.

Schmitt, Karl M. "The Clergy and the Independence of New Spain." *Hispanic American Historical Review* 34 (1954): 289–312.

Stein, Stanley J., and Barbara H. Stein. *The Colonial Heritage of Latin America: Essays on Economic Dependence in Perspective.* New York: Oxford University Press, 1970.

Tambs, Lewis A. "The Inquisition in Eighteenth Century Mexico." *The Americas* 22 (1965): 167–81.

Tutino, John. *From Insurrection to Revolution in Mexico: Social Bases of Agrarian Violence, 1750–1940.* Princeton, N.J.: Princeton University Press, 1986.

Whitaker, Arthur P. "The Elhuyar Mining Missions and the Enlightenment." *Hispanic American Historical Review* 31 (1951): 557–85.

Wolf, Eric. "The Mexican Bajío in the Eighteenth Century." *Middle American Research Institute Publications* 17 (1969): 85–113.

Young, Eric Van. "Urban Market and Hinterland: Guadalajara and Its Region in the Eighteenth Century." *Hispanic American Historical Review* 59 (1979): 593–635.

16

The Wars for Independence

Hidalgo and Early Success

Born in 1753 of moderately well-to-do criollo stock, Miguel Hidalgo y Costilla spent his first twelve years on the Hacienda de San Diego Corralejo in Guanajuato, where his father served the owner as *mayordomo* (resident manager). Encouraged by his father, the boy moved with his older brother, José Joaquín, to Valladolid (today Morelia) and matriculated at the Jesuit College of San Francisco Javier. The brothers had been at their studies only two years when shocking news reached the city: King Charles III of Spain had banished the Jesuits from New Spain and all Spanish possessions in the New World. Left without teachers, the boys had to interrupt their schooling, but within a year they had enrolled in the diocesan College of San Nicolás Obispo, also in Valladolid, and one of the nineteen colleges and seminaries in Mexico that prepared students for degrees eventually to be awarded by the Royal and Pontifical University in Mexico City. Young Miguel Hidalgo steeped himself in rhetoric, Latin, and Thomistic theology, and, in the tradition of generations of Mexican priests before him, found time to study Indian languages. His bachelor's degree was awarded by the University of Mexico in 1774, and he immediately began preparations for the priesthood. The bishop celebrated his sacrament of ordination in the fall of 1778.

Enthusiastic and self-assured, the twenty-eight-year-old priest returned to Valladolid to teach at the College of San Nicolás Obispo, where he eventually became rector. But he was scarcely exemplary from the church's point of view. Before the turn of the century the Holy Office of the Inquisition had been apprised, by rumor and fact, of a curate whose orthodoxy was suspect, who questioned priestly celibacy, who read books proscribed by the *Index Expurgatorius*, who indulged in gambling and enjoyed dancing, who challenged the infallibility of the Most Holy Father in Rome, who doubted the veracity of the virgin birth, who dared to suggest that fornication out of wedlock was not a sin, who referred to the Spanish king as a tyrant, and who—alas!— kept María Manuela Herrera as a mistress and procuress. Hidalgo was hailed before the Inquisition in 1800, but nothing could be proved. The testimony was carefully filed, however, to be used later.

Hidalgo's future fortunes and misfortunes were cast when, in 1803, he accepted the curacy of the small parish of Dolores. Devoting only minimal time to the spiritual needs of his parishioners, Father Hidalgo concerned himself primarily with improving their economic potential. He introduced new industries in Dolores: tile making, tanning, carpentry, wool weaving, beekeeping, silk growing, and wine making. He preferred to spend his spare time reading and engaging his fellow criollos in informal debate rather than listening to the confessions of his Indian charges. A few years after his arrival in Dolores, Hidalgo's path crossed that of Ignacio Allende, a thirty-five-year-old firebrand who was a captain in the Queen's Cavalry Regiment in nearby Guanajuato. Allende took the priest into his confidence and introduced him to a coterie of friends: Juan de Aldama, also a military man; Miguel Domínguez, a former corregidor of Querétaro, and his wife, Doña Josefa Ortiz de Domínguez, remembered in Mexican history as *La Corregidora*; Epigmenio González, a grocer; Marino Galván, a postal clerk; and a few others.

The group had organized a "literary club," but the members were less interested in disputing the latest tour de force of Goethe, Schiller, Wordsworth, or Chateaubriand than in plotting the separation of the New Spain from the old. As converts were attracted and the plans matured, a date was set for the uprising—December 8, 1810. Although the conspirators were all admonished to hold their tongues, Marino Galván, the postal clerk, leaked the news to his superior who, in turn, informed the audiencia in Mexico City. The forewarned Spanish authorities moved on September 13, when they searched the house of Epigmenio González in Querétaro, found bountiful arms and ammunition, and ordered the arrest of the panic-stricken owner. The events of the next few days are known to every Mexican schoolchild, for they

Miguel Hidalgo y Costilla (1753–1811). One of the most renowned individuals in nineteenth-century Mexican history, Father Hidalgo provided the initial spark for the Independence movement.

are repeated every September 16 amidst a wide array of Independence Day celebrations.

Doña Josefa entrusted Ignacio Pérez with the task of carrying the news of the arrest to Ignacio Allende in San Miguel. Not finding him at home, the messenger relayed the news to Juan de Aldama, who immediately set out to inform Father Hidalgo in Dolores. When, about two o'clock on the morning of September 16, he arrived at the priest's house, Aldama found Allende there also. The three realized that orders for their own arrest had probably been issued and decided to strike out for Independence at once. Hidalgo rang the church bells summoning his parishioners to mass earlier than usual that morning. Assembled at the little church in Dolores the Indians and mestizos, including a group of prisoners already released from the local jail, were harangued about matters of this world, not the next. The exact words of this most famous of all Mexican speeches are not known, or, rather, they are reproduced in almost as many variations as there are historians to reproduce them. But the essential spirit of the message is this:

> My children: a new dispensation comes to us today. Will you receive it? Will you free yourselves? Will you recover the lands stolen three hundred years ago from your forefathers by the hated Spaniards? We must act at once. . . . Will you not defend your

religion and your rights as true patriots? Long live our Lady of Guadalupe! Death to bad government! Death to the gachupines!

The immediate response to the *Grito de Dolores* was enthusiastic. With Hidalgo at their head, the motley band of poorly armed Indians and mestizos struck out for San Miguel, picking up hundreds of recruits along the way. When they stopped for a rest about noon at the hamlet of Atotonilco, Hidalgo entered the local church and emerged carrying a banner of the Virgin de Guadalupe—the dark-skinned lady who had appeared to Juan Diego almost three centuries before. The priest adopted this Virgin as the emblem of his crusade, but for reasons less religious than political. How better appeal to the Indian population who would make up the rank and file of his revolutionary army? What better contrast to the Spanish gold-brocaded Virgin de los Remedios than the humbly robed Indian Virgin de Guadalupe?

By dusk Hidalgo's band had taken San Miguel without difficulty, for the local militia joined the rebels. The day's dramatic events should have ended with the imprisonment of the local Spanish populace, but as night fell the unpredicted happened. The Indians were not ready to rest on their laurels and bed down for the night. If it were true that the Spaniards were to blame for everything that had befallen the aboriginal population of Mexico since the arrival of Cortés in 1519, then it was time that they be held accountable. Hidalgo's army became a mob. Bent on destruction, they moved through the streets with their clubs, slings, machetes, bows and arrows, lances, and occasional firearms, and they pillaged in blind despair. Hidalgo could not reason with them, and only Ignacio Allende, racing through the streets on horseback and warning prompt retribution, was able to contain the passions of the crowd. By morning chaos had begun to subside, but the problem would prove monotonously recurrent during the next few months. From San Miguel the rebels moved on Celaya, and after taking the town the mob again subjected the gachupín population to pillage. But Celaya was merely a rehearsal for a major encounter at Guanajuato, where the rebel army would be seriously opposed for the first time.

Hidalgo asked the intendant of Guanajuato, Juan Antonio de Riaño, to surrender the city, and he offered full protection to the Spanish citizenry in return. But the news from San Miguel and Celaya had already reached Guanajuato, and Riaño knew that Hidalgo could give no such assurance. He felt it better to make a stand and congregated the Spanish population in the Alhóndiga de Granaditas, the public granary. Although his people were greatly outnumbered, he believed they could hold out until reinforcements from Mexico City arrived.

Shortly before noon on September 28 Hidalgo began his approach to Guanajuato. He was joined by hundreds of workers from the surrounding silver mines. As the first wave of Indian foot soldiers rushed the improvised fortress, Riaño gave the order to open fire. Hundreds of Indians were cut down by the intendant's artillery. Before the second assault began, Riaño led a group of soldiers outside the wall to position them strategically. Just as he was about to re-enter the granary through the huge wooden gate, he took a musket ball on the side of the head and fell dead on the spot. But it would not have mattered at any rate. The attackers gathered up a bunch of soft pine torches used in the mines and laid them at the foot of the wooden gate. They set fire to them, and, as the gate was consumed, a few Indians charged through into the central patio. They were quickly followed by hundreds, perhaps even a thousand. Within the hour most of the gachupines were dead. They were stripped, and their naked bodies dragged unceremoniously through the streets to the nearby cemetery of Belén, where they were buried in makeshift graves. It was then time for the looting.

An eyewitness to the events of that day was eighteen-year-old Lucas Alamán, later one of Mexico's most renowned conservative statesmen and historians. In his multivolume history of Mexico he recollected:

> This pillage was more merciless than would have been expected of a foreign army. The miserable scene of that sad night was lighted by torches. All that could be heard was the pounding by which doors were opened and the ferocious howls of the rabble when the doors gave way. They dashed in in triumph to rob commercial products, furniture, everyday clothing, and all manner of things. The women fled terrorized to the houses of neighbors, climbing along the roof tops without yet knowing if that afternoon they had lost a father or husband at the granary. . . . The plaza and the streets were littered with broken pieces of furniture and other things robbed from the stores, of liquor spilled after the masses had drunk themselves into a stupor.[1]

It took a day and a half to restore order. The casualty figures were tremendous: over five hundred Spaniards and two thousand Indians killed. Hidalgo and Allende now felt strong enough to

1. Lucas Alamán, *Historia de México* (Mexico, 1942), 1: 403–04.

split their army into two striking forces, and within a month they had captured Zacatecas, San Luis Potosí, and Valladolid. By late October Hidalgo had an army of about eighty thousand marching on Mexico City. The anticipated battle took place on October 30 at the Monte de las Cruces, and there Hidalgo proved that sheer numbers could overcome a small, well-equipped, and disciplined professional army. The Spaniards were forced to retreat back into the city, and as Hidalgo camped on the hills overlooking the capital, he pondered what to do next.

A decisive strike at the capital might have ended the Wars for Independence after only a month and a half of fighting. But Hidalgo had taken heavy losses at Las Cruces, he was short on ammunition, and he was uneasy about turning his mob loose on Mexico City—they would have devastated the capital. Over Allende's objections he therefore decided to order a retreat rather than follow up his victory; as a consequence the Wars for Independence would drag on for eleven more years.

Moving northwest toward Guadalajara many of the rebel troops, their greatest opportunity denied, began to desert. At the same time Spanish forces under General Félix Calleja started to regroup. Guadalajara fell to the insurgents unopposed, but in January 1811 the royalist troops from the south caught up with the rebels and engaged them at the Puente de Calderón on the Río Lerma. Again Hidalgo and Allende had the numerical superiority, but General Calleja conducted his operations superbly and, in addition, was aided by a battlefield accident. A Spanish artillery shot hit a rebel ammunition wagon, and the resulting explosion caused a grass fire in the midst of Hidalgo's army. Panic ensued, and thousands of rebels broke rank and fled. The retreat turned into a rout. Hidalgo, Allende, and a number of other leaders recognized the futility of trying to regroup their forces and so moved northward, hoping to obtain relief in Coahuila and Texas. But their days were numbered. In March 1811, near the scorched desert town of Monclova (Coahuila), they were ambushed by a Spanish detachment that had been forewarned they were going to pass that way. Captured by Governor Manuel Salcedo of Texas, the rebels were marched in chains to Chihuahua, where Allende and the other nonclerical leaders were immediately executed as traitors. Hidalgo, because he was a priest, was subjected to an arduous trial conducted under the auspices of the Holy Office of the Inquisition. Finding him guilty of heresy and treason, the court defrocked him and turned him over to the secular arm for execution. At dawn on July 31 the firing

José María Morelos (1765–1815). With Hidalgo's execution in 1811, Morelos assumed the leadership of the Independence movement.

squad did its job. Hidalgo's corpse was decapitated, and his head, fastened to a pole, was displayed on the charred wall of the granary in Guanajuato as an object lesson to potential rebels.

Morelos and the Decline of Rebel Fortunes

With the death of Hidalgo the rebel leadership was assumed by another parish priest, José María Morelos y Pavón, a mestizo. But by this time sympathy for the cause of Independence had waned considerably. Many wealthy criollos had become alarmed at the radical twist the revolution seemed to be taking. The mob attacks on aristocratic property made some apprehensive and others openly hostile. Shut off for centuries from the decision-making positions in both church and state and obliged to compete for minor posts, the criollos favored the elimination of their Spanish rivals (and realized that Independence was the way to do it) but not at the expense of being swept up in some kind of social revolution. They recognized that to the downtrodden Indians and mestizos their white skin, if not their social position, was indistinguishable from that of the gachupines.

When the mantle of insurgent leadership fell on Morelos he knew full well that he could not count on criollo support. Unlike his predecessor, he trained a small but effective army that relied primarily on guerrilla tactics to keep the enemy off guard. Dividing his attention almost equally between military and political matters, he devised a strategy that called for the encirclement of Mexico City. By the spring of 1813 the circle was completed, and the capital was isolated from both coasts. Morelos then called for a congress to meet in Chilpancingo (Guerrero) to discuss plans for the nation once the Spaniards were driven out.

Some of the conservative criollos were still unsure of the direction in which Morelos wished to move, but his speech to the delegates at Chilpancingo cleared the air. If the Conquest of Mexico by Cortés represented a negation of Indian values by the Spanish, the Wars for Independence represented a negation of Spanish values by the Indians. Morelos invoked the names of the ancient emperors, Moctezuma and Cuauhtémoc, and implored the delegates to avenge the shameful disgrace of the last three centuries. The chains that enslaved the native population in Tenochtitlán in 1521 would be broken in Chilpancingo in 1813.

When Morelos finished, the delegates got down to work, first issuing a definitive Declaration of Independence. Those persons in the country opposing the declaration were considered guilty of high treason. The delegates further agreed upon a series of principles that should be incorporated into a new constitution: sovereignty should reside in the people and male suffrage should be universal; slavery and all caste systems should be abolished; government monopolies should be abolished and replaced by a 5 percent income tax; all judicial torture should be abolished. The nineteenth-century liberalism of the delegates was tempered only by their insistence that Roman Catholicism should be made the official religion of the new state.

But while the delegates at Chilpancingo engaged in political debate, General Calleja and his Spanish army assumed a new military offensive. In six months' time the Spaniards broke the circle around Mexico City and captured Valladolid, Oaxaca, Cuernavaca, Cuautla, Taxco, and even Chilpancingo itself. The delegates hurriedly packed their bags and moved to the more secure environs of Apatzingán, where they promulgated the constitution they had already largely agreed upon. But the document is little more than historical memorabilia for what it promised the Mexican masses on paper the viceroy's army denied them on the field of battle. With each defeat the insurgent army dwindled in size, and Morelos became more of a fugitive than the commander of an organized rebel force. And in the fall of 1815 he was captured by an enemy detachment and escorted to Mexico City,

TERRITORY UNDER INSURGENT CONTROL, 1811–13

where he was tried for treason and, like Hidalgo before him, shorn of his religious vestments and executed by a firing squad.

With the execution of Morelos the Independence movement had reached its nadir. Five years had elapsed since the Grito de Dolores, and the viceregal forces seemed stronger than ever. Neither Hidalgo nor Morelos had been able to attract much criollo support, and in 1816 the rebels could not even rally around one national leader. The entire idea of independence from Spain seemed to have lost rather than gained support.

For the next five years the Independence movement consisted of little more than sporadic guerrilla fighting. A number of independent bands, inadequately supplied and without any meaningful coordination, operated in isolated mountain pockets and the heavily foliaged areas of the coast. The loyal army consistently cut their numbers until only two of the guerrilla chieftains commanded respectable fighting forces able to sustain their efforts: Guadalupe Victoria with two thousand ragged troops in the mountains of Puebla and Veracruz and Vicente Guerrero with a thousand men in Oaxaca. By 1819 the Spanish viceroy in Mexico City, Juan Ruiz de Apodaca, was able to report to his sovereign, King Ferdinand, that the situation was so well under control that he anticipated no further need for reinforcements. To hasten the final victory he published an *indulto* (pardon) for all those who would lay down their arms. The following year, however, the rebel cause received an unexpected shot in the arm from an apparently unrelated but fortuitous event in the mother country.

Iturbide and the Plan de Iguala

In order to quell the seemingly more portentous revolutions for independence in Spanish South America, King Ferdinand assembled a powerful fighting force for service in the New World. While the troops underwent the final preparations, Colonel Rafael Riego proclaimed himself in revolt against his sovereign and was promptly seconded by thousands of troops. The Spanish insurgents demanded that Ferdinand swear allegiance to the Spanish Constitution of 1812, a liberal document that affirmed the sovereignty of the people, contained several mildly anticlerical provisions, and enunciated a liberal bill of rights. When the conservative criollos in New Spain learned that King Ferdinand had yielded to Riego's demands and accepted the Constitution, many for the first time decided to cast their lot with the revolution for Independence. Ironically, a conservative colony would thus gain independence from a temporarily liberal mother country.

Of the numerous defections from the cause of Spain to that of an independent Mexico the most significant was that of Agustín de Iturbide. Born in Valladolid of conservative Spanish parents in 1783, Iturbide early displayed an interest in pursuing a military career. He entered the army at the age of fourteen and soon received a royal commission as a lieutenant in the infantry regiment of Valladolid. When Father Hidalgo issued his Grito de Dolores in 1810, Lieutenant Iturbide decided to support the crown in its fight against the rabble that followed the banner of Guadalupe. For almost a decade he fought against the insurgents and on several occasions distinguished himself in the zeal with which he persecuted the enemy.

In the fall of 1820 Viceroy Apodaca invited Iturbide, by then a colonel, to discuss plans for a new offensive against Vicente Guerrero. Iturbide was placed in charge of twenty-five hundred men and left Mexico City for the south in late November. After a few indecisive skirmishes he asked Guerrero to a meeting during which he proposed to make peace—not war. Iturbide's price for the treason he was contemplating was to dictate the terms of Independence. But Guerrero was not easily convinced of either Iturbide's sincerity or his ideas for an independent Mexico. A series of conferences had to be held before the guerrilla warrior and the new convert could issue, on February 24, 1821, their *Plan de Iguala.*[2] Unlike the United States Declaration of Independence, which berated the mother country in a tirade of denunciations, the Plan de Iguala had an entirely different orientation and appeal. In order to attract conservative support it praised the Spanish endeavor in the New World and held out Spain as the most Catholic, holy, heroic, and magnanimous of nations. But after three hundred years of tutelage it was time for Mexico to strike out on its own. The plan contained twenty-three articles but only three major guarantees: first, the independent Mexican nation would be organized as a constitutional monarchy, and the crown would be offered to King Ferdinand or some other appropriate European prince; second, the Roman Catholic religion would be given a monopoly on the spiritual life of the country and its clergymen would retain all the rights and privileges they currently enjoyed; and, third, criollos and peninsulares would be treated equally in the new state. In order to uphold the promises a new army, the *Ejército de las Tres Garantías* (the Army of the Three Guarantees) would be placed directly under Iturbide's command.

In the Plan de Iguala Iturbide played his cards with consummate skill. The proposal was imaginative, even brilliant, in its conception. Mexicans were weary of a decade of war, and many of stout heart had given up hope. The liberal Constitution of Apatzingán had failed to attract sufficient support, and it was clear that to succeed the movement needed help from the conservatives. With liberalism temporarily manifesting itself in the mother country, the timing was perfect. In seeking to reconcile the interests of opposing factions, the plan changed the nature of the fight for Independence. Instead of urging death to the gachupines, Iturbide curried their favor. He recognized and capitalized upon the fact that both liberals, who favored the establishment of a republic, and conservatives, who preferred an absolute monarchy, could compromise on this plan as it held out the best hope for Independence, something that both groups wanted most.

Within several weeks the broadly based plan began to yield its

2. In Mexican history revolutionary movements are almost always preceded by a plan that outlines the principles to be embraced and seeks to widen the base of support.

first dividends as converts began to arrive. Military contingents throughout the country joined the Army of the Three Guarantees; priests urged cooperation from the pulpits; Masonic groups pledged support; and thousands of drifters again took up the cause. But, most important, the community of Spaniards, some fifty thousand strong, found in the Plan de Iguala the promise of a good future in a newly independent Mexico; as a result they, too, pledged support. When Guanajuato, Puebla, Durango, Oaxaca, Querétaro, and Zacatecas all fell to the insurgents, Viceroy Apodaca tendered his resignation. The Spanish crown, however, was unprepared to accept the inevitability of a rebel victory and appointed a replacement, Juan de O'Donojú, as Captain–General of New Spain. O'Donojú quickly perceived that Apodaca had assessed the situation correctly. New Spain was irrevocably lost, and there was little to be gained by not recognizing the fact. At the town of Córdoba, Iturbide and O'Donojú affixed their signatures to a treaty that, for the most part, accepted the terms of the Plan de Iguala. The highest-ranking Spanish official in New Spain had thus recognized Mexican Independence. But Iturbide, thinking of the future, incorporated into the Treaty of Córdoba one important modification. If no suitable European monarch could be persuaded to accept the Mexican crown, a Mexican congress could choose a New World emperor instead. The commander of the Army of the Three Guarantees had begun to feather his own nest.

The Effects of the Wars for Independence

Iturbide's triumphal entry into Mexico City in September of 1821 marked the end of eleven years of war. The *Gaceta Imperial de México* proclaimed theatrically that not even Rome in its days of grandeur had ever witnessed such an exultant spectacle. Upon receiving gold keys to the city the commander-in-chief explained that they would be used to lock the doors of irreligion, disunion, and despotism and to open the doors of general happiness. But the first door Iturbide opened in Mexico City was that of the great cathedral on the central plaza. Cementing his future relationship with the archbishop, he received communion and listened to a Te Deum offered in his honor.

From the campaigns, Mexico acquired not only its share of heroes and traitors but also a legacy of political violence and economic devastation. The wars exerted an incalculable influence on Mexico's future. The army had converted the dream of Independence into reality and was by no means ready to step aside and allow civilians to control the nation's destiny. For a full century the Mexican military would be very much involved in the political processes of government and would bargain with opposing factions for a greater and greater share of the nation's wealth. The military clique would constitute a ready instrument for unscrupulous politicians to use for their own purposes. More important yet, the basic issues separating different segments of society had not been resolved. Competing groups had cooperated long enough to achieve a common end, but, once Independence was achieved, the alliance called together by the Plan de Iguala proved very transitory. For some the revolution was simply anticolonial in nature and therefore it was over; others wanted its momentum to be carried into the arena of political and economic reform. The internal struggles between liberals and conservatives, between republicans and monarchists, between federalists and centralists, and between anticlericals and proponents of clerical privilege would consume the energies of the neophyte nation for much longer than the most pessimistic political analyst would have dared to predict.

But in 1821 only few Mexicans could have had premonitions of the drama that was about to unfold. The large majority of the population had not been affected directly by the wars, and the illiterate masses most assuredly did not know that a change, important at least for those on the threshold of power, had taken place. The nineteenth century would vindicate the general apathy of the rural Mexican, for his life would change little, if at all. The fate of the Mexican Indian continued to rest totally in the hands of others, as it had for the last three hundred years. His privations went unnoticed. He could take little solace in the fact that the politically articulate groups in Mexico City that completely overlooked his interests demonstrated precious little ability to govern even themselves.

Recommended for Further Study

Almaraz, Felix D. "Governor Antonio Martínez and Mexican Independence in Texas." *Permian Historical Annual* 15 (1975): 44–55.

——. *Tragic Cavalier: Governor Manuel Salcedo of Texas, 1808–1813.* Austin: University of Texas Press, 1971.

Anna, Timothy E. *The Fall of Royal Government in Mexico City.* Lincoln: University of Nebraska Press, 1978.

Archer, Christon I. "The Royalist Army in New Spain: Civil–Military Relationships, 1810–1821." *Journal of Latin American Studies* 13 (1981): 57–82.

Benson, Nettie Lee. "The Contested Mexican Election of 1812." *Hispanic American Historical Review* 26 (1946): 336–50.

———, ed. *Mexico and the Spanish Cortes, 1810–1822.* Austin: University of Texas Press, 1966.

Fisher, Lillian Estelle. *The Background of the Revolution for Mexican Independence.* Gainesville: University of Florida Press, 1966.

Gronet, Richard W. "The United States and the Invasion of Texas, 1810–1814." *The Americas* 25 (1969): 281–306.

Hamill, Hugh M. "Caudillism and Independence: A Symbiosis?" In *The Independence of Mexico and the Creation of the New Nation*, edited by Jaime E. Rodríguez O., pp. 163–74. Los Angeles: UCLA Latin American Center, 1989.

———. *The Hidalgo Revolt: Prelude to Mexican Independence.* Gainesville: University of Florida Press, 1966.

———. "Royalist Propaganda and 'La Porción Humilde del Pueblo' During Mexican Independence." *The Americas* 36 (1980): 423–44.

Hamnett, Brian R. "Royalist Counterinsurgency and the Continuity of Rebellion: Guanajuato and Michoacán, 1813–20." *Hispanic American Historical Review* 62 (1982): 19–48.

Lewis, William Francis, III. "Xavier Mina and Fray Servando Mier: Romantic Liberals of the Nineteenth Century." *New Mexico Historical Review* 44 (1969): 119–36.

Lieberman, Mark. *Hidalgo: Mexican Revolutionary.* New York: Praeger, 1970.

Lombardi, John V. *The Political Ideology of Fray Servando Teresa de Mier, Propagandist for Independence.* Cuernavaca: Centro Intercultural de Documentación, 1968.

Robertson, William S. *Iturbide of Mexico.* Durham, N.C.: Duke University Press, 1952.

Rodríguez O., Jaime E. "From Royal Subject to Republican Citizen: The Role of the Autonomists in the Independence of Mexico." In *The Independence of Mexico and the Creation of the New Nation*, edited by Jaime E. Rodríguez O., pp. 19–43. Los Angeles: UCLA Latin American Center, 1989.

Rydjord, John. *Foreign Interest in the Independence of New Spain.* Durham, N.C.: Duke University Press, 1935.

Schmitt, Karl M. "The Clergy and the Independence of New Spain." *Hispanic American Historical Review* 34 (1954): 289–312.

TePaske, John Jay. "The Financial Disintegration of the Royal Government of Mexico during the Epoch of Independence." In *The Independence of Mexico and the Creation of the New Nation*, edited by Jaime E. Rodríguez O., pp. 63–84. Los Angeles: UCLA Latin American Center, 1989.

Timmons, Wilbert H. "Los Guadalupes: A Secret Society of the Mexican Revolution for Independence." *Hispanic American Historical Review* 30 (1950): 453–79.

———. *Morelos: Priest, Soldier, Statesman of Mexico.* El Paso: Texas Western College Press, 1963.

Woodward, Margaret L. "The Spanish Army and the Loss of America, 1810–1824." *Hispanic American Historical Review* 48 (1968): 586–606.

17

The First Mexican Empire

Pomp and Circumstance

In the best of circumstances nation building is a precarious business, but how does one create a nation out of a newly independent state when the economy is in shambles and the political atmosphere is pervaded by acrimony and mistrust? The question obsessed many Latin American leaders in the nineteenth century once parental authority had been successfully challenged. Iturbide did not have all of the answers, but he felt that he had one reliable formula. Identify the head of government with the state, subsume the two into one, and by some miraculous metamorphosis a nation will emerge. But the crucial element in the process, he believed, was to identify a dynamic, resourceful, and charismatic leader. Not worried about overstepping the bounds of modesty, he could identify only one Mexican possessed of all these redeeming prerequisites.

Joel Poinsett, an American who would later become the first United States minister to Mexico, met Iturbide in the fall of 1822 and recorded his impressions.

> I will not repeat the tales I hear daily of the character and conduct of this man. . . . He is accused of having been the most cruel and blood-thirsty persecutor of the Patriots, and never to have spared a prisoner. . . . in a society not remarkable for strict morals, he was distinguished for his immorality. . . . To judge from Iturbide's public papers, I do not think him a man of talents. He is prompt, bold and decisive, and not scrupulous about the means he employs to obtain his ends.[1]

1. Joel R. Poinsett, *Notes on Mexico Made in the Autumn of 1822, Accompanied by an Historical Sketch of the Revolution* (New York, 1969), pp. 68–69.

As provided by the Plan de Iguala, Iturbide named a provisional junta to govern the country. This junta, completely dominated by conservative criollo interests, in turn named him to serve as its presiding officer. The first order of business was to select a five-man regency to exercise executive functions until an emperor could be designated. The junta chose Iturbide as one of the five. But the presidency of the junta and membership on the regency was deemed an insufficient tribute to the leader of the Independence movement, so the group awarded him a new military title, *Generalísimo de Tierra y Mar*, and, to go along with it, a salary of 120,000 pesos annually.

While the junta, the regency, and Iturbide threw flowers in each other's path, an independent Congress, also dominated by conservatives, debated Mexico's future. Although a small group of recalcitrants tried to muster sympathy for a republic, Iturbide's conservative cohorts controlled the organizational proceedings. While they beat back all attempts at republicanism they began to waver on a series of economic and military issues. When the Congress, though divided, decided to cut back on the size of the Army of the Three Guarantees and decreed that no member of the regency could simultaneously hold military office, Iturbide realized that his ranks were being thinned and that time was no longer on his side. If he failed to act decisively the crown he wanted so desperately might be denied him.

On the evening of May 18 the Generalísimo staged a dramatic demonstration in his own behalf. Troops were ordered out of the barracks and into the streets. Firing muskets and rockets into the air and shouting "Viva Agustín I, Emperor of Mexico!" they enticed other soldiers to join them. As the frenzy grew in the downtown business district, thousands of civilians accompanied the mob on its way to Iturbide's residence. Once there, the multitudes demanded that their favorite declare himself emperor at once. Iturbide told friends who were in his home at the time that he wanted to go out on his balcony and turn them down. But he later wrote:

> If I restrained myself from appearing before them for that purpose, it was solely in compliance with the counsel of a friend who happened at the moment to be with me. "They will consider it an insult," he scarcely had time to say to me, "and the people know no restraint when they are irritated. You must make this fresh sacrifice to the public good: the country is in danger; remain a moment longer undecided, and you will hear their acclamations

turned into death shouts." I felt it necessary to resign myself to circumstances.[2]

With good reason historians have concluded that Iturbide's reluctance was feigned, that his submission to the inevitable was not so stoic, and that the sergeant orchestrating the event had acted under his explicit instructions. The following morning Iturbide appeared personally before the Congress, and, with his mob in the galleries shouting, the intimidated body named him constitutional emperor of Mexico. He demonstrated no concern that a legal quorum was missing. In his oath of office he swore before God and the Holy Evangels to uphold and defend the Roman Catholic religion at the exclusion of all others and to enforce all laws and decrees promulgated by the Congress that chose him.

With the throne thus occupied, the Congress set to work, not on the conspicuous demands of the Mexican nation, but on defining proper etiquette and protocol in an obvious attempt to emulate the greatest imperial regime the world had ever known. It would not only appropriate for the emperor all of the prerogatives of the Spanish nobility but would add to them. In June the Congress refined the organizational structure of the monarchy, declaring it to be hereditary. The heir was Iturbide's eldest son, Señor Don Agustín, who was designated "Prince Imperial," while the other sons and daughters of the emperor were to be Mexican princes and princesses. Iturbide's father would carry the title "Prince of the Union" and his sister, Doña Nicolasa, "Princess of Iturbide." May 19, the day of Iturbide's proclamation, was declared a national holiday, as were his birthday and the birthdays of his children. Defining the accouterments of regality took months and at times prompted the most ludicrous debate, such as that concerning whether the motto appearing below Iturbide's bust on the new metal coinage should be in Latin or Spanish. The Congress opted for *Augustinus Dei Providentia* on one side and *Mexici Primus Imperator Constitutionalis* on the other.

The greatest preparations of all were made for the official coronation ceremonies in July. Although several liberal deputies argued that kissing of the hand and bending of the knee were repugnant to the dignity of free peoples, their voices were lost to the monarchist majority. The efforts were all based on a French

2. Quoted in William Spence Robertson, *Rise of the Spanish-American Republics as Told in the Lives of Their Liberators* (New York, 1961), p. 130.

model, and the Congress hired a French baroness who had designed the costumes for Napoleon Bonaparte some twenty-two
years before. Serious thought was given to ordering a national
fast for the three days prior to the ceremonies, but the idea was
finally dismissed as impractical to enforce outside of prisons and
convents. The Congress did, however, authorize a new Mexican
order, the Knights of Guadalupe, to participate in the coronation.
As the day of the coronation approached, jewelry was borrowed,
thrones were erected, banners and flags were hung from church
towers, and teams of peasants were engaged to scour the streets.
The citizenry of the capital were being prepared for the most
pretentious spectacle ever to occur in Mexico City.

At 8:00 A.M. on Sunday, July 21, 1822, amidst the din of artillery salvos and the clamor of several military bands, the imperial
cortège worked its way along a carpeted and flower-strewn path
to the provisional palace, and the royal family was escorted to
the central cathedral by an honor guard recently designated by
the Congress. At the door the emperor and empress were met by
two bishops who blessed them with holy water and led them to
the two thrones placed on the altar. When the lesser dignitaries,
including the diplomatic corps, were seated according to the
complicated body of protocol, the bishop of Guadalajara celebrated high mass and consecrated the emperor and empress with
sacred oil. With tremendous solemnity the president of the Congress placed the crown on Iturbide's head and he, in turn, placed
a slightly smaller one on the head of the empress. The bishop
then intoned *Vivat Imperator in aeternum*. It was time for the
bishop of Puebla to participate, and his contribution, ending
the ceremony, was a long eloquent speech eulogizing the new
emperor.

While the outer trappings of the empire were pretentious to
the absurd, they were not entirely without purpose and meaning.
Iturbide's understanding of Mexico's past, while by no means
profound, was acute enough. He realized that the entire governmental system of the colonial period had been predicated upon
loyalty to the king and the crown. Even provincial and local officials decreed and implemented ordinances in the king's name.
Independence obviously undercut the personal loyalty that sealed
Mexican society together, but the emperor wanted to capitalize
upon the time-tested tradition. He wanted to reap advantages
from the fact that Mexico was not immune to the forces of history. While he became emperor in name, in fact he became a
caudillo, a military leader with a personal following. The Con-

Agustín de Iturbide (1783–1824). Changing allegiance from the Spanish to the insurgent cause, Iturbide successfully concluded the fight for Independence and had himself named emperor of Mexico.

gress had given him the legal base he considered vital; the ostentation that engulfed his person helped to reinforce the mystique of his indispensability and to blur the distinctions between the man and the office. The words *Augustus Dei Providentia Mexici Primus Imperator Constitutionalis*, even if they were not understood, sounded enough like the unintelligible locutions of the Sunday mass to inspire awe in the large unsophisticated portion of the citizenry. Iturbide worked hard to identify the new state with his own person and, for a while, seemed to be succeeding.

Problems Facing the New Empire

The empire was huge. Embracing much of the old viceroyalty of New Spain, it stretched in the north to California and the present-day Southwest of the United States and to the south included all of Central America with the exception of Panama. Long subject to what they considered the autocratic rule of Guatemala, many Central Americans favored union with the Mexican empire, but when rebellious elements in Honduras, El Salvador, and Costa

Rica demurred, Iturbide sent in an army of six hundred men to ensure adhesion. That was sufficient.

A more serious problem occurred with the neighbor to the north. The new regime quite naturally wished to secure the official recognition of the United States. The cultivation of harmonious relations was deemed vital to the security of Mexico's northern provinces (the United States had already exhibited expansionist tendencies) and could lead to extensive commercial ties. In addition, the boundary between the two countries had never been properly defined and needed to be drawn. Most of all the Mexican monarch hoped for a loan of $10 million to help his new government meet its obligations. But President James Monroe's explicit purpose in extending diplomatic recognition to the newly independent Latin American states was to promote the establishment of free republican governments. When the Mexican Congress named Iturbide emperor, Monroe was discouraged and ventured the opinion that the monarchy could not last long.

Iturbide took the lead when he dispatched Manuel Zozaya as minister to Washington. Reception of the Mexican would, in effect, recognize the Mexican regime. With mixed emotions the United States president urged the Congress to authorize recognition in December of 1822. To reject Zozaya would impair relations with Mexico from the beginning, and business interests in the United States wanted to cultivate trade relations. In January 1823 Monroe appointed Joel Poinsett as minister to Mexico even though Poinsett had expressed serious reservations about the Mexican regime. Iturbide, through no concerted effort of his own, had won a minor diplomatic victory.

But all was not well in Mexico City. The showy imperial façade rested on vulnerable socioeconomic foundations. Mexico's eleven years of war had cost more than most governmental officials, the emperor not excepted, were willing to admit. Most serious of all was the perilous state of the Mexican economy.

Mexico's colonial economy was overwhelmingly dependent upon the gold and silver mines in the central part of the country. But it was in precisely this area that the Wars for Independence had exacted their highest toll. During the years of internecine strife mine workers left their jobs to join the fight, mine owners and operators were killed, machinery was damaged, and many of the mines were flooded. Without sufficient bullion reaching the mints, coinage was curtailed. Over $26 million was minted in 1809; in 1821, less than $6 million. Without operation of the mines, unemployment was rampant in the mining centers, and the situation was aggravated by the mustering out that began shortly after the military campaigns ended.

The impact of the wars on Mexico's agricultural output was similar. Both Spanish troops and insurgents destroyed fields, commandeered crops, and killed off cattle and sheep that might have been of benefit to the enemy. Many an hacendado was killed, and those who escaped could likely have seen their haciendas in flames if, during their flight, they had time to glance over their shoulders. Mexico was a rural country at the time of Independence, but thousands in Mexico City (population 155,-000), Puebla (population 60,000), Guadalajara (population 50,-000), and other cities suffered as the price of agricultural products rose steadily in 1822.

The average citizen in the city felt the impact of the economic decline, and the government did too. In an attempt to make the cause of Independence even more popular, the Congress lowered many old taxes, such as those on pulque and tobacco, and eliminated others altogether. But commerce and the revenues to be derived therefrom stagnated as trade with Spain ended and free trade with new areas was slow to take up the slack.

To ensure loyalty soldiers and bureaucrats had to be paid and officers promoted, but the depleted revenues could not begin to cover the extravagant expenses of the imperial regime. Month after month expenses exceeded income. Virtually nobody was willing to invest in the shaky economy or loan money to the government. Available capital was largely in the hands of the Spaniards, and most of them began to depart soon after Independence. The few moneylenders around proposed interest rates that were nothing short of exorbitant. In response to the growing crisis the Congress decreed a forced loan on ecclesiastical properties, but this measure was no more than a temporary expedient. Several issues of paper currency, not backed by hard reserves and not trusted by anyone, caused more problems than they solved, and, as the wheels of the economy ground into ominous stagnation, Mexicans became more and more critical of their new regime.

Criticism was leveled at the emperor from many quarters: from disgruntled veterans who found no employment, from deputies in the Congress who really never accommodated themselves to the concept of monarchy, and from a number of courageous journalists who exposed the burlesque aspects of Mexico's empire. Sensitive to criticism, in the summer the emperor suppressed several liberal newspapers that espoused republican ideals and even one conservative one that favored monarchy but argued that the throne should be offered to a European prince. With the newspaper suppressions a group of liberals in the Congress, led by Fray Servando Teresa de Mier, an accomplished orator, and Carlos María de Bustamante, began to conspire. Through a government spy who infiltrated congressional circles Iturbide was able to secure an accurate list of his leading enemies and, on August 20, 1822, had them all arrested. The Congress protested, and even some of Iturbide's staunchest supporters in the legislative body defended their arrested colleagues. The opposing positions were irreconcilable, and the debates in the fall were heated; their substance was less significant than the fact that they demonstrated a steadily growing majority against the emperor and the imperial concept itself. Even Guadalupe Victoria, Iturbide's erstwhile ally, denounced him as a tyrant with all the fiery eloquence he could command. On October 31 Iturbide became the first Mexican chief executive to dissolve the legislative branch of government. The precedent, once established, would be repeated many times before the nineteenth century ran its course.

The reaction in both Mexico City and the provinces was resolute. The antimonarchists found their ranks swelling, and a specific plot crystalized in Veracruz. The self-acclaimed leader was Iturbide's commander in the port city, Antonio López de Santa Anna. Although it is possible that Santa Anna had been schooled in the virtues of republicanism by Carlos María de Bustamante, whom he had met and befriended a few years before, his decision to lead a revolt against the monarchy seems to have had a more fundamental root. As commander of Veracruz, Santa Anna had been assigned the task of driving the last remaining Spanish troops from San Juan de Ulloa, the harbor fortress they still held. But Iturbide believed that Santa Anna was not pursuing the enemy forcefully enough and was even considering turning Veracruz over to them. As a result he ordered Santa Anna to Mexico City where he could be closely observed. But Santa Anna would countenance no such move. On December 1, 1822, at the head of some four hundred troops, he rode through the streets of Veracruz proclaiming a republic. A few days later he formally launched his revolt under the Plan de Veracruz. Within a month Vicente Guerrero, Nicolás Bravo, and Guadalupe Victoria had joined the movement, enhancing its prestige. Iturbide recognized the seriousness of the problem; it was one thing for deputies in the Congress to attack the regime with words and quite another for army officers to attack it with arms and ammunition.

Placing José Antonio Echáverri, the captain general of Vera-cruz, in charge of the imperial campaigns, Iturbide felt that he had little to fear. Echáverri and Santa Anna had been at each other's throats for months over the most expeditious means for driving the Spaniards out of San Juan de Ulloa. But Echáverri decided to give the emperor a little of his own medicine. Much as Iturbide had made common cause with Vicente Guerrero when dispatched to engage him, Echáverri joined Santa Anna. On February 1, 1823, Echáverri and thirty-three cohorts pro-claimed the *Plan de Casa Mata*. Santa Anna, not having en-countered much military success in recent months, and realizing that the Plan de Casa Mata was not inconsistent with his own Plan de Veracruz, accepted the new plan. Two antiimperial movements now became one.

One military contingent after another swore allegiance to the Plan de Casa Mata. One province after another fell to the insur-gents, and they began marching on Mexico City. They did not have to take the capital by force, however. Realizing that his ex-periment with monarchy had ended in failure, Iturbide abdi-cated his throne in the middle of February 1823, some ten months after coming to office, and accepted a generous pension that would have enabled him to live comfortably. In his resigna-tion address he stated he did not desire to have his name become a pretext for civil war. Then with his family he made his plans to go into European exile. The rebel army marched into Mexico City unopposed.

An Assessment

The first Mexican empire had been a dismal failure. In concep-tion it had merely substituted a new criollo oligarchy for the old gachupín oligarchy and indeed had satisfied many Mexicans hostile to the innovations of nineteenth-century liberalism. The royal household, with all of its gaudy trappings, underscored that very little had changed since New Spain won control of its own destiny. The diplomatic initiatives, the loan from the United States, and an equitable settlement of the boundary had lan-guished.

With the advantage of historical hindsight, the revolt, fought under the banner of the Plan de Casa Mata, is laden with irony. The entire antimonarchy fight was made in the name of the Congress, which Iturbide had emasculated from the day it accepted his oath of office. One would have thought that at best legislative supremacy, and at worst legislative equality, would have been the political dictum of the nineteenth century. In fact, just the opposite was true. Executive dominance and legislative subservience may have been bequeathed to Mexico during the three centuries of colonial tutelage, but they were sufficiently enforced during the empire never to be successfully challenged again. Few practical lessons in nation building derived from the empire. Administrative and legislative experience was still in short supply. The Mexican elite did not yet consider the fact that successful leadership in the Wars for Independence was by no means synonymous with statesmanship. In the period following the empire Mexico would once again turn to military heroes who had emerged from the campaigns with more than life-sized stature.

But in at least one respect the collapse of the empire marked the beginning of a new day. It brought to power for the first time the criollo middle class, which had early supported the Independence movement only to be outflanked by the conservatives after the Riego revolt in Spain. These criollos were not social revolutionaries in any sense. While on occasions they attacked intrenched interests, their objectives were political, not social. In all innocence they seemed to believe that the docility of the lower classes had no bounds and that the poor would endure their privations forever.

As Mexico prepared to embark upon its second experiment as an independent nation, only one major question had been answered. The monarchists had been so thoroughly discredited that virtually nobody, at least for a while, harbored serious notions about reviving the concept. Iturbide's wasteful pomp had converted more monarchists to republicans than could have been persuaded by a team of skillful rhetoricians. Mexico would be organized as a republic; the nature of that republic would now be the issue at stake. It would provoke violent debate, near anarchy, and finally civil war.

Recommended for Further Study

Anna, Timothy E. "The Iturbide Interregnum." In *The Independence of Mexico and the Creation of the New Nation*, edited by Jaime E. Rodríguez O., pp. 185–200. Los Angeles: UCLA Latin American Center, 1989.

————. "The Rule of Agustín de Iturbide: A Reappraisal." *Journal of Latin American Studies* 17 (1985): 79–110.

Beezley, William H. "Caudillismo: An Interpretive Note." *Journal of Inter-American Studies* 11 (1969): 345–52.

Benson, Nettie Lee. "The Plan of Casa Mata." *Hispanic American Historical Review* 25 (1945): 45–56.

————, and Charles R. Berry. "The Central American Delegation to the First Constituent Congress of Mexico, 1822–1823." *Hispanic American Historical Review* 49 (1969): 679–702.

Cotner, Thomas E. *The Military and Political Career of José Joaquín de Herrera, 1792–1854*. Austin: Institute of Latin American Studies, 1949.

Harrison, Horace V. "The Republican Conspiracy against Agustín de Iturbide." In *Essays in Mexican History*, edited by Thomas E. Cotner and Carlos E. Castañeda, pp. 142–65. Austin: Institute of Latin American Studies, 1958.

Kenyon, Gordon. "Mexican Influence in Central America, 1821–1823." *Hispanic American Historical Review* 41 (1961): 175–205.

Lewis, William Francis, III. "Xavier Mina and Fray Servando Mier: Romantic Liberals of the Nineteenth Century." *New Mexico Historical Review* 44 (1969): 119–36.

Lombardi, John V. *The Political Ideology of Fray Servando Teresa de Mier, Propagandist for Independence*. Cuernavaca: Centro Intercultural de Documentación, 1968.

McElhannon, Joseph Carl. "Relations between Imperial Mexico and the United States." In *Essays in Mexican History*, edited by Thomas E. Cotner and Carlos E. Castañeda, pp. 127–41. Austin: Institute of Latin American Studies, 1958.

Poinsett, Joel R. *Notes on Mexico Made in the Autumn of 1822, Accompanied by an Historical Sketch of the Revolution*. New York: Praeger, 1969.

Robertson, William S. *Iturbide of Mexico*. Durham, N.C.: Duke University Press, 1952.

Tenenbaum, Barbara. "Taxation and Tyranny: Public Finances during the Iturbide Regime." In *The Independence of Mexico and the Creation of the New Nation*, edited by Jaime E. Rodríguez O., pp. 201–14. Los Angeles: UCLA Latin American Center, 1989.

Villoro, Luis. "The Ideological Currents of the Epoch of Independence." In *Major Trends in Mexican Philosophy*, edited by Mario de la Cueva et al., pp. 185–219. Notre Dame, Ind.: University of Notre Dame Press, 1966.

V THE TRIALS
OF NATIONHOOD, 1824-55

18

The Early Mexican Republic, 1824-33

The Constitution of 1824

With the collapse of the empire, a three-man junta governed
Mexico provisionally. All three—Nicolás Bravo, Guadalupe Victoria, and Pedro Celestino Negrete—were military men. The
precedent of miscasting soldiers as statesmen was now well established. The first order of business was to call elections for delegates to a constitutional congress that would be charged with
framing the new charter. The constituent body met for the first
time on November 27, 1823, and before the week was out the
lines of combat had been drawn. The focus narrowed to a question that on the surface seemed simple enough: should the new
republic be federalist or centralist?

Although there were some exceptions to the general alignment
of forces, the centralists found their strength among the clergy,
the hacendados, and the army officers, while the federalist fire-
brands drew support from those liberal criollos and mestizos
who considered themselves intellectual heirs of the French and
American revolutions and students of the United States Constitution and the liberal Spanish document of 1812. The chief
spokesmen for the federalists were Miguel Ramos Arizpe from
Coahuila and Valentín Gómez Farías from Zacatecas. The centralist cause was championed by Fray Servando Teresa de Mier
and Carlos María de Bustamante. When Ramos Arizpe presented
the body with a working paper modeled very closely after the
Constitution of the United States, Fray Servando, an iconoclast
who once questioned the authenticity of the Virgin of Guadalupe, responded with an eloquent speech. He observed that the

experience of the northern neighbor had been entirely different
from that of Mexico, and, while a federal system might well be
suited to the needs of the United States, it could not work in Mexico for it would weaken the country just when strength from
union was required. Speaking of the thirteen colonies to the
north, Fray Servando argued:

> They were already separate and independent one from another.
> They federalized themselves in union against the oppression of
> England; to federalize ourselves, now united, is to divide ourselves
> and to bring upon us the very evils they sought to remedy with
> their federation. They had already lived under a constitution
> that, when the name of the king was scratched out, brought forth
> a republic. We buckled for three hundred years under the weight
> of an absolute monarch, scarcely moving a step toward the study
> of freedom. We are like children barely out of diapers or like
> slaves who have just unshackled their chains. . . . We might say
> that nature itself has decreed our centralization.[1]

Fray Servando was not speaking for rhetorical effect. But his
arguments, although having much to commend them, failed to
persuade. Ramos Arizpe and his federalist cohorts also drew upon
the irrefutable lessons of history but interpreted them quite differently. Centralism they equated with despotism. As examples
they pointed to the three hundred years of colonial rule, which
were centralistic and despotic, and the ten months of monarchy,
which were also centralistic and despotic. They preferred the dispersion of powers inherent in the federal structure and argued
that such a system was more in harmony with Mexico's recently
won liberties. A would-be dictator could be thwarted in his ne-
farious attempts to subject the people only if the states and localities enjoyed a respectable measure of independent power. Arizpe's plea appealed more to emotion than to rigorous logic, but
nevertheless he carried the day. It was simply too irresistible for
some to attribute the tremendous progress recorded by the United
States since its independence to its federal form of government.

Under the Constitution of 1824 the Estados Unidos Mexicanos
were organized as a federal republic composed of nineteen states
and four territories. In the separation-of-powers clause delineat-
ing governmental authority into the executive, legislative, and
judicial branches, the philosophical influence of Montesquieu

1. Quoted in *Antología del pensamiento social y político de América Latina* (Washington, D.C., 1964), pp. 242–43.

THE MEXICAN REPUBLIC IN 1824

States		Territories
1. Chiapas	11. Querétaro	20. New Mexico
2. Chihuahua	12. San Luis Potosí	21. Old California
3. Coahuila y Texas	13. Sonora y Sinaloa	22. New California
4. Durango	14. Tabasco	23. Tlaxcala
5. Guanajuato	15. Tamaulipas	
6. México	16. Veracruz	
7. Michoacán	17. Jalisco	
8. Nuevo León	18. Yucatán	
9. Oaxaca	19. Zacatecas	
10. Puebla		

Adapted from Romeo Flores Caballero, *Counterrevolution: The Role of the Spaniards in the Independence of Mexico* (Lincoln: University of Nebraska Press, 1974), p. 85.

and the practical influence of the United States Constitution of 1787 are both patent. The legislature was made bicameral, the upper house designated as the Senate and the lower house as the Chamber of Deputies. Each state was represented by two senators and one deputy for every eighty thousand inhabitants. In at least one respect the federal system established in 1824 went beyond its United States model and gave the states even greater power than those to the north: both the president and the vice-president were to be elected not by popular vote or an electoral college but by the state legislatures, for a term of four years.

While the federalists thus won on the major points of governmental organization, in an important sense they gave up as much as they gained. The centralists regrouped and scored at least three victories of their own. First and foremost, the Catholic Church retained its three-hundred-year monopoly on Mexico's spiritual life. Many Mexican conservatives still held that religious toleration was somehow incompatible with public morality. In addition, the president of the country was given extraordinary powers in times of emergency, powers that could convert him into a dictator while at the same time investing him with the sanction of law. The word *emergency* in the nineteenth century came to be interpreted rather loosely. Finally, the Constitution guaranteed members of the clergy and the military their special *fueros*. This time-worn Spanish institution exempted clergymen and military personnel from having to stand trial in civil courts, even if they were charged with the violation of civil law.

The Victoria Presidency

In Mexico's first presidential election the state legislatures chose as president Guadalupe Victoria and as vice-president Nicolás Bravo. The new president, a man of goodwill, was honest and unassuming. He always had time to meet the public and had proven his courage on the battlefield, but he was not a particularly talented individual. In a mood of compromise he invited several conservatives to serve in the cabinet. They accepted, not for purposes of reconciliation but to secure a power base within the government. The president sought to be impartial, but his attempts at fairness degenerated into indecision. Those in whom he placed trust took advantage of him. The problems that beset him were immense. Woefully unprepared by education or tem-

Guadalupe Victoria (1785–1843). Mexico's first president, Victoria found his term disrupted by the internal chaos that came to dominate the country's political life in the first half of the nineteenth century.

perament, he was not only unable to kindle popular imagination but proved unequal to the task.[2]

The debates of the empire and over the nature of the new republic had bequeathed an intensely political atmosphere, pervaded by mistrust, self-righteousness, rancor, and despair. Those in high office, including the president himself, found a constant friend a rare thing. While exaggerated jealousies magnified trifles, basic ideological cleavages emerged as well and began to manifest themselves in a unique manner. Both of the major political factions identified themselves and their efforts with a branch of freemasonry. The federalists attached themselves to the York Rite Masons (*Yorquinos*) and the centralists to the Scottish Rite (*Escoseses*). Masonic meetings, of course, were held in secret, and, because the lodges were inviolable, all manner of cabal could be plotted behind closed doors with little fear of exposure.

One of the more unfortunate incidents to occur during the Victoria presidency was the execution of the former emperor,

2. Recent scholarship has suggested it is not unlikely that a series of physical impairments gradually took their toll and left Victoria mentally unfit for the high office he held. See Elmer W. Flaccus, "Guadalupe Victoria: His Personality as a Cause of His Failure," *The Americas* 23 (1967): 297–311.

Agustín de Iturbide. Taking up residence first in Italy and later in England, the exiled monarch heard rumors that the restored Spanish king, Ferdinand VII, backed by the Holy Alliance, was about to undertake a reconquest of Mexico. Early in 1824 he offered his services to the republican government. He had defeated the Spanish army once and was prepared to do battle again in the name of Mexican Independence. Congress turned down his good offer and, in fact, passed legislation stipulating that should he dare return to Mexico he would be considered a traitor and, as such, would face immediate execution. Impatient and imprudent as ever, Iturbide did not wait for an answer. On May 11, 1824, he left England with his family and retainers for the New World. Disembarking at Soto la Marina, north of Tampico, he was soon recognized by the local military commander. The Tamaulipas state legislature met in hurried session and decreed that it must enforce the order of treason handed down by the national Congress the month before. On July 19, 1824, standing before a firing squad at the small town of Padilla, Iturbide could not resist making one final rambling and emotional speech protesting his innocence to his executioners: "Mexicans! Even in this act of my death I recommend to you love of our fatherland and observance of our holy religion. . . . I die for having come to assist you, and I die happy because I die among you. I die with honor, not as a traitor."[3]

The execution of Iturbide was really incidental to the Victoria presidency. The administration scored high marks in foreign policy. Not only was Mexico's Independence formally recognized by most of Europe, but several treaties of amity and commerce were concluded as well. A treaty with the United States pledged both countries to accept the Sabine River as the eastern boundary of Texas, thus ostensibly settling the boundary question. But President Victoria found representatives of foreign nations to be more reasonable than his opponents at home and international problems more soluble than domestic imbroglios.

The Victoria administration was unable to do much about the new nation's steadily worsening financial situation. For years prior to Independence the criollos had argued that the weakness of Mexico's economy was a result of poor management by the gachupines. But now in power themselves, the criollos could do no better. Not concerned that a large standing army could be a menace to civil liberties, to any hope of future civilian govern-

3. Quoted in Lucas Alamán, *Historia de México* (Mexico, 1942), 5: 736–37.

ments, and to a healthy economy, the president kept over fifty thousand men under arms at all times. The new government assumed all national debts from the late colonial period and the monarchy (over 76 million pesos) and sought to support itself by means of import taxes, sales taxes, and new government monopolies. The import duties were largely circumvented by rampant smuggling; the sales taxes were largely avoided by failure to report transactions; and the monopolies, after collection expenses, brought in little cash. Not only were the revenues insufficient to pay installments on the debt, but they were unequal to the day-to-day costs of government. Yet the deficit was less significant than the fact that the entire fiscal structure was unsound. Loans from England were deemed to be the salvation and small amounts were received. These minor infusions of foreign capital were insufficient to stimulate the economy but did mark the first step of Mexican economic dependency.

While efforts to heal the breach between rival factions foundered, the political and economic pressures merged in 1827 and expressed themselves in an armed revolt against President Victoria. The leader of the insurrection was none other than Vice-President Nicolás Bravo, who drew upon the Scottish Rite lodges for support. The Yorquinos rallied around the president, and ultimately the revolt was suppressed by Generals Santa Anna and Guerrero. But the precedent of the military coup had been set.

Domestic Turmoil and a Spanish Invasion

Passions had not yet subsided when the new presidential elections were held in September of 1828. The liberal candidate, Vicente Guerrero, an uneducated hero of the wars, was opposed by conservative Manuel Gómez Pedraza, an accomplished scholar who had served in the Victoria cabinet as secretary of war. The election results showed that Gómez Pedraza carried ten of the nineteen state legislatures, but the liberals, feeling no obligation to pay homage to the Constitution, charged that he had used his influence with the army to intimidate the legislators. Rather than turn the government over to their enemies, the liberals opted instead for revolution. Once again they found their champion in Antonio López de Santa Anna, but on this occasion the odds were strongly against him. Through persuasion and deception he gradually won others over to the liberal cause. When

Juan Alvarez rose up in Acapulco and Lorenzo de Zavala in the environs of Mexico City, the government army had to disperse its forces and the rebels made such headway that the president-elect, already disgusted with partisan abuse, announced that he was giving up the fight. As a result the defeated candidate, Vicente Guerrero, became president and Anastasio Bustamante, a compromise conservative, vice-president. Santa Anna, for his efforts, was awarded a division generalship, the highest military rank in the country.

The second president of Mexico was much more active and decisive than the first. He was not the least troubled that he alienated various segments of the population in pursuit of goals he considered worthwhile. The most progressive measure he undertook was the abolition of slavery. The bill, signed in September 1829, was accepted without protest except in Texas, where the institution of slavery had actually been encouraged by previous Mexican legislation.

Scarcely comfortable in the presidential chair, the new president received word that Spain, which had not yet recognized Mexico's independence, was indeed planning a reconquest of Mexico. The Spanish timing seemed to be excellent. The same day that the Congress named Guerrero president it decreed the enforcement of a law, passed under the previous administration, expelling almost all remaining Spaniards from Mexico. The country was rent with factionalism and considerably weakened. Just as the first Spanish conquest in 1519 had been served admirably by internal dissension, maybe the second, three hundred and ten years later, could profit as well.

The Spanish expedition of some three thousand troops left Havana, Cuba (one of the few remaining Spanish possessions in the New World), in July 1829 under the command of General Isidro Barradas. Landing on the coast of Tamaulipas at the height of summer, the Spaniards were exhausted and demoralized by intense heat, yellow fever, and an acute scarcity of water. To their amazement, however, they found that Tampico had been evacuated in anticipation of a much larger expedition, and they took the forfeited prize.

President Guerrero decided to place government operations in the hands of the man who had ostensibly saved the nation several times, the new division general, Antonio López de Santa Anna. On August 21 Santa Anna attacked Tampico but was repulsed by Barradas's well-intrenched forces. But the Spaniards had not established any sure line of supply, and Santa Anna opted for a long siege, which, he reasoned, would take its toll. As inadequate provisions and yellow fever taxed Spanish resistance, General Barradas decided to surrender. By October most of the Spanish troops were on their way home. The attempted reconquest was Spain's last Mexican hurrah. It touched off a series of reprisals against the few remaining Spaniards in the country, and they began leaving hurriedly. The exodus of these middle-class Spanish merchants further weakened Mexico's economy.

Santa Anna had saved Mexico again. By 1830 there were few in the country who could rival his popularity. Honorific but unremunerative titles began to flow in from all corners of the republic: *Vencedor de Tampico* (Victor of Tampico) and *Salvador del País* (Savior of the Country). And the national Congress authorized a medal inscribed "At Tampico he defeated Spanish arrogance" and officially named him *Benemérito de la Patria* (Benefactor of the Fatherland). Undoubtedly, he could have taken advantage of his position immediately if he had wanted to. But he was not quite ready.

The Federalist–Centralist Struggle Continues

With the Spanish threat removed, the Mexican liberals and conservatives now returned to anathematizing one another. When President Guerrero refused to relinquish the extraordinary powers Congress gave him to cope with the threat, Vice-President Bustamante posed as the champion of constitutionalism. For the second time in Mexico's brief republican history a conservative vice-president led an armed revolt against a liberal president. But where Nicolás Bravo had failed, Bustamante, largely because of his influence with the army, succeeded.

With Bustamante in the presidential office, the conservatives were back in power for the first time since the overthrow of the empire. But their promises would be so totally unredeemed as to imply that promises were made only for the pleasure of breaking them. All along the conservatives had been substituting catchy syllogisms for penetrating analyses of Mexico's problems, and when they found themselves in power they did not know what to do. Although they cut back on the size of the army and renegotiated the English loan, Bustamante was no more able to bring about stability and progress than had his liberal predecessors. And he compounded his shortcomings by giving his fellow Mexicans their first real lessons in military dictatorship.

Repressions taken against the Yorquinos were grossly intemperate. Freedom of the press was suppressed as only those presses upholding the government were allowed to roll. The federal legislature and the judiciary were badgered into acquiescence. Political corruption, not unknown in Mexico's past, reached new heights. But the incident that occasioned the greatest public outrage was the capture and execution of the former president, Vicente Guerrero. After his ouster by the Bustamante army, Guerrero gradually made his way to Acapulco, where he accepted passage on the *Colombo*, a ship flying the Italian flag. But Captain Picaluga, a Genoese citizen, had already made a trip to Mexico City and for $50,000 had agreed to sell Guerrero to the government. As soon as the former president boarded the *Colombo*, he was bound hand and foot and turned over to federal authorities. He was subsequently tried, convicted of treason, and on January 14, 1831, executed.

The execution had a sobering effect as Mexicans began to tally up. Of the five outstanding leaders of the Wars for Independence, four—Miguel Hidalgo, José María Morelos, Agustín de Iturbide, and now Vicente Guerrero—had died before the firing squad. Only Guadalupe Victoria escaped this fate. The word *traitor* had come to be used too easily and the charge invariably carried the supreme penalty. As a nation, Mexico was unsure of itself. It had drifted and vacillated since Independence. National, state, and local governments were plagued by civil disorder and insolvency. The state was still little more than an abstraction, and the criollo leadership had not served it well. The social structure had not changed in any meaningful way. Abolishing the caste system scarcely abolished poverty. Emancipating the slaves did not eliminate malnutrition and illiteracy. It seemed time for a change of direction, and there was one Mexican now ready to seize the opportunity. Santa Anna marshaled his forces once again, overthrew the Bustamante government, and returned to Veracruz to revel in his latest victory and await the outcome of the 1833 presidential elections.

Recommended for Further Study

Arrom, Silvia M. "Popular Politics in Mexico City: The Parián Riot, 1828." *Hispanic American Historical Review* 68 (1988): 245–68.

Benson, Nettie Lee. "Servando Teresa de Mier, Federalist." *Hispanic American Historical Review* 28 (1948): 514–25.

Callcott, Wilfrid H. *Church and State in Mexico, 1822–1857*. Durham, N.C.: Duke University Press, 1926.

Campbell, Randolf. "Henry Clay and the Poinsett Pledge Controversy of 1826." *The Americas* 28 (1972): 429–40.

Cline, Howard F. "The Aurora Yucateca and the Spirit of Enterprise in Yucatán, 1821–1847." *Hispanic American Historical Review* 27 (1947): 30–60.

Costeloe, Michael P. "Guadalupe Victoria and a Personal Loan from the Church in Independent Mexico." *The Americas* 25 (1969): 223–46.

Flaccus, Elmer W. "Commodore David Porter and the Mexican Navy." *Hispanic American Historical Review* 34 (1954): 365–73.

———. "Guadalupe Victoria: His Personality as a Cause of His Failure." *The Americas* 23 (1967): 297–311.

Flores Caballero, Romeo. *Counterrevolution: The Role of the Spaniards in the Independence of Mexico*. Lincoln: University of Nebraska Press, 1974.

Gardiner, C. Harvey. "The Role of Guadalupe Victoria in Mexican Foreign Relations." *Revista de Historia de América* 26 (1948): 379–92.

Gilmore, N. Ray. "Henry George Ward, British Publicist for Mexican Mines." *Pacific Historical Review* 32 (1963): 35–47.

Green, Stanley. *The Mexican Republic: The First Decade, 1823–1832*. Pittsburgh: University of Pittsburgh Press, 1987.

Hale, Charles A. *Mexican Liberalism in the Age of Mora, 1821–1853*. New Haven, Conn.: Yale University Press, 1968.

Hutchinson, C. Alan. "The Mexican Government and the Mission Indians of Upper California, 1821–1835." *The Americas* 21 (1965): 335–62.

Lamar, Quinton Curtis. "A Diplomatic Disaster: The Mexican Mission of Anthony Butler, 1829–1834." *The Americas* 45 (1988): 1–18.

Macune, Charles W. "The Impact of Federalism on Mexican Church–State Relations, 1824–1835: The Case of the State of Mexico." *The Americas* 40 (1984): 177–90.

Rippy, J. Fred. *Joel R. Poinsett, Versatile American*. Durham, N.C.: Duke University Press, 1935.

Rodríguez, Jaime O. "The Conflict Between Church and State in Early Republican Mexico." *New World* 2 (1987): 93–112.

Weber, David J. *The Mexican Frontier, 1821–1846: The American Southwest Under Mexico*. Albuquerque: University of New Mexico Press, 1982.

Winn, Wilkins B. "The Efforts of the United States to Secure Religious Liberty in a Commercial Treaty with Mexico, 1825–1831." *The Americas* 28 (1972): 311–32.

19

Santa Anna and the Centralized State

Santa Anna is the first of three towering Mexican political figures who would leave a preponderant imprint on their country's nineteenth-century historical experience. His contributions, corrosive perhaps, were quite at variance with those of his successors, Benito Juárez and Porfirio Díaz, but they were no less pronounced for he, too, was an event-making man. His intelligence, resolution, and temperament, his sins and ambitions, charted the course Mexico was to follow from the early 1830s to the middle 1850s. Mexican history from 1833 to 1855 constantly teetered between simple chaos and unmitigated anarchy. Victories were only slightly less barren than defeats. The country needed an "Era of Good Feelings" like that to the north but instead entered a phase of intense mutual recrimination. Nobody seemed willing to admit that some measure of compromise was essential to the system of government that had been inaugurated in 1824. Between May 1833 and August 1855 the presidency changed hands thirty-six times, the average term being about seven and a half months. Santa Anna occupied the presidential chair on eleven different occasions, and his whim was Mexico's imperative. Even when he was out of office he was a powerful force to be reckoned with and a constant danger to the incumbent regime and to anyone aspiring to the succession.

Santa Anna: The Expediency of Political Principles

Antonio López de Santa Anna Pérez de Lebrón was born on February 21, 1794. His schooling in Veracruz left much to be desired, but the criollo youth showed no real flair for books anyway. Shortly after his sixteenth birthday he joined the army and within a year received his baptism of fire in a small engagement against a band of pro-Hidalgo rebels. For the next decade the young royalist cavalry officer staunchly supported the crown's efforts in New Spain and not only won special commendation for his heroics but also, for a short time, became an aide-de-camp to Viceroy Apodaca in Mexico City. But in 1821 Santa Anna, like many of his criollo comrades, followed Iturbide's lead and switched allegiance; in the process they sealed Spain's fate.

The highlights of Santa Anna's career in the period immediately following Independence have already been touched upon. In 1823, under the banner of the Plan de Casa Mata, he led the republican forces against the empire and contributed in no small way to the overthrow of Iturbide. When Mexico's first vice-president, conservative Nicolás Bravo, proclaimed a revolt against President Victoria, Santa Anna took the lead in suppressing the movement and, following the next presidential election, saw to it that the defeated liberal candidate, Vicente Guerrero, was installed in office. In 1829, when Spain tried to bring its former colony back into the fold, it was Santa Anna again who defeated the Spanish forces at Tampico to save the infant republic and, in 1832, when the Bustamante dictatorship became intolerable, he overthrew it. On the surface, at least, his entire career seemed to constitute an unbroken chain of victories in the defense of Mexican liberalism. As the accolades mounted, Santa Anna fell victim to the greatest temptation of the wartime hero. He would change the field of battle from the military to the political front.

When the state legislatures cast their presidential votes in 1833, no one was surprised at the outcome. Santa Anna won by the largest majority in Mexican history. The vice-presidency went to Valentín Gómez Farías, a man of intellectual distinction and a politician whose liberal credentials were impeccable. Because both the new president and the new vice-president had upheld the cause of liberalism for years, Mexico seemed not to have to fear still another revolt of a vice-president against a president because of ideological disputation.

Santa Anna had coveted the presidency for a decade, but once he achieved the goal he quickly wearied of the daily routine, long hours, and general tedium of presidential business. The excitement was in getting there, not being there. For the first time in his career he could not devote himself to the strenuous life, flitting around the country on his white charger and making or unmaking presidents. Moreover, as the champion of liberalism, he was expected to embark upon a series of far-reaching reforms long called for by his liberal cohorts. Such reforms were bound to prompt controversy, divide the society once again, and erode his tremendous popularity. Santa Anna's response was unique but not entirely out of character. He decided to return to his magnificent estate, Manga de Clavo, in Veracruz, leaving the office in the hands of Vice-President Gómez Farías. The presidency was, it seemed, a toy to be cast aside when he tired of playing the game.

The vice-president, in good nineteenth-century liberal fashion, immediately began to sponsor a number of reforms aimed at two intrenched institutions: the army and the church. The military reforms were modest. To curtail the inordinate influence of the army, the Gómez Farías administration reduced the size of the military and legislated the abolition of the military fueros; army officers would now have to stand trial in civil courts. The clerical reforms were much more wide-ranging, as the liberals maintained that the Mexican clergy, if not having outlived its usefulness, was contributing less to the spiritual needs of the community than ever before. The initial step was a hesitant one, designed perhaps to test the wind. Clergymen throughout the country were advised that they should limit their directives and admonitions from the pulpit to matters of religion. Emboldened by the lack of a forceful rejoinder, the Congress, under the prodding of Gómez Farías and his liberal theoreticians José María Luis Mora and Lorenzo de Zavala, then voted to secularize education. One of the first steps taken in the name of educational progress was to close down the University of Mexico because its faculty was made up primarily of priests. In addition, all future clerical appointments in the republic would be made by the government rather than by the papacy. But the anticlerical reforms were just beginning. Within the month the government struck out at the church where it really hurt—the ecclesiastical treasury. The mandatory payment of the tithe was declared illegal. The individual was asked to search his own conscience and respond as he would. In addition, in the name of individual freedom (a concept much in vogue with nineteenth-century liberals) the Congress enacted legislation permitting nuns, priests, and lay brothers, who had taken oaths to spend their entire lives as brides and servants of Christ, to forswear their vows. And in one final measure the Franciscan missions in California were secularized and their funds and property sequestered.

General Antonio López de Santa Anna (1794–1876). The dominant figure of the first half of the nineteenth century, Santa Anna actually served in the presidency on eleven different occasions. A master politician, nobody understood Mexico's political dynamics better.

The response from the vested interests was almost predictable. To the rallying cry of *Religión y Fueros* the church, the army, and other conservative groupings banded together and called for the overthrow of the government. The conservatives scouted the country for a figure to protect their prerogatives and lead them to victory and turned to the maker and unmaker of presidents par excellence—Antonio López de Santa Anna. Again thirsting for public acclaim the retired president jumped at the new opportunity for action and agreed to lead the movement against his former vice-president, Gómez Farías. Not embarrassed by lack of consistency, the embattled champion of all liberal causes since 1821 suddenly began denouncing anticlerical atheists, York Rite Masons, naive federalists, subversive anarchists, Jacobins, Gómez Farías, and his liberal cohorts. The insurrection, although hampered by a cholera epidemic among the troops, succeeded, and within a short time Santa Anna made his second sortie into the presidency and rescinded most of the Gómez Farías reforms.

The new Santa Anna regime was openly conservative, Catholic, and centralist. The president's response to the perplexities of making a more perfect union was to abolish the federalist Constitution of 1824 and replace it with one more to his liking. The new charter, consisting of seven main parts, is remembered in Mexico's constitutional evolution as the *Siete Leyes*, or the Con-

stitution of 1836. In a feature designed to ensure centralist organization, the states of the old federal republic were transformed
into military departments governed by political bosses hand-
picked by the president himself. The presidential term was
extended from four years to eight, but no president under the
Constitution was to serve so long. The right to hold high political
office was extended only to those with a high annual income
($1,500 to be eligible for election to the Chamber of Deputies,
$2,500 for the Senate, and $4,000 for the presidency). The financial qualifications for voting and officeholding gave the Siete
Leyes an aristocratic flavor that obviously pleased the regime's
conservative backers.

Foreign Affairs and Finances

Santa Anna's decision to abolish the federal republic and to replace it with a centralist state precipitated a series of interrelated
events that were to dominate his life and his country for the next
twelve years. The switch to centralism was well received by some,
as the concept of federalism had already lost much of its magic
appeal, but liberal politicians in many parts of Mexico were dismayed, and several led revolts against him. The most serious opposition by far came from the northern province of Texas, which,
in turn, provoked a disastrous war with the United States. These
matters are of such importance as to be treated separately.

Even leaving the Texas issue temporarily aside, foreign relations during the age of Santa Anna were troubled, for in 1838
Mexico became involved in a war with France. The conflict was
deeply rooted in the internal chaos that had marked Mexican political life since Independence. During the unremitting series of
revolts and counterrevolts, the property of foreign nationals was
often damaged. Foreign governments then submitted claims in
behalf of their own citizens. Among the numerous French claims
were those of a French pastry cook whose delicacies were appropriated and consumed by a group of hungry Mexican soldiers in
1828. In ridicule of the event that followed, Mexican journalists
immediately dubbed the episode the Pastry War.

Conflicting property evaluations, rapid changes in the Mexican government, and the always near-bankrupt state of the Mexican treasury prevented resolution of the French claims for years.
In early 1838 the French king, Louis Philippe, demanded pay-

ment of $600,000. Because a favorable reply was not immediately forthcoming, in March a French fleet appeared off the coast of Veracruz, and the French minister, Baron Deffaudis, issued an ultimatum demanding payment of the claims by April 15, a series of assurances for French citizens residing in Mexico, and a few trading concessions. The Mexican government replied that it could not countenance any demands made with the French squadron anchored menacingly in Mexican waters. The deadline arrived and passed, whereupon France broke diplomatic relations and announced a blockade of Veracruz. When King Louis Philippe decided to increase the size of the French fleet to twenty-six vessels and over four thousand men, the Mexicans decided that it was time to negotiate. In October they agreed to pay the $600,000 but, to their surprise, found that the matter could no longer be resolved so easily. The French minister calculated that the blockade had cost his government about $200,000; the total bill was now $800,000. On this point the Mexican government could not yield. A thousand men were dispatched to reinforce the twelve hundred stationed at the venerable, moss-mottled fortress of San Juan de Ulloa in the harbor of Veracruz.

The French initiated their bombardment on the afternoon of November 27, rending a portion of the fortress walls, exploding supplies of ammunition inside, and forcing the Mexican troops to abandon their first line of defense. As night fell the Mexican commander opted to give up the fortress as indefensible. With Mexico's invincible Gibraltar abandoned, Veracruz seemed at the mercy of the French. As an incensed Mexican citizenry bemoaned incompetence and intimated treason, it was time for Santa Anna, temporarily out of the presidency, to exert himself once again. Proclaiming that God and justice were on the side of Mexico and that honor demanded he take up the challenge, he offered his services to the fatherland. They were accepted immediately as the Mexican Congress declared war on France.

Santa Anna arrived at Veracruz on December 4; the following morning some three thousand French troops made a landing. In the street fighting that ensued Santa Anna led his troops personally and drove the French back toward the coast. In one of the assaults the Mexican commander had his horse shot out from under him and, in the process, was severely wounded in the left leg. A few days later it was amputated below the knee. The French, however, had been driven back to their ships and, rather than prolong the venture, they agreed to accept the $600,000 as earlier offered by the Mexican government.

INCOME AND EXPENDITURES, 1839–46

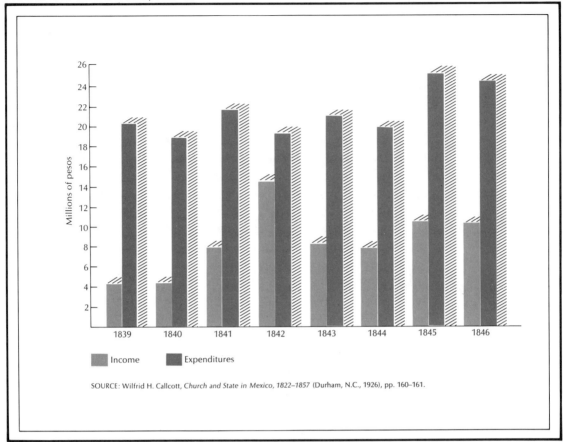

SOURCE: Wilfrid H. Callcott, *Church and State in Mexico, 1822–1857* (Durham, N.C., 1926), pp. 160–161.

The Mexicans could take some heart from having defeated the legions of King Louis Philippe, but there was little time for rejoicing. The liberal-conservative struggle continued unabated. Larger and larger armies (a standing army of ninety thousand by 1855) and a huge civilian bureaucracy drained the treasury, while industry and commerce stagnated. Successive governments tried every imaginable expedient to replenish the coffers. Old currencies were recalled and new ones issued; forced loans were made on businesses and on nunneries and other ecclesiastical corporations; voluntary loans were obtained from private money lenders called *agiotistas*; properties were confiscated; new taxes were levied on carriages, coach wheels, all internal trade, and even on dogs, pulque shops, and the gutters of houses; old taxes on real estate and imports were raised; lucrative mining concessions were sold to the British. In addition, the government declared a head tax of one and one-half pesos annually on all males between the ages of sixteen and sixty. But while Santa Anna raised more money than his predecessors, he also spent more. The average government deficit between 1839 and 1846 was 12.7 million pesos annually.

The Legacy of Santa Anna

Through it all Santa Anna somehow managed to keep Mexico afloat. As a military boss he managed at the same time to create a type of caudillo state that is almost unrivaled in the annals of nineteenth-century Latin American history. With contemptuous disregard of public opinion, his government reduced peculation to a veritable science. The protection racket became a government monopoly, and the dictator always collected his fair share. Fraudulent contracts and rebates were commonplace. Bribery was the calling card of those seeking concessions. Santa Anna quickly became a millionaire as he accumulated riches with the greed of poverty remembered. He bought new haciendas and charged high rents for grazing rights. His land holdings in 1845 totaled some 483,000 acres, and over forty thousand head of cattle bore the ALSA brand. Because those officials in the states and municipalities did not fail to profit from the lessons of their superiors in Mexico City, the graft and corruption soon penetrated all levels of government. Contraband was rampant and, indeed, was encouraged by venal port officials.

Even allowing for the exaggerations of his critics, one must conclude that Santa Anna's lust for power and quest for glory knew no bounds. Until the middle of the nineteenth century, Mexican presidents had been called simply "His Excellency." But because Santa Anna felt that too many reprobates had already held that title, he had his official designation changed to "His Most Serene Highness." He arranged for gala balls and banquets to be staged in his honor. When a sumptuous new theater was constructed in Mexico City at a cost of 350,000 pesos, it was named the Gran Teatro de Santa Anna. His busts and statues adorned public parks and streets. The presidential home in Tacubaya became a palace and, with its furniture, rugs, and tapestries newly imported from Europe and the Near East, it would have made even Iturbide comfortable.

Salvos of artillery fire and twenty-one-gun salutes preceded the dictator and announced his presence everywhere he went.

Congress declared that the small presidential bodyguard was insufficient for a man of his stature and authorized a new guard of twelve hundred men, styled the Lancers of the Supreme Power. Santa Anna's saint's day became a national holiday; while all private and public business came to a screeching halt, friends and favor seekers brought him gifts, totaling several tens of thousands of pesos on a good year. Favorite journalists grasped the occasions to lavish eulogistic editorials, while sycophants in the government delivered orations in honor of His Most Serene Highness. When Santa Anna made awards to others he signed them with an ostentatious display of titles. In 1853 one certificate of merit presented to José Angel Benavides was signed by "Santa Anna, Savior of the Fatherland, General of Division, Knight of the Great Cross of the Royal and Distinguished Spanish Order of Charles III, President of the Mexican Republic, Grand Master of the National and Distinguished Order of Guadalupe."[1]

But the most bizarre episode of all occurred in the fall of 1842. Santa Anna ordered the disinterment of his amputated leg from its quiet repose on his hacienda of Manga de Clavo. The mummified member was transported to Mexico City and, after an impressive procession through the streets of the capital in which the presidential bodyguard, the army, and the cadets from the Chapultepec Military Academy all participated, it was taken to the cemetery of Santa Fe where it was placed in a specially designed urn and set atop a huge stone pillar. The ceremony was typically Santanesque. Conducted at the site of the shrine, it was attended by the entire cabinet, the diplomatic corps, and the Congress. The speeches, songs, and poems offered in Santa Anna's honor paled all previous efforts at sanctification as the leg shattered by the French cannonball was now being offered to the fatherland.

The Santa Anna dictatorship exacted a heavy price. The only immutable law of the period was that the liberals and conservatives would never agree or compromise on matters of substance. A series of governments concerned more with show than with development, officials pilfering the treasury with impunity, political factions rife with internal dissension, an economy mired in its own inertia, all militated against progress. Time after time the country ignited in conflagration. Santa Anna himself must bear much of the responsibility. Often clever but never wise, he

1. Quoted in Oakah L. Jones, Jr., *Santa Anna* (New York, 1968), p. 125.

An 1845 lithograph depicting a one-legged Santa Anna standing on a Manga de Clavo built on extortions of various kinds.

set an example of dishonesty, deception, and complete failure to adhere to any set of principles. All of his loyalties were mercurial, and the tone he established for the age proved contagious. He was always able to muster sufficient military support to seize the moment but never sufficient political support to seize the hour. The intelligentsia cried out for constructive leadership but did not receive it. By the middle of the nineteenth century some of the obligations of Mexican nationhood had been defined, but precious few had been implemented. The political atmosphere was still charged with mistrust. Revolts and counterrevolts were accepted as inevitable concomitants of the social order. Some material improvements had been recorded, at least in the larger cities. The textile industry had developed rapidly during the 1840s and 1850s but the retrogressions in the political and economic orders were more noteworthy. Roads were in disrepair, mines were still abandoned, fertile agricultural fields lay vacant, industrialization was but a vague hope for the future, foreign trade was notable only for its absence, and the national debt was growing.

But by far the greatest misfortune of the age of Santa Anna has not yet been discussed. The loss of Texas and the war with the United States contributed more to Mexico's impoverishment, its apparent sterility, its xenophobia, its lack of self-esteem, and its general demoralization than any other event of the nineteenth century. These episodes warrant separate consideration.

Recommended for Further Study

Callcott, Wilfrid H. *Church and State in Mexico, 1822–1857.* Durham, N.C.: Duke University Press, 1926.

———. *Santa Anna: The Story of an Enigma Who Once Was Mexico.* Norman: University of Oklahoma Press, 1936.

Costeloe, Michael P. *Church and State in Independent Mexico: A Study of the Patronage Debate, 1821–1857.* London: Royal Historical Society, 1978.

———. "Federalism to Centralism in Mexico: The Conservative Case for Change, 1834–1835." *The Americas* 45 (1988): 173–86.

———. "The Triangular Revolt in Mexico and the Fall of Anastasio Bustamante, August–October, 1841." *Journal of Latin American Studies* 20 (1988): 337–60.

Gilmore, N. Ray. "The Condition of the Poor in Mexico, 1834." *Hispanic American Historical Review* 37 (1957): 213–26.

Harris, Charles H., III. *The Sánchez-Navarros: A Socio-Economic Study of a Coahuilan Latifundio, 1846–1853.* Chicago: Loyola University Press, 1964.

Jones, Oakah L., Jr. *Santa Anna.* New York: Twayne, 1968.

Lavrin, Asunción. "Mexican Nunneries from 1835 to 1860: Their Administrative Policies and Relations with the State." *The Americas* 28 (1972): 288–310.

Mayo, John. "Consuls and Silver Contraband on Mexico's West Coast in the Era of Santa Anna." *Journal of Latin American Studies* 19 (1987): 389–411.

Randall, Robert W. *Real del Monte: A British Mining Venture in Mexico.* Austin: University of Texas Press, 1972.

Robertson, William S. "French Intervention in Mexico in 1838." *Hispanic American Historical Review* 24 (1944): 222–52.

Samponaro, Frank N. "Santa Anna and the Abortive Anti-Federalist Revolt of 1833 in Mexico." *The Americas* 40 (1983): 95–108.

Sanders, Frank J. "José María Gutiérrez Estrada: Monarchist Pamphleteer." *The Americas* 27 (1970): 56–74.

Santa Anna, Antonio López de. *The Eagle: The Autobiography of Santa Anna.* Edited by Ann Fears Crawford, and translated by Sam Guyler and Jaime Platón. Austin: Pemberton Press, 1967.

Tenenbaum, Barbara. *The Politics of Penury: Debts and Taxes in Mexico, 1821–1856.* Albuquerque: University of New Mexico Press, 1986.

Walker, David W. "Business as Usual: The Empresa del Tabaco in Mexico, 1837–44." *Hispanic American Historical Review* 64 (1984): 707–36.

20

The Loss of Texas and the War with the United States

Discontent in Texas

Throughout the colonial period Texas was one of the northern provinces of New Spain. It was sparsely populated, and the Franciscan missionaries who penetrated the area found the Indian population intractable. At the beginning of the eighteenth century the Texas territory had fewer than three thousand sedentary colonists and, a hundred years later, only seven thousand. Because the Spanish crown wanted to populate and colonize the territory, in 1821, just prior to the winning of Mexican Independence, the commandant general in Monterrey granted Moses Austin, an American pioneer, permission to settle some three hundred Catholic families in Texas. Austin died and Mexico became independent before the project could be initiated, but Austin's son, Stephen F. Austin, took up the idea, had the concession confirmed by the new Mexican government, and began the colonization at once. Under the terms of the new concession Stephen Austin was authorized to bring in as many as three hundred families the first year provided that they were of good moral character, would profess the Roman Catholic religion, and agreed to abide by Mexican law. No maximum was set on future immigration into Texas, and, in fact, other concessionaires were awarded similar grants.

The influx of Americans into Texas was tremendous. The land was practically free—only ten cents an acre as opposed to $1.25 an acre for inferior land in the United States. Each male colonist over twenty-one years of age was allowed to purchase 640 acres for himself, 320 acres for his wife, 160 acres for each child and, significantly, an additional 80 acres for each slave that he brought with him. As a further enticement the colonists were given a seven-year exemption from the payment of Mexican taxes. By 1827 there were 12,000 United States citizens living in Texas, outnumbering the Mexican population by some 5,000. By 1835 the immigrant population had reached 30,000, while the Mexican population had barely passed 7,800.

The Mexican government originally believed that immigrants from the United States could be integrated into the Mexican community and passed a number of laws to foster this integration. In addition to the requirement that the colonists be Roman Catholic, all official transactions were to be concluded in the Spanish language, no foreigners would be allowed to settle within sixty miles of the national boundary, and foreigners who married Mexican citizens could be eligible for extra land. All governmental efforts to encourage peaceful integration failed, however, as tensions rose between the Mexicans, always more and more in the minority, and the immigrants. The colonists who came were not, by and large, Roman Catholics, although they knew how to make the proper declaration if asked. Very few bothered to learn Spanish. In addition, the political traditions of the two groups were far from kindred. Political, religious, and cultural conflict did not take long to surface.

One major grievance of the Texans was that the province was appended politically to the state of Coahuila, which had nine times its population. Although Texas was represented in the state legislature with one, then two, and finally three representatives (out of a total of twelve), they were easily outvoted by the Coahuilans on issues they considered crucial. In addition, all appellate courts were located far away in Saltillo, and the time and expense involved in carrying out an appeal completely discouraged the use of the judicial machinery.

But the Mexicans had serious grievances as well. A number of filibustering expeditions from the United States prompted genuine fear that the United States government was bent on securing the Texas territory for itself. The most serious of these forays saw James Long, a Tennesseean, invade Texas with a private army, capture Nacogdoches, declare Texas independent, name himself president, and affirm that Texas really belonged to the United States. Although Long's army was subsequently defeated by the Mexicans, clamor in the U.S. Congress and in the American press for changing the boundary or for acquiring much or all of

Texas through a new treaty or by stealth excited apprehensions in Mexico City.

As Mexican politicians began to realize that their problems in Texas were getting out of hand, they plotted a remedial course of action. The first important piece of legislation designed to prevent a further weakening of Mexican control was President Guerrero's emancipation proclamation of 1829. Because slavery was not important anywhere else in the republic, the measure was clearly directed at Texas. Although manumission was not immediately enforced, it was hoped that the decree itself would make Mexico less attractive to colonists from the U.S. South and would thus arrest future immigration. More important was the colonization law of April 6, 1830, which explicitly forbade all future immigration into Texas from the United States and called for the strengthening of Mexican garrisons, the improvement of economic ties between Texas and the remainder of Mexico by the establishment of a new coastal trade, and the encouragement of increased Mexican colonization. If the colonists already there could not be displaced, an intensive Mexican colonization could at least hope to re-establish the population balance.

None of the plans curtailed the growing antagonism between the two groups of colonists, for the Texans considered them not accommodative but sternly repressive. The last straw, as far as the Texans were concerned, was receipt of the news from Mexico City that Santa Anna had arbitrarily annulled the federal Constitution of 1824. The centralist tendencies of the new regime meant that, instead of having a greater voice in the management of local affairs, the Texans were to have no voice at all. As the Texas leaders began to debate their future course of action, they were urged to separate themselves not only by United States expansionists, who argued theatrically that the Texans should detach themselves from the yoke of dictatorship, but also by a number of Mexican liberals opposed to everything Santa Anna stood for. Among the latter, the most active was Lorenzo de Zavala, a leader of the Constitutional Congress of 1823–24, a founder of the York Rite lodges, and most recently a Mexican minister to France. When Santa Anna took all governmental powers into his own hands, Zavala advised the Texans that the dictator had forfeited all claims to obedience. The Texans needed little prompting, however; they had decided on independence and subsequently chose David Burnet as president of the Lone Star Republic and Zavala as vice-president.

The War for Texas Independence

It was time for Santa Anna to take the field again, and with no false modesty he later explained his decision in his memoirs.

> I, as chief executive of the government, zealous in the fulfillment of my duties to my country, declared that I would maintain the territorial integrity whatever the cost. This would make it necessary to initiate a tedious campaign under a capable leader immediately. . . . Stimulated by . . . courageous feelings I took command of the campaign myself, preferring the uncertainties of war to the easy and much coveted life of the palace.[1]

In the winter of 1835 Santa Anna moved north at the head of some six thousand troops. But because of innumerable difficulties during the long trek it was not until early March of 1836 that he reached the outskirts of San Antonio de Béxar (today San Antonio) and found that the Texans, under the command of William Barrett Travis, had taken refuge in the old Franciscan mission of the Alamo. Among them were such Texas luminaries as Davy Crockett and Jim Bowie. The essentials of what happened on March 6 are known to every schoolchild both north and south of the Rio Grande (called the Río Bravo in Mexico), though the distortions of nationalism have taken their toll on the history in both countries.

For several days prior to March 6, 1836, Santa Anna had laid siege to the Alamo. The high, stout walls seemed impregnable, and the defenders were not about to surrender to the greatly superior Mexican force. On the late afternoon of March 5 the Texans might have heard a bugle, but most assuredly they did not recognize the sounds coming over the walls as the *degüello*, a battle call used since the time of the Spanish wars against the Moors to signal that the engagement to follow was to be to the death, with no quarter to be shown the enemy. The order had come directly from Santa Anna, and he planned to enforce it.

The next morning the Mexican commander threw waves of soldiers against the adobe fortress. In the face of heavy artillery the Mexicans attacked bravely. Hundreds were cut down, but after the first hour the numerical superiority of the attackers began to tell. Several breaches were opened in the wall, and the fighting continued inside. The defenders also comported them-

---

1. Antonio López de Santa Anna, *The Eagle: The Autobiography of Santa Anna*, ed. Ann Fears Crawford, trans. Sam Guyler and Jaime Platón (Austin, 1967), pp. 49-50.

selves with great heroism. They were killed to the last man, including five who were executed as prisoners after the fighting had ended. The high toll on both sides did nothing to diminish resolve—to the contrary, it underscored that a peaceful settlement was impossible.

While the battle of the Alamo is famous in the military annals and folklore of the Texas Revolution, a much more significant episode took place several weeks later. General José Urrea engaged a force of Texans under the command of Colonel James W. Fannin at the small town of Goliad. Surrounded and outnumbered, Fannin surrendered in the belief that he and his men would be afforded the recognized rights of prisoners of war. Realizing that the tenor of the war had been set at the Alamo, General Urrea wrote to Santa Anna urging clemency for Fannin and the other prisoners. Urrea then moved on to another engagement and left the Texas prisoners in the charge of Lieutenant Colonel Nicolás de la Portilla. Using the national law of piracy as his authority, Santa Anna sent his reply to Portilla on March 23.

> I am informed that there have been sent to you by General Urrea, two hundred and thirty-four prisoners . . . as the supreme government has ordered that all foreigners taken with arms in their hands, making war upon the nation shall be treated as pirates, I have been surprised that the circular of the said supreme government has not been fully complied with in this particular. I therefore order, that you should give immediate effect to the said ordinance. . . . I trust that, in reply to this, you will inform me that public vengeance has been satisfied by the punishment of such detestable delinquents.[2]

Santa Anna had his figures slightly wrong. There were 365 prisoners. Nicolás de la Portilla found himself in the position of many a military commander from the Peloponnesian War to Vietnam. His military duty conflicted directly with his moral principles, but he was of insufficient moral fiber to reject the illegal order. In his diary he recorded his two terrible days.

> March 26. At seven in the evening I received orders from General Santa Anna by special messenger, instructing me to execute at once all prisoners taken by force of arms agreeable to the general orders on the subject. . . . At eight o'clock, on the same night, I received a communication from Gen. Urrea by special messenger in which among other things he says, "Treat the prisoners well,

2. Quoted in Wilfrid H. Callcott, *Santa Anna: The Story of an Enigma Who Once Was Mexico* (Norman, 1936), pp. 132–33.

especially Fannin." . . . What a cruel contrast in these opposite instructions! I spent a restless night.

March 27. At daybreak I decided to carry out the orders of the general-in-chief because I considered them superior. I assembled the whole garrison and ordered the prisoners, who were still sleeping, to be awakened. There were [365]. . . . The prisoners were divided into three groups and each was placed in charge of an adequate guard. . . . I gave instructions to these officers to carry out the orders of the supreme government and the general-in-chief. This was immediately done.[3]

The month following the battles of the Alamo and Goliad was one of reorganization for the Texas army. Although Santa Anna could take heart from the early military campaigns, and although he had Sam Houston and the Texans on the run, his victories proved to be costly ones. The excesses committed by his troops in both engagements, but especially the execution of the prisoners at Goliad, crystalized opposition to Mexico in the United States. Supplies and men began to pour into Texas, and by the third week in April Houston felt strong enough to make a stand. He chose his own ground and, in the middle of the afternoon on April 21, caught Santa Anna's troops off guard near the San Jacinto River. Within half an hour the Mexican army was routed, and Santa Anna himself fled for safety. Two days later he was captured by one of Houston's patrols.

The Lone Star Republic

As a prisoner Santa Anna signed two treaties, one public and one private, with Texas President David Burnet. In the public treaty he agreed that he would not again take up arms against the movement for Texas independence nor would he try to persuade his fellow Mexicans to do so. All hostilities between Mexico and Texas were to cease immediately, and the Mexican army would be withdrawn across the Rio Grande. Prisoners of war in equal numbers would be exchanged. From the Mexican point of view, the secret agreement, later made public, was much more controversial. In return for his own release and transportation to Veracruz, Santa Anna agreed to prepare the Mexican cabinet to receive a peace mission from Texas so that the independence of the Lone Star Republic could be formally recognized.

3. Quoted in Carlos E. Castañeda, ed. and trans., *The Mexican Side of the Texas Revolution* (Dallas, 1928), p. 236n.

Santa Anna as a prisoner of Sam Houston. The Mexican victory at the Alamo was offset by Santa Anna's defeat and capture following the battle of San Jacinto.

When he returned to Mexico, Santa Anna must have been shocked at the reactions his treaties had prompted. While the great masses were apathetic, the intellectual community, the liberals, and many ardent nationalists rejected them as the grossest blasphemy. His sensitivities dazed, Santa Anna was on the defensive, and from his seclusion at Manga de Clavo he offered the best excuses he could. He did nothing in the name of the nation, he argued. The promises he made as an individual, to secure his release, were not binding on the government. Where was the treason? he asked. The legislature responded by enacting a law stipulating that any agreement reached by a Mexican president while held prisoner should be considered null and void. No peace commission from Texas was to be received, and no recognition would be extended.

Texas remained independent as the Lone Star Republic from 1836 to 1845. On the surface it would appear preposterous that without the direct support of the United States, Texas should have been able to retain this independent status in face of greatly superior Mexican resources and manpower. But Mexico was so racked with internal convulsions during these nine years that it was unable to bring Texas back into the fold. The Texas issue, in fact, served to magnify political tensions in Mexico. The ultimate fate of Texas, however, would be decided not on the battlefields of northern Mexico but on the desk tops of Washington, D.C.

The United States recognized the independence of Texas in March of 1837. Although there was a good deal of sympathy for immediate annexation in both Texas and the United States Congress, calmer heads prevailed for eight years. Not only did many congressmen believe that annexation would provoke war with Mexico, but the matter became inexorably entangled in the slavery issue. If Texas entered the Union it would come in as a slave state, and, as a result, annexation was generally opposed by the North. In 1844, however, James K. Polk won the presidency on a platform that included annexation. After the election, but prior to Polk's inauguration, President John Tyler had an annexation measure introduced as a joint resolution of Congress. It passed both houses in early 1845. The stage was set for a major conflict, and Mexico was clearly being swept into the vortex of war.

The Prelude to War

As soon as the joint resolution annexing Texas passed the U.S. Congress, the Mexican minister in Washington lodged a formal protest and asked for his passport. Within a month his counterpart in Mexico City had received his passport as well. As diplomatic relations were ruptured, both countries began preparing for war. The Mexican government sought to negotiate a new loan, the proceeds of which would be directed into the war effort, if, indeed, the conflict occurred. It also authorized the formation of a new voluntary civilian militia to reinforce regular army units. President Polk ordered army troops into the border region and dispatched naval vessels to the Mexican coast. But, not particularly relishing the thought of being branded a warmonger, at the same time he made one belated effort to settle the dispute through negotiation. He asked the Mexican president, José Joaquín Herrera, to receive a special envoy in Mexico City, and Herrera agreed to receive John Slidell.

The specific issue Slidell was asked to negotiate was a boundary dispute in Texas. Throughout the entire colonial period the western boundary of Texas had been the Nueces River. When Moses Austin had received his grant to settle in Texas the western boundary of Texas was still the Nueces River; so, too, when Stephen Austin's contract was reaffirmed. But in spite of thousands of Spanish colonial documents, Mexican documents, and all reliable maps, in December of 1836 the Congress of the Republic of Texas claimed the Rio Grande as the western boundary. The Texans based their claim on two flimsy grounds. During the period of Texas colonization the Mexican government had allowed some United States immigrants to settle in the territory between the Nueces and the Rio Grande. It was all Mexico, so it really did not matter. Second, and even more important for the Texas argument, when Santa Anna agreed to withdraw his troops following his stunning defeat at San Jacinto, he ordered them back across the Rio Grande, tacit admission, so the Texans cried, that the western boundary was indeed the Rio Grande. At stake were not merely the 150 miles between the Nueces and the Rio Grande where they entered the Gulf of Mexico. The Rio Grande meandered aimlessly not north, but northwest, and the Texans claimed it to its source. Thousands and thousands of square miles of territory, indeed, half of New Mexico and Colorado, fell within the claim. When Texas entered the Union as the twenty-eighth state, the Polk administration decided to support the Texan pretensions. Albuquerque, Santa Fe, and Taos belonged to the United States as well as San Antonio, Nacogdoches, and Galveston.

But the American president wanted still more. Slidell also carried secret instructions to secure California and the rest of New Mexico. Five million dollars was deemed a fair price for the New Mexico territory and twenty-five million, or even more, for California. But diplomatic secrets had a way of leaking out, even in the middle of the nineteenth century. The Mexican press, learning the true nature of the Slidell mission, was understandably indignant. Appealing to Mexican nationalism, newspapers, circulars, and broadsides threatened rebellion if President Herrera negotiated with the ignominious Yankee pirates. The Herrera administration, like most of the caretaker governments during the age of Santa Anna, was not very secure, and the president promptly informed President Polk that he had nothing to discuss with John Slidell.

Not even in the face of a potentially calamitous war with the

U.S.-TEXAS BORDER DISPUTE

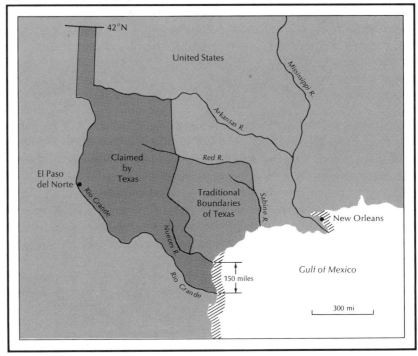

United States could the Mexicans lay aside their internal differences and present a united front. While Mexico's antagonist in the White House plotted his next course of action, General Mariano Paredes, dispatched north to reinforce Mexican troops along the border, decided to use his army on his own president instead. He overthrew the government and was himself installed in the highest office. What an inviting picture northern Mexico presented to the expansionists of the United States!

When Slidell returned to Washington, President Polk held a special cabinet meeting to weigh war feeling. Influential voices cautioned against precipitate action, but the president had already made up his mind. In his diary for May 9, 1846, he noted the following:

> I stated to the Cabinet that up to this time, as we knew, we had heard of no open act of aggression by the Mexican army, but that the danger was imminent that such acts would be committed. I said that in my opinion we had ample cause of war, and that it

was impossible that we could stand in *status quo,* or that I could remain silent much longer.[4]

Secretary of the Navy George Bancroft and Secretary of State James Buchanan would not vote for a declaration of war unless the United States was attacked by Mexico. By a strange quirk of history, hostilities began that very day. Polk had already ordered General Zachary Taylor into the disputed territory between the Nueces and the Rio Grande. The Mexican commander ordered him to withdraw, but instead Taylor penetrated all the way to the Rio Grande. While the cabinet was meeting, a skirmish broke out between Taylor's dragoons and General Mariano Arista's cavalry. On the evening of May 9 Taylor reported to Washington that sixteen of his men had been killed or wounded. Polk now had the perfect excuse. He went before the Congress and delivered a war message that bore little resemblance to the truth. The message was remarkable for its distortion and provocative to the absurd.

> We have tried every effort at reconciliation. The cup of forbearance had been exhausted even before the recent information from the frontier of the Del Norte. But now, after reiterated menaces, Mexico has passed the boundary of the United States, has invaded our territory, and shed American blood on American soil. She has proclaimed that hostilities exist, and that the two nations are now at war.[5]

With a provision limiting debate to two hours, the declaration of war was stampeded through Congress. How different things looked from Mexico City: not only had the Americans taken Texas, but they had changed the traditional boundary to double its size! When the Mexicans sought to defend themselves against the additional encroachment, the Yankees cried that Mexico had invaded the United States! But there was little time for contemplation of moral issues, and the Mexican nation was as divided as ever. President Paredes declared that the centralist Constitution was of no use, but years later Justo Sierra, Mexico's leading educator, philosopher, and historian of the late nineteenth century, noted wryly that "what was actually of no use was the army,

---

4. James K. Polk, *Polk: The Diary of a President, 1845–1849,* ed. Allan Nevins (New York, 1968), p. 81.
5. Quoted in Armin Rappaport, ed., *The War with Mexico: Why Did It Happen?* (New York, 1964), p. 6.

debased into an instrument of cynical ambitions."[6] Yet it was this army that would have to defend the nation against the invasion everyone knew was on its way. The army seemed less concerned with the war in the north than with politics in the south. It took out time to overthrow President Paredes and invite Santa Anna back from his most recent exile. The general who had fought the Spanish in 1829, the Texans in 1836, and the French in 1838 would lead his fellow countrymen against the Americans in 1846.

The Course of the War

Because President Polk, in spite of a good deal of opposition, was able to move more decisively than the ephemeral governments in Mexico City, Mexico from the outset was on the defensive. The American strategy called for a three-pronged offensive. The Army of the West would occupy New Mexico and California; the Army of the Center would be sent into northern Mexico; and the Army of Occupation would carry the battle to Mexico City. General Stephen W. Kearny, commanding the Army of the West, got under way first. Leaving Ft. Leavenworth, Kansas, with some fifteen hundred men in June of 1846, he began the nine-hundred-mile trek toward Santa Fe. Governor Manuel Armijo, not a favorite in the Mexican history textbooks, either accepted a bribe or was afraid to make a stand. He ordered his three thousand troops to evacuate the town shortly before the Americans arrived on August 19. New Mexico had fallen without the firing of a single shot.

Kearny then divided his Army of the West into three. One contingent, under Colonel Sterling Price, continued the occupation of Santa Fe; a second, under Alexander Doniphan, was dispatched directly south to Chihuahua; Kearny himself led the third west to California. California was almost a repeat of New Mexico. By the time Kearny arrived it was already in American hands, having fallen to Naval Commodore John D. Sloat and Colonel John C. Frémont with little opposition. Doniphan, on the other hand, had to engage the enemy in Chihuahua. The major battle, fought on the Sacramento River on the outskirts of Chihuahua City, was an artillery duel. The Mexican artillery pieces

6. Justo Sierra, *The Political Evolution of the Mexican People*, trans. Charles Ramsdell (Austin, 1969), p. 235.

UNITED STATES INVASION, 1846–48

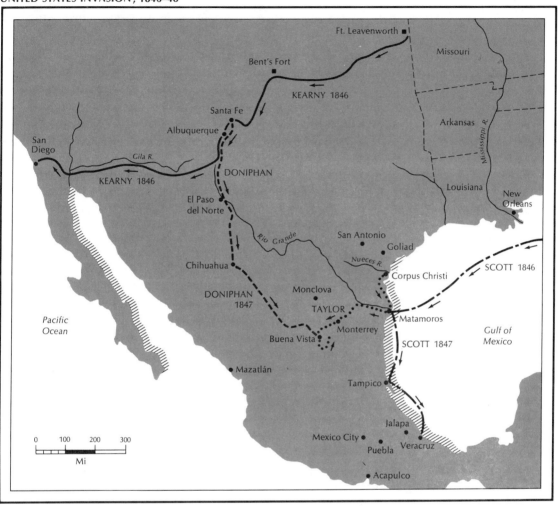

were grossly inadequate, and the supply of powder was not reliable either. Doniphan won the battle, and by February 1847 Chihuahua was under American control. Chihuahuenses were treated to the spectacle of American troops bathing in public fountains, cutting down boulevard shade trees for firewood, and singing "Yankee Doodle" in the Plaza de la Constitución.

The successes of Zachary Taylor's Army of the Center were not so easily won. Taylor's force, some six thousand strong, moved on Monterrey in August 1846. By September they were in sight of the city but were blocked off by the seven thousand Mexicans under General Pedro de Ampudia guarding the entrance. Three days of fierce battle were recorded in the middle of the month. Heavy losses were sustained on both sides before Ampudia sent up the white flag and surrendered the city. By this time Santa Anna had raised an army of about twenty thousand men and was training them in San Luis Potosí. The hard march to Saltillo was disastrous. Insufficient food and water supplies and an unusually harsh winter not only weakened the men but prompted thousands of desertions along the way. Preliminary fighting on February 21 saw Santa Anna force Taylor to pull in his perimeters. The following morning Santa Anna brazenly demanded that Taylor surrender. His messenger informed the American commander that twenty thousand seasoned troops (an exaggeration) were poised to cut his army to pieces. "Tell Santa Anna to go to Hell," Taylor barked to an aide, but the message actually sent observed proper military niceties and read, "In reply to your note of this date summoning me to surrender my forces at discretion, I beg leave to say that I decline acceding to your request."[7]

The battle of Buena Vista began in earnest later in the day. Santa Anna's assaults on Taylor's well-fortified positions did a good deal of damage, but all were repulsed. Evening found a stalemate. Santa Anna could have attacked again the following morning but instead decided to gather up a few war trophies— a few flags and three cannons—and carry them back to Mexico City as proof of his smashing victory. Northeast Mexico was lost to the invaders.

The major United States offensive, however, was waged by General Winfield Scott's Army of Occupation. Mexico's losses in the north and the constant bickering in the capital had not predisposed its leaders to abandon the fight. The United States therefore resolved to carry the battle to Mexico's heartland and to the capital itself. Making his amphibious landing on March 9, 1847, slightly to the south of the harbor of Veracruz, General Scott and his ten thousand men were not opposed as they established their beachhead. Veracruz, for centuries an object of foreign invasion and attack, was a walled city currently garrisoned by four thousand troops. The fortress of San Juan de Ulloa, in the harbor, held an additional twelve hundred. Unlike the French nine years earlier, Scott decided to avoid the fortress altogether. By ordering his troops to surround the city and attack from the rear, he not only neutralized the fortress but also cut off

7. Quoted in Charles L. Dufour, *The Mexican War: A Compact History* (New York, 1968), p. 172.

The U.S. Navy's bombardment of Veracruz resulted in extremely high civilian casualties.

the city's source of land supplies and all avenues of exit. Militarily sound, but morally questionable, the plan of attack called for a heavy mortar bombardment of the city; coincidentally it meant that hundreds of innocent civilians with no possibility of escape would be sacrificed to the apparent exigencies of war.

For the next forty-eight hours Scott devastated the city and refused all implorations of foreign consuls to allow women, children, and other noncombatants to evacuate. He would countenance no manner of truce not accompanied by unconditional surrender. Another day of intense fighting with heavy bombardment ensued.

With military and medical supplies diminished, hundreds of civilian corpses building up in the streets, fires gutting buildings, hospitals destroyed, and the frightening specter of a yellow-fever epidemic mounting, Veracruz surrendered on March 27. A total of sixty-seven hundred shells had been lobbed into the beleaguered city. The Eagle and Serpent came down the flagpole and the Stars and Stripes were hoisted up. Sixty-seven Americans had been killed or wounded, while the toll of Mexican dead within the city was between one thousand and fifteen hundred. Civilian casualties outnumbered military casualties almost two to one.

Santa Anna had reached Mexico City when news of the loss of
Veracruz arrived. He set out to block General Scott's expected
advance on the capital. The opposing forces met in the middle of
April at the mountain pass of Cerro Gordo, some twenty miles
east of Jalapa. Santa Anna had selected a seemingly excellent
position. He could command the entire road as the Americans approached. But Scott's reconnoitering scouts had noted the possibility of bypassing the entrenched Mexicans on the left flank.
While a small advance force feigned an attack along the road,
the bulk of the Americans skirted the left flank and attacked
from the rear. In the confusion that followed, the Mexican defenders broke and fled, and Santa Anna himself barely escaped
capture. He wanted to make one more stand, at Puebla, but the
citizenry there not only declined his offer of defense but informed him that they would not cooperate. Scott took the city
unopposed.

As Scott rested in Puebla the citizens of Mexico City began
bracing themselves for the imminent attack. The destruction of
Veracruz was well known, and apprehension set in. But not even
in the light of this crisis did the politicos in Mexico City join
forces. The war proved as divisive as the internal struggles that
had preceded it. The states would not provide money and men
for a national government they distrusted. The city council in
the capital originally pledged the support of all municipal employees in the work of constructing fortifications but then withdrew the pledge, arguing to the federal government that there
was no way to defend Mexico City. The government simply
placed the Federal District under martial law and began con-
scripting a civilian work force to help in the defense preparations. Santa Anna argued with his leading generals and with the
national Congress. He condemned the legislature for not giving
him the support he needed and they, in turn, chastised him for
his obvious failures on the military front.

As might be expected, the battles for control of Mexico City
were the most monumental of the war. The major preliminary
engagements were fought in the districts of Contreras and Churubusco on the outskirts, and in both cases the Americans proved
superior in leadership, armament, and tactics. At Churubusco,
however, the Mexicans had their finest hour. Fighting bravely,
they refused to yield ground to the larger and better-equipped
fighting force. The issue was finally resolved by intense hand-to-
hand combat in which the Mexicans were at last worn down.
On August 20, with the doors to the city ajar if not open, Scott

asked for a surrender. Santa Anna agreed to negotiate and used the respite to shore up his defenses within the city itself. When the armistice expired without positive result, Santa Anna was in a position to do battle again.

On the morning of September 7, Scott's cavalry charged Mexican positions at Molina del Rey, and the infantry moved in behind. It was the bloodiest single encounter of the war, as the Mexicans suffered over two thousand casualties and the Americans over seven hundred. When the position fell there was only one fortified position left in the city—Chapultepec Castle. Located at the crest of a two-hundred-foot hill and surrounded by a thick stone wall, the castle was defended by some one thousand troops and the cadets of the Military Academy. After a furious artillery barrage failed to dislodge the defenders, Scott ordered that the castle be stormed on the morning of September 13. The Mexican land mines failed to explode, and the attackers were able to breach the walls with pickaxes and crowbars. The scaling ladders arrived, and the Americans poured over the top and initiated the bitter hand-to-hand combat. Reputedly the last defenders were the cadets—the *Niños Héroes*—and many died rather than surrender. The battle of Chapultepec ended the war, and the United States government prepared to negotiate a tough peace.

The Treaty of Guadalupe Hidalgo and the Aftermath of War

After a series of difficult negotiations, the treaty ending the war was signed on February 2, 1848, at the village of Guadalupe Hidalgo, just outside of Mexico City. The treaty confirmed United States title to Texas and ceded the huge California and New Mexico territories as well. In return Mexico was to retain everything south of the Rio Grande. The United States agreed to make a cash payment of $15,000,000 to the Mexican government and to assume $3,250,000 in claims that United States citizens had against that government. For a total of $18,250,000—less than one year's budget—Mexico's territory was reduced by half.

When the United States signed the Treaty of Guadalupe Hidalgo it did more than annex half of Mexico. The war and its treaty left a legacy of hostility that would not be easily overcome. While many Mexican intellectuals had not been hesitant to praise the United States, its culture and institutions, prior to

1846, such commendations were increasingly infrequent in the second half of the nineteenth century. Mexicans had to be fatalistic about the year 1848, which Mexican positivist Justo Sierra lamented was proof of Darwin's theory of the survival of the fittest. From the middle of the sixteenth century, Mexican expeditions had been seeking the Gran Quivira in the north, and finally it was found, at Sutter's Fort, but a few months too late. The gold of California would not make Mexican fortunes or pay its share of Mexico's industrial revolution.

The war reinforced the worst stereotypes that each country held about the other, and these stereotypes in turn contributed to the development of deep-seated prejudices. United States historians rationalized, justified, and even commended the decision to wage the war as well as the prosecution of it. On grounds ranging from regenerating a backward people to fulfilling a preordained destiny, they went so far as to use this war of aggression for the purpose of instilling historical pride in generations of American children. Mexican historians, too, stereotyped and distorted. Not content with an understandably vigorous condemnation of the United States government, they pinned responsibility on the American people and the congenital defects of their Anglo-Saxon heritage.

It is almost axiomatic that wars nurture the development of xenophobia, especially on the part of the country that is dismembered. This particular war yielded its own particular variety—a virulent, almost pathological, Yankeephobia. The fears and hatred of the United States ran deep and were disseminated and popularized in the traditional Mexican *corrido*, the folk song of the common people. And the Yankeephobia was given additional respectability by the intellectual community's tirades against Yankee imperialism. But the war had at least one positive effect as well; it contributed to the development of a genuine nationalism in Mexico for the first time. This was a small consolation, perhaps, but not insignificant in a country still trying to become a nation. The Niños Héroes came to symbolize all that was best in the Mexican people, especially the young cadet Juan Escutia who reputedly wrapped himself in the Mexican flag and threw himself over the battlements rather than surrender to the enemy. Every September 13 pilgrimages are made to the monument erected in honor of the boy cadets at the entrance to Chapultepec Park.

The treaty signed at Guadalupe Hidalgo left a stunned and despondent Mexico, but the national humiliation brought no more unity than had the war itself. Local revolts kept the national government constantly on the defensive. Governors and presidents passed offices on to one another as though they were personal patrimony. In 1853 the Santanistas rallied for what turned out to be the last hurrah. With the $15 million from the United States already spent, President Santa Anna, not yet humbled by the defeats of his armies, decided that the treasury (and his own office) could be saved only by selling some more of Mexico to the United States. The United States wanted the Mesilla Valley (today southern New Mexico and Arizona) as it offered the best location for building a railroad to newly acquired California. Santa Anna agreed to sell and negotiated what is known in United States history as the Gadsden Purchase. For $10 million he alienated thirty thousand square miles of territory, but, more important, he alienated the liberal opposition so thoroughly that they would be rid of him for the eleventh and last time. The revolution the liberals proclaimed, the Revolution of Ayutla, was a new kind of movement, one in which for the first time ideology was clearly more important than personalities. It would usher in a new breed of Mexican politician who would try to set the country on a new course.

Recommended for Further Study

Bacarisse, Charles A. "The Union of Coahuila and Texas." *Southwestern Historical Quarterly* 61 (1958): 341–49.

Barker, Eugene C. *Mexico and Texas, 1821–1835.* Dallas: Turner, 1928.

Berge, Dennis E. "A Mexican Dilemma: The Mexico City Ayuntamiento and the Question of Loyalty, 1846–1848." *Hispanic American Historical Review* 50 (1970): 229–56.

Castañeda, Carlos E. "Relations of General Scott with Santa Anna." *Hispanic American Historical Review* 29 (1949): 455–73.

———, ed. and trans. *The Mexican Side of the Texas Revolution.* Dallas: Turner, 1928.

Costeloe, Michael P. "Church–State Financial Negotiations in Mexico during the American War, 1846–1847." *Revista de Historia de América* 60 (1965): 91–124.

Graebner, Norman A. "The Mexican War: A Study in Causation." *Pacific Historical Review* 49 (1980): 405–26.

Griswold del Castillo, Richard. "Mexican Views of 1848: The Treaty of Guadalupe Hidalgo Through Mexican History." *Journal of Borderlands Studies* 1 (1986): 24–40.

Hale, Charles A. "The War with the United States and the Crisis in Mexican Thought." *The Americas* 14 (1957): 153–73.

Hutchinson, C. Alan. "Valentín Gómez Farías and the Movement for the Return of General Santa Anna to Mexico in 1846." In *Essays in Mexican History*, edited by Thomas E. Cotner and Carlos E. Castañeda, pp. 169–91. Austin: Institute of Latin American Studies, 1958.

Jones, Oakah L., Jr. *Santa Anna*. New York: Twayne, 1968.

McWhiney, Grady, and Sue McWhiney, eds. *To Mexico with Taylor and Scott, 1845–1847*. Waltham, Mass.: Blaisdell, 1969.

Miller, Howard. "Stephen F. Austin and the Anglo-Texan Response to the Religious Establishment in Mexico, 1821–1836." *Southwestern Historical Quarterly* 91 (1988): 283–316.

Pletcher, David M. *The Diplomacy of Annexation: Texas, Oregon and the Mexican War*. Columbia: University of Missouri Press, 1973.

Polk, James K. *Polk: The Diary of a President, 1845–1849*. Edited by Allan Nevins. New York: Capricorn Books, 1968.

Richmond, Douglas, ed. *Essays on the Mexican War*. College Station: Texas A & M University Press, 1986.

Rives, George L. *The United States and Mexico, 1821–1848: A History of the Relations between the Two Countries from the Independence of Texas to the Close of the War with the United States*. 2 vols. New York: Scribner, 1913.

Robinson, Cecil, ed. *The View from Chapultepec: Mexican Writers on the Mexican-American War*. Tucson: University of Arizona Press, 1979.

Ruiz, Ramón Eduardo, ed. *The Mexican War: Was It Manifest Destiny?* New York: Holt, Rinehart and Winston, 1963.

Santa Anna, Antonio López de. *The Eagle: The Autobiography of Santa Anna*. Edited by Ann Fears Crawford, and translated by Sam Guyler and Jaime Platón. Austin: Pemberton Press, 1967.

Santoni, Pedro. "A Fear of the People: The Civic Militia of Mexico in 1845." *Hispanic American Historical Review* 68 (1988): 269–88.

Singletary, Otis. *The Mexican War*. Chicago: University of Chicago Press, 1960.

Smith, George W., and Charles Judah, eds. *Chronicles of the Gringos: The U.S. Army in the Mexican War, 1846–1848*. Albuquerque: University of New Mexico Press, 1968.

Smith, Justin H. *The War with Mexico*. 2 vols. Gloucester, Mass.: Peter Smith, 1963.

Tyler, Daniel. "Gringo Views of Governor Manuel Armijo." *New Mexico Historical Review* 45 (1970): 23–36.

Tyler, Ronnie C. "The Mexican War: A Lithographic Record." *Southwestern Historical Quarterly* 77 (1973): 85–110.

Vásquez, Josefina. "The Texas Question in Mexican Politics, 1836–1845." *Southwestern Historical Quarterly* 89 (1986): 309–44.

21

Society and Culture in the First Half of the Nineteenth Century

It is ironic, yet understandable, that historians seeking to understand how a people lived often rely upon the accounts of foreign travelers. That which is commonplace to a local inhabitant is often colorful or unique to a foreigner. The young Frenchman Alexis de Tocqueville related to the citizens of the United States much that they did not know about themselves, and a series of perceptive visitors to Mexico during the first half of the nineteenth century did the same for its people. While their analyses often reflected their own prejudices, their commentaries are invaluable. One has only to disregard their chauvinism and naïvely antiseptic view of the world to read these accounts with pleasure and profit.

Population

The Mexican Wars for Independence, although small in comparison with other world conflicts, nevertheless took their toll. Accurate casualty figures do not exist, but reliable estimates suggest that a half a million deaths, or about one-twelfth of Mexico's population, is not an exaggeration. The battles left tens of thousands of orphans, widows, cripples, and infirm. The dislocations occasioned by war were not quickly overcome. Impending engagements caused civilians to flee, shopkeepers to close their doors, mothers to pull their children out of school, and those who could afford it to hoard supplies. Many who left a town or city did not return, and families were permanently separated. Sev-

MEXICAN POPULATION GROWTH, 1800–50

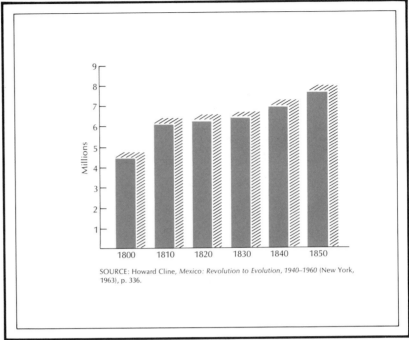

SOURCE: Howard Cline, *Mexico: Revolution to Evolution, 1940–1960* (New York, 1963), p. 336.

eral years after the wars ended visitors to Veracruz reported desolate, grass-grown streets and a generally ruinous appearance. Mexico's rate of population growth, which was rapid prior to 1810, leveled off dramatically for the next twenty years.

Although recovery was slow, change in the prevailing social structure was even slower. As one reads the accounts of travelers from the late colonial period and compares them to accounts in the nineteenth century, he is struck by how little conditions actually changed. To be sure, the gachupines were eliminated at the top of the social structure, but the criollos simply stepped into the vacuum. The population grew from 4.5 million in 1800 to over 7.5 million fifty years later, but the social categories of that population remained amazingly static.

Indian Pueblos

Mexico was a rural country in the first half of the nineteenth century. The Indians, making up over a third of the population, lived for the most part in thousands of tiny villages, socially and economically isolated from the remainder of the country. Although these pueblos varied physically from one climate to another, they presented a uniform cultural pattern. Pueblos were the most tradition-bound unit in Mexican society. Each maintained a system of internal government that had changed very little since the early colonial period. With the exception of an occasional parish priest, a white or mestizo rarely lived in the village. In south and central Mexico the huts were made of split reeds covered with thatched roofs. In the north adobe was more common, but in both cases dogs, pigs, and chickens shared the quarters with the family. In 1850 Carl Sartorius, a German natural scientist traveling in Mexico, drew a composite interior from the many Indian dwellings he had seen.

> Inside the hut, upon a floor of earth just as nature formed it, burns day and night the sacred fire of the domestic hearth. Near it, stands the *metate* and *metapile*, a flat and cylindrical stone for crushing the maize, and the earthen pots and dishes, a large water pitcher, a drinking cup and a dipper of gourdshell constitute the whole wealth of the Indian's cottage, a few rude carvings, representing the saints, the decoration. Neither table nor benches cumber the room within, mats of rushes or palm leaves answer for both seat and table. They serve as beds too for their rest at night, and for their final rest in the grave.[1]

Only the larger Indian towns had churches; practically none had schools. Spanish was unknown except to the select few. Medical care, as it existed, was entrusted to the questionable hands of the local *curandero*. The Indian agriculturalist lived outside the monetary economy. His own garden provided his daily needs—corn, beans, chile, and, occasionally, in some areas, squash and a few other vegetables and fruits. The craftsman sometimes had money pass through his hands as he could sell his wares at a neighboring market. But he was scarcely better off than the farmer in the next hut because, if his money did not vanish in momentary extravagance, he was easy prey to the unscrupulous gambler, pulque vendor, or highwayman as he returned to the pueblo.

The woman in the Indian village was much more than a housekeeper. Even when kept pregnant, she often worked in the field and shared in the physical labor as well as performed all the expected domestic functions. Foreign travelers frequently commented on the heavy loads of firewood the Indian women

1. Carl Sartorius, *Mexico about 1850* (Stuttgart, 1961), p. 69.

carried to the hut. Because daily life was difficult, the Indian woman was an integral part of the whole apparatus of survival; nevertheless, rural society was highly patriarchal and the male was the dominant, authoritarian figure in the household as well as in the community. The woman by tradition was expected to be faithful, reverential, and completely obedient in the entire conjugal relationship, and she seldom broke out of this mold, at least in public. She enjoyed a reputation of frugality and from the village tradition, for practical as well as metaphorical considerations, a phrase was born: *Donde las mujeres comen, las hormigas lloran* (Where women eat, the ants cry).

Rural Towns

The larger rural towns of from a thousand to perhaps thirty-five hundred housed primarily mestizos and Indians who had accommodated themselves to the Hispanic way of life. Spanish was the language of the street and the home. Market day, sometimes weekly and sometimes biweekly, attracted Indians by the hundreds from the surrounding pueblos and provided a festive air. The plaza would be filled with vendors trafficking in cloth, clothing, pottery, cutlery, trinkets, earthenware, and blankets, and with Indian women bent over charcoal fires preparing food for passersby. The day's work finished, the evening hours would be given over to gambling, cards, dancing, and perhaps wagering at the local cockfight. The towns generally had one or two *pulquerías* where hours could be idled away sipping the fermented juice of the century plant, the maguey. For those who found the local shop too depressing or the stench too unbearable, itinerant vendors with full jars on their heads made house calls. Invariably, the church was the most prominent architectural structure in the town. Adorned with a respectable number of saints and a few paintings, the gilded altar stood out in crass contrast to the impoverished surroundings.

If life in the rural towns was somewhat easier than in the Indian pueblo, it still left much to be desired. The streets were dirt, causing dust in the dry season and awful quagmires during the rains. The schools, in those few towns that had them, were equipped with the crudest of facilities, and the teachers were often only slightly more literate than those who sat at their feet. The one-story houses were constructed of adobe or stone and usually left unpainted. Travelers found no hotels, inns, or public

The village of Chalco, southeast of Mexico City, looked much as it had during the colonial period until the railroad passed through during the second half of the nineteenth century.

restaurants; they were generally put up for the night in the town hall or in the house of a relatively affluent resident who took pity on them. Joel Poinsett, a man who enjoyed his comforts, was not impressed with the facilities he found in a small Veracruz town as he was working his way to Mexico City in 1822.

> We supped on our cold provisions, and stretched ourselves out on the landlady's bed, which did not prove a bed of rest. It consisted only of canes laid lengthways, and covered with a blanket. This, and even the smell of raw meat, might have been endured, but we were visited by such swarms of fleas, sancudos, and musquitos [*sic*] that we rejoiced when we saw the light of day beaming through the cane enclosure that constituted the walls of the hut.[2]

The poor males in the towns had one concern that did not trouble those in the Indian village: like their counterparts in the larger cities, they were subject to the dreaded *leva*. A system of forced conscription directed at the uneducated masses (the Indi-

2. Joel R. Poinsett, *Notes on Mexico Made in the Autumn of 1822, Accompanied by an Historical Sketch of the Revolution* (New York, 1969), pp. 23–24.

ans in the villages were generally excluded simply because they did not speak Spanish), the leva was used by local commanders to fill their military quotas. Troublemakers, vagabonds, and prisoners were taken first, but as the demands of the Wars for Independence, and then the civil wars, continued in the first half of the nineteenth century, tens of thousands of illiterate males were picked up off the streets and pressed into long periods of service without even being allowed to return home to say good-by to wives, children, and parents.

Both in the Indian village and the small rural town there was little conception of the larger Mexico. Those loyalties that existed were to the locality—to the patria chica. Contact with the outside world was limited to the occasional traveler passing through or to a body of soldiers on horseback. Mexico was an abstraction not easily fathomed, and even neighbors in the next village were not really trusted.

Provincial Cities

One had to visit the larger provincial cities, generally the state capitals, to find any evidence whatsoever of culture, wealth, and sense of nationalism. Ranging in population from seven or eight thousand to seventy-one thousand (Puebla in 1852), these cities were well laid out in the classic Spanish pattern. The main streets, paved and well lighted, led into the central plaza surrounded on four sides by the main cathedral, the state or municipal office buildings, and several rows of good shops, generally under a stone arcade. In addition to an impressive selection of native products from many parts of the country, the shops also stocked foreign merchandise; the sizable merchant class thrived. The dreary, repetitive life of the smaller towns was averted by a bullring, a theater, traveling sideshows with tightrope walkers and jugglers, decent book stores, and a wide array of public and religious festivals. Unlike in the pueblo or the rural town, many criollo faces could be picked out of the crowd, and, in fact, if one wandered from the grisly slums to the better residential areas, the complexions of the property owners lightened appreciably. A few provincial aristocrats led lives of primitive plenty, but they were exceptions even among the criollo population. The schools were not bad, but they were only for the wealthy. In 1842, for example, there were only about thirteen hundred

A nineteenth-century woodcut depicting the central plaza of Mérida, Yucatán, about 1850.

schools in all of Mexico. Total enrollment was barely sixty thousand, or less than 1 percent of the population. Only about one-third of the schools were free.

Most of the state capitals grew rapidly in the first half of the nineteenth century. Aguascalientes doubled in population, and Mérida tripled. Veracruz and Guanajuato were almost alone in declining, the former because of constant warfare and heavy bombardments from naval vessels in the harbor and troops on the shore, and the latter because of the generally depressed character of the surrounding mines. By mid-century Puebla and Guadalajara were competing for second place on the nation's population rosters, with Puebla holding a slight lead.

Mexico City: The Rich and the Poor

Mexico City was a world unto itself, where all of the richest and many of the poorest in the country seemed to congregate. It was the focal point of the entire nation and exerted an influence on the country quite out of proportion to its size or its political

POPULATION OF SELECTED CITIES, 1794–1859

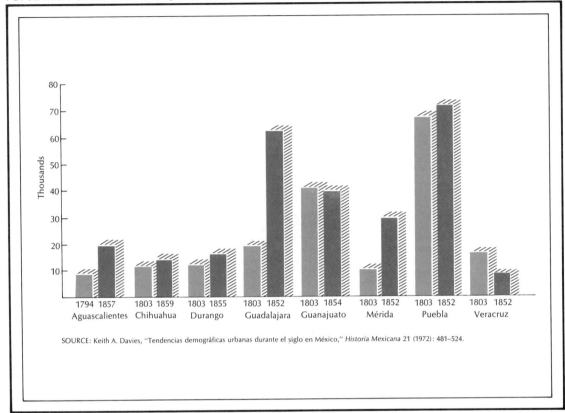

SOURCE: Keith A. Davies, "Tendencias demográficas urbanas durante el siglo en México," *Historia Mexicana* 21 (1972): 481–524.

prominence as the national capital. From a population of 137,000 at the turn of the century, it grew to 160,000 at the time of Independence and to 170,000 by 1852. Its wide, clean streets (better lighted than those in New York or Philadelphia) were crowded with expensive imported carriages, a status symbol among the rich. The main cathedral on the central plaza, the zócalo, could certainly rival any in Europe. The very bustle of the city set it apart from any other place in the republic. Street urchins hawked newspapers and pamphlets, scribes sitting on the sidewalks penned out messages for the illiterate, gentlemen on horseback paraded their finest mounts, and foreign artists gathered on park benches to sketch Chapultepec Castle or the snow-covered volcanoes of Popocatépetl and Iztaccíhuatl. In addition to numerous primary and secondary schools (again reserved largely for the affluent), Mexico City housed the venerable University, a school of mines, the Art Academy of San Carlos, a well-endowed botani-

cal garden, libraries, museums, and a surprising number of public parks. By the middle of the century a thriving opera was an
integral part of the city's cultural life. The literacy rate, for both
men and women, rose modestly during the first half of the nineteenth century.

The Mexico City aristocracy, like their counterparts throughout the world, enjoyed their amenities and were conspicuous in
their display of wealth. Many of the homes were truly luxurious.
For security and privacy they were generally enclosed by high
walls. Interior walls boasted fine imported tapestries. Aristocratic
women, whether attending the theater, the opera, or even a high
mass, displayed the immodest clothes designed by their favorite
French *modiste*, and the men, while not outdoing their wives in
fanciful dress, prided themselves on their ability to duplicate the
latest fashions from Paris or London. The accumulation of wealth
was greatly facilitated by the consistent intermarriage of *la gente
decente*.

Describing a ball she attended in 1840, the wife of the Spanish
minister to Mexico City noted the female costume.

> One, for example, would have a scarlet satin petticoat, and over
> it a pink satin robe, trimmed with scarlet ribbons to match. An-
> other, a short rich blue satin dress, beneath which appeared a
> handsome purple satin petticoat. . . . All had diamonds and

The urban aristocracy, secular and religious, looked good and lived well in
spite of the political chaos that engulfed Mexico in the twenty-five years
following Independence.

pearls . . . I did not see one without earrings, necklace, and broach.[3]

The poorest of the poor Indian population was concentrated in the Mexico City districts of Santiago Tlatelolco and San Juan Teochtitlán, but they spilled over into other areas of the capital. When the upper class filed out of the theater or left the opera they could not fail to see the *léperos*. Described variously in the literature as beggars, vagabonds, panhandlers, riffraff, and outcasts, thousands of them could be seen in the streets of Mexico City every day. Although there were undoubtedly some fakers and reprobates among them, most were genuinely wretched physical specimens: children with bloated bellies, men and women crippled by war or accident or suffering serious genetic deformities, and those of all ages and both sexes in constant drunken stupors. Not unknown in the colonial period, the léperos became institutionally endemic in the first half of the nineteenth century. No foreign traveler to Mexico City failed to notice them. In 1822, for example, Joel Poinsett recorded:

> In front of the churches and in the neighborhood of them we saw an unusual number of beggars, and they openly exposed their disgusting sores and deformities to excite our compassion. I observed one among them wrapped in a large white sheet, who, as soon as he perceived that he had attracted my attention, advanced towards me, and unfolding his covering, disclosed his person perfectly naked and covered from head to heel with ulcers. . . . No city in Italy contains so many miserable beggars, and no town in the world so many blind.[4]

Life for the urban poor who worked rather than begged offered few material rewards. Domestic service, though remuneration was small, was highly sought by both sexes because it generally offered a clean room in which to sleep and food enough to sustain one well. In the streets the most visible employee was the *cargador*, a direct descendant of the tameme of the colonial period and nothing more than a human beast of burden. In the cities, and between the cities, the sight described by Edward Tayloe, Joel Poinsett's private secretary, was common.

> There are no carts or drays for the transportation of goods, so that everything is carried upon the backs of these poor creatures, who are enabled to carry a load of 300 lbs. by means of a leather band

3. Fanny Calderón de la Barca, *Life in Mexico: The Letters of Fanny Calderón de la Barca*, ed. Howard T. Fisher and Marion Hall Fisher (Garden City, N.Y., 1970), pp. 132–33.
4. Poinsett, *Notes on Mexico*, p. 73.

The cargadores, a legacy of the colonial tamemes, carried everything on their backs.

or strap, the cargador leaning forward at an angle of about 45°, the burden resting on the back supported by this strap. With so heavy a load they travel great distances, moving in a brisk walk or trot.[5]

But the cargador carrying supplies into the city or delivering on his back an imported French piano had little to complain about in comparison to his counterpart who was taken from the city to work in the mines. Employed to bring the ore out of the deep shafts and paid by the pound, the cargadores often carried extremely heavy loads on their backs as they worked their way up ladders. Accidents were frequent; the widows might sometimes be given a small share of the last load.

The Indians and mestizos, whether they lived in a small village or in Mexico City, constituted Mexico's labor force: farmers, servants, day laborers, cargadores, vendors, military recruits, craftsmen, and errand boys. Women worked as domestic servants, spinners in the textile mills, food preparers, waitresses, and as vendors on the streets and in the marketplaces. And much as in the colonial period, the labor force enjoyed no real rights that the white population felt obliged to respect. If accused of a crime, the word of the employer was generally taken and the worker had no recourse. Held in filthy prisons, often without

5. Edward Thornton Tayloe, *Mexico, 1825–1828: The Journal and Correspondence of Edward Thornton Tayloe*, ed. C. Harvey Gardiner (Chapel Hill, 1959), pp. 50–51.

formal charges, the father who stole a loaf of bread was confined in the same common cell with the convicted murderer, the young boy with the hardened criminal, and the pregnant prostitute with the mentally insane. If Mexican politicians in the first half of the nineteenth century did little to change the fabric of society, if they were strangers in their own land, it was not because the intelligentsia failed to urge a new course of action. And it was this very talented group of Mexican writers, musicians, artists, and scholars that made Mexico City so different from the remainder of the republic.

Intellectuals and Artists

The prime literary current in Mexico, as in all of Latin America, in the period following Independence was romanticism. Intensely concerned with freedom and individualism, the Mexican romantics, in both prose and poetry, set out to explore the meaning of their newly won independence and to foster a distinctive culture. They turned their backs on Spain and sought to define a new form of national artistic expression. But to understand and convey the nascent nationalism they had to understand their Mexico, and thus they began writing with great emotion and sentimentality about the aboriginal heritage, the physical environment, the wars of Conquest, and, of course, the recent movement for Independence.

In 1836 the young novelists, poets, and dramatists began meeting in the newly formed Academia de San Juan de Letrán, and for the next twenty years the academy midwifed the birth of Mexican national literature. Of the early romantic coterie who met there regularly, only two left indelible impressions on the romantic movement itself: Fernando Calderón (1809–49) and Ignacio Rodríguez Galván (1816–42). Calderón, a sometime soldier and liberal politician, experimented with lyric poetry, then turned to drama, both comedy and tragedy. His amusing satirical plays, some with veiled criticism of the Santa Anna dictatorship, were performed on the leading stages of Mexico in the 1840s and 1850s and earned him his place among Latin American romantic dramatists. Rodríguez Galván was a better poet than Calderón but less successful as a dramatist. Self-taught and constantly poverty stricken, he penned patriotic verse and described the Mexican landscape, but, most important, lamented the Spanish injustices against the Indian populations. In the process he won his position as Mexico's foremost lyrical poet of the first half of the nineteenth century. His *Profecía de Guatimoc* (1839) has been called the masterpiece of Mexican romanticism. The passion, the sentimentality, and the anti-Spanish, pro-Indian orientation are exemplified in the following verse:

> Nada perdona el bárbaro europeo.
> Todo lo rompe, y tala, y aniquila
> Con brazo furibundo.
> Es su placer en fúnebres desiertos
> La ciudades trocar (¡Hazaña honrosa!).
> Ve el sueño con desdén, si no reposa
> Sobre insepultos muertos.[6]

Mexican music, like its literature, rejected its Spanish parentage in the early post-Independence years. Nowhere is this more graphically illustrated than in the decision of José Mariano Elízaga (1786–1842), Mexico' most famous composer of the second quarter of the nineteenth century, to drop the title "Don" (signifying the Spanish gentleman) from his name. Once the Spanish army was driven back across the Atlantic, the composer informed the Mexican populace that henceforth he preferred to be called simply Citizen Elízaga.

By sheer chance Elízaga, during the Wars for Independence, was the piano tutor to Anna María Huarte, who subsequently married Agustín de Iturbide. With the defeat of the Spanish and the establishment of the empire, Iturbide brought him to Mexico City and underwrote the preparation of Elízaga's theoretical treatise, *Elementos de música*. But Elízaga is remembered less as a musical theoretician than for his original compositions and great organizing skills. His compositions were all designed for use in the churches, but the liturgy was much too radical for the conservative, Spanish-thinking hierarchy. As a result his masses and lamentations were never performed within the walls of the church. But Citizen Elízaga did encounter success in an important ancillary venture. In 1824 he founded Mexico's first philharmonic society, and the following year this group initiated

6.   The barbarous European forgives nothing.
    He breaks and he destroys and he annihilates
    With a frenzied aim.
      He takes pleasure in converting cities
    Into desert wastes (Honorable, indeed!).
    He views sleep with contempt if he cannot rest
    On unburied bodies.
    Quoted in John Lloyd Read, *The Mexican Historical Novel, 1826–1910* (New York, 1939), p. 59.

Mexico's first national conservatory, the Academia de Música.

The Mexican artistic community strove for a type of new nationalistic expression as well. Scarcely had the new republican government of Guadalupe Victoria been established when Pedro Patiño Ixtolinque, the general director of the Art Academy of San Carlos and Mexico's most famous sculptor, set to work on a monument honoring Father Morelos. An early American visitor to the academy was impressed with its facilities but, displaying a common anti-Catholic bias, also found fault: "Connected with this academy is a disgusting sort of work shop, where gods and saints are manufactured in wood and stone for the churches in town and country."[7]

Both in painting and the plastic arts the rejection of Spain and many things Spanish was abundantly evident, much more in the choice of theme, however, than in esthetic innovation. If the emulation of Spanish technique bordered on the abject, the selection of subject matter showed the budding of a Mexican consciousness. Although the young republic housed a few artists of unusual talent, the three decades following Independence were not particularly distinguished years for Mexican art. Within the century, however, the experimentation with native Mexican themes would pay dividends.

Of all the great Mexican historians of the post-Independence years only one—Lucas Alamán (1792–1853)—did not allow an anti-Spanish bias to vitiate his historical scholarship, but he was no less partisan than his ideological foes. A criollo aristocrat, a convinced monarchist, and a firsthand witness to the excesses committed by Hidalgo's Indian army in Guanajuato, he came to the defense of the Spanish officials and, by logical extension, of the Spanish crown. His five-volume *Historia de México* (1849–52) indicates clearly that he considered Cortés the conveyer of civilization and religion and the founder of the Mexican nation. Spain's imperial system in the New World was benevolent and progressive. The Wars for Independence, according to Alamán, had to be viewed in two stages. The early stage, that of Father Hidalgo, he censured as insane attack on property and civilization itself. But the conservative conclusion of the Independence movement by Iturbide could be rationalized. The mother country, defying all true Hispanic values, had turned disturbingly liberal with King Ferdinand's acceptance of the Constitution of 1812. The leadership of the Independence movement in the colo-

7. Tayloe, *Mexico, 1825–1828*, p. 58.

nies was actually defending traditionally Hispanic values but had to sever political ties to do so.

But Lucas Alamán stands almost alone in the historiography of the 1830s and 1840s. His contemporaries, Carlos María de Bustamante, Lorenzo de Zavala, and José María Luis Mora, viewed history quite differently. While they could not agree among themselves on many of the intricacies of the Wars for Independence, they all viewed the movement as a struggle against three centuries of Spanish tyranny. The Black Legend, stressing the avarice, inhumanity, and bigotry of the Spaniards, is not difficult to spot. The Independence movement was a repudiation of Spain, and the three histories mirroring this repudiation contributed in their own way to the cultural disavowal of the Hispanic part of the Mexican spirit. This pervasive anti-Hispanism was strongly reinforced by Spain's attempted reconquest in 1829.

The greatest weakness of Mexico's post-Independence culture was its essentially negative quality. The new nationalism was defined primarily in terms of what it was not—it was not Spanish. Mexico, the linguistic purist insisted, should be written not with the Spanish *j* but with an *x*, considered more Indian. The cultural nationalism expressed dissatisfaction with the past and, by extension, with much of the present but did not spell out precisely the direction in which Mexico ought to move. It was sufficient for the time being to propose that an anti-Hispanic intellectual emancipation should follow the political emancipation begun by Hidalgo. The more positive approach in defining the cultural essence of the new nationality would have to wait another generation of Mexican intellectuals and artists.

Recommended for Further Study

Arrom, Silvia Marina. *The Women of Mexico City*. Stanford, Calif.: Stanford University Press, 1985.

Brushwood, John S. *Mexico in Its Novel: A Nation's Search for Identity*. Austin: University of Texas Press, 1966.

Calderón de la Barca, Fanny. *Life in Mexico: The Letters of Fanny Calderón de la Barca*. Edited by Howard T. Fisher and Marion Hall Fisher. Garden City, N.Y.: Doubleday, 1970.

Caponigri, A. Robert, trans. *Major Trends in Mexican Philosophy*. Notre Dame, Ind.: University of Notre Dame Press, 1966.

Fernández, Justino. *Mexican Art*. London: Spring Books, 1965.

Ferry, Gabriel. *Vagabond Life in Mexico*. New York: Harper and Brothers, 1856.

Gilmore, N. Ray. "The Condition of the Poor in Mexico, 1834." *Hispanic American Historical Review* 37 (1957): 213–26.

Green, Stanley C. *The Mexican Republic: The First Decade, 1823–1832*. Pittsburgh: University of Pittsburgh Press, 1987.

Hale, Charles A. *Mexican Liberalism in the Age of Mora, 1821–1853*. New Haven, Conn.: Yale University Press, 1968.

Lyon, G. F. *Journal of a Residence and Tour in the Republic of Mexico in the Year 1826*. 2 vols. Port Washington, N.Y.: Kennikat Press, 1971.

Poinsett, Joel R. *Notes on Mexico Made in the Autumn of 1822, Accompanied by an Historical Sketch of the Revolution*. New York: Praeger, 1969.

Rosaldo, Renato. "The Legacy of Literature and Art." In *Six Faces of Mexico*, edited by Russell C. Ewing, pp. 245–310. Tucson: University of Arizona Press, 1966.

Sartorius, Carl. *Mexico about 1850*. Stuttgart: F. A. Brockhaus Komm, 1961.

Shaw, Frederick J. "The Artisan in Mexico City (1824–1853)." In *Labor and Laborers through Mexican History*, edited by Elsa Cecilia Frost, Michael C. Meyer, and Josefina Zoraida Vásquez, pp. 399–418. Mexico City and Tucson: El Colegio de México and University of Arizona Press, 1979.

Stevenson, Robert. *Music in Mexico: A Historical Survey*. New York: Crowell, 1971.

Tayloe, Edward Thornton. *Mexico, 1825–1828: The Journal and Correspondence of Edward Thornton Tayloe*. Edited by C. Harvey Gardiner. Chapel Hill: University of North Carolina Press, 1959.

Ward, Henry G. *Mexico in 1827*. 2 vols. London: Colburn, 1828.

VI LIBERALS AND CONSERVATIVES SEARCH FOR SOMETHING BETTER, 1855-76

22

From Ayutla to the Reform

The Revolution of Ayutla

The Revolution of Ayutla, the armed movement that ousted Santa Anna from power in 1855, brought together some of the most original and creative minds in Mexico. Far from being ivory tower scholars, they were a group of writers and intellectuals who syncretized their own creative work with a spirit of public service, a sense of social consciousness, and a profound desire to see Mexico emerge at last from its long night of political shame. Humiliated by the war with the United States, they sought to re-evaluate the Mexican national conscience and redefine national goals. Secularly oriented and antimilitarist, they deeply mistrusted the church hierarchy and had little use for the ambitious, self-serving Mexican army.

Melchor Ocampo was introduced to the works of Voltaire, Rousseau, and Balzac while a student in Mexico, but when he traveled to Europe Pierre Proudhon caught his fancy. He translated many of the Frenchman's works into Spanish, and his editions were subsequently published in Mexico City. Returning to Mexico in 1842, Ocampo practiced law, began farming scientifically, cataloged flora and fauna, studied Indian languages, and collected one of the best private libraries in Mexico. He also made the decision to enter politics. In the 1840s and 1850s he served as governor of Michoacán and as a congressman in the national legislature. Shortly after the war with the United States he won acclaim when he became involved in a virtual death struggle with the clergy of Michoacán. The issue—the refusal of a local curate to bury the body of a penniless peón because the widow could not pay the sacramental fees—became a *cause célèbre* and was used effectively by Ocampo to demonstrate the ineptitude and decadence of the ecclesiastical effort.

Santos Degollado, another law professor in Morelia, shared Ocampo's interest in French philosophy and natural history. He followed Ocampo in the governorship of Michoacán for a term and, like his predecessor, spoke out against corruption in both church and state. In a short time he found himself in serious difficulties with the Santanistas in the Mexican capital. He took refuge in neighboring Jalisco and patiently bided his time.

Guillermo Prieto, the son of a Mexico City baker, received a scanty education but had a natural talent for writing. After serving as editor of the progovernment *Diario Oficial* for several years, disillusionment set in, and he moved to the camp of the opposition. In his new post as chief editor of *El Siglo xix* he experimented with new poetic forms and attacked Santa Anna. He was arrested on a number of occasions, only to be released when the Santanistas were thrown out of office temporarily. When the caudillo returned for the last time in April 1853, Prieto was sent back to his jail cell. Although he did not play an active role in the rebellion that would force Santa Anna from office two years later, he had, through his writings and personal example, popularized the cause.

But the real leader of the young, socially motivated intellectuals, and the personification of Mexican history in the two decades following mid-century, was Benito Juárez, a Zapotec Indian from the state of Oaxaca. Born on March 21, 1806, in the mountain village of San Pablo Guelatao, Juárez was orphaned at the age of three and raised by an uncle. Only a handful of the 150 villagers knew any Spanish, and Juárez had learned but a few words when, at the age of twelve, he left the adobe hut in the Zapotec village and walked forty-one miles to the state capital. An older sister working as a cook in Oaxaca City found employment for the boy in the home of a Franciscan lay brother who was a part-time bookbinder. In return for daily chores in the house and helping in the bindery, the Franciscan paid Juárez's tuition so that the boy could begin his schooling. At his benefactor's insistence he entered the seminary in Oaxaca but quickly realized that the priesthood was not his calling. He opted instead for the law and worked his way through law school.

The lawyer's certificate Juárez was awarded in 1831 not only sanctioned his judicial competence but, in effect, constituted his passport to politics. The year he was graduated he entered political life as an alderman in the Oaxaca City Council and subsequently served in the state legislature. But he did not abandon his career as a barrister and defended, without fee, groups of poor villagers challenging the exorbitant rates charged by the clergy for the sacraments or protesting the arbitrary dictates of the local hacendado class. Not notably successful in his legal campaign to make the lives of the poor easier, Juárez slowly began to realize that only structural alteration of the system could effect the changes he envisioned, and his liberalism strengthened.

When war broke out between Mexico and the United States, Juárez, a delegate in the national Congress in Mexico City, was recalled to his home state to serve a term as provisional governor. Later the defeated and disgraced Santa Anna sought refuge in Oaxaca, but Governor Juárez let him know he was not welcome there. While Santa Anna would never forgive him this indiscretion, the Oaxaqueños did, and in 1848 they elected Juárez to a full term as constitutional governor.

The Juárez governorship was far from revolutionary, but he did give the state a genuine lesson in energetic, honest, and sound management. Not only did he preside over the construction of fifty new rural schools and encourage female attendance, but he also sought to open the state up to world trade by rehabilitating the abandoned Pacific port of Huatulco (today Puerto Angel). Even more amazing for mid-nineteenth-century Mexico he cut back markedly on the huge state bureaucracy and was able to accomplish his material advances while making regular payments on the state debt. It was the kind of performance that was worthy of emulation on a broad scale.

Not long after Juárez completed his term as governor the Santanistas made their final entrance into Mexico City. Although Juárez had done little as governor to excite conservative passions, he was arrested by order of Santa Anna—the dictator certainly remembered Juárez's refusal to grant him asylum following the war. In addition, Melchor Ocampo's fiery public exchange with Santa Anna's clerical allies made this last regime hypersensitive to the liberal threat. After being kept in prison for several months, Juárez was escorted to Veracruz and subsequently placed aboard an English vessel bound for Havana and New Orleans. When he arrived in the Louisiana city he found that other Mexicans of his ilk had already taken refuge there. José María Mata and Ponciano Arriaga were active members of a revolutionary clique that was led by Melchor Ocampo. Juárez joined the exiles in plotting to overthrow the dictatorship when they decided to cast their lot with an old guerrilla chieftain, Juan Alvarez, then leading an antigovernment rebellion in the state of Guerrero. Early in 1854 they offered their support to Alvarez and sent him a statement of principles. A few months later Alvarez's lieutenants, Florencio Villareal and Ignacio Comonfort, published the *Plan de Ayutla*, which closely paralleled the statement of principles provided by exiles. After setting forth a long list of grievances against Santa Anna, the plan called for the convocation of a liberal junta to designate an interim president to replace the dictator.

The Revolution of Ayutla rapidly gained strength. In Jalisco, Santos Degollado gathered a formidable rebel army around him. In Nuevo León, Santiago Vidaurri and in Guanajuato, Manuel Doblado pronounced against the dictatorship and joined the Ayutla movement. The exiles in New Orleans helped with arms and ammunition, and in the early summer of 1855 they sent Juárez to Acapulco to join Alvarez as a political aide.

The Revolution of Ayutla enjoyed a wider base of support than most previous antigovernment movements. Santa Anna's indecisive attempts to ease up on his dictatorship dissuaded none of the enemy. The rebellions throughout the country were, at best, loosely coordinated but effective nevertheless. By August 1855 Santa Anna, his reputation tarnished and his popularity at its lowest ebb, recognized the futility of continuing the fight. He tendered his resignation and went into exile for the last time.

The Reform Laws

The government established in Mexico was composed primarily of luminaries of the Ayutla Revolution. Juan Alvarez became provisional president; Ignacio Comonfort, secretary of war; Melchor Ocampo, secretary of the treasury; Miguel Lerdo de Tejada, secretary of development; and Benito Juárez, secretary of justice. The provisional presidency of Alvarez marks the beginning of a period in Mexican history remembered as the Reform. For the first time since the Gómez Farías administration in 1833 the liberals set themselves in earnest to the task of destroying the sustaining structures of the conservative state.

The first significant piece of legislation to emerge from the Reform bore the name of the secretary of justice. *Ley Juárez*

Ignacio Comonfort (1812–63). A bureau-
crat of minor importance for most of his
life, Comonfort was thrust into the presidency in 1855 and found himself caught
in the endless liberal-conservative struggle.

abolished the military and ecclesiastical fueros, the special dis-
pensations exempting soldiers and clerics from having to stand
trial in civil courts. Ley Juárez did not, as is sometimes contended, abolish all military and ecclesiastical courts; rather, it
placed stringent restrictions on their jurisdictions. The ecclesiastical and military courts were now competent to sit only on cases
involving the alleged transgression of canon or military law. If,
on the other hand, a cleric or a soldier were charged with a violation of civil or criminal law, he would be required, like everyone
else, to stand trial in a state or federal court.

The acrimony occasioned by Ley Juárez should not have come
as a surprise. Mexico's entire historical experience belied the notion of a homogeneous and harmonious society. The church, with
understandable emotion but scant logic, cried out that religion
had again been attacked in Mexico. Conservatives throughout the
country searched through attics and pulled out dusty old banners
proclaiming *Religión y Fueros*. But, most important, the furor
generated by the new law proved schismatic within the ranks of
the newly victorious revolutionaries of Ayutla, and it did not take
long to recognize that the movement itself represented disparate,
if not contradictory, interests. The moderates (*moderados*) favored backing down, while the more staunchly liberals (*puros*)
refused. Before the month was out President Alvarez and most
of the cabinet had resigned. The presidency devolved on Ignacio
Comonfort, who was more of a compromiser than a firebrand.

In June of 1856 President Comonfort's secretary of the treasury, Miguel Lerdo de Tejada, drafted an important new law that the radicals hoped would weaken the church and the moderates hoped would increase national revenues. *Ley Lerdo* prohibited ecclesiastical and civil institutions from owning or administering real property not directly used in day-to-day operations. The Roman Catholic Church could retain its church buildings, monasteries, and seminaries and local and state units of government their meeting halls, jails, and schools, but both had to divest themselves of other urban and rural property. The massive holdings the church had gradually acquired through the centuries were to be put up for sale at public auction.

Ley Lerdo indicates that neither the puros nor the moderados of the nineteenth century were thinking in terms of social revolution. The properties were not to be distributed to the landless peón but were to be sold. Only the wealthy or at least those in a position secure enough to obtain credit were able to buy. Even if an occasional peón could have obtained financing to purchase a small plot, threats of ecclesiastical penalty from the local priest were enough to dissuade him from pursuing the idea. The radicals were still making simple anticlericalism synonymous with progress, and the moderates were concerning themselves with administrative and economic reform. In practice, the enforcement of Ley Lerdo worked to the detriment of the rural masses. One of the civil corporations forced to sell its property was the *ejido*, the communal landholding of the Indian village. While the extent to which Indian communities lost their traditional lands has not been adequately studied, many were forced to turn over their properties for sale at the various auctions.[1] In the first six months property worth over $23 million had been adjudicated, $20 million of which had belonged to the church.

The reformers were not yet finished. In January 1857 President Comonfort signed into law a statute taking the powers of registry out of the hands of the church and giving them to the state. All births, marriages, adoptions, and deaths were henceforth to be registered by civil functionaries. At the same time cemeteries were taken out of church jurisdiction and placed under the control of a Department of Hygiene. Still another blow

1. Many of the generalizations about the Reform Laws have been brought into question in a provocative article by Charles R. Berry, "The Fiction and Fact of the Reform: The Case of the Central District of Oaxaca," *The Americas* 26 (1970): 277-90. Because we do not have comparable studies for other areas, however, we do not know whether the case of Oaxaca's central district is unique or whether the generalizations themselves are invalid.

at the church was struck a few months later. *Ley Iglesias* prohibited the church from charging high fees for administering the sacraments. The poor were to receive their sacramental blessings at no charge, and those who could afford to pay were to be charged modestly.

The Constitution of 1857

The internal tensions provoked by the Reform Laws were in full evidence when, as provided by the Plan de Ayutla, delegates met to draft a new constitution. Because the conservatives had opposed the Revolution of Ayutla, they were largely unrepresented in the constitutional assembly. The debates would be between moderados and puros.

The federal Constitution of 1857 in many ways was modeled after its ancestor of 1824. The major difference in political structure was provided by an article setting up a unicameral national legislature. For purposes of economy and efficiency the framers of the document believed that a single house was sufficient, but the main reason for switching from two houses to one was neither of these. Mexico's experience since the time of Independence, like that of most of Latin America, demonstrated the perils of executive dominance and legislative subservience. It would be better, many believed, to have one strong house, instead of two weak ones, as a bulwark to dictatorship. But Mexican history showed as well that a strong national government was mandatory if the country were to escape the perils of exaggerated regionalism. The Reform liberals were not nearly so federalist as some have believed. As recent scholarship has demonstrated, on a number of key issues they took powers away from the states and gave them to the government of the nation.[2]

The Constitution of 1857 represented much more of a liberal victory than its federal predecessor of 1824. Most of the liberal legislation of the Reform, including Ley Juárez, Ley Lerdo, and Ley Iglesias, was actually incorporated into the Constitution, and, in addition, Mexico was given its first genuine bill of inalienable rights. The first thirty-four articles of the document spelled out in detail equality before the law and freedom of speech, of the press, of petition, of assembly, of the mails, and of education. They further abolished slavery, other compulsory

2. Richard N. Sinkin, "The Mexican Constitutional Congress, 1856–1857: A Statistical Analysis," *Hispanic American Historical Review* 53 (1973): 1–26.

service, and all titles of nobility and guaranteed the rights to carry arms and to have bail and of *habeas corpus*.

The articles that prompted the most heated debate were, of course, those which in some way touched upon the religious issue. While the Constitution contained no article specifying freedom of religion, it did not establish Roman Catholicism as the state church and thus provided for the exercise of other cults. Church defenders had their opportunity to express their views on several articles of the bill of rights. Freedom of education, they argued, conflicted with Christ's directives to the priesthood to "go and teach all nations"; freedom from compulsory service suggested that nuns and priests could renounce their vows; and freedom of the press could invite all manner of attack against the church. The inclusion of Ley Juárez and Ley Lerdo brought the church defenders to their feet again, but they met with defeat after defeat. When the question of religious liberty itself reached the floor the moderates and the few conservatives allied to hand the puros their only major setback. Emotional attacks against Protestantism garnered some votes, eloquent rhetoric won others, while precise Jesuitical logic convinced still more. The sophistry of the argumentation could be, at one and the same time, technically correct and banefully absurd, as in the argument that religious toleration would nullify the abolition of slavery and allow thousands of Muhammadan immigrants to enter the Mexican republic with their concubines! Others warned that freedom of religion would lead to the disintegration of the family and eventually provoke rebellion and anarchy. The puros were gradually worn down. In the end a vote on religious freedom was never taken, as a majority of the delegates voted to remove the article from debate.

Did the church believe that its defenders had done a sufficient job? Most assuredly not. The Mexican hierarchy issued decree after decree in an attempt to nullify the new Constitution. Those Catholics who took advantage of Ley Lerdo by purchasing church property were threatened with excommunication as were those who swore allegiance to the objectionable articles of the Constitution. Bishop Clemente de Jesús Munguía of Michoacán and Archbishop Lázaro de la Garza of Mexico City specified that the faithful could not accept, among other articles, those which provided for freedom of education, freedom of speech, freedom of the press, freedom of assembly, and, of course, Ley Juárez and Ley Lerdo. Pope Pius IX lent the support of the Holy See when, in an extraordinary statement, he declared:

> The Chamber of Deputies, among the many insults it has heaped upon our Most Holy Religion . . . has proposed a new constitution containing many articles, not a few of which conflict with Divine Religion itself. . . . For the purpose of more easily corrupting manners and propagating the detestable pest of indifferentism and tearing souls away from our Most Holy Religion, it allows the free exercise of all cults and admits the right of pronouncing in public every kind of thought and opinion. . . . And so that the Faithful who reside there may know, and the Catholic world may understand, that We energetically reprove everything the Mexican government has done against the Catholic Religion . . . We arise our Pontifical voice in apostolic liberty . . . *to condemn, to reprove, and declare null and void the said decrees and everything else that the civil authority has done in scorn of ecclesiastical authority and of this Holy See.*[3]

Although many of the charges were palpably untrue, the strong reaction of the church created a real quandary for Mexicans. If they did not swear allegiance to the Constitution they would be considered traitors to the state, and if they did they would be heretics in the eyes of the church. The quandary was not merely theoretical, however. Civil servants who refused to take the oath of allegiance to the Constitution lost their jobs; soldiers who took it were not treated in Catholic hospitals; if they died they did not receive the last rites nor were they buried in the proper ground. Priests who offered the sacraments to communicants who had not forsworn the Constitution were suspended. By pitting brother against brother and father against son, the Reform Laws and the Constitution divided Mexican society into two hostile and completely uncompromising camps. As tensions mounted Mexicans realized that they were beyond pragmatic compromise and began girding themselves for yet another civil war.

The War of the Reform

The War of the Reform, the civil conflict that engulfed Mexico from 1858 to 1861, was in many ways the culmination of the ideological disputations, the shuffling of constitutions, the church-state controversies, and the minor civil wars that had shattered the peace periodically since Independence. Mexicans had not yet defined the kind of society they wanted to the satisfaction of one

3. Quoted in Lesley Byrd Simpson, *Many Mexicos* (Berkeley, 1952), pp. 244–45.

another, and the intense passions of the age precluded the possibility of a rapprochement without still another resort to arms. The war began, as most Mexican wars, with a new plan, this time the *Plan de Tacubaya*, proclaimed by conservative general Félix Zuloaga. Emboldened by promises of clerical and military support, Zuloaga promptly dissolved the Congress and arrested Benito Juárez, the chief liberal spokesman within the Comonfort government. Juárez had recently been elected chief justice of the Mexican Supreme Court, a position that, according to the new Constitution, made him next in line for the presidency should a vacancy occur in the top office. President Comonfort believed in compromise but proved himself unequal to the task of blending the diverse views. As he vacillated, liberals in the provinces announced their support of the Constitution and the Reform Laws it embodied. Finding himself caught between the two extremes and not really sure who were his friends and who his enemies, the president resigned. When the army declared Zuloaga as the new president, Juárez managed to escape north to Querétaro, where his liberal cohorts proclaimed him president. With two presidents, two governments, and two uncompromising ideologies, Mexico plunged headlong into the most passionate and horrifying civil war to date.

The opposing sides in the three-year war defy the simple classification historians have traditionally given. It was not Indians versus whites and the country versus the cities. While it is true that the clergy and the army generally supported the Zuloaga government in Mexico City, the Indian masses were found in both camps. Some Indian communities, convinced correctly that their ejido lands had been taken away by the liberals under Ley Lerdo, were persuaded that their future rested with the conservatives. Led by Indian caciques such as Tomás Mejía of Querétaro, they gave the conservatives an important source of strength scarcely counted on. But the conservatives' principal leadership came from the army generals such as Miguel Miramón and Leonardo Márquez. And the liberals certainly were not without Indian support of their own, as many leaders convinced their people that their interests would best be served by casting their lot with their fellow Indian, Benito Juárez. These chieftains placed themselves and their followers under the orders of liberal commanders Santos Degollado, Santiago Vidaurri, and Manuel Doblado.

The liberals eventually succeeded in establishing their capital in Veracruz, where they could control the customs receipts and obtain military supplies from the outside world. From there Juárez and his government issued manifestos damning the enemy, enticing support, seeking the recognition of foreign governments, and outlining military strategy. At the same time in Mexico City the Zuloaga administration declared the Reform Laws null and void, swore allegiance to the Holy See, took communion in public, and planned military campaigns.

For the first two years of the war the liberals had a hard time holding their own. The conservative army, better trained, equipped, and led, won most of the major engagements and held the most populous states of central Mexico. But when, in the early spring of 1859, General Miramón attempted to dislodge the liberals from Veracruz, he was beaten back. The fighting throughout the republic was vicious, and noncombatants were subjected to wanton depredation by overzealous commanders of both armies. The conservatives shot captured prisoners in the name of holy religion, and the liberals did the same in defense of freedom and democratic government. In a particularly intemperate incident after a battle for the control of Mexico City, General Márquez, flushed with victory, ordered the execution of all doctors and medical aides who had treated wounded liberal soldiers. For this daring bit of bravado he won himself the sobriquet *El Tigre de Tacubaya*. But the liberals were far from guiltless themselves. Churches were desecrated with childish enthusiasm. Priests who refused the sacraments to the liberal rank and file were placed summarily before firing squads.

The intensity of the military campaigns manifested itself in the political arena as well. The Juárez government issued a series of decrees from Veracruz that made the earlier Reform Laws seem innocuous by comparison. The liberals who had felt shortchanged by the Constitution would now be satisfied. Births and marriages were made civil ceremonies, all cemeteries were secularized, monastic orders were outlawed, no new nuns could be admitted to the nunneries, all church properties and assets were nationalized, the number of official religious holidays was curtailed, religious processions in the streets were severely limited, and, most important, church and state were separated. The reforms tried to rivet together a society in which the church would be indisputably subordinate to the state.

By 1860 the tide of the battle had turned in favor of the liberals. Juárez found two excellent field commanders in Ignacio Zaragoza and Jesús González Ortega, while the enemy unwittingly aided the liberal cause by bickering among themselves. In

August, Zaragoza and González Ortega combined their forces at Silao to hand General Miramón his first serious defeat. Within the next two months Oaxaca fell to the rebels, and Zaragoza gave General Márquez a stunning setback at Guadalajara. With the conservatives disheartened from the series of reverses, the final battle occurred three days before Christmas when González Ortega crushed Miramón's army of eight thousand at the little town of San Miguel Calpulalpan. The newly victorious army, some twenty-five-thousand strong, entered Mexico City to a tumultuous welcome on New Year's Day. Juárez arrived ten days later.

Recommended for Further Study

Bazant, Jan. *Alienation of Church Wealth in Mexico: Social and Economic Aspects of the Liberal Revolution, 1856–1857*. Cambridge: Cambridge University Press, 1971.

Berbusse, Edward J. "The Origins of the McLane-Ocampo Treaty of 1859." *The Americas* 14 (1958): 223–46.

Berry, Charles R. *The Reform in Oaxaca, 1856–1876: A Microhistory of the Liberal Revolution*. Lincoln: University of Nebraska Press, 1981.

Brading, D. A. "Liberal Patriotism and the Mexican Reforma." *Journal of Latin American Studies* 20 (1988): 27–48.

Broussard, Ray F. "Vidaurri, Juárez and Comonfort's Return from Exile." *Hispanic American Historical Review* 49 (1969): 268–80.

Cadenhead, Ivie E., Jr. *Jesús González Ortega and Mexican National Politics*. Fort Worth: Texas Christian University Press, 1972.

Johnson, Richard A. *The Mexican Revolution of Ayutla*. Rock Island, Ill.: Augustana College Library, 1939.

Knapp, Frank A., Jr. "Parliamentary Government and the Mexican Constitution of 1857: A Forgotten Phase of Mexican Political History." *Hispanic American Historical Review* 33 (1953): 65–87.

Knowlton, Robert J. *Church Property and the Mexican Reform, 1856–1910*. DeKalb: Northern Illinois University Press, 1976.

Olliff, Donathan C. *Reforma Mexico and the United States: A Search for Alternatives to Annexation, 1854–1861*. University: University of Alabama Press, 1983.

Powell, T. G. "Priests and Peasants in Central Mexico: Social Conflict during La Reforma." *Hispanic American Historical Review* 57 (1977): 296–313.

Roeder, Ralph. *Juárez and His Mexico*. 2 vols. New York: Viking Press, 1947.

Scholes, Walter V. *Mexican Politics during the Juárez Regime, 1855–1872*. Columbia: University of Missouri Press, 1957.

Sinkin, Richard N. *The Mexican Reform, 1855–1876: A Study in Liberal Nation Building*. Austin: Institute of Latin American Studies, 1979.

23

The French Intervention

With the War of the Reform finally over, Mexico desperately needed a period of uninterrupted peace. Juárez and the liberals needed time for reflection and for the convalescence of their war-torn country. The desolation left in the wake of the civil conflict showed on the landscape dotted with burned haciendas and mills, potted roads, unrepaired bridges, neglected fields, and sacked villages. But, more important, it was epitomized in the minds and bodies of tens of thousands of exhausted, crippled, and aggrieved Mexicans. Soldiers slowly drifted back to their villages to find no work. Bandits continued to infest the highways. Frustration set in quickly. Only the national government could be expected to smooth the transition, but the tired nation was to have no relief. The liberal victory in 1861 proved to be but a brief respite from the ravages of war. The armies would soon begin marching again, but on this occasion one would wear foreign uniforms.

Discontent

Among the numerous legacies bequeathed by the war there emerged a pronounced mistrust within the victorious liberal party. Although Juárez won the presidential elections held in March 1861, the liberals were badly split on many issues, especially on what type of punishment should be meted out to their erstwhile enemies. Some favored harsh retribution, but the president opted instead for a more conciliatory policy. Only a few

Benito Juárez (1806–72). The presidential terms of Mexico's most note-worthy politician of the mid-nineteenth century were disrupted by civil wars and foreign interventions.

bishops and leading conservative generals were not included in his sweeping amnesty declaration. The moderate stance he assumed presaged difficulties with radicals in the new Congress, men such as Francisco Zarco, Sebastián Lerdo de Tejada, Ignacio Altamirano, and Ignacio Ramírez. They could see little sense in treating the conservatives with kid gloves. Allied with the corrupt and exploitative clergy, had not these same conservatives been responsible for the holocaust from which Mexico had just emerged? Should not they be made to pay for their sins?

But President Juárez was not easily swayed, and he continued to be magnanimous in his use of the presidential power of commutation of sentences. Benito Juárez believed in the chastening impact of open debate. He considered opposition in an open forum a healthy political development in Mexico, and he would not muzzle the barbed criticism in the Congress. But congressional bickering in his own party, coupled with pressure from the opposition, prompted several cabinet resignations and kept the administration in a constant state of turmoil. On one occasion a congressional vote taken to demand Juárez's resignation lost by a single vote.

Troubled Finances and Foreign Intervention

In the final analysis, however, it was economic rather than political difficulties that precipitated the next war. Juárez inherited a bankrupt treasury and an army, a corps of civil servants, and a police force that had not been paid. The income from the sale of church property had been considerably less than expected because during the desperate days in Veracruz much of it had been sold at a fraction of its true worth. Commerce was stagnant, and most of the customs receipts were already pledged. The nation's transportation system was woefully inadequate, as merchandise was still being conveyed by pack mules, oxen, and human cargadores. Transportation was slow, costly, and inefficient.

In the spring of 1861 the monthly treasury deficit amounted to $400,000, and there was practically no currency in circulation. Worst of all, Mexico's European creditors began clamoring for the repayment of debts, some half a century old. Fully sensitive to the dangers his action might portend, Juárez declared a two-year moratorium on the payment of Mexico's foreign debt. Although he took care to stress that his action was not a repudiation, but simply a suspension in time of stress, the outcry in Europe was predictably anguished.

The large majority of the English, French, and Spanish claims were quite legitimate, for foreign citizens had suffered outrages and losses of life and property. Foreign legations had been destroyed and foreign silver shipments had been stolen on the roads from the mines to the ports.

On October 31, 1861, representatives of Queen Isabella II of Spain, Queen Victoria of Great Britain, and Emperor Napoleon III of France affixed their signatures to the Convention of London. The three nations agreed upon a joint occupation of the

Mexican coasts to collect their claims. The specific plan they envisioned was to occupy the customshouse at Veracruz and apply all customs receipts on the debt. Article II of the Convention pledged: "The high contracting parties bind themselves not to seek for themselves, in the employment of coercive measures foreseen by the present convention, any acquisition of territory, or any peculiar advantage, and not to . . . impair the right of the Mexican nation to choose and freely to constitute the form of its own government."[1]

England and Spain were apparently sincere in their pledge not to seek special advantage in Mexico, but France had other plans. The enigmatic Louis Napoleon Bonaparte, nephew of Napoleon I, won the presidency of the French republic in 1848 but craved for the imperial status of his famous uncle. Ever since 1852, when a French plebiscite approved the title and dignity that he desired, Emperor Napoleon III had embarked upon an aggressive foreign policy. In the name of the Second French Empire he reinforced earlier claims to Algeria, established a protectorate in Indochina, landed troops in Lebanon, founded French colonies on the west coast of Africa, and helped to defeat Russia in the Crimean War. But, most important, the emperor dreamed of planting the Tricouleur in the New World and of reincarnating France's lost empire in America. By coming to the rescue of the church in Mexico he could also hope to curry favor with the strong Catholic element in France. The Mexican imbroglio seemed to present him with a perfect opportunity.

The Spanish troops actually landed in Veracruz first. In December 1861 some six thousand Spaniards disembarked in the port. Seven hundred British marines and two thousand French troops arrived early the next month. The commissioners of the three nations initiated a series of conferences during the course of which it became obvious that the French harbored notions of conquest. Acrimonious notes were exchanged between the three governments, and the queens of Spain and Great Britain decided to order their respective troops home.

The French Occupation

Within a month after the Spanish and British withdrawal the French army, reinforced with an additional forty-five hundred

---

1. The Spanish text of the Convention is reproduced in Ernesto de la Torre Villar et al., eds., *Historia documental de México* (Mexico, 1964), 2: 314–15.

Porfirio Díaz as a young man. Later to serve as president of Mexico for a third of a century, Díaz was catapulted to national fame because of his role in the victory over the French on May 5, 1862.

troops, began to march inland on its war of occupation. The French minister in Mexico City informed the invading commander, General Charles Latrille, that the French would be welcomed with open arms in Puebla and that the local clergy would not only shower them with magnolia blooms but would offer a special Te Deum in their honor. But Puebla, although conservative and proclerical, was not to be such an easy prize. President Juárez had assigned the defense of the city to General Ignacio Zaragoza. Encountering unexpected opposition on the morning of May 5, 1862, Latrille attacked recklessly, and within two hours the French had expended half of their ammunition. The French troops, many weakened by the affliction that sometimes smites the foreign visitor to the Mexican countryside, did not acquit themselves well. General Zaragoza, on the other hand, managed his troops with rare aplomb. The decisive maneuver of the day was carried out by young Brigadier General Porfirio Díaz, commanding the Second Brigade. Late in the afternoon Díaz repelled a determined French assault on Zaragoza's right flank. The dejected invaders, many veterans from more glorious days in Crimea, retreated to lick their wounds in Orizaba. May 5 —*Cinco de Mayo*—would be added to the national calendar of holidays in honor of the Mexican victory.

Not all Mexicans rejoiced at the news of the French defeat. Many conservative monarchists and just as many church officials not only succored the recuperating French army but openly exhorted other Mexicans to lend assistance. President Juárez was furious that priests were using their. pulpits to urge their communicants to collaborate with the enemy against his godless government. On August 30, 1862, he issued the following presidential decree:

> In use of the broad powers with which I have been invested, I have found it proper to declare that
>
> Article 1: Priests of any cult who, abusing their ministry, excite hate or disrespect for our laws, our government, or its rights, will be punished by three years' imprisonment or deportation.
>
> Article 2: Because of the present crisis all cathedral chapters are suppressed, except for that of Guadalajara because of its patriotic behavior. . . .
>
> Article 3: Priests of all cults are forbidden from wearing their vestments or any other distinguishing garment outside of the churches. . . . All violators will be punished with fines of ten to one hundred pesos or imprisonment from fifteen to sixty days.[2]

Upon hearing of the disaster at Puebla, Napoleon, with a sizable reservoir of manpower to draw upon, ordered some thirty thousand reinforcements. It took fully a year before the French army was prepared to march again. Once more they encountered their heaviest resistance at Puebla, but on this occasion the result would be quite different. On the untimely death of General Zaragoza, Juárez had placed General Jesús González Ortega in charge; the new commander immediately began constructing a series of fortifications around the city. In the middle of March the French encircled Puebla and launched a heavy bombardment. The mortars and artillery pounded away for days. Only when the walls surrounding the city had been reduced to rubble did the French infantry attack, but they were beaten back by the Mexican defenders. The siege that ensued lasted almost two months. Juárez's plans to resupply and reinforce the city were unsuccessful, for the invaders were able to interdict and repel the supply trains sent out from Mexico City. With the civilian and military population of Puebla finally reduced to nourishing themselves on rodents, pets, and leaves, González Ortega agreed to turn the city over to the French.

2. Quoted in Ernesto de la Torre Villar, *La intervención francesa y el triunfo de la república* (Mexico, 1968), 2: 159.

President Juárez realized that the fall of Puebla opened the doors to Mexico City, but he initially resolved to make a final stand in the capital. Only after consulting with his leading military advisers did he admit that the lack of troops available to him made the defense of Mexico City impossible. On May 31, his decision to evacuate Mexico City well known, he received a strong vote of confidence and a grant of extraordinary powers from the Congress. He answered by assuring the Congress that the evacuation of the capital was not tantamount to abandoning the fight. "Adversity," he exhorted the deputies, "discourages none but contemptible peoples."[3] As Juárez, his cabinet, and what was left of his army withdrew for San Luis Potosí, the French army entered the Mexican capital unopposed. The Te Deum that had been promised in Puebla over a year before was now offered in the great cathedral in Mexico City.

The New Government

Much of Mexico's conservative leadership was less concerned with their country's recent loss of sovereignty than with how the conservatives might profit from the demise of Benito Juárez and his liberal government. It did not take them long to learn. On June 16, 1863, the French commander selected a provisional government consisting of thirty-five Notables. The conservative orientation of the group was clearly manifest when it selected its executive triumvirate: General Juan Almonte, a disgruntled Santanista who had already met secretly with Napoleon in Paris to peddle monarchist schemes; General Mariano Salas, who had previously served the conservatives as provisional president of the republic during the era of Santa Anna; and Pelagio Antonio de Labastida, the bishop of Puebla and archbishop-elect of Mexico, who had been exiled to Europe by Ignacio Comonfort for opposing the Reform Laws.

Napoleon III had already made up his mind about the future of Mexico. Having conferred with numerous conservative Mexican émigrés, he had decided that if a monarchy was good for France, it would be good for Mexico as well. The French emperor and his conservative Mexican allies agreed that the Austrian archduke, Ferdinand Maximilian of Hapsburg, would be a perfect emperor. Napoleon had discussed the possibility with Maximilian even before the Convention of London. In October

3. Quoted in Charles Allen Smart, *Viva Juárez!* (London, 1964), p. 276.

1863 a delegation of Mexican conservatives visited Maximilian at Miramar, his magnificent palace on a promontory overlooking the Adriatic near Trieste. The Mexicans, led by José Miguel Gutiérrez Estrada, a monarchist for many years, and Father Francisco Javier Miranda, leader of the arch-conservatives, offered Maximilian the crown on behalf of the Assembly of Notables. Maximilian accepted only on the condition that his emperorship be approved by the Mexican people themselves. As strange as his stipulation must have sounded to the conservative monarchists, they agreed to indulge Maximilian in this folly. The plebiscite, held under the auspices of the French army and among the illiterate and indifferent masses, was a farce; when Maximilian was informed that the Mexican people had voted overwhelmingly in his favor, he accepted the throne.

Before leaving for Mexico, Maximilian entered into an agreement with his benefactor, Napoleon III. The Convention of Miramar pledged the new Mexican emperor to pay all expenses incurred by the French troops during their fight for control of the country. Maximilian also agreed to pay the salaries of the French troops, twenty thousand of whom were to remain in Mexico until the end of 1867, and to assume responsibility for payment of all the claims. In return Napoleon gave Maximilian full command over the French expeditionary force in Mexico. The new emperor, by signing the Convention of Miramar, had tripled Mexico's foreign debt before even setting foot on Mexican soil. But Maximilian was eager to begin a new life in a new world. He had his wife Charlotte hire a Spanish tutor; after the first lesson she had mastered a few salutations and had learned that her name henceforth, would be Carlota.

The Arrival of the Monarchs

Ferdinand Maximilian Joseph and Marie Charlotte Amélie Léopoldine arrived in Veracruz aboard the Austrian frigate *Novara* at the end of May 1864. He was thirty-two years old and she only twenty-four when they set out to mount the imperial throne. The most distinguished blood of Europe ran through their veins. He was descendant from the Josephs, Leopolds, and Francis of Austrian Hapsburg fame and ultimately from Charles V, and she from Queen Louise of Orléans, Louis Philippe, and the French Bourbons. They were products of European education at its best, schooled in the etiquette of court life, and accustomed to the niceties, proprieties, and extravagances of Viennese aristocratic society; their first glimpse of Mexico came as a shock.

Veracruz was not fondly remembered by visitors in the 1860s. Though carefully laid out, it was a dirty, depressing, and disease-ridden town of fewer than ten thousand where the flies never slept. In the hot, sultry temperature, the surrounding swamplands festered with mosquitoes carrying malaria and yellow fever. Hardly a visitor failed to note the horrible *zopilotes*, the black birds that hovered over the entire town. They constituted, in effect, the only garbage collection system in the port.

The welcome the emperor and empress received in Veracruz was as cold as the weather was hot. Traditionally liberal, the Veracruzanos refused to come out of their whitewashed adobe houses to greet their new monarchs. The dignitary scheduled to meet the couple, General Juan Almonte, arrived late. By the time the small royal party, accompanied by a few minor French officials and conservative leaders dispatched from Mexico City, reached the railroad station to begin the tedious journey, Carlota was in tears. As the train wound its way toward Mexico City, the weather cooled and the scenery improved. But the railroad tracks ended at the little pueblo of Totalco, and the royal party made the rest of the trip by stage. Maximilian had brought his own ornate carriage from Vienna, and, while it would catch many eyes on the good streets of Mexico City, it was scarcely designed for the atrocious tracks that passed for roads in the mountains of rural Mexico. After several breakdowns the imperial party wisely moved from the carriage to the stage for the remainder of the journey The carriage would be saved for the triumphal entry into the capital. Cordially received in Córdoba, Orizaba, and Puebla, the cavalcade finally reached Mexico City on June 12. On their way into the city they stopped to hear mass at the Basílica de Guadalupe. Maximilian had been advised that it would be wise for the blond Austrian to pay his obeisance early to the brown virgin. Not only was the appeal to the Indian masses obvious, but the clergy was pleased as well. Eleven Mexican prelates released a pastoral letter proclaiming that the days of godless radicalism were over.

Because the national palace was deemed unsuitable, the royal family established their magnificent imperial court at Chapultepec Castle, built originally for the Spanish viceroys at the end of the eighteenth century. Maximilian's salary was set at $1,500,000 annually, with an additional $200,000 for Carlota. But unlike Agustín I, Mexico's first emperor, Maximilian made

A mass was celebrated for Maximilian and Carlota when they reached Mexico City after the difficult journey from Veracruz.

himself accessible to the people. Once a week he opened the palace to his subjects, and in many small ways he tried hard for acceptance. To acquaint himself with Mexico's problems he toured the provinces and, on occasion, even donned the regional costume and ate the local food. Upon his return he shocked his conservative friends by suggesting that many priests he had met could profit from some basic lessons in Christian charity.

Believing that magnanimity would serve him well and win him converts, Maximilian declared a free press and proclaimed a general amnesty for all political prisoners serving terms of less than ten years. When aides suggested to him that a marble arch should be built and dedicated to Empress Carlota, he demurred and countered with the suggestion that a new monument honor Mexican Independence.

The emperor was pleased with the first few months of his reign, especially when diplomatic recognition began to come in from Europe. And before he fully realized that his conservative backers had placed him in a completely untenable position, he was also pleased with his new life. In the summer he wrote his younger brother an enthusiastic letter.

I found the country far better than I expected . . . and the people far more advanced than supposed at home. Our reception was cordial and sincere, free from all pretence and from that nauseating official servility which one very often finds in Europe on such occasions. The country is very beautiful, tropically luxuriant in the coast lands. . . . The so-called entertainments of Europe, such as evening receptions, the gossip of teaparties, etc., etc., of hideous memories, are quite unknown here, and we shall take good care not to introduce them. The Mexicans only enjoyment is to ride about his beautiful country on his fine horse and go to the theatre frequently; I too naturally treat myself to the latter.[4]

Internal Divisions and External Interference

But Maximilian's position was scarcely as idyllic as he imagined. His first serious problem, strangely enough, came from his conservative supporters rather than from the liberals who had been driven out of Mexico City to make room for him. The conservatives, led by Juan Almonte, naturally expected that the emperor would immediately set about to suspend the Reform Laws and return the church properties seized by Benito Juárez. Archbishop Labastida called upon Maximilian early to remind him of the need for the prompt restitution of church lands. When a papal nuncio arrived from Rome with credentials from the pope and a list of demands, the conservatives believed that the church question would be promptly settled to their complete satisfaction. But Maximilian refused to entertain seriously the pontiff's exactions. The emperor was a Mason and, in many respects, fancied himself a liberal and certainly not in the mold of the Hapsburg champions of the Counter Reformation. He would countenance no demands from Rome. Hoping to attract some liberal support to his government he not only refused to return church lands, re-establish Roman Catholicism to the exclusion of all other creeds, and decree education a church monopoly, but, when he found himself in a financial squeeze similar to that of his republican predecessors, he even levied several forced loans against the church. If conservative enthusiasm was dampened by Maximilian's church policy, his allies were aghast when he named José Fernando Ramírez, a moderate liberal, as secretary of foreign relations.

The liberals could well understand sectarian quarrels and

4. Quoted in Egon Corti, *Maximilian and Charlotte of Mexico* (New York, 1928), 2: 431–32.

were not impressed; few of them were persuaded that Maximilian's mildly anticlerical posture and winks at liberalism should occasion a change of attitude on their part. A monarchy, supported by foreign arms and headed by a foreigner, had been established in Mexico, and it was their duty as honorable citizens to overthrow it. Maximilian's position was not unlike that of Ignacio Comonfort a few years before. By attempting to find a middle ground between the liberals and the conservatives, he succeeded only in alienating both.

When Juárez withdrew from Mexico City before the French onslaught, he established his government first in San Luis Potosí and then in Chihuahua. But French troops sent out by Marshal François Bazaine pushed him and his small loyal army north until it found refuge only in El Paso del Norte (today Ciudad Juárez) on the United States border. But the French hold on the country was tenuous as the Juaristas quickly taught the Europeans the meaning of guerrilla warfare. While the French invariably won the few battles that were fought, they could not completely pacify the country, nor could they hold onto territory once the troops moved on.

In late 1864 and early 1865 the empire was at its strongest. Bazaine defeated Porfirio Díaz in Oaxaca and temporarily secured that pivotal southern state. In October of 1865 Maximilian's French advisers informed him, incorrectly, that Juárez had finally given up the fight and had fled the country, seeking refuge in the United States. Believing that the country was almost completely pacified and desiring to avoid a relapse into civil war, the emperor was importuned to issue a controversial and extremely significant decree. The death penalty was made mandatory for all captured Juaristas still bearing arms, to be carried out without appeal within twenty-four hours of capture. The October decree was implemented a few days after it was issued when two republican generals were captured by the French army and put to death. Maximilian had been given and had followed bad advice. In signing the decree he had also signed his own death warrant. Juárez had not abandoned the country and repeatedly promised his supporters that he had no intention of giving up the fight. He realized, however, that he needed substantial help and was gradually convinced by his cabinet and advisers that it could come only from north of the Rio Grande.

The government of Abraham Lincoln had been more than casually interested in France's Mexican venture from the outset. In 1823 President Monroe had intoned his famous doctrine declaring that the American continents were henceforth not to be considered as subjects for future colonization by European powers; any attempt to do so would be viewed as an unfriendly act toward the United States. In the years subsequent to its promulgation the Monroe Doctrine was disregarded incessantly by various countries in western Europe but never so blatantly as in 1862 and 1863 when the French army overran central Mexico, overthrew the Juárez government, and placed Maximilian on the Mexican throne. But Napoleon III had chosen his time well; six months prior to the signing of the Convention of London the shots fired at Fort Sumter had initiated the Civil War in the United States. Convulsed with difficulties far more serious than ever before, the government in Washington was able to do little but look askance and issue a few mild protests. The Union hardly wanted to push France into an alliance with the Confederacy. When it came time to consider recognition of the Mexican empire, however, the Lincoln administration refused. Juárez's government in exile was considered by Washington to be the legitimate representative of the Mexican people.

As the fortunes of the North improved and those of the Confederacy declined, Juárez embarked upon an all-out campaign to secure assistance from the United States. He was encouraged when in April of 1864 the House of Representatives passed a resolution declaring that the Congress of the United States was not an indifferent spectator to the deplorable events transpiring in Mexico and that it was not U.S. policy to view with inaction the establishment of monarchical governments, backed by European powers, on the ruins of republican ones. Juárez charged the head of the Mexican legation in Washington, Matías Romero, a young but forceful diplomat, with the task of securing some implementation of the resolution; at approximately the same time he dispatched an entire team of secret agents to the United States to secure financial and military aid and to begin recruiting American soldiers of fortune. Romero, who had been partially responsible for securing the earlier House resolution, opened discussions with representatives of the Lincoln administration. Progress was slow, and before any firm resolution could be reached, Lincoln was assassinated and Romero was forced to open a new round of negotiations with the government of Andrew Johnson.

The end of the Civil War brought about a major change in United States policy. The North had over nine hundred thousand men under arms when Lee surrendered to Grant at Appomattox, a formidable fighting force as the South had discovered. No longer fearful of offending the French, Secretary of State William Seward began applying pressure to Napoleon III. At the same time the government in Washington, prompted by Romero, closed its eyes to violations of neutrality legislation and allowed Juarista agents to purchase arms and ammunition in California for shipment to west coast Mexican ports under republican control. If an occasional zealous official tried to obstruct the shipments, Romero would use his considerable influence with Secretary Seward or General Grant to put the offending official in his proper place. Within a matter of a few months some thirty thousand muskets reached the Juaristas from the Baton Rouge arsenal alone. Juárez's agents were also allowed to pass back and forth across the international line without hindrance from customs officials or border patrols. Some three thousand Union veterans, attracted by good pay and a promised land bonus, joined the Juarista army. With the diplomatic atmosphere heating up, with the military potential of Juárez's army considerably bolstered, and with a new threat to French security in Europe in the form of Otto von Bismarck, Napoleon made his belated decision to begin withdrawing his foreign legion in November 1866.

The gradual withdrawal of the French troops in late 1866 and early 1867 left Maximilian in an impossible position. He sent a series of envoys to Paris to convince Napoleon that he should honor the commitment he had made in the Convention of Miramar. When the envoys reported that the French emperor would not admit the error of his ways, Maximilian toyed with the idea of abdicating his throne. Carlota, however, appealed to his sense of Hapsburg dignity and convinced him that he must stay on. She would travel to Europe herself and appeal directly to Napoleon for a countermand of his withdrawal order. But Napoleon was no less obdurate with her than he had been with the previous emissaries. She thereupon traveled to Rome for an audience with Pope Pius IX. While she pleaded with the pope to use his influence with Napoleon, he wondered why Maximilian had taken no steps to restore the church lands in Mexico. Carlota's impassioned plea was rejected, and she soon lost her mind.

The Republican Victory and the Aftermath

Spurred on by the fortuitous combination of events in Europe and America and recognizing that the underpinnings of the empire were collapsing, Juárez and his republican army assumed the offensive in the spring of 1866. General Luis Terrazas captured Chihuahua City while General Mariano Escobedo shattered a strong French column between Matamoros and Monterrey. During the summer the republicans recaptured Saltillo, Monterrey, Tampico, Guaymas, and Durango, and by the end of the year they added Guadalajara and Oaxaca to the list of reoccupied territories. With the French army pulling out of Mexico, the treasury empty, and Carlota sick in Europe, Maximilian, perhaps thinking that he could plead French deception to the world, for a second time planned to abandon his thankless task and abdicate. But again his pride overshadowed his reason, and he decided to make one last stand.

Mexico's second empire collapsed in the colonial city of Querétaro while the last installment of French troops were marching toward Veracruz for their European embarkation. Maximilian decided to take command of a few thousand Mexican imperial troops but quickly found himself surrounded by a republican army four times as strong. Hostilities commenced on February 19, 1867. Although prolongation of the inevitable made little sense, the imperial defenders inside the walls of the city held off the attackers for almost a hundred days. By the second week in May, with the aqueduct carrying the city's water supply cut and food and ammunition in short supply, the situation was desperate. Although careful plans had been laid for the emperor's escape, he preferred the solemn dignity of surrender. Maximilian turned over his sword to General Escobedo on May 15.

Juárez immediately decided Maximilian's fate; the emperor would be tried by court-martial, and the state would request the death penalty. In spite of a rain of pleas for clemency from European monarchs, New World presidents, and delegations of tearful, supplicating women, Juárez remained adamant. Thirteen accusations were leveled against Maximilian, including violation of Mexico's sovereignty, but the most important was that he had signed the infamous decree of October 1865 resulting in the death of innumerable Mexican citizens. The chief defense attorneys, Mariano Riva Palacio and Rafael Martínez de la Torre, were brilliant advocates; they ardently denied the competence of the court to sit on the case and argued that the leniency shown to Jefferson Davis in the United States after the Civil War should serve as a precedent. The verdict, however, was based more on political considerations than on legal ones. After the War of the Reform Juárez had been magnanimous in his use of executive

A contemporary woodcut depicting the execution of Maximilian on the Hill of the Bells outside Querétaro.

clemency, and he now believed that Mexico had paid a terrible price as a result. He wanted to demonstrate to the world that Mexico's existence as an independent nation would not be left to chance or to the goodwill of foreign heads of state. Three members of the six-man court voted guilty, with banishment from Mexico for life. The other three voted guilty, with the death penalty. The tie-breaking decision fell to the president of the court, Lieutenant Colonel Platón Sánchez. Fully cognizant of Juárez's wishes, he voted for the death penalty. The final appeal to President Juárez was automatic, as was his response: "The petition for clemency, and all other requests for lenience, having been carefully examined, as the gravity of this case demands, the Honorable President of the republic makes known: that he cannot honor them as the most serious considerations of justice and the need to assure public peace require that he reject them."[5]

On the morning of June 19, after having received the last sacrament, Maximilian was led by his executioners to the Hill of the Bells on the outskirts of Querétaro. There he was shot

5. Quoted in Vicente Riva Palacio, *México a través de los siglos* (Mexico [1940?]), vol. 5, pt. 2, p. 855.

along with several Mexican conservative officers who had been tried with him. As tragic and senseless as the event might have appeared from the calm of abroad, fifty thousand Mexicans had just as surely lost their lives fighting the French.

The price of the French Intervention, however, cannot be assessed solely in terms of the lives lost. The attempt to tamper with Mexico's sovereignty had ended in dismal failure, and, as a result, Mexican nationalism and self-esteem began to grow perceptibly for the first time. The United States had helped in a small way but it had been Mexicans who drove out the French. The republican victory was, at least in part, a vindication of the Constitution of 1857 and the principles it had espoused. The clerical party had been defeated, and although the country had not seen the last of its major church-state struggles, the church and its defenders in the future would seek goals much more modest than the establishment of a theocracy. The conservatives were discredited, at least for the time, because liberalism in the popular mind became identified with moral authority and independence from foreign aggression.

On the other hand, the Intervention and the empire, in spite of Maximilian's best efforts, had left Mexican commerce, industry, and agriculture in a quagmire. Education had suffered immeasurably, and the treasury was still empty. The years without a single, central authority reinforced tendencies toward localism and blunted the nationalism that the victory began to abet. Thousands of armed men roamed the countryside. In short, the dramatic events of the years 1861 to 1867 contributed markedly to Mexico's lack of political stability and economic growth in the nineteenth century.

Recommended for Further Study

Anderson, William Marshall. *An American in Maximilian's Mexico, 1865–1866: Diaries of William Marshall Anderson.* Edited by Ramón Eduardo Ruiz. San Marino, Calif.: Huntington Library, 1959.

Barker, Nancy Nichols. *The French Experience in Mexico, 1821–1861: A History of Constant Misunderstanding.* Chapel Hill: University of North Carolina Press, 1979.

Blasio, José Luis. *Maximilian, Emperor of Mexico: Memoirs of His Private Secretary.* Translated by Robert Hammond Murray. New Haven, Conn.: Yale University Press, 1934.

Blumberg, Arnold. "The Italian Diplomacy of the Mexican Empire, 1864–1867." *Hispanic American Historical Review* 51 (1971): 497–509.

Cadenhead, Ivie E., Jr. "González Ortega and the Presidency of Mexico." *Hispanic American Historical Review* 32 (1952): 331–46.

———. *Jesús González Ortega and Mexican National Politics.* Fort Worth: Texas Christian University Press, 1972.

Corti, Egon. *Maximilian and Charlotte of Mexico.* 2 vols. New York: Knopf, 1928.

Dabbs, Jack A. *The French Army in Mexico, 1861–1867.* The Hague: Mouton, 1962.

Delaney, Robert W. "Matamoros, Port for Texas during the Civil War." *Southwestern Historical Quarterly* 58 (1955): 473–87.

Egan, Clifford L. "The United States and the Spanish Intervention in Mexico, 1861–1862." *Revista de Historia de América* 63–64 (1967): 1–12.

Goldwert, Marvin. "Matías Romero and Congressional Opposition to Seward's Policy toward the French Intervention in Mexico." *The Americas* 22 (1965): 22–40.

Gordon, Leonard. "Lincoln and Juárez: A Brief Reassessment of Their Relationship." *Hispanic American Historical Review* 48 (1968): 75–80.

Hanna, Alfred Jackson, and Kathryn Hanna. *Napoleon III and Mexico.* Chapel Hill: University of North Carolina Press, 1971.

Miller, Robert R. "Matías Romero: Mexican Minister to the United States during the Juárez–Maximilian Era." *Hispanic American Historical Review* 45 (1965): 228–45.

———. "Plácido Vega: A Mexican Secret Agent in the United States, 1864–1866." *The Americas* 19 (1962): 137–48.

Robertson, William S. "The Tripartite Treaty of London." *Hispanic American Historical Review* 20 (1940): 167–89.

Roeder, Ralph. *Juárez and His Mexico.* 2 vols. New York: Viking Press, 1947.

Schoonover, Thomas D. *Dollars over Dominion: The Triumph of Liberalism in Mexican–United States Relations, 1861–1867.* Baton Rouge: Louisiana State University Press, 1978.

———. *Mexican Lobby: Matías Romero in Washington, 1861–1867.* Lexington: University Press of Kentucky, 1986.

Sheridan, Philip J. "The Committee of Mexican Bondholders and European Intervention in 1861." *Mid-America* 42 (1960): 18–29.

Smart, Charles Allen. *Viva Juárez!* London: Eyre and Spottiswoode, 1964.

Tyler, R. Curtis. "Santiago Vidaurri and the Confederacy." *The Americas* 26 (1969): 66–76.

———. *Santiago Vidaurri and the Southern Confederacy.* Austin: Texas State Historical Association, 1973.

Weber, Frank G. "Bismarck's Man in Mexico: Anton von Magnus and the End of Maximilian's Empire." *Hispanic American Historical Review* 46 (1966): 53–65.

24

The Restored Republic, 1867-76: Nascent Modernization

Modern Mexican history begins with the liberal victory of 1867.[1] In a very real sense the republic became a nation. Concerned with the growth of political democracy in Mexico, Juárez and his republican cohorts would try for a decade to consolidate their victory by implementing the letter and spirit of the Constitution of 1857 and, at the same time, by setting Mexico on the path of modernization. The sailing was far from smooth, but the political process did show definite signs of maturation. The scars from the recent wars of the Reform and the Intervention were deep, and, while the conservatives endeavored to eliminate the distinctions between victors and vanquished, the liberals set out to inaugurate a new era of peace and material progress. They both had to overcome the deeply engrained suspicion that differences of opinion, ideology, and practical politics should inevitably be settled by force rather than by reason. And while all antagonisms did not dissipate during the Restoration, bellicosity became at least less of a reflex action. But, more important, this nine-year period established the guidelines for the profound changes that would occur in Mexico during the last quarter of the nineteenth century.

Juárez's Third Term

In marked contrast to Maximilian's entrance into Mexico City in his ornate European carriage in 1864, Juárez entered the capital

---

1. Daniel Cosío Villegas, ed. *Historia moderna de México*, 9 vols. (Mexico, 1955–72). The first three volumes treat the restored republic.

on July 15, 1867, in a stark black coach. Cheers welled up from the thousands who lined the streets. His reception was triumphant, as it well should have been, but although Juárez enjoyed the display of camaraderie and goodwill, he recognized that it was no time to rest on past laurels. He immediately called for presidential elections, announcing himself as a candidate for a third term. Under the circumstances, few knowledgeable politicians believed that a third term was excessive. Most of the first two had been spent on the run with virtually no chance of implementing a progressive program. While preparing himself for the elections, the president undertook an important political reform. In order to manifest the primacy of civilian over military rule, he reduced the size of the Mexican army from sixty thousand to twenty thousand men.

In October Juárez won the presidential election and late in the year was sworn into office for a third term. In one respect he was faced with a situation not unlike that which he had encountered in 1861 when he returned to office following the liberal victory in the War of the Reform. The administration had to enunciate a policy toward the conservatives who had supported the French-imposed monarchy. During the fight against the empire, the decrees issued from the Juarista headquarters concerning French sympathizers had been harsh indeed. The no-nonsense policy was reaffirmed in Querétaro with the trial and execution of Maximilian. But by late 1867 few liberals were still crying for revenge, and it seemed time to adopt a more conciliatory policy. In a gesture of goodwill Juárez set free many political prisoners and reduced the sentences of others.

Economic and Educational Reforms

The new administration wisely directed its energies into two main fields: a revamping of the economy and a restructuring of the educational foundations of the country. Juárez named Matías Romero, who had served his exiled government so effectively in Washington, as secretary of the treasury. Romero formulated a plan for economic development that called for the improvement of transportation facilities and the fuller exploitation of natural resources through the attraction of foreign capital. He believed that Mexico's economic future rested largely on the revitalization of the mining industry rather than upon industrialization. The key to increased mineral production was a major revision of

Mexico's tax and tariff structure. Despite much congressional opposition, through hard work and thrift Secretary Romero succeeded in bringing some order out of the economic chaos by 1872, but the dividends he expected in the form of substantial capital investment would not be noticeable for several years.

While tariff and tax revision were important, other factors still discouraged the potential investor. Mexico had an image to live down. Political instability, minor rebellions, the presence of private armies and groups of bandits for whom lawlessness had become a way of life, all dissuaded foreign capitalists seeking lucrative investment fields. Travel on Mexico's roads and shipment of merchandise were precarious. One of the answers was found in a relatively new concept of public security. Prior to the French Intervention, Benito Juárez had authorized the establishment of a rural police force, the *rurales*, modeled in some ways on the Spanish *guardia civil*. But jurisdiction over the security guard was divided between two government departments: War and Interior. The overlapping and often confusing jurisdictions undermined the effectiveness of the organization, and it did not amount to much. After the overthrow of the empire, however, Juárez's Congress authorized an increased budget for the rurales, and, in 1869, placed them under the sole jurisdiction of the Department of Interior. With more adequate funds and with the organizational problem resolved, the rurales began to play a major peace-keeping role. Patrolling the roads, assisting the army, guarding special shipments of bullion and merchandise, and policing local elections, they contributed toward stabilization of life in the countryside.

Without question the most important economic development to occur during the early years of the Restoration was the completion of the Mexico City–Veracruz railroad. The enterprise had begun in 1837, and short segments of a couple of kilometers had been completed periodically since that time. But in 1860, when the United States had over 30,000 miles of track in operation, Mexico had barely 150 miles. The stage between Mexico City and Guadalajara (a distance of some 425 miles) often took more than a week even if it was not mired in the mud or assaulted by bandits. To be sure, construction in the rugged terrain between the Mexican capital and Veracruz on the Gulf was an engineering nightmare, for the roadbed had to rise from sea level to over nine thousand feet and had to be built across huge canyons and precipices. But railroad technology was clearly ahead of Mexico's determination to see the project through.

Spanning the Metlac Ravine was an engineering achievement of major proportions.

During the period of the empire the concession rights were held by the Imperial Mexican Railway Company, a corporation registered in London. The British engineers who worked for Maximilian made considerable progress in laying portions of the roadbed, but by 1866 the company was almost bankrupt and all work stopped. Upon the restoration of the republic Juárez articulated his profound concern for completion of the line. He exempted the company from the forfeiture legislation that applied to all who had supported Maximilian on the condition that construction be resumed. Realizing that the company was broke, Juárez also agreed to pay it an annual subsidy of 560,000 pesos for twenty-five years. The agreement reached by the government and the company produced considerable bombast in the Mexican

Congress. Among the leading stockholders was Antonio Escandón, a conservative who had been a member of the Mexican delegation that visited Miramar in October 1863. Cries of governmental favoritism to traitors were heard in the Congress, but Juárez believed that the railroad was more important than partisan politics and went ahead with his plans.

In an attempt to soothe passions the company was renamed the Ferrocarril Mexicano (Mexican Railroad Company). The British engineers did a fantastic job of construction, digging endless tunnels and breaching the Barranca de Metlac, a chasm 900 feet across and 375 feet deep. Gradually all the gaps were closed, the rails tied to one another, and the job finished on December 20, 1872. The line was officially inaugurated on January 1 of the following year. Archbishop Pelagio Antonio de Labastida formally blessed the new project at the Buenaventura station in Mexico City, signifying a reduction in tensions between church and state. Church endorsement of a liberal government enterprise a decade before would have been unthinkable. The successful completion of the railroad whetted the appetite, encouraging others to begin thinking of the desirability, indeed the necessity, of constructing other major lines.

Education, too, began to move in a new direction with the restoration of the republic. In the fall of 1867 Juárez appointed a five-man commission to reorganize the entire educational structure of the country. The committee was headed by Gabino Barreda, a medical doctor who had studied in France and become a devotee of the positivist philosophy of Auguste Comte. While positivism would not become the official state doctrine in Mexico for another fifteen years, its roots most definitely can be found in Barreda's educational values. The curriculum recommended by the committee and adopted by the Congress in late 1867 placed heavy emphasis on arithmetic, the rudiments of physics and chemistry, and practical mechanics in the primary schools, and further emphasis on mathematics and the natural sciences in the secondary schools. The arts and the humanities, while not entirely ignored, were subordinated to an understanding of the physical world.

More important to Juárez than the curriculum itself was the fact that primary education in Mexico was made free and obligatory for the first time. All towns with a population of over five hundred were to have one school for boys and one for girls. Two more schools were to be built for every additional two thousand

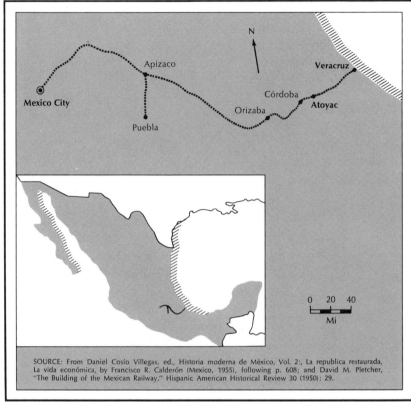

SOURCE: From Daniel Cosío Villegas, ed., Historia moderna de México, Vol. 2:, La republica restaurada, La vida económica, by Francisco R. Calderón (Mexico, 1955), following p. 608; and David M. Pletcher, "The Building of the Mexican Railway," Hispanic American Historical Review 30 (1950): 29.

inhabitants. But, as had been the case in Mexico since the arrival of the Spaniards in 1519, theory and practice, the law and the reality, seldom merged. Universal primary education remained but a liberal dream.

Juárez and his secretary of foreign relations, Sebastián Lerdo de Tejada, took special care to cultivate friendly diplomatic relations with Mexico's neighbors and with the powers of Europe, most of which had recognized the empire of Maximilian. In his first address to the Congress in 1867 the president acknowledged the sympathy and support the United States had given him during the recent unpleasantness. The relationship between the two countries was further cemented when William Seward visited Mexico in 1869, and the two countries agreed to lay claims, accumulated since the Treaty of Guadalupe Hidalgo, before a mixed claims commission. Gradually relations with Europe were renewed as well.

Division among the Liberals and the Death of Juárez

Juárez's third term was his best, and in the presidential elections of 1871 he decided, against the advice of many friends, to seek a fourth. The onetime pillar of constitutional liberalism had become prey to the nineteenth-century Latin American political myth of indispensability; he had allowed his very human desire for power and accomplishment to impugn his earlier ideals. His popularity had been ebbing for at least a year. The election of 1871 was one of the most hotly contested of the nineteenth century as two former supporters ran against him: Porfirio Díaz, who had won his military laurels in the wars against the French; and Sebastián Lerdo de Tejada, the brother of the author of Ley Lerdo. The election thus occasioned a three-way split in the undisciplined liberal party—Juaristas, Porfiristas, and Lerdistas. Juárez still enjoyed a wide base of popular support and, in addition, had most of the federal bureaucracy working in his behalf. Lerdo counted on the strong backing of the professional classes and many of the socially prominent and wealthy, while Díaz was supported by some of the military outcasts from the conservative party and a vast entourage of disappointed office seekers.

A caricature by Santiago Hernández of Juárez and his opposition. Entitled "Little Fingers," it illustrates how the opposition whittled away at Juárez's power.

Both the Lerdistas and the Porfiristas attacked the concept of constant re-election as a violation of the republican principles Juárez had always espoused.

When the ballots were counted after the June election, none of the three candidates received the requisite majority of the votes. The choice, according to the Constitution of 1857, thus fell upon the Congress. The Juaristas had done well in the congressional elections and dominated that body when it convened in the early fall. After a number of bitter credentials fights the new delegates were seated, and when the important vote was taken, Juárez was elected. Of the two defeated candidates, Díaz accepted the decision with less grace. On November 8, 1871, he proclaimed himself in revolt against the Juárez regime.

The *Plan de la Noria* proclaimed that indefinite re-election of the chief executive repudiated the principles of the Revolution of Ayutla and endangered the country's national institutions. It was necessary to overthrow those who considered national office to be their personal prerogative. No officeholder who exercised national jurisdiction of any kind in the year preceding presidential elections should be eligible to run for that high position. Those who accept the plan, Díaz proclaimed, "will fight for the cause of the people and the people will be the only victors. The Constitution of 1857 will be our banner and less government and more liberty our program."[2] But Díaz's fellow citizens were not yet ready for another armed insurrection, and Díaz was disappointed at the lack of interest his plan generated. While a few local caciques declared for the movement, Díaz had not struck a responsive chord. The army he put in the field was quickly defeated by the federals.

The revolt of La Noria was in complete disarray when, on July 19, 1872, Juárez suffered a coronary seizure and died in office. Sebastián Lerdo de Tejada, the chief justice of the Supreme Court, became acting president and scheduled new elections for October. Lerdo enjoyed a reputation for keen intelligence, great administrative ability, and unquestionable republican sympathies. In public speeches and debates he often attained forensic perfection. He decided to run against Porfirio Díaz in the elections and defeated him easily. Since Díaz's revolution against Juárez had been predicated almost entirely on the principle of no-re-election, the caudillo from Oaxaca accepted the outcome.

2. Quoted in Ernesto de la Torre Villar et al., eds., *Historia documental de México* (Mexico, 1964), 2: 361.

Pilgrimages were made to Juárez's Tomb in Mexico City long after his death in 1872.

Lerdo's Presidency

President Lerdo believed that the foundation of Mexico's future progress rested heavily on the establishment of peace. The material progress he envisioned was impossible without order, and order was impossible without firm executive control. The national government had to curb disruptive localism and weaken the army. Mexican liberalism was undergoing a significant change. It was becoming increasingly elitist and was no longer antithetical to centralism and dictatorship. When political disputes occurred in the states, Lerdo did not hesitate to intervene with federal forces.

Lerdo wisely retained many Juaristas in his government and, in seeking his goals, followed the same general policies that had been formulated by his famous predecessor. He used the rurales to patrol and protect the Mexico City–Veracruz railroad. To foster communications development he let railroad contracts for the construction of a new line north from Mexico City to the United States border. A company made up of both Mexican and British investors—the Central Railroad of Mexico—obtained the concession. A United States concern, headed by Emile la Sere of New Orleans, received promise of a subsidy of 12,500 pesos for each mile of track it laid down across the Isthmus of Tehuantepec. And, finally, the government encouraged feeder lines to connect with the recently completed Ferrocarril Mexicano and negotiated other contracts for the construction of telegraph lines. Lerdo's goal—to connect all of the state capitals to Mexico City by telegraph—was not reached, but he did add over sixteen hundred miles of telegraph line.

In the field of education Lerdo surpassed the efforts of his predecessor. Augmented federal and local funds resulted in a sharp increase in school construction but only a gradual increase in school enrollment. Between 1870 and 1874 the number of schools in Mexico almost doubled, but even in the latter year the 349,000 students represented only one out of nineteen school-age children. And years of tradition had established another pattern that was difficult to break; of these only 77,000 were female.

School construction grew much more rapidly than enrollment, and many school seats remained empty: availability of classroom space was not the answer. An available school seat did not mean that a competent teacher would be found or that a poor father would sacrifice the meager supplement to the family income that

SCHOOLS AND STUDENT ENROLLMENT 1844–74

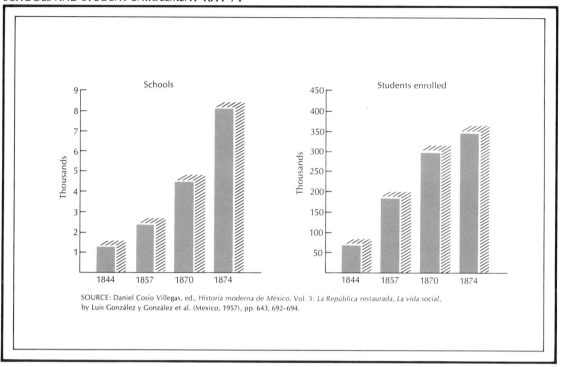

SOURCE: Daniel Cosío Villegas, ed., *Historia moderna de México*, Vol. 3: *La República restaurada, La vida social*, by Luis González y González et al. (Mexico, 1957), pp. 643, 692–694.

three or four small children working in the fields, shining shoes, or selling newspapers might provide.

The Lerdo administration made progress in other areas. The government added France to the list of European countries with which diplomatic relations had been restored. Secretary of the Treasury Romero continued his work on tariff revision and was able to codify his efforts. Lerdo also broke ground on one important political reform. The unicameral national legislature provided by the Constitution of 1857 had been under attack for years. The president proposed that a second house be added, and the legislative branch responded to the request in 1875. A Senate was added to the Chamber of Deputies, bringing the legislature back to the formula that had been first tested in 1824. Lerdo wanted the second, more elite body because he believed that it could be useful to him in his centralization efforts.

Lerdo's administration turned out to be one of the better ones that Mexico had yet experienced. But as any man of action, he could not emerge from the Mexican presidency unscathed. The enemies mounted, the press assailed him mercilessly, and prominent politicians of both parties spoke out strongly against him. The rumors were vicious. He had at one time studied for the priesthood and was even charged with making up for lost time as a celibate. When Lerdo announced that he was planning to seek re-election in 1876, Porfirio Díaz perceived that history was finally on his side. In March of 1876, five years after his unsuccessful attempt to overthrow Benito Juárez under the Plan de la Noria, Díaz was ready to try again. He issued the *Plan de Tuxtepec*, charging that Lerdo had repeatedly violated the sovereignty of the states and the municipalities, sacrificed Mexico's best interests in negotiating the railroad contracts, reduced the right of suffrage to a farce, and squandered public funds. But, most important, the plan established no-re-election of the president and the governors of the states as the supreme law of the land. Effective suffrage and no-re-election were to be the guiding principles of the Mexican political process.

The Revolution of Tuxtepec was decided in one decisive battle as soldiers in a score of states flocked to the new banner. The opposing forces met on November 16 at Tecoac in the state of Tlaxcala; Díaz, reinforced by cohort Manuel González, carried the day. Recognizing that the path to Mexico City was wide open, the president, with little disposition to carry on, abandoned the struggle and made his way to Acapulco where a steamer was waiting to carry him to the United States. Porfirio Díaz occupied Mexico City on November 21, 1876; he would control the country, directly or indirectly, for the next third of a century.

The restored republic has never received the kind of attention it deserves in the survey literature of Mexican history. One general synthesis classifies it as part of a more general period of "marking time."[3] It was almost anything but that. Careful examination of the Restoration period reveals it to be a critical transition between the demise of the empire and the establishment of the Díaz dictatorship. For the first time in Mexican history the administrations in power seemed more to pull the country together than to drive it apart. All of the major changes generally attributed to Díaz and his successive cabinets in the last quarter of the nineteenth century and first decade of the twentieth are firmly rooted in the years 1867 to 1876: tax and tariff reform; increased public security, especially in the rural areas;

3. Charles C. Cumberland, *Mexico: The Struggle for Modernity* (New York, 1968), pp. 141–89.

recognition of the need to attract foreign capital; the improvement of transportation and communication facilities; the cultivation of better relations abroad; a slightly less antagonistic relationship between church and state; and increased centralism disguised as federalism. Juárez and Lerdo, especially the former, laid the foundations, and Porfirio Díaz would construct the edifice. But modern Mexico did begin in 1867. Díaz's subsequent accomplishments were possible because his two predecessors in the presidential chair had paved the way.

Recommended for Further Study

Acuña, Rodolfo F. *Sonoran Strongman: Ignacio Pesqueira and His Times.* Tucson: University of Arizona Press, 1974.

Bazant, Jan. *Alienation of Church Wealth in Mexico: Social and Economic Aspects of the Liberal Revolution, 1856–1875.* Cambridge: Cambridge University Press, 1971.

Berbusse, Edward J. "General Rosecrans' Forthright Diplomacy with Juárez's Mexico, 1868–1869." *The Americas* 36 (1980): 499–514.

Falcone, Frank. "Benito Juárez Versus the Díaz Brothers: Politics in Oaxaca, 1867–1871." *The Americas* 34 (1977): 630–51.

Glick, Edward B. *Straddling the Isthmus of Tehuantepec.* Gainesville: University of Florida Press, 1959.

Knapp, Frank A. *The Life of Sebastián Lerdo de Tejada: A Study of Influence and Obscurity.* Austin: University of Texas Press, 1951.

Pletcher, David M. "The Building of the Mexican Railway." *Hispanic American Historical Review* 30 (1950): 26–62.

———. "General William S. Rosecrans and the Mexican Transcontinental Railroad Project." *Mississippi Valley Historical Review* 38 (1952): 657–78.

Scholes, Walter V. *Mexican Politics during the Juárez Regime, 1855–1872.* Columbia: University of Missouri Press, 1957.

Sinkin, Richard N. *The Mexican Reform, 1855–1876: A Study in Liberal Nation Building.* Austin: Institute of Latin American Studies, 1979.

Smart, Charles Allen. *Viva Juárez!* London: Eyre and Spottiswoode, 1964.

Steward, Luther N., Jr. "Spanish Journalism in Mexico, 1867–1879." *Hispanic American Historical Review* 45 (1965): 422–33.

Vanderwood, Paul. "Genesis of the Rurales: Mexico's Early Struggle for Public Security." *Hispanic American Historical Review* 50 (1970): 323–44.

Weeks, Charles A. *The Juárez Myth in Mexico.* University: University of Alabama Press, 1987.

25

Society and Culture in the Middle of the Nineteenth Century

Rural Life

Mexico was still overwhelmingly rural in the 1850s, 1860s, and 1870s, and life for the average citizen changed very little. Those who resided in the Indian pueblo or the mestizo village lived much like their parents or their grandparents. In terms of earning power, standard of living, diet, life expectancy, and education, the life of the rural Mexican during the empire and the restored republic closely mirrored that which two earlier generations of independent Mexicans had experienced. In almost every important respect he remained outside of the mainstream of national society, and his life was one of privation.

The gap separating brown and white Mexico, poor and rich Mexico, was not bridged in the middle of the century. It might even have grown more pronounced. The dichotomy of Mexican worlds in 1865 was described by Francisco Pimentel.

> The white is the proprietor; the Indian the worker. The white is rich; the Indian poor and miserable. The descendants of the Spaniards have within their reach all of the knowledge of the century and all of the scientific discoveries; the Indian is completely unaware of it. The white dresses like a Parisian fashion plate and uses the richest of fabrics; the Indian runs around almost naked. The white lives in the cities in magnificent houses; the Indian is isolated in the country, his house a miserable hut. They are two different peoples in the same land; but worse, to a degree they are enemies.[1]

1. Quoted in Daniel Cosío Villegas, ed., *Historia moderna de México*, vol. 3: *La república restaurada, La vida social*, by Luis González y González et al. (Mexico, 1957), p. 151.

Foreign travelers to Mexico found the main roads slightly better than they would have a generation earlier, but most others were still an abomination. They were all very dangerous because of the bandits who continued to infest the highways. Scarcely a visitor to the country failed to note this institutionalized ill. The wife of Prince Salm-Salm, one of Maximilian's confidants, described the anxieties of passengers of the stagecoach from Veracruz to Mexico City as follows:

> It occurs very frequently that the diligence is attacked and plundered by robbers, and many horrible adventures of that kind are recorded, furnishing the passengers not very reassuring matter for conversation, and keeping them in a continual excitement. . . . The coachman does not even attempt to escape or resist; it is his policy to remain neutral, for if he acted otherwise it would not only be in vain, but cost him his life—a bullet from behind some bush would end his career on the next journey. . . . Though the escort now and then furnished by the authorities is mostly absent when needed, it sometimes happens that they are at hand, and to escape such danger the robbers are compelled to act without any ceremony. Whilst one of them takes care of the team, two others, cocked pistol in hand, invite the passengers to descend and to undress, as it is well known that they generally try to conceal their valuables in their clothes. The terror and confusion created by such an order may be imagined, especially if there are ladies amongst the passengers.[2]

Overnight lodging in the larger towns, while generally not elegant, had improved since the early post-Independence years. But villages and Indian pueblos remained unchanged. William Marshall Anderson, a United States citizen who visited Mexico during the empire, found in one southern village "no shelter or place to rest but a miserable grass covered shanty, no bigger or better than my sheep pen." As he moved north the architecture changed but not the amenities. "Unplastered stone walls and a dirt floor constitute the comfort and elegance of our accommodation.[3]

By the 1850s and 1860s rural Mexicans were certainly long accustomed to the indignities of an army marching through their village or, if they were unfortunate, stopping for food or supplies. But the Intervention and Restoration periods added several new

2. Princess Felix Salm-Salm, *Ten Years of My Life* (London, 1876), 1: 183–85.
3. William Marshall Anderson, *An American in Maximilian's Mexico, 1865–1866: The Diaries of William Marshall Anderson*, ed. Ramón Eduardo Ruiz (San Marino, Cal., 1959), pp. 15, 80.

Saltillo, the capital of Coahuila, hardly grew at all in the 1860s and 1870s, but it was one of the more charming provincial capitals of the north.

ingredients. The French troops comported themselves even worse than their American predecessors of 1846–48. They treated the Mexican peasants with utmost disdain and were far from polite in their solicitation of female indulgence. Common sense defies that the generation of blue-eyed, light-skinned babies born in Mexico in the 1860s were all the product of French debauchery, but the not-too-subtle physiognomic changes in those villages hosting a French garrison, or having one nearby, suggest that to the victor belong the spoils.

The social consequences of war did not end with the expulsion of the French. When President Juárez cut back on the size of the Mexican army, tens of thousands of former soldiers were left jobless and hundreds of miles from home. Not a few of them formed bands, and, with a horse, gun, and tattered uniform still bearing military insignia, many took out their frustrations on rural villages or hacienda complexes. The newspapers of the period were filled with stories of brigandage and plunder. Lawlessness became a social cancer reaching epidemic proportions.

Population and Social Problems

As might be expected during a period of foreign war and domestic turmoil, the population of Mexico grew very slowly during the middle of the nineteenth century. Some of the state capitals even lost inhabitants, and northern Mexico still supported only a scanty population. From a figure of 7,860,000 in 1856, the census counters could find only 8,743,000 Mexicans in 1874. The slow rate of growth cannot be attributed to a low birth rate. To the contrary, the birth rate was high, but war casualties and a very high infant mortality rate kept the population down.

Policy makers during both the empire and the restored republic wished to open up new lands, and some even spoke of the need to encourage the development of a new class of independent farmers. Because of the slow rate of population growth, however, European immigration was deemed to be the answer. In spite of Mexico's one sad experience with foreign immigrants in Texas, laws were put on the books in the 1850s and 1860s to encourage immigration from Europe. But religious intolerance, political instability, and much administrative mismanagement all mitigated against a successful program. When the liberals consoli-

POPULATION OF SELECTED CITIES, 1849–78

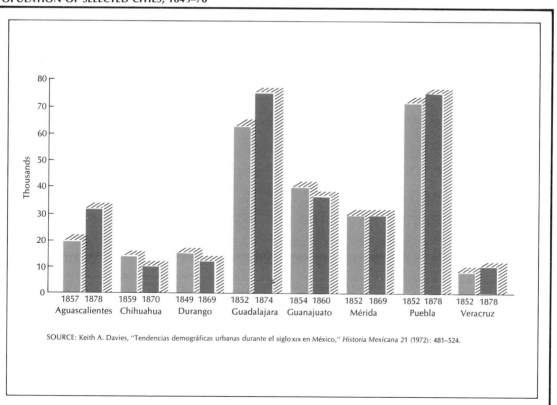

SOURCE: Keith A. Davies, "Tendencias demográficas urbanas durante el siglo xix en México," *Historia Mexicana* 21 (1972): 481–524.

The turbulence of the French Intervention and the Restoration made it inevitable that soldiers would be found congregating in Mexico City.

dated their victory after the expulsion of the French, they believed that the basic problems were resolved and that part of the flow of immigrants to Argentina, Chile, Brazil, and the United States would be diverted to Mexico. But their project met with no more success than had earlier ones. Mexico had not yet lived down its reputation, and the three thousand immigrants from western Europe, the United States, and China who began to arrive annually during the Restoration did not even offset the emigration of Mexicans to the United States. In 1876 only about twenty-five thousand people in Mexico were foreign-born, and they almost all resided in the larger cities.

Mexico City's population grew to two hundred thousand during the Restoration, and in the process the city experienced increased social problems. Prostitution had long been accepted as a necessary evil in Mexico, but when the women of the street began openly soliciting clients at the entrance to the main cathedral and the hundreds of smaller churches, a public uproar followed. Those who called for a crackdown pointed to the burgeoning rate of venereal disease and the perversion of the young and innocent. The defenders argued somewhat theatrically that the institution had to be retained as a safeguard of the chastity of honorable women who would be deflowered on the street if the virile *machos* of the capital had no such release. A sensible compromise was reached. The women of pleasure were pushed into

well-defined red-light zones so as not to offend the casual pas-
serby and were made subject to periodic medical inspection to
arrest the rate of venereal disease.

The Roman Catholic Church had always made alms giving a
virtue, and by the middle of the nineteenth century mendicancy
was as institutionalized as prostitution. While léperos could be
found in all of the larger towns and cities, they congregated by
the thousands in Mexico City. Men and women with one hand
extended—cripples, the blind, alcoholics, even abandoned children—were found everywhere in the capital. If unsuccessful on
the streets or in the churches, they moved from door to door in
both residential and business zones. Government attempts to
curb mendicancy included the establishment of new charitable
institutions and hospitals for the poor, but such efforts, as well
intentioned as they might have been, accomplished little.

The Three Classes

The lot of the urban working class at mid-century was in some
ways even worse than that of the beggars. Workers could not
count on private charity, church support, government aid, or
welfare institutions. Job security was nonexistent, the worker
being completely subject to the whims of his employer. While
the industrial revolution had scarcely touched Mexico, the capital did have its share of factories producing textiles, soap, cig-
arettes, flour, and alcoholic beverages. The thousands working in
these small industries enjoyed but few protective laws. Legislation regulating child labor, safety precautions, and other working conditions was scant, and those laws on the books were seldom enforced. Slightly better off were people who worked for
themselves, the tens of thousands of street vendors each with a
distinctive call hawking tortillas, sweet bread, fruit, flowers,
water, ice, candy, pottery, straw baskets, tamales, pulque, roasted
corn, milk, ice cream, rosaries, crucifixes, pictures of the Virgin
of Guadalupe, and an endless variety of other goods. But their
diet was grossly deficient and their life expectancy short; they
were all illiterate and lived in shacks on the outskirts of Mexico
City.

One of the best jobs the illiterate city dweller could hope for
was domestic service. As a generation earlier, the maids, garden-
ers, doorkeepers, valets, stable masters, chambermaids, and
nanas did relatively well. They received up to fourteen or fifteen

pesos a month without food, or three or four with. But they were at least assured a clean room in which to live and, in spite of long hours, tolerable working conditions in one of the nicer residential districts of the capital.

The still tiny middle class—composed of shopkeepers, merchants, small independent entrepreneurs, professional men, government officials, and other white-collar workers—lived comfortably but without amenities. The houses (often rooms above their stores) were small but adequately furnished with locally made products. Tiles or straw mats covered the floor; rugs were unusual. Because of a grossly inadequate water supply system, very few smaller homes had private baths. Public bathing facilities were scarce and inconvenient enough that neither daily nor weekly bathing was common; the trade in cheap perfumes and colognes was good.

The palatial residences of the wealthy families were mainly in the district of Tacubaya, at the western end of the city. It was a genuine showplace, described by an English visitor in the 1860s as a district where "all the men with heavy purses build villas and country houses, to which they retire in the summer months. . . . It is really a very pretty place. . . ."[4]

The façades of the houses were often decorated by students or professors from the Art Academy of San Carlos. Elegant patios, marble staircases, carved doors, crystal chandeliers, gold candelabra, imported pianos and carpets, rosewood furniture, and old Spanish paintings were staple items in every aristocratic home. Most also had private chapels with the patron saints of the family's members represented. The real marks of distinction, however, were the resplendent private baths, decorated with imported French fixtures. Many of these aristocratic homes required twenty or twenty-five servants to keep them going. Some of the affluent required fewer but hired more in unabashed ostentation.

Women who visited Mexico in the 1860s and 1870s often commented upon the general ignorance of the ladies of the genteel aristocracy they found there. Princess Salm-Salm dwelled upon the subject in her memoirs, but the best description comes from Countess Paula Kollonitz, a lady-in-waiting to Empress Carlota.

> I never saw any book in the hand of a lady, except her prayer book. . . . They write letters, for the most part, with an unpractised hand. Their ignorance is complete; they have not the smallest idea of geography and history. Europe to them consists of

4. J. F. Elton, *With the French in Mexico* (London, 1867), pp. 37-38.

Growing from a squalid Indian community to the most fashionable suburb of Mexico City, by 1850 Tacubaya often housed Mexican presidents, cabinet ministers, bishops, and all of the wealthiest residents of the capital, both Mexican and foreign. At mid-century its population stood at 5,000, but vacationers swelled the count to 6,500 during the summer months.

> Spain, from whence they sprang; Rome, where the Pope rules; and Paris, from whence come their clothes. They have no conception of other countries or other nations, and they could not comprehend that French was not our native tongue.[5]

One wonders just how much the ladies of Europe knew about Mexico, Argentina, or Chile, much less Honduras, Ecuador, or Bolivia, but the point should not be lost. Women, even aristocratic women, had received short shrift in the educational system, and the results were patent.

Social Amusements and Cultural Achievements

Everyday diversion was one of the few activities that could easily cut across class lines. Members of the lower, middle, and upper strata could be seen enjoying the promenades around the Alameda, the great central park in the downtown business district, which was equipped with hydrogen gas lamps in 1873. Everyone enjoyed the free concerts staged in the bandstands of the public parks, and all partook of secular or religious fiestas. Public fairs

5. Countess Paula Kollonitz, *The Court of Mexico* (London, 1868), pp. 160–61.

and touring circuses from Europe or the United States also attracted all elements of society, as did games of dice played on outdoor tables. But the greatest social leveler of all was the bullfight, a spectacle where the cabinet minister could converse with his shoeshine boy and the aristocrat from Tacubaya could debate the awarding of ears and tails with his gardener.

The bullfight was introduced in Mexico in the early sixteenth century and quickly became a cultural institution. The main ring used in Mexico City in the middle of the century was the Plaza del Paseo Nuevo. Built in 1851 at a cost of almost a hundred thousand pesos, it seated ten thousand and was filled each time a fight was held. To be sure, the more affluent sat in the shade and the masses in the sun, the rich drank cognac and the poor pulque, but they all saw the same show. Toreros Bernardo Gaviño, Pablo Mendoza, and Ignacio Gadea were the rage of the era. But not all of the performances were good, and after one particularly bad fight in 1867, during which several horses were killed and blood filled the ring, the press began a concerted campaign for abolition of the sport. Emphasizing the brutality of the spectacle, the opponents succeeded in having the Congress pass legislation outlawing bullfighting in the Federal District over which it had jurisdiction. But the owners of the bullrings, the raisers of fighting stock, the performers, and the thousands of fans argued for reconsideration. The law remained on the books for twenty years, but, meanwhile, ingenuity accomplished what congressional lobbying could not. In 1874 a new ring was dedicated in Tlalnepantla, just outside the Federal District but not so far as to deter the avid aficionados of Mexico City. The placards announcing the Sunday spectacles were plastered all over the walls of the capital.

If popular culture reached virtually everyone, "high culture" was obviously not directed to the illiterate masses. Yet in many ways the arts of the mid-nineteenth century were socially aware and embodied much more than the rejection of the Spanish past that had typified creative endeavors in the first three decades after Independence. The social awareness of the 1850s, 1860s, and 1870s did not generally manifest itself as a series of pleas for the impoverished masses. Rather it called for the establishment of a new, stronger, secular, more developed, and progressive Mexico. It began to inculcate pride in the concept of mexicanidad and to show what patriotism could mean. Further, it tried to overcome the damage that had been done to Mexico's self-image.

A Sunday bullfight at the Plaza de Toros de San Pablo, near Mexico City.

In literature the romantic novel was not superseded but did assume a distinctly new flavor. The new novel, while no less moralistic than the old, was more instructive. To a generation that had witnessed many civil wars and two foreign wars, the cultural orientation was historical, and the historical novel lent itself perfectly to the goals of the new intelligentsia. Armies, and especially foreign ones, marching through poor native villages, raping and looting on their way, provided an abundance of subject matter for historical novelists like Juan A. Mateos, Ireneo Paz, and Vicente Riva Palacio. These writers evoked compassion in the reader not because the Indians and mestizos were poor and subject to abuse but because they were Mexican and subject to abuse.

The literary giant of the period was Ignacio Manuel Altamirano (1834–95). Born to Indian parents in Tixtla, Guerrero, he went to school first in the pueblo and later in Mexico City, but his education was interrupted by the wars of the Reform and the French Intervention. In 1861 he had been elected to the Congress, where he voiced radical opinions. After the expulsion of the French he edited several literary journals and then turned his attention to the novel, a literary form he believed should be didactic. In 1869 and 1871 he published two widely acclaimed short novels, *Clemencia* and *La Navidad en las montañas* (translated as *Christmas in the Mountains*). Set in Guadalajara during the French Intervention, *Clemencia* propounded the ideal of patriotism through the characterization of an officer in the republican army. The social content of *La Navidad en las montañas*, however, is still more apparent. In it the author attacked forced conscription (the leva), urged the development of a new educational system, and denounced the clergy for its failure to meet the real needs of the Mexican community.

The period of Maximilian's empire could have been a productive one for Mexican music and art. The Hapsburg emperor had polished and refined cultural interests and lent his personal support and that of his office to the fine arts. He even underwrote the production costs of an opera by Melesio Morales, Mexico's foremost mid-century composer. But not even the fine arts could escape the intense partiality of the age. The old Art Academy of San Carlos, subsequently changed to the National Academy, was redesignated the Imperial Academy by Maximilian. Dedicated Juarista liberals in the academy could not serve Maximilian in good conscience, and many resigned their posts. When the French were expelled, the academy was reorganized again, this time as the National School of Fine Arts, and many of those artists who had painted for the French found it expedient to step down.

Mexican art in the 1850s, 1860s, and 1870s was dominated by two figures of primary importance: Pelegrín Clavé (1810-80) and Juan Cordero (1824-84). Clavé, a Spaniard by birth, taught at the academy for almost twenty years. He was a portrait painter of the first class; his most famous work was a portrait of Benito Juárez, which today hangs in the Chapultepec Museum. Cordero, almost a generation younger than Clavé, studied in Italy. When he returned to Mexico he keenly resented that Clavé, a Spaniard, should have been named director of the academy. Out of his deep sense of mexicanidad, something he shared with the other young intellectuals of the age, he rejected the assistant directorship of the academy. Cordero was Mexico's first great muralist, and in the late 1850s he began decorating church domes with oils and temperas. But as the anticlericalism of the Reform converted him, he turned his attention to the walls of public buildings instead.

Cordero, much like the historical novelists of the period, was comfortable with historical and philosophical themes that taught a message. In 1874 he completed a mural in the main staircase of the National Preparatory School entitled *Triumph and Study*

Gabino Barreda (1818–81). Barreda, who founded the National Preparatory School in 1867, also introduced Mexico to the positivism of Auguste Comte and in the process provided the philosophical underpinnings for Mexican *cientificismo*.

over Ignorance and Sloth. It depicted Mexican progress in terms of science, industry, and commerce. This trilogy, he believed, would destroy ignorance and greed. The new muses, Electra and Vaporosa, did not toy with harps but rather with a magnetic compass and an apparatus that converted water into steam. A locomotive pulling heavy freight cars depicted the benefits of science. It is not surprising that the positivist creed is clearly present in this work; it was commissioned by Gabino Barreda, the director of the National Preparatory School.

The music of social awareness also followed on the heels of the collapse of Maximilian's empire. Aniceto Ortega's two most famous marches, both completed in 1867, celebrated the defeat of the invader. They were appropriately entitled *Marcha Zaragoza* and *Marcha Republicana*.

Nowhere is the mid-century culture of a new Mexico better illustrated than in the field of philosophy, and seldom can the beginning of a philosophical movement be so accurately pinpointed as Mexican positivism. On September 16, 1867, in an Independence Day celebration in Guanajuato, Gabino Barreda delivered an eloquent speech subsequently known as the "Civic Oration." As a student of Auguste Comte, Barreda had read and observed widely. He interpreted Mexican history as a struggle between a negative spirit (represented most recently by the alliance of the conservative and the French) and a positivist spirit (embodied by the liberal republican forces). The combative phase of the struggle had ended with the execution of Maximilian, and the country was now prepared to embark upon the constructive phase. Barreda was optimistic. Mexico's material regeneration could be achieved through the most prudent application of scientific knowledge and the scientific method. He ended his speech by coining a new slogan for the new Mexico: "Liberty, Order, and Progress." Within a short time, however, Mexican liberals would sense that Liberty was not an equal partner in the positivist trinity. It would be sacrificed, almost meticulously, to Order and Progress. The liberal party would split asunder over the positivist issue, and the moderates, who placed their faith in Order and Progress, would gain the upper hand.

Recommended for Further Study

Altamirano, Ignacio Manuel. *Christmas in the Mountains.* Translated by Harvey L. Johnson. Gainesville: University of Florida Press, 1961.

Brushwood, John S. *Mexico in Its Novel: A Nation's Search for Identity.* Austin: University of Texas Press, 1966.

Elton, J. F. *With the French in Mexico.* London: Chapman and Hall, 1867.

Kollonitz, Countess Paula. *The Court of Mexico.* London: Saunders, Otley, and Company, 1868.

Raat, William D. "Leopoldo Zea and Mexican Positivism: A Reappraisal." *Hispanic American Historical Review* 48 (1968): 1–18.

Read, John Lloyd. *The Mexican Historical Novel, 1826–1910.* New York: Instituto de las Españas, 1939.

Rosaldo, Renato. "The Legacy of Literature and Art." In *Six Faces of Mexico,* edited by Russell C. Ewing, pp. 245–310. Tucson: University of Arizona Press, 1966.

Salm-Salm, Princess Felix. *Ten Years of My Life.* 2 vols. London: Richard Bentley & Son, 1876.

Stevenson, Robert. *Music in Mexico: A Historical Survey.* New York: Thomas Y. Crowell, 1971.

Wilson, Robert A. *Mexico: Its Peasants and Its Priests.* New York: Harper and Brothers, 1856.

Zea, Leopoldo. *The Latin American Mind.* Norman: University of Oklahoma Press, 1963.

———. *Positivism in Mexico.* Translated by Josephine H. Schulte. Austin: University of Texas Press, 1974.

VII THE MODERNIZATION OF MEXICO, 1876-1910

26

The Making of the Porfiriato

Porfirio Díaz controlled the destiny of the Mexican nation for a third of a century. These were interesting and vital years in the entire western world. Innovation characterized the era—in technology, political and economic systems, social values, and artistic expression. Otto von Bismarck transformed the German states into a nation. William Gladstone introduced England to a new kind of liberalism. The leading powers of Europe partitioned Africa unto themselves. The United States emerged as a world power, and Spain lost Cuba, Puerto Rico, and the Philippines— the last remnants of its once-glorious empire. Russia experienced a revolution that, though abortive, presaged things to come in 1917. Émile Zola and Anatole France came heroically to the defense of Captain Dreyfus, and Pope Leo XIII enunciated *Rerum Novarum*, proclaiming that employees should be treated more as men than as tools. Thomas Hardy and Thomas Mann revolutionized the world of fiction, while Renoir and Monet did the same for art. But even in a world of profound change, Porfirio Díaz's Mexico must be considered remarkable.

Mexico in 1876

When Díaz assumed control of Mexico in 1876 the country was hopelessly backward. It had scarcely been touched by the scientific, technological, and industrial revolutions or the material conquests of the nineteenth century. The benefits and comforts of civilization, as they were found in Mexico, were confined to a handful of the larger cities. While much of western Europe and the United States had been transformed in the last fifty years, Mexico had languished, less out of inertia than because of the intermittent chaos and resultant exhaustion. In the fifty-five years since Independence the presidency had actually changed hands seventy-five times. For every constitutional president there had been four interim, provisional, or irregular presidents. Continuity of policy had been clearly impossible.

Although Presidents Juárez and Lerdo during the Restoration had pointed Mexico in a new direction and had given some indication of what had to be done and how it could be accomplished, they themselves had not been in office long enough, or continuously enough, to see their plans fully implemented. In 1876 Díaz inherited an empty treasury, a long list of foreign debts, and a huge bureaucratic corps whose salaries were in arrears. Mexico's credit rating abroad was abominable, and its politics had become somewhat of a joke in Europe. The value of Mexican imports consistently exceeded the value of exports, presenting a serious balance-of-payments problem. It was virtually impossible to secure sorely needed infusions of foreign capital, and the Mexican affluent, knowing the precarious nature of the political process, would not invest their own resources to any large degree. Because of graft, ineptitude, and mismanagement the public services were poorly run. The mail, if it arrived at all, came inexcusably late.

Mining had never really recovered from the chaotic and dour days of the Wars for Independence. Only a few of the proven mines had been drained and retimbered. Those mines in operation in 1876 were, for the most part, exploited in a haphazard fashion. Extraction and smelting techniques were dated and inefficient. The patio process of the sixteenth century was still the most common method of extracting silver from silver ore. Quite often the cost of production from the mine to the silver bar was over 25 percent of the final value. Some of the marginal mines had been operated at a loss for years, and no coordinated efforts at new geological exploration had been undertaken.

The economic situation of agriculture was much the same. Many implements still in use dated from the early colonial period. The most modern reapers and threshers and newly developed chemical fertilizers were still oddities. Even metal hammers and nails were luxuries. Practically nothing had been done to improve the breeding of stock animals.

When Díaz came to the presidency the iron horse had just

started to compete with the oxcart, the mule train, and the coach. Telegraph construction had barely begun. The dock facilities on both coasts were in sad disrepair, and many of the most important harbors were silted with sand. Veracruz was so unsafe for shipping that some favored abandoning it altogether. The rurales had not yet been able to contain banditry; rural violence consistently demonstrated contempt for law and authority. A tremendously high infant mortality rate testified to the lack of modern sanitation and health facilities even as the last quarter of the nineteenth century began. Yellow fever plagued the tropical areas of the Gulf coast, particularly in the immediate environs of Veracruz.

Mexico City had a special health problem. Situated in a broad valley, it was surrounded by mountains and a series of lakes, almost all of which were at a higher elevation than the city. Heavy rains invariably brought flooding. In addition to extensive property damage (floods often caused adobe walls to crumble), the waters then stagnated in low-lying areas for weeks and months. Disease, reaching epidemic proportions, frequently followed on the heels of a serious flood. Projects to provide an adequate drainage system for the city had been proposed since the seventeenth century. The height of the surrounding mountains, however, thwarted proposals for a foolproof system of drainage canals and dikes, and the projects initiated from time to time were never fully successful.

Order and Progress under Díaz

If Mexico were to emerge from its doldrums, if progress were to displace stagnation, Díaz believed it would be necessary first to change Mexico's image drastically and to remove the stigma popularly associated with Mexican politics. Only if the potential investors from the United States and Europe were convinced that stability was supplanting turbulence, that firmness was replacing irresolution and chaos, and that the political process was maturing could they be expected to offer their dollars and pounds sterling, for profit, in the chore of national development and modernization. The task, then, as Díaz perceived it, was first to establish the rule of law; from it incalculable benefits would accrue. He was fully prepared to accept the positivist dictum of Order and Progress, in that order.

Díaz's liberal credentials and personal integrity were impeccable. Born to a family of modest means in the city of Oaxaca in 1830, he studied first for the priesthood and then for the law. But the boy was not cut out to do well in the classroom, and politics got under his skin before he finished his law degree. There were only two avenues open to political prominence in nineteenth-century Mexico—the law and the army—and Díaz chose the latter. Joining the Oaxaca National Guard in 1856, he fought under the liberal banner during the War of the Reform. With the liberal victory promotions came with startling rapidity, and by the time of his history-making defeat of the French in Puebla on May 5, 1862, he was a thirty-two-year-old brigadier general. During the period of the empire he won additional military fame championing the cause of liberal republicanism as a guerrilla fighter against the French army. Not even his abortive revolt of La Noria against Benito Juárez or his successful revolt of Tuxtepec against Lerdo de Tejada tarnished his liberal reputation. Both were fought in defense of the liberal principle of no-re-election and against liberal apostates who had prostituted it.

During his first term, which lasted until 1880, Díaz was faced with a number of insurrections. Agrarian rebellions protesting seizure of village lands flared in many states, but not all the revolts were of an agrarian nature. Some, such as the rebellion of General Manuel Márquez de León in Sinaloa, were prompted by Díaz's failure, after he came to office, to reward former supporters adequately; others, such as that of General Diego Álvarez in Guerrero, ignited when the local populace objected to presidential appointments in the state. But the most serious were a number of revolts launched along the United States border in support of exiled president Lerdo de Tejada. These military movements not only threatened the success of Díaz's pacification program but also damaged his efforts to cultivate more friendly relations with his northern neighbor. But Díaz was not hesitant in meeting force with force. Rebel leaders who were not shot down on the field of battle were disposed of shortly after their capture. Characteristic of Díaz's attitude toward those who would disrupt the national peace was his reaction to a revolt in Veracruz during his first year in office. When Governor Luis Mier y Terán asked for instructions concerning captured rebels in that state, Díaz reportedly telegraphed him, *Mátalos en caliente* (Kill them on the spot). Such lessons were not lost on potential revolutionaries elsewhere. Mexico was not as tranquil in the post-1880 period as often portrayed. The claim of the government that a blond woman in a short skirt could walk unmolested from the

United States to the Guatemalan border is sheer nonsense. Yet the peace was not shattered as often or as violently as in the past. Over eight hundred corpsmen had been added to the rurales to curb brigandage. Order was gradually coming, and progress would accompany it.

Within a couple of years of his assumption of the presidency Díaz had been recognized by most of western Europe and Latin America, but the United States held out pending the satisfactory resolution of several outstanding problems. The mixed claims commission established under Presidents Juárez and Grant had labored for almost seven years with little to show for its efforts. Many United States congressmen, feeling pressure from their constituents, were restless. But a breakthrough in the negotiations finally occurred in late 1876. Díaz agreed to the terms set forth by a special umpire. Mexico would pay almost $4,000,000 in claims, in annual installments of $300,000. The first payment was met in January 1877 and augured well for future United States–Mexican relations, but the Hayes administration had one further grievance. Groups of Mexican bandits and Indians occasionally crossed the border, attacked settlements in the United States, and drove herds of cattle back into Mexico. The Mexican government, in the name of national sovereignty, refused to grant permission to United States forces to cross over into Mexico in pursuit. In the summer of 1877 border depredations brought the two nations almost to the brink of war. Díaz was at his best at this crucial juncture. While he would not permit American troops to enter Mexican territory, he did dispatch additional troops of his own to the border region to prevent further encroachments. Tensions gradually subsided, and President Hayes was slowly convinced that the Díaz administration meant to establish order and meet its foreign obligations. In an extremely significant step he authorized recognition of the Díaz regime in the spring of 1877.

During his first administration Díaz also began to put Mexico's economic house in order. As a symbolic gesture he reduced his own salary and then ordered similar reductions for other government employees. Thousands of useless bureaucrats were eliminated from the rolls altogether. In addition, the administration attacked a problem endemic since the colonial period— smuggling. To prevent the annual loss of hundreds of thousands of dollars in import and export duties along the United States border and in Mexico's leading ports, Díaz announced a new, tough government policy. Private individuals caught trying to circumvent the payment of duties would be subject to five years' imprisonment; government employees would be subject to ten years' for the same crime; and commercial establishments trafficking in smuggled goods would receive no government contracts. To stimulate additional commerce with the United States three new Mexican consulates were opened along the border, at Rio Grande City, Laredo, and Eagle Pass. But the economic reforms, though well intentioned, were insufficient to provide a surplus in the treasury.

As Díaz's first term drew to a close, several of the states urged that the no-re-election law be amended so that Díaz could be eligible to serve another term. But Díaz preferred the law as it was; it provided that neither the president nor the state governors were eligible for immediate re-election but could serve again after the lapse of an intervening term. The Revolution of Tuxtepec, built on the foundations of no-re-election, was still too recent to attempt a change; he dutifully retired from office. The peaceful passage of power from one president to another was no common occurrence in nineteenth-century Mexico. By voluntarily stepping aside Díaz could give further substance to the growing conviction abroad that Mexico had begun to mature politically. As the term ended, Díaz threw his support behind forty-seven-year-old Manuel González, an imposing military man who had rendered yeoman service in the fight against Lerdo and who was currently serving as secretary of war. González won the election with a large majority.

The González Presidency

The González presidency was controversial. The new president wanted to follow the patterns established by Díaz and, in fact, even brought his predecessor into the government for a short time as head of the Department of Development. Revenues increased, but so did expenditures as the administration plunged headlong into further development. Modernization was expensive. Railroad construction continued, but the companies required large subsidies from the government—as high as $9,500 for each kilometer of track laid. The government also fostered new steamship lines and established the first cable service in the country. But González had overextended his regime and found himself without sufficient funds to meet government obligations; rather than neglect foreign debts or railroad subsidies, he stopped the salaries of many government officials. The outcry was predictable, but its intensity was not.

Stories of graft and corruption began filling the press, and political pamphlets denouncing the regime circulated on the streets of Mexico City. If one believed the enemies of the regime, not since the days of Santa Anna had Mexico witnessed such debauchery in high government places. The president and his cabinet were charged with negotiating illegal contracts and receiving rebates, selling government properties to administration favorites for practically nothing, and stealing from the treasury at a fantastic rate. The president's personal life also came under vicious attack as he was accused of a wide array of sexual improprieties. The public turned against him.

The charges were either fabrications or gross exaggerations. It could be fairly argued that the bureaucracy's talent for peculation outstripped its administrative qualifications, but that González consented or personally benefited has never been documented. The suggestion that Díaz fabricated the stories to discredit González is more fanciful and cynical than accurate; the best recent scholarship suggests forcefully that Manuel González was not a puppet of Porfirio Díaz.[1] González called his own shots and, in fact, must be given credit for encouraging the developmental process that had begun timidly with the restoration of the republic. But perhaps the most important lesson to be drawn is that the attacks against the president, as intense as they were, did not occasion any serious armed insurrection. The vituperations certainly could have tarnished Mexico's changing image, but when elections, rather than a new revolutionary plan, followed, many were convinced that the country had finally turned the corner.

The Return of Díaz

Díaz used his four years out of office to relax and to build a new political machine. He served for a brief time in the González cabinet and for slightly over a year in the governorship of his native state of Oaxaca. His first wife, Delfina Ortega, had died in 1880, and the following year he married Carmen Romero Rubio, the daughter of Manuel Romero Rubio, a Lerdista statesman and cabinet member. She was eighteen; Díaz had just celebrated his

1. Donald M. Coerver, *The Porfirian Interregnum: The Presidency of Manuel González of Mexico, 1880–1884.* (Fort Worth: Texas Christian University Press, 1979.)

fifty-first birthday. They traveled to the United States on their honeymoon as Mexico's representatives to the New Orleans World's Fair; newspapermen often mistook her for his daughter. But the well-bred, sensitive, and perfectly-prepared-to-be-a-first-lady Señora Díaz began to educate her husband in the social graces. She performed her task admirably, and within a couple of years Díaz was much more the polished gentleman than the crude warrior who had catapulted himself into the presidency in 1876.

All knowledgeable Mexican politicians realized that Díaz would run for the presidency again in 1884, and most knew that he would win. Liberals and conservatives, and various factions thereof, began to gather around him in the year prior to the elections. He wisely held out vague promises to all but made very few definite commitments. In September Díaz swept to victory. From this time forward he would not feel the need to step out of office after completing each term and would remain in the presidency continually until 1911. The conditions that greeted him in 1884 were a far cry from those of 1876. He not only was ready to transform the face of the nation, but had a definite plan of action.

Recommended for Further Study

Beals, Carleton. *Porfirio Díaz: Dictator of Mexico.* Philadelphia: Lippincott, 1932.

Coatsworth, John. "Railroads, Landholding, and Agrarian Protest in the Early Porfiriato." *Hispanic American Historical Review* 54 (1974): 48–71.

Coerver, Donald M. *The Porfirian Interregnum: The Presidency of Manuel González of Mexico, 1880–1884.* Fort Worth: Texas Christian University Press, 1979.

Cosío Villegas, Daniel. *The United States versus Porfirio Díaz.* Lincoln: University of Nebraska Press, 1963.

Creelman, James. *Díaz: Master of Mexico.* New York: Appleton, 1916.

García Cubas, Antonio. *The Republic of Mexico in 1876.* Mexico: La Enseñanza Printing Office, 1876.

Godoy, José F. *Porfirio Díaz: President of Mexico.* New York: Putnam, 1910.

Gregg, Robert D. *The Influence of Border Troubles on Relations between the United States and Mexico, 1876–1910.* New York: De Capo Press, 1970.

Hannay, David. *Díaz.* Port Washington, N.Y.: Kennikat Press, 1970.

27

The Process of Modernization

Economic Reform and the
Improvement of Mexico's Image

As Porfirio Díaz consolidated his political position and stabilized the country, Mexico entered a period of sustained economic growth the likes of which it had never before experienced. In the process, Mexico entered the modern age. Steam, water, and electric power began to replace animal and human muscle. A number of new hydraulic- and hydroelectric-generating stations were built as the modernization process tied itself to the new machines it supported. The telephone arrived amid amazement and wonder in the 1880s. The Department of Communications and Public Works supervised and coordinated the installation of the wireless telegraph and submarine cables. A hundred miles of electric tramway connected the heart of Mexico City to the suburbs.

A major breakthrough in health and sanitation occurred when Díaz hired the British firm of S. Pearson and Son, Ltd., to bring modern technology to the drainage problem of Mexico City. For 16 million pesos the English engineers and contractors, with the experience of the Blackwell Tunnel under the Thames and the East River Tunnel in New York behind them, successfully completed a thirty-mile canal and a six-mile tunnel that relieved the Mexican capital of the threat of constant flooding and resultant property damage and disease. At approximately the same time the face of the country was scoured to bolster the country's own self-respect and its image abroad. A public building spree changed the contours of boulevards, parks, and public buildings. Monuments and statues were dedicated to the world's leading statesmen, intellectuals, and military figures. A new penitentiary costing 2.5 million pesos opened in 1900, and a 3-million-peso post office in 1907. A new asylum for the insane, a new municipal palace, and a new Department of Foreign Relations were dedicated prior to the centennial celebrations of 1910. The white marble National Theater, however, missed the centennial target date, and the heavy structure began to sink into the spongy subsoil of Mexico City before it could be finished. Each time a new project was completed, it was formally dedicated in an elaborate and well-planned ceremony to which foreign diplomats, dignitaries, and businessmen received special presidential invitations. Their impressions of Mexico, relayed to colleagues back home, would help effect the change of image.

Mexico's own adaptation of positivism provided the philosophical underpinning of the regime, and the scientific method had great appeal in a prescientific society. The *científicos*, as those who followed in the footsteps of Gabino Barreda came to be known, were not all orthodox Comteans. Some blended Comte with John Stuart Mill, and others added a large dose of Herbert Spencer. A few of the científicos called for modest programs ushering the Indian masses into a rapidly modernizing world, but many were paternalistic toward the Indian at best and elitist at worst, believing that Mexico's future lay solely with the criollo class. Some felt that they might eventually be willing to share political and economic power with the aboriginal population, but, they contended, the time was not yet at hand. According to Justo Sierra, a científico spokesman, Mexico had to pass through a period of "administrative power" (a euphemism for dictatorship) before it could attain nationhood. Then the time would be ripe to discuss the broadening of the participatory base.

The president and his científico advisers realized first of all that a series of structural reforms were needed to place Mexico's economic house in order, and they were fortunate to find an economic genius in their midst. José Ives Limantour, soon renowned in European financial circles, was the son of a French émigré. A man of many talents, he was a scholar, an accomplished jurist, and a dedicated linguist. But he rejected the life of studious solitude for public service. First as subsecretary and then secretary of the treasury, he applied the best positivist thought of the day to the reorganization of the country's finances, which offered a fertile field for his talents. For Limantour, Mexico's future was

José Limantour (1854–1935). An advocate of positivism, Limantour, as secretary of the treasury, brought order and reason to Porfirian finances.

fully dependent upon its economic regeneration. To be sure, Matías Romero, during the Restoration, had begun work on a revision of the tariff, but much remained to be done. Gradually, during the 1880s and 1890s Secretary Limantour lowered or eliminated the duties on many imports and permitted special tariff exemptions for economically depressed areas of the country. He also negotiated a series of loans at favorable rates of interest and, most important for the economic well-being of the country, shifted Mexico from the silver to the gold standard.

As significant as any of the individual reforms was Limantour's decision to overhaul the nation's administrative machinery so that the reforms could be properly implemented. While it would be foolhardy to suggest that all graft and corruption were eliminated, Limantour did improve the situation markedly, at least at the lower echelons of government. The tariff laws were enforced; useless bureaucrats, or those who were derelict in the performance of duty, were eliminated; and at least some dishonest officials were fined, arrested, and removed from office. The dividends were startling. In 1890 the last installment of the debt to the United States, growing out of the mixed claims settlement, was paid, and four years later Mexico had not only balanced its budget for the first time in history but actually showed that revenues were running slightly ahead of expenditures. When Díaz left office in 1911 the treasury had about 70 million pesos in cash reserves.

The image abroad did change. As Limantour applied his skills to the reorganization of the treasury and Mexico met its foreign obligations on a regular basis, diplomatic relations were opened with all of Europe, and new treaties of friendship, commerce, and navigation were signed with Great Britain, France, Norway, Ecuador, and Japan. For the first time Mexico began to participate actively in international conferences. The country ceased to be the butt of jokes. To the contrary, foreign heads of state were lavish in their praise of the Díaz regime. By the late 1880s and early 1890s Díaz had begun to receive medals and decorations from foreign governments.

The Railroad Boom

Díaz was fully prepared to take advantage of the good economic indicators and the new reputation he had so assiduously cultivated. His government embarked upon a multifaceted program to attract foreign capital into the transportation and mining sectors of the economy. The most dramatic improvement in transportation was the rapid growth of the railroads, the only solution to Mexico's mountainous and broken terrain. During Díaz's first term the federal government began to subsidize the Mexican states in their effort to construct new lines, but the program proved to be something less than a smashing success. Not only did the states drag their heels, but many of the short lines completed were shoddily constructed and constituted more of a danger than a boon to travel. By the 1880s it was obvious that foreign investment and technology were better equipped to do the job.

The Mexican Central Railroad Company, backed by a group of Boston investors, received the concession to construct the major line north from Mexico City to El Paso, Texas. Work began from both terminal points, and the 1,224-mile project was completed in an amazingly short four-year period. The Central was soon flanked by two other new lines to its east and west. In 1888 the Mexican National Railroad Company, originally chartered under the laws of Colorado but subsequently purchased by a group of French and English entrepreneurs, successfully completed a new narrow-gauge line between Mexico City and Laredo, Texas, a distance of eight hundred miles and the shortest route from the

Porfirio Díaz (1830–1915). As soldier, rebel, statesman, and president, Díaz dominated his country as no previous figure in the nineteenth century.

Mexican capital to the United States border. Shortly after the turn of the century it was converted to standard gauge. Finally the Sonora Railroad Company, headed by Thomas Nickerson, built the line between Guaymas, on the Pacific Ocean, and Nogales, Arizona. By 1890 the total trackage of these three major companies approached two thousand miles.

Efforts to connect the country from east to west did not proceed so smoothly. The old Lerdo de Tejada concession to Emile la Sere to build the line across the Isthmus of Tehuantepec eventually passed into the hands of Chandos S. Stanhope. Stanhope completed a line across the Isthmus in 1894, but the construction work and terminal facilities were grossly inadequate. Díaz was forced to grant a new concession to S. Pearson and Son, Ltd., the famous British concern. Sir Weetman Dickinson Pearson (later raised to the peerage as Lord Cowdray) drove an especially hard bargain, and when finally completed the line proved to be one of the most costly in Mexican history. In 1907 the trains were running regularly between Puerto México on the Gulf coast and Salina Cruz on the Pacific, but many wondered if the price was worth it after all. The Panama Canal was already under con-

The arrival of the daily train triggered a burst of activity in hundreds of Mexican towns. This station scene was captured by American photographer Sumner W. Matteson in the station of Amecameca in 1907.

struction, and the Tehuantepec Railroad would soon be rendered obsolete.

Numerous lesser lines were undertaken in the 1880s and 1890s. A line in the south connected Mexico City with Guatemala, and short feeder lines connected most of the state capitals with the major trunks running between Mexico City and the United States border. By the end of the Díaz regime railroads interlaced the entire country; from about four hundred miles of track in 1876, Mexico in 1911 could boast fifteen thousand. Approximately 80 percent of the capital outlay came from the United States. In 1908, however, under the constant prodding of Limantour, the Díaz government purchased the controlling interest in the major lines.

Not all of the lines were laid in the most desirable areas, and not all were of first-rate quality. Yet they contributed in no small way to the tremendous economic transformation of the country.

As the cities were linked to the outlying areas, raw materials could be shipped to industries and finished goods distributed to a greatly expanded domestic market. As products could be quickly transported to population centers and the leading ports, new agricultural lands, specializing in commercial agriculture, were opened, and land values increased.[1] Mexico's textile industry, for example, relied primarily upon imported cotton at the beginning of the Díaz period, but with the opening of new lands in the north, near the railroad lines, cotton production by 1910 not only doubled but made the country almost self-sufficient. When the railroad arrived in Morelos the sugar planters began importing new machinery and setting up new mills to expand production. The larger market for locally produced products drove the costs down and, at least theoretically, widened the base of consumer use. Communities isolated by geography and centuries of tradition were gradually brought into greater contact with one another, and, as a result, the phenomenon of patria chica was challenged seriously for the first time.

The Revival of Mining

The railroads were a means to many ends, and not least among these was the revival of Mexico's potentially wealthy mining industry. The railroads, of course, offered the only practical and economical means of transporting massive shipments of ore. But, equally important, the Díaz-controlled legislature passed a new mining code in 1884. In order to appeal to the foreign investor the code made no mention of traditional Hispanic jurisprudence reserving ownership of the subsoil for the nation. Further, the proprietor of the surface was explicitly granted ownership of all bituminous and other mineral fuels. Several years after the mining code was enacted, the mining tax laws were revised, exempting certain minerals altogether and lowering the tax rates on others. United States and European investors recognized that the potential profits were great and entered Mexico in increasing

1. Arthur P. Schmidt, Jr., "The Railroad and the Economy of Puebla and Veracruz, 1877–1911: A Look at Agriculture," paper presented at the Fifty-first Annual Conference of the Southwest Social Science Association, March 22, 1973. A recent analysis of some fifty-five agrarian protests during the early Porfiriato indicates that over ninety percent occurred at a distance of less than forty kilometers from a new or projected railroad line. See John Coatsworth, "Railroads, Landholding, and Agrarian Protest in the Early Porfiriato," *Hispanic American Historical Review* 54 (1974): 55–57.

PRODUCTION OF SILVER AND GOLD IN MEXICO, 1877–1908

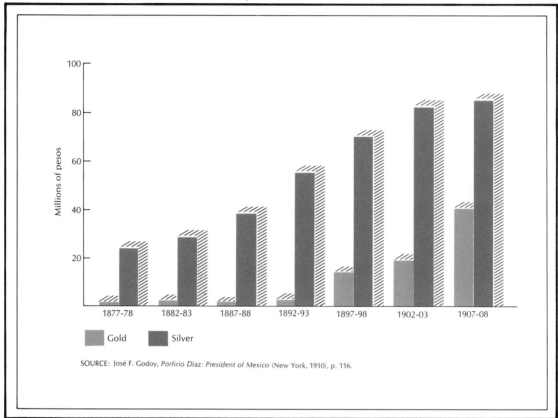

SOURCE: José F. Godoy, *Porfirio Díaz: President of Mexico* (New York, 1910), p. 116.

numbers in the 1880s and 1890s. The new miners introduced modern machinery and new processes of extracting the metal from the ore. Before the century was out they were responsible for radical transformation of the entire industry.

Between 1880 and 1890 three large mining developments were initiated by foreigners in Mexico: Sierra Mojada in Coahuila; Batopilas in Chihuahua; and El Boleo in Santa Rosalía, Baja California. Within a few years the Sierra Mojada region was yielding a thousand tons of silver and lead per week, and Batopilas had made a fortune for its owners. El Boleo, under French and German ownership, proved to be one of the richest copper mining areas in North America.

The introduction of the cyanide process, which made it profitable to extract metal from ores containing only a few ounces of metal to the ton, revolutionized the mining of gold and silver. Largely because of new explorations and the adoption of modern mining techniques, the value of gold production rose from about 1.5 million pesos in 1877 to over 40 million pesos in 1908. Silver production followed a similar pattern. From a production of 24.8 million pesos in 1877, over 85 million pesos worth of silver was being mined in 1908.

Some of the foreign investment came in the form of huge conglomerates. The Guggenheim interests, for example, spread out over much of Mexico and entered numerous interrelated mining activities. They owned the American Smelting and Refining Company, based in Monterrey but with large plants in Chihuahua, Durango, and San Luis Potosí as well. The Aguascalientes Metal Company, the Guggenheim Exploration Com-

Colonel William Greene's town of Cananea, Sonora, was the hub of Mexico's copper production and a symbol of the foreign domination of the country's natural resources.

pany, and the Mexican Exploration Company were either partially or totally owned and controlled by Daniel Guggenheim
and his six brothers. In addition, the Guggenheims acquired
many already proven mines, such as the Tecolote silver mines
and the Esperanza gold mine, as well as new mines in Durango,
Chihuahua, Coahuila, and Zacatecas. By 1902 Guggenheim investments in northern Mexico totaled some $12 million.

Other foreign investors came to Mexico with practically nothing and built multi-million-dollar businesses. Perhaps the best
example is Colonel William Greene, the copper king of Sonora.
In 1898 Greene obtained an option on a Sonora copper mine for
forty-seven thousand pesos from the widow of Ignacio Pesqueira,
a former governor of the state. Greene sold stocks for his mining
venture on Wall Street, and within a few years his Cananea Consolidated Copper Company was one of the largest copper companies in the world, operating eight large smelting furnaces and
employing thirty-five hundred men. With some of the profits
Greene became a lumber factor and a rancher as well; one of his
ranches grazed some forty thousand head of cattle.

Oil Fields and Other Industrial Enterprises

American and British investors engaged in a spirited competition
for the exploitation of Mexico's oil. The first wells were sunk in
areas where surface seepages clearly indicated the presence of
petroleum reserves, but after the turn of the century systematic
geological exploration began in earnest. The American interests
were led by Edward L. Doheny, an American who had successfully developed oil fields in California; he now purchased over
six hundred thousand acres of potentially rich oil lands around
Tampico and Tuxpan. Within a short time his Mexican Petroleum Company brought forth Mexico's first commercially feasible gusher, El Ebano.

The British answer to Doheny was Sir Weetman Dickinson
Pearson, who had worked on the drainage of Mexico City, the
modernization of the Veracruz harbor, the reconstruction of the
Tehuantepec Railroad, and the building of the terminal facilities
at Puerto México and Salina Cruz. Enjoying cordial relations
with Díaz, Pearson in 1901 secured an option on oil lands in the
vicinity of San Cristóbal (today San Cristobal de las Casas, or
Las Casas) on the Isthmus. But the Isthmian fields proved disappointing, and within a few years the regime granted Pearson

drilling concessions in Veracruz, San Luis Potosí, Tamaulipas, and Tabasco. Progress came slowly at first to Pearson's El Aguila Company, but a dramatic hit brought forth the Potrero del Llano, Number 4, a gusher that, when successfully capped, produced more than a hundred million barrels in eight years. To cement the most friendly possible relations with the regime, Pearson appointed the dictator's son, Porfirio Díaz, Jr., to the board of directors of El Aguila. Doheny's Mexican Petroleum Company and Pearson's El Aguila Company dominated the petroleum industry in the early twentieth century and within a few years made Mexico one of the largest petroleum producers in the world.

It would be an exaggeration to suggest that Mexico experienced a profound industrial revolution during the Díaz years, but the industrial process did make itself felt. In 1902 the industrial census listed fifty-five hundred manufacturing industries. The volume of manufactured goods doubled during the Porfiriato. The process began in Monterrey, Nuevo León, where, in addition to the huge Guggenheim interests, other American, French, German, and British investors backed industrial enterprises. Attracted by excellent transportation facilities and by the progressive policies of Governor Bernardo Reyes, which included tax exemptions for industries, foreign and domestic capital was directed into Mexico's first important steel firm, the Compañía Fundidora de Fierro y Acero de Monterrey. Within a few years the company was producing pig iron, steel rails, beams, and bars, and by 1911 it was making over sixty thousand tons of steel annually. Monterrey was soon dubbed the Pittsburgh of Mexico.

In 1890 José Schneider, a Mexican of German extraction, founded the Cervecería Cuauhtémoc, which quickly became the largest and most important brewery in the country. Among its products was Carta Blanca, the number-one selling beer in Mexico. Its initial production capacity of ten thousand barrels and five thousand bottles of beer a day outstripped the available supply of bottles, so the company soon entered the glass business as well. By 1900 it was also producing other kinds of glassware, bottle caps, and packing cartons for both local use and national consumption.

Other industrial concerns based in Monterrey constructed new cement, textile, cigarette, cigar, soap, brick, and furniture factories, as well as flour mills and a large bottled-water plant. Capital investment in the city grew steadily throughout the Díaz regime but most dramatically during the first decade of the new century, when it rose from under 30 million to over 55 million pesos. Smaller fledgling textile and paper mills, cement factories, leather works, soap, shoe, explosives, and tile manufacturers, and a host of lesser firms located themselves in other areas of the country, but by 1910 Monterrey was without question the industrial capital of Mexico.

The improvement of harbor and dock facilities during the Porfiriato opened Mexico up to world commerce on a grander scale than ever before. Millions of pesos spent on Veracruz transformed it in a decade from a port many urged abandoning to one of prime importance. In 1876 Tampico, located at the mouth of the Panuco River, was inaccessible to ships drawing over nine feet. Díaz invited in United States engineers, and, when the harbor was properly dredged and the dock facilities modernized, the port began welcoming ships drawing as much as twenty-five feet. The city of Tampico grew rapidly as a business and commercial center and challenged Veracruz in volume handled. Similar improvements were made in the harbors of Mazatlán, Manzanillo, Puerto México, and Salina Cruz. By the turn of the century the number of serviceable ports had increased to ten on the Gulf coast and fourteen on the Pacific side. Partially because of the improvements in port facilities, and partially because of Limantour's reforms in the tariff structure, Mexico's foreign trade (exports and imports) increased from about 50 million pesos in 1876 to about 488 million pesos in 1910.

Although many of the trappings of traditional society were still to be found, the Mexico of the first decade of the twentieth century was a far cry from that of 1876. Improved public services and modern transportation and communication facilities opened the country to new ideas and challenged the concept of patria chica. The railroads began to drive some human carriers off the road, thus undoing, for the first time, the cargador system descended from the tamemes of the colonial period. The economy boomed, and dynamism permeated the atmosphere. Technology in general and mechanization in particular made tremendous strides. Foreign travelers for the first time marveled more than they criticized, for peace and growth allowed them the luxury of contemplating the many natural beauties Mexico had to offer. Mexico's foreign credit rating was firmly established throughout the world. But perhaps the most important product of the modernization process was that Mexicans, especially urban Mexicans, began to view themselves differently. Self-confidence replaced the embarrassment occasioned by the dec-

GROWTH OF FOREIGN TRADE, 1877–1910

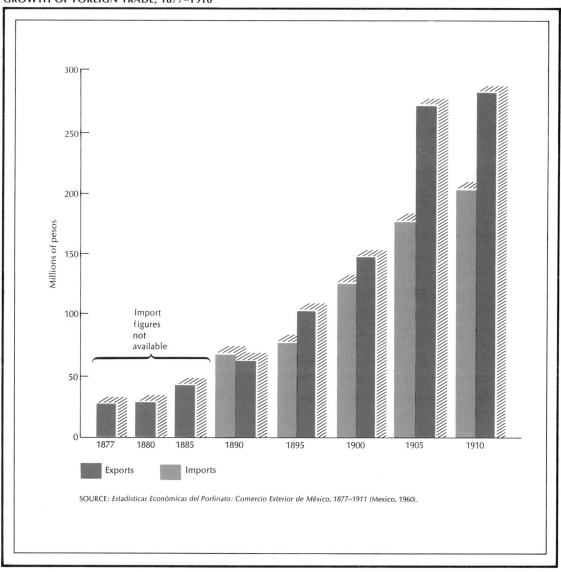

SOURCE: *Estadísticas Económicas del Porfiriato: Comercio Exterior de México, 1877–1911* (Mexico, 1960).

ades of internecine strife. For a third of a century there were no major civil wars, no major liberal-conservative struggles, and no major church-state controversies. Mexico was assuming its rightful position in the twentieth-century world. Very few yet questioned the costs the transformation had exacted because the material dividends seemed so self-evident. But the price paid was great, and the rapid modernization contained seeds of self-destruction.

Recommended for Further Study

Beato, Guillermo and Domenico Síndico. "The Beginning of Industrialization in Northeast Mexico." *The Americas* 39 (1983): 499–518.

Benjamin, Thomas and William McNellie, eds. *Other Mexicos: Essays on Regional Mexican History, 1876–1911*. Albuquerque: University of New Mexico Press, 1984.

Bernstein, Marvin D. "Colonel William C. Greene and the Cananea Copper Bubble." *Bulletin of the Business History Society* 26 (1952): 179–98.

———. *The Mexican Mining Industry, 1890–1950: A Study of the Interaction of Politics, Economics, and Technology*. Albany: State University of New York Press, 1964.

Coatsworth, John. "Railroads, Landholding, and Agrarian Protest in the Early Porfiriato." *Hispanic American Historical Review* 54 (1974): 48–71.

Davis, Thomas B. "Porfirio Díaz in the Opinion of His North American Contemporaries." *Revista de Historia de América* 63–64 (1967): 79–116.

Hoffman, Fritz L. "Edward L. Doheny and the Beginnings of Petroleum Development in Mexico." *Mid-America* 24 (1942): 94–108.

Juárez, José Roberto. "The Use of Counter-Oaths in the Archdiocese of Guadalajara, Mexico, 1876–1911." *Journal of Church and State* 12 (1970): 79–87.

Kroeber, Clifton B. *Man, Land and Water: Mexico's Farmland Irrigation Policies, 1885–1911*. Berkeley: University of California Press, 1984.

McNeely, John H. "The Railways of Mexico: A Study in Nationalization." *Southwestern Studies* 2 (1963): 1–56.

Meyers, William K. "Politics, Vested Rights, and Economic Growth in Porfirian Mexico." *Hispanic American Historical Review* 57 (1977): 425–54.

Pletcher, David M. *Rails, Mines, and Progress: Seven American Promoters in Mexico, 1867–1911*. Ithaca: Cornell University Press, 1958.

Powell, T. G. "Mexican Intellectuals and the Indian Question, 1876–1911." *Hispanic American Historical Review* 48 (1968): 19–36.

Raat, William D. "Leopoldo Zea and Mexican Positivism: A Reappraisal." *Hispanic American Historical Review* 48 (1968): 1–18.

Randall, Robert W. "Mexico's Pre-Revolutionary Reckoning with Railroads." *The Americas* 42 (1985): 1–28.

Schiff, Warren. "The German in Mexican Trade and Industry during the Díaz Period." *The Americas* 23 (1967): 279–96.

Tischendorf, Alfred. *Great Britain and Mexico in the Era of Porfirio Díaz*. Durham: Duke University Press, 1961.

Wasserman, Mark. *Capitalists, Caciques and Revolution: The Native Elite and Foreign Enterprise in Chihuahua Mexico, 1854–1911*. Chapel Hill: University of North Carolina Press, 1984.

Wells, Allen. *Yucatan's Gilded Age: Haciendas, Henequen and International Harvester*. Albuquerque: University of New Mexico Press, 1985.

28

The Costs of Modernization

Dictatorship by Force

Modernization came to Mexico during the Díaz regime not simply as the result of positivist theory and careful economic planning. The peace and stability that made it all possible were at least in part attributable to brute force. Díaz maintained himself in power from 1876 to 1911 by a combination of adroit political maneuvering, threats, intimidation, and, whenever necessary, callous use of the federal army and the rurales.

Throughout the thirty-four years the dictator maintained the sham of democracy. Elections were held periodically at the local, state, and national levels, but they were invariably manipulated in favor of those candidates who held official favor. The press throughout the epoch was tightly censored; journalists who dared to oppose the regime on any substantive matter found themselves in jail or exile, while recalcitrant editors found their newspapers closed down. Filomeno Mata, the editor of the *Diario del Hogar*, suffered imprisonment over thirty times for his anti-re-electionist campaigns. While a few persistent critics were killed, the large majority of the journalists were bludgeoned into submission and ceased to constitute a problem.

The dictator played off political opponents against one another, or bought them off. Potentially ambitious generals or regimental commanders were shifted regularly from one military zone to another to assure that they would be unable to cultivate a power base. State governors were invited to assume the same position in other states or to become congressmen, cabinet secre-

taries, or diplomats to remove their influence at home. Not even
members of the Díaz family were immune. When the dictator's
nephew, Félix Díaz, decided to run for the governorship of Oaxaca against Don Porfirio's wishes, he shortly found himself on a
ship bound for Chile, where he was given a diplomatic post and
allowed to cool off. Most influential Mexicans cooperated with
the regime and were rewarded with political favors and lucrative
economic concessions. Díaz himself never accumulated a personal fortune, but many of his civilian and military supporters in
high positions had ample opportunity for graft. The científico
advisers, for example, always seemed to know in advance the
route of a new boulevard or railroad line, the property could
thus be bought up at a low price and sold back to the government
for a profit.

When Díaz needed to use force it was provided by the army
and the rurales. He recognized the need for professionalizing
the army, and, although he did not invite foreign military missions into the country, he did send military observers to West
Point and to the French officer's school at St. Cyr. The recently
reorganized Colegio Militar de Chapultepec provided formal
instruction for the officer corps and made use of the most current
European training manuals. By the turn of the century about
half of the active officers (but very few of the generals) were
graduates of the Chapultepec academy. The cadets, resplendent
in snappy uniforms, were highlighted at the frequent military
parades during which Díaz took the opportunity to display the
latest armament obtained from France or Germany.

The rurales, Díaz's praetorian guard, also constituted an important enforcement tool for the *Pax Porfiriana*. The dictator
strengthened the corps considerably, not simply to curtail brigandage in the rural areas but to serve as a counterpoise to the
army itself. By the end of the regime the strength of the rurales
had been increased to over twenty-seven hundred men. While
the force was not large, it was used to good advantage by the dictator. In addition to its original patrolling functions, Díaz had
rural corpsmen guard ore shipments from the mines, support
local police forces, escort prisoners, enforce unpopular court decisions, and guard public payrolls and buildings. Recent scholarship has demonstrated that the rurales were neither as harsh nor
as efficient as generally thought. While Díaz did not, as commonly understood, deliberately induct known bandits into the
corps, neither did he try to set straight their image for cruelty

To reinforce the desired image, the rurales were always featured during military parades. Sumner Matteson photographed this salute to President Díaz on May 5, 1907.

and excess.[1] The myth served his purposes well, for the rurales were feared by brigands, marauders, political opponents, and recalcitrant villagers. When trouble flared it was often more prudent to send in the nearest corps than to allow a distinguished federal general the chance to enhance his reputation.

Díaz used the military not only to force compliance with the dictates of Mexico City but to administer the country as well. By the mid-1880s it was not unusual for military officers, most often generals of unquestionable loyalty, to dominate the state governorships and to be well represented among the three

1. Paul Vanderwood, "Mexico: The Porfirian Rurales," paper presented at Thirty-eighth Annual Meeting of the Southern Historical Association, November 17, 1972.

The federal artillery corps, well trained and well equipped, was the pride of the Díaz army.

hundred *jefes políticos* (local political bosses). In 1900, although relative peace had already been achieved, Díaz was still spending almost one-fourth of the total budget on the military establishment. He believed it was worth it because the modernization process was so intertwined with his concept of enforced peace. The relationship has been summarized by one scholar of Mexican militarism as follows: "The Díaz system was self-reinforcing. The military provided the order necessary for economic development, and economic development provided the revenues necessary to keep the military loyal. Economic growth also built a modern communications network, which made it far easier for the army to stamp out disorders in the outlying areas."[2]

Díaz's científico advisers have been labeled racist for their conscientious denigration of the Indian population. But the generalization has certain flaws, for it presupposes a monolithic philosophical framework within the científico community.[3] José

2. Edwin Lieuwen, *Mexican Militarism: The Political Rise and Fall of the Revolutionary Army* (Albuquerque, 1968), p. 3.
3. The revisionist position is cogently argued in William D. Raat, "Los intelectuales, el positivismo y la cuestión indígena," *Historia Mexicana* 20 (1971): 412–27; and in Raat, "Ideas and Society in Don Porfirio's Mexico," *The Americas* 30 (1973): 32–53.

Limantour was less a follower of Comte than of Darwin. He adapted notions of natural selection and survival of the fittest to Mexican reality as he understood it and emerged from his introspection calling for an aristocratic elite to reorder society. Little or no help could be expected from the Indian population. Francisco Bulnes, a prolific historian and apologist for científico rule, was more openly racist. Five million (white) Argentines, he argued, were worth more than fourteen million Mexicans. The Mexican Indian was sullenly intractable and hopelessly inferior, not because of innate corruption of his genes but because his grossly deficient diet sapped his mental, moral, and physical vitality. He responded more to the logic of force than to the art of persuasion. Less biologically oriented was Justo Sierra, the most famous científico of them all. Cofounder of the conservative newspaper, *La Libertad*, author of *Evolución política del pueblo mexicano*, secretary of education during part of the Porfiriato, and first rector of the national university, Sierra argued forcefully that social and cultural forces, not biological ones, had shaped the Indian's inferior position. And unlike Limantour and Bulnes, Sierra asserted the Indian's educability.

In the political sense the científicos may have had a point. Perhaps Mexico was not yet ready for democracy, and perhaps it was too early to broaden the participatory base. But their impassioned defense of the need for "administrative power" implied at best self-deception and at worst blatant hypocrisy. If they truly believed that the Indian masses could be prepared for a more active role in the political life of the Mexican nation, the logical place to begin the preparation process was an educational system that reached the people. But the schools built during the Porfiriato, even when the Department of Education was in Justo Sierra's hands, were almost all located in the cities where the criollos lived, not in the rural areas where they might serve the Indian and mestizo population. At the end of the Porfiriato Mexico still had two million Indians not speaking Spanish: They had been left aside.

The Hacendados

Mexico was still overwhelmingly a rural country when the twentieth century arrived, and the rural peasantry bore most of the costs of modernization. The payment was exacted in fear of the rurales, intimidation by local hacendados, constant badgering by jefes políticos and municipal officials, exploitation by foreign entrepreneurs, and, most important, seizure of private and communal lands by government-supported land sharks.

Life in rural Mexico had been dominated by the hacienda complex since the colonial period, but the abuses of the system were exacerbated markedly during the Díaz regime as railroad construction pushed land values up. The problem of exaggerated land concentration was directly attributable to a new land law enacted in 1883. This law, designed to encourage foreign colonization of rural Mexico, authorized land companies to survey public lands for the purpose of subdivision and settlement. For their efforts the companies received up to one-third of the land surveyed and the privilege of purchasing the remaining two-thirds at bargain prices. If the private owners or traditional ejidos could not prove ownership through legal title, their land was considered public and subject to denunciation by the companies.

The process that ensued was predictable. Very few rural Mexicans could prove legal title. All they knew for sure was that they had lived and worked the same plot for their entire lives, and their parents and grandparents had done the same. Their boundary line ran from a certain tree to a certain stream to the crest of a hill. The few who could produce documents, some dating back to the colonial period, were convinced by the speculators and their lawyers that the papers had not been properly signed, or notarized, or stamped, or registered. But not even those communal ejidos that could produce titles of indisputable legality were immune. The Constitution of 1857 with its Reform Laws was once again applied to the detriment of the ejidos, and with greater vigor than ever before.

Within five years after the land law became operative, land companies had obtained possession of over 68 million acres of rural land and by 1894 one-fifth of the total land mass of Mexico. Not yet completely satisfied, the companies received a favorable modification of the law in 1894, and by the early twentieth century most of the villages in rural Mexico had lost their ejidos and some 134 million acres of the best land had passed into the hands of a few hundred fantastically wealthy families. Over one-half of all rural Mexicans lived and worked on the haciendas by 1910.

The Mexican census of 1910 listed 8,245 haciendas in the republic, but a few wealthy individuals, often tied together by a marriage network of family elites, owned ten, fifteen, or even twenty of them. Though varied in size, haciendas of forty or fifty thousand acres were not at all uncommon. Fifteen of the richest

Mexican hacendados owned haciendas totaling more than three hundred thousand acres each. The state of Chihuahua affords a classic example of how the hacienda system operated and brought wealth and prestige to one extended family. Throughout the Díaz regime the fortunes of that north central Mexican state were guided by the Terrazas-Creel clan. Don Luis Terrazas, the founder of the dynasty, had served as governor prior to the French Intervention and fought with Juárez against the French in the 1860s. His land acquisitions began shortly thereafter, when he obtained the estate of Don Pablo Martínez del Río, a French sympathizer. In the 1870s, 1880s, and 1890s, in and out of the gubernatorial chair, he acquired additional haciendas, profiting immensely from the land laws of the Díaz government. By the early twentieth century Terrazas owned some fifty haciendas and smaller ranches totaling a fantastic seven million acres. Don Luis was the largest hacendado in Mexico and perhaps in all of Latin America; his holdings were eight times the size of the legendary King Ranch in Texas. He owned 500,000 head of cattle, 225,000 sheep, 25,000 horses, 5,000 mules, and some of the best fighting bulls in the western hemisphere. Encinillas, northwest of Chihuahua City, was the largest of his haciendas, extending to some 1,300,000 acres and employing some 2,000 peones. San Miguel de Babícora was over 850,000 acres, while San Luis and Hormigas were over 700,000 acres each.

But the wealth and power of the Terrazas family cannot be judged in terms of landholding and its related activities alone. Don Luis also owned textile mills, granaries, railroads, telephone companies, candle factories, sugar mills, meat packing plants, and several Chihuahua mines. Each of his twelve children was married with the care characteristic of Renaissance nobility. Daughter Angela Terrazas married her first cousin, Enrique Creel, the son of an American consul in Chihuahua and a man of wealth, erudition, and prestige. Enrique Creel also served several times in the state governorship and, in addition, was Mexico's secretary of foreign relations in 1910–11. Creel's own haciendas totaled more than 1,700,000 acres. He was also one of the founders and directors of the Banco Minero de Chihuahua, which gradually absorbed many of the other banks in the state. He was a partner, furthermore, in many of his father-in-law's enterprises and directed or owned iron and steel mills, breweries, granaries, and a coal company. Other daughters and sons also married well. The sons, as to be expected, became hacendados and entrepreneurs. Sons Alberto and Juan each had haciendas totaling over

600,000 acres, and son-in-law Federico Sisniega held some 260,-000 acres and was a director of the Banco Nacional de Chihuahua. To strengthen the already strong Terrazas-Creel ties, son Alberto married his niece, Emilia Creel, the daughter of his sister Angela and Enrique Creel. Son Federico Terrazas married into the Falomir family and daughter Adela into the Muñoz family, two of the other most wealthy and prestigious families in the state.

It is virtually impossible to calculate the extent of either the fortune or the power wielded by the Terrazas-Creel clan. Luis Terrazas himself probably did not know how much he owned. He surely did know, however, that the value of rural land in Chihuahua rose from about $.30 per acre in 1879 to about $9.88 per acre in 1908. Had he been able to liquidate only his personal, nonurban landholdings on the eve of the Mexican Revolution, he would have carried over $69 million to the bank.

One can be certain that little of major importance occurred in Chihuahua without the approval of patriarch Don Luis Terrazas. During the Díaz regime members of the extended family sat for a total of sixty-six terms in the state legislature and twenty-two terms in the national legislature. Because residency requirements were loosely defined, Enrique Creel and Juan Terrazas became national senators from other Mexican states. Municipal and regional officialdom bore either the Terrazas-Creel names or their stamp of approval. The immense power was built upon a foundation of land, and the state of Chihuahua was a microcosm of what was happening throughout the Mexican republic.

The state of Morelos was dominated not by one extended family but rather by a handful of powerful sugar families: the García Pimentels, the Amors, the Torre y Miers, and a few others. To fund the purchase of expensive new machinery these families had to increase production and so began expanding into new lands. As no public lands were available, they completely encircled small ranches and even villages, thereby choking off all infusions of economic lifeblood. Some towns stagnated, while others vanished from the map altogether. The town fathers of Cuautla could not even find sufficient land for a new cemetery and were reduced to burying children in a neighboring village.

The Peones

The millions of rural Mexicans who found themselves in dying villages or subsisting as peones on the nation's haciendas were worse off financially than their rural ancestors a century before. The average daily wage for an agricultural worker remained almost steady throughout the nineteenth century—about thirty-five centavos. But in the same hundred-year period the price of corn and chile more than doubled, and beans cost six times more in 1910 than in 1800. In terms of purchasing power correlated with the price of corn or cheap cloth, the Mexican peón during the Díaz regime was twelve times poorer than the United States farm laborer.

Working conditions varied considerably from region to region and even from hacienda to hacienda, but they were generally poor. Peones often availed themselves of the talents of a scribe to spell out their gamut of complaints. While it was not uncommon for the peón to be allotted a couple of furrows to plant a little corn and chile and on occasion he might receive a small ration of food from the hacienda, he worked from sunrise to sunset, often seven days a week, raising crops or tending cattle. Sometimes he was allowed to cut firewood free; on other occasions he paid for the right. The scant wages he received most often were not paid in currency but in certificates or metal discs redeemable only at the local *tienda de raya*, an all-purpose company store located on the hacienda complex. Credit was extended liberally, but the prices, set by the hacendado or the mayordomo were invariably several times higher than those in a nearby village. For the hacendado the situation was perfect. The taxes on his land were negligible; his labor was, in effect, free, for all the wages that went out came back to him through the tienda de raya with a handsome profit. The peón found himself in a state of perpetual debt, and by law he was bound to remain on the hacienda so long as he owed a single centavo. Debts were not eradicated at the time of death but passed on to the children. Should an occasional obdurate peón escape, there was scarcely any place for him to go. Many states had laws making it illegal to hire an indebted peón.

The bookkeeping procedures in the tienda de raya always seemed to work to the disadvantage of the illiterate peón. Goods charged against his account were more expensive than they would have been had he been able to pay cash. And other items were often debited to his account. Charges for a marriage ceremony or a funeral often exceeded the monthly wage. Fines for real or imagined crimes on the hacienda were added; forced contributions for fiestas and interest on previous debts were tallied. And, in the most ignominious charge of all, some hacendados

For a couple of centavos the rural, illiterate Mexicans could hire a scribe to scratch out a few lines to a relative or friend.

even added a monthly fee for the privilege of shopping at the tienda de raya.

Stories of corporal punishment of the peón (petty theft could bring two hundred lashes) and sexual violation of the young women on the haciendas are commonplace, but they are virtually impossible to prove or disprove. It is certain that conditions on the henequen haciendas of Yucatán were the worst in the republic. Because many of the peones in Yucatán were deportees from other parts of Mexico (some were recalcitrant Yaqui Indians from Sonora, and others were convicted criminals), they were forced to work in chains, and flogging was not uncommon. There is little evidence, however, that this type of physical maltreatment was widespread throughout Mexico. Surely the peón and his family were everywhere subject to the personal whims of the hacendado or the mayordomo, but hacienda records and correspondence to local, state, and even national officials reveal that complaints, while frequent, rarely contained charges of physical abuse. More common are complaints of intolerable working conditions, violence in the peón community itself, and dishonest record keeping in the tienda de raya—and always the sense of poverty, powerlessness, and hopelessness. During especially busy times like planting or harvesting, the permanent work force was augmented by temporary workers, often from surrounding villages. New arrivals, frequently earning a slightly higher wage than the resident peones seemed to break the socioeconomic equilibrium, and violence between the two groups of workers was a constant threat.

The dichotomies of nineteenth-century Mexican life, especially those of wealth and poverty, are almost all to be found on the hacienda. The main hacienda house was sumptuous, externally and internally. But the hacendado would seldom spend more than a few months a year there. Most often he had other haciendas to attend, inevitably businesses to manage in the cities, and then he had to visit his children in their fine European or United States boarding schools. The hacienda provided, in addition to its income, a summer vacation home, a change of pace, and social status. The hacendado's teen-age children, remarkable for their conspicuous consumption, used trips to the hacienda to impress their friends. The extended families could be comfortably accommo-

In 1907, photographer Sumner Matteson was surprised to find burros, horses, mules, and people sharing quarters in this pulque hacienda, where the stench of animals was rivaled only by the stench of fermenting pulque.

dated, and young boys, donned in charro costume and mounted on carefully bred and well-groomed horses, could fancy themselves country squires. Birthdays, saints' days, and feast days were reason enough to move the family from the state capital to the hacienda for an outing, and on special occasions, like an eighteenth birthday or a wedding, entire train cars could be reserved to carry guests, musicians, local dignitaries, and domestics.

The contrast between the hacendado and those who worked the hacienda and made it live is so stark as to be absurd. Because all "justice" on the hacienda was administered by the mayordomo, the peón had no genuine judicial rights or legal recourse. If a mayordomo overreacted in punishment of some real or imagined offense, he was accountable to nobody. Within a mile of the grand hacienda house were miserable, one-room, floorless, windowless adobe shacks. Water had to be carried in daily, often from long distances. The individual plots allotted to the peón were worked often after sunset, when the important work of the day had been completed. Twice a day a few minutes would be set aside to consume some tortillas wrapped around beans and chile, washed down with a few gulps of black coffee or pulque. Protein in the form of meat, fish, or fowl, even on the cattle haciendas, was a luxury reserved for a few special occasions during the year. Infant mortality on many haciendas exceeded 25 percent.

Diversion in the form of a local fiesta might occur once a year. An amateur bullfight could be staged in the hacienda corral, and resident aficionados would try their hand with a half-grown fighting bull that somehow looked bigger as it got closer. The peones, fortified with pulque or mescal, who found momentary escape entertaining their friends often paid dearly for their bravado, but a broken arm or a punctured thigh was a small matter when one had nothing to look forward to but the drab existence and appalling squalor of the next twelve months.

Porfirio Díaz had developed his country at the expense of his countrymen. He hermetically sealed himself off from the stark realities of Mexican masses. The great material benefits of the age of modernization in no way filtered down to the people. They were still an amorphous mass destitute of hope. Their lives were not in the least changed because the new National Theater was built in Mexico City or because José Limantour was able to borrow money in London or Paris at 4 percent. In fact, for them the cost of modernization had been too great.

Recommended for Further Study

Anderson, Rodney D. *Outcasts in Their Own Land: Mexican Industrial Workers, 1906–1911*. DeKalb: Northern Illinois University Press, 1976.

Beals, Carleton. *Porfirio Díaz: Dictator of Mexico*. Philadelphia: Lippincott, 1932.

Beezley, William H. "Opportunity in Porfirian Mexico." *North Dakota Quarterly* 40 (1972): 30–40.

Flandrau, Charles M. *Viva Mexico*. Urbana: University of Illinois Press, 1964.

Hu-Dehart, Evelyn. *Yaqui Resistance and Survival: The Struggle for Land and Autonomy, 1821–1910*. Madison: University of Wisconsin Press, 1984.

Joseph, Gilbert, and Allen Wells. "Summer of Discontent: Economic Rivalry Among Elite Factions During the Late Porfiriato in Yucatán." *Journal of Latin American Studies* 18 (1986): 255–82.

Katz, Friedrich. "Labor Conditions on Haciendas in Porfirian Mexico: Some Trends and Tendencies." *Hispanic American Historical Review* 54 (1974): 1–47.

Kitchens, John W. "Some Considerations on the Rurales of Porfirian Mexico." *Journal of Inter-American Studies* 9 (1967): 441–55.

Raat, William D. "Agustín Aragón and Mexico's Religion of Humanity." *Journal of Inter-American Studies* 11 (1969): 441–55.

———. "Ideas and Society in Don Porfirio's Mexico." *The Americas* 30 (1973): 32–53.

Ruiz, Ramón. *The People of Sonora and the Yankee Capitalists*. Tucson: University of Arizona Press, 1988.

Sandels, Robert. "Silvestre Terrazas and the Old Regime in Chihuahua." *The Americas* (1971): 192–205.

Schiff, Warren. "German Military Penetration into Mexico during the Late Díaz Period." *Hispanic American Historical Review* 39 (1959): 568–79.

Schmitt, Karl M. "The Díaz Conciliation Policy on State and Local Levels, 1876–1911." *Hispanic American Historical Review* 40 (1960): 513–32.

Stabb, Martin S. "Indigenism and Racism in Mexican Thought, 1857–1911." *Journal of Inter-American Studies* 1 (1959): 405–23.

Vanderwood, Paul. *Disorder and Progress: Bandits, Police and Mexican Development*. Lincoln: University of Nebraska Press, 1981.

Walker, David. "Porfirian Labor Politics: Working Class Organizations in Mexico City and Porfirio Díaz." *The Americas* 37 (1981): 257–90.

Wasserman, Mark. "The Social Origins of the 1910 Revolution in Chihuahua." *Latin American Research Review* 15 (1980): 15–38.

Wells, Allen. "Family Elites in a Boom-and-Bust Economy: The Molinas and Peóns of Porfirian Yucatán." *Hispanic American Historical Review* 62 (1982): 224–53.

Womack, John, Jr. *Zapata and the Mexican Revolution*. New York: Knopf, 1968.

29

Society and Culture during the Porfiriato

The changes in Mexican society and culture during the Porfiriato were every bit as profound as those in the political and economic realms. Most noteworthy perhaps was the fact that Mexicans began to view themselves differently. Self-esteem replaced the sense of shame that had characterized the introspective diagnoses of the past. For the first time Mexico had shown her potential and had begun to catch up with a rapidly changing world. Optimism had replaced pessimism, and xenophilia at least challenged xenophobia.

Population

The stability of the Porfiriato resulted in Mexico's first period of prolonged population growth. In the absence of war and its social dislocations and with modest gains recorded in health and sanitation, the population grew from 8,743,000 in 1874 to 15,160,000 in 1910. From 1810 to 1874 the average annual population growth had been about 43,000, but during the Díaz era population increased at an average of 180,000 per year. Mexico City and the state capitals grew even more rapidly than the population at large, increasing some 88.5 percent during the epoch. From a population of 200,000 in 1874, Mexico City in 1910 was the home of 471,066 Mexicans.

Railroad development, mining activities, and port improvements caused a number of tiny villages to burgeon into towns and cities. Torreón, at the intersection of the Mexican Central

POPULATION OF SELECTED MEXICAN CITIES DURING THE PORFIRIATO

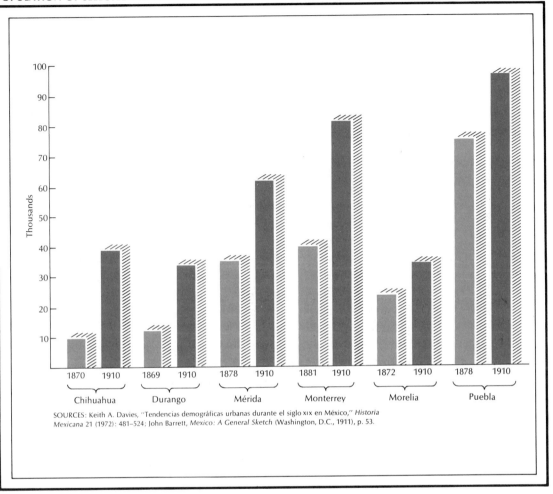

SOURCES: Keith A. Davies, "Tendencias demográficas urbanas durante el siglo xix en México," *Historia Mexicana* 21 (1972): 481–524; John Barrett, *Mexico: A General Sketch* (Washington, D.C., 1911), p. 53.

Railroad and the International Railroad (running from Eagle Pass, Texas, to Durango), jumped from fewer than 2,000 inhabitants in 1876 to over 43,000 in 1910; Sabinas, Coahuila, from 788 to 14,555; and Nuevo Laredo from 1,283 to almost 9,000. The two port terminuses of the Tehuantepec Railroad recorded similar gains. Puerto México had only 267 inhabitants in 1884 but reached 6,616 by 1910, while Salina Cruz grew from 738 in 1900 to almost 6,000 ten years later. Colonel Greene's copper town of Cananea hardly existed at the beginning of the Porfiriato. From a population of about 100 in 1876, it catapulted to almost 15,000 in 1910.

Urban Improvements

The rapid growth of towns and cities throughout the republic was accompanied by an obvious dynamism in society. The sleepy Mexico that caught the visitor's eyes earlier in the century had awakened from its slumber. Travelers were astonished by the amount of construction going on everywhere. By 1910 all the state capitals had electricity, and most had tramways. Weekly newspapers became dailies, potable water systems and sewage systems were extended, hospitals were constructed, and new hotels sprang up to cater to the greatly increasing tourist trade. Even small, out-of-the-way towns improved their facilities. Whereas travelers during the first fifty years after Independence were often horrified at Mexico's hotels and inns, tourists late in the Díaz regime were pleasantly surprised.

On occasion growth got out of hand. When Mexico City held its Independence Day celebrations in September 1882, the forty thousand tourists who descended on the capital simply could not all be accommodated. But the lesson was not lost. In 1910, during the more elaborate centennial celebrations, there were rooms for everyone.

The transportation system in the capital was excellent, with first-, second-, and third-class streetcars and cabs carrying passengers throughout the city. The streetcars were sometimes put to strange uses. One caught the eye of an Irish visitor during the late Porfiriato.

> A curious feature of the streets is the electric tramway hearse. Frequently one sees a funeral consisting of a number of cars on the rails; first comes an open one like a long low truck with a black catafalque covering, under which reposes the coffin and the wreaths; the next may be another piled up with wreaths and crosses, and then follows car after car with the mourners. This of course stops all the tramway traffic for the time being.[1]

But to many the most dramatic change was in the field of law and order. Scarcely a traveler in the late nineteenth century failed to comment upon the relative absence of obvious crime and political upheaval. Most were astute enough to realize that payment for law and order was exacted in fear of the army, rurales, and local law-enforcement agencies; they considered the result worth the price. Perhaps once Mexico had passed through the difficult transition from a law-breaking to a law-respecting society, the intimidating atmosphere could be relaxed.

1. Mary Barton, *Impressions of Mexico with Brush and Pen* (London, 1911), pp. 45–46.

The changing face of urban Mexico was accompanied by a not-too-subtle modification of the value structure. Porfirio Díaz recoiled at English and United States suggestions that the time-honored tradition of the Mexican bullfight was nothing more than a cruel and barbarous spectacle. It was the epitome of a clash of values. The phenomenon has been perfectly captured by historian William Beezley, who wrote that while most Mexicans saw "the ballet of cape and animal," foreigners "saw only blood and sand." Díaz ultimately placed a higher premium on international respect than on preserving this part of Mexico's Hispanic heritage and, although he later reversed himself, during his first administration prohibited bullfighting in the Federal District, Zacatecas, and Veracruz, areas where tourists would be most likely to witness the Sunday event. An American import soon offered itself as a substitute. Abner Doubleday's baseball made its Mexican debut in the 1880s and had caught on beyond anyone's expectations by the turn of the century. Not a few Mexican traditionalists lamented the exchange of the bat, the ball, and the baggy pants for the cape, the sword, and the suit of lights.[2]

Social Classes

The Porfiriato also witnessed some improvement in the lot of women as a select few began to enter professions hitherto regarded as the sole preserve of men. The medical school in Mexico City graduated its first woman doctor in 1887, and by the turn of the century others had followed. In the 1890s and early 1900s women began to make significant inroads into dentistry, law, pharmacy, higher education, and journalism. A new commercial school for women was inaugurated in 1903, and shortly thereafter its classes were filled. But Mexico was not yet quite ready for an active feminist movement designed to challenge in depth the traditional roles of the sexes. The prerogatives of the males were not to be questioned. The Admiradoras de Juárez, a militant feminist organization founded in 1904 by Laura Torres, was attacked by Justo Sierra as a refuge for old and ugly women whose only recourse was to try to become men. His advice to the women was to leave politics and law to the opposite sex and to concentrate instead on creating a better social atmosphere in

2. These themes are developed in William H. Beezley, *Judas at the Jockey Club and Other Episodes of Porfirian Mexico* (Lincoln, 1987), pp. 13–25.

which Mexicans could live more happily. In spite of Sierra, however, many talented Mexican women no longer felt the need to confine themselves exclusively to the home.

Of course, not everything changed from 1876 to 1910. There was certainly more crime and alcoholism than the foreign visitors saw in the tourist zones of the cities. The léperos and cargadores continued to attract their attention. Although most visitors were not aware of the working conditions in the factories throughout the republic, the plight of the urban laborer had changed little, but there were many more of them. A few employers initiated modest reform early in the twentieth century. The Cervecería Cuauhtémoc in Monterrey, a Mexican-owned and Mexican-managed enterprise, was the first major industrial concern to adopt the nine-hour day. Few other Mexican industries, however, and practically none owned by foreigners, followed suit. Even at the end of the Porfiriato the workweek for the large majority of **urban laborers was seven days and the workday eleven or even twelve hours. Pensions were almost unknown, as was compensation for accidents suffered on the job.**

The diet of the lower classes—day laborers, rank-and-file soldiers, beggars, domestics, street vendors, and the unemployed—remained monotonous and constantly inadequate. Corn, beans, chile, and pulque still constituted the staples; meat was almost totally absent. The grossly deficient diet and unsanitary living conditions made the masses susceptible to a wide array of debilitating diseases, and the large majority passed their entire lives without a single visit to a qualified doctor. Life expectancy remained constant—about thirty years. Infant mortality remained unacceptably high, averaging 30 percent for most of the Porfiriato. A Protestant missionary in Díaz's Mexico recalled his impressions.

> I used to ask, "How many of you, fathers and mothers, have children in heaven?" Usually all hands would promptly go up, while the replies came, *"Tengo cinco." "Tengo ocho."* . . . Deplorable ignorance as to proper sanitary conditions in the home and the care of children is responsible for a large proportion of this death harvest among the little ones. Children's diseases, as measles and scarlet fever, carry multitudes away.[3]

The lower-class barrios of Mexico City—La Merced, La Palma, and Nonoalco—were so bad that some suggested they be burned

3. Alden Buell Case, *Thirty Years with the Mexicans: In Peace and Revolution* (New York, 1917), pp. 61–62.

Modernization occurred at the expense of the poor, in both urban and rural settings.

to the ground. There was no indoor plumbing in these districts, and only one public bathhouse per fifteen thousand people. Garbage collection was sporadic at best. Only the completion of Mexico City's drainage canal registered a positive impact on the lower-class neighborhoods, as the masses at least were able to escape the ravages of seasonal flooding.

Consumption of pulque and other alcoholic beverages among the lower classes did not increase during the Porfiriato, but the public and private outcry against alcohol did. Because alcoholism was unempirically linked to robberies, sex crimes, child abandonment, and mendicancy, temperance societies sprang up throughout the country. The Catholic press initiated a journalistic campaign, and state and local governments enacted legislation to curtail the use of alcoholic beverages. But limiting the

Life for the peón on the hacienda was bad; living in a city slum was even worse. But nowhere was it more difficult than in the mines.

hours of pulquerías and restricting new openings seemed to do little good, so the establishments were made as uncomfortable as possible. To discourage the patron from squandering away too much time and money, pulquerías were to have no windows, no chairs, no music, and, most important, no women. But profuse legislation did not accomplish its goal. Both alcoholism and toxemia from the high bacterial content of the pulque were widespread as the nineteenth century gave way to the twentieth.

The most dramatic change in the social structure was the expansion of the middle class. The earning power of skilled artisans, government bureaucrats, scribes, clergymen, low-ranking army officers, and professional men had increased. They demonstrated no class solidarity, but their lives were perceptibly different from the lower classes whence they had sprung. The booming economy made it possible for many a small businessman and neighborhood merchant to move his family from the drab room above the store or from his parents' residence into a larger and more comfortable apartment or house. The extension of water and sewage facilities provided many the luxury of indoor plumbing for the first time in their lives. The middle-class diet included meat and soup several times a week.

With middle-class status, creating the proper impression became important. It was not unusual for the monthly wage or monthly profit to be idled away on a single night of entertainment for friends. While the middle-class wife was beginning to break out of the home, she generally resigned herself to her husband's marital infidelity and to having but a small voice in the family's decision-making process. Seemingly possessed of infinite patience, she found some solace in the church and endured her submissive role with remarkable stoicism.

Middle-class children were taught to make class distinctions based upon outward appearances. If a well-dressed person appeared at the door they were expected to report to their parents *Allí está un señor*, but if the caller was dressed poorly the proper announcement was *Allí está un hombre*.[4] Although only recently sprung from the lower class themselves, many members of the middle class could be callous in their appreciation of the problems of the downtrodden.

While the poor continued to live in misery and a new, small middle class emerged in the cities, the rich became more convinced than ever that upon the pillar of private property civilization itself was braced. The pinnacle of social acceptance during the Porfiriato was to be invited, for a monthly dues of seven hundred pesos, to enjoy the amenities of the Jockey Club in Mexico City. The club was located in the Casa de Azulejos, the most opulent mansion in the capital. One could enjoy a sumptuous dinner there, spend an hour at the baccarat table, and hope to see cabinet ministers, governors, military zone commanders, or perhaps even Don Porfirio and Doña Carmen themselves.

The true measure of aristocratic success was to see how French one could become in taste and manners. The advantages of a French education and a French governess for aristocratic children were beyond debate. Beautiful Spanish colonial furniture was stored away, and modern French furniture adorned the houses. When Mexican composer Gustavo E. Campa wrote an opera based on the life of Nezahualcoyótl, "the Poet King of Texcoco," he entitled it not *El Rey Poeta* but *Le Roi Pòete* and prepared the libretto in French. Membership in the Sociedad Filarmónica y Dramática Francesa assured one of brushing el-

---

4. Jesús Silva Herzog, *Una vida en la vida de México* (Mexico, 1972), p. 9.

José Guadalupe Posada (1852–1913), México's most famous printmaker, parodies a fashionable lady during the Porfiriato.

bows with the most Frenchified members of Mexican society at a concert or a ball and might even garner one an invitation to attend one of the famous soirées at the Lyre Gauloise. The Paseo de la Reforma was redecorated to look like the Champs Elysées, while architectural design aped *fin-de-siècle* Paris. When Mexican millionaire Antonio Escandón donated a statue of Columbus to adorn the fashionable avenue, he commissioned the Parisian sculptor Charles Cordier to do the work. Having no notion of the revolution that would soon engulf Mexico, the aristocracy blissfully celebrated Bastille Day, July 14, with almost as much enthusiasm as their own Independence Day.

French cuisine reigned supreme in the capital. The best and most expensive restaurants were the Fonda de Recamier and the Maison Doreé. Between the Consommé Brunoise Royale and the Tournedos au Cèpes, one could sip imported French wine and listen to the orchestra play "Bon Aimée," "Amoureuse," "Rendezvous," or some other tune everyone knew to be *à la mode*. For the athletic there was also membership in the French Polo Club and for the more sedate a season ticket to the French comic opera to partake of such quickly forgettable productions as *Les cloches de*

Corneville or *La Fille de madame Angot*. Those who had pretensions to both music and athletics adopted the cancan, a French import that took Mexico by storm in the 1880s.

Cultural and Intellectual Life

Literary expression during the Porfiriato found nineteenth-century romanticism yielding first to realism and almost simultaneously to modernism. The realists of the period, unlike their romantic predecessors, were not interested in instruction or moralizing. Hoping that the enforced stability of the Porfiriato would encourage the development of the arts, they early made their peace with the regime. Not a socially conscious group, the realists viewed the poor not as oppressed but rather as lazy and shiftless. On occasion a crusader emerged from the realist ranks, such as Arcadio Zentella who decried the evils of the hacienda system in his novel *Perico* (1885). But Zentella was the exception.

More typical was José López Portillo y Rojas (1850–1923), perhaps Mexico's best realist novelist of the nineteenth century. Born to a prominent Guadalajara family, he studied law and traveled widely in Europe, imbibing the French spirit, before dedicating himself to literature. In his novel *Nieves* (1887) López Portillo did recognize that an occasional hacendado might brutalize a peón, but he found no fault with the system that conditioned the relationship or anything reprehensible in a society that tolerated it. His solution was a simplistic one. It was all a matter of volition. The poor of Mexico simply had no desire to improve themselves. "Our workers will come out of their abject condition," he wrote in *Nieves*, "when they aspire to eat well, to dress decently, and to acquire the comforts of life."[5]

The realistic period in Mexican literature was briefly prolific but not very distinguished. Much more important were the modernists of the Porfiriato. Culturally mature, stylistically innovative, and concerned with refinements in the language and a new kind of imagery, the modernists stood in favor of a symbolic revolt not against Porfirian society but against nineteenth-century culture. While the modernists generally also turned their backs on political, economic, and social problems as they sought refuge in the world of imagination, they succeeded in transforming Mexican literature into an art. Modernist literature was elitist—

5. José López Portillo y Rojas, *Cuentos completos*, vol. 1: *Nieves, El primer amor* (Guadalajara, 1952), p. 41.

it was designed for the upper class—but without question it was literature of vitality, perception, and grace. Just as Limantour's balancing of the budget had yielded economic confidence, just as Díaz's quelling of rebellion had yielded political confidence, the modernist movement brought forth genuine cultural confidence.

The best and most versatile of the modernist fiction writers was Amado Nervo (1870–1919). After studying briefly for the priesthood, Nervo left the seminary and became a journalist in Mazatlán. At the turn of the century he moved to Paris—for Mexicans a cultural mecca—where he met the founder of the Latin American modernist movement, the Nicaraguan poet Rubén Darío. Before his literary career had ended, Nervo had to his credit more than thirty volumes—novels, poetry, short stories, plays, essays, and criticism.

The theme of Nervo's first novel, *El bachiller* (1895), was sensational and even horrifying. A young priest, tempted by physical love, castrates himself to avoid seduction. But the theme was developed with such skill and grace that few took umbrage or reproved the licentious plot. If Mexicans really wanted to be wordly they had to understand that the French were not offended by Gustav Flaubert's even more salacious *Madame Bovary*. In much of his work Nervo showed himself a perceptive amateur psychologist. His insight into the motivations of the protagonists he created and his appreciation of the conflicts between the material and the spiritual captivated his readers. Like most of his contemporaries, he was not interested in analyzing broad social problems but rather in probing personal problems of both a psychological and a philosophical nature.

Mexican artists during the Porfiriato, unlike their literary colleagues, did not make their peace with the regime. The Art Academy of San Carlos continued to dominate the artistic community, but it was poorly supported by the government. The future giants of Mexican art—Diego Rivera and José Clemente Orozco—were students at the academy and began perfecting the techniques that would win them world acclaim two decades hence. While heavy emphasis was placed upon copying European models, a few of the students began to break with tradition and experiment with Mexican themes.

Díaz and his científico advisers, in art as in so many other areas, continued to show preference for all things foreign. To celebrate the centennial of Mexico's Independence, the government constructed a new building to house a Spanish art display and provided a subvention of thirty-five thousand pesos for the

Spanish show. When the Mexican artists at the academy protested that they wanted to put on a national art show to coincide with the celebrations, they were forced to limp along with their old building and a paltry three thousand pesos to realize their efforts. Those who saw the Mexican exhibition probably understood why the regime chose not to support it. It was youthful, exuberant, and iconoclastic in both technique and theme. Gerardo Murillo, who changed his name to Dr. Atl, a Náhuatl word meaning *water*, had experimented with wax, resin, and oil in several scandalous bacchanals, while other young artists developed Indianist themes. Many of Mexico's most promising artists exhibited there for the first time and seemed to take special pride in their bold departures from staid European models. Slums and brothels decorated canvases, and somber Indian faces depicted the stark reality of Mexican life. This was not the impression of the stable, conservative, white, progressive Mexico that Díaz wanted portrayed.

The Porfiriato also distinguished itself as a productive period in Mexican historical scholarship. The best of the historians put polemic behind them and moved into the archives for painstaking research. Manuel Orozco y Berra and Luis González Obregón interested themselves primarily in the colonial period and produced seminal works on the society and culture of New Spain. Perhaps the greatest historian of the epoch was Joaquín García Icazbalceta (1825–94), who collected and edited several monumental series of colonial documents and prepared a bibliography of the sixteenth century—*Bibliografía mexicana del siglo xvi*—listing and annotating all of the books published in Mexico between 1539 and 1600. But his most distinguished work was a four-volume biography of the first bishop and archbishop of Mexico, Fray Juan de Zumárraga.

Of those historians not concerned with the colonial period, one name stands out far above the rest. Justo Sierra (1848–1912) set himself to the task of attempting a new interpretive synthesis of Mexican history. The result would occupy a unique niche in Mexican historiography. *Mexico: Su evolución social* was published at the turn of the century and shows Sierra as an eclectic. Though the book was written during the period of positivist domination of Mexican intellectual thought, one can still detect the impact of historical romanticism on the author. Unlike the historians who preceded him, Sierra, from a new perspective, could view Mexican history with optimism. The chaotic and unseemly events of the early nineteenth century were, for him, necessary steps in the progress of mankind. Criticism of past Mexican politicians and institutions was abundant but never indulged. Sierra's analysis of his contemporary Mexico was especially brilliant: even Díaz did not emerge completely unscathed. Sierra trod a path between a tolerably mild censure and the apologia that Díaz undoubtedly would have preferred. While Sierra could not overlook the authoritarianism of the regime, on balance he found it worthwhile. For Justo Sierra the Díaz regime, much like the early nineteenth century, was simply a step in Mexico's evolutionary process. It, too, had to yield to something else. And in the best nineteenth-century liberal tradition, the ultimate goal was not a more equitable distribution of wealth but rather liberty.

Mexico's cultural and intellectual life flourished from 1876 to 1910. When it did not come into direct conflict with the goals of the dictatorship, it received encouragement and even direct support. The novelist could concern himself with refining the language, the artist with painting a landscape, and the historian with probing Mexico's colonial heritage, all with little to fear. But artistic and intellectual expression that ran contrary to the all-important image so assiduously cultivated by the regime did not fare so well. Freedom of expression existed for those who accepted the dictatorship for what it was and who, because of personal interests or intellectual commitment, could continue to pursue their individual tasks.

During the three and one-half decades of peace and economic growth a younger generation of liberal intellectuals gradually emerged. As they began to test the cultural atmosphere with matters of honest concern, and as they began to expose some of the obvious shortcomings of the regime, they encountered no benevolent patronage or passive resignation. The more passionate and direct their indictments, the more likely they were to experience harsh retribution. In spite of harassment, intimidation, and incarceration, these young intellectuals were not easily dissuaded from their goals and contributed in no small way to the outbreak of revolutionary activity in Mexico in 1910.

Recommended for Further Study

Arnold, Channing, and Frederick J. Tabor Frost. *The American Egypt: A Record of Travel in Yucatán.* New York: Doubleday, Page & Company, 1909.

Barton, Mary. *Impressions of Mexico with Brush and Pen.* London: Methuen, 1911.

Beezley, William H. *Judas at the Jockey Club and Other Episodes of Porfirian Mexico.* Lincoln: University of Nebraska Press, 1987.

Bishop, W. H. *Old Mexico and Her Lost Provinces.* New York: Harper and Brothers, 1883.

Brushwood, John S. *Mexico in Its Novel: A Nation's Search for Identity.* Austin: University of Texas Press, 1966.

Case, Alden Buell. *Thirty Years with the Mexicans: In Peace and Revolution.* New York: Fleming H. Revell, 1917.

Charlot, Jean. *The Mexican Mural Renaissance, 1920–1925.* New Haven, Conn.: Yale University Press, 1967.

Gillpatrick, Wallace. *The Man Who Likes Mexico.* New York: Century, 1912.

McCarty, J. Hendrickson. *Two Thousand Miles through the Heart of Mexico.* New York: Phillips & Hunt, 1888.

Ober, Frederick A. *Travels in Mexico and Life among the Mexicans.* Boston: Estes and Lauriat, 1884.

Raat, William D. "Ideas and Society in Don Porfirio's Mexico." *The Americas* 30 (1973): 32–53.

Sierra, Justo. *The Political Evolution of the Mexican People.* Translated by Charles Ramsdell. Austin: University of Texas Press, 1969.

Tweedie, Mrs. Alec. *Mexico as I Saw It.* London: Hurst and Blackett, 1901.

Tyler, Ron, ed. *Posada's Mexico.* Washington, D.C.: Library of Congress, 1979.

VIII THE REVOLUTION: THE MILITARY PHASE, 1910-20

30

The Liberal Indictment

The Liberal Leadership

The opening of the twentieth century found Mexico a far different place than it had been only twenty-five years earlier. It would be sheer folly to gainsay the tremendous material benefits that had accrued in the industrial, commercial, and mining fields. But there is no Ciudad Porfirio Díaz in Mexico today, no public school or street bears his name, and it is hard to find a public statue or monument erected in his honor. Porfirian capitalism shunned the masses; the economic surplus generated by the dynamic economy had been appropriated by the few. Fifty years earlier nobody would have batted an eye, but new ideological currents had swept through the western world in the second half of the nineteenth century and had begun to lay bare the social malaise of the old regimes. A system that perpetuated itself for the sake of order and economic progress, and atrophied in the process, became less and less palatable to an increasing number of young, socially aware Mexicans.

When a handful of astute observers began to balance the progress against the costs, they at first manifested greater interest in political abuse than in social stagnation. The federal Constitution of 1857, with its theoretical guarantees, had been violated incessantly. Elections at all levels of government were a farce. The administration of justice in rural Mexico was a euphemism for the capricious whims of the local jefe político. Freedom of the press did not exist, and the restrictions of the Reform limiting the participatory role of the clergy were not enforced. To those who were concerned with the longevity of the regime, Don Porfirio became "Don Perpetuo," while those more concerned with the brutality dubbed him "Porfiriopoxtli."

The intelligentsia as a class did not abandon the regime with the advent of the twentieth century. The científicos continued to be loyal apologists for the dictatorship, as it well behooved them. They had convinced themselves that to attack the Díaz system was to attack the foundation of civilization itself. But a younger generation of intellectual activists, embracing a new faith and unwilling to be intimidated by the arrogance of the científicos, began to question the effete dictatorship.

One of the first to speak out for reform was Wistano Luis Orozco, a jurist from Guadalajara. Unlike the majority of liberal malcontents, he was concerned with social, not political, issues. As early as 1895 he had written a volume criticizing the Díaz land laws and the land companies that profited from them. He conjectured that "the large accumulation of land in a single hand causes the ruin and degradation of peoples."[1] The regime was shirking its responsibilities in the rural areas. To reverse the ever increasing trend, he argued that the government should break up and sell all public lands and begin buying up some of the huge haciendas for the same purpose. But Orozco was not propagandizing for revolution. He believed the reforms he envisioned could be effected from within the administration.

In San Luis Potosí, Camilo Arriaga, a mining engineer by profession, rejected the positivist doctrine he had learned in the schools and by the turn of the century counted himself in the small anti-Díaz camp. A typical nineteenth-century liberal, Arriaga moved into the opposition fold because of Díaz's *modus vivendi* with the Roman Catholic Church. In late 1900 he called for the organization of liberal clubs throughout Mexico and summoned a national liberal convention to meet in San Luis Potosí early the next year. The response was better than expected, and fifty delegates attended. Although the resolutions adopted were narrowly conceived and primarily anticlerical, the malcontents had been brought together for the first time. Emboldened by one another, they would gradually broaden the base of their antigovernment attack.

The least timid members of the liberal movement in the early twentieth century were the Flores Magón brothers—Jesús, Ri-

1. Quoted in Arnaldo Córdova, *La ideología de la Revolución Mexicana: Formación del nuevo régimen* (Mexico, 1973), p. 115.

cardo, and Enrique. In August of 1900 the brothers began publication of *Regeneración*, a Mexico City weekly. Not yet ready to preach the injustice of private land ownership, through its columns they supported the nascent liberal movement in San Luis Potosí and decried the excesses of Porfirismo. While their early pamphleteering might have brought the regime into some disrepute, their activities were not yet seditious.

For attacking a local jefe político in Oaxaca in the columns of *Regeneración*, the brothers were arrested in the late spring of 1901 and confined to Belén prison for a year. Their arrest served to invigorate the liberal movement as freedom of the press and suppression of the jefes políticos became new causes the liberals could add to their militant anticlericalism. Through his own intemperate action in arresting the brothers, Díaz himself had contributed to converting the narrowly based anticlerical movement into an anti-Díaz movement. By the time the Flores Magón brothers were released Camilo Arriaga had been arrested, as had other leaders of the liberal cause. The brothers renewed their attacks, this time in the columns of *El Hijo de Ahuizote*; six months later they were in prison once again. A release and a third brief arrest convinced them of the futility of trying to conduct their campaign from Mexican soil; in January 1904, broke and disheartened, they crossed over into the United States to attack the Díaz regime from exile.

From San Antonio, Texas, the Flores Magón brothers and Arriaga, who joined them shortly, began soliciting funds from liberals to reinstitute *Regeneración*. Former subscribers and liberal clubs throughout Mexico made small contributions, and an unexpected benefactor was found in Francisco I. Madero, son of a wealthy Coahuila hacendado. The first issue of the newly revived tabloid came off the press in the fall of 1904. The *Regeneración* published from San Antonio was much more militant and belligerent; attacks against Díaz were more categorical and vicious and the remedies more radical. In one editorial Enrique lashed out as follows:

> Forever—for as long as Mexico can remember—today's slavery will be identified with the name of the devil that made it all possible. His name is Porfirio Díaz, and his bestiality is being carried out in Mexico. . . . The jefes políticos do not send thieves and other criminals to jail—rather they sell them as slaves. . . . You may say that Díaz does not benefit directly from this human commerce. . . . But what about the governors of Veracruz, Oaxaca,

Cartoon from *El Hijo de Ahuizote* entitled "The Governors Praying for Díaz Support."

Hidalgo, and other states and their cronies who do benefit? Who appointed these governors? Porfirio Díaz. . . . But the day of liberation is coming. Prepare yourselves my fellow citizens.[2]

San Antonio proved to be a little too close to the Mexican border for comfort. Díaz dispatched a would-be assassin to the Texas city to end once and for all his problem with the Flores Magón brothers. The assassination attempt failed, but the liberals in exile decided it would be wiser to move deeper into the heartland of the United States where agents of the Díaz dictatorship could not so easily blend into the local populace and where local law enforcement agencies, with their deeply engrained anti-Mexican prejudices, might not be so vigilant. The exiles chose St. Louis, Missouri, and in 1905 not only again began publishing *Regeneración* but also organized a revolutionary junta for the expressed purpose of overthrowing the Díaz dictatorship. But the local St. Louis authorities were no more friendly than those in San Antonio; they arrested the Flores Magón brothers, charging them with violating United States neutrality laws. A friendly campaign waged in their behalf by the St. Louis press, however, hastened their release.

2. Quoted in Samuel Kaplan, *Peleamos contra la injusticia: La epopeya de los hermanos Flores Magón* (Mexico, 1960), 1: 162–65.

In the summer of 1906 the junta in St. Louis published its
Liberal Plan. Part of it was a simple rehash of nineteenth-century liberal concerns. It called for freedom of speech, freedom of
the press, suppression of the jefes políticos, the complete seculari-
zation of education, and the nationalization of all church property. But the Liberal Plan of 1906 added a series of new concepts
manifesting graphically that a new age of liberalism had finally
dawned. Socially oriented measures included the abolition of the
death penalty (except for treason), educational reform in favor
of the poor, and prison reform emphasizing rehabilitation rather
than punishment. More revolutionary yet was the call for a
nationwide eight-hour workday and a six-day workweek, the
abolition of the tienda de raya, the payment of all workers in
legal tender, and the prohibition of child labor. The rural areas
of Mexico were not overlooked as they had been so often in the
past. All uncultivated lands were to be taken over by the state
and redistributed to those who would work them. To enable the
small farmer to take advantage of the new law, an agricultural
credit bank would be established to provide low-interest loans.
And, finally, special emphasis would be placed on restoring the
ejido lands seized illegally from the Indian communities.

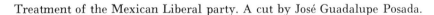

Treatment of the Mexican Liberal party. A cut by José Guadalupe Posada.

The discontent over the political abuses of the Díaz dictator-ship had been gradually transmuted into a new gospel of social reform. For the first time in Mexican history an articulate and organized minority, albeit a small one, had displayed genuine concern for the plight of the masses. Mexico had received its first application of classical capitalism late, and, as a result, the social-ist, anarchist, and syndicalist strictures of that system had also been late in making their appearance. While the Mexican exile community produced no social prophets of the stature of Karl Marx, Louis Blanc, or Mikhail Bakunin, the liberal leaders in exile had immersed themselves in European social thought and had begun to apply the lessons to Mexican reality as they under-stood it. In the thousands of copies of *Regeneración* smuggled into Mexico monthly, the Flores Magón brothers and their liberal compatriots in exile exposed the regime as intellectually impov-erished and socially bankrupt and so contributed immeasurably to the growth of the anti-Díaz movement.[3] They received their first promising news from the fatherland in the summer of 1906. It came from Cananea, Sonora.

Labor Unrest

On June 1, 1906, the Mexican workers at Colonel William Greene's Cananea Consolidated Copper Company went out on strike. The liberal junta had not planned the strike, but young socialist activists in Cananea—Manuel Diéguez, Estéban Calde-rón, and Francisco Ibarra—had been in correspondence with the exiles, had formed an affiliate liberal club in Cananea, and had agitated the workers, distributing copies of *Regeneración*.

The grievances of the miners at Cananea were manifold. Mex-icans were paid less than their United States counterparts for performing the same jobs. Qualified Mexican laborers were con-signed to undesirable posts, while the technical and managerial positions were staffed entirely by United States personnel. The workers elected a delegation, including Diéguez and Calderón, to negotiate these matters, and salary and hours, with the man-

3. A differing interpretation on the influence of the Flores Magón brothers on the nascent labor movement is found in Rodney D. Anderson, "Mexican Workers and the Politics of Revolution, 1906–1911," *Hispanic American Historical Review* 54 (1974): 94–113. Examining letters, flyers, petitions, and workers' newspapers, Anderson concludes that the impact of the Mexican liberals on the workers' move-ment has been overstated.

Mothers, wives, sisters, and daughters supported the miners' demands by demonstrating in Cananea.

agement. When Colonel Greene refused to arbitrate, the activists decided to stop all company operations.

The violence began in the company lumberyard. Disgruntled but unarmed workers attempted to force their way through a locked gate, and the resident manager ordered high-pressure water hoses to be turned on them. When the gate finally buckled and the workers swarmed into the yard, they were greeted with several volleys of rifle fire. During the chaos of the next hour several dozen Mexicans and two United States managers were slain. The remaining workers retired, leaving the lumberyard in flames. The atmosphere was explosive as the workers marched into Cananea, robbed two pawnshops of guns and ammunition, and exchanged fire with American residents. Colonel Greene informed Governor Rafael Izábal of the danger and telephoned friends across the border in Arizona to raise a volunteer force in his behalf. When the governor was apprised that the rurales could not arrive until late the next day, he gave permission for 275 Arizona Rangers to cross the border to patrol the streets of Cananea. To veil the violation of Mexico's neutrality, Izábal did not allow the Rangers to enter the country as a force. They crossed over individually and were subsequently sworn in as Mexican volunteers.

The situation in Cananea was still tense when the American force arrived, together with Governor Izábal. While no major military engagements ensued, the Rangers and the workers did exchange fire on several occasions, and deaths resulted on both sides. Late in the day a detachment of rurales arrived under the command of Colonel Emilio Kosterlitzky. "Justice" was quick for those workers Kosterlitzky considered ringleaders: they were rounded up, escorted out of town, and hanged from trees. The strike was broken, and the workers, threatened with induction into the army, returned to their jobs.

The Mexican workers at Cananea were not Molly Maguires, yet their fate was the same. But the strike did serve a purpose. It focused attention on the Díaz policy of protecting foreigners at the expense of Mexicans. United States troops had been allowed to cross into Mexican territory and kill Mexicans to guard the interests of an American mining magnate. More important yet, for the first time the masses had been organized for a show of strength.

The discontent of the miners at Cananea proved not to be an isolated phenomenon. Even as the strike in Sonora was being suppressed, liberal leaders among the textile workers in Veracruz organized the Gran Círculo de Obreros Libres and began seeking affiliate clubs in neighboring states. The last six months of 1906, with the echos of Cananea still fresh, witnessed the most intense labor conflict of the entire Porfiriato, but Díaz treated the disturbances as a political rather than a social problem. Late in the year textile strikes supported by the Gran Círculo occurred in Puebla, Orizaba, and Tlaxcala, but the major showdown was postponed until January 1907.

Working conditions in the Río Blanco textile mills were nothing short of horrible. The common workday was twelve hours, the wages were grossly inadequate, and, on top of everything else, the workers were required to pay for the normal depreciation of the machinery they used. Children of eight and nine years of age performed physically demanding work. All publications distributed among the workers had to be approved by management officials, and all strikes were illegal. Workers whose affiliation with the Gran Círculo became known were subject to immediate dismissal. The abuses seemed so patent that the workers agreed to lay their complaints directly before President Díaz for his arbitration. The dictator agreed to hear the complaints, but when he issued his decision he supported the textile owners on almost every count. On Sunday, January 6, the workers held a mass meeting and decided to strike the following day.

The trouble set in at the grocery counter of the tienda de raya. Several of the wives of the striking workers were refused credit for food. Insults led to pushing and shoving, then fisticuffs, and finally shooting. The enraged strikers put the tienda de raya to flame, and the local jefe político ordered in the rurales and the federal troops. When the troops arrived they fired point-blank into the crowd and killed several women and children along with numerous workers. The crowd dispersed, but when some of the workers returned later to collect the bodies of the dead they were again assaulted by the troops and even more were killed. The exact number of worker deaths at Río Blanco is impossible to calculate because the censored press gave no detailed account, but contemporary observers, including the nearby United States consuls, placed the figure at over one hundred.

The government reaction to the textile strike at Río Blanco was the grossest evidence of mass suppression yet. It was easy—too easy—to blame labor unrest entirely on liberal agitators in the United States without questioning seriously whether the grievances had any basis in fact. The regime showed itself no more willing to face up to the country's social maladies in 1907 than it had been in 1876. Again law and order was assured at the expense of personal liberty and social justice.[4]

Heightened Political Activity

In spite of the liberal indictment and in spite of the suppression of the nascent labor movement, most Mexican politicians believed that a revolution could be avoided and that change could be effected through the political process. The moderates were encouraged when in early 1908 the dictator granted an interview to the United States journalist James Creelman. Full of self-assurance, Díaz defended his governing philosophy to Creelman and then let loose a bombshell.

> No matter what my friends and supporters say, I retire when my presidential term of office ends, and I shall not serve again. I shall be eighty years old then. I have waited patiently for the day when

4. The labor crisis is carefully analyzed in Rodney D. Anderson, "Díaz y la crisis laboral de 1906," *Historia Mexicana* 19 (1970): 513–35.

the people of the Mexican Republic should be prepared to choose and change their government at every election without danger of armed revolution and without injury to the national credit or interference with the national progress. I believe that day has come. I welcome an opposition party in the Mexican Republic.[5]

Díaz's surprise announcement that he did not plan to seek reelection in the upcoming presidential elections of 1910 ushered in a rash of political activity and intellectual ferment. Shortly after this interview the Mexican literati went to work. The Yucatecan sociologist Andrés Molina Enríquez, a positivist but not a Porfirista, published an important volume entitled *Los grandes problemas nacionales* (translated as *The Great National Problems*). A brilliant analysis of contemporary Mexican society, the work called for a penetrating program of reform, especially in the rural areas. Molina Enríquez knew that agrarian discontent had already manifested itself in sporadic outbreaks of violence, and he feared that if positive steps were not taken the movement might fall into radical or anarchist hands.[6]

A still more influential book, *La sucesión presidencial en 1910* (translated as *The Presidential Succession in 1910*), came from the pen of Francisco I. Madero. Unlike Molina Enríquez, Madero held that Mexico's problems were primarily political in nature. The greatest danger to Mexico, as Madero perceived it, was continued military dictatorship with its concomitant absolutism. Although Madero himself did not believe that Díaz was going to step down voluntarily, he urged Mexicans to take the dictator at his word and to begin forming an opposition party, an anti-reelectionist party dedicated to the principles of effective suffrage and no-re-election. He was convinced that the desired change could be effected through the ballot box. *La sucesión presidencial en 1910* cannot compare to Molina Enríquez's *Los grandes problemas nacionales* in its scholarship, originality, or social significance. Yet it proved to be much more important historically as, together with the Creelman interview, it set into motion the political forces that would ultimately lead to the conflagration in the fall of 1910.

The political activity of 1909 and 1910 was quite unlike anything Mexico had known since the Revolution of Tuxtepec. Within the administration itself various factions began to vie for

5. Quoted in Frederick Starr, *Mexico and the United States* (Chicago, 1914), p. 253.
6. For a perceptive discussion of early agrarianism, see John M. Hart, "Agrarian Precursors of the Mexican Revolution: The Development of an Ideology," *The Americas* 29 (1972): 131–50.

the mantle of succession. The followers of General Bernardo Reyes, the capable and energetic former governor of Nuevo León and secretary of war, pushed their hero as a logical successor to Díaz. If Díaz should change his mind and run for office again, then Reyes should at least be placed on the official ticket as the vice-presidential candidate. However, the científicos within the administration, led by José Limantour, had a different candidate and opposed the steadily growing Reyista cause. At the national convention of the official party they urged another term for Porfirio Díaz and declared their belief that Ramón Corral, a former governor of Sonora and currently vice-president, should be retained for the number two position on the ticket. Without qualms the president and vice-president accepted the mandate.

The Reyista movement counted on a good deal of support from the army and from a number of active political clubs, but Reyes himself never agreed to offer himself as a candidate—for either president or vice-president. Some accused the general from Nuevo León of cowardice, but he always considered himself a loyal Porfirista. He had his disagreements with the regime but believed that reform could be effected from the inside. He wanted to avoid an open split within official circles at a time when pressure from without was beginning to build up noticeably. Díaz himself, however, was willing to take no chances. To test the general's loyalty he asked him to undertake a military study mission in Europe. Reyes's acceptance of the contrived assignment in November 1909 was tantamount to political exile.

Madero and the Anti-Re-electionist Cause

The political opposition to Díaz in the 1910 presidential elections would come, at any rate, from outside the official party, as Francisco I. Madero dedicated himself to the Anti-Re-electionist cause. Born in Coahuila in 1873 to a family of wealth and prestige, young Madero received the best education that money could provide. The family had garnered a fortune in mining, land speculation, cattle, and banking; Madero's father was happy to send his teen-age son to Paris and then to Berkeley, California, for proper grooming. Upon his return to Coahuila, Madero was placed in charge of some of the family haciendas and quickly developed an unusual interest in the welfare of the peones who worked them. He not only observed the gross social inequities firsthand but took time to ponder the pathetic written complaints that crossed his desk daily. Stories of physical abuse at the hands of the mayordomos were not as frequent as tales of poverty that left children without shelter or food, of sickness without the possibility of medical care, of military conscription as a means of punishment, and of incarceration without the formalities of law.[7] He did what he could on the family properties, but he realized fully that the Madero haciendas were simply a microcosm of rural Mexico.

Shortly after the turn of the century, as liberals throughout the country were increasingly manifesting their discomfort, Madero entered politics on a small scale. Throwing his support behind antiadministration politicians in Coahuila, he tasted defeat in 1904 and 1905 when Díaz intervened to assure the election in the state of his own favorites. The problem was thus, from Madero's point of view, primarily political—nothing could change until democratic processes had a chance to work their miraculous cures. Though Madero had initially contributed to the cause of the Flores Magón brothers, he became estranged from them as they grew more radical. In the spring of 1908 he set to work on his manuscript, *La sucesión presidencial en 1910*. The publication of the book early the next year launched not only the Anti-Re-electionist movement but also Madero's political career.

To foment anti-re-electionism and to test the political winds, Madero toured Mexico in the last half of 1909. During the summer and early fall he made public appearances in Orizaba, Veracruz, Progreso, Mérida, Campeche, Tampico, Monterrey, and Torreón. If the receptions were not always as enthusiastic as he would have liked, he did leave each city with assurances that an active group of liberals would be working there in his behalf. And although he did not realize it at the time, he was also building a revolutionary network to which he would later appeal. The winter months were no less hectic as Madero, his close confidants, and his wife continued their political tours to Querétaro, Guadalajara, Manzanillo, Mazatlán, and into the northern states of Sonora and Chihuahua. Gaining confidence and stature along the way, Madero offered himself as an energetic, capable, and articulate young leader in stark contrast to a tiring and decrepit regime—not a member of Díaz's cabinet was under sixty; many of the state governors were in their seventies. Especially well re-

7. The nature of the complaints that crossed Madero's desk are described in Michael C. Meyer, "Habla por ti mismo Juan: Una propuesta para un método alternativo de investigación," *Historia Mexicana* 22 (1973): 396–408.

ceived in Chihuahua, Madero held several meetings with Abraham González, an ardent foe of the dictatorship and president of the Centro Anti-Re-eleccionista Benito Juárez. After Madero's departure, González polled the various clubs in the state and decided to nominate Madero for the presidency at the upcoming Anti-Re-electionist convention in Mexico City.

The convention met in April 1910 with broad geographical representation. The 120 delegates in attendance, following the lead of Abraham González and his Chihuahua colleagues, officially nominated Madero for the presidency. The following afternoon the vice-presidential nomination was given to Dr. Francisco Vásquez Gómez, a distinguished physician but a lukewarm liberal at best.

The philosophy of the Anti-Re-electionist party came out gradually during the campaign that carried the candidate to twenty-two of the twenty-seven Mexican states. Madero simply expanded upon the ideas contained in his book. Political reform, predicated upon free and honest elections, was basic to the entire program. Social benefits might then accrue, but democracy was the one imperative. During a campaign speech in San Luis Potosí, Madero was interrupted by a question voiced from the audience asking why he did not break up his own haciendas. Madero's answer epitomized his philosophy. The Mexican people, he responded, did not want bread; they wanted liberty.

The campaign ended abruptly in Monterrey. A huge group of admirers broke through a police barricade to attend a demonstration in front of Madero's house. Madero shared the speakers' platform with cohort Roque Estrada, who criticized the police for trying to hamper the rally. The following day the police tried to arrest Estrada, but Madero detained them, allowing his companion to escape. Madero himself was then arrested for abetting a fugitive from justice. In reality his only crime had been to dare to oppose Díaz in the 1910 presidential elections.

Election day, June 21, 1910, found Madero in prison in San Luis Potosí and thousands of his Anti-Re-electionist colleagues in jails throughout the republic. Nobody was surprised when the government announced that Díaz and Ramón Corral had been overwhelmingly re-elected for still another term. The Madero family was able to arrange for Madero's release on bail with the proviso that he confine himself to the city of San Luis Potosí. He did remain in the city for several months, but in early October, when the rigor of his confinement was relaxed, he boarded a northbound train in disguise and escaped to the United States.

The Last Hurrah

Soon after the election Díaz began preparations for his final extravaganza. In September he would celebrate his eightieth birthday and Mexico the hundredth anniversary of its Declaration of Independence. The entire month was given over to pageants, celebration, and commemoration. A soaring column capped by a gold angel was unveiled on the Paseo de la Reforma in honor of the Independence movement. An equally impressive monument to the Niños Héroes was dedicated at the entrance to Chapultepec Park. Distinguished guests from abroad had their expenses paid to partake of the festivities. Gala balls were held in their honor, and imported French champagne flowed like water. Flags were displayed everywhere, banquets followed banquets, parades crowded the streets, fireworks lit up the night skies, and *mariachis* (folk musicians) strolled the downtown avenues. Foreign governments took part as well. The American colony, thinking of no better way of commemorating the heroic deeds of Father Hidalgo, sent Díaz and the Mexican people a statue of George Washington, and the Italians—not to be outdone—sent one of Giuseppe Garibaldi. In a rare display of *entente cordiale* the Third French Republic returned the keys to the city of Mexico that had been ingloriously sequestered by the army of Napoleon III a half-century before. King Alfonso XIII demonstrated the lasting confraternity of the Spanish people by returning the uniforms of José María Morelos.

The centennial celebrations epitomized everything that was right and everything that was wrong with the Díaz regime. Beggars were pushed off of the streets of the capital city for the duration so that the guests would receive the proper impressions of a prosperous Mexico. The cost of the celebrations exceeded the entire educational budget for the year 1910. Mexico was at last enjoying its place in the international sun—respect was no longer lacking. But while the champagne was flowing for a few, tens of thousands were suffering from malnutrition. While guests were treated to young female companions, Indian women in Yucatán were dying in childbirth. While European waiters served at the banquets, urban Mexicans were unemployed. While letters of congratulation arrived on time, 85 percent of the population was still illiterate. While visitors rode in shiny new motorcars on well-paved streets in the center of the city, mud and filth engulfed the workers' barrios in the suburbs. In September 1910

Mexico appeared to many to be enjoying its finest hour. But with social reform still alien to the Porfirian mentality, the peace would soon prove to be fragile and the showy façade would collapse with it.

Recommended for Further Study

Axelrod, Bernard. "St. Louis and the Mexican Revolutionaries, 1905–1906." *Bulletin of the Missouri Historical Society* 28 (1972): 94–108.

Brown, Lyle C. *The Mexican Liberals and Their Struggle against the Díaz Dictatorship, 1900–1906*. Mexico: Mexico City College Press, 1956.

Cadenhead, Ivie E., Jr. "The American Socialists and the Mexican Revolution of 1910." *Southwestern Social Science Quarterly* 43 (1962): 103–17.

Cockcroft, James D. *Intellectual Precursors of the Mexican Revolution, 1900–1913*. Austin: University of Texas Press, 1968.

Creelman, James. *Díaz: Master of Mexico*. New York: Appleton, 1916.

Cumberland, Charles C. *Mexican Revolution: Genesis under Madero*. Austin: University of Texas Press, 1952.

———. "Precursors of the Mexican Revolution of 1910." *Hispanic American Historical Review* 22 (1942): 344–56.

Hart, John M. "Agrarian Precursors of the Mexican Revolution: The Development of an Ideology." *The Americas* 29 (1972): 131–50.

———. *Revolutionary Mexico: The Coming and Process of the Mexican Revolution*. Berkeley: University of California Press, 1987.

Knight, Alan. *The Mexican Revolution*. Vol. 1: *Porfirians, Liberals and Peasants*. New York: Cambridge University Press, 1986.

Raat, William D. "The Diplomacy of Suppression: *Los Revoltosos*, Mexico and the United States, 1906–1911." *Hispanic American Historical Review* 56 (1976): 529–50.

Ross, Stanley R. *Francisco I. Madero, Apostle of Mexican Democracy*. New York: Columbia University Press, 1955.

Smith, Cornelius C. *Emilio Kosterlitzky: Eagle of Sonora and the Southwest Border*. Glendale, Calif.: Clark, 1970.

Turner, John Kenneth. *Barbarous Mexico*. Austin: University of Texas Press, 1969.

31

The Overthrow of Díaz

The Plan de San Luis Potosí

For years Francisco Madero had resisted the prodding of liberals who exhorted that Díaz must be overthrown by force. But when he escaped from San Luis Potosí and made his way north to the sanctuary of the United States border, he realized that the time had come at last. He had tried to unseat the dictator by constitutional means, but force had been used against him and his followers. He was finally ready to expose the inadequacies of enforced peace, and now he would call his fellow Mexicans to arms in the task of national redemption.

In the middle of October 1910, as supporters gathered around him in San Antonio, Texas, he began drafting a revolutionary plan. To avoid any possible international complications with the United States, he dated the plan October 5, the last day he had been in San Luis Potosí, and, in fact, called it the *Plan de San Luis Potosí*. He made his appeal emotionally.

> Peoples, in their constant efforts for the triumph of the ideals of liberty and justice, find it necessary at certain historical moments to make the greatest sacrifices. Our beloved fatherland has reached one of those moments. A tyranny that we Mexicans have not been accustomed to suffer since we won our independence oppresses us in such a manner that it has become intolerable. In exchange for that tyranny we are offered peace, but it is a peace full of shame for the Mexican nation, because it is based not on law but on force; because its goal is not the enrichment and prosperity of the country, but the enrichment of a small group. . . .
>
> But this violent and illegal system can no longer exist. I know

Aquiles Serdán and his family in Puebla. A cut by Fernando Castro Pacheco.

very well that if the people have designated me as their candidate for the presidency it is not because they have had an opportunity to discover in me the talents of a statesman or a ruler, but the vigor of a patriot ready to sacrifice himself, if necessary, to obtain liberty and to help the people free themselves from the odious tyranny that oppresses them. . . .

I declare the last election illegal and accordingly the republic, being without rulers, I assume the provisional presidency of the republic until the people designate their rulers pursuant to the law. . . .

I have designated Sunday, the 20th day of next November, for all the towns in the republic to rise in arms after 6 o'clock P.M.[1]

The Plan de San Luis Potosí, like *La sucesión presidencial en 1910* before it, demonstrates amply that Madero's concerns were primarily political. The few references to Mexico's social maladies were vague and ill conceived. Yet the boldness of the statement and the self-confidence it reflected struck a responsive chord. Once having received copies of the plan, the leaders who

1. The text of the plan can be found in Isidro Fabela, ed., *Documentos históricos de la revolución mexicana* (Mexico, 1960–73), 6: 69–76.

had previously worked for the Anti-Re-electionist party began preparing themselves for November 20.

The revolution actually began two days prematurely in the town of Puebla. There the local liberal leader, Aquiles Serdán, had stored arms and ammunition in his home. An informant notified the police, and the fight was on. Serdán and his family became the first martyrs of the new cause. Madero himself crossed over into Mexico on the evening of November 19, but, when his expected rebel army failed to rendezvous, he crossed back into the United States without firing a shot. The self-designated provisional president had no real assurance that anyone in Mexico would respond to his urgent call, but he would not be despondent for long. The masses immediately rallied to the cry of ¡Viva la Revolución!

The Rise of Rebel Armies and the Resignation of Díaz

Names that are remembered more in local corridos than in history texts took up arms everywhere on the stipulated day. But nowhere did the sparks fly as in Chihuahua. Town after town responded on November 20 and 21. Toribio Ortega marched on Cuchillo Parado, Gaspar Durán on Calabacillas, José de la Luz Blanco on Santo Tomás, Guadalupe Gardea on Chuviscar, Feliciano Díaz on Témores, Cástulo Herrera on Temósachic, Guillermo Baca on Hidalgo del Parral, Pancho Villa on San Andrés, and Pascual Orozco on San Isidro and Miñaca.

The rebel armies were not armies, but neither were they merely peasant mobs. There were peones, to be sure, but in addition servants, shopkeepers, mechanics, beggars, miners, federal army deserters, lawyers, United States soldiers of fortune, young and old, bandits and idealists, students and teachers, engineers and day laborers, the bored and the overworked, the aggrieved and the adventuresome, all constituted the rank and file. Some were attracted by commitment to the cause and some by the promise of spoils; some joined impulsively and others with careful forethought. Some preferred Flores Magón radicalism and some Madero liberalism; many had heard of neither. Even among the politically astute some viewed the November movement as a fight against hacendados, others decided to offer their lives to oppose local jefes políticos, while still others saw the Revolution as a chance to recapture Mexico from the foreign capitalists. But they all had one thought in common: Díaz was the

The Mexican guerrilla at the beginning
of the Revolution would soon be im-
mortalized in legend and song.

symbol of all Mexico's ills, and they were convinced that almost
any change would be a change for the better. Thus they were
willing to strap cartridge belts on their chests, find, buy, or steal
rifles somewhere, and become *guerrilleros*. Indifferently armed,
without uniforms, with no notion of military discipline, the disparate rebel bands lived off the land and attacked local authorities and small federal outposts in tiny pueblos. Sometimes they
were successful, and sometimes they were driven off to fall upon
a still weaker prey. It did not take them long to realize that they
enjoyed a dormant but fortuitous asset—the cooperation of much
of rural Mexico. Madero's communications network began to inform him that his recent efforts had not been in vain.

The Díaz regime was by no means prepared to lay down and
roll over. Unwilling to admit to himself that his system had
grown obsolescent, Díaz determined to hold on. With more
frenzy than care, army units and corps of rurales were dispatched on scattered missions in Mexico's ten military zones, and
slowly they began to curtail the spread of the rebellion. Only in
Chihuahua did the rebel movement continue to grow. The military leadership there had devolved upon Pascual Orozco, Jr., a
tall, gaunt mule skinner whose business had suffered because he

did not enjoy the favor of the Terrazas-Creel machine. When Orozco was contacted by Abraham González, the leader of the Anti-Re-electionists in the state, he had already been reading copies of *Regeneración* and did not have to be convinced that he should begin recruitment in Guerrero District and be ready to move on November 20. González supplied some modest funds and a few weapons. By the scheduled day Orozco had attracted about forty men to the cause. During the next two weeks, striking rapidly from the almost inaccessible *sierras* of western Chihuahua, he garnered four victories. Pancho Villa, José de la Luz Blanco, Cástulo Herrera, and other local leaders placed themselves under his command, and the Orozco army increased by twentyfold.

The new year opened well as on January 2, 1911, the Chihuahua rebels ambushed and almost totally destroyed a large federal convoy sent to pursue them. Now cocksure, Orozco stripped the dead soldiers of their uniforms, wrapped up the articles of clothing, and sent them to Don Porfirio with a graphically descriptive taunt: *Ahí te van las hojas; mándame más tamales* (Here are the wrappers; send me some more tamales).

In February Madero decided to cross over into Mexico for the second time and, although he had no special military talent, to assume military as well as political command. The next month he personally led an attack on Casas Grandes but, without Orozco's troops to support him, suffered the most punishing defeat of the entire northern campaign. The federal army not only routed the attackers but captured sixteen wagons of supplies and ammunition and three hundred horses. Madero realized that he had better leave the day-to-day fighting to Orozco, Villa, and the other guerrilla leaders who had already proved themselves on the field of battle.

Soon the insurrection began to bear fruit in Sonora, Coahuila, Sinaloa, Veracruz, Zacatecas, Puebla, Guerrero, and Morelos. In Baja California the Flores Magón brothers and their followers had the government on the run. Picking their own ground and their own time of battle, the small rebel contingents throughout the country kept the federals constantly off balance. The sparks were flying everywhere at the same time, and the vulnerabilities of the federal army became more acute. The military bureaucracy was inflexible, the government campaigns uncoordinated, the communications network tenuous, and the supply system inadequate. The rebels, on the other hand, moved in smaller units, lived off the land, and generally enjoyed the sympathy and cooperation of the local populace. They found it easier to smuggle in ammunition from the United States than federal commanders did to requisition it from Mexico City.

In the late spring of 1911 Orozco and Villa convinced Madero that the northern rebels should expend all their energy on capturing Ciudad Juárez, the border city across the Rio Grande from El Paso, Texas. By early May the most seasoned rebel troops had congregated on the outskirts of the city and were ready to attack. Suddenly, however, Madero changed his mind. Fearing that stray rebel shells might fall on El Paso and thus occasion United States intervention, he ordered a retreat. In direct violation of his commander's order, Orozco ordered the attack. Although the advantage of manpower and firepower lay with the rebels, the federal defense of the city, entrusted to General Juan Navarro, was stubborn. Thousands of El Paso residents climbed to their rooftops to watch the proceedings and cheer on their favorites. May 8 and 9 were indecisive, as most of the rebel assaults were blunted. But on the morning of May 10 the tide turned against the defenders of the city. Low on ammunition and completely encircled by the enemy, General Navarro decided to surrender and in the early afternoon hoisted a white flag over the federal barracks.

Madero did not know whether to be grateful, angry, or embarrassed. Against his order Orozco had handed him an important city, an official port of entry from the United States, and a provisional capital. When a few days later the provisional president named his cabinet, Orozco's name was curiously absent. The showdown took place on May 13 during a meeting of the new provisional government. Revolvers in hand to emphasize their point, Orozco and Villa burst into the room with a series of demands: General Navarro, who had executed captured rebel prisoners, must be tried as a war criminal; a new cabinet must be named from among those who had participated in the fighting; and Orozco's troops must be given their back pay. After a few tense moments cooler heads prevailed. Orozco and Villa were gradually convinced that Navarro could not receive a fair trial in the heated atmosphere following the battle for control of the city. Madero alone, by virtue of his position as provisional president, had the right to designate the cabinet. Only on their third demand were Orozco and Villa successful, as Madero wrote out a check to pay the troops lest they mutiny.

But the affair had significance that no one present could have foreseen. Though only five months old, the revolutionary coalition was already falling apart. The military's challenge to the civilian leadership would be repeated regularly for the next chaotic decade. But more important yet, the affair portended an age of bitter factionalism that exacerbated personal rivalries, turned Mexican against Mexican, extended the war, exacted a tremendously high toll of life, and increased the pain and anguish for hundreds of thousands.

The immediate results of the capture of Ciudad Juárez were less ominous. Rebels throughout the country took heart and redoubled their efforts. Tehuacán, Durango, Hermosillo, Cananea, Torreón, and Cuautla fell into revolutionary hands. Business fell victim to the trauma of uncertainty, and merchants bemoaned the lack of trade. The press became increasingly outspoken in criticism of the dictator and the sycophants who surrounded him, and the hour was too late to charge journalists again with seditious libel. Federal troops, who had not acquitted themselves too badly to this point, began deserting to the revolution *en masse*. Díaz slowly realized that an age was ending, and he agreed to dispatch a team of negotiators to treat with Madero and his staff. The Treaty of Ciudad Juárez provided that Díaz and

The battle of Ciudad Juárez (May 1911) proved to be the decisive engagement for control of the north.

The revolutionary leadership following the capture of Ciudad Juárez. The coalition would soon fall apart.

Vice-President Corral would resign before the month was out. Francisco León de la Barra, the secretary of foreign relations and an experienced diplomat, would assume the interim presidency until new elections could be held. The dictator did not wait until the end of the month. He signed his resignation and submitted it to the Congress on May 25.

A longtime United States resident in Mexico City described the mood as word of Díaz's resignation reached the public.

> Within an hour the news had traveled to the furthest corner of the capital and the peones who had been quiet all day now mustered into line. There was management in this, not accident, not spontaneous movement; yet all was joy. By eight o'clock that night a monster parade wound through the capital streets. . . . Cheers for Madero rent the heavens. The revolution had won.[2]

Díaz had indeed been overthrown, but the Revolution had scarcely triumphed. It had barely yet begun. The conviviality and jubilee of the next few days soon gave way to acrimonious debate as Mexicans began to ask themselves, what, exactly, they had won. Their answers, of course, were predicated upon what had motivated them to join the movement at the outset. As the dictator sailed away into European exile the one bond that had held them together vanished from sight. An old age had ended without a new age beginning.

2. Edward I. Bell, *The Political Shame of Mexico* (New York, 1914), pp. 82–83.

The Interim Presidency and Division within the Rebel Ranks

The interim presidency of León de la Barra (May to November 1911) turned out to be a crucial period. Madero's radical supporters, including the Flores Magón brothers, were unhappy enough with the choice of the interim president, but they were even more displeased when the provisional cabinet named by León de la Barra included a majority of Porfiristas. Emiliano Zapata in Morelos adopted a cautious wait-and-see attitude. Orozco in Chihuahua was still bristling from his recent encounter with Madero following the battle of Ciudad Juárez.

Unaware that the rumblings within his ranks were serious, in early June, Madero left the north for Mexico City. His seven-hundred-mile journey by train was truly triumphant, as thousands of enthusiastic admirers greeted him at large and small stations along the way. His reception in the capital was no less spectacular, as recorded by Edith O'Shaughnessy, the wife of the United States chargé d'affaires in the Mexico City embassy.

> There was a great noise of *vivas*, mingling with shouts of all kinds, tramping of feet, and blowing of motor horns. I could just get a glimpse of a pale, dark-bearded man bowing to the right and left. I kept repeating to myself: *"Qui l'a fait roi? qui l'a couronné?— la victoire."* . . . There were three days of continual plaudits and adoration, such as only the Roman emperors knew. . . . People came from far and near, in all sorts of conveyances or on foot, just to see him, to hear his voice, even to touch his garments for help and healing. . . .[3]

Among those there to greet Madero and talk to him was the most famous revolutionary of all—Emiliano Zapata. Like Orozco in the north, Zapata had never been a peón. His family had passed on a little land to him, and he supplemented his modest income as a muleteer, a horse trainer, and a stable master. Elected in 1909 to local office by the villagers of Anenecuilco, Morelos, he was regularly exposed to the full array of tragedies that had beset rural Mexico during the late Díaz regime. More concerned with local land problems than with the national movement to unseat the dictator, he did not call his villagers to support the Plan de San Luis Potosí on November 20, 1910. But within a few months he had linked the future of his own people

---

3. Edith O'Shaughnessy, *Diplomatic Days* (New York, 1917), p. 53.

Emiliano Zapata (1879–1919). Although Zapata played only a minor role in the fight again Díaz, his stature as a revolutionary grew steadily until his assassination in 1919.

with that of the Maderista cause and began recruiting an insurgent army. When appropriate, he made his appeal to local inhabitants in Náhuatl rather than in Spanish. A teen-age girl in Milpa Alta remembered when the Zapatistas first rode into the village.

> When he entered the village all of his men wore white clothes: white shirts, white pants, and *huaraches*. All of these men spoke Náhuatl, almost as we spoke it. Señor Zapata also spoke it, and as a result when those men came into Milpa Alta everyone understood them. . . . Señor Zapata went to the front of his men and spoke to all of the people of Milpa Alta.
>
> Notlac ximomanaca! Nehuatl onacoc; oncuan on ica tepoztli ihuan nochantlaca niquinhuicatz. Ipampa in Totazin Díaz aihmo ticnequi yehuatl techixotiz. Ticnequi occe altepetl achi cuali. Ilhuan totlac ximomanaca ipampa amo nechpactia tlen tetlaxtlahuia. Amo conehui ica tlacualo ica netzotzomatiloz. Noihqui nicnequi nochtlacatl quipiaz itlal: oncuan on quitocaz

ihuan quipixcaz tlaoli, yetzintli ihuan occequi xinachtli. Tlen nanquitoa? Namehuan totlac namomanazque?[4]

Zapata's military contributions to the overthrow of the Díaz dictatorship were not great, but he had scored a couple of victories over the federal forces by the time Díaz submitted his resignation in May 1911. With the new day now supposedly arrived, Zapata wanted to talk to Madero about the one matter that concerned him most—the land problem in Morelos. To Zapata the overthrow of Díaz had genuine meaning only if land were immediately restored to the pueblos. The encounter between the two men was dramatic. Zapata, with a large sombrero on his head and his carbine in his hand, gestured to the gold watch Madero sported on his vest and then made his point.

> Look, Señor Madero, if I, taking advantage of being armed, steal your watch and keep it, and then we meet again sometime and you are armed, wouldn't you have the right to demand that I return it?
> Of course, General, and you would also have the right to ask that I pay you for the use I had of it.
> Well, this is exactly what has happened to us in Morelos where some of the hacendados have forcibly taken over the village lands. My soldiers, the armed peasants, demand that I tell you respectfully that they want their lands returned immediately.[5]

With characteristic caution Madero would make no immediate commitment. He urged faith and patience, and to quiet Zapata's qualms he agreed to visit Morelos within a week to assess the situation firsthand. The visit turned out badly. Madero insisted that Zapata demobilize his army as a prerequisite to reducing tensions in the state. Zapata detected something absurd in the request. The revolutionaries had won; yet while the federal army remained intact, the victorious rebels were asked to disband. To show good faith the southern rebel reluctantly agreed, even though in doing so he was undermining his own bargaining posi-

---

4. "Join me. I rose up. I rose up in arms and I bring my countrymen. We no longer wish that our Father Díaz watch over us. We want a much better president. Rise up with us because we don't like what the rich men pay us. It is not enough for us to eat and dress ourselves. I also want for everyone to have his piece of land so that he can plant and harvest corn, beans, and other crops. What do you say? Are you going to join us?"

The Spanish and Náhuatl texts are found in Fernando Horcasitas, *De Porfirio Díaz a Zapata: Memoria Náhuatl de Milpa Alta* (Mexico, 1968), p. 105.

5. Quoted in Gildardo Magaña, *Emiliano Zapata y el agrarismo en México* (Mexico, 1934–52), 1: 160.

tion. But when interim President León de la Barra determined that the mustering out of the Zapatista troops was not proceeding with all good speed, he decided to send federal troops into the state to enforce the demobilization order. Madero was furious when he learned that federal General Victoriano Huerta had exchanged fire with a band of Zapatistas north of Cuernavaca. He pleaded with the interim president to withdraw the troops, but the tenuous peace had already been shattered and, with it, Zapata's faith in Madero. By August the state of Morelos was again in angry revolt, and Madero, perhaps through no fault of his own, could add Zapata's name to his growing list of enemies.

When the campaign for the 1911 presidential elections got under way, the political atmosphere was already tense. Madero's party met in Mexico City in August and gave him the nomination by acclamation. But the vice-presidential nomination divided the convention. Madero decided to dump his 1910 running mate, Francisco Vásquez Gómez, in favor of a Yucatecan lawyer and journalist, José María Pino Suárez. The convention gave Madero his choice, but Vásquez Gómez and his followers would never reconcile themselves to their sudden political demise.

The opposition candidate around whom many of the old regime could rally, albeit without enthusiasm, was General Bernardo Reyes. Reyes returned from his European study mission in June and within a month had made up his mind to run against Madero for the presidency. By early fall the election was in full swing and the debate heated. In September a group of Madero's supporters, without their leader's knowledge or approval, physically attacked Reyes at a Mexico City rally. The Reyista party protested vigorously and petitioned the Congress to postpone the elections because of the unfair treatment afforded their candidate. But the Congress turned down the request, and Reyes, perhaps realizing that his campaign stood little chance of victory anyway, withdrew from the race and went into a self-imposed exile in San Antonio, Texas. Another powerful enemy was on the list.

The election was held without further incident on October 1, 1911. Only minor candidates opposed Madero, and he swept to an overwhelming victory. With relief interim President León de la Barra turned over the office on November 6. Madero's faith in democracy would soon be put to the test, and, while his faith would remain unshaken, democracy would fall victim to the rancor and passion of the day.

Recommended for Further Study

Beezley, William H. *Insurgent Governor: Abraham González and the Mexican Revolution in Chihuahua.* Lincoln: University of Nebraska Press, 1973.

Bell, Edward I. *The Political Shame of Mexico.* New York: McBride, Nast, 1914.

Berbusse, Edward J. "Neutrality Diplomacy of the United States and Mexico, 1910–1911." *The Americas* 12 (1956): 265–83.

Blaisdell, Lowell L. *The Desert Revolution: Baja California, 1911.* Madison: University of Wisconsin Press, 1962.

Cumberland, Charles C. *Mexican Revolution: Genesis under Madero.* Austin: University of Texas Press, 1952.

Grieb, Kenneth J. "Standard Oil and the Financing of the Mexican Revolution." *California Historical Society Quarterly* 49 (1971): 59–71.

Guzmán, Martín Luis. *Memoirs of Pancho Villa.* Translated by Virginia H. Taylor. Austin: University of Texas Press, 1965.

Henderson, Peter V. N. "Mexican Rebels in the Borderlands, 1910–1912." *Red River Valley Historical Review* 2 (1975): 207–19.

Johnson, William Weber. *Heroic Mexico: The Violent Emergence of a Modern Nation.* Garden City, N.Y.: Doubleday, 1968.

McNeely, John H. "Origins of the Zapata Revolt in Morelos." *Hispanic American Historical Review* 46 (1966): 153–69.

Meyer, Michael C. *Huerta: A Political Portrait.* Lincoln: University of Nebraska Press, 1972.

————. *Mexican Rebel: Pascual Orozco and the Mexican Revolution, 1910–1915.* Lincoln: University of Nebraska Press, 1967.

Ross, Stanley R. *Francisco I. Madero, Apostle of Mexican Democracy.* New York: Columbia University Press, 1955.

Taylor, Lawrence D. "The Great Adventure: Mercenaries in the Mexican Revolution, 1910–1915." *The Americas* 43 (1986): 25–46.

Womack, John, Jr. *Zapata and the Mexican Revolution.* New York: Knopf, 1968.

32

Madero and the Failure of Democracy

In late May of 1911, on his way to Veracruz and ultimate exile, Porfirio Díaz reputedly told Victoriano Huerta, the commander of his military escort, "Madero has unleashed a tiger. Now let's see if he can control it." The remark, both prophetic and reflective of Díaz's keen perception of his fellow countrymen, augured ominous consequences. For the next decade Mexico would be torn apart, and the catharsis would be slow in coming. There would be little time to repair the devastation of war or to refashion the contours of society.

Disappointing Reforms

Bursting with optimistic idealism, Madero approached his presidential challenge with all the fresh enthusiasm of the novice. Mexico was embarking upon a democratic era, and democracy, Madero contended, would be equal to the task. But Madero the president, unlike Madero the revolutionary, found himself quickly besieged with demands from all sides. Only when established in the presidential office did he begin to realize fully that the Revolution had profoundly different meanings to different groups of Mexicans. The spurious alliance began to break up irretrievably. Of the disparate elements he had previously counted in his ranks, those of nineteenth-century liberal persuasion, interested in political reform and the growth of democracy, supported him with unabashed devotion. But both the aristocratic elite he displaced and the social revolutionaries he embraced

Francisco I. Madero (1873–1913). President of Mexico in the crucial period following the overthrow of Díaz, Madero had a faith in democracy that proved ill suited to the political realities of the day.

were increasingly displeased with the modest steps he undertook. The press began to assail him mercilessly, but, in the best democratic tradition, he gave it full rein and stoically accepted the barbed criticism and cruel satires.

It was only natural that Madero should be more responsive to the prodding of his former supporters. Although he could defy anyone to show him where he had ever promised sweeping reform, he did, nevertheless, embark upon a meager and imperfect program to restructure the prevailing social order. Though unwilling to accede to Zapata's urgent demand that land be immediately restored to the villages, the president appointed a National Agrarian Commission, under the chairmanship of his conservative cousin Rafael Hernández, to study the land question. Hernández urged that the government begin purchasing a few private estates for subdivision and sale to the small farmer. But only 10 million pesos were allocated to the project, and the hacendados demanded such high prices for the land that even this modest plan was soon abandoned in favor of restoring some of the ejido lands that had been seized illegally during the late Porfiriato. The burden of proof, however, fell on the villages, and few village leaders were able to cope with the bewildering legal arguments thrown in their faces by the hacendados' lawyers. A handful of cases were settled in favor of the villages, but progress on the agrarian question was meager.

The story was much the same in the field of labor reform. Late in 1912 the Congress authorized the formation of a Department of Labor but placed it, too, under the jurisdiction of conservative Hernández, a man whose quixotic faith in the law of supply and demand was never shaken. The budget for the Department of Labor was a paltry forty-six thousand pesos. After a convention with government officials in Mexico City, a group of textile factory owners promised to initiate a ten-hour day, but in practice the working schedules did not change.

Perhaps the greatest benefit accruing to labor during the Madero presidency was that labor organizers no longer felt so intimidated as they had in the past. Encouraged by the possibilities of revolutionary change, a group of radicals under the leadership of Juan Francisco Moncaleano, a Spanish anarchist, founded the Casa del Obrero Mundial. Not properly a union, the Casa served as a place where labor leaders could meet, exchange views, and, through their official newspaper *Luz*, disseminate propaganda favorable to the cause. But the government, caught between business interests and labor demands, was jittery. Madero feared labor strikes, and, although no labor massacres on the scale of Cananea and Río Blanco were recorded, government troops and local police authorities were used to disperse striking workers on a number of occasions. Hernández interpreted the strikes as inspired by agitators rather than resulting from intolerable conditions and finally had Moncaleano expelled from the country. But the strikes continued, and labor unrest began to disrupt the Mexican economy, growing shaky once again. The gains by labor as a result of these strikes were negligible.[1]

In the field of education the social reformers were again disap-

1. Ramón Eduardo Ruiz, "Madero's Administration and Mexican Labor," in *Contemporary Mexico*, ed. James W. Wilkie, Michael C. Meyer and Edna Monzón de Wilkie (Berkeley, 1976), pp. 187–203.

pointed. Although Madero had promised to broaden the educational base during the presidential campaign, the annual budget for 1911 to 1912 allocated only 7.8 percent for educational programs, as opposed to 7.2 percent during the last year of the Porfiriato. The new president did manage to build some fifty new schools and to initiate a modest program of school lunches for the underprivileged. But his education program is really more notable for what it did not do. No dramatic increase in expenditures was requested, nor was any project for revising the científico curriculum advanced.

In sum, the liberals of the twentieth-century stripe felt swindled by Madero as the administration failed at both the national and state levels. As the disappointed asked themselves why the president did not do more, some most assuredly must have realized that he believed that reform should proceed at a slow and gradual pace so as not to disrupt the fragile economy. But another factor was involved as well. Madero's hands were tied and his energies diverted by a series of revolts that broke out against him before he even had a chance to make himself comfortable in the presidential chair. The Revolution's lack of ideological cohesion had begun to exact a terrible toll and in the process imperiled the administration itself.

Revolts against the New Government

Emiliano Zapata was the first to pronounce against the new regime. In November 1911 the Zapatistas promulgated their famous *Plan de Ayala.* The general principles were those of Zapata himself, but the development and articulation were the work of Otilio Montaño, a schoolteacher from Ayala. After withdrawing recognition of Madero and recognizing Chihuahuan Pascual Orozco as titular head of the rebellion, the plan spelled out its program of agrarian reform.

> The lands, woods, and water that the landlords, científicos, or bosses have usurped . . . will be immediately restored to the villages or citizens who hold the corresponding titles to them. . . . The usurpers who believe they have a right to those properties may present their claims to special courts that will be established on the triumph of the Revolution. Because the great majority of Mexicans own nothing more than the land they walk on, and are unable to improve their social condition in any way . . . because lands, woods, and water are monopolized in a few hands . . . one-third of these properties will be expropriated, with prior in-

demnification, so that the villages and citizens of Mexico may obtain ejidos, townsites, and fields.[2]

The armed conflict began immediately and quickly spread from Morelos to the neighboring states of Guerrero, Tlaxcala, Puebla, Mexico, and even into the Federal District. When Madero's federal commanders were unable to contain the spread of the rebellion, they were replaced by others who promised to conduct a more vigorous campaign. But the Zapatista army continued to grow, and Madero was unable to thwart it. By early 1912 Zapata had disrupted railroad and telegraph service and taken over a number of towns; he had repeatedly defeated the federals and had the government on the run.

At approximately the same time General Bernardo Reyes launched a second movement in the north. In some ways Madero was more concerned with the Reyistas than with the Zapatistas. He feared that General Reyes still enjoyed a wide base of support among the army. Reyes crossed over into Mexico from the United States in the middle of December 1911 but found few Mexicans willing to rally to his banner. Unlike Zapata, Reyes was associated in the public mind with the old regime, and the northern Mexicans were not prepared to embrace his movement, even if many believed that Reyes had been treated unfairly in the recent presidential elections. Realizing that his sluggish revolution was not garnering sufficient support, on Christmas Day Reyes surrendered to a detachment of rurales. The commander of Mexico's third military zone, General Jerónimo Treviño, sent him first to prison in Monterrey and then had him transferred to the Prisión Militar de Santiago Tlaltelolco in Mexico City to await trial for treason.

At the end of the year a third revolt broke out against Madero in Chihuahua. Emilio Vásquez Gómez, believing that he and his brother Francisco had been unfairly treated in the last elections, launched his movement calling for Madero's ouster from office. At the end of January Madero was shocked to learn that the Vasquistas had captured Ciudad Juárez. The president knew full well the significance of this border city—he had seen his own revolt triumph there. Realizing the popularity that Pascual Orozco enjoyed in the north, Madero commissioned the Chihuahua commander to take charge of the government campaigns. For the rank and file of the Vásquez Gómez army Orozco—not Madero

2. The entire plan is quoted in Jesús Silva Herzog, *Breve historia de la Revolución mexicana* (Mexico, 1962), 1: 240–46.

—had been responsible for the overthrow of Díaz. Orozco had recruited the troops and led them in battle. He was the symbol of Chihuahua manhood and living proof that a poor, indifferently educated northerner could humble a professional army trained in the big city. The Vasquistas did not want to fight Orozco, so they agreed to meet with him. In the simple, folksy idiom of the north, Orozco made an impassioned speech calling for national unity in an hour of crisis, and he persuaded the rebel army to lay down arms without firing another shot.

But a few months later the most serious antigovernment movement broke out in the north. Its leader was the same man who had just called for national unity and saved Madero from the Vasquista offensive—Pascual Orozco. The Orozco rebellion was complex. While it combined nineteenth- and twentieth-century liberalism, it enjoyed the conservative financial support of the Terrazas clique in Chihuahua, who believed they could control the movement once it triumphed.

The *Plan Orozquista*, dated March 25, 1912, was the most comprehensive call for reform yet voiced from Mexican soil. It caustically attacked Madero for failing to abide by his own principles as set forth to the Mexican nation in the Plan de San Luis Potosí. Government corruption was still in evidence at the state and local levels, and nepotism and favoritism were more exaggerated in 1912 than they had been at any time during the Porfiriato. Not only had Madero's cousin, Rafael Hernández, been awarded the critical cabinet position of secretary of development, but his uncle, Ernesto Madero, had been made secretary of the treasury; a relative by marriage, José González Salas, was secretary of war; brother Gustavo Madero and four other members of the family were in the Congress; brother Raul Madero was given a series of government-supported military assignments; another relative was on the Supreme Court, two were in the postal service, and yet another was an undersecretary in the cabinet. Government army uniforms came from cotton cloth manufactured in Madero mills, while ammunition was purchased from cousin José Aguilar's munitions plant in Monterrey.

The Plan Orozquista, however, was more concerned with social than political reform. Drawing its inspiration from the Liberal Plan of 1906, it called for a ten-hour workday, restrictions on child labor, improved working conditions, higher wages, and the immediate suppression of the tiendas de raya. Anticipating the surge of economic nationalism that would sweep over Mexico in the next two decades, it called for the immediate nationalization of the railroads and the utilization of Mexican nationals in their operation. Agrarian reform also figured prominently. Persons who had resided on their land for twenty years were to be given title to it, while all lands illegally seized from the peasantry were to be returned. All lands owned by the government were to be distributed, and, most important, land owned by the hacendados, but not regularly cultivated, would be expropriated.

With alarming speed Orozco amassed a large army—some eight thousand strong—and began marching south to Mexico City. Capturing federally held towns along the way the rebels prepared themselves for a major showdown. The anticipated battle occurred at Rellano, close to the Chihuahua-Durango border. Madero's secretary of war, José González Salas, opted to command the government forces personally, and the army career officer was humiliated by Orozco's untrained rebels. As the federals retreated in disarray, González Salas, fearful of public rebuke, committed suicide. With panic growing in Mexico City, Madero named Victoriano Huerta to head a new government offensive. Huerta planned his campaigns with much deliberation, and by late May 1912 felt strong enough to meet the rebels face to face. By sheer chance the artillery duel once again occurred on the fields of Rellano, but on this occasion the results were different. Not only was Huerta a better field commander than his predecessor, but the Orozquistas were handicapped by lack of ammunition. Huerta pushed them back to the north and in the process temporarily saved the teetering Madero government.

Madero had no time for rejoicing, for his woes were not yet over. In early October 1912 a fifth serious rebellion broke out against him. This time it was Félix Díaz, the nephew of Don Porfirio, who called an army together in Veracruz. The Felicista movement was clearly counterrevolutionary in orientation and comprised many disgruntled supporters of the former dictator. Félix Díaz appealed to the army and suggested that Madero had trampled on its honor by passing over many competent career officers and placing self-made revolutionary generals in charge of key garrisons. The troops stationed in Veracruz came to Díaz's support, but his appeal to other army units throughout the republic went unheeded. Late in October loyal army troops isolated the rebels in Veracruz and forced their surrender. A hastily conceived court-martial found Díaz guilty of treason and sentenced him to death. But Madero reviewed the sentence and, believing his enemies to be pitied rather than executed, commuted it to imprisonment. Díaz was taken under arms to the capital and

A federal machine gun nest awaits the rebel advance.

placed in the Federal District penitentiary. Madero's generosity
was in no way reciprocated. Within two months Félix Díaz in
one Mexico City prison had established contact with Bernardo
Reyes in another, and the two were plotting to overthrow the
government. This sixth rebellion would succeed, and Madero
would lose not only his office but, a victim of his own ideals, his
life as well.

The Overthrow of Madero

Planned for several months, the military coup that began in
Mexico City on February 9, 1913, drastically altered the course
of the Mexican Revolution. The capital had thus far been spared
the ravages of the war that had engulfed much of the nation
since November 1910. Now Mexico City residents would be given
practical instruction in the full destructive significance of civil
war. Early in the morning of February 9, General Manuel Mon-
dragón, supported by several artillery regiments and military

cadets, released Bernardo Reyes and Félix Díaz from their respective prisons and marched on the National Palace. Reyes, sporting a fancy military uniform and mounted on a white horse, led the charge and was felled by one of the first machine gun blasts. The rebel leadership then devolved on Félix Díaz. When loyal government troops repulsed the assault on the National Palace, Díaz led his troops westward across the city and installed his army in the Ciudadela, an old and well-fortified army arsenal. Madero, disregarding the advice of several confidants, named General Victoriano Huerta to command his troops. It proved to be a momentous decision.

For the next ten days—the *Decena Trágica*—Mexico City became a labyrinth of barricades, improvised fortifications, and trenches. Artillery fire exchanged between the rebels in the Ciudadela and the government troops in the National Palace destroyed buildings and set fires. As commercial establishments were forced to close their doors for the duration, consumer goods became scarce and people panicked. Downtown streets were strewn with burning cars, runaway horses, and abandoned artillery pieces. Live electric wires dangled precariously from their poles. Looters broke store windows and carried off wares with complete impunity. On one occasion an artillery barrage opened a breach in the wall of the Belén prison and hundreds of inmates scurried through the opening to freedom. A few surveyed the chaos outside and decided to remain.

With neither side able to gain a clear military advantage, civilian casualties mounted into the thousands and bodies began to bloat in the streets. Foreign residents sought the sanctuary of embassies, but not all made it in time. Most traffic came to a halt as only ambulances, military vehicles, and diplomatic automobiles, identified by special flags, moved on the streets. On February 17, after nine days of constant fighting, Madero summoned Huerta and asked when the fighting could be expected to cease. Huerta assured him that peace would be restored to the beleaguered city the following day. The residents of the capital were awakened early on the morning of February 18 by the sounds of artillery and machine gun fire, just as they had been for the previous nine days. But in the afternoon the clamor of war stopped. Huerta had decided to change sides. He withdrew recognition of the federal government and dispatched General Aureliano Blanquet to the National Palace to arrest the president. Blanquet encountered Madero in one of the patios and, with revolver in hand, proclaimed, "You are my prisoner, Mr. President." Madero retorted, "You are a traitor." But Blanquet simply reaffirmed, "You are my prisoner."[3] Within a half hour Vice-President Pino Suárez, Madero's brother Gustavo, and most of the cabinet had been arrested as well.

The agreement according to which Huerta joined the rebels is known as the Pact of the Embassy because the final negotiations were conducted under the aegis of the American ambassador in Mexico City, Henry Lane Wilson. A typical diplomat of the age of dollar diplomacy, Wilson saw his role as protector of United States business interests. Throughout the Madero presidency he had meddled shamelessly in Mexico's internal affairs, and during the Decena Trágica he played an active part in charting the course of events. On one occasion, in concert with the British, German, and Spanish ministers, he even demanded Madero's resignation, alleging as his reason the tremendous damage to foreign property in Mexico City. After being rebuffed by the Mexican president, Wilson changed his tactics and worked actively to bring Huerta and Díaz to an accord. On the evening of February 18 the two generals met with Wilson at the American embassy and hammered out the pact that was made public the following day.

> In the city of Mexico, at nine-thirty in the evening on February 18, 1913, Generals Félix Díaz and Victoriano Huerta met in conference. . . . General Huerta stated that because of the unbearable situation created by the government of Mr. Madero, he had, in order to prevent the further shedding of blood and to safeguard national unity, placed the said Madero, several members of his cabinet, and various other persons under arrest. . . . General Díaz stated that his only reason for raising the standard of revolt was a desire on his part to protect the national welfare, and in that light he was ready to make any sacrifice that would prove beneficial to the country. . . . From this time forward the former chief executive is not to be recognized. The elements represented by Generals Díaz and Huerta are united in opposing all efforts to restore him to power. . . . Generals Díaz and Huerta will do all in their power to enable the latter to assume . . . the provisional presidency.[4]

Wishing to cloak his assumption of power in some semblance of legality, Huerta first secured the official resignations of Madero and Pino Suárez and then convened a special evening ses-

3. Quoted in Michael C. Meyer, *Huerta: A Political Portrait* (Lincoln, 1972), p. 57.
4. The Pact of the Embassy has been translated and included in its entirety in ibid., pp. 235–36.

sion of the Congress. The resignations were accepted by the legislative body with only five dissenting votes, and the presidency legally passed to the next in line, Secretary of Foreign Relations Pedro Lascuráin. Sworn into office at 10:24 P.M., Lascuráin immediately appointed General Huerta as secretary of interior and at 11:20 P.M. submitted his own resignation. The Constitution of 1857 provided that in the absence of a president, a vice-president, and a secretary of foreign relations, the office passed to the secretary of interior. Huerta, clad in a formal black tuxedo, was sworn into office shortly before midnight. Madero-style democracy had ended in derision as Mexico had its third president in one day.

The political charade perpetrated before the Congress was not the greatest indignity Mexicans were called upon to suffer in February 1913. On the evening of February 21, Francisco Madero and José María Pino Suárez were transferred from the National Palace, where they had been held prisoners since the day of their arrest, to the Federal District penitentiary. The capital city newspapers the following day blared an improbable tale. A group of Madero's supporters attacked the convoy escorting the prisoners, attempted to free them, and during the ensuing melee both the former president and vice-president were killed.

Virtually no one believed this official version, but few Mexicans knew what really happened. Madero and Pino Suárez had been taken to the penitentiary under the guard of Francisco Cárdenas, a major in the rurales. When the convoy reached the prison, Cárdenas ordered the captives out of the cars and, by prearranged signal, the spotlights high on the wall were turned off. The hapless men were then shot point-blank. Perhaps Victoriano Huerta ordered the assassinations, or perhaps it was Félix Díaz, or even Aureliano Blanquet. The nature of the available evidence simply precludes positive determination. But what cannot be doubted is that the senseless murders of Madero and Pino Suárez set the tone of the Revolution for at least the next five years.

Recommended for Further Study

Beezley, William H. *Insurgent Governor: Abraham González and the Mexican Revolution in Chihuahua.* Lincoln: University of Nebraska Press, 1973.

Blaisdell, Lowell L. "Henry Lane Wilson and the Overthrow of Madero." *Southwestern Social Science Quarterly* 43 (1962): 126–35.

Calvert, Peter. *The Mexican Revolution, 1910–1914: The Diplomacy of the*

Anglo-American Conflict. Cambridge: Cambridge University Press, 1968.

Cumberland, Charles C. *Mexican Revolution: Genesis under Madero*. Austin: University of Texas Press, 1952.

Harris, Charles H., and Louis R. Sadler. "The Underside of the Mexican Revolution: El Paso, 1912." *The Americas* 39 (1982): 69–84.

Henderson, Peter V. N. *Félix Díaz, The Porfirians and the Mexican Revolution*. Lincoln: University of Nebraska Press, 1981.

Knudson, Jerry W. "The Press and the Mexican Revolution of 1910." *Journalism Quarterly* 46 (1969): 760–66.

LaFrance, David G. "Failure of Reform: The Maderistas in Puebla, 1911–1913." *New World* 1 (1986): 44–64.

McNeely, John H. "Origins of the Zapata Revolt in Morelos." *Hispanic American Historical Review* 46 (1966): 153–69.

Meyer, Michael C. *Huerta: A Political Portrait*. Lincoln: University of Nebraska Press, 1972.

———. *Mexican Rebel: Pascual Orozco and the Mexican Revolution, 1910–1915*. Lincoln: University of Nebraska Press, 1967.

Niemeyer, Victor. "Frustrated Invasion: The Revolutionary Attempt of General Bernardo Reyes from San Antonio in 1911." *Southwestern Historical Quarterly* 67 (1963–64): 213–25.

Ross, Stanley R. *Francisco I. Madero, Apostle of Mexican Democracy*. New York: Columbia University Press, 1955.

Turner, Frederick C. "Anti-Americanism in Mexico, 1910–1913." *Hispanic American Historical Review* 47 (1967): 502–18.

Wilson, Henry Lane. *Diplomatic Episodes in Mexico, Belgium and Chile*. Garden City, N.Y.: Doubleday, Page, 1927.

Wolfskill, George, and Douglas W. Richmond, eds. *Essays on the Mexican Revolution: Revisionist Views of the Leaders*. Austin: University of Texas Press, 1979.

Womack, John, Jr. *Zapata and the Mexican Revolution*. New York: Knopf, 1968.

33

Huerta
and the Failure of Dictatorship

Huerta

Victoriano Huerta was born of a Huichol Indian mother and a mestizo father in a small Jalisco village. Attending a poor local school run by the parish priest, he learned to read and write and showed some natural talent for science and mathematics. As a teenager he was taken on as an aide by General Donato Guerra, a career officer who had fought against the French. Guerra used his influence in Mexico City to have Huerta accepted at the National Military Academy. In spite of his mediocre educational background, he did well as a cadet and received his commission in 1876 as a second lieutenant assigned to the army corps of engineers.

Huerta's prerevolutionary career coincided almost exactly with the Díaz dictatorship, and he became an effective agent of Don Porfirio's system of enforced peace. During the thirty-four-year Porfiriato Huerta fought in the north against the Yaqui, in the south against the Maya, and in the central part of the country against other Mexicans unhappy with the autocratic regime. Encountering much success on the field of battle, he rose rapidly in the ranks and by the turn of the century had been awarded his brigadier-general stars. National prominence and some notoriety engulfed him for the first time in the summer of 1911 when interim President León de la Barra dispatched him to Morelos to enforce the demobilization of the Zapatista troops. His relationship with Madero was never good again.

When Bernardo Reyes and Félix Díaz planned the military

coup of February 1913, their emissaries approached Huerta and solicited his support. He refused the invitation, however, not out of loyalty to the Madero administration but rather because he wanted the leadership for himself. When Bernardo Reyes was killed during the first major encounter, the situation changed. Huerta dallied for a week and, having determined that he would be able to control Félix Díaz, made his decision to change sides. Sworn into the presidential office a few days later, Huerta was sure he had made the proper choice.

Within a few days federal generals and state governors began to pledge support of the new regime. A group of talented states-men and intellectuals accepted cabinet portfolios. Sanitation workers started to scour the bloodstained streets of the capital and to attack a ten-day backlog of garbage. Red Cross units tried to identify hundreds of decaying corpses, and electricians repaired wires dangling dangerously from their poles.

Rebellion and Militarization

The first genuinely ominous sign came from the northeast where Coahuila Governor Venustiano Carranza, an ardent Madero supporter, announced his decision not to recognize the new regime. Carranza issued a circular telegram to other state governors exhorting them to follow his good example. Within a few weeks he found support in Chihuahua and Sonora. Pancho Villa assumed military leadership of the anti-Huerta movement in Chihuahua, while Alvaro Obregón, a man of considerable military talent, took charge of the antigovernment operations in neighboring Sonora. The alliance of the northern revolutionaries, and their formal pronouncement of defection, was sealed in late March when representatives from the three states affixed their signatures to the *Plan de Guadalupe*. After withdrawing recognition of the Huerta government, the plan named Venustiano Carranza as "First Chief" of the Constitutionalist Army and provided that he, or someone designated by him, would occupy the interim presidency upon Huerta's defeat. An exclusively political document, the plan embodied no program of social reform.

In southern Mexico Huerta encountered an implacable enemy of a different sort. Emiliano Zapata angrily rejected Huerta's invitation to pledge support of the government. In fact, the southern rebel arrested and subsequently executed the federal peace commissioners sent to garner his allegiance. Zapata, unlike the

Modern technology is brought to warfare. In one of the first military uses of aircraft, Huerta employed 80-horsepower planes similar to these in reconnaissance and bombing raids against the Villistas in the north.

Constitutionalists in the north, did not denounce Huerta for having overthrown Madero. While he found treason in Huerta's sudden shift of sides during the Decena Trágica, he declared himself in rebellion because he saw no hope that the federal government under Huerta would begin to restore the village lands in Morelos. Not trusting the Constitutionalist dedication to agrarian reform either, Zapata never allied himself with the anti-Huerta movement in the north. But by forcing the government to divert some of its war effort from the north to the south, Zapata placed additional military pressure on the new regime.

Facing rebellion in the north and in Morelos, Huerta's first priority was pacification. With a federal army numbering about fifty thousand, the president announced brazenly to the Congress that he would re-establish peace, "cost what it may." But pacification proved elusive on the field of battle. In March and April the Constitutionalists scored impressive victories in Sonora and Chihuahua, while in the south Emiliano Zapata had done the same. The psychology of the civil war changed drastically in May when First Chief Carranza, in a singularly intemperate decree, announced that federal soldiers who fell into rebel hands would be executed summarily. The Constitutionalists thus declared that they intended to give no quarter, and by the summer of 1913 Huerta had concluded that pacification would come only if he militarized Mexico to the teeth.

Factories and stores not related to the war effort were required to close on Sundays so that civilian employees could be given military training. Railroads left civilian passengers and freight standing in the stations so that military personnel and hardware could be shipped to where it was needed. The National Arms Factory, the National Artillery Workshops, and the National

Powder Factory received new equipment to increase their productive capacities. Military decorations were passed out in wholesale lot to the president's cronies, and new military awards were authorized to compensate favorites or to win over those of doubtful loyalty. Most important, the president decreed constant increases in the size of the federal army—from 50,000 to 100,000 to 200,000 and finally to a quarter of a million, or about twelve times the number of troops available to Porfirio Díaz when the Revolution broke out.

When small pay increases failed to attract enlistees in large numbers, Huerta fell back on a time-honored tradition—the leva, a system of forced conscription directed exclusively at the indigent masses. Tens of thousands of illiterate men were picked up off the streets of the barrios in the large cities and from the surrounding countryside and sent into the field. The crowds emerging from a bullfight or staggering out of a cantina closing its doors for the night were favorite targets, as were criminals in jail for minor offenses. But the effects of the leva were disastrous. The quality of the federal army declined steadily. The lack of adequate training meant no *esprit de corps*, no discipline, and tremendously high desertion rates. In the fall of 1913 it was not unheard of for entire units of new recruits to turn themselves and their equipment over to the enemy without firing a single shot.

The toll of the civil war in 1913 and 1914 was tremendous. The military presence was obvious everywhere. The population of a village could double or triple overnight as a large unit moved in to camp. Because there was no advance notice, a week's stay could deplete stores of food, supplies, and other basic necessities, thus aggravating the obscenities of war. When the troops withdrew, villages were often on the verge of starvation. The receipts a local merchant might receive as the troops emptied his store were scarcely worth the paper they were hastily scrawled on.

With his military position deteriorating, Huerta became increasingly impetuous, egotistical, and dictatorial. Cabinet secretaries could not work with him for very long, and turnovers followed one another in rapid succession. Recognizing the potential value of a controlled press, Huerta initiated an extensive policy of censorship. Editors who adopted hostile attitudes were removed from their positions, sent into exile, or jailed. A vast network of secret agents and spies reported on the activities of real and potential enemies, and by the fall of 1913 the jail cells in

Mexico City and many of the state capitals were crowded with political prisoners.

Without question the most reprehensible facet of the Huerta dictatorship was its unbridled use of political assassination. After the senseless slaying of Madero and Pino Suárez, Maderista Governor Abraham González was the next to be killed. Army officers, congressmen, professional men, and even petty bureaucrats who manifested their discontent were sacrificed to the ill-conceived exigencies of the day. The most celebrated case of all was that of Senator Belisario Domínguez from Chiapas, an outspoken critic of the regime. In late September 1913, against the good counsel of friends in the Senate, Domínguez asked for the floor to read a prepared statement.

> Peace, cost what it may, Mr. Victoriano Huerta had said. Fellow Senators, have you studied the terrible meaning of those words . . . ? The national assembly has the duty of deposing Mr. Victoriano Huerta from the presidency. He is the one against whom our brothers in the north protest with so much reason. . . . You will tell me, gentlemen, that the attempt is dangerous; for Mr. Victoriano Huerta is a bloody and ferocious soldier who assassinates without hesitation anyone who is an obstacle to his wishes; this does not matter, gentlemen! The country exacts from you the fulfillment of a duty, even with risk, indeed the assurance, that you are to lose your lives.[1]

Two weeks later Belisario Domínguez was dead from an assassin's bullet. The morally outraged Senate passed a resolution requesting full information from the president and resolving to remain in permanent session until the case be closed. Two days later Huerta responded by dissolving both houses of the legislature and arresting the majority of the congressmen.

Economic Problems and Foreign Relations

The war Huerta was fighting against the Constitutionalists in the north and the Zapatistas in the south was costly, and the regime had inherited an empty treasury. By relying on the leva to fill the ranks of the federal army, Huerta depleted the work force in both the cities and the countryside. With no pickers, cotton rotted in the fields, coffee beans fell off the trees, and sugarcane remained unharvested on the large plantations. Mines closed

1. Quoted in Michael C. Meyer, *Huerta: A Political Portrait* (Lincoln, 1972), pp. 137–38.

Together with several other kinds of scrip, this 20-peso note from Chihuahua state was used by the Constitutionalists in late 1913 and early 1914.

operations; cattlemen in the north lost thousands of head to the
rebels; and fruit growers, realizing their perishable products
were extremely vulnerable to transportation delays, cut back
production. As food and manufactured goods became scarce, a
black market began to flourish in the larger cities, and the entire
economic structure of the country was severely tested.

The first government expedient was to issue paper money
without adequate hard reserves to back it up. The new paper issue depreciated almost as soon as it rolled off the press. Not to be
outdone, the Constitutionalists and the Zapatistas issued their
own currency, as did a number of states and large mining and
industrial concerns. Late in 1913 there were at least twenty-five
different kinds of paper currency in circulation, and nobody was
able to ascertain accurately the fluctuating exchange rates. Coun-
terfeiters, of course, had a field day, while bankers and tax collectors were driven almost to insanity.

In addition to his military and economic problems, Huerta
faced one other dilemma as well. The United States not only
refused to recognize his regime but adopted a frankly hostile
attitude toward him. Woodrow Wilson came to the United States
presidency almost simultaneously with Victoriano Huerta's rise
to power. While the American ambassador to Mexico, Henry
Lane Wilson, urged recognition, President Wilson and his newly
appointed secretary of state, William Jennings Bryan, both with
an abiding faith in the concept of the democratic state, refused.
To the White House, Huerta, who came to power by forcefully
ejecting the previous regime, was a symbol of all that was wrong

with Latin America. Unprepared by temperament or training to understand the complexities of the Mexican Revolution, President Wilson decided to apply his own standards of political ethics to the situation. The moral judgment, as abstractly admirable as it was diplomatically impractical, once made proved unshakable.

Demonstrating little faith in the reports received from Ambassador Wilson, the president and the secretary of state decided to dispatch special agents to Mexico to report on the nature of the growing conflict. The first chosen for the special assignment was William Bayard Hale. Speaking no Spanish, Hale relied heavily on the United States business community for his information, but he managed interviews with several high-level Mexican officials as well. As his reports to the White House began, he noted that the businessmen in Mexico favored early recognition of the regime, but, sensing what the American president wanted to hear, he indicated that he himself did not. Appealing to President Wilson's sense of moral rectitude, Hale characterized Huerta as "an ape-like man, of almost pure Indian blood. He may be said to subsist on alcohol. Drunk or only half drunk (he is never sober) he never loses a certain shrewdness."[2] The American president was impressed with Hale's findings; he would not have written the report any differently, he claimed, had he gone to Mexico City himself. By summer Ambassador Wilson had been recalled and the White House had another special emissary in Mexico—John Lind, a former governor of Minnesota and a longtime friend of Secretary Bryan.

If there was ever any hope for a reconciliation between the United States and Mexico in the late summer and fall of 1913, Lind's reports to Washington eliminated it. Speaking no more Spanish than Hale and being even less conversant with Mexican politics, his dispatches were haughty, bellicose, inaccurate, and often laden with anti-Catholic and anti-Indian slurs. His characterization of the Mexican cabinet ("a worse pack of wolves never infested any community") reveals more about Lind than about Huerta's advisers. Given President Wilson's insistence that Huerta had to go, there were only two genuine avenues open: Wilson could intervene militarily in Mexico, or he could intervene indirectly by channeling United States aid to the Constitutionalists in the north. He chose the second alternative first, and, when that did not work, he opted for military intervention.

2. Quoted in Larry D. Hill, *Emissaries to a Revolution: Woodrow Wilson's Executive Agents in Mexico* (Baton Rouge, 1973), p. 31.

Domestic Reforms

Amazingly, in spite of the military, economic, and diplomatic pressures the regime faced, Huerta and his advisers found some time for domestic programs. The enemies of the dictatorship labeled them counterrevolutionary, an attempt to reincarnate the age of Díaz. But examination of the regime's social programs reveals that they were anything but that. While Porfirio Díaz had never allocated over 7.2 percent of his budget for education, and Madero had raised the percentage slightly to 7.8 percent, Huerta projected a 9.9 percent allocation for educational services. The funds were still inadequate, but Huerta did manage the construction of 131 new rural schools with seats for some ten thousand new students. Secretary of Education Nemesio García Naranjo, impressed with Henri Bergson's philosophical assault on positivism, decided to initiate a new curriculum at the National Preparatory School. Breaking sharply with the positivist tradition of Gabino Barreda, García Naranjo made more room for the study of literature, history, and philosophy. He did not abandon the sciences but argued persuasively that the other branches of learning should not be sacrificed to them. By creating a reasonable balance between the arts and the sciences, the secretary struck an important first blow at the científico philosophy of education.

The anticientífico posture of the regime manifested itself in Indian policy as well. Administration spokesman Jorge Vera Estañol was an early champion of *indigenismo*. National unity, he argued, was impossible when millions of Indians were estranged from the rest of the population by language, customs, diet, and life expectancy. The rural education program was well intended but was not sufficiently expansive to bring the Indian into the mainstream of national life. Huerta's secretary of interior, Aureliano Urrutia, a full-blooded Indian, began dispatching teams of government consultants into the pueblos to organize community projects that could make small but meaningful changes in the patterns of daily life. But again the program was so small as to make scarcely a dent in the prevailing structure.

It is in the matter of agrarian reform that the Huerta dictatorship has been most widely misrepresented. The regime initiated its program modestly by distributing free seed to anyone who asked for it and by expanding the activities of the agricultural school in Mexico City. Of greater practical significance Huerta authorized the restoration of seventy-eight ejidos to the Yaqui and Mayo Indians of Sonora. In the late spring of 1913 the president upgraded Madero's National Agrarian Commission to a cabinet department and instructed Eduardo Tamariz, Mexico's secretary of agriculture, to begin studying the problem of land redistribution. Tamariz could find nothing in the Constitution of 1857 that even faintly authorized the expropriation of land, so he had to devise another scheme. He found his solution in the taxation provisions of the Constitution. If taxes were increased on the large haciendas, the land would be less valuable for speculative purposes and hacendados would have to consider sale. Congressional authorization was not forthcoming, but Huerta went ahead on his own and decreed an increase in land taxes.

In the areas of labor, church policy, and foreign relations the Huerta regime also departed drastically from the models of the Porfiriato. The programs the administration sponsored did not add up to a social revolution. The reforms bore little demonstrable relationship to one another, no attempt at syncretization was made, and social mobility for the masses did not, as a result, increase. But the regime was no counterrevolution; it was in many ways, more farsighted than that of Madero. Huerta and his advisers allowed themselves to be tossed around by the winds of twentieth-century change and harbored no notions of pegging themselves to a Porfirian status quo. While it is true that Huerta's abuse of political power can justifiably be likened to Don Porfirio's authoritarianism, nevertheless, in the larger social sense both Huerta and his advisers recognized that the days of Díaz were gone forever.

United States Intervention and the Fall of Huerta

By the spring of 1914 Huerta was losing his wars on both the military and the economic fronts. But the final blow was precipitated by his steadily deteriorating relationship with the White House. Early in 1914 President Wilson beefed up the American fleet stationed off Mexican waters. In April a seemingly insignificant event augured the most serious United States–Mexican dispute since the war of the middle of the nineteenth century. Captain Ralph T. Earle of the USS *Dolphin*, stationed off the coast of Tampico, ordered a small landing party to go ashore to secure some badly needed gasoline. Tampico was still in government hands, but the Constitutionalists had attacked several days before and the federal forces were awaiting a more concerted assault. The United States sailors wandered into a restricted dock area and were arrested on the spot.

Within an hour orders came for the sailors' release, accompanied by an official apology. But Rear Admiral Henry T. Mayo, commander of the naval forces off Tampico, considered the apology insufficient and demanded something more elaborate. Since the boat carrying the sailors to shore allegedly flew the American flag, Mayo demanded, among other things, that the Mexican government hoist the American flag at some prominent place on shore and present a twenty-one gun salute to it. President Wilson considered the demands reasonable and prepared himself to make the incident a *casus belli* should Huerta not publicly recant in exactly the manner prescribed. Huerta's secretary of foreign relations insisted that the small landing craft had not carried the flag but agreed to the salute on the condition that the United States return the salute to the Mexican flag. The White House considered the rejoinder impertinent, for both President Wilson and Secretary of State Bryan realized that a United States salute to the Mexican flag could be considered tantamount to recognizing the Huerta regime.

With neither side knowing exactly what to do next, the stalemate was broken when the United States consul in Veracruz wired Washington that a German ship, the *Ypiranga*, was scheduled to arrive in that port on April 21 with a large shipment of arms for Huerta. President Wilson gave immediate orders for a naval occupation of Veracruz. The marines took the city but Mexican casualties mounted into the hundreds, including many noncombatants of both sexes. The public outcry in Mexico City was understandably indignant. Congressmen denounced the United States, and mobs looted American-owned businesses, tore down the statue of George Washington, and threatened tourists. Mexican newspapers urged retaliation against the "Pigs of Yanquilandia." In Monterrey the United States flag was ripped from the consulate and burned on the spot. But the Stars and Stripes, which had precipitated the furor in the first place, was subjected to even greater indignities in the capital. Tied to the tail of a donkey, it was used to sweep clean the streets of the central plaza.

President Wilson's attempt to rid Mexico of a dictator and himself of a self-made enemy almost backfired. Venustiano Carranza and the majority of his Constitutionalists, the supposed beneficiaries of the Veracruz intervention, expressed their strong disapproval of the blatant violation of Mexican sovereignty. Huerta,

U.S. Navy "bluejackets" engage Mexican defenders at Veracruz in April 1914.

however, was unable to capitalize upon their displeasure, and his call for all Mexicans to lay aside internal differences and present a united front went unheeded. Even the initial indignation expressed in Mexico City soon dissipated as the United States troops, in spite of rumors to the contrary, did not march on Mexico City as they had in 1847.

As Huerta called in his troops to make a show of force against the Americans, the Constitutionalists in the north and the Zapatistas in the south quickly moved into the military vacuums. By the early summer, with Pancho Villa's capture of Zacatecas, Huerta's military position had become completely untenable. The continued occupation of Veracruz meant that revenues from the customhouse were stopped before they reached the federal treasury. Recognizing that the diplomatic, economic, and military pressures had all conspired to his disadvantage, Huerta made his decision to resign on July 8, 1914. In his statement of resignation he placed the prime responsibility for what had happened to Mexico on the Puritan who resided in the White House.

It is true that Woodrow Wilson was in large measure responsible for Huerta's overthrow. He had meddled shamelessly in Mexico's internal affairs and, without the semblance of a threat to United States security, had shed innocent Mexican blood to effectuate the foreign policy objectives he deemed opportune. But Wilson cannot be held accountable for the larger calamity that had struck the Mexican nation. Not all Mexico's domestic ills were orphans of United States bullets. Mexicans had not yet agreed on the meaning of their Revolution. Francisco Madero's well-meaning but ineffectual experiment with democracy had failed when he had urged caution and moderation on the burning social issues of the day. But Huerta's dictatorship failed as well. While he was not unwilling to give the social reformers the chance to institute change, many Mexicans could no longer bring themselves to accommodate another brutal dictatorship that exalted order at the expense of liberty. The number of options still open were gradually being reduced, but the better day had not yet dawned.

Recommended for Further Study

Blaisdell, Lowell L. "Henry Lane Wilson and the Overthrow of Madero." *Southwestern Social Science Quarterly* 43 (1962): 126–35.

Calvert, Peter. *The Mexican Revolution, 1910–1914: The Diplomacy of the Anglo-American Conflict.* Cambridge: Cambridge University Press, 1968.

Cumberland, Charles C. *Mexican Revolution: The Constitutionalist Years.* Austin: University of Texas Press, 1972.

Grieb, Kenneth J. *The United States and Huerta.* Lincoln: University of Nebraska Press, 1969.

Hart, John M. "The Urban Working Class and the Mexican Revolution: The Case of the Casa del Obrero Mundial." *Hispanic American Historical Review* 58 (1978): 1–20.

Hill, Larry D. *Emissaries to a Revolution: Woodrow Wilson's Executive Agents in Mexico.* Baton Rouge: Louisiana State University Press, 1973.

Knight, Alan. *The Mexican Revolution.* Vol. 2: *Counter Revolution and Reconstruction.* New York: Cambridge University Press, 1986.

Meyer, Michael C. "The Arms of the *Ypiranga*." *Hispanic American Historical Review* 50 (1970): 543–56.

———. *Huerta: A Political Portrait.* Lincoln: University of Nebraska Press, 1972.

———. "The Militarization of Mexico, 1913–1914." *The Americas* 27 (1971): 293–306.

Quirk, Robert E. *An Affair of Honor: Woodrow Wilson and the Occupation of Veracruz.* New York: Norton, 1967.

Vanderwood, Paul J. "The Picture Postcard as Historical Evidence: Veracruz: 1914." *The Americas* 45 (1988): 201–26.

Wilson, Henry Lane. *Diplomatic Episodes in Mexico, Belgium and Chile.* Garden City, N.Y.: Doubleday, Page, 1927.

34

The Illusory Quest for a Better Way

The Convention of Aguascalientes and Near Anarchy

The years following Victoriano Huerta's ouster are the most chaotic in Mexican revolutionary history as the quarrels among erstwhile allies began. In 1914 First Chief Venustiano Carranza allowed that a convention should be held to determine, among other questions, who should be the provisional president of Mexico until such time as national elections could be scheduled. A proper choice, he believed, could finally put an end to the fragmentation that had characterized the Revolution almost from the beginning. The town of Aguascalientes, in neutral territory, was selected to host the convention, and invitations were extended to all the important revolutionary factions, the number of delegates being apportioned according to how many troops had been deployed in the recent anti-Huerta campaigns.

The military delegates, in a wide array of uniforms and most carrying rifles with full cartridge belts, began to arrive in Aguascalientes in early October. At one of the early sessions Alvaro Obregón, the First Chief's official spokesman, presented the Convention with a Mexican flag inscribed with the words, "Military Convention of Aguascalientes." Each of the delegates then went to the podium, placed his signature on the flag, and swore allegiance to the Convention, some offering a few garrulous remarks. The impressive display of confraternity was not destined to last for long, however. When the Zapatista delegation arrived, a few days late, its leader Paulino Martínez, asked to speak. In a deliberate affront to Carranza and Obregón he recognized Villa and Zapata as the genuine leaders of the Revolution. Manifesting the typical Zapatista aversion to gradualism, he argued that "effective suffrage and no-re-election" had no meaning for the vast majority of Mexicans. The Revolution had been fought for land and liberty. The speech presaged a serious schism in the Convention between Villistas and Zapatistas on the one hand and Carrancistas and Obregonistas on the other. The debates were not sectarian squabbles; rather they reflected fundamental differences of opinion on the direction the Revolution should take.

Martínez was followed to the rostrum by the vice-chairman of the Zapatista delegation, Antonio Díaz Soto y Gama. A thirty-year-old socialist and a polished orator, he delineated future lines of combat.

> I come here not to attack anyone but to evoke patriotism and to stimulate shame. I come to excite the honor of all of the delegates to this assembly. . . . Perhaps it is necessary to invoke respectable symbols [gesturing to the Convention flag], but I fear that the essence of patriotism does not lie in the symbols, which are, after all, quite similar to the farces of the church. . . . I believe that our word of honor is more valuable than all of the signatures stamped on this flag. In the last analysis this flag represents nothing more than the triumph of the clerical reaction championed by Iturbide. I will never sign this flag. . . . That which we called Independence was not independence for the Indian, but independence for the criollo, for the heirs of the conquerors who continue infamously to abuse and cheat the oppressed Indian.[1]

Soto y Gama's speech was continuously interrupted from the floor both by those who cheered him and by those who were livid at his ridicule of Mexican history and defamation of the flag. Not yet ready to embrace the chastening influence of open debate, some of the delegates even pointed pistols in his direction. The acrimony occasioned by the impassioned speech was not easily abated, and as the Convention set to work on naming a provisional president the underlying issue was whether the Revolution was going to follow the politically oriented plans of San Luis Potosí and Guadalupe or the agrarian Plan de Ayala.

When, against Carranza's wishes, the Convention chose Eulalio Gutiérrez as provisional president of Mexico, the First Chief, haughty as ever, disavowed the action and, from Mexico City, ordered his followers to withdraw. Some, including Alvaro Obregón, obeyed, while others made common cause with the Zapatistas and Villistas. As Villa's troops marched on the capital to install Gutiérrez in the presidency, it was obvious to all that

1. Quoted in Isidro Fabela, ed., *Documentos históricos de la revolución mexicana* (Mexico, 1960–73), 23: 181–82.

Mexico was on the verge of still another civil war. Carranza believed it was better not to make a stand in Mexico City and withdrew his Constitutionalist government to Veracruz. The United States government had agreed to pull out its troops just in time for Carranza to make the Gulf port his provisional capital.

Multiple Civil Wars

In early December 1914 Carranza's two principal antagonists, Pancho Villa, "the Centaur of the North," and Emiliano Zapata, "the Attila of the South," staged a dramatic meeting at Xochimilco on the outskirts of Mexico City. While their followers had knotted the bonds of intellectual camaraderie at the Convention, the two leaders had never before met. The historian Robert Quirk has recreated the encounter from eyewitness accounts.

> Villa and Zapata were a study in contrasts. Villa was tall and robust, weighing at least 180 pounds, with a florid complexion. He wore a tropical helmet after the English style. . . . He was clad in a heavy, brown woolen sweater, which was loosely woven, with a large roll collar . . . khaki military trousers, army leggings and heavy riding boots. Zapata, in his physiognomy, was much more the Indian of the two. His skin was very dark, and in comparison with Villa's his face was thin with high cheek bones. He wore an immense sombrero, which at times hid his eyes. . . .
>
> The conference began haltingly . . . both were men of action and verbal intercourse left them uneasy. . . . But then the conversation touched on Venustiano Carranza and suddenly, like tinder, burst aflame. They poured out in a torrent of volubility their mutual hatred for the First Chief. Villa pronounced his opinion of the middle class revolutionaries who followed Carranza: "Those are men who have always slept on soft pillows. How could they ever be friends of the people, who have spent their whole lives in nothing but suffering?" Zapata concurred: "On the contrary, they have always been the scourge of the people. . . . Those *cabrones!* As soon as they see a little chance, well, they want to take advantage of it and line their own pockets! Well, to hell with them!"[2]

But while Villa and Zapata could agree enthusiastically about their profound disdain for Carranza, their alliance was short lived. After a brief visit to Mexico City Zapata returned to Morelos and Villa turned north. Although each had promised to support the military engagements of the other, cooperation

2. Robert E. Quirk, *The Mexican Revolution, 1914–1915: The Convention of Aguascalientes* (New York, 1963), pp. 135–38.

Pancho Villa (left) and Emiliano Zapata (right) meet in Mexico City. The camaraderie was more apparent than real.

against Carranza was noticeable only by its absence. The early months of 1915 saw the Mexican Revolution degenerating into unmitigated anarchy. Civil wars ravaged many states. At times the Constitutionalists seemed to gain the upper hand only to be set back by internal bickering, badly planned campaigns, or the defection of important contingents. Civilian casualties mounted as atrocities were committed on all sides.

With his own Conventionist coalition falling apart as well, provisional President Gutiérrez abandoned Mexico City and Obregón took the capital unopposed. But nothing was thereby settled. Gutiérrez, still claiming to be president, established a new government in Nuevo León; Carranza, claiming national executive control as first chief, continued to govern from Veracruz; the Zapatistas supported Roque González Garza as president; while Pancho Villa, pretending to speak for the entire nation, ruled from Chihuahua. None of the governments recognized the paper money, coinage, or legal contracts of the others.

The muddied political waters were cleared somewhat in the

most famous military engagement of the Revolution—the battle of Celaya—in April of 1915. While Pancho Villa prepared to put his slightly tarnished record of military victories on the line, Alvaro Obregón had immersed himself in the battle reports from war-torn Europe. He had learned, among other things, that one of the best ways to blunt a concerted cavalry charge was to encircle carefully laid out defensive positions with rolls of barbed wire. In early April, when Villa attacked with a force estimated at twenty-five thousand men, Obregón was ready. He had planned his defenses with consummate skill, and, when Villa launched a furious cavalry charge, Obregón's well-placed artillery and machine guns began cutting the attackers to pieces. Villa was forced to retreat, but in the middle of the month tried again to dislodge Obregón's forces. The second Villista offensive was even less successful than the first; in fact, it was a disaster. Bent upon victory even at exorbitant costs, Villa threw his cavalry against the barbed-wire entrenchments only to see wave after wave massacred. When it all ended, thousands of bodies were strewn across the fields of Celaya and impaled on the barbed wire. Obregón's official report listed over 4,000 Villistas dead, 5,000 wounded, and 6,000 taken prisoner. He calculated his own losses at only 138 dead and 227 wounded.

The battle of Celaya did not immediately destroy Villa's capacity to make war, but it did presage his ultimate defeat. By the summer and fall of 1915 First Chief Carranza was clearly gaining the upper hand as both the Villistas in the north and the Zapatistas in the south found themselves increasingly isolated and without national support. In the White House President Wilson decided to throw the official support of the United States behind the Constitutionalists. He extended diplomatic recognition to the Carranza regime in October. Pancho Villa, who had courted the United States for years and who had not even criticized the invasion at Veracruz, was incensed. Determined not to turn the other cheek, he began to take his vengeance on private United States civilians.

The first serious incident occurred at Santa Isabel (today General Trías), Chihuahua. The strange scenario began on January 9, 1916, at El Paso, Texas, where a group of United States mining engineers and technicians from the Cusi Mining Company boarded a train for Mexico. Assured of a safe conduct and Mexican government protection, they set out to reopen the Cusihuiriachic mine. At the hamlet of Santa Isabel the train was stopped

Pancho Villa (1878–1923). Never an "armchair general," Villa often led his troops into battle.

by a barrier laid across the tracks. A band of Villistas boarded the car carrying the Americans, dragged them off, and murdered fifteen of them on the spot.

But an even more outrageous incident occurred exactly two months later. Early in the morning of March 9, 1916, Villa dispatched 485 men across the border from Palomas, Chihuahua, and attacked the dreary, sun-baked adobe town of Columbus, New Mexico. One of the first shots stopped the large clock in the railroad station at 4:11 A.M. For the next two hours the Villistas terrorized the town's four hundred inhabitants. Shouting *¡Viva Villa!* and *¡Muerte a los Gringos!* they shot and burned and looted. Troopers from the Thirteenth Cavalry succeeded in driving them off by daybreak, but eighteen Americans had been killed, many were wounded, and the town was burned beyond recognition.

The clamor for United States intervention was immediate and predictable. Senator Albert Bacon Fall of New Mexico called for a half-million men to occupy all of Mexico. President Wilson was not willing to go that far, but he did agree to dispatch a small punitive expedition under the command of General John J. Pershing, an army man who years before had chased the Apache chief, Geronimo, through the same northern Mexican desert. It took a week for Pershing to organize his expedition, and that was more than enough time for Villa to cover his tracks. Approximately six thousand United States army troops wandered hot and thirsty through the rough terrain in a futile effort to locate their prey. Little if any help could be expected from the rural Mexican, and as the Americans entered small pueblos they were often greeted with shouts of *¡Viva Mexico, Viva Villa!* As the expedition cut south into Mexico, First Chief Carranza began to get nervous and ordered Pershing to withdraw. Not yet ready to admit defeat, Pershing engaged a group of Carrancista troops ordered to forestall his southward thrust. When hostilities began he received orders to withdraw gradually to the north, but the expedition was not pulled out of Mexico until January 1917. By

General Pershing's cavalry expedition into northern Mexico may have hardened his troops for the upcoming war in Europe, but his effort to capture Pancho Villa was in vain.

that time the United States had spent $130 million in its unsuccessful attempt to catch and punish the Columbus raiders.

The Constitution of 1917

The failure of the Pershing punitive expedition notwithstanding, Villa got progressively weaker and Carranza gradually consolidated his position in Mexico City. The First Chief's advisers convinced him that the time had come to give some institutional basis to the Revolution that had engulfed the nation for almost six years. In an attempt to legitimize the Revolution he reluctantly agreed to convoke a congress to meet in Querétaro for the purpose of drawing up a new constitution. Remembering how he had lost control of the Convention of Aguascalientes, he vowed not to repeat the error in Querétaro. No individual or group who had opposed the Constitutionalist movement would be eligible to participate; thus no Huertistas, Villistas, or Zapatistas were included among the delegates when the first session convened in November 1916. But First Chief Carranza quickly learned what he should have already known; the Constitutionalists themselves were scarcely in ideologic agreement.

The delegates at Querétaro represented a new breed of Mexican politician and, in a sense, constituted a new social elite. Unlike the Convention of Aguascalientes, military men constituted only 30 percent of the delegates. Over half had university educations and professional titles. The large majority were young and middle class; because they had been denied meaningful participation during the Porfiriato, many were politically ambitious.[3]

With every intention of controlling the proceedings, Carranza submitted to the Querétaro Congress a draft of a new constitution he himself approved. It showed him to be a liberal in the best nineteenth-century tradition. His draft differed little from the Constitution of 1857, although it contained a series of sections strengthening executive control. It occasioned an inevitable split in the Congress between those moderates who supported Carranza and the radicals (called Jacobins by their opponents) who desired something more likely to harbinger rapid social reform.

3. The social background of the delegates and their votes on a number of key issues have been analyzed statistically in Peter H. Smith, "La política dentro de la Revolución: El congreso constituyente de 1916–1917," *Historia Mexicana* 22 (1973): 363–95.

The debates in Querétaro were laden with acrimony. After the first few votes had been taken, it was clear that the radicals held the majority. Led by thirty-two-year-old Francisco Múgica, they succeeded in pushing through a number of anticlerical provisions and three extremely significant articles that came to embody the fundamental orientation the Revolution was to assume in the 1920s and 1930s.

The anticlericalism of the Congress was even more intense than it had been during the height of the liberal-conservative struggle during the nineteenth century. All of the old arguments were heard, but, in addition, the church was now seen to be blocking the path of the social revolution. Article after article limited the powers of the church. Marriage was declared a civil ceremony; religious organizations would enjoy no special legal status, and, as a result, priests were considered ordinary citizens; public worship outside the confines of the church was banned; state legislatures could determine the maximum number of priests to be allowed within state boundaries; all priests in Mexico had to be native born; clergymen were prohibited from forming political parties; priests had to register with civil authorities; and new church buildings had to be approved by the government. The anticlerical tenor of the Querétaro Congress also surfaced in one of the three most important articles.

The drafting of Article 3 was assigned to Múgica's committee on education, and his proposal touched off passionate exchanges on the floor of the Congress. Few took umbrage at the principle that primary education should be free and obligatory in the Mexican republic, but Múgica and his radical cohorts had one additional criterion to add. Education should be secular. The lessons of history convinced Múgica that the clergy had sacrificed all claim to obedience.

> I am an enemy of the clergy because I consider it the most baneful and perverse enemy of our country. . . . What ideas can the clergy bring to the soul of the Mexican masses, or to the middle class, or to the wealthy? Only the most absurd ideas—tremendous hate for democratic institutions, the deepest hate for the principles of equity, equality and fraternity. . . . Are we going to turn over to the clergy the formation of our future? . . . Fellow deputies, what morality can the clergy transmit as learning to our children? We have ample testimony: only the most corrupting and terrible morality.[4]

4. Quoted in *Diario de los debates del Congreso Constituyente, 1916–1917* (Mexico, 1960), p. 642.

The responses of Félix Palavicini and other Carranza supporters in the Congress were just as terse, personal, and caustic. But when the final vote was taken, Francisco Múgica's Article 3 passed by a margin of almost two to one. With the radicals' dominance well established, two other major issues were resolved in their favor. And if the debates on education reminded many of the anticlerical rhetoric of the Reform, the ensuing disputation on land and labor left no doubt that a new age of liberalism had dawned.

Article 27 addressed itself to Mexico's endemic land problem and can be considered a direct outgrowth of Díaz's alienation of Mexico's subsoil rights and his policy of allowing the land companies to appropriate the old communal lands. While the Zapatistas were not present in Querétaro, the issue that had made them a potent force had to be squarely faced. Article 27 required that lands seized illegally from the peasantry during the Porfiriato be restored and provision be made for those communities that could not prove legal title. Equally as important, the private ownership of land was no longer considered to be an absolute right but rather something of a privilege. If land did not serve a useful social function, it could be appropriated by the state: "The nation shall at all times have the right to impose on private property such limitations as the public interest may demand, as well as the right to regulate the utilization of natural resources . . . in order to conserve them and to ensure a more equitable distribution of public wealth." A special section of Article 27 deeply disturbed foreign nationals who owned property in Mexico.

> Only Mexicans by birth or naturalization have the right to acquire ownership of lands, waters, . . . or to obtain concessions for the exploitation of mines or waters. The state may grant the same right to foreigners, provided that they agree before the Department of Foreign Relations to consider themselves as nationals in respect to such property, and bind themselves not to invoke the protection of their governments.[5]

The last, precedent-breaking article treated the labor question and sought to provide a reasonable balance between labor and management. Article 123 provided for an eight-hour workday, a six-day workweek, a minimum wage, and equal pay for equal work regardless of sex or nationality. Most important, it gave

5. Ibid.

both labor and capital the right to organize for the defense of their respective interests and allowed that the workers had the right to bargain collectively and go on strike.

The Constitution of 1917 was not nearly as radical as many contemporary observers found it, but it did mark the repudiation of nineteenth-century laissez faire liberalism. Although ideologically indebted to the Liberal Plan of 1906, the Plan Orozquista, and the Plan de Ayala, it was more reformist than revolutionary. Carranza accepted it with great reluctance. It bore scant resemblance to the draft he had proposed, but he had set the requirements for delegates himself and, more important, wanted to become constitutional president after having served as First Chief for four years.

The Carranza Presidency

Carranza handily won the special elections that were held in March 1917 and took the oath of office on May 1. Not only was the country far from pacified, but the economy was in a state of acute distress. The banking structure had been shattered, in part because of the general chaos but also as a direct result of the worthless paper money that had inundated the commercial markets. Mining suffered enormous losses, with gold production declining some 80 percent between 1910 and 1916 and silver and copper production falling off 65 percent during the same period. Industrial production fell off as well, and wages were depressed. The communication and transportation networks in which Díaz had taken so much pride were in shambles. Agricultural shortages pushed food prices up, and the inflation took a terrible toll on poor urbanites trying to live on a monetary economy.

Carranza quickly let it be known that, although he had accepted the Constitution of 1917, he had no idea of enforcing it. Confusing change in government with change in society, he believed the Revolution to be over. In fact, it had scarcely begun. Still prompted by the inviolability of private property, under Article 27 Carranza distributed only 450,000 acres of land, a paltry sum when one considers that many hacendados had more than this and Luis Terrazas alone owned in excess of seven million acres. In addition, the land Carranza did distribute had been taken away from his political enemies. This was neither the spirit nor the intent of Article 27.

The record of the administration on labor was no better. Even before the new Constitution was enacted, Carranza's labor policy was known. In the fall of 1915, when workers in Veracruz struck protesting payment of wages in worthless paper currency, Carranza used his army to put down the strike. A year later, when railroad workers declared a strike, Carranza found it treasonous and arrested the leaders. Mexican labor leaders, hoping for a better day with the adoption of Article 123, were disappointed as well. On a few occasions innocuous concessions were granted to labor, but the labor movement did not have an advocate in the presidential chair.

Though without his blessings or support, an event did occur during Carranza's presidency that was a landmark in the Mexican labor movement. In 1918 the labor leader Luis Morones founded Mexico's first nationwide union, the Confederación Regional Obrera Mexicana (CROM). The gains made by the labor movement in the next two years were marginal, but the establishment of the confederation did lay the foundation for future progress.

There can be no doubt that Carranza's presidency was complicated by World War I. The eventual entrance of the United States into the European conflagration was a foregone conclusion, and the Mexican government was anxious that it be sooner rather than later. Perhaps Washington would then be too concerned with trans-Atlantic matters to intervene again in Mexican affairs. But Mexico's own position had to be carefully defined. Many Latin American nations were prepared to follow the lead of the United States and break diplomatic relations with Germany. Should not Mexico also align itself with its Western Hemisphere counterparts? While many prominent Mexicans urged this course of action, others argued with understandable passion that, unlike France, England, and the United States, Germany had never landed troops on Mexican soil; Germany had not stolen half of the national territory or presumed to dictate how Mexico should manage its own affairs.

As Carranza himself weighed the alternatives, he received a strange proposal from the German foreign secretary, Arthur Zimmermann. In return for a formal alliance with Germany, on the successful conclusion of the war Mexico would receive back the lands it had lost to the United States in the middle of the nineteenth century. However tempting the offer sounded, Carranza had to turn it down. Germany, he realized, was much too

Venustiano Carranza (1859–1920). The First Chief of the Constitutionalist Army assumed the presidency in 1917 but, in spite of revolutionary rhetoric, moved slowly on the issues of social reform.

bogged down in Europe to come to Mexico's assistance in a war with the United States. The best course for Mexico to follow, Carranza determined, was to maintain strict neutrality during the war.

Although the European conflict was disquieting to Mexico and resulted in some economic dislocation, the slow pace of the reform program cannot properly be attributed to it. Carranza did not want to accelerate the pace of the Revolution. Of all the disillusioned groups of revolutionaries in Mexico, the Zapatistas were most dismayed. The president sent thousands of federal troops into Morelos under trusted General Pablo González. Conducting a very competent campaign, González took a number of Zapatista towns, but the guerrilla chieftain himself eluded capture. The fighting in Morelos was relentless—perhaps the most terrible of the entire Revolution. Thousands of innocent civilians were charged with succoring Zapatistas and executed. Entire towns were burned, crops methodically destroyed, and cattle stolen. The Zapatistas responded in kind and on one occasion blew up a Mexico City–Cuernavaca train, killing some four hundred passengers, mostly civilians.

In March of 1919 Zapata directed an open letter to Carranza. It was a passionate statement but one that helps to explain why Zapata had fought every Mexican head of state for a full decade.

It was not written to the president whom he did not recognize, nor to the politician whom he did not trust, but to Citizen Carranza.

> As the citizen I am, as a man with a right to think and speak aloud, as a peasant fully aware of the needs of the humble people, as a revolutionary and a leader of great numbers, . . . I address myself to you Citizen Carranza. . . . From the time your mind first generated the idea of revolution . . . and you conceived the idea of naming yourself Chief . . . you turned the struggle to your own advantage and that of your friends who helped you rise and then shared the booty—riches, honors, businesses, banquets, sumptuous feasts, bacchanals, orgies. . . .
>
> It never occurred to you that the Revolution was fought for the benefit of the great masses, for the legions of the oppressed whom you motivated by your harangues. It was a magnificent pretext and a brilliant recourse for you to oppress and deceive. . . .
>
> In the agrarian matter you have given or rented our haciendas to your favorites. The old landholdings . . . have been taken over by new landlords . . . and the people mocked in their hopes.
>
> EMILIANO ZAPATA[6]

Carranza was not about to retire in the face of polemical thunder. He had one more plan for ending his problem with Zapata. The president discussed with General Pablo González a daring plot to deceive Zapata and then to kill him. The scheme was put into operation at once. Colonel Jesús Guajardo, one of González's subordinates in the Morelos campaigns, wrote to Zapata that he wanted to mutiny and to turn himself, some five hundred men, and all of their arms and ammunition over to the Zapatistas. Zapata demanded proof of Guajardo's sincerity, for tricks had been played in the past, and asked that several former Zapatistas, who had previously defected to the federal cause, be tried by court-martial and executed. Colonel Guajardo agreed and carried out the order. Zapata was still not fully convinced when news reached him from his own network of spies that Guajardo had captured the town of Jonacatepec in the name of the Zapatistas. Zapata at this juncture agreed to meet the defecting federal officer. A conference was set for April 10, 1919, at the Hacienda de Chinameca in Zapata's home territory. With only a few men accompanying him, Zapata rode into the hacienda in the early afternoon. A young eyewitness later described what happened.

6. Quoted in Fabela, ed., *Documentos históricos de la revolución mexicana*, 21: 305–10.

Ten of us followed him just as he ordered. The rest of the people stayed [outside the walls] under the trees, confidently resting in the shade with their carbines stacked. Having formed ranks, [Guajardo's] guard looked ready to do him honors. Three times the bugle sounded the honor call; and as the last note died away, as the General in Chief reached the threshold of the door . . . at point blank, without giving him time even to draw his pistols, the soldiers who were presenting arms fired two volleys, and our unforgettable General Zapata fell never to rise again.[7]

While Carranza had thus ridded himself of his most implacable adversary, he did not have much time left himself, as he would also die by the bullet. In 1920, when the president attempted to name his successor in the high office, Alvaro Obregón allied himself with fellow Sonorans Adolfo de la Huerta and Plutarco Elías Calles and declared himself in revolt. Under a new revolutionary banner, the *Plan de Agua Prieta*, a new army of northerners began marching on Mexico City. In May, Carranza was forced to flee the capital and, on his way into exile, was assassinated by one of his own guards in the squalid village of Tlaxcalantongo. The assassin was a loyal Obregonista, but evidence directly linking Obregón to the murder is scanty.

The Carranza regime has not yet received the type of careful historical evaluation it merits. When it is subjected to the tests of archival research it might very well prove to be the period of counterrevolution in the Mexican social upheaval. Carranza was so imbued with hatred for Victoriano Huerta, his predecessor, that he not only repudiated everything Huerta did but, in fact, nullified in the name of the Constitutionalist Revolution many of the more progressive measures undertaken by that dictatorship in the period 1913–14. Having determined that Huerta had raised teachers' salaries, Carranza reduced them to their former levels at the very time that inflation had pushed consumer prices up. Land that Huerta had begun to redistribute to the communal ejidos was restored to its Porfirian proprietors. While Francisco Madero had projected 7.8 percent of his total budget for education, and Huerta 9.9 percent, the figure under Carranza had slipped, by 1919, to an appalling .09 percent. Expenditures for all social programs dropped from 11.6 percent in 1913 to 1.9 percent in 1919.

While the counterrevolutionary thesis must remain a thesis pending further investigation, what is certain is that the social

7. Quoted in John Womack, Jr., *Zapata and the Mexican Revolution* (New York, 1968), p. 326.

revolution did not find a protagonist in the First Chief. Carranza would never have admitted that laissez faire could conflict with social welfare. One should not be misled by the fact that the socially oriented Constitution of 1917 was enacted during the Carranza years. Carranza was unhappy with its progressive articles and reacted to them by applying the old colonial maxim, *Obedezco pero no cumplo*. He simply failed to take into account the aspirations of the social reformers.

Mexico had finally rounded the corner by 1920. The violence was not yet completely spent, but generally the struggles in the post-1920 period became less chaotic and more deliberative as national politicians found more constructive releases for their energy and fervor. A gradual stabilization of the political order, coupled with a modest implementation of the new Constitution, would begin to change the contours of society in the 1920s. As the shock of carnage receded into the past, the goals of a better life began to be realized, but progress was slow and arduous. Not until the 1930s would Mexico inaugurate a president undeterred by centuries of tradition or by the vested interests.

Recommended for Further Study

Bailey, David C. "Alvaro Obregón and Anti-clericalism in the 1910 Revolution." *The Americas* 26 (1969): 183–98.

Braddy, Haldeen. *Pershing's Mission in Mexico*. El Paso: Texas Western College Press, 1966.

Chacón, Ramón D. "Salvador Alvarado and the Roman Catholic Church: Church–State Relations in Revolutionary Yucatán, 1914–1918." *Journal of Church and State* 27 (1985): 245–66.

Clendenen, Clarence C. *The United States and Pancho Villa: A Study in Unconventional Diplomacy*. Ithaca, N.Y.: Cornell University Press, 1961.

Coerver, Don M., and Linda B. Hall. *Texas and the Mexican Revolution: A Study in State and National Border Policy, 1910–1920*. San Antonio: Trinity University Press, 1984.

Cumberland, Charles C. *Mexican Revolution: The Constitutionalist Years*. Austin: University of Texas Press, 1972.

Garner, Paul. "Federalism and Caudillismo in the Mexican Revolution. The Genesis of the Oaxaca Sovereignty Movement (1915–20)." *Journal of Latin American Studies* 17 (1985): 111–33.

Gerlach, Allen. "Conditions along the Border—1915: The Plan de San Diego." *New Mexico Historical Review* 43 (1968): 195–212.

Gilderhus, Mark T. *Diplomacy and Revolution: U.S.–Mexican Relations under Wilson and Carranza*. Tucson: University of Arizona Press, 1977.

————. "The United States and Carranza, 1917: The Question of De Jure Recognition." *The Americas* 29 (1972): 210–31.

Hall, Linda B. *Alvaro Obregón: Power and Revolution in Mexico, 1911–1920.* College Station: Texas A & M University Press, 1981.

Harris, Charles H., and Louis R. Sadler. "The Plan of San Diego and the Mexican–United States War Crisis of 1916: A Reexamination." *Hispanic American Historical Review* 58 (1978): 381–408.

Hart, John M. *Revolutionary Mexico: The Coming and Process of the Mexican Revolution.* Berkeley: University of California Press, 1987.

Katz, Friedrich. *The Secret War in Mexico: Europe, the United States and the Mexican Revolution.* Chicago: University of Chicago Press, 1981.

Machado, Manuel A., and James T. Judge. "Tempest in a Teapot? The Mexican–United States Intervention Crisis of 1919." *Southwestern Historical Quarterly* 74 (1970): 1–23.

Martínez, Oscar J. *Fragments of the Mexican Revolution: Personal Accounts from the Border.* Albuquerque: University of New Mexico Press, 1983.

Meyer, Michael C. "The Mexican-German Conspiracy of 1915." *The Americas* 23 (1966): 76–89.

Monticone, Joseph R. "Pancho Villa and American Security: Woodrow Wilson's Mexican Diplomacy Reconsidered." *Journal of Latin American Studies* 13 (1981): 293–311.

Niemeyer, E. V., Jr. "Anti-Clericalism in the Mexican Constitutional Convention of 1916–1917." *The Americas* 11 (1954): 31–49.

————. *Revolution at Querétaro: The Mexican Constitutional Convention of 1916–1917.* Austin: University of Texas Press, 1974.

Quirk, Robert E. *The Mexican Revolution, 1914–1915: The Convention of Aguascalientes.* New York: Citadel Press, 1963.

Richmond, Douglas W. *Venustiano Carranza's Nationalist Struggle, 1893–1920.* Lincoln: University of Nebraska Press, 1984.

Sandos, James. "German Involvement in Northern Mexico, 1915–1916: A New Look at the Columbus Raid." *Hispanic American Historical Review* 50 (1970): 70–88.

Womack, John, Jr. *Zapata and the Mexican Revolution.* New York: Knopf, 1968.

35

Society and Culture during the Age of Violence

The Impact of the Revolution on the Masses

The rapid changes in the presidential chair, the heated debates in Aguascalientes and Querétaro, and the redounding phrases of the Constitution of 1917 surely had little immediate meaning to the Mexican masses. It was the violence of that first revolutionary decade which most dominated their lives and left Mexico a country without charm or gaiety. For every prominent death—Francisco Madero, José María Pino Suárez, Pascual Orozco, Emiliano Zapata, or Venustiano Carranza—a hundred thousand nameless Mexicans also died. By any standard the loss of life was tremendous. Although accurate statistics were not recorded, moderate estimates calculate that between 1.5 and 2 million lost their lives in those terrible ten years. In a country with a population of roughly 15 million in 1910, few families did not directly feel the pain as one in every eight Mexicans was killed. Even Mexico's high birthrate could not offset the casualties of war. The census takers in 1920 counted almost a million fewer Mexicans than they had found only a decade before.

Some of the marching armies were equipped with small medical teams, and Pancho Villa even fitted out a medical train on which battlefield operations could be performed. But medical care was generally so primitive that within a week after a major engagement deaths of wounded often doubled or tripled losses sustained immediately on the battlefield. And in more cases than one likes to recount captured enemy prisoners, both federals and rebels, were executed rather than cared for and fed. Civilian deaths rose into the hundreds of thousands as a result of indiscriminate artillery bombardments and, in some cases, the macabre policy of placing noncombatants before firing squads in pursuit of some imperfectly conceived political or military goal.

It is axiomatic that war elicits not only the worst in man but often psychotic behavior in otherwise normal human beings. While Mexican history does not have names such as Andersonville, Dachau, Auschwitz, or My Lai to connote atrocity, the cumulative stress of exhaustion and constant exposure to death did produce its psychiatric casualties during the first decade of the Revolution and, on occasion, led to behavior that can only be termed sadistic. The inhumanity visited upon civilians by soldiers became legendary in the folklore of the Revolution. One could pass off stories of mutilated prisoners hanged from trees or telephone posts as exaggerations had not scores of eager photographers captured hundreds of horrifying scenes for posterity. Bodies with hands or legs or genitals cut off were a grotesque caricature of a movement originally motivated by the highest ideals.

A cost so outrageous and so cataclysmic exacted burning resentment and tremendous fear in the civilian population. An ap-

Execution without benefit of trial was common during the violent decade of 1910–20. Bodies were left hanging for weeks as object lessons.

proaching unit invariably meant trouble for poor, rural Mexicans. The best that could be hoped for was a small band demanding a meal. But often the demands were more outrageous as the war could not lend itself to decency or compassion. In northern Mexico tens of thousands of rural Mexicans joined their middle class and wealthy counterparts in seeking the security of the United States. On a single day in October 1913 some eight thousand refugees crossed the border from Piedras Negras, Coahuila, to Eagle Pass, Texas. While the vast majority left the country with the idea of returning once the situation stabilized, most remained in the United States. But in central and southern Mexico there was virtually no place to run, and the civilian population had no choice but to keep their heads low and resign themselves to the worst. The documentary evidence from the period suggests forcefully that the excesses of war cannot be attributed simply to one side or another. Both federals and rebels were guilty. A recent community study of a village in Morelos corroborates the contemporary sources. Informants who had lived through the revolutionary period declared that both sides posed an equal threat.[1]

Fear in the rural areas was challenged only by frustration. Two months spent clearing a field and planting crops under a burning sun could be wiped out in five minutes as an army of five hundred horsemen galloped through the carefully tilled rows of corn and beans. Then they might stop at the one-room hut and confiscate the one milch cow and four turkeys that held out some promise for a slightly less redundant diet in the six months to follow.

There is precious little published evidence upon which to assess the impact of the early Revolution on life in rural Mexico. But the findings of Professor Luis González, in his perceptive and beautifully written account of the Michoacán village of San José de Gracia (population about 1,200 in 1910) are probably not atypical. By 1913, when violence engulfed the region for the first time,

> Don Gregorio Pulido had given up taking local products to Mexico City, for bands of revolutionaries made the roads unsafe for travel. The San José area began to return to the old practice of consuming its own products. Trade declined. Padre Juan's goal of increasing prosperity receded in the distance. From 1913 on, increased poverty was the rule. . . . Everything in San José shifted into re-

1. Lola Romanucci-Ross, *Conflict, Violence and Morality in a Mexican Village* (Palo Alto, Cal., 1973), pp. 15–16.

verse. The revolution did no favors for the town or the surrounding *rancherías*. . . . Parties of rebels often came to visit their friends in San José, either to rescue the girls from virginity, or to feast happily on the delicious local cheeses and meats, or to add the fine horses of the region to their own. . . . They summoned all the rich residents and told them how much money in gold coin each was to contribute to the cause. In view of the rifles, no one protested.[2]

The "armies" the peones of rural Mexico saw and feared did not look much like armies. Standard uniforms were unheard of among the rebels, and weapons consisted of whatever could be found or appropriated. Sometimes makeshift insignias identified rank but gave slight clue as to group affiliation. Anonymity served rebel commanders well as it left them unconcerned with the niceties of accountability, but it caused problems for the rural *pacífico* wanting to respond correctly to the question, "Are you a Huertista, a Villista or a Carrancista?"

For Mexican women the Revolution often had a degrading personal meaning. With husbands, fathers, and sons serving somewhere in the ranks, they were subjected to the terror and indignity of wanton assault. But many did not mope or simply stay home to become the target of rape. Freeing themselves from the eternal task of grinding corn, thousands joined the Revolution and served the rebel armies in the capacity of spies and arms smugglers. So active were the women in smuggling ammunition across the border in Ciudad Juárez that the United States Customs Bureau was forced to employ teams of female agents to search the undergarments of suspicious, heavy-looking ladies returning from shopping sprees in El Paso.

Perhaps the most noteworthy role assumed by women was that of *soldadera*. The soldaderas were more than camp followers. They provided feminine companionship, to be sure, but because neither the federal army nor the rebel armies provided commissary service, they foraged for food, cooked, washed, and, in the absence of more competent medical service, nursed the wounded and buried the dead. Both sides were dependent upon them, and in 1912 a federal battalion actually threatened mutiny when the secretary of war ordered that the women could not be taken along on a certain maneuver. The order was rescinded. Not infrequently, the soldaderas actually served in the ranks, sometimes with a baby slung in a *rebozo* or a young child clinging to their

2. Luis González, *San José de Gracia: Mexican Village in Transition* (Austin, 1974), pp. 124–25.

Among the disparate revolutionary contingents in Mexico, the Yaqui Indians of Sonora figured prominently in the campaigns of the northwest.

skirts. Women holding officer ranks were not uncommon in the rebel armies.

The soldadera endured the hardships of the campaign without special consideration. While the men were generally mounted, the women most often walked, carrying bedding, pots and pans, food, firearms, ammunition, and children. Often the men would gallop on ahead, engage the enemy in battle, and then rest. By the time the women caught up, they were ready to move again, and the soldadera would simply trudge on. Losing her special "Juan" in battle, she would wait an appropriately decent period and then take on another, to prepare his favorite meal and share his bed.

The hard life of the soldadera was a relative thing. A fascinating oral history of a Yaqui woman from Sonora who was deported to Yucatán, cut her hands raw on the henequen plants, and saw her babies die from lack of adequate care, reveals that she was thrilled to become a soldadera. She later recalled that "her personal misery decreased by impressive leaps and bounds. . . . At no point during the next several years did she view her life as anything but a tremendous improvement after the years . . . in Yucatán."[3]

While, with the protection of anonymity, men could treat women as virtual slaves, public displays were more often marked by the type of chivalric indulgence so long identified with the Hispanic tradition. One traveler to Mexico City in 1918 was especially amused by the sign he found posted in the streetcar:

> GENTLEMEN: When you see a lady standing on her feet you will not find it possible to remain sitting with tranquility. Your education will forbid you to do so.
>
> GENERAL MANAGER OF THE RAILWAYS[4]

In an oblique and unintended sort of way the Revolution contributed to the emancipation of the Mexican woman. As the shortage of adult males in the cities contracted the labor supply, women began to make some inroads into the business world. At first their contributions consisted of the simplest type of work in the stores, but once escaped from the confines of the house they would not be persuaded easily to return. In Yucatán, at least, a concerted policy of women's liberation was initiated by Governor Salvador Alvarado. A farsighted revolutionary, Alvarado de-

3. Jane H. Kelly, "Preliminary Life History of Josefa (Chepa) Alvarez" (mimeographed, 1970), p. 16.
4. Quoted in P. Harvey Middleton, *Industrial Mexico: 1919 Facts and Figures* (New York, 1919), p. 6.

Armies had to be fed, and the task of grinding corn for the daily supply of tortillas continued as it had for centuries.

A familiar sight between 1910 and 1920, the soldaderas experienced both the excitement and privations of life on the military campaign.

clared: "I have always believed that if we do not elevate the role of women we will find it impossible to build a country."[5] Not only did he lower the age of majority of women from age thirty-one to twenty-one, but he actively began placing women in open positions in state government. In 1916 he sponsored a Congreso Femenino in Mérida, Yucatán. Four major themes were discussed: the social means to be employed to remove the yoke of tradition; the role of primary education in women's liberation; the arts and occupations the state should support to prepare the women for a fuller life; and the social functions women should employ to contribute toward a better society.

The Revolution, to be sure, had different meanings to different Mexicans during those years of greatest violence. But a most recurrent theme is the fear of the leva, the institution that snatched away the male population for service in the military. One corrido, popular in 1914, capsulized the problem in the doggerel of the masses.

> La leva, la odiosa leva
> que sembró desolación
> en todo el suelo querido
> de nuestra noble nación.
> Al obrero, al artesano
> al comerciante y al peón,
> los llevaban a las filas
> sin tenerles compasión.[6]

Edith O'Shaughnessy, the wife of the United States chargé in Mexico City, described the leva in her memoirs.

> I was startled as I watched the faces of some conscripts marching to the station today. On so many was impressed something desperate and despairing. They have a fear of . . . eternal separation from their loved ones. They often have to be tied in the transport wagons. There is no system about conscription here—the press gang takes any likely looking person. Fathers of families, only sons of widows, as well as the unattached, are enrolled, besides women to cook and grind in the powder mills.[7]

Among those who suffered most were foreign residents of Mexico. Because the Revolution was in part a reaction against Díaz's coddling of foreign interests, not a few revolutionaries took out

5. Salvador Alvarado, *Actuación revolucionaria del General Salvador Alvarado en Yucatán* (Mexico, 1965), p. 49.

6. Quoted in Merle E. Simmons, *The Mexican Corrido as a Source for Interpretive Study of Modern Mexico (1870–1950)* (Bloomington, 1957), p. 121.

7. Edith O'Shaughnessy, *A Diplomat's Wife in Mexico* (New York, 1916), p. 58.

THE VIOLENCE TAKES A TOLL

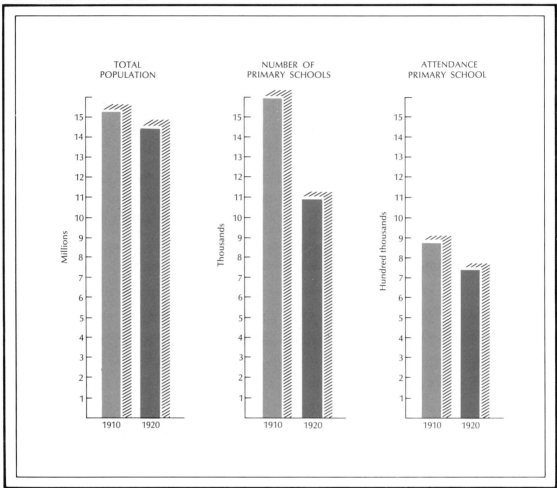

TOTAL POPULATION

NUMBER OF PRIMARY SCHOOLS

ATTENDANCE PRIMARY SCHOOL

their wrath on the foreign community. Cast in the role of exploiters, foreign oilmen and miners were forced to pay not only taxes to the government but tribute to various groups of rebels and bribes to local bandits. But other frugal and industrious foreigners, without the slightest claim to exploitation, suffered worse. After a battle for control of Torreón in 1911 over two hundred peaceful Chinese residents were murdered simply because they were Chinese. A few years later Spanish citizens in Torreón were expelled from the country and their property confiscated by Pancho Villa. Colonies of United States Mormons in Chihuahua and Sonora were terrorized to such an extent that they finally packed up those belongings they could carry and left their adopted home.

City dwellers, too, were subject to the ravishments of war. Almost all of the larger cities in the country hosted battles at some time between 1910 and 1920, and some witnessed three or four major engagements and were turned into debris before the decade ran its course. The sight of burning buildings, the sound of wailing ambulances, and the nausea of mass burials brought home in tangible terms the most immediate meaning of the Revolution. Starvation reached major proportions in Mexico City, Guadalajara, and Puebla.

The construction boom of the Porfiriato ended shortly after the outbreak of hostilities. While a few unfinished public projects were completed, for the most part those workmen who could be spared from the ranks were kept busy clearing debris, repairing damaged structures, knocking down gutted buildings, and trying to put the railroad lines back in operation.

The early Revolution took a terrible toll in education. Hundreds of schools were destroyed and hundreds of others abandoned. In the Federal District alone the number of primary schools in operation declined from 332 in 1910 to 270 ten years later. The story repeated itself in city after city, town after town. Total primary school attendance in the country declined from 880,000 to 740,000 in the same ten-year period.

Intellectuals and Artists

The first decade of the Revolution, as violent as it was, nevertheless spawned a new generation of Mexican intellectuals and artists. During the last year of the Porfiriato a group of young thinkers had banded together to form the Ateneo de la Juventud. Among its charter members were a small group that would come to dominate early revolutionary thought: Antonio Caso, Alfonso Reyes, José Vasconcelos, and Martín Luis Guzmán. Meeting fortnightly, the members of the Ateneo began to formulate a philosophical assault on materialism in general and on positivism in particular. Impressed with Immanuel Kant and Arthur Schopenhauer, but most especially with Henri Bergson's masterpiece *L'Evolution créatrice* (1907), they lashed out against the científicos and launched a movement for ideological and educational reform based on a healthy respect for the humanities.

By 1912 the members of the Ateneo were ready to give some practical application to their antipositivist posture. Interested in moving into areas that Díaz had ignored, in December 1912 they founded a "people's university," the Universidad Popular Mexicana, and took their message to the factories and shops in Mexico's leading population centers. Mexico's future happiness, they preached, was not dependent upon commercial or industrial growth but rather upon social progress. The Universidad Popular Mexicana did not offer degrees; rather it tried to bring humanistic knowledge to those who would not otherwise receive it. Stressing lessons in citizenship and patriotism as well as practical instruction in hygiene and stenography, the *ateneístas* who constituted the faculty not only lectured but sponsored weekend tours to art galleries, museums, and historical and archeological sites. They all served without pay.

The winds of change shook the literary and artistic communities as well. A new age in the Mexican novel was born in 1915 when Mariano Azuela (1873–1952) wrote *Los de abajo* (translated as *The Underdogs*). A classic in twentieth-century Mexican literature, *Los de abajo* is a social novel and marked the beginning of a trend that would last for thirty years. Azuela was deeply concerned with the progress of the Revolution and through the character of Demetrio Macías probed its meaning. Historical novels were not new in Mexico, but Azuela added new ingredients. The story is related not in the sophisticated dialogue of the French school but in the colloquial language of the Mexican masses. Avoiding the intrusion of secondary plots, Azuela tells the story of real revolutionaries, not those who intellectualized the movement and coined its resounding phrases. Demetrio Macías is caught up in the struggle without really knowing why, yet when confronted with complex decisions is able to make proper choices with amazing spontaneity. Luis Cervantes, a middle-class federal deserter, joins Macías's guerrilla band and tries to articulate the revolutionary goals for him, but the uneducated Macías recognizes the shallowness and hypocrisy of Cervantes's explanations and the inherent opportunism in his actions.

The day-to-day dehumanizing realities of the Revolution are all there—pillage, looting, burning, destruction, theft, and general debauchery. Illustrative of the passion the Revolution evoked is Azuela's description of the battlefield after a struggle for control of Zacatecas: "The three-hundred-foot slope was literally covered with dead, their hair matted, their clothes clotted with grime and blood. A host of ragged women, vultures of prey, ranged over the tepid bodies of the dead, stripping one man bare, despoiling another, robbing from a third his dearest possessions."[8] The novel ends where it began—at the Canyon of Juchilpa. Demetrio Macías, by this time a general, is killed where he first ambushed a federal convoy. The circle has been completed, and nothing has really changed. After all the suffering and killing, the Revolution seems to be back where it began. While social programs have been shunted aside and forgotten, the Revolution has become almost self-perpetuating—it just goes on and on. Shortly before he dies Demetrio's wife asks him why he must continue fighting. He answers by tossing a rock over a precipice and responding with a beautifully appropriate metaphor: *Mira esa piedra cómo ya no se para* (Look at that rock—it just keeps rolling).

Mexican music, too, changed its tone as a new nativist movement was introduced by Manuel Ponce (1882–1948), a talented young pianist and composer from Zacatecas. Ponce decried that Mexican salons in 1910 should welcome only foreign music. He urged the acceptance of the native folk tradition and believed that the Revolution was already beginning to usher it in. In an essay he attacked the stodgy salons.

> Their doors remained resolutely closed to the *canción mexicana* until at last revolutionary cannon in the north announced the imminent destruction of the old order. . . . Amid the smoke and blood of battle were born the stirring revolutionary songs soon to be carried throughout the length and breadth of the land. *Adelita*, *Valentina*, and *La Cucaracha*, were typical revolutionary songs soon popularized throughout the republic. Nationalism captured music at last. Old songs, almost forgotten, but truly reflecting the national spirit, were revived, and new melodies for new corridos were composed. Singers traveling about through the republic spread far and wide the new nationalistic song; everywhere the idea gained impetus that the republic should have its own musical art faithfully mirroring its own soul.[9]

Ponce was a major contributor to the movement he described. In 1912 and 1913 he composed his *canciones mexicanas*, including the famous *Estrellita*. And at approximately the same time

8. Mariano Azuela, *The Underdogs*, trans. E. Munguía (New York, 1963), pp. 80–81.
9. Quoted in Robert Stevenson, *Music in Mexico: A Historical Survey* (New York, 1971), pp. 233–34.

he was training the individual destined to become the most illustrious name in twentieth century Mexican music—Carlos Chávez.

Of all the intellectual and artistic groups in the country, Mexican painters showed themselves to be most restless. Having already embarrassed the Díaz regime at the centennial celebrations of 1910, these recalcitrant artists continued to scandalize staid society during the first decade of the Revolution. When neither interim President León de la Barra nor Francisco Madero was willing to remove the Porfirian director of the Art Academy of San Carlos, the artists took matters into their own hands. Not only did they go out on strike demanding the resignation of the director but on one occasion pelted the poor soul with rotten tomatoes. The desired change came with Victoriano Huerta, who named Alfredo Ramos Martínez, an impressionist, as director. Ramos Martínez reformed the curriculum, de-emphasizing the stifling classroom training in copying and formal portrait work that strived for photographic precision. Instead he encouraged the students to venture out into their Mexican world and paint what they saw and what they felt.

When the Constitutionalists came in, Ramos Martínez went out but his innovative ideas were not to be overturned. The new director, Dr. Atl (Gerardo Murillo), was even less conventional than his predecessor. Politically a loyal Carrancista but artistically a free spirit, Dr. Atl wanted to convert the academy into a popular workshop for the development of the arts and crafts. But when Pancho Villa marched his army into Mexico City following the Convention of Aguascalientes, the director and his loyal students, including José Clemente Orozco and David Alfaro Siqueiros, fled to Orizaba. The days of Mexican academic art were over.

The second decade of the twentieth century was still an experimental period for the Mexican artist. Diego Rivera spent most of his time in France and Spain, dabbling with some success in cubism. Siqueiros abandoned the brush for the gun and served in the Carrancista army for several years, storing up penetrating impressions of camp life, battles, and death, all of which he would later recreate. Orozco spent much of his time painting posters and sketching biting political cartoons and caricatures for Carrancista newspapers. In different ways these three giants of twentieth century Mexican art were preparing themselves for an artistic renaissance and the most important development in Latin American painting—the muralist movement of the 1920s and 1930s.

Social Change

Even during the chaos of violence certain unstructured social change was occurring in Mexico. Internal migrations took place, northerners and southerners came into more frequent contact with one another, and distinct regional language patterns began to yield to a more homogeneous national tongue. Increased travel, even that occasioned by the leva, provided a broader conception and a deeper appreciation of Mexico. Greater physical mobility brought about by the war tended to increase miscegenation and began to homogenize previously isolated zones. Thousands of Mexicans escaped obscurity and rose to positions of tremendous power in the various armies. Even though they did not always exercise their newfound influence with moderation, for them the Revolution was an agent of social change.

By 1920 a new kind of revolutionary nationalism had begun to emerge. The dead heroes had become martyrs to a young generation of Mexicans who did not always realize that their favorite protagonists had been killed fighting one another. The heroes loomed larger in death than in life, and their errors of judgment and human frailties could be overlooked. Madero became a symbol of democracy, Orozco of Mexican manhood, Carranza of law and justice, and Zapata of land for the humble. The newly developing revolutionary nationalism had its antiheroes as well: Porfirio Díaz, who had caused the holocaust; and Victoriano Huerta, the very incarnation of treachery and deceit.

In concrete terms, life for the great majority did not improve in the decade 1910 to 1920. In fact, because of the violence, it deteriorated in many ways. But the base of power in the republic had shifted into new hands, and the country was finally on the threshold of better times.

Recommended for Further Study

Azuela, Mariano. *The Underdogs.* Translated by E. Munguía. New York: New American Library, 1963.

Brushwood, John S. *Mexico in Its Novel: A Nation's Search for Identity.* Austin: University of Texas Press, 1966.

Charlot, Jean. *The Mexican Mural Renaissance, 1920–1925.* New Haven: Yale University Press, 1967.

Flower, Elizabeth. "The Mexican Revolt against Positivism." *Journal of the History of Ideas* 10 (1949): 115–29.

González, Luis. *San José de Gracia: Mexican Village in Transition.* Austin: University of Texas Press, 1974.

Guzmán, Martín Luis. *The Eagle and the Serpent*. Translated by Harriet de Onís. Gloucester: Peter Smith, 1969.

Innes, John S. "The Universidad Popular Mexicana." *The Americas* 30 (1973): 110–22.

Langford, Walter M. *The Mexican Novel Comes of Age*. Notre Dame: University of Notre Dame Press, 1971.

Macías, Anna. "Women and the Mexican Revolution, 1910–1920." *The Americas* 37 (1980): 53–82.

O'Shaughnessy, Edith. *A Diplomat's Wife in Mexico*. New York: Harper and Brothers, 1916.

Robe, Stanley L. *Azuela and the Mexican Underdogs*. Berkeley: University of California Press, 1979.

Romanell, Patrick. *Making of the Mexican Mind*. Lincoln: University of Nebraska Press, 1952.

Rutherford, John. *Mexican Society during the Revolution: A Literary Approach*. New York: Clarendon Press, 1971.

Simmons, Merle E. *The Mexican Corrido as a Source for Interpretive Study of Modern Mexico (1870–1950)*. Bloomington: Indiana University Press, 1957.

Sommers, Joseph. *After the Storm: Landmarks of the Modern Mexican Novel*. Albuquerque: University of New Mexico Press, 1968.

Stevenson, Robert. *Music in Mexico: A Historical Survey*. New York: Thomas Y. Crowell, 1971.

IX THE REVOLUTION: THE CONSTRUCTIVE PHASE, 1920-40

36

Alvaro Obregón Cautiously Implements the Constitution

Domestic Reforms

With the election of Alvaro Obregón to a four-year presidential term in 1920, Mexican politicians set to work on implementing the Constitution that had been drafted and promulgated at Querétaro in 1917. The war-torn country was closer to peace than it had been for a decade. Zapata had been killed, and, just a few weeks before Obregón assumed the high office, even the indomitable Pancho Villa had accepted a peace offering from the federal government. A good-sized hacienda, Canutillo, was given to him as an assurance that he would not again break the peace. The rigorous defender of the poor had grown tired, and he swallowed his pride to settle down in the comfortable role of an hacendado.

Obregón immediately turned his attention to the pressing problems of national reconstruction. A powerful and persuasive orator, he enjoyed a wide base of popular support. He was far from being a radical, but, unlike the nineteenth-century liberals, he was concerned with more than political reform. Unfortunately, the beginning of his administration coincided with the post–World War I economic slump. Prices of gold, silver, copper, zinc, henequen, and cattle were depressed. Unemployment was rampant in these industries, and the government's foreign exchange from these products fell off drastically. Hunger and general privation were more evident than they had been during the late Porfiriato. Only the price and demand for oil remained stable, and by 1921 Mexico was producing 193 million barrels, making it the world's third largest producer of petroleum. Oil

ARIZONA

NEW MEXICO

Mexicali

Tucson

TEXAS

El Paso

Nogales

Agua Prieta

Ciudad
Juárez

Cananea

BAJA CALIFORNIA NORTE

SONORA

Casas Grandes

CHIHUAHUA

Rio Grande

Hermosillo

Chihuahua

Piedras Negras
(Porfirio Diaz)

COAHUILA

Guaymas

C. Camargo

BAJA CALIFORNA SUR

Navojoa

Jiménez

Monclova

Nuevo Laredo

Cuatrociénegas

Reynosa

M

Los Mochis

Sinaloa

SINALOA

Gómez Palacio

Torreón

Saltillo

Monterrey

NUEVO LEÓN

Culiacán

DURANGO

La Paz

Durango

ZACATECAS

Ciudad
Victoria

Pacific   Ocean

Mazatlán

Fresnillo

SAN LUIS
POTOSÍ

TAMAULIPAS

Zacatecas

AGUASCALIENTES

San Luis Potosi

Tam

NAYARIT

San Blas

Tepic

Guadalajara

Atotonilco

JALISCO

Colima

Tuxpan

México D.F. ✱

Manzanillo

MICHOACÁN

Chilpancingo

GUERRERO

Oax

Acapulco

See inset map

Inset Map

León

Dolores Hidalgo

VERACRUZ

San Miguel

QUERÉTARO

Guanajuato

Papantla

GUANAJUATO

Querétaro

HIDALGO

Celaya

Pachuca

Morelia

Tlalnepantla

Texcoco

TLAXCALA

México D.F. ✱

Tlaxcala

MICHOACÁN

Toluca

Puebla

MEXICO

Cuernavaca

Yautepec

Cuautla

PUEBLA

Taxco

MORELOS

INSET MAP

0   Miles   100

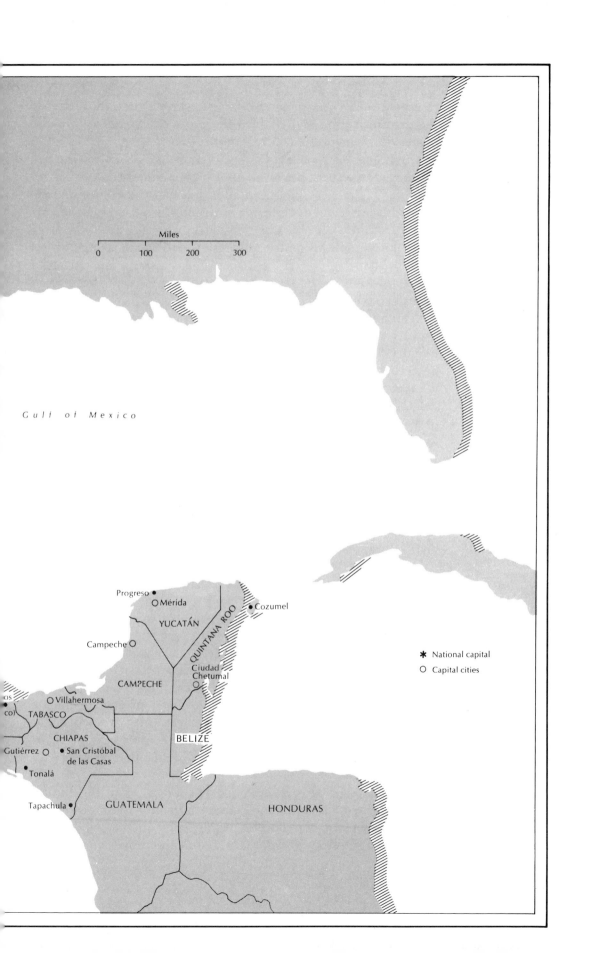

Miles

0   100   200   300

Gulf   of   Mexico

Progreso •
○ Mérida
•Cozumel

YUCATÁN

QUINTANA ROO

Campeche ○

Ciudad
Chetumal
○

CAMPECHE

○ Villahermosa

os
co)
TABASCO

CHIAPAS

BELIZE

Gutiérrez ○   • San Cristóbal
de las Casas

• Tonalá

Tapachula •   GUATEMALA   HONDURAS

✱ National capital
○ Capital cities

reserves, even with an inadequate taxation structure, sustained the administration and enabled the president to embark upon a modest implementation of the Constitution of 1917.

To implement Article 3 Obregón named José Vasconcelos, one of Mexico's most illustrious men of letters, to be secretary of education. Vasconcelos had been educated in Mexico City and received his law degree at the age of twenty-three. Late in the Porfiriato his antipositivist rebellion led him to join the Ateneo de la Juventud, and he shortly distinguished himself as one of the most brilliant minds in Mexico. An enthusiastic supporter of Francisco Madero, he became a Constitutionalist at the time of Huerta's coup and subsequently served in Eulalio Gutiérrez's Convention government. With the flight of Carranza from Mexico City in 1920, Vasconcelos briefly served as rector of the National University, but Obregón wanted him in the cabinet and he accepted the portfolio of education shortly after Obregón's inauguration.

If Nemesio García Naranjo, Huerta's secretary of education, had provided the initial impetus for the anticientífico revision of the curriculum, Vasconcelos was the patron of the rural school. With dramatically increased federal funds placed at his disposal, he sent dedicated teachers into hundreds of hamlets with a basic curriculum: reading, writing, arithmetic, geography, and Mexican history. Because the economic realities of rural Mexico dictated that children would attend only a few years of school, there simply was not much time for frills.

Vasconcelos had to inspire the teachers with a deep sense of national mission because life in rural Mexico, for many of them, was a type of cultural exile. Some of the villages were a two- or three-days' ride by horseback from the nearest railroad station, most lacked electricity, and few amenities of the comfortable life were to be found. In addition, the new teachers were not always welcomed with open arms. They often encountered deep hostility from villagers who did not want to change their traditional ways and from local priests who resented government encroachments into what they considered a church preserve. But the teachers did go into the hamlets and labored with dedication. Children attended during the day, while many adults consented to attend classes at night.

Vasconcelos's plan was designed not to segregate the Indian but through education to incorporate him into the mainstream of mestizo society. Vasconcelos would subsequently undergo a tremendous intellectual *volte-face*, but at this time he called for

FEDERAL EXPENDITURES FOR EDUCATION

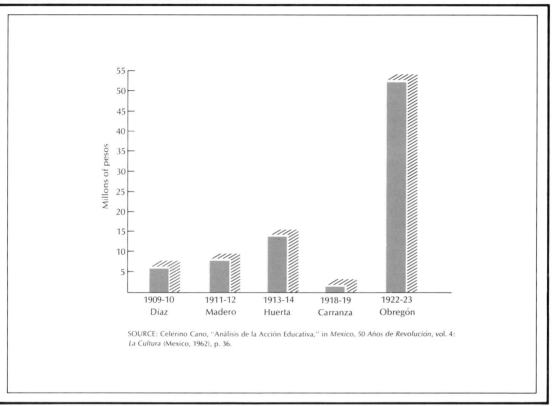

SOURCE: Celerino Cano, "Análisis de la Acción Educativa," in *Mexico, 50 Años de Revolución*, vol. 4: *La Cultura* (Mexico, 1962), p. 36.

the incorporation of the Indians into a raza cósmica. In his memoirs he described the process as follows:

> I also set up auxiliary and provisional departments, to supervise teachers who would follow closely the methods of the Catholic missionaries of the Colony among Indians who still do not know Spanish. . . . Deliberately, I insisted that the Indian Department should have no other purpose than to prepare the native to enter the common school by giving him the fundamental tools in Spanish, since I proposed to go contrary to the North American Protestant practice of approaching the problem of teaching the native as something special and separate from the rest of the population.[1]

Over a thousand rural schools were built in Mexico between 1920 and 1924, more than had been constructed during the previous fifty years. To support the new endeavor, the secretary of education began a program of public libraries. Almost two thou-

1. José Vasconcelos, *A Mexican Ulysses: An Autobiography*, trans. William Rex Crawford (Bloomington, 1963), p. 152.

sand libraries had been established by 1924, most of them stocked with books designed to reinforce the humanist tradition of Mexico's new intelligentsia. Government presses printed millions of primary readers for both the schools and the libraries. A library set for a typical rural school consisted of about fifty books packed in special crates that could be transported on muleback.

Vasconcelos believed in the utility of informal education as well and employed some of Mexico's leading artists—Diego Rivera, José Clemente Orozco, and David Alfaro Siqueiros—to begin ornamenting the walls of public buildings with murals. The murals were designed for the people rather than for the art critics, but they received world acclaim as well. The themes were anthropological and historical for the most part and, with no shortage of polemicism, sought to instruct the literate and illiterate alike in the truths that the Revolution had come to hold dear.

Article 3 of the Constitution had stipulated, of course, that education should be secular and free, but President Obregón found this provision impossible to implement in full. The church was not removed entirely from the educational field because the state had neither the funds nor the teachers to educate all the children in Mexico. Both the president and the secretary of education opposed church education strongly, but, when confronted with an apparent impasse, they allowed that under guarded conditions it was preferable to no education at all. To assure that the church would not misconstrue the government's tolerant attitude toward Catholic education, however, Obregón encouraged the work of Protestant missionaries in Mexico. He openly endorsed the work of the YMCA (Asociación Cristiana de Jóvenes) and even supported its activities with state funds. The church naturally opposed this new development, but, with a few exceptions, open hostilities were avoided. Few realized in the early 1920s that church-state relations were undergoing a lull before a terrible storm.

Obregón's labor policy favored Luis Morones and the newly formed CROM. Because labor development had been so long stifled, Obregón leaned in the opposite direction, at least as far as the CROM was concerned. Nor did Luis Morones view the CROM as a government adversary. Realizing that Obregón had the power to crush the nascent labor movement if he wished, Morones worked to establish a balance between labor and capital rather than to attack the structure of the capitalist system. These modest goals were fully consonant with government policy, and, as a result, Morones and Obregón worked hand in hand and the

Alvaro Obregón (1880–1928). President of Mexico from 1920 to 1924, Obregón is shown here recovering from the amputation of his right arm following the battle of Santa Rosa (1915).

union offered the government stellar support. In turn, the administration financed the CROM's national labor conventions and provided free railroad passes for anyone who wished to attend. Blessed with government benevolence, membership in the union rose steadily from fifty thousand in 1920 to an estimated 1.2 million in 1924.

Other developing unions did not fare so well, however. Two radical labor groups, the Communist Federation of the Mexican Proletariat and the anarchist-led Industrial Workers of the World tried unsuccessfully to gain a foothold in the labor movement. In addition to the burdens of foreign leadership, which ran counter to the newly developing revolutionary nationalism, they both quickly incurred the strident opposition of the administration. Obregón expelled a number of foreign labor leaders from the country and declared strikes of the radical unions illegal. But it was not simply the radicalism of these unions that bothered the president; he was equally obdurate with the conservative Roman Catholic union movement.

Many Mexican labor leaders, however, had expected more because Obregón's followers had helped draft Article 123 and because the president had been sympathetic to labor's interests during his military career. But in his attempt to placate diverse interests in the country, labor often found itself shunted to one side. When asked to intervene in labor's behalf, the president time after time responded that the issue in dispute should be resolved at the state or local level. In states with progressive governors labor did not fare too badly, but in those with conservative administrations it languished. Obregón had decided that Article 123 of the Constitution would be implemented according to his understanding of Mexican reality, and he had decided that only the CROM represented legitimate workers' goals.

On the matter of agrarian reform Obregón again showed himself as a compromiser. He was aware that Mexican economy, for better or for worse, was still tied to the hacienda system and that a rapid redistribution of land would result in reduced agricultural productivity. The rural population would produce enough to feed itself but not enough to feed the nonagrarian sector of the society. On the other hand, Obregón had traveled in rural Mexico and had been touched by the abject poverty he had encountered there.

He decided not to declare all-out war on the hacendados of the republic. Rather, he moved with caution and deliberation, hoping that the modest redistribution he did sponsor would not be too disruptive. By the time his term expired in 1924 he had distributed some 3 million acres to 624 villages. The land went to the communal ejidos rather than outright to individuals, but the number of villagers directly benefiting was calculated at 140,000. The radical agrarianists, such as Antonio Díaz Soto y Gama, were understandably disappointed. They believed that the president's agrarian logic was specious. Luis Terrazas alone still owned as much land as the total distributed by the administration. Obregón had failed to strike while the agrarian iron was hot. It was true that he had multiplied by nine times the amount distributed by Carranza, but in 1924, seven years after the adoption of the Constitution, Article 27 had not yet benefited the overwhelming majority of rural Mexicans.

Why had Obregón not moved faster in the agrarian field? Without question he himself believed in the wisdom of a moderate course. In a speech made before the Congress he declared:

> We must act so carefully as to solve the problem without endangering our welfare and our economical interests. If we begin by destroying the big estates in order to create afterwards the small property, I sincerely believe we have made a blunder. . . . We must not destroy the big estates before creating the small one, as

an unbalanced state might follow leading us to dearth. I am of the opinion that we must act cautiously.[2]

Obregón was a cautious man but not simply as a matter of personal predilection. He felt it necessary to re-establish the political stability absent since the overthrow of Díaz. In addition, overshadowing many of his policy decisions was the specter of possible United States intervention to protect the interests of its citizens owning property in Mexico. The fears were not idle ones as United States troops had been in Mexico twice since the Revolution began, once in Veracruz and two years later in the north in the futile attempt to capture Pancho Villa.

Relations with the United States

Obregón's presidential term coincided with the Republican administration of Warren G. Harding in the United States. Supported by big business,, Harding had won the presidency by a landslide and believed that his government's prime responsibility was the encouragement of private enterprise, both at home and abroad. Of all the corporate enterprises that dominated the Republican convention of 1920, none rivaled the oil interests of Harry F. Sinclair, Edward L. Doheny, and Jake Hammon. Within a couple of years the extent of petroleum influence in the administration would be exposed to the world in the scandal of Teapot Dome. But the petroleum interests were at work from the beginning.

For several years, through powerful lobby groups such as the National Association for the Protection of American Rights in Mexico and the Oil Producer's Association, under the chairmanship of Edward Doheny, American businessmen had been urging the United States government to become more active in the defense of their Mexican interests. Not encountering much success during the Wilson presidency, they found a much more receptive audience in President Harding and Secretary of State Charles Evans Hughes. Often working through Secretary of Interior Albert Bacon Fall (later arrested in the Teapot Dome scandal), they presented their case to the American president. Their Mexican oil properties, they contended, were about to be seized out from under them by Article 27, and, accordingly, the United States should not recognize the Obregón regime. Secretary Fall

2. Quoted in Eyler N. Simpson, *The Ejido: Mexico's Way Out* (Chapel Hill, 1937), pp. 87–88.

had long considered Americans living in Mexico as his special constituency and had won for himself, over the years, a reputation of being extremely well versed in Mexican affairs. When he wrote, "So long as I have anything to do with the Mexican question, no government of Mexico will be recognized, with my consent, which does not first enter into a written agreement promising to protect American citizens and their property rights in Mexico,"[3] President Harding was willing to be persuaded. From 1920 to 1923 Obregón was not recognized by the United States.

The United States oil interests, supported by the Harding administration and fully aware that any oil stoppage would cripple Obregón, argued that Article 27, if applied retroactively, would constitute an international wrong of the gravest proportions. Although Obregón needed the oil revenues, he could not buckle under to United States pressure; it would have been political suicide. The apparent impasse was averted by the Mexican Supreme Court. When, in September 1921, the Texas Company challenged the retroactive application of Article 27 in the Mexican courts, the Supreme Court handed down a decision propounding the doctrine of "positive acts." The oil lands could not be seized under Article 27 if the company in question had performed some "positive act" (such as erecting drilling equipment) to remove oil from the soil prior to May 1, 1917, the date on which the Constitution went into effect. If the company had not engaged in such a "positive act" prior to May 1, 1917, or if the concession had been granted after that date, Article 27 could be invoked at the pleasure of the state. This decision greatly relieved American oil interests, but, according to Mexican legal practice, five consecutive concurring decisions were necessary to establish a binding precedent. By the following year the four additional decisions had been rendered, and President Obregón then believed that he could enter into negotiations with the United States without being accused of treason.

In the spring of 1923 both countries named commissioners who agreed to meet on Bucareli Street in Mexico City during the summer. Under the terms of the agreements they reached, the Mexican government in essence agreed to uphold the doctrine of "positive acts" in its future relations with all the oil companies, and the Harding administration promised, in return, to extend diplomatic recognition. In addition, both countries agreed to establish a mixed claims commission to adjudicate the claims United

3. Quoted in John W. F. Dulles, *Yesterday in Mexico: A Chronicle of the Revolution, 1919–1936* (Austin, 1961), p. 159.

States citizens had brought against Mexico for damages suffered during the Revolution.

Political Tensions and Rebellion

At about the same time that the commissioners of the two countries were meeting on Bucareli Street in the capital, an extraordinary event occurred on Gabino Barreda Street in Parral, Chihuahua. The retired General Pancho Villa had just traveled from Canutillo to the little village of Río Florido to participate in the christening of an old comrade's baby son. After the ceremony Villa went on to Parral, where he decided to spend the night with a lady friend before returning to his famous hacienda. Early the following morning, surrounded by his bodyguards, he began the return trip to Canutillo. As his Dodge touring car turned onto Calle Gabino Barreda, eight men armed with repeating rifles burst out of a corner house and peppered the automobile. Within seconds Villa and several of his companions were dead.

Responsibility for the assassinations was not easy to fix; in fact, historians are not yet in complete agreement. Some contemporaries considered the murder to have been a personal affair in which a group of aggrieved citizens took vengeance for prior Villista depredations. But most believed that the murder was politically motivated, as Mexican politics had begun to heat up once again during the summer of 1923 and Villa had threatened to come out of retirement.

The assassination of Villa tended to exacerbate an already tense political atmosphere. The nationalists were unhappy with the Bucareli Agreements. Obregón, they contended, had truckled to the American oil men and their White House representatives. Their dissatisfaction was kept in check for a few months, however, until it merged with other disaffections in the Mexican community. The time was approaching when a decision had to be made concerning the presidential succession of 1924, and Obregón chose to support his fellow Sonoran and secretary of interior, Plutarco Elías Calles. This choice touched off political violence.

The revolution that began in Mexico in late 1923 combined the antagonisms of various interest groups. Many conservatives, including a number of wealthy hacendados and Catholic leaders, feared that Plutarco Calles was a genuine radical and sought to head him off before the upcoming elections. They were joined by

military men, disgruntled at Obregón's reduction of the federal
army for purposes of economy. Each carried important federal
garrisons into the rebel ranks. But the rebellion was not simply
an alliance of conservatives, as many ardent nationalists, unhappy with the Bucareli Agreements, pledged their support of
the new movement, as did a number of labor leaders who had
not been included within the ranks of the CROM. The opposition
coalesced around still another leading figure from Sonora, Adolfo
de la Huerta. De la Huerta was an experienced politician; he had
served as interim president a few years earlier and had been Obregón's secretary of the treasury, a position he had managed—
later charges notwithstanding—with rare aplomb.

In spite of the wide base of opposition, Obregón was not without his own sources of strength. Those unions under CROM control
supported him unabashedly, as did a number of peasant organizations. Although some key army garrisons went over to the
rebel side, many significant ones remained loyal to the government. But, most important, the recent diplomatic recognition by
the United States provided Obregón's government not only with
the moral support of Washington but also with an ample supply
of war matériel. The war itself lasted only a few months, but it
was a grueling episode for those who thought the days of violence had passed, and the toll of lives was tremendous. Some
seven thousand Mexicans were killed before the rebels of de la
Huerta admitted their defeat.

Obregón had been able to assert the dominance of the national
government in the face of tremendous odds. Inheriting a country
in financial peril and a citizenry with now-whetted aspirations,
he emerged, if not unscathed by the political antagonisms of the
day, at least with a good measure of dignity and respect, and his
administration could take some pride in having put down a major antigovernment uprising. But, as the president neared the
end of his term, some of the Mexican intelligentsia, indulging in
self-criticism, realized that he had been slow to implement the
reforms promised by the Constitution. They knew that through
shrewd pragmatism he had co-opted the radical thrust of the
Revolution, and, while occasionally yielding to the rhetoric of
reform, he had not done much to alter the sustaining structure of
society. On the other hand, many Mexican intellectuals, politicians, and journalists were willing to rationalize that in the early
1920s Mexican progress should be measured by Mexican stand-

ards. Since 1884 every Mexican president had been assassinated or driven from office by revolution. When Plutarco Calles won the presidential elections in 1924 and was inaugurated later that year, the ceremony marked the first time in forty years that the office was handed over peacefully from one chief executive to the next. Mexicans in their early sixties could perhaps remember that Manuel González had yielded peacefully to Díaz, but not a living soul could recall another instance. Political stability was returning to revolutionary Mexico, and with it Mexicans could not only afford the luxury of greater social experimentation but began to demand more from their leadership.

Recommended for Further Study

Beelen, George D. "The Harding Administration and Mexico: Diplomacy of Economic Persuasion." *The Americas* 41 (1984): 177–90.

Clark, Marjorie. *Organized Labor in Mexico*. Chapel Hill: University of North Carolina Press, 1934.

Dulles, John W. F. *Yesterday in Mexico: A Chronicle of the Revolution, 1919–1936*. Austin: University of Texas Press, 1961.

Gilderhus, Mark T. "Senator Albert Bacon Fall and 'The Plot against Mexico.'" *New Mexico Historical Review* 48 (1973): 299–311.

Haddox, John H. *Vasconcelos of Mexico*. Austin: University of Texas Press, 1967.

Hall, Linda B. "Alvaro Obregón and the Politics of Mexican Land Reform." *Hispanic American Historical Review* 60 (1980): 213–38.

Hansis, Randall. "The Political Strategy of Military Reform: Alvaro Obregón and Revolutionary Mexico, 1920–1924." *The Americas* 36 (1979): 197–232.

Lieuwen, Edwin. *Mexican Militarism: The Political Rise and Fall of the Revolutionary Army*. Albuquerque: University of New Mexico Press, 1968.

Ruiz, Ramón Eduardo. *Mexico: The Challenge of Poverty and Illiteracy*. San Marino, Cal.: Huntington Library, 1963.

Schoenhals, Louise. "Mexico's Experiments in Rural and Primary Education, 1921–1930." *Hispanic American Historical Review* 44 (1964): 22–43.

Scholes, Walter V. "Secretary of State Hughes' Mexican Policy." *Jahrbuch für Geschichte von Staat, Wirtschaft und Gesellschaft Lateinamerikas* 7 (1970): 299–308.

Tannenbaum, Frank. *Peace by Revolution: Mexico after 1910*. New York: Columbia University Press, 1966.

Vasconcelos, José. *A Mexican Ulysses: An Autobiography*. Translated by William Rex Crawford. Bloomington: Indiana University Press, 1963.

Wilkie, James W. *The Mexican Revolution: Federal Expenditure and Social Change since 1910*. Berkeley: University of California Press, 1967.

37

Mexico under Plutarco Calles, 1924-34

For a full decade beginning in 1924 Mexico found itself in the firm grip of General Plutarco Elías Calles. Though more popular among reformist groups in 1924 than Alvaro Obregón, ten years later his name was anathema to Mexican liberals. Born in Guaymas, Sonora, in 1877 to a poor family, Calles attended normal school in Hermosillo, did quite well in the classroom, and upon graduation, became a primary school teacher in the public school system. His political career began with the Revolution, and he served in a number of minor political and military capacities before becoming provisional governor of his home state in 1917. His loyal support of Obregón over a ten-year period won for him official endorsement for the presidency in 1924, and, with labor and agrarian support, he carried the election easily.

Calles's Domestic Program

Conservative elements in Mexico were far from elated by the election that year, for Calles enjoyed a liberal, even a radical, reputation. Landowners, both domestic and foreign, feared loss of property; industrialists anticipated higher wages for their workers; and church leaders recognized the new president as a confirmed anticleric. Each fear, it appeared, was grounded in understandable fact, and Calles soon let it be known that his domestic policy would not be characterized by the compromise and caution so typical of his predecessor. He was not only willing to ride the swelling tide of social revolution but sincerely believed, at least at the outset, that its course was inevitable. Better to be out in front, he conjectured, than to be dragged along.

Calles was the most strong-willed president since Díaz. He had an abiding faith in his own political instinct and, over his years in office, became increasingly domineering. Outspoken but often eloquent in public oratory, Calles was untormented by scruple when treating with his enemies. As the years passed he became less and less tolerant, more openly dictatorial, and relied heavily on the army to dispatch government foes. Deviation from presidential fiat was not tolerated during the Calles years. Political prisoners began filling the jails, and an alarming number "committed suicide." That the excesses were gross cannot be denied, but they were not, as enemies of the regime later charged, comparable to Jacobin or Stalinist purges following the French and Russian revolutions.

Calles inherited a more prosperous Mexico than had Obregón. The postwar economic slump was over and had given way to a sustained economic growth. Mexican raw materials were again in much demand from a recovered world economy. With a solid public treasury, Calles stepped up land distribution, just as the hacendados feared that he would do. Where Obregón had distributed some three million acres, Calles distributed eight million between 1924 and 1928. The vast majority of the land was granted to the communal ejidos rather than outright to individual heads of families. Because the uneducated peasant could not alienate his land through cheap sale, he was not subject to the machinations of the local land speculators. To try to stem a decline in agricultural productivity, the administration initiated a series of irrigation projects, established a number of new agricultural schools, and began to extend agricultural credit to the small farmer. While the radical agrarians had hoped that Calles would do still more, the pace of agrarian reform had accelerated demonstrably.

Calles's labor policy continued to favor Luis Morones and the CROM; in fact, Morones was brought into the cabinet as secretary of labor and quickly became the president's most intimate confidant. Other highly placed CROM officials served in the Congress, in the state legislatures, and even held state governorships. Hundreds of independent unions were brought into the CROM, and hundreds of new unions were organized. By 1928 CROM membership had reached 1.8 million, and the parent organization had affiliates in most of the states. The influence of the CROM became pervasive and its support of the government un-

A prosperous Luis Morones came to dominate the Mexican labor movement under
President Calles. At one time considered
a possible successor to Calles, charges of
corruption put an end to his political ambitions.

abashed. The confederation even prevented printers from type-
setting anti-Calles publications. The president returned the favors by supporting the CROM against employers and, more
important, against other unions. Wages rose gradually, though
never enough to constitute a serious burden to management. But
by 1928 many sincere labor leaders had begun to worry about
Morones. He was becoming a very wealthy man, and most believed that his diamond rings, new automobiles, and vast holdings in urban real estate had been acquired with union funds
and through various extortion schemes.

In the area of education Calles had inherited a new, well-
constructed foundation from Obregón and Vasconcelos. In 1924
there were approximately one thousand federally supported rural schools in operation. Calles and his able secretaries of education, José Manuel Puig Casauranc and Moisés Sáenz, continued
the emphasis of rural education. Before the presidential term
expired in 1928 they had added two thousand additional rural
schools. To facilitate the acculturation of the Indian, heavy emphasis was placed on the teaching of Spanish. Only if Spanish became the language of the village, they believed, could the Indian
be made a part of the national culture.

The government's health and sanitation program was built almost from scratch. When the Revolution broke out in 1910, sanitation conditions in Mexico were hardly better than they had
been during the colonial period. Calles was appalled and gave
his support to a newly organized Department of Public Health.

The department superintended the establishment of a new sanitary code designed to ensure cleaner markets and purer public milk supplies. For the first time in Mexican history major vaccination campaigns were undertaken. In 1926 alone over five million Mexicans were inoculated against smallpox. The government also began regular inspections of bakeries, butcher shops, dairies, cantinas, and barber shops. Those establishments that did not meet prescribed sanitary standards were closed down and their owners fined.

Relations with the United States

Relations with the United States still centered around oil. The Bucareli Agreements notwithstanding, United States Ambassador James Sheffield sought further assurances that foreign property interests would be protected. When Calles refused to go beyond the promises made on Bucareli Street, Sheffield started to bombard the U.S. State Department with Red scare dispatches. Gradually he convinced his superior, Secretary of State Frank B. Kellogg, that a Bolshevik plot was about to divest United States citizens of their just property rights. In the summer of 1925 Secretary Kellogg made a remarkable statement to the press. After reporting that an anti-Calles revolution was pending in Mexico, he continued:

> It should be made clear that this Government will continue to support the Government in Mexico only so long as it protects American lives and American rights and complies with its international obligations.
> The Government of Mexico is now on trial before the world. We have the greatest interest in the stability, prosperity, and independence of Mexico. . . . But we cannot countenance violation of her obligations and failure to protect American citizens.[1]

Calles expressed his strong displeasure with Kellogg's statement, for it appeared that the United States was once again nourishing aggressive designs. In a terse rejoinder the Mexican president declared that his government was well aware of its international obligations, but he rejected outright the inherent threat to Mexico's sovereignty in the secretary's pronouncement. He would never allow that any nation should create in Mexico a privileged position for its nationals.

1. Quoted in David Bryn-Jones, *Frank B. Kellogg: A Biography* (New York, 1937), p. 176.

In order to indicate that he would countenance no tampering with Mexico's sovereignty, Calles had his legislature enact a new petroleum law in December 1925. The legislation required all oil companies to apply to the government for a confirmation of their concessions. To determine whether or not to grant the confirmations, Mexico would apply the doctrine of "positive acts," as had been provided under the terms of the Bucareli Agreements, but the concessions would be granted only for a period of fifty years. As Calles began to enforce the new petroleum law, relations between Mexico City and Washington almost reached the breaking point.

In 1927 President Calvin Coolidge replaced Ambassador Sheffield in Mexico City with an old friend from Amherst College, Dwight Morrow, a partner in the famous financial firm of J. P. Morgan. Mexicans were, of course, convinced that the United States had sent yet another representative of Wall Street to press the case for the oil companies. But Morrow turned out to be a pleasant surprise. He did not make the Mexicans suspect that he was actually receiving his paychecks from Standard Oil. His first formal address in Mexico City presaged a more harmonious diplomatic atmosphere: "It is my earnest hope," he advised his Mexican audience, "that we shall not fail to adjust outstanding questions with that dignity and mutual respect which should mark the international relations of two sovereign and independent states."[2]

From the outset Morrow demonstrated a genuine interest in everything Mexican. He and his family lived in a Mexican-style house and shopped in the open marketplaces, marveling at native pottery and textiles. The ambassador visited the rural areas, taking special interest in new schools and irrigation projects and inquiring generally about the progress of the social revolution. He even began to study Spanish—not common for United States ambassadors in the 1920s—and invited Charles Lindbergh to Mexico on a goodwill tour. Morrow's relationship with Calles was unusually informal. The president and the ambassador began having breakfast together, and in this relaxed atmosphere, unencumbered by the bevy of official aides, they set to work on the sticky diplomatic problems besetting the two countries.

When the oil controversy first came up, Morrow did not warn that Mexico was on trial before the world; rather, in soft, diplomatic language he told Calles that he believed the issue should

2. Quoted in David C. Bailey, *Viva Cristo Rey: The Cristero Rebellion and the Church-State Conflict in Mexico* (Austin, 1974), p. 176.

be settled in the Mexican courts and expected no special consideration for United States citizens. Calles was impressed and quite possibly used his influence to see that the courts rendered a compromise decision. The Supreme Court ultimately held that the oil companies did have to apply for new concessions from the government, that the doctrine of "positive acts" would apply, but that the new permits would not expire at the end of fifty years. Both sides had given a little, but the genuine significance lay in the response of the U.S. Department of State. Remembering Calles's sensitivity to the question of sovereignty, an official release noted that the petroleum controversy had been resolved by the Mexican government and that any future controversies would also be resolved by the Mexican government without any interposition from the United States. For the first time Washington had formally recognized Mexico's full legal sovereignty, even when the interests of United States citizens were involved.

The Cristero Rebellion and the Assassination of Obregón

Calles's most serious problem turned out to be not with the United States but rather with the Roman Catholic Church. Whereas Obregón had turned his back on the anticlerical articles of the Constitution, Calles decided to enforce them. Although tensions had been building up gradually throughout the early 1920s, the event that triggered new hostilities was an interview José Mora y del Río, the archbishop of Mexico, gave to the press in February 1926. Reacting to the implementation of anticlerical provisions in a number of states, the archbishop argued that Roman Catholics could not in conscience accept the Constitution. Their opposition to it was stronger than ever, and their position was unshakable. The recalcitrant declaration served no purpose. Calles used the excuse to strike with both fists. He first disbanded religious processions, then began deporting foreign priests and nuns and closing church schools, monasteries, and convents. He also decreed that all Mexican priests had to register with civil authorities. The response of the church was both unique and unexpected. On July 31, 1926, the archbishop declared a strike, and on the following day, for the first time since the arrival of the Spaniards four centuries earlier, no masses were celebrated in Mexico.

The strike lasted for three full years; babies went unbaptized and the old died without receiving the last rites. It was not a peaceful strike. As Calles became more intemperate, gross, and even obscene in his denunciations of the clergy and the pope, Catholic leaders in Michoacán, Puebla, Oaxaca, Zacatecas, Nayarit, but especially in the backcountry of Jalisco, began organizing the masses to resist the godless government in Mexico City. To the cry of *¡Viva Cristo Rey!* Anacleto González Flores, René Capistrán Garza, and Enrique Gorostieta led bands of Cristeros against government outposts. There were sordid excesses on both sides. The Catholic guerrillas burned down the new government schools, murdered teachers, and covered their bodies with crude banners marked *VCR*. In April 1927 the Cristeros dynamited a Mexico City–Guadalajara train, killing over a hundred innocent civilians. Not to be outdone, the government troops tried to kill a priest for every dead teacher, encouraged children to throw rocks through stained glass windows, looted churches, and took great pleasure in converting them into stables. Cristeros, or suspected Cristeros, were shot perversely without benefit of trial, some swearing to the last moment that an enemy had painted *¡Viva Cristo Rey!* on their houses. The Cristeros could not withstand the military superiority of the federal army and gradually were worn down. But when Calles's presidential term expired in 1928, the rebellion was not yet completely suffocated.

The presidential election of 1928 and its immediate aftermath were shocking. The Constitution of 1917 had recently been amended to provide for a six-year presidential term and, with Alvaro Obregón specifically in mind, the possibility of re-election if it were not immediate. As the electoral process began to unfold, Calles threw his support behind the former president, no doubt thinking that Obregón would return the favor in 1934. Two opposition candidates also entered the fray: General Francisco Serrano, a former secretary of war, and General Arnulfo Gómez, a capable military man who had performed yeoman service in quelling the de la Huerta rebellion of 1923. Serrano and Gómez did not expend much energy attacking one another, they both concentrated their efforts on Obregón and attacked the principle of re-electionism. When Serrano and Gómez convinced themselves that the election of 1928 was not going to be fair, they rebelled against the government and the contemplated succession of Obregón. But within two months both of the opposition candidates had been captured and executed.

Obregón's victory brought no relief, however, for he never assumed office. On the afternoon of July 17, 1928, he attended a garden banquet in Mexico City's plush district of San Angel.

Many dignitaries whom he wanted to join the new administration were in attendance. While the guests were dining, a twenty-six-year-old artist, José de León Toral, sketched caricatures of those sitting at the head table. After showing some of his better drawings to several guests, he moved toward the head table to show the president his work. As soon as Obregón nodded his approval, Toral took a pistol from his pocket and fired five shots into the president-elect's head.

Some of the irate guests beat young Toral almost beyond recognition. That he was not killed on the spot by the hysterical mob reflected the good sense of several officials who immediately realized that the full circumstances behind the assassination had to be determined. At the police station following the assassination, Toral refused to answer any questions. Torture did not suffice to loosen his tongue, and only the threat of torture to his family elicited the desired information. In subsequent weeks, as the story began to unfold, it became increasingly apparent that this senseless act of violence was also an offshoot of Mexico's never-ending conflict between church and state.

Toral was a deeply religious man who lost touch with reality and became a mystic when the Cristero Rebellion broke out. A few months prior to the assassination he had been introduced to a nun, Sister Concepción Acevedo de la Llata, remembered in Mexican history simply as Madre Conchita. When the church declared its strike she offered spiritual consolation to the faithful in her own home, and it was in this capacity that her path crossed that of Toral. The young zealots who met regularly at Madre Conchita's house became increasingly militant as the rebellion grew more outrageous. They began manufacturing bombs and even discussed plans for killing Obregón. Finally Toral was chosen, or assumed responsibility, for implementing a mission they all considered to be divinely inspired. But just to make sure everything went as planned Toral began target practice in early July with a pistol borrowed from one of Madre Conchita's friends. Shortly after his confession, Madre Conchita and a number of others were arrested as well.

The trial, conducted in November, was a great public spectacle and undoubtedly the most sensational judicial inquiry since the trial of Maximilian. In a gesture of unparalleled magnanimity Obregón's widow asked the court to show Toral mercy, but the state was in no mood to turn the other cheek. The prosecuting attorney and the attorney general who testified in behalf of the state were warmly applauded by the gallery. On the other hand, the defense attorney, Demetrio Sodi, was heckled, disparaged, and shouted down with cries of "Death to the Assassin!" and "Death to the Prostitute Concha!" Jurors, fearful for their lives, came to the courtroom armed with pistols. Taunts of mockery and threats of lynching interrupted the proceedings, as did promises of reprisals to the jurors should they vote to acquit. The crowd became so agitated during the summation of Attorney Sodi that he was unable to conclude his defense. The court would not be used as a platform for Catholic views. The verdict was a foregone conclusion. Toral's act, after all, had been witnessed by many; he implicated Madre Conchita during his testimony, and her denials were unconvincing. Toral received the death sentence, and Madre Conchita, because Mexican law forbade the execution of women, was given a prison sentence of twenty years.

The Maximato and the Shift to the Right

Obregón's assassination created a political vacuum, and only Calles commanded sufficient respect to fill it. He decided not to assume the presidential office himself but would control the nation's destiny as the power behind the scenes. The Congress, charged with choosing an interim president until new elections could be held, selected Calles's man, Emilio Portes Gil, a lawyer and former governor of Tamaulipas. Portes Gil proved to be the first of three puppets to fill out Obregón's term, but Calles, as "the Supreme Chief" (*Jefe Máximo*), clearly called the shots. By the time the election of 1929 occurred, Calles had organized a new, widely based political party, the Partido Nacional Revolucionario (PNR). Mexican presidents never again would be elected by temporary coalitions that would splinter soon after tasting the fruits of victory. The official party would change its name on several occasions, but its control over the Mexican political process would remain permanently intact.

When the special election occurred, Calles and his newly organized PNR ran Pascual Ortiz Rubio for the presidency. The opposition candidate, running under the rubric of the National Anti-Re-electionist party, was the more experienced and much better known José Vasconcelos. Vasconcelos directed his campaign against the Jefe Máximo rather than against Ortiz Rubio and argued that a vote for Ortiz Rubio was a vote for Calles. But the strategy was useless. When the government announced the results, Ortiz Rubio was declared the winner by the unbelievable margin of 1,948,848 to 110,979. He served only two years. Shortly after he attempted to oppose Calles on several policy decisions, he picked up a morning newspaper to read that he had resigned. On this occasion the Jefe Máximo picked General Abelardo Rodríguez, a man with less administrative talent than relish for power, as puppet number three of the *Maximato.*

In spite of the musical chairs played in the presidential office, the years 1928 to 1934 were not barren of accomplishment. An important step forward was made in professionalizing and depoliticizing the Mexican army. Calles had actually initiated the process during his own term in office, but the job was completed under the puppets. By giving the military a major voice within the PNR there was less reason for revolt in support of some disgruntled politician. While the army was by no means taken out of politics, it was co-opted by being brought into the political process. Military expenditures were curtailed during the six-year Maximato, but, since military men themselves participated in the decisions, they accepted the budgetary belt-tightening with admirable restraint.

Equally important to the political well-being of the nation was the resolution of the Cristero Rebellion. Ambassador Morrow played a major but unofficial role in the reconciliation as he arranged a series of meetings between Calles, Portes Gil and Father John Burke, a prominent Catholic leader in the United States. In early June 1929 Father Burke convinced the Mexican leaders that they should allow several exiled bishops to return to the country so that they, too, could participate in the negotiations. By late June a compromise had been hammered out. The church agreed that priests would have to register with the government and that religious instruction would not be offered in the schools. The government declared publicly that it had no intention of destroying the integrity of the church and even allowed that religious instruction would not be prohibited within the confines of the churches themselves. As a result, the hierarchy ordered the Cristeros to lay down their arms and the priests to resume religious services. Mexico's long-standing church-state controversy was not yet completely over, but it would never again reach the grotesque proportions of the Cristero Rebellion.

The Calles puppetship witnessed a dramatic shift of the Revolution to the right. The social reform programs that were conceived in the early Revolution, formalized in the Constitution of 1917, and gradually implemented during the years 1920 to 1928, were all but abandoned shortly after the assassination of Obregón. Land redistribution after 1928 slowed to a snail's pace. The state of Chihuahua affords a good example. The Terrazas family had been forced to sell most of its huge land holdings during the Obregón presidency but now was allowed to buy them back. Although the Terrazases paid a somewhat higher price than they had received earlier, they bought back only the best lands that they previously owned. The rural education program suffered, and the labor movement was abandoned as the government withdrew its support of the CROM. Luis Morones surely had profited at the public trough. While he might have been beneath contempt and above the law, his personal peculation scarcely justified the all-out attack on the labor movement itself. Other highly placed officials also dipped into the treasury with impunity. With handsome sinecures many bought luxurious homes in Cuernavaca on what the contemporary pundits labeled "the Street of the Forty Thieves." The honest revolutionaries were aghast at this new clique of "millionaire socialists," and the raconteurs celebrated their corruption with hundreds of sardonic anecdotes.

As the Revolution shifted to the right, the regime and its supporters grew more and more sensitive to any form of radicalism. Virtual war was declared on the small, inconsequential Mexican Communist party. The leaders were unceremoniously deported to the penal colony on Islas Tres Marías. The anti-Communist hysteria reached its apex in 1930 and 1931, years that witnessed the appearance of the Gold Shirts, a fascist-inspired organization of thugs whose self-appointed task was to terrorize all Communists and Jews.

The Revolution: An Assessment in the 1930s

Something drastic had happened to the Revolution and its leadership. Honest, idealistic men, dedicated to principles of social reform, had been not only diverted from tasks of high priority but corrupted as well. The phenomenon has never been adequately studied, but a provocative sociological hypothesis was posited by Professor Frank Tannenbaum.

> This period [1928–34] . . . is most perplexing. If it were possible to discover what had taken hold of the leadership of Mexico in those debased and clouded years, it would illumine much of Mexican history. Here was a group of new men, most of whom

had come from the ranks of the Revolution and had risked their
lives in a hundred battles for the redemption of the people from
poverty and serfdom. . . . and yet, at the first opportunity, each
fell an easy victim to pelf and power. . . .

Their difficulty lay in the fact that they had come to power suddenly and without preparation, either morally, psychologically,
politically, or even administratively. They were taken from their
villages as barefooted youngsters who had slept on the floor and
could barely read, and after a few years spent on the battlefields
found themselves tossed into high office and great responsibility.
This new world was filled with a thousand temptations they had
not dreamed of. . . . Here, at no price at all, just for a nod, all
their hearts desired was offered them in return for a favor, a signature, a gesture, a word.[3]

There is much to be said for Professor Tannenbaum's understanding of those perplexing years. While the hypothesis must
remain tentative, it does have the ring of reality. At the same
time, however, something more tangible was also involved—the
Great Depression of 1929–32.

Mexico weathered the depression better than most Latin American countries, as the treasury had about 30 million pesos ($15
million) in cash reserves in 1930. But no country in the world
emerged from the great crash unscathed. Important Mexican exports, especially oil and metals, reflected the structural weaknesses of the world market, and, as a result, national income
from taxes declined and the value of the peso began to fall.
While in 1930 two pesos bought a dollar, by 1932 the cost of the
dollar was 3.50 pesos. The entire treasury surplus, and more,
was used up in 1931, as government revenues fell 80 million pesos short of expenditures. As a result of the unhealthy economic
atmosphere, capital began to flee the country in search of more
secure investment fields elsewhere. Many industries were para-
lyzed because of monetary deflation and tight credit. Emergency
tax measures helped the government a little, but programs had
to be cut back in many areas. Government workers were fired,
wage reductions averaged over 10 percent, and departments were
ordered to reduce their expenditures. Given this dreary set of circumstances, the social revolution simply could not progress.

In a more general sense the depression discredited the set of
revolutionary principles that had become sacrosanct to many.
Poverty cut deeply, and government leaders decided to experi-

3. Frank Tannenbaum, *Mexico: The Struggle for Peace and Bread* (New York,
1956), pp. 69–70.

ment with new, shortsighted approaches. But the leadership had misread the economic indicators and gave up too easily to a slothful defeatism. The depression had not singled out Mexico; it was not partial to one or another ideology or economic system. The principles upon which the Revolution had been founded were still sound, and in 1934 a new, dynamic leader would give them the opportunity to run their course.

The Mexican revolutionary generation had not yet demonstrated any real political genius. In the Calles decade the question of presidential succession had continued to provoke violence, a president-elect had been assassinated, and the presidential chair had had three occupants in a single term. But by 1934 the worst was over. While day-to-day political conduct would not always be exemplary, Mexico had witnessed its last successful revolt. Mexican presidents would never again leave office without finishing their terms. There would be no more interim or provisional presidents. Presidents would never again try to succeed themselves in office and presidential succession would no longer occasion armed insurrection. In 1934 the political process would stabilize itself, and the social revolution would find a new protagonist.

Recommended for Further Study

Bailey, David C. *Viva Cristo Rey: The Cristero Rebellion and the Church–State Conflict in Mexico*. Austin: University of Texas Press, 1974.

Berbusse, Edward J. "The Unofficial Intervention of the United States in Mexico's Religious Crisis, 1926–1930." *The Americas* 23 (1966): 28–62.

Bernstein, Marvin D. *The Mexican Mining Industry, 1890–1950: A Study of the Interaction of Politics, Economics, and Technology*. Albany: State University of New York Press, 1964.

Carr, Barry. "The Mexican Communist Party and Agrarian Mobilization in the Laguna, 1920–1945: A Worker–Peasant Alliance?" *Hispanic American Historical Review* 67 (1987): 371–404.

Clark, Marjorie. *Organized Labor in Mexico*. Chapel Hill: University of North Carolina Press, 1934.

Dulles, John W. F. *Yesterday in Mexico: A Chronicle of the Revolution, 1919–1936*. Austin: University of Texas Press, 1961.

Levenstein, Harvey A. "The AFL and Mexican Immigration in the 1920's: An Experiment in Labor Diplomacy." *Hispanic American Historical Review* 48 (1969): 206–19.

Lieuwen, Edwin. *Mexican Militarism: The Political Rise and Fall of the Revolutionary Army*. Albuquerque: University of New Mexico Press, 1968.

Mabry, Donald J. "Mexican Anticlerics, Bishops, *Cristeros* and the Devout during the 1920s: A Scholarly Debate." *Journal of Church and State* 20 (1978): 81–92.

Miller, Barbara. "The Role of Women in the Mexican Cristero Rebellion: *Las Señoras y las Religiosas*." *The Americas* 40 (1984): 303–24.

Quirk, Robert E. *The Mexican Revolution and the Catholic Church, 1910–1929*. Bloomington: Indiana University Press, 1973.

Ross, Stanley R. "Dwight Morrow and the Mexican Revolution." *Hispanic American Historical Review* 38 (1958): 506–28.

———. "Dwight W. Morrow, Ambassador to Mexico." *The Americas* 14 (1958): 373–89.

Ruiz, Ramón Eduardo. *Mexico: The Challenge of Poverty and Illiteracy*. San Marino, Calif.: Huntington Library, 1963.

Simpson, Eyler N. *The Ejido: Mexico's Way Out*. Chapel Hill: University of North Carolina Press, 1937.

Tannenbaum, Frank. *Mexico: The Struggle for Peace and Bread*. New York: Knopf, 1956.

Tuck, Jim. *The Holy War in Los Altos: A Regional Analysis of Mexico's Cristero Rebellion*. Tucson: University of Arizona Press, 1982.

Wasserman, Mark. "Strategies for Survival of the Porfirian Elite in Revolutionary Mexico: Chihuahua During the 1920s." *Hispanic American Historical Review* 67 (1987): 87–107.

Wilkie, James W. "The Meaning of the Cristero Religious War against the Mexican Revolution." *Journal of Church and State* 8 (1966): 214–33.

38

Cárdenas Carries the Revolution to the Left

Cárdenas

The many Mexicans impatient with the progress of the Revolution in 1934 were delighted with the election of Lázaro Cárdenas to the presidency in that year. His revolutionary career was typical of many who worked their way rapidly through the military ranks, ultimately reaching the grade of brigadier general by the end of the first violent decade. But Cárdenas was a civilian at heart. Not an imposing figure physically, he was attractive as a pensive, methodical man of principle and deep conviction. An avid reader, he was intensely interested in social reform and had that special charismatic quality of evoking passionate enthusiasm among many and strong dislike among some. And he was no run-of-the-mill politician. Supporting first Obregón and then Calles, he became, in the 1920s, a dominant force in his home state of Michoacán.

Cárdenas's governorship in Michoacán from 1928 to 1932 offered Mexicans a preview of what they might expect. The governor allowed himself to be confronted by the people and listened more than he spoke. He actually made important policy decisions, not on the advice of his confidants, but on the direct information received from the public. During years when the national government was shirking its educational responsibilities, Cárdenas opened a hundred new rural schools in Michoacán, inspected many classrooms personally, and made sure that the teachers received their salaries on time. He also encouraged the growth of labor and peasant organizations and even managed a modest redistribution of land at the state level. Throughout it all he continued to live modestly.

As the presidential elections of 1934 approached, Calles decided to throw his support behind Cárdenas, fully believing that the forty-year-old governor would be puppet number four. With the official endorsement of the Jefe Máximo, Cárdenas carried the 1933 PNR convention easily and was elected to the presidency in July of the following year. Immediately he broke with tradition as he cut his own salary in half and refused to move into the presidential mansion in Chapultepec. Instead, he kept his own modest home. Cárdenas had observed the six-year Maximato with some discomfort and once in office determined that he was going to free himself of Calles's domination, revitalize the Revolution, and carry it back to the left. Aware that Calles's control over Portes Gil, Ortiz Rubio, and Rodríguez had rested heavily on army support, the new chief executive assiduously began to cultivate promising junior officers. Not only did he raise salaries and benefits, but he also supported an improved system of education within the army and, in addition, sponsored a far-reaching internal reform of the entire military structure. Confident of the army by 1935, Cárdenas began to remove Calles supporters from the cabinet and other high governmental posts and even relieved Callista generals from their commands. When Calles discovered that he could not manipulate this president as he had the previous three, he began to speak out vociferously against the administration. By the spring of 1936 Cárdenas had had enough. He ordered that Calles and a few of his close supporters be arrested. They were placed aboard a special plane bound for the United States and informed that they should not return to Mexico.

Only once during his term was Cárdenas threatened with a serious internal revolt. Saturnino Cedillo, the conservative political boss of San Luis Potosí, withdrew recognition of the government and declared himself in open rebellion. Although Cedillo had the strong backing and financial support of conservative interests, both domestic and foreign, Cárdenas's army remained loyal and quelled the rebellion within a matter of weeks. The president would not be faced with similar problems again.

Once installed in the presidency Cárdenas did his utmost to keep close contact with the public. While cabinet secretaries and foreign dignitaries fidgeted fretfully in the presidential waiting room, Cárdenas would receive delegates of workers or peasants and patiently listen to their problems. A contemporary observer recounted that one morning the president's secretary laid before him a list of urgent matters and a telegram.

> The list said: Bank reserves dangerously low. "Tell the Treasurer," said Cárdenas. Agricultural production falling. "Tell the Minister of Agriculture." Railroads bankrupt. "Tell the Minister of Communications." Serious message from Washington. "Tell Foreign Affairs." Then he opened the telegram which read: My corn dried, my burro died, my sow was stolen, my baby is sick. Signed, Pedro Juan, village of Huitzlipituzco. "Order the presidential train at once," said Cárdenas. "I am leaving for Huitzlipituzco."[1]

The story is undoubtedly apocryphal; yet that it circulated in a sophisticated capital indicates the reputation the president enjoyed. More deeply committed to social reform than any previous Mexican head of state, Cárdenas came to the presidency at a time when a new, young generation of revolutionaries was beginning to displace the old veterans of the days of violence. Some of the familiar figures continued to serve in the national and state governments, but many names were heard for the first time. The younger generation had kept faith with the revolutionary principles enunciated in the years following the overthrow of the Díaz dictatorship but believed that it was finally time for a statist revolution to give them full rein.

Domestic Reforms

Agrarian reform more than anything else dominated the administration's concern during the first few years. Since the initiation of the land redistribution program some 26 million acres of land had been parceled out, but the figure appeared more impressive on paper than in Mexico's rural zones. Millions of Mexican peasants still owned no land at all and felt cheated by two decades of revolutionary rhetoric. Cárdenas early made up his mind to fulfill twenty years of promises. Unprepared to tarry leisurely, by the time his term expired he had distributed 49 million acres, about twice as much as all his predecessors combined. By 1940 approximately one-third of the Mexican population had received land under the agrarian reform program. In fact, most of Mexico's arable land had been redistributed. Only the large cattle haciendas on arid or semiarid land remained untouched.

---

1. Quoted in Anita Brenner, *The Wind That Swept Mexico: The History of the Mexican Revolution, 1910–1942* (Austin, 1971), p. 91.

PERCENTAGE OF LAND DISTRIBUTION BY ADMINISTRATION, 1915–40

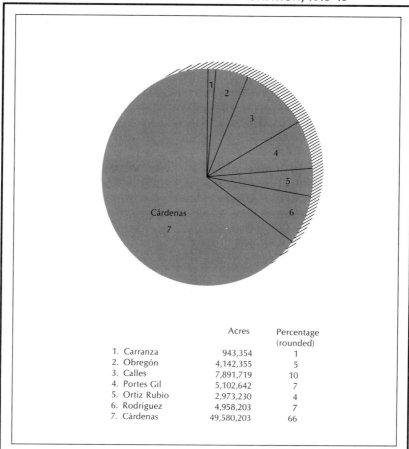

	Acres	Percentage (rounded)
1. Carranza	943,354	1
2. Obregón	4,142,355	5
3. Calles	7,891,719	10
4. Portes Gil	5,102,642	7
5. Ortiz Rubio	2,973,230	4
6. Rodríguez	4,958,203	7
7. Cárdenas	49,580,203	66

The vast majority of the land distributed did not go to individuals or even heads of households but rather to the communal ejidos. The land was held in common by the communities, sometimes to be reapportioned to individuals for their use and sometimes to be worked by the community as a whole. The largest and most important of the ejidos dating from the Cárdenas redistribution was the huge Laguna cotton ejido, some eight million acres on the Coahuila-Durango border. The thirty thousand families that worked the Laguna ejido cooperatively engaged primarily in the cultivation of long-staple cotton but also grew large amounts of wheat, alfalfa, and maize for commercial sale. Most of the families also held small individual plots on which they grew their own subsistence crops. But the Laguna experiment consisted of much more than the mere redistribution of land. Government-supported schools were established, social services in the area were extended, and a modern ejido hospital was built in Torreón, in the center of the Laguna operation. Although the Laguna ejido was the biggest single cooperative land venture initiated by Cárdenas, other large ejidos were established as well. These ventures required large-scale financing, and for this reason the administration founded the Banco de Crédito Ejidal. During the Cárdenas years this agrarian bank made loans available to some thirty-five hundred ejidos.

The ejido was no economic or social panacea, however. A rapid population growth in rural Mexico tended to offset many of the gains, and the Banco de Crédito Ejidal did not possess sufficient capital to meet the continually growing demands. In addition, much favoritism and some corruption circumscribed the distribution of ejido loans. But more important yet, production of many ejidos, even the Laguna ejido, which received adequate loans from the agrarian bank, declined. Cotton production fell by almost nine thousand tons from 1936 to 1938, and henequen production on the new Yucatecan ejidos dropped by forty-five thousand tons during the same period.

Was the ejido program then a failure? The economists answered yes, but the administration was well aware that the redistribution of land would cause an initial decline in productivity. Cárdenas embarked upon the ejido program to meet a social, not an economic, need. The critics were harsh in their denunciation of cooperative agriculture, but what they could not deny was the unalterable fact that Cárdenas's dedication to agrarian reform spelled the demise of the traditional hacienda complex in Mexico. Millions of peasants were given a new faith in the revolutionary concept. While some argued with understandable conviction that the amount of land apportioned to each family under the ejido program was insufficient, and others suggested more theatrically that one form of peonage had simply replaced another, the fact remains that the type of servitude that had bound hacendado and peón for centuries was broken by 1940. Life in rural Mexico scarcely became idyllic as a result. Per capita income, infant mortality, and indeed life expectancy lagged behind that of the cities, but the gap in the quality of life between rural and urban Mexico began to be closed for the first time. If the ejido system was an economic failure, it was a political and social success.

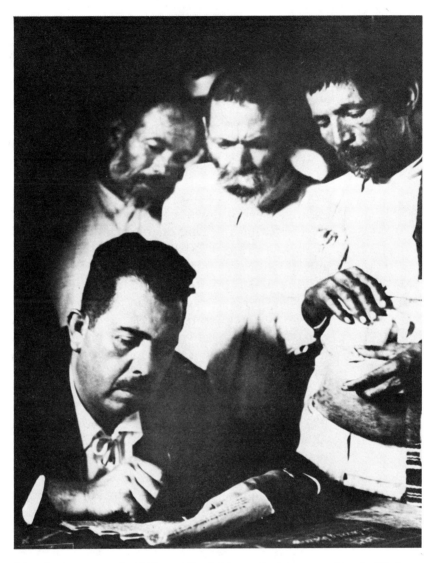

Distributing more land than all of his predecessors combined, Cárdenas here assigns a land title to a group of peasants.

The relationship between the administration and the church was conditioned almost entirely by Cárdenas's determination to implement Article 3 of the Constitution. There was no doubt that the president was an anticleric; during his campaign he had attacked the church frequently. In the state of Tabasco he had declared, "Man should not put his hope in the supernatural. Every moment spent on one's knees is a moment stolen from humanity."[2] When the PNR met in 1933 to nominate Cárdenas for the presidency, it adopted a platform that, among other things, called for the teaching of socialist doctrine in the primary and secondary schools. A new curriculum had previously been developed by the secretary of education, Narciso Bassols. The church was already incensed, but, when the hierarchy learned that sexual education would be offered in the public schools, parents were threatened with excommunication should they send their children to the anti-Catholic schools. Secretary Bassols resigned his position during the controversy, and the administration backed down somewhat on sexual instruction but not on socialist ideals. That another church strike or Cristero Rebellion was avoided is testimony to the good sense of both Cárdenas and the archbishop of Mexico, Luis María Martínez. In an important pastoral letter the archbishop implored the Mexican clergy to show more concern for the socioeconomic welfare of the masses. At the same time Cárdenas allowed that socialist education should be positive—it need not encompass antireligious propaganda in the classroom. Education itself, he believed, would eradicate fanaticism.

The federal expenditure for education in 1936 surpassed 10 million pesos for the first time in Mexican history; by 1940 it had reached 11.3 million pesos. Cárdenas earmarked twice as much for rural education as any previous president. But although more Mexicans could read and write than ever before, illiteracy was not curtailed. Inflation coupled with a high rate of population growth outran the educational budget, and, as a result, in 1940 there were two million more illiterates in Mexico than there had been only a decade before.

President Cárdenas also worked hard to strengthen the organized labor movement and to dominate it. Annoyed at the deep-seated corruption that had beset organized labor under Luis Morones, the president supported Vicente Lombardo Toledano, a onetime CROM lieutenant, in his effort to form a new national union. Much more intellectually oriented than Luis Morones, Lombardo Toledano embraced the Marxian class struggle as best explaining Mexico's historical reality and called for the establishment of a dictatorship of the proletariat. But, while he held that man was excessively acquisitive and competitive, Lombardo

---

2. Quoted in Albert L. Michaels, "The Modification of the Anti-Clerical Nationalism of the Mexican Revolution by General Lázaro Cárdenas and Its Relationship to the Church-State Detente in Mexico," *The Americas* 26 (1969): 37.

Toledano was no orthodox Communist. He never completely abandoned the humanism he had learned at the feet of Antonio Caso, and when forced to accept an anti-Marxist position he would explain that Mexico's problems were so unique as to require Mexican solutions. While he might have preferred public ownership of all property, he was practical enough to realize that partial socialization was better suited to the Mexican situation in the 1930s.

Lombardo Toledano succeeded in joining together some three thousand unions and six hundred thousand workers to form the Confederación de Trabajadores de México (CTM). The CTM made Lombardo Toledano its secretary general, and although Cárdenas did not give the secretary general a government position, he pledged to support his efforts. Within two years the membership had passed one million.

The CTM in its capacity as spokesman for the workers engaged in many different activities. It sponsored health and sanitation projects and organized a series of sports and recreational programs. But, most important, it concerned itself with improving the wage structure of the country. A survey in 1930 had estimated that the minimum daily wage on which a head of household might adequately support his family was four pesos and revealed, at the same time, that the average minimum wage in Mexico was one peso, six centavos. As Lombardo Toledano sought to rectify the wage structure in the country, he found himself blocked at every step by both Mexican and foreign management. Only by concerted effort did he finally succeed in having a new minimum wage of three pesos, fifty centavos adopted on a nationwide basis.

Nationalization of Oil Companies

Without question Cárdenas's most dramatic encounter during his six-year presidential term was the oil controversy with the United States, a matter that had ostensibly been resolved by his predecessors. The dispute began, innocently enough, as a conflict between labor and management within the petroleum industry. In 1936 Mexican workers struck for higher wages and better working conditions. While the oil workers were paid quite well in comparison to other Mexican laborers, the oil companies were extracting huge profits from the country and refused to negotiate seriously with union representatives. Worse yet, company policies more often than not demeaned the Mexican worker. To many, little had changed since the miners struck Colonel Greene's Cananea Consolidated Copper Company in 1906. As the strike in the oil industry began to weaken the Mexican economy, President Cárdenas ordered that the dispute be settled by an industrial arbitration board. The board examined the records of the companies and the living conditions of the workers and issued a decision ordering an increase in wages by one-third and an improved pension and welfare system. The companies, claiming that the order meant an increase in operating costs of over $7 million, appealed the decision to the Mexican Supreme Court, which ultimately upheld the original decision of the arbitration board. When the foreign-owned companies refused to obey the Supreme Court decision in its entirety, President Cárdenas held that they had flagrantly defied the sovereignty of the Mexican state and on March 18, 1938, signed a decree nationalizing the holdings of seventeen oil companies.

The nationalization decree became an immediate *cause célèbre*. Cárdenas received congratulatory telegrams from many other Latin American heads of state and evoked the patriotism of the vast majority of Mexicans. A few days after the decree was signed, a huge celebration was held in Mexico City to honor the stride for economic independence.

Cárdenas was reassured by the support he garnered, for he realized that the reaction would be quite different in the United States. Many United States newspapers expressed outrage, and not a few politicians called for intervention to head off a Communist conspiracy on the very borders of the United States. But there would be no intervention on this occasion, as Franklin D. Roosevelt had come to the United States presidency enunciating a new policy of nonintervention in Latin America. His ambassador to Mexico, Josephus Daniels, did his utmost to ensure that the oil companies negotiated in good faith. The compensation issue was fraught with difficulty, for the companies, led by Standard Oil of New Jersey, bombarded the United States public with articles and pamphlets vilifying Cárdenas and labeling the expropriation as common theft. While the companies claimed the value of the expropriated properties to be in the neighborhood of $200 million (and the British companies claimed an additional $250 million), Cárdenas countered that, since the original investment had been recovered several times and since the subsoil belonged to the Mexican nation, a just figure for the American companies was $10 million. Ultimately a mixed claims

Mexico's "Women's Workers' Army" supports the Cárdenas oil expropriation decree during the May Day celebration in 1938.

commission agreed upon a figure of almost $24 million, plus 3 percent interest effective from the day of expropriation.

A Change in Orientation

Shortly after the expropriation Cárdenas decided to alter the structure of the PNR, which Calles had created in 1929. Realizing that Mexico was embarking upon difficult economic times, the president wanted an even more broadly based national party and for that reason established the Partido Revolucionario Mexicano (PRM), with representation from four sectors of society: the military, labor, agrarian, and popular. Much like its predecessor, the PRM was the official party and would encounter no serious opposition in either state or national elections.

In 1938 the leftist revolution began to lose some of its thrust, and, in retrospect, the oil expropriations climaxed the socialist and nationalist orientation of Cárdenas's program. The president's last two years were characterized by severe economic difficulty. Wealthy Mexicans, fearful of the establishment of a communist state, refused to invest in the Mexican economy, and foreign capitalists looked elsewhere for lucrative investment fields. Cárdenas created a government oil company, Petróleos Mexicanos (PEMEX), to run the industry, but, inheriting antiquated machinery and a lack of trained technicians, it got off to a shaky start. The situation worsened when Cárdenas learned that he could not buy spare parts in the United States. As oil revenues declined, the national debt rose and confidence in the government lagged. Worst of all, rampant inflation set in. Between 1935 and 1940 food prices alone rose by a staggering 49.39 percent.

The reform program—school construction, benefits for labor, agrarian reform—was expensive, and cuts had to be made somewhere. As early as 1936 the president abandoned his experiments with socialist education. Land redistribution slowed down markedly after 1938 as Cárdenas implemented agrarian reform only when he needed political support. At the same time, he became more and more sensitive to labor agitation and strikes. Almost imperceptibly, the Mexican Revolution was shifting into a new phase. The change in policy was formalized in 1939 when the recently formed PRM met to choose its presidential candidate. It was expected that Cárdenas would throw his support to his long-time political ally, Francisco Múgica, but instead the president, believing it was time to change the orientation of the Revolution, supported his secretary of war, Manuel Avila Camacho, a conservative. Cárdenas's support assured Avila Camacho of the nomination, and the nomination assured him of victory.

As the Mexican Revolution was about to embark on a new course not all of the old problems had been resolved, but the Cárdenas administration was remarkable, nevertheless, for what it had done. It saw the end of one age and the beginning of another. Cárdenas had finally broken the back of the hacienda system, had fostered an impressive program of rural education, had seen that the labor movement was cleaned up and that it was reorganized into a new, powerful union, and had struck a sharp blow for Mexican economic nationalism when he failed to be bludgeoned by the oil companies. He had demonstrated that reform could progress without bringing the church crashing to its knees and without resorting to strong-arm tactics. With most critics, persuasion, he learned, yielded greater dividends than coercion. But, perhaps most important, by avoiding pivotal mistakes and not sacrificing principles to expediency, he won a new respect for the office he held as well as the plans he espoused.

By 1940 most of the goals envisioned by the revolutionaries of 1910 had been reached, and they would have considered Cárdenas's efforts a vindication of their sacrifices. But just as societies are seldom static, revolutions, if they are to be worthy of the name, must be continuing. The thirty years intervening since 1910 had begun to leave a legacy of new problems, and it was now time to reorder priorities and seek new solutions.

Recommended for Further Study

Ashby, Joe C. *Organized Labor and the Mexican Revolution under Cárdenas.* Chapel Hill: University of North Carolina Press, 1967.

Becker, Marjorie. "Black and White and Color: Cardenismo and the Search for a Campesino Ideology." *Comparative Studies in Society and History* 29 (1987): 453–65.

Britton, John A. "Teacher Unionization and the Corporate State in Mexico, 1931–1945." *Hispanic American Historical Review* 59 (1979): 674–90.

Brown, Lyle C. "Mexican Church–State Relations, 1933–1940." *Journal of Church and State* 6 (1964): 202–22.

Cronon, E. David. *Josephus Daniels in Mexico.* Madison: University of Wisconsin Press, 1942.

Daniels, Josephus. *Shirt-Sleeve Diplomat.* Chapel Hill: University of North Carolina Press, 1947.

Hilton, Stanley E. "The Church–State Dispute over Education in Mexico from Carranza to Cárdenas." *The Americas* 21 (1964): 163–83.

Koppes, Clayton R. "The Good Neighbor Policy and the Nationalization of Mexican Oil: A Reinterpretation." *Journal of American History* 69 (1982): 62–81.

Michaels, Albert L. "The Crisis of Cardenismo." *Journal of Latin American Studies* 2 (1970): 51–79.

————. "Fascism and Sinarquismo: Popular Nationalisms against the Mexican Revolution." *Journal of Church and State* 8 (1966): 234–50.

————. "The Modification of the Anti-Clerical Nationalism of the Mexican Revolution by General Lázaro Cárdenas and Its Relationship to the Church–State Detente in Mexico." *The Americas* 26 (1969): 35–53.

Michels, Elizabeth F. "Standard Oil of New Jersey Fights Mexican Expropriation, 1938–1942." Occasional Paper no. 1, Georgetown University Latin American Studies Program, 1980.

Millon, Robert P. *Mexican Marxist: Vicente Lombardo Toledano.* Chapel Hill: University of North Carolina Press, 1966.

Rippy, Merrill. "The Economic Repercussions of Expropriation: Case Study, Mexican Oil." *Inter-American Economic Affairs* 5 (1951): 52–70.

Ruiz, Ramón Eduardo. *Mexico: The Challenge of Poverty and Illiteracy.* San Marino, Calif.: Huntington Library, 1963.

Townsend, William Cameron. *Lázaro Cárdenas: Mexican Democrat.* Ann Arbor: Wahr, 1952.

Weyl, Nathaniel, and Sylvia Weyl. *The Reconquest of Mexico: The Years of Lázaro Cárdenas.* New York: Oxford University Press, 1939.

Wilkie, James W. *The Mexican Revolution: Federal Expenditure and Social Change since 1910.* Berkeley: University of California Press, 1967.

39

Society and Culture
from Obregón to Cárdenas

Daily Life in Countryside and City

Between 1920 and 1940 the lives of average Mexicans changed more rapidly than they had in any previous twenty-year period. The population decline of the decade of violence stopped, and, with the greater political stability of the 1920s and 1930s, the number of people began to climb rapidly. When Obregón came to office in 1920 the total population of the country was slightly over 14 million, but when Cárdenas turned over the presidency to his successor twenty years later the total had almost reached 20 million.

Mexico was not yet an urban country when Cárdenas's term ended, although the percentage of population living in communities with fewer than twenty-five hundred people had slipped from about 70 percent in 1920 to some 65 percent in 1940. It was in the rural areas that the change in life-style was most dramatic. The percentage of people who wore neither shoes nor sandals declined markedly, as did the percentage of illiterates. By 1940 cultural anthropologists found it difficult to find many of those quaint Indians who spoke a native tongue exclusively.

The new *ejidatario* in rural Mexico, unlike his peón forefather, was no longer bound to the hacienda. He could travel as freely as his pocketbook allowed. It was no longer necessary to purchase daily necessities in the tienda de raya, but if he did shop in the ejido store he would likely find prices somewhat lower than those in the nearby community. The old mayordomos, of course, were gone, and in most cases ejido officials were elected by the ejidatarios themselves.

Thousands of families who had fled their villages in search of security during the early Revolution returned to find that some impressive changes were taking place. Blacktop highways began to supplant bumpy dirt roads, and buses rolled over them with more or less regularity. Bicycles began to push burros off the highways. Tractors challenged the ox-drawn plow. Gasoline engines, rather than mules or horses, turned the mills that ground the corn, and gasoline pumps drew the water from nearby streams. Electricity arrived even in some small towns.

Some of the major changes in Tzintzuntzan, Michoacán, in the 1930s were recorded by the anthropologist George M. Foster.

> The first major cultural impact of modern times occurred . . . in the spring of 1931. General Lázaro Cárdenas, then Governor of Michoacán, sent a Cultural Mission consisting of teachers who specialized in plastic arts, social work, music, home economics, physical education, and "small industries," and a nurse-midwife and an agricultural engineer. . . . Most villagers were reluctant to cooperate, to help find living quarters, and to aid staff members and rural teachers. . . . In spite of such difficulties, however, the Mission had a big effect. A number of the more progressive families agreed to whitewash their houses, to improve the appearance of the village, and the present plaza, then a barren wasteland with a few houses, was cleaned up, sidewalks were marked out, flowering jacaranda trees were planted, a fountain . . . was built . . . and place was cleared for a bandstand. At the end of the first month there was an open house exposition of arts, crafts, sports, and civic betterments, to which General Cárdenas came as guest of honor. . . . Changes now began to come more rapidly. . . . Electricity was brought in from Pátzcuaro in 1938 and running water . . . was installed about the same time. . . . By 1938 the road was graded, and in 1939 it was paved. Tzintzuntzan was now an hour from the state capital, Morelia, instead of a very long day's walk or ride. . . . In 1939 the new and modern *Escuela Rural 2 de Octubre*, named to commemorate the date of Tzintzuntzan's independence, opened its doors, and for the first time village children had ready access to the full six years of primary schooling.[1]

The rural school in the 1920s and 1930s became the focal point of village life. Economic and social activity centered on programs initiated by the rural teachers, and cultural life for the first time was dominated more by the school than the church. Daily tasks became somewhat easier, and, with the gradual extension of

---

1. George M. Foster, *Tzintzuntzan: Mexican Peasants in a Changing World* (Boston, 1967), pp. 26–29.

medical facilities into the village, life expectancy improved and the infant mortality rate dropped from 222 deaths per thousand in 1920 to 125 twenty years later. But by no means did all of the essentials of the good life come to rural Mexico between 1920 and 1940. Poverty continued to be the single most pervasive characteristic of rural life. Although it was no longer accurate to suggest that rural Mexicans continued to live as they had since the days of the Conquest, most had not yet really been incorporated into the mainstream of national life.

City life became more pleasant, at least, for some, as the amenities of technology became increasingly commonplace. Mexico's first commercial radio station began transmission in 1923, and scores huddled around each neighbor lucky enough to own or have access to a receiver. Two years later the Department of Education established its own radio station and began beaming educational broadcasts to primary schools recently equipped with receivers. By the mid-1930s the commercial cinema had begun to challenge the bullfight for pre-eminence in entertainment. The most interesting films were those of patriotic content depicting the glories of the Revolution, like Ezequiel Carrasco's *Viva México* (1934) and Luis Lezama's *El Cementerio de los Aguilas* (1938). But the greatest commercial success was Fernando de Fuentes's musical *Allá en el Rancho Grande* (1936), starring Tito Guízar and Esther Fernández. The extraordinary box office profits of this film led to a cinematographic genre of folk films, soon to be dominated by two towering figures of popular culture, Jorge Negrete and Pedro Infante.

Without question, it was the internal combustion engine that most changed the life style of the urban areas. The motor car had arrived in Mexico shortly before the outbreak of hostilities in 1910, but, because of the tremendous dislocations of that first revolutionary decade, it did not begin to transform Mexican life until after 1920. By 1925 fifty-three thousand motor vehicles were digesting thirty-five million gallons of gasoline annually; fifteen years later the number of vehicles had tripled and gasoline consumption had quadrupled. In the early 1920s the motor vehicle was still a prestige symbol, carrying a select few to and from their offices or their families on an occasional weekend outing. Later in the decade motor car racing became popular, and often left a toll of killed or injured. But by the 1930s, with a tremendous increase in the number of trucks and buses, the internal combustion engine had transformed commercial life as well as disrupted staid social patterns. Automobiles, trucks, and buses

As Mexico left the era of the silent film and moved into the age of sound Fernando de Fuentes's *Allá en el Rancho Grande* awoke world interest in the Mexican cinema.

required an expanded highway network, and Mexican engineers and day laborers completed several thousand miles of new, hard-surface roads during the twenty-year period.

The growth of Mexico City was nothing short of spectacular. The high national rate of population growth, coupled with an internal migration from rural to urban areas, gave Mexico City with a population of 1,726,858 in 1940, an increase of more than one million in only two decades. The dramatic growth yielded its share of social problems as neither the job market nor the school system could absorb the tremendous influx. Those fleeing to the capital in search of a better life were more often than not disappointed. Rapid growth in other cities also caused difficulties for tens of thousands of recent arrivals. While Mexicans laughed with derision at the prohibition experiment in the United States, alcoholic consumption rose sufficiently in Mexico in the 1920s to cause alarm in the medical and scientific communities.

Life for the Mexican woman was slow to change, and her special burdens inevitably evoked compassion from foreign visitors. Verna Carleton Millan, a North American, was appalled at what she found.

> The American woman who marries into a Mexican family has a gigantic task of readjustment before her; by the mere act of crossing the border, she slips into a world that has many features of the middle ages. . . . Her first psychological shock will take place

when she realizes that in Mexico women are still considered inferior beings, unfit to manage their own lives or assume any position of responsibility. . . . The Mexican woman of today, the woman of the towns and larger cities, has this enormous burden of race and tradition upon her shoulders; product of a mestizo culture, she is caught in the mesh of not one but two traditions, both equally repressive. The Spaniards brought to Mexico the strict Catholicism that has held women in a subjective, passive role for centuries. On the other hand, the Indian tribes since time immemorial have crushed the spirit of their women beneath iron-clad taboos and repressions. . . . Within the home, the man reigns supreme, a heritage from the middle ages. The daughters are taught absolute obedience not only to their fathers but to their brothers as well. If there is a little money in the family, the sons are educated at the expense of the daughters. . . . Marriage is considered the supreme goal of every woman's life. The mother's marriage may have been a life-long tragedy, but she can conceive of no other fate for her daughters, on the theory that any kind of marriage is better than none because at least one thus fulfills the Christian command to multiply.[2]

The censure was essentially correct, but without the advantage of historical perspective Mrs. Millan could not have known that change, albeit almost imperceptible change, was taking place. More and more women were entering the worlds of business, education, government service, and medicine. Between 1920 and 1924 only 223 Mexican women received university degrees; ten years later the figure had doubled. By 1930 women were participating more actively in civic work than at any previous time, and hundreds of thousands had successfully rebelled against family-arranged marriages. In 1900 a woman in Mexico City would not have dreamed of carrying a placard of protest in a parade. By the time Cárdenas left office such activities were commonplace.

The feminist movement in Mexico was amorphous until 1935, when the United Front for Women's Rights was founded in Mexico City. With a membership of more than fifty thousand by 1940, the Front coordinated the efforts and defined the goals on a national basis. More important than anything else was the campaign to win for women the right to vote. Arguing the absurdity of disenfranchising women along with former convicts, fugitives from justice, and inmates of insane asylums, the Front assumed the offensive and, with Cárdenas's support, did manage to win the right to vote in a number of states. Woman's suffrage

2. Verna Carleton Millan, *Mexico Reborn* (Boston, 1939), pp. 148–58.

in national elections would have to wait a few more years, but the predisposition was clearly set by 1940.

The Intelligentsia of the Revolution

Mexican culture during the period 1920 to 1940 came to the service of the Revolution. The artistic, literary, and scholarly communities, with an abiding faith in the new thrust of Mexican life, supported revolutionary ideals by contributing their unique talents to awakening the consciousness of the new social order. The process is nowhere better illustrated than in the cultural achievements of Mexico's most famous painters.

The restlessness of Mexico's artistic community had been apparent during the late Porfiriato and during the first revolutionary decade, but Mexican art came into its own and won world acclaim after 1920. While secretary of education, José Vasconcelos commissioned leading artists to fill the walls of public buildings with didactic murals, and Mexico's artistic renaissance occurred in the process. Art was no longer directed to the privileged few who could afford to buy a canvas; it was for the public. If Mexico was not yet able to provide a classroom and a

A detail from Rufino Tamayo's *Allegories of Music and Song* (1933).

David Alfaro Siqueiros, *Head of an Indian.*

Juan O'Gorman, *Enemies of the Mexican People.*

seat for every child in the country, some measure of popular education could be provided by a muralist movement carried out on a scale grander than any the world had yet known.

Vasconcelos, while supplying the government subsidy, was too much the free intellectual to place any constraints on the artists. Coordinating his efforts with the artists' union, the Syndicate of Technical Workers, Painters, and Sculptors, he instructed the artist simply to paint Mexican subjects. To be sure, youthful enthusiasm carried some astray, but giants such as Jean Charlot, Rufino Tamayo, Juan O'Gorman, David Alfaro Siqueiros, Fernando Leal, and Roberto Montenegro emerged in the process as well. Two of the muralists began to dominate the movement and set themselves apart from their talented compatriots.

During the 1920s and 1930s Diego Rivera (1885–1957) became the most renowned artist in the western hemisphere and one of the most imposing artists of the twentieth century. A man of boundless talent and energy, he used the Indian as his basic motif. Rivera's realistic murals did not invite freedom of interpretation, and he depicted humanistic messages for the illiterate masses on the walls of the Agricultural School in Chapingo, the Cortés Palace in Cuernavaca, the National Preparatory School, the Department of Education, and the National Palace in Mexico City. The Spaniard during the colonial period, and his criollo offspring during the nineteenth century, had enslaved the Indian and had kept him in abject poverty. It was now time to incorporate the Indian into the mainstream of society just as Rivera was incorporating him into the mainstream of his murals. Although Rivera was more interested in content than in form, he was without rival in technique. His symmetry was near perfect, but his genius emerged even more clearly in his use of line and color. The Indians were invariably depicted in soft, gentle lines, with earthen red and brown tones, while the oppressors, white foreigners and white Mexicans, were portrayed in sharp lines and harsh colors.

Rivera's greatest masterpiece was composed at the Agricultural School at Chapingo, formerly the private hacienda of President Manuel González. With esthetic originality and flamboyance, Rivera spelled out his appreciation of the new revolutionary ideology. Not only did his frescoes display the virtues of land

Details from Diego Rivera's mural in the Agricultural School at Chapingo.

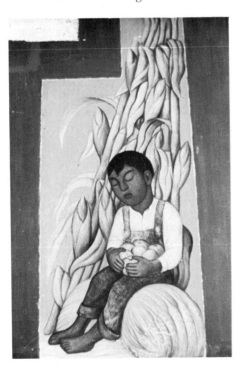 

Diego Rivera's *Awaiting the Harvest* (1923), a fresco in the Court of Labor, Department of Education.

Diego Rivera's *The Billionaires*, a mural in the Department of Education, satirizes international capitalism.

redistribution, but they instructed in the lessons of sociopolitical reality. On one wall he portrayed bad government—the peasants betrayed by false politicians, fat capitalists, and mercenary priests. But the opposite wall was one of revolutionary hope—a scene of agricultural cultivation, a rich harvest, and a liberated peasantry. Just in case the message might be lost, he painted over the main stairway of the building, "Here it is taught to exploit the land, not man."

Only slightly less famous than Rivera, but no less a genius, was José Clemente Orozco (1883–1949). As the violent decade passed, Orozco abandoned his career as a biting political caricaturist for mural art. Less a realist than Rivera, Orozco could be more forceful, expressive, and passionate. He was willing to experiment with new techniques as well as themes. His brutal and

José Clemente Orozco's *Modern Migration of the Spirit* (1933) from the fresco *Quetzalcóatl and the Aspirations of Mankind* was painted at Dartmouth College.

distorted Christs, grotesque depictions of God, and nude Madonnas pilloried all religious piety and brought forth a storm of protest. Some of his frescos were mutilated by angry crowds, but Vasconcelos did not interfere with Orozco's freedom of expression. Orozco's scenes of violence during the Revolution bring to mind Francisco Goya's *Horrors of War*, and he might well have had the Spanish master in mind when he conceived them.

Orozco had his tender moments too. During the 1920s, when he could see the first hesitant steps of social progress, some of his murals portray hope. His famous fresco, *Cortés and Malinche*, shows two nude and carnal figures sitting over the figure of the old, prostrate Mexico, and represents the miscegenation process, the biological and spiritual origin of the Mexican people. But in the 1930s, even as the pace of social reform began to accelerate, Orozco became increasingly disillusioned with the progress being made. After spending several years in the United States, he returned to his native Jalisco, and in the Instituto Cabañas in Guadalajara he decided to return to the theme of the Conquest. The new Cortés he portrayed was a powerful, violent conqueror in full armor and with sword in hand. The only hope held out is that the spirit whispering in Cortés's ear might convince him to use his power and technology for good rather than for evil.

The painters were not alone in transforming a national art into a nationalistic one. The literary community contributed as well with its novels of the Revolution. Two of the best came from the pen of Martín Luis Guzmán (1887–1976), who published *El águila y la serpiente* (translated as *The Eagle and the Serpent*) in 1928 and *La sombra del caudillo* the following year. The first constitutes a novelized personal memoir of the young Guzmán who left the comfortable life of a university student to join the Revolution and found himself a Villista. Captivated by Villa's personality, yet always afraid of his violence, Guzmán sketched the Centaur of the North most vividly in his discussion of revolutionary justice.

> This man wouldn't exist if his pistol didn't exist. . . . It isn't merely an instrument of action with him; it's a fundamental part of his being, the axis of his work and his amusement, the constant expression of his most intimate self, his soul given outward form.

José Clemente Orozco's fresco, *Cortés and Malinche.*

> Between the fleshy curve of his index finger and the rigid curve of the trigger there exists the relation that comes from the contact of one being with another. When he fires, it isn't the pistol that shoots, it's the man himself. Out of his very heart comes the ball as it leaves the sinister barrel. The man and the pistol are the same thing.[3]

Villa did not turn out to be the ideal man Guzmán had hoped for. The intellectual simply could not communicate with the people's hero and ultimately took his leave. Guzmán never abandoned his revolutionary faith, but he began to wonder whether the goals could be attained without all the violence.

Guzmán's disenchantment with the politics of the Revolution is even more evident in *La sombra del caudillo*, a novel inspired by the presidential election of 1928, which saw opposition candidates Francisco Serrano and Arnulfo Gómez both dead by election day. Mexico's most powerful novel decrying dictatorship, *La sombra del caudillo* is written with truculence and righteous indignation. But even here Guzmán does not give up on the Revolution. To the contrary, the passionate condemnation was directed against Calles for having betrayed the ideals of the movement.

The Indianist novel of the Revolution reached its apex in 1935 with Gregorio López y Fuentes's *El Indio*. Without naming a single character or place, López y Fuentes is able to portray the Indian, not as the noble savage, but as a man beset with social problems that society can help to overcome. The plot is not intricate, as the author was more interested in atmosphere. He admirably succeeded not only in illustrating the wide chasm between Indian and white society but also in making intelligible the deepest suspicions of whites harbored in the Indian community. López y Fuentes was awarded Mexico's first National Prize for Literature for this perceptive novel.

The cultural nationalism focusing on the Indian was carried into the arena of music by Carlos Chávez (1899–1978). After studying in Europe and the United States, in his late twenties Chávez returned to Mexico to become director of the National Conservatory of Music and to begin a brilliant career as a conductor, pianist, musical scholar, and composer. His *Sinfonía India* (1935) and *Xochipili-Macuilxochitl* (1940) were scored for pre-Columbian instruments, but, realizing that not all performing orchestras would be able to acquire such esoteric accouterments as strings

---

3. Martín Luis Guzmán, *The Eagle and the Serpent*, trans. Harriet de Onís (Garden City, N.Y., 1965), p. 210.

of deer hooves, he made provision for modern substitutes. But both rhythmically and melodically the compositions were inspired by Mexico's aboriginal heritage. Though Chávez was Mexico's most distinguished musician, he, like the muralists, wanted to reach the people, and he composed two important works, *Llamadas* (1934) and *Obertura republicana* (1935), based upon familiar Mexican tunes. As a result, Chávez enjoyed a popular as well as a sophisticated audience.

Anthropologists led the way among social scientists in the redefinition of cultural values. With the publication in 1922 of Manuel Gamio's highly important three-volume *La población del valle de Teotihuacán*, Mexican archeologists, ethnologists, and social anthropologists began to take a new look not only at antiquities but at contemporary Indian problems as well. Rejecting theories of racial inferiority and the anti-Indian posture of many nineteenth-century intellectuals, they set out to depict the glories of the Indian past, to restore Indian arts and crafts, and in general to revitalize contemporary Indian culture. Their efforts were greatly facilitated in 1936 when the government established a Departamento Autónomo de Asuntos Indígenas and three years later the Instituto Nacional de Antropología e Historia.

While artists, novelists, musicians, and even anthropologists could mature and prosper with the overriding ideological assumptions of the Revolution, historians encountered problems in their quest for historical truth. Rejecting the positivist tradition that had permeated historical scholarship during the late nineteenth century, the historian of the 1920s and 1930s found no new ideological peg on which to hang his hat. As his discipline was called upon to serve as one of the many vehicles for the apotheosis of the Revolution, he was confronted with an apparently irreconcilable dichotomy: should he serve the interests of the movement or of historical scholarship in those cases in which reality suggested that the two did not converge? The overwhelming majority chose to be loved rather than candid.

Once accepting that the Revolution embodied all virtue, it was necessary to deprecate the real or imagined enemies of the movement in the most scathing terms. The pervading frame of reference thus became prorevolutionary, the historians disagreeing with one another only on the question of which of the many revolutionary protagonists was most orthodox in his revolutionary commitment. Crimes of the Revolution were dismissed on grounds of political necessity, while those of the opposition were portrayed as barbarisms of the worst kind. The Díaz regime, of course, was denounced in the harshest terms with scarcely a redeeming phrase offered in its defense. But the important questions of the day—the goals of the Revolution and the means of implementing these goals—were never brought into sharp focus. One must conclude that historical scholarship did not meet the standards of other cultural endeavors.

In spite of the mediocre record of Mexican historians from 1920 to 1940, the country's overall cultural production was remarkable during those two decades. With contempt for convention, the intelligentsia suffused the environment with a new confidence. The illiterate, the petit bourgeois, the pseudosophisticate, and the intellectual could all take genuine pleasure in the tremendous flowering of culture. It was no time for the romantic landscape, the vaporous abstraction, or the unintelligible dream-sequence novel. Art and literature, as well as the social sciences, had to come to the service of the Revolution, repudiating the traditions of the recent past, satirizing the heresies of the present, and commending the material and social conquests of tomorrow.

Unequaled in Latin America, those twenty years of cultural vitality and strength captured the Mexican spirit and yielded a sense of national purpose and pride. The intellectual community did not portray Mexico as an idyllic world or expect a perfect state to arise from imperfect men. But most agreed with the philosopher Antonio Caso, who suggested forcefully in his eloquent *Principios de estética* (1925) that a meaningful morality had to be based on sacrifice and love. The enthusiasm of the intellectuals rested with their realization that after centuries of indelible stigmata, Mexico had embarked upon a compassionate social experiment that drew its strength from the best of human instincts. Although tangible progress was admittedly slow, the system had not proved to be incorrigible. Self-assured by world acclaim, the Mexican intelligentsia could never again feel constrained to look toward Europe for hallowed cultural standards. But, more important, the revolutionary beneficence they portrayed penetrated Mexican society deeply. The fighting was now over, and from that sorrow and adversity something positive had been born.

Recommended for Further Study

Beals, Ralph L. "Anthropology in Contemporary Mexico." In *Contemporary Mexico: Papers of the IV International Congress of Mexican History*, edited by James W. Wilkie, Michael C. Meyer, and Edna

Monzón de Wilkie, pp. 753–68. Berkeley: University of California Press, 1975.

Brenner, Anita. *Idols behind Altars: The Story of the Mexican Spirit.* Boston: Beacon Press, 1970.

Brushwood, John S. *Mexico in Its Novel: A Nation's Search for Identity.* Austin: University of Texas Press, 1966.

Charlot, Jean. *The Mexican Mural Renaissance, 1920–1925.* New Haven, Conn.: Yale University Press, 1967.

Fernández, Justino. *A Guide to Mexican Art: From Its Beginnings to the Present.* Chicago: University of Chicago Press, 1969.

Guzmán, Martín Luis. *The Eagle and the Serpent.* Translated by Harriet de Onís. Garden City, N.Y.: Doubleday, 1965.

Hale, Charles, and Michael C. Meyer. "Mexico: The National Period." In *Latin American Scholarship since World War II*, edited by Roberto Esquenazi-Mayo and Michael C. Meyer, pp. 115–38. Lincoln: University of Nebraska Press, 1971.

Johnson, William W. "The Tumultuous Life and Times of the Painter Diego Rivera." *Smithsonian* 16 (1986): 36–51.

López y Fuentes, Gregorio. *El Indio.* New York: Ungar, 1961.

Millan, Verna Carleton, *Mexico Reborn.* Boston: Houghton Mifflin, 1939.

Mora, Carl J. *Mexican Cinema: Reflections of a Society, 1896–1980.* Berkeley: University of California Press, 1982.

Reed, Alma. *Orozco.* New York: Oxford University Press, 1956.

Salmerón, Francisco. "Mexican Philosophers of the Twentieth Century." In *Major Trends in Mexican Philosophy*, edited by Mario de la Cueva et al., pp. 246–87. Notre Dame, Ind.: University of Notre Dame Press, 1966.

Siqueiros, David Alfaro. *Art and Revolution.* London: Lawrence and Wishart, 1975.

Sommers, Joseph. *After the Storm.* Albuquerque: University of New Mexico Press, 1968.

Stevenson, Robert. *Music in Mexico: A Historical Survey.* New York: Crowell, 1971.

Turner, Frederick C. *The Dynamic of Mexican Nationalism.* Chapel Hill: University of North Carolina Press, 1968.

Wolfe, Bertram D. *The Fabulous Life of Diego Rivera.* New York: Stein and Day, 1969.

X THE REVOLUTION SHIFTS GEARS: MEXICO SINCE 1940

40

From Revolution to Evolution, 1940-46

The Administration of Avila Camacho

To some, Mexico's presidential election of 1940 marked the end of the Revolution; to others that same political exercise was simply the harbinger of a new approach to problem solving. Many contemporary political pundits predicted that Cárdenas would give his support to Francisco Múgica, an aging radical with impeccable revolutionary credentials. The conservatives, terrified at the prospect of further socialization of the country, rallied behind Juan Andreu Almazán. A wealthy Catholic landowner who even attracted fascist support to his camp, Almazán won the endorsement of the Partido de Acción Nacional (PAN), a conservative party later to be dominated by urban industrialists. But the official party candidate supported by Cárdenas turned out to be not Múgica but Secretary of War General Manuel Avila Camacho, an honest moderate and scarcely a social revolutionary.

The Mexican citizenry knew little about Avila Camacho prior to the 1940 presidential campaign; in fact, he was nicknamed "the Unknown Soldier." Avila Camacho had joined the Revolution in 1914 and gradually worked his way up through the military ranks. His reputation in the army was one of a compromiser rather than a forceful leader. During the course of the campaign, when asked about his feelings toward the church, he answered with the words, *Soy creyente* (I am a believer). The candid response presaged things to come. It meant specifically, of course, that anticlericalism was not going to be a part of his administration, but more generally it meant that the orientation of the Revolution was about to undergo a fundamental change. No longer would the implementation of Articles 3, 27, and 123 be considered the touchstone of social progress. If the Mexican people were surprised that a candidate for the presidency dared to confess his faith so openly, the leaders of the PRM were not. The politicians who gave Avila Camacho the nomination knew that he was much more conservative than Cárdenas. With the war in Europe threatening the Mexican economy, they, like their leader, felt it was time to change the direction of the movement. Cárdenas himself had recognized the need to slow down during his last year and a half in office.

Official party nomination meant victory on election day. Avila Camacho defeated Almazán soundly and, on December 1, 1940, became the fifty-seventh president of Mexico. His inaugural address, read with United States Vice-President Henry Wallace attending the ceremony, suggested that the Revolution was over, that its tasks had been completed and that Mexico was moving from a period of revolution to a period of evolution. To be sure, he took pride in what had been accomplished since 1910, but Mexico could no longer afford to look backward. It was now time to look to the future. "Each new epoch," he instructed the nation, "demands a rebirth of ideas. The clamor of the entire republic now demands the material and spiritual consolidation of our social conquests in a prosperous and powerful economy. It demands an era of construction of abundant life, of economic expansion."[1]

Because the new president was determined to embark upon new programs, he began to phase out some of the old. Land redistribution did not stop entirely, but the pace certainly slowed. Whereas Cárdenas had distributed over 49 million acres, Avila Camacho parceled out fewer than 12 million. In addition, because he favored small, private ownership, emphasis was no longer placed on distribution to the ejido but rather to the heads of individual families.

Avila Camacho's educational program also reflected a change of direction. First of all, the ideology of the socialist school was abandoned, and great emphasis was placed on private initiative. Under the slogan "Each one teach one," the president and his secretary of education, Jaime Torres Bodet, had the Congress enact a law exhorting each literate Mexican to instruct one or more illiterates in the fundamentals of reading and writing. The program began amidst great fanfare with the president, his cabinet

1. Quoted in Betty Kirk, *Covering the Mexican Front: The Battle of Europe vs. America* (Norman, 1942), p. 320.

secretaries, and much of the federal and state bureaucracy setting aside an hour each day to give practical reading instruction.
To encourage compliance, some public employees were fined for
failure to cooperate. States initiated incentive plans of various
kinds; Oaxaca promised a new school for the village that compiled the best record, and Michoacán reduced the sentences of
prisoners who learned to read and write. Soon, however, the original enthusiasm lagged, and the program slacked off. Obviously,
private initiative was not going to achieve what neither church
nor state had been able to accomplish over centuries—the elimination of illiteracy.

The president replaced Marxist labor leader Vicente Lombardo Toledano with the much more conservative Fidel Velásquez. Lombardo Toledano's departing speech was caustic and
indicated his anger at the recent turn of events. "I leave this
office a rich man," he declared, "rich in the hatred of the bourgeoisie."[2] The press, for some time having portrayed Lombardo
Toledano as inordinately egotistical, pointed out that he had used
the word *I* sixty-four times in the farewell address and took the
occasion to dub him "the Yo-yo Champion."

Under Velásquez's leadership, government support of the CTM
was held to a minimum. Rejecting what he judged to be Communist domination of the confederation, Velásquez supported
moderate elements within the union, and their requests to him
were modest indeed. Although small increases in wages were
won by the new labor leader, they did not keep pace with the
rapidly growing inflation that engulfed the Mexican economy.
All areas of the country were hit, but especially Mexico City.

COST OF LIVING IN MEXICO CITY
(Base year 1939 = 100)

Year	Food	Clothing	Services
1939	97.6	104.1	111.8
1940	97.0	114.4	102.9
1941	106.0	127.2	143.3
1942	119.1	156.4	153.9
1943	161.4	217.6	219.7
1944	188.8	241.9	235.7
1945	225.6	261.8	239.9

Source: Jorge Vera Estañol, *Historia de la revolución mexicana: Orígenes y resultados* (Mexico, 1967), p. 737.

2. Quoted in ibid., p. 90.

The entire philosophy of the union movement changed. Velásquez did not even protest vigorously when the administration
enacted measures limiting the use of strikes. Progressive and radical affiliates of the confederation were displeased with the new
leadership, and in 1942 workers from the textile and building
trades industries withdrew from the CTM. The most important
potential benefit to accrue to the workingman was the creation
of a social security agency, the Instituto Mexicano de Seguro Social (IMSS), in 1943, but the initial coverage was so limited
that only a small percentage of the workers fell under the program at this time. When Avila Camacho left office fewer than
250,000 workers were participating.

World War II

World War II broke out in Europe while Lázaro Cárdenas was in
the last year of his term, and the president left it to his successor
to define Mexico's position. After the Russo-German nonaggres-
sion pact of 1939, both the Mexican left, led by Lombardo Toledano and Múgica, and the right, led by Almazán, adopted a pro-
German position. But when in the summer of 1941 Hitler broke
his promises and ordered the Wehrmacht toward Moscow and
Leningrad, the Mexican left could no longer support the Axis
cause. President Avila Camacho enunciated an unmistakably
pro-Allied course of action, and only a few Mexican fascists and
neo-fascists failed to support him. One day after the Japanese attack on Pearl Harbor, Mexico broke diplomatic relations with
the Axis powers and Secretary of Foreign Relations Ezequiel Padilla took the lead in urging other Latin American countries to
support the Allies.

Most Mexicans were satisfied that breaking diplomatic relations was sufficient and that the ultimate step of declaring war
was unnecessary. The United States and Mexico appointed members to a joint defense board, and Avila Camacho deported German, Italian, and Japanese diplomats from Mexico. In March
of 1942, when the president participated in the opening of the
new Benjamin Franklin Library in Mexico City, he pointed to
the stark cultural contrast between free societies who valued
books and the Nazis who burned them. But Mexico would not
have entered the war had not Germany forced its hand. On the
night of May 14 a German submarine operating in the Caribbean torpedoed and sank the *Potrero de Llano*, a Mexican tanker

that was fully lighted and properly identified. Although a number of leftist organizations favored an immediate declaration of war, Avila Camacho instead sent an ultimatum to Germany demanding full satisfaction and proper indemnification. Germany's answer was forthcoming. On May 24 a second Mexican tanker, the *Faja de Oro*, was torpedoed. Thereupon the president went before the Congress and announced that, although Mexico had tried to avoid war, the country could no longer accept dishonor passively. He asked for and, without serious debate, received his declaration of war.

Many Mexican intellectuals were less shocked at being at war than they were embarrassed at being formally allied with the United States. But on September 16, 1942, on the 132nd anniversary of the Grito de Dolores, an amazing and unprecedented display of camaraderie occurred on the balcony of the National Palace. Six former presidents—Adolfo de la Huerta, Plutarco Elías Calles (invited to return from the United States), Emilio Portes Gil, Pascual Ortiz Rubio, Abelardo Rodríguez, and Lázaro Cárdenas—linked arms with Avila Camacho to indicate that past antagonisms had been forgotten and that Mexico was fully united in time of war.

Secretary of Interior Miguel Alemán was charged with eliminating subversive activity within the national boundaries. Once a stiff espionage act passed the Congress, he began seizing German, Italian, and Japanese properties including banks, drug firms, hardware stores, and coffee plantations to prevent them from being used as bases of propaganda or espionage. Several German agents, most notably Gestapo officers George Nicolaus and Karl Hellerman, were arrested, and Alemán's secret service also rooted out several enemy agents operating clandestine radio stations relaying instructions to German submarines in the Atlantic. Mexico's valuable oil fields and munitions factories were placed under strict military control. Some modernization of the Mexican army occurred as military supplies were received through the Lend-Lease program of the United States.

The Avila Camacho administration also moved to provide a small military contingent for service with the Allies. After consultation with the members of the joint defense board it was decided that an air force squadron—Squadron 201—should be prepared for duty in the Far East. The Mexican aviators and support personnel received their training in the United States and were assigned to the Fifth Air Corps in the Philippines. Squadron 201 participated in bombing and strafing raids in the Philippines

May Day demonstrators destroy a Nazi flag in front of a German-owned electric company.

Mexican nurses march in support of the war effort.

and Formosa in early 1945, and some Mexicans lost their lives. After the war the squadron received commendations from General Douglas MacArthur and a hero's welcome upon return to Mexico.

More important than token military support were the strategic war materials Mexico provided for the Allied war effort. Zinc, copper, lead, mercury, graphite, and cadmium flowed into United States war plants and were transformed into military products. The increased demand for these raw materials could have caused prices to soar, but the Mexican government instituted price controls as further testimony of its cooperation.

The most unique, and ultimately the most controversial, contribution to the war effort was the mutual decision made by Avila Camacho and Franklin D. Roosevelt to allow Mexican laborers (*braceros*) to serve as agricultural workers in the United States Southwest. The draft in the United States had depleted the work force, and the Mexicans in many ways picked up the slack as they began to harvest major crops. The terms of the agreement were carefully spelled out: the workers were to receive free transportation to and from their homes; they were not to displace United States workers or to be used to suppress wages; minimum wages were set at 46 cents an hour (later raised to 57 cents); and Mexican labor officials were authorized to make periodic inspections to certify that the rules were being enforced. By the spring of 1943, in spite of the opposition of organized labor in the United States, the program was expanded to include nonagricultural labor as well. When the war ended, the bracero program was well entrenched as some three hundred thousand Mexicans had worked in twenty-five different states, some as far north as Minnesota and Wisconsin. But innumerable difficulties had beset the program, for the regulations were not always enforced and the workers encountered deep-seated prejudices in the United States.

Industrialization

Although it would be an exaggeration to suggest that Mexico's support during World War II materially influenced the outcome, nevertheless its contribution was more substantial than that of any other Latin American country. Moreover, the war was of singular importance for Mexico's internal development. It marked improved relations with the United States and an end to

With thousands of men working as braceros in the United States, Mexican women were called upon to serve the country by working in industry, in the fields, and at home.

the intense and bitter factionalism that had been born with the Revolution. But most important, it contributed in a major way to the acceleration of the country's economic development.

Wartime shortages in the United States and Europe deprived Mexico of its normal source of imported manufactured goods and convinced even the doubters of the need for industrialization. The goal was not simply to meet the demands of the domestic market but to produce a surplus of manufactured goods for export to other Latin American countries. Even during the last years of the Cárdenas administration, Mexican social scientists had begun to argue the absurdity of dividing the same pie into smaller and smaller pieces. For the Revolution to realize its ultimate goal of providing a better life for the vast majority of the people, it was imperative that the country's economic base be expanded, and this could be accomplished only through a major program of industrialization. The program not only would provide additional employment for a rapidly growing population but, through increased productivity, would generate wealth and improve the standard of living for the masses.

To foster industrial expansion the Avila Camacho administration established the Nacional Financiera, a government-owned bank created primarily to provide loans to industry but also to oversee the industrial process. In each year of the administration the favorable loans of the Nacional Financiera increased dramatically, reaching a total of 286.8 million pesos by 1945.

In addition, other incentives, such as tax exemptions and tariff protection, persuaded potential investors that the risks were acceptable. With the CTM in the hands of moderate Fidel Velásquez, the wage structure of the country was not going to change markedly; in fact, Velásquez pledged his support to the new industrialists. Native Mexican capital did begin to pour into new industrial pursuits, but, because the program was such an ambitious one, in 1944 the Congress passed legislation allowing foreign participation in industrialization with the proviso that Mexican capital own the controlling stock in any mixed corporation. In spite of the oil expropriations of the previous decade, the wartime alliance seemed to have initiated an era of good re-

INDUSTRIAL LOANS OF THE NACIONAL FINANCIERA, 1940–45

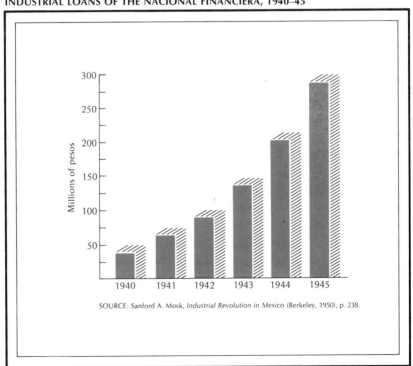

SOURCE: Sanford A. Mosk, *Industrial Revolution in Mexico* (Berkeley, 1950), p. 238.

lations, and some United States investors jumped at the opportunity. Credits were also extended through the Export-Import Bank in the United States.

The new and often young industrialists took it upon themselves to educate Mexican politicians, and indeed the public, in the virtues of industrial growth. In 1942 they founded the Cámara Nacional de la Industria de Transformación to develop an industrial consciousness in the country and to convince policy makers that without industrialization the masses were doomed to perpetual privation. During the Avila Camacho years industrialization became as important to the national self-conception as agrarian reform had been during the Cárdenas administration. Its lure was irresistible, and stories of new factories pushed political news off the front pages of the newspapers. The Cámara became not only an effective propaganda agency and lobby but, in essence, the recognized spokesman for the manufacturing industries.

There is no doubt that Cámara members convinced themselves that what was good for industry was good for the nation. Without it, they argued, Mexico would always be at the mercy of economic vicissitudes abroad. Their initial goal was to foster those industries which relied on Mexican raw materials, for example, cereal processing, edible oil from agricultural products, sugar, alcohol, and the manufacture of fibers and chemicals. The ultimate goal was to make Mexico completely self-sufficient in all manufactured goods consumed in large volume and to begin exporting these products as well.

The industrial revolution gathered momentum throughout the war years as a wide range of old industries were expanded and new ones initiated. The textile, food processing, chemical, beer, and cement industries grew rapidly. Pig iron production increased from 99,200 metric tons in 1930 to 240,300 metric tons in 1946, and during the same period steel increased from 142,200 metric tons to 257,900 metric tons. Electrical capacity rose by 20 percent, and the industrial proletariat grew steadily in size.

As predicted, industrialization generated much new wealth. The national income almost tripled, from 6.4 billion pesos in 1940 to 18.6 billion in 1945. Per capita income jumped from 325 pesos the year Avila Camacho was inaugurated to 838 pesos during his last year in office. As social critics quickly pointed out, however, increased per capita income does not necessarily mean a more equitable distribution of wealth or increased earning power for the poor. In fact, the middle class was growing in numbers and in earning power, but the large majority of the lower class was not benefiting fully from the improved economic indicators.

The emphasis of the Revolution had certainly changed. Those who had believed—and with some reason—that the semifeudal society inherited by the Revolution would be replaced by socialism had to re-examine their expectations. It now appeared increasingly certain that the post-Cárdenas period would be typified not by socialism but by industrial capitalism. The basic change in outlook became institutionalized in January 1946 when the PRM met to choose a candidate for the presidency.

For almost a decade the party had gradually been opened up. By 1946 it was no longer dominated by intellectuals, agrarian reformers, and ardent defenders of the labor movement. The business and industrial communities were now represented, as were economists and technicians. To symbolize that it endorsed the new thrust of the Revolution the party decided to change its name to the Partido Revolucionario Institucional (PRI). Of equal significance, to signify that the old Revolution was over, the official party for the first time endorsed a civilian, Miguel Alemán, as its presidential candidate. There would now be no turning back. Mexico's conception of modernity had been made synonymous with the industrial state.

Recommended for Further Study

Alvarez, José. "A Demographic Profile of the Mexican Immigrant to the United States, 1910–1960." *Journal of International American Studies* 8 (1960): 471–96.

Call, Tomme Clark. *The Mexican Venture*. New York: Oxford University Press, 1953.

Cline. Howard. *Mexico: Revolution to Evolution, 1940–1960*. New York: Oxford University Press, 1963.

———. *The United States and Mexico*. New York: Atheneum, 1963.

Galarza, Ernesto. *Merchants of Labor: The Mexican Bracero Story*. San Jose, Cal.: Rosicrucian Press, 1964.

Kirk, Betty. *Covering the Mexican Front: The Battle of Europe vs. America*. Norman: University of Oklahoma Press, 1942.

Leaming, George F., and Walter H. Delaplane. "An Economy of Contrasts." In *Six Faces of Mexico*, edited by Russell C. Ewing, pp. 209–43. Tucson: University of Arizona Press, 1966.

McWilliams, Carey. *North from Mexico: The Spanish-Speaking People of the United States*. New York: Greenwood Press, 1968.

Mosk, Sanford A. *Industrial Revolution in Mexico*. Berkeley: University of California Press, 1950.

Powell, J. R. *The Mexican Petroleum Industry, 1938–1950.* Berkeley: University of California Press, 1956.

Tannenbaum, Frank. *Mexico: The Struggle for Peace and Bread.* New York: Alfred A. Knopf, 1956.

Wilkie, James W. *The Mexican Revolution: Federal Expenditure and Social Change since 1910.* Berkeley: University of California Press, 1967.

41

The Institutionalized Revolution, 1946-58

For a dozen years following the Second World War, Mexicans were instructed by concrete example that the profound changes which had occurred with the Avila Camacho presidency were not to be transitory in nature but, in fact, had become institutionalized within the governmental structure. The next two chief executives, Miguel Alemán (1946–52) and Adolfo Ruiz Cortines (1952–58), both pledged to foster economic growth in general and large-scale industrialization in particular. That they were not diverted from this task is evidenced by the fact that Mexico's gross national product doubled during their twelve years in office. At the same time the agrarian revolution languished. Productivity on most of the ejidos had not lived up to expectations, and, as a result, government planners decided not to experiment further with communal agriculture.

The Presidency of Miguel Alemán

The election of Miguel Alemán, the first civilian president since Venustiano Carranza and the first to have played no illustrious role in the early Revolution, signified that the days of the soldier-politician were over. The new president reduced the military's share of the budget to less than 10 percent of the total for the first time in the twentieth century, and the generals accepted the decision, scarcely batting an eye. Over the years the military share of the budget had been gradually reduced, and, more suc-

PERCENTAGE OF MILITARY EXPENDITURE IN THE TOTAL BUDGET, 1917–52

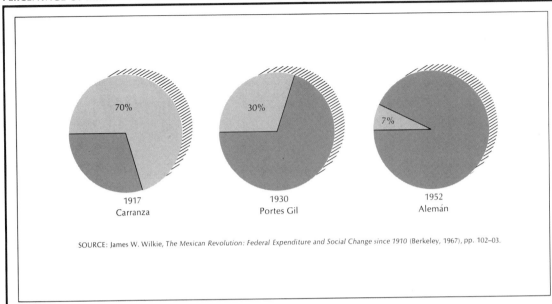

1917
Carranza

1930
Portes Gil

1952
Alemán

SOURCE: James W. Wilkie, *The Mexican Revolution: Federal Expenditure and Social Change since 1910* (Berkeley, 1967), pp. 102–03.

cessfully than its Latin American neighbors, Mexico curbed the problems of rampant militarism.[1]

With a healthy dollar reserve turned over to him by his predecessor, Alemán launched an impressive number of public works projects designed both to provide work for a steadily growing labor force and to meet a series of crucial developmental needs. Most important was the construction of dams to control flooding, increase arable land acreage, and supply ample power for the modernization impulse. The Morelos Dam on the Colorado River near Mexicali worked agricultural wonders in the northwest as some seven hundred thousand arid acres were reclaimed and converted into a rich truck-farming zone. In the northeast work was initiated, in cooperation with the United States, on the Falcón Dam in the lower Rio Grande Valley. Completed in 1953, the year after Alemán left office, the Falcón project yielded substantial agricultural benefits as well. The major project in the south was the harnessing of the Papaloapan River in the states of Puebla, Veracruz, and Oaxaca. Not only were tens of thousands of acres added to the agricultural base of the nation, but a series

1. The process is described in Edwin Lieuwen, *Mexican Militarism: The Political Rise and Fall of the Revolutionary Army* (Albuquerque, 1968).

of hydroelectric stations contributed to the tripling of Mexico's electrical output capacity by 1952.

Other large-scale public works centered on improving the communications network. In addition to modernizing the railway system, Alemán completed Mexico's segment of the Pan-American Highway in 1951. This all-weather road made possible automobile travel between the United States and Guatemala. Of equal importance commercially was the completion of the Isthmian Highway, which connected Puerto México and Salina Cruz across Tehuantepec. To cater to the tourist traffic, an increasingly important source of foreign exchange, Alemán ordered the construction of a four-lane superhighway between the capital and the Pacific resort town of Acapulco. In total, paved roads increased from about twenty-five hundred miles in 1946 to over ten thousand by 1952.

Postwar Mexico was prosperous and booming. If the working class did not share proportionately in the benefits of an expansive economy, the middle class continued to grow. Hundreds of small factories, not only in Mexico City but in Monterrey, Guadalajara, Puebla, and San Luis Potosí, took advantage of the cheap and abundant source of electric power and began to transform the economy and also the face of the nation. Low taxes and high rates of profit encouraged both Mexican and foreign capital to continue investing in the industrial sector of the economy. PEMEX expanded its activities; new pipelines and refineries, coupled with accelerated drilling, made it possible for the state-owned corporation to double its production between 1946 and 1952.

The most impressive construction project of all was the new University City built to house the National University of Mexico. Dedicated in 1952, the campus of three square miles was one of the most modern in the world. The architectural and artistic achievements at University City were unparalleled: the plans were conceived by leading artists such as Juan O'Gorman (1905–1982), the buildings designed by talented architects such as Félix Candela, and the walls adorned with anthropological and historical murals by Rivera and Siqueiros. Alemán considered the University a monument to his own presidency, and the first thing visitors encountered when entering the campus in the 1960s was a huge statue of Alemán himself.

Relations between the United States and Mexico continued to be cordial during the Alemán years. Accepting an invitation

The main library at the National University of Mexico, University City.

from President Truman, Alemán became the first Mexican head of state to visit Washington, and Truman also called upon the Mexican president in Mexico City and delighted his hosts by placing a wreath at the monument of the Niños Héroes, the boy cadets who had fallen fighting United States troops a hundred years before. Both congresses voted to return all trophies of war sequestered in the middle of the nineteenth century. The outward manifestations of goodwill had practical effects as well. The United States was able to count on Mexican support in the cold war, and loans from the Export-Import Bank flowed into Mexico at an accelerated pace. United States tourists (over four hundred thousand in 1952 alone) left hundreds of millions of dollars in the country, and trade relations became more interdependent than ever before.

On the surface Mexico seemed healthier than at any time in her history. But, behind the showy façade Alemán had created,

A mural by José Chávez Morado at the Faculty of Science Building, University City.

President Harry S. Truman visits the Pyramid of the Sun during his trip to Mexico City.

serious problems had begun to sap the strength and vitality of his institutionalized Revolution. Corruption beset his administration, and many new millionaires emerged between 1946 and 1952.[2] The displays of sprawling mansions, yachts, and airplanes, paid for with bribes, brought to mind the venality of the days of Santa Anna. The library at the new University City, while a marvel to gaze at, was embarrassingly short of books. The row after row of empty shelves were symbolic of the building spree that failed to cope with basic issues and emphasized form rather than content.

While PRI politicians continued to mouth pleasant-sounding revolutionary euphemisms, the little man had been shunted aside. The labor movement was not crushed, but it was intimidated. Lombardo Toledano lamented to oral historians James and Edna Wilkie that under Alemán "the workers didn't dare to call large strikes because Alemán had embarked upon the cold

---

2. Estimates of dollars deposited in foreign banks by highly placed officials in the administration run between $500 million and $800 million. See William S. Stokes, *Latin American Politics* (New York, 1959), p. 390.

war and shared few sympathies with the working class."[3] While Lombardo Toledano cannot be considered an impartial observer, the facts nevertheless bear him out. When in April 1950 Secretary of the Treasury Ramón Beteta exhorted the industrialists of Monterrey to keep their costs down so that Mexican industry could become competitive, he was, in effect, inviting them to keep wages depressed. When petroleum workers struck, army troops were dispatched to patrol the fields and fifty union leaders were dismissed from their posts. In spite of John Maynard Keynes's revolution in economic theory, the Mexican worker was not yet to be confused with a consumer.

While new primary and secondary schools were built throughout the country, teachers' salaries were so paltry that it was almost impossible to staff them with qualified professionals. School attendance remained low. Of the 6 million schoolchildren in the age bracket six to fourteen, fewer than 2.25 million attended classes on a regular basis. In spite of the emphasis successive administrations since 1920 had placed on rural education, the 1950 census revealed that only .5 percent of rural children finished the sixth grade. Certainly it would be unfair to hold President Alemán responsible for all of the shortcomings of four decades of Revolution; yet his administration did not move in a direction suited to overcome them.

The Presidency of Ruiz Cortines

When PRI officials met to choose Alemán's successor, many believed it crucial to rekindle confidence in the integrity of the party. It would be necessary to repudiate the peculation of the Alemán administration by selecting as a presidential candidate one whose personal honesty and devotion to service were impeccable. Sixty-one-year-old Adolfo Ruiz Cortines fit the bill. During his governorship of Veracruz and tenure as secretary of interior under Alemán he had garnered a reputation for party loyalty, efficiency, and integrity. Although his campaign speeches enraptured nobody, with official party support he won over his leading opponent, Miguel Henríquez Guzmán, by a margin of almost five to one.

Ideologically much akin to his predecessor, the hard-working but unspectacular president did not disappoint those who had

3. Quoted in James W. Wilkie and Edna Monzón de Wilkie, *México visto en el siglo xx: Entrevistas de historia oral* (Mexico, 1969), p. 314.

urged a cleansing of bureaucratic corruption. He announced in his inaugural speech that he would demand strict honesty and ordered all public officials to make public their financial holdings. During the next several years he fired a number of notorious grafters. In an even more significant political reform he pushed through the Congress legislation fully enfranchising the Mexican woman. This long overdue measure culminated years of active campaigning by women's organizations throughout the country.

The Mexican economy remained dynamic during the Ruiz Cortines years as industry continued to receive government support and, in turn, established an entire series of new records for production. A devaluation of the peso in 1953 (to a rate of 12.50 to the dollar) helped stabilize the economy and prompt new foreign investment. United States capital, encouraged by the healthy economic indicators, poured into the country unhesitatingly, and United States visitors in the larger cities saw familiar signs advertising General Motors, Dow Chemicals, Pepsi-Cola, Coca-Cola, Colgate, Goodyear, John Deere, Ford, Proctor and Gamble, Sears, Roebuck, and other corporate giants who would not have dared to invest their stockholders' dollars in Mexico twenty years earlier. It was not easy to categorize the Mexican economy. Some observers viewed it as statist, some as socialist, and others as free enterprise. In reality it was a mixed economy comprising all three, and, in terms of development, it seemed to work.

Believing that Alemán had overtaxed the idea of public works, the new Mexican president did not initiate many grandiose construction schemes, but he did see hundreds of his predecessor's projects through to completion. Ruiz Cortines was content to serve the country by consolidating the gains made before he took office, and, as a result, many of the plaques he unveiled on public projects announced that they had been initiated during the presidential administration of Miguel Alemán. Whereas Alemán had built huge dams, Ruiz Cortines sponsored smaller projects; whereas Alemán had built superhighways, Ruiz Cortines paved two-lane roads to help the farmers get their products to a suitable market.

For the first time since its foundation in 1943, the IMSS expanded its coverage sufficiently to constitute an agency of genuine social importance. Ruiz Cortines's director, Antonio Ortiz Mena, not only obtained increased funding but moved the services into the countryside for the first time. The number of IMSS-sponsored clinics rose from 42 to 226 and hospitals from 19 to

105. Rural services did not yet approximate urban ones, but a beginning was at least made as about a hundred thousand rural persons received some kind of social security coverage for the first time. The basic issue of low wages was not resolved. Although salaries did rise by an average of 5 percent a year in the period from 1952 to 1958, the workers lost their increases to inflation, which rose annually at a rate of 7.3 percent.

Throughout his term of office Ruiz Cortines found himself caught up in a situation over which he had no direct control. Mexico's population was growing at a rate that began to alarm not only social scientists but also his political advisers. When Lázaro Cárdenas came to power the population of the country was only about 16 million. But by 1958 it had soared to more than 32 million. The population had doubled in only twenty-four years, and the dire consequences of this rapid and sustained growth were being felt for the first time. The population explosion was compounded by a concomitant trend toward urbanization. While the national growth rate had reached 3.1 percent a year by 1955 (as opposed to 1.9 from 1930 to 1940), the growth rate of the major cities approached 7 percent a year. The Federal District jumped from 3 million in 1952 to an amazing 4.5 million only six years later.

Drawn by the lure of industry, hundreds of thousands of rural Mexicans flocked to the cities in hope of a better life, but few found it. The industrial revolution required skilled, not unskilled, labor. The need for more jobs, schools, health services, sewage disposal plants, streets, and houses in the cities was now taxing even the extraordinary postwar prosperity. Although by 1958 a million and a half Mexicans were earning their living from industry, the laboring force was growing faster than industry could provide jobs. At precisely the time when the apparent thrust of the country was directed toward modernization, Ruiz Cortines found it necessary to order the use of hand labor rather than machinery on public works just to keep the new work force occupied. Allowing twenty men to work while an expensive machine stood idle seemed to meet a pressing social demand, but the scheme was directed toward the symptom rather than the disease.

The Revolution: An Assessment at Mid-Century

Ruiz Cortines considered himself a custodian of the Revolution as he announced repeatedly that he had full faith in revolutionary institutions. But surely his policies would have repulsed the heroes of the 1910 movement. The postwar generation of Mexican politicians had redefined priorities and concluded at mid-century that the programs of 1910 no longer had meaning. The burdens of industrial development fell most heavily on those who were least able to bear them. The president's economic advisers were aware of this problem, but they suggested that a temporary lack of equity constituted an important investment in the future. **These advisers had an abiding faith in the perfectibility of a system that would ultimately produce abundance. Mexico simply had to continue flexing its industrial muscles.**

From the very outset the Revolution had been criticized from both the left and the right. As it turned more conservative in the postwar years, however, the majority of the critics were isolated on the left. More wealth was being generated, but the proceeds were not being distributed. Mexican radicals were alienated by the new trends, but, more important, the moderate left was becoming increasingly apprehensive about the burgeoning population and the heavy emphasis on technology as the key to a more abundant life. If something were not done in the near future to arrest the tremendous rate of population growth, all discussion of the quality of life would be beside the point. For the first time in Mexican history social scientists began seriously to ponder the Malthusian theory of impending starvation. To be sure, the prophets of doom constituted only a small majority in 1958, but they addressed a serious problem that would concern more and more in the 1960s, 1970s, and 1980s.

On another important issue the left and right could agree. The official party, the PRI, had pre-empted the political life of the country. Party nomination was tantamount to election. Though the party itself was broadly based and incorporated many segments of society, its complete domination of the political process produced nothing less than a contradiction in terms—a one-party democracy.

When Mexico's distinguished political critic and respected scholar, Daniel Cosío Villegas, delivered his often-quoted Montgomery Lecture on Contemporary Civilization at the University of Nebraska, he provided a brilliant analysis of what was happening to the Mexican Revolution.

> The drive and energy of the Revolution were consumed much more in destroying the past than in constructing the future. As a result the past certainly disappeared, but the new present came

into being and began to develop haphazardly, so that, for lack of another image to imitate, it finally ended by becoming equal to the destroyed past. . . . The economy is sound, judged from a classical liberal point of view, so much so that it is often commented that Mexico has made phenomenal progress in recent years. . . . Strictly speaking the only problem of great magnitude is the rate at which the population and the national product grow. . . . It is possible that this population increase may very well strain the country's physical, human and economic resources, and that if energetic measures are not taken, it may present a very serious problem. . . . The political situation is decidedly less satisfactory. . . . The election [of the president, governors, and local authorities] is far from popular, being decided by personalist forces that rarely or never represent the genuine interests of large human groups. The economic and political power of the president of the Republic is almost all-embracing and . . . it is impossible for one man to know the special needs of each city or town and which person or persons are most suitable to resolve them.[4]

Ruiz Cortines's last message to the Congress was atypical of Mexican politicians of the twentieth century. He, too, had begun to hear the voices of criticism, and rather than exalt revolutionary successes, he took the occasion to pinpoint at least some of the shortcomings. The social imperfections of the system troubled him more than the deficiencies of one-party rule or executive dominance. The Mexican masses, the outgoing president conceded, had not benefited from the revolutionary process as much as he had anticipated. Many of the revolutionary promises were yet to be fulfilled. Illness, ignorance, and poverty had not been overcome. The desired balance between economic development and social justice had tipped in favor of the former.

PRI officials had to agree. The pace of the social movement had slowed and, since 1940, had almost ground to a halt. Perhaps a moderate shift to the left would mute government critics and reinstill some faith in revolutionary ideals. They were willing to give it a try.

4. Daniel Cosío Villegas, *Change in Latin America: The Mexican and Cuban Revolutions* (Lincoln, 1961), pp. 30–33.

Recommended for Further Study

Brandenburg, Frank. *The Making of Modern Mexico*. Englewood Cliffs, N.J.: Prentice-Hall, 1964.

———. "Organized Business in Mexico." *Inter-American Economic Affairs* 12 (1958): 26–50.

Call, Tomme Clark. *The Mexican Venture*. New York: Oxford University Press, 1953.

Cline, Howard. "Mexico: A Maturing Democracy." *Current History* (1953): 136–142.

———. *Mexico: Revolution to Evolution, 1940–1960*. New York: Oxford University Press, 1963.

Lewis, Oscar. "Mexico since Cárdenas." In *Social Change in Latin America Today*, edited by Richard N. Adams et al., pp. 285–345. New York: Vintage Books, 1960.

Mosk, Sanford A. *Industrial Revolution in Mexico*. Berkeley: University of California Press, 1950.

Padgett, L. Vincent. "Mexico's One Party System: A Re-evaluation." *American Political Science Review* 51 (1957): 995–1008.

Pérez López, Enrique, et al. *Mexico's Recent Economic Growth: The Mexican View*. Austin: University of Texas Press, 1967.

Ross, Stanley R., ed. *Is the Mexican Revolution Dead?* New York: Alfred A. Knopf, 1966.

Scott, Robert E. *Mexican Government in Transition*. Urbana: University of Illinois Press, 1959.

Taylor, Philip B. "The Mexican Elections of 1958: Affirmation of Authoritarianism?" *Western Political Science Quarterly* 13 (1960): 722–44.

Tucker, William P. *The Mexican Government Today*. Minneapolis: University of Minnesota Press, 1957.

Vernon, Raymond. *The Dilemma of Mexico's Development: The Roles of the Private and Public Sectors*. Cambridge, Mass.: Harvard University Press, 1963.

Wilkie, James W. *The Mexican Revolution: Federal Expenditure and Social Change since 1910*. Berkeley: University of California Press, 1967.

42

Adolfo López Mateos: The Lull Before the Storm, 1958-64

Prior to the presidential elections of 1958, some Mexican political analysts predicted that Luis H. Alvarez, the candidate of the conservative, proclerical PAN, stood a good chance to make a strong showing against the PRI candidate. For the first time in Mexican history women were fully enfranchised, and the church urged them not to follow the lead of their husbands blindly but rather to consider carefully the qualifications of the conservative opposition. The political temper of the country proved difficult to measure, but in the end the Mexican people, both men and women, were not about to turn the PRI out of office for a candidate who enjoyed the support of the church. The PRI nominee, Adolfo López Mateos, the well-educated son of a small-town dentist, won the presidency with about 90 percent of the total vote. The women's vote increased the total ballots cast but scarcely changed the official party's margin of victory.

Domestic Policy

President López Mateos presented a stark contrast to his sixty-seven-year-old predecessor. Only forty-seven at the time of his election, he was dynamic, energetic, and personally attractive. Having served as secretary of labor during the Ruiz Cortines administration, he had won a reputation as a liberal for his management of labor disputes; only a few of the thirteen thousand cases he handled degenerated into strikes. He enjoyed the backing of Lázaro Cárdenas and seemed to be just the right man at the right time. More intellectually oriented than presidents of recent vintage, he indicated during the campaign that he planned to nudge the Mexican Revolution back to the left. Hundreds of thousands of young Mexicans, disheartened with the slow progress in the social field since the Second World War, identified with López Mateos, much as the youth of the United States would, a few years later, identify with President John F. Kennedy. In fact, López Mateos was the last Mexican president to win the enthusiastic endorsement of the country's young.

Shortly after his inauguration the new president was asked to comment on his political philosophy and he answered with the words, "I am left within the Constitution." Mexican Communists, and other radicals whom he judged to be left *of* the Constitution, were not treated with kid gloves. López Mateos removed Communist leadership from the teachers' union and the railroad union and imprisoned Mexico's internationally known muralist and Communist, David Alfaro Siqueiros, on charges of "social dissolution," an amorphous kind of sedition. But just as local and foreign businessmen and industrialists sat back and relaxed, thinking that they had an unexpected friend in the presidential chair, López Mateos also began to demonstrate that he intended to depart markedly from the conservative, business-oriented policies of Manuel Avila Camacho, Miguel Alemán, and Adolfo Ruiz Cortines.

Land redistribution, almost forgotten as a revolutionary goal by the end of World War II, was stepped up once again, on both an individual and a collective basis. During his six-year term López Mateos parceled out some 30 million acres, more than any president except Lázaro Cárdenas. He also cleared and opened up new agricultural lands in extreme southern Mexico, which relieved land tension in the south.

State intervention in the economy accelerated from 1958 to 1964 as the administration purchased controlling stock in a number of foreign industries. In 1962, for example, the government gained control of the United States and Canadian electric companies and, not being able to divine a future in which energy would become a luxury, authorized huge, wasteful electric signs proudly announcing *La electricidad es nuestra* (The electricity is ours). At about the same time the government also purchased the motion picture industry, the production and distribution of which had been largely under United States domination. The president pledged to keep the price of tickets low so that all people could avail themselves of this medium of entertainment. So-

Even after the emphasis on agrarian reform programs, life for workers on the maguey plantations of Yucatán remained difficult.

cial welfare projects, most notably medical care and old age pensions, were expanded, and the IMSS program for rural Mexico was stepped up markedly. By 1964 public health campaigns had significantly reduced tuberculosis and polio rates, while malaria was almost completely eliminated.

Like his predecessors, López Mateos continued to skirt the issue of birth control, even as a million Mexican babies were born in 1962 and almost a million and a half in 1963. But he did recognize the tremendous dislocations occasioned by rapid urbanization. For the first time in history the government entered the housing business on a large scale. Low-cost housing projects were initiated in the major industrial cities, many of which had become encircled with shanty towns of indescribable misery and poverty. One of the largest housing developments in Mexico City covered some ten million square feet of a former slum, housed a hundred thousand persons, and contained thirteen schools, four clinics, and several nurseries. The rents were modest: $6.00 a month for a one-bedroom apartment and $16.00 a month for a three-bedroom unit. To be sure, it was impossible to build large, multiple units rapidly enough to absorb the dramatically increasing population, but at least the problem had been acknowledged and a start made. To complement public housing, the president also developed an incentive program designed to en-

A major campaign to eradicate malaria
in 1962 and 1963 yielded positive results.

Curious villagers inspect the newly completed sewer system in the state of
Chiapas.

URBAN-RURAL POPULATION DISTRIBUTION

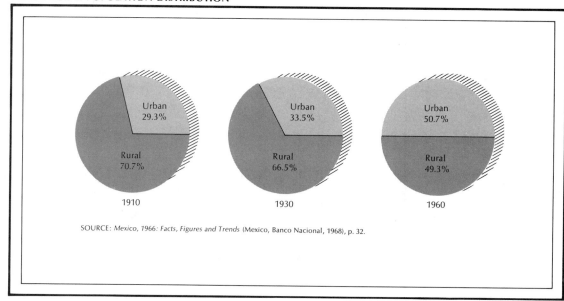

SOURCE: *Mexico, 1966: Facts, Figures and Trends* (Mexico, Banco Nacional, 1968), p. 32.

courage industry to stay away from the greater Mexico City environs. The emphasis on urban problems reflected a new reality in the demographic potpourri. In 1960, on the fiftieth anniversary of the Revolution, Mexico's urban population surpassed its rural population for the first time.

López Mateos's labor supporters were visibly shaken in 1959 when the president used federal troops to put down a major railroad strike. Arguing that the strike threatened to paralyze the country, he arrested a number of leaders, including Demetrio Vallejo, the head of the union. It was a bad start on the labor front. But the movement judged the new president too quickly and too harshly. His sympathies lay more clearly with the working class than any president since Mexico's industrial revolution began, and he set out to allay workers' fears. In an interesting move he decided to implement an almost forgotten article of the Constitution of 1917 that called for labor to share in the profits with management. In 1962 a special commission, the Comisión Nacional para el Reparto de Utilidades, was convoked to implement the profit-sharing plan. The formula agreed upon was complicated, dependent upon the amount of capital investment and the size of the labor force within each industry. But by 1964 many Mexican laborers were earning an extra 5 to 10 percent a year under the profit-sharing law.

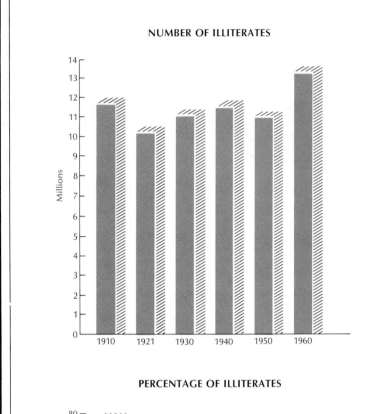

NUMBER OF ILLITERATES

PERCENTAGE OF ILLITERATES

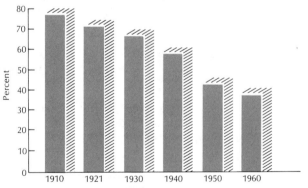

SOURCE: James W. Wilkie, *The Mexican Revolution: Federal Expenditure and Social Change since 1910* (Berkeley, 1967), p. 208.

The educational policy of the López Mateos administration renewed the emphasis on the rural school. By 1963 education had become the largest single item in the Mexican budget, and the educational outlay was twice that allocated for national defense. The dramatic increase was made necessary by the revelation of some startling statistics in 1960. While the percentage of illiteracy in Mexico had been cut from some 77 percent in 1910 to less than 38 percent in 1960, the population explosion in a very real sense had nullified the results. In absolute numbers there were more illiterates in 1960 (13,200,000) than there had been at the time of the Plan de San Luis Potosí (11,658,000).

To attack illiteracy the president and his secretary of education, Jaime Torres Bodet, who had also served under Avila Camacho, launched a two-pronged assault. Through an ingenious system of prefabricated schools costing only $4,800 per unit, the number of rural classrooms increased rapidly. The government provided the building materials and the technical assistance, and the individual communities were called upon to provide the land and the actual labor. In this way villages were given a genuine stake in the educational process. Each unit contained unpretentious living quarters for the teacher, an important factor in convincing qualified teachers to venture into the rural areas.

Together with renewed emphasis on school construction, López Mateos decided to initiate a system of free and compulsory

In an attempt to reduce illiteracy, López Mateos revived the idea of adult reading classes.

textbooks. On this program he encountered opposition. Although the books were prepared in consultation with some of the leading scholars in the country, they did reflect the historiographical preconceptions that had grown up with the Revolution, and the Roman Catholic Church took umbrage at the treatment afforded many of its efforts throughout Mexican history. The National Union of Parents Association, a conservative organization supported by the PAN and a number of leading clerics, led demonstrations against the books, insisting that their imposition on a mandatory basis constituted a totalitarian act designed to standardize thought in the Mexican republic. At the same time radical leftists opposed the textbooks because they exalted revolutionary accomplishments and overlooked the shortcomings. But López Mateos was not intimidated, and the books were adopted throughout the country over the protests.

If Mexico's rate of economic growth under López Mateos did not quite keep pace with that under Miguel Alemán and Adolfo Ruiz Cortines, the economy remained strong. British and French capital poured into PEMEX's new petrochemical division. Private initiative constructed luxury hotels, and tourists came in droves to Acapulco and the newly developed resort town of Puerto Vallarta—and left behind millions of dollars that were put to good use. By 1964 Mexico was self-sufficient in iron, steel, and oil. Local capital no longer felt the need to seek investment fields elsewhere and, indeed, purchased controlling stock in the Mexican telephone network. And in 1963 Mexican bonds were sold on United States and European markets for the first time since the Díaz regime. The country was still in its period of sustained economic growth.

Foreign Policy

Mexico's foreign policy from 1958 to 1964 showed López Mateos not unsympathetic to concerns of the left. Coming to the presidency only a few months before Fidel Castro's July 26 revolution ousted rightest Cuban dictator Fulgencio Batista, López Mateos occupied himself with defining the Mexican position on the most crucial Latin American issue of the postwar period. To the chagrin of the United States, he opted for a policy of total nonintervention in Cuba's internal affairs. Arguing the national sovereignty and juridical equality of all states, Mexico refused to condemn the Castro regime, voted against Cuba's expulsion from the Organization of American States, did not endorse economic sanctions, and, most important, remained the only country in the Western Hemisphere to retain air service and diplomatic relations with Cuba. But the Mexican government was not prepared to accept dictates from Moscow either, and López Mateos condemned the Soviet Union in 1962 for placing offensive missiles in Cuba. Roll call votes in the United Nations verify that Mexico did not tie itself to either bloc but maintained an independent course. When French President Charles de Gaulle visited Mexico City in the spring of 1964 and was accorded the honor of being the first foreign head of state ever to speak from the presidential balcony overlooking the Plaza de la Constitución, the two leaders congratulated one another on escaping the tutelage of the superpowers. Mexico's independent foreign posture was a theme relayed in a series of trips that López Mateos and his close associates made to Yugoslavia, Poland, Indonesia, India, Canada, and a number of African countries.

By his own reckoning, López Mateos's greatest diplomatic victory concerned the final resolution of a century-old boundary dispute with the United States—the Chamizal controversy. At the end of the war with the United States the boundary had been set at the Rio Grande. But because of the sandy texture of the soil, especially in the area of El Paso, the river periodically shifted its bed. In 1864 it moved suddenly to the south, leaving some six hundred acres of Mexican territory north of the river in the state of Texas. Mexico, of course, claimed that this land, the Chamizal, was part of the national domain, but the various arbitration commissions had been unable to reach an accord suitable to the United States government. When President John F. Kennedy visited Mexico City in 1962, he was informed that the Chamizal continued to be a reminder of Yanqui imperialism and ordered the United States ambassador, Thomas Mann, to enter into new negotiations with the Mexican government for its final resolution. In the summer of 1963 the United States agreed to return the disputed territory to Mexico, to reimburse the El Paso residents for their lost property, and to share the costs of building a new international bridge and a concrete-lined channel to eliminate possible future disputes.

The Mexican public was elated when López Mateos appeared on a nationwide television news special to announce that "justice has come at last. . . . There is nothing left except to congratulate ourselves on the victory of law and reason."[1] An assassin's

1. Adolfo López Mateos, *El chamizal ya es Mexicano* (Mexico, 1964), pp. 47–51.

bullet took John Kennedy's life before he could sign the agreement, but his successor, Lyndon Johnson, met López Mateos at the Chamizal in September 1964 and formalized the arrangement amid sincere displays of goodwill. Through adroit diplomacy the Mexican president was considered a good friend of the United States—in spite of his failure to endorse a hostile policy toward Cuba, in spite of articulating an independent foreign policy, and in spite of his victories in the resolution of the Chamizal dispute.

Criticism of the One-Party System

Criticism of the PRI's monopoly on government continued to build during the López Mateos administration. His election in 1958 with 90 percent of the total vote marked thirty consecutive years of rule by the official party. The party not only had won every contest for the presidency but also had captured all of the senatorial and gubernatorial races. While electoral fraud might have contributed to some of the early victories, since 1934 there was no need to rig elections. The PRI had succeeded in identifying itself with the Revolution, and the Revolution was practically synonymous with the state. The PRI's colors—red, white, and green—were identical to those on the national flag; they appeared on its symbol on the ballot, and the lesson was not lost on even the illiterate. In addition, the party was able to mobilize bountiful resources to get its message across.

For many years Mexicans were willing to accept the PRI on its own terms, but by the early 1960s an increasingly sophisticated electorate began to question the bossism, favoritism, and corruption that had beset the PRI officialdom. A party without any genuine opposition was accountable to nobody. A party that could embrace the leftist policies of Cárdenas and the business-oriented policies of Alemán was ideologically bankrupt. How could it be expected to embark upon a meaningful redistribution of wealth designed to close the still gigantic gap between rich and poor? Alienation was broadly based, cutting across many class lines and most ideological persuasions. Effective democratization, in spite of potential obstacles, was deemed crucial. Properly conceived and skillfully channeled, it could lead to a developmental attitude that sought not only to increase the national product but to redistribute it. Pablo González Casanova, a distinguished Mexican social scientist, pinpointed this specific need when he argued in his perceptive *Democracy in Mexico:* "It is not enough to establish democratization formally in the under-developed countries in order to accelerate development, nor to imitate all of the specific forms of classic democracy in order to have democracy: democracy exists to the extent that the people share the income, culture, and power; anything else is demo-cratic folklore or rhetoric."[2]

López Mateos was not only willing to listen to criticism of the system; he was sensitive to it. Therefore he sponsored an amend-ment to the Constitution that altered the electoral procedures in the Chamber of Deputies. In order to broaden the opposition in the lower house of the legislature, his amendment provided that any party winning 2.5 percent of the national vote was entitled to five congressmen whether or not the candidates actually won their respective races. For every additional .5 percent of the vote these parties would receive an additional congressman, up to a total of twenty, each of whom would occupy a new seat, not re-place an elected congressman. Because of the new law the PAN received twenty congressional seats in the 1964 elections and the Partido Popular Socialista (PPS), ten seats. The electoral revi-sion by no means ended the debate on the shortcomings of Mex-ican democracy, but it did demonstrate a liberalizing tendency on the part of the presidential incumbent.

López Mateos is the most fondly remembered president of the postwar era. Like his contemporary in the United States, John F. Kennedy, part of his appeal undoubtedly lies in his style and charisma. But when the occasion demanded it, he exerted force-ful leadership. At the same time he was not doctrinaire and ap-preciated the value of compromise. Yielding to appeals and peti-tions, he made it a point to pardon muralist Siqueiros before he left office. Equally important to the favorable reputation he con-tinues to enjoy is the fact that he served his term at the right time, prior to the worldwide movement of social dissidence and student radicalism from which no head of state could emerge completely unscathed. Almost as soon as he left office he suffered a severe stroke and lay in a coma for six years until his death in 1970. He was eulogized as a nationalist who defended Mexican interests in the world community and a humane statesman who appreciated the concerns of the powerless masses at home. It is not difficult to agree on both counts. But Mexico in 1970 was a

2. Pablo González Casanova, *Democracy in Mexico* (New York, 1970), p. 194.

far different country from what it had been in 1964. In the post–
López Mateos years it was subjected to new tensions and the
spectacle of political violence once again.

Recommended for Further Study

Brandenburg, Frank. *The Making of Modern Mexico*. Englewood Cliffs,
    N.J.: Prentice-Hall, 1964.

Brown, Lyle C., and James W. Wilkie. "Recent United States–Mexican
    Relations: Problems Old and New." In *Twentieth Century Foreign
    Policy*, edited by John Braeman et al., pp. 378–419. Columbus: Ohio
    State University Press, 1971.

Cline, Howard F. *Mexico: Revolution to Evolution, 1940–1960*. New York:
    Oxford University Press, 1963.

Faust, John R., and Charles C. Stansifer. "Mexican Foreign Policy in the
    United Nations: The Advocacy of Moderation in an Era of Revolu-
    tion." *Southwestern Social Science Quarterly* 44 (1963): 121–29.

González Casanova, Pablo. *Democracy in Mexico*. New York: Oxford Uni-
    versity Press, 1970.

Hundley, Norris, Jr. *Dividing the Waters: A Century of Controversy be-
    tween the United States and Mexico*. Berkeley: University of Cali-
    fornia Press, 1966.

Johnson, Kenneth F. *Mexican Democracy: A Critical View*. Boston: Allyn
    and Bacon, 1971.

Liss, Sheldon. *A Century of Disagreement: The Chamizal Conflict, 1864–
    1964*. Washington, D.C.: University Press of Washington, D.C., 1965.

López Mateos, Adolfo. "Philosophy and Program of the Revolutionary
    Party." In *Is the Mexican Revolution Dead?* edited by Stanley R.
    Ross, pp. 169–74. New York: Knopf, 1966.

Machado, Manuel. *An Industry in Crisis: Mexican–United States Coopera-
    tion in the Control of Foot-and-Mouth Disease*. Berkeley: University
    of California Press, 1968.

Needler, Martin C. *Politics and Society in Mexico*. Albuquerque: Univer-
    sity of New Mexico Press, 1971.

Padgett, L. Vincent. *The Mexican Political System*. Boston: Houghton
    Mifflin, 1966.

Ross, Stanley R. "Mexico: Cool Revolution and Cold War." *Current History*
    41 (1963): 89–94, 116–17.

Schmitt, Karl M. *Mexico and the United States, 1821–1973*. New York:
    Wiley, 1974.

Vernon, Raymond. *The Dilemma of Mexico's Development: The Roles of
    the Private and Public Sectors*. Cambridge, Mass.: Harvard Univer-
    sity Press, 1963.

43

Sparks, Fire, and Smoldering, 1964–76

In spite of major breakthroughs in science and medicine and the space spectaculars that saw the United States place men on the moon, the late 1960s and early 1970s found a world full of tensions and hate. Modernization in general, and communications technology in particular, interlaced nations and dramatically shrank the globe. Word of Martin Luther King's assassination reached Angola only minutes after it reached Atlanta, and Robert Kennedy's assassination was known in Sao Paulo almost as soon as it was known in San Francisco. By the end of the 1960s the entire literate world knew that the United States had dropped a greater tonnage of bombs on Vietnam than the total dropped on all fronts during World War II. Massive marches for peace, for civil rights, and for the right of agricultural workers to organize were reported on the front pages of the world's press.

Mexicans in their living rooms, watching the evening news, saw the destruction of the black ghetto in Washington, the burning of Watts, and riots in Tokyo, Prague, and Berlin; they saw Parisian students pelting police on the Boulevard St. Michel and the senseless killing of students at Kent State University. Mexico's entire history demonstrates amply that Mexicans needed no foreign instruction in standing up for change or, if necessary, putting their lives on the line. And while the late 1960s did not witness any worldwide conspiracy of the young, there was a youthful commonality of interests that transcended national borders. The international pantheon of heroes, with a few national adaptations, included Che Guevara, Ho Chi Minh, Malcolm X, and Mao Tse-tung. The intellectually inclined devoured Herbert Marcuse, while others opted for the simpler, more doctrinaire answers of Fidel Castro. But, however an older generation might have been repulsed by the rebellion, shocked by its rhetoric, and disgusted by its tactics, many of the issues were real and deserved a fair hearing. In Mexico, as well as elsewhere, the sparks would soon begin to fly.

Díaz Ordaz and Political Discontent, 1964–70

When the PRI leadership chose Gustavo Díaz Ordaz as the presidential candidate for 1964, it badly misread the temper of the times. Díaz Ordaz had served as secretary of interior in the López Mateos cabinet and was badly tinged with policy decisions that reform-minded groups could not stomach. It had been he who applied the laws of "social dissolution" against David Alfaro Siqueiros and other radicals. Born in Puebla, the most Catholic state in Mexico, Díaz Ordaz was reputed to be the most conservative official party candidate of the twentieth century. But after winning the election by the customary official party margin, he pledged to carry out the policies initiated by his predecessor.

The electoral reform law that provided for minority representation in the lower house was interpreted to allow the seating of several minority parties in addition to the PAN—the PPS and, although it did not quite reach 2.5 percent of the vote, the Partido Auténtico de la Revolución Mexicana (PARM). But the PAN, the only genuine opposition party, received a very unfavorable ruling in the congressional elections. The congressional seats they actually won from PRI candidates would now be subtracted from the total of twenty they were allowed under López Mateos's constitutional amendment. The decision represented a rejection of the liberalizing tendency many hoped would continue to flourish. If there were any doubts about the trend, the sad and disappointing case of Carlos Madrazo removed them.

Shortly after coming to office, President Díaz Ordaz appointed Madrazo, a reform-minded liberal, to be president of the PRI. Championing a series of far-reaching innovations designed to promote internal democratization of the party, increase rank-and-file participation, reduce the vast power of local and state bosses, and bring more women into the organization, he ran headlong into the vested interests. In the spring of 1965, when Madrazo introduced new reforms designed to purify nomination procedures at the local level, the state political machines rose up in rebellion and, amid tremendous political uproar, prevailed upon Díaz Ordaz to fire him. That the president yielded to party pressure provided further testimony that the party liberalization urged by López Mateos was a thing of the past. As a matter of fact, just the opposite occurred. When PAN candidates won the mayoralties of Tijuana and Mexicali in Baja California, Norte, the government annulled the elections because of "irregularities." Opposition leaders who recalled that Díaz Ordaz had recently stated, "To us, political democracy is a living formula, even more, a way of life based on liberty,"[1] were once again reminded of the colonial maxim, *Obedezco pero no cumplo*. The official party, they contended, was stealing elections with total impunity. The party leadership had lost touch with the people and served simply as a vehicle for the realization of personal political ambitions.

Student Protests and the Olympic Games

Discontent with the official party was not limited to campaign headquarters. Campus after campus exploded with strikes and violence as local university issues merged with national political unrest. A massive strike at the National University in the spring of 1966 resulted in the resignation of the rector. Federal troops were dispatched to restore order on university campuses in Michoacán and Sonora. A major showdown was about to ensue, and the students picked their time very carefully. Mexico was planning its greatest extravaganza since the centennial celebrations of 1910.

When the International Olympic Committee accepted Mexico's bid to host the summer games in 1968, the world was informed that the Olympiad was to be held in Latin America and in a developing country for the first time. The challenge for Mexico was clear, for the Japanese had done a superb job in 1964 and it was incumbent upon the Mexicans to match their effort. Athletes, trainers, representatives of the press, and hundreds of thousands of visitors from the entire world would descend on Mexico and subject it to scrutiny. Construction of athletic facilities, hotels, housing projects, tourist facilities, and a new modern subway system preceded the games, and, amid some amazement, construction workers on round-the-clock shifts finished the

1. Quoted in Alfonso Corona del Rosal, ed., *Gustavo Díaz Ordaz: A Portrait of the President of Mexico for 1964–1970* (Mexico, n.d.), p. 32.

One of the most modern subways in the world, the Mexico City system was running to capacity and beyond within a few months of its completion. In 1990, more than 5 million Mexico City passengers were using the eighty-seven miles of the metro's double tracks every day. Plans to add an additional thirty-seven miles of track were cancelled because of financial exigencies.

Excavation for the subway uncovered hundreds of priceless pre-Columbian artifacts.

major installations on time. To add a unique flavor to the international sports spectacular, a cultural Olympics was scheduled simultaneously, featuring international art exhibitions, book displays, lectures, concerts, and plays. Early charges from critics that the costs were exorbitant for a country such as Mexico were fended off by administration spokesmen who argued that not only would the visitors leave behind tens of millions of dollars but the facilities themselves would be put to good use once the Olympic torch was extinguished. The party and the president were placing all their prestige on the line. The country, they insisted, would show itself as a prosperous and stable republic.

The trouble began almost innocently in July 1968 with a fight between the students of two Mexico City schools, a college preparatory school and a nearby vocational school. The principal of the high school called for police help, and the mayor of the Federal District, General Alfonso Corona del Rosal, erred badly in sending out the *granaderos*, a despised paramilitary riot force. The granaderos stopped the intramural fight but in the process politicized a large portion of the student population in Mexico City. A few days later, as leftist students gathered to celebrate the July 26 anniversary of the Cuban Revolution, they met the granaderos again, and on this occasion a full-scale street riot ensued. But nobody had yet been killed.

August 1968 was a very bad month in Mexico. As city workers were putting the finishing touches on the various construction projects, tensions between the students and the government reached the breaking point. Huge demonstrations were held on the campuses of the National University and the National Polytechnic Institute, and a National Student Strike Committee was formed. A list of demands accentuated tensions; students insisted that all political prisoners be released, that the chief of police be fired, that the granaderos be disbanded, and that the law of "social dissolution" be repealed. Secretary of Interior Luis Echeverría agreed to enter into private discussions with the student leadership, but when the students demanded that the dialogue be broadcast publicly on radio and television, negotiations broke down. On August 27 the National Student Strike Committee brought together in the Zócalo an estimated half a million people, the largest organized antigovernment demonstration in Mexican history. The rally lasted well into the night, and when the government moved tanks and armored cars into the downtown area, violence and the first verified student death resulted.

President Díaz Ordaz's State of the Union address on September 1, 1968, was not full of typical revolutionary platitudes. With the Olympic Games a little over a month away, he had to address himself to the issue of student unrest and respond to the demands.

> It is obvious that hands other than those of students were involved in the recent disturbances; but it is also a fact that . . . a good number of students took part in the affair. . . . I do not admit that there are "political prisoners." A "political prisoner" is one who has been deprived of his freedom *exclusively* because of his political ideas, without having committed any crime. Nevertheless, if I am informed of the name of any person who has been incarcerated without due process of law . . . orders will be given for his immediate unconditional release. . . . With regard to Articles 145 and 145b of the Penal Code, the first of which refers to the crime known as "social dissolution," the abolition of which is requested, let me make it clear that:
>
> The abolition of a law is not within the powers of the President. . . .
>
> We have caused Mexico to appear in the eyes of the world as a country in which the most reprehensible events may take place; for the unfair and almost forgotten image of the Mexican as a

violent, irascible gunman to be revived; and for slander to be mixed with painful truth in the same news reports.[2]

While some of the speech was conciliatory, most of it was hard line. The students were concerned with lack of freedom and the president with lack of security. The worst was yet to come. In the middle of September, with the capital bedecked with Olympic flags and signs of welcome and the students occupying the campus of the National University, Díaz Ordaz ordered ten thousand army troops, in full battle dress, to seize the campus. Some five hundred demonstrators were thrown into jail, and the new rector of the university, Javier Barros Sierra, resigned in protest of the army occupation of his campus. For two weeks, bands of disgruntled students and other malcontents who were in no way associated with the university roamed Mexico City streets, periodically seizing and burning buses, barricading streets, and pillaging. The climax came on October 2, 1968, at a place that will not be forgotten in Mexican history—Tlatelolco.

Strike organizers called for still another outdoor rally at the Plaza de las Tres Culturas in the District of Tlatelolco. The purpose was to berate the government for its failure to comply with the earlier demands. The rally was not large by recent standards, perhaps only five thousand, including many women, children, and innocent spectators. The speeches were emotional, but the demonstration was peaceful. At about 6:30 P.M., army and police units arrived in tanks and armored vehicles. When the demonstrators failed to disband as ordered, the granaderos moved in and began to disperse them with billy clubs and tear gas. What happened next will never be completely clarified. The government version, carried the next day in the Mexican press, claimed that terrorists in nearby apartment buildings began firing on the police. Others insisted that the police opened fire first and that only then did snipers in the buildings begin to shoot. At any rate, when the army units uncovered their high-caliber machine guns and other automatic weapons, thousands of innocent people were caught in the cross fire. Helicopters dropped flares into the crowds, and the troops sprayed indiscriminately from short range. Official government statistics admitted first eight, then eighteen, and finally forty-three deaths, but few knowledgeable Mexicans accepted mortality figures under three or four hundred. Ambulances wailed through the night as hospi-

2. Gustavo Díaz Ordaz, "State of the Union Address, September 1, 1968," in *Models of Change in Latin America*, ed. Paul E. Sigmund (New York, 1970), pp. 38–44.

The Plaza de las Tres Culturas, a tourist attraction for thousands, became a battleground for hundreds in October 1968. *Courtesy of James W. Wilkie.*

tals and clinics filled beyond capacity with the wounded and dying. By the next morning, Mexico City jails held over two thousand new prisoners.

One has only to recall the trauma that engulfed the United States after Kent State, a tragedy of much lesser proportion, to appreciate the anger and despair that Mexicans felt as the story was gradually pieced together over the next few days. But despair quickly gave way to recriminations as Carlos Madrazo attributed the killings to police brutality. The decision had been a political one, and it greatly altered public perception of the country's leadership.

The Olympic Games themselves were notably free of turbulence, and it appeared that the violence had spent itself. The year that followed was a period of reflection for many Mexicans. But in October 1969, on the anniversary of the tragedy at Tlatelolco, Mexicans became aware that urban guerrilla groups had been planning to renew their fight with the administration. Terrorist bombs ripped newspaper offices and government buildings. It was a bad omen as Díaz Ordaz neared the end of his term. The fire of Tlatelolco had been largely extinguished, but social smoldering would continue to choke the country for years. It would become increasingly apparent that much of the PRI's legitimacy had been eroded at the Plaza de las Tres Culturas.

Díaz Ordaz had fostered a number of important social and economic programs during his tenure as president. Federal expenditure for education reached over 26 percent of the total budget, one of the highest rates in the entire world. Urban renewal projects in the northern border cities catered to the tourist trade, and tourists left record amounts of money in Ciudad Juárez, Tijuana, Nogales, Piedras Negras, and Matamoros. The economy remained healthy, registering 6 percent annual increases in the gross national product. Mexico took the lead in international conferences, securing pledges that Latin America should be declared a nuclear free zone. Under other circumstances, Díaz Ordaz might have been remembered for these accomplishments, but, just as the administration of Richard M. Nixon will be remembered less for finally extricating the United States from Vietnam than for the shame of Watergate, the name of Díaz Ordaz will always be associated with the unpardonable tragedy at Tlatelolco.

The Presidency of Echeverría

The political atmosphere had not returned to normal when Mexico held its 1970 presidential election. PRI candidate Luis Echeverría had been secretary of interior during the recent Olympic trouble, and the Mexican left held him largely responsible for the government's overreaction. With a reputation for inflexibility and intolerance, he scarcely seemed the man to foster an atmosphere of national consensus. Echeverría decided to campaign vigorously, yet he failed to capture public imagination and left many wondering when he declared that Mexico, a country that had experienced an increase in population of some 14 million since 1960, had no need for family planning.

During the first year of his term, President Echeverría showed himself as a man of boundless energy; he put in long hours and demanded the same of those who surrounded him. He nurtured himself on face-to-face dialogue with farmers in dusty villages and workers in urban factories. Not nearly as inflexible as portrayed, he quickly began to counter his reputation by moving to the center and then to the left. To the chagrin of the conservative business community, he began renewing initiatives in rural Mexico and even announced that perhaps industrialization had to slow down. A major emphasis was placed on extending the rural road system and rural electrification. Caught in the worldwide inflation of the early 1970s, he tried to minimize its impact on the poor by ordering rigid price controls of basic commodities; at the same time, luxury items were hit with a new tax of 10 percent, and a 15 percent surtax was added to all bills in first-class restaurants and night clubs. Echeverría even moderated his stand on family planning and halfway through his administration gave a cautious endorsement to birth control. But Echeverría surprised his critics most when he released the majority of Mexico's student prisoners in early 1971.

The transition from Díaz Ordaz to Luis Echeverría seemed to be going well until in late 1971 and early 1972 Mexicans learned that the violent legacy of Tlatelolco was not yet over. A series of bank robberies in the fall were traced to the Movimiento Armado Revolucionario (MAR) when gunmen bragged that their exploits were in behalf of the coming revolution. Other robberies and political kidnappings followed: Jaime Castrejón, rector of the University of Guerrero, and Julio Hirschfield, director of the nation's airports, both fell into rebel hands. But there was still more to come. Terrance Leonhardy, United States consul general in Guadalajara, was kidnapped, as were the British honorary consul, Anthony Duncan Williams; Fernando Aranguren, a wealthy Guadalajara businessman; and Nadine Chaval, the daughter of the Belgian ambassador. A wealthy Monterrey industrialist, Eugenio Garza Sada, was killed during a kidnapping attempt, and a train carrying tourists was assaulted in southern Sonora, resulting in the deaths of four travelers. In the summer of 1974, President Echeverría's father-in-law, Guadalupe Zuno Hernández, a former governor of Jalisco, was captured and held for ransom by a group calling themselves the Fuerzas Revolucionarias Armadas del Pueblo (FRAP).

In the mountains of Guerrero, Lucio Cabañas, a flamboyant former schoolteacher, gathered a guerrilla army, had the police chief of Acapulco assassinated, and began attacking small army outposts stationed in the state. The eyes of the nation focused on Cabañas when guerrillas under his command kidnapped Guerrero senator Rubén Figueroa, at the time a candidate for governor. Ten thousand army troops were dispatched to Guerrero to capture the guerrillas, but it took them over a year to do the job.

Luis Echeverría (b. 1922). The most active president since Cárdenas, Echeverría was interested primarily in foreign policy, but his energies were directed to the country's serious economic woes.

Cabañas and twenty-seven of his men were killed in gun battles with the army, but most observers were convinced that another guerrilla leader would simply pick up his banner.

When United States ambassador Joseph John Jova told the Mexican Chamber of Commerce in September 1974 that "there is no large scale opposition to the federal government,"[3] one might have been reminded that in November 1910 Ambassador Henry Lane Wilson had made similar statements. But where Wilson was wrong, Jova was essentially correct. In spite of the impressions one might receive in the morning newspapers, Mexico was not yet falling apart at the seams. Pressures were building, but Echeverría had made major attempts to accommodate the interests of youth. He brought more young people into important positions in the government than any previous head of state. The voting age was lowered to eighteen, the age for holding a Senate seat from thirty-five to thirty, and for holding membership in the Chamber of Deputies from thirty to twenty-one. Other administration programs should have been well received by youth. Mexico granted diplomatic asylum to Hortensia Allende, widow of the murdered Chilean president. In 1972 the administration nationalized the tobacco and telephone industries. Echeverría's foreign travels opened new avenues of trade and, by extension,

3. Joseph John Jova, "American Business and Mexican Development," address to the Mexican Chamber of Commerce, September 11, 1974 (mimeographed, 1974).

sought to lessen dependence upon the United States. Yet all these measures were ineffectual palliatives.

Alienation had set it, and the roots went deep. To be sure, part of the problem could be attributed to the inflation rate, which topped 20 percent in both 1973 and 1974. But to ascribe the alienation simply to rate of inflation or even to the gradual demise of Mexico's postwar economic miracle would be to miss the point. In at least one sense some of the Revolution's successes, rather than its shortcomings, contributed to the growing tensions in Mexican society. As Stanley R. Ross noted in an article assessing the stresses in Mexico in the early 1970s:

> There is a fair amount of evidence which suggests that rapid economic growth may of and by itself adversely affect societal stability. Specifically it disrupts the existing social structure and increases the numbers who are gainers and losers. Rising literacy, exposure to mass communications, and other advances in integrating the nation produce rising demands on the political system. Equally important is the creation of rising expectations that soon outdistance the capacity of even a rapidly expanding economy to satisfy them.[4]

Other factors contributed to the alienation as well, and not least among them was the manner in which the Revolution had propagandized itself over the years. By the late 1960s and early 1970s, the young, sophisticated generation of Mexican students had absorbed an incredible amount of revolutionary rhetoric. A not untypical Sunday outing in Mexico City could include a car or taxi ride by the Monument to the Revolution and then on to Avenida 20 de Noviembre, where the book stores carried posters not of Sophia Loren and Farrah Fawcett-Majors but of Emiliano Zapata and Pancho Villa. Then, on Avenida Francisco I. Madero the walls would be plastered with billboards propagandizing the Partido Revolucionario Institucional. And on Sunday evening every radio station in the country carried "La Hora Nacional," a musical and cultural presentation interspersed with three- to four-minute orations on themes such as "The Pride of Being Mexican," "One Must Defend the Revolution," and "The March of Revolutionary Progress."

The spate of revolutionary euphemisms became more than the young intellectual could easily accept. Fewer and fewer Mexicans were content to look south toward Guatemala and beyond

---

4. Stanley R. Ross, "México: Las tensiones del progreso," *Latinoamérica* 4 (1971): 9–21.

and, by comparison, to feel gratitude for their own Revolution. Disquieting everyday realities denied the easy revolutionary platitudes. And when late in his term President Echeverría attempted to address a student convocation at the National University, he was driven off the campus by an angry, rock-throwing mob, calling for forceful action, not mindless rhetoric. But even in December 1975, Luis Echeverría most assuredly could not have realized that a year later he would leave office under a tremendous cloud of controversy. His successor would inherit a dispirited country, one in which cynicism had become a hallmark. The roots of the problem were economic, but they meshed with ideological postures and social realities to produce an unparalleled crisis of confidence.

The 1970s found Mexico suffering a large balance of payments deficit. The rate of industrial growth had been impressive, but that expansion had rested on the foundation of government protection. Mexican industry, it turned out, was not cost effective and was not generally competitive on world markets. It was unable to turn the balance of payments tide. With imports outstripping exports by almost $3.5 billion in 1975 alone, Echeverría, currying Third World support in a bid for the secretary-generalship of the United Nations, ordered his ambassador in the world organization to cast two votes equating Zionism with racism. The result was unanticipated, as in early 1976 Jewish groups in the United States organized a tourist boycott of Mexico. Empty resort hotels dramatically testified that a substantial proportion of Mexico's tourist industry of $2.5 billion had been curtailed. Other factors, such as shortages of electric power, steel, and transportation facilities, contributed to a decline in the rate of economic growth. Echeverría had repeatedly lectured his citizenry on the need for democratization in Mexico and the value of a free press. As the economic situation deteriorated, however, he found himself attacked on all sides. When criticism from Mexico's largest daily newspaper, *Excelsior*, became too severe, the administration removed its editor, Julio Scherer García. By the summer of 1976, rumors were rampant that for the first time in twenty-two years Mexico would have to devalue the peso. The president's repeated assurances to the contrary did not prevent the flight of huge amounts of pesos as wealthy Mexicans exchanged their currency for dollars and investment in the United States and Europe. Capital flight in 1976 alone might have topped $6 billion. Mexican pundits quickly coined a new pejorative to deride their unpatriotic countrymen. *Sacadólares* (dollar extractors) would enter the day-to-day parlance.

The decision to devaluate came in September, and the peso fell from 12.50 to 20.50 to the dollar, a 60 percent devaluation. Once the initial shock subsided, Mexicans accepted the devaluation stoically, as they were assured that the resultant reduction of imports and growth of exports would combine to shore up the economy. But Mexican policy makers had not allowed the peso to float long enough to reach its true level. A month later a second devaluation of an additional 40 percent was announced in Mexico City. Psychologically, the second was more painful than the first, for it pointed up financial mismanagement of major proportions.

With the country still in shock, a serious old problem surfaced once again. Thousands of landless Sonora peasants moved onto privately owned lands in the rich Yaqui Valley and seized several hundred thousand acres from some eight hundred owners. Although the land seizures were being adjudicated in the Mexican Supreme Court, Echeverría, with not two weeks remaining in his presidential term, took matters into his own hands. He declared the seizures legal and gave the peasants 250,000 acres for communal development. The uproar could have been expected; Mexican industrialists and businessmen joined the former landowners in a huge protest strike. Yet to the more ardent agrarian radicals of the 1970s the presidential expropriation decree was tokenism of the worst kind, a ploy to gain Echeverría a historical niche in the Cárdenas tradition.

The twelve years encompassed by the Díaz Ordaz and Echeverría administrations, 1964 to 1976, were difficult ones in Mexico's post–World War II experience. Since the onset of the institutional revolution in the early 1940s, Mexican confidence had been bolstered repeatedly by the country's political stability and remarkable economic success. Mexico seemingly had separated itself from the systemic problems of its neighbors to the south. But by 1975 and 1976, it was obvious to Mexicans and foreigners alike that the political system and economic structure had proved themselves to be quite fragile. This fragility would be severely tested in the years to come.

Recommended for Further Study

Anderson, Bo, and James D. Cockcroft. "Control and Co-optation in Mexican Politics." In *Dependence and Underdevelopment*, edited by James D. Cockcroft et al., pp. 220–43. Garden City, N.Y.: Doubleday, 1972.

Blough, William J. "Political Attitudes of Mexican Women: Support for the Political System among a Newly Enfranchised Group." *Journal of Inter-American Studies and World Affairs* 14 (1972): 201–24.

Cochrane, James D. "Mexico's New Científicos: The Díaz Ordaz Cabinet." *Inter-American Economic Affairs* 21 (1967): 61–72.

"Documents on the Student Revolt of 1968." In *Models of Political Change in Latin America*, edited by Paul Sigmund, pp. 33–44. New York: Praeger, 1970.

Eckstein, Susan. *The Poverty of Revolution: The State and the Urban Poor in Mexico*. Princeton, N.J.: Princeton University Press, 1977.

Erb, Richard D., and Stanley R. Ross, eds. *U.S. Policies toward Mexico: Perceptions and Perspectives*. Washington, D.C.: American Enterprise Institute for Public Policy Research, 1979.

Grindle, Merilee S. *Bureaucrats, Politicians, and Peasants in Mexico: A Case Study in Public Policy*. Berkeley: University of California Press, 1977.

Hansen, Roger D. *The Politics of Mexican Development*. Baltimore: Johns Hopkins University Press, 1971.

Johnson, Kenneth F. *Mexican Democracy: A Critical View*. Boston: Allyn and Bacon, 1971.

Liebman, Arthur. "Student Activism in Mexico." *Annals of the American Society of Political and Social Science* 395 (1971): 159–70.

Lomnitz, Larissa Adler. *Networks and Marginality: Life in a Mexican Shantytown*. New York: Academic Press, 1977.

Needler, Martin C. *Politics and Society in Mexico*. Albuquerque: University of New Mexico Press, 1971.

Paz, Octavio. *The Other Mexico: Critique of the Pyramid*. New York: Grove Press, 1972.

Pellicer de Brody, Olga. "Mexico in the 1970's and Its Relations with the United States." In *Latin America and the United States*, edited by Julio Cotler and Richard R. Fagen, pp. 314–33. Stanford, Calif.: Stanford University Press, 1974.

Ross, Stanley, ed. *Views Across the Border*. Albuquerque: University of New Mexico Press, 1978.

Sepúlveda, César. "Student Participation in University Affairs." *American Journal of Comparative Law* 17 (1969): 384–89.

Shapira, Yoram. *Mexican Foreign Policy Under Echeverría*. Beverly Hills, Calif.: Sage, 1978.

Williams, Edward J. *The Rebirth of the Mexican Petroleum Industry*. Lexington, Mass.: Heath, 1979.

Womack, John, Jr. "The Spoils of the Mexican Revolution." *Foreign Affairs* 48 (1970): 677–87.

44

Mexico since 1976:
The Tensions of Development
and Democratization

José López Portillo and Petropolitics

On December 1, 1976, José López Portillo, the presidential candidate of the PRI, replaced Luis Echeverría in the Mexican presidency. While a few Mexicans evidenced optimism on that inauguration day, the vast majority found little cause for celebration. Sixty-six years had passed since Francisco Madero's Plan de San Luis Potosí, but many believed that the same old problems had emerged once again.

Prior to the famous Arab oil embargo in the early 1970s, the world thought little about energy, conservation, or the influence of petroleum and petroleum by-products on inflation and power politics. But these issues dominated the national and international press in the late 1970s and early 1980s. In some circles it became archaic to speak of the First, Second, and Third worlds. It seemed more appropriate to categorize nations as oil producers and oil consumers, and this, in turn, necessitated new conceptualizations of dependency and interdependency.

The large petroleum discoveries made in southeastern Mexico (primarily in the state of Tabasco and Chiapas and offshore in the Gulf of Mexico) antedated the inauguration of President José López Portillo in 1976, but their extent and influence grew markedly during his administration and came to overshadow every-

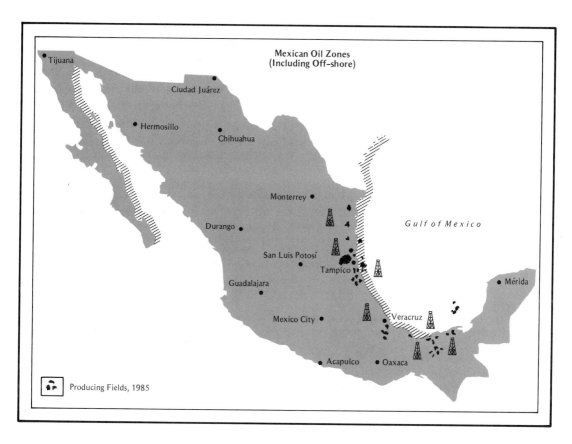

Mexican Oil Zones
(Including Off-shore)

Gulf of Mexico

Producing Fields, 1985

thing else. The figures for proven and probable reserves have varied tremendously since the discoveries were first announced in 1974. But in 1980, López Portillo verified that proven reserves topped 60 billion barrels, while probable reserves approached 200 billion.

From the outset, López Portillo followed a policy of gradual, not dramatic, daily increase. Although Mexico had the necessary capital and technology to increase production with great rapidity, it resisted pressures from the United States and other foreign powers to do so. The economic infrastructure was not prepared to digest suddenly huge infusions of foreign capital without negative side effects. More important, it then seemed obvious that the price of petroleum in the future was not doing to decline. Oil production rose steadily but sensibly during the López Portillo years, growing from about 800,000 barrels per day in 1976 to 2.3 million barrels a day in 1980. In 1981 Mexico became the world's fourth largest producer. The tripling of production during the administration did not reveal the whole story of how petroleum influenced the Mexican economy. For two reasons, Mexico's earning of petrodollars rose much more rapidly than the increased production figures would seem to suggest. First, a large percentage of the increase was destined for the international, not the domestic, market. Even more important was the steadily spiraling price of a barrel of crude. During the same period that production tripled, earnings from petroleum sales increased twelve-fold, from $500 million in 1976 to about $6 billion in 1980. Prospects for a healthy and dynamic economy never looked better.

Mexican petroleum wealth had an incalculable impact on how the country viewed itself and how it related to others in the international community. In an energy-hungry world, petroleum production carried unusual international prestige. Mexico's new oil muscle was flexed repeatedly in its relations with the United

GROWTH OF THE MEXICAN PETROLEUM INDUSTRY

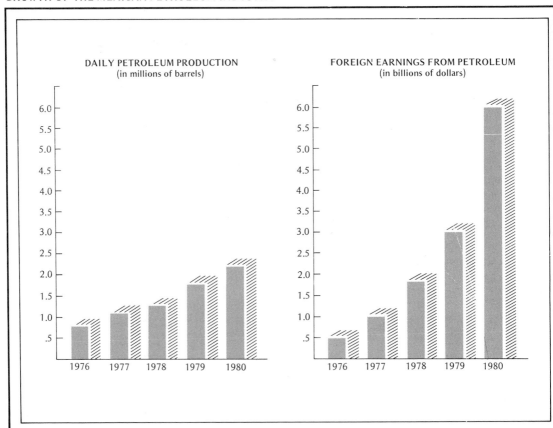

States. Standing up to Washington and Wall Street, even in the face of threats, was nothing new in the history of the Mexican Revolution. What was different was the self-assurance Mexico carried into the international arena. The United States of Jimmy Carter had to learn that Mexico's support of foreign policy initiatives from Washington could not be taken for granted unless they were judged by Mexicans to be in Mexico's best interests. In a dramatic but symbolic gesture, López Portillo was one of the first Latin American heads of state to announce that his country could not support the Carter administration's boycott of the Moscow Olympics. When the United States and Mexico could not agree on the price of natural gas, the Mexican president simply decided to burn off excess gas rather than sell to the United States at a figure judged to be inequitable.

Mexico's new international posture was most graphically displayed during President Carter's goodwill visit to Mexico City in 1979. López Portillo used the occasion to chastise the United States for its historical record in Mexico, to criticize his guest for being insensitive to Mexican dignity, and to warn Carter against "surprise moves or sudden deceits." The new administration of Ronald Reagan quickly learned that outward manifestations of friendship and goodwill would not change Mexico's foreign policy. In 1981 Mexico joined France in a declaration recognizing rebel guerrillas in El Salvador as a representative political force. In spite of public reaction, none of these incidents can be fairly interpreted as Mexican hostility to the United States. They were reflections of the new petroleum equation in United States–Mexican relations.

Only the most naïve considered petroleum a panacea for Mexico's sundry social and economic problems, but few realized the dangers that petro-dependency portended for the future. The first indications of trouble were faint and subtle. By the late 1970s, López Portillo was faced with an unemployment rate of almost 25 percent and an underemployment rate of almost 50 percent of the country's work force. Petroleum was a capital-intensive, not a labor-intensive industry. With continuing increased production it could absorb perhaps 150,000 new workers each year, but by 1980, 800,000 Mexicans were entering the job market annually. Jobs would have to be created in other sectors of the economy.

Industry maintained healthy growth during the López Portillo administration, but agricultural production could not keep pace with the increase in population. Fearful that the newly found petrodollars could all be expended on food imports, in March

Between 1980 and 1982, Presidents José López Portillo and Ronald Reagan met on four occasions. The public cordiality of the visits notwithstanding, the two countries found it difficult to agree on important issues such as undocumented workers and the revolutionary turmoil in Central America.

1980 the president announced the formation of Sistema Alimentario Mexicano (SAM), the Mexican Food System. The first major coordinated effort to increase agricultural production in the postwar period, SAM's goals called for agricultural growth of 4 percent a year and self-sufficiency in basic grains by 1985. A few months after SAM was proclaimed, the World Bank approved a loan of $325 million, the largest loan that agency ever made, to help implement the program. SAM was an extremely important undertaking. Increased agricultural production not only promised to improve the standard of living in rural areas, but by eliminating the need for huge food imports would greatly improve Mexico's unfavorable balance of trade. The goals were certainly sound, but the success rate fell short of spectacular. Several years after López Portillo left office, Mexico was still importing about 10 million tons of food annually.

Mexico's 1980 census, conducted two-thirds through the López Portillo administration, revealed one very promising trend. In the early postwar years, the percentage of illiterates in Mexico was constantly reduced, but because of the population explosion, the absolute number of illiterates rose. The 1980 census documented not only a decline in the percentage of illiterates from 28 percent in 1970 to 17.1 percent in 1980, but a drop of 1.5 million in the absolute number of illiterates. The education efforts of all the postwar administrations had finally left their mark.

The Economic Slide Begins

López Portillo led Mexico on an unparalleled spending spree. Government construction, public works, social welfare projects, and government subsidies of consumer goods all meant an increased government participation in the economy. Although national income was insufficient to cover the costs, Mexico's vast petroleum reserves made the international banking community willing, indeed eager, to extend large loans. Mexico's massive deficit spending was predicated on the supposition that continuing rises in the price of oil would allow the country to generate new wealth and repay its foreign obligations. But contrary to all expectations, petroleum prices did not rise. Because of the world oil glut of the early 1980s, they began to decline, and this fact changed the nature of the Mexican political equation. López Portillo was forced to retreat from his assertive foreign policy and adopt a more moderate stance.

In 1982, during the last year of his administration, López Portillo found himself in a position which seemed similar to that of Luis Echeverría in 1976. Actually it was much worse. The Mexican rate of inflation greatly exceeded that in the United States, and the peso was again over-valued in relation to the dollar. As Mexican businessmen lost confidence in the economy, they began investing abroad and opening new bank accounts in the United States. To stop the monetary flight, in February the president ordered the Central Bank to stop buying and selling dollars and to allow the peso to find its true worth. Within a few days, it had lost one-third of its former value as it slipped from 26 to 37 pesos to the dollar, and by summer of 1982 had sunk to 100 pesos, marking the peso's lowest value ever. Concomitant price increases and tight currency controls created near panic in both business and government circles. It was only the tip of the iceberg.

In the last analysis, López Portillo applied the brakes too late, after he had first tried to squander Mexico into prosperity. The oil miracle had become the oil nightmare, and the president came under severe fire for mishandling the economy and demonstrating a lack of judgment and leadership. His response was un-anticipated as he accused the country's private banks of looting, of greed, and of disloyalty for their participation in the flight of Mexican capital in the amount of $22 billion. He had found a perfect scapegoat. In September 1982, without first soliciting any advice from his cabinet, the president, with high drama, announced that he was nationalizing fifty-nine of the country's banks. He used the occasion to lecture his countrymen:

> A group of Mexicans, led, counseled, and aided by the private banks, has taken more money out of the country than all the empires that have exploited us since the beginning . . . we cannot, with dignity do anything else. We cannot stand with our arms crossed while they tear out our entrails.[1]

But the nationalization of the banks was more an act of bravado than a rational solution to Mexico's economic ills.

As López Portillo's administration came to an end, Mexicans were incensed to learn that the president, in spite of his pious incantations about others, had taken care of himself prior to the expiration of his term of office. He had constructed four large mansions for himself and his family on prime land. The lofty site of the López Portillo compound was dubbed "Dog Hill," a sarcastic reminder of the president's earlier remarks that he would defend the peso "like a dog." As he departed Mexico for an extended vacation in Europe, he left behind Mexico's worst economic crisis of the twentieth century.

Miguel de la Madrid: From Crisis to Crisis, 1982–88

When forty-seven-year-old Miguel de la Madrid was told that he had won the Mexican presidency, he reportedly quipped to a friend, "Fraud, fraud!" If he did repeat those words, one could scarcely have blamed him. He faced the sobering prospect of inheriting the leadership of a country beset with economic problems so serious that they threatened to disrupt the social order.

Educated at the Universidad Nacional Autónoma de México and subsequently at Harvard University, Miguel de la Madrid's rise to his country's highest office was nothing short of meteoric. In spite of his relative youth, his formal education and previous

---

1. Quoted in Judith Adler Hellman, *Mexico in Crisis* (New York, 1983), p. 225.

Elected in July, 1982, Miguel de la Madrid succeeded López Portillo as president. He recognized that he would face difficult times but could not have predicted that the country was on the verge of economic collapse.

experience in public administration prepared him better for the tasks that lay ahead than most of his twentieth-century predecessors. He had campaigned on a firm pledge of moral renovation, a promise to eliminate the corruption so endemic in the Mexican public sector. He was given ample opportunity to carry out this pledge. During his first year in office, revelations of corruption during the administration of López Portillo were carried in the front pages of the press almost on a daily basis. Although President de la Madrid did not prosecute his predecessor, he did strike out against other high-ranking government officials. In one spectacular case, Jorge Díaz Serrano, the former director of PEMEX, was indicted for embezzlement of $43 million. Serrano was convicted and sentenced to a ten-year jail term. Even more outrageous were the alleged crimes of Arturo Durazo, Mexico City's chief of police and a friend of López Portillo since childhood. "El Negro Durazo" was charged with fifty murders, trafficking in drugs, and extortion of superlative proportions. His luxurious residence in the coastal resort of Zihuatanejo was nicknamed "The Parthenon," to which it bore some resemblance. His palatial home near Mexico City came complete with its own discotheque, modeled after New York City's famous Studio 54. Weekend guests, flown to the $2.5 million estate in police helicopters, marvelled at Durazo's string of race horses, nineteen collector's automobiles, casino, gymnasium, and cellar of vintage wines. Not even the most shrewd businessmen, they opined, could have accumulated this kind of fortune on a government salary of $65 per week. But Durazo escaped prosecution by fleeing the country prior to the order for his arrest. United States law enforcement officials arrested him in Puerto Rico and sent him to Los Angeles to await extradition papers from Mexico City, but the process was delayed endlessly as the money in Durazo's foreign bank accounts, reported to total some $600 million, permitted him to hire one of the most prestigious law firms in California to fight the legal process. They delayed Durazo's extradition until the spring of 1986, when he was returned to Mexico and subsequently convicted.

The president received his share of accolades for his two highly publicized victories against the egregious dishonesty of Díaz Serrano and Durazo, but the battle against governmental malfeasance had scarcely been won. The country's comptroller general, Ignacio Pichardo, synopsized the issue with perfect insight when he stated that Mexican corruption was like garbage: it had to be removed daily. He was calling for a type of moral stamina that was difficult to find.

An equally persistent dilemma was the country's deepening economic crisis. The peso began to slip against the dollar in 1984 and then began a veritable plunge on the free market. Many stood in disbelief as it plummeted from 150 to 200, and then to 380 to the dollar during the summer of 1985, but the bottom had not been reached. By autumn 1986, currency houses and money brokers along the U.S.–Mexican border were exchanging the peso at an incredible 800 to 1. The year 1987 was even more catastrophic for the peso. When the year opened it took 950 pesos to purchase a dollar, but by December the exchange rate was an incredible 2,300 to 1. The relationship between the two countries' currencies was so out of kilter in the summer of 1987 that a U.S. tourist could ride the Mexico City metro over two thousand times for one dollar or make ten thousand calls on a pay phone for the same amount. The 20-centavo coins were worth so little that owners of hardware stores in Sonora drilled holes in their middles and sold them as washers.

Mexico's foreign debt under Miguel de la Madrid grew in geometric proportion. Although the president was able to arrange a rescheduling of payments on the debt, the pressure on him was tremendous. Political parties, peasant groups, and labor unions of the left, following the lead of Cuba's Fidel Castro, urged him to repudiate the debt or at a minimum to declare a unilateral

THE EXCHANGE RATE, PESOS TO THE DOLLAR, 1955-90

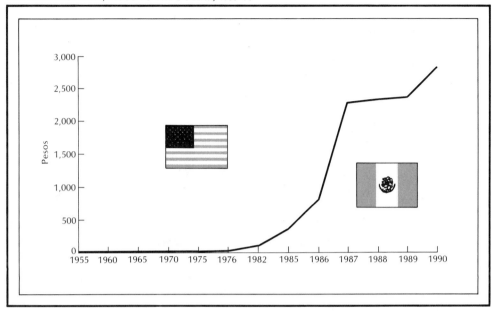

moratorium on repayment. The lessons of Mexican history cautioned against such precipitous action: a similar action in 1861, for no less dire reasons, had occasioned a foreign intervention and ultimately the establishment of a French empire in the valley of Anáhuac. And though de la Madrid feared no such intervention and undoubtedly agreed that the interest rates being paid on Mexico's debt were excessive, he did realize the necessity of rekindling some degree of confidence in the world's banking community and financial markets. He opted for economic austerity, not repudiation. It was a calculated risk: asking the Mexican masses to tighten their belts once again was asking them to accept their miserable squalor.

Recognizing that government expenditures had to be drastically reduced, de la Madrid not only curtailed many new projects but also announced reductions in federal subsidies, the sale of inefficient and unprofitable state-owned enterprises, and a freeze on federal employment. Using the considerable influence of the presidential office, he did his best to limit the size of wage increases in the labor force. Finally in a bold move, the president eliminated some 51,000 federal jobs and cut back the salaries of other government employees whose positions could not be eliminated. The economic reforms seemed to be paying dividends, for in late 1984 the international banking community not only applauded his efforts but indicated that Mexico was dealing with the debt crisis more effectively than any other Latin American country. Progress had been made, and there was room for cautious optimism.

Then, suddenly, tragedy struck during the morning rush hour on September 19, 1985, as Mexico paid the price of sitting at the juncture of three of the earth's tectonic plates. An earthquake registering in excess of 8 on the Richter Scale devastated the capital, leaving more than eight thousand dead, many more injured, and damage estimated at $4 billion. This latest test for the Mexican citizenry was met with fortitude and heroism, but the calamity not only made payments on the foreign debt impossible, but presented dismal prospects for continued progress on the economic front.

The last years of the de la Madrid administration saw Mexico slip deeper and deeper into the economic morass. In addition to the collapse of the peso, inflation soared to unprecedented heights. Official inflation rates, released by Mexico's Central Bank, reported 63.7 percent in 1985, 105.7 percent in 1986, and 159 percent in 1987. The man on the street swore that the actual figures were even higher. Increases in the cost of gasoline, corn, wheat, and electricity led the assault on the consumer price index, but no product or service emerged unscathed. The only thing that could match the rapid rise in prices was the rapid growth of the foreign debt. When de la Madrid left office in December 1988, the Mexican government owed foreigners a whopping $105 billion in outstanding debts.

United States–Mexican Relations

Two major problems defying easy solution dominated United States–Mexican relations in the 1970s and 1980s. Both of them concerned movement across the common border, and both of them had national significance that transcended the international line that divides the two countries.

Since the 1950s, the United States–Mexican border region has witnessed one of the most profound demographic shifts in world history not conditioned by either war or epidemic disease. The result of a high birthrate and massive northern migration in Mexico and the equally telling Sunbelt phenomenon in the United States, the population has soared unremittingly on both sides of the border. In 1940, only about 16 million persons occupied the four U.S. states and six Mexican states that share

Damage in Mexico City was extensive, and the clean-up task monumental, after the earthquake of September 19, 1985.

For young and old alike, the chain-link boundary line separating Nogales, Arizona, from Nogales, Sonora, is little more than a daily inconvenience.

the international line. At the beginning of 1990, the estimated population of the same ten states was over 60 million. The swell has been so dramatic that it not only dominates day-to-day human relations of the region but drives international relations as well. The border between the countries is permeable, and not only to people. Disease, polluted water, contaminated air, to cite but a few examples, refuse to respect the artificial line drawn by nineteenth-century politicians to ratify the work of nineteenth-century generals.

Of the major problems growing out of a common international boundary, the most protracted one is that of the undocumented worker. Beginning in the 1970s unemployment, underemployment, persistent poverty, and the undeniable lure of the United States prompted hundreds of thousands of Mexican workers to cross the border illegally into the United States each year in pursuit of gainful employment. The number of undocumented workers in the United States at any given time cannot be calculated accurately, but most serious estimates range between 4 and 6 million.

The undocumented worker phenomenon is an emotion-charged topic that has precipitated much national and international debate. Everyone agrees that the United States has the right to enforce its immigration laws and to regulate entries into the country. But there is no consensus on precisely what should be done and how. Few United States citizens would feel comfortable living in a country that convinced itself that there was no alternative but to guard its southern boundary with mine fields, electrically charged barbed wire, or a human fence of soldiers stationed along that porous two-thousand-mile border at intervals of two hundred yards.

Realistic solutions are complicated by the fact that an undocumented worker mythology is current in the United States and is nurtured by vested interest groups. Contrary to popular opinion, the undocumented workers do not constitute a drain on social services. The best evidence suggests forcefully that most of them have federal and state taxes deducted from their wages but do not reap the benefits of the tax system for fear of being detected and reported to immigration authorities. In reality, undocumented workers subsidize social services and use them only infrequently. Equally evident is the myth that a great many displace United States workers and in a major way contribute to unemployment north of the international boundary. Undoubtedly some United States workers have been displaced, but the large majority of the undocumented fill positions that would remain vacant at wage levels falling below minimum scale. It is true that because many undocumented workers will accept jobs below the minimum wage they tend to depress the labor market. For this reason, a broad spectrum of labor organizations in the United States began calling for tighter controls while an equally broad spectrum of employers, in both rural and urban areas, favor the maintenance of the status quo.

A solution of sorts was reached in 1986 when the United States Congress passed the Immigration Reform and Control Act (the Simpson-Rodino Act). The main features of the legislation provided for a tighter enforcement of immigration policy, sanctions against those who knowingly employed undocumented workers, and an amnesty for those workers who could establish continued residence in the United States since 1982. But Simpson-Rodino did not solve the undocumented worker problem because it addressed only those factors that pulled the Mexican workers toward the United States, ignoring those that pushed them out of Mexico. The undocumented continued to come, albeit in smaller numbers, as there was no shortage of United States employers willing to offer work in spite of threatened sanctions. The fundamental problems remained. In 1989, Jorge Bustamante, Mexico's leading border specialist, reported that earnings sent back to

Mexico by undocumented workers totaled $1.25 billion annually, making this source of income the country's third largest source of foreign exchange.

If Mexican workers are performing useful labor, if they are able to earn money with which to support their families, if they are not contributing in a major way to unemployment in the United States, and if they do not constitute a burden on social services, why are they considered to be a problem? The answer in part rests with the plight of the undocumented workers themselves as revealed in the countless human tragedies that occur each year. Crossing the border illegally immediately converts a law-abiding citizen into a fugitive from justice with no protection from the varied forms of human exploitation. Those Mexicans, called *coyotes*, who contract with individual workers for surreptitious entry and transportation to a job have been known to collect their fees and deliver their human cargo to U.S. immigration authorities. United States employers have been known to set up two-week pay periods, and, after receiving thirteen days of labor from an entire work force, call in the border patrol, thus relieving themselves of the need to meet the payroll. In the Southwest, groups of vigilantes have taken "law enforcement" into their own hands and have terrorized and physically brutalized undocumented workers as object lessons to those who would follow them. Unintended tragedies also abound as evidenced by two dozen undocumented workers asphyxiated in an air-tight van or thirteen more dying of dehydration trying to cross the Arizona desert by foot in the burning heat of summer. When thousands of sick people fear to go to a hospital or thousands of victims of assault and robbery fear to go to the police, when an entire group is made the scapegoat for a complicated potpourri of social ills, a compassionate society must be concerned.

The second and more serious problem that plagued the generally good relations between Washington, D.C., and Mexico, D.F., and that contributed to a politically charged atmosphere, was the unremitting flow of drugs across the United States–Mexico border. The smuggling of contraband between the two countries certainly was nothing new. Arms and ammunition, automobiles, trucks, agricultural equipment, household items, and scores of other products had long evaded the eyes, regulations, and taxing authority of the customs agents. What made the problem so volatile in the late 1980s was the especially insidious nature of the illegal cargo. The international drug traffic, both sides agreed, not only left its legacy of abuse and dependence, but also fostered an entire host of parasitic crimes, especially in the border region. Authorities from the two countries, however, agreed on little else. The public was soon treated to the most bizarre misapplication of the theories of the Scottish economist Adam Smith: United States officials found the problem to be simply one of supply, while their Mexican counterparts retorted that it was simply one of demand.

Following the murder of U.S. Drug Enforcement Administrative agent Enrique Camarena near Guadalajara, in 1986 and 1987 the United States Congress held formal hearings on terrorism and drugs. These hearings prompted the most intemperate statements on Mexico's alleged lack of cooperation on the drug issue in spite of indications to the contrary from the United States ambassador in Mexico City. By 1988, Mexico-bashing had become a favorite pastime of those who could think of no other reasons for the United States failure to win its much publicized war on drugs. In that year, the U.S. Senate failed to certify Mexico for economic assistance because it was not doing enough to intercept the flow of drugs before they crossed the border.

The strident rhetoric continued until early 1989 when crimes of violence became so outrageous in the border region that law enforcement officials on both sides had to stop shouting and start talking. In addition to many drug-related individual murders, execution-style killings in the spring of 1989 claimed six lives in Caborca, Sonora; four in Navojoa, Sonora; twelve in Agua Prieta, Sonora; five in Tucson, Arizona; and twelve in Matamoros, Tamaulipas. The binational cooperation in the investigation of these killings and the prompt extradition of suspects augured well for the future, but much remained to be done.

Democratization and the Elections of 1988

The 1980s were a decade of democratization or redemocratization throughout much of Latin America. In most of the region, this phenomenon meant replacing military dictatorships with civilian governments chosen in an open or a relatively open electoral process. In Mexico, democratization was something very different. The army had ceased to call the political shots in Mexican politics decades earlier. Democratization in Mexico meant opening up the political system, recognizing that it had systemic weaknesses, and making it more responsive to the Mexican citizenry. The process was far from innocuous, for it meant that the influential political bosses in the country would have to share their power with others.

The basic problem was not new to the 1980s. Because of circumstances unique to Mexico's twentieth-century experience, one political party had gained almost absolute dominance. This official party, under different names, had won every election for president and every election for the thirty-one governorships since its foundation in 1929. If an occasional member of an opposition party could be found occupying a seat in the national Congress, it was probably not because he or she had won a congressional race but because Mexico's electoral law permitted the seating of a limited number of defeated candidates based on the percentage of votes cast for their respective parties in the last election.

As the official party became almost synonymous with the government, and thus commanded huge resources as well as incredible patronage, elections became a farce. Mexico's democracy was a one-party system in which the citizens, for all practical purposes, were denied the element of choice, the most fundamental democratic right of all. In the 1980s, several opposition parties (conservative in the north and leftist in the south), capitalizing on increasing dissatisfaction with the performance of the official party, began to score some modest victories in state and local elections. With some regularity, the official party overturned the electoral results and had its own candidates installed in office. In this process, the PRI began to lose its sense of legitimacy. The growing challenges to the system were clearly evident in the presidential elections of 1988.

The conservative position was articulated by the PAN and its presidential candidate, Manuel Clothier, a millionaire industrialist. Clothier ran on a platform calling for a closer relationship with the United States, a more limited role for the government in the economy, a more vigorous private sector, and, of course, an end to electoral fraud by the PRI. The leftist opposition came from Cuauhtémoc Cárdenas, the son of former president Lázaro Cárdenas and a former PRI governor of Michoacán. Cárdenas, who had harbored presidential ambitions for some time, broke with the official party over the issue of how presidential candidates were chosen from among those judged to be *presidenciable*. He ran on the Frente Democrático Nacional, a coalition that was able to temporarily unite a broad spectrum of leftist parties. Cárdenas agreed with Clothier on one platform plank—the need to bring an end to the PRI's electoral fraud—but differed sharply

MEXICAN PRESIDENTIAL ELECTIONS, 1958-88
PRI CANDIDATES' PERCENTAGE OF VOTES

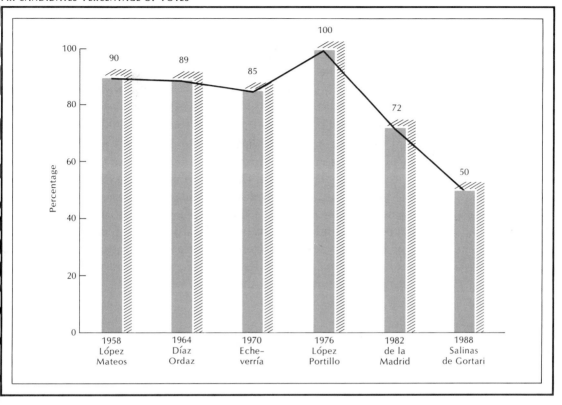

on other issues. He called for greater independence from the United States and indicated that if elected he would declare a moratorium on the repayment of Mexico's gigantic foreign debt.

The PRI candidate, Carlos Salinas de Gortari, was the epitome of the successful technocrat. He had earned a doctorate in economics from Harvard University and in the de la Madrid cabinet was secretary of planning and budget. Never having served in elective office, however, he was unaccustomed to political campaigning, and his effort in this regard was lackadaisical. For the first time in recent memory, the press gave extensive coverage to the opposition. Election day was a surprise even to the most astute political observers. The election was close enough for all three candidates to claim victory. Salinas ultimately was declared the winner, but his was the worst showing of an official party candidate since 1929. The political stock of PRI had fallen so precipitously that Salinas barely received a majority of the votes cast.

During his first year in office, after very briefly flirting with the left, Salinas determined that he had to bolster his support from conservatives and, as a consequence, began nudging Mexico to the right. In a statement that recalled Manuel Avila Camacho's *Soy creyente*, Salinas argued that it was now time for the government to seek a new accommodation with the church. During his second month in office, he struck out against the powerful oil workers' union and arrested its leader, Joaquín Hernández Galicia. To labor outrage, the president answered that Hernández Galicia had been arrested because of fraud and corruption in union activities, but some saw the dramatic move as an object lesson to other union leaders who might demand more on the wage front than the government was willing to concede. Finally, the new president began openly courting foreign investment as one solution to the ever deepening economic crisis. He decreed the end of the 49 percent limit on the foreign ownership of many businesses. Whether or not these measures would help Mexico emerge from its economic doldrums was unclear as President Salinas entered the second year of his six-year term.

The Mexican Revolution: An Assessment for the 1990s

Had the Mexican Revolution thus been a failure? Was it a myth? Had it been more an invention of historians than a social reality? The alienated minority would answer all these questions in the affirmative. When U.S. scholar Ramón Ruiz synthesized the movement in a book published in 1980, he preferred not to use the word *revolution* and entitled his study *The Great Rebellion: Mexico, 1905–1924*. Some distinguished intellectuals would begin·to argue forcefully than Mexico was in the throes of a neo-Porfiriato. The government had again become repressive, the scenario continued, and a small group was again enriching itself at the expense of the many. Social priorities, including the redistribution of land, had been laid aside in favor of economic development. Censorship, as evidenced in the celebrated *Excelsior* case, had become political reality once again. Economic exploitation in the form of the multinational corporation was even more pervasive than under the mining and petroleum companies of the early twentieth century. Bourgeois technocrats had replaced the científicos, but all the inadequacies of the closed society remained intact.

These judgments contain many truths, but many flaws as well; they obscure much more than they enlighten. While mili-

tary force had been used irresponsibly and unpardonably at Tlatelolco, while the army had hunted down and killed Lucio Cabañas, and while political prisoners were taken at the time of
the Olympic demonstrations, it is pure folly to imply that presidential tenure in the postwar period rested primarily or even
largely on the force of arms, as it had under Díaz. Although private enterprise was flourishing, the state had intervened actively
enough to challenge laissez faire economics. Can one imagine
Porfirio Díaz, shortly after the turn of the century when rich oil
fields were discovered in Mexico, telling a president of the
United States "no special consideration for your consumers"? Yet
this was precisely Echeverría's message to Gerald Ford when the
two met on the Arizona–Sonora border in 1974. The United
States would not use Mexico to weaken OPEC. In the 1980s,
López Portillo and de la Madrid politely informed Ronald Reagan that Mexico's foreign policy, especially regarding Central
America, would not be instructed from Wall Street or Pennsylvania Avenue. While some members of the intelligentsia had
been co-opted with largess, in the 1970s Daniel Cosío Villegas
could argue the neo-Porfirian theorem and excoriate the administration—indeed, the system—with neither a trip into exile nor
a sojourn in a Mexico City prison. His terse stricture was not
greeted as treason. Had Díaz's father-in-law, Manuel Romero
Rubio, been kidnapped in 1884 rather than Guadalupe Zuno
Hernández ninety years later, many innocents would have perished in the search for information and the guilty would have
been dispatched without even the formality of trial. And had a
cache of arms been uncovered in Veracruz in 1900, Díaz might
well have ordered again: *Mátalos en caliente.*

But all historical analogies tax intellectual sensibilities. The
critics might do better to vent their displeasure on the obvious.
The Mexican Revolution simply did not midwife the socialist
state, nor did it usher in the millennium. The catalog of shortcomings was far from small. Poverty still abounded to all with
open eyes. Several recent studies have concluded that the gulf
between rich and poor widened rather than narrowed in the postwar years. Studies undertaken in the 1980s indicated that the
lowest 20 percent of the population shared only 3 percent of the
national wealth, while the upper 20 percent shared a whopping
54 percent. The manifestations of this stilted distribution of
wealth were obvious. Millions were still illiterate; wages were
low, and unemployment was high; housing was inadequate;
medical care, especially in the rural areas, was grossly insuffi-

cient; and the industrial and vehicular smog of the Federal District choked the Mexican capital and threatened health problems of major consequences. One Mexico City barrio, Ciudad Nezahualcóyotl, with a population of 3 million, was the largest slum in the world. In the rural areas, a million peasants still worked plots too small to sustain themselves and their families. Only one-third of all Mexicans had access to running water in their place of residence. Real income declined in the 1980s as inflation consistently outran rises in the minimum wage. Worst of all, in 1987 the International Society of Public Health reported that 40 percent of all Mexicans still suffered from malnutrition.

But the Revolution had occurred; it had broken the back of neo-feudalism, had eliminated the hacendado class, and had abolished the rurales. After ten years, it had yielded to a system of political stability without the daily use of force, to economic growth with a minimum of foreign participation, and to a broadened political base without the fragilities of traditional democracy or the repugnant liabilities of dictatorship. While the gulf separating the rich and the poor was as wide as ever, Mexico was no longer a country of two social poles. The caloric intake in the average diet doubled between 1910 and 1970; the infant mortality rate (deaths before the age of one year) fell from thirty deaths per hundred children to about five; and, concomitantly, life expectancy soared. The average Mexican lived only about thirty-six years in 1930; in 1990, life expectancy had reached seventy years, not much below that of the developed countries. To be sure, these particular breakthroughs were more scientific than socioeconomic, but one must realize that, since most other developing countries cannot match the twentieth-century record, it is the implementation of scientific advances that is crucial.

The overall goal of the Revolution had been to ensure a better life for the Mexican citizenry. In spite of persistent poverty and multiple imperfections in the system, in spite of many chores left half finished, more Mexicans were living better in the 1980s than ever before. Millions had ascended to the middle class, and the corner had been turned in the fight against illiteracy. It is naïve to expect that Mexico could completely eradicate the degradations of poverty. Nations that opened the twentieth century far ahead have not succeeded either. But the first task after economic recovery is a more equitable distribution of the emoluments of a productive society. The benefits of dynamic growth must be funneled to those for whom the Revolution invoked a historical pride but left without an adequate diet, a meaningful life, or a hope for a better future.

Recommended for Further Study

Brannon, Jeffrey, and Eric N. Baklanoff. *Agrarian Reform and Public Enterprise in Mexico: The Political Economy of Yucatán's Henequen Industry*. University: University of Alabama Press, 1987.

Domínguez, Jorge I., ed. *Mexico's Political Economy: Challenges at Home and Abroad*. Beverly Hills, Calif.: Sage, 1982.

Falk, Pamela, ed. *Petroleum and Mexico's Future*. Boulder, Colo.: Westview Press, 1987.

Gentleman, Judith, ed. *Mexican Politics in Transition*. Boulder, Colo.: Westview Press, 1987.

Grayson, George W. *Oil and Mexican Foreign Policy*. Pittsburgh: University of Pittsburgh Press, 1988.

Hellman, Judith Adler. *Mexico in Crisis*. New York: Holmes and Meier, 1983.

Levy, Daniel, and Gabriel Székely. *Mexico: Paradoxes of Stability and Change*. Boulder, Colo.: Westview Press, 1983.

Martínez, Oscar J. *Troublesome Border*. Tucson: University of Arizona Press, 1988.

Middlebrook, Kevin J. "Political Liberalization in an Authoritarian Regime: The Case of Mexico." In *Elections and Democratization in Latin America, 1980–85*, edited by Paul W. Drake and Eduardo Silva, pp. 73–104. San Diego: Center for Iberian and Latin American Studies, University of California, 1986.

Purcell, Susan Kaufman. *Mexico in Transition: Implications for U.S. Policy*. New York: Council on Foreign Relations, 1988.

Reynolds, Clark W., and Robert K. McCleery. "The Political Economy of Immigration Law: Impact of Simpson-Rodino on the United States and Mexico." *Journal of Economic Perspectives* 2 (1988): 117–31.

Riding, Alan. *Distant Neighbors: Portrait of the Mexicans*. New York: Knopf, 1985.

Smith, Peter. *Mexico: The Quest for a United States Policy*. New York: Foreign Policy Association, 1980.

Thorup, Cathryn L., ed. *The United States and Mexico: Face to Face with New Technology*. New Brunswick, N.J.: Transaction Books, 1987.

Urquidi, Victor L. "Economic and Social Developments in Mexico." In *Mexico Today*, edited by Tommie Sue Montgomery, pp. 77–87. Philadelphia: Institute for the Study of Human Issues, 1982.

Velasco-S., Agustín. *Impacts of Mexican Oil Policy on Economic and Political Development*. Lexington, Mass.: Lexington Books, 1983.

45

Society and Culture
Since World War II

In the period after World War II, Mexico became more fully integrated into the international community than ever before. The country's charter membership in the United Nations at the close of the world conflict symbolized an end to the exclusive concern for parochial matters and a more profound interest in great world issues. Mexican presidents traveled widely carrying Mexico's message to Europe, Africa, the Orient, and South America. They were determined to begin exerting leadership in the Third World. This new world outlook effected a basic change in self-image. The strident nationalism of the revolutionary era did not entirely abate but did give ground to a new internationalism. Many perceived that the problems faced by the nation—rapid population growth, urbanization with its attendant social dislocations, persistent poverty, serious pollution, and ecological imbalance—were not only Mexican but global. Through science, technology, and economy the world had become increasingly interdependent, and solutions to these problems were scarcely possible within the confines of the national boundaries.

Population

The social and cultural changes of the postwar years were every bit as dramatic as those that had characterized the Porfiriato. The population growth was nothing short of fantastic, doubling in the twenty-three-year period between 1940 and 1963 and con-

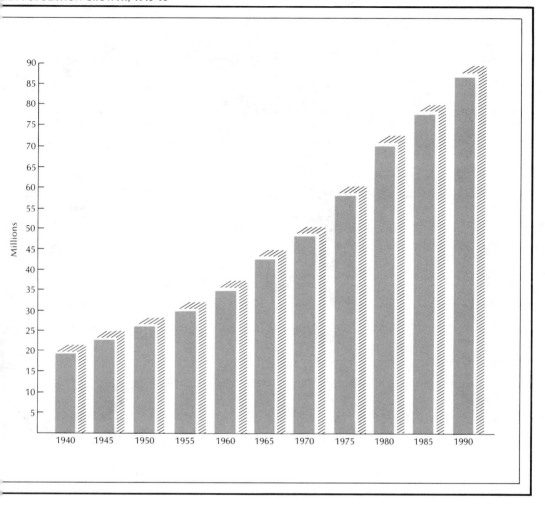

tinuing to burgeon in geometric proportion. At the end of World War II, the population of the country numbered some 22 million; by 1990, it had soared to about 87 million. At the current rate of growth (2.1 percent annually), Mexico will pass the 100 million mark in 1997.

The capital had only 3 million inhabitants in 1950, but in 1990, according to some counts, greater Mexico City had swelled to a depressing 20 million. Like a giant magnet, it draws people from the countryside, adding hundreds of thousands to its population each year, and in the process becomes less uniquely Mexican and more like New York, Paris, or London. Those who enthusiastically approved of the changes argued that the nation's

Flanked by huge office buildings and tourist hotels, Mexico City's Paseo de la Reforma carries as much traffic as any boulevard in the world.

capital had at last become cosmopolitan; those who preferred the simplicity and charm of earlier days suggested that, as each colonial structure was torn down to make room for a skyscraper or a freeway, the capital had—alas!—ceased to be Mexican. New elegant restaurants and ostentatious nightclubs catered to the thousands of tourists brought in each day by scores of jumbo jets. By 1985, the sprawling metropolis had passed Tokyo for the distinction of being the most densely populated region on earth and had developed the most acute traffic and smog problems in the Western Hemisphere. In 1990, almost 3 million vehicles traveled the crowded streets of the Federal District, and the poisonous atmosphere caused over one hundred thousand deaths annually. The U.S. government considers embassy assignments in Mexico City hazardous duty, and its diplomats stationed there are given two years' credit toward retirement for each year served. The noxious air spreads for hundreds of miles so that even the isolated ruins of Palenque and Uxmal are suffering the corrosive effects of acid rain.

In spite of the difficulties, Mexico City dominated the entire country as never before. Over 50 percent of the country's industries were located in the capital, and more than 70 percent of the country's daily banking transactions occurred there. Provincial Mexicans resented not only the exaggerated centralism emanating from Mexico City but also what they believed to be the arrogant attitudes of those from the nation's capital. They coined derogatory epithets for them, *Chilangos* and *guachos*, and in the state capitals decorated the walls of buildings with uncharitable graffiti inviting them all to go home.

In 1986, the World Bank estimated that Mexico City, with an estimated three thousand new arrivals from the rural areas every day, would house 31 million people by the turn of the century. The United Nations Fund for Population Activities considered this estimate to be too conservative. It predicted a Mexico City population of 37 million by the year 2000. The pace of life had become hectic. Professional men held two and three jobs to keep up with the spiraling cost of living. Huge working-class housing projects brought hundreds of thousands together into closer proximity than they would have imagined possible. Juvenile delinquency and adult crime rates soared. By 1988 Mexico City was recording 242 robberies and thirteen murders every day. Over 1 million youths belonged to street gangs (the Vikings, Sex Rats, Savages, Street Machine, and the like) that terrorized innocent passersby. With the thought of forestalling some Malthusian tragedy, Mexican urban planners began to consider seriously the building of an entirely new capital, much as the Brazilians had done in the late 1950s. But there was more talk than action as people rationalized that these costs of modernization were inevitable. Octavio Paz synopsized it well when he lamented that after centuries of struggle Mexico was finally a contemporary of all mankind.

While the provincial capitals were slightly more successful in retaining some of their local flavor, they, too, fell victim to the homogeneity of technological proficiency conditioned by electronic circuitry, pocket calculators, and large, sophisticated computers. One had to travel to the small village to encounter some of the charm of an age now past, but there, behind the façade of what seemed quaint to the foreign eye, the disabilities of under-

THE TEN LARGEST MEXICAN CITIES (1990 ESTIMATES)

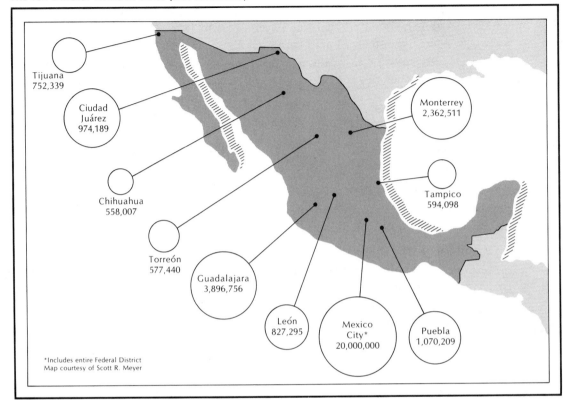

Tijuana
752,339

Ciudad
Juárez
974,189

Chihuahua
558,007

Torreón
577,440

Guadalajara
3,896,756

León
827,295

Mexico
City*
20,000,000

Puebla
1,070,209

Monterrey
2,362,511

Tampico
594,098

*Includes entire Federal District
Map courtesy of Scott R. Meyer

development remained stark. While more rural children were in school than ever before, they returned in the afternoon to hovels barren of comforts.

Mexican advocates of population control had their ups and downs in the postwar period. They were crushed by the 1968 papal encyclical banning all methods of artificial contraception because they recognized the awful truth in the quip that the rich get richer and the poor get children. During the presidential campaign of 1970, Luis Echeverría, the father of eight, announced that Mexico did not need to limit family size. In that same year, some six hundred thousand Mexican women underwent illegal abortions, and thirty-two thousand died. In 1972, in face of incontrovertible evidence, the Council of Mexican Bishops performed a remarkable *volte-face* and issued a pastoral letter declaring that Mexican couples should in good conscience make responsible decisions about the size of their families. The president agreed, and government-sponsored clinics began making birth control information available to those who requested

MEXICAN POPULATION, DISTRIBUTION BY AGE AND SEX (1990 ESTIMATES)

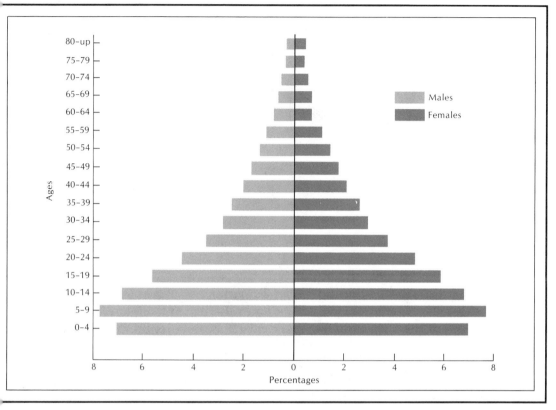

it. The program began in a small way; the sell was very soft, but by 1980 López Portillo had earmarked over 500 million pesos annually for the family planning program and some dividends had been recorded. A population growth rate that had hovered between 3.2 and 3.4 percent during the 1970s had been cut to about 2.1 percent in 1988. Over six thousand family planning centers, funded by the government, were in operation. There was no general rejoicing, however, as Mexican demographers expressed deep concern about the age distribution of the population. In 1990, fully 43 percent of Mexico's 87 million people had not yet reached fifteen years of age, and the female population about to reach childbearing age was enormous. In spite of the fact that more women than ever were visiting family planning clinics, some demographers predicted that the birth rate might actually begin to ascend once again. A 3.2 percent rate of growth in the decade between 1990 and 2000 would leave Mexico with a population of almost 127 million at the turn of the century.

The movement for women's rights built up steam during the

THE TWO-CHILD FAMILY

La familia pequeña vive mejor
decida la suya . . .
(The small family lives better
decide on yours . . .)

Posters such as this, with an unmistakable message, became increasingly common in Mexican cities in the 1970s and 1980s.

postwar years. The full enfranchisement of women in 1955 was just the beginning. More important was the feminist victory scored in 1974. While the Equal Rights Amendment languished in the United States, President Echeverría sent a bill to the Congress asking that Mexican men give women their full stake in society. The law that passed promised women equal job opportunities, salaries, and legal standing. Throughout the 1970s and 1980s, with political activist Guadalupe Rivera, federal senator Aurora Ruvalcaba, federal deputy Silvia Hernández, and labor leader Magda Monzón in the forefront, the feminist movement began seriously to challenge laws and social practices denigrating the role of women. For the first time in its ninety-nine years, the prestigious Mexican Academy of the Language admitted a woman, Dr. María del Carmen Millán. Griselda Alvarez Ponce de León became governor of the state of Colima, and Dr. Rosa Luz Algería was chosen to serve in the cabinet as secretary of tourism.

In 1984 and 1985, women were incorporated into various municipal police forces, not only because they could perform equally with men but also because they were thought to be less corruptible than their male counterparts. A few years later, Socorro Díaz, after establishing a brilliant record as a journalist, was elected to Congress and became the first woman to serve as president of the Chamber of Deputies. She was not alone in Congress. In 1988, ten of the sixty-four Mexican senators and fifty-five of the five hundred members of the Chamber of Deputies were women. The legal victories scored by the feminist movement were certainly impressive, but they were unable to seriously undermine the deeply ingrained cultural pressure of Mexican machismo. Behind a veil of anonymity, male attitudes toward women could be openly insensitive and degrading. The touching, grabbing, and verbal abuse suffered by women on the Mexico City metro became so intolerable in the 1980s that a radical solution was instituted. The Mexico City system became the only subway in the world where the individual cars were segregated by gender.

The Americanization of Mexico

Mass communication, and most especially television, changed not only patterns of leisure but the information level of the urban citizenry. By the mid-1960s, Mexican television was no longer the sole preserve of the middle and upper classes. Television antennas sprouted from the most decaying of urban slums and attested to the vastness of the audience. In the summer of 1969, millions of Mexicans watched in amazement as Neil Armstrong took his first tentative steps for mankind on the surface of the moon. And although some judged the telecast a gigantic hoax, most would soon have opinions about how nations, weak and strong, should allocate their limited resources. The great educational and cultural potential of the medium was approximated no more in Mexico than elsewhere in the Western world, but the possibilities were so substantial that in the summer of 1985 the Mexican government contracted with NASA to carry Mexico's first television satellite into space. Successfully launched in an orbit 22,000 miles above the earth, *Morelos A* brought advanced telecommunications to the most remote parts of the country.

United States cultural influences overwhelmed Mexico in the postwar period, occasionally for the better but generally for the worse. If anything, these new cultural inroads were more pervasive than those of the French during the late Porfiriato. To the chagrin of those who prized traditional Hispanic values, advertisements and commercials assumed a distinct United States flavor, and hundreds of Anglicisms invaded the language. Somehow *el jit, el jonron, el extra inin* seemed more palatable, and certainly more understandable, than *okay, bay-bay, chance, jipi, biznes,* and *parquear.* Linguistic syncretism bequeathed its share of amusing redundancies, such as the cocktail lounge that dis-

In spite of the anticlericalism embodied in revolutionary ideology, the faithful continued their pilgrimage to the Basilica de Guadalupe in the postwar period.

played a sign reading "4:00–5:00, La Hora de Happy Hour" and the tourist restaurant whose menu proudly advertised "Chile con Carne with Meat." Quick lunches (*quik lonches*) and the coffee break (*kofi breik*) replaced heavy noon meals and afternoon siestas; beer supplanted pulque as the favorite alcoholic drink of the lower classes, while Scotch whisky took the place of cognac among the middle and upper classes.

American-style football did not really challenge the pre-eminence of soccer, but thousands of Mexicans became enthralled with professional football, telecast to Mexico City on Sundays. The January 1988 spectacular, Superbowl XX, between the Osos de Chicago and the Patriotas de Nueva Inglaterra seemed especially to captivate the Mexican sports fan. Mexican businessmen joined the Rotary and the Lions Club. Installment buying on Mexican versions of Visa and MasterCard placed families in a new kind of debt but gave them the opportunity of acquiring furnishings and accouterments for the home that would have been unusual two decades before. *Supermercados* with plastic packaging and individually priced items began to replace the traditional marketplace in all the larger cities. Stocked with corn flakes, Campbell's soup, Heinz 57 Steak Sauce, Cap'n Crunch cereal, Van Camp's pork and beans, and Coca-Cola, Mexican supermarkets were distinguished from their North American counterparts only by the absence of huge parking lots.

Multinational chains were everywhere. The tourist in Mexico City could rent a car from Avis, Hertz, Budget, or Thrifty and drive on Goodyear, Firestone, or Uniroyal tires to a fast food outlet called Denny's, Shakey's, or Pizza Hut. When the McDonald's chain opened its first restaurant on the southern edge of the sprawling capital in October 1985, eight Mexico City policemen were kept busy for days directing traffic in front of the golden arches. United States music dominated most of Mexico City's twenty-four radio stations, while television audiences were treated to reruns of "Mannix," "Hawaii Five-O," "Los Dukes de Hazard," and "The Flintstones." The latest teen-age dance fads reached Mexico City from California months before they caught on in Nebraska or South Dakota. Some cried understandably for spiritual independence, others more modestly for *taco sí, hamburguesa no;* but faced with such cultural imperialism, most realized that in the absence of a vast program of government censorship the process was inevitable.

Literature, Art, and Scholarship

Mexico became a country of vibrant intellectual ferment in the forty-five years following World War II. Mexico City was clearly the cultural capital of the country and in 1985 could boast twenty daily newspapers and 250 periodicals. The television and film industries were based in the capital, as were the most outstanding art galleries and museums.

Throughout the postwar period, new literary journals and magazines of social protest provided the grist for healthy cultural debate. The postwar years saw the demise of both indigenismo and the novel of the Revolution as Mexican writers began their quest for the universal. While nobody could question the Mexicanidad of Octavio Paz, his writing revealed greater concern for ecumenical matters than for the heroes and apostates of the great Revolution. Born in Mexico City four years after the Revolution broke out, he was, by the 1950s, one of the most profound and prolific members of the new intelligentsia. As with many of the great intellects of the postwar period, it was often difficult to pinpoint where his philosophy ended and his literature began. In essays, in drama, and, above all, in poetry, he sought to link the Mexican experience with that of all humanity through the common denominators of suffering and tragedy. His most penetrating study, *El laberinto de la soledad* (translated as *The Labyrinth of Solitude*) (1950), is a psychological study of the Mexican character but was conceived in the United States, where Paz was able to observe Mexicans in a foreign milieu. Solitude for Paz was a condition that Mexicans had to comprehend to understand themselves, but the inquiry into the Mexican psyche revealed his more basic interest in the human condition.

> Solitude—the feeling and knowledge that one is alone, alienated from the world and oneself—is not an exclusively Mexican characteristic. All men, at some moment in their lives, feel themselves to be alone. And they are. To live is to be separated from what we were in order to approach what we are going to be in the mysterious future. Solitude is the profoundest fact of the human condition.[1]

Paz's criticism of the Revolution was far from mundane. The intellectual paucity of the movement troubled him, especially the failure of the intelligentsia to relate the Mexican experience to the human enterprise at large.

While Octavio Paz broke out of the mold many considered properly Mexican, Juan José Arreola in a number of works turned his back on Mexican themes. Four years younger than Paz, Arreola developed a sharp, biting satire of the bourgeois values of postwar Mexican society. Culturally indebted to Bertolt Brecht and Albert Camus, he was sarcastic, irreverent, hyperbolic, humorous to the point of cruelty, and blatantly sexist.

1. Octavio Paz, *The Labyrinth of Solitude: Life and Thought in Mexico*, trans. Lysander Kemp (New York, 1961), p. 195.

Arreola jabbed mercilessly at the pomposity and deceptions of his world. In one notably wicked short story, he invented a plastic woman and advertised her as would befit the merchandising practices of the new Mexico.

> Wherever the presence of woman is difficult, onerous, or prejudicial, whether in the bachelor's bedroom or in the concentration camp, the use of Plastisex is highly recommended. The army and the navy, as well as some directors of penal and teaching establishments, provide their inmates with the services of these attractive, hygienic creatures. . . . We will furnish you with the woman you have dreamed about all your life: she is manipulated by automatic controls and is made of synthetic materials that reproduce at will the most superficial or subtle characteristics of feminine beauty. Tall and slim, short and plump, fair or dark, redhead or platinum blonde—all are on the market. . . . The mouth, nostrils, inner parts of the eyelids, and other mucous regions are made of very soft sponge, saturated with hot, nutritive substances of variable viscosity and with different vitamin and aphrodisiac contents extracted from sea weeds and medicinal plants. . . .
>
> Our Venuses are guaranteed to give perfect service for ten years—the average time any wife lasts—except in cases where they are subjected to abnormal sadistic practices. . . . Though submissive, the Plastisex is extremely vigorous, since she is equipped with an electric motor of one-half horse power. . . . Nude, she is simply unexcelled; pubescent or not, in the flower of youth, or with autumn's ripe opulence, according to the particular coloring of each race or mixture of races.[2]

Perhaps the most creative of the postwar writers was novelist Carlos Fuentes. Born in 1928 to a middle-class family, Fuentes took a law degree at the National University and then studied international law at Geneva. His most famous novel, *La región mas transparente* (*Where the Air Is Clear*), published in 1958, is a cynical story of disillusionment with the Revolution. But it is scarcely a novel of the Revolution in the classic sense. While those familiar with the outlines of Mexican history in the twentieth century might find it easier than others to comprehend, more than anything else it is a Marxist critique of human nature and a creative condemnation of capitalism. The names and the places are clearly Mexican, but the major themes—the abuses of power, the self-serving opportunism of the bourgeoisie, the pointless existence of the *nouveau riche*, and the tendency of the new

2. Juan José Arreola, *Confabulario and Other Inventions*, trans. George D. Shade (Austin, 1974), pp. 134–39.

society to accept all things foreign—clearly have an applicability transcending Mexico. The lesson of postwar Mexico for Fuentes was that it reflected the same degenerate bourgeois values that characterized most of the Western world.

The tragedy of Tlatelolco initiated a protracted national debate and spawned its own impressive body of literature in the 1970s. Tlatelolco literature found expression in the essay, poetry, short story, and novel. While Octavio Paz and Carlos Fuentes dominated the outpouring of perceptive political essays, the fictional responses are best epitomized by Carlos Monsiváis's *Días de guardar* (1970), Arturo Azuela's *Manifestación de silencios* (1979), Luis Spota's *La plaza* (1977), and Gonzalo Martre's *Los símbolos transparentes* (1978). No matter what the specific genre, the body of literature itself testified eloquently to the fact that the Mexican intelligentsia insisted that such an untoward episode should be neither repeated nor forgotten. Tlatelolco, in essence, became not only a backdrop but a major point of departure for the best Mexican literature published in the decade following the infamous events of 1968.

Mexican art in the postwar period also rejected—in fact, rebelled violently against—the nationalistic indigenismo. Although Mexican painters of the 1950s and 1960s never achieved the stature of the great revolutionary muralists, some of the new experiments with abstract expressionism and even op art were exciting to some and completely bewildering to others. Leading the *avant-garde* was José Luis Cuevas, who epitomized the rejection of traditional muralism when he stated that what he wanted for his country's art was "broad highways leading to the rest of the world rather than narrow trails connecting one adobe village to another."[3] Many of his contemporaries agreed, and the new generation, including Olga Costa, Jesús Reyes, Pedro Coronel, and Carrillo Gil, executed paintings that could have been conceived anywhere in the Western world. They did not believe it necessary to reaffirm their Mexicanidad or to instruct the masses. But it was Juan Soriano who depicted the movement best, and in 1957 a distinguished jury of artists at the Salón de la Plástica Mexicana gave him the first prize ever awarded to a Mexican abstract painting. Soriano later articulated his views on the new Mexican art to Elena Poniatowska in a celebrated interview.

> Siqueiros limits himself to one country—Mexico. And to one political idea. I'm interested in ideas that are much broader. . . .

3. José Luis Cuevas, "The Cactus Curtain," *Evergreen Review* 2 (1959): 120.

Siqueiros . . . wants to create a strongly nationalistic art. And I believe that his art is excellent because it expresses him. But I want, and have always wanted to be universal. . . . Those murals are only tourist bait. They're the same kind of thing as those gigantic posters of the travel agencies: *Visit Mexico.* Furthermore those murals reveal nothing. They're a chronicle and not a poetic creation. Diego Rivera created a completely bureaucratic art. He made himself a propagandist of the victorious revolution. . . . I reproach him for having completely prostituted the pictorial language, reducing it to little more than a caricature, vulgarizing it. Because, don't you see, the caricature is a creation of the bourgeoisie. . . . I'm not concerned with my nationality. I can assure you I don't carry it like a chip on my shoulder, nor do I have to remind myself daily that I'm a Mexican.[4]

To the amusement of some and to the shock of others, Mexican painting turned iconoclastic in the 1970s and 1980s. Artistic impiety was epitomized by the sacrilegious work of Rolando de la Rosa. His 1988 art exhibit featured the superimposed face of Marilyn Monroe on the image of the Virgin of Guadalupe and the face of actor Pedro Infante similarly substituted for that of Christ in his rendition of the Last Supper. A generation or two earlier this type of mocking materialism would have occasioned major outcries, but most viewers simply shrugged their shoulders.

Historical scholarship had not fared well in the two decades prior to World War II, for historians often found it impossible to reconcile their faith in the Revolution with documentary evidence available to them. But in the postwar years historical scholarship came of age. Between 1940 and 1951, three important institutions—El Colegio de México, the Escuela Nacional de Antropología e Historia, and the Instituto de Historia of the National University—were founded and devoted major effort to improving historical training. Reacting against the blatant partisanship of the prorevolutionary school that had emerged in the 1920s and 1930s, the new generation of historians was much more concerned with methodology, archival research, careful bibliographical preparation, and documentary publication. The preparation of excellent regional histories and microhistories put the scholarly community on notice that in the future Mexico and Mexico City would not be considered synonymous terms.

Contributing to the maturation of historical scholarship were

4. Quoted in Elena Poniatowska, "Interview with Juan Soriano," *Evergreen Review* 2 (1959): 144–49.

seven important conferences in which Mexican historians came together with their United States and European counterparts. Meeting in Monterrey, Nuevo León, in 1949; in Austin, Texas, in 1958; in Oaxtepec, Morelos, in 1969; in Santa Monica, California, in 1973; in Pátzcuaro, Michoacán, in 1977; in Chicago in 1981; and in Oaxaca in 1985, historians from around the world who specialized in Mexican history, both established hands and young aspirants, submitted the fruits of their research to one another, tested new ideas, pinpointed lacunae, analyzed historiographical trends, disputed the latest trends in methodology, and

An architectural and anthropological achievement of gigantic proportions, the new Museum of Anthropology in Mexico City (above and on opposite page) became a prime tourist attraction in the 1970s.

published their proceedings. While the conferences were far from barren of vigorous controversy, polemical acrimony was noticeable mainly for its absence. The debates were healthy ones and augured well for the future of Mexican historiography.

One of the most remarkable historical endeavors undertaken in Mexico in the postwar era was the project of Daniel Cosío Villegas. In the late 1940s, he began work on an ambitious, multivolume history of modern Mexico. Twenty-five years later the ninth and final volume appeared, and the project had received acclaim as perhaps the most significant Latin American historical enterprise of the twentieth century. The *Historia moderna de México* covers the years from the restoration of the republic in 1867 to the outbreak of the Revolution, with separate volumes treating the political, economic, social, and international aspects of the period. Cosío planned the project with extreme care, founding in 1950 the Seminar on Modern Mexican History at El Colegio de México. This workshop brought together a group of talented researchers who, under Cosío's direction, prepared extensive bibliographies; compiled statistical data; searched out the major manuscripts, printed documentation, and newspapers; and cooperated in the production of the finished volumes.

Although thirteen scholars contributed sections, Cosío's conception of history permeated the entire enterprise and his guiding hand ensured a high quality. Eschewing the notion that history should be a tool for the apotheosis of the Revolution, Cosío did not find it necessary to excoriate Porfirio Díaz and his regime. He proposed that the birth of modern Mexico was properly attributable to the restored republic rather than to the Porfiriato. He held no special brief for the abuses of the Díaz dictatorship, but, in the tradition of classical nineteenth-century scientific history, he was content to let the facts speak for themselves. When conclusions were offered, however, they were clearly supported by the evidence. The picture that emerged was clear and objective, unflawed by the distortions of prorevolutionary presupposition. The historian Charles A. Hale prepared a penetrating view of Cosío's work in a long review essay. His conclusions are particularly appropriate:

> By breaking through the seemingly impenetrable ideological barrier thrown up by the Revolution of 1910, by eschewing the centennial impulse in historiography, and by basing interpretations on serious research, Daniel Cosío Villegas and his collaborators have given new life to the professional study of modern and contemporary Mexico, both within the country and abroad.[5]

Mexico's cultural and intellectual community viewed the future with a mixture of skepticism and hope, but there was little general euphoria with the direction the Revolution had taken and even less faith in the beneficence of party leadership. Without question, the art and letters of the period exuded more pessimism and even anxiety than confidence. But there was no serious call for barricades in the streets. Vociferous critics of the weaknesses of the system, men such as Octavio Paz, Carlos Fuentes, Juan Soriano, and Daniel Cosío Villegas, for different reasons enjoyed scant support among the rebellious youth, and all were referred to disparagingly as *vendidos* (sellouts). But in the last analysis, their reasoned judgments were more sensitive and sensible, their preoccupations more central, than those who took to the streets or who became guerrillas in the mountains.

One need not excuse the unconscionable excesses of 1968 and

---

5. Charles A. Hale, "The Liberal Impulse: Daniel Cosío Villegas and the *Historia moderna de México*," *Hispanic American Historical Review* 54 (1974): 498.

their aftermath, or disguise his outrage, to suggest that in Mexico, as elsewhere, ahistorical notions of revolution, by their limited vision, are often romanticized. Posters of Pancho Villa and Emiliano Zapata may well symbolize resistance to oppression, but they are too quixotic to portray the ghastly suffering and devastation of a real revolution. When Francisco Madero called his countrymen to arms, he expounded eloquently that at certain historic moments peoples are called upon to make the greatest personal sacrifices. Because Madero had a vision of the sweep of history, he knew that the cataclysmic moment had arrived in November 1910, but as Mexico looked beyond 1990, in spite of a few protestations to the contrary, the need for violent change had not reappeared. Democratizaton offered itself as an alternative not available to the revolutionaries of 1910.

Recommended for Further Study

Alisky, Marvin. "Mexico versus Malthus: National Trends." *Current History* 66 (1974): 200–203, 227–30.

Arreola, Juan José. *Confabulario and Other Inventions.* Translated by George D. Shade. Austin: University of Texas Press, 1974.

Bailey, David C. "Revisionism and the Recent Historiography of the Mexican Revolution." *Hispanic American Historical Review* 58 (1978): 62–79.

Brody, Robert, and Charles Rossman, eds. *Carlos Fuentes: A Critical View.* Austin: University of Texas Press, 1982.

Brushwood, John S. *Mexico in Its Novel: A Nation's Search for Identity.* Austin: University of Texas Press, 1966.

Carr, Barry. "Recent Regional Studies of the Mexican Revolution." *Latin American Research Review* 15 (1980): 3–14.

Chavarría, Jesús. "A Brief Inquiry into Octavio Paz." *The Americas* 27 (1971): 381–88.

Cuevas, José Luis. "The Cactus Curtain." *Evergreen Review* 2 (1959): 111–20.

Duncan, J. Ann. *Voices, Visions and a New Reality: Mexican Fiction Since 1970.* Pittsburgh: University of Pittsburgh Press, 1986.

Fuentes, Carlos. *The Death of Artemio Cruz.* Translated by Sam Hileman. New York: Noonday Press, 1966.

———. *Where the Air Is Clear.* Translated by Sam Hileman. New York: Ivan Obolensky, 1960.

Goldman, Shifra M. *Contemporary Mexican Painting in a Time of Change.* Austin: University of Texas Press, 1981.

———. "Rewriting the History of Mexican Art: The Politics and Economics of Contemporary Culture." In *Mexico: A Country in Crisis,* edited by Jerry R. Ladman, pp. 96–115. El Paso: Texas Western Press, 1986.

Hale, Charles A. "The Liberal Impulse: Daniel Cosío Villegas and the *Historia moderna de México.*" *Hispanic American Historical Review* 54 (1974): 479–98.

————, and Michael C. Meyer. "Mexico: The National Period." In *Latin American Scholarship since World War II*, edited by Roberto Esquenazi-Mayo and Michael C. Meyer, pp. 115–38. Lincoln: University of Nebraska Press, 1971.

Hayner, Norman S. *New Patterns in Old Mexico.* New Haven, Conn.: Yale University Press, 1966.

Langford, Walter M. *The Mexican Novel Comes of Age.* Notre Dame, Ind.: University of Notre Dame Press, 1971.

Lewis, Oscar. *The Children of Sánchez: Autobiography of a Mexican Family.* New York: Vintage Books, 1961.

————. *Five Families.* New York: Science Editions, 1962.

————. *Pedro Martinez: A Mexican Peasant and His Family.* New York: Vintage Books, 1967.

Lipp, Solomon. *Leopoldo Zea: From Mexicanidad to a Philosophy of History.* Waterloo, Ontario: Wilfrid Laurier University Press, 1980.

Meyer, Michael C. "A Venture in Documentary Publication: Isidro Fabela's *Documentos Históricos.*" *Hispanic American Historical Review* 52 (1972): 123–29.

Paz, Octavio. *The Labyrinth of Solitude: Life and Thought in Mexico.* Translated by Lysander Kemp. New York: Grove Press, 1961.

Poniatowska, Elena. "Interview with Juan Soriano." *Evergreen Review* 2 (1959): 141–52.

Sáenz, Gustavo. "New Trends in Mexican Literature: A Response to Change." In *Mexico: A Country in Crisis*, edited by Jerry R. Ladman, pp. 116–31. El Paso: Texas Western Press, 1986.

Schmidt, Henry C. "Hector Aguilar Camín and the Interpretation of the Mexican Revolution." *New World* 1 (1986): 82–93.

Sommers, Joseph. *After the Storm.* Albuquerque: University of New Mexico Press, 1968.

Wilkie, James W. "Alternative Views in History: Historical Statistics and Oral History." In *Research in Mexican History: Topics, Methodology, Sources and a Practical Guide to Field Research*, edited by Richard E. Greenleaf and Michael C. Meyer, pp. 49–62. Lincoln: University of Nebraska Press, 1973.

————, Michael C. Meyer, and Edna Monzón de Wilkie, eds. *Contemporary Mexico: Papers of the IV Congress of Mexican History.* Berkeley: University of California Press, 1976.

Young, Dolly J. "Mexican Literary Reactions to Tlatelolco, 1968." *Latin American Research Review* 20 (1985): 71–85.

APPENDIX: MEXICAN HEADS OF STATE

The Aztec Empire

Tenoch	?
Queen Ilancueitl	1349–75
Acamapichtli and Queen Ilancueitl	1375–83
Acamapichtli	1383–96
Huitzilíhuitl	1396–1417
Chimalpopoca	1417–27
Itzcóatl	1427–40
Moctezuma Ilhuicamina (Moctezuma I)	1440–69
Axayácatl	1469–81
Tizoc	1481–86
Ahuítzotl	1486–1502
Moctezuma Xocoyótzin (Moctezuma II)	1502–June 1520
Cuitláhuac	June–October 1520
Cuauhtémoc	October 1520–August 1521

Immediate Post-Conquest Period

Fernando Cortés	1521–24
Crown Officials	1524–26
Residencia Judges	1526–28
First Audiencia	1528–31
Second Audiencia	1531–35

Viceroys of the Colonial Period

Antonio de Mendoza	1535–50
Luis de Velasco (the elder)	1550–64
Gastón de Peralta	1566–68
Martín Enríquez de Almanza	1568–80

Lorenzo Suárez de Mendoza	1580–83
Pedro Moya de Contreras	1584–85
Alvaro Manrique de Zúñiga	1585–90
Luis de Velasco (the younger)	1590–95
Gaspar de Zúñiga y Acevedo	1595–1603
Juan de Mendoza y Luna	1603–7
Luis de Velasco (the younger)	1607–11
Fray García Guerra	1611–12
Diego Fernández de Córdoba	1612–21
Diego Carrillo de Mendoza y Pimentel	1621–24
Rodrigo Pacheco y Osorio	1624–35
Lope Díaz de Armendáriz	1635–40
Diego López Pacheco Cabrera y Bobadilla	1640–42
Juan de Palafox y Mendoza	1642–48
Marcos de Torres y Rueda	1648–49
Luis Enríquez y Guzmán	1650–53
Francisco Fernández de la Cueva	1653–60
Juan de Leyva y de la Cerda	1660–64
Diego Osorio de Escobar y Llamas	1664
Antonio Sebastián de Toledo	1664–73
Pedro Nuño Colón de Portugal	1673
Fray Payo Enríquez de Rivera	1673–80
Tomás Antonio de la Cerda y Aragón	1680–86
Melchor Portocarrero Lasso de la Vega	1686–88
Gaspar de Sandoval Silva y Mendoza	1688–96
Juan de Ortega y Montañez	1696
José Sarmiento Valladares	1696–1701
Juan de Ortega y Montañez	1701
Francisco Fernández de la Cueva Enríquez	1701–11
Fernando de Alencastre Noroña y Silva	1711–16
Baltasar de Zúñiga y Guzmán	1716–22
Juan de Acuña	1722–34
Juan Antonio Vizarrón y Eguiarreta	1734–40
Pedro de Castro y Figueroa	1740–41
Pedro Cebrián y Agustín	1742–46
Francisco de Güemes y Horcasitas (subsequently first Count Revillagigedo)	1746–55
Agustín Ahumada y Villalón	1755–60
Francisco Cajigal de la Vega	1760
Joaquín de Monserrat	1760–66
Carlos Francisco de Croix	1766–71
Antonio María de Bucareli	1771–79
Martín de Mayorga	1779–83
Matías de Gálvez	1783–84
Bernardo de Gálvez	1785–86
Alonso Núñez de Haro y Peralta	1787
Manuel Antonio Flores	1787–89
Juan Vicente de Güemes Pacheco y Padilla (second Count Revillagigedo)	1789–94
Miguel de la Grúa Talamanca y Branciforte	1794–98
Miguel José de Azanza	1798–1800

Félix Berenguer de Marquina	1800–1803
José de Iturrigaray	1803–8
Pedro Garibay	1808–9
Francisco Javier de Lizana y Beaumont	1809–10
Francisco Javier de Venegas	1810–13
Félix María Calleja del Rey	1813–16
Juan Ruiz de Apodaca	1816–21
Francisco Novella	1821
Juan O'Donojú	did not assume office

Independence Period and Early Republic

Emperor Agustín de Iturbide	1822–23
Guadalupe Victoria (Félix Fernández)	1824–29
Vicente Guerrero	1829
José María Bocanegra (interim)	1829
Pedro Vélez, Luis Quintanar, and Lucas Alamán, triumvirate	1829
Anastasio Bustamante	1830–32, 1837–39, and 1842
Melchor Múzquiz (interim)	1832
Manuel Gómez Pedraza	1833
Antonio López de Santa Anna	variously from 1833 to 1855
Valentín Gómez Farías	1833, 1834, and 1847
Miguel Barragán	1835–36
José Justo Corro	1836–37
Nicolás Bravo	variously from 1839 to 1846
Javier Echeverría	1841
Valentín Canalizo	1844
José Joaquín Herrera (interim)	1844, 1845, and 1848–51
Mariano Paredes Arrillaga	1846
Mariano Salas	1846
Pedro María Anaya	1847 and 1848
Manuel de la Peña y Peña	1847 and 1848
Mariano Arista	1851–53
Juan Bautista Ceballos (interim)	1853
Manuel María Lombardini	1853
Martín Carrera (interim)	1855
Rómulo Díaz de la Vega	1855

The Reform and the French Intervention

Juan Alvarez	1855
Ignacio Comonfort	1855–58

Liberal Government

Benito Juárez	1855–72

Conservative Government

Félix Zuloaga	1858 and 1859
Manuel Robles Pezuela	1858

Miguel Miramón	1859–60
Ignacio Pavón	1860
Conservative Junta	1860–64
Emperor Maximilian von Hapsburg	1864–67

Post-Reform Period

Sebastián Lerdo de Tejada	1872–76
Porfirio Díaz	1876–80 and 1884–1911
Juan N. Méndez	1876
Manuel González	1880–84

Revolutionary Period

Francisco León de la Barra (interim)	1911
Francisco I. Madero	1911–13
Pedro Lascuraín (interim)	1913
Victoriano Huerta (interim)	1913–14
Francisco S. Carbajal (interim)	1914
Venustiano Carranza	1914 and 1915–20
Eulalio Gutiérrez (interim, named by Convention)	1914
Roque González Garza	1914
Francisco Lagos Cházaro	1915
Adolfo de la Huerta (interim)	1920
Alvaro Obregón	1920–24
Plutarco Elías Calles	1924–28
Emilio Portes Gil (interim)	1928–30
Pascual Ortiz Rubio	1930–32
Abelardo L. Rodríguez (interim)	1932–34
Lázaro Cárdenas	1934–40

Period of Institutional Revolution

Manuel Avila Camacho	1940–46
Miguel Alemán Valdés	1946–52
Adolfo Ruiz Cortines	1952–58
Adolfo López Mateos	1958–64
Gustavo Díaz Ordaz	1964–70
Luis Echeverría Alvarez	1970–76
José López Portillo	1976–82
Miguel de la Madrid	1982–88
Carlos Salinas de Gortari	1988–

Source: Adapted from Richard E. Greenleaf and Michael C. Meyer, eds., *Research in Mexican History: Topics, Methodology, Sources and a Practical Guide to Field Research* (Lincoln, 1973), pp. 221–24.

SELECTED BIBLIOGRAPHY
FOR THOSE WHO READ SPANISH

Part I *Pre-Columbian Mexico*

Bernal, Ignacio. *Bibliografía de arqueología y etnografía: Mesoamérica y Norte de México, 1514–1960*. Mexico, 1962.
———. *Tenochtitlán en una isla*. Mexico, 1972.
———, et al. *Historia general de México*. 4 vols. Mexico, 1976.
Bosch García, Carlos. *La esclavitud prehispánica entre los aztecas*. Mexico, 1944.
Carrasco, Pedro. *Estratificación social en la Mesoamérica prehispánica*. Mexico, 1976.
Caso, Alfonso. *Culturas mixteca y zapoteca*. Mexico, 1941.
Dahlgren Jordan, Barbara. *La mixteca*. Mexico, 1954.
Florescano, Enrique. *Memoria mexicana: Ensayo sobre la reconstrucción del pasado: Época prehispánica–1821*. Mexico, 1987.
González Obregón, Luis. *Cuauhtémoc, Rey heróico mexicano*. Mexico, 1955.
Jiménez Moreno, Wigberto. "Síntesis de la historia precolonial del valle de México." *Revista Mexicana de Estudios Antropológicos* 14 (1954–55): 219–36.
Lameiras, José. *Los déspotas armados. Un aspecto de la guerra prehispánica*. Zamora, Mexico, 1985.
León-Portilla, Miguel. *La filosofía Náhuatl*. Mexico, 1956.
———. *Trece poétas del mundo azteca*. Mexico, 1972.
Leonard, Carmen Cook de, ed. *Esplendor del México antiguo*. 2 vols. Mexico, 1959.
Lombardo de Ruiz, Sonia. *Desarollo urbano de México-Tenochtitlán según las fuentes históricas*. Mexico, 1973.
López Austin, Alfredo. *Juegos rituales aztecas*. Mexico, 1967.
———. *Medicina Náhuatl*. Mexico, 1971.
———. "Organización politica en el altiplano central de México durante el posclásico." *Historia Mexicana* 23 (1974): 515–50.
Marquina, Ignacio. *Arquitectura prehispánica*. Mexico, 1951.
Martí, Samuel. *Instrumentos musicales precortesianos*. Mexico, 1955.
Martínez, José Luis. *Nezahualcóyotl*. Mexico, 1971.
Martinez del Río, Pablo. *Los orígenes americanos*. Mexico, 1943.
Muria, José María. *Sociedad prehispánica y pensamiento europeo*. Mexico, 1973.

Palerm, Angel. *Agricultura y sociedad en mesoamérica.* Mexico, 1972.

———, and Eric Wolf. *Agricultura y civilización en mesoamérica.* Mexico, 1972.

Tibón, Gutierre. *Mujeres y dioses de México.* Mexico, 1970.

Vogt, Evon Z., and Alberto L. Ruz, eds. *Desarrollo cultural de los mayas.* Mexico, 1964.

Westheim, Paul. *Arte antiguo de México.* Mexico, 1950.

Wright, David. *Conquistadores Otomies en la guerra Chichimeca.* Querétaro, Mexico, 1988.

Part II   The Spanish Conquerors

Argensola, Bartolomé Leonardo de. *Conquista de México.* Mexico, 1940.

Bataillon, Marcel. "Zumárraga, Reformador del clero seglar. (Una carta inédita del primer obispo de México)." *Historia Mexicana* 3 (1953): 1–10.

Bosch García, Carlos. *Sueño y ensueño de los conquistadores.* Mexico, 1987.

Chevalier, François. "El Marquesado del Valle." *Historia Mexicana* 1 (1951): 48–61.

Cortés, Hernando. *Cartas de relación de la conquista de la Nueva España escritas al Emperador Carlos V, y otros documentos relativos a la conquista, años de 1519–1527.* Codex Vindobonensis 1600. Edited by Josef Stummvoll, Charles Gibson, and Frans Unterkircher. Graz, 1960.

———. *Relaciones de Hernán Cortés a Carlos V sobre la invasión de Anáhuac.* Edited by Eulalia Guzmán. Mexico, 1958.

Díaz del Castillo, Bernal. *Historia verdadera de la conquista de la Nueva España.* 2 vols. Mexico, 1942.

Dorantes de Carranza, Baltasar. *Sumaria relación de las cosas de la Nueva España con noticia individual de los descendientes legítimos de los conquistadores y primeros pobladores españoles.* Mexico, 1902.

Durand, José. "El ambiente social de la conquista y sus proyecciones en la colonia." *Historia Mexicana* 3 (1954): 497–515.

García Icazbalceta, Joaquín. *Don Fray Juan de Zumárraga primer obispo y arzobispo de México.* 3 vols. Mexico, 1947.

Gurria Lacroix, Jorge. *Itinerario de Hernán Cortés.* Spanish–English edition. Mexico, 1973.

Icaza, Francisco A. de. *Diccionario autobiográfico de conquistadores y pobladores de Nueva España.* 2 vols. Madrid, 1923.

Iglesia, Ramón. *Cronistas e historiadores de la conquista de México: El ciclo de Hernán Cortés.* Mexico, 1942.

Jiménez Moreno, Wigberto. "La conquista: Choque y fusión de dos mundos." *Historia Mexicana* 6 (1956): 1–8.

León-Portilla, Miguel. "Quetzalcóatl-Cortés en la conquista de México." *Historia Mexicana* 24 (1974): 13–35.

López Portillo y Weber, José. *La conquista de la Nueva Galicia.* Mexico, 1935.

Pérez Embid, Florentino. *Diego de Ordás, Compañero de Cortés, y explorador del Orinoco.* Seville, 1950.

Rico González, Victor. *Hacia un concepto de la conquista de México.* Mexico, 1953.

Romero Vargas e Yturbide, Ignacio. *Moctecuhzoma X o Moctecuhzoma el magnífico y la invasión de Anáhuac.* 3 vols. Mexico, 1964.

Vasconcelos, José. *Hernán Cortés, Creador de la nacionalidad.* Mexico, 1941.

Warren, J. Benedict. *La conquista de Michoacán, 1521–1530.* Morelia, Mexico, 1977.

Yáñez, Agustín. *Crónicas de la conquista de México.* Mexico, 1937.

Zavala, Silvio. *Los esclavos indios en Nueva España.* Mexico, 1968.

———. *La filosofía política en la conquista de América.* Mexico, 1947.

———. *Los intereses particulares en la conquista de Nueva España.* Mexico, 1964.

Part III   *The Colony of New Spain*

Aguirre, Carlos, et al. *Fuentes para la historia de la ciudad de México y bibliografía sobre el desarrollo urbano y regional.* Mexico, 1976.

Alberro, Solange. *Inquisición y sociedad en México, 1571–1700.* Mexico, 1988.

Artis Espriu, Gloria. *Regatones y maquileros: El mercado de trigo en la ciudad de México (siglo xviii).* Mexico, 1986.

Bazant, Jan. *Cinco haciendas mexicanas: Tres siglos de vida rural en San Luis Potosí (1600–1910).* Mexico, 1975.

Benedict, Bradley. "El estado en México en la época de los Habsburgo." *Historia Mexicana* 23 (1974): 551–610.

Benítez, Fernando. *Los demonios en el convento: Sexo y religión en la Nueva España.* Mexico, 1985.

Berthe, Jean-Pierre. "El cultivo del 'pastel' en Nueva España." *Historia Mexicana* 9 (1960): 340–67.

Boyer, Richard Everett. *La gran inundación: Vida y sociedad en la ciudad de México (1629–1638).* Mexico, 1975.

Brown, Thomas A. *La Academia de San Carlos de la Nueva España.* 2 vols. Mexico, 1976.

Calderón, Francisco R. *Historia económica de la Nueva España en tiempo de los Austrias.* Mexico, 1989.

Carrera Stampa, Manuel. "Las ferias novohispanas." *Historia Mexicana* 2 (1953): 319–42.

Carroll, Patrick. "Estudio sociodemográfico de personas de sangre negra en Jalapa, 1791." *Historia Mexicana* 23 (1973): 111–25.

Cervantes de Salazar, Francisco. *México en 1554.* Mexico, 1939.

Chaunu, Pierre. "Veracruz en la segunda mitad del siglo xvi y primera de xviii." *Historia Mexicana* 9 (1960): 521–57.

Couturier, Edith B. *La hacienda de Hueyapan, 1550–1936.* Mexico, 1976.

Estrada, Julio, ed. *La música de México.* Vol. 1: *Historia.* Vol. 2: *Período virreinal, 1530–1810.* Mexico, 1986.

Feijoo, Rosa. "El tumulto de 1634." *Historia Mexicana* 14 (1964): 42–70.

———. "El tumulto de 1692." *Historia Mexicana* 14 (1965): 656–79.

Florescano, Enrique. *Estructuras y problemas agrarios de México (1500–1821).* Mexico, 1971.

———. *Precios del maíz y crisis agrícolas en México, 1708–1810.* Mexico, 1969.

Florescano, Sergio. "La política mercantilista española y sus implicaciones económicas en la Nueva España." *Historia Mexicana* 17 (1968): 455–68.

García Martínez, Bernardo. *El Marquesado del Valle: Tres siglos de régimen señorial en Nueva España*. Mexico, 1969.

Gemelli Carreri, Juan F. *Viaje a la Nueva España*. 2 vols. Mexico, 1955.

Gonzalbo, Pilar. *Las mujeres en la Nueva España: Educación y vida cotidiana*. Mexico, 1987.

González Sánchez, Isabel. *Haciendas y ranchos de Tlaxcala en 1712*. Mexico, 1969.

Gringoire, Pedro. "Protestantes enjuiciados por la Inquisición." *Historia Mexicana* 11 (1961): 161–79.

Guadalupe Victoria, José. *Pintura y sociedad en Nueva España, siglo xvi*. Mexico, 1986.

Holmes, Jack D. L. "El mestizaje religioso en México." *Historia Mexicana* 5 (1955): 42–61.

Horcasitas, Fernando. *El teatro Náhuatl*. Mexico, 1975.

Huerta Preciado, María Teresa. *Rebeliones indígenas en el noreste de México en la época colonial*. Mexico, 1966.

Jiménez Moreno, Wigberto. *Estudios de historia colonial*. Mexico, 1958.

Lavrin, Asunción. "La congregación de San Pedro—una cofradía urbana del México colonial—1640–1730." *Historia Mexicana* 29 (1980): 562–601.

López Cámara, Francisco. "La conciencia criolla en Sor Juana y Sigüenza." *Historia Mexicana* 6 (1957): 350–73.

López Miramontes, Alvaro, and Cristina Urrutia. *La minería de Nueva España en 1743*. Mexico, 1976.

López Sarrelangue, Delfina Esmeralda. *La nobleza indígena de Pátzcuaro en la época virreinal*. Mexico, 1965.

———. "La población indígena de la Nueva España en el siglo xviii." *Historia Mexicana* 12 (1963): 515–29.

Lozano Armendares, Teresa. *La criminalidad en la Ciudad de México, 1800–1821*. Mexico, 1987.

McCarty, Kieran R. "Los franciscanos en la frontera chichimeca." *Historia Mexicana* 11 (1962): 321–60.

Matesanz, José. "Introducción de la ganadería en Nueva España, 1521–1535." *Historia Mexicana* 14 (1965): 533–66.

Miranda, José. *Las ideas y las instituciones políticas mexicanas: Primer parte, 1521–1820*. Mexico, 1978.

———. "Las mercedes de tierras en el siglo xvi." *Historia Mexicana* 3 (1954): 442–44.

Miranda Godínez, Francisco. *El Real Colegio de San Nicolás de Pátzcuaro*. Cuernavaca, 1967.

Moreno Toscano, Alejandra. "Tres problemas de la geografía del maíz, 1600–1624." *Historia Mexicana* 14 (1965): 631–55.

Mörner, Magnus. *Estado: Razas y cambio social en la Hispanoamérica colonial*. Mexico, 1974.

Muriel, Josefina. "Notas para la historia de la educación de la mujer durante el virreynato." *Estudios de Historia Novohispana* 2 (1968): 25–34.

Ordóñez, Plinio P. "Las misiones franciscanos del Nuevo Reino de León (1575–1715)." *Historia Mexicana* 3 (1953): 102–12.

Ortiz Macedo, Luis. *El arte del Mexico virreinal*. Mexico, 1972.

Ouweneel, Arij, and Cristina Torales Pacheco, eds. *Empresarios, indios y estado: Perfil de la economía mexicana (siglo xviii)*. Amsterdam, 1988.

Porras Muñoz, Guillermo. *Personas y lugares de México, siglo xvi*. Mexico, 1986.

Rojas Garcidueñas, José. *El teatro de Nueva España en el siglo xvi*. Mexico, 1973.

Sarabia Viejo, María Justina. *Don Luis de Velasco: Virrey de Nueva España, 1550–1564*. Seville, 1978.

Semo, Enrique, et al. *Siete ensayos sobre la hacienda mexicana*. Mexico, 1976.

TePaske, John, et al. *La hacienda real de Nueva España: La caja real de México, 1576–1816*. Mexico, 1976.

Venegas Ramírez, Carmen. *Régimen hospitalario para indios en la Nueva España*. Mexico, 1973.

Zavala, Silvio. *Ensayos sobre la colonización española en América*. Mexico, 1971.

Zepeda, Tomás. *La educación pública en la Nueva España en el siglo xvi*. Mexico, 1972.

Part IV Reform and Reaction: The Move to Independence

Alamán, Lucas. *Historia de Méjico desde los primeros movimientos que preparon su independencia en el año de 1808, hasta la época presente*. 5 vols. Mexico, 1849–52.

Arcila Farías, Eduardo. *Reformas económicas del siglo xviii en el reinado de Carlos IV*. 2 vols. Mexico, 1974.

Benedict, H. Bradley. "El saqueo de las misiones de Chihuahua, 1767–1777." *Historia Mexicana* 22 (1977): 24–33.

Benítez, Fernando. *La ruta de la libertad*. Mexico, 1963.

Benson, Nettie Lee. *La diputación provincial y el federalismo mexicano*. Mexico, 1955.

Brading, David A. "Gobierno y elite en el México colonial durante el siglo xviii." *Historia Mexicana* 23 (1974): 611–45.

———. *Los orígenes del nacionalismo mexicano*. Mexico, 1973.

Bravo Ugarte, José. "El clero y la independencia." *Abside* 15 (1961): 199–218.

Bulnes, Francisco. *La guerra de independencia: Hidalgo–Iturbide*. Mexico, 1910.

Bushnell, David. "El Marqués de Branciforte." *Historia Mexicana* 2 (1953): 390–400.

Bustamante, Carlos M. *Cuadro histórico de la revolución de la América mexicana*. 6 vols. Mexico, 1823–32.

Calderón Quijano, José Antonio, ed. *Los virreyes de Nueva España en el reinado de Carlos IV*. 2 vols. Seville, 1972.

Carrera Stampa, Manuel. "Hidalgo y su plan de operaciones." *Historia Mexicana* 3 (1953): 192–206.

Castillo Ledón, Luis. *Hidalgo: La vida del héroe*. 2 vols. Mexico, 1948.

Chávarri, Juan. *Historia de la guerra de independencia de 1810–1821*. Mexico, 1960.

Flores Caballero, Romeo. "La consolidación de vales reales en la economía, la sociedad y la política novohispanas." *Historia Mexicana* 18 (1969): 334–78.

Florescano, Enrique. *La época de las reformas borbónicas y el desarrollo económico, 1750–1808.* Mexico, 1974.

———. *Precios de maíz y crisis agrícolas en México, 1708–1810.* Mexico, 1969.

———. "El problema agrario en los últimos años del virreinato, 1821." *Historia Mexicana* 20 (1971): 477–510.

———, and Isabel Gil, comps. *Descripciones económicas generales de Nueva España (1764–1817).* Mexico, 1973.

González, Luis. "El optimismo nacionalista como factor en la independencia de México." In *Estudios de historiografía americana,* pp. 155–215. Mexico, 1948.

González Navarro, Moisés. "Alamán y Hidalgo." *Historia Mexicana* 3 (1953): 217–40.

Hera, Alberto de la. *El regalismo borbónico en su proyección indiana.* Madrid, 1963.

Hernández y Dávalos, Juan E., ed. *Colección de documentos para la historia de la guerra de independencia.* 6 vols. Mexico, 1877–82.

Lemoine Villicaña, Ernesto. *Morelos: Su vida revolucionaria a través de sus escritos y de otros testimonios de la época.* Mexico, 1965.

Lerner, Victoria. "Consideraciones sobre la población de la Nueva España (1793–1810) según Humboldt y Navarro y Noriega." *Historia Mexicana* 17 (1968): 327–48.

Macías, Anna. *Génesis del gobierno constitucional en México: 1808–1820.* Mexico, 1973.

María y Campos, Armando de. *Allende: Primer soldado de la nación.* Mexico, 1964.

Meier, Matt S. "María Insurgente." *Historia Mexicana* 23 (1974): 466–82.

Miranda, José. *Vida colonial y albores de la independencia.* Mexico, 1972.

Morales, Francisco. *Clero y política en México, 1767–1845.* Mexico, 1975.

Nava Oteo, Guadalupe. *Cabildos y ayuntamientos de la Nueva España en 1808.* Mexico, 1973.

Ocampo, Javier. *Las ideas de un día: El pueblo mexicano ante la consumación de su independencia.* Mexico, 1969.

Pompa y Pompa, Antonio. *Orígenes de la independencia mexicana.* Guadalajara, 1970.

Riley, James D. "San Lucía: Desarrollo y administración de una hacienda jesuíta en el siglo xviii." *Historia Mexicana* 23 (1973): 238–83.

Rubio Mañé, J. Ignacio. "Los Allende de San Miguel el Grande." *Boletín del Archivo General de la Nación.* 2d ser. 2 (1961): 517–56.

———. "Iturbide y sus relaciones con Estados Unidos de América." *Boletín del Archivo General de la Nación.* 2d ser. 6 (1965): 251–407, 757–845.

Silva Herzog, Jesús. "Fray Servando Teresa de Mier." *Cuadernos Americanos* 154 (1967): 162–69.

Tavera, Xavier Alfaro. *El nacionalismo en la prensa mexicana del siglo xviii.* Mexico, 1963.

Teja Zabre, Alfonso. *Vida de Morelos: Nueva versión.* Mexico, 1959.

Torre Villar, Ernesto de la. *La constitución de Apatzingán y los creadores del estado mexicano.* Mexico, 1964.

Urquizo, Francisco Luis. *Morelos, Genio militar de la independencia.* Mexico, 1945.

Velásquez, María del Carmen. *El estado de guerra de Nueva España, 1760–1808.* Mexico, 1950.

Villoro, Luis. *El proceso ideológico de la revolución de independencia.* Mexico, 1967.

Zavala, Lorenzo de. *Ensayo histórico de las revoluciones de Méjico desde 1808 hasta 1830.* 2 vols. Paris, 1931–32.

Part V   The Trials of Nationhood, 1824–55

Arnaíz y Freg, Arturo. "El Dr. José María Luis Mora: 1794–1850." *Memoria de la Academia Mexicana de la Historia* 25 (1966): 405–25.

Arrangoiz y Berzábal, Francisco de Paula. *Méjico desde 1808 hasta 1867.* 4 vols. Madrid, 1871–72.

Arrom, Silvia M. *La mujer mexicana ante el divorcio eclesiástico (1800–1857).* Mexico, 1976.

Bazant, Jan. "Peones, arrendatarios y aparceros en México, 1852–1853." *Historia Mexicana* 23 (1973): 330–57.

Berninger, Dieter George. *La inmigración en México (1821–1857).* Mexico, 1974.

Bocanegra, José María. *Memorias para la historia de México independiente, 1822–1846.* 2 vols. Mexico, 1892–97.

Bosch García, Carlos. *Historia de las relaciones entre México y los Estados Unidos.* Mexico, 1961.

Córdova, Luis. "Proteccionismo y libre cambio en el México independiente, 1821–1847." *Cuadernos Americanos* 175 (1970): 135–57.

Davies, Keith A. "Tendencias demográficas urbanas durante el siglo xix en México." *Historia Mexicana* 21 (1972): 481–524.

Díaz Díaz, Fernando. *Caudillos y caciques: Antonio López de Santa Anna y Juan Alvarez.* Mexico, 1972.

Estrada, Dorothy T. "Las escuelas lancasterianas en la ciudad de México, 1822–1842." *Historia Mexicana* 22 (1973): 494–513.

Filisola, Vicente. *Memorias de la historia de la guerra de Tejas.* 2 vols. Mexico, 1968.

Flores Caballero, Romeo. *La contrarevolución y la independencia: Los españoles en la vida política, social y económica de México, 1804–1838.* Mexico, 1969.

Flores Mena, Carmen. *El General Don Antonio López de Santa Anna, 1810–1833.* Mexico, 1950.

Fuentes Mares, José. *Santa Anna: Aurora y ocaso de un comediante.* Mexico, 1956.

García Rivas, Heriberto. *Historia de la cultura en México.* Mexico, 1970.

González Navarro, Moisés. *El pensamiento político de Lucas Alamán.* Mexico, 1952.

Hale, Charles A. "Alamán, Antuñano y la continuidad del liberalismo." *Historia Mexicana* 11 (1961): 224–45.

Hutchinson, C. Alan. *Valentín Gómez Farias, la vida de un republicano.* Guadalajara, 1983.

Jiménez Rueda, Julio. *Letras mexicanas en el siglo xix.* Mexico, 1944.

Juárez, José Roberto. "La lucha por el poder a la caída de Santa Anna." *Historia Mexicana* 10 (1960): 72–93.

López Cámara, Francisco. *La genesis de la conciencia liberal en México.* Mexico, 1964.

Macune, Charles W. *El Estado de México y la federación Mexicana, 1832–1835.* Mexico, 1978.

Moreno Toscano, Alejandra. "Cambios en los patrones de organización en México, 1810–1910." *Historia Mexicana* 22 (1972): 160–87.

Mosley, Edward H. "Los planes de Ayutla y Monterrey." In *Estudios de historia del noroeste*, pp. 209–27. Monterrey, 1972.

Potash, Robert. *El Banco de Avio de México.* Mexico, 1959.

Roa Barcena, José M. *Recuerdos de la invasión norteamericana, 1846–1848.* 3 vols. Mexico, 1947.

Rodríguez, Jaime F. "Oposición a Bustamante." *Historia Mexicana* 20 (1970): 199–234.

Samponaro, Frank. "Mariano Paredes y el movimiento monarquista mexicano en 1846." *Historia Mexicana* 32 (1982): 39–54.

Sánchez Lamego, Miguel A. *La invasión española de 1829.* Mexico, 1971.

Sims, Harold. *Descolonización en México: El conflicto entre mexicanos y españoles, 1821–1831.* Mexico, 1982.

Staples, Anne. *La iglesia en la primera república federal mexicana (1824–1835).* Mexico, 1976.

Thomson, Guy P. C. "La colonización en el departamento de Acayucan: 1824–1834." *Historia Mexicana* 21 (1972): 481–524.

Tornel y Mendivil, José M. *Breve reseña histórica de los acontecimientos más notables de la nación mexicana desde de año de 1821 hasta nuestros dias.* Mexico, 1852.

Torre Villar, Ernesto de la, ed. *Correspondencia diplomática franco-mexicana, 1808–1839.* Mexico, 1957.

Valadés, José C. *Alamán, Estadista e historiador.* Mexico, 1938.

———. *Orígenes de la República Mexicana.* Mexico, 1972.

———. *Santa Anna y la guerra de Texas.* Mexico, 1936.

Vásquez de Knauth, Josefina. *Mexicanos y norteamericanos ante la Guerra del 47.* Mexico, 1960.

Vigness, David M. "La República del Río Bravo." In *Estudios de historia del noroeste*, pp. 181–95. Monterrey, 1972.

Part VI   *Liberals and Conservatives Search for Something Better, 1855–76*

Aguirre, Manuel J. *La intervención francesa y el imperio en México.* Mexico, 1969.

Arnáiz y Freg, Arturo, and Claude Bataillon, eds. *La intervención francesa y el imperio de Maximiliano cien años después, 1862–1962.* Mexico, 1965.

Bazant, Jan. *Los bienes de la iglesia en México, 1856–1875.* Mexico, 1971.

Berry, Charles R. "La ciudad de Oaxaca en vísperas de la Reforma." *Historia Mexicana* 19 (1969): 23–61.

Blasio, José Luis. *Maximiliano íntimo: El emperador Maximiliano y su corte.* Mexico, 1960.

Blásquez Domínguez, Carmen. *Veracruz liberal, 1858–1869.* Mexico, 1986.

Broussard, Ray F. "Comonfort y la revolución de Ayutla." *Humanitas* 8 (1967): 511–28.

⸺. "El regreso de Comonfort del exilio." *Historia Mexicana* 16 (1967): 498–515.

Bulnes, Francisco. *Juárez y las revoluciones de Ayutla y de la Reforma.* Mexico, 1905.

Corti, Egon C. *Maximiliano y Carlota.* Mexico, 1944.

Cosío Villegas, Daniel. *Historia moderna de México.* Vol. 1: *La república restaurada, La vida política.* Mexico, 1955.

⸺, ed. *Historia moderna de México.* Vol. 2: *La república restaurada, La vida económica,* by Francisco R. Calderón. Mexico, 1955.

⸺, ed. *Historia moderna de México.* Vol. 3: *La república restaurada, La vida social,* by Luis González y González et al. Mexico, 1957.

Cosío Villegas, Emma. "El diario de Matías Romero." *Historia Mexicana* 8 (1959): 407–23.

Cué Canovas, Agustín. *La reforma liberal en México.* Mexico, 1966.

⸺. *El tratado McLane-Ocampo: Juárez, los Estados Unidos y Europa.* Mexico, 1956.

Davies, Keith A. "Tendencias demográficas urbanas durante el siglo xix en México." *Historia Mexicana* 21 (1972): 481–524.

Díaz Díaz, Fernando. *Caudillos y caciques: Antonio López de Santa Anna y Juan Alvarez.* Mexico, 1972.

Díaz López, Lilia, ed. *Versión francesa de México: Informes diplomáticos.* 4 vols. Mexico, 1963–67.

Fraser, Donald J. "La política de desamortización en las comunidades indígenas, 1856–1872." *Historia Mexicana* 21 (1972): 615–52.

Fuentes Mares, José. *Juárez y los Estados Unidos.* Mexico, 1961.

⸺. *Juárez y la intervención.* Mexico, 1963.

⸺. *Juárez y la república.* Mexico, 1965.

García Granados, Ricardo. *La constitución de 1857 y las leyes de Reforma en México.* Mexico, 1906.

Hart, John M. "Miguel Negrete: La epopeya de un revolucionario." *Historia Mexicana* 24 (1974): 70–93.

Hernández Rodríguez, Rosaura. *Ignacio Comonfort: Trayectoria política, documentos.* Mexico, 1967.

Keremitsis, Dawn. "La industria textil algodonera durante la Reforma." *Historia Mexicana* 21 (1972): 693–723.

Knowlton, Robert J. "La iglesia mexicana y la reforma: Respuesta y resultados." *Historia Mexicana* 18 (1969): 516–34.

McGovern, Gerald L. *Prensa y poder, 1854–1857: La revolución de Ayutla y el Congreso Constituyente.* Mexico, 1978.

McLean, Malcolm D. *Vida y obra de Guillermo Prieto.* Mexico, 1960.

Perry, Laurens Ballard. "El modelo liberal y la política práctica en la república restaurada, 1867–1876." *Historia Mexicana* 23 (1974): 646–94.

Pompa y Pompa, Antonio. "La reforma liberal en México." *Memorias y Revista de la Academia Nacional de Ciencias* 1–2 (1960): 115–45.

Powell, T. G. "Los liberales, el campesinado indígena, y los problemas agrarios durante la reforma." *Historia Mexicana* 21 (1972): 653–75.

Rivera Cambas, Manuel. *Historia de la intervención europea y norteamericana en México y del imperio de Maximiliano de Habsburgo.* Mexico, 1968.

Romero, Matías. *Diario personal, 1855–1865.* Mexico, 1960.

Sierra, Justo. *Juárez: Su obra y su tiempo.* Mexico, 1948.

Tamayo, Jorge L. "El tratado McLane-Ocampo." *Historia Mexicana* 21 (1972): 573–614.

Torre Villar, Ernesto de la. *La intervención francesa y el triunfo de la república.* Mexico, 1968.

Valadés, José C. *Don Melchor Ocampo, Reformador de México.* Mexico, 1954.

Zarco, Francisco. *Historia del Congreso Extraordinario Constituyente de 1856–1857.* Mexico, 1956.

Zayas Enríquez, Rafael de. *Benito Juárez: Su vida y su obra.* 3d ed. Mexico, 1971.

Part VII   *The Modernization of Mexico, 1876–1910*

Aguirre, Manuel J. *Cananea: Garras del imperialismo en las entrañas de México.* Mexico, 1958.

Albro, Ward S. "El secuestro de Manuel Sarabia." *Historia Mexicana* 18 (1969): 400–407.

Anderson, Rodney D. "Díaz y la crisis laboral de 1906." *Historia Mexicana* 19 (1970): 513–35.

Bazant, Jan. "Peones, arrendatarios y parceros, 1868–1904." *Historia Mexicana* 24 (1974): 94–121.

Bryan, Anthony. "El papel del General Bernardo Reyes en la política nacional y regional de México." *Humanitas* 13 (1972): 331–40.

Bryan, Susan E. "Teatro popular y sociedad durante el Porfiriato." *Historia Mexicana* 33 (1983): 130–69.

Bulnes, Francisco. *El verdadero Díaz y la Revolución.* Mexico, 1967.

Coatsworth, John H. *Crecimiento contra desarrollo: El impacto económico de los ferrocarriles en el porfiriato.* 2 vols. Mexico, 1976.

Cortés, Enrique. *Relaciones entre México y Japón durante el Porfiriato.* Mexico, 1980.

Cosío Villegas, Daniel. *Historia moderna de México.* Vols. 5 and 6: *El porfiriato, La vida política exterior.* Mexico, 1960–63.

———. *Historia moderna de México.* Vols. 8 and 9: *El porfiriato, La vida política interior.* Mexico, 1970–72.

———. *Porfirio Díaz y la revuelta de la Noria.* Mexico, 1953.

———, ed. *Historia moderna de México.* Vol. 4: *El porfiriato, La vida social,* by Moisés González Navarro. Mexico, 1957.

———, ed. *Historia moderna de México.* Vol. 7: *El porfiriato, La vida económica,* by Nicolau d'Olwer et al. 2 vols. Mexico, 1965.

Díaz de Ovando, Clementina. "La ciudad de México en 1904." *Historia Mexicana* 24 (1974): 122–44.

Espinosa de los Reyes, Jorge. *Relaciones económicas entre México y los Estados Unidos, 1870–1910.* Mexico, 1951.

Fuentes Mares, José. *Y México se refugió en el desierto: Luis Terrazas, Historia y destino.* Mexico, 1954.

García Rivas, Heriberto. *Historia de la cultura en México.* Mexico, 1970.

Godoy, José F. *Porfirio Díaz, Presidente de México.* Mexico, 1967.

González Navarro, Moisés. *La colonización en México, 1877–1910.* Mexico, 1960.

————. *Las huelgas textiles en el porfiriato*. Mexico, 1970.

————. "Las ideas raciales de los científicos, 1890–1910." *Historia Mexicana* 37 (1988): 565–84.

Hamon, James L., and Stephen Niblo. *Precursores de la revolución agraria en México: Las obras de Wistano Luis Orozco y Andrés Molina Enríquez*. Mexico, 1975.

Hart, John M. *Los anarquistas mexicanos, 1860–1900*. Mexico, 1974.

Iturribarría, Jorge Fernando. "Porfirio Díaz ante la historia. México, 1867–1914." *Historia Mexicana* 23 (1974): 700–721.

Lloyd, Jane Dale, ed. *Porfirio Díaz frente al descontento popular regional (1891–1893): Antología documental*. Mexico, 1986.

Luna, Jesús. *La carrera pública de don Ramón Corral*. Mexico, 1975.

Martínez Jiménez, Alejandro. "La educación elemental en el Porfiriato." *Historia Mexicana* 22 (1973): 514–52.

Montes Rodríguez Ezequiel. *La huelga de Río Blanco*. Veracruz, 1965.

Niemeyer, Victor. *El General Bernardo Reyes*. Monterrey, 1966.

Prida, Ramón. *Los sucesos de Río Blanco en 1907*. Mexico, 1970.

Raat, William D. "Los intelectuales, el positivismo y la cuestión indígena." *Historia Mexicana* 20 (1971): 412–27.

————. *El positivismo durante el porfiriato (1876–1910)*. Mexico, 1975.

Romero, Matías. *Reciprocidad comercial entre México y los Estados Unidos: El tratado comercial de 1883*. Mexico, 1971.

Sims, Harold D. "Espejo de caciques: Los Terrazas de Chihuahua." *Historia Mexicana* 18 (1969): 379–99.

Thorup, Cathryn. "La competencia económica británica y norteamericana en México (1887–1910)." *Historia Mexicana* 31 (1982): 599–641.

Valadés, José C. *El porfirismo: Historia de un régimen*. 3 vols. Mexico, 1941–47.

Vanderwood, Paul J. "Los rurales: Producto de una necesidad social." *Historia Mexicana* 22 (1972): 34–51.

Villegas, Abelardo. *Positivismo y Porfirismo*. Mexico, 1972.

Wasserman, Mark. "Oligarquía e intereses extranjeros en Chihuahua durante el porfiriato." *Historia Mexicana* 22 (1973): 279–319.

Part VIII   *The Revolution: The Military Phase, 1910–20*

Aguilar Camín, Hector. *La frontera nómada. Sonora y la Revolución Mexicana*. Mexico, 1977.

Amaya, Juan Gualberto. *Madero y los auténticos revolucionarios de 1910*. Mexico, 1946.

————. *Venustiano Carranza: Caudillo constitucionalista*. Mexico, 1947.

Amaya C., Luis Fernando. *La soberana convención revolucionaria, 1914–1916*. Mexico, 1966.

Blanco Moheno, Roberto. *Pancho Villa que es su padre*. Mexico, 1969.

Calreo, Manuel. *Un decenio de política mexicana*. New York, 1920.

Calvert, Peter. "Francis Stronge en la Decena Trágica." *Historia Mexicana* 15 (1965): 57–69.

Carr, Barry. *El movimiento obrero y la política en Mexico, 1910–1929*. 2 vols. Mexico, 1976.

Cervantes, Federico. *Francisco Villa y la Revolución*. Mexico, 1960.

Coker, William S. "Mediación británica en el conflicto Wilson–Huerta."
    Historia Mexicana 18 (1968): 244–57.

Fabela, Isidro, ed. *Documentos históricos de la revolución mexicana*. 27
    vols. Mexico, 1960–73.

Falcón, Romana. *Revolución y caciquismo: San Luis Potosí, 1910–1938*.
    Mexico, 1984.

González Navarro, Moisés. "El Maderismo y la revolución agraria." *His-
    toria Mexicana* 37 (1987): 5–28.

Harrison, John P. "Henry Lane Wilson, El trágico de la decena." *Historia
    Mexicana* 6 (1957): 374–405.

Lara Pardo, Luis. *Matchs de dictadores*. Mexico, 1942.

Lerner, Victoria. "La suerte de las haciendas: Decadencia y cambio de
    propietarios." *Historia Mexicana* 36 (1987): 661–98.

Magaña, Gildardo. *Emiliano Zapata y el agrarismo en México*. 5 vols. Mex-
    ico, 1934–52.

Márquez, Sterling M. *Los últimos días del Presidente Madero*. Mexico,
    1958.

Mendoza, Vicente. *El corrido de la Revolución mexicana*. Mexico, 1956.

Meyer, Jean. "Los obreros en la Revolución mexicana: Los Batallones
    Rojos." *Historia Mexicana* 21 (1971): 1–37.

Meyer, Michael C. "Habla por ti mismo Juan: Una propuesta para un
    método alternativo de investigación." *Historia Mexicana* 22 (1973):
    396–408.

Palacios, Porfirio. *El Plan de Ayala: Sus orígenes y su proclamación*. Mex-
    ico, 1969.

Palavicini, Félix. *Historia de la constitución de 1917*. 2 vols. Mexico, 1938.

Prida, Ramón. *De la dictadura a la anarquía*. Mexico, 1958.

Roman, Richard. *Ideología y clase en la Revolución mexicana: La con-
    vención y el congreso constituyente*. Mexico, 1976.

Ross, Stanley R. "La muerte de Jesús Carranza." *Historia Mexicana* 7
    (1957): 20–44.

Silva Herzog, Jesús. *Breve historia de la Revolución mexicana*. 2 vols. Mex-
    ico, 1962.

Smith, Peter H. "La política dentro de la Revolución: El congreso con-
    stituyente de 1916–1917." *Historia Mexicana* 22 (1973): 363–95.

Sotelo Inclán, Jesús. *Raíz y razón de Zapata*. Mexico, 1970.

Ulloa, Berta. *La revolución intervenida: Relaciones diplomáticas entre
    México y Estados Unidos, 1910–1914*. Mexico, 1971.

———. *Veracruz, Capital de la nación, 1914–1915*. Mexico, 1986.

Valadés, José. *Imaginación y realidad de Francisco I. Madero*. 2 vols. Mex-
    ico, 1960.

Part IX   The Revolution: The Constructive Phase, 1920–40

Britton, John A. *Educación y radicalismo en México: Los años de Bassols
    (1913–1934)*. Mexico, 1976.

———. *Educación y radicalismo en México: Los años de Cárdenas (1934–
    1940)*. Mexico, 1976.

———. "Moisés Saenz: Nacionalista mexicano." *Historia Mexicana* 22
    (1972): 78–97.

Cabrera, Luis. *Veinte años después*. Mexico, 1937.

Campbell, Hugh G. *La derecha radical en México, 1929-1949*. Mexico, 1976.

Cárdenas, Lázaro. *Ideario político*. Mexico, 1972.

Córdova, Arnaldo. *La ideología de la Revolución mexicana*. Mexico, 1973.

Dooley, Francis P. *Los cristeros, Calles y el catolicismo mexicano*. Mexico, 1976.

Fernández, Justino. *El arte moderno en México*. Mexico, 1937.

Fowler, Heather. "Orígenes laborales de la organización campesina en Veracruz." *Historia Mexicana* 20 (1970): 240–64.

———. "Los orígenes de las organizaciones campesinas en Veracruz: Raíces políticas y sociales." *Historia Mexicana* 22 (1972): 52–57.

Gilly, Adolfo. *La revolución interrumpida*. Mexico, 1972.

Gómez, Marte R. *La reforma agraria de México: Su crisis durante el período 1928-1934*. Mexico, 1964.

González Navarro, Moisés. *La Confederación Nacional Campesina*. Mexico, 1968.

González Ramírez, Manuel. *La revolución social de México*. 2 vols. Mexico, 1960–66.

Horn, James J. "El embajador Sheffield contra el Presidente Calles." *Historia Mexicana* 20 (1970): 265–84.

Keremitsis, Dawn. "Del metate al molino: La mujer mexicana de 1910 a 1940." *Historia Mexicana* 33 (1983): 285–302.

León Portilla, Miguel. *Los Manifiestos en Náhuatl de Emiliano Zapata*. Mexico, 1978.

Lozoya, Jorge Alberto. *El ejército mexicano, 1911-1945*. Mexico, 1970.

Medin, Tzvi. *Ideología y praxis política de Lázaro Cárdenas*. Mexico, 1972.

Meyer, Eugenia. *Luis Cabrera: Teórico y crítico de la Revolución*. Mexico, 1972.

Meyer, Lorenzo. "El estado mexicano contemporáneo." *Historia Mexicana* 23 (1974): 722–52.

———. *México y Estados Unidos en el conflicto petrolero (1917–1942)*. Mexico, 1968.

Michaels, Albert L. "Las elecciones de 1940." *Historia Mexicana* 21 (1971): 80–134.

———. "El nacionalismo conservador mexicano desde la Revolución hasta 1940." *Historia Mexicana* 14 (1966): 213–38.

Novo, Salvador. *La vida en México en el período presidencial de Lázaro Cárdenas*. Mexico, 1965.

Olivera Sedano, Alicia. *Aspectos del conflicto religioso de 1926 a 1929*. Mexico, 1966.

Portes Gil, Emilio. *Quince años de política mexicana*. Mexico, 1941.

Raby, David L. *Educación y revolución social en México, 1921–1940*. Mexico, 1974.

Ramírez Plancarte, Francisco. *La revolución mexicana: Interpretación independiente*. Mexico, 1948.

Sáenz, Aarón. *La política internacional de la revolución: Estudios y documentos*. Mexico, 1961.

Scholes, Walter V., and Marie V. Scholes. "Gran Bretaña, los Estados Unidos y el no reconocimiento de Obregón." *Historia Mexicana* 19 (1970): 388–96.

Silva Herzog, Jesús. *La expropiación del petróleo en México*. Mexico, 1963.

Taracena, Alfonso. *La verdadera revolución mexicana.* 17 vols. Mexico, 1960–65.

Tibol, Raquel. *Historia general del arte mexicano: Epoca moderna y contemporánea.* Mexico, 1964.

Vasconcelos, José. *Obras completas.* 4 vols. Mexico, 1957–61.

Wilkie, James W., and Edna Monzón de Wilkie. *México visto en el siglo xx: Entrevistas de historia oral.* Mexico, 1969.

Part X   *The Revolution Shifts Gears: Mexico since 1940*

Alba, Victor. *Las ideas sociales contemporáneas en México.* Mexico, 1960.

Bermúdez, María Elvira. *La vida familiar del mexicano.* Mexico, 1955.

Beteta, Ramón. *Pensamiento y dinámica de la Revolución mexicana.* Mexico, 1950.

Brushwood, John S. *La novela mexicana (1967–1982).* Mexico, 1985.

Carreño, Alberto María. "Las clases sociales en México." *Revista Mexicana de Sociología* 12 (1950): 333–50.

Carrillo Flores, Antonio. "La política exterior de México." *Foro Internacional* 6 (1965): 233–46.

Chávez Orozco, Luis. *El presidente López Mateos visto por un historiador.* Mexico, 1962.

Cosío Villegas, Daniel. *Ensayos y notas.* 2 vols. Mexico, 1966.

———. *Labor periodista: Real e imaginaria.* Mexico, 1972.

Esser, Elisabeth. "La posición de México frente al regionalismo." *Foro Internacional* 7 (1967): 331–55.

Glade, William P., and Stanley R. Ross, eds. *Críticas constructivas del sistema político mexicano.* Austin, 1973.

González, Raúl. "El comercio exterior de México y el imperialismo norteamericano, 1956–1965." *Historia y Sociedad* 7 (1966): 69–80.

González Casanova, Pablo. *La democracia en México.* Mexico, 1965.

González Navarro, Moisés. *México: El capitalismo nacionalista.* Mexico, 1970.

Hernández, Salvador. *El PRI y el movimiento estudiantil de 1968.* Mexico, 1971.

Krauze, Enrique. *Daniel Cosío Villegas: Una biografía intelectual.* Mexico, 1980.

Madrazo, Carlos. *Madrazo: Voz postrera de la Revolución.* Mexico, 1971.

Mendieta y Núñez, Lucio. "La clase media en México." *Revista Mexicana de Sociología* 17 (1955): 517–31.

Moreno Sánchez, Manuel. *Crisis política de México.* Mexico, 1970.

Navarrete, Alfredo. *Alto a la contrarevolución.* Mexico, 1971.

Novo, Salvador. *La vida en México en el período presidencial de Miguel Alemán.* Mexico, 1967.

Ortiz Mena, Antonio. *Las finanzas públicas: El desarrollo socioeconómico de México.* Mexico, 1969.

Pellicer de Brody, Olga. *México y la revolución cubana.* Mexico, 1972.

Ponce, Bernardo. *Adolfo Ruiz Cortines.* Mexico, 1952.

Poniatowska, Elena. *La noche de Tlatelolco: Testimonios de historia oral.* Mexico, 1971.

Ramírez, Ramón. *El movimiento estudiantil de México, julio/diciembre de 1968.* 2 vols. Mexico, 1969.

Ross, Stanley R. "México: Las tensiones del progreso." *Latinoamérica* 4 (1971): 9–21.

Schmidt, Samuel. *El deterioro del presidencialismo mexicano: Los años de Luis Echeverría.* Mexico, 1986.

Solis, Leopoldo. "La política económica y el nacionalismo mexicano." *Foro Internacional* 9 (1969): 235–48.

Torres Ramírez, Blanca. *México en la segunda guerra mundial.* Mexico, 1979.

Urquidi, Victor L., and Adrián Lajous Vargas. *Educación superior, ciencia y tecnología en el desarrollo económico de México.* Mexico, 1967.

Valadés, José C. *El presidente de México en 1970.* Mexico, 1969.

Valdés, Carlos. *José Luis Cuevas.* Mexico, 1966.

Ygarza G., Alberto. "El futuro de la política fiscal en México." *Investigación Económica* 31 (1971): 13–22.

SOURCES OF ILLUSTRATIONS

We gratefully acknowledge the following persons and institutions for the photographs and illustrations in this book.

List of Abbreviations

AMNH American Museum of Natural History, New York
AIA Archaelogical Institute of America, New York
ASHS Arizona State Historical Society, Tucson
BL The Bancroft Library, University of California, Berkeley
HRC The Humanities Research Center, The University of Texas at Austin
HL Henry E. Huntington Library, San Marino, California
LC Library of Congress, Washington, D.C.
MMA The Metropolitan Museum of Art, New York
MNTC Mexican National Tourist Council, New York
MNA Museo Nacional de Antropología, Mexico
NA National Archives, Washington, D.C.
NYPL New York Public Library
OAS Organization of American States, Washington, D.C.
SMM The Science Museum of Minnesota, St. Paul
UAL University of Arizona Library, Tucson

Chapter 1. p. 7, AMNH; 10, MNA; 11, LC; 12, left–Brooklyn Museum, lent by Mr. Robin B. Martin, right–MMA, Michael C. Rockefeller Mem. Coll. of Primitive Art. *Chapter* 2. p. 15, MMA, Rockefeller Coll; 19, above and lower left–AMNH, lower right–MMA, Rockefeller Coll; 21, MNTC; 22, AIA; 23, MNTC; 25, MNA; 26, Leslie Hewes; 28, Jeffrey House; 30, MMA, Rockefeller Coll; 32, above–AMNH, below–MNTC; 33, MNA; 34, left–MNA, right–Dumbarton Oaks, Washington, D.C. *Chapter* 3. p. 40, AIA; 42, above–NYPL, below–Alan Bates; 44, left–MMA, Rockefeller Coll, right–MNTC, below–MNA; 45, 46, Leslie Hewes; 47, above–AIA, below–Bradley Smith: 49, AMNH; 50, MNTC; 51, Thomas Laging. *Chapter* 4. p. 57, LC; 62, 64, AMNH. *Chapter* 5.

p. 68, OAS; 70, Biblioteca, MNA; 71, BL; 72, Dumbarton Oaks, Washington, D.C.; 77, LC; 83, 84, MNA; 88, AMNH; 90, left–Bradley Smith. *Chapter* 6. p. 97, above left–MMA, Rogers Fund, 1904, right–MMA, Gift William H. Riggs, 1913, below left–MMA, Gift Abraham Silberman, 1937, right–MMA, Rogers Fund, 1921; 100, Hospital de Jesús, México; 102, BL; 105, British Museum; 110, NYPL. *Chapter* 7. p. 119, above–Los Angeles County Museum of Natural History, below–MMA, Gift William H. Riggs, 1913; 123, NYPL; 125, Biblioteca, MNA; 127, above–after a model in the John W. Higgins Armory, Worcester, Mass. *Chapter* 8. p. 132, MNTC; 134, OAS; 141, from Justo Sierra, *Mexico, Its Social Revolution*, 1900; 144, BL. *Chapter* 9. p. 163, LC; 165, MMA. Gift William H. Riggs, 1913. *Chapter* 10. p. 171, Pan Amer. Development Foundation; 173, Weidenfeld & Nicolson, London; 175, NA; 178, upper left–Philadelphia Museum of Art, upper right and below–MMA, Gift Mrs. Robert W. de Forest, 1911; 179, from Carlos Nebel, *Viaje pintoresco y arqueológico sobre . . . la República Mexicana . . .*, 1839; 181, American Numismatic Society, N.Y. *Chapter* 11. p. 185, LC; 187, MNTC; 189, LC; 190, 192, Jeffrey House; 191, LC; Museo Nacional de Historia, México; 193, 196, 197, 198, Vicente Riva Palacios, *México a través de los siglos*, 1887–89; 194, LC; 200, Elsie Y. Haack. *Chapter* 13. pp. 222, 223, 226, from Justo Sierra, *Mexico, Its Social Revolution*, 1900; 228, 232, LC; 233, BL; 234, MNA; 235, Leslie Hewes; 238, 239, Hispanic Society of America, N.Y.; 242, from *México y sus Alrededores*, Editorial Valle de México, 1980. *Chapter* 14. p. 252, Bruckmann–Art Reference Bureau; 262, from *México y sus alrededores*, Editorial Valle de México, 1980. *Chapter* 15. p. 265, OAS; 266, LC; 267, from Carlos Nebel, *Viaje pintoresco y arqueológico sobre . . . la República Mexicana . . .* ; 269, Weidenfeld & Nicolson, London; 271, Vicente Riva Palacios, *México a través de los siglos*, 1887–89; 272, The Brooklyn Museum; 273, BL; 280, MMA, Bequest Mrs. H. O. Havemeyer, 1929; 282, BL. *Chapter* 16. p. 287, LC; 291, Bettmann Archive. *Chapter* 17. p. 303, from *Gobernantes de México, 1325–1911*, Artes de México No. 175, año XXI, p. 59. *Chapter* 18. p. 317, from Justo Sierra, *Mexico, Its Social Revolution*, 1900. *Chapter* 19. p. 327, BL; 333, NYPL. *Chapter* 20. p. 341, BL; 349, NA. *Chapter* 21. pp. 359, 361, from Vicente Riva Palacios, *México a través de los siglos*, 1887–89; 363, 365, from B. Mayer, *Mexico, Aztec, Spanish and Republican*, 1852. *Chapter* 22. p. 377, BL. *Chapter* 23. p. 386, BL; 389, ASHS; 394, 400, from M. de los Torres, *El archiduque Maximiliano de Austria en México*, 1867. *Chapter* 24. p. 406, HRC; 409, NYPL; 411, HL. *Chapter* 25. p. 418, from Vicente Riva Palacios, *México a través de los siglos*, 1887–89; 420, BL; 423, from *México y sus alrededores*, Editorial Valle de México, 1980; 425, NYPL; 427, from Justo Sierra, *Mexico, Its Social Revolution*, 1900. *Chapter* 27. p. 441, HRC; 443, BL; 444, SMM; 447, ASHS. *Chapter* 28. p. 455, SMM; 456, UAL; 462, HL; 463, SMM. *Chapter* 29. p. 471, HRC; 472, ASHS. *Chapter* 30. p. 486, Hemeroteca Nacional de México; 489, BL. *Chapter* 31. p. 501, UAL; 504, HRC; 505, ASHS. *Chapter* 32. p. 512, HRC; 518, NA. *Chapter* 33. p. 525, HL; 533, LC. *Chapter* 34. p. 538, HRC; 540, 541, LC; 547, HRC. *Chapter* 35. p. 553, ASHS; 556, LC; 558, above–HL, below–HRC. *Chapter* 36. p. 575, HRC. *Chapter* 37. p. 584, NYPL. *Chapter* 38. pp. 601, 605, NA. *Chapter* 39. pp. 614, 615, LC; 616, Pan Amer. Development Foundation; 617, LC; 618, Dartmouth College Museum, Hanover, N.H.; 619, National Preparatory School, México.

Chapter 40. pp. 632, 634, NA.   *Chapter* 41. pp. 642, 643, Editorial Photo-color Archives; 644, NA.   *Chapter* 42. 653, MNTC; 654, OAS; 657, MNTC. *Chapter* 43. pp. 666, 667, MNTC; 670, James W. Wilkie.   *Chapter* 44. p. 682, Diego Goldberg/Sygma; 685, Secretaría de información y propaganda del Partido Revolucionario Institucional; 689, Alejandro Castañeda, Mexico D.F., 1985; 690, Photograph by David Burckhalter, *Journal of the Southwest* 32 (Spring 1990).   *Chapter* 45. p. 702, MNTC; 708, OAS; 714, 715, MNTC.

INDEX

XXV